CARROLL & GRAF

THE BIOGRAPHICAL ENCYCLOPEDIA

OF THE

NEGRO BASEBALL LEAGUES

THE
BIOGRAPHICAL
ENCYCLOPEDIA
OF THE
NEGRO
BASEBALL
LEAGUES

JAMES A. RILEY

Foreword by MONTE IRVIN

CARROLL & GRAF PUBLISHERS
NEW YORK

THE BIOGRAPHICAL ENCYCLOPEDIA OF THE NEGRO BASEBALL LEAGUES

Carroll & Graf Publishers
An Imprint of Avalon Publishing Group Incorporated
161 William Street, 16th Floor
New York, NY 10038

First Carroll & Graf cloth edition 1994
First Carroll & Graf trade paperback edition 2002

Library of Congress Cataloging-in-Publication Data is available.

ISBN: 0-7867-0959-6

Printed in the United States of America
Distributed by Publishers Group West

This book is dedicated to my wife Dottie, without whose love and support this volume would not have been possible

Contents

Acknowledgments

This encyclopedic volume is the result of twenty years of research by the author, but many people have contributed to the successful completion of this landmark publication. Foremost, the author would like to thank former Negro League players Buck Leonard, Ray Dandridge, Leon Day, Monte Irvin, Buck O'Neill, and Felix "Chin" Evans for the many hours they shared through the years in helping to preserve for posterity the memory of their fellow players.

Other former players providing invaluable assistance toward the completion of this project were Ted "Double Duty" Radcliffe, Piper Davis, Edsall Walker, Gene Benson, Mahlon Duckett, Bill Cash, Byron Johnson, Quincy Trouppe, and Eugene Smith.

Also contributing information were Max Manning, Rufus Lewis, Saul Davis, Verdell Mathis, Jim Zapp, Marlin Carter, Roy Campanella, Joe Black, Willard Brown, Josh Johnson, Bobby Robinson, Cowan "Bubba" Hyde, and Wilmer "Red" Fields. And Bill Wright, Sam Jethroe, Johnny Britton, James "Red" Moore, Cy Morton, Jimmie Hill, James "Lefty" LaMarque, Butch McCord, Al Fennar, and Josh Gibson, Jr.

Posthumous accolades for their many contributions go to Willie Wells, David Barnhill, Johnny Davis, Jimmy Crutchfield, Judy Johnson, "Cool Papa" Bell, Bill Byrd, Juanelo Mirabal, and Chet Brewer. Also to Bob Harvey, Jake Dunn, Othello "Chico" Renfroe,

Ford Smith, Hilton Smith, Bus Clarkson, Bill Harvey, Johnny Taylor, and Frank "Doc" Sykes.

And to all other former players who graciously shared their time and memories over the years, please accept a sincere thank you for the help provided. A complete list of players who made contributions to this volume appears in the appendix.

In addition to the former players, heartfelt appreciation goes to the baseball researchers and historians within SABR (Society for American Baseball Research) who are working to preserve a complete and accurate legacy for the veterans of the Negro Leagues. A special thanks is due Dick Clark for helping provide roster continuity, and Baylor Butler for his help with the minor-league data for players who entered organized baseball. Thanks also go to Jerry Malloy for his assistance with the nineteenth-century players; to Luis Alvelo and Luis Munoz for providing additional information for Latin American players; and to John Holway, Todd Bolton, Larry Hogan, Merl Kleinecht, Bob Peterson, Bob Davids, Al Ritter, Mike Mastrangelo, Larry Lester, Phil Dixon, and Tweed Webb for providing additional player data.

More than anyone, mention needs to be made of the invaluable contributions of my wife, Dottie Riley, who has helped, from beginning to end, in every phase of research and manuscript preparation necessary to make this volume become a reality. A word of appreciation is also in order for my sons, Josh Riley and Jube Riley, and to my nephew, Mike Riley, who have helped at crucial times by locating and copying box scores and news items relating to the Negro Leagues.

A final thanks to the countless other historians, researchers, and media center employees who have been most helpful through the years.

Foreword
Memories of the Negro Leagues

Monte Irvin

My interest in baseball started when I was a youngster on a farm down South. After they finished work, most of the farmhands would choose up sides and start to play baseball. And I remember sitting on the sidelines when I was six years old watching how much fun they had while they played.

I was particularly impressed with my brother Bob. He was ten years older than I was, and he threw the ball as hard as Satchel Paige. In fact, after we left the South and moved to New Jersey, a team called the Jacksonville Redcaps came through and they had heard about him and gave him a tryout. They wanted him to go with them, but my mother wouldn't let him go because they played ball on Sunday, and she thought that was a sin. It was a shame because he was a natural.

During that time, there was a local white team about twenty miles from Newark, called the East Orange B.B.C. All the Negro League teams that came to Newark loved to stop there and play because it was not far from Ruppert Stadium, the Newark Eagles' home field. I saw the Crawfords, Philadelphia Stars, Bacharach Giants, Lincoln Giants, and all the other teams that came through.

As I got older, I started to play with the local team in Orange, New Jersey, and one scout told me, "The way you can throw the ball, you ought to be a pitcher." And I would pitch and do okay. But I wanted to play every day and be in on every play, so I started to

catch. Lennie Pearson, who later became my teammate, moved to Orange from Akron, Ohio, and he could throw the ball as hard as I could. So we would take turns pitching and catching. One day I would pitch and he would catch and the next day he would pitch and I would catch, and we developed into an almost unbeatable duo and built quite a reputation.

We were the same age, but he dropped out of high school early and joined the Newark Eagles. I couldn't join them until I graduated, but when the Eagles played at home, I would work out with them and sit in the stands. But on the road, they would let me play, because that way I would not lose my amateur standing. I saw some of the best players of that time— John Henry Lloyd, John Beckwith, Oscar Charleston, Dick Lundy, Chino Smith, Cool Papa Bell, and last but not least, Turkey Stearnes. The first time I saw Turkey Stearnes play, he was the leadoff batter and he hit the first pitch over the center-field fence at Sprague Field in Bloomfield, New Jersey.

The most impressive left-hander I ever saw at that time was Slim Jones. He was very impressive because he was tall and threw the ball very hard. And I saw the great catcher Biz Mackey just a little past his peak. And I saw other greats who inspired me to want to be a ballplayer.

I'm just sorry I didn't get a chance to see more of the players. I didn't see Smokey Joe Williams, Bullet Rogan, or Willie Foster. I did see Dick Redding, but he was well past his prime.

When I finally joined the Newark Eagles, I was playing with the best. King Richard Lundy was our manager, and we also had Willie Wells, Ray Dandridge, Dick Seay, and Mule Suttles. They were called the million-dollar infield. Pitching was our ace, Leon Day, as well as Terris McDuffie, Max Manning, and Jimmy Hill. That was a terrific staff.

As I think back now, the Negro Leagues served a great purpose by entertaining the downtrodden people who came to see them. At that time, we didn't have too many heroes. Remember this was before Joe Louis came along, and before Jesse Owens and Sugar Ray Robinson. I guess Jack Johnson and Harry Wills were the big heroes of that time. There weren't too many heroes to look up to, so these great baseball players filled this need.

Great tribute has to be paid to the early baseball players. Not only were they naturals, but also most of them were self-taught and were big and strong. They developed through trial and error, and they learned how to play by talking and watching other players. Sometimes they would go to major-league parks and watch how major-leaguers did it. And when the black players would go to Cuba, Mexico, Puerto Rico, Venezuela, and Santo Domingo, they would gain more expertise about inside baseball.

Now, after some of the fellows started to play white clubs, a rapport was developed and they talked inside baseball with them. Some players were friendly and gave tips about making certain plays and shared all those little points that helped them improve their game, including where to obtain the best bats, balls, and gloves.

I understand Rube Foster was a great teacher as well as a great pitcher. There must have been a lot of guys like him who had that kind of natural ability and became quite good, and who also studied the game and passed the knowledge on to others. I salute all those early fellows.

When I got to Newark, I was a right-field hitter and sometimes I would get fooled because I would lunge at the ball. Dick Lundy tried to help me, and suggested that I copy Joe DiMaggio's style. He said, "One of these days go over and watch him." So I went over to Yankee Stadium and watched him, and became a wrist hitter. When spring training time came, I practiced it constantly and I became a wrist hitter like Joe. By the time spring training was over I had it perfected and became a much better hitter. Pitchers didn't fool me anymore and I was ready for a fastball, change-up, or curve.

Now, the team that impressed me after I got to know baseball was the Homestead Grays. They had a great club, with Josh Gibson and Buck Leonard. Also they had Raymond Brown, Roy Partlow, Howard Easterling, Jerry Benjamin, Lick Carlisle, Jelly Jackson, Boojum Wilson, Blue Perez, Big Tom Parker, and all the rest. They had a perfect team. They had speed and power. David Whatley could go to first base as fast as anybody I've ever seen. And Vic Harris was not a power hitter, but he was one of the best clutch hitters of all time. He was one of the key reasons why they were champs so long, along with that great pitching staff.

I saw the Kansas City Monarchs play the Homestead Grays at Griffith Stadium while I was in the Army in 1943. It was baseball at its best. Not only did the Monarchs have Satchel Paige, Booker McDaniels, and Hilton Smith pitching, they also had Frank Duncan, Willard Brown, and just a great club all around. It was as good a brand of baseball as you ever wanted to see, with lots of talent. And all of them played so natural. They knew how to play, and they would sometimes do the unexpected. A favorite play was, with a man on first the batter would bunt down the third-base line and the runner would almost always end up on third—a play seldom used today.

The Baltimore Elites had a good team, featuring Bill Byrd and Bill Wright. Bill Wright was a switch-hitter but was big and strong and could run like a deer, similar to the present-day Dave Parker. He avoided slumps because when he batted left-handed he bunted the ball between the pitcher, second baseman, and first baseman, and invariably beat the play at first base. I must have seen him do it a hundred times.

In Cuba I saw Martin Dihigo, Silvio Garcia, "Walla Walla" Oms, and some of the other great Cuban players. And you would learn a lot just by watching them. And the same thing applied when you played in Cuba, Mexico, Puerto Rico, Santo Domingo, or Venezuela.

As you got older, you got to the point where you thought, "All I need is a chance to make the majors. These guys can't play any better than we can." Black Teams would barnstorm against the major leaguers, and everybody made a lot of money. Judge Landis stopped it because the black teams started to win too many games, and that became embarrassing to the lords of baseball. Consequently no teams could play with more than three players from a major-league club.

Just a few white players would resent playing against black teams. I think that an athlete enjoys seeing the excellence of another player. Look at the way almost everybody rooted for Michael Jordan because they had never seen anybody play basketball like that before. He was a scoring machine. People used to root for Josh Gibson the same way. He had the power to hit the ball out of any ballpark. Satchel was also a very prominent and popular player at that time. But there were other good players who never got much publicity.

When Jackie got the chance with the Dodgers and really opened things up, most of the players were very happy, but rather envious because they wished they had gotten the chance fifteen or twenty years earlier. I was

just going into the Army and I didn't get a chance to play during the war, when I was in my prime. And when I came out I practically had to start all over again. I knew that younger players would follow him. And that's precisely what happened when Willie Mays, Hank Aaron, Frank Robinson, Larry Doby, and all the rest of these guys came along. If Jackie had not made it, it would only have delayed the process, because there was Roy Campanella and Don Newcombe who would have stepped in and filled the role.

All of us were grateful that Jackie made it because he made it better for everybody. Not only athletically, but also financially, socially, and politically. And in every other way. He caused things to be desegregated, and a lot of black folks finally got a lot of well-deserved respect. We'll always be grateful for the great pioneering job he did, and may God bless him forever.

After Jackie made it, the major-league owners saw the potential talent in the Negro Leagues. All they had to do was sign them and let them train with the various farm clubs and learn the major-league system of doing things.

I say that the baseball I saw when I first started playing in the Negro Leagues was very impressive. Most of the players simply had natural talent, and you have to pay tribute to those men, who were extraordinarily gifted and who simply loved the game. They would almost have played for nothing, and most of the time they did.

Finally I say, thank God that there were the Negro Leagues although they were not organized the way they should have been. But at least they served a purpose. If it were not for the Negro Leagues, there would not have been a place for black Americans to develop their baseball skills properly.

Preface
Odyssey Through the Shadows

When Jackie Robinson walked on the field in a Brooklyn Dodger uniform on opening day of the 1947 season, the exodus of black Americans from the Negro Leagues was immediate and irreversible. The defection was also destructive, and the demise of black baseball was rapid and inevitable. For almost a quarter of a century the history of the parallel world of black baseball was virtually forgotten and in danger of being lost.

Like most Americans, my first introduction to this segment of baseball history came from Bob Peterson's excellent book *Only the Ball Was White*. But after my appetite was whetted for more information, I found that there were no other books on the subject. At first my interest and research were on a personal level, but gradually, as I realized the dearth of information available on the subject, I began to expand the perimeters of my research to encompass a goal of preserving a complete and accurate history of the Negro Leagues, with a special emphasis on the men who were destined to spend their careers in the shadows of relative obscurity.

My efforts to achieve this goal assumed a dual approach. Foremost, I considered it imperative to contact living players from the Negro Leagues to secure both personal histories and evaluations of their deceased contemporaries who had passed away without leaving an account of their own baseball memories. As I

traveled across the country speaking with these men, I was encouraged by their caring and sharing attitude and by their genuine appreciation of finally being remembered for their contributions to baseball.

Also essential to learning more about the men who played in the sundown shadows of the Negro Leagues was utilization of archival resources for contemporary accounts of games and events from this segment of baseball history. Countless hours spent in studied analysis of microfilms of black newspapers from the era produced additional information that contributed to a more complete understanding of the special spirit of black baseball that made it truly a unique piece of Americana.

In rediscovery of this spirit, other publications have maintained a broader perspective and presented an overview of black baseball, or focused on sociological conditions that contributed to the existence of the Negro Leagues.

Individual players, with the exception of a select number of stars, have been neglected and remain unknown to the American sports world. Previously, no source existed for an interested reader to learn about these forgotten specters from the shadows of the past. In filling this void, *The Biographical Encyclopedia of the Negro Baseball Leagues* stands as a landmark publication.

James A. Riley

A Brief History of
the Negro Leagues

In the beginning, baseball was a gentlemen's game, played by amateur athletic clubs for leisuretime recreation. Among the early amateur teams in the game's evolution toward professionalism were black aggregations. However, after the close of the 1867 season, the National Association of Baseball Players voted to exclude any club with a black player. Thus the sport remained a predominantly white pastime.

In 1869, although not bound by the amateur agreement, baseball's first recognized professional ballclub, the Cincinnati Red Stockings, fielded an all-white team. The Red Stockings' diamond success led to an increased interest in baseball, and professionalism spread rapidly. In 1871 the first professional league was formed, but again all the players were white.

Within a year, however, the complexion of the game changed when Bud Fowler became the first black professional player, albeit with a nonleague team. Other Americans of African ancestry followed in his footsteps, and soon there were numerous black professional ballplayers playing on otherwise all-white teams. Fleet Walker, a black catcher, even appeared with a major-league ballclub in 1884. Such situations were not devoid of racial incidents, and Cap Anson's refusal to play against a black pitcher, George Stovey, in 1887 is representative of the era's prevalent mind-set.

In that same year, the International League's Board of Directors voted not to approve any subsequent contracts with black players. This official action postdated baseball's national agreement and, although some black players continued to play with other teams, the league's position eventually led to the "gentlemen's agreement" of total exclusion of black players from baseball. This unwritten understanding carried the same impact of enforcement as a written policy, and was firmly entrenched in baseball tradition in 1946, when Jackie Robinson reintegrated America's game.

With black players experiencing restricted access to white ballclubs, the first black professional team, the Cuban Giants, was organized in 1885. In some instances during their formative years, the Cuban Giants and other early black teams played as a city's representative in an otherwise white league.

The nadir of black baseball occurred in the early 1890s, when only one professional black ballclub was operating. As more black teams began to organize and interest expanded two hubs of black baseball emerged, one centered around Chicago in the Midwest and another along the Philadelphia-New York City axis in the East. During the deadball era, black teams continued to operate as independent ballclubs, playing series with each other and also booking white semipro teams as well.

In 1920, Rube Foster founded the first enduring black baseball league, popularly christened the Negro National League. Acting as a virtual czar, he nurtured the league into maturity and was almost solely responsible for the success the league enjoyed. After Foster's debilitating illness and death in 1930, the league became rudderless from a void in leadership and, following the 1931 season, fell victim to the Depression.

A second league, the Eastern Colored League, was organized in 1923 and enjoyed a half decade of relative prosperity before imploding in 1928. During the league's tenuous existence, four Negro World Series (1924–27) were played between the two black major leagues. A replacement league, the American Negro League, was formed the following year but disbanded after only one season, returning the eastern teams to an independent status.

The Depression years weighed oppressively on black baseball franchises, creating chaotic conditions. The 1932 season suffered most extensively from the country's economic problems, as teams dissolved and players scattered in all directions trying to relocate with a solvent franchise. Those ballclubs that survived either maintained a delicate economic balance by "scuffling" across the country on barnstorming tours or by affiliation with a new league.

One attempt to continue black baseball on the previous organizational level was the formation of the East-West League, but the effort collapsed in midseason. Another haven for players proved to be the Negro Southern League, a previously minor league. With the influx of players from the defunct Negro National League, the Negro Southern League was accorded major-league status for the 1932 season.

The next year some stability was renewed, primarily through the efforts of Gus Greenlee, when the second Negro National League was established and the East-West All-Star game inaugurated. The All-Star game became an annual classic and proved to be the biggest single event in black baseball each season, surpassing even the Negro World Series in interest and attendance.

In 1937 the Negro American League was constituted, consisting of teams from the Midwest and the South. A corresponding change in the Negro National League's composition resulted in its realignment as an eastern league. This structure, patterned along the lines of the white major leagues, lasted for a dozen seasons, until the Negro National League disbanded after the 1948 season. During this time the Negro World Series was reinstated and seven World Series (1942–48) were played between the champions of the two leagues.

After the demise of the Negro National League, the Negro American League absorbed some of the surviving franchises and divided into two divisions in an effort to resuscitate black baseball. Although the league struggled on through 1960, most historians agree that the 1948 season was the last year that the Negro Leagues were of major-league quality.

Once the color line in organized baseball was eradicated, the end of black baseball was inevitable. For all practical purposes, the end of the Negro Leagues came with the stroke of a pen when Jackie Robinson signed a Brooklyn Dodgers contract.

Logic suggests that baseball expansion was a natural outgrowth of integration and that a measure of the essence of black baseball still lives through the assimilation of black players into the major leagues.

James A. Riley

Introduction

Baseball is our national pastime. It is America's game—played, loved, and passed on from father to son, from generation to generation. Its lore possesses a special quality, a timelessness, that forms a bond that defies definition. One that supersedes age differences and eradicates class distinctions. And one that provides a common ground, a proving ground—a leveling field of dreams. It is a history to be shared and savored in all its richness and fullness by every American.

But there is a segment of baseball history that remains an unmined repository of baseball lore and that reflects a unique slice of Americana with a style and flavor all its own, waiting to be resurrected from the ashes of the past, like the phoenix in rebirth. The history of the Negro Leagues, once neglected to the point of invisibility, is now becoming romanticized and, somewhere in the process, the reality of black baseball is in danger of being lost.

It is the story of a world populated by thousands of ballplayers who remain undiscovered by the American sports world. A story that preserves the reality of a shared experience in a singular era in our country's history, that captures the essence, and that transcends the baseball diamond to instill a feeling of identity with this generation of men who were destined to spend their careers in the parallel world of black baseball.

They never played in the recognized major leagues, never earned big salaries, and were rarely mentioned by the leading sports pages. But they formed a big league of their own, scuffled to make a living, and made a reluctant sporting world take notice by the brand of baseball they played. Pushing the door to the major leagues ajar for Jackie Robinson to step through, they were the sowers, and all who followed were the reapers. With but few exceptions, they remain enigmatic specters still hidden in the sundown shadows of baseball history.

Through an aurora of biographical vignettes, this essential part of baseball history is being salvaged for future generations. In the preservation of this essence, we follow the flow of forgotten waters and, as we walk the banks in rediscovery, we become part of a unique renaissance—a fusion, returning the lost soul to our national pastime. It is a story for all Americans, for all times.

The Biographical Encyclopedia of the Negro Baseball Leagues blossoms as a rich blend of anecdotal archives and player profiles; it envelops the statistical skeletons with flesh and blood to reconstruct ballplayers who will be remembered as *real* people. And more than just a name in an obscure boxscore or bits of dust caught in the cobwebs of an old man's memories.

Explanatory Notes

The Biographical Encyclopedia of the Negro Baseball Leagues is designed as a complete but easy-to-use reference book, with the interests of the reader in mind. The format facilitates access to specific areas of interest, making it possible to identify quickly individual players or specific years, teams, and positions. Included is every player who played with a team of major-league quality, or whose career had historical significance. Over four thousand players are included, with careers ranging from 1872 through 1950. Hundreds of others were omitted because their careers failed to meet the established parameters.

Player Names

Names are alphabetized, with full names given when possible and nicknames in parentheses. The name by which the player was best known is indicated by boldface type, and italics indicate an infrequently used nickname or one that may have been generated by the media. In instances where a player was sometimes identified by a different name during his career, the alternate identification is listed underneath his common name following the designation a.k.a. (also known as). This alternate name may be a real one or simply an incorrect listing by the media, but is included to facilitate location of the proper player.

Career

The career lists the beginning and ending dates for which the individual was an active player with a black ball club of *major-league* quality. This does not necessarily imply continuity throughout the interval with a major-league club for the duration of the time indicated. Nor should it be interpreted as being all-inclusive constraints for his career. Alternate years listed following a semicolon indicate a secondary career in a nonplaying capacity (e.g., manager, umpire, executive).

Position

The positions played by the individual are listed in order of frequency of appearances. Boldface type indicates the position at which a player is most strongly identified. Normal print indicates positions that he played on a reasonably regular basis at some time in his career. Italicized type indicates a position played infrequently in his career, with his appearance possibly resulting only from injury to another player or other special circumstances relating to the team situation.

Teams

The teams are listed chronologically, with the years with that team listed parenthetically when this degree of specificity is available. Boldface type indicates a team strongly identified with the player. For career continuity, some teams are listed that are not of major-league caliber, and these are indicated by italicized type. When a year listed for a team is italicized, but the team is not, it indicates that although the team was of major-league caliber for most of his tenure, the indicated season was not of the same quality. In some instances teams are listed separately, although in actuality there was simply a franchise shift and not a different ballclub. Teams listed following a semicolon indicate that a player was with the team in a nonplaying capacity, and a year listed following a semicolon inside parentheses has the same connotation.

Bats/Throws

When known, this information is included. In rare instances when a player batted as a switch-hitter for only part of his career, the distinction is indicated in the body of the biography.

Height/Weight

When known, this information is included for their prime playing career. In instances when a slight variance existed from different sources, the data deemed the most credible were selected for inclusion.

Born/Died

When known, the birth date, birthplace, death date, and deathplace are included. Again, in instances of conflicting data, the source determined to be most reliable was used.

Biographical Sketch

Each biographical sketch is intended to stand alone. Designed as a brief synopsis of a player's life with a special emphasis on his baseball career, the content also includes an analysis of his individual baseball skills and highlights of his diamond experience. Also included are sufficient statistics, where available, to assist in accurately depicting his baseball abilities.

Statistics

There is no single source for complete and accurate Negro League statistics. Anyone delving into the miasmic quagmire of this area of research has encountered conflicting and often confusing data. Some sources purporting to be valid representations of Negro League statistics are tainted from flawed research techniques. The statistics used in this volume are drawn from diverse sources, including contemporary press accounts and reconstructed data from box scores, scorebooks, and written summaries, and represent the data with the highest degree of reliability and validity that currently exists. Because of the diversity of performance data, semantic qualifiers are utilized to present a more comprehensive basis for analysis. Also used for proper perspective is a much-overlooked statistical tool, the batting order, which conveys inherent characteristics of players' skills and peer esteem.

Sources

Primary sources were interviews with former players and contemporary press accounts of the era. Special collections provided secondary sources from which additional information was gleaned, while tertiary sources included books and articles of more recent vintage. A bibliography and a listing of players interviewed are included in the appendix.

THE
BIOGRAPHICAL
ENCYCLOPEDIA
OF THE
NEGRO
BASEBALL
LEAGUES

Team Histories
In addition to biographies of all Negro League players, team histories are also presented for all Negro League teams, independent black ballclubs of major-league quality, and other selected teams of historical significance. A listing of the teams included follows:

Algona Brownies
All Nations
Argyle Hotel Athletics
Atlanta Black Crackers
Atlantic City Bacharach Giants
Baltimore Black Sox
Baltimore Elite Giants
Birmingham Black Barons
Brooklyn Eagles
Brooklyn Royal Giants
Chicago American Giants
Chicago Columbia Giants
Chicago Giants
Chicago Leland Giants
Chicago Unions
Chicago Union Giants
Cincinnati Buckeyes
Cincinnati Clowns
Cincinnati-Indianapolis Clowns
Cincinnati Tigers
Cleveland Bears
Cleveland Browns
Cleveland Buckeyes
Cleveland Cubs
Cleveland Elites
Cleveland Giants
Cleveland Hornets
Cleveland Red Sox
Cleveland Stars
Cleveland Tate Stars
Cleveland Tigers
Cole's American Giants
Columbus Blue Birds

Columbus Buckeyes
Columbus Elite Giants
Cuban Giants
Cuban House of David
Cuban Stars (East)
Cuban Stars (West)
Cuban X-Giants
Dayton Marcos
Detroit Stars
Detroit Wolves
Ethiopian Clowns
Harrisburg Giants
Harrisburg-St. Louis Stars
Havana Red Sox
Hilldale Daisies
Homestead Grays
Houston Eagles
Indianapolis ABCs
Indianapolis Athletics
Indianapolis Clowns
Indianapolis Crawfords
Jacksonville Red Caps
Kansas City Kansas Giants
Kansas City Monarchs
Long Branch Cubans
Louisville Black Caps
Louisville Buckeyes
Louisville White Sox
Memphis Red Sox
Milwaukee Bears
Mohawk Giants
Monroe Monarchs
Montgomery Grey Sox

Nashville Elite Giants
New Orleans-St. Louis Stars
New York Black Yankees
New York Cubans
New York Gorhams
New York Harlem Stars
New York Lincoln Giants
New York Lincoln Stars
Newark Browns
Newark Dodgers
Newark Eagles
Newark Stars
Page Fence Giants
Pennsylvania Red Caps of New York
Philadelphia Giants
Philadelphia Stars
Philadelphia Tigers
Pittsburgh Crawfords
Pittsburgh Keystones
St. Louis Giants
St. Louis Stars
St. Paul Gophers
Stars of Cuba
Toledo Crawfords
Toledo Tigers
Washington Black Senators
Washington Elite Giants
Washington Pilots
Washington Potomacs
Wilmington Potomacs
Zulu Cannibal Giants

A

Aaron, Henry Louis (**Hank**)
Career: *1952*   Position: **ss**
Teams: *Indianapolis Clowns ('52), minor leagues ('52–'53),* major leagues ('54–'76)
Bats: Right   Throws: Right
Height: 6'0"   Weight: 180
Born: Feb. 5, 1934, Mobile, Ala.

In 1952, as a skinny, crosshanded-batting eighteen-year-old, the future home-run king played shortstop for the Negro American League's Indianapolis Clowns under manager Buster Haywood for about three months. Aaron had been signed in April for $200 per month by Bunny Downs, the Clowns' business manager, after being discovered the previous season (1951) while playing with the semipro Mobile Black Bears in an exhibition game against the Clowns. During the time he was with the Clowns, he was scouted by both the New York Giants and the Boston Braves and, although the Giants were unimpressed, the Braves bought his contract from Clowns' owner Syd Pollock.

The fledgling shortstop finished the season at Eau Claire in the Northern League, hitting .336 with nine home runs in the remaining 87 games. The following season he was switched to second base at Jacksonville in the Sally League, and he responded by leading the league in almost every category except home runs. His .362 batting average topped the league, as did his hits (208), runs (115), RBIs (125), doubles (36), putouts (330), assists (310), and errors (36). He also contributed 14 triples and 22 homers.

The next season he made the transition to the major leagues with the Milwaukee Braves, was shifted to the outfield, and hit 13 home runs. The rest is history. Twenty-three years later he retired as the all-time home-run king with 755 homers and a lifetime .305 batting average. Along the way he lead the league in home runs ('57, '63, '66–'67) and in RBIs ('57, '60, '63, '66) four times each, won three Gold Gloves ('58–'60) and two batting titles ('56, '59), was selected to the All-Star team ('54–'76), and voted the National League's MVP ('57). He was inducted into the Baseball Hall of Fame in 1982 to cap an illustrious career.

Aballi
Career: 1930   Position: p
Team: Cuban Stars
Bats: Right   Throws: Right

He was a right-handed pitcher with the Cuban Stars in 1930, his only season in black baseball.

Abbott
Career: 1906–08   Position: of, p
Teams: Cuban Giants ('06), Genuine Cuban Giants ('07–'08), Brooklyn Royal Giants ('08)

A pitcher turned outfielder, he began his career in 1906 as a pitcher with the Cuban Giants and after a season on the slab, played two seasons with the Genuine Cuban Giants and Brooklyn Royal Giants as an outfielder.

Abernathy, Robert William (*James*)
Career: 1945–48   Position: lf
Teams: Kansas City Monarchs ('45), *Boston Blues ('46)*, Indianapolis Clowns ('46-'47), *San Francisco Sea Lions ('47)*, New York Cubans ('48)
Bats: Right   Throws: Right
Height: 5'9"   Weight: 175
Born: July 12, 1918, Columbia, Tenn.

The outfielder began his career as a wartime reserve center fielder with the Kansas City Monarchs in 1945, and continued playing after the end of World War II until a broken leg in 1948 ended his career. He had salary problems with the Monarchs and left the team in 1946. After a stint with the Boston Blues in the United States League, a league of lesser status, he signed with the Indianapolis Clowns. In 1947 he played left field and batted in the cleanup spot for the Clowns. A line-drive hitter with respectable power, he was swift on the bases and was a dependable fielder with good range and a strong arm. He was still in his prime years, playing with the New York Cubans, when the injury occurred. After a triple, he scored on a ground ball to the pitcher, but when he tried to break his slide at the plate, he broke his leg instead.

As a youngster he began playing sandlot games in Nashville with the N & T Tigers and other teams until he went to California in 1940 to work on a defense job. Meanwhile, he continued playing with semipro teams on the West Coast during the summer months, until signing with the Monarchs. After he ended his career, he returned to Nashville and worked in a dry-cleaning business. After retiring, he encountered health problems, and lost both legs during the '80s from diabetes.

Abreau, Eufemio
a.k.a. Abreu
Career: 1919–34   Position: **c**, 3b, of, 1b, *ss, p*

Teams: **Cuban Stars (West)** ('20–'25, '30), Cuban Stars (East) ('30), Cuban Stars ('32–34)
Bats: Right   Throws: Right
Born: Cuba

The Cuban catcher began his career in the United States in 1919 and a year later was batting eighth in the lineup as a regular with the Cuban Stars in the inaugural Negro National League season. The following winter, in his homeland, he played with Almendares in a series against the New York Giants, but batted only .188. Returning to the United States in the spring with the Cuban Stars, he continued his fifteen-year career in the Negro Leagues. In addition to his receiving duties, he also saw action at both corners of the infield and in the outfield. At various stages of his career the Cubans' franchise played as an independent team and was a member of three different leagues: the Negro National League, the Eastern Colored League, and the East-West League.

Acosta, Jose
Career: 1915   Position: p
Team: Long Branch Cubans ('15), Minor leagues ('16), Major leagues ('20–'22)
Bats: Right   Throws: Right
Height: 5'7"   Weight: 140
Born: March 4, 1891, San Antonio, Rio Blanco, Cuba

A white Cuban player, the little right-hander was the best pitcher for the Long Branch Cubans in 1915, his only season in black baseball. The team played out of Long Branch, New Jersey, and dissolved after only two seasons. Acosta signed with Vancouver of the Northwest League in 1916 and later played in the major leagues with the Washington Senators and Chicago White Sox (1920–22), compiling a lifetime 10–10 record with a 4.51 ERA. Prior to playing in the major leagues, while pitching with Havana, he twice led the Cuban winter league in wins with 16 (1918–19) and 6 (1920–21). In the latter season he played against the New York Giants when they traveled to Cuba for postseason exhibitions.

Adams, Emery (Ace)
Career: 1932–46   Positions: **p,** *lf, rf*
Teams: Memphis Red Sox ('32, '37), **Baltimore Elite Giants** ('39–'42), New York Black Yankees ('43–'46)
Bats: Right   Throws: Right
Height: 5'8"   Weight: 160
Born: 1911, Collierville, Tenn.

The diminutive right-hander assumed the role of the ace of the Baltimore Elite Giants' pitching staff in 1940 when Bill Byrd opted to play in Latin America. That season he compiled a 10–7 record with a 3.16 ERA and followed with a 5–2, 2.87 ERA season in 1941, but after dropping to a .500 winning percentage in 1942, he was released to the New York Black Yankees for the 1943 season. He remained with the New York club through 1946, when he closed a fifteen-year career that began with the Memphis Red Sox in 1932.

Adams (Packinghouse)
Career: 1938   Position: 3b
Team: Kansas City Monarchs

He received very limited playing time as a substitute third baseman for the Kansas City Monarchs in 1938.

Addison, J.
Career: 1910–11   Positions: ss, c
Team: Philadelphia Giants

He was a weak-hitting shortstop-catcher with the Philadelphia Giants in 1910–11, when the once-great ballclub was in decline. On at least one occasion the three Addisons all played in the same game for the Philadelphia Giants in 1911. It is not known if they were related.

Addison, K.
Career: 1911–12   Position: 3b
Teams: Philadelphia Giants ('11), *Pittsburgh Giants* ('12)

He played as a third baseman with the Philadelphia Giants when the once-great ballclub was in decline, and also with the Pittsburgh Giants, a lesser team. On at least one occasion the three Addisons all played in the same game for the Philadelphia Giants in 1911. It is not known if they were related.

Addison, T.
Career: 1911   Position: ss
Team: Philadelphia Giants

He was a weak-hitting shortstop with the Philadelphia Giants in 1911, when the once-great ballclub was in decline. On at least one occasion the three Addisons all played in the same game for the Philadelphia Giants in 1911. It is not known if they were related.

Adkins, Clarence
Career: 1931   Position: of
Team: *Nashville Elite Giants*

He was a reserve outfielder with the Negro Southern League's Nashville Elite Giants in 1931, the year between seasons when the Elites were members of a major league.

Adkins, Stacy
a.k.a. Atkins
Career: 1950   Position: p
Team: Chicago American Giants

He pitched in three games for the Chicago American Giants in 1950 without a decision.

Agnew, Clyde
Career: 1950   Position: p
Team: Baltimore Elite Giants

The pitcher was with the Baltimore Elite Giants briefly in 1950 but had no record in league competition.

Ahrens
Career: 1930   Position: p
Team: Cuban Stars

The pitcher was on the Cuban Stars' roster in 1930, but his playing time was minimal.

Albertus
Career: 1932   Position: p
Team: Cuban Stars (East)

In his only season in black baseball, he

pitched briefly with the Cuban Stars (East) in 1932.

Albrecht, R.
a.k.a. Albright
Career: 1928–29   Position: p
Team: Atlantic City Bacharach Giants

He pitched briefly with the Bacharachs in 1928–29, but was not in the starting rotation and was winless the latter season, while hitting only .143 in limited play.

Albright, Thomas (Pistol **Pete**)
Career: 1936   Position: p
Team: New York Cubans
Bats: Right   Throws: Right
Height: 5'10"   Weight: 225
Born: Dec. 23, 1909, Crockett, Tex.

The hefty Texan pitched with the New York Cubans in 1936. Earlier in his career he played with the Denver White Elephants, the only black team in the Denver City League, and pitched them to the 1930 championship, striking out eleven batters in the title game.

Albritton, Alexander (**Alex**)
a.k.a. Al Britton
Career: 1921–25   Position: p
Teams: *Washington Braves ('21)*, Atlantic City Bacharach Giants ('21–'23), Hilldale Daisies ('21), Baltimore Black Sox ('22–'23), Washington Potomacs ('23–'24), Wilmington Potomacs ('25)
Born: 1894, Philadelphia, Pa.
Died: Feb. 16, 1940, Philadelphia, Pa.

During a five-year span in the early '20s, he pitched with five different eastern teams, but despite being a hard worker and always ready to pitch, never really made it big. With Hilldale in 1921, pitching against all competition, he had a 7–2 record with a 3.73 ERA and batted .286. He was a fair pitcher and could beat the white semipro teams but was not effective against the black major-league teams. His best season came in 1924 after he was secured by the Washington Potomacs from the semipro Brooklyn All-Stars and placed in the starting

rotation. In 1940, fifteen years after leaving baseball, he was beaten to death in a mental hospital.

Alderette
Career: 1918   Position: p
Team: Cuban Stars (East)

He was a second-line pitcher with the Cuban Stars (East) in 1918, his only year in black baseball.

Alexander
Career: 1918–21   Positions: of, 1b, 2b
Teams: Dayton Marcos ('18–'20), Columbus Buckeyes ('21), Chicago Giants ('21)

Primarily an outfielder, he also played first base and second base for the Dayton Marcos, Columbus Buckeyes, and Chicago Giants during his four-year career, usually batting in the lower part of the batting order.

Alexander, Chuffy
Career: 1927–32   Positions: **of**, 3b, 1b, 2b, ss
Teams: Memphis Red Sox ('27), Birmingham Black Barons ('27–'28), Monroe Monarchs ('32)
Bats: Right   Throws: Right
Height: 5'0"   Weight: 125

The diminutive outfielder stood barely five feet tall but was fast afoot, and also played each infield position during his half-dozen seasons with southern teams. Playing most of the 1927 season with the Memphis Red Sox, he batted .265, but was also a utility player with the second-half Negro National League champions Birmingham Black Barons part of that season.

Alexander, Freyl
Career: 1912   Position: officer
Team: Homestead Grays

He served as president of the Homestead Grays in 1912, when the team was in its formative stages.

Alexander, Grover Cleveland (**Buck**)
Career: 1923–26   Position: p

Teams: Chicago Giants ('23), Detroit Stars ('23–'25), Indianapolis ABCs ('25–'26), Cleveland Elites ('26)

A mediocre pitcher who struggled to stay in the lineup with top clubs, the most successful part of his career was when he pitched in the Detroit Stars' regular rotation. In his last year in the Negro National League, with the Cleveland Elites in 1926, he won only a single game while losing six and finished with a meager .091 batting average.

Alexander, Hub
Career: 1913   Position: c
Team: Chicago Giants

He was a catcher with the Chicago Giants in 1913, during his only season in black baseball.

Alexander, Joe
Career: 1950   Position: c
Team: Kansas City Monarchs

He was a reserve catcher with the Kansas City Monarchs in 1950 but played in fewer than ten games.

Alexander, Spencer
Career: 1940–41   Positions: rf, 1f
Team: Newark Eagles

He was a light-hitting substitute outfielder playing in the side pastures with the Newark Eagles in 1940–41, batting .161 and .176. Later in the decade he played with lesser teams, including the Asheville Blues in 1949.

Alexander, Ted (Red)
Career: 1940–49   Position: p
Teams: New York Black Yankees ('39), Cleveland Bears ('39–'40), *Palmer House All-Stars* ('40), Chicago American Giants ('41), Newark Eagles ('40), **Kansas City Monarchs** ('43–'47), Homestead Grays ('48), Birmingham Black Barons ('49)
Bats: Right   Throws: Right
Height: 5'10"   Weight: 185

Although only an average pitcher with the standard three-pitch (fastball, curve, and change of pace) repertory, Ted had the distinc-tion of pitching for the two great teams of the '40s, the Kansas City Monarchs and the Homestead Grays, and appearing in a World Series with each team. After a 9–4 record with the 1946 Monarchs, he had a 2.70 ERA in the Series, but lost his only decision in two games as the Monarchs lost to the Negro National League Newark Eagles in the closely contested seven-game Series. He had a bit more luck in the 1948 Series, when he split his two deci-sions as the Grays won the Negro Leagues championship by defeating the Negro American League pennant-winning Birmingham Black Barons. During the regular season, avail-able statistics show a 2–0 mark with the Grays.

Earlier in his career, before joining the Mon-archs, he spent two seasons with the Cleveland Bears and pitched briefly with the Palmer House All-Stars, a Chicago-based independent team of less than major-league caliber. Incom-plete statistics from these earlier years show him to be a .500 pitcher.

Alfonso, Angel
a.k.a. Alphonso
Career: 1924–30   Positions: ss, 2b, 3b
Teams: **Cuban Stars (West)** ('24–'26, '30), Cuban Stars (East) ('27–'29)
Bats: Left   Throws: Right

The versatile Cuban infielder played second base, shortstop, and third base for the Cuban Stars in three different leagues: the Negro Na-tional League, the Eastern Colored League, and the American Negro League. Offensively he demonstrated good speed on the bases and hit .321, .344, and .280 in 1927, 1929, and 1930, respectively, while showing average power at the plate and usually batting either in the lead-off spot or in the lower part of the order. Off the field, the infielder was a loner with para-noid tendencies and did not cultivate friends.

Algona Brownies
Duration: 1902–03   Honors: Western Champions ('03)
Affiliation: Independent

Based in Algona, Iowa, and comprised of

former members of the Union Giants and Chicago Unions, this short-term ballclub won the Western championship in 1903.

All Nations

Duration: 1912–18   Honors: None
Affiliation: Independent

A ballclub comprised of multinational players (including Indians, Orientals, and Latin Americans as well as black and white Americans) that toured the Midwest during the mid-teens. The team was organized and owned by J. L. Wilkinson, a white businessman from Kansas City, and J. E. Gall. At various times the team featured John Donaldson, José Mendez, and Christobel Torriente, and when any of these outstanding black players were in the lineup, the club competed on a par with the top black teams of the era, especially when Donaldson was in his prime. The team faltered during World War I, when most of their better players were drafted, and it was disbanded in 1918. When Wilkinson organized the Kansas City Monarchs and entered them in the Negro National League in 1920, the All Nations club never regained its former glory.

Allen

Career: 1887–88   Position: c
Team: Cuban Giants

He was a catcher with the Cuban Giants, the Colored champions in 1887 and 1888, and was considered one of the top players at his position at the time. The Cuban Giants were the first black professional team, organized two years earlier as an extension of the Argyle Hotel Athletics, formed in 1885 by Frank P. Thompson, the headwaiter at Long Island's Argyle Hotel in Babylon, New York, to play for the entertainment of the summer guests.

Allen

Career: 1936   Position: ss
Team: *Memphis Red Sox*

The shortstop played with the Memphis Red Sox one season before they became charter members of the Negro American League.

Allen

Career: 1940–43   Position: of
Teams: Birmingham Black Barons ('40), New York Black Yankees ('43)

An outfielder named Allen played with the Birmingham Black Barons and the New York Black Yankees during the early years of the 1940s. It is thought that they are the same player.

Allen, Clifford (Crooks, Clyde)

Career: 1932–38   Positions: p, *of*
Teams: Baltimore Black Sox ('32), Hilldale Daisies ('32), Atlantic City Bacharach Giants ('32), Philadelphia Stars ('33), Homestead Grays ('37), Memphis Red Sox ('38)

The pitcher began and ended his seven-year career with championship teams, tailoring a 3–1 record with the Baltimore Black Sox, who were leading the East-West League in 1932 when the league disbanded, and finishing as a pitcher-left fielder with the 1938 Memphis Red Sox, first-half champions of the Negro American League. In between he served tours of duty with three other eastern teams, including the 1937 Homestead Grays when they won the first of nine consecutive Negro National League pennants.

Allen, David (Dave)

Career: 1887   Positions: c, 1b
Teams: *Pittsburgh Keystones ('87)*, Cuban Giants ('87)

He was a first baseman for the Pittsburgh Keystones, one of eight teams that were charter members of the League of Colored Baseball Clubs in 1887. However, the league's existence was ephemeral, lasting only a week. Later in the season, he was a catcher and utility player for the Cuban Giants, who were representing Trenton, New Jersey, in the Middle States League.

Allen, Homer

Career: 1932   Position: p
Team: Monroe Monarchs

He was a pitcher with the Monroe Monarchs

in 1932, when the Negro Southern League was designated major-league status.

Allen, Hoses (Buster)

Career: 1942–47   Positions: **p,** of

Teams: Jacksonville Red Caps ('42), Cincinnati Clowns ('43), Cincinnati-Indianapolis Clowns ('45), Cleveland Buckeyes ('46), Indianapolis Clowns ('47), Memphis Red Sox ('47)

During the '40s he pitched without distinction for several Negro American League teams, primarily with the Clowns at their various franchise locations.

Allen, Major

Career: 1919–22   Positions: **2b,** ss, 3b

Teams: Brooklyn Royal Giants ('19), New York Lincoln Giants ('19–'20), *Madison Stars ('20), Washington Braves ('21)*, Baltimore Black Sox ('22)

A light hitter, he was a part-time starter with the 1919 New York Lincoln Giants as a middle infielder, splitting his playing time between shortstop and second base and hitting .241 against all opposition. A Howard University man, after leaving the Lincoln Giants he played with lesser teams until joining the Baltimore Black Sox in 1922 and closing out his career when he quit the team in June.

Allen, Newton Henry (Newt, Colt)

Career: 1922–44; 1947 Positions: **2b,** 3b, ss, of, 1b, manager

Teams: *All Nations ('22)*, **Kansas City Monarchs** ('22–'44), St. Louis Stars ('31), Detroit Wolves ('32), Homestead Grays ('32), *voluntarily retired ('45–'46)*; Indianapolis Clowns ('47)

Bats: Right   Throws: Right
Height: 5'8"   Weight: 160
Born: May 19, 1901, Austin, Tex.
Died: June 11, 1988, Cincinnati, O.

Considered the best second baseman during the 1920s and early 1930s, the wide-ranging, slick-fielding middle infielder had quick hands and was superb on the pivot in turning a double play. Although playing primarily at the keystone sack, he was a fine infielder at any position. He was quick in the field and on the bases, and was an aggressive base runner and a rough slider who utilized his speed to take extra bases as well as to steal bases. An excellent bunter and consistent hitter with good bat control who went with the pitch, he was an ideal player to have hit in the second slot in the lineup.

His twenty-three-year career was spent almost entirely with the Kansas City Monarchs. His progression to the Monarchs was rapid. While attending Lincoln High School in Kansas City, he helped organize an amateur team, the Kansas City Tigers, and soon graduated to the semipro ranks with the Omaha Federals in 1921, where he was discovered by J. L. Wilkinson, owner of both the Monarchs and the All Nations ballclub. Allen was assigned to the All Nations team, but at the end of his first season, 1922, he was promoted to the Monarchs.

In the first phase of his career, the second sacker sparked the defense and served as captain as the Monarchs captured Negro National League pennants in 1923–25 and 1929. In 1924, the first World Series was held between the Negro National League and the Eastern Colored League, and Allen hit .282 with seven doubles as the Monarchs edged Hilldale in a hard-fought best-of-nine series that featured four one-run games and a tie. In a rematch the following season, Allen hit .259 as the Monarchs lost to Hilldale, after having defeated the St. Louis Stars in a playoff for the Negro National League flag. The next season the Monarchs lost their bid for a fourth straight pennant when they lost the league playoff to the Chicago American Giants by dropping a doubleheader on the last day, needing only one victory to win the pennant.

Three years later the Monarchs won their last Negro National League flag by decisively winning both halves of the split season. No World Series was held that season, and a year later the Monarchs disbanded temporarily. In addition to his Golden Glove performance in the field, the slender infielder hit for averages of .277, .308, .259, .334, .280, .330, and .345 for the previous seven seasons with the Monarchs (1924–30).

The following season, Allen joined the St. Louis Stars, where he paired with fellow Austinite Willie Wells to form the best double-play combination in baseball. The Stars went on to win the last Negro National League pennant, with Allen returning to the Monarchs in late summer when they reorganized. He hit for a combined .274 average for the season, following with a .326 average the next year.

But the Depression years were hard ones for Allen and the Monarchs, as they began touring as an independent team after the demise of the Negro National League. During those years, records are sketchy, but the slick fielder hit .290 in 1936, the last season for the Monarchs as a traveling independent club.

In 1937 the Monarchs entered the newly formed Negro American League and promptly dominated it, winning five of the first six pennants, with Allen contributing averages of .363, .273, .255, .323, .305, and .272, respectively, during this last phase of his playing career. Just as he had played in the first World Series between the Eastern Colored League and the original Negro National League in 1924, he also played in the first World Series played between the Negro American League and the new Negro National League in 1942. The Monarchs defeated the great Homestead Grays, with Allen contributing a .267 batting average while playing third base.

Popular with the fans even in the latter years of his career, he was selected to the East-West All-Star game four times, 1936–38 and 1941, playing both second base and shortstop in the annual classic but going hitless for his four appearances.

Having served a stint as manager of the Monarchs in 1941, he took the reins of the Indianapolis Clowns for the 1947 season, his last year in the Negro Leagues. The superior gloveman proved to be more than adequate

with a bat as well, finishing with a lifetime batting average of .290, being credited with a .301 average against major leaguers in exhibitions, and showing a .278 average for two winter seasons in Cuba. Allen's two winters on that island were separated by a dozen years, with him hitting .313 with Almendares early in his career (1924–25) and .269 with Havana in the latter part of his career (1937–38). During his career Allen also played winters in California, Mexico, Puerto Rico, and Venezuela and toured the Orient in 1935–36 with the Monarchs, playing exhibitions while touring Japan and the Philippines. After retiring from baseball, he participated in Kansas City Democratic Party politics.

Some controversy remains about whether Allen was a switch-hitter, but evidence indicates that while he probably batted from both sides early in his career, he abandoned the practice later in his career.

Allen, Todd

Career: 1911–25   Positions: **3b,** manager
Teams: **Indianapolis ABCs** ('11–'15, '25), Bowser's ABCs ('16), Jewell's ABCs ('17), New York Lincoln Giants ('18–'19), Chicago American Giants
Bats: Right   Throws: Right

A good line-drive hitter who "choked up" on the bat for better contact, the solid-fielding third baseman began his career in the black big time with C. I. Taylor's Indianapolis ABCs in 1915, batting .255 with four home runs and 18 stolen bases in 41 games, despite missing some playing time due to a split finger. The following season, when a management schism split the franchise into two ballclubs, he went with owner Thomas Bowser's ABCs squad, while C. I. Taylor installed his brother Candy Jim Taylor as the hot corner on the other ABCs team. After Bowser's team fragmented, Allen anchored third base and batted cleanup for Jewell's ABCs in 1917.

In addition to his stints with the various ABCs teams, he also played with the Chicago American Giants and the New York Lincoln

Giants, where he hit .343 against all levels of opposition in 1919, before returning to Indianapolis in 1925 to manage the ABCs. During his tenure as skipper, he pinch hit and occasionally filled in as an outfielder. That was to be his last year with a top black baseball club.

Allen, Toussaint L'Ouvertre (**Tom**)
Career: 1914–26   Positions: **1b**, 3b
Teams: Havana Red Sox ('14, '17), *Pop Watkins' All-Stars ('16), Pittsburgh Stars of Buffalo ('17), Philadelphia Giants ('17), Military Service ('18),* **Hilldale Daisies** ('19–'24), Wilmington Potomacs ('25), Newark Stars ('26)
Bats: Right   Throws: Left
Born: 1896, Atlanta, Ga.

Although he was a good-fielding first baseman and was not noted for his hitting, he managed a .306 average against all levels of competition in 1919, his first year with Hilldale. He also hit for averages of .283, .344, .261, and .275, respectively, in 1921–24, and was on the club's pennant-winning teams in 1923 and 1924, the first two years of the Eastern Colored League's existence. In the latter year he played in the first Negro World Series between the Eastern Colored League and the Negro National League.

Although primarily identified with Hilldale, he also played with other, lesser-known teams during his thirteen-year career. After entering the Army during World War I, he served overseas in the French Army's 349th Battalion. He was a heavy drinker and later in life may also have developed a drug addiction.

Allen, William
Career: 1887   Position: player
Team: *Cincinnati Browns*

He played on one of the earliest black teams, the Cincinnati Browns, one of eight teams that were charter members of the League of Colored Baseball Clubs in 1887. However, the league's existence was ephemeral, lasting only a week. His position is uncertain.

Allison
Career: 1915–25   Positions: c, 1b, 2b
Teams: Chicago American Giants ('15–'17), Chicago Union Giants, Nashville Elite Giants ('21), Indianapolis ABCs ('25)

A nondescript player during a checkered ten-year span, he appeared at a variety of positions, but primarily as a catcher, for a variety of teams, mostly in the Chicago area, but never performed with any appreciable consistency. In 1915, with Rube Foster's Chicago American Giants, he hit only .173 as a reserve catcher.

Almas
Career: 1925   Position: p
Team: Cuban Stars (West)

He pitched with the 1925 Cuban Stars of the Negro National League, but his playing time was limited.

Almeida, Rafael D.
a.k.a. Almeyda
Career: 1904–05   Position: 3b
Team: All Cubans
Bats: Right   Throws: Right
Height: 5'9"   Weight: 164
Born: July 30, 1887, Havana, Cuba

A white Cuban, he was a graceful fielder and demonstrated good speed and average power as a third baseman with the 1905 All Cubans team. He later played three seasons (1911–13) in the major leagues with the Cincinnati Reds, batting .313 in 1911 and averaging .270 for his career.

Almenteros, Juan Pablo
a.k.a. Armentero
Career: 1916   Position: p
Team: New York Cuban Stars

He was one of the top pitchers on owner Alejandro Pompez's New York Cuban Stars in 1916, his only season in black baseball.

Almeyda
[see Almeida, Rafael D.]

Alonzo, Rogelio
Career: 1925–30   Positions: p, rf, 1f
Team: Cuban Stars (West)

He was a pitcher-outfielder with the 1925–30 Cuban Stars (West) of the Negro National League. As a pitcher, incomplete statistics show losing records for the last four seasons, exclusive of 1928. As a hitter, he hit .209 and .274 in 1927 and 1929, respectively, while demonstrating good speed and average power.

Alsop
Career: 1920–22   Position: p
Team: Kansas City Monarchs

A pitcher from Salina, Kansas, he was an infrequently utilized member of the Kansas City Monarchs' pitching staff during the first three seasons of the Negro National League's existence.

Alvarez, Raul
Career: 1924–33   Position: p
Teams: Cuban Stars (West) ('24–'27), Cuban Stars (East) ('28), Cuban Stars ('31–'32)
Bats: Right   Throws: Right

During his ten-year career the right-hander pitched with the Cuban Stars when they were affiliated with three different leagues: the Negro National League, the Eastern Colored League and the East-West League.

Amoros, Edmundo Isasi (Sandy)
a.k.a. Amoro
Career: 1950   Position: of
Teams: New York Cubans ('50), *minor leagues ('52–'54, '58–'59, '61)*, major leagues ('52, '54–'57, '59–'60), *Mexican League ('62)*
Bats: Left   Throws: Left
Height: 5'8"   Weight: 170
Born: Jan. 30, 1930, Havana, Cuba
Died: June 27, 1992, Miami, Fla.

The youngster came along near the end of the Negro Leagues, playing first base and outfield for the New York Cubans in 1950 and hitting .338 for the season. Later signed with the Dodgers, he is best remembered for his catch down the left-field line, robbing Yogi Berra of a double in the 1955 World Series, when the Dodgers won their first World Championship.

That year marked his first full season in the majors, after spending the previous two seasons in the International League, where he hit .353 in 1953 (and led Montreal hitters in batting average, doubles, hits, runs, and total bases) and followed with a .352 average in 1954. He earned his first call to the parent club after hitting .337 for St. Paul of the American Association in 1952. After being sent down again in 1958, he returned to the majors for brief and unproductive stints with the Los Angeles Dodgers and Detroit Tigers, and finished his major-league career in 1960 with a .255 BA and three World Series under his belt. He returned to the minors for two more years and, in his last season in organized ball, hit .305 with Mexico City in 1962, finishing with a career minor-league average of .308.

Playing with Havana in the Cuban winter league, he won the batting title in 1952–53 with a .373 average. Beginning in 1950–51, he registered averages of .286, .333, .373, .322, and .307 for five consecutive winters and finished with a lifetime Cuban winter league average of .330.

Anderson
Career: 1908–12   Positions: p, 3b
Team: Cuban Giants

He made two appearances with the Cuban Giants, first as a pitcher in 1908 and as a third baseman in 1912.

Anderson, Lewis
Career: 1930–33   Position: c
Teams: Chicago American Giants ('30), Baltimore Black Sox ('33)

He held spots on the rosters as a reserve catcher for the Chicago American Giants and the Baltimore Black Sox during his brief career.

Anderson, Ralph
Career: 1932   Position: of

Teams: *Nashville Elite Giants ('27)*, Indianapolis ABCs ('32), Homestead Grays ('32)

After gaining experience in the Negro Southern League with the Nashville Elite Giants in 1927, the outfielder made an appearance in the big time in 1932 with the Indianapolis ABCs and the Homestead Grays.

Anderson, Robert James (**Bobby**)
Career: 1915–25   Positions: **ss, 2b,** 3b,
                                              of, *p*
Teams: Chicago Giants ('16, '20, '25), *Peters' Union Giants* ('15), Chicago American Giants, *Gilkerson's Union Giants, Philadelphia Giants*

Often with marginal teams during his career, he played shortstop and second base for over a decade, mostly with Chicago-based teams. In 1920, the inaugural season of the Negro National League, he was a reserve infielder and gleaned some playing time at shortstop with the Chicago Giants when John Beckwith played behind the plate.

Anderson, Theodore (**Bubbles**)
Career: 1922–25   Positions: **2b,** c
Teams: Kansas City Monarchs ('22–'23), Washington Potomacs ('24), Birmingham Black Barons ('24), Indianapolis ABCs ('25)

A good fielder with average speed and long-ball capability, he began his career with the Kansas City Monarchs in 1922. After two years in Kansas City, he moved East and started the 1924 season at second base for the Washington Potomacs but soon was released and not reserved for 1925. He eventually landed a spot with the ABCs, but after having contracted a social disease, he was sent home and never returned to the ballclub. He died in Denver in the latter years of the '20s.

Anderson, William
Career: 1927–31   Position: of
Teams: Nashville Elite Giants ('27, '30), Birmingham Black Barons ('31)

The outfielder made brief appearances with the Nashville Elite Giants, both in the Negro Southern League and the Negro National League, hitting .290 with average power in limited play as a right fielder in 1930. He closed his short career in 1931 as a right fielder with the Birmingham Black Barons, a year after the club dropped out of the Negro National League.

Anderson, William (**Bill**)
Career: 1940–47   Position: p
Teams: **New York Cubans** ('41–'47), Cuban Stars, Brooklyn Royal Giants ('40), Philadelphia Stars
Bats: Right   Throws: Right
Height: 5'10"   Weight: 181
Born: 1911

Anderson was a starting pitcher for the New York Cubans during the 1940s. Most seasons, he enjoyed only modest success and was basically an average pitcher with a good curve and control. In addition to his curve, he employed a fastball, drop, slider, and a change-up, but in 1941 the Homestead Grays accused him of having another (and illegal) pitch in his arsenal, alleging that he was "cutting" the ball and "making it do funny things." Their contention was never proven conclusively. His record against league competition that season was 2–3 with a 3.72 ERA.

After World War II he had a 3–2 record in 1946, and the next season the Cubans won the Negro National League pennant and World Series. At the plate he was a good-hitting pitcher and signed to play winter ball in Venezuela in 1944–45, but returned to the New York Cubans for the regular season. His eight-year career also included stays with the Cuban Stars, Brooklyn Royal Giants, and Philadelphia Stars.

Andrews, Herman (**Jabo**)
a.k.a. Jabbo
Career: 1930–43   Positions: **rf, 1f**, cf, 1b,
                                              p, manager
Teams: Birmingham Black Barons ('30, '40), Memphis Red Sox ('30–'32), Indianapolis ABCs ('31–'32, '39), Detroit Wolves ('32), Homestead Grays ('32), Pittsburgh Crawfords ('32, '37), Columbus Blue Birds ('33), New

York Cubans ('36), Washington Black Senators ('38), Cleveland Bears ('39), Jacksonville Red Caps ('42), Chicago American Giants ('42), Philadelphia Stars ('43)

Bats: Left   Throws: Left
Height: 6'3"   Weight: 190

A big, tall, slender outfielder, he was a good hitter with power and very fast afoot but only a fair defensive player. A well-traveled player, his bat kept him in the lineup and he proved to be a solid outfielder for many seasons with numerous ballclubs, averaging almost a team per season during his fourteen-year career.

He began his career with southern teams, hitting .388 for the 1930 season, and the next year he was playing right field and hitting third for manager Candy Jim Taylor's Indianapolis ABCs. In 1932 he divided the season among three teams, starting the season with the Detroit Wolves, who were leading the East-West League when they consolidated with the Homestead Grays, and also playing with the Pittsburgh Crawfords, where he hit .482 with nine doubles and six triples in only 17 games. The next season, with the Columbus Blue Birds, he hit .383, and he showed a .308 batting average in 1936.

After the 1938 season, with his skills fading, he worked hard all winter to get himself back in shape by playing on the shop team in Birmingham, and in the early spring of 1939, apparently facing the new season without the prospect of a job, he wrote Abe Manley, asking for a tryout with the Newark Eagles. His desperation was evident in his indication that if he made the team, there would be no money problem. However, Manley did not seek his services, and the veteran outfielder signed on with the Atlanta Black Crackers, who moved to Indianapolis in 1939 and played as the ABCs. Andrews batted cleanup and hit 13 homers for the season.

In his rookie season, while splitting the year between the Memphis Red Sox and the Birmingham Black Barons, he also pitched, going winless in his few outings, and intermittently throughout his career, continued to pitch on infrequent occasions. Late in his career he contracted tuberculosis, left the baseball scene, and was forgotten.

Andrews, Pop
Career: 1905–19   Positions: **p**, of, 1b, 2b
Teams: **Brooklyn Royal Giants** ('05–'12, '14), Pittsburgh Stars of Buffalo ('16, '19), Philadelphia Giants ('13), Havana Red Sox

A slowball pitcher for the Brooklyn Royal Giants in the deadball era, he was one of the most notable players on the team, oftimes playing in the outfield or infield when not on the mound.

Anthony, Lavance Peter (**Pete**)
Career: 1950   Position: c
Teams: Houston Eagles ('50), New York Cubans ('50)

A reserve catcher with the Houston Eagles in 1950, he lacked defensive skills and, in limited action, batted only .148 with a high strikeout frequency.

Anthony, Thad
Career: 1950   Position: c
Team: Baltimore Elite Giants

He was a reserve catcher for a brief time with the Baltimore Elite Giants in 1950, and his playing time was severely restricted.

Arango, Angel
Career: 1913   Positions: 2b, ss
Team: Long Branch Cubans

A white player, he was a middle infielder with the Long Branch, New Jersey, Cubans in 1913, his only year of participation in black baseball.

Arango, Luis (Pedro)
a.k.a. Orango
Career: 1925–39   Positions: **3b**, 1b, ss
Teams: **Cuban Stars (West)** ('25–'31), Cuban Stars ('32–'34), New York Cubans ('35–'39)
Bats: Right   Throws: Right
Born: Cuba

Playing on both corners, primarily at the hot

corner, he was a good ballplayer for the Cuban Stars and New York Cubans. He was a good hitter with some power and usually batted in the heart of the order. Early in his career, in 1926, he hit .317, but partial statistics indicate a declining average during the latter years of his career. In 1935, when the New York Cubans won the second-half Negro National League title and faced the Pittsburgh Crawfords in the championship playoffs, he slipped to .200 for the season. However, the paucity of available statistics from the Depression years precludes this from being considered as absolute.

He played in Santo Domingo in 1936, splitting time afield between shortstop and third base, and hit fourth in the batting order for the Eastern Stars. In his prime, playing in the winter league in his homeland, the Cuban infielder helped Cienfuegos win the 1929–30 Cuban championship.

Arbuckle
Career: 1918   Position: p
Team: Chicago American Giants
He pitched one game for the Chicago American Giants in 1918, without a decision.

Archer
Career: 1919–24   Positions: p, *c*
Teams: New York Lincoln Giants ('19–'20), Baltimore Black Sox ('22), *Philadelphia Giants ('24)*
The Buffalo native pitched without distinction for a trio of teams for a half-dozen seasons, with his best effort coming in 1922, when he was 5–3 with the Baltimore Black Sox when they were still playing as an independent ballclub.

Arencibia, Eduardo (Edward)
Career: 1948   Position: of
Team: New York Cubans
Bats: Left   Throws: Left
In 1948, his only year in the Negro Leagues, the Latin American left-hander was a reserve right fielder for the New York Cubans.

Arguelles, Martinano
[see Martinano Arguelles Garay]

Argyle Hotel Athletics
Duration: 1885   Honors: None
Affiliation: *Independent*
Organized by headwaiter Frank P. Thompson, the team was regarded as the springboard for the first professional black baseball club. Comprised of players from the Philadelphia Keystones (a strong amateur club) who doubled as waiters, the team represented the Argyle Hotel of Babylon, New York, and played for the enjoyment of summer tourists at the Long Island resort community. Encouraged by a successful summer (6 wins, 2 losses, and 1 tie), and playing under the management of white entrepreneur John F. Lang, the team added numerous new players from the Philadelphia Orions and the Manhattens of Washington, D.C., and began touring as the Cuban Giants.

Ariosa, Mario (Homero)
Career: 1947–49   Positions: **of**, 2b, 3b
Team: New York Cubans
Bats: Right   Throws: Right
Height: 6'0"   Weight: 175
Born: Sept. 12, 1920, Remedios, Cuba
He was an outfielder with the New York Cubans in 1947–49. In limited action during the championship season of 1947, he batted only .194, but by 1949 he had raised his average to .260. He headed south of the border to Mexico during the 1949 campaign and played in the Mexican League for the remainder of his career, finishing twenty years later with a lifetime average of .314. In general he was an able base stealer and had above-average power. His best year was 1955, when he hit .335 with 22 home runs in 103 games.

Armistead, Jimmie
a.k.a. Armstead
Career: 1938–49   Positions: **of**, p
Teams: Indianapolis ABCs ('38), St. Louis

Stars ('38–'39), Baltimore Elite Giants ('40–'46), Philadelphia Stars ('49)

A reserve outfielder for the Baltimore Elite Giants during the 1940 season, he played briefly in right field and batted .294. He began his career as a pitcher with the Indianapolis ABCs and St. Louis Stars in 1938, and closed out his career as an outfielder with the Philadelphia Stars in 1949.

Armentero
[see Juan Pablo Almenteros]

Armour
Career: 1933   Positions: p, 3b
Team: Detroit Stars

He was a reserve third baseman and also pitched without a decision for the Detroit Stars in 1933.

Armour, Alfred (Buddy)
Career: 1936–50   Positions: **lf**, rf, cf, ss,
                                         3b
Teams: **St. Louis Stars** ('36–'39), Indianapolis ABCs ('38), New York Black Yankees ('40), New Orleans-St. Louis Stars ('40–'41), Harrisburg-St. Louis Stars ('43), Cleveland Buckeyes ('44–'46), Chicago American Giants ('47–'48), Homestead Grays ('50), *Canadian League ('49–'51)*
Bats: Left   Throws: Right
Height: 5'9"   Weight: 170
Born: 1915, Jackson, Miss.

A left-handed batter, he was a fine hitter with a good eye and hit well over .300 many seasons, but without much power. An accomplished base stealer, he also utilized his speed on the bases to stretch singles into doubles. As an outfielder, he had good range and a fine throwing arm, which he coupled with his quickness to plug a hole at shortstop for the St. Louis Stars in 1939 and 1941. He was no stranger to the position, having played there in 1938 with the ABCs before the franchise abandoned Indianapolis for St. Louis. He was the second-place hitter for the ABCs but moved into the third slot with the Stars. He

played with the Stars when the franchise shared home sites with New Orleans and Harrisburg, leaving after the 1943 season to join the Cleveland Buckeyes. There, he played left field and hit .299 while batting in the cleanup slot for much of the 1944 season.

He followed with a .325 average as the Buckeyes won the Negro American League pennant and then swept the Homestead Grays in the World Series to claim the 1945 Negro Leagues championship. In the third game of the Series he had three hits, including two doubles and two RBIs, to spark the Buckeyes to a 4–0 victory, and finished with a .308 average for the Series. In 1946 he slipped to a .245 batting average for the Buckeyes, but rebounded the following season to make the all-star squad. During his 12 years in the Negro Leagues he played in three All-Star games, hitting an even .500 with five hits in ten times at bat. His appearances were with the St. Louis Stars ('41), Cleveland Buckeyes ('44), and Chicago American Giants ('47).

He left the Negro Leagues to play with Farnham in the Canadian Provincial League, leading the league in batting in 1949 with a .342 average. He remained in Canada with Granby for two more seasons, and although his average dropped (.290 and .262), he maintained a good on-base percentage and continued his impressive base thefts. After he left baseball, he returned to his home in Carbondale, Illinois.

Armstead, Jimmie
[see Jimmie Armistead]

Armstrong
Career: 1913   Position: c
Team: Chicago Giants

He was a catcher with Frank Leland's Chicago Giants in 1913, his only season in black baseball.

Arnet
Career: 1921   Position: p
Team: Atlantic City Bacharach Giants

He was undistinguished as a pitcher with the

Bacharachs in 1921, when they were still playing as an independent team.

Arnold, Paul
Career: 1926–36   Positions: 1f, cf
Teams: Hilldale ('26), Brooklyn Royal Giants ('27), Newark Browns ('31–'32), Newark Dodgers ('34–'35), *Atlantic City Bacharach Giants ('36)*
Bats: Left   Throws: Right

The light-complexioned outfielder was a good hitter, averaging about .300, with a modicum of power. Defensively he was a good hustler, but demonstrated only average ability in running, fielding, and throwing. He began his career in the Eastern Colored League with Hilldale, hitting only .200 in extremely limited play, but after moving to the Brooklyn Royal Giants the following season, he was installed in left field and hit .304 while batting in the leadoff position.

He later played with the Newark Dodgers during their two seasons in the Negro National League (1934–35) and was selected for the East squad in the 1935 All-Star game, playing as a replacement in center field for Martin Dihigo when the big Cuban was called in from center field as a relief pitcher in the late innings.

Arumis, Aran (Arumi)
Career: 1920   Positions: rf, 2b
Team: Kansas City Monarchs

In his only season in the Negro Leagues, he was a reserve player with the Kansas City Monarchs in 1920, the first year of the Negro National League, and played both second base and right field.

Asbury
Career: 1918   Position: p
Team: New York Lincoln Giants

A pitcher of unproven capability, he pitched without a decision for the 1918 Lincoln Giants.

Ascanio, Carlos
Career: 1946   Position: 1b
Team: New York Black Yankees
Bats: Left   Throws: Left

The left-hander played first base for the 1946 Black Yankees on occasions when Bud Barbee, the starting first baseman, pitched or played in the outfield. When he was in the lineup, Ascanio usually batted in the second slot in the order.

Ash, Rudolph
a.k.a. Rudolph
Career: 1920, 1926   Positions: **rf**, 1f, *p*
Teams: Chicago American Giants ('20), Newark Stars ('26), Hilldale Daisies ('26), *Chappie Johnson's Stars ('27)*

He was a reserve outfielder throughout his career, playing briefly with the Chicago American Giants in 1920 and the Newark Stars and Hilldale Daisies in 1926. He was sometimes listed in box scores under his first name.

Ashby, Earl
Career: 1945–48   Position: c
Teams: Cleveland Buckeyes ('45), Homestead Grays ('47), Birmingham Black Barons ('47), Newark Eagles ('48), *Canadian League ('50)*
Bats: Right   Throws: Right
Height: 5'11"   Weight: 185
Born: 1921, Havana, Cuba

In 1945, as a twenty-four-year-old rookie during his first year in the United States, the Havana-born player was the backup catcher for the Negro American League champion Cleveland Buckeyes. The free swinger hit for a .286 average in his backup role.

Two years later he became one of the players the Homestead Grays tried as a possible replacement for Josh Gibson after the great slugger's death. But his arm was erratic, his overall defensive skills lacking, his foot speed unimpressive, his batting mediocre (.254), his power at the plate only average, and, like the others, he was unable to fill the void adequately.

Later in the season, he was "loaned" to the Birmingham Black Barons, and he remained in the Negro Leagues through the 1948 season.

In 1950 he played in the Canadian Provincial League, registering a .292 average for his year north of the border.

Ashford
Career: 1944   Position: c
Team: Newark Eagles

He was a wartime reserve catcher for the Newark Eagles in 1944, his only year in the Negro Leagues. He was fourth on the depth chart, and consequently his playing was severely restricted.

Ashport
Career: 1913   Position: 3b
Team: *Havana Red Sox*

He played third base for the 1913 Havana Red Sox, a team of marginal quality.

Askari
[see Rogers Pierre]

Atame
Career: 1920   Position: p
Team: Kansas City Monarchs

He pitched in two games with the Kansas City Monarchs in 1920, the first year of the Negro National League and his only year in the Negro Leagues.

Atkins, Abe
Career: 1923   Positions: ss, 3b
Team: Toledo Tigers

In his only season in the Negro Leagues, he played shortstop and third base with the Toledo Tigers, who disbanded in July of 1923, their only season in the Negro National League.

Atkins, Joseph O. (**Joe**, Leroy)
Career: 1947   Positions: 1f, rf, 3b
Teams: *Pittsburgh Crawfords ('46)*, Cleveland Buckeyes ('47), *Canadian League ('48–51), minor leagues ('52–'54)*
Bats: Right   Throws: Right
Height: 6'1"   Weight: 190
Born: 1922, Pittsburgh, Pa.

A combination outfielder-third baseman, he was a good all-around player, although with only average speed. Offensively he was a free-swinger with good power and respected by pitchers, who pitched to him carefully. In 1947, as a rookie with the Negro American League's pennant-winning Cleveland Buckeyes, he hit .330 with a league-high ten home runs.

The following season, he jumped to Farnham in the Canadian Provincial League and hit .378 and 26 home runs. Still in Canada three years later, he hit 18 homers with Drummondville, but managed only a .268 average. The next season, 1952, he joined Tampa in the Florida International League but hit only .210 in limited play. The following season he played with Carman in the Mandak League and displayed good power along with his .294 average.

In 1954 he appeared in eight games with Ottawa in the International League and then disappeared from organized ball, ending a career begun in 1946 with the Pittsburgh Crawfords in the United States League and that included stays in Latin American leagues. His best performance in the tropics was in 1948–49, when he recorded his best average (.325) with Ponce in the Puerto Rican winter league.

Atkins, Stacy
[see Adkins, Stacy]

Atlanta Black Crackers
Duration: 1938   Honors: Second-half champions ('38)
Affiliations: Independent, NSL, NAL ('38)

Although the team played mostly in the Negro Southern League, during their one-year venture (1938) in the Negro American League, they won the second-half championship. At the beginning of the spring there were two separate teams vying to represent Atlanta in the Negro American League, but after the two squads finally merged into a single team carrying the name of the Atlanta Black Crackers, they continued to improve until they copped the second-half title. In the scheduled playoff against the first-half champion Memphis Red Sox, they lost the first two games played, but after conflict due to game cancellations, the league president ruled the unfinished series a "no contest," and a league champion was undetermined.

The following season, for financial reasons, the franchise moved to Indianapolis and played in the Negro American League under the name of the Indianapolis ABCs. However, once again financial difficulties led to their dropping from league play and disbanding. They later reorganized and returned to play in the Negro Southern League.

Augustine, Leon
Career: 1923   Position: umpire
League: Negro National League
In 1923, he was an umpire in the Negro National League.

Augustus
Career: 1927   Position: p
Team: Memphis Red Sox
He pitched briefly as one of the many young pitchers used by the 1927 Memphis Red Sox, losing his only decision.

Aussa
Career: 1938–42   Positions: **2b**, c, 3b
Team: Ethiopian Clowns
A second baseman, he sometimes also played as a catcher and third baseman with the Ethiopian Clowns. It is difficult to identify properly many of the Clowns' players by their real name because ofttimes a name would belong to a position rather than to an individual, with different players sharing the same "Clown name" from year to year and sometimes from game to game.

Austin, Frank Samuel (Pee Wee, Junior)
Career: 1944–48   Position: ss
Team: Philadelphia Stars
Bats: Right   Throws: Right
Height: 5'7"   Weight: 168
Born: May 22, 1922, Panama Canal Zone
Died: Jan. 15, 1960, Panama City, Panama

The Panamanian was a smart base runner, excellent bunter, and good contact hitter who could execute the hit-and-run. Although he had only an average arm, he was one of the best shortstops afield, and his quickness made him dependable and thrilling to watch. A high average hitter but with only mediocre power at the plate, the Philadelphia Stars' rookie won the batting title in 1944 with an average of .390. He avoided the "sophomore jinx," finishing in the top ten batters with a .354 average and finishing fourth in stolen bases to earn a spot on the 1945 All-Star team. He continued his fine play in 1946–48 with .328, .284, and .316 batting averages, respectively, and made two more All-Star appearances the latter two years. The shortstop whiz finished his five-year career in black baseball with a lifetime .333 batting average. In 1945 he was compared to Jackie Robinson as a big-league prospect, but although he played ball winter and summer for the next ten years, he never got the chance to break into the majors.

Beginning in 1949, he signed with Newark of the International League but played only 19 games before being transferred to the Pacific Coast League, where he played for the next eight seasons. All except the last year was with Portland, with his best season on the Coast coming in 1951, when he hit .293. Except for the 1952 and 1953 seasons, his stolen base totals fell off dismally. His last season in organized ball was 1956, when he hit .285 with Vancouver. In the winter leagues, he always played impressively. During the winter of 1945–46 he played with Venezuela and Panama, and both clubs won championships. Most of his years in Panama were spent with Chesterfield, and his best season was in 1946–47, when he hit .357. In his last year in Panama (1954–55) he hit .331.

Austin, John
Career: 1887   Position: player
Team: *Cincinnati Browns*
He was a player with one of the earliest black professional teams, the Cincinnati

Browns, one of eight teams that were charter members of the League of Colored Baseball Clubs in 1887. However, the league's existence was ephemeral, lasting only a week. His position is uncertain.

Austin, Tank

Career: 1930–32   Position: p
Teams: Nashville Elite Giants ('30), Birmingham Black Barons ('30), *Atlanta Black Crackers ('32)*

Showing a 1–2 worksheet for his first season in the Negro National League, he pitched unimpressively for a trio of southern teams during his three-year tenure, but is best identified with the Birmingham Black Barons.

Averett

Career: 1943   Position: of
Team: New York Black Yankees

A wartime player, he appeared briefly as a reserve outfielder with the Black Yankees in 1943, his only year in the Negro Leagues.

Awkard, Russell

a.k.a. Russell
Career: 1940–41   Positions: cf, rf, *2b, ss*
Teams: New York Cubans ('40), Newark Eagles ('40–'41), *military service ('41–'45)*
Bats: Left   Throws: Right
Height: 5'10"   Weight: 145
Born: Oct. 7, 1917, Howard County, Md.

During his abbreviated two-year career, the Newark native played outfield for the New York Cubans and Newark Eagles, sometimes being listed by his first name in box scores. An outstanding fielder with an adequate arm, he had good range afield and sufficient speed to steal some bases. Usually batting at the top of the order, he was a spray hitter without significant power, and hit mostly to left field before learning to pull the ball late in the 1940 season.

As a youngster in Rockville, Maryland, he was late developing and did not play ball until his last year in high school, and then not as a regular. After graduation, he played sandlot ball until joining a semipro team managed by Ben Taylor. The team had an agreement with Clark Griffith for use of a park, and he earned $10 a week playing on Sundays. The next year, Taylor was coaching with the New York Cubans and recommended him to the Cubans, but the Eagles also wanted him. He opted for the Eagles, but during spring training, Eagles' owner Abe Manley loaned him to the New York Cubans for a season, and he finished with a .250 batting average for the year.

In 1941 Manley exercised his recall option, and Awkard opened the season in center field for the Eagles, but the next day was called to Washington, D.C., and inducted into the Army. He was replaced by Leon Day, who left the pitching rotation to play as an everyday player.

Entering the Army, he was assigned to the Quartermaster Corps and was shipped overseas in 1945, serving in England, Belgium, and France. After being discharged, he did not return to league play, choosing to work at a regular job and confine his baseball to the sandlot play. Initially he worked in the trucking business before gaining employment at the Navy Ordnance Laboratory, where he worked until retiring in 1980.

Aylor, James

Career: 1887   Position: player
Team: *Philadelphia Pythians*

Although his playing position is uncertain, he played with one of the earliest black professional ballclubs, the Philadelphia Pythians, one of eight teams that were charter members of the League of Colored Baseball Clubs in 1887. However, the league's existence was ephemeral, lasting only a week.

B

Bacharach Giants

Duration: 1916–34   Honors: ECL Pennants ('26–'27)

Affiliations: Independent ('16–'22, '30–'33), ECL ('23–'28), ANL ('29), NNL ('34)

The team originated in Jacksonville, Florida, as the Duval Giants and, in 1916, moved intact to Atlantic City, New Jersey, where they assumed the name Bacharach Giants in honor of the city's mayor, Harry Bacharach. Two black Atlantic City politicians, Tom Jackson and Henry Tucker, were responsible for moving the team North and bankrolling the team. They quickly became one of the top independent teams in the East, and when the Eastern Colored League was formed in 1923, the Bacharachs became a charter member and copped consecutive pennants in 1926 and 1927. In each of the ensuing Negro World Series, the Bacharachs lost to the Negro National League champion Chicago American Giants in a hotly contested Series.

The Bacharachs became the last Eastern Colored League pennant winner when the league folded during the 1928 season. The following year, 1929, the Bacharachs joined a replacement league, the American Negro League, which operated only a single season before falling victim to the Depression. The team struggled on as an independent ballclub until joining the Negro National League as a second-half addition in 1934. After this last league appearance, the team dropped dramatically in quality and soon disbanded. In later years a team of lesser status and quality of play took the name Bacharach Giants, but this was a completely different franchise.

Bagley

Career: 1937   Position: c
Team: Cincinnati Tigers

He was one of four catchers used as a backup for Cincinnati Tigers' manager Ted "Double Duty" Radcliffe, who doubled as the team's regular catcher in 1937.

Bailey

Career: 1910   Position: c
Team: Chicago Giants

A catcher from Honduras, he was with the Chicago Giants very briefly in 1910, but performed very poorly when given an opportunity to start behind the plate and had to be replaced during the game by pitcher Johnny "Steel Arm" Taylor.

Bailey

Career: 1932   Position: of
Team: Hilldale Daisies

He appeared briefly as a reserve outfielder with the Hilldale team in 1932, the club's last season of existence.

Bailey, Alonza

Career: 1935   Position: p
Team: Newark Dodgers

He pitched briefly with the Newark Dodgers in 1935, his only year in the Negro Leagues, but was not present when the Dodgers were consolidated with the Brooklyn Eagles to form the Newark Eagles in 1936.

Bailey, D.

Career: 1916–20   Positions: **of**, 3b, 2b, ss
Teams: New York Lincoln Stars ('16), Pennsylvania Red Caps of New York ('17–'20, '26–'28)

Most of his five-year career was spent in the deadball era, beginning his career with the Lincoln Stars in 1916 as a substitute, playing shortstop and in the outfield. When the franchise folded, he was among many ex-Stars who joined the Pennsylvania Red Caps of New York, a team comprised of railway redcaps working at New York's Pennsylvania Station. With the "ringers" signed from the Stars, the team fielded a highly competitive ballclub for a few seasons. With the Red Caps he played as a regular for three seasons, playing mostly third base and center field, while batting near the bottom of the order. In 1918 he hit .286 against all levels of competition, and although he continued to play with the team throughout the decade of the '20s, the Red Caps were not a major-league-caliber ballclub during the new decade.

Bailey, Otha S. (Bill)

Career: 1950   Position: c
Teams: Birmingham Black Barons ('50, '52–'59), *Chattanooga Choo Choos* ('50), Cleveland Buckeyes ('50), Houston Eagles ('50), *New Orleans Eagles* ('51)
Bats: Right   Throws: Right
Height: 5'6"   Weight: 150
Born: June 30, 1930, Huntsville, Ala.

The catcher made the jump from the sandlots to the black majors at a time when the quality of play in the Negro Leagues was declining. After playing with the Huntsville Pirates and the Huntsville Stars in 1949, he had a tryout with the Birmingham Black Barons, but was released in the spring of 1950. He then signed with manager Jim Canada's Chattanooga Choo Choos before joining the Negro American League's Cleveland Buckeyes. Leaving the Buckeyes, he joined the Houston Eagles, and stayed with the club when they relocated in New Orleans in the spring of 1951.

The scrappy little catcher had an accurate arm and was quick behind the plate, often beating the runner to first base while backing up a play. He also called a good game, studying the opposing hitters during batting practice to learn their weaknesses. He was fast enough to steal a few bases, and was a line-drive hitter without much power. In 1952 he found a spot on the Birmingham Black Barons' roster for the remainder of the decade. However, during these years the Negro Leagues were no longer quality leagues. One of the pitchers on the ballclub was Charlie Pride, who later became a country music star.

During the early '50s he barnstormed against major leaguers, and was scouted by the Boston Red Sox, but his size was against him. On another occasion he overslept and missed his tryout with the Dodgers. Finally, in 1959, he left baseball and took a regular job with Connor Steel in Birmingham.

Bailey, Percy (Bill)

Career: 1927–34   Position: p
Teams: Baltimore Black Sox ('27), Nashville Elite Giants ('33), Detroit Stars ('33), Cole's American Giants ('34), New York Black Yankees ('34)

He pitched in the Negro Leagues for eight seasons for a host of teams, beginning in 1927 with the Baltimore Black Sox and closing out his career in 1934 with the New York Black Yankees. In 1933 he registered a combined 7–3 worksheet while playing with both the Nashville Elite Giants and the Detroit Stars.

Bainerd

Career: 1919   Position: player
Team: Brooklyn Royal Giants

He played in one game with the Brooklyn

Royal Giants in 1919, collecting two hits in four at-bats. His position is uncertain.

Baird, Thomas Y. (**Tom**)
Career: 1920–50   Position: officer, owner
Team: Kansas City Monarchs
Died: July 2, 1962, Kansas City, Mo.

A white business associate of J. L. Wilkinson, he was connected with the Kansas City Monarchs for many years in several capacities, as a booking agent, officer, and coowner. In addition to his position with the Monarchs, he served as the booking agent for Negro American League exhibition games. Eventually, following the 1948 season, he bought out Wilkinson's interest in the franchise and transferred the operation across the state line to Kansas City, Kansas.

As a young man he played semipro ball in Kansas City, Kansas, but his career ended when he injured his leg in a railroad accident in 1918, leaving him with a permanent limp. He organized the T. Y. Baird Club and won two city championships. He began his association with J. L. Wilkinson in 1919, a year before Wilkinson organized the Kansas City Monarchs.

Initially Baird openly criticized Branch Rickey's signing of Jackie Robinson without compensating the Monarchs for relinquishing their rights. Under pressure from both the media and the public, he relented and publicly supported Robinson's entry into the major leagues, but privately he still resented not being paid for Robinson's contract.

Despite successfully recruiting, developing, and selling young players, he still was unable to compete financially with the major leagues, and after operating at a loss for several seasons, he sold the Monarchs during the '50s to Ted Rasberry, a former educator turned baseball businessman.

Afterward, working for the House of David, Baird showcased Babe Didrikson and Grover Cleveland Alexander for their gate appeal.

Baker, Bud
Career: 1937   Position: p
Team: New York Black Yankees

In 1937 the pitcher from Durham, North Carolina, was a twenty-one-year-old rookie for the New York Black Yankees, but he failed to break into the regular rotation and did not figure prominently in their season.

Baker, Edgar
Career: 1945–46   Position: p
Teams: Memphis Red Sox ('45), *Cleveland Clippers ('46)*

A wartime player, his career lasted only two years, beginning with a chance on the mound for the Memphis Red Sox in 1945, when he was winless against three losses. The next season he pitched with the Cleveland Clippers of the U.S. League.

Baker, Eugene Walter (**Gene**)
Career: 1948–50   Position: ss
Teams: Kansas City Monarchs ('48–'50), *minor leagues ('50–'53, '61–'62)*, major leagues ('53–'58, '60–'61), *voluntarily retired ('59)*
Bats: Right   Throws: Right
Height: 6'1"   Weight: 170
Born: June 15, 1925, Davenport, Ia.

Joining the Monarchs in 1948, in the last few years of black baseball's existence on a major-league level, he promptly hit .293 and fielded his position with sufficient prowess to earn consideration soon as the best shortstop in the Negro Leagues. Although the "sophomore jinx" dropped his average to .236 the following year, he still excelled afield and quickly caught the eye of major-league scouts. After beginning the 1950 season with the Monarchs, he was signed by the Chicago Cubs and assigned to their Des Moines farm club in the Western League, where he compiled an impressive .321 batting average to earn a promotion to the Los Angeles Angels of the Pacific Coast League.

With Los Angeles in the Pacific Coast League, 1950–53, he registered averages of .280, .278, .260, and .284, respectively, prior to joining the parent Chicago Cubs late in the 1953 season as a second baseman. In 1954 the versatile infielder mastered the transition to second base and earned a starting position pairing with Ernie Banks to form the first black keystone combination in major-league history. That season Baker hit .275 with 13 home runs and 32 doubles. After three years as the starting second baseman, he was traded to the Pittsburgh Pirates during the 1957 season and finished his eight-year major league career in 1961 with a .265 lifetime average.

Most of 1961 was spent with Batavia in the New York-Pennsylvania League, where he hit .387. He finished his professional baseball career with Columbus of the International League in 1962, and remained in baseball as a scout for the Pirates.

Baker, Henry
Career: 1925–32   Positions: rf, lf, 1b
Teams: Indianapolis ABCs ('25, '32), Dayton Marcos ('26), St. Louis Stars

A speedy outfielder, he began and ended his career in the side pastures with the ABCs, usually batting in either of the first two slots in the order, but he played at first base as a part-time starter with the Dayton Marcos in 1926, their only season in the Negro National League.

Baker, Howard (Home Run)
Career: 1910   Position: player
Team: Chicago Giants

He appeared briefly with Frank Leland's Chicago Giants in 1910.

Baker, Lamar
Career: 1950   Position: p
Team: New York Black Yankees

He was listed as a pitcher with the New York Black Yankees in 1950, when the Negro American League was struggling to survive the loss of players to organized baseball, but his playing time has not been confirmed by season statistics.

Baker, Norman (Bud)
Career: 1937   Position: p

Teams: Newark Eagles ('37), New York Black Yankees ('37)

The Washington, D.C., native pitched briefly with the Eagles and Black Yankees in 1937, his only year in the league.

Baker, Rufus (Scoop)
Career: 1943–50   Positions: ss, c, 2b, 3b, of
Team: New York Black Yankees

A versatile player, he was an excellent fielder but a weak hitter. In a partial season in 1943 he had only a .191 average, but in 1944, facing his first full season in the Negro National League, he was considered a whirlwind sensation at shortstop and was thought to have a long and bright future with the New York Black Yankees and in the Negro Leagues. But he had another dismal year at the plate, hitting only .173.

The following winter he completed a highly successful season of winter baseball in Puerto Rico, hitting with great confidence and continuing as a phenomenal fielder. His hitting carried over to the 1945 season, when he hit .241 for the Black Yankees. Unfortunately, he was not able to maintain even a semblance of that mark and returned to his previous level, with averages of .183 and .195 in 1946 and 1947, respectively. Despite his weak bat, in 1948 he was one of only eight players returning to the Black Yankees from the previous season. He also played outfield and even performed behind the plate as a receiver on occasion during his eight years with the Black Yankees.

Later in life he made his home in Bridgeport, Connecticut, where he was active with both the Boys' Club and Girls' Club.

Baker, Sam (Sammy)
Career: 1950   Position: p
Team: Chicago American Giants

The pitcher was listed with the Chicago American Giants in 1950, when the Negro American League was struggling to survive the loss of players to organized baseball, but his playing time has not been confirmed by season statistics.

Baker, Tom

Career: 1940   Position: p
Team: Baltimore Elite Giants

He pitched for the Elite Giants in 1940, but his playing time was severely restricted.

Baker, W. B.

Career: 1937–38   Position: business
                         manager
Team: Atlanta Black Crackers

In 1937–38 he was the business manager of the Atlanta Black Crackers, who played their only season in the Negro American League in his second season in this capacity.

Baldwin, Robert

Career: 1925–26   Positions: 2b, ss
Teams: Indianapolis ABCs ('25), Cleveland Elite Giants ('26), Detroit Stars ('26)

During his two seasons with three midwestern teams in the Negro National League, the middle infielder played shortstop for Cleveland and second base for Detroit, hitting a composite .200 in 1926.

Ball, George Walter

a.k.a. The Georgia Rabbit, The Black Diamond
Career: 1903–1923   Positions: p, of
Teams: *Augusta, Ga.*, Chicago Union Giants ('03, '05), Cuban X-Giants ('04), Philadelphia Giants, Brooklyn Royal Giants ('05, '13), **Leland Giants** ('05–'09), Quaker Giants ('06), St. Paul Colored Gophers ('07), *Keystones* ('08), **Chicago Giants** ('10–'11, '17–'21), St. Louis Giants ('12), Chicago American Giants ('12, '15), Mohawk Giants ('13), New York Lincoln Giants ('14), Milwaukee Giants
Bats: Right   Throws: Right
Born: Sept. 13, 1877, Detroit, Mich.
Died: Dec. 15, 1946, Chicago, Ill.

He was one of the best pitchers of the early years of black baseball. At the end of the first decade of the century, he, Rube Foster, Dan McClellan, and Harry Buckner were considered "head and shoulders above" other moundsmen. He was a smart pitcher with good control, and made frequent use of the spitball, but was not a power pitcher. Off the field, the premier hurler was noted for his sartorial splendor, wearing tailored suits and earning a reputation as the "swellest" dresser.

Ball pitched for eighteen years (1906–23), primarily on Chicago-based teams, including the Leland Giants, Chicago Giants, Chicago Union Giants, and Chicago American Giants. He also played with the Milwaukee Giants and was one of the first black pitchers to play in the Cuban winter league, spending three winters on the island and compiling a 9–16 record.

He began his baseball career in 1893 in St. Paul, Minnesota, on the Young Cyclones team and continued his formative baseball career playing with the Occola team in the City League and with other city teams. In 1899 he pitched for the Grand Forks, North Dakota, team in the Red River Valley League (later changed to the Northern League), and in his first season pitched 28 games and won 25 to lead the team to the North Dakota championship. After two seasons the young pitcher left Grand Forks and split the 1901 season with two teams, beginning with the Lakota, North Dakota, team before leaving to captain the York, North Dakota, team during the last half of the season. The following season, 1902, he pitched the St. Cloud, Minnesota, team to the championship of eastern Minnesota.

Returning to Grand Forks for the winter, Ball was contacted by manager Frank Leland and signed to play with the Chicago Union Giants for the 1903 season. This was the first black team with whom Ball had ever been associated. Previously he had been the only black player on white teams.

Ball's excellent play in Chicago attracted the attention of E. B. Lamar, manager of the famous Cuban X-Giants of New York. Signing with Lamar, Ball went East for the 1904 season, but after only one year he joined the Brooklyn Royal Giants for the first half of the 1905 season. At midseason he returned West to reunite with Leland as a starting pitcher for the Leland Giants, in their first year of existence. During the last half of the season, Ball's hurling contributed significantly to a winning streak of forty-eight games.

In 1906 Ball went back to New York, this time with the Quaker Giants, but the team disbanded on the first of July, and once again he returned to Chicago, finishing the season with the Leland Giants. In 1907, at the behest of St. Paul, Minnesota, businessmen Reid and Hirshfield, Ball organized, managed, and played for the St. Paul Colored Gophers. However, after a short while he again returned to Chicago to finish the season with Leland's team. The latter part of this season the Leland Giants played a series of games with an All-Star club at the White Sox grounds. Often playing in the outfield when not pitching, Ball made a phenomenal catch in right field in the last game, saving the championship for the Leland Giants.

In 1908 he went to Minnesota with the Keystones, but manager Leland again succeeded in getting Ball to return to his team, securing Ball's release from Keystones' owner Mitchell so he could finish the season in Chicago with the Leland Giants. After the season, Ball departed in December 1908 for Havana, Cuba, to play with the Fe club in the winter league. He pitched good ball on the island, losing only three games out of fifteen and snapping Almendares's five-year string of pennants.

The Cuban winter season closed March 31, 1909, and Ball returned to the United States, joining the Leland Giants in Memphis, Tennessee, in April. During the team's southern tour the star hurler did not suffer a single defeat. He opened the regular season May 1, 1909, for the Leland Giants, and during the season pitched twenty-five games in the City League, losing only once to top the league in winning percentage and lead the Lelands to a pennant. Records credit Ball with a 12–1 record for the season, with 70 strikeouts, 34 walks, 12 hit batsmen, and 1 wild pitch to go with a batting average of .238.

During the season, the Kansas City, Kansas

Giants arranged a three-game challenge series to determine the Colored Championship and offered a $1,000 purse to the winners. In the first game, Ball shut out the Kansas aggregation 5–0. Unfortunately, his fellow moundsmen could not duplicate his feat and lost the next two contests. Despite the Kansas team's claims, this was a midseason series, and by year's end other claimants for the title arose, including the St. Paul Colored Gophers, and a postseason Series was scheduled for the Western Championship. Rube Foster was injured and could not pitch in the Series, so the burden fell on Ball and Pat Dougherty. Ball pitched in two games but dropped his only decision as the Lelands lost the title. In a postseason exhibition series against the Chicago Cubs, he lost a 4–2 decision to Mordecai "Three Finger" Brown.

When owner Frank Leland and manager Rube Foster split in 1910, Ball remained with Leland and hit .359 for Leland's new team, the Chicago Giants, but injured his kneecap late in the season. He remained with Leland's Chicago Giants in 1911, but the following season he pitched with the St. Louis Giants, where he won 23 straight games against all levels of opposition. Three years later, in 1915, he was a member of Rube Foster's Chicago American Giants mound corps. One source indicates that he may also have pitched briefly with the Chicago American Giants in 1912 before joining the St. Louis Giants. Most of his later years were spent with lesser teams, including the Chicago Giants, who were in their declining years. With Chicago, fragmentary records show a 1–2 record against top teams in 1917 and a 0–3 ledger in league action in 1921.

Ballard
Career: 1910   Position: p
Team: Chicago Giants

He made a brief appearance as a pitcher with the Chicago Giants in 1910.

Ballesteros
Career: 1916   Position: p
Team: Long Branch Cubans

He pitched with the Long Branch Cubans in 1916 and is thought to have possibly been white, but not much is known about him.

Ballestro, Miguel (Pedro)
a.k.a. Ballester
Career: 1948   Positions: **ss**, 2b, 3b, 1b
Teams: New York Cubans ('48), *Canadian League ('51, '54), minor leagues ('52–'53), Mexican League ('55)*
Bats: Right   Throws: Right
Height: 5'8½"   Weight: 160
Born: 1925

A light hitter who could play any infield position, he played mostly as a middle infielder throughout his career. In 1948, his only season in the Negro Leagues, he played shortstop for the New York Cubans. He played two winters in Cuba, where he failed to hit impressively.

Beginning in 1951 he entered organized baseball with Sherbrooke of the Canadian Provincial League, where he batted .282 with some power, slapping 23 homers and 24 doubles. However, he failed to exhibit the same degree of prowess at Keokuk of the Three-I League in 1952, where he hit only .220, with ten homers. In successive stops in the Wisconsin State League, Provincial League, and Mexican League, he hit adequately (.315, .285, and .281, respectively), but failed to win a promotion to the big leagues. After the 1955 Mexican League season there is no record of him in baseball.

Ballew
Career: 1930   Position: p
Team: *Louisville White Sox*

He pitched for the Louisville White Sox in 1930, a year before they entered the Negro National League.

Baltimore Black Sox
Duration: 1916–34   Honors: League pennants ('29, '32)
Affiliations: ECL ('23–'28), ANL ('29), EWL ('32) independent ('16–'22, '30–'31), NNL ('33–'34)

The Black Sox started as an independent team in 1916 but was clearly not of major-league caliber at the onset. During the latter years of the deadball era, under the ownership and guidance of white businessmen George Rossiter and George Spedden, the ballclub improved the quality of play on into the early '20s, and attained major-league quality before joining the Eastern Colored League in 1923.

After becoming charter members of the league, the Black Sox fielded strong teams each season, but a pennant always eluded them. However, after the league folded during the 1928 season, a new league with essentially the same configuration but with a different name, the American Negro League, was organized, and the Black Sox won the pennant in 1929, the league's only year of existence, with a composite mark of 49–21 for the year.

The Black Sox then returned to independent status until joining the ill-fated East-West League in 1932. Baltimore started strong and was in first place, but unfortunately the league did not last through the season. Under new owner Joe Cambria, the Black Sox joined the new Negro National League when it was resurrected in 1933. The team moved to Bugle Field for their home games, and Cambria took the players off salaries and operated on a percentage basis in an effort to remain fiscally solvent during the Depression years. Following a poor performance, they dropped out of the league at the beginning of 1934, but were added for the second half of the season. After another dismal showing both on the field and financially, the franchise folded after the 1933 season.

In 1934 Jack Farrell, a black sportsman from Chester, Pennsylvania, appropriated the team name for his franchise and entered the Negro National League for the second half of the season. After a dismal performance the franchise folded following the season, leaving Baltimore without a major black team until the Elite Giants moved there in 1938.

Baltimore Elite Giants

Duration: 1938–50   Honors: Playoff champions ('39), League Championship Series ('49)

Affiliations: NNL ('38–'48), NAL ('49–'50)

Owner Tom Wilson's franchise originated in Nashville in 1921, evolving from the Nashville Standard Giants, and entered the Negro National League in 1930, but in search of a large population base for financial support, the team was subsequently moved to Columbus in 1935 and to Washington, D.C., in 1936–37, before finding a home in Baltimore in 1938.

The ballclub remained a fixture in the city for the next thirteen years. During the Elites' years in the Negro National League, the Homestead Grays was the dominant team, claiming nine consecutive titles, and competition was fierce between the two teams. The Elites battled them every year for league supremacy, and in 1939 the Elites claimed a tainted championship when they defeated the pennant-winning Grays in a four-team postseason tournament.

When the league folded after the 1948 season, the Elites joined the Negro American League, which assimilated the four remaining solvent franchises from the defunct Negro National League. In 1949, the first season of the restructured league and under the tutelage of new manager Lennie Pearson, the Elites won both halves of the split season to capture the Eastern Division title, and swept the Western Division's Chicago American Giants in four straight games to claim the league championship.

Tom Wilson was the force behind the Elites for a quarter century but, in declining health, he sold the franchise to longtime associate Vernon "Fat" Green in 1946. The franchise was floundering under his leadership, but he placed Dick Powell in charge of the team's operations in 1948. After Green's death Powell continued to run the team under power of attorney from Green's widow, and he temporarily resurrected the team for a final hurrah in 1949. But after slipping to second place in the East in 1950

and suffering financial problems, the club was sold to William Bridgeforth in the spring of 1951 for $11,000. After returning the team to Nashville for a final season, the team was dissolved and the Elite Giants' identity was lost.

Bames, Harry

Career: 1937   Position: c
Team: Birmingham Black Barons
Bats: Right   Throws: Right

The stocky catcher played with the Birmingham Black Barons in 1937, the inaugural year of the Negro American League.

Bankes, James

Career: 1950   Positions: **p**, rf, 1b
Teams: Baltimore Elite Giants ('50), *Memphis Red Sox ('51–'58)*

He pitched with the Elites in 1950, when the Negro American League was struggling to survive the loss of players to organized baseball. The following season he moved to the Memphis Red Sox and continued playing through the 1958 season as a pitcher, outfielder, and first baseman, but during the '50s the quality of the Negro American League was strictly at a minor-league level.

Bankhead, Daniel Robert (**Dan**)

Career: 1940–47   Positions: **p**, of
Teams: Chicago American Giants, **Birmingham Black Barons** ('40–'42), military service ('43–'45), **Memphis Red Sox** ('46–'47), *minor leagues ('47–'49, '51–'52)*, major leagues ('47, '50–'51), *Canadian League ('53), Mexican League ('54–'65)*
Bats: Right   Throws: Right
Height: 6'1"   Weight: 184
Born: May 3, 1920, Empire, Ala.
Died: May 2, 1976, Houston, Tex.

One of the five Bankhead brothers who played in the Negro Leagues, the hard-throwing right-hander had a blazing fastball and a tantalizing screwball. He capitalized on these attributes to earn a pitching spot in three All-Star games (1941, 1946, and 1947) during the 1940s, and was the winning pitcher in the 1947 contest. That year was a good one for Bankhead, as he defeated the New York Yankees in the spring while pitching with Caguas, Puerto Rico, and joined the Brooklyn Dodgers later in the season to become the first black pitcher in the major leagues. Bankhead was also a good hitter, and in his first major-league at-bat, he hit a home run. But that was a false promise, and he was pounded pretty hard in his handful of pitching appearances during the remainder of the season.

After the inauspicious trial with the Dodgers at the end of 1947, he spent the next two seasons regrouping. In 1948 he chalked up impressive stats at Nashua (20–6, 2.35 ERA, and a no-hitter), and St. Paul (4–0), following in 1949 with a 20–6 mark (while batting .328) at Montreal in the International League to earn another shot with the Dodgers. His second season in Brooklyn, 1950, was his most productive major-league season, as he compiled a 9–4 ledger despite a 5.50 ERA. Off to a poor start the next year, losing his only decision, he was farmed to Montreal, where his run of hard luck continued and he ended the season with a 2–6 record. Bankhead was never to return to the major leagues, and during his short major-league career he registered a lifetime 9–5 record.

After another unproductive year on the mound at Montreal in 1952, where he lost his only decision, he signed with Drummondville in the Canadian Provincial League and attempted a transition to an everyday player. Always fairly handy with the stick, he hit .275 with respectable power. However, as a batter he was good enough to be a good-hitting pitcher but not good enough to play as a regular in the major leagues. With his batting average he would have had to have generated more power and cut down significantly on his strikeouts to warrant a legitimate shot at the major leagues.

He continued to try to mix both pitching and hitting without concentrating on one position and, in 1954, he began a long career in Mexico. For a dozen seasons he played with an assortment of Mexican teams, playing as a pitcher-first baseman-outfielder and building a respectable record, hitting over .300 five times and compiling a lifetime pitching record of 32–19. His best years on the slab were 1961–62, when he was 8–2 and 9–6 despite high ERAs of 5.14 and 4.06.

Touted early in his career as another Satchel Paige, he could match Paige's speed but not his control, and Bankhead's early promise was never fully realized. He began his career in the Negro Leagues with the Birmingham Black Barons and, in league contests, had records of 6–1 and 3–0 in 1941–42. However, he was better identified with the Memphis Red Sox, where he had records of 6–2 and 4–4 in 1946–47 and was the highest-paid player on the ballclub. His salary escalated because he was bold in asking for raises when other ballplayers would not. His attention to money matters carried over to the major leagues, and when he signed with the Dodgers, he had an agent negotiate the contract for him. During this time, pitching with Caguas in the Puerto Rican League, he was compiling impressive strikeout totals, whiffing 179 and 131 in the winter seasons of 1946–47 and 1949–50.

Bankhead, Fred

Career: 1936–48   Positions: **2b**, 3b, 1b, ss
Teams: Birmingham Black Barons ('36–'38), **Memphis Red Sox** ('38–'47), New York Black Yankees ('48)
Bats: Right   Throws: Right
Height: 5'11"   Weight: 170
Born: Nov. 23, 1912, Empire, Ala.
Died: December 17, 1972, Miss.

One of the five Bankhead brothers who played in the Negro Leagues, Fred was overshadowed by brothers Sam and Dan. Primarily a second baseman, the sure-handed infielder made difficult plays look easy and could play any infield position. Offensively he was a pretty fair hitter, was a good bunter, and was fast on the basepaths.

He began his career as a reserve infielder, and played as a second baseman with the 1938 Memphis Red Sox, winners of the Negro

American League's first-half championship. The following season he moved into a starting position at third base, and remained in the starting lineup for the next nine seasons, primarily at second base, and usually batting in one of the top two spots in the batting order. In 1942 he hit .235 and made his only East-West All-Star appearance, entering the game as a pinch runner. In 1944–46 he hit for averages of .282, .242, and .204.

Before he began playing baseball professionally, he attended Daniel Payne College in Selma, Alabama. Bankhead was killed in an automobile accident when his car skidded on an icy road on the way to the airport to pick up his mother for a visit during the Christmas holidays.

Bankhead, Garnett

Career: 1947–49   Position: p
Teams: Memphis Red Sox ('47), Homestead Grays ('48, '49)
Bats: Right   Throws: Right
Height: 6'1"   Weight: 175
Born: June 27, 1928, Empire, Ala.
Died: September 15, 1991, Detroit, Mich.

The youngest of the five Bankhead brothers who played in the Negro Leagues, he spent a couple of weeks on the pitching staff of the Homestead Grays in 1948. The Grays went on to win the Negro National League pennant and World Series. The following season, after the Grays had dropped out of the Negro National League and were no longer a formidable ballclub, he rejoined the team. But the Grays at that time were playing against much weaker opposition. He had also pitched briefly with the Memphis Red Sox prior to joining the Grays. Bankhead died from a gunshot wound precipitated by an argument.

Bankhead, Joe

Career: 1948   Position: p
Team: Birmingham Black Barons
Bats: Right   Throws: Right
Height: 5'7"   Weight: 175
Born: Sept. 8, 1926, Empire, Ala.

Died: Feb. 4, 1988, Empire, Ala.

A member of the famous Bankhead clan, he was a fair little pitcher and took a few turns on the mound with the 1948 Negro American League champion Birmingham Black Barons, but wasn't able to stick with the team. He entered organized baseball with Grand Rapids in the Central League that same season, but there is no record of his baseball career afterward. Severely failing health caused him to be admitted to a VA hospital in 1987, and he died a year later.

Bankhead, Samuel Howard (Sam)

Career: 1930–50   Positions: **ss, cf, 2b, 1f, rf, 3b,** *p*
Teams: Birmingham Black Barons ('29, '31–'32, '38), Nashville Elite Giants ('30, '32–'34), Louisville Black Caps ('32), Kansas City Monarchs ('34), **Pittsburgh Crawfords** ('35–'36, '38), *Santo Domingo ('37)*, Memphis Red Sox ('38), Toledo Crawfords ('39), **Homestead Grays** ('39, '42–'50), *Mexican League ('40–'41), Canadian League ('51)*
Bats: Right   Throws: Right
Height: 5'8"   Weight: 175
Born: Sept. 18, 1905, Empire, Ala.
Died: July 24, 1976, Pittsburgh, Pa.

A hustling, all-around ballplayer, he was an outstanding fielder with a wide range and good hands but was best known for his exceptional throwing arm. On the bases he had good speed and could take an extra base, and was also a proficient base stealer. A good clutch hitter with moderate power, he could pull the ball and was always a threat at the plate. He was a players' player who was at home as a middle infielder or as an outfielder and excelled at whatever position he was placed. He was selected to the East-West All-Star team seven times, representing three different teams (Elites, Crawfords, and Grays), and starting at five different positions (2b, ss, 1f, cf, rf) while batting .346 in the classics. In a 1952 *Pittsburgh Courier* poll, he was selected as the first-team utility player on the all-time Negro Leagues all-star team.

Sam was an integral part of the great Pittsburgh Crawfords of the mid-'30s and the Homestead Grays' dynasty of the late '30s and '40s. He possessed one of the strongest arms in the Negro Leagues and was a solid hitter, with a .318 lifetime batting average. In 1937 he jumped to Santo Domingo along with Satchel Paige to play with the Ciudad Trujillo team, hitting .309 to help them win the championship. During the ensuing winter he led the Cuban League with a .366 average, and in his four seasons on the island, 1937–41, produced a lifetime .297 average. He also is credited with a .342 average in exhibition games against major leaguers. Even late in his career, Bankhead was still regarded as one of the top players in the Negro National League, and had averages of .287, .282, and .277 in 1944–46, and also hit .350 in the 1944 World Series against the Birmingham Black Barons.

As a youngster in Empire, Alabama, a mining town near Birmingham, Bankhead worked in the coal mines and played pickup baseball games in his free time. After several years he began his professional career with the Birmingham Black Barons in 1929, and played with the Nashville Elite Giants in 1930 before returning to the Black Barons, where he established himself early in his career as a superb utility man, playing infield and outfield. The Alabaman even did a little catching, and in 1932 took a few turns on the pitching slab with the Black Barons, Elite Giants, and Louisville Black Caps. However, pitching did not prove to be his best position, as available records show a 2–6 ledger for the year.

After the season he traveled to the West Coast to play in the California winter league, where he hit .371 and .344 with good power for the next two winters, 1932–33, while also ranking high in stolen bases each year. Back with the Elites as a shortstop, he hit .338 in 1934 to earn his first All-Star assignment.

The next season he signed with Gus Greenlee's Pittsburgh Crawfords, a team that fielded five Hall of Famers and is generally conceded to be the greatest black team of all time. Bankhead fit right in with the other superstars, batting .354 and .324 in 1935 and 1936.

In 1938, Memphis Red Sox manager "Double Duty" Radcliffe picked up Bankhead and David Whatley from the Birmingham Black Barons for the Negro American League playoffs against the Atlanta Black Crackers. The next season both of these players were signed by the Homestead Grays, defending champions of the Negro National League. Joining the Grays as a second baseman, he hit .377 as the Grays won their third consecutive pennant.

Bankhead interrupted his tenure with the Grays to accompany his friend Josh Gibson to Monterrey, Mexico, in 1940 and 1941, where Bankhead hit .318 and .351 while again showing good power and stolen-base totals, leading the league with 32 stolen bases in 1940. He and Gibson returned to the Grays for the 1942 season and, at age 38, moved into the lineup at shortstop as the Grays won the next four straight pennants and Bankhead made four more All-Star appearances out of his first five seasons back in the fold.

While with the Grays, he played winters with Ponce in the Puerto Rican League, batting .351 in 1941–42 and .271 and .290 in 1944–46. Back in the United States, Bankhead hit .284 as the Grays won another pennant in 1948, the last one before the Negro National League folded. During the latter years of the league, Bankhead played a winter each in Venezuela (1946) and in Panama (1948). The next year, as the Grays became a traveling independent team, he managed them for two seasons before they disbanded.

Sam had four younger brothers (Dan, Fred, Joe, and Garnett) who played in the Negro Leagues, but he also developed a close friendship with Josh Gibson and, after Gibson's death, Bankhead became a surrogate father for Josh, Jr. He signed the youngster to play with the Grays during this time and took him under his wing, teaching him about both baseball and life. In 1951 he took the younger Gibson to Canada with him when he managed Farnham in the Provincial League, becoming the first black man to manage a white ballclub. While at the helm, his team finished in seventh place with a .423 winning percentage, with the skipper batting .274 at age forty-seven.

In the off-season of 1949–50 he had worked for the refuse department for the city of Pittsburgh, and after retiring from baseball, he and Josh, Jr., took full-time jobs there. Some observers contend that Bankhead served as the model for the character Troy Maxson in the broadway play *Fences*. Later Bankhead worked as a hotel porter at the William Penn Hotel in Pittsburgh. He was a hard drinker and, while working there, his death resulted from a gunshot wound inflicted by a friend after Bankhead had provoked an argument that escalated into a drunken fight.

Banks

Career: 1917   Positions: **of**, 3b
Teams: Atlantic City Bacharach Giants ('17), *Madison Stars ('20–21)*

He played center field and batted second in the order as a part-time starter with the Bacharachs in 1917, during their second season in Atlantic City. Later he played with lesser teams, including the Madison Stars, for whom he played third base.

Banks

Career: 1896   Position: p
Team: Cuban X-Giants

In 1896, his only season in black baseball, he was a pitcher with the Cuban X-Giants, one of the leading teams of the era. The team originally consisted of former Cuban Giant ballplayers under new management and quickly surpassed their predecessor as the dominant team in black baseball.

Banks

Career: 1930   Position: 2b
Team: Hilldale Daisies

In his only year in black baseball he appeared briefly as a reserve second baseman for Hilldale in 1930.

Banks, Ernest (**Ernie**)

Career: 1950   Position: ss
Teams: Kansas City Monarchs ('50–'53), *military service ('51–'52)*, major leagues ('53–71)
Bats: Right   Throws: Right
Height: 6'1"   Weight: 180
Born: Jan. 31, 1931, Dallas, Tex.

An all-around athlete, he starred in football, basketball, and track in high school and at age seventeen signed to play semipro baseball with a barnstorming black team for $15 a game. Cool Papa Bell saw him and signed him for the Kansas City Monarchs. Playing shortstop for the Monarchs under manager Buck O'Neill, he hit .255 in 1950 but, after two years in the Army, improved to .347 in 1953.

Late in the season he was discovered by the Chicago Cubs, signed to a contract, and sent directly to the major leagues, the first black player in the franchise's long history. He hit .314 with the Cubs in only ten games, but the following season, as the regular shortstop, he hit .275 while stroking 19 homers. His power kicked into high gear in 1955 when he nailed 44 homers while batting .295. His best major-league seasons came in 1957–60, when he hit more than 40 homers each season (winning two home-run titles and two RBI titles) and hitting for averages of .285, .313, .304, and .271. The middle two years (1958–59) he was voted back-to-back National League MVP awards.

He also played in eleven All-Star games and picked up a Golden Glove award in 1960. In the early '60s, while beginning to slow in the field, Banks moved to first base for the remainder of his career. The right-handed slugger, who became known as Mr. Cub, spent his entire nineteen-year major-league career with the franchise, and ended with a .274 batting average and 512 home runs. He was elected to the National Baseball Hall of Fame in 1977, in his first year of eligibility.

Banks, G.

a.k.a. F. Banks
Career: 1914–17   Positions: **p**, rf, *c*

Teams: *Philadelphia Giants ('14)*, New York Lincoln Giants ('14–'17)

Bats: Left   Throws: Left

After breaking in with the once-proud Philadelphia Giants, who had fallen on leaner years, the college kid pitched with the New York Lincoln Giants for parts of four seasons, 1914–17. He was regarded as a fairly good left-handed pitcher but played primarily against weaker teams. It is thought that he is the same player listed as F. Banks who pitched in a game in 1915.

Banks, Johnny

Career: 1950   Position: p

Teams: Philadelphia Stars ('50), Baltimore Elite Giants ('50)

In 1950 he was listed as a pitcher with both the Philadelphia Stars and the Baltimore Elite Giants, but he pitched in only one game, without a decision.

Banks, Norman **Earl**

Career: 1945   Positions: 2b, 3b

Team: Newark Eagles

The light-hitting infielder hit a meager .135 as a wartime player with the 1945 Newark Eagles, playing second base and third base while batting in the eighth spot in the order.

Banks, S.

a.k.a. J. Banks

Career: 1915–16   Positions: c, *p*

Teams: New York Lincoln Giants ('15), *Philadelphia Giants ('16)*

He was a catcher with the New York Lincoln Giants in 1915, playing primarily against weaker teams. The following year, after leaving the Lincolns, he played with the once-proud Philadelphia Giants, who had fallen on leaner years. It is thought that he is the same player listed as J. Banks who appeared in a game in 1915.

Banton

Career: 1914   Position: p

Teams: Chicago American Giants ('14), West Baden Sprudels ('14)

In 1914 the Detroit native was considered one of Chicago American Giants' manager Rube Foster's "finds" and he pitched briefly, winning his only recorded decision, but did not remain with the club, finishing the season with the Sprudels of West Baden, Indiana, a team of lesser quality.

Baptiste

a.k.a. Bapiste

Career: 1923–24   Positions: of, p

Teams: Atlantic City Bacharach Giants ('23), *Philadelphia Giants ('24)*

He was an outfielder with the Bacharach Giants in 1923 and then pitched with manager Danny McClellan's Philadelphia Giants the following year. The Philadelphia Giants, once a top club, was generally regarded as a minor team during the 1920s.

Baranda

Career: 1915–18   Positions: 3b, of, 1b

Teams: Long Branch Cubans ('16), Jersey City Cubans, Cuban Stars ('18)

He played in the outfield and on the infield corners (third base and first base) for the Long Branch Cubans and the Jersey City Cubans in 1915–16, usually batting sixth in the order, and was a reserve player for the Cuban Stars in 1918.

Barbee, Lamb (**Bud**)

a.k.a. Barboo

Career: 1937–49   Positions: **p, 1b**, of, manager

Teams: **New York Black Yankees** ('37, '40–'41, '46–'49), Baltimore Elite Giants ('40), Philadelphia Stars ('42), Ethiopian Clowns ('42), Cincinnati-Indianapolis Clowns ('45), Indianapolis Clowns ('46), *Raleigh Tigers ('48)*

Bats: Right   Throws: Right

Height: 6'3"   Weight: 212

Born: 1917

The big right-hander was a versatile player who played both as a pitcher and an everyday player for the Black Yankees and other teams during his twelve-year career beginning in 1937. Although he was primarily known as a pitcher, he was also a good hitter with power, but was slow afoot and, at best, a mediocre fielder at the initial sack. As a pitcher he basically relied on two pitches, fastball and curve, but neither of the pitches was exceptional. He also utilized a change-up, but it was not very effective.

In 1937, with the Black Yankees, he jumped off to a torrid start with the bat, hitting a lofty .607 through June, including a team-leading 4 homers, but cooled off later in the season. In the early '40s his hitting was more in line with the norm, batting .225, .276, and .234 in 1940, 1943, and 1946, respectively.

On the mound he showed a 5–3 ledger for 1940, with most of his wins coming with the Elite Giants before moving back to the Black Yankees. But his ledger showed a deficit for the remainder of the decade, including a 1–8 record for the Black Yankees in 1947.

He played with the Chesterfield team in Panama during the following winter of 1947–48 and starred as both a pitcher and first baseman, averaging .300 with the bat. He returned to the Black Yankees for the '48 season. In addition to the Black Yankees, he played with the Elites and Philadelphia Stars in the East and with the Indianapolis Clowns in the West.

He also tried his hand at the managerial reins with the Raleigh Tigers, a team of lesser status. His younger brother, Quincy, played in the Negro Leagues and was also given the nickname "Bud," which creates a degree of difficulty in tracing their careers.

Barbee, Quincy (Bud)
Career: 1943–49   Positions: **of**, 1b
Teams: Baltimore Elite Giants ('43), Louisville Buckeyes ('49), Kansas City Monarchs ('49), *Canadian League ('49–'51, '54), minor leagues ('52–'55)*
Bats: Right   Throws: Right
Height: 6'0"   Weight: 195

The younger brother of Lamb Barbee, who also played in the Negro Leagues, he played briefly as an outfielder with the Louisville Buckeyes and Kansas City Monarchs in the Negro American League in 1949, but spent most of the season in the Canadian Provincial League, where he hit 23 home runs for St. Jean and followed in 1950 with 11 home runs to go with a .284 batting average. In his third year in the league, with Granby, he hit .289, with 8 home runs. During his three seasons in the league he played mostly at first base but also saw some duty in the outfield.

In 1952 he entered organized baseball, playing with Minot in the Mandak League and with Pampa in the West Texas-New Mexico League. Two years later he played with four teams in four leagues, including a return to the Provincial League, but his hitting was subpar in all of them. He finished his organized ball career with Texas City in the Big State League in 1955, batting only .233 in 13 games.

His first year in the Negro Leagues was with the Baltimore Elite Giants in 1943, where he batted fifth and played first base. He had good home-run power and consequently walked and struck out more than average, but he was slow on the bases. Many of his characteristics were similar to those of his brother.

Barber, Bull
Career: 1920–25   Position: 2b
Teams: Hilldale Daisies ('20), Harrisburg Giants ('23), Kansas City Monarchs ('25)

He was a second baseman who played with the Hilldales in 1920 and Kansas City Monarchs in 1925.

Barber, Jess
[see Barbour, Jess]

Barber, Sam
Career: 1946–50   Positions: **p**, of
Teams: Birmingham Black Barons ('40–'41), *Cleveland Clippers ('46)*, Cleveland Buckeyes ('42, '46–'50)
Born: Sept. 17, 1919

After two seasons of semipro ball in the Birmingham, Alabama, City League with the Stockham Valve Fitting Company and Acipco Pipe Company in 1938–39, he began his professional baseball career with the Birmingham Black Barons in 1940–41 before joining the Cleveland Buckeyes in 1942. After World War II he rejoined the Buckeyes following a brief stint with the Cleveland Clippers of the U.S. League, and stayed with the Buckeyes through 1950. The following season he returned to the Birmingham City League for two more seasons.

Barbette
Career: 1918   Position: 1b
Team: Cuban Stars (East)
This first baseman played with the 1918 Cuban Stars in his only season with a top team.

Barbour, Jess
a.k.a. Barber
Career: 1909–24   Positions: **lf**, rf, cf, ss, 1b, 2b, 3b
Teams: Philadelphia Giants ('09–'10, '25–'26), **Chicago American Giants** ('11–'19), Chicago Giants ('11), Indianapolis ABCs ('16), Atlantic City Bacharach Giants ('20–'21), Hilldale Daisies ('21), Detroit Stars ('22), Pittsburgh Keystones ('22), Harrisburg Giants ('22–'24), St. Louis Giants, *Quaker Giants*
Bats: Left   Throws: Right
Much of his seventeen-year career (1910–26) was spent as an outfielder for Rube Foster's Chicago American Giants during their glory years of the second decade of the century. He was extremely fleet of foot, and benefited from many infield hits when he would chop down on the ball and beat the throw to first. He was also an excellent base stealer and a good hitter and bunter. Defensively he was versatile afield, playing every infield position in addition to the outfield. He played winters with Foster's Royal Poinciana team in the Florida Hotel League between regular seasons with the Chicago American Giants.

He joined Foster's ballclub in 1911 as a shortstop, after two seasons with the Philadelphia Giants, but when John Henry Lloyd rejoined the team in 1914, the tall infielder moved to first base, where his fielding of bunts earned comparison to Hal Chase. He also contributed a .314 batting average for the year. The next two seasons, batting leadoff, he hit for averages of .288 and .283 and moved to the outfield during the latter year. In 1917 he temporarily "lost his batting eye," a condition that may have been caused by his fondness for the bottle, but regained his "eye" before the end of the season while still batting a disappointing .205.

He was with the American Giants in 1918 but was above draft age for World War I, and provided a veteran presence on the diamond as a balance for the younger players' inexperience during the wartime seasons. During these two seasons his batting average dropped to .235 and .277, and with his playing time also diminishing, he moved East after the war to join the Bacharachs in 1920. The next season he was with Hilldale briefly but "walked into a cigar store and never came out," returning to Atlantic City. He became their leadoff hitter and batted .277 in 1921, but after two seasons with the Bacharachs he joined former American Giants' teammate Bruce Petway's Detroit Stars. Although Barbour hit .284 with the Stars, his drinking problems persisted, and when Petway found him intoxicated at the ballpark, he moved Clint Thomas to center field, and Barbour never got back into the regular lineup.

Afterward, Barbour bounced around, playing with the Pittsburgh Keystones and Harrisburg Giants before returning to the Philadelphia Giants to close out his career where it had begun. But in 1925–26 the Giants were no longer a quality team.

Barcello
a.k.a. Barcelo
Career: 1921   Position: p
Team: Cuban Stars (East)
Bats: Right   Throws: Right

In his only year in the Negro Leagues, he was a right-handed pitcher with the Cuban Stars (East), who were representing Cincinnati in 1921.

Barker, Marvin (Hack, Hank)
Career: 1935–50   Positions: **cf, 1f**, rf, 2b,
                       3b, 1b, manager
Teams: Newark Dodgers ('35), Bacharach Giants ('36), **New York Black Yankees** ('36–'41, '43–'50), Philadelphia Stars ('42)
Bats: Right   Throws: Right
Height: 5'9"   Weight: 178

He started his career as an outfielder with the Newark Dodgers in 1935, but when the club was consolidated with the Brooklyn Eagles, he left to join the New York Black Yankees. There he utilized his superior hitting qualities and versatility to be always in the lineup. Batting in the leadoff position, he got off to a good start in 1937 and was hitting .318 through June. The following year he finished at .296 and, although his average dropped in 1940, with partial statistics showing a .209 mark, he made his first East-West All-Star game appearance, as an outfielder.

In 1945 the versatile veteran hit .310 and was considered the league's best center fielder but was also a good infielder and started the All-Star game that season as a third baseman. His two All-Star appearances produced a composite .429 batting average for the midseason classic. Aside from his All-Star season, his hitting had fallen off during the '40s, with available statistics showing marks of .143, .203, .248, and .234 for the seasons of 1942–43, 1944, and 1946. During these lean years he continued to bat in key slots (second, third, or fifth) in the lineup. The 1942 season that he spent with the Philadelphia Stars was the only year during fifteen straight seasons that he was not with the Black Yankees. In 1948 his loyalty was rewarded when he was appointed playing manager.

Barkins, W. C.
Career: 1928   Position: officer
Team: Cleveland Stars

He was an officer with the 1928 Cleveland Stars during their only season in the Negro National League.

Barnes
Career: 1906   Position: 3b
Team: Philadelphia Giants

In 1906 he played briefly as a reserve infielder with the Philadelphia Giants.

Barnes
Career: 1925   Position: p
Team: Kansas City Monarchs

He pitched briefly with the Kansas City Monarchs in 1925, his only season in the Negro Leagues.

Barnes
Career: 1937   Position: p
Team: Birmingham Black Barons

In 1937, his only year in the Negro Leagues, he was a pitcher with the Birmingham Black Barons.

Barnes, Arthur
Career: 1932   Position: owner
Team: New York Black Yankees

In 1932, as a coowner, he helped bankroll the New York Black Yankees in their first season of existence. The team operated on a percentage basis and, since his reputation was not above suspicion, he remained behind the scenes without taking a cut of the profits.

Barnes, Ed (Sam)
Career: 1937–40   Position: p
Teams: Kansas City Monarchs ('37–'38), Satchel Paige's All-Stars ('39), Baltimore Elite Giants ('39–'40)

He split his four-year pitching career between an eastern team, the Baltimore Elite Giants, and a western team, the Kansas City Monarchs. After beginning with the Monarchs in 1937, he appeared briefly with Satchel Paige's All-Stars before making the transition to the Elite Giants, where he was winless against three losses in 1940, his last season.

Barnes, Fat
[See Barnes, John]

Barnes, Frank
Career: 1947–50   Position: p
Teams: Kansas City Monarchs ('49–'50), *minor leagues ('50–'52, '54–'62, '65), voluntarily retired ('53)*, major leagues ('57–'58, '60), *Mexican League ('63–'67)*
Bats: Right   Throws: Right
Height: 6'1''   Weight: 185
Born: August 26, 1928, Longwood, Miss.

A right-hander with a good fastball, Barnes was a leading pitcher on the Monarchs' staff during the late 1940s, before entering organized baseball. He was a weak hitter and a poor base runner, so his only avenue for success in organized ball was on the mound. His last two years with the Monarchs show records of 8–6 in 1949, and 9–4, with a 2.41 ERA, in 1950. The latter season he signed with Muskegon in the Central League and finished the year there, with an 8–4 record and a 2.23 ERA.

In 1951 he was 15–6 with a 3.22 ERA, earning a promotion to Toronto of the International League, where he lost his only decision in two appearances. After a 7–3 record at Scranton in 1952 he earned another trial with Toronto, where he pitched only one game. Following a season away from baseball in 1953, he spent the entire 1954 season with Toronto and compiled a 9–8 record.

Barnes perservered in his quest to make the major leagues and, after two respectable seasons at Omaha in the American Association (13–5 and 12–10), he earned a shot at the big leagues with the Cardinals at the end of 1957 and 1958. The first time up, in only four games he lost his only decision, and in his next shot he split two decisions despite a high ERA. After winning 15 games at Omaha in 1959, he spent most of the 1960 season with San Diego in the Pacific Coast League and earned another chance with the Cardinals. In his third and last time in the majors, he again lost his only decision, to finish with a career major-league record of 1–3.

The remainder of his career was spent with minor-league teams and, after another season on the West Coast with San Diego and Portland, he played with Buffalo in the International League in 1962. Resigning himself to not receiving another chance at the majors at his age, he spent the last five years of his career with Reynosa in the Mexican League, registering winning records each season. His best year in Mexico was 1966, when he earned a 17–8 record with a 2.10 ERA. He finished his organized baseball career in 1967 with a 6–5 record for Reynosa. He did leave Mexico once for a final effort in the United States, when he pitched in two games with Seattle of the Pacific Coast League in 1965 without a decision but with a ballooned 19.80 ERA.

Barnes, Harry (Mooch, Tack Head)
Career: 1937–49   Position: c
Teams: Birmingham Black Barons ('35–'38), *Birmingham All-Stars ('39–44), Atlanta Black Crackers ('45), Chattanooga Choo Choos ('46–'47), Asheville Blues ('48)*, Memphis Red Sox ('49)
Bats: Right   Throws: Right
Born: Aug. 19, 1915

Most of his career was spent in the Negro Southern League, but he had two stints in the black big leagues, first with the Birmingham Black Barons in 1937–38 and again in 1949 with the Memphis Red Sox. He began his professional career with the Black Barons in 1935 and was still with the club when they became charter members of the Negro American League in 1937. After two seasons in the Negro American League, the catcher spent the next decade with lesser southern teams, including the Atlanta Black Crackers, before playing with the Memphis Red Sox in 1949.

Barnes, Jimmy
[See Barnes, William]

Barnes, Joe
Career: 1950   Position: p
Teams: Memphis Red Sox ('50–'51), *Kansas*

City Monarchs ('51), Indianapolis Clowns ('52)
Born: Oct. 8, 1926

The beginning of his career coincided with the onset of the Negro Leagues' decline. He joined the Memphis Red Sox in 1950 and split the next season between the Sox and the Kansas City Monarchs, before winding up his career with the Indianapolis Clowns in 1952.

Barnes, John (**Fat**, Tubby)
Career: 1922–31   Positions: **c**, 1b
Teams: Cleveland Tate Stars ('22–'23), Toledo Tigers ('23), Cleveland Browns ('24), Detroit Stars ('24), St. Louis Stars ('25, '31), Indianapolis ABCs ('26), Cleveland Elite Giants ('26), Cleveland Hornets ('27), Cleveland Tigers ('28), Memphis Red Sox ('30)

In a career that stretched across a decade, the heavy catcher played with an equal number of different teams, including five different ballclubs based in Cleveland. He was the regular catcher for the Tate Stars in 1922, his first year with a league ballclub. In 1924 he was one of three catchers who shared the receiving duties for the Detroit Stars, and in 1926 he was a reserve catcher for the ABCs. In his last two seasons he hit .258 with the Memphis Red Sox in 1930 and was the backup catcher with the 1931 Negro National League champion St. Louis Stars. Throughout his career he usually hit in the lower part of the batting order when in the lineup. He also accumulated an assortment of monikers, being called "Tubby" in the South, but was more generally referenced as "Fat" in the Midwest.

Barnes, Mute
Career: 1938   Position: p
Team: Atlanta Black Crackers
Bats: Left   Throws: Left
Height: 6'1"   Weight: 195

He was a big left-handed pitcher who was on the early spring roster for the 1938 Atlanta Black Crackers but did not stick for the season.

Barnes, O.
Career: 1932   Position: officer
Team: New York Black Yankees

He was an officer with the New York Black Yankees in 1932, their first full season playing under that name.

Barnes, Sam
[see Barnes, Ed]

Barnes, Tobias
Career: 1937   Position: 3b
Team: Chicago American Giants

The third sacker was a reserve infielder with the Chicago American Giants for a short time in 1937.

Barnes, Tom
Career: 1950   Positions: p, of
Teams: Memphis Red Sox ('50, *'54–55), Canadian League ('51), minor leagues ('52)*
Bats: Right   Throws: Right
Born: June 29, 1930

After beginning his career with the Memphis Red Sox in 1950, he played with Drummondville of the Canadian Provincial League in 1951 and was in the Yankee chain with Three Rivers, Canada, in 1952. He returned to Memphis and finished his career back with the Red Sox in 1954–55 after the decline of the Negro American League.

Barnes, Tubby
[see Barnes, John]

Barnes, V.
Career: 1940   Position: of
Team: Kansas City

He appeared briefly as a reserve outfielder with the Kansas City Monarchs in 1940, his only year in the Negro Leagues.

Barnes, William (Bill, Jimmy)
Career: 1941–47   Position: p
Teams: Baltimore Elite Giants ('41–'42, '46),

Memphis Red Sox ('43), *military service ('44–'45)*, Indianapolis Clowns ('47)
Bats: Right   Throws: Right
Height: 6'1"   Weight: 195
Born: Birmingham, Ala.

He had a combined 4–4 league record for the last three years before World War II. After a stint in the armed forces, the big right-handed hurler returned to the Baltimore Elite Giants for the 1946 season before closing out his career with the Indianapolis Clowns.

Barnhard

Career: 1914   Position: of
Team: Philadelphia Giants

The outfielder played with the Philadelphia Giants at a time when the club was struggling to maintain a quality team.

Barnhill, David (Dave, Impo, Skinny)

Career: 1937–49   Position: p
Teams: *Miami Giants ('36)*, Zulu Giants ('37), Ethiopian Clowns ('37–'40), **New York Cubans** ('41–'49), *minor leagues ('49–'53)*
Bats: Both   Throws: Right
Height: 5'7"   Weight: 145
Born: October 30, 1914, Greenville, N.C.
Died: January 8, 1983, Miami, Fla.

A small, fireballing strikeout artist, the New York Cuban ace threw "aspirin tablets" and was one of the top pitchers in the East during the early '40s. With sensational records of 18–3 for the 1941 campaign and 26–10 (11–3 in league play) for 1943, he was selected to start the 1943 East-West All-Star game against Satchel Paige. The two star hurlers had met twice previously in the season, each time at Yankee Stadium, with Barnhill coming away with a split, losing the first encounter but spinning a shutout to even the score. Having been credited with the victory over Paige in the previous year's All-Star game, this outing also marked the little right-hander's third consecutive All-Star appearance, for which he had an aggregate six strikeouts to show for his nine innings pitched.

It was during these prime years that Barnhill received a telegram regarding the possibility of becoming the first black in the major leagues. Barnhill was called the "Tommy Bridges of the Negro Leagues" and rated as a "surefire" major-league prospect. A tryout had been arranged for Barnhill, Roy Campanella, and Sammy T. Hughes with the Pittsburgh Pirates, but owner Ben Benswanger reneged on his pledge, and the opportunity did not materialize.

He stayed with the Cubans and eventually helped pitch them to a Negro National championship in 1947. During this season he did not lose a game in league play, posting a 4–0 mark, and polished off the season with a shutout victory over the Cleveland Buckeyes in the World Series.

Barnhill began his baseball career on the sandlots of North Carolina, where his semipro opponents included Buck Leonard and Ray Dandridge. In the town of Wilson, the small, slender hurler earned both the nickname "Skinny" and the designation as ace of the staff. When playing teams from other towns, they would refuse to start a game without him. They would say, "Wait until Skinny gets here."

Barnhill was discovered by the touring Miami Giants when they were barnstorming through North Carolina in 1936, and Barnhill beat them 2–1. Later, after he had been signed, the team evolved into the Ethiopian Clowns and he acquired his Clown name, "Impo," and stayed with the team for three years as their star attraction. Buck Leonard had wanted the Homestead Grays to sign him, but the Grays favored big players and said he was too small. So "Impo" became a member of the Clowns, who were part baseball and part show biz and who included a shadow ball routine and "clowning" skits to entertain the fans. Although he spent most of his early professional career with the Clowns, he also played briefly with the rival Zulu Giants in the early spring of 1937. The Zulus donned wigs and makeup and also did comedic routines to delight the fans.

During this time, the diminutive hurler demonstrated his wizardry in Latin America, fashioning an 11–9 record and leading the league with 193 strikeouts while pitching for Humacao, Puerto Rico, in the winter of 1940–41. The following spring he joined the New York Cubans and remained with Alejandro Pompez's club until going into organized baseball.

He quickly became a sensational performer and gate attraction with the New York Cubans. In 1943 Barnhill pitched against Satchel Paige twice at Yankee Stadium, losing the first game 6–3 but winning the second encounter by a shutout. After three super seasons with the Cubans, he suffered from an unspecified malady that kept him idle most of the 1944 season. In actuality he was stabbed by teammate Fred Wilson, but this was kept quiet. In 1945, Barnhill was fully recovered and again in top form.

The winter after the Cubans won the 1947 Negro World Series, Barnhill embarked for his first of three successive winters in Marianao, Cuba, and led the league in strikeouts, while compiling a record of 10–8 with a 2.26 ERA. The following winter, 1948–49, his excellence on the mound continued as he led the league in victories and complete games while compiling a 13–8 record with an 2.81 ERA. He began tailing off in the last year there, losing the only three games he pitched, to end his Cuban career with a three-season total of 23–19 for a .548 winning percentage.

Meanwhile, in 1949, after his first two winter seasons, Barnhill was signed by the New York Giants along with Ray Dandridge. Assigned to the Giants' AAA franchise in Minneapolis, Barnhill compiled an 11–3 record to help the Millers to the championship in 1950. At Minneapolis he was accused of "cutting" the ball, and opposing managers watched his every move, trying to catch him. When they couldn't find any evidence to support their claim, they accused third baseman Ray Dandridge of doing it for him. Dandridge maintained his innocence and Barnhill maintained his secret.

During his three seasons with Minneapolis in the American Association, 1949–51, he compiled records of 7–10, 11–3, and 6–5, with corresponding ERAs of 5.75, 3.60, and 4.46. In addition to pitching, he could also help his team in other ways, by fielding, hitting, or running the bases. He was quick off the mound and was regarded as a good-fielding pitcher. He was also a good-hitting pitcher, with batting averages of .213, .226, and .204, and he was sometimes used as a pinch hitter. Despite his size, he hit three homers while at Minneapolis, with two of his round-trippers coming in 1951. He was also a fleet base runner and stole 8 bases in only 54 times at bat.

By then his age kept him from getting a shot at the majors, but he played with Miami Beach in the Florida International League, where he was 13–8 with a 1.19 ERA in 1952, while playing under Pepper Martin. Barnhill spent the next year with Fort Lauderdale in the same league, and split two decisions in only four games pitched. That was his last year in organized ball, and after leaving the baseball diamond in 1953, he lived his last thirty years in Miami, working in the city's recreation department until his retirement.

Barnhill, Herbert (**Herb**)
Career: 1938–46   Position: c
Teams: Jacksonville Red Caps ('38, '41–'42), Cleveland Bears ('39–'40), Kansas City Monarchs ('43), Chicago American Giants ('44–'46)
Bats: Right   Throws: Right
Height: 6'0"   Weight: 175

He was an adequate catcher who stretched his talent into a nine-year career in the Negro American League, spent with four teams. He began his career with the Jacksonville Red Caps, sharing the starting assignments for a season before being relegated to backup duties for the next four seasons, including the two years the Red Caps were based in Cleveland and playing under the banner of the Bears.

Joining the Kansas City Monarchs in 1943, he gained more playing time, again sharing the regular receiving responsibilities. The following season he moved to the Chicago American Giants and was their irregular receiver for three seasons, although sharing the duties at times. Defensively he was an average receiver in every phase of the game but was a weak hitter, batting .270, .259, and .198 in 1944–46. A typical catcher, he was slow on the bases. He was not related to pitcher Dave Barnhill.

Barnwell, Ernest (Gator)
Career: 1937   Position: p
Team: Ethiopian Clowns ('37)
Bats: Right   Throws: Right
Height: 6'2"   Weight: 171
Born: June 9, 1910, Titusville, Fla.

The tall hurler could break a curve that could "knock a man out from behind a post," and he threw both his fastball and curve with the same motion. He pitched more than 200 games during his nineteen-year career during the '30s and early '40s, almost entirely with semipro teams in Florida. But he was also sought to pitch as a "ringer" with professional teams, including the Ethiopian Clowns when they were based in Miami.

Born in Titusville, Florida, he moved to Vero Beach in 1918 and played on the school's baseball team. Later, as a teenager, while playing for the Vero Beach Hornets, he was taught to throw a curveball by a man named Anthony Davis, and also played with other teams, including the West Indian Royals. With these semipro teams, they traveled in battered buses and cars, and passing the hat, with the winner getting 60 percent of the take. Sometimes the team would play against the inmates at Raiford State Prison but Barnwell never minded, as long as they let him out after the game. While he was playing baseball, he worked intermittently as a fruit picker, but never held a full-time job. He also was a catcher on occasion, but eventually he quit baseball for a steady job to make more money.

Baro, Bernardo
Career: 1913–30   Positions: **lf, rf, cf,** 1b
                                    p, c
Teams: Cuban Stars ('13), New York Cuban Stars, ('16), **Cuban Stars (West)** ('17–'21), **Cuban Stars (East)** ('22–'29), Kansas City Monarchs ('30)
Bats: Left   Throws: Left
Born: Cuba
Died: June 1930, Cuba

A brilliant outfielder, he could make all the plays but "showed off" too much in the field. The small, light complected Cuban starred in center field with the Cuban Stars in the Eastern Colored League, and in 1923–24 he formed, with Pablo Mesa and Alejandro Oms, one of the greatest outfields in black baseball history. A left-handed batter, the veteran outfielder was a five-point player, a player who can run, field, throw, hit, and hit with power. (These are the five points that scouts look for in a player.) He was an excellent hitter who hit to all fields with extra-base power and was a good bunter. He was very fast and a great base runner, and had wide range in the field and a good arm.

He was a violent man, edgy, quick-tempered, and ready to fight. He once threatened an opposing player with a bat. In retaliation, he was hit by a fastball by Juanelo Mirabal and broke his ankle. In 1924 he suffered a compound fracture of the leg while running into the stands to get a foul ball, and it was feared that his career would be over. Surgery was required, and after the last operation, it was reported that one leg would be shorter and that he would have a limp. However, although he had lost his once exceptional speed, the gritty competitor refused to give up and continued to play for another half-dozen seasons.

The Cuban began his career as a pitcher in 1915 with Almendares in his homeland. The following year he came to the United States as the regular right fielder on owner Alejandro Pompez's 1916 Cuban Stars, but also did some pitching. However, existing statistics from five seasons show his combined record to be 2–6.

At the plate he was much more productive, hitting .337, .347, .381, and .364 for the years 1920–23.

Returning after his injury, he played first base for the first two seasons back in the lineup, but moved back to the outfield and hit .300, .292, and .275 for the years 1927-29 to conclude his career with the Cuban Stars in both leagues.

Playing in his homeland during the winter seasons, primarily with Almendares, he had a lifetime Cuban League batting average of .313 for an intermittent eleven-year career that spanned the period of 1915–29. His best year came in 1922–23, when he led the league with a .401 average. Other sterling seasons showed averages of .364 and .352 (1918–20), two consecutive seasons of .309 (1925–27), and .311 (1928–29). Playing with Almendares in a 1920 series against the New York Giants, he hit .405, with 1 home run and 6 doubles in 37 at-bats for a slugging average of .649. In honor of his great career, he was elected to the Cuban Hall of Fame in 1945.

In 1929, while playing in the Negro Leagues, Baro suffered a "mental collapse" and had to be restrained with a straitjacket. The next year, he closed out his Negro Leagues career with a lifetime batting average of .302, after appearing with the Kansas City Monarchs for a portion of the season. After leaving the Monarchs he returned to Cuba, and a short time later, in June 1930, he died suddenly in his homeland.

Barr

Career: 1921–22   Positions: ss, 3b
Teams: Kansas City Monarchs ('21), Cuban Stars ('22)

A reserve infielder for a couple of years, he saw action at shortstop and third base for the Kansas City Monarchs and the Cuban Stars.

Barrett, Pearl

Career: 1917   Position: 1b
Team: Havana Stars ('17)

She was a female first baseman signed by the Havana Stars in 1917 as a gate attraction, and promoted as the first female in the world to play baseball at this level.

Barrow, Wesley

Career: 1945–47   Position: manager
Teams: *New Orleans Black Pelicans ('45), Nashville Cubs ('46)*, Baltimore Elite Giants ('47)

After directing the New Orleans Black Pelicans and Nashville Cubs earlier in his career, he was the manager of the Baltimore Elite Giants in 1947.

Barry

Career: 1915   Position: p
Team: Chicago American Giants ('15)

He pitched briefly with the Chicago American Giants in 1915, but had control problems and did not stick with the team.

Bartamino

Career: 1904   Position: manager
Team: All Cubans ('04)

He was manager of the 1904 All Cubans, the best Cuban team playing in the United States during the early years of the century.

Bartlett, Howard (Homer, Hop, Sapho)

Career: 1914–25   Position: p
Teams: **Indianapolis ABCs** ('11–'14, '18–'25), Bowser's ABCs ('16), Jewell's ABCs ('17), Kansas City Monarchs ('24–'25)

Beginning his professional career in 1911 with the ABCs, when they were not a quality ballclub, he remained with the team when they attained a level comparable to the major leagues in 1914. He was not with the Indianapolis ABCs during their two outstanding seasons of 1915–16, but played with both Bowser's ABCs and Jewell's ABCs during parts of the 1916–17 seasons. Although not a first-line pitcher, he continued his baseball career through 1925, when he finished his last season with a 0–2 record with the Kansas City Monarchs.

Barton, Sherman
Career: 1896–1911   Positions: 1f, cf, rf,
3b, p
Teams: Chicago Unions ('96), Page Fence Giants ('98), Chicago Columbia Giants ('99–'00), Algona (Iowa) Brownies ('02–'03), Chicago Union Giants ('04–'06, '11), Leland Giants ('05), Cuban X-Giants, *Quaker Giants of New York*, St. Paul Colored Gophers ('09), Chicago Giants ('11)

Beginning his career in the nineteenth century, he spent most of his sixteen seasons in the Midwest, primarily with Chicago-based teams. He played in the outer gardens for two championship teams during the first decade of the century, as the regular left fielder for the 1903 Algona (Iowa) Brownies and then, a half a dozen seasons later, as the center fielder for the 1909 champion St. Paul Colored Gophers. Sandwiched between these two championship seasons he joined the Leland Giants in their first year of existence, 1905, as the starting third baseman. He was with Frank Leland during his last season as well, but was batting in the bottom half of the lineup as the center fielder with Leland's Chicago Giants in 1911.

Bashum
Career: 1932   Position: c
Team: Indianapolis ABCs

He was a catcher with the 1932 Indianapolis ABCs of the Negro Southern League in his only year in top-level competition.

Baskin, William
Career: 1890–92   Position: 2b
Team: Chicago Unions ('90–'92)

Beginning in 1890, this nineteenth-century infielder played only three seasons in black baseball but was the regular second baseman for the Chicago Unions each season.

Bass, Leroy (Red)
Career: 1938–40   Position: c
Teams: Pittsburgh Crawfords ('38–'39), Homestead Grays ('40)

Bats: Right   Throws: Right
Height: 6'0"   Weight: 170

One of the candidates for Josh Gibson's replacement in 1940 when Gibson left the Grays for Mexico, Bass started the spring with a bang but leveled off with a .250 batting average and never earned the starting position, being dropped by the club early in the season. He had played with the Pittsburgh Crawfords the previous two seasons (1938–39).

Bassett, Lloyd (Pepper)
Career: 1936–50   Position: c
Teams: *New Orleans Crescent Stars ('34)*, Homestead Grays ('36–37), Pittsburgh Crawfords ('37–'38), Toledo Crawfords ('39), Chicago American Giants ('39–41), *Mexican League ('40)*, Ethiopian Clowns ('42), Cincinnati Clowns ('43), Cincinnati-Indianapolis Clowns ('44), **Birmingham Black Barons** ('44–'52), Philadelphia Stars, *Memphis Red Sox ('53), Detroit Stars ('54)*
Bats: Both   Throws: Right
Height: 6'3"   Weight: 220
Born: Aug. 5, 1919, Baton Rouge, La.

Touted as another Josh Gibson when he joined the Pittsburgh Crawfords as Josh's replacement, Bassett never lived up to that billing, but was a productive player over a seventeen-year period. He made four East-West All-Star game appearances, stretching from 1937 with the Crawfords to 1950, when he was with Birmingham. Bassett hit .395 and .308 for the Crawfords in 1937 and 1938, but received a letter from owner Gus Greenlee stating that the Crawfords were disbanded and that Bassett was a free agent. The new circumstances left him unable even to cash his final $53 check from the Crawfords.

After playing with the Baltimore Elite Giants in the California winter league, the big catcher signed with the Chicago American Giants, making two All-Star appearances (1939 and 1941) during his three years in Chicago. Interestingly, although he was an all-star performer in Chicago, he usually hit in the lower part of the batting order, as he did throughout his career. Sandwiched between his two All-Star seasons in Chicago was a year with Nuevo Laredo in Mexico, where he hit .230 with 8 home runs. After leaving the American Giants, he spent two full seasons with the Clowns and became a popular gate attraction known as "the rocking chair catcher" because he would catch part of the game while sitting in a rocking chair. He had first originated the rocking chair routine in 1936 at the request of Grays' owner Cum Posey, and continued the practice while with the Pittsburgh Crawfords.

In 1944 he signed with the Birmingham Black Barons and, despite a .212 batting average as a part-time starter, helped the Black Barons repeat as the Negro American League champions, although they lost the World Series to the Homestead Grays. After a woeful .177 average the following season, he bounced back with a respectable .260 mark in 1946 and, in 1948, he enjoyed one of his best years ever, hitting a hefty .350 as the Black Barons captured another Negro American League pennant but lost again to the Grays in the World Series.

During the next two years he hit .298 and .271 and continued playing with the Black Barons on into the early '50s, when the Negro American League was in decline, finally closing out his career in 1954, twenty-one years after it had started with the New Orleans Crescent Stars.

Batson
Career: 1908–09   Position: of
Teams: Genuine Cuban Giants ('08), Philadelphia Giants ('09)

In his only two seasons in black baseball, he was an outfielder with the 1908 Genuine Cuban Giants and the 1909 Philadelphia Giants.

Battle, Ray
a.k.a. Battles
Career: 1944–45   Position: 3b
Team: Homestead Grays ('44–'45)
Bats: Right   Throws: Right
Height: 5'11"   Weight: 155
Born: Rocky Mount, N.C.

A light hitter and mediocre fielder, Battle was a wartime replacement for the Homestead Grays' third baseman Howard Easterling, who was called into military service. Battle developed into a fairly good player at the hot corner in 1944, hitting .294. But the following season, due to his light hitting, he was embroiled in a battle with Robbie Robinson for the regular third-base job. Although he retained the starting position, his finished the season with a woeful .185 batting average. He was discovered by the Grays while playing in Rocky Mount, North Carolina, a hometown he shared with the Grays' superstar Buck Leonard.

Battle, William (Bill)
Career: 1947–49   Position: p
Teams: Homestead Grays ('47), Memphis Red Sox ('49)

He was a pitcher for the Homestead Grays and Memphis Red Sox during the latter years of the Negro Leagues' existence as a major league.

Battles
Career: 1924   Positions: c, 3b, ss
Team: Harrisburg Giants

A youngster from "out West," he was signed in the latter part of 1924 by Harrisburg, who was having a problem with their catching corps, to finish the season as a backup catcher and occasional utility infielder.

Bauchman, Harry
Career: 1910–23   Positions: 2b, ss, 1b
Teams: Chicago Giants ('10–'14, '23), **Chicago American Giants** ('15–'21), Chicago Union Giants
Bats: Right   Throws: Right
Born: c. 1891, Omaha, Neb.
Died: June 20, 1931, Chicago, Ill.

A light hitter but an excellent gloveman and a good base stealer, he was the starting second baseman on Rube Foster's American Giants during most of the century's second decade, until being replaced by Bingo DeMoss in 1917. His career stretched from 1915 to 1923, and he also played shortstop and first base. His entire baseball career was spent in Chicago, where he played with the Chicago Union Giants and the Chicago Giants in addition to the Chicago American Giants.

He came to Chicago from Omaha in 1910, playing with Frank Leland's Chicago Giants. But baseball at this time was not his exclusive avocation, since, in 1912 at Denver, he fought four rounds with heavyweight boxer Fireman Jack Flynn, one of most prominent heavyweights of the time.

In 1915 Bauchman stepped into the starting second-base spot and held it for two years, usually batting in the lower part of the batting order. He hit .230 in his first season with Foster's squad, but dropped to a weak .151 in 1916, with a decrease in power and an increase in strikeouts. In both years the American Giants were embroiled in a hotly contested battle with C. I. Taylor's ABCs for the western championship, winning the first year and losing the second.

After losing his regular position with the American Giants, he generally played with lesser teams, although he did return to Foster's team for short stints. Bauchman retired from baseball following the 1923 season and a year later was married. Life then looked bright to Bauchman and his bride, Octavia, but he had only seven more years to live. He died of heart disease at age forty in Chicago after a two-week illness.

Baum
Career: 1906   Position: of
Team: Brooklyn Royal Giants

In 1906 he was an outfielder with the Brooklyn Royal Giants, one of the top black teams of the era.

Bauza, Marcellino
a.k.a. Marcelline Bauzz
Career: 1930   Position: ss
Teams: Cuban Stars (West)
Bats: Right   Throws: Right

A light-hitting shortstop for the Cuban Stars (West) in 1930, he had a weak .160 batting average for his only year in the Negro Leagues.

Baxter
Career: 1899   Position: ss
Team: Cuban Giants

He was a shortstop for the Cuban Giants during his only season with a recognized ballclub.

Baxter, Al
Career: 1898   Position: lf
Team: *Celeron Acme Colored Giants*

He was an outfielder with an all-black team, dubbed the Acme Colored Giants, formed in 1898 by Harry Curtis, a white man, to represent Celeron, New York, in the Iron and Oil League. Both the team and the league folded in July, and it was to be the last time a black team played in a white league.

Bayliss, Henry J. (Hank)
Career: 1948–50   Positions: **3b**, 2b, *c*
Teams: Chicago American Giants ('48), Baltimore Elite Giants ('49), Birmingham Black Barons ('49–'50), *Kansas City Monarchs ('51–'55), minor leagues ('56–57)*
Bats: Right   Throws: Right
Height: 5'9"   Weight: 178
Born: 1927, Topeka, Kan.

In 1948, his first season in the Negro Leagues, the slap-hitting infielder batted .320, but without much power, for the Chicago American Giants. He experienced some difficulty hitting breaking pitches, and the next two years his averages dropped off to .284 and .270, while playing with the Birmingham Black Barons. He joined the Kansas City Monarchs for five years in the early '50s and eventually found his way into organized baseball in 1956, hitting .263 as the regular third baseman with El Paso in the Southwestern League.

The following season was a nomadic year for Bayliss as he split his time among three teams (El Paso and Tucson in the Arizona-Mexico League, and Yakima in the Northwest League). However, most of the season was with Tucson, where he hit an even .300. That was his last season in organized ball.

A good athlete who was accomplished as both a baseball and basketball player, his versatility permitted him to fill in as a catcher on occasion. During his career he was not issued many free passes by pitchers, and he struck out slightly more than an average player.

Baynard, Frank
Career: 1916–28   Positions: rf, cf, 1f, 3b, c
Teams: *Pittsburgh Stars of Buffalo ('16)*, Atlantic City Bacharach Giants ('16–18), Havana Red Sox ('17), *Pennsylvania Red Caps of New York ('18–'28)*, New York Lincoln Giants ('19), Newark Stars ('26), *Philadelphia Quaker City Giants ('28)*

An outfielder, he played as a reserve with the Bacharachs and Lincoln Giants during the latter years of the deadball era. Between his stints with these two well-known teams, he played center field for the Havana Red Sox in 1917 and subsequently played a decade with the Pennsylvania Red Caps of New York, a team of lesser status.

Bea, Bill
Career: 1940   Position: rf
Teams: Philadelphia Stars, New York Black Yankees
Bats: Left   Throws: Right
Height: 6'0"   Weight: 200

A protégé of Gene Benson, the Philadelphia native was a good hitter, batting .317 with displays of power, but was mediocre in the field. Like many players who did not like traveling, he did not want to leave Philadelphia to play ball, choosing instead to concentrate on a more stable job.

Beal, G. (Lefty)
Career: 1947   Position: p
Team: Newark Eagles
Bats: Left   Throws: Left
Height: 5'10"   Weight: 175

The left-hander had a good fastball and a fair curve but poor control, and was released for more seasoning after pitching briefly and without distinction with the Newark Eagles in 1947.

Beale, Harry
Career: 1929   Position: manager
Team: Pittsburgh Crawfords

In the formative stages of the Pittsburgh Crawfords, while they were a struggling young ballclub, he booked games and, along with Bill Harris, ran the team. By 1929 he had taken control of the team and was handling public relations and serving as manager.

Beavers, Ben (Rail)
Career: 1941–42   Positions: ss, 2b
Teams: *Dayton Marcos ('31–32), College Park Indians ('31–'35), Macon Peaches ('36–'38)*, Jacksonville Red Caps ('39–'42)
Bats: Right   Throws: Right
Born: Sept. 12, 1911

The middle infielder played with the Jacksonville Red Caps in 1941–42 but previously spent a decade with sandlot, semipro, and minor-league teams, including the Dayton Marcos when they were playing independent ball. He played with Jacksonville in 1939–40, but they were not in the Negro American League until 1941.

Bebley
Career: 1925   Position: p
Team: Birmingham Black Barons

He pitched briefly with the Birmingham Black Barons in 1925, when they were members of the Negro National League.

Bebop, Ralph (Spec)
a.k.a. Ralph Bell (real name)
Career: 1950   Position: clown
Team: Indianapolis Clowns ('50–'60)
Bats: Right   Throws: Right
Height: 4'6"   Weight: 160

Bebop was the midget who was prominently featured in the comic routines of the Indianapolis Clowns during their barnstorming trips. Although listed on the roster, he was more a showbiz personality than a ballplayer. He and King Tut were the most popular gate attractions on the team and paired together on routines, such as their famous "rowboat" routine. Bebop had a serious drinking problem and caused owner Ed Hamman much consternation during the years he was with the Clowns.

Becker
[see Hocker, Bruce]

Beckwith, John

Career: 1916–38   Positions: **ss, 3b, c,** of, 1b, *2b, p,* manager

Teams: *Montgomery Grey Sox ('16),* Chicago Union Giants ('16), **Chicago Giants** ('16–'23), Havana Stars ('17), Chicago American Giants ('22–'23), **Baltimore Black Sox** ('24–'26, '30–'31), Harrisburg Giants ('26–'27), Homestead Grays ('24, '28–'29, '35), New York Lincoln Giants ('29–'30), Atlantic City Bacharach Giants, Newark Browns ('31–'32), New York Black Yankees ('33–'34), Newark Dodgers ('34), *Palmer House Indians ('36),* Brooklyn Royal Giants ('38)

Bats: Right   Throws: Right
Height: 6'3"   Weight: 220
Born: 1902, Louisville, Ky.
Died: 1956, New York, N.Y.

The right-handed pull hitter was a powerful and consistent hitter whose slugging prowess was extraordinary. Despite facing a severely overshifted defensive alignment, he maintained a high batting average and proved that nothing could stop his prodigious blasts out of the ballpark. Two of his most memorable tape-measure drives still generate awe. In Cincinnati he was the first player to hit a ball over the roof and completely out of Redland Field (1921), and in Washington, D.C., he hit a ball over the left-field bleachers that struck an advertising sign, 460 feet from home plate and 40 feet above the ground.

When he wasn't swinging his 38-inch bat, the hulking 220-pounder could play any position on the field. He began his career as a shortstop-catcher, progressed to a third

baseman-shortstop during his prime seasons, and was a third baseman in his waning years. While demonstrating his prodigious power, the free-swinger tried to pull everything to left field and developed a vulnerability to sidearm curveballs, increasing his frequency of strikeouts.

His temperament and basic approach to the game contributed to his making the rounds of a variety of teams during his twenty-two-year career. Beckwith began playing baseball in the Sunday School leagues in Chicago as a youngster, and turned professional in 1916 as a catcher with the Montgomery Grey Sox before playing with both the Union Giants and Chicago Giants later in the year. Except for a short tour of duty as captain of the Havana Stars the following spring, he remained with Chicago through 1921, when he hit .419, second best in the Negro National League.

Soon afterward he was signed by Rube Foster and, playing on the corners and hitting .302 while batting in the fifth and sixth spots in the order, he helped the American Giants win their third straight NNL pennant. The next season he hit .323 but, after less than two full seasons with the American Giants, he got into trouble with the law and left Chicago. Traveling East, Beckwith joined owner Cum Posey's Homestead Grays in 1924. But after proving to be unreliable and lacking in self-discipline, he was unconditionally released by Posey in midseason. He was quickly signed by the Baltimore Black Sox to fill a weak spot at shortstop and shortly after his arrival was made captain, with the team's success the remainder of the season being attributed largely to his presence. His versatility was one of his strong points, but his hitting prowess was the attribute that really set him apart from other players of the day. Ben Taylor considered him to be a "demon at bat," and Beckwith's stats (.452 batting average and 40 home runs against all competition and .403 in league play) corroborate this assessment. Beckwith followed in 1925 with a .402 average while finishing second in home runs.

That season he displaced Pete Hill as manager and moved himself to third base to fill the void left by the death of star third sacker Henry Blackman, who died while still in his prime. By late July Beckwith lead all Negro Leagues with 22 homers but shortly thereafter was suspended for severely beating an umpire and avoided arrest only by leaving town before a warrant was served. In August, engaged in a contract dispute, he quit as player-manager of the Black Sox without notice.

Rube Foster wanted to sign him for the 1926 season but Baltimore refused to release him, even after Foster offered star pitcher Juan Padron and two other players as compensation. Beckwith applied to the Negro National League commissioner to let him play in Chicago, where he owned a poolroom and where he was spending his time since quitting Baltimore. His efforts to relocate in Chicago were unfruitful, and in the spring of 1926 he was back with the Baltimore Black Sox.

However, his stay was short, and soon after Ben Taylor took over from Pete Hill, who had resumed the managership, Beckwith was traded to Harrisburg in midseason. Despite the turbulence generated by his personality, he managed a composite .361 batting average for the season. With the Harrisburg Giants in 1927 he hit .335 and again finished second in home runs for league play, while being credited with 72 home runs against all levels of competition. Back with the Homestead Grays again in 1928, he had 31 homers before the end of June and is credited with 54 home runs for the year. The following season, the Grays joined the American Negro League and Beckwith hit .443, second best in the league, while slamming 15 home runs. In 1930, playing with the Lincoln Giants, he won the unofficial eastern batting title with a .480 average and hit 19 home runs in 50 games against top black teams, despite missing almost two months with a broken ankle. Playing against all levels of opposition, he was credited with an almost unbelievable .546 average for the year. The Lincolns had an outstanding team that season but lost the playoff for the eastern championship to the Homestead Grays. Beckwith returned to the Black Sox late in the season, and in 1931, while splitting his playing time between the Sox and the Newark Browns, he hit .347.

Winding down his career during the Depression years with a series of teams as his skills eroded, he ended his career with a stupendous .366 lifetime batting average in Negro Leagues competition, and a .337 average in exhibitions played against major leaguers.

The numbers he accumulated during his career are impressive but, unfortunately, his contributions to a team with his natural ability were offset by negative intangibles. Beckwith was moody, brooding, hot-tempered, and quick to fight. Combined with a severe drinking problem, and an often lazy, unconcerned attitude about playing, his character deficiencies often negated his performance value. Sometimes he would play in an inebriated condition or exhibit meanness on the field. On one occasion, when Beckwith's error cost a game, pitcher Bill Holland tossed his glove in disgust and, in the clubhouse after the game, Beckwith responded by knocking the pitcher unconscious.

After his playing skills began to erode, he dropped out of the lineups of top teams but hung on as manager of a team of dubious quality, the Crescents of White Plains, New York. When he left baseball entirely, he worked briefly as a policeman in New York, but eventually reverted to activities on the other side of law enforcement that involved loose women, dice games, and bootlegging.

During his prime Beckwith was regarded as one of the top players by his peers, and he possessed sufficient versatility afield to play almost any position. However, he did not excel at any position, and his team value, lessened by his temperament, was often considered suspect.

Bejerano, Augustin (Pijini)
Career: 1928–29   Position: of
Teams: Cuban Stars (East) ('28–'29), *Mexican League ('37–'54)*
Bats: Left   Throws: Left
Born: Cuba

A consistent batter with exceptional speed, the left-handed outfielder played two seasons in the late '20s with the Cuban Stars (East), the first year in the Eastern Colored League and the second in the American Negro League, where he hit for a .381 average. The Cuban also played with Marianao in his homeland in the winter of 1943–44 and stole 14 bases.

However, he earned most of his baseball honors in Mexico, where he played for 15 seasons, playing on seven championship teams while leading the league in stolen bases four times, topping the .300 mark eight times and finishing with a .312 lifetime batting average. Beginning his Mexican career in 1937, he hit for averages of .404, .364, and .368 in his first three seasons. After a year's absence from the Mexican League, he returned to bat .366 for the 1941 champion Veracruz team, and continued with marks of .369, .281, .313, .322, .328, .297, .263, .254, .294, .278, and .256 through 1952. After another year's absence he returned for a final season in 1954 before closing out his baseball career. He was elected to the Mexican Hall of Fame in 1972.

Bell
Career: 1918   Positions: rf, lf
Team: *Baltimore Black Sox*
He was a reserve outfielder with the Baltimore Black Sox for a season during their formative years.

Bell
Career: 1946   Position: ut
Team: Philadelphia Stars
He was a utility player for the 1946 Philadelphia Stars in his only year in the Negro Leagues.

Bell, Charles (Lefty)
Career: 1948   Position: p
Team: Homested Grays
Bats: Left   Throws: Left
The left-hander was a second-line pitcher with the 1948 champion Homested Grays but fashioned a perfect 3–0 record.

Bell, Clifford (**Cliff,** Cherry)
Career: 1921–31   Positions: **p,** *of*
Teams: **Kansas City Monarchs** ('21–'26, '32), **Memphis Red Sox** ('27–'30), Cleveland Cubs ('31), Nashville Elite Giants ('31)
Bats: Right   Throws: Right
As a hurler for the Kansas City Monarchs, Cliff Bell started two games in each of the 1924 and 1925 World Series, and fashioned ERAs of 3.86 and 2.46. He began his career with the Monarchs in 1921 with a 4–3 league record, and during the championship seasons he is credited with records of 4–1 and 4–6. After a .500 season in 1926, he left the Monarchs for the Memphis Red Sox, and his record reflected the loss of the Monarchs' potent offense and sterling defense, as he dropped to records of 8–10, 1–13, and 6–14 during his three seasons with Memphis. During the 1929 season Cliff and his brother Fred Bell pitched together for the Red Sox in 1929. He closed out his career in 1931, splitting the year between the Negro National League Cleveland Cubs and the Nashville Elites of the Negro Southern League. During his career he also pitched in the Cuban winter league, and in four winters in Cuba he recorded a 15–17 ledger.

Bell, Frank
Career: 1888–91   Position: of
Teams: New York Gorhams ('88–'89), Cuban Giants ('91)
This nineteenth-century player was an outfielder with the Cuban Giants and the New York Gorhams. The two teams played in otherwise white leagues as representatives of a host city. The Cubans represented Ansonia in the Connecticut State League in 1891, while the Gorhams played in the Middle States League for two seasons, 1888–89.

Bell, Fred (Lefty)
Career: 1922–29   Positions: **p,** of
Teams: Birmingham Black Barons ('23), Toledo Tigers ('23), St. Louis Stars ('23–'24), Harrisburg Giants ('24–'25), Washington Poto-

macs ('24), Detroit Stars ('25–'27), Memphis Red Sox ('29)

Bats: Left **Throws:** Left

The left-handed pitcher was Cool Papa Bell's brother and was credited with having an outstanding fastball when he began his professional career in St. Louis. The youngster was picked up from the St. Louis Stars by Harrisburg of the Eastern Colored League in midseason 1924 in an effort to bolster a weak pitching staff. However, his stay was brief and, although he made a fair showing, he was not reserved for 1925. After leaving Harrisburg he also pitched briefly with the 1924 Washington Potomacs, but was released after only a month for more seasoning. He then joined the Detroit Stars and later the Memphis Red Sox, where he pitched together on the same team with his brother in 1929. He also logged some playing time in the outfield during his short career and hit .299 in 1926.

Bell, Herman

Career: 1943–50 Position: c
Team: Birmingham Black Barons
Bats: Right Throws: Right
Height: 5'9" Weight: 195

The stocky catcher was a good receiver with a strong but not consistent arm, and was a reliable performer behind the plate for the Birmingham Black Barons for most of the decade of the '40s. However, his hitting lacked consistency and power. Beginning as a backup in 1943, he hit for averages of .277 and .194 in 1945–46. He assumed more playing time in 1947, sharing the regular catching duties for the next three seasons, and hitting for averages of .261 and .196 in 1948–49.

Bell, James (Steel Arm)

Career: 1932–40 Positions: c, p
Teams: Montgomery Grey Sox ('32–'33), Indianapolis Crawfords ('40)

Playing during the '30s, he began his career as a pitcher for the Montgomery Grey Sox and closed it as a catcher for the Indianapolis Crawfords.

Bell, James Thomas (Cool Papa)

Career: 1922–46 Positions: cf, lf, *1b*, p
Teams: **St. Louis Stars** ('22–'31), Detroit Wolves ('32), Kansas City Monarchs ('32, '34), **Homestead Grays** ('32, '43–'46), **Pittsburgh Crawfords** ('33–'38), Memphis Red Sox ('42), *Santo Domingo ('37), Mexican League ('38–'41)*, Chicago American Giants ('42), *Detroit Senators ('47), Kansas City Stars ('48–'50)*
Bats: Both Throws: Left
Height: 5'11" Weight: 150
Born: May 17, 1903, Starkville, Miss.
Died: March 7, 1991, St. Louis, Mo.

The fastest man ever to play baseball, Cool Papa Bell rode the crest of the publicity from his incredible speed and colorful nickname into the Hall of Fame. The lean racehorse once was clocked circling the bases in an amazing 12 seconds. Cool Papa used his speed and daring to become the foremost base stealer in baseball and to "leg out" extra-base hits, thus offsetting his lack of real power at the plate.

Numerous stories are told of his feats on the basepaths. Many no doubt are true, such as consistently hitting two-hoppers to the infield and beating the throw to first for a hit, going from first to third on a bunt, scoring from second on a sacrifice fly, stealing two bases on one pitch, and once scoring from first base on a bunt against Bob Lemon and a team of major-league all-stars. Other stories are simply colorful exaggerations. Such accounts have Cool Papa hitting a single up the middle and being declared out when hit by his own batted ball as he slid into second base; and, of course, the most repeated story of how he could switch off the light and get into bed before the room was dark.

While some stories may be exaggerated, his speed was real. He once stole 175 bases in just under 200 games. He also utilized his speed in the field, with his great range allowing him to play a shallow center field and still run down pitchers' mistakes.

His speed going from home to first is described by former teammates, "If he bunts and it bounces twice, put it in your pocket,'' says ''Double Duty'' Radcliffe. ''If he hits one back to the pitcher, everyone yelled, 'Hurry!' '' claims Jimmie Crutchfield. When Jackie Robinson was a shortstop with Kansas City, Bell proved that Robinson didn't have the arm to play the position in the major leagues, by hitting two-hoppers to Robinson's right and beating them out. In an exhibition game against major leaguers on the West Coast, Bell scored from first on a bunt by Satchel Paige.

His grandfather was an Oklahoma Indian and his father was a farmer, living in Starkville, Mississippi, and Bell began playing pickup games on the sandlots of the area. In 1920 there was neither a high school nor available jobs in his hometown, so he went to St. Louis to stay with his older brothers while attending high school for two years. He also worked in a packing plant and played baseball with the Compton Hill Cubs. A left-handed thrower, he was discovered and signed by the St. Louis Stars for $90 a month. At that stage of his career he was a pitcher with a knuckler, screwball, and curve, and threw all of his pitches with three different motions. He was still a pitching prospect when he earned his nickname in 1922 by retaining his poise while striking out Oscar Charleston in a clutch situation. His manager, Bill Gatewood, observed how ''cool'' the nineteen-year-old had been under pressure and added the ''Papa'' to make the name sound better. Although the nickname became permanent, his pitching career was short-lived, being ended by an arm injury that left him without the strong throwing arm he had had previously. After moving to the outfield in 1924, he used a quick release to compensate adequately for the loss of arm strength. That year he also learned to be a switch-hitter; previously he had hit from the right side only.

Cool Papa played on three of the greatest teams in the history of black baseball: the St. Louis Stars, who won championships in 1928, 1930, and 1931; the great Pittsburgh Crawfords teams of 1932–36, often called the best team ever in black baseball; and after returning from five years ''south of the border,'' the Homestead Grays of 1943–45 for the last three of their nine consecutive championships

The switch-hitting Bell had good bat control and hit for a high average. After he became a full-time outfielder, existing records show season averages of .354, .362, .319, .332, .312, .332, and .322 with the Stars (1925–1931); .362, .317, .341, and .329 with the Crawfords (1933–36); and .356, .373, .302, and .396 with the Grays ('43–'46). Transitory seasons show averages of .384 in 1932, split between the Detroit Wolves and Kansas City Monarchs, and .370 in 1942, spent with the Chicago American Giants. Bell maintains that in his last year, 1946, he had ''given'' the batting title to Monte Irvin to enhance his chance of playing in the major leagues.

Bell was a selfless player and fans recognized and appreciated this quality in his character. Cool Papa's popularity was evident—he was voted to the East-West All-Star game every year from its inception in 1933 through 1944, except for the years when he was playing in Latin America.

In 1937 he went to Santo Domingo with Satchel Paige and hit .318 to help win the championship for Trujillo's ballclub. The following season was the first of four summers spent in Mexico, where he earned $450 a month. Beginning with Tampico in 1938, he hit for averages of .356, .354, .437, and .314 during his stay south of the border. During his second year with Tampico, he was selected to play in the All-Star game, but in 1940, while splitting the season between Veracruz and Torreon, he enjoyed his best year in the Mexican League, winning the Triple Crown with a .437 batting average, 12 home runs, and 79 RBIs, while also leading the league in runs (119) and triples (15) and finishing with 29 doubles and 28 stolen bases, each third best in the league. Although his average slipped the following year, he still led the league in doubles in his last year before returning to the United States.

In addition to those prime summers that he spent in the Mexican League, he played 21 winter seasons in Cuba, Mexico, and California. His Cuban stats show a .292 batting average for four winter seasons. His last four seasons in baseball were spent as a playing manager with teams of lesser quality, the Detroit Senators in 1947 and the Kansas City Stars, a farm club of the Kansas City Monarchs, in 1948–50. The following season he declined an offer from the St. Louis Browns as a player, but accepted a position as a part-time scout with the organization until the franchise was moved to Baltimore in 1954. He closed his baseball career with a lifetime batting average of .341 for a quarter century in black baseball. Further indications of his exceptional batting skills are a .391 batting average in exhibition games against major leaguers.

After the end of his baseball career he worked as a custodian and night security officer at the St. Louis City Hall, retiring in 1970. Bell was honored for his long and distinguished baseball career by being inducted into the National Baseball Hall of Fame in 1974.

Bell, Julian (Jute)
Career: 1924–30   Positions: **p**, of
Teams: Detroit Stars ('24), Memphis Red Sox ('27–'28), Birmingham Black Barons ('29–'30)
Born: May 30, 1900, Jellico, Tenn.
Died: December 7, 1991, Knoxville, Tenn.

A pitcher for seven seasons in the Negro Leagues, playing primarily with southern teams, he was called the black Tommy Bridges for his great curve and good control. Pitching with the Memphis Red Sox in 1927, he suffered through a 3–8 season. Joining the Birmingham Black Barons two years later, he was 5–11 and 4–10 in 1929–30.

After completing his professional baseball career, he embarked on a long and distinguished career in education as a teacher, coach, and administrator. Among the players he coached was Goose Tatum. He was a graduate of Tennessee State University, the University of Michigan, and Indiana University, with additional studies at Springfield College, the University of Illinois, and the University of Tennessee. He was on the faculty, coaching staff, and served as the athletic director at Lane College in Jackson, Tennessee; at Fisk University in Nashville, Tennessee; and for twenty years (1952–73) he taught, coached basketball, and was athletic director at Knoxville College. He retired in 1973, was active in civic activities and politics, and served as an officer of the Southern Intercollegiate Athletic Association. In 1977, four years after his retirement, he was inducted into the Tennessee Sports Hall of Fame.

During World War II he served as director of YMCA–USO operations at Camp Forest in Tullahoma and in the Pacific Northwest.

Bell, Ralph
[see Bebop, Ralph (Spec)]

Bell, William
Career: 1902–04   Positions: **p**, of
Team: Philadelphia Giants ('02–'04)

A player with the Philadelphia Giants in 1902–04, he was utilized as both a pitcher and an outfielder.

Bell, William, Jr. (Lefty)
Career: 1949–50   Position: p
Teams: Kansas City Monarchs ('49–'54), Birmingham Black Barons ('50)
Bats: Left   Throws: Left

Beginning his career with the Kansas City Monarchs in 1949, at a time when the Negro American League was in decline, the left-hander pitched with both the Monarchs and the Birmingham Black Barons in 1950, and he continued with the Monarchs on into the early '50s, when the league was strictly a minor league.

Bell, William, Sr.
Career: 1923–37, '48 Positions: **p**, of
                         manager
Teams: **Kansas City Monarchs** ('23–'30), Harlem Stars ('31), Detroit Wolves ('32), Homestead Grays ('32), Pittsburgh Crawfords

('32–'35), Newark Dodgers ('35), Newark Eagles ('36–'37; '48)

Bats: Right   Throws: Right
Height: 5'11"   Weight: 185
Born: Lavaca County, Tex.
Died: 1979, El Campo, Tex.

Bell was a clutch pitcher with a moving fastball, a good curve and change, a slider, and excellent control. A workhorse for the pennant-winning Kansas City Monarchs of 1924 and 1925, the ledger shows marks of 10–2 and 9–3 for the regular season. He started three games in the 1924 World Series, winning his only decision and compiling a 2.63 ERA, and in the 1925 World Series he pitched in three games, including two starts, and had a 1.13 ERA. The following year he is credited with a 16–3 record, as the Monarchs lost their bid for a third consecutive pennant in a league playoff against the Chicago American Giants. In 1927–28 he logged records of 13–6 and 10–7. Still in his prime, he spent the 1928–29 winter with Havana in the Cuban League and tied with Dolph Luque for the lead in wins with nine. The next two years, back in the United States with the Monarchs, he fashioned work sheets of 14–4 and 9–3.

In 1932, after the demise of the Negro National League the previous season, he joined the Detroit Wolves. When the Detroit franchise was absorbed by the Homestead Grays, he signed with the Pittsburgh Crawfords and compiled a 16–4 record for the 1932 season. From the Crawfords he went to the Newark Dodgers, and when that franchise was merged with the Brooklyn Eagles to form the Newark Eagles, he became the Eagles' manager in 1936–37. He was a good teacher, and, with his mastery of the three basic pitches, was a positive role model for young pitchers. Bell also was a decent hitter for a pitcher, batting .321 and .286 in 1927 and 1929, and fielded his position adequately, but was slow on the bases. His last appearance in black baseball was as a manager of the Eagles in 1948.

Bema
Career: 1929   Position: ph
Team: Cuban Stars (West)

He appeared as a pinch hitter with the Cuban Stars (West) in 1929, in his only appearance in the Negro Leagues.

Benjamin, Jerry Charles
a.k.a. Christopher
Career: 1932–48   Positions: cf, *manager*
Teams: Memphis Red Sox ('32), Detroit Stars ('33), Birmingham Black Barons ('34), **Homestead Grays** ('35–'48), Newark Eagles ('39), Toledo Crawfords ('39), New York Cubans ('48)

Bats: Both   Throws: Right
Height: 5'9"   Weight: 165
Born: Nov. 9, 1909, Montgomery, Ala.

As the center fielder for the Homestead Grays' dynasty of 1937–45, his prime seasons coincided with the Grays' glory years, when they rolled up nine consecutive pennants. A speedy base runner, good fielder, and steady hitter, he joined the Grays in 1935 and hit .320 and .344 in his first two seasons in Homestead. The next year began the Grays' skein of Negro National League pennants, and Benjamin contributed an all-star performance to their initial success. For the next three seasons, he hit for successive averages of .328, .300, and .298 as the Grays copped a trio of additional titles.

Although the Grays took the next two flags, Benjamin's offense dropped off, hitting .235 and .240, but he bounced back in 1943 with one of his best seasons, hitting .485 in home contests to finish with an overall .392 average and earn his second trip to the East-West All-Star game. In 1944 he continued his solid hitting with a .305 average, and moved into the top ten with a .329 average in 1945. He also tied with Cool Papa Bell for second place in stolen bases, only one behind the league leader, and earned his third trip to the All-Star game.

The Grays won three more pennants during these years, and defeated the Birmingham Black Barons in the World Series in the first two years, before losing to the Cleveland Buckeyes in the 1945 Series. Benjamin had another solid season in 1946 with a .296 performance at the plate, but the Grays failed to win the pennant for the first time in a decade. In 1947 Benjamin's average slipped to .208 and his long association with the Grays was ended.

He first joined the Homestead Grays from the Birmingham Black Barons in 1934, but his tenure with the Grays was interrupted in 1939, when he was traded by owner Cum Posey to the Newark Eagles for Ray Dandridge. But Benjamin refused to report and played ball for Oscar Charleson's Toledo Crawfords under the alias of Christopher. Posey threatened to take some of the West's players in retaliation, and Benjamin was soon back with the Grays. Dandridge, who had jumped to Venezuela and was unaware of the trade, remained the property of the Newark Eagles.

When Cool Papa Bell joined the Grays, arguments developed among the fans about which outfielder was faster, but Benjamin remained in center, with Bell taking a side pasture. However, Benjamin did not often employ either the bunt or the hit-and-run to capitalize on his speed, and did not protect a base runner on a steal attempt as much as some thought he should. During an exhibition game in Buffalo he suffered a broken ankle when he tripped over a guy wire holding the portable lights in place.

In 1948, after leaving the Grays, he played briefly with the New York Cubans before taking the helm as manager of the Norfolk-Newport News Royals in the Negro American Association and guiding the team to 23 straight victories.

Bennett
Career: 1913–14   Position: of
Team: New York Lincoln Giants

He was a substitute outfielder with the New York Lincoln Giants in 1913, batting .308 in very limited play in left field. The next season he again was a reserve player, filling in at second base in addition to playing the outfield.

Bennett
Career: 1930   Position: player
Team: Birmingham Black Barons

A marginal player of undetermined position, he appeared briefly with the Birmingham Black Barons in 1930, his only season with a quality ballclub.

Bennett, Bradford
Career: 1940–46   Positions: of, 1b
Teams: New Orleans-St. Louis Stars ('40), St. Louis Stars ('41), New York Black Yankees ('42), *Boston Blues ('46)*
Bats: Right   Throws: Right
Height: 6'0"   Weight: 175
Born: 1922, Fulton, Ky.

At age seventeen, the fleet-footed Fulton, Kentucky, product jumped from the sandlots and, as a teenage wonder, was playing left field for the 1941 St. Louis Stars. Unfortunately, his batting and fielding skills did not match his speed, and his career was relatively short. When the St. Louis franchise folded, he played first base with the New York Black Yankees in 1942, hitting .224, and finished his career with the Boston Blues in the U.S. League.

Bennett, Don
Career: 1926–34   Positions: 2b, rf
Teams: Dayton Marcos ('26), Cleveland Cubs ('32), Memphis Red Sox ('34)

He enjoyed a brief career as a second baseman, beginning with the Dayton Marcos as a reserve in 1926 and also playing with the Cleveland Cubs and Memphis Red Sox in the early years of the Depression.

Bennett, Frank
Career: 1918   Position: manager
Team: Atlantic City Bacharach Giants

He served a season as manager of the Bacharach Giants in 1918, following their move to Atlantic City, New Jersey, from Jacksonville, Florida.

Bennett, Jim
Career: 1945–48   Position: p
Teams: Cincinnati-Indianapolis Clowns ('45), Indianapolis Clowns ('46–'48)

He pitched with the Clowns for four seasons

during the '40s, and also pitched with the Havana La Palomas in 1947. In his last season in the Negro American League, he won his only decision in three games pitched.

Bennett, John
Career: 1932   Position: of
Team: Louisville Black Caps

In his only season in the Negro Leagues, he played outfield with the Louisville Black Caps in 1932.

Bennett, Sam
Career: 1911–25   Positions: **of**, c, 1b, 2b
Teams: **St. Louis Giants** ('11–'21), Mohawk Giants, St. Louis Stars ('22–'25)
Died: Jan. 30, 1969, St. Louis, Mo.

Moving North from Austin, Texas, he began his career with the St. Louis Giants in 1911, playing center field and batting cleanup. He remained in this capacity for the next two seasons as the Giants won the City League Championship. As an outfielder he would turn his back and run to where the ball was coming down, then turn and make the catch. Later in the decade he moved to the right-field position, and also played first base and catcher. He was an excellent hitter and had a good throwing arm that served him well when he began catching. Bennett also served a stint as manager of the Giants during his fifteen years with St. Louis teams, playing with the Stars during his latter years. His style and playing characteristics were compared to those of Sam Crawford, and he is reported to have divulged some pointers on outfield play to Tris Speaker.

Bennette, George Clifford (Jew Baby)
a.k.a. Bennett
Career: 1920–36   Positions: of, *c*
Teams: Columbus Buckeyes ('20–'21), Detroit Stars ('22), Pittsburgh Keystones ('22), Memphis Red Sox, Indianapolis ABCs, Chicago American Giants, Chicago Union Giants ('36), *Atlanta Black Crackers ('35)*

During a seventeen-year career as an outfielder and fill-in catcher, he played with a host

of teams located mostly in the Midwest. In 1935, during the waning years of his career, he was appointed manager of the Atlanta Black Crackers but was fired after only ten days.

Benning
Career: 1937   Position: 2b
Team: Indianapolis Athletics

In his only year in the Negro League, he was a reserve second baseman with the 1937 Indianapolis Athletics.

Benson
Career: 1937–40   Position: p
Teams: Washington Elite Giants ('37), Memphis Red Sox ('40)

He pitched briefly in each league, appearing in the Negro National League in 1937 with the Washington Elite Giants, and in the Negro American League in 1940 with the Memphis Red Sox.

Benson, Eugene (**Gene**, Spider, *Elwood*)
a.k.a. Bention
Career: 1933–49   Positions: **cf**, lf, *1b*
Teams: *Santop's Bronchos ('32)*, Brooklyn Royal Giants ('33), *Boston Royals ('34), Atlantic City Bacharach Giants ('34–'36)*, Washington Elite Giants ('36), **Philadelphia Stars** ('37–'48), Pittsburgh Crawfords ('38), Homestead Grays ('38), Newark Eagles ('42)
Bats: Left   Throws: Left
Height: 5'8"   Weight: 180
Born: October 2, 1913, Pittsburgh, Pa.

The left-handed outfielder for the Philadelphia Stars was an accomplished fielder with good speed and great range, who popularized the basket catch years before Willie Mays joined the Negro Leagues. Gene was noted for picking line drives off of his shoetops and also for turning his back to the ball and running back to turn just in time to catch a long fly hit directly over his head. This was a matter of practice and experience. Benson and other black outfielders did not trail the ball as today's outfielders do, but just ran to the spot where the ball was judged to come down, and turned and caught the ball.

Once using this technique, Benson made a catch under circumstances that were extraordinary. The Stars played their home games at Forty-fourth and Parkside, and beyond right field was the roundhouse of the main yard of the Pennsylvania Railroad. When a train rolled into or out of the roundhouse, it belched black smoke as thick as a blanket that covered the field in semidarkness. One summer night in 1937, in a game between the Philadelphia Stars and the Homestead Grays, slugger Josh Gibson hit a fastball to deep center field, and Benson went back to the tennis courts beyond center field and disappeared from sight. He reappeared holding a ball high above his head. Gibson accused him of hiding a ball in his pocket.

A natural hitter, the left-handed line-drive hitter hit left-handers better than right-handers. A big RBI man, he was a good fastball hitter and had an unorthodox stance that looked like he was not ready, but the slap hitter was a bad-ball hitter and went with the pitch, usually hitting to left field. His easy swing produced batting averages of .327, .370, and .345 for the years 1944–46. Benson appeared in the East-West games in each of the two latter years (two games were played in 1946), bringing his total All-Star appearances to four. His first appearance was in 1940, when he played center field and batted in the leadoff spot for the East squad, and responded with a pair of hits.

He moved from Moundsville, West Virginia, to West Philadelphia in his early teens and played baseball at Sulzberger Junior High School, but when he went to West Philadelphia High School, he couldn't play on the school team because of his color and had to play on the sandlots.

In 1932 he played first base with Santop's Bronchos, and the following year he and Buck Leonard, both first basemen, tried out with the Brooklyn Royal Giants, but with veteran High-pockets Hudspeth ensconced at first base, had to play in the outfield, although neither had

ever played the outfield before. Originally Benson fancied himself a power hitter, but he struck out so much that he adjusted his stance and became a contact hitter. With the Royals Benson received some playing time in left field, often batting in the leadoff position, but in 1934 he was ready for more playing time and signed with the Boston Royals, who left him stranded in Kalamazoo, Michigan. Finding his way back to Philadelphia, he joined manager Otto Briggs' Bacharachs, a semipro team of younger and less accomplished players whose only connection with the original Bacharachs was their name.

While playing with the Bacharachs, he was discovered by the Philadelphia Stars and signed in 1937. His ability to hit Slim Jones in an exhibition game between the two teams helped him earn a place on the Stars' roster. He hit a solid .280 in his rookie year and, for some inexplicable reason, during his first season with the Stars the local press referred to him as Elwood Benson. But once with the Stars, manager Oscar Charleston, the greatest center fielder in black baseball history, taught him to play center field and the fleet-footed youngster soon was the key man in the outfield. He was credited with irregular averages of .240, .367, .300, .272, .234, and .343 for the next six seasons (1938–43) after his rookie season.

During his career with the Stars, he sometimes played in Latin American leagues, including winters in San Juan in Puerto Rico (1939), Venezuela (1945), and Cuba (1947), and a summer with Torreon in the Mexican League (1941), where he hit .340 with 8 triples in 153 at-bats.

While with the Stars, Benson was also involved in some interesting roster transfers, which can perhaps best be described as trades that turned out to be nontrades due to circumstances. In 1936 he was added to the Washington Elite Giants' squad for the playoffs against the Pittsburgh Crawfords, but the Series was never completed because of player defections and management replacement procedures. In 1938 he was traded from the Philadelphia Stars to the Pittsburgh Crawfords, but when he arrived in Pittsburgh, the Crawfords were out of town and he played for the Homestead Grays, who were favorably impressed and wanted to keep him. On the other occasion, in April 1942, he was traded to the Newark Eagles but refused to report to his new team. In each instance he was returned to the Philadelphia Stars.

Remaining by choice in Philadelphia, when a black all-star team was selected to barnstorm through Venezuela during the winter of 1945–46, he was chosen as one of the outfielders after having just completed a .370 season. On the team was the Kansas City Monarchs' rookie shortstop, Jackie Robinson, who became Benson's roommate in Caracas. Before the team left the airport on their exhibition trip, Branch Rickey had signed Robinson to a contract with the Dodger organization. Heeding Rickey's request, Robinson did not discuss the matter with his teammates until after the official announcement had been made. From that time on, Benson and Robinson spent many long evenings together talking about the importance and far-reaching impact of the now historic contract. Manager Felton Snow had assigned Robinson to room with Benson so he could take advantage of the counseling sessions that reached far into the nights, with Benson talking to Robinson, trying to encourage him.

Robinson, with only one season of Negro League baseball under his belt, had doubts about his ability to play at the major-league level. But Benson assuaged his anxieties and assured him he could make it in the big leagues, telling him that if he could hit in the Negro Leagues, he could hit in the major leagues.

After returning to the United States, Benson continued his own career in impressive fashion, rapping the ball for a .345 average. After the season, he joined Satchel Paige's All-Stars to tour the country playing against Bob Feller's All-Stars. The two all-star teams ended their cross-country tour with Feller's All-Stars only one game ahead, proving that black players could compete on an equal basis with white major leaguers. But for Benson, who was successful batting against the Cleveland Indians' right-hander, it also proved that he could hit the best pitcher in the major leagues in his prime.

In 1947 he hit .286 and added another full season with the Stars before finally leaving baseball in 1949. With his diamond career behind him, Benson worked as a stevedore on the waterfront; operated a poolroom in North Philadelphia; and, beginning in 1961, worked in the transportation department for the school district of Philadelphia until his retirement in 1979.

Bention
[see Benson, Gene]

Benton
Career: 1950   Position: p
Team: Memphis Red Sox

He was listed as a pitcher with the Memphis Red Sox in 1950, when the Negro American League was struggling to survive the loss of players to organized baseball, but his playing time was severely restricted.

Benvenuti, Julius
Career: 1939   Position: officer
Team: Chicago American Giants

In 1939 he served as vice president of the Chicago American Giants for one season.

Bergin, Jimmy
Career: 1949   Position: 1b
Team: Kansas City Monarchs

He played as a reserve first baseman in 1949, when the Negro American League was struggling to survive the loss of players to organized baseball.

Berkeley, Randolph
Career: 1919   Position: c
Team: Hilldale Daisies ('19)

A reserve catcher, he was with Hilldale briefly in 1919, and played the following season with the Madison Stars, a team of lesser quality.

Berkley

Career: 1941   Position: p
Team: New Orleans-St. Louis Stars

He was a pitcher with the 1941 New Orleans-St. Louis Stars, but his playing time was limited.

Bernal, Blacedo

a.k.a. Bernard
Career: 1941   Position: p
Team: New York Cubans

The right-hander pitched briefly with the New York Cubans in 1941, losing his only decision.

Bernard

[see Bernal, Blacedo]

Bernard

Career: 1911–17   Positions: of, c
Teams: New York Lincoln Giants ('12, '17), Philadelphia Giants ('13), Pittsburgh Giants ('11), New York Lincoln Stars ('15), Hilldale Daisies ('17), Cuban Giants

For seven seasons prior to World War I, he was an outfielder-catcher with several eastern teams in the New York and Philadelphia areas. With the Lincolns he was a reserve right fielder and his playing time was severely restricted.

Bernard, Pablo

Career: 1949–50   Positions: ss, 2b
Teams: Louisville Buckeyes ('49), Cleveland Buckeyes ('50), *minor leagues ('50–'57), Mexican League ('58–'61)*
Bats: Right   Throws: Right
Height: 5'11"   Weight: 158
Born: Panama, 1927

Beginning his career just as the Negro Leagues were ending as a major-league organization, the light-hitting middle infielder played both shortstop and second base with the Buckeyes when they were in Louisville and Cleveland. However, most of his baseball career was spent in the minor leagues, and he spent a dozen years in the minors beginning in 1950.

After hitting .242 in 1949 in his only full season in the Negro Leagues, he began the 1950 season with the Buckeyes but soon entered organized ball with Ventura in the California League, where he hit .284 for the remainder of the year. The following year he hit an even .300 with Ventura to earn a move to Denver in the Western League.

His travels in organized ball took him to Billings in the Pioneer League, Tulsa in the Texas League, and Havana in the International League, where he hit .271 in 1956. In 1957 he was with three teams, beginning with Havana and ending with Austin in the Texas League. His best season in organized ball was 1954 with Billings, where he hit .334 and stole 40 bases.

His last four seasons were spent in Mexico in the summer and Panama in the winter (excluding the 1959–60 winter). In 1958, with Nuevo Laredo, he led the league in batting average (.371), hits (182) and runs (106). The final two years were spent with Vera Cruz, where he ended his career in 1961 with a .292 batting average for the season.

Berry

Career: 1943   Position: p
Team: Baltimore Elite Giants

A wartime player, he pitched briefly without distinction for the Baltimore Elite Giants in 1943, his only season in the Negro Leagues.

Berry, Bubber (Bubbles)

Career: 1938   Position: p
Teams: Ethiopian Clowns ('38), Atlanta Black Crackers ('38)

He pitched with the Ethiopian Clowns in 1938 but was obtained for the playoffs by the second-half pennant-winning 1938 Atlanta Black Crackers. He started one game for the Black Crackers against the Memphis Red Sox but was ineffective and suffered the loss.

Berry, E.

Career: 1930   Positions: ss, 2b

Teams: Memphis Red Sox ('30), Detroit Stars ('30)

The middle infielder split the 1930 season between the Memphis Red Sox and Detroit Stars, playing both shortstop and second base.

Berry, John Paul
Career: 1935–37, '45   Positions: **p**, 1b
Teams: Kansas City Monarchs ('35–'36, '45), St. Louis Stars ('37)

He was a pitcher with the St. Louis Stars and the Kansas City Monarchs during the late '30s, and returned for a final wartime season as a first baseman in 1945.

Berry, Mike (**Red**)
Career: 1947   Position: p
Team: Kansas City Monarchs
Bats: Right   Throws: Right
Height: 5'11"   Weight: 170

A mediocre pitcher with a pretty good fastball but not much else, he pitched with the 1947 Kansas City Monarchs.

Bert
[see Best]

Best
a.k.a. Bert
Career: 1904–06   Position: p
Teams: Brooklyn Royal Giants ('04), Famous Cuban Giants ('05–'06)

He pitched with the Brooklyn Royal Giants and the Famous Cuban Giants for three seasons during the early years of the twentieth century. A pitcher listed as Bert pitched with the 1906 Famous Cuban Giants and is thought to be the same player.

Betts
Career: 1938   Position: of
Team: Kansas City Monarchs

He was briefly a substitute outfielder with the Kansas City Monarchs in 1938.

Betts, Russell B.
Career: 1950   Position: p
Team: Kansas City Monarchs

He was listed as a pitcher with the Kansas City Monarchs in 1950, when the Negro American League was struggling to survive the loss of players to organized baseball.

Beverie
[see Beverly, Green (Wooger)]

Beverly, Charles (**Charlie**)
Career: 1915   Position: p
Team: Chicago American Giants

As a rookie in 1915 with Rube Foster's great Chicago American Giants, the left-hander with a smoking fastball twirled a no-hitter. He had been discovered by Foster after excelling in the Texas-Louisiana League.

Beverly, Charles (Hooks)
Career: 1924–36   Position: p
Teams: Cleveland Browns ('24), Birmingham Black Barons ('25), *Nashville Elite Giants ('27)*, **Kansas City Monarchs** ('31–'35), Cleveland Stars ('32), Pittsburgh Crawfords ('32), *New Orleans Crescent Stars ('34)*, Newark Eagles ('36), Philadelphia Stars ('36)
Bats: Left   Throws: Left
Height: 6'0"   Weight: 180
Died: Brookshire, Tex.

The tall, slender left-hander pitched for nine different teams during his thirteen-year career but is best identified with the Kansas City Monarchs. He primarily utilized breaking pitches, earning the name "Hooks" because of his good curveball. Unfortunately, his prime years came during the Depression, when the Monarchs were barnstorming across the Midwest as an independent team, and records are scarce from this period. In 1932, while splitting the season between the Cleveland Stars and the Pittsburgh Crawfords, he fashioned a combined 6–4 record.

He began playing baseball in Houston, Texas, with a longshoremen's team called the Morgan Line, and later barnstormed in San Francisco against Bob Feller in the latter '30s. His last year in league play was in 1936, when he played in the East, dividing his time between the Newark Eagles and the Philadelphia Stars. His brother, Green Beverly, was also a player in the Negro Leagues.

Beverly, Green (**Wooger**)
a.k.a. Beverie
Career: 1939   Position: 3b
Teams: Baltimore Elite Giants ('39), New York Black Yankees ('39)

After leaving home in 1932, he played with several teams before arriving as the third baseman with the Baltimore Elite Giants in 1939. During his career he also played with the New York Black Yankees and other teams, but was listed under the name Beverie because he was illiterate. He had a rifle arm and would sometimes play hard shots by letting the ball hit his legs that he had padded with three layers of socks, and then pounce on the ball and throw the runner out at first. Both his brother, Charles, and his son, William, also played in the Negro Leagues.

Beverly, William (Bill, **Fireball**)
Career: 1950   Positions: **p**, of, 1b
Teams: Houston Eagles ('50), *New Orleans Black Pelicans ('51), New Orleans Eagles ('51), Chicago American Giants ('51–'52), military service ('52), Canadian League ('53), Birmingham Black Barons ('54–'55)*
Bats: Right   Throws: Right
Height: 6'0"   Weight: 185
Born: May 5, 1930, Houston, Tex.

A hard-throwing right-hander, his bread-and-butter pitch was his fastball, but he also had a curve, slider, and change-up. The beginning of his career coincided with the decline of the Negro Leagues, pitching with the Houston Eagles in the Western Division of the Negro American League in 1950, where he registered a 5–1 record with a 4.63 ERA. By the end of the season, the Negro Leagues were no longer of major-league caliber and were not attracting crowds in Houston, and owner Allen Page moved the team to New Orleans, where the franchise name changed from the Black Pelicans to the New Orleans Eagles.

Moving North during the 1951 season, he joined the Chicago American Giants, where he remained until late in the 1952 season, when he entered military service. After his discharge, he played with the Thetford Miners in the Canadian Provincial League in 1953. Returning after a year, he played with the Birmingham Black Barons for two more seasons, 1954–55, before closing out his career. After leaving the baseball diamond, he worked for an oil well company in Houston.

Bibbs, Junius A. (**Rainey**, Sonny)
Career: 1933–44   Positions: **2b**, ss, 3b, *1b*
Teams: Detroit Stars ('33), Cincinnati Tigers ('36–'37), **Kansas City Monarchs** ('38–'41), Chicago American Giants ('38, '44), Indianapolis Crawfords ('40), Cleveland Buckeyes ('44)
Bats: Both   Throws: Right
Height: 5'10"   Weight: 180
Born: Oct. 10, 1910, Henderson, Ky.
Died: 1979

A good line-drive hitter who sprayed the ball to all fields, the switch-hitting second baseman hit .404 in 1936 with the Cincinnati Tigers, and after being selected to the West squad in the All-Star game, doubled in his only time at bat. He was also a good bunter and hit-and-run batter, but had only average speed on the bases. Although he was versatile afield and could play any infield position, he did not excel at any of them. After the Tigers dropped out of league play, he signed with the Chicago American Giants in 1938, and was playing as their regular second baseman and batting in the leadoff spot when he jumped to the Kansas City Monarchs during the season.

After joining the Monarchs, he played on three straight Negro American League pennant winners (1939–41), hitting for averages of .231 and .259 in the first and last seasons of the triad. During the middle season he began the year with the Indianapolis Crawfords as their cleanup hitter before returning to Kansas City. In 1944, the last of his dozen years in the Negro Leagues, he began the season with the

Monarchs and finished with the Cleveland Buckeyes, hitting .309 to close out his career.

He began his career with the Detroit Stars in 1933 and, prior to playing professional baseball, starred in college as a football player. Reared in Terre Haute, Indiana, Bibbs died from a heart attack in 1979.

Bilgar

Career: 1914   Position: c
Team: Chicago Giants

He shared a regular catching position with the Chicago Giants in 1914, his only year in black baseball.

Billings

Career: 1946   Position: c
Team: Homestead Grays

In 1946, the last season before Josh Gibson's death, Billings was one of the Grays' backup catchers.

Billings, William

Career: 1921   Position: p
Team: Nashville Elite Giants

He pitched with the Nashville Elite Giants in 1921, his only year in black baseball.

Billingsley, John

Career: 1950   Position: c
Team: Memphis Red Sox

He was listed as a catcher with the Memphis Red Sox in 1950, when the Negro American League was struggling to survive the loss of players to organized baseball, but league statistics do not confirm his playing time.

Billingsley, Sam

Career: 1950   Position: p
Team: Memphis Red Sox

He was listed as a pitcher with the Memphis Red Sox in 1950, when the Negro American League was struggling to survive the loss of players to organized baseball, but league statistics do not confirm his playing time.

Binder, James (**Jimmy**)

Career: 1930–37   Positions: **3b**, 2b
Teams: Memphis Red Sox ('30), Indianapolis ABCs ('31–'32), Detroit Stars ('33), **Homestead Grays** ('33–'35), Washington Elite Giants ('36), Pittsburgh Crawfords ('37)
Bats: Right   Throws: Right
Height: 5'11"   Weight: 180

An average player who manned the hot corner for the Homestead Grays during the early 1930s. He first attracted attention from better teams in 1927 when he hit .317 with the Argos (Indiana) Colored Giants. With the top clubs, he was only an average hitter with no significant power, a fair base runner, and an adequate fielder with an average arm. He began his career with the Memphis Red Sox and hit for a respectable .273 average.

After stints with the Indianapolis ABCs and Detroit Stars, he signed with the Grays in 1933 and stepped into the third slot in the batting order, moved up to the leadoff position in 1934, but in 1935, with partial statistics showing a batting average of only .188, dropped to the seventh slot. The next year he played with the Washington Elites, hitting .266 in a substitute capacity for the Elites, winners of the first-half Negro National League title before dropping to the cellar in the second half. The following season he closed out his career playing with the Pittsburgh Crawfords as a reserve infielder, mostly at second base. Throughout his career the infielder quietly performed his job in a workmanlike manner without attracting attention.

Binga, Jess E.

Career: 1887   Position: player
Team: *Washington Capital Citys*

He was a player with the 1887 Washington Capital Citys, one of eight teams that were charter members of the League of Colored Baseball Clubs in 1887. However, the league's existence was ephemeral, lasting only a week. His position is uncertain.

Binga, William

Career: 1895–1910   Positions: 3b, of, c

Teams: **Page Fence Giants** ('95–'98), *minor leagues ('95)*, Columbia Giants ('99–'00), Chicago Union Giants ('02, '04), Philadelphia Giants ('03), Leland Giants ('05), St. Paul Colored Gophers ('09), Kansas City Kansas Giants ('10)

He was regarded as one of the top third basemen in the early history of black baseball and played third base for some of the great teams of the latter part of the nineteenth century and the first decade of the twentieth century. He began his career with the Page Fence Giants in 1895, batting .286 for the season. That season Binga, who made his home in Lansing, Michigan, also played three games with Adrian in the Michigan State League as a replacement for the injured Vasco Graham.

After the Page Fence Giants disbanded, he joined the Columbia Giants in 1899 as the regular third baseman during their two years of existence, before they merged with the Chicago Unions in 1901 to form the Chicago Union Giants under manager Frank Leland. When Leland formed his new team that carried his name, the Leland Giants, Binga joined them in their first year of existence, 1905, playing both third base and left field. He also played with the St. Paul Colored Gophers when they won the western championship in 1909, and closed out his baseball career with the Kansas City, Kansas, Giants in 1910.

Bingham, William (**Bingo**)
Career: 1910–21   Position: of
Teams: West Baden Sprudels ('10), Chicago Union Giants ('16–'21), Chicago Giants ('21)

An outfielder in the Midwest during the deadball era, he began his career with the West Baden Sprudels in 1910, but played most of his career with the Chicago Union Giants. In 1916 he was a part-time starter in right field and usually batted fifth in the order when in the lineup. In 1921, his last season in black baseball, he was a reserve outfielder with the Chicago Giants.

Biot, Charles (**Charlie**)
Career: 1939–41   Position: cf
Teams: Newark Eagles ('39), New York Black Yankees ('39–'40), Baltimore Elite Giants ('41)
Bats: Right   Throws: Right
Height: 6'3"   Weight: 180
Born: Oct. 18, 1917, Orange, N. J.

A fast base runner and outstanding fielder, Biot hit for averages of .305 and .278 in 1940–41. He began his career as a pitcher, but was switched to the outfield early in his career. The speedy outfielder made two plays that stand out in his memory, one with the bat and one with the glove. While with the Black Yankees in 1940, he hit a two-run home run off Ace Adams in the bottom of the ninth inning to win the game, and while with the Baltimore Elites in 1941, he made a great catch off the Grays' Buck Leonard on a ball hit between light towers in Bugle Field, to save the game.

In the 1940 California winter league, he played against Babe Herman's All-Stars, also featuring Gerry Priddy, Lou Novikoff, and Lou Stringer. In six weeks of play, his team won 11 of 12 games from the major leaguers. While there he met Jackie Robinson (who was at the time a college football star) and gave him a pass to come see a game.

His professional baseball career was interrupted by the U. S. entry into World War II. Biot entered military service in 1942 and was captain of the Army baseball team for the 93rd Division of the 369th Regiment. After the war he never played with the top teams again. After leaving baseball he worked in a plastics factory for ten years, and when they closed down, worked for P. S. Electric for fifteen years.

Biran, Jack
a.k.a. Biron
Career: 1916   Position: 2b
Team: Chicago American Giants

He was listed as an infrequently used substitute infielder in 1916 for the Chicago American Giants.

Birmingham Black Barons

Duration: 1924–50   Honors: Second-half champions ('27), NAL pennants ('43–'44, '48)

Affiliations: NNL ('24–'25, '27–'30), NSL ('26, '31–'36), NAL ('37–'38, '40–'50)

Except for 1926, when they played in the Negro Southern League, the Black Barons were members of the Negro National League from 1924 through 1930; and except for 1939, they were members of the Negro American League from 1937 through 1950. Actually the franchise continued as members of the Negro American League on into the '50s, but the league was strictly a minor operation then, and the focus here is on the teams before the doors of organized baseball were opened to the best black athletic talent in the country.

The first significant success enjoyed by the Black Barons was their second-half title in the 1927 Negro National League split season, before losing the League Championship Series in a four-game sweep by the Chicago American Giants. The high points of Birmingham's nineteen-year black baseball history were the three Negro American League pennants in 1943, 1944, and 1948. Unfortunately, each time they lost the Negro World Series to the Homestead Grays.

Bissant, Bob

Career: 1938   Positions: 2b, ss

Teams: *Zulu Cannibal Giants ('35–'39)*, Miami Ethiopian Clowns ('38), *Nashville Cubs ('40), New Orleans Black Pelicans ('41–'45)*

Bats: Right   Throws: Right

Born: Aug. 20, 1913

The middle infielder played briefly with the Miami Ethiopian Clowns in 1938. Previously he had been with the Zulu Cannibal Giants, a team similar to the Clowns but with less talented ballplayers. Subsequently he played with several minor teams during the '40s, including the Nashville Cubs and the New Orleans Black Pelicans.

Bissant, John L.

Career: 1934–48   Positions: **lf, rf, cf,** 2b, p

Teams: Coles American Giants ('34), *Shreveport Acme Giants ('35–'36)*, Cincinnati Tigers ('37), *New Orleans Black Pelicans ('38)*, **Chicago American Giants** ('39–'48), Birmingham Black Barons ('40), *Chicago Brown Bombers ('42)*

Bats: Right   Throws: Right

Height: 5'8"   Weight: 180

Born: Feb. 19, 1914

A good outfielder, he could run and throw, but is probably better known for his hitting. He played left field for the Chicago American Giants in 1947 and hit .354 while serving as team captain under manager Jim Taylor. Bissant was appointed to continue in that capacity by Quincy Trouppe when he assumed the managerial reins the following season.

He began his career with Coles American Giants in 1934 before joining the Acme Giants in Shreveport, Louisiana, in 1935. After two seasons there, he played with the Cincinnati Tigers and the New Orleans Black Pelicans before joining the Chicago American Giants in the Negro American League in 1939. He played in a reserve role while posting averages akin to the .185 he hit in 1942, until breaking into the starting lineup in 1943. Playing left field, he hit .249, .304, and .235 for the 1944–46 seasons, while batting variously in the second, third, fifth, and sixth spots in the batting order over the next four seasons. Before entering professional baseball, the New Orleans native was a college star and was considered one of the best athletes ever to play at Wiley College.

Bivins

Career: 1948   Position: p

Team: Memphis Red Sox

He pitched briefly with the Memphis Red Sox in 1948, losing his only recorded decision.

Bix

Career: 1921   Position: p

Team: St. Louis Giants

A pitcher with the St. Louis Giants in 1921, he did not garner much playing time during his only season in the Negro Leagues.

Bizzle
Career: 1947   Position: of
Team: Birmingham Black Barons

He appeared as a reserve outfielder with the Black Barons in 1947, his only season in the Negro Leagues.

Black
Career: 1926   Position: p
Team: Cleveland Elite Giants

He pitched briefly without a decision for the Cleveland Elites in 1926, the team's only season in the Negro National League.

Black, Joseph (Joe)
Career: 1943–50   Position: p
Teams: Baltimore Elite Giants ('43–'50), *military service ('43–'45), minor leagues ('51, '54, '57)*, major leagues ('52–'57)
Bats: Right   Throws: Right
Height: 6'2"   Weight: 210
Born: Feb. 8, 1924, Plainfield, N.J.

In 1947, pitching for the Baltimore Elite Giants, the big, strong, hard-throwing right-hander split 18 decisions while leading the league in games pitched. After three more years as the Elites' workhorse, where he registered seasons of 10–5, 11–7, and 8–3, he was selected as the starting pitcher for the East in the 1950 All-Star game.

An all-around athlete at Morgan State College, he had a natural slider that aided him when he made the transition to professional baseball. However, soon after graduation in the summer of 1943, he was drafted into the Army and his baseball career was structured around his military responsibilities. With the Elite Giants in 1944 he split six decisions but had only one start in 1945 before remaining inactive for the duration of World War II. Back with the Elite Giants in 1946, he was 4–9 in his first full season after military service but was beginning to mature as a pitcher. Signed

after three good years with the Elite Giants, he entered organized ball in 1951. He split the season with Montreal in the International League (7–9, 3.85 ERA) and St. Paul in the American Association (4–3, 2.25 ERA). A winter season (1951–52) with Cienfuegos in the Cuban winter league produced a record of 5–7 and a 4.22 ERA.

While the numbers were not impressive, Black's velocity was, and in the spring of 1952 the big fireballer debuted with the Brooklyn Dodgers, having a sensational rookie year, winning 15 games and saving a like number while losing only 4 games. His contributions to the Dodgers' pennant success earned him Rookie of the Year honors. In the World Series that year he started the opening game, winning 4–2, the first victory by a black pitcher in a World Series. He continued his Herculean efforts as he started two other games and compiled a 2.53 ERA for the Series in a losing cause as the Dodgers dropped a hard-fought seven-game series to the Yankees.

That winter (1952–53) in Cuba, Black's improvement as a pitcher was amplified with a 15–6 record (tops for the league in wins) and a 2.42 ERA. His numbers further reflected remarkable improvements in other areas from the previous winter. His control, hit ratio, and ERA were all significantly lower. This gave him a combined 20–13 work sheet for the two Cuban winter seasons.

In the spring of 1953, while trying to expand his repertory of pitches, he lost a measure of the control that he had demonstrated the year before and, although he pitched for five more major-league seasons with Brooklyn, Cincinnati, and Washington, he was never able to regain the dominance from his rookie season. He finished his baseball career in 1957 by going down to Seattle in the Pacific Coast League and then to Tulsa in the Texas League. He ended his six years in the major leagues with a 30–12 lifetime record.

After leaving the baseball diamond, he continued his college education with postgraduate studies at Seton Hall and Rutgers universities, and served as vice president of special markets with the Greyhound Corporation.

Black, William
Career: 1938   Position: of
Team: Atlanta Black Crackers

The outfielder from Jackson, Mississippi, was on the Atlanta Black Crackers' spring roster in 1938, but his stay with the team was very brief.

Blackburn, Hugh
Career: 1920   Positions: p, *1b*
Team: Kansas City Monarchs

He was a pitcher with the Kansas City Monarchs in 1920, their first year of league play.

Blackman, Clifford (Cliff, Speed)
Career: 1937–41   Position: p
Teams: Chicago American Giants ('37). Birmingham Black Barons ('38), Memphis Red Sox ('39), Indianapolis ABC's ('39), New Orleans-St. Louis Stars ('41), New York Cubans ('41), Homestead Grays ('41)
Bats: Right   Throws: Right

In 1937, the rookie right-hander for the Chicago American Giants was regarded as a "clever pitcher," but he was unable to stick with any ballclub for very long, playing with seven different teams, mostly in the Midwest and South during the five seasons prior to World War II.

Blackman, Henry
Career: 1920–24   Positions: **3b**, *c, 1b*
Teams: *San Antonio Black Aces ('20),* New York Lincoln Giants ('20), **Indianapolis ABCs** ('20, '22–'23), *Colored All-Stars ('21),* Baltimore Black Sox ('24)
Bats: Right   Throws: Right
Height: 6'2"   Weight: 185
Born: 1888, Hillsboro, Tex.
Died: August 8, 1924, Baltimore, Md.

Although his career was short, the Indianapolis ABCs' hot-corner star is mentioned among the best of his era. He had a wide range, a strong and accurate arm, and was very quick afield. He excelled in fielding bunts and making the throw to first base without raising up. In the California winter league of 1921 he finished with the second-highest batting average (.408). His untimely death while still a top player at his position voided what might well have been a Hall of Fame career. At the time of his demise, he was hitting .333 with the Baltimore Black Sox in the Eastern Colored League.

The youngest of five children, he honed his baseball skills on the ball diamonds of Texas, and in July 1917 he was the third baseman with the Texas All-Stars. Three years later, while playing with a team called the San Antonio Black Aces, he left the Lone Star State to join C. I. Taylor's ABCs in 1920. While with the ABCs he earned a reputation as one of the cleanest fielders and had one of the best and snappiest arms in baseball, rarely making a bad throw. He was a fair hitter, with averages of .224 and .264 in 1922–23, and a fair base runner. He was good-natured, likable, and popular with the fans, and earned the nickname "the Galloping Ghost."

Manager Pete Hill of the Baltimore Black Sox signed the Texan in 1924, but Blackman didn't report, and business manager Charles Speeden caught a train and went West to bring him back East personally. After reporting to the Sox, the smooth-fielding third sacker was considered the peer of Judy Johnson and Oliver Marcelle and quickly became a crowd favorite.

Blackman played a game against Hilldale on July 26, performing in usual fashion, and two weeks later he was dead. His death took place in the office of Dr. Montague on Madison Avenue in Baltimore. He had gone there because of a throat ailment that later developed into complications that caused his death, listed as a liver ailment. Over a thousand fans followed his bier as his remains were taken to the Pennsylvania Railroad Station to be sent to Texas for interment.

Blackstone, William

Career: 1887   Position: player
Team: *Cincinnati Browns*

He played with the 1887 Cincinnati Browns, one of eight teams that were charter members of the League of Colored Baseball Clubs in 1887. However, the league's existence was ephemeral, lasting only a week. His position is uncertain.

Blackwell

Career: 1934   Position: p
Team: Philadelphia Stars

A fringe player, he pitched briefly with the Philadelphia Stars in 1934, but his playing time was severely restricted.

Blackwell, Charles (John, Rucker)

Career: 1915–29   Positions: lf, rf, cf
Teams: West Baden Sprudels ('15), Bowser's ABCs ('16), Jewell's ABCs, ('17), Indianapolis ABCs ('17), **St. Louis Giants** ('16–'21), **St. Louis Stars** ('22–'24, '28), Birmingham Black Barons ('25), Detroit Stars ('26), Nashville Elite Giants ('28–'29)
Bats: Left   Throws: Right
Height: 5'8"   Weight: 150
Died: May 12, 1935, Chicago, Ill.

An excellent contact hitter, he had a good eye at the plate and seldom struck out, but also had good power. He had a drinking problem but still hit on those occasions when playing under the residual influence of alcohol. He also had good speed, both in the field and on the bases. Blackwell began his career with the West Baden Sprudels but joined the St. Louis Giants in 1916 and was batting in the cleanup spot the following season when the team folded in May. Leaving the Giants, he signed on with the ABCs for the remainder of the season, hitting .286.

He rejoined the St. Louis Giants in 1919, batting cleanup and, while playing in the accommodating Car Barn Park after the lively ball was introduced, he rang up some impressive statistics, hitting .322 in 1920 as a prelude to his best season ever in 1921, when he hit .448, with a .729 slugging percentage and 27 stolen bases in 62 games. The next season the Giants became the St. Louis Stars, and Blackwell was in center field for the Stars in their first game ever played in St. Louis. With the Stars he hit for averages of .382, .311, and .258 for his last three years in St. Louis (1922–24), and afterward he hit .307 with the Birmingham Black Barons in 1925 and .276 with the Detroit Stars in 1926. Three years later, in 1929, he closed out his career, with the Nashville Elite Giants, with a lifetime .329 batting average.

Blair, Garnett E.

Career: 1942–48   Position: p
Teams: Homestead Grays ('42, '45–'48), *military service ('43–45), Richmond Giants ('49–52), minor leagues ('53)*
Bats: Right   Throws: Right
Height: 6'3"   Weight: 215
Born: July 31, 1921, Carnegie, Pa.

The young speedballer was discovered by the Homestead Grays playing sandlot ball with the Pittsburgh Monarchs, and after signing with the Grays, pitched briefly without a decision during their 1942 championship season. Entering military service at the end of the season, he returned to the Grays after two years of Army life and posted a 7–1 record for the 1945 season. He continued his mound work for three more seasons, recording a 3–2 league ledger for the 1948 season as the Grays annexed the last Negro National League flag and defeated the Birmingham Black Barons in the World Series to claim the championship.

Following the demise of the Negro National League after the 1948 season, he left the Grays to pitch for the Richmond Giants, a lesser team. After four years, he left the team and entered organized ball briefly, pitching two games without a decision for the Richmond Colts in the Piedmont League in 1953.

The elongated athlete also excelled in basketball, starring as a college player on the hardwood. His brother Lonnie also played with the

Grays for a short time but was less talented than his older brother.

Blair, Lonnie (Chico)
Career: 1947–50   Positions: **p, 2b,** *of, ss*
Team: Homestead Grays
Bats: Right   Throws: Right
Height: 5'6"   Weight: 170
Born: Oct. 30, 1929
Died: Jan. 27, 1991, Pittsburgh, Pa.

A brother of Garnett Blair, he joined the Homestead Grays in 1947 while still in high school but was not on the traveling squad, and pitched mostly in exhibition games. After the demise of the Negro National League following the 1948 season, he stayed with the Grays for two more seasons while they played as an independent ballclub, sometimes "passing" because of his light complexion to buy food for the team as they traveled throughout the South. Earning a salary of $300 per month with the Grays, he declined a tryout with the Cleveland Indians, and after the Grays broke up in 1950, he joined the Air Force. After leaving the service, he worked as a meatcutter and foreman in the Pittsburgh area prior to his death in 1991 from heart disease.

Blair, William, Jr.
Career: 1948   Position: p
Teams: *Detroit Senators ('47),* Birmingham Black Barons ('48)

After playing the 1947 season with the Detroit Senators, a minor team, the youngster from Dallas, Texas, joined the Birmingham Black Barons the following spring, vying for a position on their pitching staff.

Blake, Frank (Big Red)
Career: 1932–35   Position: p
Teams: Baltimore Black Sox ('32), New York Black Yankees ('34–'35), New York Cubans ('35)

A hard thrower with rather severe control problems, the big right-hander pitched primarily for New York-based teams during his four-year career.

Blanchard, Chester
Career: 1926   Positions: **ss,** 2b, lf, *p*
Team: Dayton Marcos ('26–*'33*)

A light-hitting infielder, his versatility won him a spot as a part-time starter, playing at both keystone positions and in the outfield, with the Dayton Marcos in 1926. He hit .235 that season, the Marcos' last in the Negro National League. Afterward they played a less demanding schedule.

Blanco, Carlos
Career: 1938–41   Positions: 1b, 3b
Teams: Cuban Stars, New York Cubans ('41), *Mexican League ('43–'52)*
Bats: Right   Throws: Right
Born: Cuba

He was the brother of Heberto Blanco and played first base for the New York Cubans in 1941, hitting .246. However, most of his career was spent in Mexico, where he appeared in five All-Star games, including his first four years in the league, 1943–46. Beginning with Torreon in 1943, he hit .339 before joining Nuevo Laredo for the next three All-Star seasons and batting .305, .319, and .327. For the next six years he played in Mexico, except for the 1949 season, and changed teams each year. He had average power, a good eye at the plate, and good speed on the bases, while recording averages of .321, .343, .260, .319, and .276.

Blanco, Heberto (Harry, Henny)
a.k.a. Herberto
Career: 1941–42   Positions: **2b,** ss, *lf*
Teams: New York Cubans ('41–'42), *Mexican League ('43–'46, '48, '50–'52, '55), minor leagues ('56)*
Bats: Right   Throws: Right
Height: 5'7"   Weight: 168
Born: Oct. 17, 1920, Bayamo, Oriente Province, Cuba

A smooth-fielding second baseman with good speed, the Cuban was only an average hitter and did not have much power, batting .219 and .292 during his two seasons with the New York Cubans in the Negro Leagues

(1941–42), and played in the East-West All-Star game the latter year. When the color barrier fell, he was regarded as one of the top prospects and was scouted by the New York Yankees.

In his native country, his best year was in 1942–43, when he hit .294. Playing primarily with Havana during his ten-year Cuban career, he had a lifetime batting average of .258 and showed less than average power (rarely hitting a home run) but a good stolen-base ratio.

In 1943 the slick fielder took his glove to Monterrey in the Mexican League and recorded consecutive seasonal batting averages of .263, .300, .330, and .279. After a year away from Mexico, he returned to hit .260 in 1948, and continued playing on into the '50s, with averages of .276 and .269 with Nuevo Laredo in 1950–51. His best offensive years were in 1952 with Monterrey (.333 BA) and 1955 with Vera Cruz (.294 BA). His last year in organized baseball was in 1956 with Roswell in the Southwest League, where he hit .342 while playing in only ten games.

Blattner, Frank
Career: 1921   Positions: 1b, 2b, of
Team: Kansas City Monarchs
He was a first baseman for the 1921 Kansas City Monarchs, but also played other positions, both infield and outfield, during his only year in the Negro Leagues.

Blavis, Fox
a.k.a. Fox
Career: 1936   Position: 3b
Team: Homestead Grays
In 1936 he played a few games at third base, but without distinction, for the Homestead Grays, who were trying to fill a weak spot at the hot corner.

Bleach, Larry
Career: 1937   Position: 2b
Teams: Detroit Stars
He was a second baseman for the Detroit

Stars in 1937, his only year in the Negro Leagues.

Bledsoe
Career: 1937   Position: player
Team: St. Louis Stars
He was listed on the roster of the 1937 St. Louis Stars, but his position is uncertain.

Blount, John T. (Tenny)
Career: 1919–33   Positions: owner, officer
Team: Detroit Stars
A numbers banker who ran a gambling establishment, he was the owner and officer of the Detroit Stars from their inception through their final season. A friend of Rube Foster's when the Negro National League was formed, he served as the league's vice president, but later had a disagreement with Foster that ended their close relationship.

Blueitt, Virgil
a.k.a. Bluett; Bluitt
Career: 1916–18;   Positions: 2b, umpire
1937–49
Team: Chicago Union Giants
Died: April 29, 1952, Chicago, Ill.
He played second base for the Chicago Union Giants for three seasons, beginning in 1916, when he was a part-time starter, batting fifth in the lineup. Later in his career he became an umpire in the Negro American League when it was organized in 1937, and he arbitrated for thirteen seasons.

Bluett
[see Blueitt, Virgil]

Bluford
Career: 1931   Position: cf
Team: *Newark Browns*
He was a center fielder with the Newark Browns in 1931, a year before they joined the East-West League.

Blukoi, Frank
Career: 1916, 1920   Position: 2b
Teams: All-Nations Team ('16–'19), Kansas City Monarchs ('20)

The infielder began his professional career in 1916 with Wilkinson's All-Nations Team and then joined Wilkinson's Kansas City Monarchs when they became charter members of the Negro National League in 1920.

Boada, Lucas
Career: 1921–25   Positions: p, of, 1b, 3b
Teams: Cuban Stars (West) ('21–'25), Cuban Stars (East)
Bats: Right   Throws: Right

He was both a pitcher and a position player with the Cuban Stars during the early '20s. Beginning his career with the Cuban Stars when they were based in Cincinnati in 1921, he posted a 5–5 record on the mound, while playing primarily in the outfield when not pitching. He also pitched in the Cuban winter league, registering a league-high 10–4 mark for the champion Marianao team in 1922–23.

Boardley
Career: 1919   Position: of
Team: Baltimore Black Sox

He was an outfielder with the Baltimore Black Sox in 1919 during the team's formative years.

Bobo, James
[see Leonard, James (Bobo)]

Bobo, Willie
Career: 1923–30   Positions: 1b, of, p
Teams: All Nations ('23), Kansas City Monarchs ('24), **St. Louis Stars** ('24–'28), Nashville Elite Giants ('28–'30)
Born: Phoenix, Ariz.
Died: March 1, 1931, San Diego, Calif.

The slugger was also a very good fielder and was the starting first baseman for the St. Louis Stars for four seasons, beginning in 1924. He usually hit in the third slot in the batting order, and registered a .344 average in 1926. The next season he hit a dramatic home run over the car-barn shed in left field to give the St. Louis Stars a 1–0 victory in one of the most memorable contests ever played in the ballpark.

He began his professional baseball career with J. L. Wilkinson's All-Nations team in 1923, joining the Kansas City Monarchs the following spring for a short time, before the Stars secured his services for their ballclub. Giving way to Mule Suttles in 1928, he joined the Nashville Elites and hit .304 and .289 in his last two seasons, 1929–30.

He was still a productive player until his untimely death, which was related to an unsavory association with the bootlegging business. During the 1930 California winter league season, he and two teammates made a trip across the border to Tijuana, Mexico, where he apparently consumed a quantity of wood alchohol, and died the next day, shortly after returning to the United States.

Boggs, G.
Career: 1923–34   Positions: **p**, of
Teams: Detroit Stars ('23), Milwaukee Bears ('23), Dayton Marcos ('26), Cleveland Tigers ('28), Baltimore Black Sox ('28)

For a dozen years he was a pitcher and outfielder, primarily with teams having short tenures in the Negro National League.

Bolden, Edward (**Ed**, Chief)
Career: 1910–50   Positions: owner, officer (NNL, ECL, ANL)
Teams: **Hilldale Daisies**, *Darby Phantoms*, Philadelphia Stars
Died: September 17, 1950, Darby, Pa.

A gentlemanly little man, he worked in the Philadelphia post office, and was the owner of the two best-known Negro Leagues teams in the Philadelphia area, the Hilldale Daisies and the Philadelphia Stars. A shy, quiet, and modest man who preferred working in the background instead of in the spotlight, the longtime executive is best known as the owner of the Hilldale team that won the first three Eastern Colored League championships in 1923–25, and the

1925 World Series over the Kansas City Monarchs. As founder of the Eastern Colored League, he was responsible for the player raids by eastern teams on the more established Negro National League.

He took over the operations for the ballclub in 1916, when the team was a semipro team in Darby, Pennsylvania. The team attained major-league status the following season and won a championship in 1921; then came the Eastern Colored League and the three straight pennants. He suffered a nervous breakdown in 1927, and without his leadership the league folded the following spring.

After he recovered his health he organized the Philadelphia Stars in 1933, with the financial backing of white booking agent Ed Gottlieb. After appointing Webster McDonald as manager, Bolden again raided other clubs for players, and entered the Negro National League in 1934, winning the pennant in the first season in the League. In the championship playoff the team defeated the Chicago American Giants. He remained at the head of the Stars until his death in 1950.

In addition to contributions to black baseball as a team executive, he also served as an officer in three different leagues: the Eastern Colored League, the American Negro League, and the Negro National League.

Bolden, Jim (Fireball)
Career: 1946–47   Position: p
Teams: Cleveland Buckeyes ('46), Birmingham Black Barons ('47, '52), *Chattanooga Choo Choos ('48), New Orleans Creoles ('49), Brooklyn Cuban Giants ('50), minor leagues ('51)*
Born: Feb. 8, 1923

He broke in with the Cleveland Buckeyes in 1946, and after half a season with the Birmingham Black Barons in 1947, spent the remainder of his career with teams of lesser quality, including the Chattanooga Choo Choos, the New Orleans Creoles, the Brooklyn Cuban Giants, and the Elmwood Giants of the Mandak League. He finished his career with

the Birmingham Black Barons in 1952, but by that time the Negro Leagues were not of major-league caliber.

Bolden, Otto
Career: 1910, 1920   Positions: p, c
Team: Chicago Giants ('10, '20)

He had an odd career, making appearances on each end of the battery ten years apart, as a catcher in 1910 and as a pitcher in 1920.

Bond, Timothy
Career: 1935–40   Positions: ss, 3b
Teams: Pittsburgh Crawfords ('35), Newark Dodgers ('35), **Chicago American Giants** ('37–40)
Bats: Left   Throws: Right
Height: 5'7"   Weight: 140

A good gloveman with good speed on the bases, his stickwork was generally his weakness, although partial statistics show a .333 batting average for 1935, when he played briefly with the Pittsburgh Crawfords. He finished the season with the Newark Dodgers and joined the Chicago American Giants in 1937, when the franchise became a charter member of the Negro American League. That season he batted in the leadoff spot while holding down the starting shortstop position, but in his last year, with the American Giants in 1940, he played third base and hit in the second slot in the batting order. The remainder of his career was spent with lesser teams.

Bonds
Career: 1927   Position: c
Team: Cleveland Hornets

He was a backup catcher with the Cleveland Hornets in 1927, the team's only year in the Negro National League.

Bonner, Robert
Career: 1921–26   Positions: 1b, c, 2b
Teams: Cleveland Tate Stars ('22), Toledo Stars ('23), St. Louis Stars ('23), Cleveland Browns ('24–'25), Cleveland Elite Giants ('26)

Playing mostly with Cleveland-based teams

that were one-year entries in the Negro National League, he began his career in 1922 as a first baseman, hitting only .194 while batting sixth in the order, with the Cleveland Tate Stars, and closed out his career in 1926 with the Cleveland Elite Giants, batting in the cleanup spot while dividing his playing time between first base and catcher. In between he also played with the Cleveland Browns during their only year in the league. Altogether he played half a dozen seasons with five different teams.

Booker, Billy
Career: 1898   Position: 2b
Team: *Celeron Acme Colored Giants*

He was a second baseman for the all-black team dubbed the Acme Colored Giants and formed in 1898 by Harry Curtis, a white man, to play in the Iron and Oil League as representatives of Celeron, New York. Both the team and the league folded in July, and it was to be the last time a black team played in a white league.

Booker, Dan
Career: 1909   Position: p
Team: Kansas City Royal Giants

He was a pitcher with the Kansas City, Missouri, Royal Giants in 1909.

Booker, James **(Pete)**
Career: 1905–19   Positions: c, 1b
Teams: Philadelphia Giants ('05–'06, '13), **Leland Giants** *('07–'10), New York Lincoln Giants ('11–'12), Mohawk Giants ('13), Brooklyn Royal Giants ('13), Chicago American Giants ('14), Chicago Giants ('15–'18), Indianapolis ABCs ('19)*
Bats: Right   Throws: Right

Pete Booker had been an outstanding catcher and was the starting receiver for the Leland Giants for the previous three seasons, but in 1910, when Bruce Petway joined the team, he moved to first base in deference to Petway's skills and developed into a solid first baseman while hitting .317.

Booker came to the Lelands from the Philadelphia Giants along with Rube Foster and left the team in 1911 along with John Henry Lloyd to join the New York Lincoln Giants. The big husky catcher-first baseman had good power and hit for averages of .340 and .383 for the 1911 and 1912 Lincoln Giants. In 1913 Booker played with a trio of teams in the East, including the Brooklyn Royal Giants and the Mohawk Giants. Back with Foster's American Giants in 1914, records show a .326 batting average, but his batting skills began to erode and he played with the Chicago Giants and finished his career with the Indianapolis ABCs in 1919. During his career Booker played on most of the great black teams of the deadball era.

Boone
Career: 1910   Position: cf
Team: St. Louis Giants

In his only season in black baseball, he was with the St. Louis Giants in 1910 as a reserve outfielder.

Boone, Alonzo D. **(Buster)**
Career: 1929–50   Positions: p, manager
Teams: Memphis Red Sox ('29–'30), Cleveland Cubs ('31), Birmingham Black Barons ('32, '44–'45), Cleveland Bears ('39–'40), Cincinnati Buckeyes ('42), **Cleveland Buckeyes** ('43, '45–'48, '50), Chicago American Giants, Louisville Buckeyes ('49)
Bats: Right   Throws: Right
Height: 5'10"   Weight: 195
Born: 1909
Died: April 8, 1982, Cleveland, O.

A pitcher of average effectiveness who threw a "heavy" ball but with pretty good control, he contributed a 5–1 record to the Cleveland Buckeyes' drive to the Negro American League pennant in 1947 and managed the team from 1948 until the franchise folded following the 1950 season.

He began with the Buckeyes when the franchise was based in Cincinnati in 1942, and was with the team in September, escaping with minor injuries, in the car wreck in which Buckeye teammates Ulysses "Buster" Brown and Raymond "Smoky" Owens were killed. The car, driven by Brown and carrying six players, was struck from behind by a truck, while reentering the highway after they had stopped to change a flat tire. The accident occurred at 3:00 A.M. just west of Geneva, Ohio, while the team was returning home from a series against the New York Black Yankees. Three others were also injured, with Eugene Bremmer and Herman Watts being hospitalized, and owner Wilbur Hayes escaping with minimal injuries.

The next season he had a 3–1 record with the Buckeyes but spent a two-year war time hiatus with the Birmingham Black Barons, where he had seasons of 2–1 with a 3.83 ERA and 4–0 with a 3.67 ERA in 1944–45. The former year saw the Black Barons win the Negro American League pennant, although they lost to the Homestead Grays in the World Series, with Boone pitching in only one game, in relief.

In 1946 he rejoined the Buckeyes, who were now playing in his hometown of Cleveland. The Buckeyes played in League Park when the Indians were out of town, and Boone earned the distinction of winning the Buckeyes' first game ever played there, and finished the season with a 5–1 league record. The Buckeyes also traveled extensively, and he was more at home on a bus than in a bed, but despite having been in tough conditions, later in life he remembered them as fun years.

His father was said to have been a left-handed pitcher with the Kansas City Monarchs, and Boone ran away from a Knoxville, Tennessee, boarding school to follow in his father's footsteps. He began his career with the Memphis Red Sox in 1929 as a .500 pitcher and finished with the Cleveland Buckeyes twenty-two years later, in 1950, with a 0–3 record and a 9.24 ERA.

After his days on the diamond were over, Boone worked in the custodial department of the Cleveland Museum of Art, then in 1970 took a job with the city streets department, issuing permits for streetwork, until he retired in 1981. Within a year he passed away, at age seventy-two.

Boone, Charles (Lefty, Bob)
Career: 1941–46   Position: p
Teams: New Orleans-St. Louis Stars ('41), New York Black Yankees ('42), Harrisburg-St. Louis Stars ('43), *Pittsburgh Crawfords ('45)*, Jacksonville Red Caps, Cleveland Buckeyes ('46), *Boston Blues ('46)*
Bats: Left   Throws: Left
Height: 6'3"   Weight: 210

The big left-hander was one of the Big Four pitchers with the St. Louis Stars in 1941, his first year in the Negro Leagues. The Stars disbanded at the end of the season and, although he retained his home is St. Louis, he was one of several ex-Stars to sign with the New York Black Yankees for the 1942 season. He had a good fastball and mediocre breaking pitches but was afflicted with a lack of control and suffered from poor support from the Black Yankees, who were the doormats of the Negro National League. Boone himself was a poor hitter and only a fair fielder and fit in with the overall ineffectiveness of the team. After suffering through a bad season in the East, he rejoined the Stars, who were playing out of Harrisburg and St. Louis, but the team dropped out of league play early in the spring of 1943 to barnstorm against Dizzy Dean's team. In 1946 he pitched briefly with the Cleveland Buckeyes but closed his career that same season with the Boston Blues, a team in the lesser U.S. League.

Boone, Oscar
Career: 1939–42   Positions: c, 1b
Teams: Atlanta Black Crackers ('39), Indianapolis ABCs ('39), Baltimore Elite Giants ('39), Birmingham Black Barons ('40), Ethiopian Clowns ('40), Chicago American Giants ('41–'42)

The catcher-first baseman didn't stay in one place very long during his four-year career. In 1939 the Atlanta Black Crackers, champions of the Negro American League's second half, moved their franchise to Indianapolis and played as the ABCs. In July Boone and four other former Atlanta players (Chin Evans, Ed Dixon, Pee Wee Butts, and Red Moore) were sold to the Baltimore Elite Giants. However, his stay there was short, and the following spring found him with manager Jim Taylor's Birmingham Black Barons, which he jumped in April to join the Ethiopian Clowns. He joined the Chicago American Giants in 1941, where he shared the regular catching assignments, hitting seventh in the batting order when in the lineup.

Boone, Robert
Career: 1923–28, 1946   Position: umpire
League: NNL

He was an umpire in the Negro National League during the '20s, then went back behind the plate for one last hurrah in 1946.

Boone, Steve (Lefty)
Career: 1940   Position: p
Team: Memphis Red Sox

He was a left-handed pitcher with the Memphis Red Sox in 1940, and it is thought that this may have been Charles (Lefty) Boone with a mistaken listing.

Borden, J.
Career: 1932–33   Positions: ss, of, p
Team: Birmingham Black Barons

A utility player whose best position was shortstop, he played with the Birmingham Black Barons for two years.

Bordes, Ed
Career: 1940   Positions: ss, 2b, 3b
Team: Cleveland Bears

Although primarily a shortstop, he was a utility infielder with the Cleveland Bears in 1940, his only year in the Negro Leagues.

Borges
Career: 1904–05   Position: 2b
Team: All Cubans

He played second base for the All Cubans

team for two years in the early part of the century.

Borges
Career: 1928   Positions: ss, 3b, 2b
Team: Cuban Stars (West)

Playing briefly as a utility infielder with the Cuban Stars (West) in the Negro National League in 1928, he proved to be a versatile player.

Borselo
a.k.a. Borotto
Career: 1921   Positions: p, c
Team: Cuban Stars (East)

In 1921 he appeared both as a pitcher and catcher with the Cuban Stars team based in the East and playing under the name All Cubans.

Bostick
Career: 1924   Position: of
Team: St. Louis Giants

He was a reserve outfielder with the St. Louis Giants in 1924, his only year in the league.

Bostock, Lyman Wesley, Sr.
Career: 1940–49   Positions: **1b**, of *ss*
Teams: Brooklyn Royal Giants ('38–'39), **Birmingham Black Barons** ('40–'42, '46), *military service ('42–'45)*, Chicago American Giants ('47, '49), New York Cubans ('48), *Mexican League ('48)*, *minor leagues ('50–'54)*
Bats: Left   Throws: Right
Height: 6'1"   Weight: 215
Born: March 11, 1918, Birmingham, Ala.

Bostock was a solid player both offensively and defensively, and equally adept at first base or in the outfield. A very good fielder with average speed, the left-handed pull hitter demonstrated both consistency and power at the plate. He began his career in 1938 as a first baseman with the Brooklyn Royal Giants, but joined the Birmingham Black Barons in 1940 and played in the 1941 East-West All-Star game, rapping a hit in his first trip to the plate.

After his All-Star season he was off to another good start, hitting over .300 early in the new season, when his baseball career was interrupted for a four-year wartime stint in the U.S. Army.

When he returned in 1946, he had to overcome a weight problem and a military mindset to get back into playing shape, and was slow returning to his previous playing form. The next four years were spent rounding back into form while playing with a trio of teams. After finishing the 1946 season with a .265 batting average for Birmingham, he played with the Chicago American Giants in 1947 and 1949, hitting .336 in the latter year. The two years in Chicago were sandwiched around a season split between the New York Cubans and Guaymas in the Mexican League. In the fall of 1948 he toured with Jackie Robinson's All-Star team.

In 1950, when integration left the Negro Leagues short of players and of funds, he signed with the newly organized Canadian baseball league and played four more years north of the border with the Winnipeg Buffalos in the Mandak League in 1950–51, and the Carman Cardinals in 1952–53.

Eventually he traded his pursuits on the baseball diamond for employment in the postal service, where he worked for twenty-eight years, before retiring to the life of an artist. His son, Lyman Bostock, Jr., played in the major leagues and was still in his prime when he was tragically killed in 1978 by a gunshot wound inflicted by his ex-wife.

Boston, Bob
Career: 1948   Position: 3b
Team: Homestead Grays ('48)
Bats: Right   Throws: Right
Height: 6'4"   Weight: 204
Born: July 4, 1922, Gaston, Ala.

The light-hitting youngster played third base for the Homestead Grays in 1948. He earned a tryout with the Grays after leading the East Liverpool (Ohio) City League in fielding and batting in 1947 and impressed manager Vic

Harris in spring camp the following spring to earn the third-base position vacated by Howard Easterling.

Boswell
Career: 1939   Position: p
Team: Toledo Crawfords

He pitched with manager Oscar Charleston's Toledo Crawfords, who joined the Negro American League for the second half of the 1939 season, Boswell's only year in the Negro Leagues.

Bounds
Career: 1933   Position: p
Team: Philadelphia Stars

He was on the pitching staff of the Philadelphia Stars in their first year of existence, when they were playing as an independent team.

Bowe, Randolph (Bob, **Lefty**)
Career: 1938–40   Position: p
Teams: Kansas City Monarchs ('38–'39), Chicago American Giants ('39–'40), Indianapolis Clowns ('40)
Bats: Left   Throws: Left
Height: 6'3"   Weight: 200

After two years with the Kansas City Monarchs, the hard-throwing youngster was a sensation when he joined the Chicago American Giants in 1940. But the lefthander had only an average curve and change-up and experienced considerable control problems, which limited his effectiveness. In August 1940, after managing only a 2–2 record, he jumped the American Giants to travel with the Indianapolis Clowns, using the identity of "Lefty" with their club.

Bowen
Career: 1940   Position: of
Team: Philadelphia Giants

He was a reserve outfielder with the Philadelphia Giants in 1904.

Bowen
Career: 1950   Position: p
Team: Indianapolis Clowns

He was listed as a pitcher with the Indianapolis Clowns in 1950, but league statistics do not confirm his playing time.

Bowen, Chuck
Career: 1937–1943   Position: of
Teams: Indianapolis Athletics ('37), *Chicago Brown Bombers ('43)*

An outfielder with the Indianapolis Athletics in the inaugural Negro American League season of 1937, he later played left field with the Chicago Brown Bombers, a team of lesser status.

Bowers
Career: 1887   Position: of
Team: *Philadelphia Pythians*

He was an outfielder with the Philadelphia Pythians, one of eight teams that were charter members of the League of Colored Baseball Clubs in 1887. However, the league's existence was ephemeral, lasting only a week.

Bowers, Chuck
Career: 1926   Positions: p, ss
Team: Baltimore Black Sox

He was with manager Ben Taylor's Baltimore Black Sox briefly in 1926, playing both as a pitcher and shortstop.

Bowers, Julius (**Julie**)
Career: 1947–50   Position: c
Team: New York Black Yankees

He was a reserve catcher for the New York Black Yankees during the last two seasons before the demise of the Negro National League. When the Black Yanks continued as an independent ballclub, he remained with the team for an additional pair of seasons.

Bowman, Bill
Career: 1903   Positions: p, c, 3b, ss
Team: Cuban X-Giants

Although primarily a pitcher, he was an all-purpose player with the Cuban X-Giants, the top team of the era.

Bowman, Emmett (**Scotty**)
Career: 1905–16   Positions: p, c, ss, 3b, 1b, of

Teams: Philadelphia Giants ('05–'06), Leland Giants ('08), Brooklyn Royal Giants ('09–12), Chicago American Giants ('16)

One of the best players of the early part of the century, Bowman was a remarkably versatile player who could pitch or play every day. When not on the mound, he was in the lineup as a catcher, infielder, or outfielder. As one of the best players on the squad, he helped make the Brooklyn Royal Giants a formidable team during the deadball era. The team was the eastern champions in 1909–10, with Bowman playing first base and batting fifth in the order in the latter season.

Bowser, Thomas
Career: 1914–16   Position: owner
Teams: Indianapolis   ABCs   ('14–'15), Bowser's ABCs ('16)

He was the owner of the Indianapolis ABCs but split with C. I. Taylor in 1916 and two ABC teams were formed. His ballclub became known as Bowser's ABCs.

Boyd, Benjamin W. (**Ben**)
Career: 1885–90   Positions: cf, 2b, ss
Teams: *Argyle Hotel ('85),* **Cuban Giants** ('86–'91)
Born: April 8, 1858

He played at second base and in the outfield for the first black professional team. While doubling as a waiter at the Argyle Hotel in 1885, he was one of the top players on their baseball team. After the summer season, the team added more players and toured professionally as the Cuban Giants. Boyd stayed with the team for their first six seasons, 1885–90.

The little bottle-shaped player from Washington, D.C., had learned his baseball skills as an amateur, playing third base for the Manhattans (a Washington, D.C., club) in 1874, second base for the Mutuals in 1875, and for other amateur clubs. While with the Cuban Giants, the team represented various towns in white leagues, including York, Pennsylvania, of the Eastern Interstate League in 1890, Trenton, New Jersey, of the Middle States League in 1887 and 1889, and Ansonia of the Connecticut State League in 1891. He also played against the New York Giants and Philadelphia A's while a member of the Cuban Giants.

Boyd, Fred

Career: 1920–22   Positions: **of**, ss
Teams: Chicago American Giants ('20), Cleveland Tate Stars ('22)

His career lasted for three years during the early '20s. He was a reserve outfielder with the Chicago American Giants for a short time in 1920, and was a part-time starter in left field for the Cleveland Tate Stars in 1922, batting fifth in the order when in the lineup.

Boyd, James

Career: 1946   Position: p
Team: Newark Eagles

As a pitcher for the 1946 Newark Eagles, his pitching time was very restricted.

Boyd, Lincoln

Career: 1949   Position: of
Teams: Louisville Buckeyes ('49), *Indianapolis Clowns ('50–'52), minor leagues ('53–'56)*
Bats: Right   Throws: Right
Height: 6'3"   Weight: 180
Born: 1933

His only season in the Negro Leagues was in 1949, as an outfielder with the Negro American League Louisville Buckeyes. The franchise had moved from Cleveland for a single season. In the early '50s he was playing with the Indianapolis Clowns, but the Negro Leagues were strictly minor leagues at that time. Organized baseball had been opened to everyone, and in 1953 he signed to play with Leesburg of the Florida State League. Although hitting only .238, he demonstrated his base-stealing capability in his first outing in organized ball. The next three seasons (1954–56) were spent at Clovis of the West Texas–New Mexico League, where the free-swinger hit .315, .340, and .302 with good power (30, 44, and 21 home runs) and had high walk and strike-out numbers.

Boyd, Ollie

Career: 1933   Positions: of, p
Team: 1933 Kansas City Monarchs

He was an outfielder with the 1933 Kansas City Monarchs when they were touring as an independent team.

Boyd, Robert Richard (**Bob**, The Rope)

Career: 1946–50   Position: 1b
Teams: Memphis Red Sox ('46–'50), *minor leagues ('50–'55, '62–'64),* major leagues ('51, '53–'54, '56–'61)
Bats: Left   Throws: Left
Height: 5'9"   Weight: 168
Born: Oct. 1, 1926, Potts Camp, Miss.

During his four full years in the Negro American League, he registered averages of .339, .376, .375, and .356, for a career average of .362. He began his career as a walk-on with the Memphis Red Sox and was quickly signed, farmed out, and then recalled. During his first full season (1947) he was batting .340 at the All-Star break and demonstrated good speed and a good glove in the field. The following season he finished with 9 triples, the second-highest in the league, and was selected to start for the West squad in the East-West All-Star game, responding with two hits in the contest. In 1949 the Sox star repeated as the West's starting first baseman in the All-Star game.

He was the first black signed by the White Sox, and in 1950 he split the season between the Negro American League and Colorado Springs in the Western League, where he hit .373. In 1951, with Sacramento, he led the Pacific Coast League with 41 stolen bases while hitting .342 to earn a trial with the White Sox, but he was sent back down and, playing with Seattle in 1952, he led the Pacific Coast League in batting with a .320 average.

He was thirty years old when he finally made it to the major leagues to stay, and once there, his frozen line drives earned him the nickname "The Rope." During his nine-year major-league career he compiled a lifetime .293 average. His best year came in 1957, when he hit .318, as the first Oriole regular player to hit .300. This was sandwiched between two other .300 seasons (the first was as a part-time starter) that he enjoyed for the Baltimore Orioles.

He also rang up some impressive seasons in Latin America, batting .374 with Ponce in Puerto Rico (1951–52) and .305 with Cienfuegos in Cuba (1954–55) and finishing with a lifetime Cuban batting average of .300.

Boyd finished his career in the majors in 1961, splitting his playing time between the two leagues, with Kansas City (AL) and Milwaukee (NL). Always able to swing an impressive bat, he played three more seasons in the high minors, compiling impressive credentials. He hit .326 in 1962 while playing in AAA ball with Louisville (American Association) and Oklahoma City (Pacific Coast League). Then he followed with a .336 average in the Texas League. Finally his bat lost its sting, and in 1964 he finished his career as a pinch hitter with Oklahoma City, without a hit in nine games.

Bracken, Herbert (Herb, **Doc**)
Career: 1940–47   Position: p
Teams: St. Louis Stars ('40), *military service ('44–'45)*, Cleveland Buckeyes ('46–'47)
Bats: Left   Throws: Right
Height: 6'3"   Weight: 185

The hard throwing righthander had a good fastball, curveball and control. While pitching with the 1940 St. Louis Stars, he defeated every Negro American League team he faced, including the Champion Kansas City Monarchs, and although he was offered a handsome salary by teams from the Negro Leagues and Mexico, he preferred to stay at home in St. Louis. His impressive mound work continued, and he was still considered a hot young pitching prospect for the Cleveland Buckeyes in 1944, but entered the U.S. Navy and played for the Great Lakes Naval Base, registering a 13–1 record. His only loss was a 1–0, 14-inning two-hitter that he lost to Mickey Cochranes's All-Star squad. His service baseball credentials were further enhanced when he beat the Carioca Stars 6–2 on a four-hitter after being selected to play with the Navy All-Stars in Hawaii.

In 1946, after completing his military service, he was the most sought-after pitcher in black baseball. He joined the staff of the Cleveland Buckeyes for the 1946–47 seasons, despite an attempt by the Brooklyn Brown Dodgers to gain title to Bracken by buying the St. Louis Giants' franchise. However, his two seasons on the Buckeyes' roster failed to produce more than a .500 winning percentage in only a few mound appearances.

Bradford, Charles
Career: 1912–26   Positions: p, of, coach
Teams: *Pittsburgh Giants ('10–'12), Philadelphia Giants ('13–'16),* New York Lincoln Giants ('12, '22–'26), *Philadelphia Colored Giants of New York ('28)*

He was a pitcher, outfielder, and coach during his career with the Lincoln Giants. Before joining the Lincolns he played with two teams of lesser quality, the Pittsburgh Giants and the once-proud but declining Philadelphia Giants. He first appeared with the Lincolns in 1912 as a center fielder with limited playing time, and when he reappeared in the lineup during the '20s he was a pitcher, although not logging many innings on the mound.

Bradford, William (**Bill**)
Career: 1938–43   Positions: lf, rf, cf, *2b*
Teams: Indianapolis ABCs ('38), St. Louis Stars ('39), New Orleans-St. Louis Stars ('40), Memphis Red Sox ('40–'42), Chicago American Giants ('41), Birmingham Black Barons ('42), New York Black Yankees ('43)
Bats: Right   Throws: Right
Height: 6'2"   Weight: 195

He began his career with the Indianapolis ABCs in 1938, playing right field and batting sixth in the order. The next season, the ABCs franchise moved to St. Louis, playing as the Stars, and he held the same position and spot in the batting order at the new location. In 1940 he moved to Memphis, sharing an outfield position that season before being relegated to a substitute position for the parts of the next two seasons that he was with the Sox. In each of those seasons he was with other teams part of the time, playing as a reserve second baseman with the Chicago American Giants in 1941 and as a part-time right fielder with the Birmingham Black Barons in 1942. Curiously, the next season, his last, he batted third in the order while playing as the regular left fielder for the New York Black Yankees. Incomplete statistics show a disparity of batting averages, with .326 and .205 for the seasons 1942–43.

Bradley
Career: 1931   Position: lf
Team: *Newark Browns*

The outfielder played with the Newark Browns when they were playing as an independent team and still a year away from competing in the East-West League.

Bradley, Phil
Career: 1905–19   Positions: c, 1b, of, ss
Teams: Famous Cuban Giants ('05–'06), Brooklyn Royal Giants ('07–'10, '14), New York Lincoln Giants ('11), Smart Set ('12), Mohawk Giants ('13), Philadelphia Giants ('15), Pittsburgh Stars of Buffalo ('16–'19), *Pittsburgh Colored Stars, Pop Watkins Stars*

With a career that stretched over parts of three decades, he was a star of the deadball era, playing primarily with New York-based teams. After beginning his career with the Famous Cuban Giants in 1905, he joined the Brooklyn Royal Giants in 1907, sharing the catching assignments in his first year with the team before assuming the backstopping chores on a regular basis. In 1909 and 1910 the Royals were the eastern champions, with Bradley moving from the seventh slot in the batting order to the third spot in the latter season.

Although primarily a catcher, a position he also played with the Lincoln Giants in 1911 (while hitting .342) and the Smart Set in 1912, he was versatile and could play a variety of positions, including first base. Many of the

teams that he played with were of marginal major-league caliber or below. He managed the Schenectady Mohawk Giants in 1913, probably their best season.

Bradley, *Province* Frank (Red, Dick)
Career: 1937–43   Position: p
Teams: **Kansas City Monarchs** ('37, '42–'43), Cincinnati Tigers ('37), Memphis Red Sox ('39)
Bats: Right   Throws: Right
Height: 6'0"   Weight: 195

He was basically a one-pitch pitcher with an outstanding fastball with good control but little else. He was discovered while playing with the Benton Eagles of the Los Angles City League in 1937 and toiled in the Negro Leagues for seven seasons, with the Kansas City Monarchs, Cincinnati Tigers, and Memphis Red Sox, closing out his career in 1943.

Bradshaw
Career: 1926   Position: ph
Team: Dayton Marcos

He made one appearance, as a pinch hitter for the Dayton Marcos in 1926.

Brady, John
Career: 1887   Position: of
Team: *Pittsburgh Keystones*

He was an outfielder with the Pittsburgh Keystones, one of eight teams that were charter members of the League of Colored Baseball Clubs in 1887. However, the league's existence was ephemeral, lasting only a week.

Brady, Lefty
Career: 1921   Position: p
Team: *Cleveland Tate Stars*

He was a pitcher with the 1921 Cleveland Tate Stars, a year before they played in the Negro National League.

Bragana, Ramon (El Professor)
Career: 1928–47   Positions: **p**, of
Teams: Cuban Stars (East) ('28–'30), Stars of

Cuba, New York Cubans, *Mexican League ('38–'55)*, Cleveland Buckeyes ('47)
Bats: Right   Throws: Right
Height: 5'11"   Weight: 180
Born: May 11, 1909, Havana, Cuba

The strong-armed power pitcher starred for several Cuban teams playing in the Negro Leagues during the late '20s and '30s including the Cuban Stars, Stars of Cuba, and New York Cubans. The right-hander had a 90-mph fastball, a devastating curve, a tremendous drop, and an effective slider, and he used good control to keep them down.

When he was not pitching, he frequently played in the outfield, where he proved an average fielder, but with a strong and accurate arm. He was an average base runner. In 1928 he was in the regular lineup with the Cuban Stars in right field, and batted in the lower part of the order. The next year he was suspended for not reporting to the team, but the Cuban was an excellent hitter with good power, as he demonstrated in Mexico when he hit .299 with 17 home runs in 1942 while winning 22 games as a pitcher. He preferred the Latin Leagues to the Negro Leagues because he was treated better there than in the States. He is ranked with Dihigo and Luque as the three best Cuban pitchers ever.

Playing in Havana in the spring of 1937, he pitched Almedares to victory over the defending National League champion New York Giants. Again pitching with Almedares in the Cuban winter league of 1941–42, he led that league with 9 wins. During two other winters in his native country, he matched that victory total for the short winter season, compiling records of 9–5 in 1936 and 9–6 in 1945. He also showcased his versatility in the Venezuelan winter league, where he was 8–4 as a pitcher and hit .318 for the 1936–37 winter.

He spent most of his career in the Mexican League, where he was a star pitcher during the '40s. Bragana first went to Mexico in 1938 and hit .303 and was 8–5 as a pitcher. He played in Mexico on through 1955, with his best year as a pitcher coming in 1944, when he was 30–8

with a 3.30 ERA. Other good years were 1940–43, when he was 16–8, 13–8, 22–10, and 17–16. In 1946 he was involved in a dispute with owner Jorge Pasquel centering around allegations that former Dodger Mickey Owen, now manager of Vera Cruz, was biased against black players. Bragana was suspended temporarily but returned in good favor to take the managerial reins after Owen had been deposed.

However, after two losing seasons with Vera Cruz, he returned to the States in 1947 for part of the season (5–5 with the Cleveland Buckeyes with one World Series win in relief), but returned to finish 18–12 with Vera Cruz for the season. Altogether he played with Vera Cruz from 1940 to 1951 and then played an additional three years with other teams before finally giving up baseball.

Bragg, Eugene
Career: 1925   Position: c
Team: Chicago American Giants

He was a substitute catcher for a brief time with the Chicago American Giants in 1925.

Bragg, Jesse
Career: 1908–18   Positions: **3b**, 2b, ss, of
Teams: Cuban Giants ('08–'09), **Brooklyn Royal Giants** ('10–'12, '14, '17–'18), Mohawk Giants ('13), New York Lincoln Giants ('15–'18), *Philadelphia Giants ('16, '18), Pennsylvania Red Caps of New York ('19)*

One of the more enduring third basemen in the East during the '10s, he was a substitute infielder for much of his career and often also played second base. After beginning with the Cuban Giants in 1908, he played with two of the top eastern teams, the Brooklyn Royal Giants and New York Lincoln Giants. He joined the Royal Giants in 1910 in a reserve role but broke into the starting lineup in 1914, batting eighth in the order. His best years came after joining the Lincoln Giants, where he held down a regular position in the infield for two years, 1915–16. The first year he started at third base, and he moved over to second base the latter season. Both years, he hit in the second slot in the batting order. During the next two years he split playing time between the Lincolns and the Royals, and he is credited with a composite .231 batting average in 1917. His last year with a quality team was in 1918; he played with lesser teams afterward.

Braithwaite, Alonzo (**Archie**, Hiram)
Career: 1944–48   Positions: **rf**, cf, *1b*
Teams: Newark Eagles ('44), Philadelphia Stars ('47–'48), *Mexican League ('51, '59), Canadian League ('51–'55), minor leagues ('55–'58)*
Bats: Right   Throws: Right
Height: 5'11"   Weight: 180
Born: Panama

Although an average player in the field, on the bases, and at the plate, he could hit with power when he made contact. The outfielder began his career during World War II, hitting .282 as the seventh-place batter with the Eagles in 1944. Joining the Philadelphia Stars in 1947, he hit .277 and moved into the third slot in the batting order the following season.

After closing his five-year Negro Leagues career, he subsequently played in the Canadian Provincial League for five seasons (1951–55) as a middle infielder, playing both second base and shortstop. His batting average generally hovered around .250, but he hit a lusty .332 with Burlington in 1955.

He entered organized baseball with Johnstown in the Eastern League later in the season, but hit only .184 in 98 at-bats. In 1956 he split the season with Columbia in the Sally League and Abilene in the Big State League as a first baseman and hit .268 and .273, respectively. In 1958 he hit only .218 while playing in the Three-I League. He ended his career in Mexico in 1959 batting .270 for the year. That marked the second time he had played in the Mexican League, having batted .332 in a partial season with Vera Cruz in 1951. He shared the same hometown in Panama as the star shortstop for the Philadelphia Stars Pee Wee Austin, and also played eleven winters in his home country, averaging .311 for his career.

Bram
Career: 1930   Position: p
Team: Hilldale Daisies

In 1930, his only year with a top black ballclub, he was a pitcher with Hilldale when they played an independent schedule.

Brammell
Career: 1932   Position: c
Team: Indianapolis ABCs

He was a backup catcher with the Indianapolis ABCs in 1932.

Branahan, J. Finis (Slim, Legs)
Career: 1922–31   Position: p
Teams: Cleveland Tate Stars ('22–'23), Toledo Tigers ('23), Chicago American Giants ('23), Harrisburg Giants ('24), Homestead Grays ('24), New York Lincoln Giants ('24), Detroit Stars ('25), St. Louis Stars ('25), Cleveland Elite Giants ('26), Cleveland Hornets ('27), Indianapolis ABCs ('31)

A journeyman pitcher with several midwestern teams during the '20s, he began his career as the mainstay of the Cleveland Tate Stars in 1922–23. In 1924 he signed with the Homestead Grays, but jumped to Harrisburg until being released in the late summer for indifferent work, and was picked back up by the Grays. In 1925 he split time between the St. Louis Stars and the Detroit Stars, and in the next two years he played with the Cleveland entries in the Negro National League, posting records of 0–7 and 2–6 in 1926–27 with the Elites and Hornets, respectively. After a four-year absence from the lineup of league teams, he appeared with the Indianapolis ABCs in 1931 to close out his career.

Branham, Luther H.
Career: 1949–50   Positions: 2b, 3b, of, *ss*
Teams: Birmingham Black Barons ('49), Chicago American Giants ('50), *Canadian League ('51), minor leagues ('51–53)*
Bats: Right   Throws: Right
Height: 5'6½"   Weight: 160
Born: Jan. 5, 1924

A versatile but light-hitting infielder, he began his career with the 1949 Birmingham Black Barons before joining the Chicago American Giants in 1950, where he hit .245 without demonstrable power or consistent contact. However, he did show a good eye at the plate and a measure of ability running the bases. With the Negro Leagues in rapid decline, he departed for the Canadian Provincial League in 1951 and hit only .204 with Drummondville. The next two seasons were spent with Victoria in the Western International League, where he hit .288 and .266 and registered some pretty good stolen-base numbers, but this was his last appearance in organized baseball.

Branham, Slim
a.k.a. Brannon
Career: 1917–26   Position: p
Teams: Jewell's ABCs ('17), Dayton Marcos ('20), Toledo Tigers ('23), Cleveland Tate Stars ('22–'23), Cleveland Elite Giants ('26)

The Nashville native's pitching career with several midwestern teams bridged the deadball and modern eras, with his best season coming in 1922 with the Cleveland Tate Stars.

Brannigan
[see Brannigan, George]

Brannigan, George
a.k.a. Branigan
Career: 1926–27   Positions: p, *of*
Teams: Cleveland Elite Giants ('26), Cleveland Hornets ('27)

He began his career in 1926 as a pitcher with the Cleveland Elite Giants, was credited with two wins without a loss, and continued with their successors, the Cleveland Hornets, in 1927.

Brannon
[see Branham, Slim]

Brantley, Ollie
Career: 1950   Position: p
Teams: Memphis Red Sox ('50–'53), *minor leagues ('53–70)*
Bats: Right   Throws: Right

Height: 6'2½"   Weight: 178
Born: 1932, Lexon, Ark.

He began his career in the Negro Leagues with the Memphis Red Sox in 1950, when the Negro American League was struggling to survive the loss of players to organized baseball. He continued with the Memphis Red Sox into the 1953 season before eventually finding his way into organized baseball that same season with Colorado Springs and Wisconsin Rapids and registered a combined 8–11 ledger, and for the next 17 years he played with a dozen different teams in a dozen different leagues. His best seasons came with Dubuque (13–7 in 1954) in the Mississippi–Ohio Valley League, Eugene (22–15 and 3.65 ERA in 1957) in the Northwestern League, Colorado Springs (15–6 in 1958), and Orlando (15–8 and 1.62 ERA in 1965) in the Florida State League. The highest classification in which he played was AAA with San Diego of the Pacific Coast League, where he played in only three games in 1960.

Bray, James
Career: 1922–31   Positions: c, of
Teams: Chicago Giants ('22), Chicago American Giants ('25, '27, '30), Chicago Columbia Giants ('31)
Bats: Left   Throws: Right
Height: 5'11"   Weight: 185
Died: 1931

Bray was a good hitter and had a good arm but possessed some deficiencies as a receiver. To keep his bat in the lineup he sometimes played in the outfield during his abbreviated career in the '20s, spent exclusively with Chicago-based teams. He joined Rube Foster's Chicago American Giants in 1925 as a backup catcher and essentially remained in that role throughout his career, except for the 1927 season, when he shared the regular receiving responsibilities and contributed a .294 batting average to the American Giants' pennant race. After winning the Negro National League flag, the American Giants defeated the Eastern Colored League Bacharachs in the World Series. After Foster's death, Bray joined David Malarcher's Chicago Columbia Giants in 1931, again in a backup role, for what became his last season in baseball. Off the field Bray was considered a hard case and was killed by teammate Johnny Hines when their drinking led to an argument and a fight.

Brazelton, Clarkson
a.k.a. Clarkson
Career: 1915–17   Position: c
Teams: Chicago Giants ('15–'16), Chicago American Giants ('16–'17)

He began his career with the Chicago Giants and was picked up as a backup catcher for the Chicago American Giants during the winter of 1915–16, and stayed with the ballclub during the regular season when Bruce Petway was incapacitated and manager Rube Foster had to find a replacement. During Brazelton's stint behind the plate he hit for a .211 average.

Breda, William **(Bill)**
Career: 1950   Positions: rf, lf
Teams: Kansas City Monarchs ('50–'51), *Birmingham Black Barons ('54)*

He was an outfielder with the Kansas City Monarchs in 1950, when the Negro American League was struggling to survive the loss of players to organized baseball. He hit .268 with average power and continued with the Monarchs through the next season. He played with the Birmingham Black Barons in 1954, but during the '50s the league was strictly at a minor-league level of play.

Breen
Career: 1928   Position: 1b
Team: Philadelphia Tigers

He was reserve first baseman with the Philadelphia Tigers in 1928, his only year in black baseball.

Bremble
Career: 1931   Position: 2b
Team: Birmingham Black Barons

A second baseman with the Birmingham Black Barons in 1931, his only year in black

baseball was sandwiched between two seasons when the Black Barons were playing in a recognized major league.

Bremer, Gene
[see Bremmer, Eugene (Gene)]

Bremmer, Eugene (Gene)
a.k.a. Bremer
Career: 1932–48   Position: p
Teams: *New Orleans Crescent Stars ('32–'34), Shreveport Giants ('35),* Cincinnati Tigers ('36–'37), Memphis Red Sox ('38–'40), *Mexican League ('39), voluntarily retired ('41), Cincinnati Buckeyes ('42),* **Cleveland Buckeyes** ('43–'48), *minor leagues ('49)*
Bats: Right   Throws: Right
Height: 5'8"   Weight: 160
Born: June 16, 1915, New Orleans, La.

The right-hander had a good overhand curve, utilized a no-windup delivery, and was one of the best-fielding pitchers in the league. Gene compiled a 25–12 record for the Cincinnati Tigers in 1936, and under manager Ted "Double Duty" Radcliffe, the Tigers entered the Negro American League in 1937, with Bremmer posting a 4–0 league ledger. The next season, when Radcliffe signed to manage the Memphis Red Sox, Bremmer went with him, and the Red Sox captured the first-half championship.

Incomplete records show an up-and-down pattern to his mound performance, going from a pennant in 1938 to a winless season (0–5) and jumping to Monterrey, Mexico, to pitch in seven games during a short stint south of the border in 1939, before returning to an All-Star performance (5–2) in 1940. Selected as the starting pitcher for the West squad, he encountered control problems, walking five batters and yielding two runs to suffer the loss.

After being out of baseball in 1941, he signed with the Cincinnati Buckeyes in 1942, fashioning a 5–1 record and making a second appearance in the East-West All-Star game. All was going well with the new team until September, when he was one of four players injured in the car wreck in which teammates

Ulysses "Buster" Brown and Raymond "Smoky" Owens were killed. Bremmer suffered a fractured skull and brain concussion and was hospitalized.

When the franchise moved to Cleveland the following season, he stayed with the club, spending the remainder of his Negro Leagues career with the Buckeyes. He started strong in 1943, finished with a 9–3 league record, and remained with the Buckeyes in 1944 after being rejected for military service. Using his complete repertory of pitches, he recorded a 10–6 (2.81 ERA) season in 1944, followed with an 8–4 (2.44 ERA) record in the championship season of 1945, and pitched in the All-Star game both seasons, making a total of four All-Star appearances.

The latter year, he teamed with the Jefferson brothers to pitch the Buckeyes to the Negro American League Pennant and a four-game sweep of the favored Homestead Grays in the World Series. A good hitter, he won his own game in the second game of the 1945 World Series by knocking in the winning run in the bottom of the ninth inning for a 3–2 victory. The Buckeyes won the Negro American League pennant again in 1947, but he had only a 2–3 slate and absorbed a complete-game loss in his only start the World Series as the Buckeyes lost to the New York Cubans. His pitching skills were beginning to fade a bit, and in 1948 his numbers showed a 3–5 slate and a 3.63 ERA for his last Negro Leagues season.

He started his baseball career in his hometown, with the New Orleans Crescent Stars in 1932. Three years later he joined the Shreveport Giants, under W. S. Welch, for a season before moving up in competition to play with the Cincinnati Tigers. He ended his career after one year in organized baseball with Cedar Rapids in 1949, where he had an uncharacteristically poor 2–7 record with a 6.38 ERA.

Brenner

Career: 1917   Position: p
Team: Chicago American Giants
The pitcher appeared briefly with Rube Fos-

ter's Chicago American Giants in 1917, considered to be the best team during the decade.

Brewer Chester Arthur (**Chet**)

Career: 1925–48   Position: p
Teams: *Gilkerson Union Giants* ('24), **Kansas City Monarchs** ('25–'35, '37, '40–'41, '46), *Crookston, Minn. ('31)*, Washington Pilots ('32), Brooklyn Royal Giants ('35), *Bismarck, N.D. ('35–'36)*, New York Cubans ('36), *Dominican Republic ('37)*, *Mexican League ('38–'39, '44)*, Philadelphia Stars ('41), Cleveland Buckeyes ('42–'43, '46–'48), Chicago American Giants ('46), *minor leagues ('52)*
Bats: Both   Throws: Right
Height: 6'4"   Weight: 187
Born: Jan. 14, 1907, Leavenworth, Kan.
Died: Mar. 26, 1990, Whittier, Calif.

An outstanding finesse pitcher with good control and a retentive memory, he spotted the ball, mixing a wide repertory of pitches that included a live running fastball, a sweeping curve, an overhand drop, a deep sinker, an emery ball, and a good screwball. He also learned to throw a cut ball from Emory Osborne and "Double Duty" Radcliffe, and would not hesitate to hit a batter to establish respect. Brewer toiled on the mounds of black baseball for twenty-four years with an assortment of teams throughout the world, including China, Japan, the Philippines, Hawaii, Canada, Mexico, Panama, Puerto Rico, Haiti, Santo Domingo, and in forty-four of the forty-eight continental United States.

The tall, lanky right-hander had his first outstanding season in 1926, his second year with the Kansas City Monarchs, when he teamed with Bullet Rogan to pitch the Monarchs to the first half of the Negro National League championship. Brewer is credited with 20 victories against all competition, and carried an 11–3 league record into the hard-fought seven-game playoff against the victorious Chicago American Giants, but was not utilized in the Series.

Although his marks the next two seasons (8–7 and 7–9) were not indicative of his talent, Brewer continued his impressive hurling and put together his best year (17–3) in 1929, while pitching the Monarchs to the Negro National League pennant. While fashioning his exquisite .850 winning percentage, he hurled 31 consecutive scoreless innings in league play. The next season, 1930, playing under the Monarchs' portable light system against the Homestead Grays, Brewer locked up with an aging Smokey Joe Williams in a 12-inning pitching duel in which Brewer struck out 19 batters, including 10 straight during one stretch, only to have Williams strike out 27 Monarchs and allow only one hit to win 1–0. Both Williams and Brewer were accused of "doctoring" the balls in this game. Similar allegations plagued Brewer throughout his career.

After the Negro National League folded, the Monarchs played as an independent team, barnstorming across the country. Against league competition his ledger shows a combined 15–11 mark for the first three years of the '30s, but against all levels of competition Brewer was credited with winning 30 games on three occasions (30 in 1930, 34 in 1933, and 33 in 1934). In the latter season, Brewer won 16 straight games for the Monarchs to earn a berth in the East-West All-Star game. Succumbing to the lure of more money, many of his prime years were spent in Latin American leagues. In 1937 he went to Santo Domingo, logging a 2–3 record for the Aguilas Cibaenas team, and hurled a one-hitter against Satchel Paige and the Ciudad Trujillo team, featuring Josh Gibson and Cool Papa Bell.

When the Dominican season ended, he joined an All-Star team that won the *Denver Post* Tournament, striking out 19 batters in one contest, albeit losing to Paige 2–1. Two years earlier, in 1935, he and Satchel had pitched together for Bismarck, North Dakota, and won the Wichita Tourney. Brewer spent two years in Bismarck, but spent part of the last season with the New York Cubans, logging a 5–2 record while pitching in the Big Apple.

As the first black American to play in Mexico, he fashioned an 18–3 record with a 1.82 ERA for Tampico in 1938, and followed with a 16–6, 2.50 ERA season while pitching 40 scoreless innings and two no-hitters. Five years later, in 1944, he returned for his last season in the Mexican League, and endured an 8–12 season and a 5.11 ERA with Mexico City.

Returning to the United States, he rejoined the Monarchs for their 1940 pennant-winning campaign, and years later, pitching for the Cleveland Buckeyes, Brewer posted a 12–6 ledger as he helped pitch the team to the 1947 Negro American League pennant. At midseason, thirteen years after his first appearance, he again pitched in the All-Star game. And in postseason play he pitched in the World Series against the New York Cubans, losing his only start. In 1948 he split 10 decisions in league games and, during the span of three seasons (1947–49) with the Buckeyes, he is credited with starting and completing 41 games.

Also in 1947, pitching with Caguas in the Puerto Rican winter league, he suffered a broken hand in the first half of the season, but came back to log a 7–3 record and help the team win the second-half title. In the final drive to the flag he won a 1–0 game in 103-degree weather and won the finale 6–5 to nail down the championship. In an earlier year, in Puerto Rico, Brewer was released because management thought he did not strike out enough players, and he was replaced with Satchel Paige. Brewer then signed with another team and came back and beat Satchel. Fans were so incensed that the team manager who had released Brewer had to be escorted back to the hotel by soldiers.

Brewer also played in other foreign locales, splitting four decisions in Cuba in the winter of 1930–31, touring the Orient in 1933, and pitching two years in Panama, winning the Caribbean Series in his second season.

His career covered a wide experiential range, including playing against major leaguers in exhibition games. In 1934 he pitched against an all-star team that included Jimmie Foxx and Heinie Manush, and later was manager of the Kansas City Royals, who played in the Los

Angeles winter league against Bob Feller and other major leaguers.

His father was a minister and, as a youngster, Brewer learned early the value of hard work. He attended Western High School in Des Moines, Iowa, where he played football and basketball, and in the summers he played baseball for a team called the Tennessee Rats. His professional baseball career started when he signed with the Gilkerson Union Giants, playing out of Joliet, Illinois, in 1924, but after playing briefly with Gilkerson's team, at age twenty, he joined manager José Mendez's Kansas City Monarchs.

The record book is not complete but, from existing data, the underpublicized hurler is credited with a 127–79 record for his long career in the Negro Leagues. After he closed out his career in black baseball, he entered organized baseball in 1952, playing in the Southwest International League, where he was 6–5, and with Visalia in the California League, where he was 1–4, for a combined 7–9 record in his last year in baseball.

After retiring from baseball, he was a major-league scout and instructor for the Pittsburgh Pirates for almost thirty years (1957–74), developing a very close relationship with Roberto Clemente, and later worked with the Major League Scouting Bureau. Later in life, in recognition of his contributions to baseball, Chet Brewer Field in Los Angeles was dedicated in his honor.

Brewer, Luther
Career: 1918–21   Positions: 1b, of
Team: Chicago Giants ('18–'21)

He was a first baseman-outfielder with the Chicago Giants of 1918–21, beginning when they were an independent team and remaining with the club when they entered the Negro National League as a charter member in 1920.

Brewer, Sherwood (Sherry, Woody)
Career: 1948–50   Positions: of, ss, 2b, 3b
Teams: New York Cubans ('48), Indianapolis

Clowns ('49–'51), *minor leagues* ('52, '55–'56), *Kansas City Monarchs ('53–'54)*
Bats: Right   Throws: Right
Height: 5'8"   Weight: 168
Born: Aug. 16, 1923, Clarksdale, Miss.

His career was beginning just as the Negro Leagues were declining. He joined the New York Cubans in midseason of 1948 from the Harlem Globetrotters' baseball team, and then spent three seasons playing both outfield and infield with the Indianapolis Clowns, batting .279 and .298 in 1949–50. In the former season he made his only East-West All-Star appearance, getting one hit in two at-bats and scoring a run in the East's 4–0 victory.

In 1952 he made his debut in organized baseball with Ardmore of the Sooner State League, batting .238. However, he returned to the Negro Leagues with the Kansas City Monarchs in 1953–54, although the Negro American League was then strictly a minor-league operation. Taking another shot at organized baseball, his best years were in 1955 and 1956 with San Angelo, where the second baseman hit .288 and .268. Although not hitting for high averages, the contact hitter exhibited average power and was a good base stealer.

Brewster, Samuel
Career: 1950   Position: of
Team: Cleveland Buckeyes

He was a reserve outfielder with the Cleveland Buckeyes in 1950, but his playing time was severely restricted.

Brewton
[see Bruton, Charles John]

Bridgeforth, William (Soo)
Career: 1950   Position: owner
Teams: Baltimore Elite Giants ('50), *Birmingham Black Barons ('51–'54)*
Born: March 23, 1907, Athens, Ala.

A lifelong baseball fan, he was an owner during the declining years of the Negro American League. A numbers banker, he owned and operated a nightclub in Nashville, and bought the Baltimore Elite Giants from Dick Powell in 1950 for $11,000. The Elites had originated in Nashville under the direction of entrepreneur Tom Wilson but had been subsequently relocated in Baltimore. After Bridgeforth assumed ownership, the franchise was not attracting customers and, after only one year, he took decisive action in an effort to salvage his investment. In 1951 he purchased the Birmingham Black Barons from Tom Hayes, and melded the personnel from the two franchises, with the Elite Giants losing their identity. The owner allowed manager Paul Jones to direct operation of the ballclub, and the team struggled on for a few years at a time when attendance was declining drastically because of the exodus of players to organized ball. Bridgeforth finally divested himself of the team, practically giving the franchise away. During his last season, 1954, he spent $90 on baseballs, and the team failed to generate enough income to recover even that cost.

Born into a baseball family in Athens, Alabama, he played ball on school teams as a youngster until leaving town at age eighteen. Arriving in Nashville, he played semipro baseball before turning to the business world for employment. Encouraged by Homestead Grays owner Cum Posey, he entered the numbers business as an avenue for accumulating sufficient capital to finance a franchise.

Bridgeport, R.
Career: 1932   Position: officer
Team: Cleveland Cubs
He was an officer with the Cleveland Cubs in 1932.

Briggs, Otto (*Mirror*)
Career: 1915–34   Positions: **rf**, cf, lf, 2b, *p*, mgr
Teams: *West Baden Sprudels ('14–'15)*, Indianapolis ABCs ('15, '17), **Hilldale Daisies** ('17–'28, '30, '34), *Madison Stars ('20)*, Dayton Marcos, *Quaker Giants*, Atlantic City Bacharach Giants ('32–'34), *Santop's Bronchos*
Bats: Right   Throws: Right

Height: 5'7"   Weight: 155
Born: 1891, Kings Mountain, N. C.
Died: Oct. 28, 1943, Philadelphia, Pa.

The leadoff hitter for the great Hilldale teams of the 1920s, the speedy little outfielder was one of the smartest players in the game. He would wear uniforms that had big sleeves so he could get hit by a pitch by letting the ball tip his floppy sleeve. He became the starting center fielder when Jess Barbour jumped to the Bacharachs, and proved to be a steady .300 hitter. After rapping out a .393 batting average in 1922, he followed with a .342 batting average and 54 stolen bases as Hilldale won the first Eastern Colored League pennant in 1923. After Hilldale repeated as pennant winners the following two years, he garnered an even dozen hits in each World Series. The latter year, his .414 batting average was the best on the team as they won the World Series against the Kansas City Monarchs in 1925.

Early in his career, in very limited play, he hit a meager .182 in 1915 as a reserve second baseman for the Indianapolis ABCs, but after coming East in 1917 he became the captain for the Hilldale team during their formative years and, with the exception of service in World War I with the 368th Infantry Regiment of the 92nd Division in France, he remained with Hilldale until 1934. He played mostly in right field, and had good range but a poor throwing arm.

Late in his career he managed the Philadelphia Bacharachs, taking over for John Henry Lloyd during the 1932 season, while still an active player. He continued managing the next year without playing as a regular, and in 1934 he returned to Hilldale to assume the position of manager there. After his baseball years were behind him, he also managed a girls' softball team and both boys' and girls' basketball teams. He married into the family who owned and operated the *Philadelphia Tribune*, with his wife assuming the duties of president while he became circulation manager.

Brigham
Career: 1924   Position: p
Team: Harrisburg Giants

The pitcher appeared briefly with the Harrisburg Giants in 1924, his only year in the Negro Leagues.

Bright, John M.
Career: 1888–1909   Positions: owner, manager
Teams: Cuban Giants, Famous Cuban Giants ('05–'06)

One of the early owners of black baseball teams, he loved the game and was a shrewd businessman who was highly successful in generating both revenue and publicity to support his ballclub, the Cuban Giants. On occasion, if attendance was higher than anticipated, he would hold up the game while demanding a larger cut of the gate. For two decades, beginning in 1888, the white sportsman was the force behind the Cuban Giants. However, in 1895, his players deserted him to rally around the leadership of E. B. Lamar, Jr. Lamar acted as booking agent and manager for the players, who formed a new team and appropriated the name Cuban X-Giants. This left Bright with a lesser talented group of players and, although they continued to attract crowds, they were not as successful as the newly formed Cuban X-Giants.

Brisker, William
Career: 1950   Position: officer
Team: Cleveland Buckeyes

He was the general manager of the Cleveland Buckeyes in 1950, the last season for the franchise.

Britt, Charles (**Charlie**)
Career: 1927–33   Position: 3b
Team: Homestead Grays

A substitute third baseman for the Homestead Grays during the late '20s, he was sometimes mistaken for George Britt, an all-purpose player who was also with the Grays.

Britt, George (**Chippy**)
a.k.a. George Britton; George Brittain

Career: 1920–44   Positions: **p, c**, 3b, 1b, 2b, ss, of
Teams: *Madison Stars ('20)*, Dayton Marcos ('20), Columbus Buckeyes ('21), Harrisburg ('22), **Baltimore Black Sox** ('22–'26), *Philadelphia Royal Giants ('25)*, **Homestead Grays** ('26–'33), Hilldale Daisies ('29), Detroit Wolves ('32), Newark Dodgers ('34), Columbus Elite Giants ('35), Washington Black Senators ('38), Baltimore Elite Giants ('39), Brooklyn Royal Giants ('40), Jacksonville Red Caps ('42), Chicago American Giants ('42), Cincinnati Buckeyes ('42), Cleveland Buckeyes ('43–'44)
Bats: Right   Throws: Right
Height: 5'8"   Weight: 175
Born: 1891, Kings Mountain, N. C.

A tough competitor who could both pitch and catch, he forged a twenty-five-year career in black baseball. An ideal utility man, he was an all-purpose player who could play every position and look good at all of them. With the 1924–25 Baltimore Black Sox he was a great catcher and above average as a hitter, batting .315 and .345. But he was most valuable to the Black Sox as a pitcher, earning a 5–4 slate the latter year. He split the 1926 season between the Sox and the Homestead Grays. After doing triple duty with the Grays, he was traded in 1929 with Martin Dihigo, to Hilldale for Jake Stevens and Rev Cannady. Britt had a composite .242 batting average for the 1929 season and was used more sparingly on the mound.

The right-handed curveball pitcher returned to the Grays and played on their outstanding teams of 1930–31. With Josh Gibson behind the plate, Britt was used mostly as a pitcher on these squads. The statistics from that era suffer from a dearth of data, but a three-year composite for 1930–32 shows an 8–2 record. The next year, 1933, he was selected to play in the inaugural East-West All-Star game, pitching two innings and yielding a run, but also getting a hit in his only at-bat and scoring a run.

He was given the nickname "Chippy" because that is what he called everyone else. He learned to catch from Chappie Johnson, and used to cut out padding from his mitt and put a sponge in the pocket. He was known as a tough man, both on the field and off. In 1930, when Ted Page and George Scales got in an argument that led to blows, Britt broke up the fight by grabbing each of them in one arm and separating them. Britt was one of the four "big bad men" of black baseball (along with Jud Wilson, Oscar Charleston, and Vic Harris), and no one on the team challenged him because, as one observer explained, "He could whip the whole ballclub." During a game in Mexico City he won the title of "Public Enemy Number One" when he dared a detachment of armed revolutionaries to come down out of the stands and fight.

During a career that can only be tracked with a road map, he played with 18 different teams, beginning in 1920, with teams of marginal quality struggling to make it in the Negro National League. Playing as a pitcher-catcher combination, he found little support from the Dayton Marcos during the last part of 1920 and is credited with a 1–3 pitching record for the year. With the Columbus Buckeyes the next year he had an 8–9 record in his first full season. For the next dozen seasons he enjoyed a measure of stability, playing with the Baltimore Black Sox and Homestead Grays most of this time. During the late '30s and early '40s his longest stop at any franchise was his last three seasons, when he played with the Buckeyes.

After retiring from baseball, he worked as a doorman at a cabaret operated by Buckeyes' owner Ernie Wright. Originally from Cincinnati, Britt made his home in Jacksonville, Florida, during the latter stages of his career.

Brittain, Al
[see Albritton, Alexander (Alex)]

Brittain, George
[see Britt, George (Chippy)]

Britton
Career: 1923   Positions: **p**, c, 1b, 2b, of
Team: Baltimore Black Sox

A very versatile player, he was utilized at several disparate positions for the 1923 Black Sox. Although his playing characteristics are similar to those of Chippy Britt, who was also on the squad, he is definitely not the same player, since they once appeared in the same lineup and both batted in the same inning according to the inning-by-inning account of the game.

Britton, George
[see Britt, George (Chippy)]

Britton, John (**Johnny**, Jack)
Career: 1940–50   Position: 3b
Teams: *Minnesota Gophers ('40),* Ethiopian Clowns ('40–'42), Cincinnati Clowns ('43), **Birmingham Black Barons** ('43–'49), Indianapolis Clowns ('50), *minor leagues ('51), Japanese League ('52–'53)*
Bats: Left   Throws: Right
Height: 5'8"   Weight: 160
Born: April 21, 1919, Mt. Vernon, Ga.

A left-handed batter, he was a good line-drive hitter who sprayed the ball to all fields and hit with consistency but not with power. Not noted for his fielding ability, he preferred playing on grass rather than "skin" infields like some parks had, especially in Puerto Rico.

He was the Birmingham Black Barons' third baseman during their pennant-winning years of 1944 and 1948 but was often overshadowed by his better-known teammates. His first full season was in 1944, and he stepped into the third slot in the order, hitting .324, .333, .262, .336, .289, and .242 for the next six seasons. In 1948 he moved to the second slot in the batting order and the Black Barons won another Negro American League pennant, but also again lost the World Series to the Homestead Grays, as they did in 1944.

Britton played in only one game in that Series because he was involved in an automobile accident while traveling between cities hosting the games. He suffered a dislocated left hand in the same wreck that broke Tommy Sampson's legs, and missed the remainder of the World Series games.

He came to the Black Barons from the Cincinnati Clowns in a trade for Hoss Walker, whom the Clowns wanted as manager. While with the Clowns he played shadow ball and engaged in a few of their comedy routines. The one best received by the fans involved his wig. He had a clean-shaven head, but wore a wig and, as part of a comedic routine, after a bad call by the umpire would take his hat off and throw it on the ground in mock anger while arguing the ump's call, and then would take his wig off and do the same with it. Then he would pick the wig and hat back up and put them on his head. The crowds loved it.

He joined the Clowns on the advice of Abe Saperstein, for whom he was playing on a team called the Minnesota Gophers. Both the Homestead Grays and the Clowns wanted to sign him, but he went with the Clowns. He also toured with Satchel Paige's All-Stars one winter and played winter ball in Mexico (1945) and in Puerto Rico (1947). After leaving the Negro Leagues, he played in the Mandak League and spent two years in Japan with the Hankyu Braves, batting over .300 each season. He and Jimmy Newberry went over together, the first black Americans to play on a Japanese team.

Broadnax, Maceo (Baby Boy)
a.k.a. Brodnax
Career: 1932   Position: p
Team: Kansas City Monarchs

He was a pitcher for the Kansas City Monarchs for one season, 1932, when the club was touring as an independent team.

Broadnax, Willie (Broadway)
Career: 1928–29   Positions; **p**, of
Team: Memphis Red Sox

He pitched with the Memphis Red Sox for two seasons, logging a 2–3 record in 1929, and also played in the outfield occasionally.

Broiles
a.k.a. Broyles
Career: 1925–27   Position: p
Team: St. Louis Stars

He was a second-line pitcher with the St. Louis Stars for three seasons during the '20s.

Brooklyn Eagles
Duration: 1935   Honors: None
Affiliation: Negro National League ('35)

A forerunner of the Newark Eagles, the Brooklyn Eagles existed for one season, 1935, and finished in the second division of the Negro National League. The following year, Abe Manley bought both the Eagles and another ailing ballclub, the Newark Dodgers, and consolidated them into a single franchise, the Newark Eagles.

Brooklyn Royal Giants
Duration: 1905–42   Honors: Eastern championship ('09, '10, '14, '16)
Affiliations: Independent ('05–'22, '34–'41), ECL ('23–'27), NNL ('33)

Organized in 1905 by John Connors, the portly black owner of the Brooklyn Royal Café, they were one of the best ballclubs in the East during the first decade of the century, and claimed eastern championships in 1909, 1910, 1914, and 1916. In 1914 they lost a challenge playoff against the western champion Chicago American Giants.

Before the onset of World War I, Connors sold the team to Nat Strong, a white booking agent in New York City. He was a good promoter and was a powerful figure in black baseball. When the Eastern Colored League was organized in 1923, the Royals became charter members, finishing third with an even .500 winning percentage, their highest finish during their stay in the league. After dropping to the second division in 1924–25, they dropped to the cellar for the next two seasons, and dropped out of the league after the 1927 season. They continued as an independent team and in 1933 were an associate member of the Negro National League, but after Strong died of a heart attack, the quality of both the administration of the team and the level of play dropped below major-league standards, and during the late thirties and afterward they played mostly against white semipro teams.

Brooks

Career: 1887   Position: player
Team: *Louisville Falls City*

He was a player with Louisville Falls City, one of eight teams that were charter members of the League of Colored Baseball Clubs in 1887. However, the league's existence was ephemeral, lasting only a week. His position is uncertain.

Brooks

Career: 1928   Position: c
Team: Memphis Red Sox

He was a catcher with the Memphis Red Sox in 1928, a year between seasons in the Negro National League.

Brooks, Alex (Alvin)

Career: 1934–40   Positions: of, 3b
Teams: Philadelphia Stars ('34–'35), New York Black Yankees ('36–'39), Brooklyn Royal Giants ('40)

An outfielder during the '30s with a trio of eastern teams, during his seven-year career he was most identified with the New York Black Yankees. In 1938 he shared a starting berth in right field, batting sixth in the order, but returned to a reserve role the following season. He broke in as a reserve outfielder with the 1934 Negro National League champion Philadelphia Stars, batting .222 in very limited play, and closed his career as the regular left fielder, hitting fifth in the lineup, with the Brooklyn Royal Giants in 1940, when they were trying to renew a major-league level of play.

Brooks, Ameal

a.k.a. Emil; Macon
Career: 1929–47   Positions: c, of

Teams: Chicago American Giants ('29), Cole's American Giants ('32), Cleveland Cubs ('32), Columbus Blue Birds ('33), Homestead Grays ('33, '41), New York Black Yankees ('37), Cuban Stars, New York Cubans ('38, '42–'45), Ethiopian Clowns ('42), Cincinnati Clowns ('43), Newark Eagles ('47), Brooklyn Royal Giants
Bats: Left   Throws: Right
Height: 5'10"   Weight: 165
Born: 1906, New Orleans, La.

Embued with a highly competitive spirit, he played in the Negro Leagues for almost twenty years. He was a solid catcher and a very dangerous hitter who was often added to a roster to add punch to the lineup, sometimes even playing in the outfield. The Grays secured him for this purpose during the 1941 Negro National League playoffs against the New York Cubans, and he responded with a .313 batting average. The next year the Cubans added him to their squad, and he shared the catching duties for two years, batting in the lower part of the order, before being relegated to backup service in 1944–45.

Earlier in his career, incomplete statistics show an average of .351 with the Columbus Blue Birds in 1933. During his brief time with the Clowns, he played under the name "Macon." He also played with LaGuaira, Venezuela, and in Puerto Rico, and was with the New York Black Yankees in 1937 when they trained in Havana, Cuba.

Brooks, Beattie

Career: 1918–1921   Positions: 2b, ss, c
Teams: Brooklyn Royal Giants ('18–'19, '21), Philadelphia Giants ('18), New York Lincoln Giants

The infielder enjoyed a four-year career, mostly with New York-based teams, and was a regular second baseman for the 1918–19 Brooklyn Royal Giants. He was a fair hitter at this stage of his baseball development and usually batted in the seventh slot in the order. It is believed by some that this is the same player as Chester Brooks.

Brooks, Charles
Career: 1919–26   Positions: **2b**, p, of,
                                3b, 1b
Teams: St. Louis Giants ('19–'21), St. Louis Stars ('22–'24), Homestead Grays ('24), Detroit Stars ('24), Dayton Marcos ('26)

During the '20s he played with several midwestern ballclubs but is most identified with St. Louis clubs. Primarily an infielder, he pitched with the Detroit Stars in 1924.

Brooks, Chester (Irvin)
Career: 1918–33   Position: **cf**, rf, *2b, p*
Team: Brooklyn Royal Giants
Bats: Right   Throws: Right
Born: Nassau, Bahamas

During the 1920s he was one of the best all-around ballplayers and also one of the most underpublicized stars. A strong right-handed hitter, his consistency at the plate didn't command the attention it should have because he played with a losing ballclub. He was an outstanding hitter: Available averages show marks of .304 and .330 for 1924–25 and correlate with the type of hitter oral histories attribute him to be. A good outfielder defensively, the West Indian toiled his entire 16-year career with the Brooklyn Royal Giants.

A Nassauan, one source indicates that he began his career as a pitcher and was discovered by Rube Foster in the Florida Keys in 1917. He was signed as a pitcher but hurt his arm and, although he continued to pitch for a few more years, he played more often as an outfielder. A broken ankle sustained in 1923 still caused him trouble and hampered his base running in 1924, but he was still regarded as the best utility man in the East. As the regular right fielder for the Brooklyn Royal Giants that season, he was their cleanup hitter.

Brooks, E.
Career: 1936   Position: p
Team: Kansas City

He was a pitcher with the Kansas City Monarchs in 1936, while they were still touring as an independent team.

Brooks, Edward (Eddie)
Career: 1949–50   Position: 2b
Teams: Houston Eagles ('49–'50), Memphis Red Sox ('50), *New Orleans Eagles ('51), Birmingham Black Barons ('52–'55)*

He was a second baseman with the Memphis Red Sox and Houston Eagles in 1949–50, when the Negro American League was struggling to survive the loss of players to organized baseball. He hit .235 with average power for Houston in 1950 and remained with the Eagles after they moved to New Orleans in 1951. He continued in the league, playing with the Birmingham Black Barons in 1952–55, but during the '50s the level of play was strictly of minor-league caliber. During this time singer Charlie Pride was with the Black Barons for a short time, and when Pride would sing on the bus trips, Brooks would complain about his style of songs.

Brooks, Gus
Career: 1894–95   Position: of
Teams: Chicago Unions ('94), Page Fence Giants ('95)

An outfielder with the Chicago Unions, a team under the management of W. S. Peters that was a continuation of the Unions organized in 1887, he joined the strong Page Fence Giants of Adrian, Michigan, in 1895, batting .346 for the season.

Brooks, Irvin
[see Brooks, Chester (Irvin)]

Brooks, James
Career: 1887   Position: player
Team: *Lord Baltimores*

He was a player with the Lord Baltimores, one of eight teams that were charter members of the League of Colored Baseball Clubs in 1887. However, the league's existence was ephemeral, lasting only a week. His position is uncertain.

Brooks, James
Career: 1938   Position: p
Team: Atlanta Black Crackers

The pitcher was added to the Atlanta Black Crackers' roster during the second half of the 1938 season but received little playing time.

Brooks, Jesse
Career: 1934–37   Positions: **3b**, of
Teams: Cleveland Red Sox ('34), Kansas City Monarchs ('37)
Bats: Right   Throws: Right
Height: 5'11"   Weight: 185

An adequate but undistinguished player, the rotund recruit patroled the hot corner for the Kansas City Monarchs during their first year in the Negro American League in 1937. His range was restricted, but otherwise he was an average fielder. Although not a strong hitter, he showed glimpses of home-run power, and also played in the outfield during his short career.

Brooks, John O.
Career: 1942   Position: p
Team: Memphis Red Sox

He was a pitcher for the Memphis Red Sox in 1942, his only season in the Negro Leagues.

Brooks, Wallace
Career: 1948   Position: p
Team: Baltimore Elite Giants

A pitcher for the Baltimore Elite Giants in 1948, his playing time was very limited.

Broom
Career: 1941–42   Position: p
Team: Jacksonville Red Caps

He was a pitcher for the Jacksonville Red Caps during the last two years before the team disbanded in midseason of 1942.

Broome, J. B.
Career: 1947   Position: of
Team: New York Black Yankees

He was an outfielder with the New York Black Yankees in 1947, but his playing time was very limited.

Browcow
Career: 1905–06   Position: 2b
Team: Brooklyn Royal Giants

During the first decade of the modern era, a player with this name was listed as a second baseman for the Brooklyn Royal Giants for two years.

Brown
Career: 1886   Position: p
Team: Cuban Giants

He pitched one game for the Cuban Giants in 1886 and was ineffective. Previously he had pitched for S. K. Govern for four years (1881–84) when Govern managed the Washington, D.C.-based Manhattans ballclub.

Brown
Career: 1910–13   Position: 1b
Teams: Cuban Giants ('10–'12), Mohawk Giants ('13)

He was a first baseman for the Cuban Giants and the Mohawk Giants for four years during the deadball era.

Brown
Career: 1905–16   Positions: rf, cf
Teams: Brooklyn Royal Giants ('05–'12), Lincoln Stars ('14–'16)

The outfielder broke in with the Brooklyn Royal Giants in 1905, the first year of the team's existence. The next season, he played right field but batted at the bottom of the order. He continued with the Royals, appearing as a substitute centerfielder in 1912, before closing his active days on the diamond as a reserve player with the Lincoln Stars in 1916.

Brown
Career: 1924   Position: of
Teams: Washington Potomacs ('24), *Philadelphia Giants ('24)*

Formerly with the Washington Potomacs of

the Eastern Colored League, he played right field for the 1924 Philadelphia Giants, a team of lesser quality.

Brown
Career: 1927   Positions: 1b, lf
Team: Memphis Red Sox
He was a reserve player for the Memphis Red Sox in 1927, and could play either first base or outfield.

Brown
Career: 1930   Position: p
Team: Hilldale Daisies
He pitched briefly and without distinction for Hilldale in 1930.

Brown
Career: 1938   Position: p
Team: Newark Eagles
In 1938 he pitched for the Newark Eagles against both league (1–2) and nonleague (4–2) opponents.

Brown
Career: 1943   Positions: ss, of
Team: Baltimore Elite Giants
A wartime reserve player for the Baltimore Elite Giants in 1943, he played shortstop but could also play in the outfield.

Brown, A.
Career: 1923   Position: c
Team: *Birmingham Black Barons*
He was a catcher for the Birmingham Black Barons in 1923, a year before they entered the Negro National League.

Brown, Arnold
Career: 1921–22   Positions: ss, 2b
Teams: *Washington Braves ('21)*, Hilldale Daisies ('21), Atlantic City Bacharach Giants ('22), Harrisburg ('22)
Appearing in one game with Hilldale in 1921, the middle infielder was a marginal player, and appeared briefly with both the

Bacharachs and Harrisburg the following season before dropping out of black baseball.

Brown, Barney (Brinquitos)
a.k.a. Brownez
Career: 1931–49   Positions: **p**, of
Teams: Cuban Stars (West) ('31–'32), New York Black Yankees ('36–'39), **Philadelphia Stars** ('37,'42–'49), *Mexican League ('39–'41, '45, '50–'52), military service ('43), minor leagues ('52–'53)*
Bats: Left   Throws: Left
Height: 5'9"   Weight: 165
Born: Kimball, W.V.
One of the best left-handed hurlers in the Negro National League, his screwball, good control, and competitive spirit made the slick southpaw a leading pitcher during the late 1930s and the 1940s. Brown pitched in five East-West All-Star games in four years, appearing in both games played in 1946. His first two years as an All–Star (1938–39) was as a representative of the New York Black Yankees, while the remainder of the games (1942, 1946) came in the uniform of the Philadelphia Stars.

He began his professional career in 1931 and, before joining the Black Yankees, played with the Cuban Stars of the East-West League in 1932. In an apparent effort to add a little Spanish flavor to the Cubans' lineup, he was sometimes listed as Brownez. His record for his season in the ill-fated league was 2–5, setting a pattern that continued through much of his career in the Negro Leagues. He pitched good ball for bad teams, and consequently his numbers are not as impressive as they would have been otherwise.

Playing winters in Latin America, he led the Puerto Rican League in victories twice (1941–42 and 1946–47); in the latter year he won 16 games and had an ERA of 1.24 with San Juan. But the next winter he was only 2–4 with Ponce in the same league. He won 16 games during four winter seasons in Cuba.

Always a good hitter with reasonable power at the plate, he had a high walk ratio as a batter. He sometimes played in the outfield or pinch-hit to utilize his bat in the lineup. He also fielded his position well, and as an outfielder he had good range and an accurate arm. He was a quick base runner but was not a skilled base stealer.

In 1937, playing with the New York Black Yankees, he got off to a good start with the bat, hitting .430 through June, and was 2–2 on the mound for the Negro National League's perennial doormat. The next two years he was selected to represent the Black Yankees in the East-West All-Star game and not only pitched excellent ball but also rapped out two hits in his three at-bats.

The following season, the All-Star portsider heard the rustle of pesos from south of the border and skipped to Mexico, where he recorded consecutive seasons of 16–5, 2.49 ERA, .318 batting average; 16–7, 3.97 ERA, .281 batting average; and 16–5, 3.94 ERA, .323 batting average for the years 1939–41, the last two with Vera Cruz.

He was the best pitcher in Mexico in 1941, with a record of 19–4, and after finishing the season he pitched for Guayama in the Puerto Rican winter league. While there he offered his services to the Newark Eagles for $200 a month. Willie Wells, who was to manage the Eagles in 1942, beseeched owner Abe Manley to sign Brown, but Manley failed to act decisively, and the Eagles lost the pitcher who could have meant a championship for them.

Instead, he signed with the Philadelphia Stars for the 1942 season and is credited with a record of 23–8 against all levels of opposition (but with a 5–7 league ledger) and earned another All-Star appearance. Brown wore uniform number 1 with the Philadelphia Stars, indicative of his status as ace of the mound corps. Meanwhile, World War II was reaching its height, and during the ensuing winter he was called into military service. However, attending circumstances enabled him to remain active in the Negro Leagues, playing in the States for most of the war's duration. He is credited with a 3–1 league record in 1943 and

a 3–1 ledger in 1945 before going back to Mexico City later in the season.

He was not as successful on the mound (6–8, 4.52 ERA) as in his previous stint in the Mexican League, but he batted .318. After that season he returned to the Philadelphia Stars and posted contrasting records for the next two years, going 8–4 in 1946 and 2–8 in 1947. He remained with the Stars through the 1949 season, returning to Mexico in 1950 to play with Torreon for three seasons, with pitching records of 12–10, 2.82 ERA, 15–12, 3.11 ERA and 3–6, 4.88 ERA, while batting .295, .275, and .233 for the years 1950–52. His lifetime Mexican totals were 84–53 with 3.58 ERA as a pitcher while hitting .302. After leaving Mexico he played two years (1952–53) in the Mandak League and was 9–4 the last season, with a .306 batting average.

Brown, Ben
Career: 1899–1900   Positions: p, of
Teams: Cuban Giants ('99), Genuine Cuban Giants ('00)

Around the turn of the century, he was a pitcher-outfielder with two of the black franchises bearing the popular name Cuban Giants.

Brown, Benny
Career: 1932   Position: ss
Teams: Newark Browns ('32), Atlantic City Bacharach Giants ('32)

In his only year with a major-league team, the light-hitting shortstop batted at the bottom of the order with the Newark Browns of the East-West League in 1932. After the league folded, he played with the Bacharach Giants, an independent team of declining quality.

Brown, (Black Rider)
Career: 1938   Position: p
Team: Atlanta Black Crackers

He pitched for the hometown Atlanta Black Crackers in the spring of 1938, but his real first name is uncertain.

Brown, C.
Career: 1925–30   Position: c
Team: Brooklyn Royal Giants

The catcher made two appearances with the Brooklyn Royal Giants, first in 1925, when the team was a member of the Eastern Colored League, and again in 1930, when the team was playing as an independent ballclub.

Brown, Charles
Career: 1886–87　　　Position: p
Teams: Cuban Giants ('86), Pittsburgh Keystones ('87)

He began his career pitching with the Cuban Giants in 1886 and, after a season, he joined the Pittsburgh Keystones, one of eight teams that were charter members of the League of Colored Baseball Clubs in 1887. However, the league's existence was brief, lasting only a week.

Brown, Country
[see Brown, Elias (Country)]

Brown, Curtis
a.k.a. Browne
Career: 1947–50　　　Position: 1b
Team: New York Black Yankees

The first baseman made two appearances as a reserve player with the New York Black Yankees, first in 1947 and again in 1950.

Brown, D.
Career: 1925　　　Position: p
Team: St. Louis Stars

He was a pitcher with the St. Louis Stars in 1925, his only year in the Negro Leagues.

Brown, David (Dave, Lefty)
Career: 1918–25　　　Position: p
Teams: *Dallas Black Giants ('17–'18)*, Chicago American Giants ('18–'22), New York Lincoln Giants ('23–'25), *Gilkerson's Union Giants ('26)*
Bats: Left　　　Throws: Left
Height: 5'10"　　　Weight: 170
Born: 1896, San Marcos, Tex.
Died: Denver, Colo.

Mixing outstanding speed, a good curve, a hard drop, and excellent control in a relatively short but sterling career, the smart left-hander was the ace of Rube Foster's dominating Chicago American Giants clubs of the early '20s. His clutch pitching in 1920–22 (10–2, 11–3, and 8–3 in league contests for a composite .784 winning percentage) was a primary factor in the club winning the first three Negro National League championships. In 1921 he is credited with three victories in a playoff against the Bacharach Giants.

After leaving the American Giants, Brown and Ed Rile jumped to East Coast clubs when the Eastern Colored League was formed in 1923. His first year, after moving East to the New York Lincoln Giants, was disappointing as he suffered a losing season (4–7), but his resilience manifested itself in 1924 as his superb control continued to make him a consistent and effective pitcher, being almost unbeatable when he was right, which was most of the time. He defeated the Brooklyn Royal Giants' Cannonball Dick Redding 3–1 for the New York City championship. Following the 1924 season, veteran player and manager Ben Taylor regarded Brown and Nip Winters as being "without doubt . . . our greatest left-handers."

There was always a mystery about Brown, even dating back to when he was pitching with the Dallas Black Giants in 1917–18. During the intervening winter he was involved in a highway robbery before he was first picked up by Rube Foster the following spring. Stories persisted that he was a fugitive from justice even then, and Foster put up a $20,000 bond to get Brown a parole from the highway robbery conviction.

Despite his reputation for having difficulty obeying the law, he is reputed not to have been a troublemaker and was described by some teammates as being a "gentleman," a "timid, nice guy," and a "kind, wonderful fellow." Others called him "jolly" and "joking all the time." Whatever his true character, the popular pitcher was a good fielder but a weak hitter.

But he was in demand even in Cuba, and showed a 17–12 composite record for his three

Cuban winter league seasons. His most notable Cuban performance came in the winter of 1923–24, when he posted a 7–3 record for the Santa Clara team that is considered the greatest Cuban team of all time. After he returned to the United States he was listed on the roster of the Lincoln Giants during the early spring, but had made his exit before the opening of the season.

He began his career in the black major leagues in 1918, after a brush with the law, and ended it abruptly, in like manner, when he again ran afoul of the law in 1925. After killing a man in a barroom fight that year, apparently in an argument involving cocaine, he dropped out of sight to avoid arrest on a murder charge. Oliver Marcelle and Frank Wickware were with him when the fight started. The next day at the ballfield they were picked up, but Brown was not there. While the FBI was searching for him, it is reported that he traveled throughout the Midwest, playing for semipro teams under the alias "Lefty Wilson." Sometimes he toured with Gilkerson's Union Giants, as he did in 1926, and in 1927 he was with a white team in Bertha, Minnesota. He was also reported to have pitched with teams in Sioux City, Iowa, in 1929 and Little Falls, Minnesota, in 1930. Unverified reports also persist that he died in Denver, Colorado, under mysterious circumstances.

Brown, E.
Career: 1916–18   Positions: 3b, p
Team: Chicago Union Giants

Beginning his career as a pitcher with the Chicago Union Giants in 1916, he finished his three seasons with them as a third baseman in 1918.

Brown, Earl
Career: 1923–26   Positions: p, of
Teams: New York Lincoln Giants ('23–'26), Harrisburg Giants ('24), Baltimore Black Sox ('25)

A star pitcher with Harvard in 1923–24, he appeared briefly with the New York Lincoln Giants in '23 and again for about three weeks in 1924 after graduation. But he then gave up baseball and went into real estate. After a year away from baseball, he signed again with the Lincoln Giants in June 1926. He also played in the outfield.

Brown, Edward
Career: 1920–21   Position: p
Teams: Detroit Stars ('20), Indianapolis ABCs ('20), Chicago American Giants ('21)

A pitcher for three Negro National League teams during the first two years of its existence, his playing time was limited with each team.

Brown, Elias (Country)
Career: 1918–33   Positions: **3b**, lf, rf, 2b
Teams: Hilldale Daisies ('18), **Atlantic City Bacharach Giants** ('18–'21, '24–'26), New York Bacharach Giants ('22), Washington Potomacs ('23–'24), Wilmington Potomacs ('25), **Brooklyn Royal Giants** ('27–'33)
Bats: Left   Throws: Left

During the '20s he was one of the best outfielders, and he had good speed on the bases. During his sixteen-year career he doubled as a comedian who kept the fans amused at all times. Recognized as a comedic entertainer, he provided antics designed to please the fans while also playing a basically sound game of baseball. Most of his "clowning" was confined to the coaching box or for occasions when the game tension was minimal, but he sometimes would bat while on his knees and get a hit. Once he got a shovel and pretended to dig the umpire's grave. His "act" was in the same vein as the Ethiopian Clowns, who came later. In his later years with the Brooklyn Royal Giants, his drinking became a problem, and on one occasion when it was time for his "act," he was found in a car outside the ballpark in an inebriated condition and had to be carried onto the field, where he performed his routine to the delight of the unsuspecting crowd.

His wife was an actress and, in the off-season,

he pulled the curtain for her. Brown was involved in a tragic altercation with his wife's brother that resulted in his brother-in-law's death. When Brown knocked the man down, his head struck the sidewalk and the impact killed him.

Playing right field with the Washington Potomacs in 1924, Brown's veteran status made him an asset to any ballclub. Not only was he one of the oldest players, he was also one of the best hitters on the ballclub, hitting .322 for the Potomacs in 1925. Ben Taylor, manager of the Potomacs, also had managed Brown on the New York Bacharachs of 1919, a team that claimed the eastern championship by defeating Hilldale.

Brown had begun his career with Hilldale in 1918, before joining the Bacharachs in 1920 for his first tour of duty with the Atlantic City club. While playing in the side pastures and hitting fifth in the batting order in 1920–21, he hit .271 the latter year. During his second stint with the team, he hit .241 while the regular left fielder and leadoff batter for the Bacharachs as they won the Eastern Colored League championship in 1926. The next year he joined the Brooklyn Royal Giants, batting .319 in his initial season in Brooklyn and remaining with the club until closing out his career following the 1933 season.

Brown, Elmore **(Scrappy)**
Career: 1918–32   Positions: ss, 3b
Teams: New York Lincoln Giants ('18), *Washington Red Caps,* ('18), Hilldale Daisies ('20), *Madison Stars ('20),* **Baltimore Black Sox** ('20–'22, '27), Homestead Grays ('23–'24), *Chappie Johnson's Stars ('25–'27),* Brooklyn Royal Giants ('30–'32)

The young shortstop from Baltimore was very fast on the bases, a flash in the field, a good hitter, and popular with the fans. He began his career as a reserve with the Lincoln Giants in 1918, but first landed a starting assignment with Hilldale in 1920, replacing Dick Lundy, who jumped to the Bacharachs. But the great John Henry Lloyd was due to join Hilldale sometime in late September, which made

Brown expendable, and he jumped to the Baltimore Black Sox, where he hit .276 while batting seventh in the order. In 1922 he helped the Sox sign Jud Wilson and, when Wilson's homesickness caused him to jump the team early in the year, Brown went to Washington, D.C., and brought him back.

As the Black Sox continued to strengthen their team preparatory to joining the Eastern Colored League, Brown was reduced to part-time status and joined the Homestead Grays in 1923 for a two-year stint before joining Chappie Johnson's Stars. Brown liked to have a good time, and the style of Chappie's team suited him pretty well. After three years he returned for the 1927 season to the Black Sox, where he hit .244. He closed out his career with the Brooklyn Royal Giants, who were playing as an independent team and had sustained a decline in quality. An all-around athlete, Brown was also regarded as one of the country's best basketball players.

Brown, F.
Career: 1918   Position: 2b
Team: Chicago Union Giants

He was a second baseman with the Chicago Union Giants in 1918, his only year in black baseball.

Brown, G.
Career: 1925–27   Position: p
Team: St. Louis Stars

He pitched for the St. Louis Stars for three years during the '20s, with his best season coming in 1926, when he posted a 6–3 record.

Brown, George
Career: 1910–28   Positions: lf, rf, cf, 1b,
                                        manager
Teams: West Baden Sprudels ('10–'15), Indianapolis ABCs ('16), Jewel's ABCs ('17), **Dayton Marcos** ('18–'20), St. Louis Giants, Detroit Stars ('21, '28), Columbus Buckeyes ('21)

He fashioned a fourteen-year career with several teams in the Midwest as an outfielder and manager. In 1916 he played right field for the western champion ABCs, and hit .298 while batting in the eighth slot in the order, but inexplicably left the team during the playoffs against the Chicago American Giants in October and went home to Metropolis, Illinois. He broke in with the West Baden Sprudels as a center fielder in 1910 and played the same position ten years later while batting leadoff for the Dayton Marcos in 1920, when they were in the Negro National League.

Brown, George
Career: 1939–45   Positions: of, *p*
Teams: Ethiopian Clowns ('39), Cincinnati Buckeyes ('42), Cleveland Buckeyes ('45)

He was a reserve outfielder with the Ethiopian Clowns and the Buckeyes' ballclub at both franchise locations, Cincinnati and Cleveland.

Brown, H.
Career: 1913–15   Position: p
Teams: Mohawk Giants ('13), Brooklyn Royal Giants ('15)

A pitcher during the deadball era for teams in New York State, he pitched with the Mohawk Giants of Schenectady, New York, in 1913, their best year, and also hurled for the Brooklyn Royal Giants in 1915.

Brown, J.
Career: 1939   Position: p
Team: Homestead Grays

He was listed as a pitcher with the Homestead Grays in 1939.

Brown, James
Career: 1939–48   Positions: **p**, of
Teams: Newark Eagles ('39, '41–'43, '48), Indianapolis Clowns ('47)
Bats: Left   Throws: Right
Height: 6'0"   Weight: 180
Born: May 14, 1919, Laurenburg, N.C.

He joined the Eagles as an outstanding prospect, both as a pitcher and an everyday player, but he showed the most promise on the mound. He had a good fastball, a quick curve, an ability to change speeds effectively, and good control. As an outfielder he had good defensive skills, a strong arm, and a good bat with some power, hitting .304 in 1941 in limited play. However, the Eagles had difficulty keeping him in Newark because of his domestic situation. He had married a girl from his adopted hometown, Sharpsburg, North Carolina, and kept jumping the team to go to North Carolina to be with his new wife.

Brown, James
Career: 1938   Position: p
Team: Atlanta Black Crackers

The Tennessean was on the Atlanta Black Crackers' spring roster in 1938 but was dropped in early May.

Brown, James (Jim)
Career: 1918–35   Positions: **c, 1b**, of, *3b,* manager
Teams: **Chicago American Giants** ('18–'30), Chicago Columbia Giants ('31), Louisville Black Caps ('32), Cleveland Cubs ('32), Cole's American Giants ('33–'35), *Palmer House All-Stars, Minneapolis-St. Paul Gophers ('42)*
Bats: Both   Throws: Right
Height: 6'0"   Weight: 205
Died: Jan. 21, 1943, San Antonio, Tex.

A catcher with a good arm, he played for Rube Foster's great Chicago American Giants teams of the '20s. At the plate he was a big, strong switch-hitter who could also bunt and run in the style of the American Giants. He was especially adept at executing a successful drag bunt. A fast man for a catcher, he also played first base, and was a key player for the American Giants as they won five Negro National League pennants (1920–22 and 1926–27) in an eight-year span.

He and Dave Brown were from the same hometown in Texas and during World War I formed a "Brown" battery in the Lone Star State, where the pair were discovered and signed at the same time by the Chicago American Giants. Beginning with his second season with Foster's club, 1920, Brown moved into the starting lineup, batting fifth in the order behind Christobal Torriente, as the Giants won the first three pennants in the history of the Negro National League. He contributed consistent clutch hitting and, in the middle season, a .288 batting average to the team's successful pursuit of the trio of pennants.

In 1926 Brown began playing more at first base and, with Torriente gone, had to pick up a larger part of the offensive burden; he responded to the challenge by hitting .335 while leading the team in home runs as the American Giants won another Negro National League pennant and defeated the Eastern Colored League Bacharach Giants in the World Series. A year later he hit .293 as the Giants repeated as Negro National League Champions and, in a rematch from the previous year, batted .314 and slugged two home runs as the Giants defeated the Bacharachs in the World Series. The following season, 1928, he lost playing time when he underwent a midsummer operation and was in the hospital for almost two weeks. His absence from the lineup contributed to the team narrowly missing a third straight pennant, but they salvaged part of the title by winning the second half of the 1928 Negro National League split season.

In 1929 he was named manager of the Chicago American Giants and, as his batting average plummeted (.237) and the team's winning percentage dropped, he proved to be hard to get along with in the clubhouse. A disciplinary dispute caused him to suspend Stanford Jackson and Buck Miller, who were signed by the Grays. In 1930 he rebounded at the plate, hitting .323, but Rube Foster's death that year caused an unsettled situation with the franchise. Brown signed with David Malarcher's Chicago Columbia Giants in 1931 but was used in a reserve role. The years had taken their toll, and his playing time was curtailed for the remainder of his career, although he still managed a .341 batting average in limited play in 1933. He retired as an active player after the 1935 season. He later managed the Palmer House All-Stars and the St. Paul Gophers.

Brown enjoyed nightlife and liked to gamble, and it eventually led to his death. In an incident relating to his gambling he was thrown out of a moving car and died from a broken neck.

Brown, Jerome
Career: 1949   Position: if
Team: Houston Eagles
He was a reserve infielder with the Houston Eagles in 1949, when the Negro American League was struggling to survive the loss of players to organized baseball.

Brown, Jesse J. (Jess, Lefty, Professor)
Career: 1938–42   Positions: **p**, of
Teams: Newark Eagles ('38–'39), New York Black Yankees ('38, '40), Baltimore Elite Giants ('40–'42)
Bats: Left   Throws: Left
Height: 5'8"   Weight: 160
Born: 1913, Cleveland, O.
Died: May 25, 1980, Wellesley, Mass.
Jesse was a slender left-handed pitcher with a modicum of skill but with a repertory of disconcerting windups and a terrific sinker that hit the outside corner to right-handed batters and inside to left-handers. He began his career in 1938, pitching with the Newark Eagles and New York Black Yankees before joining the Baltimore Elites. His record in Baltimore was not impressive, with seasons of 0–2, 1–3, and 0–3 for the years 1940–42. The latter season was his last in the Negro Leagues. During his five-year career he proved to be a good fielder but only a fair hitter.

Brown, John W.
Career: 1944–49   Position: p
Teams: *St. Louis Giants ('42–'43),* **Cleveland Buckeyes** ('44–45, '48), Chicago American Giants ('46–'47), Houston Eagles ('49)
Born: 1919, Crossett, Ark.
The Arkansan started his career with the Greensville Bucks in 1936-37 and played with the Norfolk, Virginia, Stars in 1938. After being out of baseball in 1939, he returned to

the diamond with the Oklahoma Indians (1940) and the Bastrop, Louisiana, Blues (1941). Moving up a notch in competition, he played with the St. Louis Giants for two years before signing with the Cleveland Buckeyes in 1944. In his first Negro American League season he finished with a 2–5 work sheet and a 4.04 ERA, but improved to 6–2 with a 3.46 ERA in 1945, when the Buckeyes won the Negro American League pennant and swept the Homestead Grays in the Negro World Series. The next year he was 0–2 with the Chicago American Giants but returned to the Buckeyes in 1948 to fashion a 4–1 mark with a 3.38 ERA. A year later he closed out his career with the Houston Eagles.

Brown, Julius
Career: 1946   Position: p
Team: Indianapolis Clowns

In 1946, his only year in the Negro Leagues, he pitched briefly with the Indianapolis Clowns.

Brown, L.
Career: 1914   Position: 2b
Team: Indianapolis ABCs

He was a second baseman with the Indianapolis ABCs in 1914, their first year of major-league caliber.

Brown, L. A.
Career: 1926–27   Position: officer
Team: St. Louis Stars

He served as an officer for the St. Louis Stars in 1926–27.

Brown, Larry (*Iron Man*)
Career: 1919–49   Positions: c, manager
Teams: Birmingham Black Barons, ('19), Indianapolis ABCs ('21–'23), Pittsburgh Keystones ('22), **Memphis Red Sox** ('23–'25, '27–'29, '31, '38–'48), Detroit Stars ('26), Chicago American Giants ('27, '29, '40), New York Lincoln Giants ('30), Harlem Stars ('31), New York Black Yankees ('32), Cole's American Giants ('32–'35, Philadelphia Stars ('36–'38)

Bats: Both   Throws: Right
Height: 5'8"   Weight: 180
Born: September 5, 1905, Pratt City, Ala.
Died: April 7, 1972, Memphis, Tenn.

An outstanding receiver with a quick release and an arm to be envied, Larry Brown was a master behind the plate. In the field, whether smothering dirt balls or handling pop flies, he was tops but was noted for the peculiar practice of not removing his catcher's mask on pop-ups. A conscientious, hard worker popular with the fans but rough on umpires, he was a durable workman credited with catching 234 games in 1930 for the New York Lincoln Giants, earning the nickname "Iron Man." In addition to his superior defensive skills, the husky catcher was a smart ballplayer who became a successful playing manager during the 1940s with the Memphis Red Sox. He played on three championship teams and in six All-Star games, which are indicative of his value to a team.

His first championship came after he and Nate Rogers joined the Chicago American Giants late in the 1927 season from Memphis. He was the starting catcher in the Negro World Series rematch against the Eastern Colored League's Bacharach Giants, a team that had stolen 19 bases in the previous Series without Larry behind the plate. In the 1927 Series he neutralized their running game as he gunned down four of the eight attempted base stealers. After the World Series was over, he and Rogers were ruled by Negro National League president Hueston to be the property of the Memphis Red Sox.

Six years later, Brown returned to the American Giants to provide stability behind the plate as they won the Negro National League championship in 1933 and came within a game of repeating in 1934, losing a hard-fought, seven-game playoff to the Philadelphia Stars. These two seasons also marked the first two East-West All-Star games, and he was selected to start the All-Star game for the West squad in each of these years.

In the spring of 1938 he rejoined the Memphis Red Sox and help them annex the first-half Negro American League title. That year also marked the first of a string of four more consecutive All-Star appearances (1938–41) and, although he was not noted for his hitting, he had a .308 average to show for his six All-Star games. Generally he maintained respectable batting averages, with marks of .292 and .289 in 1928–29. Partial statistics show identical .431 averages for two years with Cole's American Giants, 1932 and 1934, but more characteristic of his batting skills are averages from some of the better teams he played with during his career, including .253 (1927 American Giants), .256 (1930 Lincoln Giants), and .262 (American Giants). He is credited with a .259 lifetime average for his 31 seasons in black baseball.

Although he is most closely identified with the Memphis Red Sox, Brown played with ten different teams during his career. He was a heavy drinker, which possibly also contributed to his frequency of uniform changes.

He was best known for his defensive skills, and his cannonlike arm generated a story that, although unsubstantiated, persists. Oral tradition insists that while playing against Ty Cobb in Cuba in the winter of 1926, Brown threw out the legendary base stealer on five consecutive attempts to steal second base. According to the story, Cobb was sufficiently impressed to try to get the light-skinned Brown to pass as a Cuban and play in the major leagues. The story has not been conclusively proven or disproven. Similar stories insist that Rogers Hornsby wanted to pass him off as a Cuban, but Brown objected to the plan.

Brown, Lawrence James (**Lefty**)
Career: 1932–39   Position: p
Teams: Memphis Red Sox ('33–'37), *Claybrook Tigers*

The left-hander pitched for the Memphis Red Sox during the '30s and also played with the Claybrook Tigers, a team of lesser quality.

Brown, M.
Career: 1918–22   Position: rf

Teams: Atlantic City Bacharach Giants ('18), Baltimore Black Sox ('22)

In 1918, during the formative years of the Bacharach Giants, he was the regular right fielder, batting second in the lineup, with incomplete and sporadic statistics indicating a .438 average against all levels of opposition. In 1922, under similar circumstances, when the Baltimore Black Sox were building a stronger team, he was recruited for the Sox but did not become a regular.

Brown, Maywood
Career: 1921–25   Position: p
Team: Indianapolis ABCs

He was a pitcher with the Indianapolis ABCs for the first half of the '20s but was not a leading pitcher.

Brown, Oliver
Career: 1932   Position: business manager
Team: Newark Browns

He was the business manager with Newark Browns in 1932, when they were in the East-West League.

Brown, Oscar
Career: 1939   Position: c
Teams: Indianapolis ABCs ('39), Baltimore Elite Giants ('39)

A reserve catcher, he appeared with both the Indianapolis ABCs and the Baltimore Elite Giants in 1939.

Brown, Ossie
Career: 1934–39   Positions: p, of
Teams: Cole's American Giants ('34–'35), Indianapolis Athletics ('37), Indianapolis ABCs ('38), St. Louis Stars ('39)

Primarily a pitcher, he also received some playing time in the outfield with midwestern teams during the late '30s but never distinguished himself at either position. The best team that he appeared with was Cole's American Giants, but most of the teams he played with were struggling to maintain a place in the

Negro American League, including the Indianapolis Athletics and Indianapolis ABCs, who moved their franchise to St. Louis in 1939 and played as the St. Louis Stars.

Brown, Raymond
Career: 1939–40   Position: c
Team: Brooklyn Royal Giants

He was a catcher with the Brooklyn Royal Giants for two years, when the team was playing as an independent ballclub and declining in quality.

Brown, Raymond (Ray)
Career: 1930–48   Positions: **p**, of,
                       manager
Teams: Dayton Marcos ('30), Indianapolis ABCs ('31), Detroit Wolves ('32), **Homestead Grays** ('32–'45, '47–'48), *Mexican League ('39, '46–'49), Canadian League ('50–'53)*
Bats: Both   Throws: Right
Height: 6'1"   Weight:195
Born: February 23, 1908, Ashland Grove, O.
Died: 1968, Dayton, O.

The Homestead Gray's ace had a sinker, slider, and a fine fastball, but his curveball was his best pitch. So confident was Ray in all of his pitches that he would throw a curve with a 3–0 count on the batter. Later in his career he developed an effective knuckleball, and he had good control of all his pitches. During his nineteen-year career he pitched in two East-West All-Star games (1935 and 1940) without a decision. As the mainstay of the Homestead Grays during their dynasty period, Ray pitched a total of seven games in the World Series of 1942–45, earning a 3–2 World Series ledger. This included a one-hit shutout of the Birmingham Black Barons in the 1944 World Series. However, the workhorse's best pitching gem was yet to come, when he pitched a perfect game in a seven-inning contest against the Chicago American Giants in 1945.

Before turning to professional baseball, Brown played high school baseball in Indian Lake, Ohio, and attended Wilberforce University, but left before graduation to sign with the Homestead Grays. He continued his studies in the off-season, and after graduating in 1935, the handsome hurler married the daughter of Grays' owner Cum Posey in a ceremony at home plate on the Fourth of July. The slender, light-complected athlete was a steel-armed competitor and always ready to play. But the hard drinker was considered temperamental by some and, as Posey's son-in-law, was thought by others to receive preferential consideration.

In 1935 he sported a 12–3 pitching ledger, but Brown was not only an outstanding pitcher, he was also a good hitter from both sides of the plate, and often played the outfield when not toeing the rubber. When he first joined the Grays, he played center field and batted in a prominent spot in the batting order, but as the years passed, he concentrated more on his pitching. In 1936 he was selected for the Negro National League All-Star team that devastated the opposition in the *Denver Post* Tournament, winning the title easily without a loss.

With the great offensive support generated by the powerhouse bats in the Grays' lineup, he enjoyed a high degree of success and ranks high in winning percentage among Negro League pitchers of all time. Throughout his career he had long winning streaks, including one stretch in 1936–37 when he won 28 straight games over two seasons.

In 1938 the Grays fielded the strongest team of their nine straight pennant winners, and he was picked for the East-West All-Star game but was withheld from participation by the club and the East lost, causing some owners to demand that the best players be allowed to represent their league in future contests. Brown finished the season with a 10–2 record and was one of five players designated by the *Pittsburgh Courier* as certain major-league stars and recommended to the Pittsburgh Pirates to sign if they wanted to be guaranteed a pennant. The other players identified were Josh Gibson, Buck Leonard, Cool Papa Bell, and Satchel Paige. Few baseball historians doubt that with these five stars added to the Pittsburgh roster (giving them a total of seven Hall of Famers) the Pirates would have more than overcome the 2-game deficit by which the Chicago Cubs won the pennant when Gabby Hartnett hit his famous "homer in the gloaming."

In May 1939, after playing winter ball and angry at the Grays' contract offer for the coming season, Brown wrote Newark Eagles' owner Abe Manley, offering to play with the Eagles for $215 per month. With Manley not accepting his offer, he opted instead to pitch in Mexico and posted a 15–8 record before returning to the Grays late in the season. Rejoining the rotation, he won four of his five decisions as Homestead annexed another of their nine straight pennants, albeit a tainted one, as they lost a postseason tournament to the Baltimore Elite Giants.

The 1940 season brought another All-Star year for Brown (18–3, 2.53 ERA) and another pennant for the Grays. In 1941 the big right-hander was credited with 27 straight wins against all competition (10–4, 2.72 ERA in league contests) as the Grays won their fifth straight Negro National League flag. In the league championship playoffs against the New York Cubans, he tossed a shutout in the deciding contest, and contributed three hits, including a home run and a double, to the offense. In 1942 he was 13–6 as the Grays swept to another pennant but lost to the Kansas City Monarchs in the World Series. The next two years, Brown posted marks of 8–1 and 9–3 and the Grays won both the pennant and the World Series each season. Although he dropped to a 3–2 record in league play, the 1945 season brought another pennant, extending the Grays' skein to nine straight flags.

Brown made his home in Homestead during the off-season, except when he was playing in the Latin American Leagues. A favorite in Cuba, he won more games in the winter leagues than any other black American pitcher, having a 46–20 record to show for his five seasons there, while batting .266. With Santa Clara in 1936–37, he led the Cuban League in wins, posting a 21–3 record and spinning a no-hit, 7–0 victory over Havana on November 7,

1936. The next winter (1937–38) he again led the league in wins, with 12, and pitched Santa Clara to the championship. Pitching for Ponce in the winter of 1941–42, he also led the Puerto Rican League in victories, when he posted a 12–4 ledger with a 1.82 ERA. Six winters later he was still pitching effective ball, as he registered a 1.05 ERA in Puerto Rico. The next winter, 1948–49, he was the manager for Caracas in the Venezuelan League.

In 1946 he left the Grays for another stint in Mexico, where he was 13–9 with a 3.52 ERA for Tampico, and followed with marks of 10–12, 13–4, and 15–11 with respective ERAs of 3.24, 3.53, and 3.40 in 1947–49. Leaving the Mexico City ballclub after the 1949 season, he went to Shebrooke in the Canadian Provincial League and was 6–1 and 11–10 in 1950–51, also playing outfield the latter year as the club won the provincial championship. In 1953 he pitched two games for the Thetfore Miners' ballclub and won his only decision. Apparently this was his last baseball decision ever, and he went out a winner. After his baseball career ended, he remarried and settled in Canada for several years, but had returned to the United States by the time of his death.

Brown, Robert
Career: 1887   Position: player
Team: *Boston Resolutes*

He was a player with the Boston Resolutes, one of eight teams that were charter members of the League of Colored Baseball Clubs in 1887. However, the league's existence was ephemeral, lasting only a week. His position is uncertain.

Brown, Ronnie
Career: 1943   Position: 1b
Team: Harrisburg-St. Louis Stars

He was a wartime reserve first baseman for the Harrisburg-St. Louis Stars in 1943, when the team withdrew from the Negro National League in the spring to barnstorm against a white team headed by Dizzy Dean.

Brown, Roosevelt

Career: 1938   Position: p

Team: Atlanta Black Crackers

A native Tennessean, the pitcher was on the Atlanta Black Crackers' spring roster in 1938.

Brown, Roy

Career: 1928–31   Positions: p, of

Team: Kansas City Monarchs

The pitcher-outfielder made two appearances with the Kansas City Monarchs, first in 1928 and again in 1931

Brown, Scrappy

[see Brown, Elmore (Scrappy)]

Brown, T. J. (Tom)

Career: 1939–50   Positions: **ss**, 3b, 2b

Teams: Memphis Red Sox ('39–'45, '47–'50), Harrisburg-St. Louis Stars ('43), *military service ('46),* Cleveland Buckeyes ('50), Indianapolis Clowns ('47), Louisville Buckeyes ('49), *minor leagues ('52–'53)*

Bats: Right   Throws: Right

A hustler with a wide range and a good arm, the small, bowlegged Memphis Red Sox shortstop held down a regular spot for seven years before entering the Army and missing part of the 1946 season. His best season during his stint with Memphis was 1942, when he hit .316 and was selected to play in the East-West All-Star game. Not a strong hitter, he usually batted in the lower part of the order, recording averages of .211 and .105 in 1944–45 and being credited with a .292 average in 1949. He also played with the Buckeyes and Clowns in the latter years of his Negro Leagues career, and played two seasons in organized baseball with Danville of the Mississippi-Ohio Valley League in 1952–53, where he hit .241 and .163. Brown's eye for the ladies was as good as his eye at the plate, and he married a bathing beauty queen.

Brown, Theo

Career: 1911   Position: 3b

Team: Chicago Union Giants

He was a third baseman with the Chicago Union Giants in 1911.

Brown, Tom

Career: 1917–19   Position: p

Teams: Brooklyn Royal Giants ('17), Chicago American Giants ('19), New York Lincoln Giants ('19)

He pitched for three years during the World War I era, beginning with a brief appearance with the Brooklyn Royal Giants at the end of the 1917 season and including stints with the New York Lincoln Giants and the Chicago American Giants. In 1921 he played as a right fielder with the Madison Stars, a team of lesser caliber.

Brown, Ulysses (**Buster**)

Career: 1937–42   Positions: **c**, of

Teams: Newark Eagles ('37–'39), Jacksonville Red Caps ('38), Ethiopian Clowns ('40–'41), Cincinnati Buckeyes ('42)

Bats: Right   Throws: Right

Height: 6'2"   Weight: 200

Died: Sept. 7, 1942, Geneva, O.

He was a catcher with an average arm and was not a good base runner, but he was considered a dangerous man at the plate and a distance hitter. A native of Jacksonville, Florida, he learned his baseball skills on the sandlots of the city. He signed with the Eagles in 1937 and was credited with a .267 average in his first year, but was relegated to a reserve role for a couple of seasons prior to being released in the spring of 1939. Nicknamed "Buster," he was a hard case with the reputation of being evil. Two years later he was with the Ethiopian Clowns when they won the *Denver Post* Tournament in 1941.

The following season he was the regular catcher with the Cincinnati Buckeyes when he was killed in an automobile accident while driving home after a series with the New York Black Yankees. On September 7, 1942, a car he was driving, with five Cincinnati Buckeyes teammates as passengers, was struck from behind by a truck, and Brown and Raymond "Smoky" Owens were killed instantly. Four others were injured, with Eugene Bremmer and Herman Watts being hospitalized, and with Alonzo Boone and owner Wilbur Hayes escaping with minimal injuries. The accident occurred at 3:00 A.M. just west of Geneva, Ohio, when their car was reentering a highway after they had stopped to change a flat tire.

Brown, W.

Career: 1939   Position: ss
Team: Memphis Red Sox

He was listed as a shortstop with the Memphis Red Sox in 1939.

Brown, W. (Mike)

Career: 1913–15   Positions: **p**, 1b, of
Teams: Mohawk Giants ('13), Philadelphia Giants ('13–'15)

Although primarily a pitcher, he played three different positions for three seasons with the Mohawk Giants and the Philadelphia Giants.

Brown, Walter S.

Career: 1887   Positions: manager, officer

Team: *Pittsburgh Keystones*

In 1887 the manager of the Pittsburgh Keystones served as the president of the League of Colored Baseball Clubs. The Keystones was one of eight teams that were charter members of the League of Colored Baseball Clubs. However, the league's existence was ephemeral, lasting only a week.

Brown, Willard Jesse (Home Run, Esse Hombre, Willie, Sonny)

Career: 1935–50   Positions: **cf**, lf, ss
Teams: *Monroe Monarchs ('34)* **Kansas City Monarchs** ('35–'43, '46–'51), *Mexican League ('40), military service ('44–'45),* major leagues ('47), *minor leagues ('50, '53–'56)*
Bats: Right   Throws: Right
Height: 6'0"   Weight: 195
Born: June 26, 1911, Shreveport, La.

Black baseball's premier home-run hitter of the 1940s was a bundle of unlimited and largely unfulfilled potential. Willard Brown was a slugger who was exceptionally fast in

the field, a good base runner, and an excellent gloveman with a great arm. Noted as a big-game player, he was at his best in front of a large crowd.

Nicknamed "Esse Hombre" in Puerto Rico, where he played winter ball, he hit for a lifetime .350 batting average and won three consecutive batting titles (1946–50), with averages of .390, .432, and .353. During this span he also won three home-run titles, establishing the all-time record of 27 in the winter of 1947–48 and following with totals of 18, 16, and 14. He began his Puerto Rican career in 1941–42 with Humacao as a second baseman and hit for a .410 average. After service in World War II, he returned to Puerto Rico as an outfielder with Santurce for the rest of his career. Beginning in 1946 he had consecutive averages of .390, .432, .323, 353, .325, .295, .342, and .265. After a two-year absence, he played a final season with Santurce in 1956–57 but hit only .261. He also played in Mexico for a season, jumping the Monarchs early in the 1940 season to play with Nuevo Laredo, where he hit .351 with eight home runs in 70 games.

A free-swinger and notorious bad-ball hitter, the big, strong slugger considered anything that left the pitcher's hand a strike and often swung at bad pitches. He hit with power to all fields, used a 40-ounce bat, and often hit tape-measure shots. On at least one occasion, he hit a home run off a pitch that arrived at home plate on one bounce. Had he been more patiently selective, he may have accumulated even more impressive statistics.

In the United States, "Home Run" Brown played on the great Monarch teams that dominated the Negro American League from 1937 to 1942, winning five pennants in six years, contributing averages of .371, .356, .336, .337, and .365 to the pennant efforts, exclusive of 1940, when he opted to play in Mexico. In 1942, one of his best years, Willard was hitting .429 at the All-Star break and batted cleanup for the West squad in the East-West All-Star game. After the midseason classic, he continued his slugging as the Monarchs captured another pennant and met the Negro National

League champion Homestead Grays in the first World Series between the Negro American League and the Negro National League. With Brown continuing his hot bat, hitting .412 and a home run, the Monarchs swept the Grays four straight.

The next season, Brown hit .345 and made another All-Star appearance before entering military service for two years (1944–45), but the Monarchs had lost too many players to the service to secure another pennant. In the Army, Brown was among those in the five thousand ships that crossed the English Channel during the Normandy invasion. A member of the Quartermaster Corps, he was not in combat but was engaged in hauling ammunition and guarding prisoners. After being transferred to Special Services, he began playing baseball and played in the G.I. World Series, banging two home runs over the center-field fence off Ewell Blackwell to help Leon Day earn the victory over an Army team of major leaguers.

After his discharge Brown had little difficulty readjusting to baseball, batting .348 and clubbing a league-high 13 home runs in 1946 while leading the Monarchs to another pennant. In the ensuing World Series against the Newark Eagles, who had dethroned the Grays, he added two round-trippers in a losing cause as the Monarchs lost in a closely contested seven-game Series.

The following year, 1947, Jackie Robinson made his major-league debut with the Brooklyn Dodgers, and once the color barrier was lifted, Brown and Hank Thompson were signed by St. Louis Browns' owner Bill Veeck. Batting .353 with eight homers in 46 games at the time, he was labeled a "can't miss" prospect by major-league scouts and sent directly to the Browns without an adjustment period in the minor leagues, as Robinson had received for the new "experiment." Both he and Thompson were questionable personality types and needed this interim period much more than Robinson. However, the husky outfielder was not given this opportunity nor adequate time to make the transition at the major-league level and, after

playing briefly (21 games) and hitting only .179 with one homer, he and Thompson were released unconditionally. Brown thought that they should have been farmed out after their release, and given another chance after a period of adjustment. Thompson did get a second chance, with the New York Giants, and made good on his second opportunity, but Brown never received a second chance.

A footnote to his major-league career was that his lone home run was the first ever hit in the American League by a black player. A second footnote deals with a different aspect of the home run. Brown hit the homer with a bat that belonged to a teammate, and the player broke the bat rather than allow Brown ever to use it again.

After his release, he returned to the Monarchs, where he hit .336 for the remainder of the year. In 1948 he resumed his barrage on Negro American League pitching with a .374 average while slugging a league-leading 18 home runs. In 1949 he hit .371 before going into organized ball, ending his career in the Negro Leagues with a .355 lifetime batting average and six All-Star appearances.

The next year he played in the Border League with Ottawa, where he hit .352. In the twilight of his career, he moved to the Texas League for four years (1953–56), where he hit .310, .314, .301, and .299 with 23, 35, 19 and 14 home runs, respectively. In two of his four seasons he led his team to the Texas League pennant, first with Dallas in 1953 and with Houston the following year, and gained a popularity so lasting that he continues to be an area favorite. The latter season he also played for a short time with the Topeka club in the Western League and hit .294 with 3 homers, leaving him with a lifetime .305 average for his combined minor- and major-league career. His final appearance in professional baseball was with Santurce in Puerto Rico during the following winter (1956–57), but he hit only .261 with 2 home runs in 23 at-bats.

Brown first began playing baseball as a youngster in Shreveport, Louisiana, and in

1934 he signed with the Negro Southern League's Monroe Monarchs for $10 a week as a shortstop and pitcher. After only one year, he was grabbed by Kansas City Monarchs' owner J. L. Wilkinson, who offered Brown a $250 bonus, $125 per month and $1 a day meal money. He made his first All-Star appearance as a shortstop in the 1936 East-West game. But after two years as the Monarchs' regular shortstop, slick-fielding Byron Johnson was installed at shortstop in 1937, and Brown was moved to the outfield. He was selected to the All-Star team that season at his new position.

A natural athlete, Brown was very talented but lacked drive. He loved to play to large crowds but was lazy, stubborn, and very relaxed, "saving his strength" and playing hard only when he thought it necessary. He was also lackadaisical at times, and often would carry a copy of *The Reader's Digest* in his hip pocket to read in center field during a game. Off the field, he was congenial, fun-loving, and enjoyed a long-lasting popularity from his playing days in the Texas League. After retiring from baseball, he settled in Houston and continued to enjoy life until he was hospitalized in 1989 with Alzheimer's disease.

Brown, William H.
Career: 1887   Position: 1b
Team: *Pittsburgh Keystones*

He was a first baseman with the 1887 Pittsburgh Keystones, one of eight teams that were charter members of the League of Colored Baseball Clubs. However, the league's existence was ephemeral, lasting only a week.

Brown, William M.
Career: 1931–32   Position: officer
Team: Montgomery Grey Sox

A club officer for the Montgomery Grey Sox, his service with the team extended through 1932, when the Negro Southern League was considered a major league.

Browne, Hap
Career: 1924   Position: p
Team: Cleveland Browns

He was a pitcher with the Cleveland Browns in 1924, his only year in the Negro Leagues.

Bruce, Clarence
Career: 1947–48   Positions: **2b**, 3b
Teams: Homestead Grays ('47–'49), *Canadian League ('50)*
Bats: Right   Throws: Right
Height: 6'1"   Weight: 170
Born: Sept. 26, 1926, Pittsburgh, Pa.
Died: Jan 23, 1990, Pittsburgh, Pa.

A mediocre hitter without significant power and lacking consistent contact, he was also an average defensive player. After hitting .246 as a part-time starter in 1947, he assumed the role as the regular second baseman for the Homestead Grays when Luis Marquez was moved to center field the following season. Bruce batted .255 as the Grays won the 1948 Negro National League pennant in the league's last year of existence, and defeated the Negro American League champion Birmingham Black Barons. After leaving the Grays, he played with Farnham in the Canadian Provincial League in 1950, managing only a .222 batting average without any demonstrable power.

Bruce, Lloyd
Career: 1940   Position: p
Team: Chicago American Giants

He was a pitcher with the Chicago American Giants in 1940, his only year in the Negro Leagues.

Bruton, Charles John (**Jack**)
a.k.a. Brutton; Brewton
Career: 1936–1941   Positions: **p**, of, 1b,
                                    3b, *2b*
Teams: Birmingham Black Barons ('36–'38, '40), Philadelphia Stars ('38), Cleveland Bears ('39), New York Black Yankees ('40), New Orleans-St. Louis Stars ('40–'41)

A native of Cordova, Alabama, he played outfield and filled in as a backup first baseman for the St. Louis Stars in 1941. Earlier in his career he pitched and played both as an outfielder and infielder for several ballclubs, including the Birmingham Black Barons. At the plate he had good power and was dangerous in the pinches.

Bryant, Allen, Jr. (**Lefty**)
Career: 1937–47   Position: p
Teams: *All-Nations ('37–'38),* Memphis Red Sox ('37, '40), Kansas City Monarchs ('39–'41, '43, '45–'47), *military service ('41–'44), Canadian League ('48–'49)*
Bats: Left   Throws: Left
Height: 5'11"   Weight: 160
Born: Mar. 29, 1918, Chicago, Ill.
Died: Mar. 22, 1992, Kansas City, Mo.

Pitching for the Monarchs in the early 1940s, the little left-hander was a "junkball" pitcher who mixed a wide assortment of off-speed breaking pitches effectively, including a knuckler, which was his best pitch. During a career that began in 1937, he also pitched for the Memphis Red Sox and the All-Nations team prior to joining the Monarchs in 1939. His career was interrupted by military service during World War II; he was honorably discharged from the U.S. Army as a sergeant.

He returned to the Monarchs, pitching through the 1947 season, until leaving to pitch for the Minot Merchants in Minot, North Dakota, in 1948. During the season, he joined the Edmonton Eskimos and pitched with them for two years, 1948–49. He also played with Winnipeg and the Canadian All-Stars.

His family moved to Kansas City when he was eight years old and he attended the city's public schools. After retiring from baseball, he worked as a park ranger for Missouri's Jackson County Parks and Recreation Department for fourteen years, retiring in 1979.

Bryant, Eddie
Career: 1928   Position: 2b
Team: Harrisburg Giants

He played with a semipro club, the Pittsburgh Black Sox, along with his brother Willie and the Williams brothers, Harry and Roy. They were all reunited on the Pittsburgh Crawfords in 1928, before the Crawfords became a

professional team. Later that season he signed with the Harrisburg Giants as a second baseman.

Bryant, Johnnie
Career: 1950   Postion: of
Team: Cleveland Buckeyes

He is listed as an outfielder for the Cleveland Buckeyes in 1950, when the Negro American League was struggling to survive the loss of players to organized baseball, but league statistics do not confirm his playing time.

Bryant, R. B.
Career: 1937   Position: ss
Team: Memphis Red Sox

He was listed as a shortstop for the Memphis Red Sox in 1937, his only year in the Negro Leagues.

Bubbles
[see Berry, Bubber]

Buchanan, Chester (Buck)
Career: 1937–44   Position: p
Teams: *Philadelphia Bacharach Giants ('31–'36),* Philadelphia Stars ('40–'44)
Bats: Right   Throws: Right
Height: 6'2"   Weight: 200

He was a pitcher for the Philadelphia Stars during the early '40s after spending many seasons with the Philadelphia-based Bacharach Giants, a team of lesser quality. He had a good arm but was a weak hitter and slow baserunner and was not a good fielder. He was in the pitching rotation for the Stars, registering marks of 2–5, 1–6, 2–2, and 5–3 for the first four seasons (1940–43) that he was with them. In his last season he was used less frequently and finished with fewer than 3 decisions for the year.

Buck
Career: 1923   Position: p
Team: Birmingham Black Barons

In 1923 he appeared briefly as a pitcher with

the Birmingham Black Barons, a year before they entered the Negro National League.

Buckner, Harry (Green River)
Career: 1896–1918   Positions: **p**, of, c, ss
Teams: Chicago Unions ('96–'98), Columbia Giants ('90–'00), Philadelphia Giants ('03), Cuban X-Giants ('04–'05), *Quaker Giants,* Brooklyn Royal Giants ('09–'10), New York Lincoln Giants ('11–'12), Smart Set ('12), Mohawk Giants ('13), Chicago Giants ('14–'18)

One of the leading players during the early years of black baseball, this talented and versatile athlete could pitch, catch, and play both infield and outfield. He was one of only a few Americans who played in Cuba during the first decade of the century, pitching for Almendares in the Cuban winter league of 1907. He began his career as a pitcher with W. S. Peters's Chicago Unions in 1896, and after three years joined the Columbia Giants for another two seasons on the mound. In 1901 Frank Leland combined the Unions and the Columbia Giants into a single team, the Chicago Union Giants, but Buckner opted to play in the East.

He was a smart pitcher and was called the "speed marvel" of the Brooklyn Royal Giants in 1910. That season the Royals won the eastern championship for the second consecutive year and, along with Rube Foster, Dan McClellan, and Walter Ball, Buckner was considered to be "head and shoulders above" all other pitchers. In 1909 he also was a regular behind the plate, when not pitching, and in 1917 he was the regular right fielder and batted third in the lineup. In 1911, playing with the New York Lincoln Giants, he split a pair of decisions while batting .336. He pitched the next two seasons with the Smart Set and the Mohawk Giants of Schenectady, New York, before returning to Chicago to finish his career with the Chicago Giants.

During his 23 years in black baseball, he was associated with numerous teams in both the East and the Midwest. Buckner also was a keen judge of talent; he, Rube Foster, and Sol White discovered the great John Henry Lloyd in 1905.

Buckner, James (Joe)
Career: 1946   Position: p
Teams: Chicago American Giants ('46), *Boston Blues ('46)*

The pitcher split the 1946 season between the Chicago American Giants and the Boston Blues of the lesser U.S. League.

Budbill
Career: 1950   Position: p
Team: Houston Eagles

He was listed as a pitcher for the Houston Eagles in 1950, when the Negro American League was struggling to survive the loss of players to organized baseball, but league statistics do not confirm his playing time.

Buddles
Career: 1925   Position: if
Team: Chicago American Giants

The infielder signed a contract with the Chicago American Giants in the spring of 1925 after Rube Foster released a massive group of players.

Buford
Career: 1913–14   Position: p
Team: Chicago Giants

He was a pitcher with the Chicago Giants for two seasons during the deadball era.

Buford, (Black Bottom)
Career: 1930–33   Positions: **3b**, ss, 2b, of, p
Teams: **Nashville Elite Giants** ('27–'32), Cleveland Cubs ('31), Birmingham Black Barons ('31), Detroit Stars ('33), *Louisville Red Caps ('34)*
Bats: Right   Throws: Right

The infielder with the colorful nickname could play any infield position and had pretty good power and speed. He played eight years in the Negro Leagues, mostly with the Nashville Elite Giants. Beginning with the Elites in

1927, when they were in the Negro Southern League, he hit only .229 in 1929, a year before the Elites were in the Negro National League. The next year, 1930, usually batting cleanup, he hit .283 in league play. In 1931 the franchise moved to Cleveland and played as the Cubs, but before the end of the year the team was back in Nashville playing in the Negro Southern League, with Buford playing second base and batting third in the order. The Southern League was no longer designated as a major league, and owner Tom Wilson entered the Elites in the East-West League in 1932, with Buford batting in the second slot and playing at the hot corner. However, the league encountered financial difficulties and broke up during the summer. The next season was his last year with a major-league team, when he played with the 1933 Detroit Stars as a part-time starter, usually hitting in the sixth slot in the batting order.

Bumpus, Earl

Career: 1944–48   Positions: **p**, *of*
Teams: Kansas City Monarchs ('44), Birmingham Black Barons ('44–'46), Chicago American Giants ('47–'48)
Bats: Left   Throws: Left
Height: 6'1"   Weight: 215

The big left-hander from Uniontown, Kentucky, began his career pitching with the Kansas City Monarchs, but joined the Birmingham Black Barons during the course of the 1944 season, compiling a composite 1–8 record with a 6.50 ERA. The Black Barons won the Negro American League pennant, and although Bumpus was a first-year member of the pitching staff, he was selected to start a game in the World Series against the Homestead Grays, Bumpus hurled a complete game but lost the decision, and the Black Barons lost the Series in five games.

Steady and strong, he had a good fastball, but lack of a good curve restricted his effectiveness somewhat. However, his control was sufficient to provide solid portside pitching to balance the staff. In 1945, in his first full season in Birmingham, he improved to a 4–2 record with a 3.63 ERA, but his ex-mates in Kansas City took the title. Leaving the Black Barons after another season, he signed with the Chicago American Giants, but after two seasons and losing all four decisions in 1948, he closed out his career. Overall he was a pretty good pitcher, and in addition to taking his turn on the mound, he occasionally filled in as an outfielder.

Bunel

Career: 1920   Position: c
Team: Baltimore Black Sox

He was a reserve catcher with the Baltimore Black Sox in 1920, when they were playing as an independent team but building toward entry into league play.

Bunn, Willie

Career: 1943   Position: p
Teams: Philadelphia Stars ('43) *Atlanta Black Crackers ('43)*

A wartime player, in 1943 he appeared briefly with the Philadelphia Stars in the Negro National League before pitching most of the season with the Atlanta Black Crackers in the Negro Southern League.

Burbage, Knowlington O. (**Buddy**)

Career: 1929–43   Positions: lf, rf, cf, *c*
Teams: *Ewing's All-Stars ('28), Mohawk Giants ('29, '31),* Baltimore Black Sox ('29, '32), Hilldale Daisies ('30), Pittsburgh Crawfords ('31, '37), Newark Browns ('32), Atlantic City Bacharach Giants ('33, *'36*), Newark Dodgers ('34–'35), Homestead Grays ('33, '35–'36), Washington Black Senators ('38), Brooklyn Royal Giants ('38–'42), Philadelphia Stars ('43)
Bats: Left   Throws: Right
Height: 5'6"   Weight: 160
Born: 1905
Died: Aug. 30, 1989, Philadelphia, Pa.

The diminutive speedster from South Philadelphia had been an outstanding sprinter in high school, and when he began playing semipro ball at age fifteen, the scrappy hustler utilized his speed on the bases and in the outfield. He was strong for a little man, but although he had some good years, he was generally a mediocre hitter.

He began his professional career in 1929 with the Mohawk Giants but quickly joined the Baltimore Black Sox the same season, earning $125 a month playing right field and batting in the leadoff position. Soon after joining the team he had three hits, including a home run, off the Philadelphia A's Howard Ehmke in an exhibition game. Eventually working his way up to a peak of $400 a month, Burbage hit .252 as the Sox won the American Negro League's only pennant. After the league folded, he joined the independent Hilldale ballclub, where he played left field and enjoyed his finest season, hitting .401 against all levels of competition.

The next season he joined the Pittsburgh Crawfords, where he played center field and batted leadoff, but when owner Gus Greenlee began recruiting top players to build a championship ballclub, the little outfielder became expendable. Returning to the Black Sox, now in the East-West League, he stepped into his accustomed leadoff position while patrolling the center pasture, and the Sox were on course for another pennant. When the league folded during the season, the Black Sox were perched atop the standings.

With another failed league, he signed with the Bacharachs in 1933, playing center field and batting leadoff, but the Bacharachs were a marginal ballclub. He also played with the Homestead Grays part of the 1933 season, but in a reserve role. In 1935 he batted .268 but still was not in the Grays' starting lineup. In 1937 Burbage again signed with the Pittsburgh Crawfords, who were suffering from the defection of Satchel Paige and several other Crawfords to Santo Domingo, and stepped into the center-field and leadoff spot vacated by Cool Papa Bell, who was among the defectors.

The next season he started with the Washington Black Senators, a new entry in the Negro National League, but the team folded during the second half of the season and Burbage joined the Brooklyn Royal Giants, a team in decline but striving to remain a marginal team. With the Royals he batted leadoff and played center field, but in 1941 he began also to take a turn behind the plate, and in 1943, in his last year in the Negro Leagues, he joined the Philadelphia Stars as a reserve catcher.

With the advent of World War II, he ended his baseball career and worked in the Philadelphia Naval Shipyard. Later he worked as a baggage handler at the Thirtieth Street Station in Philadelphia until illness forced him to retire in 1975. During his fifteen-year career Burbage played with a dozen teams and, as a veteran player, he was willing to share his experience with younger players.

Burch
Career: 1914   Position: p
Team: Indianapolis ABCs

He was a pitcher for the Indianapolis ABCs in 1914, the first year the club played major-league-caliber baseball, and in 1917 he pitched with the Lost Island Giants, an independent team of lesser stature that combined showbiz with baseball.

Burch, John Walter
Career: 1931–46   Positions: c, 2b, ss, p,
                              manager
Teams; Atlantic City Bacharach Giants ('31), Washington Pilots ('32), Newark Dodgers ('34), Baltimore Black Sox, Kansas City Monarchs, Homestead Grays ('36), Cleveland Bears ('39), Chicago American Giants ('40), New Orleans–St. Louis Stars ('40), St. Louis Stars ('41), Cincinnati Buckeyes ('42), Cleveland Buckeyes ('43–'44,'46)
Bats: Right   Throws: Right
Height: 6'0"   Weight: 175

During his career he was primarily a catcher, but also served as an infielder and manager. Defensively he was an average receiver, but he lacked punch at the plate. He spent almost all of his baseball career with teams in the Negro

American League, and after his playing days ended, he embarked on a managerial career. He took the reins of the Buckeyes in 1942, their inaugural season in the Negro American League, but was replaced by Parnell Woods in early summer. Burch remained with the team, batting .277 in 1944; and in 1946, his last in the Negro Leagues, he also took a few turns on the mound, splitting a pair of decisions.

Burdine, J.

Career: 1926–32   Positions: **p**, of, 3b
Teams: Birmingham Black Barons ('26–'31), Memphis Red Sox ('27–'30), Indianapolis ABCs ('32)

He pitched with the Birmingham Black Barons in 1926 when they were in the Negro Southern League, and played for another half-dozen seasons in the Negro National League as a pitcher, outfielder, and third baseman with the Black Barons, Memphis Red Sox, and Indianapolis ABCs. In 1929 he posted a 4–13 record for the Black Barons, while batting .248.

Burgee, Lou

Career: 1917   Positions: 2b, *p*
Teams: Hilldale Daisies ('17), *Madison Stars ('20)*

In 1917, with Hilldale during their formative years, he was a part-time starter at second base and hit second in the batting order. Later he played with the Madison Stars in 1920, and earlier in his career (1910), he had been a pitcher with another lesser club, but neither of these teams were of major-league caliber.

Burgess

Career: 1942   Position: p
Team: Chicago American Giants

He was a pitcher with the American Giants in 1942, his only season in the Negro Leagues.

Burgett

Career: 1920   Position: of
Team: St. Louis Giants

He was a reserve outfielder with the St.

Louis Giants in 1920, the inaugural season of the Negro National League and his only year in the Negro Leagues.

Burgin

Career: 1913   Position: rf
Team: Havana Red Sox

He played right field for the 1913 Havana Red Sox, a team of marginal quality.

Burgin, Ralph

a.k.a. Bergin; Bergen
Career: 1917–43   Positions: **2b**, 3b, ss, of
Teams: Hilldale Daisies ('17, '21, '30), Baltimore Black Sox ('30), New York Black Yankees ('31, '37–'39), Atlantic City Bacharach Giants ('32), Philadelphia Stars ('36), Pittsburgh Crawfords ('36), Brooklyn Royal Giants ('40)
Bats: Right   Throws: Right
Height: 5'10"   Weight: 180

This longtime player was an all-purpose man, playing every infield position and also in the outfield. He played with a variety of eastern teams, and although his best position was second base, he was a reserve third baseman for Hilldale in 1930, batting .375 while playing mostly against semipro opposition. In 1936 he hit .176 with the Philadelphia Stars in very limited play and, toward the end of his career, he played left field for the New York Black Yankees in 1939, batting .214. In 1940 he played right field for the Brooklyn Royal Giants, hitting in the sixth slot in the batting order, and he closed his career in 1943.

Burgos, José A.

Career: 1949–50   Position: ss
Teams: Birmingham Black Barons ('49–'50), *minor leagues ('51–'53)*
Bats: Right   Throws: Right
Height: 5'6"   Weight: 150
Born: Puerto Rico, 1928

A light-hitting shortstop for the Black Barons in 1949–50, this native Puerto Rican hit .224 and .243, respectively. Entering organized baseball, the next two seasons (1951–52) were spent in the Florida International League with Leesburg and Lakeland, where he hit .263 and .221. The next season was his last in organized baseball, and he hit .243 with Richmond in the Piedmont League. He had good speed and a good eye at the plate, but a weak bat plagued him throughout his career. He played nine winters (1946–55) with Ponce in the Puerto Rican League, where he hit .216 lifetime with a high batting average of .258 in 1950–51.

Burke, Charles

Career: 1937   Positions: ss, of
Team: Indianapolis Athletics

He played shortstop and right field as a part-time starter, batting third when in the lineup for the Indianapolis Athletics in 1937. That was the inaugural year of the Negro American League, the team's only year in the league play and his only year in the Negro Leagues.

Burke, Ernest

Career: 1947–48   Positions: p, of, 3b
Teams: Baltimore Elite Giants ('47–'48), *minor leagues ('49, '54), Canadian League ('50–'51)*
Bats: Left   Throws: Right
Height: 6'1"   Weight: 180
Born: June 26, 1924, Havre de Grace, Md.

He was a right-handed pitcher with the Baltimore Elite Giants in 1947–48, posting a 4–1 record the latter season. After entering organized baseball in 1949, he pitched less but appeared more as an everyday player. As an outfielder and third baseman for Pough-Kingston in the Western League, he batted .253 but had no decision as a pitcher. The next two seasons were spent with St. Jean in the Canadian Provincial League, where he hit .308 and .258 as a third baseman-outfielder while registering marks of 15–3 and 8–8, with a 4.33 ERA the former season. Three years later, in 1954, he appeared in eight games for Billings in the Pioneer League without a hit.

Burke, Ping

Career: 1938   Position: p
Team: Atlanta Black Crackers ('36–'38)
Bats: Right   Throws: Right
Height: 5'11"   Weight: 180

The right-handed pitcher from Greensboro, Georgia, was a fastball artist with blinding speed, a famous drop, and a fast curveball. The fireballer was sensational in 1937, his second season with the Atlanta Black Crackers, and counted among his victories was a 13-strikeout, 3-hit shutout over the Chicago American Giants. But he had difficulty signing with the ballclub in 1938 because of his salary demands, which were considered unreasonable. He played with the semipro Athens Red Sox while the negotiations continued. When he finally signed with the Atlanta Black Crackers for the second half, he lacked the stamina to hurl a complete game and tired in the late innings after pitching effectively for four or five innings.

Burke, Roy

Career: 1938   Position: p
Team: Atlanta Black Crackers
Bats: Left   Throws: Left
Height: 5'10"   Weight: 177

This left-handed pitcher was on the early spring roster for the Atlanta Black Crackers in 1938, but his stay with the team was brief.

Burnett, Fred (Tex)

a.k.a. Texas
Career: 1922–46   Positions: c, 1b, of, 3b, manager, coach
Teams: Pittsburgh Keystones ('21–'22), Indianapolis ABCs ('23), New York Lincoln Giants ('24), Harrisburg Giants ('25), Atlantic City Bacharach Giants ('25), Brooklyn Royal Giants ('26–'30, '33, '35), New York Black Yankees ('31–'32, '40–'41), Baltimore Black Sox, ('33), Homestead Grays ('33–'34), Newark Dodgers ('34), Brooklyn Eagles ('35), Newark Eagles ('36–'37, '44), *Pittsburgh Crawfords ('45), Nashville Cubs ('46)*
Bats: Both   Throws: Right
Height: 5'9"   Weight: 165

His career spanned twenty-five years with thirteen different teams as a player, coach, and manager. A mediocre hitter without appreciable power, he was slow afoot but had a pretty good eye at the plate and was a fair receiver with an average throwing arm. He also played first base, third base, and alternated in the outfield.

In 1924, as a youngster sharing the catching duties for the New York Lincoln Giants, he hit .244 while batting eighth in the lineup, and showed lots of pep but displayed a bad temper. His inability to control his disposition caused him to be dropped by the Lincoln Giants and he was not reserved for 1925. Picked up by Harrisburg, he hit .274 in 1925 while splitting his playing time with the Bacharachs. The next year he joined the Brooklyn Royal Giants, playing first base in 1926 but moving back behind the plate in 1927, with available stats showing a minuscule .156 batting average.

In 1931 he joined John Henry Lloyd's Harlem Stars, who later became the New York Black Yankees, and was a backup catcher for two years. The next year he continued his vagabond ways, beginning the season as a regular for the Black Sox; joining the Royal Giants; and, late in the year, the veteran receiver and his rookie teammate Buck Leonard joined the Homestead Grays together. The next year, 1934, Burnett was the regular catcher for the Grays, batting at the bottom of the order, and in 1935 he was back with the Royal Giants, where partial statistics show an uncharacteristic .458 batting average. The next year he was with the Newark Eagles as a backup catcher, after playing with both of the teams (the Newark Dodgers and the Brooklyn Eagles) that owner Abe Manley consolidated to form the Newark Eagles. He spent the last few years of his Negro National League career as a backup catcher for the Black Yankees and the Eagles, hitting .183 in 1944. In 1946 he closed out his baseball career with teams in the United States League, a league of lower status.

Burnham, Willie (Bee)
Career: 1932   Position: p
Team: Monroe Monarchs (*'30–'34*)

He was a pitcher with the Monroe Monarchs for the first half of the '30s, including the 1932 season, when the Negro Southern League was considered a major league.

Burns, Peter (**Pete**)
Career: 1890–1902   Positions: c, of
Teams: Chicago Unions ('94), Page Fence Giants ('95, '97–'98), *minor leagues ('95),* Columbia Giants ('99–'00), Algona Brownies ('02)

During the 1890s he was a catcher-outfielder with the best black teams in the Midwest, including the Page Fence Giants, where he hit .266 in 1895. The New Orleans native also played four games in the Michigan State League as a replacement for the injured Vasco Graham, batting .611 for his short stint with the team. He began his career with the Chicago Unions in 1894 and later joined the Columbia Giants for two seasons, 1899–1900, and closed his career after the turn of the century with the Brownies of Algona, Iowa.

Burns, William (**Willie**, Bill, Lefty)
Career: 1935–44   Position: p
Teams: *Miami Giants ('34),* Newark Dodgers ('35), Ethiopian Clowns ('39), Newark Eagles ('42), Baltimore Elite Giants ('43), Philadelphia Stars ('43), Memphis Red Sox ('43), Cincinnati-Indianapolis Clowns ('44)
Bats: Left   Throws: Left
Height: 6'0"   Weight: 175
Born: Jan. 12, 1916, West Palm Beach, Fla.

During his intermittent decade with top clubs, the left-hander pitched with several teams and also occasionally played in the outfield. He began his career in 1934 with the Miami Giants and "pitched his best ball on the northern tour." Joining the Newark Eagles in 1942, he was winless against a single loss in limited play. The next season he was 1–2 while splitting the season between the Baltimore Elite Giants and the Philadelphia Stars. While with the Stars, he was suspended in midsummer by owner Ed Bolden, who wanted to trade him. Bolden succeeded in divesting himself of

Burns and, in 1944, the pitcher was in a new league with the Cincinnati-Indianapolis Clowns, where he posted a 6.53 ERA while splitting four decisions to end his Negro League career.

Burrell
Career: 1918–20   Position: lf
Teams: Baltimore Black Sox ('18–'20), *Washington Braves ('21)*

He was a part-time starter in left field, batting near the bottom of the order, with the Baltimore Black Sox in 1918, when the Black Sox were an independent team in their formative stages and still working toward parity with league teams.

Burris, Samuel (Speed)
Career: 1937–40   Position: p
Teams: Memphis Red Sox ('37), Birmingham Black Barons ('38–'40)

This hurler earned his nickname from his fastball, but he had a short career, beginning with the Memphis Red Sox in 1937 before joining the Birmingham Black Barons for the next three seasons.

Burton
Career: 1913   Position: player
Team: Mohawk Giants

He played with the Mohawk Giants in 1913, but his position is uncertain.

Burton, Jack
a.k.a. Bruton
Career: 1940–50   Positions: p, of, 3b, 1b, 2b, ss
Teams: Birmingham Black Barons ('40), Cleveland Buckeyes ('50)

A pitcher-utility man for the Birmingham Black Barons, he was not a good hitter and was with the Black Barons for only one season, 1940. A decade later, in 1950, when the Negro American League was struggling to survive the loss of players to organized baseball, he was listed as an infielder with the Cleveland Buck-

eyes, but league records do not confirm actual playing time for him.

Busby
Career: 1933   Positions: of, 3b
Team: Detroit Stars

He was a reserve player with the Detroit Stars in 1933 and could play either in the outfield or at third base.

Busby, Maurice (Lefty)
Career: 1920–22   Position: p
Teams: Atlantic City Bacharach Giants ('20–'21), All-Cubans ('21), Baltimore Black Sox ('22)
Bats: Left   Throws: Left

During the early '20s, the left-hander pitched with the Bacharachs and All-Cubans before closing his career with an appearance with the Baltimore Black Sox in 1922.

Buset
Career: 1930   Position: player
Team: Hilldale Daisies

He played in one game with Hilldale in 1930, but his position is uncertain.

Bush
Career: 1946   Position: p
Team: Cleveland Buckeyes

He is listed as a pitcher with the Cleveland Buckeyes in 1946, but his playing time was severely restricted.

Bustamente, Luis (Anguilla, The Eel, Buster)
Career: 1904–13   Positions: **ss**, 2b, 3b, of
Teams: All-Cubans ('04–'05) **Cuban Stars** ('07–'13)

The little shortstop was regarded by Philadelphia Giants' manager, Sol White, as the best shortstop of the early years before John Henry Lloyd's arrival on the black baseball scene. John McGraw called him a "perfect shortstop." He was lightning fast on his feet, covering a wide range afield, and had a strong and accurate throwing arm. At the plate he was a good clutch hitter but without good power.

He was the leadoff batter for the Cuban Stars in 1907 and was hitting third in 1910 and captaining the team. In his last two seasons, 1912–13, he dropped to sixth in the order, while giving way to Chacon at shortstop and playing other positions: second base in 1912 and left field in 1913.

Still considered one of the greatest Cuban infielders of the first two decades of the century, he was among the first group of ten players elected to the Cuban Hall of Fame in 1939. He was best known for his superior defensive play, and his lifetime batting average for his twelve seasons (1901–12) in Cuba was only .222. His best season in his homeland was .323 in 1908 (excluding a .357 batting average in 1910 in only 12 games). In 1907 he was the league leader in three separate categories (games, at-bats, and doubles).

In the United States in 1910 he was captain of the Cuban Stars and excelled at performing comedy stunts to entertain the fans. That fall, in October, he returned to Cuba with a white bride, and that is said to have contributed to the trouble he had later in the United States. That winter, while playing third base with Havana in two games against the Detroit Tigers, he managed only a .143 batting average for the two appearances. The following winter (1911–12), playing second base with Almendares in a series against the New York Giants, he hit only .100.

Sadly, the smooth-fielding Cuban developed a drinking problem that ultimately led to his death at an early age.

Buster, Herbert
Career: 1943   Positions: ss, 2b, 3b
Team: Chicago American Giants

The wartime infielder played briefly with the Chicago American Giants in 1943, playing primarily as a middle infielder.

Butler
Career: 1917   Position: of
Team: New York Lincoln Giants

He was a right fielder with the New York Lincoln Giants in 1917, but his playing time was limited.

Butler
Career: 1937–43   Positions: 3b, ss
Teams: Pittsburgh Crawfords ('37), Newark Eagles ('43)

This seldom-used utility infielder was released by the Pittsburgh Crawfords in June 1937 and signed by the Homestead Grays, who also released him after a brief time. He reappeared in 1943 as a wartime substitute shortstop with the Newark Eagles.

Butler, Benjamin
Career: 1887   Position: manager
Team: *New York Gorhams*

He was manager of the New York Gorhams, one of eight teams that were charter members of the League of Colored Baseball Clubs in 1887. However, the league's existence was ephemeral, lasting only a week.

Butler, Doc
Career: 1950   Position: c
Team: Memphis Red Sox

He was a catcher with the Memphis Red Sox in 1950, when the Negro American League was struggling to survive the loss of players to organized baseball, but league statistics do not confirm his playing time.

Butler, Frank
Career: 1894–95   Positions: of, p
Team: Chicago Unions

During the middle of the last decade of the nineteenth century, he was an outfielder-pitcher for two years with the Chicago Unions.

Butler, Sol
Career: 1925   Position: p
Team: Kansas City Monarchs

He pitched briefly with the Kansas City Monarchs in 1925, winning his only decision.

Butts, Harry T.
Career: 1949–50   Position: p

Teams: Indianapolis Clowns ('49–'51), *minor leagues ('52–'53)*
Bats: Right   Throws: Left

He was a left-handed pitcher with the Indianapolis Clowns in 1949–50, with unimpressive records of 2–8 (5.22) and 8–8 (4.50). In 1952 he played with Brandon in the Mandak League and with Vancouver in the Western International League, where he was 0–2 in 4 games pitched. The next season, 1953, he pitched with Portsmouth-Richmond in the Piedmont League and was 3–15 with a 5.95 ERA.

Butts, Thomas (Tommy, **Pee Wee**, Pea Eye, Baby)
a.k.a. Robert
Career: 1938–50   Position: ss
Teams: Atlanta Black Crackers ('38), Indianapolis ABCs ('39), **Baltimore Elite Giants** ('39–'42, '44–'51), *Mexican League ('43), Birmingham Black Barons ('52–'53), Memphis Red Sox ('54), minor leagues ('51–'52, '55)*
Bats: Right   Throws: Right
Height: 5'7"   Weight: 145
Born: 1919, Sparta, Ga.
Died: January 1973, Atlanta, Ga.

An outstanding defensive shortstop who could do everything afield, the small second sacker was a steady, smooth gloveman with sure hands, exceptional range, and a strong and accurate throwing arm. While not a flashy fielder, he made all the plays and excelled on the double play.

Playing for the Baltimore Elite Giants, he teamed with Junior Gilliam to form an outstanding keystone combination. The best shortstop in the East during the '40s, the slick-fielding Butts was selected to the All-Star squad six years (1944 and 1946–50). Credited with an uncharacteristically high .391 average in 1940, Butts was a pesky fastball hitter, without much power, who sprayed the ball to all fields. Also a good bunter and skilled hit-and-run man, he had good speed and approached the game with a contagious enthusiasm. Team records show that Butts scored a team high 82 runs in 1941. Other averages with the Elites

show .219 and .227 marks before his 1943 sojourn to Mexico, and .308, .309, .287, .321, .281, .261, and .216 after his return from the Mexican League.

Although he was slender, he was tough and starred as a quarterback on Atlanta's Booker T. Washington High School football team. He began his professional career while still in high school, when he was signed by the Atlanta Black Crackers in 1938 for the second half of the season. As the regular shortstop, he quickly proved to be the spark the team needed to win the second-half pennant, and he enjoyed great popularity with the fans, who gave him a special "day" in appreciation.

In 1939, when the Atlanta franchise moved to Indianapolis and then began struggling for survival, the 19-year-old athlete was signed by the Elites, where he developed into the Negro National League's top shortstop and amazed fans with his scintillating play afield. He remained in Baltimore, except for a season with Monterrey, Mexico, (1943), where he hit .248, until the 1951 season, when he played with Winnipeg in the Mandak league, batting .286. The following season, he played with Lincoln in the Western League but hit a woeful .170. In 1953 he returned to the Negro American League with the Birmingham Black Barons and hit .240. But the Negro American League by then had been decimated by players going into organized baseball and was no longer of major-league caliber. In 1955, his last season in organized baseball, he hit .265 with Texas City in the Big State League.

Butts was a smart ballplayer and, although a veteran, he was still only 27 years old when Jackie Robinson broke in with the Dodgers. Playing in Cuba that winter (1947–48), he demonstrated his usual smooth game afield and hit .246 but didn't get serious consideration by major-league scouts. His only playing liability was difficulty hitting a curveball, but most observers felt that his defensive skills more than compensated for a light bat. When his double-play partner, Junior Gilliam, was signed by the Dodgers and he failed to receive an offer, he was almost devastated. Earlier in his career, his aggressive nature led to an assault on an umpire, which some feel may have hurt his chances of getting into the major leagues. He also was known for his pursuit of nightlife activities, and his off-field patterns of behavior may have added to scouts' reservations about signing the slick-fielding shortstop.

He continued in the Negro Leagues during the '50s, playing with the Birmingham Black Barons and Memphis Red Sox, before finally retiring following the 1955 season.

Byas, Richard Thomas (**Subby**, Prof)
Career: 1931–42   Positions: **c**, 1b, of, 2b
Teams: Kansas City Monarchs ('31), *Gilkerson's Union Giants ('33),* Newark Dodgers ('34), Cole's American Giants ('35–'36), **Chicago American Giants** ('37–'39), Memphis Red Sox ('41–'42)
Bats: Both   Throws: Right
Died: October 1985

In 1936 the Chicago American Giants played as an independent team, and the catcher hit .353 against all levels of competition and played in the East-West All-Star games of 1936 and 1937. Before joining the American Giants he played with Gilkerson's Union Giants in 1933 and sometimes managed the team. He was a switch-hitter but was more effective batting from the left side and, while he showed good power, he was also a capable bunter. He graduated from Wendell Phillips High School, where he was an All-City performer in both baseball and basketball, and was called "Prof" because he was regarded as an intellectual.

Byatt
[see Biot, Charlie]

Byrd
Career: 1921   Position: 1b
Team: Chicago Giants

He was a substitute first baseman with the Chicago Giants in 1921, the franchise's last year in the Negro National League.

Byrd, James F.
Career: 1927–30   Position: officer
Team: Hilldale Daisies

He served as an officer with the Hilldale club for four years, during which time the Eastern Colored League folded and the American Negro League began and folded.

Byrd, Prentice
Career: 1934   Position: officer
Team: Cleveland Red Sox

He was an officer with Cleveland Red Sox in 1934, their only season in the Negro National League.

Byrd, William (**Bill**, Daddy)
Career: 1932–50   Positions: **p**, 1b, of
Teams: Columbus Turfs ('32), Columbus Blue Birds ('33), Nashville Elite Giants ('33), Cleveland Red Sox ('34), Homestead Grays ('34), Columbus Elite Giants ('35), Washington Elite Giants ('36–'37), **Baltimore Elite Giants** ('38–'39), '41–'50), *Venezuelan League ('40)*
Bats: Both   Throws: Right
Height: 6'1"   Weight: 210
Born: July 15, 1907, Canton, Ga.
Died: Jan. 4, 1991, Philadelphia, Pa.

One of the last pitchers to have the privilege of throwing a legal "spitter," the Baltimore Elite Giants' ace was a gifted ballplayer, and his presence on the mound was one of unflinching dominance. A workhorse with lots of stamina, he once pitched and won a doubleheader with the Elites. In addition to his spitball, he had a wide variety of other pitches and had excellent control of them all. His repertory included a slow knuckler, a fast knuckler, a slider, a roundhouse curve, a fastball, and a sinker. He learned the spitball from Roosevelt Davis while playing with the Columbus Blue Birds in 1933, and would often fake throwing the pitch for psychological reasons.

When Tom Wilson's Elites moved from Nashville to Columbus for the 1935 season, he was recruited to play with the ballclub, and he remained with the franchise as it shifted to

Washington and then to Baltimore. A responsible and caring individual as he gained experience, he assumed the role of looking after the welfare of the younger players and became a father figure to some, including Roy Campanella, who called him "Daddy." He remained with the Elites for sixteen years, with the exception of part of one summer season spent in Caracas, Venezuela.

In league games from 1932 to 1949, he maintained better than a .600 winning percentage, suffering only one losing season over a fourteen-year period. In 1936 he is credited with a 20–7 record, and available statistics show league records of 5–3, 6–3, and 9–4 for the years 1937–39. After a season in Venezuela in 1940, he returned to the Elites and posted a 7–3 record with a 2.75 ERA in 1941, following with seasons of 10–2, 9–4, 8–7, and 10–6 for the years 1942–45.

After his first losing season in 14 years, he added three winning seasons in 1947–49 with records of 9–6, 11–6, and 12–3, the last of these coming in his last year in the Negro Leagues as the Elites won their only untainted pennant.

Byrd was almost a perennial member of the East squad in the East-West All-Star game. His five pitching appearances (1936, 1939, 1941, 1944, and 1946) are exceeded only by Leon Day and Hilton Smith. A good hitter, Byrd also made an All-Star appearance as a pinch hitter in 1945. He learned to hit by hitting rocks with tree branches on the family farm in Canton, Georgia, and like most pitchers, he took pride in his hitting. He had good power as a hitter and was proud of the four homers he hit while playing in the outfield. He also played on occasion at first base and was often used as a pinch hitter. Regular-season averages include marks of .318 (1936), .286 (1941), .304 (1942), and .344 (1948). But his pitching and hitting were not matched by his baserunning, and the big hurler was slow on the bases.

Throughout his career, he and Leon Day often hooked up in pitching duels—in the Negro Leagues, in Venezuela, and in Puerto Rico, where he was called "El Maestro" and led the league in victories during the winter season of 1940–41, with 15 wins. He also pitched with Santurce in the winter of 1938–39, and in both Latin American countries, Byrd had Josh Gibson as his catcher.

After beginning the 1950 season with the Elites, Byrd quickly retired, with a lifetime record of 114–72, and contented himself playing semipro ball while holding down a regular job at General Electric Company in Philadelphia, where he worked for twenty years before retiring in 1970.

C

Caballero, Luis Perez
a.k.a. Perez, Luis
Career: 1948–50   Position: 3b
Teams: *Mexican League ('45),* Indianapolis Clowns ('48), New York Cubans ('50), *minor leagues ('54–'55)*
Bats: Right   Throws: Right
Height: 5'8"   Weight: 158
Born: 1927

The light-hitting third baseman played with the Indianapolis Clowns and New York Cubans during the sunset years of the Negro leagues, 1948–50. In 1945 he played for Vera Cruz in the Mexican League and hit only .209, the same average he had for the New York Cubans in 1950. After leaving the Negro Leagues, he played in organized ball with Big Springs in 1954–55, where he proved his versatility, playing third base, shortstop, outfield, and catcher while hitting for averages of .289 and .293 and pilfering 25 and 33 bases, respectively. Otherwise he was an average player at that level in organized ball.

Cabanas, Armando
Career:1910   Positions: **2b**, 1b, of
Team: Stars of Cuba

In 1909, at Key West, he was called a Chinaman and refused admittance into the United States. However, the following season, with immigration problems resolved, he played in this country with the Stars of Cuba. The veteran was a smart baseball player and was tough in the clutch with his timely hitting. In the field the stocky infielder had quick feet and was good on ground balls. Although primarily a second baseman, he also played outfield for Almendares in the 1910 winter series against the Detroit Tigers, batting only .133.

Cabrera
a.k.a. Cabrere
Career: 1905   Positions: 1b, ss
Team: All-Cubans

A graceful fielder with a strong and accurate arm, he was a first baseman with the All-Cubans in 1905 in his only appearance in black baseball. In his home country, with Almendares in the 1907 Cuban League, he also played both first base and shortstop, showing a wide range afield at shortstop.

Cabrera, Lorenzo (**Chiquitin**)
Career: 1947–50   Position: 1b
Teams: New York Cubans ('47–'50), *Mexican League ('50), minor leagues ('51, '54–'56)*
Bats: Left   Throws: Left
Height: 6'1"   Weight: 212
Born: April 30, 1920, Cienfuegos, Cuba

The big left-handed first baseman had a fiery temperament but was a good hitter with power. In 1947 he broke in with the champion New York Cubans, hitting .352 as the club took the Negro National League pennant and Negro World Series. His play afield was undistinguished but, although not fast afoot, he had a fair amount of success stealing bases.

Once, while playing in Mexico, he became incensed at pitcher Rufus Lewis for hitting him with a pitched ball and charged the mound with a bat, knocking Lewis unconscious. Before Cabrera could do further damage, Lewis's teammate Bill Wright charged from the dugout with a bat and knocked Cabrera unconscious. The hotheaded Latin had plenty of trouble from brush-backs and beanballs throughout his career. Earlier in his career, in August 1948, he had been hospitalized after being hit in the right temple by Cleveland Red Sox pitcher Norman Reinhardt in an exhibition game at Eastside Park in Paterson, New Jersey. The pitch came with the bases loaded and none out in the top of the first inning. Cabrera was unconscious for about four minutes and was taken to Barnett Hospital, where he remained in serious condition. Meanwhile, the Cubans lost the game, 17–5.

Later, in the early '50s, playing in the Cuban winter league, future Dodger skipper Tommy Lasorda, who was then a promising left-hander in the Dodger chain, hit him with a pitch and Cabrera charged the mound with a bat, precipitating a fight. In the ensuing battle, Lasorda picked him up over his head and body-slammed him.

Between skirmishes, the Cuban had a productive baseball career that began in his homeland with a single game in 1942–43, but he began playing as a regular in 1946–47, and beginning in the winter season of 1948–49, he hit for successive averages of .314, .330, .342, .298, .314, .316, and .296. In his ten-year Cuban career, playing mostly with Marianao, he registered a lifetime average of .307.

In the United States he hit .333 in 1948, the last year before the demise of the Negro National League, and in 1949 the New York Cubans joined the Eastern Division of the Negro American League and Cabrera continued his hitting prowess with a .377 average. The next year, after starting the season with the Cubans, he spent most of the year with Mexico City,

where he hit .355. Following another good winter season in Cuba, he was assigned to AAA ball in organized ball and in 1951 he split the season between Oakland in the Pacific Coast League and Ottawa in the International League, where he hit a disappointing .205 and .236, respectively.

His next foray into organized ball was in 1954 with Del Rio in the Big State League, where he hit .345 with good power, reaching double digits in each extra-base category (31–12–12). In 1955 he was back in the same league but with a new team (Port Arthur), and both his playing time and his batting average (.308) dropped. In 1956, his last season in organized ball, he played with Tijuana-Nogales in the Arizona-Mexican League, but his average fell to .261.

Cabrera, Luis Rafael (**Villa**)
Career: 1944–50   Positions: p, of
Team: Cincinnati-Indianapolis Clowns ('44), New York Cubans ('44–'49), Birmingham Black Barons ('50)
Bats: Right   Throws: Right
Born: Cuba

He was a pitcher for the New York Cubans in the 1940s and also played in the outfield occasionally, showing batting averages of .247 and .212 of the 1944 and 1948 seasons.

Cabrera, Luis Raul (Tigre)
Career: 1948   Position: p
Team: Indianapolis Clowns ('48)
Bats: Right   Throws: Right
Height: 5'10"   Weight: 175

The right-hander was most effective when utilizing his curve and slider, but he also had a fastball to mix with his breaking pitches. With the Indianapolis Clowns in 1948, he was 8–5 with a 2.80 ERA and then signed to play in organized ball with Bristol in the Colonial League, where he had an impressive 11–1 (1.41 ERA) season in 1949. However, the next season he dropped to 3–3 (4.28 ERA) before joining St. Jean in the Provincial League for the remainder of the season, where he had a

7–6 record with a 4.37 ERA. Returning to St. Jean for the 1951 season, his performance continued to decline, dropping to a 2–8 (4.96 ERA) record. Early in his career he had pitched with some effectiveness in two Puerto Rican winters (2–3, 3.05 ERA in 1944–45 and a league-leading 75 strikeouts in 1945–46), sandwiched around a 6–16 season with Puebla in the Mexican League.

Cabrera, Sungo

[see Carrera, Clemente (Sungo)]

Cabrera, Villa

[see Cabrera, Luis Rafael]

Cabrere

[see Cabrera]

Cade, Joe

Career: 1929   Positions: p, of
Team: Atlantic City Bacharach Giants

A pitcher with the 1929 Bacharachs, he was winless in limited mound duty but sometimes filled in as an outfielder, with incomplete statistics showing a .385 average in very limited play.

Caffie, Joseph Clifford (Joe)

Career: 1950   Position: of
Teams: Cleveland Buckeyes ('50), *minor leagues ('51–'61),* major leagues ('57–58)
Bats: Left   Throws: Right
Height 5' 10½"   Weight: 180
Born: Feb. 14, 1931, Ramer, Ala.

As a nineteen-year-old, he hit .203 in 1950 with the Buckeyes in his only year in the Negro Leagues. The next year he began an eleven-year career in organized ball, including two stints with the Cleveland Indians. Coincidentally, he had identical batting averages for both his minor- and major-league careers, .291. On his way to the major leagues he developed a little more patience at the plate, cut down on his strikeouts, and increased his walk ratio, but

he still can be described as a free-swinger. In 1952, with Duluth in the Northern League, he led the league in six batting categories (at-bats, hits, triples, total bases, and batting average) to earn an advance to Indianapolis in the American Association.

He hit his peak during 1956–58, when he split his time with Cleveland in the American League and Buffalo in the International League. With Buffalo in 1956 he hit .311 to earn a promotion to Cleveland, where he hit .342 in only a dozen games. Back at Buffalo in 1957, he led the league with a robust .330 batting average to earn another shot at the bigs, where he hit .270, including 3 home runs among his 89 at-bats. But in 1958 he was back in Buffalo, where he hit .295 while leading the league with 39 doubles. Although he played three more seasons in the minors, he never had another shot at the major leagues.

Cain, Marlon (Sugar)

Career: 1937–49   Positions: **p**, *of, 1b*
Teams: *Atlantic City Bacharach Giants* ('37), Pittsburgh Crawfords ('37–'39), New York Black Yankees ('39), Brooklyn Royal Giants ('39–'40), Indianapolis Clowns ('49)
Born: Feb. 14, 1914

The pitcher with the sweet name was discovered while playing with the Black Meteors, a semipro team in Philadelphia, in 1936. The next season he advanced to the Bacharach Giants and later in the season to the Pittsburgh Crawfords. He pitched with the Crawfords in 1938, and after leaving the Crawfords during the 1939 season, he played with the Brooklyn Royal Giants, the New York Yankees, and the Indianapolis Clowns and also played winter ball in Mexico and Venezuela.

Calarai

Career: 1933   Position: p
Team: Cuban Stars

The pitcher appeared briefly with the Cuban Stars in 1933, his only year in the Negro Leagues.

Calderin

Career: 1917–24   Positions: **p**, rf

Team: Cuban Stars (East) ('11–'19, '24)

The Cuban pitcher did double duty as a reserve outfielder with the eastern-based Cuban Stars, playing as the Havana Cuban Stars in 1917 and joining the Eastern Colored League in 1924.

Calderon, Benito

a.k.a. Caleron

Career: 1926–28   Positions: **c**, 3b, p

Teams: Cuban Stars (West) ('26–'27), Homestead Grays ('28)

He was the regular catcher with the Negro National League Cuban Stars for two seasons, hitting .228 while batting in the eighth slot in his first year with the team, but improving to .266 and moving up to the fifth slot the following year. Joining the Homestead Grays in 1928, he was a backup catcher and also saw limited mound duty.

Caldwell

Career: 1933   Position: of

Team: *Birmingham Black Barons*

He was the regular left fielder, hitting sixth in the batting order, for the Birmingham Black Barons in 1933. The Black Barons were in the Negro South League and, although it had been recognized as a major league in 1932, the league no longer had that designation.

Caleron

[see Calderon, Benito]

Calhan, Rowland

Career: 1938   Position: p

Team: Washington Black Senators

He was a pitcher for the Washington Black Senators in 1938, their only season in the Negro Leagues.

Calhoun, Jim

Career: 1923   Position: 2b

Team: Toledo Tigers

In his only year in the Negro Leagues, he was a second baseman for the 1923 Toledo Tigers.

Calhoun, Walter (Walt, **Lefty**)

Career: 1931–46   Positions: **p**, of

Teams: Birmingham Black Barons ('31, '33), Montgomery Grey Sox ('32), Memphis Red Sox ('32), Pittsburgh Crawfords ('37), Indianapolis Athletics ('37), Indianapolis ABCs ('38), Washington Black Senators ('38), *Louisville Black Colonels ('38),* St. Louis Stars ('39), New Orleans–St. Louis Stars ('40–'41), New York Black Yankees ('42), Philadelphia Stars ('42), Harrisburg-St. Louis Stars ('43), Cleveland Buckeyes ('46)

Bats: Left   Throws: Left

Height: 5'9"   Weight: 180

The left-hander had excellent control and changed speeds expertly while mixing a fastball, curve, and slider. His best years came with the St. Louis Stars, and he stayed with the team during the franchise's moves to Harrisburg and New Orleans. In 1940, while with the Stars, he pitched in the East-West All-Star game. The following season he was again counted among the ''Big Four'' pitchers of the 1941 St. Louis Stars. When the Stars disbanded after the 1941 season, he jumped to the East, pitching with the Black Yankees and Philadelphia Stars in 1942, splitting four decisions during the season. When the St. Louis Stars reformed in 1943 as an entry in the Negro National League, he returned to the fold, but the franchise withdrew from the league in the spring to barnstorm with Dizzy Dean's team.

He began his career in the South, but during his sixteen-year career he pitched with a dozen different ballclubs, many of them struggling to maintain a major-league quality. Aside from his pitching, he could field his position, but offensively, while an adequate bunter, he was a poor hitter and had little speed on the bases.

Calhoun, Wesley

Career: 1950   Positions: if, of

Team: Cleveland Buckeyes

He was listed as an infielder-outfielder with the 1950 Cleveland Buckeyes, when the Negro American League was in decline, but league statistics do not confirm his playing time.

Callis. J. Joseph
Career: 1887   Position: manager
Team: *Baltimore Lord Baltimores*

He was the manager of the Lord Baltimores, one of eight teams that were charter members of the League of Colored Baseball Clubs in 1887. However, the league's existence was ephemeral, lasting only a week.

Calvo, Jacinto Gonzalez (Jack)
a.k.a. Jacinto Del Calvo (real name)
Career: 1913–15   Position: of
Teams: Long Branch Cubans ('13, '15), major leagues ('13, '20), *minor leagues ('16)*
Bats: Left   Throws: Left
Height: 5'10"   Weight: 156
Born: June 11, 1894, Havana Cuba
Died: June 15, 1965, Miami, Fla.

A white Cuban, he was an outfielder with the Long Branch, New Jersey, Cubans in 1915 and, along with José Acosta, signed with Vancouver of the Northwest League in 1916. Calvo also played, both previously (1913) and subsequently (1920), in the major leagues with the Washington Senators, and compiled a lifetime major-league average of a paltry .161.

Playing in his homeland, he hit with good extra-base power and demonstrated very good speed. In Cuba he broke in with Almendares with a .356 batting average, then joined Havana and hit .331, .300, .341, and .336 in the next four seasons. In 1923–25 he hit .317 and .342, before finishing his career in 1927 where he started, in Almendares, with a .292 average. While playing with Havana in an exhibition series against the New York Giants after the 1920 season, he hit .200. His lifetime batting average in Cuba was .310 for thirteen years (1913–27), and he was elected to the Cuban Hall of Fame in 1948.

Calvo, T.
Career: 1915–16   Positions: cf, *1b, c*

Teams: Long Branch Cubans ('15–'16), Jersey City Cubans ('16)

He was an outfielder with the Long Branch, New Jersey, Cubans and the Jersey City Cubans in the midteens. In 1916 he batted in the third slot in the order and also played occasionally at first base and catcher.

Cam
Career: 1891   Position: of
Team: Cuban Giants

He was an outfielder with the Cuban Giants in 1891, when they represented Ansonia in the Connecticut State League.

Cambria, Joe
Career: 1932–33   Positions: owner, officer
Team: Baltimore Black Sox

A white businessman who owned the Bugle Apron and Laundry Company, he was the owner of the Baltimore Black Sox in their last years of existence. After buying the franchise from George Rossiter in 1933, he entered the team in the new Negro National League in its inaugural season, moved the team to Bugle Field for their home games, took the players off salaries, and operated on a percentage basis in an effort to remain fiscally solvent during the Depression years. However, his efforts were not successful, and the franchise was losing money; the club was dissolved after the 1933 season. He then became a scout in Cuba for the Washington Senators.

Campanella, Roy (Campy, *Poochinella*)
Career: 1937–45   Positions: c, 3b, of, *p*
Teams: Baltimore Elite Giants ('37–'42, '44–'45), *Mexican League ('43), minor leagues ('46–'48),* major leagues ('48–'57)
Bats: Right   Throws: Right
Height: 5'9½"   Weight: 195
Born: November 19, 1921, Philadelphia, Pa.
Died: June 26, 1993, Woodland Hills, Calif.

Campy started playing for the Baltimore Elite Giants as a fifteen-year-old youngster and learning his trade from the great Biz Mackey, he developed into an outstanding catcher, earning a spot on the East squad in the 1941 All-Star game and being voted the game's MVP. After missing the next two East-West games because of his ventures into showcasing for the major leagues and playing in the Mexican League, Campy made two more All-Star appearances, in 1944 and 1945, seasons in which he finished in the top half-dozen hitters in the league. In 1944 he led the league in doubles and compiled a .350 batting average.

That season, Campy even took a turn on the mound, ending with a no-decision even though his team got the win. That was the end of his "pitching career," but his next season's plate encore showed a .365 batting average while leading the league in runs batted in. The aggressive receiver's composite average in All-Star competition was a resounding .364, and his lifetime average for his nine-year Negro League career was .353.

As a high-school student he was invited by the Philadelphia Phillies to work out at Shibe Park, but when he arrived and they discovered he was black, the offer was rescinded. The setback was only temporary, and he began his career with the Bacharach Giants, a semipro team unrelated to the earlier team of the same name. Later he signed with the Elites in 1937 as a third-string catcher, playing only on weekends to spell his mentor Biz Mackey. The next year he quit school and began playing baseball full-time, but still as Mackey's understudy. In 1939 Mackey left the Elites for the Newark Eagles, and Campy moved into the regular catcher's position, hitting eighth in the batting order. In a postseason four-team tournament the Elites upset the Homestead Grays to claim the playoff championship.

In 1940 he shared the catching duties with veteran Bill Perkins, and in 1941 he came of age as a hitter and catcher, moving into the fifth slot in the batting order. The next season Campanella received a telegram informing him that a tryout had been arranged with the Pittsburgh Pirates for him, teammate Sammy T. Hughes, and New York Cubans diminutive

pitching ace David Barnhill. Before it could become a reality, owner Ben Benswanger reneged on the implied arrangement. However, later in the year the three players showcased for the major leagues in an exhibition game in Ohio.

At the time he left the team, Campanella was batting cleanup and the Elites were engaged in a tight pennant race with the Homestead Grays. He was assessed a $250 fine and an indefinite suspension by the management, which may never have been paid, but he was out of the lineup for a short but crucial time. Very shortly after this dispute with owner Tom Wilson, the young catcher jumped the Elites for the remainder of the season to play in Mexico, batting .296 in 20 games with Monterrey. The next summer season was spent in Mexico, where he hit .289 with 12 homers, 5 triples, and 24 doubles.

Campanella also often played in Puerto Rico and Cuba during the winter seasons. In 1940–41, with Caguas, Puerto Rico, he hit .263 with 8 homeruns in only 171 at-bats, and the following winter (1941–42), hit .275 without a home run but with good extra-base power. After an interim in which he hit .266 in his only winter in Cuba (1943–44), he was back in Puerto Rico, where he played for Santurce (1944–45) and San Juan (1946–47) and hit .294 and .222 (in only 45 at-bats).

In October 1945 he played on a black All-Star team that played a five-game series against a major-league team managed by Charlie Dressen, and was signed by the Dodgers shortly afterward.

Most experts agree that Campy could have gone straight to the majors, but instead he had to spend two and a half years in the minors prior to joining Jackie Robinson with the Dodgers in 1948. His time in the minors was spent with Nashua (1946), Montreal (1947), and St. Paul (1948), and, coincidentally, he hit 13 home runs each year while logging batting averages of .290, .273, and .325 and winning league MVP awards in both of his two full seasons in minors. The month spent at St. Paul was an unnecessary interruption of his major-league career, and by the end of 1948 he was with the Brooklyn Dodgers to stay.

The compact right-handed slugger enjoyed a fabulous ten-year major-league career during which he was selected to the All-Star team eight consecutive years (1949–56) and earned MVP laurels three times (1951, 1953, 1955) with seasons of .325 batting average, 33 home runs, 108 RBIs; .312 batting average, 41 home runs, 142 RBIs; and .318 batting average, 32 home runs, 107 RBIs, respectively.

In January 1958, after playing on five pennant winners with the "boys of summer," his career was prematurely shortened by a near-fatal automobile accident that left him paralyzed. In 1969 Roy was voted into the National Baseball Hall of Fame for his great career in the major leagues.

Campbell, Andrew
Career: 1903–06   Position: c
Teams: Chicago Union Giants ('03, '06), Leland Giants

In 1903 he shared the catching duties of the Chicago Union Giants, and later served as a backup receiver with the club. During his short career he also caught for the Leland Giants.

Campbell, David (Dave)
Career: 1938–42   Positions: **2b**, ss, 3b, 1b, of
Teams: New York Black Yankees ('38–'39), Philadelphia Stars ('40–'42)
Bats: Left   Throws: Right
Height: 5'5"   Weight: 140

The little second baseman was a good bunter but otherwise a mediocre ballplayer both at bat and in the field. Beginning with the Philadelphia Stars in 1938, he played two full seasons each, with the Stars and the Black Yankees prior to World War II. With both teams he batted in the leadoff position and managed averages of .182, .247, .224, and .243. After only a few games in 1942, he was no longer carried on the Stars' roster and never again reappeared in the Negro Leagues.

Campbell, Grant
Career: 1887–94   Positions: 1f, cf, 2b
Teams: Unions ('87), Chicago Unions ('88–'94)

He was the starting second baseman for the Unions in 1887, but moved to left field when the team changed its name to the Chicago Unions in 1888. He remained in the outfield, including two seasons in center field, for most of his career, spent entirely with the Chicago Unions.

Campbell, Hunter
Career: 1938–42   Positions: manager, officer
Teams: Ethiopian Clowns, Cincinnati Clowns

He was an officer and manager for the barnstorming Ethiopian Clowns for five seasons beginning in 1938 and paved the way for their entry into league play in 1943 as the Cincinnati Clowns.

Campbell, Joe
Career: 1887–93   Position: p
Teams: Unions ('87), Chicago Unions ('88–'93)

This nineteenth-century hurler spent his entire seven-year career (1887–93) with the same franchise. In 1887 they were known as the Unions, but the following season they became known as the Chicago Unions.

Campbell, Joe
Career: 1922   Positions: of, 3b
Teams: Pittsburgh Keystones

He was an outfielder-third baseman for the Pittsburgh Keystones in 1922, the only year they were in the Negro National League.

Campbell, Robert (Buddy)
Career: 1931–32   Position: c
Teams: Atlantic City Bacharach Giants ('31), Cole's American Giants ('32)

He was a backup catcher with Cole's American Giants in 1932 after serving a year's apprenticeship with the Bacharachs the previous season.

Campbell, William (**Zip**)
Career: 1923–29   Position: p
Teams: *Richmond Giants ('23),* Washington Potomacs ('23), *Philadelphia Giants ('24),* **Hilldale Daisies** ('24–'29), Brooklyn Royal Giants ('27), New York Lincoln Giants ('28–'29)

A pitcher with several eastern clubs during the '20s, he played with marginal teams before joining the Hilldale ballclub in 1924. Although Hilldale won two consecutive Eastern Colored League pennants in during his first two seasons with the club, he was not utilized in either World Series. The next season, 1926, he registered a 17–8 record but was unable to sustain a winning record with Hilldale. In addition to Hilldale, he pitched in the Eastern Colored League with the Brooklyn Royal Giants and the Lincoln Giants.

Campini, Joe
Career: 1948   Position: c
Teams: Baltimore Elite Giants ('48), *minor leagues ('49–'50)*
Bats: Left   Throws: Right
Height: 5'10"   Weight: 191
Born: May 11, 1923, East Wareham, Mass.

In 1948 he was a catcher with the Baltimore Elite Giants before entering organized ball the following year. He was a free-swinger and had a high incidence of strikeouts while hitting .269 and .265 in 1949–50, playing with Sanbor-Bennick and the Border League's Watertown ballclub.

Campos, Manuel
Career: 1905   Position: manager
Team: Cuban Stars of Santiago

In 1905 he managed the Cuban Stars of Santiago, one of the better Cuban clubs of the time.

Campos, Tatica
Career: 1915–30   Positions: *p,* of, 3b, 1b, 2b, c
Teams: Cuban Stars (West) ('17–'18, '27),

Cuban Stars (East) ('20–23), Cuban Stars ('30)

Like many Cubans of the era, he was an all-purpose player for the Cuban Stars of both leagues, pitching and playing infield and outfield. In both 1917 and 1918 he won his only recorded decision as a pitcher, and in the latter year he was a regular, playing right field and third base while batting in the lower part of the order. In 1920 he jumped to the East, playing as the regular second baseman and batting in the second slot in the order. For the next two years he was the starting first baseman and leadoff batter for the Cubans. He began his career in 1915, when the Cubans played as an independent team. During his career he played every position except shortstop.

Canada, James (Jim, Cat, Flash)
a.k.a. Canady
Career: 1936–46   Position: 1b
Teams: Jacksonville Redcaps *('33–'34,* '42), Birmingham Black Barons ('36–'37, '46), Atlanta Black Crackers ('38), Baltimore Elite Giants, Memphis Red Sox ('43–'45)
Bats: Left   Throws: Right

This first baseman was a steady hitter and a dependable fielder who was considered a ballplayer's ballplayer and who spent most of his career with southern ballclubs. He began his career with the Jacksonville Redcaps in 1933 and joined the Birmingham Black Barons in 1936, when they were still in the Negro Southern League, but remained with the team as the regular first baseman, batting third in the order, when they became a member of the Negro American League in its inaugural year, 1937.

In 1938 he waged a hard-fought battle with Red Moore for the starting first-base position for the Atlanta Black Crackers, but lost out to the flashy fielder and was dropped from the squad in early May. In 1942 he returned to Jacksonville for another stint with the Redcaps, playing first base and batting sixth in the order prior to the team dropping out of the Negro American League in midsummer. The next season he joined the Memphis Red Sox and was the regular first baseman with the Sox for three seasons, hitting in the lower part of the batting order and registering averages of .206 and .209 the latter two seasons.

The next year he returned to the Black Barons and was associated with the franchise intermittently afterward through 1962. During most of this time the Negro Leagues no longer had major-league-caliber ballclubs and were serving as stepping-stones for young players. Two of the players that Canada helped during these later years were Willie McCovey and Billy Williams. Many years earlier, in 1948, during a brief managerial stint with a lesser team, the Chattanooga Choo Choos, he discovered Willie Mays playing with the semipro Fairfield Stars and signed him to play with Chattanooga. When Canada left the team a short time later, due to not being paid, he recommended Mays to Piper Davis, who was managing the Black Barons.

Canizares, Avelino
a.k.a. Canizeris; Canozeris
Career: 1945   Position: ss
Teams; *Mexican League ('44, '46–'48, '56–'58, '64),* Cleveland Buckeyes ('45), *Canadian League ('50), minor leagues ('52)*
Bats: Right   Throws: Right
Height: 5'7"   Weight: 148
Born: Nov. 10, 1919, Havana, Cuba

The Cuban star was twenty-five years old in 1945 when recruited by manager Quincy Trouppe to come to the States and play for the Cleveland Buckeyes. At the plate he hit .314, and in the field, the shortstop studied hitters, positioned himself accordingly, and served as the "glue" for the infield to help the Buckeyes win the pennant during his only full season in the Negro Leagues. That season he was compared to the Monarchs' Jackie Robinson and Birmingham's Artie Wilson, and the trio were regarded as the three best shortstop prospects. Prior to being signed by Trouppe, Canizares played winter ball with Cienfuegos ('42–43) and Almendares ('43–43) and with Tampico, Mexico, in the summer season of '44. After

seeing him play in the Mexican League, Trouppe went to Cuba in the winter of 1944 to sign him.

Following the 1945 season he returned to Mexico, where he hit .298, .281, and .270 for the next three seasons (1946–48) with Torreon, San Luis, and Vera Cruz. In 1950 he signed with Sherbrooke in the Provincial League and hit .295. Two years later, at Keokuk in the III League, he hit only .222. But the little infielder bounced back after returning south of the border, batting .302 in each 1956 and 1957, with Durango (Central Mexican League) and Mexicali (American-Mexican League). But this was not the country's top league. The next year, at age thirty-eight, he raised his average to .359 with Mexicali while playing both shortstop and third base.

The quick little shortstop had exceptional speed and was a good base stealer but lacked real power at the plate. His lifetime batting average for eleven winter seasons (1942–54) in Cuba was .251. Most of his Cuban career was spent with Almendares, where his best years were .284 (1943–44), .275 (1945–46), and .270 (1951–52). However, his best season was with Alacranes, when he hit .310. He ended his career in 1964 with Saltillo, Mexico, as a utility infielder hitting .189 in a handful of games.

Cannady, Walter (Rev)
Career: 1921–45   Positions: **2b**, 3b, ss, of, 1b, p, manager
Teams: Columbus Buckeyes ('21), Cleveland Tate Stars ('22), Homestead Grays ('23–'24, '29, '32), Harrisburg Giants ('25–'27), Dayton Marcos, New York Lincoln Giants ('26–'28, '30), Hilldale Daisies ('28, '31), Pittsburgh Crawfords ('32, '36), **New York Black Yankees** ('33–'39), Brooklyn Royal Giants ('40), Philadelphia Stars, Chicago American Giants ('42), Cincinnati-Indianapolis Clowns ('43–'44), Homestead Grays ('44), New York Cubans ('45)
Bats: Right   Throws: Right
Height: 6' 0"   Weight: 180
Born: March 6, 1904, Lake City, Fla.

Although second base was his best position, Rev was an all-purpose player who could play anywhere in the field and play the position well. He was a good fielder in all aspects of defensive play, but was best known for his hitting. Throughout his well-traveled career, he was usually placed in the heart of the batting order, regardless of the team. A bad-ball hitter, he was known as a superior curveball hitter who would wait on a curve and then "jump on it." He also had relatively good speed on the bases, although not excelling as a base stealer. Cannady was quiet but moody and "mean," and other players generally left him alone because of his unpredictability. On one occasion he attacked an umpire and, after being put out of the game, broke the umpire's car windows with a bat. At times he was also lazy and seemingly unconcerned about playing, which introduced an inconsistency in his play.

A versatile fielder and a good power hitter, at Harrisburg in 1926 he was playing shortstop and batting cleanup behind Oscar Charleston. The next season, switching to third base, he hit .317 with seven home runs, and joined with Charleston and John Beckwith to make a formidable batting triad.

Cannady's career can best be traced with a road map. Early in his career, he hit .303 with the Cleveland Tate Stars in 1922, their only year in the Negro National League. Afterward he played with the independent Homestead Grays for two seasons before joining Harrisburg in 1925, where he hit .386 with 11 home runs in 52 games. After the 1927 season he became the property of the New York Lincoln Giants, but the following April he and Red Ryan were traded to Hilldale for Nip Winters and George Carr. In turn, Hilldale traded him and Jake Stevens to the Grays for Chippy Britt and Martin Dihigo in 1929. Back home with the Grays, now a member of the American Negro League, Cannady played shortstop and pounded out a .378 batting average. In 1930 he rejoined the Lincoln Giants and was credited with a .370 batting average. By 1931 he was back with Hilldale, batting .235, but he

and Judy Johnson were sent to the Pittsburgh Crawfords in 1932, where Rev hit a respectable .309 before returning to the Grays to finish the season.

A large part of his career was spent with New York-based teams, and after hitting .328 with the Crawfords in 1936, he moved over to the New York Black Yankees during the season. With the Black Yankees in 1937 he got off to a torrid start batting cleanup and hitting .385 through midseason. The following year he hit .321 and, when top vote-getter Ray Dandridge jumped to Venezuela, Cannady started the 1938 East-West game. He responded to his only All-Star appearance with a double in three times at bat. After another year with the Black Yankees, batting third in the order while playing three different infield positions, he joined the Brooklyn Royal Giants in 1940, batting cleanup and playing second base. During the World War II years he played with four different teams, but age had begun to catch up with him and his batting average slipped to .222 in 1944 with the Clowns and the Grays. The next year he closed out his twenty-five-year career, having played every position except catcher and also serving a stint as manager.

Cannon, Richard (Speedball)
Career: 1928–34   Position: p
Teams: St. Louis Stars ('28–'29), Louisville White Sox ('30), Cleveland Cubs ('31), Nashville Elite Giants ('31–'32), Birmingham Black Barons ('32), Louisville Black Caps ('32), Louisville Red Caps ('33–'34)

The fastball pitcher maintained a good strike out ratio but had control problems while averaging a team per year during his seven seasons in black baseball. He began his career with the Negro National League champion St. Louis Stars in 1928, and split four decisions for the Stars the next season before pitching with marginal ballclubs for the remainder of his career.

Canton
Career: 1941   Position: p
Team: New York Cubans

He pitched briefly with the New York Cubans in 1941, his only year in the Negro Leagues.

Capers, Lefty

Career: 1930–32   Position: p

Teams: Louisville White Sox ('30–'31), Hilldale Daisies ('32)

The left-hander pitched with the Louisville White Sox in 1930–31 and with Hilldale in the East-West League in 1932.

Carabello, Esterio

Career: 1939   Position: rf

Team: Cuban Stars

The outfielder was the regular right fielder with the Cuban Stars in 1939 and, although he batted only .203, alternated hitting in the fourth and sixth slots in the batting order.

Card, Al

Career: 1887   Position: 3b

Team: *Pittsburgh Keystones*

He was a third baseman with the 1887 Pittsburgh Keystones, one of eight teams that were charter members of the League of Colored Baseball Clubs in 1887. However, the league's existence was ephemeral, lasting only a week.

Cardenas, P.

Career: 1924–27   Positions: **c**, of, 1b

Teams: Cuban Stars (East) ('24–'27), Cuban Stars (West) ('27)

The youngster was the second-string catcher with the 1924 Cuban Stars of the Eastern Colored League in his first year in the Negro Leagues. He was laid up part of the season, accounting for a lowly .182 batting average, but when he played he was impressive and was regarded as one of the best catchers in the league and a future star. However, the predicted stardom did not materialize, and although he improved his batting mark to a more respectable .239 in 1925, he never became a regular. He also played first base and in the outfield during his four seasons with the team.

Carey

a.k.a. Carry; Cary

Career: 1916–17,   Positions: 2b, 3b, ss,
1920–21   1b, rf

Teams: St. Louis Giants ('16, '17), *Madison Stars ('20), Dayton Marcos ('21)*

This light-hitting utility infielder broke in with the St. Louis Giants as a reserve in 1916, but earned the starting second-base assignment the following season, batting eighth in the lineup. When the team broke up in May, almost all of the regular players except he jumped to other teams. Subsequently he played with some lesser teams, including the Dayton Marcos in 1921, a year after they had withdrawn from league play.

Carlisle, Matthew (Matt, **Lick**)

Career: 1931–46   Positions: **2b**, ss, of

Teams: Birmingham Black Barons ('31), Montgomery Grey Sox ('32), Memphis Red Sox ('33), *New Orleans Crescent Star ('34)*, **Homestead Grays** ('35–'44, '46), *military service ('45)*

Bats: Right   Throws: Right
Height: 5'6"   Weight: 145

Born: Feb. 5, 1910, Wenonah, Ala.

Died: Nov. 18, 1972, Pittsburgh, Pa.

The hustling second baseman for the Homestead Grays' championship teams of the late 1930s and early 1940s, "Lick" had good speed and was one of the team's leading base stealers. Although short in stature, he contributed big plays to the Grays' success. He often batted second in the batting order and was a "place-setter" for the Grays' power tandem, Josh Gibson and Buck Leonard. With the exception of his speed, he was an average player, both in the field and at bat, but showed respectable power.

He joined the Grays in 1935, batting .326, but dropped to .236 the next year. In 1937 the Grays started their string of nine consecutive Negro National League pennants, with the 1938 team being the best in this long Gray line. Carlisle contributed a .257 average that year but was only a part-time starter in 1939.

As the decade of the '40s started, he returned to the starting lineup but was dropped to the lower part of the batting order, registering averages of .244, .288, and .237 for the seasons 1940–42. He never played as a regular again.

During World War II he was with the team in a reserve capacity except for the 1945 season, when he served in the military. After missing the entire season, he returned for a final bow in 1946 before a combination of the rigors of league play and his lack of stamina led to his retirement from baseball.

Before becoming a professional ballplayer, Carlisle worked in the coal mines near Birmingham and, before joining the Grays, played with several southern teams, including the Birmingham Black Barons, the Memphis Red Sox, the Montgomery Grey Sox, and the New Orleans Crescent Stars.

Carlson
Career: 1916   Position: c
Team: Chicago American Giants

He was a light-hitting reserve catcher with the Chicago American Giants, providing additional insurance for the injured Bruce Petway in 1916.

Carlyle, Sylvestor Junius
Career: 1945   Position: if
Team: Kansas City Monarchs

A wartime player, he was an infielder with the Kansas City Monarchs in 1945, his only season in the Negro Leagues.

Carpenter
Career: 1923–27   Position: of
Teams: *Memphis Red Sox ('23), Nashville Elite Giants ('27)*

An outfielder with southern teams prior to their entrance into the black big leagues, he appeared with the Memphis Red Sox in 1923 and the Nashville Elite Giants in 1927.

Carpenter, Clay
Career: 1926   Positions: **p**, 3b, 2b
Teams: *Philadelphia Giants ('25–'26),* Baltimore Black Sox ('26)

After hurling for a couple of seasons with the Philadelphia Giants, a lesser team, he earned a chance to pitch with the Baltimore Black Sox in 1926.

Carr, George Henry (**Tank**)
Career: 1917–34   Positions: **1b**, 3b, of, 2b, c
Teams: Los Angeles White Sox ('17–'20), Kansas City Monarchs ('20–'22), **Hilldale Daisies** ('23–'28), *Philadelphia Royal Giants ('25),* New York Lincoln Giants ('28), **Atlantic City Bacharach Giants** ('28–'29, '33), Philadelphia Stars ('33–'34)
Bats: Both   Throws: Right
Height: 6'2"   Weight: 230
Born: 1895, California

A switch-hitter who hit for both average and power, the hard-hitting first baseman for the Eastern Colored League champion Hilldale teams of 1923–25 hammered 21 home runs while batting .354 and stealing 39 bases in 1923. There was no World Series that year, but in the next two Series he hit .316 and .320, respectively, adding a home run in the 1925 World Series victory over the Kansas City Monarchs. During the regular seasons preceding the Series, he registered averages of .300 and .367. The next two seasons (1926–27) he hit .311 and .412, batting sixth and third in the order, respectively. Still swinging a big bat, he hit .416 in the intervening 1926–27 Cuban winter league.

Carr was from Los Angeles and early in his career played with the Los Angeles White Sox in the California Winter League, batting third in the lineup in 1917. When the Negro National League was formed in 1920, he left the West Coast to play with the Kansas City Monarchs hitting for averages of .296, .311, and .274. The underrated Carr blended speed with his power and was among the leaders in stolen bases, with totals of 24 and 19 in 1925–26.

Earlier in his career he was clocked in the 100-yard dash in 10 seconds. Despite all the potential that he commanded, he had one definite liability: a serious drinking problem that sometimes caused a disciplinary problem for his manager.

Although he is most identified with Hilldale, he played with several other teams during his eighteen-year career. In April 1928 he and Nip Winters were traded from Hilldale to the New York Lincoln Giants in exchange for Red Ryan and Rev Cannady, but later in the season Carr moved on to the Bacharachs, compiling a composite batting average of .307. In 1929 he returned to the Bacharachs, batting in the fourth or fifth spot in the lineup.

For the last few years of his career, his skills faded and he was only a shadow of his former self, closing out his career as a reserve with the Philadelphia Stars in 1933–34, ending his career with a .313 lifetime average. After retiring from baseball he worked as a cook for the railroad.

Carr, Wayne
Career: 1920–28; 1934 Positions: **p**, manager
Teams: St. Louis Giants ('20–'21), Baltimore Black Sox ('20–'23), Brooklyn Royal Giants ('21, '27), Indianapolis ABCs ('22), Atlantic City Bacharach Giants ('23–'24), Washington Potomacs ('23–'24), Wilmington Potomacs ('25), Newark Stars ('26), New York Lincoln Giants ('28); *Miami Giants ('34)*

He began his pitching career with the St. Louis Giants in 1920, before moving to the East and playing with the Brooklyn Royal Giants, Baltimore Black Sox, and Bacharachs through 1923. Secured from the Bacharachs by the Washington Potomacs in 1924, he was the top pitcher on the ballclub and had one of his best years. He was still young and was regarded as one of the best pitchers in the East. The next year, with the franchise moving to Wilmington, he posted a 3–4 record for a weak team. He averaged one team per year during his nine seasons in black baseball. After he

finished his playing days, he managed the Miami Giants in 1934.

Carrera, Clemente (**Sungo**)
a.k.a. Carreras
Career: 1938–41   Positions: **2b**, of, 3b
Team: New York Cubans ('38, '40–'41) Cuban Stars ('39)
Bats: Right   Throws: Right
Height, 5'10"   Weight: 188
Born: March 25, 1914, Havana, Cuba

Joining the New York Cubans in 1938, he was their regular second baseman in 1940–41, hitting .281 and .215, while batting in the third slot in the order. He played both infield and outfield for the Cubans during his four seasons in black baseball.

Carrillo
[see Castillo]

Carroll
Career: 1940   Position: p
Team: Homestead Grays

He pitched briefly with the Grays in 1940, without a decision.

Carroll, Hal
Career: 1887   Position: Player
Team: *Cincinnati Browns*

He was a player with the Cincinnati Browns, one of eight teams that were charter members of the League of Colored Baseball Clubs in 1887. However, the league's existence was ephemeral, lasting only a week. His position is uncertain.

Carroll, Sonny
Career: 1950   Position: p
Team: Baltimore Elite Giants

He was listed as a pitcher with the Baltimore Elite Giants in 1950, but league records do not substantiate any playing time.

Carry
[see Carey]

Carswell, Frank (Big Pitch)
Career: 1944–48   Position: p
Teams; Cleveland Buckeyes ('44–'48), *Indianapolis Clowns ('51–'53)*
Bats: Right   Throws: Right
Height: 6'2"   Weight: 190
Born: 1918, Atlanta, Ga.

A big, fastball pitcher with good control, he began his career in the Negro American League during World War II, posting a 2–0 record in 1944. In his second year in the league, he fashioned a 5–2 record with a 2.14 ERA to help the Cleveland Buckeyes to the 1945 pennant, and tossed a four-hit shutout against the Homestead Grays in the fourth game of the World Series to complete a sweep by the Buckeyes. The next season he slipped to a 3–5 record for the Buckeyes. His last year with the Buckeyes, 1948, he had a league ledger of 1–2.

Born in Atlanta, he moved to Albion, Michigan, when he was young and from there to Buffalo, where he was discovered by ''Square'' Moore and signed by the Buckeyes in 1944. While with the Buckeyes, he earned the nickname ''Big Pitch.'' After leaving Cleveland, he pitched with the Indianapolis Clowns for three seasons, 1951–53, when the Negro American League had declined to minor-league status.

Carter
Career: 1897–99   Position: p
Team: Cuban Giants

During the last three years of the nineteenth century, he was a pitcher with the Cuban Giants.

Carter
Career: 1917   Position: p
Team: St. Louis Giants

He was a pitcher with the 1917 St. Louis Giants before the team broke up in the late spring.

Carter
Career: 1918   Position: 2b
Team: Chicago Giants

He was a second baseman with the 1918 Chicago Giants in his only year in black baseball.

Carter, Alfred
Career: 1935–40   Positions: of, if
Teams: Nashville Elite Giants ('35), Pittsburgh Crawfords ('35), New York Cubans ('40)

Primarily an outfielder, he also filled a utility role during his abbreviated and irregular career. He began his professional career in 1935 with the Elite Giants, a Nashville-based team that moved briefly to Detroit before locating in Columbus for the season. He did not play for any substantial amount of time with any team.

Carter, Bill
Career: 1948   Position: p
Team: Newark Eagles

He pitched with the Newark Eagles in 1948, his only season in the Negro Leagues.

Carter, Bobo
Career: 1938   Position: 2b
Team: Atlanta Black Crackers

In 1938 he played second-base for the Atlanta Black Crackers in the waning days of the first half, but was dropped by the club when Gabby Kemp returned from the Jacksonville Redcaps for the second half.

Carter, Charles
Career: 1943   Position: p
Teams: Baltimore Elite Giants ('43), Homestead Grays ('43)

A wartime player, he pitched with both the Baltimore Elites and the Homestead Grays in 1943.

Carter, Charles (Kid)
Career: 1902–06   Positions: **p**, of
Teams: **Philadelphia Giants** ('02–'04), *Wilmington Giants ('05)*, Brooklyn Royal Giants ('06), *Quaker Giants ('13)*

He pitched with the Philadelphia Giants in their early years as they were developing into a eastern power during the first decade of the twentieth century, and holds the distinction of yielding the first hit of John Henry Lloyd's career. He could also play in the outfield and was with the Brooklyn Royal Giants and the Wilmington Giants during his career.

Carter, Clifford
Career: 1923–34   Position: p
Teams: Atlantic City Bacharach Giants ('23–'24, '33–'34), *Richmond Giants ('23–'24)*, Hilldale Daisies ('24, '29–'30, '32), Baltimore Black Sox ('23–'24), Harrisburg Giants ('24–'27), Philadelphia Tigers ('28), Philadelphia Stars ('33–'34)

His career got off to a rocky start when he lost twice as many games as he won (2–4) in his first season and was passed around like a hot potato, playing with four teams in 1924. He was playing at Richmond under Bill Pettus when he was picked up by Hilldale in mid-season, but was soon released and picked up by the Baltimore Black Sox but released again near the end of the season, before being secured by Harrisburg for the remainder of the year. With them, he was an "in-and-outer" but possessed lots of natural ability and was expected to develop into a good, dependable pitcher for the 1925 season. His development continued into the 1927 season, when he forged a 12–7 record with the club in their last year in the Eastern Colored League.

Carter remained in the league, however, playing with the Philadelphia Tigers in 1928, but neither the team nor the league survived the season. After the Eastern Colored League folded, he joined Hilldale in the American Negro League, remaining with the team even after the demise of the league after only a single season. Sparse statistics indicate that he was a .500 hurler with Hilldale over the next two seasons, and in 1933 with the Philadelphia Stars he continued the trend, splitting four decisions. Leaving the Stars, he closed out his career with the Bacharachs in 1934.

Carter, Elmer (Willie)
Career: 1932–37   Positions: c, 1b, ss

Team: Birmingham Black Barons ('30–'32, '37)

A versatile player, he played catcher, first base, and shortstop with the Birmingham Black Barons during the '30s. In his first two seasons, the Negro Southern League was not considered to be a major league, but in his third season with the team, the league was considered to be major. In 1937 the Black Barons joined the Negro American League in its inaugural season, and Carter played as a substitute and occasional starter.

Carter, Ernest C. (Spoon)
Career: 1932–49   Positions: p, manager
Teams: Louisville Black Caps ('32), Memphis Red Sox ('32–'33, '45–'49), Birmingham Black Barons ('32, '41, '49), Akron Tyrites ('33), Cleveland Giants ('33), Pittsburgh Crawfords ('33–'36), Cleveland Red Sox ('34), *Santo Domingo ('37)*, Philadelphia Stars ('38–'39), Toledo Crawfords ('39), Indianapolis Crawfords ('40), Newark Eagles ('40), *Mexican League ('41, '47)*, Homestead Grays ('42–'45)
Bats: Left   Throws: Right
Height: 6' 0"   Weight: 185
Born: Dec. 8, 1902, Harpersville, Ala.
Died: Jan. 23, 1974

Pitching for a dozen teams over eighteen seasons, he demonstrated good control and a wide repertory of pitches, but his most effective were his knuckler, screwball, and curve. He also had a fastball, drop, slider, and a change-up. He began his career pitching with southern teams, but in 1933 he joined the Pittsburgh Crawfords. He was used sparingly during his years with the Crawfords, and records are almost as sparse as his playing time. Incomplete statistics indicate that he lost his only two decisions in 1933, but won his only decision in 1935, the year when the Crawfords were considered to be the greatest black team of all time.

In 1942 he joined his second great black team when he signed with the Homestead Grays. In 1943–44 he posted marks of 5–0 and

7–1 (tops in the league) as the Grays added two Negro National League pennants and victories over the Birmingham Black Barons in the World Series each year. In the Series, his only decision came in 1944, when he lost his only start. Unlike most Grays pitchers, who were also good hitters, Carter lacked punch at the plate, but his fielding and baserunning were adequate.

Prior to joining the Homestead Grays, the zany hurler pitched with the Philadelphia Stars, Newark Eagles, and had another tour with the Crawfords after they departed Pittsburgh. He also made appearances in Latin American leagues, winning his only decision for the Estrellas Orientales in Santo Domingo in 1937, and playing in the Cuban League the same year. In 1941 he split two decisions in Mexico and later made a second trip to the Mexican league, in 1947.

After leaving the Grays during the 1945 season, he went back to the South, pitching with the Memphis Red Sox. After registering a 6–2 mark with a 3.15 ERA in 1948, his third full season with the Sox, he closed out his career with the Birmingham Black Barons in 1949.

Carter, Frank

Career: 1917   Position: p
Team: Havana Red Sox
Bats: Left   Throws: Left

A native of Dallas, the left-hander pitched with the Havana Red Sox in 1917.

Carter, Jimmy

Career: 1938–39   Position: p
Team: Philadelphia Stars

For two years at the end of the decade of the '30s, he was a pitcher with the Philadelphia Stars.

Carter, Kenneth

Career: 1950   Position: c
Team: Cleveland Buckeyes

He was listed as a catcher with the Cleveland Buckeyes in 1950, but league records do not substantiate his playing time.

Carter, Marlin Theodore (Mel, Pee Wee)

Career: 1932–48   Positions: **3b, ss**, 2b
Teams: *San Antonio Black Indians ('31)*, Monroe Monarchs ('32–'33), **Memphis Red Sox** *('33–'34, '38–'42, '46–'48)*, Cincinnati Tigers ('35–'37), *military service ('43–'45)*, Chicago American Giants ('48), *minor leagues ('49–'50)*
Bats: Left   Throws: Right
Height: 5' 7"   Weight: 159
Born: Dec. 27, 1912, Haslam, Tex.

A popular player for the Memphis Red Sox, the little infielder played with the 1938 Negro American League first-half champion Memphis Red Sox and made his only East-West All-Star appearance in 1942. Incomplete records indicate a batting average of .257 for the year, and after his All-Star season, his career was interrupted by World War II, during which he served in the U.S. Coast Guard, missing three entire baseball seasons ('43–'45). Before he was discharged, he saw the devastation caused by the atomic bombs at Hiroshima and Nagasaki. Returning home, he resumed his baseball career, hitting .294 in 1946 with the Red Sox and .281 in 1948 with the Chicago American Giants in his final Negro League season.

After captaining the high-school baseball team at Louisiana Collegiate Institute, the Texan turned down a scholarship at Wiley College to launch his professional baseball career in his home state with the San Antonio Black Indians in 1931. He then signed with the Monroe Monarchs, playing out of Monroe, Louisiana, and members of the Negro Southern League. In 1932, when Carter joined the team, the league was designated as a major league because of the influx of players from the clubs formerly aligned with the Negro National League, which had folded following the 1931 season. Leaving Monroe during the 1933 season, he joined the Red Sox for his first tour of duty, with the Sox being in the Negro Southern League at the time.

After two seasons in Memphis he joined the Cincinnati Tigers, where the left-handed swinger recorded a batting average of .387 in 1936, when the Tigers were playing as an independent team. In 1937 the Tigers joined the Negro American League and after one season dropped out of top-level play, with Carter rejoining the Red Sox, now also in the Negro American League. In 1939 he shared the second-base position and was the leadoff hitter, moving to third base in 1940 and batting in the second slot in the order for two years before moving into the key third slot during his All-Star season of 1942. After the war he stepped back into his familiar spot in the lineup while also playing at shortstop.

After the color barrier was lifted, he entered organized baseball with the Rochester Royals in 1949, spending two seasons with the club. While with the team, he was a popular player with the fans but was beaned, and his hearing was impaired as a result. After retiring from baseball, he entered the workforce in 1951, being employed for almost equal intervals at International Harvester, Chicago Latrobe, and Memphis's Colonial Country Club. He retired to the golf links in January 1978.

Carter, Paul (Nick)

Career: 1929–36   Position: p
Teams: Hilldale Daisies ('29–'32), Philadelphia Stars ('33–'34), New York Black Yankees ('35–'36)

A pitcher during the '30s, primarily with Philadelphia-based teams, he is credited with a 10–3 record in 1931, including a no-hitter, while pitching for Hilldale against all levels of competition. That season the team was between leagues and playing as an independent ballclub. The next year, after Hilldale joined the East-West League, he dropped to a 1–6 record. In 1933 he joined the Philadelphia Stars in their first season, but was used sparingly during his stint with them, including their Negro National League championship season of 1934. He closed his career with the New York Black Yankees in 1936.

Carter, Robert

Career: 1947   Position: p
Team: Homestead Grays

In 1947, his only year in the Negro Leagues, he pitched with the Grays without a decision.

Carter, William

Career: 1920–22   Position: c
Teams: Detroit Stars ('20–'21), Kansas City Monarchs ('22)

He played three seasons as a reserve catcher, beginning his career with the Detroit Stars in 1920 and closing it with the Kansas City Monarchs in 1922.

Carter, William

Career: 1937, 1943   Position: 3b
Teams: St. Louis Stars ('37), Harrisburg-St. Louis Stars ('43)

He was the regular third baseman for the St. Louis Stars of the Negro American League in 1937, batting in the sixth slot, and for the Harrisburg-St. Louis Stars of the Negro National League in 1943, batting in the leadoff position.

Cartmill, Alfred, Jr.

Career: 1949   Position: 2b
Team: Kansas City Monarchs ('49, '55)

He played second base with the Monarchs in 1949, the last season of the Negro American League as a quality organization, and in the league's declining years he continued with Kansas City on into the '50s, playing with them again in 1955.

Cary

[see Carey]

Cary

Career: 1927   Position: p
Team: Brooklyn Royal Giants

He pitched briefly with the Brooklyn Royal Giants in 1927, their last year in the Eastern Colored League.

Casey, Joe

Career: 1920   Position: p
Team: St. Louis Giants

He was a pitcher with the St. Louis Giants

in 1920, the first year of the Negro National League.

Casey, William **(Mickey)**
Career: 1930–43   Positions: **c**, 3b, of, manager
Teams: Hilldale Daisies ('30), Baltimore Black Sox ('30–'32), Atlantic City Bacharach Giants, **Philadelphia Stars** ('33–'37), Washington Black Senators ('38), New York Cubans ('39–'40), Baltimore Elite Giants ('42), *Baltimore Greys ('42),* New York Black Yankees ('43), *minor leagues ('50–'55)*
Bats: Right   Throws: Right

A solid journeyman ballplayer, he was a mediocre hitter, not noted for either consistency, contact ability, or power, and he was not distinguished defensively nor noted as a base-stealing threat. However, he was sufficiently capable behind the plate and versatile enough to play other positions, particularly third base and the outfield. His career encompassed the decade of the '30s and extended into the early war years, with Casey also taking a turn in the latter stages of his career as a manager.

He began his career in 1930, serving as a reserve receiver with both Hilldale and the Baltimore Black Sox, but earned a job as a part-time starter in 1932, the year the Black Sox were in the East-West League. When the Philadelphia Stars were organized in 1933, Casey joined the team as a backup for Biz Mackey, but when Mackey was injured in 1934, he assumed the starting role for a large part of the season. Although records show only a .179 average for him, the Stars won the Negro National League pennant despite Mackey's prolonged absence from the lineup. His playing time increased in 1936, as did his batting average (.277), and he earned the starting spot behind the plate in 1937. Although he hit last in the order, he is credited with a .360 batting average for the season.

In 1938 he joined Ben Taylor's Washington Black Senators as the regular catcher, but when the club folded after only one year in the Negro National League, he signed with the New York Cubans, winning the starting position behind the plate for two seasons and hitting .276 and .258.

In 1950, twenty years after he started his professional baseball career, he finally played in organized ball, playing at Eau Claire in the Northern League, where he registered a .282 average. In 1953 the veteran receiver was with Jacksonville in the Sally League, where he hit .253. The next season he split time between Jacksonville and Dallas in the Texas League, hitting an aggregate .184. His last season was split between Charlotte in the South Atlantic League (.214) and Atlanta in the Southern Association (.250), where he was used sparingly.

Cash, William Walker (**Bill,** Ready)
Career: 1943–50   Positions: **c**, of, 3b, 1b
Teams: **Philadelphia Stars** ('43–'50), *Mexican League ('50), Canadian League ('51), minor leagues ('52–'53)*
Bats: Right   Throws: Right
Height: 6'2"   Weight: 195
Born: Feb. 21, 1919, Round Oak, Ga.

A rugged receiver with a strong arm and a perfect peg to second base, he broke in with the Philadelphia Stars in 1943 with an impressive .321 batting average to go with his defensive skills. The next half-dozen seasons (1944–49) he hit .282, .244, .237, .276, .290, and .268, and earned a spot on the All-Star team the latter two years. He entered the 1948 game as a substitute, but caught the entire 1949 East-West game, calling the pitches in the East's two-hit shutout of the West Stars. In 1946 Cash was scheduled to be a member of Satchel Paige's All-Star team that barnstormed against Bob Feller's All-Stars in an autumn series, but Cash broke his thumb and was unable to play.

On opening day in 1946, Cash was involved in an incident during a closely contested game against the Newark Eagles. The Eagles' Leon Day was in the process of pitching a no-hitter, but the game was scoreless. With Larry Doby on second base, Lennie Pearson hit a one-hop shot to shortstop, and when the ball was thrown to first base, Doby rounded third and tried to score. The ball was relayed home and Cash blocked Doby off the plate and made the tag. However, the umpire ruled him safe and Cash jumped to his feet and, in protesting the call, the umpire was knocked to the ground. While the ump was on his hands and knees, Stars' manager Goose Curry, who had raced in from his spot in right field, kicked the felled arbiter. Cash was thrown out of the game, fined $25, and suspended for three days. Some observers feel that the catcher received an unwarranted stigma from the incident that may have followed him into organized baseball when he made the transition four years afterward.

In 1950, only a few games into the season, the eight-year veteran left the Philadelphia Stars to play with the Mexico City Red Devils, registering a .311 average with 15 homers. From Mexico he traveled to Granby in the Canadian Provincial League, hitting .296 with 16 homers, despite being frequently issued free passes to first base. In 1952, after the color barrier was lifted, he played in the White Sox organization, splitting an injury-plagued season between the Waterloo Whitehawks of the Three-I League (.228) and Superior of the Northern League. At Waterloo he suffered from bursitis in his shoulder and broke his leg, sliding into second base to break up a double play. In 1953 he played with the Brandon Braves in the Mandak League and hit .347. For the next three years he played in the Dominican Republic, with his best year coming with the San Diego Eagles in 1954, when he hit .297. He closed out his career the following year with Licey, batting .230. Sandwiched between these two winters was a year with Bismarck, North Dakota, a strong semipro team that featured Ray Dandridge.

During Cash's career he also played in other Latin American leagues. He hit .214 in the 1947–48 Cuban winter league. In Venezuela he played with Vargas in the winter league and with an All-Star club in Maricaibo, and in Mexico he also played with Culiacan in the Mexican Pacific Coast League.

As a youngster, Cash lived in the Meadows, an area near the Philadelphia airport. In high school he was the only black player on the school team and quit the squad, but played semipro baseball in the city for four years with the Camden Giants, Black Meteors, and Philadelphia Daisies. He was fortunate to have sound baseball men managing those teams, including Otto Briggs with the Camden team and Webster McDonald with the Daisies. When McDonald thought Cash was ready to make the step up to the black big leagues, he introduced him to manager Goose Curry, who signed him for the Philadelphia Stars. After leaving the baseball diamond, Cash returned to Philadelphia to practice the trade he had learned before baseball, working as a machinist at Westinghouse Electrical & Manufacturing Company until his retirement.

Cason, John
Career: 1918–32   Positions: **c**, of, 2b, ss, 1b
Teams: **Brooklyn Royal Giants** ('18–'27), Norfolk Stars ('20), Birmingham Black Barons ('23), Atlantic City Bacharach Giants ('28), Hilldale Daisies, New York Lincoln Giants, Baltimore Black Sox ('31–'32)

The catcher was a versatile ballplayer who made a good utility man when not in the starting lineup during his fifteen-year career. He began his career with the Brooklyn Royal Giants in 1918 as a backup catcher, with incomplete statistics showing a .111 batting average in very limited play. He continued with the Royals into the '20s, sharing the catching duties while also playing in the outfield. In 1923 he was a regular, dividing his playing time between catcher and second base and hitting .307 while batting cleanup. He remained in the starting lineup as the regular catcher through 1927, usually batting sixth in the order, while hitting .260 and .292 in 1925 and 1927, respectively. In 1928 he moved over to the Bacharachs to share the regular catching duties, batting eighth in the order. He appeared with

Hilldale and the Lincoln Giants before joining the Baltimore Black Sox as a reserve in 1931.

Castillo, Julian *(Big)*

Career: 1904–12   Positions: **1b**, p
Teams: All-Cubans ('04–'05, '11–'12), Cuban Stars ('12)
Height: 6'2"   Weight: 240

The big, heavy-hitting Cuban was hard as nails and had an equally big reputation for hitting the long ball. While he had good power, he did not distinguish himself afield and was not a good base runner. He played first base for the All-Cubans in 1904–05 and again in 1911–12, when he was a ten-year veteran and nearing the end of his career. He also played with the Cuban Stars in the early years of the '10s.

In Cuba he was a top player during the first decade of the century and held many Cuban records, including most games played in 1907; most hits in 1901, '03, '08–'09, and 1910; highest batting average in 1901 (.454), 1903 (.330), 1908–09 (.315), and 1910 (.408); most home runs in 1903, 1912, and 1913; most triples in 1903, 1904, and 1907; and most doubles in 1901, 1903, 1907, 1908–09, and 1912. Other good batting averages were 1904 (.358) and 1913 (.319) for a lifetime batting average in Cuba of .310 for his 13 years (1901–13).

Playing with Almendares (and batting fifth in the order) against the Detroit Tigers in a 1910 winter exhibition series, he was hitless in five games. According to contemporary newspaper accounts, he and Tiger pitching ace George Mullin had a "grudge" against each other, but whether it was real or just for show to draw a crowd is unclear.

He was elected to the Cuban Hall of Fame in 1943.

Castro, Antonio

Career: 1929   Position: c
Team: Cuban Stars (East)

He was a backup catcher for the Cuban Stars (East) in 1929, his only year in the Negro Leagues.

Cates, Joe (Rabbit)

Career: 1931   Positions: **ss**, 2b, 3b
Teams: Louisville White Sox ('31, *'33, '38*), *Louisville Red Caps ('34)*

The light-hitting middle infielder played with the Louisville White Sox in 1931, when they were in the Negro National League, and other top Louisville Teams during the early '30s. Primarily a shortstop, he also played second base and third base while batting in the eighth slot in the order.

Cathey, Willis (**Jim**, Bill)

Career: 1948–50   Position: p
Team: Indianapolis Clowns
Bats: Left   Throws: Left
Height: 5'10"   Weight: 170

The left-handed fastballer had good control, and pitched with the Indianapolis Clowns for three years during the declining years of the Negro Leagues. In 1948 he registered a 5–9 mark with a 4.93 ERA.

Cato, Harry

Career: 1887–96   Positions: 2b, p, of
Teams: Cuban Giants ('87–'88, '93, '96), New York Gorhams ('89), Cuban X-Giants ('93)

A versatile performer, he played infield, outfield, and pitched with the early teams of the nineteenth century, including the well-known Cuban Giants and their spin-off team, the Cuban X-Giants. Organized in 1885, the Cuban Giants were the first black professional team and were the Colored Champions in 1887 and 1888. Considered the top ballclub of the era, the Cuban Giants often played as representatives of a host city in an otherwise white league, as they did in 1887, when they represented Trenton, New Jersey. The New York Gorhams did the same, representing Philadelphia in the Middle States League in 1889.

Celada

a.k.a. Celeda
Career: 1928–29   Positions: ss, 3b
Teams: Cuban Stars (West)

The light-hitting infielder played with the

Negro National League Cuban Stars for two seasons at the end of the decade of the '20s, playing primarily at shortstop with a paltry .181 batting average to show in 1929.

Cepeda, Pedro Anibal (Perucho, The Bull)

Career: 1941   Positions: ss, 1b, of
Team: New York Cubans
Bats: Right   Throws: Right
Height: 5'11"   Weight: 200
Born: 1906, San Juan, Puerto Rico
Died: 1955, Puerto Rico

Nicknamed "The Bull" by the fans, he was a hero in his native Puerto Rico. Alejandro Pompez consistently pursued him to play with the New York Cubans and he was listed on their roster in 1941, but there is no record of him having actually played in a game for them. He had a temper and was concerned that he might encounter some problems because of the racial climate then existing in the United States. Although he changed his mind about playing with Pompez's Cubans, he unquestionably could have starred in the Negro Leagues had that been his choice. A good shortstop, he was fast for a big man and was a very good line-drive hitter who could hit the long ball but who hit primarily to the power alleys for extra-base hits. The star infielder led the Puerto Rican League in batting with back-to-back titles in the winters of 1938–39 and 1939–40 with averages of .365 and .386, respectively. Twenty years later his son, Orlando Cepeda, who starred in the major leagues, also won back-to-back batting titles in the Puerto Rican League.

In 1941 in Puerto Rico, he hit .423 and led the league in RBIs, and followed with a .464 mark in 1942. In the latter years of his career before his retirement in 1948, he played first base, the same position his son would later play, and many observers regard the father to have been the better ballplayer of the two.

Cephas

[see Cephus, Goldie]

Cephus, Goldie

a.k.a. Cephas
Career: 1925–31, 1938 Positions: ss, of
Teams: *Philadelphia Giants ('25–'27)*, Atlantic City Bacharach Giants ('31), Newark Dodgers ('34), Birmingham Black Barons ('38)

A light-hitting shortstop, he also gained some playing time in the outfield in a checkered career mostly with marginal teams, including the Philadelphia Giants and Bacharachs. In 1938, playing as Cephas, he hit eighth in the batting order as a part-time starter at shortstop with the Birmingham Black Barons.

Chacon, Pelayo

Career: 1909–31   Positions: ss, 2b, of, manager
Teams: Stars of Cuba ('10), Cuban Stars (West) ('11–'16), **Cuban Stars (East)** ('17–'28), Cuban Stars ('30–'31)
Bats: Right   Throws: Right
Height: 5'8"   Weight: 140
Born: Sept. 22, 1889, Havana, Cuba

A suburb defensive player, he was very fast in the field and on the bases and was acknowledged as one of the best shortstops in baseball. He had excellent range and an outstanding throwing arm and was a good base stealer and smart base runner. Although not a long-ball hitter, he had superb bat control and was a good hit-and-run man, and used his speed to generate extra-base hits, making him an offensive threat. And he was a smart baseball tactician, serving as captain and manager of the Cuban Stars for several years. He is the father of Elio Chacon, also a shortstop, who played in the major leagues for the Cincinnati Reds.

He first came to the United States in 1909 and throughout his career was scouted by major-league scouts who wanted to sign him but who were prohibited by his color. In 1910 he played with the Stars of Cuba, and the following season joined Tinti Molina's Cuban Stars, a team that played mostly in the Midwest. For the next six seasons he was their leadoff hitter and sparkplug. Leaving to join Pompez's

Cuban Stars, who played in the East, he was their shortstop and glue that held the team together for a dozen seasons. In his first year with the franchise, 1917, the team sometimes played under the name of the Havana Stars. In 1918 partial statistics show a .345 batting average, and when the Stars joined the Eastern Colored League, he abandoned his customary batting place in one of the two top spots in the order and moved into the cleanup slot, with available statistics showing averages of .302, .257, .260, .267, and .302 for the years 1923–27. With age, injury, and illness catching up with him, he began to suffer a loss of playing time during the late '20s.

By then he was in the latter stages of his twenty-three-year career, and had assumed managerial reins, both in the United States and in his homeland, guiding Cienfuegos to their first flag when they copped the 1929–30 Cuban championship. In his native country he played with eight different teams for a total of twenty-three years (1908–09 through 1931–32) and had a lifetime average of .246. He led the league with an average of .344 in 1920–21 and topped the .300 mark on three other occasions, .336 (1926–27), .316 (1922–23), and .302 (1914–15). He also had a trio of near misses, .294 (1929–30), .291 (1919–20), and .290 (1927–28).

He also played for Havana in two winter exhibition series against John McGraw's New York Giants, first as a youngster in 1911–12, when he hit .350, and then in 1920, when he hit .364. In 1949, in recognition of his baseball achievements, he was elected to the Cuban Hall of Fame. He also played with the Licey Tigers in the Dominican Republic in 1929, and in Venezuela in the early '30s.

Chamberlain

Career: 1889   Position: 1b
Team: New York Gorhams

He was a first baseman in 1889 with the New York Gorhams, who were playing in the Middle States League.

Chambers, *Arthur* (**Rube**)

Career: 1925–27   Position: p
Teams: Wilmington Potomacs ('25), Lincoln Giants ('26–'27)
Bats: Left   Throws: Left
Died: Feb. 7, 1928, West Palm Beach, Fla.

A smart and talented lefthander, he had a good screwball and was the best pitcher in Philadelphia during the mid–'20s. The hurler's career consisted of three seasons in the Eastern Colored league. After suffering through a winless season (0–6) with the woeful Wilmington Potomacs in 1925, he signed with the Lincoln Giants for his last two seasons. After joining the Lincolns and sitting on the bench for about a week, he finally got a chance to start and proved himself by striking out 18 batters. He was also an accomplished player in other facets of the game. Catquick in the field and a good-hitting pitcher, he hit .319 in his season with the Potomacs. Chambers's career and life were shortened when he became involved with gambling and bootlegging activities during Prohibition, and he was found in an empty boxcar in West Palm Beach, Florida, shot to death, a victim of criminal elements.

Chandler

Career: 1916   Position: p
Team: Bowser's ABCs

He was a member of the pitching staff for Bowser's ABCs in 1916, after owner Thomas Bowser split from the Indianapolis ABCs to form his own team.

Chapman, Edward

Career: 1927–31   Position: p
Teams: Detroit Stars ('27), Chicago Columbia Giants ('31)

A pitcher with David Malarcher's Chicago Columbia Giants in 1931, his only previous appearance in top competition was a brief stint with the Detroit Stars in 1927.

Chapman, Joseph W.

Career: 1887   Position: player
Team: *Cincinnati Browns*

He was a player with the Cincinnati Browns, one of eight teams that were charter members of the League of Colored Baseball Clubs in 1887. However, the league's existence was ephemeral, lasting only a week. His position is uncertain.

Chapman, John

Career: 1887   Position: player
Team: *Cincinnati Browns*

He was a player with the Cincinnati Browns, one of eight teams that were charter members of the League of Colored Baseball Clubs in 1887. However, the league's existence was ephemeral, lasting only a week. His position is uncertain.

Chapman, Leonardo Medina

[see Medina, Leonardo]

Chapman, Roy Lee (Ray)

Career: 1949–50   Position: p
Team: New York Black Yankees

He was a pitcher during the 1949–50 seasons, when the Negro American League was struggling to survive the loss of players to organized baseball, but his playing time was severely restricted.

Charleston

Career: 1942   Position: c
Team: Cincinnati Buckeyes

In his only year in the Negro Leagues, he was a backup catcher with the 1942 Cincinnati Buckeyes.

Charleston, Benny

Career: 1930   Position: of
Team: Homestead Grays

He was a brother of Oscar Charleston and played briefly and without distinction as an outfielder for the Homestead Grays in 1930.

Charleston, Oscar McKinley (Charlie)

Career: 1915–41;   Positions: **cf, 1b,**
1942–*54*   manager

Teams: **Indianapolis ABCs** ('15–'18, '20, '22–'23), New York Lincoln Stars ('15–'16), Bowser's ABCs ('16), Chicago American Giants ('19), St. Louis Giants ('21), **Harrisburg Giants** ('24–'27), Hilldale Daisies ('28–'29), **Homestead Grays** ('30–'31), **Pittsburgh Crawfords** ('32–'38), Toledo Crawfords ('39), Indianapolis Crawfords ('40), Philadelphia Stars ('41; '42–'44, '46–'50); *Brooklyn Brown Dodgers ('45), Indianapolis Clowns ('54)*

Bats: Left   Throws: Left
Height: 6'0"   Weight: 190
Born: Oct. 14, 1896, Indianapolis, Ind.
Died: Oct. 6, 1954, Philadelphia, Pa.

As a hitter, the popular barrel-chested, spindly-legged slugger *par excellence* was often compared to Babe Ruth. Earlier in his career, his speedy, slashing style on the basepaths earned him comparison with Ty Cobb, and defensively his superb play from a shallow center-field position was reminiscent of Tris Speaker. Jocko Conlon, a Hall of Fame umpire, made this comparison, calling him *"The* great Negro player of that time" and concurring that he was a beautiful center fielder, comparable to Speaker, and a great hitter. After the 1924 season, Former Charleston teammate Ben Taylor, a longtime star first baseman and manager, declared that Charleston was the "greatest outfielder that ever lived . . . greatest of all colors. He can cover more ground than any man I have ever seen. His judging of fly balls borders on the uncanny."

Much to the delight of the fans, Charleston sometimes injected "showboating" into his diamond performances. A complete ballplayer who excelled in every facet of the game, Oscar Charleston epitomized the spirit of black baseball.

Temperamentally he presented a bit of a contradiction. He was a fearless, steely-eyed brawler who could not be intimidated and whose fights both on and off the field are as legendary as are his playing skills. And yet he was protective of younger players and idolized by kids who were mesmerized by his charisma.

In his prime, the well-honed blend of power

and speed was unparalleled by any player in black baseball. One of the fastest men in the game and an instinctive, aggressive base runner, he was rough and tumble, sliding hard with spikes high. At bat he had few equals and, as an excellent drag bunter, he also used his tremendous speed to bunt his way on base. In the field his combination of great range, good hands, powerful arm, and superior baseball instincts was unsurpassed, allowing him always to get a good jump, robbing batters of ''sure'' hits.

His father was a construction worker and his mother's father was a carpenter who had been employed in the construction of Fisk University in Nashville, Tennessee. Oscar was the seventh of eleven children and, as a youngster in Indianapolis, he was batboy for the local ABCs ballclub. At age fifteen, he left home and served a stint in the Army, where he ran track (23 seconds for the 220-yard dash) and played baseball while stationed in the Philippines with the 24th Infantry. In 1914 he was the only black baseball player in the Manila League.

Returning home, the young athlete joined the Indianapolis ABCs in 1915 as a pitcher-outfielder and made a strong showing in his rookie season. His aggressive play on the diamond was evident even in his first year in top competition, when he and Bingo DeMoss were arrested for assaulting an umpire and causing a riot. Later in his career Charleston was known for engaging in fights at various times with a member of the Ku Klux Klan and several Cuban soldiers. His fearlessness was an attribute that helped the team win a championship the following year, with Charleston contributing a .360 average in the playoff series over Rube Foster's Chicago American Giants.

A fastball hitter, the sharp-eyed Charleston hit for both average and distance and utilized the entire ballpark, hitting to all fields. The left-handed swinger was always a dangerous hitter but was at his best in the clutch. The 1921 season serves best to exemplify the range and depth of his exceptional talent as he compiled a .434 batting average, and led the league in stolen bases (35), doubles (14), triples (11), and home runs (15) in only 60 league games. In an effort at a repeat performance the following season he again led the league in home runs and stolen bases while slamming out a .370 batting average.

Joining Harrisburg as playing manager in the newly formed Eastern Colored League, Charleston had superlative back-to-back performances in 1924–25, batting .411 and .445, while leading the league each year in home runs with 14 and 20. The latter season he also topped the league in doubles and hits. In 1926 he continued his offensive bombardment, and in late June he homered twice in a doubleheader against the New York Lincoln Giants, bringing his total to 19 for the young season. He finished the season with a .344 batting average, followed in 1927 with .384, while again leading the league in home runs.

That was his last year in Harrisburg, leaving to join Hilldale for the beginning of the 1928 season, which was highlighted by the early-season demise of the Eastern Colored League. After a .363 average the first year with Hilldale, he hit .396 the following year when the club joined the American Negro League in its only year of existence. With the collapse of the second eastern league in two years, he joined the independent Homestead Grays for the 1930–31 seasons. In 1930 the Grays defeated the strong New York Lincoln Giants in a ten-game series for the eastern championship, and the 1931 Grays are considered to be among the greatest teams of all time. In addition to Charleston, who hit .380, the team boasted such greats as Josh Gibson, Smokey Joe Williams, Jud Wilson, George Scales, Vic Harris, Ted Page, and Ted ''Double Duty'' Radcliffe.

He left the Grays to assume the managerial reins of the Pittsburgh Crawfords and talked Josh Gibson into going with him. After leaving the Grays, Charleston's age and weight gain prompted a move to first base, where he continued to star as playing manager for the outstanding Pittsburgh Crawfords of 1932–36. The

1935 champion Crawfords team, boasting five Hall of Famers in the lineup, are generally conceded to be the best black team of all time. Although approaching his fortieth birthday and well past his prime, Charleston hit for averages of .363, .450, .310, .304, and .356 with the Crawfords and was selected to the first three East-West All-Star games as a first baseman.

Although records are incomplete, the hard-hitting slugger ended his twenty-seven-year career credited with a .357 lifetime batting average and 151 home runs. He also fashioned a .326 batting average in exhibitions against major-league opposition and .361 batting average for nine Cuban winter seasons, including a .405 mark in 1921–22.

After his days as a playing manager ended, he continued as a bench manager with the Stars through 1950, taking a year off in 1945 to take the helm of Branch Rickey's Brooklyn Brown Dodgers. He returned to the managerial ranks in 1954, guiding the Indianapolis Clowns to a championship in his last season before falling victim to a heart attack. During his thirty-nine-year career he was associated with fourteen different teams, as player and manager. He also assisted Branch Rickey in scouting the Negro Leagues to find *the* player to break baseball's color line. He was elected to the National Baseball Hall of Fame in 1976, a fitting tribute to a man who might well have been the greatest all-around ballplayer in black baseball history.

Charleston, Porter

Career: 1927–35   Position: p
Teams: Hilldale Daisies ('27–'32), Philadelphia Stars ('33–'35)
Bats: Right   Throws: Right
Born: 1908

His nine seasons, spent primarily with Philadelphia-based teams, was a story of failed leagues and teams, as three leagues folded while he was with Hilldale, and then the Hilldale club itself disbanded. When the right-handed pitcher first signed with Hilldale in 1927 as a nineteen-year-old, he was considered the "find" of the year. Two years later, after the collapse of the Eastern Colored League, he fashioned a 6–4 record in the American Negro League, which also folded. In 1931, with Hilldale playing as an independent ballclub, he recorded a 16–4 ledger against all levels of competition. The next season Hilldale was again aligned with an ill-fated league, as the East-West League failed even to finish the season. But before its collapse, Charleston managed a 4–2 record in league play. After finishing the 1932 season, the Hilldale ballclub disbanded, with owner Ed Bolden beginning a new team called the Philadelphia Stars in 1933. Charleston was a member of the pitching staff for Bolden's new aggregation, pitching during their 1934 championship season before closing out his career in 1935.

Charleston, Red

Career: 1923–32   Positions: **c**, 2b
Teams: Birmingham Black Barons ('23), Memphis Red Sox ('24), Nashville Elite Giants ('27–'32)

A catcher for ten years, spent entirely with teams in the southern triangle, he played with the Birmingham Black Barons, Memphis Red Sox, and Nashville Elite Giants. Sparse statistics from the Depression years indicate a composite .284 batting average for three years with the Nashville Elites (1929–31), while hitting in the seventh slot in the batting order as the regular catcher the latter season. The Elites' first year in the Negro National League was 1930, sandwiched between two years in the Negro Southern League.

Charter, W. M. (*Bill*)

Career: 1941–46   Positions: 1b, c, 3b, 2b
Teams: *Detroit Black Sox ('41–'42)*, Chicago American Giants ('43, '46)

He was a regular for the Chicago American Giants for two years, one as a first baseman (1943) and the other as a catcher (1946). With the American Giants he batted in the lower part of the order and is credited with a .261 average the latter year. He also had some playing time at both third base and second base in 1943. Before joining the American Giants he played third base with the Detroit Black Sox, a lesser team, in 1941–42.

Chase
Career: 1920, 1923   Positions: p, of
Teams: Detroit Stars ('20), Chicago Giants ('20), Toledo Tigers ('23)

In the early '20s he pitched briefly and without distinction for both the Detroit Stars and the Chicago Giants and also was an outfielder with the Toledo Tigers before the team broke up during the 1923 season.

Chatman
Career: 1922   Position: p
Team: Cleveland Tate Stars

In 1922 he pitched briefly with the Cleveland Tate Stars in their only year in the Negro National League.

Chatman, Edgar
Career: 1944–45   Position: p
Team: Memphis Red Sox

He was a wartime pitcher with the Memphis Red Sox, pitching two seasons and recording a 4–10 ledger with a 3.21 ERA in 1945.

Chavous
Career: 1895–96   Positions: p, of
Teams: Page Fence Giants

In 1895–96 he played with the Page Fence Giants of Adrian, Michigan, one of the top teams of the era. His first year he played in the outfield and batted only .154, and the second season he was a pitcher with the ballclub.

Cheatham
Career: 1930–34   Position: p
Teams: Baltimore Black Sox, Pittsburgh Crawfords, Homestead Grays

A marginal player during the early years of the '30s, he pitched briefly with the Baltimore Black Sox, Pittsburgh Crawfords, and Homestead Grays over a five-year period.

Cheavier
[see Wiggins, Joe]

Cherry, Hugh
Career: 1949   Position: officer
Team: Houston Eagles

After Effa Manley sold the Newark Eagles' franchise, the ballclub was moved to Texas, and Cherry was an officer of the team during their first year in Houston.

Chester
Career: 1926   Position: of
Team: Harrisburg Giants

He was listed as a reserve outfielder with the Harrisburg Giants in 1926.

Chestnut, Henry **Joseph** (Joe)
Career: 1950   Position: p
Teams: Indianapolis Clowns, Philadelphia Stars

In 1950 the pitcher began the season with the Indianapolis Clowns, but pitched the last part of the season with the Philadelphia Stars, finishing with a 1–5 record and a 6.05 ERA.

Chicago American Giants
Duration: 1911–50   Honors: World Series ('26–'27), pennants ('20–'22, '26–'27, '32–'33), second-half NNL title ('28), first-half NNL title ('34)

Affiliations: Independent ('11–'19, '36), NNL ('20–'31, '33–'35), NSL ('32), NAL ('37–'50)

Organized by Rube Foster, who built the team into a dynasty before his demise, the organization was the longest continuous franchise in the history of black baseball. The team began in 1910 when Rube Foster and Frank Leland, who were the manager and owner, respectively, of the Leland Giants, separated and formed two different ballclubs. Foster retained the team name of Leland Giants for the first season, but beginning in 1911 the club became known as the American Giants. For the first decade of the team's existence, they won every declared western championship, losing only to the 1916 Indianapolis ABCs. The American Giants' dominance continued after Foster organized the first black professional league, the Negro National League, in 1920, winning the first three pennants.

After Foster's incapacitation from his mental illness, his white business partner, John M. Schorling, ran the ballclub, and in 1926 and 1927, with Foster's lieutenant David Malarcher at the reins, the team won both the Negro National League flag and the Negro World Series, each time facing the Eastern Colored League's champion Bacharach Giants. In the spring of 1928 Schorling sold the ballclub to William E. Trimble, a white florist, alleging that he was "squeezed out" by a conspiracy of the other owners to diminish the gates by keeping the best clubs out of Chicago.

After Foster's death and the demise of the Negro National League, the franchise again rose to prominence as Cole's American Giants, under the management of new owners Robert A. Cole and Horace G. Hall, in 1932–34, winning pennants the first two years before losing a hard-fought League Championship Series to the Philadelphia Stars in 1934. The first of the two pennants came while playing in the Negro Southern League and the second in the newly reorganized Negro National League. After dropping out of the Negro National League to play as an independent team in 1936, the American Giants prospered again under new ownership as Dr. J. B. Martin took control of the team, and the American Giants became a charter member of the Negro American League in 1937. Although the franchise encountered many difficulties during the '40s, the ballclub remained in the league even after it had ceased to be of major-league caliber.

Chicago Giants
Duration: 1910–21   Honors: None
Affiliations: Independent ('10–'19), NNL ('20–'21)

The Chicago Union Giants were organized by Frank Leland in 1901, and in 1905 the club became the Leland Giants, under Leland's managerial command until he turned the reins over to Rube Foster in 1907. In 1910 owner Frank Leland and manager Rube Foster separated and formed two distinct teams, with Foster's group winning the legal right to retain the name of Leland Giants. Leland's new team was called the Chicago Giants and continued through the deadball era, becoming a charter member of th Negro National League and fielding a league team the first two years (1920–21) of its existence. After dropping out of the Negro National League, the Chicago Giants were no longer a major-league-quality ballclub, although the team continued to function into the later '20s.

Chicago Leland Giants
[see Leland Giants]

Chicago Union Giants
Duration: 1901–04   Honors: None
Affiliation: Independent

In 1887 the team was called the Unions and played out of Chicago under the management of Abe Jones. After their initial season they became known as the Chicago Unions through the 1900 season. In 1899 the Columbia Giants had organized and quickly became a dominant team in the West. In 1901 Frank Leland combined the Chicago Unions and the Columbia Giants to form the Chicago Union Giants (1901–04), with himself as manager. They were recognized as a top team in the West, but lost a challenge playoff to the Algona Brownies in 1903 for the western championship. In 1905 they became the Leland Giants, with Frank Leland still acting as manager.

Chicago Unions
Duration: 1888–1900   Honors: Western champions ('94), western cochampions ('00)
Affiliation: Independent

In 1887 the team was called the Unions and played out of Chicago under the management of Abe Jones. After their initial season they became known as the Chicago Unions and were under the management of W. S. Peters from 1890 through the 1900 season, claiming the western championship in 1894. In 1899 they lost a challenge playoff to the Columbia Giants, and in 1900 there was a disputed championship between the same two teams. In 1901 Frank Leland ended the friction by combining the Chicago Unions and the Columbia Giants to form the Chicago Union Giants (1901–04), with himself as manager. In 1905 they assumed the manager's name and became the Leland Giants.

Childers, Wolf
Career: 1936   Position: c
Team: Cincinnati Tigers

He was a backup catcher with the Cincinnati Tigers in 1936, their last year as an independent team before joining the Negro American League for a season.

Childs, Andy
Career: 1936–45   Positions: 2b, p
Teams: St. Louis Stars ('36), Indianapolis Athletics ('37), Indianapolis ABCs ('38), Memphis Red Sox ('38, '44–'45)
Bats: Right   Throws: Right
Height: 5'7"   Weight: 140

The little, short ballplayer began his career as an infielder. He played second base and batted second in the order for the Indianapolis Athletics in 1937, and finished as a pitcher with the Memphis Red Sox, losing his only decision in 1945, his last season.

Childs, Charles
Career: 1909   Position: p
Team: Kansas City Royal Giants

In 1909, the team's best season, he was a pitcher for the Royal Giants of Kansas City, Missouri.

Chilton
Career: 1919   Position: of
Team: Detroit Stars

He was a reserve outfielder with the Detroit Stars in 1919, his only season with a top ballclub.

Chirban, Louis
Career: 1950   Position: p
Team: Chicago American Giants

He was one of three white players (along with Louis Clarizio and Al Dubetts) signed by the Chicago American Giants in 1950. In 1950 he pitched with the Chicago American Giants as a nineteen-year-old. He started against the Clowns and was hit hard, giving up five runs in only two innings. He pitched in two more games with an equal lack of effectiveness, hurling a total of only six innings, yielding 14 hits and 13 runs and losing all three decisions. He was a former Crane Tech athlete and was playing with a semipro team when signed by Ted "Double Duty" Radcliffe in late June.

Chism, Elijah (Eli, Little Chis)
Career: 1937, 1946–47 Position: of
Teams: St. Louis Stars ('37), Cleveland Buckeyes ('46), Birmingham Black Barons ('47, '51)
Died: April 4, 1982, St. Louis, Mo.

The light-hitting outfielder made his first appearance in 1937 as a reserve outfielder with the St. Louis Stars, but his playing time was very limited. Almost a decade passed before his second chance in the black big leagues, playing with the Cleveland Buckeyes and Birmingham Black Barons in the late '40s. With the Buckeyes, he is credited with a .210 batting average for the 1946 season. The following season he was the regular left fielder with the Black Barons, and hit .287 while he had good speed and was a successful base stealer, batting sixth in the order. In 1951, when the Negro American League was struggling to survive the loss of players to organized baseball, he played another season with the Black Barons.

Chretian, Ernest Joseph
Career: 1949–50   Positions: of, if
Teams: Kansas City Monarchs ('50), Philadelphia Stars ('50), *minor leagues ('53–'54)*
Bats: Right   Throws: Right

The beginning of his career coincided with the end of the Negro Leagues as a major-league caliber organization. A light-hitting utility man with a high strikeout ratio but without correlating power, he played both infield and outfield while splitting the 1950 season between the Kansas City Monarchs and the Philadelphia Stars, and batted .242. Three years later he spent two seasons (1953–54) in organized ball with the Lake Charles in the Gulf Coast League and Tallahassee in the FLorida International league. However, he hit only .232 and .135 in a utility role to close out his career.

Christian
[see Charleston, Oscar]

Christopher
[see Benjamin, Jerry]

Christopher, Ted
Career: 1949   Position: c
Team: New York Black Yankees
Bats: Right   Throws: Right
Height: 5'11"   Weight: 175

He made his only appearance with a Negro Leagues team in 1949, as a catcher with the New York Black Yankees.

Christopher, Thadist (Thaddeus, Thad, Ted)
Career: 1935–49 Positions: **of, 1b**, c
Teams: Nashville Elite Giants ('35), Washington Elite Giants ('36), Newark Eagles ('36, '41), Pittsburgh Crawfords ('37), *Santo Domingo ('37)*, New York Black Yankees ('38, '43–'46, '49), Ethiopian Clowns ('39), *Mexican League ('40)*, Cincinnati Buckeyes ('42), Cleveland Buckeyes ('43), Cincinnati Clowns ('43), Homestead Grays ('43)
Bats: Left   Throws: Right
Height: 6'1"   Weight: 185

The outfielder was a very good hitter who could pull the ball with some power, as shown in 1944, when he hit a home run completely out of the Polo Grounds. While noted for his bat, his speed, glovework, and range afield were only ordinary, and he often was placed at first base to get his bat in the lineup. He had a strong arm and was sometimes also utilized as a catcher.

Beginning his career with the Nashville Elites in 1935, he went with the franchise when it moved to Washington in 1936, but joined the Newark Eagles during the season, playing left field and hitting .257 for the year. In 1937 the Eagles traded Christopher and Harry Williams to the Pittsburgh Crawfords for Dick Seay and Jimmie Crutchfield, but Christopher jumped the Crawfords for the purported reason of going to Santo Domingo. The following spring, the outfielder was on the roster of the Atlanta Black Crackers when they secured their franchise for the Negro American League and was actively sought by the ballclub but never signed.

In 1940 he jumped again, this time to Mexico, where he hit .319 with eight homers for Torreon. After one year in the Mexican League he returned to the United States, signing with the Newark Eagles, playing in the side pastures, batting in the fifth slot, and hitting .263 for the 1941 season. Christopher was versatile, playing outfield with the Buckeyes in 1942–43 but serving as a reserve catcher for the Grays in the latter part of 1943 before the New York Black Yankees obtained him to handle the bulk of their catching duties. Once with the Black Yankees, he played more at first base and in the outfield, hitting .386 and .203 in 1944–45, and was their cleanup hitter the latter year.

Christopher claimed Miami as his hometown, and off the field, he was tall and handsome but also was a bit of a hard case, known both for carrying a knife and for his willingness to use it. Once, while with the Newark Eagles, the team was on a boat ride down the Hudson River and he got in a fight with another passenger. When his Eagles teammate Ray Dandridge got between them to try to stop the altercation, his new suit was cut to ribbons.

In 1949, after the demise of the Negro National League following the previous season, the New York Black Yankees began playing as an independent team. The quality of opposition was considerably less than when they were in the league, but that proved to be Christopher's last year in black baseball.

Cincinnati Buckeyes

Duration: 1942 Honors: None
Affiliation: NAL

Organized by Ernest Wright in 1942, the franchise was based in Cincinnati during it's initial season before moving to Cleveland for the 1943 season. Walter Burch was the first manager but was replaced by Parnell Woods during the season, making Woods the youngest pilot in the Negro Leagues at the time. No final standings were published, but the team finished the season in second place behind the Kansas City Monarchs, with an estimated record of 35–15.

Cincinnati Ethiopian Clowns

[see Miami Ethiopian Clowns]

Cincinnati Clowns

Duration: 1943 Honors: None
Affiliation: NAL

The Clowns' franchise began as the Miami Ethiopian Clowns, an outgrowth of the Miami Giants, and after years as an independent ballclub, joined the Negro American League. Some years the ballclub operated exclusively out of either Cincinnati or Indianapolis, while the two cities shared the franchise during other years. In 1943, the team's first entry into the Negro American League, Cincinnati was the home base for the team. Final standings were not published, but partial data indicate the Clowns were a losing ballclub during the 1943 season.

Cincinnati Tigers

Duration: 1934–37 Honors: None
Affiliations: Independent ('34–'36), NAL ('37)

After enjoying a measure of success playing as an independent team, especially in 1936, the club became a member of the Negro American League in its inaugural season. Under the guidance of manager Ted "Double Duty" Radcliffe, the Tigers finished in third place, with a

record of 15–11, for the first half of the Negro American League season. No final standings were published.

Cincinnati-Indianapolis Clowns

Duration: 1944–45 Honors: None
Affiliation: NAL

The Clowns' franchise began as the Miami Ethiopian Clowns, an outgrowth of the Miami Giants, and after years as an independent ballclub, joined the Negro American League. Some years the ballclub operated exclusively out of either Cincinnati or Indianapolis, while the two cities shared the franchise during other years. For two years, 1944–45, the Clowns played their home games in both cities. In 1944 the Clowns finished second in each half of the split season, with a combined record of 40–31 for a .563 winning percentage. The next season they dropped to a second-division finish with a combined record of 30–39 for a .435 winning percentage. Beginning in 1946 Indianapolis became the sole home site for the Clowns' franchise.

Clarizio, Louis

Career: 1950 Position: of
Team: Chicago American Giants

The outfielder was one of three white players (along with Louis Chirban and Al Dubetts) signed by the Chicago American Giants in 1950. He was a former Crane Tech athlete and was playing with a semipro team when signed by Chicago manager Ted "Double Duty" Radcliffe. Playing with the Chicago American Giants as an eighteen-year-old, in his first game, facing the Indianapolis Clowns, he struck out in his first two at-bats and was removed from the lineup. Soon afterward he was released by the team.

Clark

Career: 1887 Position: player
Team: *Louisville Falls City*

He was a player with the Louisville Falls City, one of eight teams that were charter members of the League of Colored Baseball

Clubs in 1887. However, the league's existence was ephemeral, lasting only a week. His position is uncertain.

Clark

Career: 1908–09   Positions: of, 2b
Teams: *Brooklyn Colored Giants ('08),* Brooklyn Royal Giants ('09)

In 1909 he was a center fielder with the Brooklyn Royal Giants, after playing second base with the Brooklyn Colored Giants the preceeding season.

Clark

Career: 1919   Position: of
Team: Brooklyn Royal Giants

He was listed as an outfielder with the Brooklyn Royal Giants in 1919, but little else is known about him.

Clark

Career: 1931   Position: of
Team: Louisville White Sox

The outfielder was a substitute and occasional starter in left field with the Louisville White Sox in 1931, their only season in the Negro National League.

Clark

Career: 1931   Position: p
Team: Kansas City Monarchs

He was a second-line pitcher with the Kansas City Monarchs in 1931 after they reorganized for the second half of the season and played as an independent team.

Clark

Career: 1950   Position: p
Team: New York Cubans

He pitched two games, winning his only decision, for the New York Cubans in 1950, when the Negro American League was struggling to survive the loss of players to organized baseball.

Clark, Albert

Career: 1919–26   Positions: **p**, c, of, ss

Teams: Dayton Marcos ('19–'20,'26), Pittsburgh Keystones ('21–'22), Cleveland Tate Stars ('22), Indianapolis ABCs ('23), Memphis Red Sox ('24), Cleveland Browns ('24)

A marginal pitcher playing mostly with teams on the periphery of the Negro National League, he began his career with the Dayton Marcos and pitched for two Cleveland entries in the Negro National League, the Tate Stars in 1922 and the Browns in 1924. During his eight years in the Negro Leagues he also played with the Indianapolis ABCs, the Memphis Red Sox, and the Pittsburgh Keystones before ending his career where it started, with the Dayton Marcos in their second entry in the Negro National League.

Clark, Albert (**A.D.**)

a.k.a. Clarke
Career: 1930–31   Positions: if, cf
Team: Chicago American Giants
Born: 1911, Fayette, Miss.

This contact hitter was a reserve outfielder with the Chicago American Giants for two seasons, 1930–31, but spent most of his career with barnstorming teams of lesser quality. The Mississippian played baseball at Alcorn College, serving as team captain, and hit a team-high .418 in his best season. Alcorn's ace pitcher was Willie Foster, who later became the greatest left-hander in the Negro Leagues. After tiring of the rigors of baseball barnstorming at age thirty-five, he continued his college studies at Atlanta University and embarked on a second career, in education as a high-school teacher and coach in Mississippi. After retiring in 1975 he moved to Baton Rouge, Louisiana.

Clark, Chiflan **Cleveland**

Career: 1945–50   Positions: **cf**, 1f, 1b
Team: New York Cubans ('45–'50)
Bats: Right   Throws: Right
Height: 5'11"   Weight: 177
Born: 1922

He joined the New York Cubans in 1945 as a twenty-three-year old center-field sensation fresh from a great year where he hit .361 with the Cuban winter league champion Almendares team. In spring training he showed tremendous power, good speed and grace, and an accurate throwing arm, but despite the promise exhibited in the spring, he managed only a .125 batting average in limited play as a reserve during his rookie season with the Cubans. In the ensuing winter (1945–46) he was on the All-Cuban team and won a starting position with the New York Cubans when he returned to the United States for the 1946 season, hitting .224 while batting in the fifth spot in the order.

The next season was his best in the Negro Leagues, as he hit .338 as the regular center fielder as the New York Cubans won the 1947 Negro National League pennant and defeated the Negro American League Cleveland Buckeyes in the World Series. Following his career season he played three more years with the Cubans, splitting his playing time between center field and left field while batting seventh in the order in 1948 and hitting .210 with average power in 1950.

Clark, Dell

Career: 1914–23   Position: ss
Teams: New York Lincoln Giants ('14, '19), St. Louis Giants ('21), Washington Potomacs ('23)

In a checkered career with top teams that began in 1914 and spanned a decade, he appeared intermittently as a reserve shortstop for the Lincoln Giants and the St. Louis Giants before earning a starting position with the Washington Potomacs in 1923. While sharing the regular shortstop position, he was the leadoff batter for manager Ben Taylor's Potomacs.

Clark, Harry

Career: 1922–25   Position: p
Teams: Brooklyn Royal Giants ('23), Hilldale Daisies, Atlantic City Bacharach Giants

He pitched four years with eastern ballclubs during the '20s in an undistinguished career.

Clark, John L.

Career: 1932–46   Position: officer

Teams: Pittsburgh Crawfords, Homestead Grays

During the '30s and '40s he was affiliated with both Pittsburgh-based teams, as business manager for the Pittsburgh Crawfords and as public relations director for the Homestead Grays. He also served as secretary of the Negro National League.

Clark, Maceo (Marty)

a.k.a. Clarke
Career: 1923–25   Positions: p, 1b
Teams; Homestead Grays ('23), Washington Potomacs ('23–'24), Wilmington Potomacs ('25), Atlantic City Bacharach Giants ('25)

He pitched and served as a reserve first baseman for manager Ben Taylor's Potomacs while the franchise was located in both Washington and Wilmington. In 1924 he pitched very briefly with the Washington Potomacs but was released during the first month of the season for more seasoning. He never really established himself with the more established league teams. He began his career in 1923, playing briefly with the Grays, and closed it with the Bacharachs in 1925.

Clark, Milton J., Jr.

Career: 1937   Position: officer
Team: Chicago American Giants

He served as secretary of the Chicago American Giants during the Negro American Leagues inaugural season.

Clark, Morten (Morten, Specs)

Career: 1910–23   Positions: ss, 3b, of, c
Teams: West Baden Sprudels ('10, '15), Brooklyn Royal Giants ('14), Indianapolis ABCs ('15–'21), Baltimore Black Sox ('23)
Bats: Right   Throws: Right

One of the first black ballplayers to wear glasses, he was a good defensive infielder and was described as "a whirlwind at shortstop" while playing with C. I. Taylor's ABC's in 1915–16. He also was a good hitter, batting fifth in the order for the ABCs in 1915 and 1916, hitting a "heavy" .227 and .274. He also contributed 25 stolen bases in 43 games in 1915 and 16 stolen bases in 40 games in 1916. His bat, baserunning, and especially his glovework were instrumental in the team's climb to the championship in 1916. The following season he suffered from eye problems and his play was affected, with his average dropping to .176. This was a different kind of problem than he had the previous season, when he had off-the-field "girlfriend problems."

Most of his career was spent in Indianapolis, and when the club joined the Negro National League in 1920, C. I. Taylor moved him to the top of the batting order, and he batted in the first or second spot until he left the ABCs after the 1921 season, when he hit for a .219 average in his final year in Indianapolis. The bespectacled infielder began his career with the West Baden, Indiana, Sprudels in 1910 and finished with the Baltimore Black Sox in 1923, sometimes playing third base or the outfield as well as his usual position.

Clark, Roy

Career: 1934–35   Position: p
Team: Newark Dodgers

He was a pitcher with the Newark Dodgers in 1934–35, but was not retained when the team was consolidated with the Brooklyn Eagles in 1936 to form the Newark Eagles.

Clark, William (Eggie, Biff)

Career: 1928   Position: of
Team: Memphis Red Sox

He was an outfielder with the 1928 Memphis Red Sox when they were in the Negro Southern League.

Clark, Wilson (Connie)

Career: 1922   Position: 2b
Team: Indianapolis ABCs

In his only year in the Negro Leagues, he was a reserve second baseman with the ABCs in 1922.

Clarke, Calvin (Allie)

a.k.a. Clark

Career: 1938   Positions: 2b, 1b, c
Team: Washington Black Senators

He was a second baseman and also played first base and catcher with the Washington Black Senators in 1938. He usually batted second in the order when in the lineup.

Clarke, Robert (Eggie, Bob, Kike)

a.k.a Clark

Career: 1923–48   Positions: c, 1b, ss, mgr
Teams: *Richmond Giants ('22–'23),* **Baltimore Black Sox** ('23–'32), **New York Black Yankees** ('33–'40), **Baltimore Elite Giants** ('41–'46), Philadelphia Stars
Bats: Right   Throws: Right
Height: 5'10"   Weight: 175
Born: 1906, Richmond, Va.

A smart player who was always thinking, he was a top-notch receiver for two decades and one of best handlers of pitchers in the league. He had a very accurate throwing arm, once beating Josh Gibson in a pregame throwing contest, when a bucket was placed at third base and Clarke hit it three times to Gibson's one successful throw. Clarke was slow afoot, which restricted him behind the plate and on the bases, but he was an asset to a pitching staff. He was a light hitter without power, but he could make contact and was considered "tricky" at the plate. Throughout his career he was generally placed at the bottom of the batting order.

After joining the Baltimore Black Sox as a backup receiver in 1923, his low batting marks restricted his playing time. But despite a .164 mark in 1925, he began sharing catching assignments in 1926, hit for respectable marks of .286 and .237 in 1927 and 1929, and remained the starting catcher through 1932 as the Sox moved through three leagues (ECL, ANL, and EWL) and a stint as an independent team.

The next season he began a long string of seasons behind the plate for the New York Black Yankees, when he was the regular catcher or shared the starting assignments for most of the eight years he was with the team. In his last season with the Black Yankees, despite a meager .129 batting average, his defensive skills warranted his selection to the East squad for the East-West All-Star game of 1940.

The next year the veteran joined the Baltimore Elite Giants and was a backup for Roy Campanella except for 1943, when Campy went to Mexico and Clarke moved into the starting position. In 1946 Campanella had signed in organized ball and Clarke again headed their backstopping corps. His batting marks are not very substantial as a backup, hitting only .145 and .164 for 1941–42, but when he was the regular receiver his mark jumped to .260 in 1943. His maintained a respectable average in 1944 with a .273 mark, but dropped back to the previous level with marks .091 and .174 in his last two years with the Elite Giants (1945–46).

The Richmond native had a big head and long hair, earning him the nickname ''Cayuka'' in Spanish-speaking countries.

Clarke, Vibert Ernesto (Webbo)
Career: 1946–50   Position: p
Teams: **Cleveland Buckeyes** ('46–'48), Louisville Buckeyes ('49), Memphis Red Sox ('50–'53), *minor leagues ('55–'57)*, major leagues ('55)
Bats: Left   Throws: Left
Height: 6'0"   Weight: 170
Born: June 8, 1928, Colón, Panama
Died: June 14, 1990, Cristobel, Canal Zone

The left-hander had a good fastball, a pretty good curve, and fair control. He pitched in the Negro Leagues for five years, breaking in with the Cleveland Buckeyes in 1946 with a record of 7–7 and attaining ace status the next season as he improved to an 11–2 record and the team cruised to their second Negro American League pennant in three years. In the losing World Series against the Negro National League New York Cubans, he pitched in two games, one in relief, without a decision. He dropped back to a 8–9 (3.67 ERA) and 4–10 (4.50 ERA) records the next two seasons and, in 1950, he moved to the Memphis Red Sox

and regained the winner's circle with a 13–10 ledger and a 2.98 ERA.

He pitched in the winter league of his native Panama for ten consecutive seasons beginning in 1945–46, compiling records of 4–3, 3–6, 6–5, 7–5, 9–5, 14–4, 5–6, 7–8, 6–8, and 1–9. His best year was in 1950–51 with the Spur Cola team, where he had 14–4 with 2.87 ERA. After a stint in organized ball he returned for two more season in Panama as his last hurrah with 2–2, 1.98 ERA in 1961–62 and 4–2, 3.09 ERA in 1963–64.

His stint in organized ball started at Charlotte in the South Atlantic League in 1955, where he was 16–12 and earned a shot at the big time with the Washington Senators. In the American League he pitched in seven games, mostly in relief, without a decision while compiling a 4.64 ERA. During his brief time in the major leagues he experienced some control problems, which contributed to his lack of effectiveness. The next two years in organized ball were split among five teams and four leagues, but he couldn't pitch well enough to warrant another shot at the big leagues, registering composite records of 7–20 and 7–12 in 1956–57.

Clarkson
[see Brazelton, Clarkson]

Clarkson, James Buster (**Bus**, Buzz)
Career: 1937–50   Positions: ss, 3b, 2b, of
Teams: Pittsburgh Crawfords ('37–'38), Toledo Crawfords ('39), Indianapolis Crawfords ('40), Newark Eagles ('40, '42), *Mexican League ('41, '46–'47)*, **Philadelphia Stars** ('42, '46, '49–'50), Baltimore Elite Giants, *military service ('43–'45), Canadian League ('48), minor leagues ('50–'56)*, major leagues ('52)
Bats: Right   Throws: Right
Height: 5'11"   Weight: 195
Born: Mar. 13, 1918, Hopkins. S.C.
Died: Jan 18, 1989, Jeannette, Pa.

A powerfully built right-handed power hitter who hit consistently and could pull the ball, he was a fine all-around fielder with a strong arm and could play any infield position. In his younger days he showed better than average speed on the bases. The Philadelphia Stars' shortstop made All-Star appearances in 1940 and 1949, and he finished his fourteen-year career in black baseball with a .359 lifetime average. In the Puerto Rican winter league he was the home-run leader in 1951 with 17 round-trippers. He belatedly made it to the major leagues at age thirty-four, as a utility infielder with the Boston Braves.

An all-around athlete, he played football and baseball at Wilberforce University, and was sought by both the Homestead Grays and the Pittsburgh Crawfords. After finishing his college schooling, he chose the Crawfords because he knew the manager, Oscar Charleston, and began his Negro League career with the Crawfords in 1937. He liked Charleston as a player and as a manager, and for the next three seasons he remained with the franchise as it was relocated in Toledo and Indianapolis. Leaving the Crawfords for the Newark Eagles in 1940, he rapped the ball for a .376 average. In 1941 he played with Tampico in the Mexican League and hit for a .334 average with 19 home runs, second only to Josh Gibson. Clarkson got off to a tremendous start in Mexico, slamming nine home runs in his first ten games, but then leveled out somewhat. As was his career pattern, the dangerous free-swinger had a high incident of both walks and strikeouts.

After only one season in Mexico, he returned to the Newark Eagles, a young and talented team with the promise of becoming an overpowering ballclub. But early in the spring, owner Abe Manley traded him to the Philadelphia Stars, where he led the team in round-trippers. In February 1943 he and Philly pitching ace Barney Brown were called to military service, and Clarkson spent three years (1943–45) in the Army during World War II.

After service, he was back in the Philadelphia Stars' lineup in 1946, batting cleanup and hitting .308 while ranking with the leading infielders in baseball. Late in the season he left

the Stars for a second stay in the Mexican sun. Playing with Veracruz, he hit .298 for the balance of the year and enjoyed another good season in 1947, batting .303 with 17 home runs to his credit. In the ensuing Cuban winter league he had an uncharacteristically poor season, batting a woeful .198. However, he was quick to rebound: Playing the '48 season with St. Jean in the Canadian Provincial League, he hit .399 with 28 home runs in 80 games.

Back with the Philly Stars in 1949, he hit .313 and made his second appearance in the East-West All–Star game. Clarkson began the 1950 season with the Stars but was signed by the Braves' organization and was sent to the Milwaukee Brewers in the American Association. In the season split between the Negro Leagues and organized ball, he hit .296 and .302, respectively. In 1951 he returned to Milwaukee for the entire season, and hit an impressive .343, and became the fans' favorite player.

The next season, after continuing his hard hitting with Milwaukee, he was brought up to the majors with the Boston Braves, where he had a cup of coffee to go with his .200 batting average in only 25 major-league at-bats. The Braves were rebuilding and had a young infield that included Eddie Mathews at third base, so Clarkson was expendable. After his brief major-league appearance he was assigned to Dallas in the Texas League, and he responded with a pair of memorable seasons (.330 batting average, 18 home runs, 87 RBIs, 100 walks; and .324 batting average, 42 home runs, 135 RBIs, 104 walks). In 1955 he was sent to Los Angeles in the Pacific Coast League and hit for a .294 average. The following season, which was to be his last, was split among three teams in three leagues (Pacific Coast League, Texas League, and Western League).

During the years that he was playing summers in organized ball, he was playing winters in Puerto Rico, where he hung up some good numbers for seven consecutive seasons, 1948–55, beginning with Ponce the first two winters (.309 and .286), and ending with Santurce the last two winters (.324 and .280).

Claxton, James E. (Jimmy)
Career: 1932   Position: p
Teams: *minor leagues ('16), Chicago Union Giants,* Cuban Stars ('32)
Bats: Left   Throws: Left
Born: 1892, Wellington, British Columbia, Canada

He was a pitcher with the Cuban Stars in the East-West League in 1932, the league's only season of existence, posting a 1–2 league record. Earlier in his career he had pitched with the Chicago Union Giants, a traveling team of lesser status, and posted a 20–1 record against all levels of opposition. Claxton's ancestry was predominantly European, but included approximately one-sixth black and an equal amount of Indian heritage. As a young man, disclaiming his African roots while acknowledging the Indian part, he passed for white and pitched with the Oakland Oaks in organized baseball in 1916.

The left-handed hurler was discovered while pitching with a black team called the Oakland Oaks by an Oklahoman named Hastings, who was part Indian and who passed Claxton off as being from his tribe. His minor-league career consisted of only five games, three starting assignments and two relief appearances, when he was released without a reason being given. Claxton felt that he was not given a fair chance by the manager to make the team, and suspects that someone informed the skipper of his true racial identity. Partial statistics indicate that he may have experienced some control problems, and he lost his only recorded decision.

He had started his amateur baseball career at age thirteen, as a left-handed catcher with a town team in Roslyn, Washington. In 1912, after five years behind the plate, he switched to the other end of the battery, pitching with the nearby Chester team. In his first outing, he registered 18 strikeouts. During his long career, he traveled all across the country, playing with a wide variety of teams. After settling in Ta-

coma, Washington, he pitched for the South Tacoma Pines at age fifty-two, and over a decade later, hurled two token innings in an old-timers' game at age sixty-three.

Clay, Albert Alton
Career: 1949–50   Position: of
Team: New York Black Yankees ('49–'50)

He was a reserve outfielder with the New York Black Yankees for parts of two seasons (1949–50), when the Negro American League was struggling to survive the loss of players to organized baseball.

Clay, William (Lefty)
Career: 1932   Position: p
Team: Kansas City Monarchs

He pitched with the Kansas City Monarchs in 1932 after they left the Negro National League and were touring as an independent team.

Clayton, Leroy Watkins (Zack)
Career: 1932–44   Positions: 1b, c
Teams: *Santop's Bronchos ('31),* Atlantic City Bacharach Giants ('32, '34, *'36),* Coles' American Giants ('35), Chicago American Giants ('37, '43), New York Black Yankees ('43–'44), *Chicago Brown Bombers*
Bats: Left   Throws: Left
Height: 5'11"   Weight: 190

He was a steady, solid player with average all-around ability in the field and on the bases, but a little light at bat. Although he was a first baseman, at times he was also pressed into service behind the plate. During his decade in the black big leagues he played in both the East and the West, but is most identified with the Chicago American Giants and New York Black Yankees. After a year with Santop's Bronchos, a semipro team of lesser quality, he joined the Bacharachs in 1932 but, with John Henry Lloyd at first base, there was not much opportunity for him to find any measure of playing time.

In 1935 he signed with Cole's American Giants, and incomplete data indicate that he experienced some difficulty at the plate. In 1937, the American Giants' first year in the Negro American League, he was the regular first baseman but batted at the bottom of the order. During the war years he moved back East, as the regular first baseman for the New York Black Yankees in 1943–44, and hit for averages of .171 and .213 while batting in the lower half of the order. Clayton was also an outstanding basketball player, even performing with the Globetrotters for a time, and is better known for his accomplishments in that sport than for his participation in baseball.

Cleage, Ralph (**Pete**)
Career: 1924; 1936   Positions: of, *1b,*
                      umpire
Teams: *Knoxville Black Giants ('20–'24),* St. Louis Stars ('24)
Bats: Left   Throws: Right
Height: 5'10"   Weight: 180
Born: 1898

After four seasons with the Knoxville Black Giants, he made the step up to the Negro National league as a reserve outfielder with the St. Louis Stars in 1924. He was not swift on the bases and did not pose a basestealing threat, and that was his only season with a top team. But although his playing career was short, he later became an umpire in the Negro National League, in 1936.

Cleveland Bears
Duration: 1939–40   Honors: None
Affiliation: NAL

The Jacksonville Red Caps moved North in 1939, using Cleveland as their home base and playing under the name Cleveland Bears in the Negro American League for two seasons, 1939 and 1940. Each season the team finished at .500 for the first half, and no final standings were published. The 1939 team was managed by Alonzo Mitchell, but he was replaced by Jim Williams for the 1940 season. The franchise moved back to Jacksonville for the 1941 season.

Cleveland Browns
Duration: 1924   Honors: None
Affiliation: NNL

During the 1920s and early 1930s Cleveland sought to have a franchise in the Negro Leagues but had no success until the Buckeyes moved to the city in 1943. The Cleveland Browns, managed by Sol White, was the city's second effort at establishing a viable league team. After their initial attempt to establish a league team in 1922, there was a season without Negro National League representation, and the Browns were an attempt to fill that void. Unfortunately, the 1924 season was a replay of the previous effort and the team finished last in an eight-team league, with a record of 15–34, and dropped from league play at the end of one season.

Cleveland Buckeyes
Duration: 1943–48,   Honors: NAL pennants
1950   ('45, '47), World Se-
                      ries champions ('45)
Affiliation: NAL

In 1942, when the franchise was first organized, some games were played in Cleveland, but a permanent move was not made until the ballclub moved from Cincinnati in 1943 and remained until 1949, when they moved to Louisville for a season before returning in 1950. The highlight of the franchise's history came in 1945, when catcher-manager Quincey Trouppe led the Buckeyes to a Negro American League pennant (winning both halves of the split season and finishing with an overall 53–16 record for a .768 winning percentage) and a sweep of the Homestead Grays in the Negro World Series. The Buckeyes, under Trouppe's tutelage, captured another flag in 1947 with a 54–23 record (.701 pct.) but lost the World Series to the New York Cubans in five games.

Cleveland Cubs
Duration: 1931   Honors: None
Affiliation: NNL

During the 1920s and early 1930s, Cleveland sought to have a franchise in the Negro Leagues, but had no success until the Buckeyes moved to the city in 1943. The city's final effort at establishing a viable league team in the first Negro National League was the Cleveland Cubs, who were owner Tom Wilson's Nashville Elite Giants relocated in Cleveland and playing under a different name. Wilson's entry into Cleveland came after three seasons without a Negro League team in the city. The team featured Satchel Paige and, although no final standings were published, incomplete records credit the Cubs with a 24–22 ledger, the first time a Cleveland team had been above .500. Unfortunately, neither the league, the team, nor Paige would survive the season. The Negro National League folded, Wilson moved his team back to Nashville, and Paige signed with Gus Greenlee's Pittsburgh Crawfords even before the season was over. With his exit, the team fell on leaner times and the franchise's exit was inevitable.

Cleveland Elites

Duration: 1926   Honors: None
Affiliation: NNL

During the 1920s and early 1930s, Cleveland sought to have a franchise in the Negro Leagues but had no success until the Buckeyes moved to the city in 1943. The city's third effort at establishing a viable league team was the Cleveland Elites, managed by Candy Jim Taylor, who had managed the city's first entry in the Negro National League in 1922. Each of the first two attempts at establishing a league team resulting in an aftermath of a season without Negro National League representation. The Elites were another attempt to fill that void. Unfortunately, the 1926 season was as unsuccessful as the two previous efforts, and at the end of the first half, the team was in last place in an eight-team league, and failed to finish the second half of the season, showing a 6–38 record for a worse winning percentage (.136) than either of its predecessors. The Elites did

not reapply for admission to the league for the next season.

Cleveland Giants

Duration: 1933   Honors: None
Affiliation: NNL

During the 1920s and early 1930s, Cleveland sought to have a franchise in the Negro Leagues but had no success until the Buckeyes moved to the city in 1943. After many unsuccessful attempts to maintain a team in the NNL, the league itself folded following the 1931 season. After a year of chaos, a new Negro National League was organized for the 1933 season. During the second half of the season, the Columbus Blue Birds dropped out of the league and the Cleveland Giants, with the addition of some of the Columbus players, became their replacement for the remainder of the season. However, the second-half schedule was not completed and no standings are available.

Cleveland Hornets

Duration: 1927   Honors: None
Affiliation: NNL

During the 1920s and early 1930s, Cleveland sought to have a franchise in the Negro Leagues but had no success until the Buckeyes moved to the city in 1943. The city's fourth effort at establishing a viable league team was the Cleveland Hornets. The Hornets were the first entry that did not follow a season without Negro National League representation, following in the year after the Elites had failed. Unfortunately, the 1927 season was as unsuccessful as all the previous efforts, and at the end of the first half the team was in last place in an eight-team league. No standings were published for the second half, but the Hornets are credited with a final record of 14–38. The Hornets were replaced in 1928 by the Cleveland Tigers, a new franchise.

Cleveland, Howard (Duke)

a.k.a. Dukes
Career: 1938–46   Position: of
Teams: Jacksonville Red Caps ('38, '41–'42),

Cleveland Bears ('39–'40), Cincinnati Buckeyes ('42), Cleveland Buckeyes ('43), Indianapolis Clowns ('46)

Playing in his hometown, the Jacksonville Red Caps' outfielder had good power at the plate and appeared in the 1941 East-West All-Star game, hitting safely as a pinch hitter. He batted in the third spot in the order in both 1941 and 1942. When the Red Caps dropped out of the league in July, he joined the Cincinnati Buckeyes, and maintained a blistering .405 batting average for the first half of the 1942 season. In 1946, his last season in the Negro Leagues, he played right field for the Indianapolis Clowns, hitting .231 while batting seventh in the order. In Cleveland he was sometimes listed in box scores as either Duke or Dukes.

Cleveland Red Sox
Duration: 1934   Honors: None
Affiliation: NNL

During the 1920s and early 1930s, Cleveland sought to have a franchise in the Negro Leagues but had no success until the Buckeyes moved to the city in 1943. Their final effort at establishing a viable Negro National League team came in 1934, when the Cleveland Red Sox joined the league. At the end of the first half of the split season, the team finished last in a six-team league and played only five games during the second half, finishing with a combined record of 4–25 and dropping from league play at the end of the season.

Cleveland Stars
Duration: 1932   Honors: None
Affiliation: EWL

During the 1920s and early 1930s, Cleveland sought to have a franchise in the Negro Leagues but had no success until the Buckeyes moved to the city in 1943. After a half dozen unsuccessful attempts to maintain a team in the Negro National League, the league itself folded. In 1932, in an effort to fill the organizational void, the East-West League was formed. The Cleveland Stars were the city's entry in the new league. Unfortunately, the league could not remain solvent and became a victim of the Depression before the season could be completed. The last published standings show the Stars with a record of 8–16, placing them sixth in a seven-team league.

Cleveland Tate Stars
Duration: 1922   Honors: None
Affiliation: NNL

During the 1920s and early 1930s, Cleveland sought to have a franchise in the Negro Leagues but had no success until the Buckeyes moved to the city in 1943. Their first effort at establishing a viable league team came in 1922, when the Cleveland Tate Stars, managed by Candy Jim Taylor, joined the Negro National League. The team finished last in an eight-team league, with a record of 17–29, and dropped from league play at the end of one season.

Cleveland Tigers
Duration: 1928   Honors: None
Affiliation: NNL

During the 1920s and early 1930s, Cleveland sought to have a franchise in the Negro Leagues but had no success until the Buckeyes moved to the city in 1943. The city's last effort in the decade at establishing a viable league team was the Cleveland Tigers, managed by former Chicago American Giants outfield star Frank Duncan. Final standings of the Negro National League's 1928 season were not published, but the Tigers are credited with a record of 19–53 and a seventh-place finish in an eight-team league. After their unsuccessful season there was not another attempt to field a Negro National League team in Cleveland for three more years.

Clifford, Luther
Career: 1948–50   Positions: c, of
Teams: Homestead Grays ('48, '50), Kansas City Monarchs ('49), *Clowns ('53)*
Bats: Right   Throws: Right
Height: 6'0"   Weight: 200

He was usually a backup catcher, but in

1948 he alternated with Eudie Napier as the regular receiver for the Homestead Grays, hitting .239 while batting in the seventh slot in the order. The Grays won the Negro National League pennant in the league's last year of existence, and defeated the Birmingham Black Barons in the World Series. The next season he played with the Kansas City Monarchs in the Negro American League for a year before returning to the Grays, who were touring as an independent team and no longer were a ballclub of major-league caliber. After the 1950 season the Grays disbanded and Clifford, who also played in the outfield on occasion, later played with the Indianapolis Clowns in 1953, but the team was then strictly a minor-league ballclub.

Clifton, Nathaniel (Nat, **Sweetwater**)
Career: 1949   Position: 1b
Teams; Chicago American Giants ('49), *Detroit Stars ('49), minor leagues ('49–'50)*
Bats: Left   Throws: Right
Height: 6'8"   Weight: 235
Born: October 13, 1922, Chicago, Ill.
Died: Sept. 2, 1990, Chicago, Ill.

The reknowned basketball great with the Globetrotters and the New York Knickerbockers also played baseball. In 1949 he played first base with four different teams in four league scenarios, the Chicago American Giants in the Negro American League, the Detroit Stars an independent black team, Pittsfield in the Can-Am League (.275 batting average), and Dayton in the Central League (.322 batting average). At Dayton he demonstrated good power but had a high strikeout total. In 1950 he played with Wilkes-Barre in the Eastern League and hit .304.

Clinton
Career: 1917   Positions: 3b, rf
Team: Atlantic City Bacharach Giants

A light hitter, he was a regular with the Bacharachs in 1917, during their formative years, and split his playing time between third base and right field while batting seventh in the order.

Close, Herman
Career: 1887   Position: manager
Team: *Philadelphia Pythians*

He was the manager for the Philadelphia Pythians, one of eight teams that were charter members of the League of Colored Baseball Clubs in 1887. However, the league's existence was ephemeral, lasting only a week.

Cobb, L.S.N.
Career: 1920–34   Position: officer
Teams: St. Louis Giants, Birmingham Black Barons, Memphis Red Sox

A club officer with three teams over a fifteen-year period in the Negro National League, he also served as secretary of the Negro National League.

Cobb, W.
Career: 1914–20, 1928 Positions: c, of
Teams: West Baden Sprudels ('14), **St. Louis Giants** ('15–'17, '20), Indianapolis ABCs ('17), Jewell's ABCs, New York Lincoln Giants ('18), Brooklyn Royal Giants ('18), St. Louis Stars ('28)

He was a catcher during the last half of the '10s, primarily with teams based in St. Louis and Indianapolis. Playing with the ABCs in the late summer of 1917, he was unable to stop Rube Foster's racehorse Chicago American Giants from stealing as they ran the bases rather freely against him. Partial statistics indicate that he had a measure of difficulty with the bat as well, showing a .185 average in limited play.

The next year he journeyed to New York for a season spent mostly with the Lincoln Giants and, with a .353 average against all levels of competition, appeared to have found his batting eye. He returned to the Midwest in 1920, joining the St. Louis Giants for the inaugural season of the Negro National League. With the Giants he shared the regular catching assignments, while hitting fifth in the batting order when in the lineup. During his career he also played occasionally in the outfield. After seven seasons he dropped out of play, but reappeared in 1928 as a reserve player with the St. Louis Stars for a final season.

Cockerell
[see Cockrell, Phil]

Cockerham, Jimmy
Career: 1939   Position: 1b
Team: Indianapolis ABCs

He was a reserve first baseman with the Indianapolis ABCs in 1939, but his playing time was limited.

Cockrell, Phillip (**Phil**, Fish)
a.k.a. Cockerell; Phillip Williams (his real name)
Career: 1917–34; 1935–46 Positions: *p*, of, manager, umpire
Teams: Havana Red Sox ('*13*–'17), New York Lincoln Giants ('18–'19), **Hilldale Daisies** ('18–'32), Atlantic City Bacharach Giants ('21, '32–'33), Philadelphia Stars ('34)
Bats: Right   Throws: Right
Height: 5'8"   Weight: 160
Born: 1898, Augusta, Ga.
Died: Mar. 31, 1951, Philadelphia, Pa.

A star spitballer for the Hilldale club during their pennant-winning years of 1923–25, the right-hander had an excellent fastball and good control to complement his spitter. He registered a 24–8 record in 1923 against all competition and posted league ledgers of 10–1 and 14–2 the latter two years. In each of these seasons Hilldale played the Kansas City Monarchs in a World Series played between the Eastern Colored League and the Negro National League, and Cockrell started two games in each Series. In the 1924 Series he started the opening game but lost to Bullet Rogan for his only Series decision that year. The two teams were evenly matched and it took ten hard-fought games before the Monarchs could claim the title. In the 1925 World Series rematch Cockrell split two decisions but won the sixth

and conclusive game to clinch the championship for Hilldale. In the two Series he compiled a composite ERA of 3.04.

He first joined Hilldale in 1918, after a stint with the Havana Red Sox, showing a 6–3 record for the season. In 1921, with the team still playing as an independent club, he registered a 14–11 season, pitching against all levels of opposition. After the string of three straight pennants, he followed with a 14–2 season in 1926, but dropped to losing marks the next two years with records of 11–13 and 8–12. After being with Hilldale as a player during their halcyon years, he replaced Oscar Charleston as manager in May 1929, when the team was in the American Negro League, and brought the team home with a strong second-place finish in the second half of the season, contributing his own 6–3 mark on the mound. However, the league folded after a single season and Hilldale returned to play as an independent team. Cockrell experienced a pair of flip-flop seasons in 1930–31, with records of 1–5 and 8–1. The next year he split the season between Hilldale and the Bacharachs, finishing with a composite 2–7 record. He closed out his playing career in 1934 with the Negro National League champion Philadelphia Stars, but was not a factor in their success, managing only one win in five decisions.

The next season he was manager of the Bacharachs and later formed his own team for a short time. During his career he was credited with four no-hitters, including a 1922 gem against Rube Foster's champion Chicago American Giants. He was also a good-hitting pitcher and, although he struck out more than average, he was sometimes utilized in the outfield or as a pinch hitter. While with Hilldale he formed a close friendship with teammate George "Dibo" Johnson that extended beyond the baseball diamond, and he and Johnson roomed together after their playing careers ended.

At the same time, Cockrell began a second baseball career, as an umpire in the Negro National League; that lasted through the 1946 season. Umpiring in the Negro Leagues could be hazardous, and Cockrell once made a call on a close play that infuriated Jud Wilson. In the locker room after the game, the enraged Wilson grabbed him by the skin of his chest and lifted him off the floor. Fortunately, cooler heads prevailed and Cockrell was rescued, and went on to complete a career that spanned thirty-four years in baseball. However, fewer than five years after his retirement, the ex-spitballer was the victim of a homicide in a case of mistaken identity, when he was shot by a jealous husband as he walked out of a bar.

Coffey, Marshall
Career: 1889   Position: 2b
Team: Chicago Unions
He was the starting second baseman for the Chicago Unions in 1889.

Cohen, James Clarence (**Jim**, Fireball)
Career: 1946–50   Position: p
Teams: *military service ('42–'46),* Indianapolis Clowns ('46–'52)
Bats: Right   Throws: Right
Height: 5'11"   Weight: 190
Born: Mar. 26, 1918, Evergreen, Ala.

A fastball pitcher with the Indianapolis Clowns in the post-World War II era, his primary asset on the mound was his fine control. While he also had a curve, slider, and change-up, he most often utilized a knuckleball as his off-speed pitch to keep batters off stride for his fastball. He logged records of 3–8 with a 3.90 ERA in 1948 and 2–3 with a 3.64 ERA in 1950. The former season, he was in uniform for the East-West All-Star game but did not get into the lineup. A second All-Star game was played that season, and he pitched a three-inning stint. The following winter, 1948–49, he played his only season in Latin American leagues, when he was with Vargas in Caracas, Venezuela.

As a youngster in Pennsylvania, he played football, basketball, and track in high school, but the school did not have a baseball team. However, he went into the coal mines after high school, and the coal camps had baseball teams, which gave him his start in baseball. He was drafted into the Army in 1942 and, while assigned to the Replacement Training Center at Camp Lee, Virginia, he played on the baseball team for four years, and was signed by the Clowns while still in service. After his discharge in January 1946, he went to spring training with Syd Pollock's Clowns.

During his years with the ballclub, he also served at times as bus driver and business manager, but when asked to take a pay cut in 1952, he quit baseball and took a regular job with the postal service in Washington, D.C., where he worked for 35 years until retiring in 1982.

Coimbre, Francisco (Frank, **Pancho**, Al)
a.k.a. Francisco Coimbre Atiles
Career: 1940–46   Position: of
Teams: New York Cubans ('40–'41, '43–'44, '46)
Bats: Right   Throws: Right
Height: 5'11"   Weight: 180
Born: Jan. 29, 1909, Coamo, Puerto Rico
Died: Nov. 4, 1989, Ponce, Puerto Rico

A five-point player, he was a strong hitter with a natural swing and sprayed hits to all fields but also had good power and could go for the long ball when needed. He was also an outstanding fielder with good range, hands, and arm. A hustler, he had good speed on the bases and was a threat to steal.

He starred for the New York Cubans during the '40s, beginning his Negro League career in 1940, playing right field and batting second in the order while hitting .330. The next year he moved into the cleanup spot and hit .353 with a slugging percentage of .500. He remained in Puerto Rico in 1942, but returned to his cleanup spot with the Cubans in 1943 and is credited with a .436 batting average. In 1944 he hit .357 and had a .510 slugging percentage to earn a berth in the starting lineup in the All-Star game, his second starting assignment for the East squad in the classic.

In Puerto Rico he was considered to have a "touch of royalty" and, prior to Roberto Clemente (with whom he had a "father-son relationship"), was regarded as the best Puerto Rican player ever. Clemente acknowledged Coimbre as his superior and, even now, Coimbre still remains one of the greatest Puerto Rican players of all time. He won the batting title in his homeland with a .342 average for th 1942–43 winter season, and again in 1944–45 with a .425 average. The previous winter in Cuba, the outfielder had hit a resounding .401.

With Ponce during the decade of the '40s (excluding the 1942–43 winter) he compiled consecutive batting averages of .401, .372, .376, 425, .333, .333, .323, and .336 and finished with a lifetime Puerto Rican batting average of .337. A member of Ponce's sports Hall of Fame, he also established the Puerto Rican record for hitting safely in the most consecutive games (22), and Satchel Paige once called him the best hitter he ever faced.

With his extraordinary vision and good eye-hand coordination, he rarely struck out. He played two consecutive Puerto Rican winter seasons (1941–42 and 1942–43) without striking out. In the 1948–49 winter he had only one strikeout in 239 at-bats during the season. In 13 years in Puerto Rico, he had 1915 at-bats and only 29 strikeouts.

In addition to his accomplishments in the United States and Puerto Rico, he also played in Venezuela, Mexico, Canada, Colombia, and the Dominican Republic. He began his baseball career in 1926 at age seventeen, and after retiring in 1951, he scouted for the Pittsburgh Pirates for twenty-five years and operated a baseball school for boys. He died tragically in 1989, at age 80, in Ponce, Puerto Rico, when a fire razed his home.

Colas, Carlos (Charles, Charlie)
Career: 1940–50   Positions: c, of
Teams: Cuban Stars ('40), New York Cubans ('41), Memphis Red Sox ('49–'52)
Bats: Right   Throws: Right

After breaking in as a catcher with the Cuban Stars in 1940, he shared the catching duties with the New York Cubans in 1941, hitting .281 while batting at the bottom of the lineup. Almost a decade later, he joined the Memphis Red Sox in 1949, hitting .242 and .268 with average power during his first two seasons with the team while pilfering 18 bases in 58 games in 1950. He continued catching with the Red Sox for two more years, although the Negro American League had declined in quality and had become strictly a minor league. At Memphis his brother José Colas was a teammate. Carlos also played in Mexico and Cuba.

Colas, José Luis
Career: 1947–50   Positions: cf, manager
Teams: Memphis Red Sox ('47–'51), *minor leagues ('52, '54)*
Bats: Right   Throws: Right
Born: Cuba

In his first year with the Memphis Red Sox, the outfielder played in the 1947 All-Star game, getting two hits in the West's 5–2 victory. As a second-year player, he was inserted into the third slot in the batting order and followed with another good season, batting .310. However, his production dropped the next two years, as he finished with averages of .247 and .268.

Colas was aggressive at the plate and infrequently walked. He spent most of the 1952 season with Brandon in the Mandak League but played briefly with Scranton in the Eastern League. His short stint was unimpressive (.152 batting average in 13 games), and his next excursion into organized ball was in 1954 with Mount Vernon in the Mississippi-Ohio Valley League, where he hit .238 as an outfielder-infielder.

At Memphis his brother Carlos Colas was a teammate. Later in his career, José was a manager with the Memphis Red Sox.

Cole
Career: 1924   Position: p
Team: Detroit Stars

In his only year in the Negro Leagues, he pitched briefly with the Detroit Stars in 1924.

Cole, Cecil
a.k.a. Coles
Career: 1946   Position: p
Team: Newark Eagles
Bats: Right   Throws: Right
Height: 5'9"   Weight: 170

A strong second-line pitcher with the 1946 Negro National League champion Newark Eagles, he finished the season with a 2–2 record. His fastball was the best of his standard three-pitch repertory, but he had only average control. He fielded his position adequately but was weak in hitting and baserunning.

Cole, Ralph (Punjab)
a.k.a. Askari
Career: 1939–46   Positions: lf, cf
Teams: Cleveland Bears ('39–'40), Jacksonville Red Caps ('41), Ethiopian Clowns ('42), Cincinnati Clowns ('43), Indianapolis Clowns ('46)

The outfielder was part-time starter with the Cleveland Bears in 1939–40, playing left field and usually batting sixth in the order. When the franchise moved back to Jacksonville and resumed playing as the Red Caps, he held his starting left field position and the same spot in the batting order. After the Red Caps dropped out of the league in 1942, he joined the Clowns.

Cole, Robert A.
Career: 1932–35   Positions: owner, officer
Team: Chicago American Giants

An undertaker with a limited knowledge and understanding of baseball, he was owner of the American Giants in 1932–35. Having gained control of the team after the demise of the Negro National League, he renamed the team after himself. Known as Cole's American Giants, the franchise again rose to prominence in 1932–34, winning pennants the first two years before losing a hard-fought League

Championship Series to the Philadelphia Stars in 1934. The first of the two pennants came while playing in the Negro Southern League and the second in the new Negro National League. He also served as treasurer of the Negro National League and vice president of the Negro Southern League.

Cole, William
Career: 1896–1899   Positions: c, p
Team: Cuban Giants

In two appearances with the Cuban Giants, one of the top teams of the era, he played as a catcher in 1896 and pitched with the team in 1899.

Coleman
Career: 1932   Position: rf
Team: Newark Browns ('31–'32)

The outfielder first appeared with the Newark Browns in 1931, a year before they entered the East-West League, and hit fifth in the batting order as their regular right fielder in 1932, until the demise of the league.

Coleman, Benny
Career: 1950   Position: p
Team: Chicago American Giants

He was a pitcher with the Chicago American Giants in 1950, when the Negro American League was struggling to survive the loss of players to organized baseball.

Coleman, Clarence (Pops)
Career: 1913–26   Positions: p, c, 1b, 2b, of
Teams: Bowser's ABCs ('16), All Nations ('17), Chicago Union Giants ('17–'18), Indianapolis ABCs ('18), St. Louis Giants ('19), Chicago Giants ('13, '20), Dayton Marcos ('20), Columbus Buckeyes ('21), Cleveland Tate Stars ('19, '22), *Gilkerson's Union Giants ('23–'24)*, New York Lincoln Giants ('26)

A literate ballplayer, Coleman was with several different teams for various seasons at a wide range of positions. Most of the teams were marginal and struggling to maintain a major-league quality of play, and he was not a central player. With the Indianapolis ABCs in 1918, partial statistics show only a .176 batting average in limited play. In 1920, the inaugural season of the Negro National League, he was a pitcher and occasional right fielder. His last year with a league team was as a reserve with the Cleveland Tate Stars in 1922, their only year in the Negro National League, but he continued playing afterward with the independent Unions Giants as a catcher.

Coleman, Gilbert
Career: 1927–33   Positions: 2b, ss, of
Teams: *Chappie Johnson's All-Stars ('27), Brooklyn Cuban Giants ('28),* Bacharach Giants ('32), Newark Dodgers ('33)
He was an infielder with the Brooklyn Cuban Giants in 1928 and was an outfielder with the Bacharach Giants in 1932.

Coleman, John
Career: 1950   Position: p
Team: Elite Giants
Beginning his career in 1950, when the Negro American League was struggling to survive the loss of players to organized baseball, he pitched with the Baltimore Elite Giants, recording a 5–2 ledger with a 3.53 ERA.

Coleman, Melvin (Slick)
a.k.a. Macon
Career: 1937–41   Positions: ss, c
Teams: Birmingham Black Barons ('37–'39), Ethiopian Clowns ('40–'41)
Beginning his career in 1937 as the regular shortstop and hitting sixth in the batting order for the Birmingham Black Barons, he stayed with the Black Barons for three seasons, during which he also logged some playing time behind the plate. In 1940 he played with the Ethiopian Clowns while listed under his Clown name of Macon.

Cole's American Giants
Duration: 1932–35   Honors: Pennants ('32–'33), first-half NNL title ('34)
Affiliations: NSL ('32), NNL ('33–'35)

This team was only an interim continuation of the Chicago American Giants, a franchise organized by Rube Foster in 1910 and which was taken over by a new owner, Robert A. Cole, who renamed the team after himself and ran it for four years (1932–35). The team won pennants the first two years before losing a hard-fought League Championship Series to the Philadelphia Stars in 1934. The first of the two pennants came while playing in the Negro Southern League and the second in the newly reorganized Negro National League. Following the 1935 season, Cole had financial difficulties and divested himself of the team. The team's accomplishments are properly included as a segment of the history of the Chicago American Giants rather than as a separate franchise. [see also Chicago American Giants]

Coley
Career: 1923–34   Position: p
Teams: Toledo Tigers ('23), Kansas City ('23), Detroit Stars ('24)
During two years in the '20s, he pitched without distinction for three different teams in the Negro National League. Prior to entering league play, he also pitched with the Madison Stars, a lesser team.

Coley
Career: 1931   Position: of
Team: Nashville Elite Giants
The reserve outfielder appeared briefly with the Nashville Elite Giants in 1931.

Collier
Career: 1928   Positions: c, rf
Team: Atlantic City Bacharach Giants
In 1928 he was a reserve player for the Bacharachs, appearing as a backup catcher and as an outfielder to provide bench strength for the team.

Colliers, Leonard
Career: 1950   Position: p
Team: Cleveland Buckeyes
He began his pitching career with the Cleve-

land Buckeyes in 1950, when the Negro American League was struggling to survive the loss of players to organized baseball, and suffered through a 0–7 season with a 9.21 ERA.

Collins

Career: 1910–18   Positions: c, 1b
Teams: *New York Black Sox,* Brooklyn Royal Giants ('10), Pennsylvania Red Caps of New York ('18), New York Lincoln Giants ('18), *Pittsburgh Giants, Philadelphia Giants*

He played with several New York-based teams during the '10s, mostly as a reserve or with marginal teams. Early in his Career (1910) he was a reserve first baseman with the eastern champion Brooklyn Royal Giants, and late in his career (1918) he was a reserve catcher with the Lincoln Giants, with partial statistics showing a .381 average in limited play.

Collins

Career: 1928   Position: p
Team: Baltimore Black Sox

The pitcher played briefly with the Baltimore Black Sox in 1928, the last year of the Eastern Colored league.

Collins, Eugene (Gene)

Career: 1947–50   Positions: **p**, of
Teams: Kansas City Monarchs ('47–'51), *minor leagues ('51–'54), Mexican League ('55–'61)*
Bats: Left   Throws: Left
Height: 5'10"   Weight: 165
Born: January 7, 1925, Kansas City, Mo.

He was a pitcher-outfielder with the Kansas City Monarchs for five years, 1947–51, when the Negro Leagues were in decline. The left-hander was primarily a pitcher during his first two seasons with the club, but the emphasis began to shift more toward his play as an everyday player during the last two seasons, a trend that continued into his years in organized ball. As a pitcher the left-hander was strong and had an excellent fastball, a good curve, and an outstanding move to first base. As an

outfielder he was a hustler with good range and an outstanding arm. He also had good speed on the bases but was only mediocre at bat, with less than average power.

His best season as a pitcher was in 1948, when he was 9–3 with a 2.23 ERA. The next season he was 8–4 with a 3.38 ERA, followed by a 3–0 log in 1950, when he was used much more as an outfielder. His corresponding batting averages were .243, .299, and .227.

In 1951 he made his entrance into organized ball at Waterloo, Iowa, in the Three-I League and was used primarily as a pitcher (7–2, 3.27 ERA). The next season was split among three different leagues, where he compiled a composite 2–2 ledger while gaining more playing time in the outfield. This pattern continued through the next season as he logged a 3–3 record while splitting his time between two leagues.

Beginning in 1955 he spent the remainder of his career in Mexico, with his best season, both on the mound and at the plate, coming his first year (7–5, 4.62 ERA; .336, 13 home runs). Used mostly as an outfielder for the remainder of his career, he hit for averages of .276, .275, .324, .281, .317, and .230 through 1961. During his career he also played one winter each in Puerto Rico (1948–49) and Pompero, Venezuela (1958–59), where he led the league with a .356 batting average.

Collins, George

Career: 1922–25   Positions: of, 2b, ss, p
Teams: Kansas City Monarchs ('22), *New Orleans Crescent Stars ('22–'23),* Toledo Tigers ('23), Milwaukee Bears ('23), Indianapolis ABCs ('25), *Nashville Elite Giants ('27)*

Beginning his league career with the Kansas City Monarchs in 1922, he also played with the Indianapolis ABCs during his spotted career with assorted teams in the Midwest and the South. Showing more versatility than talent, he played outfield, infield, and even did some pitching with ballclubs that were predominantly of marginal quality, but he was never a regular with a league team.

Collins, Nathan Fred (Nat)
Career: 1888–89   Position: p
Teams: New York Gorhams ('88–'89)

He pitched with the New York Gorhams, one of the earliest black professional teams, when they played in the Middle States League in 1888 and when they represented Philadelphia in 1889.

Collins, Sonny
Career: 1934–36   Position: p
Teams: Atlantic City Bacharach Giants ('34), New York Black Yankees ('36)

Both of his seasons in the Negro Leagues were spent with teams that began the year as an independent team but joined the Negro National League for the second half of the season. In 1934 he was a member of the Bacharachs' pitching staff in their last season in league play, and two years later he pitched with the New York Black Yankees in their first year in league play.

Collins, Walter
Career: 1947–48   Positions: p
Teams: American Giants ('47), Memphis Red Sox ('48), *Indianapolis Clowns ('51–'52)*

This pitcher began his career with the American Giants in 1947 and moved to the Memphis Red Sox in 1948, winning his only decision. While the Negro American League was struggling to survive the loss of players to organized baseball, he continued to play with the Indianapolis Clowns in 1951–52, although the Negro American League was strictly a minor league at the time.

Collins, Willie
Career: 1933   Position: of
Team: *Nashville Elite Giants*

In 1933 he was a reserve outfielder with the Nashville Elite Giants, when they were in the Negro Southern League.

Collins, Willie P. (James)
Career: 1950   Position: p
Teams: Birmingham Black Barons

He began his pitching career with the Birmingham Black Barons in 1950, when the Negro American League was struggling to survive the loss of players to organized baseball, and registered a 3–3 season with a 5.01 ERA.

Colthirst
Career: 1948   Position: ss
Team: Indianapolis Clowns

He was a reserve shortstop with the Indianapolis Clowns in 1948, his only year in the Negro Leagues.

Columbia Giants
Duration: 1899–1900   Honors: Western champions ('99), Western cochampions ('00)
Affiliation: Independent

The Columbia Giants were organized in 1899 and, operating out of Chicago, quickly became a dominant team in the West. Many of their players came from the disbanded Page Fence Giants and, in some respects, could be viewed as a franchise relocation under different management. Although existing for only two years, they were involved in the championship both seasons. In 1899 they defeated the more established Chicago Unions in a challenge playoff for the western championship, and in 1900 they again claimed the championship, but in the absence of a playoff, the title remained in dispute between the same two teams from the previous year. In 1901 Frank Leland ended the disagreement by combining the Chicago Unions and the Columbia Giants to form the Chicago Union Giants, with himself as manager.

Columbus Blue Birds
Duration: 1933   Honors: None
Affiliation: NNL

The ballclub operated only part of one season, 1933, the first year of the reconstituted Negro National League. After finishing in the cellar in the first half, the franchise folded in August and was replaced by the Cleveland Giants.

Columbus Buckeyes
Duration: 1921   Honors: None
Affiliation: NNL

A second-division ballcub finishing in sixth place in the eight-team league with a 24–38 record in 1921, the franchise completed only one season in the Negro National League.

Columbus Elite Giants
Duration: 1935   Honors: None
Affiliation: NNL

In 1935 owner Tom Wilson moved his franchise from Nashville to Columbus for a season before moving on to Washington, D.C., the following year and eventually to Baltimore. In the first half of the season they finished in second place behind the Pittsburgh Crawfords and, although they dropped to fourth place in the second-half standings, finished with a combined record of 27–21 for a .563 winning percentage. This team constituted only a franchise shift and is properly included as part of the history of the Baltimore Elite Giants

Colzie, Jim
Career: 1946–47   Position: p
Team: Indianapolis Clowns

A pitcher with the Indianapolis Clowns for two seasons in the post–World War II era, he posted a 6–1 record in 1946, his first season.

Combs, A. Clark (**Jack**)
Career: 1922–26   Position: p
Team: Detroit Stars

Spending his entire career with the Detroit Stars, he pitched for five years during the '20s, logging records of 3–3, 6–6, and 6–9 for the seasons 1923–25.

Condon, Lafayette
Career: 1887   Position: player
Team: *Louisville Falls Citys*

He was a player for the Louisville Falls Citys, one of eight teams that were charter members of the League of Colored Baseball Clubs in 1887. However, the league's existence was ephemeral, lasting only a week. His position is uncertain.

Connell
Career: 1913   Position: p
Teams: *Indianapolis ABCs*

He was a pitcher with the Indianapolis ABCs in 1913, a year before they achieved a major-league quality of play.

Connors, John W.
Career: 1905–22   Positions: owner, officer
Teams: Brooklyn Royal Giants ('05–'14), Atlantic City Bacharach Giants ('19–'22)
Born: 1878, Portsmouth, Va.
Died: July 1926

One of the early businessmen who contributed greatly to the success of the black ballclubs before there was a viable black league, he was the man behind the Brooklyn Royal Giants in the early years of the century. In addition to owning the baseball team, he was the owner of a nightclub, the Brooklyn Royal Garden, and the Porter's Club. As a youngster he ran away from home and joined the Navy; he was a veteran of the Spanish-American War.

He organized the Brooklyn Royal Giants in 1905 and ran the team for a decade, winning eastern championships in 1909–10 and 1914. In the latter season, his Royals lost a playoff to the Chicago American Giants. Soon afterward, he sold the team to Nat Strong.

A few years later the portly black entrepreneur became a coowner of the Bacharach Giants and moved the team to New York for the 1919 season, but moved back to Atlantic City after only one year. In 1926 he had a stroke and passed away at age forty-eight. Star pitcher Dick Redding, who had played under Connors with both the Royals and the Bacharachs, was a pallbearer at his funeral.

Cook
Career: 1918   Position: of
Team: New York Lincoln Giants

He appeared briefly as a right fielder with the Lincoln Giants in 1918, his only year in black baseball.

Cook, C.
Career: 1935   Position: p
Team: Pittsburgh Crawfords

His only appearance in the Negro Leagues was with a top team, as he pitched briefly with the 1935 Pittsburgh Crawfords.

Cook, Howard (Johnny)
a.k.a. Cooke
Career: 1937   Position: p
Team: Indianapolis Athletics

He was a pitcher with the Indianapolis Athletics in 1937, the inaugural season of the Negro American League and the Athletics' only year in a league.

Cook, Walter L.
Career: 1886–88   Positions: owner,
                                   officer
Team: Cuban Giants

A white businessman, he was the owner of the Cuban Giants from 1886 until his death in 1888. He gained ownership of the ballclub in May 1886 and moved the team to Trenton, New Jersey. His brother donated his estate to the YMCA to build Trenton's William Grant Cook Memorial YMCA Building, named in honor of his father.

Cooke, James (Jay)
a.k.a. Cook
Career: 1929–33   Position: p
Teams: Baltimore Black Sox ('29–'32), Atlantic City Bacharach Giants ('32–'33)

He began as a pitcher with the Baltimore Black Sox in 1929, when they were in the American Negro League, and remained with the Sox until 1932, when they were in the East-West League, claiming victories in both of his decisions before the demise of the league. During the season he joined the Bacharach Giants and played with them through the 1933 season.

Cooley, Walter
Career: 1931   Positions: c, 3b
Team: *Birmingham Black Barons*

He was a catcher and third baseman with the Birmingham Black Barons in 1931, a year after they dropped out of the Negro National League.

Cooper, Alex
Career: 1928   Position: of
Teams: Philadelphia Tigers ('28), Harrisburg Giants ('28)

He was an outfielder in the Negro Leagues for a single year, splitting the 1928 season between the Philadelphia Tigers and Harrisburg Giants.

Cooper, Alfred (Army)
Career: 1928–32   Position:p
Teams: **Kansas City Monarchs**, ('28–'31), Cleveland stars ('32)
Bats: Left   Throws: Left
Height: 6'3"   Weight: 250

The huge left-hander was a standout pitcher with the Kansas City Monarchs during the last years of the Negro National League. In the 1929 Negro National League championship season, he forged a 13–4 record as the "other Cooper" in the Monarchs' starting rotation. Left-hander Andy Cooper was the more established half of the pair of pitching Coopers for Kansas City that season. After the league folded, Army Cooper pitched for a season with the Cleveland Stars in 1932. He was a smart pitcher and, although a large man, he was gentle off the field.

Cooper, Andy (Lefty)
Career: 1920–41   Positions: **p**, manager
Teams: **Detroit Stars** ('20–'27, '30), Chicago American Giants, St. Louis Stars, **Kansas City Monarchs** ('28–'41)
Bats: Right   Throws: Left
Height: 6'2"   Weight: 220
Born: Mar. 4, 1896, Waco, Tex.
Died: June 10, 1941, Waco Tex.

This longtime star of the Kansas City Monarchs pitched in the 1936 All-Star game for the West squad at age forty. Earlier in his career the large left-hander had been the ace hurler with the Detroit Stars and the Monarchs. A smart pitcher who was a master at mixing pitches and changing speeds, he had superb control and an exceptional and effective array of breaking pitches, including a great curveball, change, slider, and screwball, that he used to finesse the batters. His move to first base was superb, and he was at his best in the clutch. His brother, Daltie Cooper, was also a pitcher in the Negro Leagues but pitched primarily in the East, while Andy pitched in the West.

Beginning his career with Detroit, he is credited with a composite 5–11 record during his first two years in the Negro National League; then began a string of impressive seasons, with marks of 14–5, 15–8, 12–5, 12–1, 12–8, and 7–3 for the years 1922–27. The next year he joined the Monarchs and had records of 13–7 and 13–3, with the latter coming in their 1929 Negro National League championship season. The next season he was involved in a car wreck with other Kansas City players and suffered cuts on his arms and legs. The last part of 1930 was spent back in Detroit, where he fashioned a 15–6 work sheet.

During the '20s he registered a 15–17 record for three years in Cuba's winter league, and in the winter of 1933–34 he toured the Orient with Lonnie Goodwin's All-Star team, playing in Japan, China, and the Philippines before arriving back Stateside. Eventually rejoining the Monarchs, who were playing as an independent team against all levels of opposition, he had a 27–8 record in 1936. The following season, with Cooper at the helm, the Monarchs became charter members of the Negro American League and won the league's first pennant. In the first-half playoffs he pitched a 17-inning, 2–2 tie against the Chicago American Giants, but the Monarchs prevailed in the Series to take the pennant. He added two more Negro American league flags in 1939–40 before passing away in the spring of 1941 at age forty-five.

Cooper, Anthony (**Ant**)
Career: 1928–41   Positions: **ss**, 2b, cf, lf, 3b
Teams: Birmingham Black Barons ('28–'30), Memphis Red Sox ('29), Louisville White Sox ('31), Cleveland Stars ('32), Homestead Grays ('32), Baltimore Black Sox ('33), Pittsburgh Crawfords ('33), Cleveland Red Sox ('34), Newark Dodgers ('35), New York Black Yankees ('41)
Bats: Right   Throws: Right
Height: 5'4"   Weight: 165

The little infielder was a nice fielder with a good arm but was a light hitter and not a fast base runner. During his career he was with a different team almost every year. He began his career with the Birmingham Black Barons in 1928, and incomplete statistics show a .253 batting average in 1929, while splitting the season as a shortstop for the Black Barons and the Memphis Red Sox. A versatile player, he could also play outfield, and in 1930 he hit .218 while playing in the outer garden for the Black Barons. The next season he split his playing time between center field and shortstop while nested in the number two slot in the batting order for the Louisville White Sox, who were entered in the Negro National League that season.

In 1932 he was back at shortstop and batting leadoff for the Cleveland Stars in the East-West league. When the league broke up in mid-year, he finished the season with the Homestead Grays, playing third base and outfield as a part-time starter and batting last in the order when in the lineup. Remaining in Pittsburgh in 1933, he joined the Crawfords and hit .288 as a part-time starter, alternating between left field and both middle infield positions. The next season he played with the Cleveland Red Sox, the city's newest entry in the Negro National League. But the team folded after only a season, and in 1935 he was with the Newark Dodgers before they were assimilated by the Newark Eagles the following year.

Throughout his career, his adaptability enabled him always to find a niche on a team somewhere. His last season in the Negro National League came in 1941, after an absence of six seasons, as a shortstop batting seventh in the order for the New York Black Yankees.

Cooper, Chief
Career: 1928   Position: umpire
Teams: NNL

He was an umpire in the Negro National League in 1928

Cooper, Daltie (Dolly)
Career: 1923–40   Positions: **p**, of
Teams: *Nashville Elite Giants ('21–'22)*, Indianapolis ABCs ('23), Baltimore Black Sox ('23, '31), Washington Potomacs ('24), Harrisburg Giants ('24–'27), New York Lincoln Giants ('26), Hilldale Daisies ('28–'29, '32), Homestead Grays ('30), Washington Pilots ('32), Atlantic City Bacharach Giants ('33–'34), Newark Eagles ('40)

In 1923, as a youngster starting his big-league career with the Indianapolis ABCs, great things were expected of him. The following year he was with Harrisburg in the Eastern Colored League and was a good pitcher, but the management found it difficult to keep him in playing condition. That might have been a contributing factor to his frequent movement among the different teams. His work sheets included marks of 6–3 in 1925 for Harrisburg, 8–8 in 1929 for Hilldale, and 5–4 in 1931 for the Baltimore Black Sox. He also pitched with the Lincoln Giants, Homestead Grays, and several other teams during his career. He was the brother of the Kansas City Monarchs' ace left-hander Andy Cooper.

Cooper, E.
Career: 1910–24   Positions: 1b, of
Teams: Leland Giants ('10) Mohawk Giants ('14), *Philadelphia Giants ('16)*, Lincoln Stars ('16), New York Lincoln Giants ('18), *Pennsylvania Red Caps ('19)* Cleveland Tate Stars ('22), *St. Louis Giants ('22–'24), Philadelphia Colored Giants of New York ('28)*

A first baseman-outfielder playing mostly as a reserve player, his career bridged the dead-ball era and modern baseball. The best-known teams that he was with include the Lincoln Stars, the New York Lincoln Giants, and the St. Louis Giants, where he closed his big-league career.

Cooper, James
Career: 1938–47   Position: p
Teams: Atlanta Black Crackers ('38), New York Black Yankees ('46), Newark Eagles ('47)

After pitching with the Atlanta Black Crackers in 1938, their only season in the Negro American League, he next appeared in the post–World War II Negro National League, pitching with the New York Black Yankees and Newark Eagles.

Cooper, Ray
Career: 1928–29   Positions: **p**, rf, 3b
Team: Hilldale Daisies

During the last two years of the '20s he was a pitcher with Hilldale, playing in the Eastern Colored League in 1928 and the American Negro League in 1929.

Cooper, Sam
Career: 1926–34   Position: p
Teams: *Richmond Giants ('23)*, Baltimore Black Sox ('26), Harrisburg Giants ('26–'27), Atlantic City Bacharach Giants ('27–'29), Homestead Grays ('30)

The pitcher was released by the Baltimore Black Sox in mid-August of 1926 and was picked up by Harrisburg to add depth to a weak pitching staff. The following season he moved to the 1927 Eastern Colored League champion Bacharachs during the season, remaining with the Atlantic City team until joining the Homestead Grays in 1930. He also pitched with the Richmond Giants in 1923 before signing with a top ballclub.

Cooper, Thomas R. (Tom)
Career: 1947–52   Positions: c, of, 1b
Teams: Kansas City Monarchs ('47–'52),

minor leagues ('53, '57), Canadian League ('54)
Bats: Both   Throws: Right
Height: 5'11"   Weight: 180
Born: 1927

During the last years of the Negro American League as a major league, he played with the Kansas City Monarchs. Although he was sufficiently versatile to play several positions, he was an average ballplayer in every phase of the game. His best seasons at bat were in 1948 (.269) and 1950 (.279). He entered organized ball in 1953 with Schenectady in the Eastern League and hit a dismal .192. The next season he played with Three Rivers in the Provincial League and batted .229. His last appearance in baseball was with Schenectady in 1957, when he went hitless in only 16 at-bats.

Cooper, William T. (**Bill**, *Dr. Jekyll*)
Career: 1938–46   Positions: c, 2b, 3b, ss,
                                              1b, of
Teams: Atlanta Black Crackers ('38), Philadelphia Stars ('39–'42), *military service ('43–'45),* New York Black Yankees ('46)
Bats: Left   Throws: Right
Height: 5'8"   Weight: 168

Extremely versatile, he played every position except pitcher and handled them adequately, but his best position was catcher. He began his career with the Atlanta Black Crackers, winners of the Negro American League's second-half flag in 1938. He was a good fielder, an average hitter, and, as a former track man, he was the fastest player on the team. Before joining the Atlanta Black Crackers, he was a star halfback on the Morris Brown College football team and was rough and tumble, earning him the nickname "Dr. Jekyll" because of the contrast in his on-field and off-field personalities.

After leaving Atlanta, he played with the Philadelphia Stars, and as a regular batting in the lower part of the order, hit .256, .224, and .217 in the last three seasons (1940–42) before entering military service. After the end of

World War II he returned to the Negro Leagues for a season, closing out his career in 1946.

Corbett, Charles (Geech)
Career: 1922–28   Position: p
Teams: Pittsburgh Keystones ('22), Indianapolis ABCs ('23), **Harrisburg Giants** ('24–'28), Hilldale Daisies ('27)

Beginning with the Pittsburgh Keystones in 1922, he was a promising pitcher with the Indianapolis ABCs in 1923 but was allowed to escape to the East, where he was signed by Harrisburg in 1924 and had an 8–1 record in 1925. In 1927 he joined Hilldale for part of the season, but returned to Harrisburg and closed out his career in 1928.

Corcoran, Tom
Career: 1942   Position: p
Team: Homestead Grays

He pitched briefly, without a decision, for the Homestead Grays in 1942.

Cordova, Pete
Career: 1921–23   Positions: 3b, ss, 2b
Teams: Kansas City Monarchs ('21), Toledo Tigers ('23), *Cleveland Tate Stars ('23), Philadelphia Giants ('24, '27)*

The infielder played primarily on the left side of the infield, either third base or shortstop, but could play any spot in the infield. He began his career with the Kansas City Monarchs in 1921 and played with the Toledo Tigers, a team entered in the Negro National League in 1923 but that disbanded in mid-July. He also played with the Cleveland Tate Stars and Philadelphia Giants, two teams of lesser quality.

Cornelius, William McKinley (Willie, **Sug**)
Career: 1928–46   Position: p
Teams: Nashville Elite Giants ('28–'29), Memphis Red Sox ('29–'31), Birmingham Black Barons ('30), Cole's American Giants ('33–'35), **Chicago American Giants** ('36–'43, '45–'46), Cincinnati Buckeyes ('42)

A crafty right-hander with good control, "Sug" had a superb curveball that he could "throw around a barrel." Other pitches in his arsenal included a good fastball, hard slider, screwball, drop, and change of pace. A member of owner Robert A. Coles's Chicago American Giants Negro National League championship team in 1933, the curveball artist had enough confidence in his curve to throw it on a 3–2 count. He fashioned an 8–3 league record for the regular season, and in the playoffs against the Philadelphia Stars the following year he made a supreme effort to stave off defeat by starting three games and relieving in another. His best season came two years later, when he was credited with a 20–4 record for the 1936 season.

He appeared in three East-West All-Star games, starting on the mound for the West squad in 1936 and 1938 and gaining the victory in relief in the 1935 game. In 1937, the only year during this period when he missed making the All-Star team, he was credited with 22 victories.

He started his career with southern teams, posting a combined 11–17 record for the 1929–30 seasons before joining the American Giants and finding a winning touch. Although his best years in Chicago were in the '30s, he still managed to produce winning results late in his career, with records of 6–5 and 5–4 (4.65 ERA) in 1943 and 1945. The next year was his last in the Negro Leagues, and he ended his nineteen-year career after the 1946 season.

Cornett, Harry
Career: 1913   Position: c
Team: *Indianapolis ABCs*

He was a catcher with the Indianapolis ABCs in 1913, before they became a top team.

Correa, Marceline (**Cho-Cho**)
a.k.a. Marcelino
Career: 1926–36   Positions: **ss**, 1f, 2b
Teams: Cuban Stars (West) ('26–'29), Cuban Stars (East) ('29), Cuban Stars ('32–'33), New York Cubans ('35–'36)
Bats: Right   Throws: Right

The Cuban shortstop with the colorful nickname "Cho–Cho" (pronounced "Shoo-Shoo") played eleven years with the New York Cubans and the Cuban Stars in four different leagues. He began his career in 1926 with Tinti Molina's Cuban Stars in the first Negro National League, batting third in the order while registering averages of .238 and .279 in his first two seasons. After moving East in 1929, he hit .317 in the American Negro League while batting cleanup for Alex Pompez's Cuban Stars. During the chaotic 1932 season, the Cubans played part of the season as the Cuban House of David but also entered in the East-West League until its demise. Pompez's New York Cubans entered the new Negro National League in 1935, and the hard-hitting shortstop was a vital member of the team, both at the plate and in the field. In 1935 he hit .281 as they won the Negro National League second-half flag but lost to the Pittsburgh Crawfords in the playoff. The next season was the last year in his Negro League career, and he hit at a .361 clip.

Cortez
Career: 1928–31   Positions: c, 1b
Teams: Cuban Stars (West) ('28–'30), Cuban Stars ('31)

A combination catcher-first baseman, he played four years with the Cuban Stars. As the regular catcher and cleanup hitter in 1929–30, he registered batting averages of .237 and .293 during the Cubans' last two years in the Negro National League. In 1931, his last year with the ballclub, the Cubans played as an independent team.

Cosa
Career: 1932   Positions: of, 1b
Team: Memphis Red Sox

An outfielder with the Memphis Red Sox in 1932, when the Negro Southern League was recognized as a major league, he often batted leadoff and sometimes played first base.

Costello
Career: 1911   Position: 1b
Team: All Cubans

He was a first baseman for the 1911 All Cubans, one of the top Cuban teams of the era.

Cottman, Darby
Career: 1887–93   Position: 3b
Teams: Unions ('87), Chicago Unions ('90–'93)

He was the regular third baseman for the Unions in 1887 under manager Abe Jones. The following season the team became known as the Chicago Unions, but Cottman did not play with the team again until 1890, when W. S. Peters took over the managerial reins, and then returned as the regular at the hot corner for the next four years.

Cottrell
Career: 1923   Position: c
Team: Hilldale Daisies

He played briefly as a backup catcher with Hilldale in 1923, his only year in the Negro Leagues.

Cowan, Eddie
Career: 1919   Position: ss
Team: *Cleveland Tate Stars*

He was a shortstop for the Cleveland Tate Stars in 1919, when they were playing as an independent team.

Cowan, John (**Johnnie**)
Career: 1942–50   Positions: 2b, 3b, *of*
Teams: Birmingham Black Barons ('34, '36, '50), *Detroit Stars ('39)*, Cincinnati Buckeyes ('42), Cleveland Buckeyes ('44–'47), Memphis Red Sox ('48–'49), *minor leagues ('50)*
Bats: Right   Throws: Right
Height: 5'11"   Weight: 165
Born: May 31, 1913, Birmingham, Ala.
Died: Oct. 24, 1993, Birmingham, Ala.

A good fielder but light hitter, noted more for his glove than his bat, he had a good arm and was a proficient double-play man. He began his professional career in 1934 with his hometown team, the Birmingham Black Barons, playing in the Negro Southern League. After being out of the league the following season, he rejoined the team in 1936, but when the Black Barons entered the Negro American League in 1937, the infielder again was dropped from the club. In 1942 he made another attempt to break into the lineup with a top team, but was a seldom-used reserve with the Cincinnati Buckeyes.

Finally in 1944, at age thirty-one, he signed with the Cleveland Buckeyes and was installed as the regular second baseman. He held the spot for the next four seasons, compiling averages of .235, .247, .225, and .210 while relegated to the eighth spot in the batting order. In 1945, however, he temporarily lost his starting position when Billy Horne was shifted from shortstop to second base. But Horne entered military service early in the season, and Cowan was the starting second baseman as the Buckeyes captured the Negro American League pennant. In their sweep over the Homestead Grays in the ensuing World Series, he had the game-winning hit in the first contest. In 1947, after capturing their second pennant in three years, the Buckeyes lost the World Series to the New York Cubans.

That was Cowan's last season with the Buckeyes, and he joined the Memphis Red Sox in 1948, playing second base for a pair of seasons and batting .235 and .213. He played the first part of the 1950 season with the Black Barons before leaving the Negro Leagues to play with the Elmwood Giants in the Mandak League for the remainder of the season. In 1951 he returned to the Stockham Valve Fitting Company in the Birmingham City League, ending his career where it had begun twenty-two years earlier.

Cox
Career: 1936   Position: c
Team: *Memphis Red Sox*

He was a catcher with the Memphis Red Sox in 1936, a year before the team entered the Negro American League in its inaugural season, but never played with the club when they were engaged in major-league competition.

Cox, Comer (**Hannibal**, Russ)
Career: 1930–31   Positions: 3b, 2b, 1f, rf
Teams: Nashville Elite Giants ('30–'31), Cleveland Cubs ('31)

A good utility player, he could play either in the infield or the outfield, and he alternated between the two during each of his seasons with the Elites franchise. Breaking in with the Nashville Elites in 1930, their first year in the Negro National League, he played third base and in the outfield. In 1931 owner Tom Wilson moved the Elites North and they played as the Cleveland Cubs, with Cox dividing his playing time between right field and second base. As a part-time starter each season, he batted leadoff when in the lineup and hit for a .317 average in 1930.

Cox, M. D. (**Alphonse**)
Career: 1938–43   Position: p
Teams: Jacksonville Red Caps ('38), Cleveland Bears ('39), Memphis Red Sox ('43)

He began his career pitching with the Jacksonville Red Caps in 1938 and remained with the team when the franchise was relocated in Cleveland and played under the banner of the Cleveland Bears in 1939. His last appearance in the Negro Leagues was during World War II, when he pitched with the Memphis Red Sox in 1943, winning his only recorded decision.

Cox, Roosevelt (Benny, Indian Joe)
Career: 1937–44   Positions: 3b, 2b, ss, c
Teams: Detroit Stars ('37), Monarchs ('38), Ethiopian Clowns ('39), New York Cubans ('42–'43)
Bats: Right   Throws: Right
Height: 5'11"   Weight: 185

An average hitter without appreciable power, he was adequate at any infield position. A hustler with average speed on the bases, his versatility was his best asset. He began his career with the Detroit Stars in 1937, batting fifth in the order while dividing his time between second base and catcher. The next year he was the regular third baseman for the Kansas City Monarchs, batting second in the order. In 1939

he joined the Ethiopian Clowns and after a stint with the independent ballclub, returned to league play, signing with the New York Cubans of the Negro National League.

In 1942–43 he was the regular at the hot corner with the Cubans, batting in the lower part of the order, with incomplete statistics showing averages of .125 and .268. The Louisianan was part Indian and light-complected, sometimes enabling him to "pass" for white to buy food for his teammates in instances when they were denied ready access.

Cox, Tom (Lefty)
Career: 1928–32   Position: p
Teams: Cleveland Tigers ('28), New York Lincoln Giants ('30–'31), *Cleveland Cubs ('32)*

The left-hander broke in with the Cleveland Tigers in 1928, their only season in the Negro National League, and after they dropped out of league play, he signed to pitch with the Lincoln Giants under John Henry Lloyd. After leaving the Lincolns, he pitched for a season, with the Cleveland Cubs, a lesser team.

Cozart, Haywood (**Harry**, Big Train)
Career: 1939–43   Position: p
Team: Newark Eagles
Bats: Right   Throws: Right
Height: 6'4"   Weight: 240

The big right-hander was a power pitcher with a good fastball and was nicknamed "Big Train." He had fair control and was a bit lacking in his breaking pitches, which restricted his overall effectiveness. Although adequate at fielding his position, he was slow on the bases and not much help offensively. During the five years he pitched with the Newark Eagles, owner Abe Manley communicated with him in the off-season by writing to the poolroom in his hometown of Raleigh, North Carolina.

Craig, Charles
Career: 1926–27   Position: p
Teams: Homestead Grays ('26), New York Lincoln Giants ('26–'27), *Brooklyn Cuban*

Giants, Harrisburg Giants ('27), *Ewing's All-Stars ('28)*

In addition to playing with teams of lesser status, he pitched without distinction for two years with quality teams in the East, including the Homestead Grays and the Harrisburg Giants, but he is best identified with the Lincoln Giants.

Craig, Dick
Career: 1940   Position: 1b
Team: Indianapolis Crawfords

He was with the Indianapolis Crawfords briefly in 1940 as a reserve first baseman.

Craig, Homer
[see Craig, John (Homer)]

Craig, John (Homer)
Career: 1935–46   Position: umpire
Teams: NNL

The arbiter was one of the better umpires in the Negro National League, spending a dozen seasons in black baseball.

Craig, Joseph (**Joe**)
Career: 1940, 1946   Positions: 1b, of
Teams: Indianapolis Crawfords ('40), Philadelphia Stars ('46)

Making two appearances in the Negro Leagues, both in reserve roles, he could play either first base or in the outfield. His first appearance was a brief one with the Indianapolis Crawfords in 1940, but in 1946 he played as a left fielder with the Philadelphia Stars, making occasional starts and hitting .299.

Crain, A. C.
Career: 1887   Position: player
Team: *Lord Baltimores*

He was a player with the Lord Baltimores, one of eight teams that were charter members of the League of Colored Baseball Clubs in 1887. However, the league's existence was ephemeral, lasting only a week. His position is uncertain.

Crawford, David
Career: 1947–48   Position: 1b
Team: Birmingham Black Barons
Height: 6'3"   Weight: 185

The big first baseman from Grambling College was vying for a position with the Birmingham Black Barons in the spring of 1948. He is credited with a .333 average in 1947.

Crawford, John
Career: 1943   Position: umpire
Teams: NNL

For one season, 1943, he was an umpire in the Negro National League.

Crawford, Sam
Career: 1910–38   Positions: p, 2b, of, manager, coach
Teams: *New York Black Sox ('10),* Brooklyn Royal Giants ('11–'12), Chicago Giants ('12), Chicago American Giants ('13–'19, '25–'28), Chicago Union Giants, Detroit Stars ('19), Kansas City Monarchs ('20–'23, '34–'35), Cleveland Tate Stars ('22), St. Louis Stars ('24), Birmingham Black Barons ('25, '38), Cleveland Tigers ('28), Chicago Columbia Giants ('31), Cole's American Giants ('36), Indianapolis Athletics ('37)

The elongated hurler from the deadball era had a good fastball and knuckleball and was considered one of the best pitchers in black baseball during the early years of the '10s. In 1912, while pitching with the Chicago Giants against the Coal Citys of Braidwood, Illinois, he pitched two no-hitters in one day, registering 27 strikeouts (15 in the first game and 12 in the second game) without allowing a base on balls in either game. The only run yielded came in the first contest, when the catcher missed the third strike on a batter and then threw wildly to first base, making the final score 4–1. Although the games were only five innings each and against opposition of lesser quality, the accomplishment was noteworthy.

Crawford was especially effective against the Cuban Stars, and by 1918 he had earned a reputation as being a "Cubans-killer" because of his consistency against the islanders. During the 1918–19 seasons incomplete statistics show a composite 3–1 ledger for Crawford, and in 1921 with the Kansas City Monarchs he registered an 8–3 record.

In 1925 Crawford returned to the Chicago American Giants, and the following year the club copped the Negro National League pennant under manager David Malarcher. In the ensuing World Series, Crawford hurled in one game in relief as the Giants took the Series over the Eastern Colored League Bacharach Giants, 5 games to 3, and 2 ties in the Series.

Intermittently throughout his career he served as a manager and coach, ranging from 1917, when he managed the Havana Red Sox, through 1935, when he managed Kansas City. In between, as a coach, he handled the Chicago American Giants in spring training in the absence of manager David Malarcher. Altogether he had a long career as player, coach, or manager (1910–38) with thirteen different teams.

Crawley
Career: 1931   Position: 3b
Team: Atlantic City Bacharach Giants

He was a reserve third baseman with the Bacharachs in 1931, his only year in black baseball.

Creacy, A. D. (Dewey)
Career: 1924–40   Position: 3b
Teams: Kansas City Monarchs ('24), **St. Louis Stars** ('24–'31), Detroit Wolves ('32), Washington Pilots ('31–'32), Columbus Blue Birds ('33), Cleveland Giants ('33), Philadelphia Stars ('34–'38), Brooklyn Royal Giants ('39–'40)
Bats: Right   Throws: Right
Height: 5'9"   Weight: 160
Born: Fort Worth, Tex.

The regular third baseman for the St. Louis Stars' teams that won three Negro National League pennants in four years (1928 and 1930–1931), he was a solid fielder and a good hitter with power, batting .308, .326, .341, .318, and .327 for his first five seasons with

the Stars, beginning in 1924. A right-handed batter, playing at home with a short left field aided his power numbers, and in 1926 he posted his best totals, banging 23 home runs in 89 games while batting cleanup for the Stars. In other years he usually batted in the sixth slot in the order while contributing to the Stars' success.

The Stars won two split-season titles during the '20s. In 1925 they won the second-half title but lost the playoff to the Kansas City Monarchs in seven games, and in 1928 they won the first-half title and bested the Chicago American Giants in the playoffs. In 1930–31 they added the last two Negro National League pennants outright before the demise of the league following the 1931 season. Creacy's hitting declined during his last three seasons with the Stars, batting .256, .285, and .206 in 1929–31.

Following the breakup of the league, the Stars also disbanded, and Creacy played with the Washingotn Pilots, Detroit Wolves, and Columbus Blue Birds during the next two seasons before landing with the Philadelphia Stars in 1934. In his first year in Philadelphia the Stars won the Negro National League flag, with Creacy batting second in the order and contributing a .223 average. For the next four seasons in Philadelphia he hit for averages of .232, .292, .224, and .281 before joining the Brooklyn Royal Giants, where he closed out his career, playing third base and batting second in the order for the independent Royals, who were struggling to maintain a quality ballclub.

Before joining the Monarchs in 1924, he had served in the 25th Infantry. During his career he proved an adequate fielder and, although he once stole 16 bases in a season, he was not noted as a good base runner.

Creek, Willie
Career: 1924–32   Positions: ss, c
Teams: Washington Potomacs ('24), Brooklyn Royal Giants ('30–'32), Atlantic City Bacharach Giants ('32)

THE NEGRO BASEBALL LEAGUES

He began his career with the short-lived Washington Potomacs in 1924 as a backup catcher and reappeared in 1930 with the Brooklyn Royal Giants as a combination shortstop-catcher for three seasons.

Crespo, Alejandro (Alex, Home Run)
Career: 1940, 1946   Position: lf
Teams: New York Cubans ('40, '46), *Mexican League ('41–'45, '47–'51), minor leagues ('55)*
Bats: Right   Throws: Right
Height: 6'1"   Weight: 206
Born: Feb. 26, 1915, Guira de Melena, Cuba

The big right-handed Cuban power hitter played only two years in the Negro Leagues, choosing to play in Mexico in the other seasons. In his first year in the Negro Leagues, the New York Cubans' outfielder hit .344 as their cleanup hitter and earned a trip to the 1940 All-Star Game, getting a triple in two at-bats in the contest. In 1946, his only other year in the league, the slugger hit for a .336 average in league play. A rough-and-tumble player who used a head-first slide, he was a pretty good base stealer and also used his speed to augment his natural power by stretching hits for extra bases.

A consistent .300 hitter, he fashioned a fine career in Mexico, hitting for averages of .361, 332, .331, .316, .311, .293, .311, .346, and .306. In 1943, playing with Toreon, he led the league in RBIs. His Mexican career totals show a .321 lifetime average for nine seasons and a .333 average for seven years in All-Star competition. In Mexico, in addition to his normal outfield post, he often played in the infield and as a catcher.

Playing in his native land for fourteen seasons, mostly with Cienfuegos, he compiled a lifetime .277 batting average. He led the league in 1948–49 with a .326 average, but that was not his highest mark; he hit .339 in his first year (1939–40) and .337 in 1942–43. On two other occasions he flirted with the coveted .300 mark, hitting .298 (1945–46) and .296 (1944–45).

He finished his baseball career in 1955, splitting the season between Hobbs and Charlotte in organized baseball.

Crespo, Alejandro Rogelio
Career: 1918–33   Positions: **2b**, 3b
Teams: **Cuban Stars (East)** ('18, '26–'27), Cuban Stars of Havana, ('19) *Gilkerson's Union Giants ('21–'25 '32–'33),* Chicago Giants
Bats: Right   Throws: Right
Born: Sept. 16, 1891, Cuba

The infielder played intermittently with the Cuban Stars, both in the Eastern Colored League and when they were operating as an independent team between 1918 and 1933. Considered a solid hitter and an all-around good ballplayer, the infielder could play almost any position, but played primarily at second base, with substantial time at third base. He began his career in 1918 with the Cuban Stars, and incomplete statistics show only a .185 batting average for his first season. In 1921 he began playing with Gilkerson's Union Giants and barnstormed throughout the Midwest, often playing against Oscar Felsch, Swede Risberg, and other "outlawed" players in the aftermath of the 1919 World Series "Black Sox" scandal. After years of touring with Gilkerson's team, he made his next appearance with the Cuban Stars in 1926, batting in the leadoff position. But he was dropped to the lower part of the order in 1927, when his average dropped to .200.

The little Cuban infielder came from a poor family and learned to play baseball in his homeland. After entering the Cuban Army in 1914, he was playing a pickup game with a group of soldiers, and was taking a turn as the catcher when he sustained a serious injury to his forehead from a foul tip off the bat of Cristobal Torriente. That episode ended Crespo's catching career. After leaving the Army, he played under manager Strike Gonzalez, and in 1922, he hit .290 to help Marianao win the pennant. In 1923 he played for Havana, batting fifth and playing third base, but was back with

Marianao, batting .262, in the 1923–24 Cuban winter league.

After baseball, he was a dishwasher in a restaurant and worked in a hospital in Chicago.

Crockett, Frank
Career: 1916–23   Positions: cf, rf
Teams: Atlantic City Bacharach Giants ('16, '22–'23), Brooklyn Royal Giants ('18), *Norfolk All-Stars ('20), Madison Stars ('21)*

In the Bacharachs' first season in Atlantic City, he played center field and hit in the second slot in the batting order. He returned to the Bacharachs in 1922, their last year as an independent team before joining the Eastern Colored League. In 1923 he played as a part-time starter in the outfield, batting in the lead-off position when in the lineup, to close out his career in black baseball. Between his two stints with the Bacharachs, he played mostly with teams of marginal quality, but also appeared as a reserve with the Brooklyn Royal Giants in 1918.

Cromatie, Leroy (Ray)
Career: 1945   Position: 2b
Team: Cincinnati-Indianapolis Clowns
A wartime player, he was a reserve second baseman in 1945 with the Cincinnati-Indianapolis Clowns.

Cross, Bennie
Career: 1887   Position: of
Team: *Boston Resolutes*

He was an outfielder with the Boston Resolutes, one of eight teams that were charter members of the League of Colored Baseball Clubs in 1887. However, the league's existence was ephemeral, lasting only a week.

Cross, Norman
Career: 1932–38   Position: p
Teams: Cole's American Giants ('32–36), Atlanta Black Crackers ('38), *Palmer House All-Stars ('40)*

He made his home in Chicago and was a pitcher with the American Giants for five years

during the Depression years, showing records of 4–1 and 6–2 for his first two years in the league, 1932–33. His last year with the American Giants was 1936, when the team dropped out of the league and played an independent schedule. When the Atlanta Black Crackers got their Negro American League franchise team in 1938, they wanted him to join their ballclub, and although he was on their early spring roster, for undetermined reasons he didn't stick with the team. Two years later he was back in Chicago pitching with the Palmer House All-Stars, an independent ballclub of marginal major-league caliber.

Crossen
Career: 1921   Position: c
Team: New York Lincoln Giants
He was a reserve catcher with the Lincoln Giants in 1921, his only year in black baseball.

Crowe, George
Career: 1947–49   Position: 1b
Teams: New York Black Yankees ('47–'49), New York Cubans ('48–'49), *minor leagues ('49–'52, '61),* major leagues ('52–'60)
Bats: Left   Throws: Left
Height: 6'2"   Weight: 210
Born: Mar. 22, 1923, Whiteland, Ind.

The big, hard-hitting first sacker hit .305 as a rookie with the New York Black Yankees in 1947 and was a holdout the following year. In 1949 he entered organized ball with Pawtucket in the New England League, hitting .354 with a league-leading 106 RBIs. The next two seasons he played at Hartford in the Eastern League and led the league in batting (.353), runs, hits, and doubles while blasting 24 home runs and 122 RBIs. In 1951 he advanced to the American Association with Milwaukee, and hit .339 with 24 home runs and a league-leading 119 RBIs, while also leading the league in hits and doubles.

After another good start at Milwaukee in 1952, he finally made it to the major leagues with the Braves and played nine years in the major leagues (three each with the Braves,

Reds, and Cardinals). He moved with the Braves to Milwaukee in 1953, then was traded to the Cincinnati Reds in 1956, enjoying his best major-league season in 1957, when he hit .270 with 31 home runs. After being dropped by the Cardinals, he finished his baseball career in the International League with Charleston in 1961, leaving behind a lifetime major-league batting average of .270. In recent years he became a recluse, living in the rural Adirondacks without modern conveniences.

Croxton

Career: 1908–09   Positions: p, c
Team: Cuban Giants

He was a combination pitcher-catcher with the Cuban Giants, a marginal team, in 1908–09.

Crue, Martin (Matty)

Career: 1942–47   Position: p
Teams: New York Cubans ('42–'43, '46–'47), Homestead Grays ('43)

He was a second-line pitcher for the 1947 Negro National League champion New York Cubans, fashioning a 4–1 record for the regular season and pitching in one World Series game in relief against the Negro American League Cleveland Buckeyes. The previous season he had a 3–1 work sheet. He began his career with the Cubans in 1942.

Crumbley, Alex (Murder Man)

a.k.a. Crumley
Career: 1937–38   Position: of
Teams: New York Black Yankees ('37), Atlanta Black Crackers ('38), Pittsburgh Crawfords ('38), Washington Black Senators ('38)
Bats: Left   Throws: Right

A big, brutal outfielder with good range in the field, he was described as being herculean, and was a consistent and dangerous pull hitter with power. He was on the Atlanta Black Cracker' roster in the early spring of 1938 but opted to play elsewhere for most of the season. After Atlanta had won the second-half title, he

was added to their roster in time for the play-offs against the Memphis Red Sox.

Crump, James

Career: 1921–22;   Positions: 2b, umpire
1925–38
Teams: *Norfolk Giants ('20), Washington Braves ('21)*, Hilldale Daisies ('21–'22), *Philadelphia Giants ('24)*

He was a peppery reserve second baseman with Hilldale for a couple of seasons during the '20s, sandwiched between stints with lesser teams. In 1922 he was credited with a .248 batting average. After his playing career he became an umpire in the Negro National League, extending his total career in baseball through the 1938 season.

Crump, Willis

Career: 1916–23   Positions: of, 3b, 2b, ss
Team: Atlantic City Bacharach Giants
Bats: Left   Throws: Right
Born: 1890, Florida
Died: Jan. 24, 1972, New York, N.Y.

The uncle of Dick Lundy, he began playing with the Jacksonville Giants in 1907 as a shortstop, and nine years later accompanied the team North to Atlantic City, where they began playing as the Bacharach Giants in 1916. In the first season he shared the left-field position and batted at the bottom of the lineup. Remaining with the team through 1923, he played as an outfielder and infielder, but primarily in a reserve role.

Crutchfield, John William (**Jimmie**)

Career: 1930–45   Positions: cf, rf, 1f
Teams: Birmingham Black Barons ('30), Indianapolis ABCs ('31), **Pittsburgh Crawfords** ('31–'36), Philadelphia Stars ('33), Newark Eagles ('37–'38), Toledo Crawfords ('39), Indianapolis Crawfords ('40), *voluntarily retired ('40)*, Chicago American Giants ('41–'42, '44–'45), *military service ('43–'44)*, Cleveland Buckeyes ('44)
Bats: Left   Throws: Right
Height: 5'7"   Weight: 150

Born: Mar. 15, 1910, Ardmore, Mo.
Died: Mar. 31, 1993, Chicago, Ill.

A gutsy hustler whose ability and team contributions were recognized by both teammates and opponents, Crutchfield was a fine all-around ballplayer and a team man. The small batsman, often called the black Lloyd Waner, was a proficient bunter, excellent hit-and-run man, fast base runner, good fielder, and consistent though not powerful line-drive hitter.

Reared in Moberly, Missouri, he attended elementary school in Ardmore, Missouri, and high school in Moberly, and he and Leroy Matlock played on a local team managed by Bill Gatewood, learning the game from the old-time pitcher. After attending Lincoln University in Jefferson City, Missouri, Crutchfield began his professional career with the Birmingham Black Barons in 1930. In his first game he played center field behind Satchel Paige and hit a home run to give Paige the victory. He finished his rookie year with a .286 batting average while playing for $90 a month.

After a brief stay with the Indianapolis ABCs, playing without a contract, he jumped to the Pittsburgh Crawfords in 1931 for the princely sum of $150 a month as they were making the transformation from a semipro team to a great professional ballclub. Records show averages of .267, .307, .280, .308, and .307 for the young Crutchfield in 1932–36. As an outfielder on the great Pittsburgh Crawfords' teams, "Crutch" started the East-West All-Star games from 1934 to 1936 and also was selected to the 1941 squad after joining the Chicago American Giants.

The fielding genius played baseball because he loved the game and would play anywhere, anytime. No outfielder had better hands, or better eyes in judging a ball than the mighty mite from Moberly. He practiced catching fly balls behind his back to entertain the fans and, under the proper circumstances, he would sometimes liven up routine outfield plays by making a behind-the-back catch in a game.

During his prime he made a couple of sojourns to Latin climates in pursuit of a baseball livelihood. He toured Mexico with the Negro All-Star team in 1935 and was the last surviving American who played in the first Puerto Rican winter season in 1938, having played with the Santurce ballclub that year.

After leaving the Crawfords, he played with the Newark Eagles, recording averages of .289 and .337 for his two seasons with Abe Manley's team. Leaving the Eagles in 1939, he returned to the Crawfords, now located in Toledo, and then began the 1940 season with them before personal reasons compelled him to leave baseball for a season.

In 1941 he joined the Chicago American Giants for two seasons before entering the Army for a year of military service. In 1944 he played with the Cleveland Buckeyes but returned to Chicago in 1945 to close out his sixteen-year career. During his last three years in the Negro Leagues his batting average had dropped off to .245, .254, and .246. Following his retirement from baseball, he worked for the postal service for twenty-six years.

Cruz
Career: 1930   Position: p
Team: Cuban Stars

He pitched briefly with the Cuban Stars in 1930, his only year in the Negro Leagues.

Cuban Giants
Duration: 1885–99   Honors: Colored champions ('87–'88), eastern champions ('94)
Affiliation: Independent ('85–'88, '92–'99), Middle States League ('89–'90), Connecticut State League ('91)

Organized in 1885, the Cuban Giants were the first salaried professional black baseball team. Frank P. Thompson, the headwaiter at Long Island's Argyle Hotel in Babylon, New York, recruited players from the Philadelphia Keystones to work at the hotel as waiters and form a baseball team to play for the entertainment of the summer guests. After the end of the tourist season, the team added more players from the Philadelphia Orions and the Manhattens of Washington, D.C., to form the Cuban Giants, and toured as the first black professional team.

The Cuban Giants were the Colored champions in 1887 and 1888, and annexed the eastern championship in 1894. They were considered the top ballclub of the era, often playing as representatives of a host city in that city's regular league. They represented Trenton, New Jersey (1889), and York, Pennsylvania (1890), in the Middle States League and Ansonia in the Connecticut State League (1891). The New York Gorhams did the same, representing Philadelphia in the Middle States League in 1889.

The Cuban Giants was the first and most successful black professional team and remained a top attraction for the remainder of the century, generating imitation teams who copied their success and who appropriated a variation of the Cuban Giants' name as their own. Several of these ballclubs played a quality of baseball close to that of the original team and flourished during the early years of the century.

Cuban Stars (East)
Duration: 1916–29   Honors: None
Affiliations: Independent ('16–'22), Eastern Colored League ('23–'28), ANL ('29)

In the early years of black baseball, a major gate attraction was two Cuban teams, each of mixed racial composition, but with one team playing primarily in the East and the other in the West. Both teams carried the name Cuban Stars. To differentiate between the two, they are usually designated by historians as the Cuban Stars (East) and the Cuban Stars (West). The eastern team, beginning as an independent team, became a charter member of the Eastern Colored League in 1923, remaining until the league's collapse in 1928. When the league folded, the Cuban Stars were the top team and finished the season with a record of 93–22. In 1929 they joined the American Negro League, which was basically a continuation of the Eastern Colored League. During their early years as an independent ballclub, the team was sometimes referred to by different designations,

being called the New York Cubans in 1916, the Havana Cuban Stars in 1917, and the All Cubans in 1921. After the Breakup of the eastern leagues, the team again lost its separate identity, with the Cuban Stars playing under the banner of the Cuban House of David during the early '30s. During this time they also played in the ill-fated East-West League in 1932 and eventually were reorganized by Alex Pompez as the New York Cubans.

Cuban Stars (West)
Duration: 1907–30   Honors: None
Affiliations: Independent ('07–'19), NNL ('20–'30)

In the early years of black baseball, a major gate attraction was two Cuban teams, each of mixed racial composition, but with one team playing primarily in the East and the other in the West. Both teams carried the name Cuban Stars. To differentiate between the two, they are usually designated by historians as the Cuban Stars (East) and the Cuban Stars (West). The western team, beginning as an independent team, became a charter member of the Negro National League in 1920, remaining through the 1930 season. In 1921 they were referred to as the Cincinnati Cubans, while representing that city in the Negro National League.

Cuban X-Giants
Duration: 1897–1907   Honors: Colored champions ('99), eastern champions ('97–'03), eastern cochampions ('00–'02)
Affiliation: Independent

Comprised of defecting Cuban Giants, the Cuban X-Giants became the dominant team during the late 1890s and early 1900s. Under manager E. B. Lamar, Jr., they won the first challenge playoff championship series between the East and the West in 1899. The trip undertaken by the X-Giants was the longest ever for a black ballclub at that time. The X-Giants continued to be the dominant team in the East until dethroned by the Philadelphia Giants in

1904, when the Philly team reversed the previous season's outcome in the playoffs.

Cuerira
Career: 1921–22   Positions: p, of
Teams: All Cubans ('21), Cuban Stars (West) ('22)

He was a combination pitcher-outfielder with the All-Cubans and Negro National League Cuban Stars in 1921–22 but did not distinguish himself at either position.

Culcra
[see Culver]

Culver
a.k.a. Colyer; Culcra
Career: 1916–22   Positions: ss, 3b, cf
Teams: Lincoln Stars ('16), Pennsylvania Red Caps of New York ('17–'19), New York Lincoln Giants ('18–'20), *Candian semipro ('21)*, Cuban Stars (West) ('22)

During the late '10s he played with New York-based ballclubs, most notably the New York Lincoln Giants. In 1918 he split the season between the Lincolns and the Pennsylvania Red Caps of New York, an offshoot of the Lincoln Stars. Incomplete statistics show a composite batting average of .294, but with most of his hits coming with the Red Caps, for whom he played center field while batting sixth in the order. In 1920 he was described as a "corking" shortstop and a reliable hitter but, because of money problems with the Lincoln Giants' owner, he left the ballclub and joined a white Canadian team. His last appearance was with the Cuban Stars (West), as a third baseman in 1922.

Cumming, Hugh S.
Career: 1887   Position: player
Team: *Lord Baltimores*

He was a player with the Lord Baltimores, one of eight teams that were charter members of the League of Colored Baseball Clubs in 1887. However, the league's existence was ephemeral, lasting only a week. His position is uncertain.

Cummings
Career: 1932   Position: c
Team: Louisville Black Caps

He was a catcher with the Louisville Black Caps in 1932, when the Negro Southern League was considered a major league.

Cummings, Napoleon (Chance)
Career: 1916–29   Positions: **1b,** 2b
Teams: **Atlantic City Bacharach Giants** ('16–'18, '22–'28), Hilldale Daisies ('18–'21), *Madison Stars ('20), Norfolk All-Stars ('20)*
Bats: Right   Throws: Right
Height: 5'11"   Weight: 175
Born: June 8, 1893, Jacksonville, Fla.

Nicknamed "Chance" from being compared to the Chicago Cubs' great Frank Chance, Cummings was the first baseman for the Bacharach Giants for eleven of his fourteen years in black baseball. Although big and awkward, he was a hard worker and from studied scrutiny of batters' tendencies, he developed an uncanny instinct for knowing where to play batters, and he became a good fielder. To some observers he appeared to be just lucky, but his luck was the residue of design. As an astute observer of the opposition, Cummings became adept at stealing signs and was a good bunter and a fair base runner.

While not a great hitter or possessing a natural hitter's raw abilities, through hard work and constant practice the bad-ball hitter became a "very tricky" batter and developed into a dangerous hitter in the clutch. After a .282 average in the 1926 regular season to help the Bacharachs to the Eastern Colored League pennant, he hit .313 in the World Series against the Kansas City Monarchs in a losing effort. The Bacharachs repeated as Eastern Colored League champions in 1927 but again lost the World Series, to the Chicago American Giants. Cummings did not enjoy a good relationship with playing manager Dick Lundy, and this might have hastened Cummings' departure from the team.

The son of a longshoreman, he quit school when his father died and worked at the United Produce Company to help support his mother but also continued to play baseball. He began his professional career in Jacksonville, Florida, with the Duval Giants and became one of the original Bacharachs when the team went North to Atlantic City in 1916. He was the starting first sacker, hitting either fifth or sixth in the batting order during the first three years at the New Jersey locale. In 1918 he jumped to Hilldale and, as a regular in 1921, registered a .223 batting average. Returning to the Bacharachs in 1924, he hit .247 and .275 in the next two seasons, preparatory to the Bacharachs' two pennant-winning teams in 1926–27. During his fourteen-year career he played both first base and second base for the Bacharachs and Hilldale.

In his early years with the Bacharachs, he "clowned" for the amusement of the fans, sometimes pretending to shoot craps and bugging out his eyes at the phantom outcome of the dice roll. In an exhibition game with a white semipro team, he gave defensive pointers to Lou Gehrig, who was then a student at Columbia University. Cummings was a sharp dresser, and after baseball he worked as a salesman, an investigator for the prosecutor's office, and became involved in politics. As a Republican and supporter of President Richard Nixon, he received criticism from some members of the black community and had his windows broken with rocks, but he remained steadfast in his position.

Cunningham
Career: 1917–20   Positions: **ss**, 2b
Teams: St. Louis Giants ('17), Indianapolis ABCs ('18), Dayton Marcos ('18–'20)

He was the regular shortstop, batting seventh in the order, for the St. Louis Giants in 1917, but the club broke up in May. The next season he was with the ABCs briefly before joining the Dayton Marcos as a part-time starter for

three seasons, playing both shortstop and second base.

Cunningham, H. (**Rounder**)
Career: 1918–31   Position: ss
Team: *Montgomery Grey Sox*

A longtime shortstop for the Montgomery Grey Sox, he began his association with the ballclub in 1918 and closed out his career in 1931, a year before the Negro Southern League was accorded major-league status for a season.

Cunningham, Harry (Baby)
Career: 1930–37   Positions: p, of
Teams: Memphis Red Sox ('30–'32, '37), Birmingham Black Barons ('32)

This pitcher began his career in 1930, registering a 5–10 ledger with the Memphis Red Sox, and also closed his career with the Red Sox in 1937, with a short stint with the Birmingham Black Barons in between.

Cunningham, L.
Career: 1933–34   Position: of
Teams: Washington Pilots ('33), Cuban Stars (East) ('33), Baltimore Black Sox ('34)

He was an outfielder with the Baltimore Black Sox in 1934, the ballclub's last year in the Negro Leagues.

Cunningham, Larry
Career: 1950   Position: of
Teams: Memphis Red Sox ('50,) Houston Eagles ('50)

He was an outfielder with the Memphis Red Sox and the Houston Eagles in 1950, batting .233 for the season.

Cunningham, Marion (**Daddy**)
Career: 1924–25   Positions: 1b, manager
Teams: Memphis Red Sox ('24–'25), *Montgomery Grey Sox ('26)*

He was a first baseman and manager for the Memphis Red Sox and the Montgomery Grey Sox for three seasons during the '20s.

Cunningham, Robert (Slim)
Career: 1950   Position: p
Team: Cleveland Buckeyes

He began his pitching career with the Cleveland Buckeyes in 1950, when the Negro American League was struggling to survive the loss of players to organized baseball, and logged a 0–2 record in 8 games pitched.

Curley, Earl C.
Career: 1925   Position: of
Team: Memphis Red Sox

In 1925 he played in the outfield with the Memphis Red Sox during his only year in black baseball.

Currie, Reuben (Rube, Black Snake)
Career: 1920–32   Position: p
Teams: *Chicago Unions ('19),* Los Angeles White Sox ('20), Kansas City Monarchs ('20–'23, '26, '28, '32), Hilldale Daisies ('24–'25, '30), *Philadelphia Royal Giants ('25),* Chicago American Giants ('26–'27), Detroit Stars ('28), Baltimore Black Sox ('30), Cleveland Stars ('32)
Bats: Right   Throws: Right
Height: 6'4"   Weight: 195
Born: 1899, Kansas City, Mo.
Died: 1969, Chicago, Ill.

A tall, right-handed curveballer with excellent control, Currie was one of the best pitchers of the '20s. After registering a 10–5 record in the Cuban winter league of 1923–24, he was a key pitcher on four consecutive pennant winners and pitched in all four of the World Series between the Negro National League and the Eastern Colored League.

First, as a member of the Hilldale staff, he pitched in three games in the 1924 Series against the Kansas City Monarchs, getting a win and recording a brilliant 0.55 ERA in a losing effort. Continuing his autumn effectiveness in following years, he had his best Series ever, earning two complete-game victories to go with a 1.29 ERA as Hilldale defeated the Monarchs in a rematch to become the world champions of black baseball.

Joining the Chicago American Giants of the rival Negro National League in the aftermath, he picked up his last World Series victory as he helped the American Giants defeat the Bacharach Giants for the 1926 championship. He made his last appearance in 1927, pitching in relief as the American Giants were repeat victors over the Bacharachs.

Prior to facing the Monarchs in the 1924 World Series, Currie had pitched four years with the Monarchs, concluding with their 1923 Negro National League championship team, and posted records of 10–12, 12–10, 12–7, and 14–7. After moving East to Hilldale, he had two vastly contrasting seasons, beginning with a 1–5 mark in 1924 before turning around the poor performance with a 13–2 work sheet in 1925. After his sterling season he was a holdout the following spring before finally reaching contractual agreement with Rube Foster's Chicago American Giants. His two seasons with the American Giants were similar to the disparate pair with Hilldale, with ledgers of 8–3 and 4–5 before the World Series encounters.

In 1928 he returned to the Monarchs, where he enjoyed his initial success, and split a dozen decisions before closing his career in 1932.

Curry, Homer (Goose)
Career: 1928–50   Positions: **lf, rf**, p, 2b, manager
Teams: Cleveland Tigers ('28), **Memphis Red Sox** ('29–'33, '37, '49–'50, '53–'55), Monroe Monarchs ('32), Nashville Elite Giants ('33–'34), Columbus Elite Giants ('35), Washington Elite Giants ('36), Indianapolis Athletics ('37), New York Black Yankees ('38–'40), Baltimore Elite Giants ('38, '40–'41), **Philadelphia Stars** ('42–'47), Newark Eagles, Louisville Black Colonels ('54), Birmingham Black Barons ('55)
Bats: Left   Throws: Right
Height: 5'10"   Weight: 175
Born: 1905, Mexia, Tex.
Died: Mar. 30, 1974, Memphis, Tenn.

He was a good contact hitter, had good speed, and was an adequate fielder but without a strong arm. He had a shrewd baseball mind and was a playing manager much of his career. He began the 1940 season as playing manager of the New York Black Yankees but joined the Elites during the season, finishing with a combined .206 average. In 1941, his first full season with the Elites, as the right fielder and leadoff batter, he tied for the team lead in both doubles (23) and stolen bases (18) and also hit 6 home runs, had 167 total bases, and scored 80 runs while batting .289. In 1942 he moved to the Philadelphia Stars as their leadoff hitter, right fielder, and manager, and hit for averages of .297 and .231 for the next two seasons before dropping himself to the sixth spot in the batting order and hitting for averages of .289, .313, and .321 in 1944–46.

As the Stars' playing manager in 1946, he was involved in a brouhaha during Newark Eagles' ace Leon Days' opening day no-hitter against his club. The incident began when the umpire called the Eagles' Larry Doby safe on a close play at the plate. Stars' catcher Bill Cash was infuriated and knocked the arbiter to the ground. Curry, who was already moving in from his position in right field to voice his objection to the call, arrived in time to kick the felled umpire while he was still on the ground. A riot ensued, with fans spilling out of the stands, necessitating the use of mounted police to clear the field. Later in the season Curry was replaced as manager, and in his last year with the Stars, 1947, his playing time was reduced but he batted an even .400 in limited play.

In another incident, Curry earned a spot in the Negro Leagues' baseball lore when he was victimized by Luis Tiant's exeptionally fine move to first base, and struck out on a ball that Tiant threw to first on a pickoff attempt.

Ironically, Curry began his career as a pitcher. In 1929–30 he registered marks of 2–8 and 5–3 for the Memphis Red Sox while also batting .302 and .327. It was soon apparent that his future was not on the pitching mound, and he moved to the outfield and eventually to a managerial position. In 1929, with the Memphis Red Sox, he was one of three managers who directed the ballclub during the season.

He continued pitching, mostly with southern teams, but began playing more in the outfield as his career advanced. Playing with the Nashville Elites in 1933, he hit .269, and after the franchise left the South and moved successively to Columbus and Washington, D.C., he was credited with a .226 average in 1936 with the Elites and, after joining the New York Black Yankees, an average of .400 in 1939.

He finished his career in the South, returning to the Memphis Red Sox in the early '50s, when the Negro American League's quality had diminished to a minor-league level. After the Sox, he spent two more seasons with the Louisville Black Colonels and the Birmingham Black Barons before retiring after the 1955 season.

Curry, Oscar J.
Career: 1887   Position: p
Team: Cuban Giants

He was a pitcher with the Cuban Giants when they represented the city of Trenton, New Jersey, in 1887.

Curtis
Career: 1932   Position: c
Team: Louisville Black Caps

The Negro Southern League was accorded major-league status in 1932, and he was a catcher with the league's Louisville Black Caps.

Curtis
Career: 1898   Position: manager
Team: Celeron Acme Colored Giants

He was the manager of the Celeron Acme Colored Giants of the Iron and Oil League in 1898. Harry Curtis, a white man, formed the all-black team to represent Celeron, New York, in the league. Both the team and the league folded in July, and it was to be the last time a black team played in a white league.

Cyrus, Herb (Baldy)
[see Souell, Herb]

D

Dabney, Milton

Career: 1885–96   Positions: of, p

Teams: *Argyle Hotel ('85)*, Cuban Giants ('85–86, '96), Cuban X-Giants ('96).

A player on the 1885 Argyle Hotel team that became the first black professional ballclub, he continued as an outfielder-pitcher with the club as it became a traveling team called the Cuban Giants and later joined the Cuban X-Giants, playing through 1896.

Dailey, James

Career: 1948   Position: p

Team: Baltimore Elite Giants

He was a second-line pitcher with the 1948 Baltimore Elite Giants in his only season in the Negro Leagues.

Dallard, William (Eggie)

a.k.a. Morris J. Dallard

Career: 1921–33   Positions: **1b, of,** c, 2b

Teams: *Madison Stars ('20–'21)*, Hilldale Daisies ('21, '28–'32), *Philadelphia Quaker Giants ('22–'24)*, Washington Potomacs ('24), Baltimore Black Sox ('24–'26, '32), Wilmington Potomacs ('25), Lincoln Giants ('25), Atlantic City Bacharach Giants ('26–'27), Philadelphia Stars ('33)

Bats: Right   Throws: Right

Born: 1899

Died: December 1933

Best known as the Hilldale first baseman

during the late twenties and early thirties, this versatile and well-traveled player was a good hitter with sufficient speed to bat in the leadoff position frequently. During his checkered career he performed at first base, second base, in the outfield, and as a catcher for numerous teams, but his longest stints were with the Baltimore Black Sox and Hilldale. After an apprenticeship with the Madison Stars, a team of lesser quality, he had his first chance with a top team with Hilldale in 1921, batting .278 in limited play. Needing more experience, he played with another lesser team, Dan McClellan's Philadelphia Quaker Giants, until 1924. That season, he joined the Eastern Colored League's Washington Potomacs as a replacement for star center fielder Chaney White, who suffered a leg injury. Given a chance to play regularly, Dallard proved to be one of the best outfielders in the league. The next season the Potomacs moved to Wilmington, Delaware, but folded early in the year. Dallard signed with the Lincoln Giants for the remainder of the season and registered a .253 batting average.

His off-field temperament sometimes superseded his on-field ability, and he was dropped from the Baltimore Black Sox in mid-August of 1926 because of a severe drinking problem. Discipline on the team was extremely lax, and fans would bring liquor to the ballpark and pass it to the players. After his release he was quickly grabbed by the Bacharach Giants. A month later he suffered internal injuries making a diving catch, and for a substantial period of time afterward he remained seriously ill.

In 1927 he was healthy again and the Bacharachs won their second straight Eastern Colored League pennant. Dallard played first base and finished with a .333 average while batting second in the order. But the Bacharachs lost the World Series to the Chicago American Giants for the second year in a row. Dallard started the 1928 season with the Bacharachs but moved back to Hilldale, where he shared the regular left-field position while batting in the sixth slot in the order.

The next four seasons he was in the regular lineup, playing left field in 1929 and first base for the next three seasons. As the team's lead-off batter he hit .349 and .303 against all levels of competition in 1930–31. In 1932 he was still with Hilldale for most of the season, the last one before the franchise folded, but he finished the season with the Baltimore Black Sox.

The following year, after completing a substandard season with the Philadelphia Stars, the thirty-four-year-old first baseman was killed along with his two-year-old son in a car accident.

Dallas, Porter (Big Boy)
Career: 1929–32   Position: 3b
Teams: Birmingham Black Barons ('29), Monroe Monarchs ('32)
Bats: Right   Throws: Right

Playing exclusively with southern teams, the big third baseman began his career with the Birmingham Black Barons in 1929, hitting .293. He played in the black big leagues for four seasons, closing his career with the Monroe Monarchs in 1932, when the Negro Southern League was recognized as a major league.

Dalton, Rossie
Career: 1940   Position: of
Teams: Chicago American Giants ('40), Birmingham Black Barons ('40)
Bats: Right   Throws: Right

In his only season, 1940, the utility player split his playing time with the Chicago American Giants and the Birmingham Black Barons.

Dandridge, John
Career: 1949   Position: p
Team: Houston Eagles ('49)

He was an undistinguished pitcher with the Houston Eagles in 1949, when the Negro American League was struggling to survive the loss of players to organized baseball.

Dandridge, Ping
a.k.a. George Dandy
Career: 1917–20   Positions: ss, 3b, 2b, p
Teams: *West Baden Sprudels ('15)*, Havana Red Sox ('17), New York Lincoln Giants ('17, '19), St. Louis Giants ('20)
Bats: Right   Throws: Right

In the later years of the deadball era, he was an infielder and pitcher with the New York Lincoln Giants and St. Louis Giants but played most of his career with teams of lesser status. In 1919 he hit .207 as a part-time starter at shortstop while batting at the bottom of the lineup. When he began his pitching career with the West Baden, Indiana, Sprudels in 1915, he had control problems and was listed in the box scores as Dandy.

Dandridge, Raymond Emmitt (**Ray,** Dannie, Hooks, Squatty, Talua, Mamerto)
Career: 1933–49   Positions: **3b,** 2b, ss, *of*
Teams: Detroit Stars ('33), Nashville Elite Giants ('33), Newark Dodgers ('33–'35), **Newark Eagles** ('36–'39, '42, '44), *Venezuelan League ('39), Mexican League ('40–'43, '45–'48),* New York Cubans ('49), *minor leagues ('49–'53)*
Bats: Right   Throws: Right
Height: 5'7"   Weight: 170
Born: Aug. 31, 1913, Richmond, Va.

There has never been a more masterful third baseman than Ray Dandridge. Relaxed, smooth as silk, and possessing a great pair of hands with a velvet touch, he could make all the plays. In addition to his quick hands, he had a powerful arm, and the versatility to excel at shortstop and second base as well as at third base.

He joined Willie Wells, Dick Seay, and Mule Suttles to form the "million-dollar infield" of the Newark Eagles during the late 1930s. Some said that a train could go through his bowlegs but that a baseball never did. And those bandy legs never kept him from running the bases; he finished third in the league in stolen bases in 1944, behind Henry Kimbro and Cool Papa Bell.

Often called "the best third baseman never to make the major leagues," Dandridge was also a good hitter for average, rapping the ball at a .370 clip during the 1944 season while leading the league in hits, runs, and total bases. A spray hitter who went with the pitch, and possessing a camera eye and good bat control, he seldom struck out and was a skilled practitioner of the hit-and-run play.

The Virginian started his professional career in 1933 by hitting .333 with Jim Taylor's Detroit Stars. During the latter part of the season he was loaned to Tom Wilson's Nashville Elite Giants for a short time but returned to Detroit, where the team was breaking up because of financial difficulties. Refusing to return to Detroit the next season, he signed with Dick Lundy's Newark Dodgers and hit .436 and .368 during his two seasons with the club. In 1936 owner Abe Manley merged the team with the Brooklyn Eagles to form the Newark Eagles. Dandridge continued as a star player with Newark for the remainder of the 1930s, hitting .354 and .305 in his first two seasons with the Eagles.

During his time in the Negro National League he compiled a lifetime .355 average in league play and played in three All-Star games, posting a lofty .545 batting average for the classics. The star infielder was also voted by the fans to start in two additional All-Star games, but he missed these due to excursions to Latin America. He also was elected for the 1938 East-West All-Star squad, but the Eagles withheld him, and the East lost the game.

His first venture to Latin America came in

August 1939, when he left the Eagles to play with Caracas's Vargas team in the Venezuelan League. After leading his club to the title, he journeyed to Mexico and, with six weeks left in the season, hit .347 to help Veracruz to another title. In October he stopped in Cuba and slapped out a .310 average for Cienfuegos. This almost pulled out a third title in a year's time, but his team fell a half game short. His average marked the second consecutive year that he had topped the .300 mark, having hit .319 the previous winter. Altogether, the sure-handed third baseman played eleven seasons in Cuba, showing a .282 lifetime batting average. He also played winters in Puerto Rico, batting .288 with Santurce in the 1941–42 season, and in the Dominican Republic, but most of his time in Latin American baseball was spent in Mexico.

The 1940 interim excursion began a long association with the Mexican millionaire and sportsman Jorge Pasquel. His Veracruz team also featured Josh Gibson, Willie Wells, and Leon Day, and they won the pennant with ease. For most of the decade of the '40s, Dandridge remained in Mexico, recording averages of .367, .310, and .354 before his single-season return to the United States in 1944, when Manley activated a plot to get him and Wells back from Mexico by having their draft exemptions revoked. However, Manley's plan failed, and Dandridge was back in Mexico in 1945 and resumed a torrid pace, setting a record with his consecutive-game hitting streak.

This was the second time that Manley attempted an act of dubious ethics. In late July 1939, after Ray had jumped to Venezuela and realizing that he had lost a player without any compensation, Manley arranged a trade with the Homestead Grays, giving them Dandridge's contract in exchange for center fielder Jerry Benjamin. But Benjamin failed to report, and Dandridge, who knew nothing about the impending deal, remained the property of the Eagles. He also remained in Mexico, forging a career that would make him a legend south of the border and earn him a place in the Mexican Hall of Fame.

In 1949, at age thirty-five, he was signed by the New York Giants' organization and assigned to their AAA farm club at Minneapolis. Upon arrival there, the right-handed batting whiz promptly compiled averages of .363, .311, and .324. A great "team man," Dandridge won the league's Most Valuable Player honors in 1950, when he led the Millers to the league championship.

However, regardless of his outstanding accomplishments, the Giants would not promote Dandridge to the parent club, nor would they sell his contract to another team. Dandridge continued in the Pacific Coast League for another year and played a final season with Bismarck, North Dakota, in 1954, before ending his diamond career.

After leaving baseball, he worked as a bartender and as a recreation director for the city of Newark before finally retiring to Florida. Dandridge was duly recognized as one of the greatest third basemen in the history of baseball when he was inducted into the Baseball Hall of Fame in 1987.

Dandridge, Troy Rasmussen (Dan)
Career: 1929   Position: 3b
Teams: Chicago Giants ('29), Dayton Marcos ('29)
Bats: Right   Throws: Right

In 1929 the third baseman split his playing time between two marginal independent teams, the once-proud Chicago Giants and the Dayton Marcos.

Dandy, George
[see Dandridge, Ping]

Daniels
Career: 1935   Position: p
Team: Newark Dodgers

He pitched briefly with the Newark Dodgers in his only season in the Negro Leagues.

Daniels, Edgar **(Eddie)**
Career: 1946–47   Positions: **p,** *of*

Teams: New York Cubans ('46–'47), *minor leagues ('50–'54)*
Bats: Left   Throws: Left

The left-hander broke in with the New York Cubans as a second-line pitcher just as the doors to organized baseball were being opened (1946–47). But three years later it was as an outfielder that he passed through those doors, hitting .325 in the Western League. In 1954, showing evidence of both respectable power and a high strikeout ratio, he batted .286 with Pampa in the West Texas-New Mexico League.

Daniels, Fred
Career: 1919–28   Positions: p, *of*
Teams: St. Louis Giants ('19), Hilldale Daisies, Birmingham Black Barons ('23–'27), New York Lincoln Giants ('24), Nashville Elite Giants ('28)

He pitched for a decade with a half-dozen teams but is best identified with the Birmingham Black Barons, where he was 1–4 in 1927, when they won the Negro National League's second-half title before losing to the Chicago American Giants in the league playoffs.

Daniels, Hammond
Career: 1924–26   Position: officer
Team: Atlantic City Bacharach Giants

He was an officer with Atlantic City's Eastern Colored League champion Bacharach Giants in 1926, his third and last season with the club.

Daniels, James George (Jim Schoolboy)
Career: 1943   Position: p
Team: Birmingham Black Barons

The wartime pitcher played with the Birmingham Black Barons in 1943, his only season in the black big leagues.

Daniels, Leon (Pepper)
Career: 1921–35   Positions: c, 1b
Teams: **Detroit Stars** ('21–'30), Harrisburg Giants ('24), Chicago Columbia Giants ('31).

Cuban Stars, Atlantic City Bacharach Giants ('33), Brooklyn Eagles ('35)
Bats: Right   Throws: Right
Died: Sept. 25, 1978, Chester, N.Y.

A very smart catcher with a complexion light enough to pass for white, the youngster played with the Detroit Stars before signing a fat contract with the Harrisburg Giants of the Eastern Colored League in 1924. After starting the season as the regular catcher, he became homesick and, although batting .375, left the team early in the season to return West. Although primarily a catcher, he also saw some action at first base. Spending most of his career with the Stars, he was a light hitter in his early years, but hit for averages of .262 and .265 in 1926 and 1930, respectively. The latter season was his last year in Detroit, and in 1931 he joined Dave Malarcher's Chicago Columbia Giants, a team that filled the void in Chicago after Rube Foster's death the previous year. Daniels was a backup catcher on the squad, which was essentially a continuation of Foster's Chicago American Giants. As he neared the end of his fifteen-year career, he also played with the Cuban Stars, Bacharach Giants, and Brooklyn Eagles.

Darden, Clarence
Career: 1938   Position: 3b
Team: Atlanta Black Crackers

An ambitious third baseman from Brooklyn, he was recruited by the 1938 Atlanta Black Crackers to fill the void at the hot corner left by the defection of Ormand Sampson to the Chicago American Giants. He made a favorable impression with his fine throwing arm but his hitting punch failed to materialize, and he was dropped from the squad in May. Meanwhile, Atlanta improved and went on to win the second-half Negro American League championship.

Darden, Floyd
Career: 1950   Positions: 2b, of
Team: Baltimore Elite Giants

He spent his playing time as a combination second baseman-outfielder with the Baltimore Elite Giants in 1950.

Davenport, Lloyd (Ducky, Bear Man)
Career: 1935–49   Positions: of, manager
Teams: *Monroe Monarchs ('34), New Orleans Crescent Stars ('34),* Philadelphia Stars ('35–'36), Cincinnati Tigers ('37), Memphis Red Sox ('38–'39), *Mexican League ('40, '45–'46),* Birmingham Black Barons ('41–'42), Jacksonville Red Caps ('42), Cincinnati Buckeyes ('42), Chicago American Giants ('43–'44, '49, *'51),* Cleveland Buckeyes ('44–'45), *Pittsburgh Crawfords,* Louisville Buckeyes ('49), *minor leagues ('51)*
Bats: Left   Throws: Left
Height: 5'4"   Weight: 150
Born: Oct. 28, 1911, New Orleans, La.

The little left-handed outfielder was an all-around good ballplayer with outstanding speed. He was extremely quick out of the batter's box and utilized his speed to advantage on the bases and in the field. Possessing a good arm to complement his great range, he was the center fielder on the 1938 Negro American League champion Memphis Red Sox team. A flat-footed hitter who could place the ball anywhere he wanted, he was also strong for his size and a hard hitter. Generally batting in one of the first three spots in the lineup, he recorded batting averages of .313 in 1936, .313 in 1937, .360 in 1942, .304 in 1944, and .345 in 1945 and during this period made five appearances in the East-West All-Star game (1937, 1942–45), representing four different teams.

Sandwiched between stints with the Memphis Red Sox and Birmingham Black Barons, Davenport made his first excursion to Mexico, batting .356 with Tampico in 1940. Signing with the Cleveland Buckeyes in 1944, he became a key player in their first-half drive toward the pennant in 1945. After playing in the All-Star game, he again succumbed to the lure of more money and jumped to Mexico late in the season, hitting .352 in 30 games with Nuevo Laredo. He returned to the same team for part of the 1946 season and registered a

.289 batting average. Playing in the Cuban winter league between the two Mexican seasons, he topped all hitters with a .332 batting average, his second consecutive season over .300 in Cuba, and finished with a .275 lifetime average to show for his five years on that island (1943–48).

The Negro League career that began in 1934 was closed out in 1949 with a .248 season with the Chicago American Giants. Nicknamed "Ducky" because of his distinctive walk and "Bear Man" because of his uncomely appearance and the way he said everything with a growl, the little outfielder also managed during the latter part of his sixteen-year career, which was spent with ten different teams. He had one last hurrah with Elmwood in the Mandak League in 1951, where he still mustered a .278 batting average.

Davidson, Charles (Specks, John)
Career: 1939–49   Position: p
Teams: New York Black Yankees ('39–'40, '46–'48), Memphis Red Sox ('46), Brooklyn Royal Giants ('40), Baltimore Elite Giants ('40, '49)
Bats: Right   Throws: Right
Height: 6'2"   Weight: 200

A pitcher with a three-quarters overhand motion, the New York Black Yankees' hurler's best pitch was a curve. He spent two stints with the Black Yankees, beginning with them in 1939 for two seasons and returning a second time following the end of World War II. In 1947 he logged an unimpressive 1–4 record with the Black Yanks but still was one of only eight holdovers in 1948. Aside from his pitching, he was of little assistance to the team effort, being rather inept as a hitter, a poor base runner, and with restricted abilities in the field. He also pitched for the Brooklyn Royal Giants, Baltimore Elite Giants, and Memphis Red Sox.

Davis
Career: 1905   Position: p
Team: Leland Giants

This pitcher joined the Leland Giants in 1905, their first year of existence.

Davis
Career: 1934   Position: of
Team: Kansas City Monarchs

He played briefly as an outfielder with the Kansas City Monarchs in 1934, during the years when they were between leagues and touring across the Midwest to survive the Depression.

Davis
Career: 1935   Position: ss
Team: Brooklyn Eagles

The infielder from Winston-Salem, North Carolina, was an ordinary player but, for a short time, he was the regular shortstop for the Brooklyn Eagles.

Davis
Career: 1935–38   Position: p
Teams: Newark Dodgers ('35), Newark Eagles ('38)

He pitched with the Newark Dodgers in 1935 and appeared again with the Newark Eagles in 1938, but was used primarily against semipro opposition.

Davis, A.
Career: 1887–91   Positions: 2b, rf,
                        manager
Teams: Boston Resolutes ('87), New York Gorhams ('88–'91)

For five seasons during the formative years of black baseball in the nineteenth century, he was a player-manager with the Boston Resolutes and New York Gorhams.

Davis, Adie
Career: 1940   Position: 3b
Team: Newark Eagles
Bats: Right   Throws: Right
Height: 5'10"   Weight: 165

In an abbreviated baseball career, the former basketball player at Shaw University played briefly and without distinction as a third baseman with the Newark Eagles. He was a mediocre player with good hustle and slightly above-average speed and fielding ability, but his development was hindered by his nightlife activities.

Davis, A. L.
Career: 1924–25   Positions: ss, of
Team: Indianapolis ABCs

A shortstop and outfielder with the Indianapolis ABCs in 1924–25, he was released a year before the team disbanded.

Davis, Albert (Gunboat)
Career: 1927–37   Position: p
Teams: **Detroit Stars** ('27–'30, '37), Baltimore Black Sox ('31)

He began his pitching career in 1927 with the Detroit Stars and, with a dearth of quality pitches but an abundance of offensive support, he posted records of 7–10 and 9–7 for the years 1929–30. Joining the Baltimore Black Sox the following season, he won his only recorded decision. Although not reknowned for his pitching skills, when the new Detroit Stars' team organized for the inaugural season of the Negro American League in 1937, he returned to the Stars for a second stint, ending his career where it started a decade earlier.

Davis, Babe (Atlas, *Dave*)
Career: 1938   Position: of
Team: Atlanta Black Crackers
Bats: Right   Throws: Right
Height: 6'2"   Weight: 190

An all-around good athlete, he was called "Atlas" because of his physique. The big, strong outfielder was a straight-away hitter and had a lot of power, usually batting about .300, and was also a good bunter. A right-hander all the way, he was the left fielder and batted cleanup for the 1938 Atlanta Black Crackers, second-half champions of the Negro American League. In addition to his hitting prowess, he had outstanding speed and was a good base stealer. In the outfield he was a bit lazy and did not have a strong arm.

Before he began playing professional baseball he was a star high-school football player in his hometown, Athens, Georgia. At the beginning of the 1938 season he was unsigned and playing with the semipro Athens Red Sox prior to reaching accord with the Black Crackers in mid-May. Once in the lineup, he provided the offensive thrust to make Atlanta a contender. By August he was leading the club with a .354 average and was also tops in RBIs. Occasionally, when the need arose, he played second base to help the ballclub.

Davis, Big Boy
Career: 1932   Position: p
Team: Indianapolis ABCs

He was a pitcher with the Indianapolis ABCs in 1932, when they were a member of the Negro Southern League. That season, following the collapse of the Negro National League, the Negro Southern League was considered a major loop.

Davis, Bill
Career: 1945–47   Position: p
Team: Philadelphia Stars

He began his pitching career with the Philadelphia Stars in 1945, but after the end of World War II, although he remained on the pitching staff for two more seasons, he was seldom used.

Davis, Country
Career: 1939   Position: of
Team: Homestead Grays

He was with the Homestead Grays briefly as an outfielder in 1939.

Davis, Dave
[see Davis, Babe]

Davis, Dwight
Career: 1930   Position: p
Team: Detroit Stars

He was a pitcher with the Detroit Stars in 1930, his only year in the Negro Leagues.

Davis, Earl (Hawk)
Career: 1930–33   Positions: **2b**, ss, 3b
Teams: *Philadelphia Giants ('27)*, Hilldale Daisies ('30), Newark Browns (*'31*–'32), Newark Dodgers ('33), *Atlantic City Bacharach Giants ('36)*

Although primarily a second baseman, he could play any infield position and, during the early '30s, he spent four seasons with teams of marginal quality on the Eastern Seaboard. In 1930 he was a reserve shortstop with the Hilldale club but, after one season, joined the Newark Browns, playing as the regular second baseman and batting second in the order, when they were in the East-West league in 1932.

Davis, Edward A. (Eddie, **Peanuts,** Nyassas)
Career: 1939–50   Position: p
Teams: Ethiopian Clowns ('39–'42), Cincinnati Clowns ('43, '45), Cincinnati-Indianapolis Clowns ('44), Indianapolis Clowns ('46–'50)
Bats: Right   Throws: Right
Height: 5'11"   Weight: 150
Born: 1917

The star pitcher-comedian for the Clowns featured a wide repertory of comedy routines and pitches, some of which were of dubious legality. Counted among his legal pitches was an excellent knuckleball. His pitching matchups with Satchel Paige were great crowd pleasers, as was a 20-inning, 3–3 duel against the Chicago American Giants' Gentry Jessup in 1946. Beginning with the independent Ethiopian Clowns in 1939, he stayed with the club throughout his twelve-year career as the franchise joined the Negro American League and changed home locations, playing variously as the Cincinnati Clowns, the Cincinnati-Indianapolis Clowns, and the Indianapolis Clowns. After leaving the Clowns he played with the Asheville Blues, a minor black ballclub. A noted ladies' man, he contracted a social disease that led to his death at an early age.

Davis, Goldie (Red)
Career: 1924–25   Positions: p, of
Team: Indianapolis ABCs

During his two-year stint with the Indianapolis ABCs during the midtwenties, the light-complexioned player began as a pitcher and finished as an outfielder but failed to impress manager C. I. Taylor sufficiently at either position.

Davis, Hy
Career: 1934   Position: 1b
Team: Newark Dodgers ('34)

In 1934, his only season with a major club, the first baseman played without distinction for the Negro National League Newark Dodgers.

Davis, J.
Career: 1945   Position: 3b
Team: Homestead Grays

A wartime player, he had a brief trial with the Homestead Grays as a third baseman in 1945.

Davis, Jack
Career: 1922–23   Positions: 3b, 2b
Teams: *Washington Braves ('21)*, Atlantic City Bacharach Giants ('22–'23), *Philadelphia Giants ('24–'25)*

He appeared briefly as a reserve third baseman for the Bacharach Giants in 1922–23 but otherwise played with lesser teams.

Davis, James
Career: 1920   Position: p
Teams: Chicago Giants ('20), New York Lincoln Giants ('20)

In 1920 he made brief pitching appearances with both the Chicago Giants and the New York Lincoln Giants.

Davis, Jimmy
[see Davis, Spencer]

Davis, John
Career: 1903–10   Position: p
Teams: Chicago Union Giants ('03), Leland Giants ('05), Cuban Giants, Philadelphia Giants ('10), St. Paul Colored Gophers ('09)
Bats: Right   Throws: Right
Among early black moundsmen, he was

noted as one of the era's effective pitchers and was one of the pitchers for the champion St. Paul Colored Gophers in the 1909 playoffs against Rube Foster's Leland Giants. Although suffering a loss in his only start, he saved the crucial fourth game to seal the Series victory. Beginning his career in 1903, he joined the Leland Giants in their first year of existence, 1905, and pitched with several other well-known teams, including the Cuban Giants, the Philadelphia Giants, and the Chicago Union Giants, until his career ended in 1910.

Davis, John Howard (**Johnny,** Cherokee, Chief)
Career: 1941–50   Positions: **of,** p
Teams: *Mohawk Giants ('40),* **Newark Eagles** *('41–'48),* Houston Eagles *('49–'50), Canadian League ('51), minor leagues ('52–'54)*
Bats: Right   Throws: Right
Height: 6'3"   Weight: 215
Born: Feb. 16, 1918, Ashland, Va.
Died: Nov. 17, 1982, Fort Lauderdale, Fla.

A mainstay on the Newark Eagles during the 1940s, the big, hard-hitting outfielder was one of the "Big Four" who powered the Eagles to the 1946 Negro championship. In the World Series victory over Kansas City Monarchs, Davis hit .292, including a game-winning double in the deciding seventh game. This came after two consecutive All-Star seasons where he had averages of .345 and .319 in 1944 and 1945, respectively. In the latter East-West All-Star game, superstar Josh Gibson refused to play unless the players got $200 each for the game.

That season the right-handed slugger finished second in home runs and was runner-up again in 1947, this time only 1 home run behind teammate and league-leader Monte Irvin. Davis was very strong and had excellent power. A pull hitter, he murdered fastballs but had a little difficulty with curves, once being hit in the head with a curve by Dan Bankhead. Davis's only other baseball deficiency was that he was a slow base runner. Davis made his

third All-Star appearance in 1949, after the Eagles moved to Houston.

After the 1946 championship season, he was a member of Satchel Paige's All-Star team that barnstormed across the country playing against Bob Feller's All-Stars. In the last game of the tour, played at Kansas City, he hit a home run off Spud Chandler to win the game, 3–2.

While known primarily as a hitter in the United States, Davis was better known as a pitcher in the Puerto Rican winter leagues, where he pitched in addition to playing the outfield. His mound accomplishments there included a no-hitter in 1944 while leading the league in strikeouts the same season. As a batter he topped the league in home runs in 1951–52. But his most memorable achievement was winning the MVP award in the winter of 1947–48. An added feature from his Puerto Rican career occurred in 1952, when he was married while in the country. He also stared in the Venezuelan winter league, batting .381 in 1950–51.

Before starting his career in the Negro Leagues, he was well known for his baseball heroics in Schenectady, New York. His association with the city resulted from a meeting in New York City's Central Park with the Brooklyn Dodgers' Al Campanis, who sent him to Schenectady to play for the Mohawk Giants while also working at the American Locomotive Company. While playing with the Mohawk Giants in 1940, his pitching prompted a letter to the *Amsterdam News* saying that Davis was a better pitcher than Satchel Paige. Eventually Davis was signed by Abe Manley, and although he was used mostly as an outfielder, he took some turns on the mound, posting .500 marks for the years 1944–45 and 1947 (3–3, 1–1, and 2–2). In one June outing in 1948, the hard-throwing right-hander struck out 15 batters.

The road to baseball stardom was not an easy one for Davis. He grew up in a series of orphanages and foster homes, including six years at the Catholic Protectory, where he was an altar boy. During this time he would run away but the police would always take him back. He did get a good education during his years at the protectory, finishing the ninth grade before being put in a foster home at age seventeen. Soon afterward he went down to the docks with a friend to become a longshoreman, but instead lied about his age and enlisted in the merchant marine. Unused to the ocean, he was seasick almost from the outset, but stayed in the merchant marine for four years until his discharge in 1939.

After his stint in the merchant marine, he had some trouble with the law and was incarcerated in a New York State penitentiary. Newark Eagles' owner Abe Manley secured his release from prison so he could play with the Eagles, signing Davis in April 1941. But Davis was on parole and could not leave New York State, and played only in the games that were scheduled there. The following season, on March 6, he wrote Effa Manley, the team's business manager, that he wouldn't be able to play with the Eagles in 1942. However, he did play another year under the same circumstances. In 1943 he was the star of the outfield in both batting and fielding, and was a favorite with the Newark fans. The media insisted that he was swinging the bat with authority and was "tearing down fences."

While with the Eagles he was a bit of a loner but at other times he was like a big, fun-loving kid who liked to drive the team bus. Once, while touring in Oklahoma, the team stopped to eat and he was taking too long to finish, so the other players moved the bus as a practical joke. When he came out of the restaurant the bus was nowhere in sight, and he thought he had been left behind. In a few minutes the bus came around the corner, with the players laughing at their teammate's discomfort.

Overcoming his early background and uneven beginning, he spent a decade in the Negro Leagues, and soon after the color bar was lifted, Johnny entered organized ball, playing with Drummondville in the Canadian Provincial League in 1951, where he hit .347 with

31 home runs and 116 RBIs despite being frequently walked. The next year he played with San Diego in the Pacific Coast League, hitting .263 with good power, and was targeted by the Chicago White Sox executives to join their team to hit behind Eddie Robinson, their top power hitter. Unfortunately, Davis broke his ankle sliding into a base and missed the impending call to the major leagues. After recuperating, he played in the Florida International League in 1953, where he hit .331 while setting the all-time league home-run record (35). In 1954, with Montgomery in the South Atlantic League, he hit .263 with 8 homers in only 40 games.

Davis Lee
Career: 1945   Position: p
Team: Kansas City Monarchs

This wartime player pitched with the Kansas City Monarchs in 1945, his only year in the Negro Leagues.

Davis, Lorenzo (**Piper**)

1942–50	Positions: **2b, 1b,** ss, manager

Teams: **Birmingham Black Barons** ('42–'50), *minor leagues ('50–'58)*
Bats: Right   Throws: Right
Height: 6'3"   Weight: 186
Born: July 3, 1917, Piper, Ala.

A star infielder for the Birmingham Black Barons from 1942 to 1949, Piper formed a great keystone combination with Artie Wilson. Equally adept at playing first base or second base, the tall, smooth infielder was a master of the double play and was considered a premier player in the league. He had outstanding hands, an accurate arm, and, while not a speedster, was proficient at executing the hit-and-run play. A good ground-ball man, he was also at home at shortstop and could play any position and often exercised this versatility during his professional baseball apprenticeship.

He turned pro with the Omaha Tigers in 1936. He played in Alabama's Coal and Iron League in 1937, was with the Yakima Indians in 1938, and was with Acipco in the Industrial League in 1939–42. It was not until 1942 that he entered the black big leagues, when he joined the Black Barons for the latter part of the season. After his arrival, the team won consecutive Negro American League pennants during Piper's first two full seasons with the team. In 1943, his official rookie season, the right-handed swinger hit .386 with good extra-base power. After the "sophomore jinx" resulted in an uncharacteristic poor showing (.142 batting average), he rebounded in 1945 with a .313 average. Noted as a good curveball hitter, during the next four campaigns (1946–49) he recorded marks of .273, .272, .353, and .378 and was selected to the East-West All-Star team each year, where he batted in the heart of the lineup and compiled a .385 average for his All-Star appearances. In 1948, as playing manager of the Black Barons, he led his team to the pennant and a World Series showdown with the Homestead Grays. As manager, Piper had a commanding presence and an abundance of patience. One of his prize pupils that season was a teenager named Willie Mays, who later became one of the greatest center fielders ever to play the game.

The versatile fielder continued in his capacity as player-manager until he became the first black player signed by the Boston Red Sox organization, in 1950, and batted .378 in the interim. Davis had been acquired by the St. Louis Browns in July 1947 at the same time that Willard Brown and Hank Thompson were signed, and was to report in thirty days with an option to buy. He was hitting .359 at the time, but the Browns wanted to option him to Elmira, but he wanted to play with the Browns and consequently the option was not exercised. This release of the option rights may have been misinterpreted by other teams who subsequently scouted Davis. When the Red Sox signed him two years later, he was also being scouted by the Yankees, whose scouting report called him a good ballplayer but stated that "if he wasn't good enough for the Browns two

years ago, he couldn't make it with the Yankees now."

Unfortunately, when he signed with the Red Sox, their rookie first sacker Walt Dropo had a super season, and Davis was assigned to Scranton in the Eastern League, where he hit .333. Subsequently he played with Ottawa in the International League (.263) and in the Pacific Coast League with the Oakland Oaks and Los Angeles Stars, with a batting average oscillating around .300. After seasons of .306, .296, .288, and .316 on the Coast, Piper played his last two baseball seasons in the Texas League. His last season, 1958, he hit .282 to wind down his baseball career. Before he retired, Piper's versatility was showcased with a special night when he played all nine positions, as he had also done in the Pacific Coast League.

Playing the year around during his prime, Piper also spent eight winter seasons in Latin America, with stays in Venezuela (1953–56); Puerto Rico (1949–50, 1950–52); and Mexico and the Dominican Republic (1956–57).

Piper received his nickname from his hometown, Piper, Alabama, where he lived while working in the coal mines. A natural athlete, he excelled at both baseball and basketball and, after being rescued from the mines because of his athletic ability, was signed by the Harlem Globetrotters. While also serving as the Globetrotters' road manager, he played both sports for two years (1943–44) before choosing baseball as a career.

That choice proved a good one, and seventeen years later, after the 1958 season as a player-coach with Fort Worth in the Texas League, at age forty-two, Piper hung up the spikes a final time. After his active diamond days were ended, he remained active in baseball, scouting for the Tigers, Cardinals, and Expos for a total of eleven years ('68–'76, '84–85).

Davis, Louis
Career: 1916   Position: p
Team: Chicago American Giants

A pitcher, he appeared in one game with the Chicago American Giants in 1916, his only year in black baseball.

Davis, Martin Luther
Career: 1945   Position: p
Team: Chicago American Giants

With a shortage of players during the waning year of World War II, he had a brief spring trial with the Chicago American Giants in 1945.

Davis, Nathaniel (**Nat**)
Career: 1947–50   Position: 1b
Teams: New York Black Yankees ('47–'48), Philadelphia Stars ('49–'50)

During the last two years of the Negro National League's existence, the first baseman appeared briefly with the New York Black Yankees as a reserve player, and joined the Philadelphia Stars, who entered the Negro American League after the demise of the Negro National League, for another pair of seasons, batting .246 in the first season with his new team.

Davis, Quack
Career: 1913–15   Position: cf
Team: Indianapolis ABCs

He began as a player with the 1913 Indianapolis ABCs, a year before they attained major-league quality. He also appeared in one game with the ABCs in their outstanding 1915 season.

Davis, Red
[see Davis, Goldie (Red)]

Davis, Robert Lomax (**Butch**)
Career: 1947–50   Position: of
Teams: Baltimore Elite Giants ('47–'50), *minor leagues ('50–'52)*
Bats: Left   Throws: Right
Height: 6'0"   Weight: 220
Died: 1990

Playing during the last few years of the Negro Leagues as a quality league, the Balti-more Elite Giants' outfielder was recognized as a good hitter with power and speed, but experienced some difficulty with left-handed pitchers. Defensively he was an adequate fielder with an average arm. In 1947 the like-able rookie from Delmont, North Carolina, hit .340 with 27 stolen bases in only 306 at-bats, and two years later he hit .371. Leaving the Elites, he played parts of two seasons with Winnipeg in the Mandak League (1950–51), walloping the ball for averages of .456 and .406. In 1951 he batted .350 with Albany in the Eastern League, and the following season, in his last year in organized ball, he went to spring training with Scranton in the Eastern League but jumped the team and played most of the year with Toledo in the American Association, where he hit .319. Davis also played in the Latin American leagues before he ended his diamond career. He was killed in an automobile accident in 1990.

Davis, Roosevelt (Rosey, Duro, Macan)
Career: 1924–45   Position: p
Teams: **St. Louis Stars** ('24–'31), Indianapolis ABCs ('31–'32), Columbus Blue Birds ('33), Pittsburgh Crawfords ('34–'35, '37), New York Black Yankees ('36–'38, '45), Newark Eagles ('38), Ethiopian Clowns ('39–'41), *Chicago Brown Bombers ('42),* Cincinnati Clowns ('43), Cincinnati-Indianapolis Clowns ('44–'45), Cleveland Buckeyes ('45), Philadelphia Stars ('45), Memphis Red Sox ('39), Brooklyn Royal Giants
Bats: Right   Throws: Right
Height: 5'10"   Weight: 180
Born: Bartlesville, Okla.

One of the best spitball and emery-ball pitchers in black baseball, he was considered a nervy pitcher who made batters look bad when he appeared to have nothing on the ball. He had good control and, although he threw a spitter most of the time, his repertory of legal pitches included a fastball, curve, drop, change-up, and screwball, but only his screwball was better than ordinary. While he was a good pitcher, his skills were limited to the mound and he was only an average fielder, a poor hitter, and a slow base runner. A well-traveled player, he pitched for fourteen ball-clubs over a twenty-two-year career, including some of the best teams. He was a member of the mounds corps for the champion St. Louis Stars of 1928 and 1930–31, the Pittsburgh Crawfords of 1934–35, and (at age 40) the pennant-winning Cleveland Buckeyes of 1945.

He started his career in 1924 with the St. Louis Stars under manager Candy Jim Taylor, posting records of 11–7, 11–3, 11–5, 7–8, and 10–7 for his first five seasons. In 1930, when the Stars captured the Negro National League pennant, he sported an 8–2 record. After the demise of the Negro National League following the 1931 season, the Stars disbanded and his next stop was with Bismarck, North Dakota, a strong white semipro team.

Leaving the semi-pro circuit after the new Negro National League was organized in 1933, he joined the league's Columbus Blue Birds, where he split six decisions and taught Bill Byrd how to throw the spitter. He was with the Pittsburgh Crawfords in 1934–35, showing an 11–3 record the latter year as the Crawfords won the Negro National League championship by defeating the New York Cubans in the league playoffs. After leaving the Crawfords he spent three seasons with the New York Black Yankees before going to Mexico in 1939.

Returning to the States the following season, he hooked up with the Ethiopian Clowns and stayed with the independent ballclub until joining the Cleveland Buckeyes early in their championship 1945 season, finishing with a combined 2–4 (4.08 ERA) record for the season. Other teams he played with during his wanderings included the Philadelphia Stars, Brooklyn Royal Giants, Chicago Brown Bombers, Indianapolis ABCs, Memphis Red Sox, and Newark Eagles.

Davis, Ross (Satchel)
Career: 1940–47   Position: p
Teams: Baltimore Elite Giants ('40), Cleveland Buckeyes ('43, '47), *military service ('44–'45), Boston Blues ('46)*
Bats: Right   Throws: Right

He joined the Baltimore Elite Giants from Louisville in 1940 as a twenty-one-year-old rookie pitcher but did not stick with the team. Three years later, still considered a promising youngster from St. Louis, he joined the Cleveland Buckeyes, but military service during World War II intervened. Following his service stint, he played one season with the Boston Blues in the United States League before returning to the Buckeyes for a final season. Pitching for the 1947 Negro American League champion Cleveland Buckeyes, he compiled a 5–1 record and added one relief appearance against the Negro National League champion New York Cubans in the Negro World Series.

Davis, Saul Henry (Sol, Rareback)
Career: 1921–31   Positions: ss, 3b, 2b, *manager*
Teams: *Houston Black Buffalos ('18–'22)*, Columbus Buckeyes ('21), Birmingham Black Barons ('23–'26), Cleveland Tigers ('28), Memphis Red Sox ('24, '27–'28, '30), Chicago American Giants ('25–'26, '29–'30), *Black House of David ('27), Jack Johnson's All-Stars ('27), Gilkerson's Union Giants ('28, '31), Chicago Giants,* Detroit Stars ('31), *Zulu Grass Skirts ('37)*
Bats: Right   Throws: Right
Height: 5'11"   Weight: 185
Born: Feb. 22, 1901, Bayou, La.

The versatile infielder could play shortstop, third base, or second base and had a strong arm and an above-average glove. Offensively he was a punch hitter with a mediocre batting average, with averages of .217 and .214 for the seasons of 1927 and 1929. He began playing baseball with a club from Hot Springs, Arkansas, in 1917 and joined the Houston Black Buffaloes the following year and played with the team for five years. Rube Foster saw him playing ball in Houston and wanted to sign him for his Chicago American Giants. Eventually they got together on the arrangements, but although he appeared briefly with Foster's teams for two seasons in the midtwenties, he did not begin to play as a regular with the American Giants until after Foster had become incapacitated by mental illness and was no longer with the team. In 1929 he moved into the starting lineup at second base while hitting in the eighth slot in the batting order. The next season he served as a utility infielder until late in the season, when he joined the Memphis Red Sox.

Davis also played intermittently with the Columbus Buckeyes, Birmingham Black Barons, Cleveland Tigers, and Detroit Stars during the '20s. Between stints with league teams, he played with traveling independent ballclubs. In 1927 he toured with the Black House of David team for part of the season and with ex-heavyweight champion Jack Johnson's All-Stars for the remainder of the year. During the next five years he barnstormed at times with Gilkerson's Union Giants and Joe Green's Chicago Giants.

Play was rough in his era, and he wore shinguards in the infield to protect himself from the filed spikes of base runners. Later in his career he was appointed manager of the Zulu Grass Skirts, a team that barnstormed and entertained across the Midwest, much like the Ethiopian Clowns did in more recent years. After he finished his baseball career he settled in the Dakotas.

Davis, Spencer (Jimmy)
Career: 1937–'42   Positions: **3b,** ss, of, *manager*
Teams: Jacksonville Red Caps ('37), Atlanta Black Crackers ('38), Indianapolis ABCs ('39), New York Black Yankees ('40–'42), *Winston-Salem Giants ('41–'48)*
Bats: Right   Throws: Right
Height: 6'0"   Weight: 165

The infielder was an undistinguished but reliable ballplayer who provided average speed and glovework for a team. Offensively, although he would pull the ball, he was only a fair line-drive hitter without much power. The North Carolinian, a former Jacksonville Red Caps infielder, was picked up by the Atlanta Black Crackers in 1938 to fill a spot at the hot corner that had become a problem. He provided steady defense and consistent hitting during the second half of the split season as the Black Crackers copped the title for the last half of the Negro American League season. When the franchise moved to Indianapolis the following year, he stayed with the club and played as both a third baseman and an outfielder. In 1940 he joined the New York Black Yankees as a shortstop to round out his playing career. Afterward he managed the Winston-Salem Giants, a black minor-league team, for eight years during the '40s.

Davis, Walter (Steel Arm)
Career: 1923–'35   Positions: of, 1b, *p*
Teams: Detroit Stars ('23), **Chicago American Giants** ('24–'30), Chicago Columbia Giants ('31), Cole's American Giants ('32–'35), Nashville Elite Giants ('34), Brooklyn Eagles ('35)
Bats: Left   Throws: Left
Height: 6'1"   Weight: 175
Born: 1902, Madison, Wis.
Died: 1935, Chicago, Ill.

Nicknamed "Steel Arm" from his early days as a pitcher, the hard-hitting veteran outfielder hit at a .438 clip as the cleanup batter on Robert Coles's 1933 Negro National League champion Chicago American Giants, earning selection to a starting position in the inaugural East-West All-Star game. Starting in left field and batting third in the order, Davis responded with two hits in three times at bat in his only All-Star appearance.

He began his career with the Detroit Stars in 1923 as a pitcher, fashioning a 5–3 record but also hitting .319. The next season he was playing with Rube Foster's Chicago American Giants and earning a spot in the outfield with his bat. In 1927 he hit .399 as the American Giants, now under manager David Malarcher, won their second straight pennant. The hard-hitting outfielder extended his batting skills into the next decade, registering averages of .336 in 1930 and .297 in 1932 as the American

Giants copped the Negro Southern League pennant.

On one occasion he hit a home run on a pitch that short-hopped to the plate. While recognized as a dangerous hitter, he was only a fair defensive outfielder, and to keep his bat in the lineup, the left-hander was sometimes used at first base. Throughout his career he played hard both on and off the field. In the summer of 1928 he lost playing time on two occasions, once from an ankle injury and the other time from a suspension for hitting an umpire. While his batting average dropped under .200 in 1935, he was still a formidable player. However, his off-field temperament eventually led to his demise that year, when he was shot and killed in a barroom fight at the Indiana Inn in Chicago.

Davis, William (W. L.)
Career: 1937–40   Positions: 3b, of
Teams: St. Louis Stars ('37), Atlanta Black Crackers ('38), Indianapolis ABCs ('39), Memphis Red Sox ('40)

Primarily a third baseman, he sometimes also played the outfield during his years in the black big leagues. After starting his career with the St. Louis Stars in 1937, he joined the Atlanta Black Crackers during the 1938 season, when they copped the Negro American League's second-half championship. He remained with the Atlanta franchise when it was shifted to Indianapolis the following season and played as the ABCs, and closed out his career in 1940 with the Memphis Red Sox.

Dawson, Johnny
Career: 1938–42   Position: c
Teams: Kansas City Monarchs ('38, '42), Memphis Red Sox ('40), Chicago American Giants ('40), Birmingham Black Barons ('41)
Bats: Right   Throws: Right
Height: 6'0"   Weight: 180

A catcher with an average arm but below average in other phases of the game, his role was primarily as a backup catcher, and he is probably best known for that role with the

Kansas City Monarchs. In 1942 he began the season with the Monarchs but was dropped from the team and was not on the World Series roster. At the plate he failed to hit with consistency or power and, in very limited play, was batting only .100 when released. The young receiver also played with the Memphis Red Sox, Chicago American Giants, and Birmingham Black Barons during his short career.

Dawson, Leroy
Career: 1946   Position: manager
Team: Philadelphia Stars

After the end of World War II he was the manager of the Philadelphia Stars for a single season.

Day
Career: 1917   Position: 1b
Team: Jewell's ABCs

While playing first base with the 1917 Jewell's ABCs, his playing ability earned him praise from the press that he "promises to be as good as Leroy Grant."

Day, Connie
[see Day, Wilson C. (Connie)]

Day, Eddie
Career: 1898   Position: ss
Team: *Celeron Acme Colored Giants*

This nineteenth-century player was a shortstop for the Celeron Acme Colored Giants in 1898. Harry Curtis, a white man, formed the all-black team to play in the Iron and Oil League as representatives of Celeron, New York. Both the team and the league folded in July, and it was to be the last time a black team played in a white league.

Day, Guy
Career: 1885   Position: c
Team: *Argyle Hotel*

He was a catcher on the Argyle Hotel team, formed in 1885 by Frank P. Thompson, the headwaiter at Long Island's Argyle Hotel in Babylon, New York, who recruited players from the Philadelphia Keystones to work at the hotel as waiters and form a baseball team to play for the entertainment of the summer guests. After the end of the tourist season the team added more players to form the Cuban Giants, the first black professional team.

Day, Leon

Career: 1934–50   Positions: **p,** 2b, of
Teams: Baltimore Black Sox ('34), Brooklyn Eagles ('35), **Newark Eagles** ('36–'39, '41–'43, '46), *Venezuelan League ('40), Mexican League ('40, '47–'48), military service ('44–'45),* Baltimore Elite Giants ('49–'50), *minor leagues ('50–'54)*
Bats: Right   Throws: Right
Height: 5'9"   Weight: 170
Born: Oct. 30, 1916, Alexandria, Va.

The most consistently outstanding pitcher in the Negro National League during the late 1930s and 1940s, Leon Day was a heady pitcher whose money pitch was his fastball. The Newark Eagles' ace right-hander had a good curve and change of pace to complement his speed. A strikeout artist, he holds the strikeout record in the Negro National League, the Puerto Rican League, and the East-West All-Star game.

Not only was Leon a great pitcher, but he was also a fast base runner (once running a 100-yard dash in 10 seconds in his baseball uniform), a good fielder (regarded as the best-fielding pitcher in the league and who functioned as a fifth infielder), a good hitter (with averages of .320, .336, .274, .469, and .271 to show for the seasons of 1937, 1941, 1942, 1946, and 1949), and a recognized team leader (and one of the most respected and best-liked players on the club).

With the exception of catcher, the versatile athlete played every position well, and when not on the mound, often started at second base, in center field, or pinch hit. In 1941 a publicity release described Day as "the most versatile and outstanding player on the team" and "the most desirable player on any club." Before the season was over, he lived up to the billing. On opening day he was the starting pitcher, but when the regular center fielder was drafted, he moved into the middle pasture for most of the season. After returning to mound duty later in the season, an injury to an infielder required him to leave the rotation again to play second base, where he formed a double-play combination with Monte Irvin that was unchallenged.

His best season record came in 1937 when, backed by the Eagles' "million-dollar infield," he finished league play with a perfect 13–0 record, with his only loss coming in an exhibition game. However, his best performance year was in 1942. Appearing in a record seven East-West All-Star games from 1935 to 1946, the Eagles' star hurler won his only decision and set an All-Star record by striking out a total of 14 batters. In the 1942 game he struck out 5 of the 7 batters that he faced, without giving up a hit.

Earlier that season he established the Negro National League strikeout record when he fanned 18 Baltimore Elite Giants while allowing only a bloop single over shortstop by the first batter in the game. In postseason play the Homestead Grays, after dropping the first three games to the Kansas City Monarchs, added Day to their World Series roster to face the Monarchs' Satchel Paige. The tough little competitor responded with a five-hit victory over his more illustrious opponent.

Available records show a 7–1 ledger for Leon in league play for that season. Following another good year in 1943, when he was described by the press as "the best pitcher in colored baseball today," despite a 5–4 ledger, Day missed two prime years when he was drafted into the Army during World War II. After two and a half years in an amphibian unit that landed on Utah Beach during the Allied invasion of France, he was discharged in February 1946.

Returning to the Eagles, he picked up where he had left off, pitching an opening day no-hitter against the Philadelphia Stars and not allowing a runner past first base. After the opening day no-hitter, Leon continued his pitching heroics, topping the league in strike-outs, innings pitched, and complete games, and finishing with a 13–4 record as the Eagles captured the pennant. Even though his arm was hurt, the veteran moundsman started two games in the World Series, and made a game-saving catch while playing center field in another game, as the Eagles edged the Kansas City Monarchs in seven games for the championship.

The hardworking competitor also played in Latin American leagues, including leagues in Venezuela, Puerto Rico, Cuba, and Mexico. Beginning with his first trip in 1935 and an All-Star team, Day played six winters in Puerto ('35–'36, '39–'42, '49–'50), establishing the league's single-game strikeout record in 1941 by fanning 19 batters in an extra-inning game. In another game, pitching with Aquadilla in January 1942, he struck out 15 in a nine-inning game and again earned the distinction as the leading pitcher in the winter league for the 1941–42 season.

In 1940 he pitched in Venezuela with the Vargas team, carving out a 12–1 record while pitching his team to the championship. After breaking up the Venezuelan League because of his dominance, Day signed with Veracruz in the Mexican League, where he logged a perfect 6–0 record, with a 3.79 ERA, and contributed a .298 batting average while annexing his second pennant of the season. He returned to Mexico again for two seasons in 1947–48 with the Mexico City Reds and also played his second winter season in Cuba that year (having played before in 1937), finishing with a composite 8–4 Cuban record.

He began playing baseball as a youngster in Baltimore's Mount Winan's district, and after quitting school after the tenth grade, he played sandlot ball with the local athletic club. In 1934 he was playing second base for the semi-pro Silver Moons ballclub, but at midseason he made his first excursion into professional baseball with the Baltimore Black Sox, playing out of Chester, Pennsylvania, where he earned $60 a month. The next season he joined the

Brooklyn Eagles, where manager Candy Jim Taylor converted him to a full-time pitcher and he recorded a 9–3 ledger for the season. His long association with the Newark Eagles began in 1936 when Abe Manley bought the Brooklyn Eagles' franchise and consolidated it with the Newark Dodgers to form the Newark Eagles. After his perfect record in 1937, he injured his arm in the winter and missed virtually all of the 1938 season. Through hard work and determination he rehabilitated the arm and was credited with 16 wins against only 4 losses in 1939.

The 1949 season, spent with the pennant-winning Baltimore Elite Giants, was his last full season in the Negro Leagues, although he spent about a month in the spring of 1950 with the team. He left the Elites early in the season to play with manager Willie Wells's Winnipeg Buffaloes in the Mandak League. During the 1951 season he left the Canadian team and entered organized baseball at age thirty-five, pitching for the Toronto Maple Leafs in the AAA International League. In 1952 he played with the Scranton Miners of the Eastern League, and the next two seasons he was with the Edmonton Eskimoes in the Western International League (1953) and the Brandon, Manitoba, ballclub in the Mandak League (1954).

In contrast to the confidence he exuded in competition, off the field he maintained a modest demeanor, but both on and off the field, Day displayed a calm temperament. After closing out his baseball career, he worked as a security guard, a mail carrier, and as a bartender in ex-teammate Lennie Pearson's lounge before opting to enjoy the life of a retiree.

Day, Wilson C. (**Connie**)
Career: 1920–32   Positions: **2b,** 3b, ss, manager
Teams: Indianapolis ABCs ('20–'23, '32, '39), Baltimore Black Sox ('24–'26), Harrisburg ('26–'28), Atlantic City Bacharach Giants ('29), Hilldale Daisies ('30)
Bats: Right   Throws: Right
A big, rangy player, the infielder was a mar-

vel on defense and was a crowd-pleaser, who "clowned around" while making catches to entertain the fans. Primarily a second baseman, he could play any infield position and was one of the best ground-ball men in the game. His exceptional range, quick hands, and throwing arm made him good on double plays. He was also known as a "rough" base runner, but the fielding whiz was weak at the plate.

He learned his baseball with the Indianapolis ABCs under C. I. Taylor, breaking in with the club when they were a charter member of the Negro National League in 1920. As a rookie he split his playing time between third base and shortstop, while hitting in the lower part of the batting order. During his second season with the team he moved over to second base and hit .236 for the year.

But after C. I. Taylor's death he jumped to the East, joining the Baltimore Black Sox of the Eastern Colored League in 1924, where he hit .237 and .260 in his first two years. With the Sox he alternated between the second slot and the lower part of the batting order. He remained as the regular second sacker until being traded to Harrisburg in late August 1926. With Harrisburg he hit in the second spot in the lineup, and in 1927, his first full season with the team, he batted .223.

Day joined the Bacharachs in 1929 as their regular second baseman and joined Hilldale in a reserve capacity the following season. In his prime he played winter ball with the Philadelphia Royal Giants in 1925, and after his playing career was over, he managed the ABC's in 1939.

Dayton Marcos

Duration: 1919–26   Honors: None
Affiliation: NNL ('20, '26)

One of the original franchises when the Negro National League was formed in 1920, they withdrew from the league after the initial season and fielded a league team in only one other year, 1926, registering a dismal .179 winning percentage. In their other years of existence, they played as an independent ballclub

and were generally below the league standard of play.

Dean, Bob

Career: 1937–40   Position: p
Teams: St. Louis Stars ('37–'39), New Orleans-St. Louis Stars ('40)
Bats: Right   Throws: Right

Basically this right-hander was a two-pitch pitcher, with a good fastball, a mediocre curve, and little else. He had average control and enjoyed a modicum of success during his four years with the St. Louis Stars, later the New Orleans-St. Louis Stars, in the Negro American League.

Dean, Jimmy

Career: 1946–50   Position: p
Teams: Philadelphia Stars ('46, '48–'50), New York Cubans ('47)
Born: Feb. 25, 1925

A pitcher with the Philadelphia Stars during the postwar '40s, his best years coincided with the last years of the black major leagues as quality leagues. He played with half a dozen semipro teams in 1946 before landing with the Philadelphia Stars at the end of the season. He began the next year with the New York Cubans, but in a very short time he was with the Santurce All Stars, a New York-based touring team of lesser caliber. In 1948 he was back with the Philadelphia Stars, where he stayed through the 1950 season.

Dean, Nelson

Career: 1925–32   Position: p
Teams: Kansas City Monarchs ('25–'26, '32), Birmingham Black Barons ('27–'28), Cleveland Hornets ('27), Cleveland Tigers ('28), Memphis Red Sox ('29), Detroit Stars ('30–'31), Cleveland Stars ('32)
Bats: Right   Throws: Right

This right-hander had a fastball, and a curve with a little break, but his good control was his strongest asset. As a rookie pitcher with the 1925 Negro National League champion Kansas City Monarchs, the right-hander registered the best record of his career, sporting a 12–4 ledger. In the Negro World Series against Hilldale of the Eastern Colored League, he was the winning pitcher in the Monarchs' only victory. The next year he split 10 decisions and then, leaving the Monarchs, fell on some lean years, suffering through seasons of 3–8 and 1–7 in 1927 and 1929. The next year he signed with the Detroit Stars, regaining the winning touch with 10–8 and 8–3 ledgers in 1930–31. In his last season, pitching for the Cleveland Stars of the East-West League, he won only one game while losing four times.

Dean, Robert
Career: 1925   Positions: 3b, 2b, ss
Teams: New York Lincoln Giants ('25), *Ewing's All-Stars ('28), Pennsylvania Red Caps of New York ('30–'32)*

This infielder could play both third base and second base and stretched out his career for almost a decade with teams in the New York area. In 1925, as a reserve infielder with the New York Lincoln Giants, he batted .217 in very limited play. Afterward he played with teams of lesser quality, including the Pennsylvania Red Caps of New York.

Deane, Alpheus (Charlie)
a.k.a. Dean
Career: 1947   Position: p
Team: New York Black Yankees

He was a pitcher with the New York Black Yankees in 1947, his only season in the Negro Leagues.

Deas, James Alvin (**Yank**)
a.k.a. Yank
Career: 1916–23   Positions: c, of
Teams: **Atlantic City Bacharach Giants** ('16–'18, '20–'23), New York Lincoln Giants ('18), *Pennsylvania Giants ('18),* Hilldale Daisies ('18–'19), *military service ('18), Richmond Giants ('23), Philadelphia Colored Giants of New York ('28)*
Bats: Right   Throws: Right
Height: 5'6"   Weight: 148

Born: January 8, 1895, Savannah, Ga.
Died: May 1972, New York, N. Y.

This little player was considered a fine hitter and was a highly regarded receiver with a great throwing arm. The Georgian began playing baseball with the Savannah Home Boys, but shipped out of his hometown after being recruited by Dick Lundy to play in Atlantic City with the ballclub that became the Bacharach Giants. Breaking into the black big leagues in 1916, he was the regular catcher with the Bacharachs, but shared catching duties with Burlin White in 1917. The youngster was an able receiver, but White had an edge on him defensively.

Drafted into service during World War I, he played on the Camp Dix baseball team while in the Army, and also played occasionally with assorted professional teams when leave from the Army made it feasible. After being discharged, he joined Hilldale in 1919 as their regular receiver and hit .221 while batting near the bottom of the order, as he did throughout his career.

The next season he returned to the Bacharachs for four years as a backup catcher. In 1921 he is credited with a .200 batting average in limited play in this role. After leaving the Bacharachs he played with lesser teams for the remainder of his career. He was sometimes listed in the box scores only by his nickname "Yank."

Debran, Roy
a.k.a. Debram
Career: 1940   Position: of
Team: New York Black Yankees

An outfielder, he played in three games with the New York Black Yankees in 1940, batting .333 in his limited playing time.

Decker, Charles (Dusty)
Career: 1932–37   Positions: ss, 3b, 2b, manager
Teams: Indianapolis ABCs ('32), Montgomery Grey Sox ('32), Memphis Red Sox ('36), De-

troit Stars ('37), *Louisville Black Colonels* (*'38*)

He began his career in 1932 as a reserve infielder with the Indianapolis ABCs, and five years later he was the regular second baseman for the 1937 Detroit Stars while batting in the lower part of the order.

Decuir, Lionel
Career: 1939–40   Position: c
Team: Kansas City Monarchs
Bats: Right   Throws: Right
Height: 5'11"   Weight: 165

A catcher with the Kansas City Monarchs in 1939–40, he was a good receiver defensively but was lacking offensively. He failed to hit for average or power and lacked speed on the bases.

Dedeaux, Russ
Career: 1941, 1946   Position: p
Teams: Newark Eagles ('41), New York Black Yankees ('41, '46)

Dedeaux (pronounced Dee-doe) pitched briefly, without a decision, for the Newark Eagles in 1941, and following World War II, he had another short stint, with the New York Black Yankees in 1946, but was lacking the necessary skills for success at that level. In later years he was killed in a car wreck.

Defried
Career: 1931   Position: c
Team: *Newark Browns*

He was a catcher with the Newark Browns in 1931, a year before they joined the East-West League.

Dejernett
Career: 1939   Position: p
Team: Indianapolis ABCs

He appeared briefly with the Indianapolis ABCs in 1939, the team that was the Atlanta Black Crackers transplanted to Indianapolis and playing under a different name.

Delaney
Career: 1910   Position: 2b
Team: Brooklyn Royal Giants

He was a reserve second baseman with the Brooklyn Royal Giants in 1910, when they won their second consecutive championship.

Delgado, Felix Rafael (Felle)
a.k.a. Delgardo
Career: 1936–41   Positions: of, 1b
Teams: Cuban Stars ('36), New York Cubans ('41)
Bats: Right   Throws: Right

An outfielder with the 1941 New York Cubans, he could also play first base. He was a very fast base runner but a weak hitter, batting only .118 for the season. Earlier in his career he was the regular right fielder with Oscar Levis's Cuban Stars in 1936.

Delman
Career: 1934   Position: ss
Team: Homestead Grays

In 1934 he made his only appearance in the Negro Leagues, as a reserve shortstop for the Homestead Grays.

DeLugo
Career: 1935   Position: p
Team: New York Cubans

The pitcher appeared with the 1935 New York Cubans in his only season in the Negro League.

DeMeza
Career: 1905   Position: p
Team: All Cubans

He was a pitcher with the 1905 All Cubans, the top Cuban team of the era.

Demmery
Career: 1941   Position: of
Team: Baltimore Elite Giants

He played in one game as an outfielder with the Baltimore Elite Giants in 1941.

DeMoss, Elwood (**Bingo**)
Career: 1910–30;   Positions: **2b,** ss, of,
1942–45   *p,* manager
Teams: *Topeka Giants ('05),* Kansas City Kansas Giants ('10), *Oklahoma Giants, West Baden Sprudels ('12–'14),* Chicago Giants ('13), **Indianapolis ABCs** ('15–'16, '26), Bowser's ABCs ('16), **Chicago American Giants** ('13, '17–'25), Detroit Stars ('27–'30), All-Cubans, Cleveland Giants ('33), *Chicago Brown Bombers ('42–'43), Brooklyn Brown Dodgers ('45)*
Bats: Right   Throws: Right
Height: 6'2"   Weight: 175
Born: Sept. 5, 1889, Topeka, Kan.
Died: Jan. 26, 1965, Chicago, Ill.

Unquestionably the greatest second baseman in black baseball for the first quarter century, Bingo DeMoss was the consummate ballplayer, excelling at all phases of the game. Very fast on the bases and quick in the field, he could make all the plays, and his style afield served as a model for those who later played the keystone position. DeMoss had quick hands and teamed with Bobby Williams on the Chicago American Giants to form a superlative double-play combination that could turn two "super quick." Demoss would often make the throw to first under his left arm without even looking at first base.

In addition to his impeccable defensive skills, the right-handed line-drive hitter was also productive with the bat, and was at his best in the clutch. Spraying hits to all fields, he recorded batting averages of .316, .316, .303, and .314, in 1915, 1919, 1926, and 1929 in the United States, and a .333 average for his play in the 1915–16 Cuban winter league.

A scientific clutch hitter with superior bat control and exceptional eye-hand coordination, he was a good contact hitter and could place the ball where he wanted. A natural right-field hitter, he was a skilled hit-and-run artist and a superb bunter, making him an ideal second-place hitter in the lineup. Jocko Conlon, who before becoming an umpire played exhibitions against the Chicago American Giants, said that DeMoss could drop a bunt on a dime. He and Foster's other players would drive Jocko's team crazy.

DeMoss began his career in 1905 with the Topeka Giants, and was a shortstop until he hurt his arm pitching and was shifted to second base for a shorter throw to first base. He made stops with other marginal teams before joining C. I. Taylor's Indianapolis ABCs in 1915.

With the ABCs he quickly established himself as a star player, batting .316 and pilfering 34 bases in 50 games, but the ABCs lost the championship in a closely contested series with Rube Foster's Chicago American Giants. The following season, with both teams being essentially the same, DeMoss finished strong to register a .250 batting average as the ABCs overcame internal management problems and defeated the American Giants in a playoff series rematch to win the 1916 western championship.

The next season he signed with Rube Foster's Chicago American Giants, where his hustle and team play were perfectly compatible with Foster's managerial style. His first year there he hit .258 and stole 24 bases in 51 games on a squad that was possibly the best black baseball team of the deadball era. That winter he played with the Royal Poinciana Hotel team in the Florida winter league, and the following season, as the combat of World War I intensified, he received a "fourth class" draft classification and was able to remain with the decimated team, but incomplete statistics show only a .201 batting average.

After the war, DeMoss replaced Pete Hill as the captain of the Chicago American Giants and held that position for six years, during which the Chicago American Giants won the first three Negro National League pennants, with DeMoss contributing his usual sterling defensive play while hitting for averages of .286, .261, and .254. Following the 1924 season, because the Indianapolis ABCs had lost so many players to raids by eastern teams, Rube Foster sent DeMoss and George Dixon to the ABCs to balance the league. With DeMoss's departure, Dave Malarcher ascended to the captaincy of the Chicago American Giants.

Playing for the two greatest managers of his day, Bingo absorbed baseball strategy from the masters. A smart, aggressive field general, his leadership contributed to the success of the teams on which he played, and in the latter stages of his career he became a manager, directing the Detroit Stars for six seasons (1926–31). At one point in his career he was rumored to be headed to St. Louis as a manager, but instead he chose to go with the Indianapolis ABCs in that capacity in the early spring of 1927. Later in his career he managed teams of lesser quality, including the Brown Bombers in 1943 and the Brooklyn Brown Dodgers in 1945.

Dennis, Wesley (Doc)
Career: 1942–48   Positions: 1b, 2b, 3b, ss, of
Teams: Baltimore Elite Giants ('42–'45, *'51*), Philadelphia Stars ('45–'48), *Nashville Stars ('49)*, Birmingham Black Barons ('50, '52–'55)
Bats: Right   Throws: Right
Height: 6'0"   Weight: 170
Born: Feb. 10, 1918, Nashville, Tenn.

An average batter, both for consistency and power, he was a versatile defensive player who could play any nonbattery position. Although primarily a first baseman, he also gained considerable playing time at second base and the outfield. He began his career in 1942 as a reserve infielder with the Baltimore Elites and continued as a substitute the next season, appearing mostly at second base. In 1944 he broke into the starting lineup, sharing the starting assignments at third base and hitting .285. The next year he moved to the other corner as the regular first baseman, hitting .232 while batting at the bottom of the order. After the end of World War II he joined the Philadelphia Stars as their regular first baseman for the next three seasons, also batting in the lower part of

their batting order and hitting for averages of .288 and .247 in 1946–47.

In 1949 he moved back home to Nashville, playing with the Nashville Stars, a team of lesser status, and then rejoined Negro American League teams during the first half of the '50s, although the league had dropped in quality and was then strictly a minor league. Altogether his diamond career lasted a total of fourteen years, his athletic ability extended beyond the baseball diamond and he also won recognition as an outstanding golfer.

Dent, Carl J.
Career: 1950   Position: ss
Team: Indianapolis Clowns

In black baseball's marginal season of 1950, when the Negro American League was struggling to survive the loss of players to organized baseball, he was listed as a shortstop with the Indianapolis Clowns, but league statistics do not confirm his playing time.

Despert, Denny
Career: 1915–16   Position: of
Teams: *Philadelphia Giants ('14)*, New York Lincoln Giants ('15), Brooklyn Royal Giants ('16)

Beginning as an outfielder with the Philadelphia Giants after they had declined in quality, he was a reserve outfielder with two of the top clubs in the East, first with the New York Lincoln Giants in 1915 and then as a substitute left fielder with the Brooklyn Royal Giants in 1916.

Detroit Stars
Duration: 1919–31,   Honors: Western
1933, 1937   Champions   ('19), second-half champions ('30)
Affiliations: Independent ('19), NNL ('20–'31, '33), NAL ('37)

Organized in 1919, the franchise fielded a team of outstanding players that defeated Rube Foster's American Giants in a showdown series and were in all probability the best team in the West that season. They became a charter member in the Negro National League in 1920 and remained an annual entry until the league's demise after the 1931 season. Afterward the Motor City made two efforts to reprieve the Stars' legacy by entering franchises in the inaugural season of new leagues, the Negro National League in 1933 and the Negro American League in 1937.

Detroit Wolves

Duration: 1932   Honors: None
Affiliation: EWL (1932)

Formed in 1932 after the Detroit Stars disbanded following the demise of the original Negro National League, the Wolves' roster was stocked with many former players from the Kansas City Monarchs and the St. Louis Stars. Although they were successful on the ballfield, the club lasted less than a full season. Entered in the East-West League, they were the top team in that league until Cum Posey consolidated the Wolves with the Homestead Grays, who played out the Wolves' remaining schedule.

Devers

Career: 1950   Position: p
Team: Houston Eagles

He pitched in one game without a decision for the Houston Eagles in black baseball's marginal season of 1950, when the Negro American League was struggling to survive the loss of players to organized baseball.

Devoe

Career: 1905–18   Positions: 1b, c
Teams: Philadelphia Giants ('05), Chicago American Giants ('15), Chicago Giants ('18)

He appeared briefly as a reserve catcher with the Chicago American Giants in 1915 after Bruce Petway reinjured his arm in late September. He also appeared as both a first baseman and catcher with other teams during his career, beginning with the Philadelphia Giants in 1905 and ending with the Chicago Giants in 1918.

Devoe, J. R.

Career: 1922   Position: officer
Team: Cleveland Tate Stars

He was business manager for the 1922 Cleveland Tate Stars, their only season in the Negro National League.

Devon

Career: 1933   Position: of
Team: Philadelphia Stars

In 1933, the first year after Ed Bolden organized the team, he appeared briefly as an outfielder with the Philadelphia Stars.

Devora

Career: 1925   Position: player
Team: Baltimore Black Sox

A Canadian, he was an excellent fielder but a weak hitter, and after appearing briefly with the Baltimore Black Sox, he was released because of his inability to hit at that level of competition.

Dewberry, William

Career: 1904   Position: c
Team: Chicago Union Giants

He was a catcher with the Chicago Union Giants in 1904, his only season in black baseball.

DeWitt, Fred

a.k.a. Dewear
Career: 1922–30   Positions: 1b, c
Teams: Kansas City Monarchs ('22–'23, '25, '27), Memphis Red Sox ('29), Hilldale Daisies ('30)

Primarily a reserve first baseman, he also played other positions during his career. After making brief appearances with the Kansas City Monarchs in the early '20s, he played more substantially in 1927 but was never able to earn a regular role. In 1929 he was a reserve first baseman for the Memphis Red Sox, and the following season he played in two games with Hilldale to close his career.

DeWitt, S. R. (Sammy, **Eddie)**
Career: 1917–28   Positions: **3b,** 2b, 1b
Teams: Dayton Giants ('17–'20), Indianapolis ABCs ('20), Columbus Buckeyes ('21), Toledo Tigers ('23), Dayton Marcos ('26), Cleveland Tigers ('28)

The light-hitting infielder played for fourteen seasons with teams in the Midwest, usually as a reserve with a struggling franchise. After beginning his baseball career with the Dayton Giants in 1917, he joined the Indianapolis ABCs during the 1920 season, playing as the regular second baseman and batting in the seventh slot in the order. He began the next season as the regular third baseman for the Columbus Buckeyes, usually batting at the bottom of the order, but was displaced during the year. Two years later he joined the Toledo Tigers and started some games at the hot corner for the struggling ballclub before the team dissolved in midsummer. In 1926 he shared the regular third-base position for the Dayton Marcos in their last effort to field a league team, and closed out his career in 1928 with the Cleveland Tigers, another marginal ballclub trying to maintain a league franchise.

Dial, Kermit
Career: 1932–37   Positions: 2b, 1b, ss, p
Teams: Cole's American Giants ('32), Columbus Blue Birds ('33), Chicago American Giants ('36), Detroit Stars ('37)

The infielder played mostly at second base during his half-dozen seasons with midwestern teams in the Negro Leagues during the '30s. He also tried his hand at pitching but met with little success, losing all of his decisions.

Dials, Alonzo Odem (**Lou)**
a.k.a. Lou Diaz
Career: 1925–36   Positions: 1b, lf, rf, cf, manager
Teams: **Chicago American Giants** ('25–'28, '36–'37), Birmingham Black Barons ('28), Memphis Red Sox ('29), Detroit Stars ('30–'31), Hilldale Daisies ('32), Homestead Grays ('32), Columbus Bluebirds ('33), Cleveland Giants ('33), Akron Tyrites ('33–'34), New York Black Yankees ('35), *Mexican League ('38–'41), Industrial League ('41–'45)*
Bats: Left   Throws: Left
Height: 5'10"   Weight: 185
Born: Jan. 10, 1904

A good hitter with respectable power, he is claimant to two disputed batting titles (1931 with a .382 batting average, and 1933 with a .370 batting average), but these averages have not been verified. Primarily an outfielder, he played in the 1936 East-West All-Star game as a representative of the Chicago American Giants, playing as a substitute in right field but going hitless in two at-bats. He was also a good first baseman and later in his career began spending more playing time at the initial sack.

He began his career in the Negro Leagues in 1925 as a reserve outfielder with the Chicago American Giants. After discontinuing baseball for most of two seasons to pursue his college education, he was unable to break into the starting lineup upon his return, and left Chicago during the 1928 season to join the Birmingham Black Barons for the remainder of the year. In 1929 he played with the Memphis Red Sox, registering a .280 batting average. The next two seasons he returned North to play with the Detroit Stars, where some reports credit him with winning batting titles both seasons. However, statistics show a batting average of .275 for the 1930 season in league play. In 1931, hitting third in the batting order in front of Turkey Stearnes, he enjoyed a big offensive season and was credited with an unconfirmed average of .382.

Following that season, both the Negro National League and the Stars folded, and Dials bounced around for the next four years, playing for short stints with the Hilldale Daisies, Homestead Grays, Cleveland Giants, Akron Tyrites, and New York Black Yankees before returning to the Chicago American Giants for the 1936 season. The American Giants were playing as an independent team and playing mostly nonleague opposition. In 1937 the American Giants joined the Negro American

League in its initial season, and Dials began the season with Chicago.

However, he soon answered the lure of pesos and was among the first black Americans to play baseball in Mexico, serving a four-year stint with Torreon (1938–40) and Pueblo (1941). In 1939 he received the MVP award, and during the last three seasons, he served as playing manager and guided Torreon to two pennants. While records show high batting averages, they also show that his playing time was limited during the last two seasons, playing only three games in 1940 (.400 batting average) and six games in 1941 (.385 batting average).

After Dials returned to the United States, Pants Rowland, general manager of the Los Angeles Angels of the Pacific Coast League, wanted to sign him and Chet Brewer in 1943, but owner Philip Wrigley vetoed the idea. With the advent of World War II, Dials played with Lockheed in the North American Industrial League in Los Angeles for the duration of the war (1941–45), and afterward spent another four years (1946–49) with the Saltillo All-Stars in Los Angeles. During this time he played two winters with the Kansas City Royals (1944–46). His last hurrah came with Tijuana in California's Sunset League in 1950, at age forty-six. He enjoyed a long career with many different teams, including eight different ballclubs from the Negro Leagues.

In 1926–27, when he took a leave of absence from baseball to concentrate on his college studies, he earned a degree in electrical engineering from the University of California. After finally retiring from baseball, he put his degree to use and worked at Lockheed as an electrician. He also scouted for eight years for four separate major-league teams: Houston, Cleveland, Kansas City, and Baltimore.

Diamond Black
[see Pipkin, Robert]

Diaz, Edolfo (**Yo Yo**)
a.k.a. Heliodoro

Career: 1926–39   Positions: **p,** of, 1b, *c*
Teams: Cuban Stars (West) ('26–'30), Cuban Stars ('33–'34), New York Cubans ('35–'36, '39)
Bats: Right   Throws: Right
The stocky right-handed Cuban pitcher had a long career with the Cuban Stars and the New York Cubans, posting records of 4–10, 6–8, and 11–7 for the seasons of 1927, 1929, and 1930. He also occasionally played at first base or in the outfield. Pitching with the Champion Cienfuegos team in his native country, he led the 1929–30 Cuban winter league with 13 wins while suffering only 3 losses.

Diaz, Fernando
[see Pedroso, Fernando Diaz]

Diaz, Pablo Mesa
Career: 1930–35   Positions: c, 1b
Teams: Cuban Stars (West) ('30–'31), Cuban Stars ('32–'35)
Bats: Right   Throws: Right
In 1930 he hit an even .300 as a combination catcher-first baseman for the Cuban Stars in the Negro National League. Two years later he was the regular catcher with the Cuban Stars of the East-West League, sometimes batting in the cleanup spot. Early in the season, before the onset of league play, the Cubans were playing as the Cuban House of David. After the league broke up during the season, the ballclub reverted to this designation at times. In 1934 he was a backup to veteran receiver José Fernandez for the Cuban Stars. Regarded as an excellent hitter in the Caribbean leagues, the Cuban receiver played for Caguas in the Puerto Rican winter league of 1939–40, batting .329.

Diaz, Pedro (**Manny**)
Career: 1943   Position: p
Team: New York Cubans
A wartime player, he pitched with the New York Cubans in 1943.

Dibut, Pedro
Career: 1923   Position: p
Team: Cuban Stars (West)

In 1923 he pitched with the Cuban Stars in the Negro National League, and also pitched with Santa Clara in the Cuban League, splitting a half dozen decisions. Three years later, pitching with Havana in the 1926–27 Cuban winter league, he tied for the lead in wins with 5.

Dickerson, John Fount (Babe)
Career: 1950   Position: p
Teams: *Asheville Blues ('49),* Homestead Grays ('50), Chicago American Giants ('50)

After a year with the Asheville Blues, a lesser team, in 1949, this pitcher appeared briefly the next season with the Homestead Grays, who had dropped out of league play and were touring as an independent team. He was also listed with the Chicago American Giants that year, but although the Negro American League was struggling to survive the loss of players to organized baseball, league statistics do not confirm his playing time with the American Giants.

Dickerson, Lou
Career: 1921   Position: p
Team: Hilldale Daisies

Pitching with Hilldale in 1921, he won his only decision and registered a 4.66 ERA while pitching mostly against lesser opposition.

Dickey, John Claude (**Steel Arm**)
Career: 1922   Position: p
Teams: *Montgomery Grey Sox ('21),* St. Louis Stars ('22)
Bats: Left   Throws: Left
Died: Mar. 13, 1923, Etowah, Tenn.

An excellent pitcher with an exceptional fastball and good control, his professional baseball career ended almost before it began. A native of Knoxville, Tennessee, where his father was a church custodian, most of his brief career was spent in the Negro Southern League. He began playing baseball in his hometown before joining the Montgomery Grey Sox, and he was called the "pride of the South." In 1921 the Grey Sox were the champions of their league and played Rube Foster's Negro National League champion Chicago American Giants in a postseason series. In a Sunday showdown between Dickey and Foster's ace Dave Brown, the southern southpaw showed great promise despite losing a 1–0 verdict. He struck out 9 batters while holding Chicago to 4 scratch hits, and lost the game in the bottom of the ninth inning on an unearned run.

Foster, a shrewd judge of pitching talent, wanted to sign Dickey, but had competition from the St. Louis Stars. Unconfirmed reports indicate that Dickey appeared in a few games with the St. Louis Stars in 1922 and was slated for duty the following season. Another unconfirmed source asserted that he could hit and throw from both sides. Tragically, he was killed in a stabbing incident in Etowah, Tennessee, while trying to break up a fight during the early spring before the start of the baseball season.

Dickins
Career: 1945   Position: p
Team: Cincinnati Clowns

He was a wartime player, pitching briefly with the Cincinnati Clowns in 1945.

Dieckert
Career: 1943   Position: 3b
Team: Cuban Stars

A wartime player, he played as a reserve third baseman with the Cuban Stars in 1943.

Dihigo, Martin
Career: 1923–45   Positions: **2b, of, p, 1b, 3b,** ss, *c,* manager
Teams: **Cuban Stars (East)** ('23–'27, '30), Homestead Grays ('28), Hilldale Daisies ('29–'31), Baltimore Black Sox ('31), *Venezuelan League ('33),* **New York Cubans** ('35–'36, '45), *Santo Domingo ('37),* Mexican League ('40–'44)
Bats: Right   Throws: Right
Height: 6'3"   Weight: 190
Born: May 25, 1905, Matanzas, Cuba
Died: May 22, 1971, Cienfuegos, Cuba

The most versatile man ever to play the game of baseball was Martin Dihigo. When he first came to the United States as a youth, he was most often played at second base. But as the years passed, his playing time at the infield corners and in the outfield increased. Later he turned more to the mound as his primary position, while still playing as an everyday player when not taking his turn in the pitching rotation. Whether playing the outfield, the infield, or pitching, he was awesome. The gifted Cuban was literally a star at every position he played. Neither before his appearance on the baseball horizon, nor since his departure from the scene, has his multitude of talents afield ever been approached by a single player.

A natural five-point player, the graceful athlete had an exceptionally strong arm, great range in the field, very good speed on the bases, and was a superior batter with power at the plate. His batting skills were quickly demonstrated during his early years with the Cuban Stars. His first season with the Cubans was 1923, the year the Eastern Colored League was organized. He led the league in home runs in 1926 and tied for the lead in 1927 while hitting .421 and .370, respectively. The following season the superb ballplayer was secured by Cum Posey to play with the Homestead Grays. After a year with the Grays, however, he was traded with Chippy Britt to Hilldale, for Jake Stevens and Rev Cannady. The change proved a good one for Dihigo, as he finished second in the American Negro League with 18 home runs while compiling a .386 batting average. In 1930 he was back with the Cuban Stars and is credited with a .393 batting average for the year. The next season he returned to Hilldale and was credited with a 6–1 pitching record.

Meanwhile, he was also playing winters in his homeland. With Havana he hit over .400 twice, posting averages of .413 and .415 in consecutive seasons (1926–28), and hit over .300 nine times during the period 1924–38, adding a tenth season over .300 in a later season. During this interval there were four seasons in the '30s that he did not play in Cuba, but when an active participant, the only time he failed to hit .300 was in 1929–30, when he hit .282 and had 12 stolen bases in 180 at-bats.

He remained primarily an everyday player until 1935–36 with Santa Clara in the Cuban League. But once he made the transition to pitching, he had four consecutive seasons (1935–39) of 11–2, 14–10, 11–5, and 14–2. In the 1943–44 winter season he was 8–1 with a 2.23 ERA. His control was good but not exceptional, nor was his strikeout ratio. His move to the mound was made when he was managing himself, winning consecutive Cuban championships in 1935–36 with Santa Clara and with Marianao in 1936–37. During the former season he had five base hits in the final game to overtake teammate Willie Wells for the batting title with a .358 average.

The preceding summer in the United States, as playing manager of the New York Cubans in one of his last seasons in the Negro Leagues before embarking on a long career in Mexico, he hit .372 and fashioned a 7–3 pitching record to lead his club to the 1935 Negro National League second-half title and a showdown with the powerful Pittsburgh Crawfords, often called the best team in the history of the Negro Leagues. In the ensuing playoffs Dihigo played well but the Cubans lost to the Crawfords in a hard-fought seven-game Series.

Earlier that season, Dihigo's versatility was showcased in the East-West All-Star game, where he started in center field, batted third in the power-laden lineup, and finished on the mound against the West's best sluggers. Unfortunately, he yielded an eleventh-inning two-out homer to Mule Suttles to lose the contest.

The tall, lanky, talented Cuban spent most of his early career (1923–36) in the Negro Leagues, except for intermittent interruptions to play seasons in Latin American countries. But afterward, except for 1945, when he again returned for a single season as a player-manager of the New York Cubans, most of his summer baseball career was spent in Mexico and other Latin American leagues.

In 1937 he played in Santo Domingo with the Aquilas Cibaenas ballclub, where he was their leading hitter and ace pitcher. In a demonstration of both his versatility and ability, he finished near the top in both hitting and pitching, losing out to Satchel Paige in victories and to Josh Gibson in batting average. At the plate he tied for the league lead in home runs while finishing with a .351 batting average, third best in the league. On the mound his 6–4 record represented the second-highest win total in the league and accounted for almost half of his team's victories in the 28-game season.

The following year, 1938, in Mexico, he led the league with a .387 batting average and also topped the league in pitching with a record of 18–2 and a 0.90 ERA. In 1940, playing with the champion Veracruz team, he hit .364 with a 549 slugging percentage while also registering an 8–6 pitching record with a 3.54 ERA. The next season he switched teams, splitting the season between Mexico City and Torreon, and although dropping off to a 9–10 ledger, he ranked in the top ten in both ERA (4.01) and strikeouts (93). In 1942 he hit .319, but was inclined more toward the pitching half of his baseball career. The increased focus resulted in a 22–7 record, with league-leading marks in both ERA (2.53) and strikeouts (211 in 245⅓ innings). Dihigo extended his inclination toward pitching as he registered a 16–8 ledger, with a 3.10 ERA and a league-high 134 strikeouts, but dropped to a .277 batting average in 1943. In addition to his batting and pitching, in 1944 he added a third duty, as he assumed the managerial reins of the Laredo team in the Mexican League.

While starring primarily as a hitter in the States, the right-hander starred as a pitcher in Latin America, pitching no-hitters in Venezuela, Puerto Rico, and Mexico. In his homeland, Cuba, his lifetime record as a pitcher was 115–60, and in Mexico, where he managed and recruited players for the Mexican League, his pitching statistics showed a 119–57 lifetime total. Incomplete records credit him with a 27–21 record in the Negro Leagues, yielding an impressive aggregate 261–138 lifetime pitching record. Hall of Famer Johnny Mize called him the best player he ever saw and remembered that when they were teammates in the Dominican Republic, opponents would intentionally walk Dihigo to pitch to him.

Dihigo displayed a warm, friendly personality blended with humor, which earned him a popularity everywhere he played and made him a national hero in Cuba, where he served as minister of sports under Fidel Castro's regime. Probably the most widely known Cuban ever to perform in the United States, he was considered by many to be the greatest all-around Negro player of all time. He was already a member of both the Cuban and Mexican Halls of Fame when he was posthumously elected to the National Baseball Hall of Fame in 1977.

Dillard

Career: 1927, 1932   Position: p
Teams: New York Lincoln Giants ('27), Atlantic City Bacharach Giants ('32)

He made two appearances in black baseball, pitching first with the New York Lincoln Giants in 1927 and again with the Bacharachs in 1932.

Dilworth, Arthur

Career: 1916–19   Positions: **p,** c, of
Teams: Atlantic City Bacharach Giants ('16–'17, '19), Hilldale Daisies ('18), New York Lincoln Giants ('18)
Bats: Right   Throws: Right

Beginning and ending his career with the Bacharachs, he was also a member of Hilldale's mound corps in 1918 and split two decisions for the season. A versatile player, he also performed at times behind the plate or in the outfield during his four seasons with top black teams.

Dimes

Career: 1926, 1933   Position: of
Teams: Dayton Marcos ('26), Akron Tyrites ('33)

A marginal player, the light-hitting outfielder was one of several players who shared playing time in left field for the Dayton Marcos' last season in the Negro National League, 1926. He also shared the center-field spot for the Akron Tyrites in their lone appearance in the Negro National League, in 1933, but when the team consolidated with Columbus to form the Cleveland Giants' entry for the second half, he was lost in the shuffle.

Direaux, Jimmy
Career: 1937–39   Position: p
Teams: Washington Elite Giants ('37), Baltimore Elite Giants ('38–'39), *Mexican League ('40–'43)*
Bats: Right   Throws: Right

This Los Angeles native first gained notoriety in 1935 when he was mentioned in Ripley's *Believe It or Not* for striking out 108 batters in 54 innings. That year he averaged 18 strikeouts per game and, after graduating from high school, played with the Phoenix Bronchos of the Arizona State League. Even though he had a sore arm, he pitched a doubleheader victory to earn the team a trip to the Wichita Tournament.

He joined the Washington Elite Giants in 1937 as a twenty-year-old rookie and played three years with the Elites but was unable to recapture the success he had had as an amateur. In 1940 he jumped to Mexico, where he encountered the same lack of pitching success as he had in the Negro Leagues. In his first year he split playing time between Monterrey and Tampico and won the only game he was to ever win in the Mexican League. Used very sparingly in his last two years with Tampico, he ended with a combined record of 1–6 for his three years in the league.

However, in Mexico he was primarily an everyday player. His first season there he hit only .210, but raised his average each of the next two years to .246 and .271. In 1942 he demonstrated more than a modicum of power for the first time and was issued a high ratio of walks. However, in 1943 his playing time was restricted and he hit only .186.

Dismukes, William (Dizzy)
Career: 1910–30;   Positions: **p,** manager,
1931–*51*   officer
Teams: West Baden Sprudels ('10–'13), St. Louis Giants ('12), Philadelphia Giants ('13), Brooklyn Royal Giants ('13–'14), Lincoln Stars ('14–'15), **Indianapolis ABCs** ('14–'18, '20–'24), *French Lick Plutos ('16),* Mohawk Giants, Chicago American Giants ('16), *military service ('17–'18),* Dayton Marcos ('18–'19), Pittsburgh Keystones ('21–'23), Birmingham Black Barons ('24, '38), Memphis Red Sox ('25, '42), St. Louis Stars ('26–'29; '36–'37); Chicago American Giants ('30, '35), Cincinnati Dismukes, Detroit Wolves ('32), Columbus Blue Birds ('33–'34), Atlanta Black Crackers ('39), Homestead Grays ('40), Kansas City Monarchs ('41–'51)
Bats: Right   Throws: Right
Born: Mar. 15, 1890, Birmingham, Ala.
Died: June 30, 1961, Campbell, O.

A right-handed submariner, he was regarded as one of the best pitchers in black baseball during the '10s and early '20s. A college man, he was a smart, studious player with a wonderful memory and was a strategist. He knew a batter's tendencies and would almost unerringly position his infielders where the batter would hit according to the pitches he was throwing. He had a variety of breaking pitches and was considered by some to be a "trick pitcher" because of the way his breaking balls moved. He was credited with teaching Webster McDonald and Carl Mays the tricks of the submarine style of pitching.

He began pitching with lesser teams, progressing from the Imperials of East St. Louis, Illinois, in 1908 to the Kentucky Unions in 1909 to the Minnesota Keystones early in 1910, before joining the West Baden Sprudels later in the season, when many of the future Indianapolis ABCs were also getting their professional careers under way under manager C. I. Taylor. Dismukes pitched intermittently with Taylor's teams over the next decade, taking time for stints with other ballclubs before settling in Indianapolis with Taylor's ABCs for many years. He was with the St. Louis Giants in 1912 before traveling East to join the Philadelphia Giants the next year. In 1914, while pitching for the eastern champion Brooklyn Royal Giants, he pitched three of the four games in the playoffs in a valiant losing effort against the Chicago American Giants.

He began the 1915 season with the Lincoln Stars but signed with the ABCs in late April. The next two years were the best ever in the history of the ABCs. With Dismukes contributing a 19–5 record, the team contended for the title before losing in a close battle with the Chicago American Giants. The following year they struggled at the onset of the season but finally overcame the adversity caused by a schism at the management level and finished strong to defeat the Chicago American Giants for the western championship. Dismukes had another outstanding season, posting a 17–6 ledger. After the showdown with the Chicago American Giants, he pitched with the French Lick Plutos in September, but returned to the ABCs the next season, with incomplete records showing only a 4–6 work sheet for the 1917 season. His baseball career was interrupted briefly while he served with the 803rd Pioneer Infantry during World War I. After leaving the ABCs to assume the role as playing manager of the Dayton Marcos in 1919, he returned after a season and, when the ABCs entered the Negro National League in 1920, he registered an 11–6 league ledger.

He continued in Indianapolis until shortly after the death of manager C. I. Taylor, and returned for a part of the 1924 season as a playing manager. Leaving during the season, he pitched with Birmingham, Memphis, and St. Louis to finish out the decade of the '20s. Pitching records show seasons of 6–4 and 3–8 for 1923–24, and the batting marks confirm his anemic hitting, which plagued him throughout his playing career.

In 1930, after a change in ownership of the Chicago American Giants following the death of Rube Foster, Dismukes took the helm of the team. He was a kindly man and, as a coach and manager, he was proficient at imparting inside baseball to young players. During the '30s and '40s he entered into the management end of baseball, also managing with Detroit (1932), Birmingham (1938), Memphis (1942), and Kansas City (1941–42) at various times.

He moved from the dugout to the front office and was traveling secretary with the Monarchs for many years, and was the personnel director for the team for over a decade, from 1942 to 1952. In this capacity he was instrumental in acquiring Jackie Robinson to play with the Monarchs in 1945. He recognized Robinson's deficiency at shortstop and asked Cool Papa Bell to convince Robinson that this was not his best position. Dismukes also served as secretary for the Negro National League during his many years in black baseball. After the color line was removed, he scouted two years for the New York Yankees (1953–54) and the Chicago White Sox (1955–56).

Dismukes toiled on the mound for almost a score of teams and spent forty years in black baseball, almost evenly split between the playing field and the management level. He retired as an active player after twenty years in the pitcher's box prior to becoming a prominent coach, manager, business manager, club officer, and league officer for an additional twenty years.

Dixie
Career: 1912   Position: cf
Team: Lincoln Giants

In 1912 he appeared briefly with the Lincoln Giants' ballclub as a center fielder.

Dixon
Career: 1938   Position: of
Team: Memphis Red Sox

He was an occasional center fielder with the Negro American League first-half champion Memphis Red Sox in 1938.

Dixon
Career: 1914–17   Position: p

Teams: Chicago Giants ('15–'17), Chicago American Giants ('16)

He stepped into the Chicago American Giants' rotation in 1916 as the fourth starter, after having teamed with Pat Dougherty as the two top pitchers for the Chicago Giants the previous season. In 1917 Dixon returned to the same team, and partial statistics indicate that he lost his only decision that year.

Dixon, Eddie, Eddie Lee (Ed, **Bullet,** Bullet Joe, George)
a.k.a. Dickson, Dickerson
Career: 1938–39   Position: p
Teams: Atlanta Black Crackers ('38), Indianapolis ABCs ('39), Baltimore Elite Giants ('39)
Bats: Right   Throws: Right
Height: 5'9"   Weight: 160

As a rookie in 1938, the right-handed fastballer was a member of the Negro American League second-half champion Atlanta Black Crackers. He was strictly a fastball pitcher with explosive speed and good control. He also had a fast curve and a "dinky" slider but did not utilize them extensively. But he pitched with sufficient effectiveness to be selected by the SNS's Negro American League All-Star team.

In the spring he shut out the U.S. Army team, 15–0, with 12 strikeouts in six innings pitched. At the plate, however, the Atlanta hurler was a very poor hitter. The following year he remained with the franchise when it was relocated in Indianapolis to play as the ABCs. When the club floundered, he was among the four players who were sold to the Baltimore Elite Giants to finish the season.

Dixon, Frank
Career: 1950   Position: p
Team: Birmingham Black Barons

In 1950, when the Negro American League was struggling to survive the loss of players to organized baseball, he pitched a total of three times in three games with the Birmingham Black Barons.

Dixon, George (Tubby)
Career: 1917–33   Position: c

Teams: **Chicago American Giants** ('17–'25), Indianapolis ABCs ('23–'26), Birmingham Black Barons ('24), Cleveland Elites ('26), Cleveland Hornets ('27), Cleveland Tigers ('28), Cleveland Cubs ('31), Cleveland Giants ('33)
Bats: Left   Throws: Right

Dixon was considered "a real find" when he arrived with the Chicago American Giants in 1917 along with Ruby Tyree as half of a much-heralded "pony battery." Initially the young left-handed-hitting backstop started strong, but he leveled off and finished with a .253 batting average, while sharing the catching assignments with the veteran Bruce Petway. The next year the two again shared the catching chores, but Dixon raised his average to an even .300 and, after two years of the shared assignments, he was installed as the regular catcher, supplanting the great receiver. At the plate, the heavy receiver had good power to accompany his .255 average, and defensively he displayed a good arm, quickness, and leadership. However, he was a slow base runner. Although he was eligible for the draft in 1918, he was not called to military service and remained with the club to provide continuity for the American Giants into the next decade.

Together with Jim Brown, he formed a catching duo that served the Chicago American Giants well during their glory years of the early 1920s, when they won the first three pennants in the Negro National League's history. In 1921, the middle season, Dixon hit .222, which, compared to the other averages on the team, was respectable. In the spring of 1925 Rube Foster did some housecleaning and unconditionally released many veteran players. Dixon was dispatched to the Indianapolis ABCs along with Bingo DeMoss to balance the league, and hit .258 in 1926, his last year in Indianapolis. After he left the ABCs, most of his remaining years were spent as a backup catcher, primarily with Cleveland-based ballclubs, where he hit .226 in 1927 with the Cleveland Hornets.

He had played in the inaugural season of the

In 1884, Fleetwood Walker (above) became the first black player in the major leagues. *(Jerry Malloy)*

(bottom, left) Raymond Brown was the ace hurler for the Homestead Grays during the years when they won nine straight pennants. *(Author collection)*

(bottom, right) Bruce Petway (standing) and Pete Hill (seated) were the top players at their positions during the deadball era and spent their best years with Rube Foster's Chicago American Giants. Petway, a catcher, excelled defensively and Hill, a consistent line-drive hitter, was the first great black outfielder. *(Author collection)*

Catcher Louis Santop was the top slugger of the deadball era and was a crowd favorite, who earned the nickname "Big Bertha." *(Author collection]*

Centerfielder Spot Poles was a consistent hitter and possessed incredible speed, making him an ideal lead-off hitter for the New York Lincoln Giants during the deadball era. He was decorated for his service in World War I. *(Author collection)*

A smart, scientific ballplayer, Bingo DeMoss was a prototype secondbaseman, excelling at all phases of the game. *(Author collection)*

(above) Sammy T. Hughes was a smooth fielding secondbaseman for the Baltimore Elite Giants. A well-
rounded ballplayer, he was also a good baserunner and
a solid hitter. *(Author collection)*

(above, right) Grant "Homerun" Johnson had a stellar career that began in the nineteenth century and extended
to the beginning of the lively ball era. *(Author collection)*

(right) Dave Brown was Rube Foster's ace lefthander and
pitched the Chicago American Giants ballclub to the first
three Negro National League championships. *(Author
collection)*

(top, left) A member of the famous Taylor clan, Ben Taylor was a smooth-fielding, sharp-hitting firstbaseman with the Indianapolis ABCs. *(Author collection)*

(top, right) As a thirdbaseman, the fiery Oliver Marcelle was spectacular and was part of the "million dollar infield" of the Baltimore Black Sox.
(Author collection)

(left) The versatile Wilbur "Bullet" Rogan starred for the Kansas City Monarchs for almost twenty years as a pitcher and outfielder. A durable workhorse on the mound, he had a good fastball and curve. Playing in the outfield when he was not pitching, he was a dangerous hitter and batted in the heart of the batting order. *(Author collection)*

(right) Ted "Double Duty" Radcliffe was given his nickname by Damon Runyon, who witnessed him catch Satchel Paige in the first game of a double header and then pitch the second game himself. *(Author collection)*

(above) Slim Jones' fastball was compared to that of Satchel Paige and Lefty Grove. However, his career was brief, cut short by his death from pneumonia. *(Author collection)*

(above, right) Pitcher Eustaquio Pedroso (left) and outfielder Christobel Torriente (right), were teammates on the Cuban Stars. Torriente was a complete ballplayer, excelling in all phases of the game. While later starring with Rube Foster's Chicago American Giants, the Cuban slugger was regarded as a franchise player. *(Author collection)*

(right) Judy Johnson was a sure-handed third-baseman with good range and a strong arm. He was elected to the Hall of Fame in 1975. *(Author collection)*

(top, left) Called the black Babe Ruth, Josh Gibson was the most prolific slugger in the Negro Leagues. He is credited with an unverified 962 career homeruns against all levels of competition. *(Author collection)*

(top) John Donaldson was a poised left-hander with pinpoint control. He won his greatest fame with the All Nations ball-club. *(Author collection)*

(left) Roy Campanella (left) and Bill Byrd (right) were teammates for the Baltimore Elite Giants in the Negro National League. Byrd was one of the last legal spitball pitchers and Campanella went on to stardom with the Brooklyn Dodgers in the major leagues. *(Author collection)*

Dick Lundy was a good hitter and a superb fielder with an exceptionally strong arm. The graceful shortstop was annointed "King Richard" for his style and skill. *(Author collection)*

Bill Wright was a star outfielder for the Baltimore Elite Giants in the Negro Leagues and for Mexico City in the Mexican League. *(Author collection)*

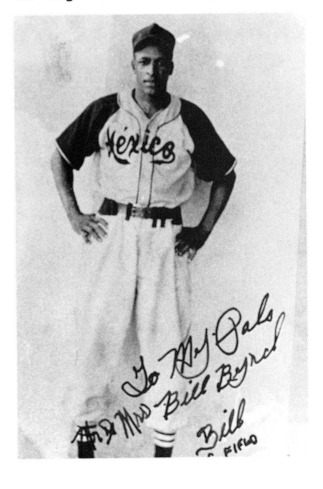

The greatest lefthanded pitcher in the history of black baseball was Willie Foster, a half-brother of the famous Rube Foster. *(Author collection)*

first Negro National League, and he finished his career with the Cleveland Giants, a second-half replacement team in the inaugural season of the new Negro National League.

Dixon, Glenn
Career: 1937   Positions: of, p
Team: St. Louis Stars

He was an outfielder and pitcher with the St. Louis Stars in 1937, the first year of the Negro American League.

Dixon, Herbert Albert (Rap)
Career: 1922–37   Positions: **rf,** cf, lf, *3b,*
                                    p, manager
Teams: **Harrisburg Giants** ('22–'28), Washington Potomacs ('24), Chicago American Giants ('26, '30–'31), **Baltimore Black Sox** ('28–'31, '34), Hilldale Daisies ('31), Pittsburgh Crawfords ('32, '34, '37), Washington Pilots ('32), Philadelphia Stars ('33), Brooklyn Eagles ('35), New York Cubans ('35), Homestead Grays ('36)
Bats: Right   Throws: Right
Height: 6'2"   Weight: 185
Born: Sept. 2, 1902, Kingston, Ga.
Died: July 20, 1944, Detroit, Mich.

A five-point ballplayer who did everything with style, the power-hitting outfielder was one of the better hitters during the 1920s and 1930s. The line-drive hitter never guessed on a pitch and was regarded as both a good two-strike hitter and a good curveball hitter. Although he could really ''rap'' the ball, his nickname derived from the Rappahannock River in Virginia. A complete ballplayer, Dixon also ranked among the best defensive outfielders. He had good speed and range, was a good judge of fly balls, and had an outstanding throwing arm. Physically he had spindly legs, small feet, bony shoulders, and a narrow waist, but well-developed arms, which gave him his power.

He played for several great teams, including the 1929 American Negro League champion Baltimore Black Sox, for whom he hit .432 with 16 homers, 25 stolen bases, and a .784

slugging percentage while also rapping fourteen straight hits in a series against the Homestead Grays. The next season, the right-handed slugger displayed his long-ball capability in the first games played between black teams in Yankee Stadium, when he hit three home runs in a doubleheader against the New York Lincoln Giants. Although sometimes temperamental, Dixon was an intelligent hitter, and hit for average as well as for power, finishing with a lifetime .340 batting average in league play and a .362 average in exhibitions against major leaguers. In 1933 he was honored by being selected to participate in the first East-West All-Star game ever played.

He started playing with the Harrisburg Giants in 1922, when they were still an independent ballclub, and two years later, when the team joined the Eastern Colored League, the young right fielder brought one of the best arms in baseball into the league. Batting cleanup behind Oscar Charleston that season, Dixon moved into the second slot the next two years, 1925–26, and hit for averages of .357 and .358. While playing on the West Coast during the intervening winter, Dixon was seen by Rube Foster, who wanted him so badly for the Chicago American Giants that he offered a top pitcher in exchange. Newspapers prematurely headlined Foster's acquisition of the hard-hitting outfielder, but he remained in the East. During the next winter, Dixon went to Japan with the All-Star team touring the Orient and was credited with hitting the longest home run ever hit in Japan. Dixon was given a cup by the emperor of Japan, honoring him for his performance on the diamond. But he returned to the Giants for the regular season.

In 1928, when Harrisburg dropped from league play, he joined the Baltimore Black Sox during the season, finishing with a combined .351 average for the two teams. In 1930 Dizzy Dismukes, manager of the Chicago American Giants, secured Dixon from the Black Sox, but two years after the Sox' 1929 championship season, he was broke and stranded in California. Because of his drinking problem and reputation as a hard case, most teams did not want to take a chance on the talented but temperamental outfielder. However, manager Judy Johnson signed him to play with Hilldale, and kept him under control by withholding praise until the end of the season and not letting him become complacent or swellheaded.

Following his short stint with Hilldale, Dixon joined Gus Greenlee's Pittsburgh Crawfords for the 1932 campaign. During the season he jumped the club for two games with the Washington Pilots but promptly jumped back to the Crawfords, where he rapped the ball for a .343 batting average and walloped 15 home runs. The next season he signed with Ed Bolden's Philadelphia Stars, playing right field and batting sixth in the order, and was credited with a .310 batting average for the Stars in their first season of existence.

That winter he went to Puerto Rico with an all-star team and injured his spine while sliding into second base, which required hospitalization for almost a half season after he returned to Philadelphia. When the new Baltimore Black Sox franchise was entered in the Negro National League for the second half of the 1934 season, Dixon was appointed manager. The ballclub did not fare well, either on the field or financially, and folded after the season. In 1935 the veteran outfielder began the season with the Brooklyn Eagles but switched to the New York Cubans and hit .344 to help them capture the second-half title before losing the playoff to the Pittsburgh Crawfords. The next season he appeared briefly with the Homestead Grays, and in 1937 he closed out his baseball career with an appearance with the Crawfords. During these years he was in bad health from consumption and was not a full-time player.

He began playing semipro baseball in 1916 with the Keystone Giants of Steelton, Pennsylvania, where his father was a steelworker. After retiring from baseball, he returned to Steelton to work for the Bethlehem Steel Company. He died from a heart attack while still a young man, in his early forties.

Dixon, John (Frank)
Career: 1950   Position: p
Teams: Chicago American Giants ('50), Birmingham Black Barons ('50)

In 1950, when the Negro American League was struggling to survive the loss of players to organized baseball, the pitcher appeared briefly with both the Chicago American Giants and the Birmingham Black Barons, but without a decision for either team.

Dixon, John Robert (**Johnny Bob**)
Career: 1926–34   Positions: **p,** *ss*
Teams: Detroit Stars ('26, '31), Cleveland Tigers ('28), Chicago American Giants ('30), Indianapolis ABCs ('31–'32), Cuban Stars ('32), Cleveland Giants ('33), Cleveland Red Sox ('34)
Died: Feb. 3, 1985, Massillon, O.

He was a pitcher with several midwestern teams who were struggling to be competitive in league play, including three different Cleveland franchises: the Tigers, the Giants, and the Red Sox. While with the Detroit Stars in 1931, he split two decisions. During his career he also played shortstop on special occasions.

Dixon, Paul Perry (Dick)
Career: 1931–38   Position: of
Teams: Atlantic City Bacharach Giants ('31–'36), Baltimore Black Sox ('32, '34), Newark Browns ('32), Philadelphia Stars ('37–'38)
Bats: Right   Throws: Right
Height: 5'11"   Weight: 180
Born: 1907

He was the brother of longtime outfield star Rap Dixon and played eight seasons during the '30s in the Negro Leagues but could not come close to matching his brother's ability. In 1934, when Rap was appointed manager of the new Baltimore Black Sox playing out of Chester, Pennsylvania, Paul was the left fielder and cleanup hitter under his brother's direction. After returning to the Bacharachs for another stint, he signed with the Philadelphia Stars in 1937 and was the regular center fielder for two years. In his first year he batted in the heart of the order but was dropped to the bottom of the order the next season. That was his last year with a major-league ballclub.

Dixon, Rap
[see Dixon, Herbert Albert (Rap)]

Dixon, Tom
Career: 1932–36   Position: c
Teams: Washington Pilots ('32), Hilldale Daisies ('32), Baltimore Black Sox ('34), *Atlantic City Bacharach Giants ('35–'36)*

He was a reserve catcher with several marginal teams struggling to maintain a major-league level of play during the Depression years. He began with the Washington Pilots in the East-West league in 1932, until the league broke up, joining the Hilldale club for the remainder of the season, the club's last year of existence. In 1934 he was the regular catcher and batted in the fifth slot for the Baltimore Black Sox, who joined the Negro National League for the second half of the season before disbanding. He finished his career with the Bacharachs, who were a minor-league club at the time.

Dobbins, Nat
Career: 1921   Positions: ss, 2b, p
Teams: Hilldale Daisies ('21), *Washington Braves ('21)*

While garnering playing time as both a pitcher and a middle infielder, he appeared briefly with Hilldale in 1921, hitting .222 in very limited play.

Doby, Lawrence Eugene (**Larry,** LD)
a.k.a. Larry Walker
Career: 1942–43,
1946–47   Positions: **2b,** *3b*
Teams: **Newark Eagles** ('42–'43, '46–'47), *military service ('44–'45),* major leagues ('47–'59), *minor leagues ('60), Japanese League ('62)*
Bats: Left   Throws: Right
Height: 6'1"   Weight: 175

Born: Dec. 13, 1923, Camden, S.C.

A hard-hitting second baseman, Larry Doby starred for the 1946 champion Newark Eagles, played in the All-Star game, and finished the season with a .341 average and only 1 home run behind the league leaders, Josh Gibson and Johnny Davis.

The following year, the fastball hitter went straight to the major leagues from the Negro Leagues, leaving behind a .414 batting average, and played a handful of games as an infielder for the Cleveland Indians. In 1948 he switched to the outfield and won a starting position, hitting .301 for the pennant-winning Indians and .318 in their World Series victory over the Braves.

Two years later, Larry recorded his best major-league batting average, hitting .326 for the season. The left-handed swinger led the American League in home runs in 1952 and 1954, with 32 round-trippers each year. The latter year he also led the league with 126 RBIs as he powered the Indians to another pennant. Altogether he had five seasons with over 100 RBIs. In a thirteen-year major league career spent mostly with the Indians, Larry belted a total of 253 home runs and hit for a lifetime average of .283.

His father was a semipro baseball player but died when Doby was eight years old. By the time he was a teenager, he was all-state in football, basketball, and baseball at Paterson (N.J.) East Side High School and attended Long Island University. In 1942, when he broke in with the Eagles, he played under the name of Larry Walker to protect his amateur standing. The next season, playing under his own name, he was a sensation in fielding the keystone position and in demonstrating power at the plate and speed on the bases.

The next two years were spent in the U.S. Navy, but he rejoined the Eagles in time to help them win a Negro National League pennant and World Series over the Kansas City Monarchs. Two years later he would again be playing on a winning World Series team, this time in the major leagues with the Cleveland

Indians. He is one of only four players, along with Monte Irvin, Willie Mays, and Satchel Paige, to play in both a Negro World Series and a major-league World Series. Doby also played in All-Star games in both leagues, appearing in the 1946 East-West game in the Negro Leagues and making six straight appearances (1949–54) in the major-league All-Star game.

After his major-league career ended, he played briefly with San Diego in the Pacific Coast League and extended his career by playing in Japan. Later he coached for the Montreal Expos, Cleveland Indians, and Chicago White Sox and managed the White Sox during the last four months of the 1978 season.

Dodson

Career: 1919   Position: of
Team: Detroit Stars

He appeared briefly with the Detroit Stars in 1919, his only year in black baseball.

Dominguez

Career: 1925   Positions: p, *rf, 3b*
Team: Cuban Stars (West)

In 1925 he was a pitcher with the Cuban Stars (West) in the Negro National League.

Donaldson, John Wesley

Career: 1913–34   Positions: **p,** of
Teams: *Tennessee Rats ('12),* **All Nations** ('13–'17), Gilkerson's Union Giants ('17), Chicago Giants, *military service ('17),* Indianapolis ABCs ('18), Brooklyn Royal Giants ('18), Lincoln Giants ('18), Detroit Stars ('19), **Kansas City Monarchs** ('20–'24, '31, '34), *independent semipro teams ('24–'30), John Donaldson All-Stars ('31–'32)*
Bats: Left   Throws: Left
Height: 6'0"   Weight: 185
Born: Feb. 20, 1892, Glasgow, Mo.
Died: Apr. 14, 1970, Chicago, Ill.

John Donaldson was a poised left-hander with pinpoint control, and his money pitch was a hard, sharp-breaking curve. He won his greatest fame in the '10s as a star for J. L. Wilkin-

son's multiracial All Nations ballclub, based in Des Moines, Iowa, and with whom he averaged almost 20 strikeouts per game. He once pitched three consecutive no-hitters, in 1913.

However, his prime seasons often were spent barnstorming across the Midwest, playing against white semipro ballclubs of dubious quality, resulting in both inflated statistics and fragmentary records. Against one of those teams, at Marchall, Minnesota, in 1913, he pitched a 12-inning one-hitter while fanning 27 batters, In 1915 he whiffed 35 batters in an 18-inning 1–0 loss to Sioux Falls. His beautiful drop and wide assortment of curves, combined with a good fastball and change-up, made him one of the best left-handers in the history of black baseball. At times he was almost unhittable, and during one stretch through mid-June 1915 he had 92 strikeouts in 56 innings pitched, and extended that to 252 strikeouts in 15 games. The next year he was credited with 240 strikeouts over a 12-game period.

In 1916 Donaldson also pitched the All Nations team to series victories over the two top black teams, Rube Foster's Chicago American Giants and C. I. Taylor's Indianapolis ABCs. At that time he was the best pitcher in black baseball.

After induction into military service and a tour of duty in France with the 365th Infantry during World War I, Donaldson did go to New York in 1918, but not to pitch for a team in a white league. After beginning the season in the Midwest with the Indianapolis ABCs, he traveled East to pitch with two of the top black eastern teams, the New York Lincoln Giants and the Brooklyn Royal Giants. In the latter part of 1918 he pitched against John McGraw's New York Giants, losing a hard-fought 1–0 encounter.

When the Negro National League was organized in 1920, the star left-hander returned to the West, reuniting with J. L. Wilkinson, who called Donaldson the most amazing pitcher he had ever seen. While playing for Wilkinson's Kansas City Monarchs during the inaugural season, he is credited with a 4–1 league ledger despite an arm that had gone dead.

Donaldson's career spanned parts of four decades. After completing the schoolwork offered at Avon Grammar School in his hometown of Glasgow, Missouri, he attended George Smith College in Sedalia, Missouri, for a year before embarking on his professional career in 1912 with a barnstorming combination of baseball and showbiz talent called the Tennessee Rats. He was signed by Wilkinson for his All Nations team after the team's female first baseman was released when she demanded more money. He later pitched for the Indianapolis ABCs, Chicago Giants, Brooklyn Royal Giants, Detroit Stars, Los Angeles White Sox, and Kansas City Monarchs. Although his last appearance with a top ballclub was in 1934, his final hurrah was in 1945, when he played with the Monarchs' traveling ballclub under manager Newt Joseph.

He was the first great black left-hander and continues to be categorized with Willie Foster, Nip Winters, and Slim Jones as one of the best left-handers in the history of black baseball. John Henry Lloyd regarded him as the toughest pitcher he had ever faced, and New York Giants' manager John McGraw assessed Donaldson's value at $50,000 had he been white. In 1917, a New York State League manager reportedly offered him $10,000 to pass as a Cuban and pitch for his team.

The tall, lean, graceful athlete abstained from strong drink and other dissipating habits, and besides being an outstanding pitcher, he possessed good all-around playing skills. Donaldson was a good bunter and could hit with a measure of authority, was a fast base runner, and fielded smoothly, often playing at shortstop or in the outfield. Many years, he played in winter leagues in Cuba, Florida, or California. During the winter of 1916–17 he was the star pitcher for the Los Angeles White Sox in the California winter league, and also played in the outfield, sometimes batting cleanup in the batting order.

His batting eye didn't wane and, after experiencing arm trouble later in his career, he continued as an everyday player, holding down the center-field spot for the Kansas City Monarchs when they entered the Negro National League in 1920. With the Monarchs he often batted in the leadoff spot to utilize his exceptional speed from the batter's box to first base. Partial statistics for 1921 show a .320 batting average while batting in the third slot in the order, but the next season he was dropped to the lower half of the batting order.

After leaving the Monarchs in 1923, he pitched with the Bertha, Minnesota, Fisherman, a white team, recording an 18–3 mark with 300 strikeouts in 1924. The next season he was 28–4 with a team in Moose Jaw, Canada, and he signed with the Lismore, Minnesota, ball club in 1926 before returning to Bertha, where he won 22 games and hit .440 in 1927. He pitched with St. Cloud, Minnesota, in 1930 and later formed his own touring baseball team, the John Donaldson All-Stars, and continued playing on into the decade, returning to the Monarchs in 1931.

After his active baseball career ended, Donaldson worked as a shipping clerk in the post office and, when the color ban was lifted, scouted for the Chicago White Sox.

Donaldson, W. W. (Billy)
Career: 1923–27   Position: umpire
Teams: Negro National League

A well-known long-time umpire, he worked behind home plate for fifteen seasons, arbitrating in both the first and second Negro National Leagues.

Donelly
Career: 1938   Position: 3b
Team: Memphis Red Sox

He received some playing time as a third baseman for the 1938 Negro American first-half champion Memphis Red Sox.

Donoso, Lino Galata
Career: 1947–49   Position: p
Teams: New York Cubans ('47–'49), *Mexican*

League ('50–'53, '56, '58–'62), minor leagues ('54–'57), major leagues ('55–'56)
Bats: Left   Throws: Left
Height: 5'11"   Weight: 160
Born: Sept. 23, 1922, Havana, Cuba
Died: Oct. 13, 1990, Vera Cruz, Mexico

After registering an 8–2 record with two shutouts in the regular season, the New York Cubans' right-hander split two decisions in the 1947 Negro World Series. After two more seasons with the New York Cubans, he joined Aguila in the Mexican League in 1950, where he fashioned four seasons of 12–11, 14–14, 18–11, and 17–9, never having an ERA over 2.55.

That earned him a chance with Hollywood in the Pacific Coast League, where he registered a 19–8 record with a .237 ERA in 1954. After beginning the 1955 season with Hollywood (4–3, 3.24 ERA), the Cuban hurler finally had a shot at the major leagues at age thirty-two, when he joined the Pittsburgh Pirates and finished the season with a 4–6 record. The next season, after pitching in three games without a decision, he was shipped back to Hollywood, and from there he returned to Mexico, with the Mexico City Tigers.

The rest of his career was spent in Mexico, with the exception of an interval in 1957, when he pitched briefly with Columbus in the International League. Pitching with Vera Cruz in 1958–61, he again strung together four double-digit winning seasons, with records of 16–14, 16–10, 13–9, and 10–6. The next season, 1962, was also the last season of his career. During the post-major-league part of his career, he also was a respectable hitter, having four intermittent seasons in Mexico with averages of .388, .310, .309, and .298.

During his career he also played five winters (1946–50 and 1954–55) in Cuba, playing mostly with Marianao, and had a lifetime 12–14 record. His last season was the winter before making the major leagues and, playing with Almendares, he recorded his only winning season (4–3 and 3.18 ERA).

Dooley
Career: 1933   Position: of
Team: Kansas City Monarchs

This outfielder appeared briefly with the Kansas City Monarchs in 1933, when they were barnstorming as an independent team.

Dorsey
Career: 1921   Position: p
Team: Baltimore Black Sox

He pitched briefly with the Baltimore Black Sox in 1921, winning his only decision. At that time the Black Sox was still playing as an independent team, and their level of performance was of marginal quality.

Dorsey
Career: 1941   Position: lf
Team: Philadelphia Stars

He was a reserve outfielder with the Philadelphia Stars in 1941, hitting only .136 in limited play during his only season in the Negro Leagues.

Dougherty
Career: 1909   Position: 1b
Team: Kansas City Royal Giants

In 1909, the team's only quality season, he was a first baseman with the Kansas City Royal Giants of Kansas City, Missouri.

Dougherty, Charles (**Pat**)
a.k.a. Doherty
Career: 1909–18   Position: p
Teams: *West Baden Sprudels ('09),* Leland Giants ('09–'10), Chicago American Giants ('11–'14, '18), Chicago Giants ('15–'17)
Bats: Left   Throws: Left
Born: 1879, Summershade, Ky.
Died: July 12, 1940

Described by the press as a "big sidewheeler," Pat Dougherty was a star left-handed pitcher for the great Leland Giants of 1909–10, who picked him up from the Sprudels of West Baden, Indiana. In 1909, when Rube Foster's injury kept the pitcher-manager out of the championship series, Dougherty stepped into the breach and the rookie won both of the Leland Giants' victories in the five-game playoffs against the St. Paul Gophers. Although he lost a tough decision in the finale, 3–2, to "Steel Arm" Johnny Taylor of the famous Taylor clan, Dougherty finished the series with 27 innings pitched and allowed only 8 hits and 4 earned runs while fanning 18. An interesting oddity involving Dougherty occurred during the Series, which resulted in the game being protested. Walter Ball had started the game and, when he got in a jam, Dougherty came in to strike out the batter, and Ball, who had left the game, returned to finish the contest.

That same year, in a postseason exhibition against the Chicago Cubs, he struck out the first three batters and shut down the Cubs after yielding a second-inning run, but lost a 1–0 duel with Mordecai "Three Finger" Brown.

The next season, when Rube Foster split with owner Frank Leland, Dougherty stayed with Foster and teamed with Frank Wickware to form an almost unbeatable mound duo for Foster's Leland Giants. Dougherty finished the 1910 season with a perfect 13–0 slate. Foster later called his team the greatest of all time, black or white. The following year the team was renamed the Chicago American Giants and Dougherty continued his sterling work, with partial records showing a 3–0 ledger. He also was a good-hitting pitcher, often helping his own cause with his stickwork. In 1913, when Wickware left the team, he assumed the role as ace of the staff and lived up to his top billing by hurling a no-hitter.

Two years later, he joined Frank Leland's Chicago Giants and encountered control problems. In 1918 he returned to the American Giants for his final appearance in black baseball. During the intermittent decade of his short career, he was the top left-hander in the game and was sometimes described as the "black Marquard."

Douglas, Eddie
Career: 1922   Position: of
Team: St. Louis Stars

He was an outfielder with the St. Louis Stars in 1922, in their first season of existence.

Douglas, Edward (**Eddie**)]
[see Douglass, Edward (Eddie)]

Douglas, George
Career: 1885–91   Position: of
Teams: *Brooklyn Remsens ('85),* Cuban Giants ('91)

He was an outfielder with the 1885 Brooklyn Remsens, one of the earliest black professional teams, and later joined the Cuban Giants in 1891 as an outfielder-pitcher when they represented Ansonia in the Connecticut State League.

Douglas, Jesse Warren
Career: 1937–50   Positions: **2b, ss,** 3b, *1b, of*
Teams: New York Black Yankees ('38), Satchel Paige's All-Stars ('39), Kansas City Monarchs ('37, '40–'41), Birmingham Black Barons ('41–'42), Memphis Red Sox ('50), **Chicago American Giants** ('44–'45, '49–'50), *Mexican League ('46–'48, 54), New Orleans Eagles ('51), minor leagues ('52–'58)*
Bats: Both   Throws: Right
Height: 5'10"   Weight: 160
Born: March 27, 1920, Longview, Tex.

Although he was primarily an infielder, he played both infield and outfield with a number of teams between the years 1937 and 1950, including the Chicago American Giants, Kansas City Monarchs, Birmingham Black Barons, and Memphis Red Sox. He was basically an average player in the field, on the bases, and at the plate. Although he lacked power at bat, he was a good bunter.

Douglas went on the road with Satchel Paige in 1939 as a nineteen-year-old second sacker, and upon returning to the Kansas City Monarchs in 1940 shared playing time at second base. The next season, with the Birmingham Black Barons, he shared an outfield position.

He served two stints with the Chicago American Giants, joining them first as a second baseman during the war years, hitting .280 and .303 in 1944–45. He left for Mexico in 1946, where he hit .270 with Mexico City, playing both infield and outfield, but returned to the Chicago American Giants for his second stint as the Negro Leagues were nearing their end, batting .287 and .331 in 1949–50.

After his second tour with the Chicago American Giants, he signed in organized baseball with Colorado Springs in the Western League, where he hit for a .262 average. The following two seasons were spent in the Mandak League, where he hit .252 in 1953. From Canada he went back to Mexico in 1954 and hit .322 with Mexicali in the Arizona-Mexican League in 1956. The last trace of him in organized baseball was in 1958, when he hit .207 with Yakima in the Northwest League.

Douglass, Edward (**Eddie**)
a.k.a. Douglas
Career: 1918–29   Positions: **1b,** manager
Teams: **Brooklyn Royal Giants** ('18–'25), New York Lincoln Giants ('18, '24)
Born: Texas
Died: New York, N.Y.

The Brooklyn Royal Giants' first baseman was regarded as the best player at his position in the East from the post-World War I era into the midtwenties. He was an excellent gloveman, a proficient base stealer, and a good hitter, who was especially dangerous in the clutch and who usually batted third in the order. The Texan began his career in Dallas in 1907 and honed his skills in the baseball hotbed of Texas before migrating to the Northeast.

Once in New York, he spent twelve years with the Royal Giants and New York Lincoln Giants. In 1918, playing primarily with the Royal Giants, available statistics credit him with a .300 batting average in his first year with a top team. After establishing himself as the premier player at his position over the next five years, he was appointed playing manager of the Royal Giants during the 1923 season, when they became a charter member of the Eastern Colored League. He continued to serve

in that capacity for the entire 1924 season but experienced less team success than he had expected. His batting average may have been affected by his managerial responsibilities, as he dropped off to a .250 average for the season, although he rebounded in 1925 with a .354 average.

During this time his services were sought in the Cuban winter league, and he hit .336 as the first sacker for the great 1923–24 Santa Clara championship team that is classed as the greatest Cuban team of all time.

After retiring from baseball he operated a poolroom in New York City for several years.

Dow
Career: 1911   Position: p
Team: Philadelphia Giants

The pitcher appeared with the Philadelphia Giants in 1911 as the franchise began a decline in quality of play.

Downer, Fred
Career: 1921   Position: lf
Teams: Pittsburgh Keystones ('21), Baltimore Black Sox ('21)

He was an outfielder with two emerging teams prior to their entrance into league play. The Keystones entered the Negro National League the following year and the Baltimore Black Sox entered the Eastern Colored League two years after his appearance on the squad.

Downs, Ellsworth
Career: 1887   Position: player
Team: *Cincinnati Browns*

He was a player with the Cincinnati Browns, one of eight teams that were charter members of the League of Colored Baseball Clubs in 1887. However, the league's existence was ephemeral, lasting only a week. His position is uncertain.

Downs, McKinley (**Bunny**)
Career: 1916–28;
1942–55   Positions: **2b,** ss, 3b,
                         1b, of, manager

Teams: *West Baden Sprudels ('15), Louisville Sox ('15),* St. Louis Giants ('16), Indianapolis ABCs ('16), **Hilldale Daisies** ('17–'22), Atlantic City Bacharach Giants ('18, '23), *military service ('18),* Lincoln Giants ('20), *Richmond Giants ('23),* Brooklyn Royal Giants ('23–'25), Harrisburg Giants ('25), Philadelphia Tigers ('26, '28), *Chappie Johnson's Stars ('27), Brooklyn Cuban Giants,* Ethiopian Clowns ('42), Cincinnati Clowns ('43), Indianapolis Clowns ('52–'55)

Bats: Right   Throws: Right
Height: 5'5"   Weight: 158
Died: North Carolina

The short little second baseman was a hustler who always got the most from his talent. He started his professional baseball career in the Midwest in 1915, joined the Indianapolis ABCs in 1916, and traveled East to play with Hilldale the following season. A good bunter and hit-and-run man, he was placed in the second slot in the batting order to utilize these skills.

He had a very light complexion and, when he played with the Bacharachs in 1918, it was alleged (but unproven) by the press that he had been on the roster of a major-league club. With the Bacharachs he formed a double-play combination with Dick Lundy, with whom he had played previously in Jacksonville, Florida. A smart player, the Morehouse College man was the captain of Hilldale's team and batting .286 when he was drafted into military service late in the 1918 season. After his discharge, he returned to Hilldale and continued his sterling glovework while hitting .245. While a good fielder, he was only a fair base runner and a fair hitter, usually batting in the lower part of the order. He still managed averages of .379, .279, and .282 and 1920–22, when the team was still playing as an independent ballclub.

When the Eastern Colored League organized in 1923, Hilldale joined the league, but Downs left the fold after an incident in Philadelphia, where he shot and killed a woman who was trying to shoot him. After being dispatched by Hilldale, he joined another Eastern Colored League club, the Brooklyn Royal Giants. With the Royals he alternated hitting in the second and sixth spots in the batting order, while his average dropped to .263 and .226 in 1924–25. But he was still recognized as one of the best black second basemen in the game in 1924 and was highly regarded by the press. His last year as an active player in the Negro Leagues was in 1928, when he played with the Philadelphia Tigers, an ill-fated entry in the Eastern Colored League during their last season before imploding. The veteran infielder could play any infield position, and often also played shortstop or third base as well as at the keystone sack.

In later years, as business manager with the Indianapolis Clowns, he scouted and helped develop a youngster named Hank Aaron. After retiring from baseball, Downs supervised an apartment complex in New York City.

Drake, Andrew
Career: 1930–32   Positions: p, c
Teams: Nashville Elite Giants ('30), Birmingham Black Barons ('32), Cole's American Giants ('32), Louisville Red Caps ('32), *Chattanooga Black Lookouts*

He began his career as a pitcher with the Nashville Elite Giants, winning his only two recorded decisions but, two years later, he was a catcher with the Birmingham Black Barons. Most of his short career was spent with southern teams, but he also played with Cole's American Giants for part of the 1932 season, when they were members of the Negro Southern League.

Drake, Reynaldo **Verdes**
Career: 1945–50   Positions: **cf,** lf, rf
Teams: Cincinnati-Indianapolis Clowns ('45), Indianapolis Clowns ('46–'54)
Bats: Left   Throws: Left
Height: 5'7"   Weight: 150

The fleet center fielder had good speed and was an excellent fielder, with great range and a good arm. Offensively he displayed only average power and usually batted in the leadoff position for the Clowns. During the latter half of the decade of the forties, he had batting averages of .232, .283, .275, .206, and .300 for the years 1945–50, exclusive of the 1947 season.

Drake, William P. (**Bill,** Plunk)
Career: 1915–30   Position: p
Teams: *Tennessee Rats ('14),* All Nations ('15), St. Louis Giants ('16–'21), St. Louis Stars ('22, '30), Kansas City Monarchs ('22–'26), Indianapolis ABCs ('26), Dayton Marcos ('26), Memphis Red Sox ('26), Detroit Stars ('27)
Bats: Right   Throws: Right
Height: 6'0"   Weight: 205
Born: June 8, 1895, Sedalia, Mo.
Died: Oct. 30, 1977, St. Louis, Mo.

A smart pitcher who used a good curve, good control, and a variety of "trick" pitches, including the emery ball, Drake was a tough competitor who earned his nickname "Plunk" because he kept batters loose in the batter's box. He is credited with hurling a no-hitter in Sioux Falls, South Dakota.

He started his professional career in 1914 with the Tennessee Rats, a touring aggregation that was a combination minstrel show and baseball team. After one season he joined the All Nations club, which consisted of fifteen players of various nationalities (Japanese, Indian, Hawaiian, two Negroes, and white players of various ethnic groups). Although they also were a barnstorming team, they played a better class of baseball and traveled in a private car. As with the previous traveling team, he stayed with the team only one season before moving up to a better team, joining the St. Louis Giants in 1916. When the Negro National League was formed in 1920, the Giants became a charter member and Drake posted a record of 9–12 in the league's inaugural season. The next year he turned in his best performance, with a 20–10 ledger.

When the Giants were sold in 1922 and became the Stars, he was traded to the Kansas City Monarchs, where he spent parts of five seasons (1922–26) without ever signing a con-

tract. During the transitional season he was 8–8, but in the three full seasons he spent with the Monarchs, he fashioned records of 9–7, 10–8, and 9–5 as they won the Negro National League pennant each season. In the latter two seasons, 1924–25, a World Series was played against the Eastern Colored League's champion Hilldale ballclub, and the tall right-hander played in six World Series games but was winless against 3 losses in the postseason games.

In 1926 he left Kansas City and joined the Indianapolis ABCs, splitting a dozen decisions during the season, and improved to a 10–8 ledger with the Detroit Stars in 1927.

Drake's career was a nomadic existence, beginning when he played with lesser teams in Springfield, Illinois, and other forgettable teams before joining the Tennessee Rats. Even after joining the Monarchs, owner J. L. Wilkinson earned more money by barnstorming through the Midwest. With the Monarchs Drake earned about $150 per month and sometimes, as in league play, the team ate and slept in the best Negro restaurants and hotels. At other times the players slept in tents, and some of their meals came from fishing in nearby streams as they traveled. During the regular season they played in Kansas City at the stadium shared by the American Association's Kansas City Blues and once beat the Kansas City Blues in a postseason series, but on the road they played on a diversity of baseball diamonds.

In winters he often played in California with the Los Angeles White Sox, playing against major leaguers including Babe Ruth and the Meusel brothers. Drake considered Ruth to be a regular guy because the Babe shared a plug of chewing tobacco with him. While Drake was with the St. Louis Giants, they played a series of games against the Cardinals and won three of the eight games played. Although Rogers Hornsby was absent from the lineup, most of other regulars did play in the series. Drake met Satchel Paige when he was with the Memphis Red Sox and Satchel was with the Chattanooga Black Lookouts.

Drake played on white semipro teams in North Dakota, even rooming with a white player, and never had any problems of any consequence, but he refused to play in the Florida Hotel League in West Palm Beach because of the social conditions in the South. In later years he relented in his reluctance to travel in the South and took a black basketball team to Atlanta to play the black college teams in the area. He remained pessimistic about the integration of baseball and never thought blacks would be allowed to play in organized ball.

He was also afraid to go to the Caribbean Leagues because of his habit of throwing at batters, a practice that earned disapproval in Cuba. He hit several of the Cuban players in the States and thought they were holding a grudge and were "laying for" him.

Off the field, Drake was always involved in some "foolishness" and joking around. And while still an active player, he gave no thought to the future and had nothing to fall back on for a second career after baseball. Consequently he didn't work at a regular job until he worked with Famous and Barr for ten years to qualify for Social Security benefits, retiring at age sixty-two. His later years were rather spartan, and he sought assistance from governmental agencies, stating that he "went to war" and expected a pension after reaching a specified age.

Dreke, Valentin
a.k.a. Drake
Career: 1918–28   Positions: cf, lf
Teams: **Cuban Stars (West)** ('18–'28), Cuban Stars of Havana ('19)
Bats: Left   Throws: Right
Height: 5'8"   Weight: 160
Born: June 21, 1898, Union de Reyes, Cuba
Died: Sept. 25, 1929

A good-hitting outfielder with speed and power, he played for a decade in the Negro Leagues. A good leadoff batter, he was a good base stealer, an adept drag bunter, and hit to all fields. He was also an excellent fielder and had a good throwing arm. He began his career with the Cuban Stars (West) in 1918, when they were still playing as an independent team. The Cubans entered the Negro National League in its inaugural season, 1920, and in his first year in league play he hit .353 while playing left field and batting second in the order. He dropped off the marks of .284 and .291 before bouncing back with a .378 average in 1923. The next year was his career best, as he hit .429 and had a slugging average of .538. For the next three years he batted in the cleanup spot and hit for averages of .319, .316, and .327.

In his home country, playing primarily with Almendares, he hit .308, .261, .354, .385, .284, and .252 for the years 1922–28, finishing his eight years in Cuba with a lifetime average of .307. He also led the Cuban League in stolen bases in 1923–24. In honor of his achievements, he was elected to the Cuban Hall of Fame in 1945.

Drew
Career: 1899   Position: 3b
Team: Cuban Giants

He played third base for the Cuban Giants, a team organized in 1885 by Frank P. Thompson and that has the distinction of being the first black professional team. The Cuban Giants were considered the top ballclub until the early 1890s, but by 1899 the quality of their play had declined.

Drew, John M. (Johnny)
Career: 1928–32   Position: officer
Team: Hilldale Daisies

He assumed the responsibility of running the Hilldale ballclub in 1928, when Ed Bolden became incapacitated. However, he failed to understand the arrangements with booking agents fully and consequently the team had difficulty securing games. He continued to serve as an officer for the ballculb during the final two years of the Philadelphia-based team's existence, 1931–32.

Drew, P.
Career: 1939   Positions: of, p
Team: Indianapolis ABCs

He appeared briefly as an outfielder-pitcher with the 1939 Indianapolis ABCs, who were in reality the transplanted Atlanta Black Crackers.

Drummer
Career: 1948   Position: c
Team: Newark Eagles
He appeared in one game as a catcher with the 1948 Newark Eagles.

Duany, Claro
Career: 1944, 1947   Positions: rf, lf
Teams: New York Cubans ('44, '47), *Mexican League ('45–'46, '50–'51), Canadian League ('48–'49, '51), minor leagues ('52)*
Bats: Left   Throws: Left
Height: 6'2"   Weight: 215
Born: Aug. 12, 1917, Caibarien, Cuba
The left-handed power hitter batted .297 while hitting in the fifth spot in the batting order as the regular right fielder with the New York Cubans' 1947 Negro League Championship team, and made his only All-Star game appearance that year. A good hitter for both average and power, he was respected by opposing hurlers and was issued more than a normal amount of free passes. As with most power hitters, the Cuban slugger was a poor bunter and not a capable hit-and-run man. Defensively he had an average arm, but limited range afield. He was slow on the bases, although he occasionally stole a base.

He began his career in 1944 with the New York Cubans by hitting an even .300 with good power, but was unable to break into the Cubans' strong outfield on a regular basis. After two powerful seasons with Monterrey in the Mexican League, where he hit a league-high .375 with 100 RBIs, followed by a .364 mark the second year, he came back in 1947 to earn a spot in the Cubans' outfield. The previous winter in Puerto Rico, he earned the sobriquet "The Puerto Rican Babe Ruth" because of a combination of his home-run power and physique. Duany was heavy, with a tendency to add too much weight, which hindered him severely as a base runner.

The big slugger also played in the Cuban winter league for 11 years (1942–55), hitting for a .282 lifetime average. From 1943 through 1951 he had averages of .273, .340, .288, .368, .300, .244, .274, .314, and .275. His .340 batting average in 1944–45 with Almendares-Marianao was good enough to lead the league.

After his 1947 season with the New York Cubans, he hit .388 (23 home runs, 17 doubles, 77 RBIs), .290 (22 home runs, 18 doubles, 99 RBIs), and .337 (23 home runs, 23 doubles, 88 RBIs) for Sherbrooke in the Provincial League in 1948–49 and 1951. He had gone back to Mexico in 1950 and part of 1951, and hit .280 and .289. In 1952 he played with Tampa-Havana in the Florida International League and managed only a .243 average in his last year in organized ball.

Dubetts, Al M.
Career: 1950   Position: p
Team: Chicago American Giants
The baseball prospect from Havana, Illinois, was one of three white players (along with Louis Clarizio and Louis Chirban) signed by manager "Double Duty" Radcliffe for the Chicago American Giants in late June 1950. However, his skills were limited and his stay with the team was very brief.

Ducey
Career: 1924–26   Positions: 3b, rf, lf
Teams: St. Louis Giants ('24), Dayton Marcos ('26)
A versatile player, he played third base with the St. Louis Giants in 1924 and outfield for the Dayton Marcos two years later, batting .224 the later season.

Ducey, Eddie
a.k.a. Ducy
Career: 1947   Position: 2b
Team: Homestead Grays
In 1947 he was a reserve second baseman with the Homestead Grays, as the franchise gave many young players a chance while the

team underwent an extensive change in playing personnel.

Duckett, Mahlon Newton (Mal)
Career: 1940–50   Positions: **2b,** ss, 3b
Teams: **Philadelphia Stars** ('40–'49), Homestead Grays ('49–'50)
Bats: Right   Throws: Right
Height: 5'10"   Weight: 170
Born: Dec. 20, 1922, Philadelphia, Pa.

Entering the Negro National League in 1940 at age seventeen, the light-hitting, smooth-fielding, versatile infielder played for the Philadelphia Stars for the duration of the '40s. After his rookie year, when he hit .234 while playing third base, he moved to shortstop. His batting average dropped considerably as the teenager encountered difficulties adjusting to major-league pitching, batting only .146 and .117 for the next two seasons. After holding down the starting shortstop position through the 1943 season, he temporarily lost his starting position in 1944 but raised his average to .233 while splitting his playing time between second base and shortstop.

That season allowed him to gain additional experience and maturity and, at age twenty-one, he regained his regular spot in the lineup in 1945, and responded with a .277 batting average. That year began four seasons as the starting second sacker for the Stars, and he registered averages of .209, .216 and .268 in 1946–48. Although usually hitting in the lower part of the batting order, Duckett was a good bunter and moved up to the number two spot in the lineup in the latter season.

Following the demise of the Negro National League, he began the 1949 season with the Stars but soon joined the Homestead Grays, who had dropped out of league play and were playing as an independent ballclub. When the Grays broke up after the 1950 season, Duckett also ended his career. He had an average arm and a modicum of speed and power, and was known more for his glove than for his bat, but

he still had his moments at the plate. He enjoyed the memory of successful forays against Satchel Paige, which he considers highlights of his career. After baseball he worked as a mail carrier for the U.S. Postal Service in Philadelphia.

Dudley, C. A.
Career: 1920–23   Position: of
Teams: St. Louis Giants ('20–'21), St. Louis Stars ('22–'23)

A fast ballplayer both in the field and on the bases, he began his career as an outfielder with the St. Louis Giants, and after the franchise restructured in 1922, he played left field for the team in their first game as the Stars.

Dudley, Edward
Career: 1925–28   Position: p
Teams: New York Lincoln Giants ('25–'27), Brooklyn Royal Giants ('28), *Chappie Johnson's Stars ('27),* Philadelphia Tigers ('28)

He was a pitcher with the New York Lincoln Giants and the Brooklyn Royal Giants in the late '20s, during the last four seasons of the Eastern Colored League.

Duff, Ernest
Career: 1925–32   Positions: rf, lf, cf, c, 2b, 1b
Teams: Indianapolis ABCs ('25–'26), Cleveland Elites ('26), Cleveland Hornets ('27), Cleveland Tigers ('28), Cuban Stars ('32)

The outfielder began his career with the Indianapolis ABCs in 1925 but also played infield while with Cleveland-based teams during his eight-year career. In 1926, with the Elites, he hit .314 while batting in the heart of the order and playing the odd combination of center field and catcher. The next season, with the Hornets, he hit .319 while batting in the second slot and playing rightfield. In 1928 he played with the Tigers, his third Cleveland team in as many years, and true to the pattern, the Tigers also dropped out of the league after one season. Most of his career was spent with teams that were marginal and folded the year after he played with them.

Duffy, Bill
Career: 1947   Position: c
Team: Kansas City Monarchs

In 1947 he was a third-string catcher with the Kansas City Monarchs and received minimal playing time.

Dukes
[see Cleveland, Howard (Duke)]

Dukes, Tommy (Dixie)
Career: 1928–45   Positions: **c**, 1b, rf, 3b
Teams: Chicago American Giants ('28, '45), Birmingham Black Barons ('31), Cuban Stars (West) ('31), Cuban Stars (East), Memphis Red Sox ('32), Nashville Elite Giants ('32–'34), Columbus Elite Giants ('35), **Homestead Grays** ('35–'38), Toledo Crawfords ('39), Indianapolis Crawfords ('40)
Bats: Left   Throws: Right
Height: 5'8"   Weight: 165

Primarily a catcher, he had a good arm and handled himself well defensively, although he was only moderately mobile behind the plate. Offensively the left-handed batter had good power but was only an average contact hitter and a fair bunter. Playing mostly with southern teams in his early years, he signed with owner Tom Wilson's Nashville Elite Giants in 1932, when the Negro Southern League was accorded major-league status. The next season, Wilson entered his team in the new Negro National League and Dukes batted cleanup and hit for a .311 batting average. Two years later Wilson moved his team to Columbus, and Dukes began the season at the new franchise location but shortly afterward signed with Cum Posey's Homestead Grays.

With the Grays he moved into the cleanup spot batting behind slugging first baseman Buck Leonard, and responded with a .375 batting average with his new team. The next year he contributed a .290 average to the Grays' attack, but in 1937 Posey signed Josh Gibson,

relegating Dukes to bench duty. The ousted receiver made playing time for himself by playing first base and right field as well as spelling Gibson behind the plate, but after two seasons as a backup, he joined the Toledo Crawfords when they entered the Negro American League for the second half of the season. With manager Oscar Charleston's team he moved into his accustomed cleanup spot, and incomplete statistics show him with a .277 average with the Crawfords.

The eighteen-year veteran closed out his career with the Chicago American Giants, hitting only .175 in 1945. Dukes occasionally saw action as a third baseman during his career, and played with a host of teams, but is probably best identified with the Homestead Grays.

Dula, Louis
Career: 1933–38   Positions: **p,** of
Teams: Homestead Grays ('33–'38), Cincinnati Tigers
Bats: Right   Throws: Right
Height: 5'11"   Weight: 180

The right-handed pitcher had good control and a varied repertory of pitches, including a fastball, curve, drop, slider, and change-up. Primarily identified with the Homestead Grays, the Depression era pitcher also played occasionally in the outfield. However, he was below par as a hitter and on the bases, but had a good arm and hustled to field his position adequately. As a pitcher his most productive years came before the Grays established their dynasty, but his tenure concluded with the first two of the Grays' nine straight Negro National League pennants. There is a dearth of statistics from the Depression era, but although incomplete, they show a composite 2–3 ledger for his first three seasons with the Grays and a 1–1 record for his last season, 1938.

Dumas, Jim
Career: 1940–41   Positions: of, 1b, 3b, p
Team: Memphis Red Sox

An all-purpose player with the Memphis Red Sox, he played outfield, on the infield corners, and pitched with the Red Sox in 1940–41. In 1940 he won his only decision on the mound and, when in the lineup as an everyday player, batted in the cleanup spot.

Dumpson, Bill
Career: 1950   Position: p
Teams: Indianapolis Clowns ('50), Philadelphia Stars ('50–'52)

He had a record of 0–2 while pitching in 5 games with the Indianapolis Clowns and Philadelphia Stars in 1950, when the Negro American League was struggling to survive the loss of players to organized baseball.

Dunbar, Ashby
Career: 1909–20   Positions: lf, rf, cf
Teams: Brooklyn Royal Giants ('09–'11, '16), New York Lincoln Giants ('12), Mohawk Giants ('13), Louisville White Sox ('15), Indianapolis ABCs ('16), Lincoln Stars ('16–'17), Pennsylvania Red Caps of New York ('17–'19), Chicago American Giants ('20)

A good fielder with good speed, the outfielder was one of the best players for the Brooklyn Royal Giants in 1910–11, batting sixth in the lineup, and played with the Lincoln Giants in 1912 as a part-time center fielder, hitting .280 in limited play. In 1916 he played left field with the ABCs for part of the season, batting .261 during his stint in the West, but finished the season with the Lincoln Stars. In 1917 he became one of several ex-Lincoln Stars who joined the Pennsylvania Red Caps of New York and was the regular left fielder and leadoff batter for the next three seasons, with partial statistics showing a .217 batting average in 1918.

Dunbar, Frank
Career: 1908   Position: of
Team: Philadelphia Giants

In 1909 he played outfield for the Philadelphia Giants, his only season with a recognized team.

Dunbar, Vet
Career: 1937   Positions: c, 3b

Teams: Memphis Red Sox ('37), Indianapolis Athletics ('37)

In 1937 the New Orleans native split the season with the Memphis Red Sox, where he was an infielder playing mostly at the hot corner, and with the Indianapolis Athletics, where he assumed the regular catching duties while batting in the lower part of the order.

Duncan, Charlie (Scottie)
Career: 1938–40   Position: p
Teams: Atlanta Black Crackers ('38), Indianapolis ABCs ('39), St. Louis Stars ('40)

The high point of his three-year career was as a pitcher with the 1938 second-half Negro American League champion Atlanta Black Crackers.

Duncan, Frank (Pete, Dunk)
Career: 1909–28   Positions: **lf**, rf, cf, manager
Teams: Philadelphia Giants ('09), Leland Giants ('10), **Chicago American Giants** ('11–'18), Detroit Stars ('19), Chicago Giants ('20), Toledo Tigers ('23). Milwaukee Bears ('23), Cleveland Elite Giants ('26), Cleveland Hornets ('27), Cleveland Tigers ('28)
Bats: Left   Throws: Right

Beginning his career with the Philadelphia Giants in 1909, the little outfielder left the team along with John Henry Lloyd and Bruce Petway to join Rube Foster's Leland Giants in 1910. In his first year with the team, Duncan, an exceptionally good bunter and a fast base runner, found himself compatible with Foster's style of play and quickly proved to be popular with the fans.

In the field he was one of the most reliable outfielders, possessing all-around ability and a great arm, but he was overshadowed by teammate Pete Hill. Regarded as the most successful leadoff man the team had ever had, Duncan proved to be an effective table-setter with his consistent hitting and base stealing. On the bases he was as nervy as Pete Hill, but his style was more in line with John Henry Lloyd's approach to base running, with no wasted motion.

The left-handed batter hit .389 against all levels of competition in his initial season with Foster's club and continued the good stickwork, while usually batting in the third slot throughout his career with the American Giants. He was credited with averages of .277, .327, .258, .230, and .222 for the years 1914–18. In addition to his good play in the States, he compiled a .345 batting average during the 1915–16 winter in Cuba and hit .382 with the Royal Poinciana team in the Florida Hotel League in West Palm Beach for the winter of 1917–18.

In 1918 he was still with the Chicago American Giants but was above draft age for World War I. Following the return of players from the service in 1919, Foster sent him to the Detroit Stars along with Hill and several other established veterans who were past their primes, but the move backfired on Foster as the Stars defeated Foster's club to lay claim to the western title.

Duncan should not be confused with the catcher of the same name who came along a decade later, but like the other Frank Duncan, he was a playing manager in the latter years of his baseball career, assuming the reins of the Cleveland Elites during the course of the 1926 season and continuing in that capacity with the Cleveland Hornets in 1927 and the Cleveland Tigers in 1928. In his first year at the helm, he also played right field on a part-time basis, batting .243, but afterward he was a pinch hitter, batting only .176 in this capacity in 1927.

Duncan, Frank, Jr.
a.k.a. Frank Duncan, Sr.
Career: 1920–48   Positions: **c,** 1b, *of*, manager
Teams: *Peters' Union Giants ('20),* Chicago Giants ('20–'21), **Kansas City Monarchs** ('21–'34, '37, '41–'47), New York Black Yankees ('31), Pittsburgh Crawfords ('32), Homestead Grays ('32), New York Cubans

('35–'37), Chicago American Giants ('38, '40), *Palmer House Stars ('39)*
Bats: Right   Throws: Right
Height: 6'0"   Weight: 175
Born: Feb. 14, 1901, Kansas City, Mo.
Died: Dec. 4, 1973, Kansas City, Mo.

Generally regarded as one of the top receivers in black baseball, Frank was a master of handling pop flies, and during his prime years with the Kansas City Monarchs he cut down would-be base stealers with one of the best throwing arms in the league. The durable receiver had a quick release but threw a "heavy" ball. With pitchers such as Satchel Paige, Bullet Rogan, Chet Brewer, John Donaldson, and José Mendez the Monarchs were always noted for their strong pitching staff. Duncan, a good handler of pitchers, caught them all. He also once caught Dizzy Dean in an exhibition game against the Monarchs after Dean personally hauled him out of a poolroom to catch the game.

A hard-nosed competitor although he was slow on the bases, he ran the bases with reckless abandon and asked no quarter on the playing field. In 1926 he precipitated a bench-clearing brawl when he "jumped" at Chicago American Giants' catcher John Hines. During the melee on the field, a policeman hit Duncan on the back of the head with his pistol butt and knocked him unconscious. While he was on the ground, Jelly Gardner kicked him in the mouth with his spikes.

A line-drive hitter, Duncan was not noted for his batting accomplishments, but he was tough in the clutch. Beginning with the Monarchs in 1921, he hit for averages of .226, .221, .212, .247, .234, and .284 during his first six seasons in league play. In 1929, when the Monarchs won their last Negro National League pennant, he hit .346 and followed with a .372 mark in 1930.

In Cuba during the intervening winter, he batted .250 for the 1929–30 champion Cienfuegos team. His first winter in the country, he hit .336 with Santa Clara in 1923–24. Records for his five seasons in the tough Cuban winter league show a .272 average, which was slightly higher than his lifetime average in the Negro Leagues. Duncan was a good bunter and, although having only average power, he could pull the ball, and in general proved to be an asset offensively.

He was playing with the Swift Packing House in St. Joseph, Missouri, when he signed with Peters' Union Giants in Chicago in 1920. After having launched his long professional career, he jumped to Joe Green's Chicago Giants later in the year, with John Beckwith moving to shortstop to make room for Duncan behind the plate. In June 1921 the young prospect was traded to Kansas City for three players and $1,000. He played with them during their first dynasty period, when they won three consecutive Negro National League pennants (1923–25) and won the first Negro World Series in 1924, defeating the Eastern Colored League's Hilldale ballclub in a hard-fought Series. Following the 1926 season he played in the California winter league and, after the close of the winter season, joined the Philadelphia Royal Giants in their tour of the Orient, playing in Hawaii, the Philippines, Japan, China, and Russia. The club featured some of the top black talent from the United States and lost only one game during the trip. Upon the team's return to the States, he rejoined Kansas City for the 1928 season.

Although he left the Monarchs on four separate occasions, he always returned to Kansas City after an interlude elsewhere. After the demise of the first Negro National League, the Monarchs disbanded and he began a pilgrimage that ultimately led back to the Monarchs. His time away from the Kansas City domicile included a stint with New York Black Yankees at the beginning of 1931, but he returned to Kansas City for the second half when Wilkinson reorganized the club. In 1932 he started with the Crawfords and then went to the Homestead Grays, but was back with Kansas City in 1933. In 1935 he joined the New York Cuban Stars, batting .172 and .234 before returning to Kansas City in 1937.

However, his stay with the Monarchs was short and, when the Chicago American Giants pressed shortstop Ormond Sampson into duty as a catcher only to have him jump the team for Mexico, Duncan left Kansas City in July to fill the Chicago American Giants' receiving void for the latter part of the season. This second trip to Chicago lasted three years, two seasons with the Chicago American Giants sandwiched around a season with Gamble's Palmer House Stars, a Chicago-based independent team that won the 1939 Illinois State semipro title.

During this respite from the Monarchs, he was selected to the All-Star team in 1938, representing the American Giants. He began the 1940 season with the Chicago American Giants as a backup catcher behind Pepper Basset, but when Monarchs' manager Andy Cooper died, he returned to Kansas City for the fourth and final time to assist Newt Allen in directing the team.

Duncan was appointed manager in 1942 and led his charges to a sweep over the Homestead Grays in the Negro World Series. The wily veteran maintained his enthusiasm and knew how to handle players, directing his team to another pennant in 1946 but losing the World Series to the Newark Eagles in a hotly contested seven-game series. In addition to handling the managerial chores, the veteran receiver continued to take his turn behind the plate when the occasion required his special expertise behind the bat, until turning the managerial reins over to Buck O'Neill in 1948. Duncan's appearances as a player in the latter stages of his career always drew big ovations from the crowd. His career closely approximated that of catcher-manager Al Lopez, who also won two pennants as a manager after a long career as a catcher.

At age forty-two he was drafted into the Army during World War II, and quickly rose to the rank of sergeant in the 371st Infantry Regiment of the 92nd Division. There he set a markmanship record, hitting thirty-one bull's-eyes in thirty-two shots in rapid firing at 200 yards. However, he served in the Army for only six months before being honorably discharged in 1943, and returned to his baseball career.

While earning a "mean" reputation on the field, he was a nice guy off the field. After retiring from baseball, he umpired the Monarchs' home games for a couple of years and ran a tavern for several years. He was married to blues singer Julia Lee. His son also played briefly in the Negro Leagues.

Duncan, Frank, III
a.k.a. Frank Duncan, Jr.
Career: 1940–47   Positions: p, *of*
Teams: Kansas City Monarchs ('40–'41), *military service ('42–'43),* Baltimore Elite Giants ('44–'47), *minor leagues ('56), Mexican League ('57)*
Bats: Right   Throws: Right
Born: Oct. 10, 1920

The son of Frank Duncan, Jr., he began his career with the Kansas City Monarchs, the same team that his father was associated with for so long. In 1940 he played right field, subbing for Ted Strong, and the following year pitched with the team prior to entering the Army. During this time he and his father formed the first father-son battery in professional baseball. After his discharge, he continued his pitching career with the Baltimore Elite Giants for four more seasons, 1944–47, but without much success. In 1945, pitching in only four games, he lost his only decision. He played with the San Angelo Colts of the West Texas-New Mexico League in 1956 and with Cordoba in Mexico in 1957.

Duncan, Melvin L.
Career: 1949–50   Position: p
Teams: Kansas City Monarchs ('49–'51, '55), *Detroit Stars ('55)*
Bats: Right   Throws: Right
Height: 5'9"   Weight: 155

A right-hander beginning his career when the Negro American League was in decline, he had average control, an average fastball, and a fair curve. He pitched with the Kansas City Monarchs for three years, 1949–51. During the midfifties, when the Negro American League was strictly a minor affair, he pitched with both the Kansas City Monarchs and Detroit Stars in 1955.

Duncan, Trees (Tall Papa, Scoot)
Career: 1938   Position: p
Team: Atlanta Black Crackers
Height: 6'6"   Weight: 195

The big, tall curveball pitcher with the 1938 Atlanta Black Crackers was in the lineup in May but apparently was released until recalled for the second half of the season.

Duncan, Warren (Joe)
Career: 1922–27   Positions: **c,** of
Team: Atlantic City Bacharach Giants

He was a reserve catcher and occasional outfielder with the Bacharach Giants during the '20s, beginning in 1922 and ending with the 1927 Eastern Colored League championship team.

Dunkin, Ishkooda (Stringbean)
a.k.a. Dunkins
Career: 1938   Position: p
Teams: Pittsburgh Crawfords ('37), Atlanta Black Crackers ('38)

He was a pitcher with the 1937 Pittsburgh Crawfords and the Atlanta Black Crackers in June 1938. Because of his physical resemblance to Satchel Paige, his appearance triggered rumors that Paige was with Atlanta.

Dunlap, Herman
a.k.a. Dunlop
Career: 1936–39   Positions: **rf,** cf, lf
Team: Chicago American Giants

An outfielder with the Chicago American Giants in the late '30s, he hit .319 with the Giants in 1936, earning a spot on the West squad for the 1936 All-Star game. In the classic contest he connected for one hit in two at-bats and scored one of the West's two runs. The next year the American Giants entered the

Negro American League as a charter member and he was a regular outfielder, hitting second in the batting order for the next two seasons.

Dunn, Alphonse (**Blue**)
Career: 1937–43   Positions: **1b,** lf, rf
Teams: Detroit Stars ('37), Ethiopian Clowns ('39), New York Cubans ('42), Birmingham Black Barons ('42–'43), Jacksonville Red Caps.

For seven seasons the first baseman played a steady game at the initial sack, beginning his career in 1937 as the leadoff batter for the Detroit Stars while playing first base and in the outfield. The high point of his career was when he shared the starting assignments at first base for the Negro American League champion Birmingham Black Barons in 1943, batting sixth in the order when in the lineup. He began the previous year with the New York Cubans but joined the Black Barons during the season, hitting a combined .219 in limited play. While only an average ballplayer on the diamond, off the field he was noted for enjoying the luxury of smoking big Cuban cigars. After finishing league play, he played with the Harlem Globetrotters' independent baseball team in 1947.

Dunn, Blue
[see Dunn, Alphonse (Blue)]

Dunn, Joseph (**Jake**)
Career: 1930–41   Positions: **ss, of,** 2b,
                                                3b, manager
Teams: Detroit Stars ('30), Washington Pilots ('32), Nashville Elite Giants ('33), Baltimore Black Sox ('33), **Philadelphia Stars** ('33–'34), *military service ('42–'45)*
Bats: Right   Throws: Right
Height: 5'11"   Weight: 195
Born: Nov. 5, 1909, Luther, Okla.
Died: July 24, 1984, Los Angeles, Calif.

A versatile player, Jake was best known as a shortstop with a strong arm, but he also covered his share of territory when pressed into duty as an outfielder, and he played in the 1937 East-West All-Star game as a second baseman.

The strong-armed infielder began his career in 1930 by hitting .279 with the Detroit Stars and traveled East in 1932 to play with the Washington Pilots in the ill-fated East-West League. In 1933 he played with three different teams, beginning as a third baseman with the Nashville Elites, then joining the Baltimore Black Sox as a shortstop and hitting in the third slot in the batting order. Finally he found a home with his third team of the season, the Philadelphia Stars, a new team organized by Ed Bolden. During their first year of existence the team played as an independent ballclub, but in 1934 Bolden entered the team in the Negro National League and Dunn won a spot in the starting lineup as the center fielder, hitting .272 while batting sixth in the order and making a valuable contribution to the success of the Stars as they won the 1934 Negro National League championship.

During the next two years he is credited with batting averages of .235 and .289. He moved back to shortstop in 1937. He was a good contact hitter and, while not known for his power, he could hit the long ball on occasion and became the Stars' cleanup hitter in 1938, responding with a .314 batting average. In 1939 he hit .277, but in late July Dunn displayed the power potential in his bat when he hit two home runs in the same inning (the lucky seventh) against the New York Black Yankees to produce one of the high points in his twelve-year career.

At the beginning of the season the veteran infielder had assumed the duties of playing manager for the Stars, succeeding Jud Wilson at the helm. One of the first moves he made as a skipper was to move himself back to the outfield, with the slick-fielding Chester Williams taking over at shortstop. But Dunn was not comfortable in the manager's seat, and he asked to be relieved of the responsibility after the season. In 1940 he hit .247 as a part-timer and, without knowing it, played his last season in baseball. He was one of the first players from the Negro Leagues to enter military service after the bombing of Pearl Harbor, and after four years of service in World War II, Dunn never returned to the Negro Leagues.

Dunn had a very light complexion, and during the midthirties, when he was with the Baltimore Black Sox, owner Joe Cambria, who also owned the white ballclub at Albany, New York, wanted him to pass for white and play for the Albany team, but Dunn refused to leave his wife, choosing to play in the Puerto Rican winter league instead.

Dunn, Willie
Career: 1942   Position: p
Team: Jacksonville Red Caps
He was a pitcher in 1942 with the Jacksonville Red Caps before the team disbanded during the season.

Durant
Career: 1932   Position: of
Teams: *Ewing's All-Stars* (*'28*), Washington Pilots ('32), Baltimore Black Sox ('32), Hilldale Daisies ('32)
After playing with Buck Ewing's traveling independent team earlier in his career, this outfielder split the 1932 season with three teams, beginning the year with the Washington Pilots and finishing with the Baltimore Black Sox.

Durvant
Career: 1923   Position: p
Team: Cuban Stars (West)
He was a pitcher in 1923 with the Negro National League Cuban Stars (West).

Dwight, Edward Joseph (**Eddie,** Pee Wee, Flash)
a.k.a. Edward Milner Dwight
Career: 1925–37   Positions: **cf,** lf, *2b*
Teams: **Kansas City Monarchs** ('25–'29, '33–'37), Indianapolis ABCs ('32)
Bats: Right   Throws: Right
Height: 5'8"   Weight: 165
Born: Feb. 25, 1905, Dalton, Ga.
Died: Nov. 27, 1975, Kansas City, Kan.
An exceptionally speedy outfielder, his speed and basestealing ability were comparable to that of Cool Papa Bell. A contact hitter without power, he was an excellent bunter with good hit-and-run ability, and usually batted in the second slot in the order when in the lineup. He managed to maintain a modicum of batting consistency, with partial statistics showing an average of .308 in 1929. An outstanding fielder with great range but an average arm, the center fielder spent his entire thirteen-year career (1925–37) in the Midwest, mostly with the Kansas City Monarchs. He won a starting assignment in the Monarchs' outfield in 1933 and held the regular spot until he left the Monarchs after the 1937 season. During this time the veteran player appeared in the 1936 All-Star game.

Dwight was reported to have died of tuberculosis. In 1962 his son became the first black American selected for training as an astronaut by NASA, and later gained further recognition as the sculptor of the Hank Aaron statue in Atlanta's Fulton County Stadium.

Dyall, Frank
Career: 1950   Position: ss
Team: Chicago American Giants
He was listed as a shortstop with the Chicago American Giants in 1950, when the Negro American League was struggling to survive the loss of players to organized baseball, but league statistics do not confirm his playing time.

Dykes, A.
Career: 1929   Position: 2b
Team: Birmingham Black Barons
He was a second baseman with the Birmingham Black Barons in 1929, but his playing time was limited.

Dykes, John
Career: 1932   Position: officer
Team: Washington Pilots
He was an officer with the Washington Pilots during their tenure in the East-West League.

Dysoin, Major
Career: 1950   Position: ss
Team: New York Black Yankees

He was a shortstop with the 1950 New York Black Yankees, who were playing as an independent team and had declined in quality.

E

Earle, Frank Charles

a.k.a. Frank Earl; Charles Babcock; Frank Peles

Career: 1906–19   Positions: **lf,** rf, cf, p. manager

Teams: Wilmington Giants ('06), Cuban Giants, Philadelphia Giants, **Brooklyn Royal Giants** ('09–'14, '16–'17), St. Louis Giants ('15), New York Lincoln Giants ('15), G.C.T. Red Caps of New York ('18–'19), Atlantic City Bacharach Giants ('19), Pennsylvania Red Caps of New York ('19)

Bats: Right   Throws: Right

A speedy outfielder who also wielded a good stick, he was one of the top outfielders in the East during the deadball era. He captained the Brooklyn Royal Giants during the '10s, and during the 1910–11 winter he also served as the captain and manager of the Royal Poinciana team in the Florida Hotel Winter League.

Before switching to the outfield, he started his career as a pitcher and was the top hurler for the 1909 Royal Giants, who were recognized as the black champions. In September of that season, with a capacity crowd on hand, he defeated José Mendez and the Cuban Stars, 2–1, in a two-hitter. Two weeks later he defeated the Cubans' star southpaw Juan Padrone 5–3 for his third consecutive win over the Cubans, to ensure the title. The win gave the Royals a 3–1 advantage in the five-game series, and the Cubans left for Havana immediately after the contest without playing the last game in the series.

In 1910 the Royal Giants repeated as champions, with Earle still pitching and playing left field when not on the mound. He hit in the second slot in the batting order, and his hitting and defensive play led to his becoming an everyday player, with his slabwork becoming secondary. However, throughout his career he continued to pitch when the occasion dictated. In 1911 he was the regular left fielder and leadoff batter for the Royals, and he remained in this capacity for the next four seasons.

In 1914 the Royals won the eastern championship and faced Rube Foster's western champion Chicago American Giants in a postseason challenge series for the Colored championship. Unfortunately, the Royals were defeated decisively in the playoffs. The following season the Royals did not field a team, and Earle was one of four players, along with Lyons, Webster, and Handy, who signed with the St. Louis Giants for the start of the 1915 season. Earle's stay in the Midwest was brief, and he played most of the year in New York as the right fielder and leadoff batter for the Lincoln Giants.

After only one year he was back in the Royals' fold for the 1916 season, pitching, playing left field, and batting cleanup, to lead the Royal Giants to another eastern championship under his captaincy. There were no playoffs against the Indianapolis ABCs, who won the western championship that year.

In 1917, his last season with the Royals,

Earle moved to center field and contributed a .308 average while batting third in the order. The next season he and several other ex-Royals joined the Grand Central Terminal Red Caps of New York, where he was the center fielder and leadoff batter. When the Bacharachs moved to New York in 1919, he signed with them but returned to the G.C.T. Red Caps during the season, which was to be his last with a quality black team. Although strongly identified with the Brooklyn Royals, he also played with the Wilmington Giants, Cuban Giants, and Philadelphia Giants earlier in his career.

Easley

Career: 1936   Position: of
Team: Memphis Red Sox

This outfielder was with the 1936 Memphis Red Sox during his only year in the Negro leagues.

Easte

Career: 1923   Position: p
Team: Hilldale Daisies

He pitched briefly with the Hilldale ballclub in 1923, when they captured the first Eastern Colored League pennant.

Easter, Luscious (Luke)

Career: 1947–48   Positions: of, 1b
Teams: *Cincinnati Crescents ('46),* Homestead Grays ('47–'48), *minor leagues ('49, '54–'64),* major leagues ('49–'54)
Bats: Left   Throws: Right
Height: 6'4½"   Weight: 240
Born: Aug. 4, 1915, Jonestown, Miss.
Died: March 29, 1979, Euclid, O.

As a rookie with the Homestead Grays in 1947, he was touted as a new Josh Gibson and was expected to provide the same home-run power at the plate as the recently departed Gibson. With Buck Leonard entrenched at first base, Easter was forced to play in the outfield. In league play, Easter hit .311 and finished third in home runs, while against all levels of opposition he was credited with 43 homers and a .382 batting average. The next year, 1948,

the big, strong slugger earned a spot on the East squad for the East-West All-Star game by hitting .403 and being credited with a league-high 13 home runs for the Grays' last pennant-winning team.

Easter began playing baseball on the sandlots of St. Louis, then was discovered by the Cincinnati Crescents before signing with the Grays. He had little speed, limited range afield, only an average arm, and couldn't bunt or execute the hit-and-run play, but he was a young, natural pull hitter with prodigious power. But he also had a reputation for fearsome skills as a gambler. A card shark, he loved playing cards and engaged in the pastime at every opportunity, often using a marked deck. Although he was fun-loving, friendly, and charismatic, his dishonest tendencies with a deck of cards often caused him trouble. Once in a card game on the Gray's team bus, he and diminutive Groundhog Thompson accused each other of cheating. Easter threatened the little man, and Thompson responded by pulling his knife and threatening to cut Easter down to his size. Fortunately, cooler heads prevailed.

That was to be Easter's last year in the Negro Leagues, as the hulking 240-pounder was signed by the Cleveland Indians during the winter of 1948–49. Easter, playing with Mayagüez, was leading the Puerto Rican League with a .402 batting average while also leading in doubles and runs scored. The Indians paid $10,000 for his contract, with an additional $5,000 promised if he made the major leagues. Easter thought he deserved the incentive bonus for himself and worked out a deal with Rufus Jackson's widow, who was then handling the Gray's financial operations. Like many Negro Leaguers, he shaved years off his age to get into organized baseball. In 1949 he began with San Diego in the Pacific Coast League and hit .363 with 25 homers in 80 games before being called up to Cleveland, where he hit .222 without a homer in 21 games. The following season, 1950, he spent the entire year as a first baseman with the Indians and hit .280 with 28 home runs. During the next two major-league seasons, the left-handed swinger hit 27 and 31 home runs, and was on the way to another good season in 1953 before being sidelined by a broken foot. Despite the injury, he still finished with a .303 batting average.

In 1954 he was limited to only six pinch-hitting appearances, which were to be his last in the major leagues. The rest of the season was spent with Ottawa (International League) and San Diego (Pacific Coast League), where he hit for a composite batting average of .315 with 28 home runs. After a season with Charleston in the American Association, where he clubbed 30 home runs, 102 RBIs, and batted .283, he joined Buffalo in the International League, where he became a local legend with consecutive seasons of 35 home runs, 106 RBI, .306 batting average; 40 home runs, 128 RBI, .279 batting average; and 38 home runs, 109 RBI, .307 batting average. Easter remained in the International League for the remainder of his career, spending the last five seasons (1960–64) with Rochester while his batting average dropped about 10 points each season as age began to catch up with him.

At age forty-nine, he ended his minor league career as he had his major league career, appearing only as a pinch hitter in a handful of games. His career stats show a lifetime .296 minor-league average, a .274 major-league record, and .336 for the Negro Leagues, as well as a lifetime total of 385 home runs.

He also played in the Latin American winter leagues, blasting 17 home runs in Puerto Rico in 1956–57 and 8 in the Venezuelan winter of 1947–48, while batting .302. Everywhere he played, he left behind stories of his gargantuan home runs. After leaving baseball, Easter worked as a security guard with Wells, Fargo and, while taking a payroll to a nearby bank, was killed by a robber.

Easterling, Howard

Career: 1936–49   Positions: **3b,** 2b, ss, of
Teams: Cincinnati Tigers ('36–'37), Chicago American Giants ('38), **Homestead Grays** ('40–'43, '46–'47), *military service ('44–'45),*
New York Cubans ('49), *Mexican League ('51, '53)*
Bats: Both   Throws: Right
Height: 5'10"   Weight: 175
Born: Nov. 26, 1911, Mount Olive, Miss.
Died: Sept. 6, 1993, Collins, Mississippi

A complete ballplayer, he could run, throw, field, and hit with power. The versatile infielder was a five-time All-Star during his fourteen-year career in the Negro leagues, batting .320 in the East-West classic contests. He was selected to the West squad as a shortstop in 1937 and to the East squad as a third baseman in 1940, 1943, 1946, and 1949. He could also play the outfield and had a strong arm and good range. However, he was better known for his hitting ability, and the switch-hitter was consistent with the bat from both sides of the plate, beginning with averages of .326 and .386 with the Cincinnati Tigers in 1936–37, his first years with a quality team. In the latter year the Tigers joined the Negro American League in its inaugural season, and three years later the star infielder joined the Homestead Grays, who were looking for someone to generate some offense to help compensate for the loss of Josh Gibson to Mexico.

His first year in a Grays' uniform was very productive, as he contributed a .358 average and the Grays took the Negro National League pennant. The Grays repeated as Negro National League champions in 1941 and 1942, with Easterling registering averages of .307 and .226. In the former season he had a 6 hits in 10 at-bats in a doubleheader during the playoff victory over the New York Cubans. In the latter season the Grays lost to the Kansas City Monarchs in the first World Series between the Negro American League and the Negro National League, but Easterling smacked a home run and registered a .332 batting average in the Series.

In 1943 he came back strong with the bat, hitting especially well at home, where he hit for a .473 average in games played at Griffith Stadium and Forbes Field. The Grays won another pennant and defeated the Negro American League champion Birmingham Black Barons in the World Series to reign as champions of black baseball. Easterling was in his prime, but while still savoring the world championship, his career was interrupted by World War II. When he received his draft notice, he was playing with the Baltimore Giants in the California winter league and, although he knew he was going into service and would not be able to play, he conned Grays' owner Cum Posey into sending him advance money for the coming season. Posey's eagerness to sign him was understandable, since the Grays had won four consecutive pennants with the third sacker's bat joining those of Josh Gibson and Buck Leonard in the heart of the lineup. Batting either third in front of the "Thunder Twins" or fifth behind the pair of sluggers, Easterling could also hit the long ball.

After returning from two years of military service, he batted .310 in 1946, but the Grays were not to win any more pennants during his last years with the team. After closing out his Negro Leagues career by hitting .302 with the New York Cubans in 1949, he extended his playing career in Mexico, where he hit for averages of .323 and .379 for Monterrey in 1951 and 1953. Playing the Venezuelan winter league, he topped the circuit in both home runs and doubles, with 9 and 16, respectively.

Eaton
a.k.a. Eatmon
Career: 1937–38   Position: p
Team: Birmingham Black Barons
Bats: Right   Throws: Right
He pitched with the Birmingham Black Barons during the first two seasons of the Negro American League's existence, 1937–38.

Eccles
[see Echols, Joe]

Echevarria, Rafael
Career: 1938   Position: 2b
Team: New York Cubans
The Cuban was a second baseman for the 1938 New York Cubans in his only season in the Negro Leagues. He also played with Caguas in the 1939–40 Puerto Rican winter season.

Echols, Joe
a.k.a. Eccles
Career: 1939   Position: of
Team: Newark Eagles
Bats: Right   Throws: Right
Height: 6'1"   Weight: 175
The speedy outfielder was a good fielder with an average arm but a light bat. The hustling player from Englewood, New Jersey, was also a good bunter, but his stint with the Eagles in 1939 was brief.

Eckelson, Juan
a.k.a. Ekelson
Career: 1925   Position: p
Teams: Cuban Stars (West)
He was a pitcher with the Negro National League Cuban Stars (West) in 1925, his only season in the Negro Leagues. Pitching with Almendares in the 1931–32 Cuban winter league, he fashioned a 5–1 record.

Edsall, George
Career: 1898   Position: rf
Team: *Celeron Acme Colored Giants*
He was an outfielder with the 1898 Celeron Acme Colored Giants, an all-black team formed by Harry Curtis, a white man, to play in the Iron and Oil league as representatives of Celeron, New York. Both the team and the league folded in July, and it was to be the last time a black team played in a white league.

Edwards, Chancellor (**Jack,** Pep)
Career: 1928   Position: c
Team: Cleveland Tigers
He was a catcher with the Cleveland Tigers in 1928, the franchise's only season in the Negro Leagues.

Edwards, Frank (**Teeny**)
Career: 1936–37   Positions: c, 2b, 3b, ss

Teams: Cincinnati Tigers ('36), St. Louis Stars ('37)

He began the 1937 season as a catcher but moved to second base to fill an empty spot when the regular at that position moved to the Chicago American Giants in midseason.

Edwards, James
Career: 1919   Position: c
Team: Atlantic City Bacharach Giants

He was a reserve catcher with the Bacharachs in 1919, when the franchise was still in its formative years.

Edwards, Jesse (**Johnny**)
Career: 1923–31   Positions: **p, 2b,** of, 3b, ss
Teams: Memphis Red Sox ('23–'24), Birmingham Black Barons ('25, '31), Nashville Elite Giants ('26–'31), Detroit Stars ('29)

During the '20s and early '30s he played as an infielder-outfielder with the Nashville Elite Giants, and also pitched with the Birmingham Black Barons, Memphis Red Sox, and Detroit Stars. In 1929, in his only year outside the South, he was 1–2 as a pitcher with the Detroit Stars and later in the season switched to the Nashville Elite Giants as a second baseman, hitting a meager .179 as a substitute at that position. In 1930 he followed with a .152 average as an utility player.

Edwards, Osee
Career: 1950   Position: cf
Team: New York Black Yankees

In 1950 he was an outfielder with the New York Black Yankees, who were playing as an independent ballclub and had become a team of marginal quality.

Edwards, Smokey
Career: 1913–17   Positions: **p,** of, c
Teams: New York Lincoln Giants ('13, '15), Mohawk Giants ('13–'14), Lincoln Stars ('16), Pennsylvania Red Caps of New York ('17–'18), *Philadelphia Giants ('22)*

During the '10s he was a pitcher-outfielder with three different New York teams. He began his career in 1913 as a pitcher with Jess McMahon's Lincoln Giants, but when he signed with McMahon's new team in 1916, he split his playing time between the mound and part-time service in the outfield for the Lincoln Stars. When the Stars broke up after the season, he was among a group of ex-Stars who joined the Pennsylvania Red Caps, where he continued to split his time between pitching and playing right field. In the fall of 1918 the club encountered financial problems and suspended play. Incomplete statistics show the hurler losing his only decision in the 1913 season and in the 1918 season.

Edwards, William
Career: 1944   Position: p
Team: Kansas City Monarchs

He was a wartime player, pitching briefly with the 1944 Kansas City Monarchs in his only appearance in the Negro Leagues.

Eggleston, Macajah Marchand (**Mack,** Egg)
a.k.a. Eggleton
Career: 1919–34   Positions: **c,** of, 3b, 2b, manager
Teams: *Dayton Giants ('17–'18), military service ('18–'19),* Dayton Marcos ('19), Detroit Stars ('20), Columbus Buckeyes ('21), Indianapolis ABCs ('22), Washington Potomacs ('23–'24), Hilldale Daisies ('25), Wilmington Potomics ('25), Harrisburg Giants ('25–'26), Atlantic City Bacharach Giants ('25, '29, '34), New York Lincoln Giants ('26), Baltimore Black Sox ('26–'28, '30, '33), Harlem Stars ('30), New York Black Yankees ('31), New York Stars ('31), Washington Pilots ('32), Homestead Grays ('32), Nashville Elite Giants ('33–'34); Philadelphia Stars ('35), Baltimore Elites ('36)
Bats: Right   Throws: Right
Height: 6'0"   Weight: 175
Born: Sept. 16, 1896, Roanoke, Va.

When Ben Taylor organized the Washington Potomacs in 1923, Eggleston went with him and, for the next two seasons, was the first-string catcher and was considered one of best catchers in the East. He was very brainy and was excellent at handling young pitchers but lacked aggressiveness. He had a good arm and was an above-average hitter, posting a .312 batting average in 1924 while hitting fifth in the order. The next season, playing with Harrisburg, he hit .301, and in 1927, with the Baltimore Black Sox, he hit .393.

The Virginian began playing baseball in 1912 in his hometown, as an outfielder with the local Roanoke ballclub. After three years he left for a pair of years in West Virginia, playing with lesser teams in Pocahontas and Montgomery. In 1917 he signed with Chappie Johnson's Dayton Giants and, after being pressed into service as a catcher in an emergency situation, became the regular catcher until entering the Army in 1918. He was stationed at Chillicothe, Ohio, and after his discharge in 1919, he signed with the Dayton Marcos. Although he began as the right fielder, he had a strong arm, and Chappie Johnson had taught him the rudiments of catching, so he soon switched to behind the plate.

Although a great catcher, he could play all infield positions and was a fair outfielder. Throughout his career he continued to be utilized at other positions to get his bat in the lineup. In 1920 he joined the Detroit Stars, where Bruce Petway instructed him in the finer points of receiving. The young catcher continued connecting with great catchers and, after a year with Columbus in 1921, he was paired with the premier receiver of the time, Biz Mackey, on the ABCs in 1922 and again in 1925, when they were both with Hilldale.

In 1926 he was traded from Harrisburg to the Baltimore Black Sox in late summer, and remained with the franchise until 1929, when he was appointed playing manager of the Bacharach Giants. Unfortunately, the team finished with the lowest winning percentage in the American Negro League, and Eggleston batted only .253 for the season. Two years and two teams later, he hit .218 while with the New York Black Yankees.

Always on the move, the receiver had a road-map career, averaging almost one team each season throughout his eighteen-year career, but he was always helpful to young players, even when he was not managing. Always a man of high principle, he became a Baptist deacon after his playing days were over.

Eggleston, William
Career: 1885   Position: ss
Team: *Argyle Hotel Athletics*

He was a shortstop with the 1885 Argyle Hotel team, which evolved into the first black professional ballclub. The team was formed for the entertainment of the guests at the hotel, located in Babylon, New York, then a Long Island resort community.

Ekelson
[see Eckelson, Juan]

Elam
Career: 1932   Position: p
Team: Atlantic City Bacharach Giants

In 1932 he appeared briefly with the Bacharachs, when the franchise was in its declining years.

Elam, Jim (Ed)
a.k.a. Elan
Career: 1943   Positions: p, *if*
Team: Newark Eagles

The elongated youth from Richmond joined the Eagles in 1943 as a rookie with blinding speed, a nice assortment of curves, and a change of pace, but he never became more than a second-line pitcher. While losing his only decision, he also gained a little playing time as an infielder for the wartime-depleted Eagles.

Ellerbe, Lacey
Career: 1950   Positions: of, ut
Team: Baltimore Elite Giants

Primarily an outfielder, he was a utility player with the Baltimore Elite Giants in 1950, but league statistics do not confirm his playing time. The Elites' franchise had joined the

Negro American League and was struggling to survive the loss of players to organized baseball.

Elliott, Jesse

Career: 1948   Position: 1b
Team: Birmingham Black Barons
Height: 6'3"   Weight: 187

The big youngster from Greensboro, North Carolina, was vying for a first-base position with the Birmingham Black Barons in the spring of 1948, but his tenure with the club was very brief.

Ellis, Albert

Career: 1950   Position: p
Team: Cleveland Buckeyes

He was listed as a pitcher with the Cleveland Buckeyes in 1950, when the Negro American League was struggling to survive the loss of players to organized baseball, but league statistics do not confirm his playing time.

Ellis, James

Career: 1921–25   Positions: 1b, 3b, ss
Teams: Dayton Marcos ('21), Nashville Elite Giants ('21), Memphis Red Sox ('23), Cleveland Browns ('25)

During his half decade with several teams in the early years of the '20s, the infielder's playing time was usually limited to playing on the corners.

Ellis, Rocky (Rube)

Career: 1926–42   Positions: **p,** of
Teams: Hilldale Daisies ('26–'28), *Philadelphia Phantoms ('30),* Atlantic City Bacharach Giants ('31), *Baltimore Grays,* **Philadelphia Stars** ('33–'39), Homestead Grays ('40), Birmingham Black Barons ('42)

This sidearm fastball pitcher was Hilldale's mascot for four years and, after hurting his arm, switched from the infield to the pitching rubber and was given a chance to pitch with the team in 1928. After the Hilldale club disbanded, Ed Bolden formed the Philadelphia

Stars in 1933, and Ellis signed with the Stars and registered a 4–3 record as a member of the mound corps when they won the 1934 Negro National League championship. The next season, both he and the Stars slipped, with the Stars falling out of contention and Ellis dropping to a 1–3 record. Remaining with the Stars, he was in the regular rotation under manager Jud Wilson in 1937–38, but both he and Wilson left the Stars after the 1939 season and joined the Homestead Grays. Ellis split two decisions with the Grays in 1940, his only year with the Grays, and closed his Negro League career with the Birmingham Black Barons in 1942, winning his only recorded decision. He was also a good hitter and sometimes played in the outfield or pinch hit. During his career, Ellis also spent several winters in Puerto Rico and the Dominican Republic.

Ellis, Spec

Career: 1934   Position: p
Team: *Jacksonville Redcaps ('34)*

Despite being frail and asthmatic, the Jacksonville hurler had sufficient stamina to pitch in the longest game played during the 1934 season. Facing Terris McDuffie and the Pennsylvania Red Caps of New York, he lost the 18-inning game on his own error.

Else, Harry

Career: 1931–40   Positions: c, *p*
Teams: Monroe Monarchs *('31–'32), New Orleans Crescent Stars ('33), New Orleans Black Creoles,* Kansas City Monarchs ('36–'38), Chicago American Giants ('40)
Bats: Right   Throws: Right
Height: 5'11"   Weight: 170

A good receiver with an average arm, this Depression era player was slow afoot and had a light bat, not hitting with either power or consistency. During his ten-year career he played with several teams, mostly as a backup, but had his best season with the Kansas City Monarchs in 1936, when he played in the East-West All-Star game as a substitute.

Embry, William R. **(Cap)**
Career: 1923   Position: umpire
League: NNL
He was an umpire in the Negro National League during the 1923 season.

Emery, Jack
Career: 1906–15   Positions: **p,** of
Teams: Brooklyn Royal Giants ('06), *Brooklyn Colored Giants ('08),* Philadelphia Giants ('09, '15), Smart Set, *Pittsburgh Colored Stars ('16)*
A pitcher during the deadball era, he began his career in 1906 with the Brooklyn Royal Giants. Many of the teams he appeared with were of marginal quality, and in addition to his mound work, he also played the outfield on occasion. The best-known team he played with was the Philadelphia Giants, but they were in decline at that time. He also played with the Smart Set and Brooklyn Colored Giants before closing out his career in 1916 with the Pittsburgh Colored Stars.

Emmett
Career: 1924   Position: p
Teams: Indianapolis ABCs
He pitched briefly with the Indianapolis ABCs in 1924, his only year in the Negro Leagues.

Emory
Career: 1889   Position: c
Team: New York Gorhams
He was a catcher with the New York Gorhams, one of the top teams of the era, when they played in the Middle States League in 1889.

English, H. D.
Career: 1932   Position: officer
Team: Monroe Monarchs
During the 1932 season, when the Negro Southern League was designated a major league, he was an officer with the Monroe Monarchs.

English, Louis
Career: 1929–34   Positions: c, of
Teams: Detroit Stars ('29), Nashville Elite Giants ('30), Louisville White Sox *('30–'33),* Louisville Black Caps ('32), *Louisville Red Caps ('34),* Memphis Red Sox ('34)
In six seasons spent primarily with Louisville-based teams, he played both as a catcher and an outfielder. Beginning his career as a reserve catcher with the Detroit Stars, he hit .229 in limited play, and the next season, with the Nashville Elite Giants, he batted .217 while playing both positions. In 1931 he joined the Negro National League's Louisville White Sox, batting fifth in the order while splitting his time between left field and catcher. After the team's only season as a member, the league folded and he signed with the Louisville Black Caps, who played in the Negro Southern League for the first half before dropping out of league play. He continued to play for two more seasons before closing out his career in 1934.

Ervin, Willie Lee
Career: 1948   Position: p
Team: New York Black Yankees
During the last year of existence of the Negro National League, the schoolboy sensation from Waco, Texas, pitched with the New York Black Yankees in the early spring.

Erye, John
Career: 1887   Position: player
Team: *New York Gorhams*
He was a player with the New York Gorhams, one of eight teams that were charter members of the League of Colored Baseball Clubs in 1887. However, the league's existence was ephemeral, lasting only a week. His position is uncertain.

Espenosia
Career: 1947   Position: p
Team: Indianapolis Clowns

He pitched with the Indianapolis Clowns in 1947, his only season in the Negro Leagues.

Estenza

Career: 1927–28   Positions: 3b, p, of, 2b, c ss

Team: Cuban Stars (West)

In 1927–28, with the Negro National League Cuban Stars (West), he was an all-purpose player, variously pitching and playing infield, outfield, and catcher. In 1927 he was a regular player, splitting his time between right field and second base and hitting .185 while batting in the sixth slot in the order.

Estrada, Oscar

Career: 1924–25, 1931 Positions: p, of, 1b

Teams: Cuban Stars (East) ('24–'25), Cuban House of David ('31)

He was a pitcher with the Eastern Colored League Cuban Stars in 1924–25 and, like many of the Cuban pitchers, he was sufficiently versatile to appear at other positions as well. During his short time in the Negro Leagues he also played in the outfield and at first base but posted only a .182 batting average in 1924. After his first two years with the Cubans he did not play in the United States again until 1931, when he pitched for the Cuban House of David team.

Etchegoyen, Carlos

Career: 1930–32   Positions: 3b, of, c

Teams: Cuban Stars (East) ('30), Cuban House of David ('31–'32)

He was the starting third baseman with the Cuban House of David in 1931–32 and also played in the outfield during his brief career in black baseball.

Evans

Career: 1916–18   Positions: 2b, ss

Team: Baltimore Black Sox

This middle infielder was a regular, batting sixth in the order, for the Baltimore Black Sox during their formative years, when they were playing as an independent team and had not yet advanced to a league level of play. In his first season he played shortstop and afterward was a second baseman.

Evans, Charles Alexander

Career: 1924–25   Position: p

Team: Atlantic City Bacharach Giants

A pitcher with the Bacharachs in 1924, he was also used as a pinch hitter and was placed on the Bacharachs' reserve list for 1925.

Evans, Clarence

Career: 1949   Position: p

Team: Homestead Grays

He was a pitcher with the Homestead Grays in 1949, a year after the demise of the Negro National League, when the Grays were an independent ballclub playing primarily against teams of lesser quality.

Evans, Felix (Chin)

a.k.a. Kalihari

Career: 1934–49   Positions: p, of, 3b, 1b

Teams: Atlanta Athletics ('34), Atlanta Black Crackers ('35, '38–39), Memphis Red Sox ('40–'48), Jacksonville Redcaps ('38), Indianapolis ABCs ('39), Baltimore Elite Giants ('39), Newark Eagles ('39), Ethiopian Clowns ('39–'40), Birmingham Black Barons ('49)

Bats: Right   Throws: Right

Height: 6'2"   Weight: 180

Born: Oct. 3, 1911, Atlanta, Ga.

Died: Aug. 21, 1993, Pompano Beach, Fla.

After starring as an all-around athlete at Morehouse College, this Atlanta athlete began his professional baseball career in 1934. A mound star for the Atlanta Black Crackers and the Memphis Red Sox throughout most of his sixteen-year career, the right-hander's best pitch was a good overhand curve, which was called his "mountain drop." A good hitter, as attested by his .295 batting average in 1949, when not taking his turn on the slab, he often played in the outfield or pinch hit when the occasion required.

In 1946, his 15–1 record at the All-Star

break earned the Memphis Red Sox star the starting assignment for the West in the midseason classic, played at Comiskey Park. The curveball artist shut out the East sluggers, yielding only 1 hit in his 3-inning stint, while registering the victory. At the end of the season, Chin was also the starting and winning pitcher in the North-South All-Star game.

In the spring of 1938, while a freshman at Morehouse College, he played baseball with the Atlanta Black Crackers, remaining home on road trips so he would not miss classes. Because he would not travel with the team, the management dropped him from the squad in May, and he subsequently joined the Jacksonville Redcaps and became a big winner. Included in his win streak was an impressive victory over his former teammates, and within a month the Atlanta Black Crackers had negotiated for his return. After returning to the fold he became one of the "Big Three" pitchers who pitched them to the second-half title. Late in the baseball season, when college football practice began, the versatile athlete doubled up and on one occasion left football practice to pitch a postseason victory over the Birmingham Black Barons.

In the playoffs against the Memphis Red Sox, winners of the Negro American League's first-half title, the lanky right-hander was called on to start the first game against "Double Duty" Radcliffe. The Red Sox won the first two games of the series, but a dispute arose between the managements of the two ballclubs, and the championship series was never completed.

The following season, the Atlanta Black Crackers' owner sold the team to some of the players, and the season became a disaster. Before the season was over, Evans would play with four different teams. After the Atlanta franchise moved to Indianapolis to play under the banner of the ABCs, the best players (including Evans) were sold to the Baltimore Elite Giants in late July, and the Black Crackers eventually disbanded. After about a week in Baltimore, the curveball artist was released and

quickly signed by the Eagles before finishing the season with the Ethiopian Clowns in the fall. In 1940, pitching under his "Clown name" of Kalihari, he was credited with a 26–4 record for the Clowns. But that season also provided his start with the Memphis Red Sox, and he remained with the Tennessee team through 1948, when he posted a 7–9 record with a 4.28 ERA. The following season he joined the Birmingham Black Barons for his final baseball season.

A good-hitting pitcher, during his career he often pinch hit and played in the outfield. He is credited with 17 home runs against all levels of competition during one season, and credits Willie Wells for making him a better hitter by teaching him to hit the curveball. After closing his active baseball career, he entered the field of education as a teacher and coach until his retirement.

Evans, Frank
Career: 1915–20   Positions: of, 3b
Teams: *Kansas City Giants ('15),* All Nations ('17), Kansas City Monarchs ('20)

Primarily an outfielder, he began his professional career in 1915 with the Kansas City Giants of Kansas City, Kansas, and joined the All Nations team two years later. After the establishment of the Negro National League in 1920, he made his last appearance in black baseball as a reserve player with the Kansas City Monarchs.

Evans, Frank
Career: 1949–50   Positions: of, *1b, p, c*
Teams: Cleveland Buckeyes ('49–'50), *minor leagues ('50)*
Born: Dec. 16, 1921

He was an outfielder with the 1949 Cleveland Buckeyes and, after beginning the '50 season with the same ballclub, left to play in the Mandak League with Brandon and the Winnipeg Buffaloes. Beginning in 1951, after the decline of the Negro Leagues, he played and managed for several black teams for another decade. For a quarter century he was affiliated with ballclubs in organized baseball as an instructor, scout, and coach.

Evans, George
Career: 1887   Position: player
Team: *New York Gorhams*

He was a player with the New York Gorhams, one of eight teams that were charter members of the League of Colored Baseball Clubs in 1887. However, the league's existence was ephemeral, lasting only a week. His position is uncertain.

Evans, John
Career: 1887–88   Position: player
Team: *New York Gorhams*

He was a player with the 1887 New York Gorhams, one of eight teams that were charter members of the League of Colored Baseball Clubs in 1887. However, the league folded after only a week, but he remained with the team for another season, as the Gorhams continued play as an independent ballclub. His position is uncertain.

Evans, Robert (Bob)
Career: 1933–43   Position: p
Teams: Homestead Grays ('33), Newark Dodgers ('34–'35), Newark Eagles ('36–'39), Toledo Crawfords ('39), New York Black Yankees ('40–'43), Philadelphia Stars ('42–'43)
Bats: Right   Throws: Right
Height: 6'2"   Weight: 190

A talented prospect with all the necessary tools, he and Ray Dandridge were good friends and signed with the Newark Dodgers together in 1934. Big things were expected of the hard-throwing right-hander. He had a good fastball, exceptional curve, and adequate control, but only a fair change-up. As a youngster he had lost vision in one eye from an injury sustained in a gang fight at a party that got out of control, and some teams bunted on him because of his visual limitations.

Evans played with the Newark Dodgers for two years, and when Abe Manley bought the franchise and consolidated it with the Brooklyn Eagles in 1936 to form the Newark Eagles, Evans was one of the players making the transition. With Evans pitching in the starting rotation along with Leon Day and Terris McDuffie, the trio formed a formidable staff.

In 1938 he compiled a 5–5 record, and the following season he was traded to the Toldeo Crawfords in early May for catcher Leon Ruffin. After finishing the season with the Crawfords, he signed with the New York Black Yankees, where he fashioned a 5–1 record with a 4.18 ERA in 1941. Although he remained in the league for a decade, he never fulfilled his early promise, and existing records show no more than a single decision for each of his other years with the Black Yankees. Off the field he was inclined toward drinking and, after leaving baseball, he was killed at a relatively young age in an off-season incident.

Evans, Tom
Career: 1938   Position: p
Team: Philadelphia Stars

The pitcher appeared briefly with the Philadelphia Stars in 1938.

Evans, Ulysses (Cowboy)
Career: 1943   Position: p
Teams: *Louisville Red Caps ('33), Chicago Brown Bombers ('43),* Cincinnati Clowns ('43)

He was a pitcher with the Cincinnati Clowns in 1943, although he played most of his career with teams of lesser status. In 1933 he appeared with the Louisville Red Caps, and a decade later, in addition to the Clowns, he pitched with the Chicago Brown Bombers.

Evans, W. P.
Career: 1920–25   Positions: of, p
Teams: Baltimore Black Sox ('20–'22, '25), Chicago American Giants ('24–25)

A reserve outfielder for a short time with the Chicago American Giants during the '20s, he was unconditionally released, along with a large number of other veteran players, by Rube Foster in the spring of 1925. He hit .286 as a part-time starter in right field with the Baltimore Black Sox in 1921, before they entered league play.

Evans, William
Career: 1903   Positions: c, **rf**
Team: Philadelphia Giants

He was a player with the Philadelphia Giants in 1903, his only year in black baseball.

Evans, William
Career: 1924–25   Position: p
Team: New York Lincoln Giants

Beginning his career on the mound as a young pitcher with the New York Lincoln Giants in 1924, he was an "in-and-outer" but was expected to move into the regular rotation as he gained more experience. However, he was never able to earn a regular spot on the pitching staf.

Evans, William Demont, II (**Bill,** Happy, Gray Ghost)
Career: 1924–34   Positions: **cf, rf,** ss, lf, 3b

Teams: *Louisville White Sox ('19), Gilkerson's Union Giants ('20–'24),* Chicago American Giants ('24), Indianapolis ABCs ('25–'26), Dayton Marcos ('26), Cleveland Hornets ('27), Brooklyn Royal Giants ('28–'29), **Homestead Grays** ('30–'34), Washington Pilots ('32), Detroit Wolves ('32), *Cincinnati Tigers ('34)*
Bats: Both   Throws: Right
Height: 6'0"   Weight: 160
Born: Mar. 30, 1899 Louisville, Ky.

Outstanding defensively, he was a light hitter but was a starting outfielder on the talent-laden 1931 Homestead Grays. Evans was an excellent bunter, fast on the bases, had a great throwing arm for both strength and accuracy, and was an instinctive player afield. Due to an injury to the regular shortstop, he moved in from the outfield and did such a good job that he stayed for most of the season.

Throughout his career, his defense kept him in the lineup at a key position, usually in center field or at shortstop. With the Grays he usually batted in the lower part of the batting order, but hit .328 in 1930 and .259 in 1933. With lesser teams he would be in the leadoff slot, as he was with the Washington Pilots in 1932 and the Cleveland Hornets in 1927, where partial statistics credit him with only a .141 batting average. The previous season he hit .270 while splitting the year between the Indianapolis ABCs and the Dayton Marcos. In 1928 he joined Nat Strong's Brooklyn Royal Giants and stayed with them until joining Cum Posey's Grays in 1930.

As a tall, skinny youngster, he gravitated toward sports and starred in both football and baseball as a schoolboy in Louisville, Kentucky. He later played at Livingston College for two years, 1917–18, before beginning as a semipro player in 1919 with the Louisville White Sox, where he pitched and played shortstop. After a year, he joined Gilkerson's Union Giants and, utilizing his college education, doubled as the team secretary. During the next few years he toured with the ballclub, often playing against Buck Weaver, Oscar Felsch, Joe Jackson, and the other banned members from Chicago's "Black Sox" scandal. Felsch and Weaver taught him how to bunt, and he developed it into an art form. In 1924 he signed with Rube Foster's Chicago American Giants but, after a short time, he jumped the team and rejoined the Unions.

During the heart of his career he played winter ball, including three years as captain of the Poinciana Hotel ballclub in West Palm Beach, Florida, and also in the 1930 California winter league. After closing out his career as a player, Evans turned to managing. In 1941 he was manager of the Chattanooga Black Lookouts and, a decade later, he managed the North American Aviation ballclub for two years. In addition to his managerial stints, he worked as a sportswriter for the *Louisville News* and as a playground director, and was the founder of the Midwest Association of Coaches.

Everett, Clarence
Career: 1927   Positions: ss, of

Teams: Kansas City Monarchs, Detroit Stars ('27)

He was a reserve shortstop in 1927, playing for a short time with both the Kansas City Monarchs and Detroit Stars, and hitting only .176 in very limted play.

Everett, Curtis
Career: 1950–51   Positions: of, c
Team: Kansas City Monarchs

In 1950, when the Negro American League was struggling to survive the loss of players to organized baseball, he was an outfielder with the Kansas City Monarchs, batting .312 for the season. He could also play as a catcher when needed.

Everett, Dean
Career: 1929   Position: p
Team: New York Lincoln Giants

He was a pitcher in 1929 with the Lincoln Giants, splitting 4 decisions and batting an even .200 in limited play during his only year in the Negro leagues.

Everett, Jimmy
Career: 1940–43   Positions: **p,** of
Teams: *Newark Browns ('31), Pennsylvania Red Caps of New York ('31), Memphis Red Sox ('36),* Newark Eagles ('40), Cincinnati Clowns ('43)

Beginning his professional career with the Newark Browns a year before they began league play, he made appearances in both the Negro National League and the Negro American League, pitching with the Newark Eagles in 1940 and with the Cincinnati Clowns in 1943. He also sometimes played in the outfield.

Ewell, Wilmer
Career: 1925   Position: c
Teams: Indianapolis ABCs ('25), *Cincinnati Tigers ('34)*

He was a catcher with the Indianapolis ABCs in 1925, and a decade later was a catcher with the Cincinnati Tigers, when they were still playing as an independent team and were not yet of league quality.

Ewing, William Monroe (**Buck**)
Career: 1920–30   Position: c
Teams: Chicago American Giants ('20), Columbus Buckeyes ('21), Cleveland Tate Stars ('22), Indianapolis ABCs ('25), New York Lincoln Giants ('25), Chappie Johnson's Stars ('25–'28), **Homestead Grays** ('28–'30)

He was a catcher with several teams during the '20s. In 1929 he hit .369 with the Homestead Grays, playing against all levels of opposition. The next season he hit .270, but is more remembered as the player replaced by Josh Gibson when a split finger kept Ewing out of the Grays' lineup one day, providing the young Gibson with his first opportunity to catch for the Grays. Ewing never returned to the starting lineup, and that proved to be his last year with top black teams. Prior to signing with the Grays he had been on the reserve list of the New York Lincoln Giants for the 1925 season, but played instead with Chappie Johnson's Stars until joining the Grays in 1928. Before he went to the major leagues, New York Giants' star Hal Schumacher pitched exhibition games against Ewing in New York during the '20s.

Eyers, Henry
Career: 1887   Position: player
Team: *Pittsburgh Keystones*

He was a player with the 1887 Pittsburgh Keystones, one of eight teams that were charter members of the League of Colored Baseball Clubs in 1887. However, the league's existence was ephemeral, lasting only a week.

F

Fabelo, Julian

Career: 1916–23   Positions: ss, 2b, 1b, 3b, of

Teams: Cuban Stars (East) ('16–'17, '20–'23), New York Cuban Stars ('16), Havana Cuban Stars ('17), Cuban Stars (West)

He broke in with Alejandro Pompez's New York-based Cuban Stars in 1916 as the starting shortstop, but the following season, when Chacon, the top Cuban shortstop, left the Cuban Stars in the West and joined Pompez's eastern aggregation, Fabelo moved to second base. The team played as the Havana Cuban Stars, with Fabelo batting third or fourth in the order. By 1920 he was splitting his playing time between the two corner positions, and he also played in the outfield during his eight-year career (1916–23) with the eastern branch of the Cuban teams.

Fabors, Thomas

[see Favors, Thomas]

Fabre, Isidro

Career: 1918–39   Positions: **p**, of, *1b*
Teams: **Cuban Stars (East)** ('18–'29), All Cubans ('21), Cuban Stars ('33–'34), New York Cubans ('39)
Bats: Right   Throws: Right
Born: Cuba

He began his career primarily as an outfielder, hitting seventh in the batting order for the Cuban Stars, but soon began taking his turn on the mound, with partial statistics showing one win against two losses in 1918, his first year in black baseball. The Stars were playing as an independent team with a limited roster and, like many Cubans, he was versatile and still played in the outfield on occasion. The right-hander was not a power pitcher but developed good control, and in 1924 was considered a young pitcher who would improve with experience. That season he also played regularly in right field when not pitching, usually hitting in the fifth or sixth spot in the batting order and registering a .249 average. He followed in 1925 with a .295 average while posting a pitching record of 4–3 for the season.

In 1921 the Cubans played under the banner of the All Cubans team, and in 1923 the Stars entered the Eastern Colored League, with Fabre hitting for a .389 average in league competition in 1927. The league broke up early in the 1928 season, and the Cubans joined the American Negro League, a replacement league for the eastern teams, in 1929. That season he continued playing both as a pitcher and an outfielder, batting .241 with a 1–3 mark for his slabwork. After two years as an independent team, the Cubans joined the new Negro National League in 1933. Fabre made his last appearance in 1939 with Alex Pompez's New York Cubans, stretching his career over a twenty-two-year period.

Playing in his homeland, he hit .273 for Almendares in a 1920 series against the New

York Giants while compiling a 2–1 record as a pitcher, including a 3-hit, 5–0 shutout win over Jesse Barnes. In another memorable game, while with the Cuban Stars in the United States, he pitched 18 innings and walked only a single batter.

Fagan, Gervis
Career: 1942–43   Positions: **ss,** 2b, 3b, 1b
Teams: Memphis Red Sox ('42), Jacksonville Red Caps ('42), Philadelphia Stars ('43), New York Black Yankees ('43)

An all-purpose infielder although shortstop was his best position, he played with the Memphis Red Sox, Jacksonville Red Caps, and Philadelphia Stars during his short career. In 1943 he was a reserve second baseman with the New York Black Yankees.

Fagan, Robert W. (**Bob**)
Career: 1920–23   Positions: **2b,** of
Teams: Kansas City Monarchs ('20–'22), St. Louis Stars ('22–'23)

One of the players from the 24th Infantry team who were signed by the Kansas City Monarchs when they became charter members of the Negro National League in 1920, he played second base with the Monarchs and St. Louis Stars in the early '20s. He also played in the winter leagues with the Los Angeles White Sox in 1920 and the Colored All-Stars in 1921.

Fallings, John
a.k.a. Falling
Career: 1947–48   Position: p
Team: New York Black Yankees ('47–'48)

A pitcher with the 1947 New York Black Yankees, he was one of only eight holdovers in 1948.

Fanell
Career: 1950   Position: p
Team: Baltimore Elite Giants

In 1950, when the Negro American League was struggling to survive the loss of players to organized baseball, he pitched with the Baltimore Elite Giants, losing his only decision.

Farmer, Greene, Jr.
Career: 1942–47   Position: of
Teams: Jacksonville Red Caps ('42), Cincinnati Clowns ('45), New York Black Yankees, ('47), Cuban Stars ('45–'47)

The light-hitting substitute outfielder with the colorful name split his playing time between the East and West during his half-dozen seasons in black baseball in the '40s. He went hitless in very limited play in 1945, and he hit .147 in 1947.

Farrell
[see Ferrell, Willie (Red)]

Farrell, Jack
Career: 1934   Position: owner
Team: Baltimore Black Sox

In 1934 he was the owner of the Baltimore Black Sox when the team was in decline and based in Chester, Pennsylvania.

Farrell, Luther
a.k.a. Luther
Career: 1919–34   Positions: **p, of**
Teams: Indianapolis ABCs ('19), St. Louis Giants ('20), Chicago Giants ('20–'23), Chicago American Giants ('22–'23), Gilkerson's Union Giants ('24), St. Louis Stars, **Atlantic City Bacharach Giants** ('24–'29, '34), New York Lincoln Giants ('20, '25, '30, '32), Hilldale Daisies ('25), New York Black Yankees ('32)
Bats: Left   Throws: Left
Height: 6'1"   Weight: 260
Died: Miami, Fla.

He was a very large and heavy man who excelled both on the mound and as a regular outfielder. Early in his career, the left-handed pitcher played under the last name of Luther in the West and posted ledgers of 3–8 and 3–6 in 1920–21. Although his success was limited, Rube Foster added him to his postseason mound staff in 1922. When he moved East in

1925, he began using his full name, but his winning percentage remained the same, as he finished with a 8–16 record. In his first year in the East, he pitched for three different teams: the Lincoln Giants, the Bacharachs, and Hilldale.

Although his mound success was restricted, he was a good power hitter, batting .328, .320, and .268 for 1925–27, and he was the regular right fielder for the 1926 Eastern Colored League champion Bacharach Giants. When the Bacharachs repeated as champions in 1927, in addition to playing in the outfield he was one of their mound stalwarts. He was credited with an impressive 17–13 mark for the season and won two of the team's 3 victories in the ensuing Negro World Series against the Chicago American Giants. Farrell finished the Series with a 2–2 slate as the Bacharachs dropped the best-of-9 Series in 8 games. The highlight of his pitching career came in the fifth game, when he pitched a no-hitter, even though it was shortened to 6⅓ innings because of darkness.

Although his pitching fell off the next season, his batting improved, as he was credited with a .368 average with 13 home runs in 43 games for the 1928 season. A year later, and only two years after his last World Series performance, he found work as a member of the Atlantic City police force, but the big hurler was not allowed to pitch for their baseball team. In his limited appearances with the Bacharachs in 1929, he finished league play winless against 2 losses. In 1930 he returned to the Lincoln Giants and fashioned an 11–4 work sheet. He was also credited with a .474 batting average in limited play, as the Lincolns fielded their strongest team since 1913.

That was the last measure of success that he was to experience in black baseball, as his only recorded mound efforts resulted in marks of 0–3 in 1932 with the New York Black Yankees and 1–3 with the Bacharachs in 1934, his last year as an active player. During his fifteen-year career he was with several teams but is best identified with the Bacharachs.

Favors, Thomas (Monk)
a.k.a. Fabors
Career: 1938–47　　Positions: p, of, 1b
Teams: Baltimore Elite Giants ('39, '42), *Atlanta Black Crackers ('46), New Orleans Creoles ('47)*, Kansas City Monarchs ('47)
Born: Dec. 29, 1920

He was with the Baltimore Elite Giants in 1939, and after two years with the Atlanta All-Stars, returned to pitch briefly with the Elite Giants in 1942. Following World War II he played with the Atlanta Black Crackers in 1946 and, after starting the next season with the New Orleans Creoles, he joined the Kansas City Monarchs in midseason as a utility player.

Faxio
Career: 1941　　Position: p
Team: Homestead Grays

Appearing briefly with the Grays in 1941, the pitcher lost his only decision.

Fearro
Career: 1938　　Position: 3b
Team: Homestead Grays

He was a third baseman for the Homestead Grays but was playing in Mexico when the Grays were playing a spring series against the Atlanta Black Crackers when he was replaced by Jim Miller. However, after the series, the Grays left Miller with the Black Crackers, in anticipation of Fearro's return, but he remained in Mexico, and the Grays sought a new man for the hot corner.

Felder, Kendall (Buck, John)
a.k.a. Feldon
Career: 1944–46　　Positions: 3b, 2b, ss, of
Teams: Chicago American Giants ('44), Memphis Red Sox ('44–'46), Birmingham Black Barons ('45)

A good utility man, his best position was third base but he could also play the middle infield positions and in the outfield. He played for a trio of Negro American League teams in 1944–46, hitting .119 with the Chicago American Giants in 1944 and .149 in 1945 with the Birmingham Black Barons.

Felder, William (James, Benny)
Career: 1946–48   Positions: **ss,** 3b
Teams: Newark Eagles ('46–'47), Indianapolis Clowns ('48), *Philadelphia Stars ('51), minor leagues ('52–'54)*
Bats: Right   Throws: Right
Height: 5'9"   Weight: 170
Born: 1925

The hustling infielder was an adequate gloveman, but at best only a mediocre hitter without appreciable power. He was a shortstop with the Newark Eagles and Indianapolis Clowns in the late '40s but could also play second base or third base. The youngster was enthusiastic but didn't possess sufficient talent, especially with a bat, to stick with the black big-league clubs, batting only .151 in 1948. He was with the Philadelphia Stars in 1951, playing both shortstop and third base, but the Negro Leagues were no longer of major-league caliber by then.

The following season, with the doors to organized baseball opened, he played with Key West in the Florida International league but managed only a meager .176 batting average. With Pampa in the West Texas-New Mexico League the following two seasons he was more consistent with the bat, recording averages of .301 and .302. During the latter part of the 1954 season he played with Artesia in the Longhorn League, in his last appearance in organized baseball, and batted .295 in 23 games.

Fellows
Career: 1937   Positions: p, c
Team: Birmingham Black Barons

Although primarily a moundsman, in 1937 Fellows did double duty with the Birmingham Black Barons as a bookend battery, both pitching and catching during his stint in Birmingham.

Fennar
a.k.a. Fern

Career: 1920   Position: p
Team: Kansas City Monarchs

He was a seldom-used pitcher with the Kansas City Monarchs in 1920, the inaugural season of the Negro National League.

Fennar, Albertus A. (Al, **Cleffie**)
Career: 1931–34   Positions: ss, 3b, 2b
Teams: Harlem Stars ('31), New York Black Yankees ('32), Brooklyn Royal Giants ('32–'33), Atlantic City Bacharach Giants ('34), Cuban Stars ('34), *Pennsylvania Red Caps ('34)*
Bats: Right   Throws: Right
Height: 5'8"   Weight: 170
Born: May 12, 1911, Wilmington, N.C.

An infielder with teams along the Eastern Seaboard during the early '30s, he was fast on the bases and sometimes batted leadoff. After graduating from DeWitt Clinton High School in New York City, he signed with the Harlem Stars, formerly known as the Lincoln Giants, in 1931. The next season Bill "Bojangles" Robinson bought the team and renamed them the Black Yankees. That season the team wore the New York Yankees' old set of uniforms, and the pair of pants that fit Fennar belonged to Lou Gehrig. Later in the year he joined the Brooklyn Royal Giants, and he appeared briefly with other teams, but most of the sixteen seasons that he played baseball were spent with industrial teams rather than league teams.

His unusual nickname resulted from his family's musical connections. Both his father and older brother were musicians, and on the night he was born the pair were playing at the Cleff Club in New York City.

Fenton
Career: 1920   Position: ss
Team: Baltimore Black Sox

He was a reserve shortstop with the 1920 Baltimore Black Sox when they were still playing as an independent team.

Fernandez, Bernard
Career: 1938–49   Position: p

Teams: Atlanta Black Crackers ('38), Jacksonville Red Caps ('39), *Pittsburgh Crawfords ('46)*, New York Black Yankees ('48–'49)

In 1938, the Cuban right-handed pitcher from Tampa was on the spring roster for the Atlanta Black Crackers but had some control problems and was dropped from the squad in early May. He played with the Jacksonville Red Caps the following season but did not appear in the Negro Leagues again until after World War II, when he played with the new Pittsburgh Crawfords, a lesser team in the U.S. League that used the Crawfords' name. He also played with the New York Black Yankees in 1948–49, when black baseball was struggling to survive the loss of players to organized baseball.

Fernandez, José Maria, Jr. **(Pepe)**
Career: 1948–50   Position: c
Team: New York Cubans
Bats: Right   Throws: Right

The son of longtime catcher-manager José Fernandez, Sr., he followed in his father's footsteps, catching with the New York Cubans in 1948–50 during the last years of the Negro National League's existence.

Fernandez, José Maria, Sr.
Career: 1916–50   Positions: **c,** 1b, of, **manager**
Teams: **Cuban Stars (East)** ('16–'29, '31–'34), Chicago American Giants ('30), **New York Cubans** ('35–'50)
Bats: Right   Throws: Right
Height: 5'10"   Weight: 175
Born: July 6, 1896, Guanabacoa, Cuba
Died: 1971

A smart catcher who was expert at handling pitchers, he spent thirty-five years in the Negro Leagues as a player and manager, beginning in 1916. Defensively he was a good receiver with an excellent throwing arm, and in 1924 he was regarded as one of the best catchers in the league. As a veteran player he also played first base and was a good average hitter but did not generate much power and was not a fast base runner. Even as late in his career as 1945, after having spent nearly thirty years in the United States and Cuba catching winter and summer, he was still considered a peerless catcher in black baseball.

In Cuba he caught some of the greatest names in baseball, black and white, including Dolph Luque and Freddie Fitzsimmons, and never had an injured finger. While playing 23 winters in Cuba, mostly with Almendares, he compiled a lifetime batting average of .277, with his best years being .333 ('27–'28), .318 ('28–'29), .306 ('35–'36), .303 ('22–'23), and .290 ('34–'35).

The light-complexioned Cuban began his thirty-five year U.S. baseball career as one of the catchers on owner Alejandro Pompez's 1916 Cuban Stars, batting eighth in the lineup. The next year he moved up in the batting order, and beginning in 1918, he was the cleanup hitter for the Cubans for the next three seasons while also playing at first base and in the outfield. In his first two years the ballclub was sometimes known as the New York Cuban Stars and the Cuban Stars of Havana. Beginning in 1922 he dropped down to the sixth and seventh spots in the batting order for the remainder of the decade, hitting for averages of .259, .263, .235, and .232 for the years 1924–25, 1927, and 1929, respectively.

In 1929, in a game against Hilldale, he showed why he was sometimes called "hot-headed." After being hit by a ball pitched by Cooper, the opposing pitcher, he threw his bat at the pitcher and was determined to settle the matter off the field after the game was over. The umpire tossed Fernandez out of the game to avoid an escalation of the rhubarb. In 1930 he left the Cubans for a season to play with the Chicago American Giants and had one of his best years at the plate, hitting .373.

When the Cuban Stars joined the new Negro National League in 1933, the wily veteran receiver was the starting catcher, and when Pompez organized the New York Cubans, Fernandez hit for averages of .217, .255, and .344 in 1939–41. In 1938 he took the managerial reins for Pompez's ballclub and remained at the helm through the 1950 season, directing the Cubans to a Negro National League pennant and World Series victory over the Negro American League champion Cleveland Buckeyes in 1947. Fernandez advocated playing hard but clean baseball and was considered a smart pilot without equal. He also became a playing manager in his home country, managing the All Cubans in 1945–46.

Although unable to play as a regular as the years began catching up with him, he was still able to come off the bench to pinch hit in a tight spot. His son, Pepe, also a catcher, followed in his footsteps but had only an abbreviated career.

Fernandez, Renaldo
Career: 1950   Position: of
Team: New York Cubans

He was an outfielder with the New York Cubans in 1950, when the Negro American League was struggling to survive the loss of players to organized baseball. He had good speed and a batting average of .283, but he also had a high strikeout frequency.

Fernandez, Rodolfo
Career: 1916, 1923   Positions: p, lf
Teams: Cuban Stars (East) ('16), Cuban Stars (West) ('23)

This pitcher made two appearances with the Cuban Stars: once in 1916, when they were an independent team and sometimes played under the name of the New York Cuban Stars, and again in 1923, when they were in the Negro National League.

Fernandez, Rodolfo (Rudy)
a.k.a. Rudolfo
Career: 1932–43   Position: p
Teams: Cuban Stars ('32–'34, '36), New York Cubans ('35, '39, '43), *Santo Domingo ('37), Venezuelan League ('37–'38), Mexican League ('40–'42), Canadian League ('46)*
Bats: Right   Throws: Right
Height: 6'1"   Weight: 190

Born: June 27, 1911, Guanabacoa, Havana, Cuba

A younger brother of Jose Fernandez, Sr., the hard-throwing right-hander had an excellent sinker, and good control of his fastball and curve. He pitched for the New York Cubans during the late '30s and served the team as a coach after his playing days ended. He was especially effective in exhibition games against major-league teams. In the spring of 1937 in Havana he defeated the defending National League champion New York Giants, 4–0, on 4 hits; defeated the Brooklyn Dodgers, 3–0, in another Cuban exhibition game; and beat the Cincinnati Reds, 2–1, in Puerto Rico.

Prior to joining the New York Cubans, managed by his brother, he played with the Cuban Stars and also played in Latin American leagues. He pitched in Santo Domingo in 1937 for the champion Ciudad Trujillo team and compiled a 4–5 record. Fernandez played a dozen winters in Cuba, all except one with Almendares. He led the league in wins with eight in 1931–32, and posted a 7–4 mark in 1939–40 as Almendares copped the championship under manager Dolph Luque.

In 1938 he played in Venezuela for two seasons and then moved to Mexico for three seasons, registering a 4–5 mark with a 4.52 ERA in 1942. In 1943 he returned to the New York Cubans for a season. He played with Havana in the Cuban winter league in 1942–43 and also played in Puerto Rico, Venezuela, and Panama, continuing as an active player through the 1947 season. In addition to his pitching, he served as a coach and manager in Cuba, Puerto Rico, Venezuela, Nicaragua, and the Dominican Republic. In 1952 he managed the Aquilas Cibaenas team to their first championship in the Dominican League. After baseball he worked in New York City's St. Luke's Hospital until his retirement.

Fernandez, T.
Career: 1941   Positions: p, of
Team: New York Cubans

He was listed as a pitcher with the 1941

New York Cubans but did not register a decision.

Ferrell, Leroy Howard (Toots)
Career: 1948–50   Position: p
Team: Baltimore Elite Giants
Bats: Right   Throws: Right
Height: 6'1"   Weight: 210

The big right-hander threw three-quarters overhand and had a standard three-pitch repertory (fastball, curve, change) but relied primarily on his fastball. He could field his position but was no help with the bat. Ben Taylor, a great first baseman and an astute judge of playing talent in later life, discovered and developed many young ballplayers and represented a father figure for Ferrell. His first season with the Elite Giants, 1948, was the last season of the Negro National League's existence. Following the league's demise, the Baltimore franchise joined the Negro American League. In their first year, with Ferrell contributing an 8–2 record, the Elites won the Eastern Division title and swept the Western Division's Chicago American Giants four straight in the championship series. Off the field he was an excellent pool player and liked to frequent places where he could display his talent with a cuestick. He was a big man with a big frame and an appetite to match. In 1950 he was invited to the Brooklyn Dodgers' spring training camp and "ate himself out of camp."

Ferrell, Willie Truehart (**Red**)
Career: 1937–43   Positions: **p,** of
Teams: Birmingham Black Barons ('37), Jacksonville Red Caps ('38), Cleveland Bears ('39–'40), Homestead Grays ('39–'40), Chicago American Giants ('41–'43), Cincinnati Clowns ('43)
Bats: Right   Throws: Right
Height: 5'10"   Weight: 165

Although not a top pitcher in their mound corps, he was with the pennant-winning Homestead Grays in 1939–40, posting a 2–1 record in league play. The Grays signed him from the Jacksonville Red Caps, and most of his seven-year career was spent with teams in the Negro American League, beginning in the league's first year, 1937, when he was with the Birmingham Black Barons. After leaving the Grays he joined the Chicago American Giants, where he recorded a 3–1 mark for the 1941 season before closing out his career as a pitcher-outfielder in the wartime season of 1943.

Ferrer, Efigenio (**Coco,** Al)
Career: 1946–48   Positions: ss, 2b, 3b
Teams: Indianapolis Clowns ('46–'48), *Chicago American Giants ('51)*
Bats: Right   Throws: Right
Height: 5'7"   Weight: 150

Primarily a middle infielder, the little Puerto Rican could also play adequately at the hot corner. The light-hitting infielder played with the Indianapolis Clowns during the Post-World War II years, beginning as a reserve in 1946 while hitting .193. After two seasons on the bench he had a chance to play as a part-time starter in 1948, batting leadoff when in the lineup and hitting .238. Three years later, after the Negro American League declined to minor-league status, he played with the Chicago American Giants in 1951.

Ferrer, Pedro
Career: 1922–25   Position: 2b
Team: Cuban Stars (East)

The light-hitting reserve infielder played four seasons as a second baseman with the Cuban Stars (East), batting .146 in 1925.

Fiales
[see Fiall, Tom]

Fiall, George
a.k.a. Fial; Fyle; File
Career: 1918–31   Positions: ss, 3b
Teams: New York Lincoln Giants ('18, '20–'22, '27), Harrisburg Giants ('23–'25, '27), Baltimore Black Sox ('24–'26), Atlantic City Bacharach Giants ('26), *Pennsylvania Red*

Caps of New York ('28), Birmingham Black Barons ('29), Brooklyn Royal Giants ('31)
Born: New York, N.Y.
Died: April, 12, 1936, New York, N.Y.

Primarily a shortstop, his quickness made him a good fielder with a very good range. He was very fast afield and on the bases but weak at the plate. He began his career with the Lincoln Giants in 1918 as a reserve middle infielder but broke into the starting lineup at third base in 1920, batting second in the order. The next year, still at the hot corner, he was dropped to the bottom of the batting order. In 1923 he joined the Harrisburg Giants as their regular shortstop, usually batting in the lower half of the order in his first season with the team, but moving into the second slot in 1924 and hitting .248 and .231 for the next two seasons. While with Harrisburg, he and Fats Jenkins were called "The Heavenly Twins" because they starred in both baseball and basketball.

The next stop for Fiall was with the Baltimore Black Sox, where he began as a reserve but ended as a part-time starter at shortstop in 1927. Two years later, incomplete stats show only a .185 average in very limited play with the Birmingham Black Barons. His last appearance in black baseball was as a third baseman with the Brooklyn Royal Giants in 1931. A good all-around athlete, he was also a basketball star for the Harlem Renaissance Five in his prime years. He died in New York City from pneumonia.

Fiall, Tom
a.k.a. Fial; Fiales; Files
Career: 1917–25   Positions: **cf**, rf lf, *c*
Teams: Cuban Giants ('17), Hilldale Daisies ('18), Pennsylvania Red Caps of New York ('19), **Brooklyn Royal Giants** ('18–'23, '31), New York Lincoln Giants ('20, '25)

He began his career with the Cuban Giants in 1917, and for the next three seasons split his playing time between the Brooklyn Royal Giants and a second team. In 1918 he was a part-time starter in center field with Hilldale

for a time, in 1919 he was with the Pennsylvania Red Caps of New York for part of the season, and in 1920 he was briefly a reserve catcher with the New York Lincoln Giants. Meanwhile, when with the Royal Giants he was starting in center field, hitting second in the batting order for four straight seasons, 1920–23. He lost his spot as the regular center fielder with the Royals in 1924, and closed out his career the following year with the Lincoln Giants, batting only .219.

Fields
Career: 1918–32   Position: p
Teams: Chicago American Giants ('18), St. Louis Giants ('21), Cleveland Browns ('24), Dayton Marcos ('26), Cleveland Elites ('26), Cleveland Hornets ('27), Cleveland Stars ('32)

He broke into the big time in 1918 with Rube Foster's World War I-weakened mound staff, with incomplete statistics showing a 2–1 ledger. His next stop was with the St. Louis Giants, where he split 6 decisions in 1921. He later pitched with the Dayton Marcos and Cleveland's various entries in the Negro National League and East-West League, the Cleveland Browns, Cleveland Elites, Cleveland Hornets, and Cleveland Stars.

Fields, Benny
Career: 1930–38   Positions: 2b, of, 3b
Teams: Memphis Red Sox ('30), Cleveland Cubs ('32), Birmingham Black Barons ('36), Atlanta Black Crackers ('38)

The second baseman broke in with the Memphis Red Sox in 1930 and played most of his career at the keystone position, but later in the '30s he also spent some playing time in center field with the Birmingham Black Barons. He was picked up by the Atlanta Black Crackers in 1938 and played briefly at second base at the end of the first half of the season before Gabby Kemp was reacquired from Jacksonville to fill the keystone position.

Fields, Buddy
Career: 1917   Position: ss
Team: *Havana Red Sox*

The shortstop from Evanston, Illinois, played with the 1917 Havana Red Sox, a team of marginal quality.

Fields, Clifford Peter
Career: 1950   Position: lf
Team: Chicago American Giants

In 1950, when the Negro American League was struggling to survive the loss of players to organized baseball, he was an outfielder with the Chicago American Giants, showing good speed while hitting .222 and accumulating a high strikeout ratio.

Fields, Tom
Career: 1946   Position: p
Team: Homestead Grays

He pitched briefly, without a decision, with the Homestead Grays in 1946.

Fields, Wilmer Leon (**Red,** Chinky, Bill)
Career: 1940–50   Positions: **p,** 3b, of, *ss, 2b, c*
Teams: **Homestead Grays** ('40–'42, '46–'50), *military service ('43–'45), Canadian League ('51, '53–'55), minor leagues ('52, '56–'57), Mexican League ('58)*
Bats: Right   Throws: Right
Height: 6'3"   Weight: 215
Born: Aug. 2, 1922, Manassas, Va.

A pitcher with a running fastball complemented by a curve and a slider, and with average control of his pitches, he was an ace on the Homestead Grays' pitching staff that won the last Negro National League championship, in 1948. That season was a good one for Fields, as he registered a 7–1 record in league games, appeared in the All-Star game, and also pitched in two World Series games, winning his only decision.

The big right-hander was a hard-throwing seventeen-year-old relying strictly on a fastball while playing with a semipro team in Fairfax, Virginia, when he was discovered by the Grays in 1940 and given a tryout. The Grays liked what they saw and added the youngster to the roster. Playing against all levels of opposition,

he fashioned a work sheet that showed seasons of 2–1, 13–5, and 15–3 for the three seasons (1940–42) prior to his entering military service during World War II.

Inducted into the Army in 1943, he was discharged in 1946 and resumed his career with the Grays, posting seasons of 16–1, 14–7, 13–5, 17–2, and 12–2 against all levels of competition until the Grays broke up after the 1950 season. During the last four seasons he also played third base and in the outfield when not pitching, and hit for averages of .233, .286, and .311 for the last three seasons of the Negro National League's existence, 1946–48.

After the Grays disbanded, Fields had five offers from the major leagues but he sent their money back. However, in 1952, owner Jack Kent Cook paid him $14,000 to play with Toronto in the International League, and he hit .299 playing at the AAA level. Sandwiched around this season, he spent four seasons in Branford, Canada, pitching and playing in the outfield, posting pitching records of 11–2, 10–2, 9–3, and 8–0, and batting averages of .382, .381, .379, and .425 while winning MVP awards in 1951, 1954, and 1955. He returned to organized baseball in 1956–57 with Fort Wayne, where he pitched and played third base and had records of 6–1 and 5–0 with batting averages of .432 and .387.

During the winters Fields played in several Latin American Leagues, including Mexico, Puerto Rico, Venezuela, Cuba, Panama, Colombia, and the Dominican Republic. In most leagues he pitched, or played thirdbase or outfield in games when he was not scheduled to pitch.

For four winters (1947–51) in the Puerto Rican League he fashioned pitching records of 5–5, 10–4, 8–4, and 5–2, and posted batting averages of .328, .330, .335, and .340. His first year was with San Juan, but the other seasons were with Mayagüez, where he won the MVP award in the winter of 1948–49.

He spent three baseball campaigns in Venezuela (1950–52), the first season with Maracaibo and the latter two with Caracas, and hit

.365, .398, and .350, but only pitched in the first season, recording a 6–2 ledger. With Caracas he won the MVP award in 1951–52, and the next winter he led the league in home runs and RBIs.

In 1953, his only season in the Dominican Republic, he was 5–2 on the mound and played in the outfield when not pitching, batting .395 for the season. In 1958, his only season in Mexico, he played exclusively in the outfield, batting .392 for the Mexico City Reds. He also won the MVP award in Colombia in 1955–56, and played briefly in Cuba and Panama.

He spent his entire Negro League career with the Grays, but continued his college education in the off-seasons while also playing football and basketball. After his active baseball career ended he worked for the government in Washington, D.C., as a counselor for alcoholics.

Fields pitched in many important games during his long baseball career, but one of the games that he best remembers was a loss. In an exhibition game in 1946, he matched up with Johnny Vander Meer in a tight pitching duel before losing, 1–0.

Fifer
Career: 1921   Position: p
Team: Indianapolis ABCs

In his only appearance in the Negro Leagues, he pitched briefly, without a decision, for the 1921 Indianapolis ABCs.

Figarola, José
Career: 1904–18   Positions: c, 1b
Teams: All Cubans ('04), Stars of Cuba ('10), Cuban Stars (West) ('11–'16), Brooklyn Royal Giants ('18)

He was considered one of the two best Cuban catchers to play in this country before 1925. A good defensive catcher, he was a light hitter and usually batted near the bottom of the batting order. He made his first appearance in 1904 with the All Cubans, one of the best Cuban teams of the first decade of the century. He next appeared as a catcher with the 1910

Stars of Cuba before joining the Cuban Stars (West) the following season. With the Stars he was their top catcher but also played first base, and held down a starting position for four years before being relegated to backup catcher and substitute first baseman during his last two seasons with the Cubans. In 1918 he played briefly with the Brooklyn Royal Giants in his last appearance in black baseball.

Figueroa, José Antonio (Tito)
Career: 1940   Position: p
Team: New York Cubans
Bats: Right   Throws: Right
Height: 6'0"   Weight: 190

The Puerto Rican hurler pitched with the New York Cubans in 1940, posting a 2–5 ledger while batting .222. A strong pitcher with a good fastball, he had excellent control and kept the ball down. He and Enrique Figueroa were brothers. He was elected to the Puerto Rican Hall of Fame in 1992.

Figueroa, Luis Enrique (Tite)
Career: 1946   Position: p
Team: Baltimore Elite Giants
Bats: Left   Throws: Left
Height: 5'11"   Weight: 180
Born: Sept. 26, 1926, Mayaguez, Puerto Rico

The Puerto Rican left-hander pitched with the Baltimore Elite Giants in 1946, where he finished with a 5–1 record for the season while batting .275. In winters he played with his hometown team in Puerto Rico. He and José Figueroa were brothers.

Files
[see Fiall, Tom]

Filmore, Joe (Fireball)
a.k.a. Fillmore
Career: 1940–50   Position: p
Teams: Philadelphia Stars ('40–'42, '45–'52), *military service* ('43–'46), *Baltimore Grays* ('46)
Bats: Right   Throws: Right
Height: 6'4"   Weight: 210

Born: Mar. 14, 1914, Victoria, Tex.
Died: Sept. 20, 1992, Los Angeles, Calif.

This big, strong right-hander's career with the Philadelphia Stars spanned the decade of the '40s, with three years out for military service in World War II. He began his career in 1940 and registered 1–6 and 2–1 records for the 1941–42 seasons. In 1943 he was projected as one of the top two hurlers on the Stars' staff, but prior to the beginning of the season he was called into military service, where he served in the Army's Special Services and played baseball. After his discharge he pitched in a few games at the end of the 1945 season, splitting 2 decisions. In 1946 he continued his pitching progress, posting a 5–2 record with the Stars. He was a good-hitting pitcher, batting .294 and .274 in 1941 and 1946, and occasionally played in the outfield, where he was a mediocre fielder without good foot speed.

He played winter ball in Latin countries, appearing with Santurce in the Puerto Rican League and served stints in Mexico both before and after World War II. In 1940 he shared playing time with Pueblo and Torreon, and in 1946 he played with Mexico City.

After the Negro National League folded following the 1948 season, the Stars joined the Eastern Division of the Negro American League, and Filmore continued in black baseball through 1952, although the quality of play had declined significantly.

Although he was born in Texas, his family moved to Los Angeles when he was very young and he attended public schools in the city, beginning in kindergarten. After his active baseball career was over he worked as a butcher in Philadelphia for many years until moving back to Los Angeles.

Finch
Career: 1933   Position: player
Team: Nashville Elite Giants

In 1933 he had one at-bat with the Nashville Elite Giants, but his position is uncertain.

Finch, Rayford
Career: 1949–50   Position: p
Teams: Louisville Buckeyes ('49), Cleveland Buckeyes ('50), *minor leagues ('50–'53)*

Toward the end of the Negro Leagues as a major-league operation (1949–50), he pitched with the Buckeyes without being credited with a victory, compiling an aggregate 0–4 record. However, most of the 1950 season was spent with Elmwood in the Mandak League, where he managed only a 2–6 record. He remained in the league for the next two seasons, improving to a 10–11 record with Elmwood in 1951 before playing with Winnipeg in 1952. His last season in organized baseball was with Danville in the Mississippi-Ohio Valley League in 1953, where he managed only a 1–2 ledger.

Finch, Robert
Career: 1926   Position: p
Teams: *Madison Stars ('20–'21)*, New York Lincoln Giants ('26)

He was a pitcher with the 1926 Lincoln Giants after having previously pitched with the Madison Stars, a lesser team, in 1920–21.

Findell, Thomas
Career: 1887   Position: player
Teams: *Washington Capital Citys*

He was a player with the Washington Capital Citys, one of eight teams that were charter members of the League of Colored Baseball Clubs. However, the league's existence was ephemeral, lasting only a week. His position is uncertain.

Fine, Charlie
[see Harmon, Chuck]

Finley, Thomas (**Tom**)
a.k.a. Finney; Findley
Career: 1922–33   Positions: **3b**, ss, 2b, *c*
Teams: Atlantic City Bacharach Giants ('22, '24–'25), Washington Potomacs ('23–'24), Wilmington Potomacs ('25), New York Lincoln Giants ('25–'26), Brooklyn Royal Giants ('27–'29), Pennsylvania Red Caps of New York ('30), New York Black Yankees ('31),

Baltimore Black Sox ('32), Philadelphia Stars ('33)

Died: 1933, New York, N.Y.

The infielder from Jacksonville, Florida, was a fair shortstop but was too weak with the bat in his early years. He spent a dozen seasons with teams along the Eastern Seaboard prior to his untimely death. In his third season he became the regular shortstop for the Washington Potomacs in 1924, until he became ill in August and never got back in the lineup, remaining out of action for the rest of the year and finishing with a meager .166 batting average.

He started the 1925 season with the Bacharachs, but was traded in midseason with Charles Mason to the New York Lincoln Giants for star third baseman Oliver Marcelle, and hit .231 for the year. The next year he was the starting third baseman for the Lincoln Giants, but hitting in the lower part of the batting order. In 1927 he joined the Brooklyn Royal Giants and split his playing time between third base and shortstop while hitting .319 but still batting in the lower half of the lineup. The next year he settled at the hot corner and moved into the third slot in the batting order.

In 1931 he joined John Henry Lloyd's New York Harlem Stars, playing third base as a part-time starter but batting in the cleanup spot when in the lineup. The next season, playing third base with the Baltimore Black Sox in the ill-fated East-West League, he hit in the heart of the batting order until the league broke up.

Changing teams again in 1933, he was a part-time starter for Ed Bolden's newly organized Philadelphia Stars, but died as the result of a spiking accident in 1933. Incomplete statistics show a .455 average at the time of the incident. Owner Ed Bolden offered a moving prayer at his funeral.

Finner, John

Career: 1919–25   Position: p

Teams: St. Louis Giants ('19–'21), St. Louis Stars ('22–'24), Milwaukee Bears ('23), Birmingham Black Barons ('25)

The pitcher broke in with the St. Louis Giants in 1919 and was also used as a pinch hitter. Two years later he registered an 11–7 record with the Giants, and the next season the team was sold and became the St. Louis Stars. He also pitched with the Milwaukee Bears and Birmingham Black Barons for short stints in his seven seasons.

Finney, Ed

Career: 1948–50   Position: 3b

Teams: Baltimore Elite Giants ('48–'50), *minor leagues ('51), Canadian League ('51)*

bats: Right   Throws: Right

Height: 5'8"   Weight: 188

Born: Nov. 4, 1924, Akron, O.

A third baseman with the Elite Giants in 1948–50, he hit for averages of .278, .320, and .333 during his three seasons. He was not a power hitter and was not issued many free passes but utilized his speed to stretch base hits into extra bases, and was a good base stealer. In 1951 he played with Brandon in the Mandak League and hit .239 in only 18 games. The last record of him in organized baseball was one hitless pinch-hit appearance with the Thetford Miners in the Provincial League.

Fisher

Career: 1909–10   Position: p

Team: Philadelphia Giants

He was a pitcher with the Philadelphia Giants in 1909–10, the last years of the once-pround franchise as a major-league-caliber ballclub.

Fisher

Career: 1932   Position: p

Team: Columbus Turfs

He was a pitcher with the Columbus Turfs in 1932, in his only appearance in the Negro Leagues.

Fisher, George

Career: 1922–23   Position: of

Teams: *Washington Braves ('21),* Richmond Giants ('22), Harrisburg Giants ('23)

After a season with a lesser ballclub, he was an outfielder with the Richmond Giants and the Harrisburg Giants for two years in the early '20s.

Fisher, Pete (The Wonder)
Career: 1886   Position: c
Team: New York Gorhams

In 1886 he was a catcher with the New York Gorhams, one of earliest black professional teams.

Fitzgerald, Gerald
Career: 1948   Position: if
Team: New York Black Yankees

The infielder from Newark, New Jersey, and his brother John both tried out with the New York Black Yankees in the early spring of 1948.

Fitzgerald, John
Career: 1948   Position: c
Team: New York Black Yankees

The catcher from Newark, New Jersey, and his brother Gerald both tried out with the New York Black Yankees in the early spring of 1948.

Flammer
Career: 1921   Position: of
Team: Hilldale Daisies

He appeared briefly with Hilldale in 1921, the only time he appeared in black baseball.

Fleet, Joseph (Joe)
Career: 1930   Position: p
Team: Chicago American Giants

He pitched briefly with the 1930 Chicago American Giants, losing his only decision.

Fleming, Buddy
[see Reedy, Fleming]

Flemming, Frank
Career: 1946   Position: p
Team: Cleveland Buckeyes

He was listed as a pitcher with the Buckeyes in 1946 but was not involved in a decision.

Flintroy, Lee
Career: 1948   Position: of
Team: Birmingham Black Barons

The youngster from Grambling College was vying for an outfield position with the Birmingham Black Barons in the spring of 1948.

Flood, Jess
Career: 1919   Position: c
Team: *Cleveland Tate Stars*

He was a catcher with the 1919 Cleveland Tate Stars, who were playing as an independent team and did not enter the Negro National League until 1922.

Flourney
Career: 1950   Position: p
Team: Cleveland Buckeyes

He pitched in one game with the Buckeyes in 1950, his only appearance in the Negro Leagues.

Flournoy, Fred
Career: 1928   Position: c
Teams: *Chappie Johnson's Stars ('27), Brooklyn Cuban Giants ('28), Pennsylvania Red Caps ('28)*

He was a catcher with a trio of marginal teams during the late '20s but never made it with a top black team.

Flournoy, Jesse Willis (Pud)
Career: 1919–33   Positions: p, *of*
Teams: Hilldale Daisies ('19–'23), Brooklyn Royal Giants ('23–'28), Baltimore Black Sox ('23, '29–'32), Atlantic City Bacharach Giants ('33)
Bats: Left   Throws: Left

The heavyset left-hander was an outstanding pitcher, with excellent speed, a variety of curves, and good control for a southpaw. Finishing the 1929 season with a strong second half, giving him a 9–5 ledger, he teamed with right-hander Laymon Yokely to pitch the Baltimore Black Sox to the American League pennant, one of the high points of Flournoy's fifteen-year career.

As a rookie with Hilldale in 1919, he pitched a no-hitter against a team of "all-stars," and in 1921 he recorded a 12–5 record with a 2.39 ERA. His last season with Hilldale was 1923, when they captured the first Eastern Colored League pennant, but he was not with them the entire season, also playing with the Baltimore Black Sox before joining the Brooklyn Royal Giants. The Royals that year had a wealth of pitching talent, as Flournoy joined a staff with Smokey Joe Williams, Dick Redding, Connie Rector, and Jesse Hubbard. Flournoy frequently played against major-leaguers in exhibitions and is credited with striking out Babe Ruth three straight times. Hal Schumacher, a star pitcher with the New York Giants, recalled pitching exhibitions against the Brooklyn Royal Giants when Flournoy was with the team.

With the Royals in 1925 Flournoy logged a 3–6 record and stayed with the team until the breakup of the Eastern Colored League. After joining the Black Sox he was credited with only a single win against 3 losses in each of his last two seasons (1931–32) with the team.

Flowers, Johnny (Jake)
Career: 1941–43   Positions: **3b,** of, ss,
                                                        2b, of
Team: New York Black Yankees

The reserve infielder was with the Black Yankees for three years in the early '40s, playing mostly at third base. In 1941, in very limited play, he is credited with a .474 batting average.

Floyd
Career: 1937   Position: p
Team: Indianapolis Athletics

He appeared briefly as a pitcher with the Indianapolis Athletics in 1937, the only year in the Negro Leagues for both him and the team.

Floyd
Career: 1913–16   Position: of

Teams: *Indianapolis ABCs ('13),* Bowser's ABCs ('16)

The outfielder appeared with the Indianapolis ABCs in 1913, a year before they began playing major-league-caliber ball, and again with Bowser's ABCs in 1916, when Thomas Bowser and C.I. Taylor formed separate teams.

Foote
Career: 1929   Position: c
Team: Detroit Stars

This catcher appeared in one game with the Detroit Stars in 1929.

Footes, Robert
a.k.a. Foots
Career: 1895–1909   Position: c
Teams: Chicago Unions ('95–'00), Chicago Union Giants ('02–'03), Philadelphia Giants ('03–'04), Brooklyn Royal Giants ('06–'09)

This catcher bridged two centuries, playing with teams in both the East and the West for fifteen years. He began his career in 1895 as the regular catcher with the Chicago Unions, holding that position for six seasons until 1901, when owner Frank Leland combined the Chicago Unions and the Columbia Giants to form the Chicago Union Giants. After a year out of the starting lineup, he was the regular receiver for the consolidated Union Giants in 1902–03. After nine seasons in Chicago, the veteran moved East to join the Philadelphia Giants, the top team of the East. In 1906 he was with the Brooklyn Royal Giants, hitting in the sixth slot in the batting order. Three years later he closed out his career in black baseball.

Forbes
Career: 1886–1901   Positions: 1b, of, 3b, c
Teams: Cuban Giants ('86, '88), Philadelphia Pythians ('87), Algona Brownies ('01)

He was signed as a first baseman by the Cuban Giants in midsummer of 1886 to replace A.G. Randolph, but also played at the hot corner and in the outfield with the Cubans. In 1887 he joined the Philadelphia Pythians, one of eight teams that were charter members of the League of Colored Baseball Clubs. Unfortunately, the league folded after only a week, and by the next season he had found his way back to the Cubans. His last appearance with a top black team was in 1901, as a catcher with the Brownies of Algona, Iowa.

Forbes, Frank (Joe, Strangler)
Career: 1913–19;   Positions: **ss,** 3b, of,
1929–43   2b, *p*, business man-
                                   ager, umpire (NNL),
                                   promoter (NNL)
Teams: Philadelphia Giants ('13 ,'22), Lincoln Stars ('14), New York Lincoln Giants ('15–'18), Pennsylvania Red Caps of New York ('18–*'20*), Atlantic City Bacharach Giants ('19), *Chappie Johnson's Stars ('27),* New York Cubans ('35)
Born: 1891
Died: Aug, 19, 1983, Philadelphia, Pa.

The light-hitting infielder began his career with the Philadelphia Giants in 1913, when the franchise was in decline, and joined the Lincoln Stars in 1914 as the regular shortstop, hitting in the lower part of the batting order. The next four seasons were spent with the Lincoln Giants, the first two as the starting shortstop. He batted last in the lineup each of these seasons (1915–16), and incomplete statistics show an average of .222 in limited play for the 1917 season. In 1918 he was earning $110 a month, and owner Jess McMahon promised him $125 if he hit .300. When he raised his average over the .300 mark and did not receive the money, he left the team and went to Canada. The next season he played with the Bacharachs as a part-time starter at third base and in right field. The remainder of his career was spent with teams of lesser status, including the Pennsylvania Red Caps of New York and Chappie Johnson's Stars.

An all-around athlete, he played basketball, football, and baseball at Central High in South Philadelphia. Later he attended Howard University, and the Lincoln Giants signed him on the advice of Doc Sykes, another Howard man. In 1914 he replaced John Henry Lloyd at shortstop when Lloyd left the team. He had excellent speed, which was reflected in his number of triples, but he seldom hit a home run. With the Lincolns he often earned extra money playing postseason exhibitions against major-leaguers. He went to Cuba in the winter of 1914–15, earning $200 per month, more than he made in the United States.

In addition to baseball, he was a professional in both basketball and boxing. He earned his nickname "Strangler" from breaking up a fight in a basketball game where he got each player around the neck and pulled them apart.

He had a variety of league and club positions in black baseball, including as an umpire and promoter with the Negro National League and as business manager for the New York Cubans in 1935. Before entering baseball, he played basketball with the original Renaissance team.

Force, William
Career: 1921–30   Positions: p, *of*
Teams: Chicago American Giants ('21), Detroit Stars ('21–'23), **Baltimore Black Sox** ('24–'29), Brooklyn Royal Giants ('30), New York Lincoln Giants
Bats: Right   Throws: Right

The right-handed pitcher had some good years in the West before coming East. A 1919 graduate of Knoxville College, he played with the Knoxville Giants as pitcher and outfielder before signing with the top black teams. After coming North he played briefly with the Chicago American Giants and then joined the Detroit Stars in 1921, posting a 13–6 record. Force was with the Stars for four years and pitched impressively.

He joined the Baltimore Black Sox in 1924 and, although still adjusting to the move East, had a good year, barely missing a no-hitter against the Washington Potomacs when, just one strike away, Ben Taylor spoiled his near-perfect outing with a hit. The next year he had a mark of 2–1 and logged an 8–5 record in

1927. He was occasionally used in the outfield, and hit for averages of .170 and .188 for those two seasons. He remained with the Black Sox throughout the '20s and by 1929 was helping younger players by acting as an unofficial pitching coach. In 1932, after his years with top clubs were over, he was playing with the Baltimore Red Sox, a semipro team and appeared with the Baltimore Stars in 1933.

Ford, C.
Career: 1917–18   Position: p
Teams: Hilldale Daisies ('17), *Pennsylvania Giants ('18)*

He was a pitcher with Hilldale in 1917, during their first year as a quality team, and the following season pitched with the Pennsylvania Giants, a lesser team.

Ford, Frank
Career: 1917–18   Position: c
Teams: Hilldale Daisies ('17), *Pennsylvania Giants ('18)*

This catcher played with Hilldale in 1917, during their first year as a quality team, and the following season played with the Pennsylvania Giants, a lesser team.

Ford, James (**Jimmy,** Jim)
Career: 1931–46   Positions: **3b, 2b,** *ss*
Teams: **Memphis Red Sox** ('31, '33–'37, '44'–'46), Baltimore Elite Giants ('38), Washington Black Senators ('38), St. Louis Stars ('39), New Orleans-St. Louis Stars ('40–'41), New York Black Yankees ('42), Harrisburg-St. Louis Stars ('43), Philadelphia Stars ('43)
Bats: Right   Throws: Right
Born: 1912

A scrappy infielder, he could play any infield position and could hit as well as run the bases, but at times he was a bit lazy. In 1941 he played third base for the St. Louis Stars and was one of the best hitters on the club, usually batting fourth or fifth in the order, and was selected to the West squad for the East-West game. The Stars disbanded after the season and Ford was one of several ex-Stars who moved

East to play with the New York Black Yankees. Partial statistics show only a .125 batting average for 1942, when he was playing third base with the Black Yankees.

The Stars reorganized in 1943, playing with dual home cities as they did in 1940–41, only with Harrisburg as the additional hometown instead of New Orleans, as it was previously. The infielder rejoined the Stars, playing second base until the team withdrew from league play in the early spring to barnstorm against Dizzy Dean's All-Star team. Soon afterward he joined the Philadelphia Stars to finish the season.

Before joining the St. Louis Stars, he was the Memphis Red Sox' second baseman during most of the '30s, hitting in the heart of the batting order, and rejoined the Red Sox in 1944, batting .279 and .204 for the next two seasons while closing out his career in the Negro Leagues in 1946. Unconfirmed reports indicate that he may have played briefly in organized ball.

Ford, Roy
Career: 1916–25   Positions: **2b,** ss, lf, rf, 3b, p
Teams: Baltimore Black Sox ('16–'25), Harrisburg Giants ('23)

He began his career in 1916 as a fledgling moundsman for the Baltimore Black Sox when they were still in their formative years, and he switched to a role as a position player in 1918, as a part-time starter in right field. Two years later he was the regular shortstop for the Sox, batting at the bottom of the lineup, and in 1921 he hit .324. In 1922–23 he moved up to the second slot in the batting order while playing second base, as the Black Sox made their entry into the Eastern Colored League the latter season. In 1924 the Sox finished a strong second in the league, with Ford moving into the starting left-field position, but dropped to the seventh spot in the batting order. The next season was his last in the Negro Leagues. In 1921 he pitched one game for the Black Sox, winning the decision.

Foreman
Career: 1921   Position: ss
Teams: *Madison Stars ('20–'21)*, Hilldale Daisies ('21)

He played with the Madison Stars, a team of lesser quality, for two years and made a brief appearance as a shortstop with Hilldale in 1921.

Foreman, F. Sylvestor (Hooks)
Career: 1921–33   Positions: **c**, of, *p*
Teams: Kansas City Monarchs ('21–'23, '25, '27, '33), Milwaukee Bears ('23), Cleveland Browns ('24), Homestead Grays ('24), Indianapolis ABCs ('26), *semipro teams ('27–'30)*, Washington Pilots ('32)

He was a backup catcher with the Kansas City Monarchs during the early '20s. After stints with the Milwaukee Bears, Cleveland Browns, and Homestead Grays, he returned to the Monarchs for the 1925 season, hitting .217 as a backup. The next season he was the regular catcher for the Indianapolis ABCs in the franchise's last season, and hit .231 while batting sixth in the order. After returning to the Monarchs for another stint as a backup in 1927, he joined a predominantly white semipro team in Little Falls, Minnesota, where he was batterymate with Webster McDonald for three years. After returning to league play, he joined the Washington Pilots in the East-West League in 1932 in a backup capacity, returning to the Monarchs in 1933 for his fourth tour of duty in Kansas City to close out his career where it had begun.

Foreman, Zack
Career: 1920–21   Positions: p, of
Team: Kansas City Monarchs

The pitcher from Parsons, Kansas, joined the Monarchs in 1920 as a pitcher, posting a 4–5 record in 1921, and also played in the outfield on occasion.

Forest, Charles
Career: 1920   Position: player
Team: St. Louis Giants

He was a player with the St. Louis Giants in 1920, but his position is undetermined.

Formenthal, Pedro
Career: 1947–50   Positions: cf, lf
Teams: *Mexican League ('44–'46)*, Memphis Red Sox ('47–'50), *minor leagues ('54–'55)*
Bats: Left   Throws: Left
Height: 5'11"   Weight: 200
Born: Apr. 19, 1915, Baguanos, Cuba

An outfielder with the Memphis Red Sox in the latter years of the Negro Leagues (1947–50), he was a good hitter (.341 in 1949), with home-run power and good speed. In the three seasons prior to joining Memphis he played with Vera Cruz and San Luis in the Mexican League, hitting .345, .362, and .384.

He was also a star in Cuba, where he compiled a lifetime batting average of .274 for 13 years, mostly with Havana. The slugging outfielder was on the All Cubans team of 1945–46, but his best years were in 1949–50, when he led the league with a .336 average, and in 1952–53, when he hit .337. These two superlative seasons were his only years over .300, but he was a good clutch hitter, and despite being frequently issued free passes with men on base, was a big RBI man. In 1952–53 he tied the Cuban single-season RBI record with 57 and also led in RBIs the previous season. He ended his Cuban career tied for the record in career RBIs (362).

In the summers of 1954 and 1955 he played with Havana in the International League, recording identical averages of .293 each season, with a winter in the Venezuelan League sandwiched between. He continued playing ball until age forty-nine, but preferred playing in the Latin American leagues because of the status of blacks in the United States at that time. Once, while with the Memphis Red Sox, he demonstrated his disdain for the prevailing social conditions by using his Cuban passport to dine at a white restaurant in Dallas, Texas.

Forrest
Career: 1919–25   Positions: of, *c*

Teams: *Havana Red Sox ('17),* New York Lincoln Giants ('19, '21–'25), *Philadelphia Giants ('28)*

He was an outfielder with the Lincoln Giants for a half-dozen seasons, sandwiched between stints with lesser teams.

Forrest, Joe
Career: 1949   Position: p
Team: *New York Black Yankees*

He pitched with the New York Black Yankees in 1949, when the team was no longer engaged in league play and was playing a lesser caliber of baseball.

Forrest, Percy (Pete)
Career: 1938–49   Position: p
Teams: Chicago American Giants ('38), New York Black Yankees ('43, '45–'46), Newark Eagles ('44), Indianapolis Clowns ('49)
Bats: Right   Throws: Right
Height: 5'11"   Weight: 180

The right-hander started and ended his career in the West but spent the intervening seasons in the East during his dozen years in the black big leagues. With the Black Yankees he was winless in his first and last seasons with the team, losing twice in 1943 and four times in 1946. In 1945, in very limited play, he hit .385.

Foster, Albert (Red)
Career: 1910   Position: 1b
Team: Kansas City, Kansas, Giants

He was a first baseman with the 1910 Kansas City, Kansas, Giants.

Foster, Andrew (Rube, Jock)
Career: 1902–26   Positions: **p,** 1b, of, **manager, executive, owner;** founder, officer (NNL)
Teams: Chicago Union Giants ('02), Cuban X-Giants ('03), Philadelphia Giants ('04–'06), Leland Giants ('07–'10), **Chicago American Giants** ('11–'26)
Bats: Right   Throws: Right
Height: 6'2"   Weight: 200

Born: Sept. 17, 1879, Calvert, Tex.
Died: December 9, 1930, Kankakee, Ill.

He was recognized as the father of the Negro Leagues, and Foster's career exemplifies the essence of black baseball. As a raw-talent rookie pitcher soon after the turn of the century, the big Texan was credited with 51 victories in 1902, including a win over the great Rube Waddell, the game in which Foster received his nickname. The son of Sarah and Andrew Foster, the youngster had been named after his minister father but would ever afterward be called by his earned nickname. Soon after completing the eighth grade in Calvert, Texas, the youthful Foster began his baseball career pitching with the Waco Yellow Jackets in his native state. In 1902 he traveled North and joined Frank Leland's Chicago Union Giants. His first appearance with the team was as an unsuccessful pinch hitter, but whatever first impression he made was quickly erased when he took the mound, as he lost only one game in three months with the team, after which he pitched briefly with a white semipro ballclub at Otsego, Michigan, before returning to the top black teams the following season.

Foster was a smart pitcher who supplemented his normal repertory of pitches with a highly effective screwball, and the big right-hander's presence on a team usually was the determining factor in a championship. In 1903 he joined the Cuban X-Giants and compiled a 54–1 record for the regular season, and won 4 games in the playoffs victory over the Philadelphia Giants. The next year, after jumping to the Philadelphia squad, Foster won 2 games in the 3-game playoffs victory over his former teammates.

In 1905 he was reported to have won 51 of 55 games from major-league and minor-league teams, and he led the Philadelphia Giants to two more championships in 1905–06 as they became the dominant team of the era.

That winter he played in Cuba with the Fe ballclub and led the league in wins with 9, while pitching half of his team's games. His natural leadership manifested itself, and he took charge of the team during the Cuban season of 1907.

Once back in the United States, he left Philadelphia in a salary dispute and returned to Chicago to begin his managerial career when Frank Leland appointed him playing manager of the Leland Giants in 1907. Foster was a stern, demanding manager but fair and tolerant with his players, and his keen mind and ability to handle men naturally lent itself to managerial success, with his team immediately becoming one of the best teams in black baseball.

In 1909 a broken leg sustained in the first inning of a mid-July game against the Cuban Stars resulted in a six-week mending period, which caused him to miss the championship series against the St. Paul Colored Gophers. His absence cost the Lelands the title as they lost the 5-game series on the final day. The following year, after a split with owner Frank Leland, he organized his own team, stocking the club with players from the old Leland Giants and the Philadelphia Giants. Rube considered his 1910 team to be the greatest baseball talent ever assembled. Featuring stars such as John Henry Lloyd, Pete Hill, Bruce Petway, Home Run Johnson, Frank Wickware, and Pat Dougherty, the team fashioned a fabulous 128–6 record. Incomplete statistics show Foster contributing a 13–2 record himself, as a moundsman. Although past his prime, he was classed with Walter Ball, Danny McClellan, and Harry Buckner in a group that was considered "head and shoulders above" other pitchers of the era in black baseball.

The next season Foster entered into a handshake partnership with John M. Schorling, a white tavern owner and son-in-law of Charles Comiskey, and arranged for the team to play at the old Chicago White Sox Park, with the proceeds being divided equally between the two men. That year, 1911, Foster renamed the team the Chicago American Giants and a dynasty was born, with the club becoming a dominant force until Foster's departure from baseball. Foster himself was phasing out his active career, with incomplete data showing records of 5–4 in 1914 and 1–0 in 1917, two of his best teams of the decade. Enormously popular at the time, he still took the mound on special occasions to enhance attendance and, more than any other individual, Rube Foster is identified with the Chicago American Giants. The team was an extension of his personality and philosophy and bore his distinct imprint. At the beginning of the second decade of the century he had already established himself as the most dominant black pitcher from the first decade, and was in the process of earning the same recognition as a manager.

With the American Giants he molded players to fit his "racehorse" style of play. Good pitching, sound defense and an offense geared to the running game became the trademarks of his teams. All of his players were required to master the bunt and the hit-and-run, and he expected runners to go from first to third on the hit-and-run and the bunt-and-run. All of his players had to master the bunt, and his runners often had a "green light" to run on their own, so the scrappy American Giants could always push across some runs and avoid prolonged team slumps. Only the 1916 Indianapolis ABCs were able to break his monopoly in the West as the American Giants won all other recorded championships from 1910 through 1922.

After establishing the best black baseball team, Foster organized the first black baseball league, the Negro National League, serving as president and treasurer while overseeing its development into a first-class enterprise. While booking games for his own team, he had encountered difficulties with East Coast promoter Nat Strong, and considered the formation of a black league as the solution to scheduling problems created by Strong's iron-handed control of teams in the East. As president of the league, Foster was unsalaried but took 5 percent of the gate receipts of every league game and distributed as he chose. Through the formation of a league, Foster became an even more powerful influence on black baseball, and through his autocratic policies, he alienated many others in positions of authority. By 1925 the opposition to his unrestricted influence had grown, and although he received a unanimous vote of confidence from the other owners, he offered to resign.

Rube wore three hats—as player, manager, and executive—and they all sat well on his head. However, it was for his contributions to baseball as a manager that he is probably best remembered. A stern disciplinarian, shrewd handler of men, developer of new talent, and ingenious innovator of baseball strategy, he instilled his philosophy and style of play in his players so that even after his deteriorating mental health forced him to leave the game, his team and his league continued to flourish until after his death in 1930.

The sharp mind that he had exhibited in his prime years began to show effects of the stressful situation under which he had labored for years, and his mental deterioration began to manifest itself in 1925, when he thought that his players had "laid down on him." In 1926 his lieutenant Dave Malarcher was placed at the helm of the team and, by early September, Foster was in a mental hospital for psychopaths, after having shown evidence of mental unbalance for several weeks. For the next four years after his nervous breakdown, he was never to leave the state asylum at Kankakee, Illinois, until his death two weeks before Christmas in 1930. Fans and admirers lined up for three days to view the casket.

Rube Foster's career covered the entire spectrum of baseball participation, from the playing field to the front office, and he excelled at each level. He was black baseball's greatest manager, the man most responsible for black baseball's continued existence, and a man almost bigger than life itself. In recognition of his contributions to baseball, Foster was voted into the National Baseball Hall of Fame in 1981.

Foster, Leland
Career: 1932–38   Position: p
Teams: Monroe Monarchs ('32–'36), Atlanta Black Crackers ('38)

He was a pitcher with the 1932–36 Monroe Monarchs, and in 1938, while a student at Morehouse College, he was on the Atlanta Black Crackers' spring roster but pitched mostly against lesser-caliber opposition before being dropped from the team.

Foster, Leonard
Career: 1938   Position: if
Team: Atlanta Black Crackers

He was an infielder with the 1938 Atlanta Black Crackers.

Foster, William Hendrick (**Willie,** Bill)
Career: 1923–38   Positions: **p,** manager
Teams: Memphis Red Sox ('23–'24, '38), Chicago American Giants ('23–'30, '37), Birmingham Black Barons ('25), Homestead Grays ('31), Kansas City Monarchs ('31), Cole's American Giants ('32–'35), Pittsburgh Crawfords ('36)
Bats: Both   Throws: Left
Height: 6'1"   Weight: 195
Born: June 12, 1904, Calvert, Tex.
Died: Sept. 16, 1978, Lorman, Miss.

A half brother of the famous Rube Foster, Willie Foster was a pitching star for the Chicago American Giants for over a decade. With near-perfect control and a wide assortment of pitches, all delivered with the same motion, the tall left-hander was at his best when the stakes were highest. With a crucial game to win, Willie was the kind of pitcher a manager wanted on the mound. He was a smart pitcher who knew how to get the most out of his vast repertory of pitches, which included a blazing fastball, a slider, a fast-breaking drop, a sidearm curve, and a masterful change of pace. According to Jocko Conlon, Foster was comparable to Herb Pennock, only faster and had beautiful control, adding that "he was really something to watch."

His mother died when he was only four years old, and the youngster was reared by his maternal grandparents in Mississippi. He attended school at Alcorn College until 1918, when he traveled North to Chicago to work in the stockyards and attempted to sign on with Rube's team as a pitcher. His half brother's refusal to allow him to play with the Chicago American Giants created a resentment that continued throughout his life. After this rejection, he returned to Mississippi and later signed with the Memphis Red Sox in 1923. However, Rube exercised his power to demand that the younger Foster be sent to Chicago. Memphis owner Bubbles Lewis capitulated, and the hot left-handed pitching prospect was signed by Rube before the end of the season. Foster divided each of his first three seasons between the American Giants and a southern team, registering marks of 5–2, 6–1, and 7–1 before playing his first complete season in Chicago in 1926, the year after Foster yielded the managerial reins to David Malarcher. That year Foster was still in college in Tennessee in the early stages of the season.

His tenure in Chicago included pennant-winning seasons in 1926, 1927, and 1933. In the 1926 season he won 26 consecutive games against all levels of competition while compiling an 11–4 league record to lead the American Giants to the second-half title. In the Negro National League playoffs against the Kansas City Monarchs, first-half winners, for the championship, the American Giants needed to win both games in a final-day doubleheader to capture the pennant. With the team's back to the wall, Foster started and won both ends of the doubleheader, defeating Bullet Rogan in each contest to claim the Negro National League flag. Foster followed this with a sensational performance in the World Series against the Eastern Colored League champion Bacharach Giants. He pitched 3 complete games while relieving in another, getting 2 victories, including a shutout, and compiling a 1.27 ERA. The following year Foster compiled a sensational 32–3 record, with a 21–3 league ledger, and was again the workhorse in the Series, pitching 2 complete games relieving in 2 others while picking up 2 more victories to go with a 3.00 ERA.

After each of the championship seasons he played winter ball, traveling to Cuba after the 1926 season, while opting for the California winter league after the 1927 season, where he finished with a 14–1 record.

The left-hander's ledger showed 14–10 and 11–7 seasons for the next two years, and after two seasons without a pennant, Foster was named manager of the Chicago American Giants for the 1930 season. Although he couldn't produce a pennant, he fashioned a 16–10 record in league play. In 1931 he was enticed away from the Giants temporarily to join the Homestead Grays, where his presence made an already good team the greatest of all time. In September, in a rare occurrence, he pitched Cum Posey's Grays to a victory over J.L. Wilkinson's Kansas City Monarchs and then, with the permission of both owners, switched teams for the remainder of the season. He is credited with a combined 9–2 record for both clubs.

Back in the Chicago fold, his league ledger showed 15–8 and 9–3 seasons for 1932–33, each producing a pennant. The first year they copped the Negro Southern League flag, and the latter year he pitched the American Giants to a pennant in the new Negro National League. His performance in 1933 made him the choice as the starting pitcher for the West squad in the first East-West All-Star game. At that time the rules did not restrict a pitcher to only three innings in All-Star competition, and Willie pitched the complete-game victory over an East lineup that read like a Hall of Fame roll call.

In 1934 the American Giants won the first-half championship but lost a tough playoff, 4 games to 3, to the second-half champion Philadelphia Stars. After a league performance of 6–3 during the 1935 season, including a victory over Satchel Paige in a late September matchup, Foster joined the Pittsburgh Crawfords in 1936, the last year of their black baseball domination, and although past his prime, he was still a formidable presence on the mound.

Although he worked out with the Memphis

Red Sox in the spring of 1938 and pitched in an April exhibition game against the Elites, the 1937 season was the left-hander's last full season with a top team in the Negro Leagues. The following season he played with the Yakima Browns, a lesser team. He always deported himself in a gentlemanly manner and commanded respect. During his baseball career, Foster had pursued his educational goals in the off-seasons and, after retiring from baseball, he became dean of men and baseball coach at Alcorn State College in 1960, a position he held until shortly before his death.

Foulkes, Erwin
[see Fowlkes, Erwin]

Fowikes, Erwin
[see Fowlkes, Erwin]

Fowikes, Samuel
[see Fowlkes, Samuel]

Fowler, John W. (**Bud**)
a.k.a. John W. Jackson (his real name)
Career: 1877–99   Positions: **2b,** p, ss, 3b, of, c, manager
Teams: *minor leagues ('77–'79, '81, '84–'99),* Page Fence Giants ('95), Cuban Giants ('98), *Smoky City Giants ('01), All-American Black Tourists ('03), Kansas City Stars ('04)*
Bats: Right   Throws: Right
Height: 5'7"   Weight: 155
Born: Mar. 16, 1858, Fort Plain, N.Y.
Died: Feb. 26, 1913, Frankfurt, N.Y.

He was the first professional black ballplayer, beginning his career in 1878, only one year after the first minor league was organized. Born John W. Jackson, the son of a fugitive hop-picker and barber, he lived in Cooperstown, New York, as a youngster, and may well have learned the rudiments of baseball on the sandlots of the region. For some undiscovered reason he took the name of Bud Fowler when he began playing professionally. Unsubstantiated reports that he played with the Washington Mutuals in 1869 and with a Newcastle,

Pennsylvania, team in 1872 cannot be confirmed and are improbable.

He began his career as a pitcher, and the first documented account of his appearing in a game was with Chelsea, Massachusetts, in April 1878. Later that month, pitching for Lynn Live Oaks of the International Association, he defeated Tommy Bond and the famed Boston Nationals, 2–1, in an exhibition game. Over the next few seasons he played with Worcester of the New England Association (1878), Malden of the Eastern Massachusetts League (1879), Guelph, Ontario (1881), and the Petrolia Imperials (1881). After 1884, when he finished with a 7–8 record with Stillwater, Minnesota, of the Northwestern League, he did not pitch substantially.

Eventually he became an everyday player and, while he could play any position, second base became his preferred spot. He continued to play in white leagues, appearing with Keokuk in the Western League (1885), Pueblo in the Colorado League (1885), Topeka in the Western League (1886), Binghamton in the International League (1887), Montpelier in the New England League (1887), Crawfordsville in the Central Interstate League (1888), Terre Haute in the Central Interstate League (1888), Santa Fe in the New Mexico League (1888), Greenville in the Michigan League (1889), Galesburg of the Central Interstate League (1890), Sterling of the Illinois-Iowa League (1890), Burlington of the Illinois-Iowa League (1890), Lincoln-Kearney of the Nebraska State League (1892), and the independent Findlay, Ohio, team (1891, 1893–94, 1896–99).

In the early days of baseball there was no official color line, and he played in organized baseball with white ballclubs until the color line became established and entrenched. However, his stays were almost always of short duration despite his playing ability—probably because of the race factor. In 1887 he was dropped from Binghamton of the International League and was forbidden to sign with any other International League team.

In the fall of 1894, the social conditions led

him to organize the Page Fence Giants, an all-black team sponsored by the Page Woven Wire Fence Company of Adrian, Michigan, and the team began play the following spring with Fowler as the playing manager and Grant "Home Run" Johnson as the shortstop and captain. That spring the Page Fence Giants played a 2-game exhibition series against the National League Cincinnati Reds but dropped both games. However, the season was a success, as they ended it with a 118–36 record for a .766 winning percentage and Fowler hit .316 for the year. Fowler had left the team before the end of the season to play with the Lansing team of the Michigan State League and hit .331 while splitting his time between second base and third base. That was to be his tenth and last season in organized baseball, a record until broken by Jackie Robinson in his last season with the Brooklyn Dodgers.

He also played with the Cuban Giants in 1898, and as his playing skills faded, he became more inclined toward organizing and managing various barnstorming black ballclubs. These teams included the Smoky City Giants (1901), the All-American Black Tourists (1903), and the Kansas City Stars (1904), and although now in his forties, Fowler continued to play himself except with the latter team. At the end of his career he asserted that he had played on teams based in twenty-two different states and in Canada.

In 1909, with Fowler in failing health, several attempts were made to play a benefit game for the ailing baseballist, but the efforts all proved unfruitful and the game never materialized. Less than three years later, the "real first"—the first black professional baseball player—died of pernicious anemia after an extended illness, just eighteen days short of his fifty-fifth birthday.

Fowlkes, Erwin
a.k.a. Fowikes, Foulkes
Career: 1947–48   Position: ss
Teams: Chicago American Giants ('47), Homestead Grays ('48)

Bats: Right   Throws: Right
Height: 5'7"   Weight: 170
A good fielder but light hitter who usually batted in the eighth spot in the lineup, he was a part-time starter at shortstop with the Homestead Grays, with incomplete statistics showing a feeble .065 batting average in their championship season of 1948.

Fowlkes, Samuel
a.k.a. Fowikes
Career: 1948–50   Position: p
Teams: Chicago American Giants ('48), Kansas City Monarchs ('50), Cleveland Buckeyes ('50)

This pitcher from Lake Charles, Louisiana, played with the Chicago American Giants in 1948 after being obtained in a trade, and also pitched with the Kansas City Monarchs and the Cleveland Buckeyes as the quality of play in the Negro Leagues declined.

Fox
Career: 1914   Position: p
Team: Brooklyn Royal Giants
This second-line pitcher was a marginal player with the 1914 Brooklyn Royal Giants and pitched primarily against teams of lesser caliber.

Fox
Career: 1943   Position: if
Team: New York Black Yankees
A wartime player, he hit .319 for the New York Black Yankees in 1943, his only year in the Negro Leagues.

Fox, Orange
Career: 1887   Position: rf
Team: Chicago Unions
He was a right fielder with the 1887 Chicago Unions in his only year in black baseball.

Francis, Del
Career: 1917–20   Position: 2b
Team: Indianapolis ABCs ('11–20)
The reserve second baseman with the Indian-

apolis ABCs in the latter years of the deadball era played infrequently, having begun his career when the franchise was not of major-league quality.

Francis, William (**Billy,** Brodie, Ducky, *The Little Corporal*)
Career: 1904–25   Positions: **3b,**   ss, manager
Teams: Philadelphia Giants ('04–'10), **New York Lincoln Giants** ('11–'13), Mohawk Giants ('13), **Chicago American Giants** ('14–'19, '25), Cuban Giants, Hilldale Daisies ('20–'22), Atlantic City Bacharach Giants ('23), Cleveland Browns ('24), Wilmington Giants ('25), Chicago Giants ('25)
Bats: Right   Throws: Right
Height: 5'5"   Weight: 140

Recognized as one of the best third basemen of the first two decades of the century, the chunky little infielder had good hands, wide range, and was a member of most of the great teams during the deadball era, including the champion Philadelphia Giants of 1906–07, the champion Lincoln Giants of 1911–13, and Rube Foster's great Chicago American Giants of 1914–19, which won titles each year except 1916. A good defensive player, Francis played a shallow third base and, without question, would have starred in the major leagues had he been given the opportunity.

The little "stump-jumper" was a combination Eddie Stanky and Ron Hunt, accumulating a large number of walks and times hit by a pitch. A smart player, he wore a loose shirt to enhance his chances of being hit by a pitch. Curiously, with Foster's team he usually batted fifth or sixth in the lineup, but with the Lincoln Giants he batted second behind speedster Spot Poles, and usually filled the same number two slot for Hilldale. With the Lincolns, playing against all levels of competition, he hit for averages of .344, .320, and .240 in 1911–13. After moving to the Chicago American Giants in 1914, he is credited with batting averages of .396, .265, .213, .207, .242, and .239 for the remainder of the decade. After returning to the

East with Hilldale in 1920, he hit for averages of .324 and .223 in 1921–22. In the winter of 1917 he played with the Royal Poinciana Hotel in the Florida Hotel League and was credited with a .300 batting average.

He was a fast and alert base runner, which served him well during his stay with Rube Foster's American Giants. According to Hall of Fame umpire Jocko Conlon, the little third baseman was one of the best of the black players of his time. In addition to third base he also could play shortstop adequately, but as manager of Hilldale in the early '20s he moved a young Judy Johnson to shortstop and positioned himself at third base. Later in his career "The Little Corporal" managed lesser teams in New England.

Franklin, William B.
Career: 1887   Position: manager
Team: Louisville Falls Citys

He was the manager of the Louisville Falls Citys, one of eight teams that were charter members of the League of Colored Baseball Clubs in 1887. However, the league's existence was ephemeral, lasting only a week.

Frazier, Albert Edwin (Al, Cool Papa)
a.k.a. O. Frazier
Career: 1932–40   Positions: **2b,** 3b
Teams: Montgomery Grey Sox ('32), Jacksonville Red Caps ('34, '38), Cleveland Bears ('39–'40)
Bats: Right   Throws: Right
Height: 6'1"   Weight: 143
Born: Jan. 23, 1915, Jacksonville, Fla.

He was a good utility infielder through part of his career. After appearing with the Montgomery Grey Sox in the Negro Southern League, the youngster broke in with the Jacksonville Red Caps in 1934 as a second baseman and earned a regular spot at third base in 1938. When the franchise moved to Cleveland the following two seasons, he won a starting spot in the infield with the Bears, playing one season each at second base and third base. He was fast on the bases, earning him the nickname "Cool Papa" after the famous speedster Cool Papa Bell, and he played with several teams during his nine-year career.

Freeman, Bill

Career: 1925, 1933   Position: p
Teams: Indianapolis ABCs ('25), Cuban Stars ('33)

This pitcher made two appearances with top black teams, with the Indianapolis ABCs in 1925 and the Cuban Stars in 1933.

Freeman, Charlie

Career: 1916, 1927–33 Positions: player, officer
Team: Hilldale Daisies

His association with Hilldale began as a player during the team's formative years, and later he served as an officer with the ballclub in 1927–30.

Freeman, William

Career: 1888–89   Position: 3b
Team: Chicago Unions

He was the starting third baseman with the Chicago Unions in 1888–89, his only two seasons in black baseball.

Friely

Career: 1922   Position: 2b
Team: Atlantic City Bacharach Giants

He was a second baseman with the Bacharachs in 1922, a year before the team entered the Eastern Colored League.

Frye, John H. (Jack)

a.k.a. Fry
Career: 1883–96   Positions: **1b**, c, p, of, 2b
Teams: Cuban Giants ('86, '88–'91), New York Gorhams ('87)

The versatile player from Harrisburg, Pennsylvania, pitched and played as an everyday player at a wide range of positions during his fourteen-year career. He played with the Cuban Giants, the leading black team of the era. His first game with the Giants was as a second baseman in an exhibition game against the major-league Cincinnati team of the American Association of July 21, 1886. The following month he pitched the Cuban Giants to the Colored championship by defeating the Gorhams of New York, 25–4.

During his years with the Cuban Giants, the team often played as representatives of a host city in that city's regular league. For three consecutive seasons, 1889–91, they represented Trenton, New Jersey, in the Middle States League ('89); York, Pennsylvania, in the Eastern Interstate League ('90); and Ansonia in the Connecticut State League ('91). In addition to playing in organized baseball when the Cuban Giants represented one of the cities in a league, he also played with various teams in organized baseball, including Reading, Pennsylvania, in the Interstate League and Lewiston, Pennsylvania, in the Pennsylvania State League.

Following the 1888 season he taught school, but not much is known about his life after baseball. Although the exact date is unknown, he died prior to 1907.

Fulchur, Robert

a.k.a. Fulcur
Career: 1940   Position: p
Teams: Chicago American Giants ('40), Birmingham Black Barons ('40)

He was a pitcher with the two teams during his only season in the Negro American League.

Fuller, Chick

[see Fuller, W. W.]

Fuller, Jimmy

Career: 1917–21   Positions: **c**, 1b
Teams: Philadelphia Giants ('14, '20–'22), Lincoln Stars ('15–'16), Cuban Giants ('17), Atlantic City Bacharach Giants ('17)

He was a backup catcher with the Lincoln Stars in 1915–16, sandwiched between stints with the Philadelphia Giants in 1914 and the Cuban Giants and Bacharachs in 1917.

Fuller, W. W. (Chick)

Career: 1916–19   Positions: **ss, 2b,** of

Teams: *Brooklyn Colored Giants ('08), New York Colored Giants ('08),* Atlantic City Bacharach Giants ('16–'17), Cuban Giants, *Pennsylvania Giants ('18–'19), Cleveland Tate Stars,* Hilldale Daisies ('18), G.C.T. Red Caps ('18–'19), *Pennsylvania Red Caps of New York*

A smooth-fielding middle infielder during the deadball era, he played shortstop with the 1916 Bacharachs, moving a young Dick Lundy to third base. Two years later he was the starting second baseman with Hilldale, hitting sixth in the batting order. Later in the year he played with the G.C.T. Red Caps, playing right field while batting in the lower part of the order for 1918–19.

Fullman
Career: 1916   Position: of
Team: Baltimore Black Sox

He was an outfielder with the Baltimore Black Sox in 1916, when the team was in its formative years and not of major-league quality.

Fumes, C.
Career: 1925–30   Positions: **lf,** 3b
Teams: Cuban Stars (West) ('25, '30), Cuban Stars (East)

He was a reserve outfielder with the Cuban Stars, both when they were in the Negro National League and when they played as an independent team.

Fuqua
Career: 1917   Position: c
Team: Havana Red Sox

He was the owner of a lesser team called the Fuqua Giants prior to joining the Havana Red Sox as a catcher in 1917.

G

Gadsden, Gus
Career: 1932   Position: **rf**
Team: Hilldale Daisies

The light-hitting outfielder was the regular right fielder, batting eighth in the order, with Hilldale in 1932, the franchise's last year of existence.

Gaichey
Career: 1948   Position: p
Team: Memphis Red Sox

He pitched briefly with the Memphis Red Sox in 1948, losing his only decision.

Gaideria
Career: 1918   Position: p
Team: Cuban Stars

The pitcher made limited appearances with the Cuban Stars in 1918, his only season in black baseball.

Gaines, Jonas Donald (Lefty, George)
Career: 1937–50   Position: p
Teams: Newark Eagles ('37), Washington Elite Giants ('37), **Baltimore Elite Giants** ('32–'42, '46–'48), *Mexican League ('40), military service ('43–'45),* Philadelphia Stars ('49–'50), *minor leagues ('51–52, '54–57), Japanese League ('53)*
Bats: Right   Throws: Left
Height: 5'9"   Weight: 158
Born: January 9, 1914, New Roads, La.

The slender left-hander pitched with the Ea-gles, Elites, and Philadelphia Stars in a career that spanned fourteen seasons (1937–50) in the Negro Leagues. Best identified with the Baltimore Elite Giants, during his prime the small hurler was regarded as a potential 20-game winner in the majors. He was an effective pitcher with good control and whose repertory of pitches included a good fastball, curve, slider, change, and an outstanding screwball. His tenure with the Elites was interrupted twice, first by a stint in Mexico in 1940, where he fashioned an 8–3 record with a 3.68 ERA with Vera Cruz, and again during World War II, when he spent three years in the Army.

Before his induction, he posted a 4–2 league ledger with a 3.14 ERA in 1941, and split 10 decisions in 1942. After returning from service, he registered marks of 6–5, 5–4, and 9–4 for the 1946–48 seasons. Despite the breaks in his career, he pitched in the East-West All-Star games of 1942, 1946, and 1950, all without a decision.

Before signing a professional contract, the Southern University graduate attracted much attention while pitching on ball diamonds of Mississippi and Louisiana and was heavily recruited by the big clubs. Finally signing with Newark in 1937, he joined a staff led by star hurlers Leon Day and Terris McDuffie, and the rookie's services were limited, as was his record, showing only a 1–3 ledger for the season.

The Elites recognized the youngster's potential and quickly acquired his services in 1938.

Soon after arriving, he and veterans Bill Byrd and Andrew Porter formed Baltimore's "Big Three." Gaines enjoyed most of his success with the Elites, but also pitched with the Philadelphia Stars, recording an unimpressive 2–3 mark in 1950.

With the decline of the Negro Leagues, he played in organized ball with Minot in the Mandak League in 1951–52 before becoming one of the first Americans to play in Japan, in 1953. After only one season in the Orient, he returned to the minor leagues with Pampa in the West Texas-New Mexico League in 1954, where he had a 16–7 record despite a 5.12 ERA. Gaines then played a year with Bismarck, North Dakota, where he posted an 8–3 mark with a 3.27 ERA, and finished his career with records of 9–7 and 6–10 for Carlsbad in the Southwestern League in 1956–57, his last year in organized ball.

A fair-hitting pitcher with less than average power, he was at best an average base runner but could field his position adequately. During his career he also played in Cuba, where he split 4 decisions in two winters on the island.

Gaines, Willie
Career: 1950–52   Position: p
Teams: Philadelphia Stars ('50–'52), *Indianapolis Clowns ('53–'55), minor leagues ('52)*
Bats: Right   Throws: Right
Height: 6'0"   Weight: 190
Born: 1931

As a pitcher with the 1950 Philadelphia Stars, he was 5–3 with a 3.33 ERA, and two years later, in 1952, he was pitching in organized baseball with Porterfield in the Southwestern League but managed only a 0–1 ledger with an 8.13 ERA.

Galata, Domingo
Career: 1949   Position: p
Team: New York Cubans

He was a pitcher with the New York Cubans in 1949, his only season in the Negro Leagues.

Galata, Raul
Career: 1949–50   Positions: **p**, 1b, of

Teams: Indianapolis Clowns ('49–'51), *Mexican League ('51–'64), minor leagues ('58)*
Bats: Left   Throws: Left
Height: 5'9"   Weight: 170
Born: Cuba, 1930

The left-hander pitched with the Indianapolis Clowns in the waning years of the Negro Leagues, registering an 11–6 record with a 2.92 ERA in 1950, while batting .313. The following season he began a long career in the Mexican League, compiling a 7–7 ledger with Monterrey. In 1955 he had his best season on the mound (14–8, 3.72) with Vera Cruz while also batting .306. However, that was his last winning season in the Mexican League in a career that lasted through the 1964 season. In 1958 he played with Chihuanca in the Arizona-Mexican League and fashioned a 12–2, 2.54 ERA mound record while hitting for an average of .310. Always a good hitter with some power, he also played first base and outfield in Mexico and later in his career became more of an everyday player rather than a pitcher, batting a .291 in 1963.

Gales
Career: 1931   Position: 1b
Team: Detroit Stars

He was a reserve first baseman with the Detroit Stars in 1931, his only appearance in the Negro Leagues.

Galey
Career: 1897   Positions: 1b, of
Team: Cuban Giants

In 1897, his only year in black baseball, he played first base and outfield with the Cuban Giants, the first black professional team, dating back to its organization in 1885.

Gallardy
Career: 1906   Position: of
Team: Cuban Giants

He was an outfielder with the 1906 Cuban Giants in his only season in black baseball. The Giants were the first black professional team and for several years was regarded as the best black team, but the franchise had declined considerably by 1906 and no longer held a place among the top clubs.

Galloway
Career: 1931   Position: 2b
Team: Bacharach Giants

He was a reserve second baseman with the Bacharachs in 1931, after they had dropped out of league play.

Galloway, Bill
Career: 1899–1905   Positions: lf, 2b
Teams: Cuban X-Giants ('00, '05) Cuban Giants, *Canadian League*

An outfielder with the Cuban Giants and the Cuban X-Giants, two of the most prominent black teams of the era, he also could play second base. In addition to the black teams, he played with Woodstock in the Canadian League.

Galvez, Cuneo
a.k.a. Cundo
Career: 1928–32   Position: p
Teams: Cuban Stars (West) ('28–'30), Cuban Stars ('32)
Height: 7'0"

The giant Cuban hurler played with Cuban teams during the years when leagues were faltering. Using an underhand delivery, he posted a 4–9 record for the Cubans in 1929, when they were in the Negro National League. When the league folded following the 1931 season, the Stars entered the East-West League in 1932, where he was winless against 3 losses when the league broke up before the season was completed. That year the team sometimes played as the Cuban House of David. In his homeland he helped pitch Cienfuegos to the 1929–30 Cuban winter league championship.

Gambel
a.k.a. Gambell
Career: 1941   Position: p
Team: Philadelphia Stars

He was listed as a pitcher with the Philadel-

phia Stars in 1941, but there is no record that he pitched in any league game.

Gamble
Career: 1917–21   Positions: of, p
Teams: Cuban Giants ('17), Columbus Buckeyes ('21)

He played as an outfielder with the Cuban Giants, an independent team, in 1917, and later reappeared as a pitcher with the Negro National League Columbus Buckeyes, in 1921.

Gamiz, Mazio
Career: 1925–29   Positions: p, c
Team: Cuban Stars (East)

He was a pitcher with the Cuban Stars in the Eastern Colored League for five years, beginning in 1925, when he pitched in 4 games for the Cubans and lost his only decision. He was also a sometime catcher. His last year was in 1929, when he was arrested by immigration authorities for violating the conditions of his entry into the United States. He was reported by Syd Pollock, owner of the Havana Red Sox, with whom he had a contract. He was released on bail soon after his arrest in August but was expected to be deported.

Gamp
Career: 1917   Position: rf
Teams: *Pittsburgh Stars of Buffalo*

He was a right fielder for the Pittsburgh Stars of Buffalo, a marginal team during the preleague era of black baseball.

Gans, Robert Edward (**Jude,** Judy)
Career: 1910–27;
1932–38   Positions: **lf**, rf, cf, p, manager, umpire (EWL, NNL)
Teams: **New York Lincoln Giants** ('11–'13, '21–'25), Smart Set ('12), Mohawk Giants ('13), Chicago American Giants ('14–'20), Chicago Giants ('17), New York Lincoln Stars ('15), Cuban Giants ('10, '17), *military service*

*('18–'19), Chappie Johnson's Stars ('26–'27),
Cuban Stars ('27)*
Bats: Left   Throws: Left

A good all-around player, the outfielder
could hit, field, and had good speed on the
bases. During the '10s he was one of the best
outfielders in black baseball and was generally
found on the best ballclubs of the era as he
jumped back and forth between New York in
the East and Chicago in the West. A good fastball hitter, while playing left field with the
great New York Lincoln Giants in 1911–13 he
batted third in the order in front of John Henry
Lloyd and recorded batting averages of .388,
.361, and .302 against all levels of opposition.
He left New York, along with Lloyd and Bill
Francis, to make Rube Foster's 1914 Chicago
American Giants a powerhouse. While he was
hitting sixth in the batting order, published statistics show that Gans had a slow start and was
hitting only .191 in August, but he improved
his productivity during the latter part of the
season, and the American Giants were the
strongest team in black baseball that year.

After a season in Chicago, he and Lloyd
returned East to play with the Lincoln Stars,
but the duo returned to Foster's team late in
the season to help the American Giants defeat
the Indianapolis ABCs for the 1915 western
title. Gans stayed in Chicago for the 1916 season, where he hit .372 as a part-time starter,
and jumped back East again to the Lincoln
Giants in 1917 and back to the American
Giants again the following year. Incomplete
statistics show averages of .269 and .245 for
the two seasons, while he was still playing on
a part-time basis.

He was eligible for the World War I draft
in 1918 and the Chicago American Giants were
concerned about his status, but he was not
called into military service until after the season was already in progress. While serving
overseas in France as a lieutenant with the 59th
French Division, he learned to speak French
fluently and, according to the press, was "a
hero to the French women." After the Armistice he was welcomed back to the United

States with a "wonderful reception" from
the fans.

Back home by the spring of 1919, he returned to the diamond, and despite batting only
.188 as a part-timer, remained with the American Giants through 1920. As he got older he
began taking more turns on the mound when
the occasion required, playing less in the outfield. During the '10s incomplete records show
an aggregate 5–3 ledger for his mound work.
In 1921 he returned East again to the Lincoln
Giants and took over the managerial reins in
1924–25. The playing manager tried to pitch
in 1924, but his arm didn't respond, and his
batting average dipped to .176. In earlier years,
the left-handed swinger hit .340 for three winters in Cuba and took an occasional turn on
the mound.

During his earlier stays in New York, the
former football star at Washington, Pennsylvania, left the Lincoln Giants for short stints with
other New York teams. In 1912 he was with
the Smart Set briefly, and he played the "sun
field" for the Lincoln Stars. When the ball was
hit to left field, fans yelled, "It's in the well
now." His last fling as a manager was with the
Cuban Stars in the Eastern Colored League in
1927. After his career as a playing manager ended,
he became an umpire, working in both the East-
West League and the Negro National League. Hall
of Famer "Judy" Johnson was given his nickname
due to his resemblance to Jude.

Gant
Career: 1887   Position: 3b
Team: *Pittsburgh Keystones*

He was a third baseman with the Pittsburgh
Keystones, one of eight teams that were charter
members of the League of Colored Baseball
Clubs in 1887. However, the league's existence
was ephemeral, lasting only a week.

Gantz
[see Gomez, Harry,]

Garay, Martiniano Arguelles (**José**)
Career: 1950   Position: p

Teams: New York Cubans ('50), *Mexican League ('56–'57)*
Bats: Right   Throws: Right

The right-handed pitcher fashioned a perfect 5–0 record with an impressive 3.06 ERA for the 1950 New York Cubans in his only year in the Negro Leagues. However, the Negro American League's quality had declined considerably by this season as the flow of younger players into organized baseball continued. The ensuing winter he had a 1.91 ERA while splitting two decisions with Almendares in the Cuban winter league. Pitching with Fresnillo in the Central Mexican League in 1956–57, he had a composite 10–18 record for the two seasons with ballooning ERAs of 5.94 and 8.35.

Garcia, Antonio Maria
Career: 1905–12   Positions: c, 1b, of
Teams: All Cubans ('05), Cuban Stars (West) ('09–'12)

He was the best Cuban player of the nineteenth century and one of the best Cuban catchers of all time. He earned election to the Cuban Hall of Fame in 1939 in recognition of his career in his homeland that spanned 24 years (1882–1905). In later years he also played first base, and he batted cleanup for the Cuban Stars (West) in 1912, his last year in the United States.

Garcia, Atires (Angel)
Career: 1945–50   Position: p
Teams: Cincinnati Clowns ('45), Indianapolis Clowns ('46–'53)
Bats: Left   Throws: Left

A pitcher for the Indianapolis Clowns during the latter seasons of the Negro American League as a viable major league, he broke into the league in 1945 with a 7–6 record and a 2.65 ERA and followed in 1946 with another winning season, posting a 7–5 record. However, he was not utilized as much for the remainder of his career, showing only a 0–3 record in 1948. In 1945–46 he hit for averages of .237 and .324.

Garcia, John
Career: 1904   Position: c
Team: Cuban Giants

He was a catcher with the 1904 Cuban Giants in his only year with a top black team.

Garcia, Manuel (**Cocaina**)
Career: 1926–36   Positions: **p**, rf, lf, 1b, *2b, 3b, ss, c*
Teams: Cuban Stars (West) ('26–'31), Cuban Stars ('33), New York Cubans ('35–'36), *Santo Domingo ('37), Mexican League ('41–'49)*
Bats: Left   Throws: Left
Height: 5'8"   Weight: 185
Born: Cuba

The little short, stocky, hard-throwing Cuban left-hander had a big curve, a good drop, and a fastball that was described as being "like lightning." He was given his nickname because his pitching was like giving the batters a dose of cocaine and putting them to sleep. He pitched in the Negro Leagues for eleven seasons, with the Cuban Stars and the New York Cubans. Beginning his baseball career in 1926, he posted a 3–6 pitching record and a .388 batting average in 1927. After the first Negro National League broke up the following the 1931 season, he returned with the Cuban Stars in the new Negro National League in 1933. Two years later he signed with Alejandro Pompez's New York Cubans, and they won the second half of the Negro National League's split season, but lost a close 7-game playoff to the Pittsburgh Crawfords.

The next season, 1936, was his last season in the United States, but he continued for many more years in the Latin leagues. In 1937, while playing with the Estrellas Orientales team in Santo Domingo, he was classed with Satchel Paige and Martin Dihigo as the "three big pitchers" in the league, and led his team in victories with a 5–3 record for the season and hit .254. Later, pitching with Havana in the Cuban winter league, he led the league in victories three years, twice in succession. In 1942–43 he led with 10 wins and tied for the lead with 12 wins the following season, with one of his victories being a 5–0 no-hitter against Marianao. He again led the league with 10 victories against only 3 losses in the winter of 1946–47, finishing his Cuban career with a lifetime record of 85–61.

After leaving the Negro Leagues, he also starred in the Mexican League during the '40s. His best seasons were in 1942–46, when he had records of 19–14, 16–12, 13–10, 18–11, and 14–10. He finished his career in Mexico with a lifetime 96–68 ledger and a 3.82 ERA.

He was a good hitter for a pitcher and, when not on the mound, he would sometimes fill an outfield position. He was credited with disparate averages of .192 and .480 for the 1935–36 seasons with the New York Cubans.

Garcia, Regino
Career: 1905   Position: c
Team: All Cubans ('05)

In 1905 he was a catcher with the All Cubans team, one of the top Cuban teams of the era.

Garcia, Romando (Cheno)
Career: 1926–27   Positions: 2b, 3b
Teams: Bacharach Giants ('26), New York Lincoln Giants ('27)

The Cuban infielder was an average player in the field and at bat, but filled a weak spot in the lineup as the starting second baseman for the Eastern Colored League champion Bacharachs in 1926, hitting .237 while batting at the bottom of the order. He played with the Lincoln Giants the following season, his last in the United States.

Garcia, S.
Career: 1904–05   Position: of
Team: All Cubans ('04–'05)

During the early years of the century he was an outfielder with the All Cubans team for two seasons.

Garcia, Silvio
Career: 1940–47   Positions: **ss**, 3b, of, p, 2b

Teams: *Santo Domingo ('37)*, Cuban Stars ('40), *Mexican League ('41–'45, '48)*, New York Cubans ('46–'47), *Provincial League ('49–'51)*, *minor leagues* ('52)
Bats: Right   Throws: Right
Height: 5'11"   Weight: 190
Born: Oct. 11, 1914, Limonar, Cuba
Died: 1978, Cuba

Beginning his career as a pitcher, he was struck on the arm by a line drive while sitting in the dugout, and was forced by the injury to become an everyday player. But for the first three years of his career he was considered a pitcher and registered a 13–12 lifetime record in Cuba, including a 10–2 mark with Marianao in 1936–37. During this time he also pitched in the Puerto Rican winter league, posting a 10–6 mark with a 1.32 ERA with Ponce in the season of 1939–40, while batting .298.

As a New York Cubans' infielder, Garcia compiled batting averages of .319 and .324 in 1946 and 1947, respectively, and played in the All-Star games each of these years. In the latter season he played a major role in the Cubans' drive to the Negro National League championship and World Series victory over the Cleveland Buckeyes.

He was a complete ballplayer who could run, field, throw, hit, and hit with power. He was a good hitter who liked the ball out over the plate and had good power to right field. According to Tommy LaSorda, who pitched against him in Cuba, he was one of the best hitters who never played in the major leagues. As a fielder he could play shortstop or third base, and was on the All Cubans team of 1945–46 as a shortstop. Leo Durocher raved about him being a great fielder. He was also a good base runner, and in 1943 New York Cubans' owner Alex Pompez regarded him as the best player in the Negro Leagues.

In Cuba he had a lifetime average of .282 for 19 years ('31–'54), spent mostly with Cienfuegos. His marks include .295, .293, .314, .351, .303, .329, .254, .288, .344, and .292 for the seasons 1937–48, exclusive of the 1939–40 winter, when he took a year off. His .351 average in 1941–42 was tops in the league. Garcia had a last Cuban hurrah in 1950–51, when he led the league with a .347 average.

As a pitcher in Cuba he had records of 1–2, 1–3, 10–2, 0–1, and 1–4 for the years 1934–39, playing with Marianao except for the last season. Although he was no longer considered a pitcher, he took the mound without a decision in both 1944–45 and 1946–47.

With Mexico City in the Mexican League he hit .366 (29 doubles, 11 triples, 5 homers) in 1941 and .364 (19 doubles, 4 triples, 11 homers) in 1942, each good for fourth place in the batting race. The next three seasons he followed with averages of .301, .314, and .350. After two years with the New York Cubans, he returned to Mexico City in 1948 and hit .295. His lifetime Mexican League average was .335.

In Santo Domingo, playing with Trujillo's championship team in 1937, he hit for an average of .297 and led the league in hits and doubles. However, he lost both of his decisions on the mound. In 1938 he played with Aguila in Mexico and hit .349. Playing third base with Sherbrooke in the Provincial League in 1949–51, he hit for averages of .315, .365, and .346, with the middle season being his best, with 21 homers and 116 RBIs in 106 games to cap the Triple Crown. He rounded out his career with Havana in the Florida International League in 1952, batting .283.

Gardner

Career: 1920–23, 1926 Positions: **of**, 3b
Teams: Baltimore Black Sox ('20), Toledo Tigers ('23), St. Louis Stars ('23), Dayton Marcos ('26)

He began his career as a reserve outfielder with the Dayton Marcos in 1920, and played for five seasons in the Negro Leagues with midwestern teams.

Gardner, Floyd (**Jelly**)

Career: 1919–33   Positions: **rf**, cf, lf, 1b
Teams: Detroit Stars ('19, '31), **Chicago American Giants** ('20–'30, '33), New York Lincoln Giants ('27), Homestead Grays ('28, '32)
Bats: Left   Throws: Right
Height: 5'7"   Weight: 160
Born: Sept. 27, 1895, Russellville, Ark.
Died: 1977, Chicago, Ill.

An outstanding defensive outfielder, Jelly Gardner had a good arm and great range. With his blazing speed, the punch hitter was an ideal leadoff man for Rube Foster's champion Chicago American Giants of the '20s. He loved to run, was a good drag bunter, and could outwait a pitcher to draw a base on balls or get a good pitch to hit. With his ability to collect "leg" hits, steal bases, take extra bases on a hit-and-run play, and sometimes to score from first base on a bunt, he could create a run with his speed. Cum Posey described his approach to the game by saying, "He could steal first base," which made him perfect for Foster's style of play. A left-handed batter, he had some difficulty hitting a left-handed pitcher's curveball. During his eleven years with the American Giants they won four pennants and a World Series.

In 1920 he joined the Chicago American Giants, and for six seasons under Rube Foster his personal performance was inversely related to the team's success. In his first three seasons, although he batted only .182, .219, and .236, the American Giants won the Negro National League pennant each year. In the next three seasons (1923–25) he hit .302, .357, and .287, but the American Giants failed to win a pennant during that interval. Finally, in 1926, with Dave Malarcher at the helm, the two factors correlated as the left-handed line-drive hitter led the team with a .376 average and hit .300 in the playoffs as the team copped a pennant and defeated the Eastern Colored League champion Bacharach Giants in the World Series.

Tough, scrappy, and very argumentative, he was quick to express himself verbally or with his fists. Gardner was a heavy drinker and liked the nightlife, and some players described him as "evil and jealous," while others cited him as being "good with his dukes." Once in a free-for-all with the Kansas City Monarchs, he kicked Frank Duncan in the mouth with his spikes, after Duncan had already been knocked unconscious by a policeman trying to quell the fighting. His disposition made him hard to get along with in the clubhouse. Foster was able to handle players of Gardner's temperament better than Malarcher, and trouble began to develop. In 1924 the right fielder had held out through the early spring of 1924, and in 1927 he jumped to the New York Lincoln Giants for part of the season. The next year he played part of the season with the Homestead Grays, who signed him after he quit the Chicago American Giants. Each year he returned to Chicago for part of the season, returning in 1929 for two more years with the American Giants until Foster died. His batting averages for the prior seasons were .289, .303, and .233.

In 1931 he played with the Detroit Stars, where he batted second in the order instead of his accustomed leadoff spot, and his average dropped off to .193. However, he still retained the same speed and baserunning skills that he had exhibited when he first began his career in black baseball in 1919, as a youngster batting seventh in the order as a part-time starter in left field for the Detroit Stars. His first year with the Detroit Stars was not amicable due to his differences with owner Tenny Blount.

Before signing with the Stars, Gardner learned the game of baseball while attending Arkansas Baptist College, where he was a cross-handed-batting infielder until the coach corrected him. In 1916–17 he played with the Longview Giants in Dallas, Texas, during the summers and returned to school in the fall. In July 1917 he was the left fielder for the Texas All-Stars when he first attracted the attention of the top black teams. He went to Chicago in 1919 and did odd jobs in addition to playing baseball.

After leaving baseball he worked in the post office, and on the Gulf, Mobile, and Ohio Railroad as a porter and waiter until retiring in 1965.

Gardner, James **(Chappy)**
Career: 1908–17   Positions: 2b, 3b
Teams: Brooklyn Colored Giants ('08), Cuban Giants ('12), Brooklyn Royal Giants, Havana Red Sox ('17)

An infielder with several teams during the deadball era (1908–17), including the Brooklyn Royal Giants, Havana Red Sox, Brooklyn Colored Giants, and Cuban Giants, later in life he was the publisher of the *Official Negro Professional Baseball Guide,* which appeared in the '40s.

Gardner, *Kenneth* **(Ping,** Steel Arm)
Career: 1918–32   Positions: p, of, if
Teams: *Chappie Johnson's Stars,* Baltimore Black Sox ('19, '21, '28), *Washington Red Caps* ('20), Brooklyn Royal Giants ('20, '31), New York Lincoln Giants ('20–'21, '24), Hilldale Daisies ('22–'23, '30), *Philadelphia Royal Stars,* Harrisburg Giants ('24–'27), Bacharach Giants ('28–'29), Cleveland Tigers ('28), Newark Browns ('32)

A product of the Washington, D.C., sandlots, he was a little fellow with an underhand delivery. The submariner was a very good pitcher when he was right, but it was hard to keep him in shape. He had a great throwing arm and occasionally played in the infield or outfield. He was also a pretty fair hitter for a pitcher, averaging .215 for a half dozen years during the '20s, but with a high of .345 in 1930. He started his baseball career with Chappie Johnson's team but went to Hilldale until Chappie persuaded him to return. He lost his only decision for the Baltimore Black Sox in 1921 before joining the Lincoln Giants during the season. His most success came with the hard-hitting Harrisburg teams of 1924–27, registering a 9–3 record in 1925. Playing with the Bacharachs in 1929, he fashioned a 2–3 record, and after rejoining Hilldale for a second stint in 1930, he was credited with a 1–3 ledger. Two years later, in his last season in the Negro Leagues with the Newark Browns in the East-West League, he had an identical record.

Garey
Career: 1925   Position: c
Team: Cuban Stars (West)
He was a reserve catcher with the Cuban Stars (West) of the Negro National League in 1925.

Garner
Career: 1886   Position: 3b
Team: New York Gorhams
He was a third baseman with the New York Gorhams, one of the earliest professional black teams.

Garner, Horace Charles
Career: 1949   Position: of
Teams: Indianapolis Clowns ('49), *minor leagues ('51–'61)*
Bats: Right   Throws: Right
Height: 6'3"   Weight: 200
Born: 1925
The outfielder began his career with the Indianapolis Clowns in 1949 and soon entered organized baseball, hitting .359 with good power, 96 RBIs, and 44 stolen bases for Eau Claire in the Northern League in 1951. The next season, with Evansville in the Three-I League, he hit .318 with 23 homers and 107 RBIs despite being walked 111 times in 112 games. This production led to a promotion to Jacksonville in the South Atlantic League, where the free-swinger hit for averages of .305, .323, and .294. Following his three seasons in Jacksonville, he split the 1956 season between Augusta of the South Atlantic League (.287) and Evansville (.354). He finished his career with Cedar Rapids in the Three-I League, batting .313 and .309 in 1958–59, with a final hitless at-bat in 1961.

Garren
Career: 1905   Position: c
Team: All Cubans
He was a catcher with the All Cubans in 1905, the top Cuban team of the era.

Garret, Al H.
Career: 1887   Position: player
Team: Columbia Giants
Nothing is known about his brief baseball career that sandwiched the beginning of the twentieth century except that he managed the Columbia Giants for two seasons, with the team being recognized as one of the top black ballclubs in the West during this time.

Garret, Frank
Career: 1887   Position: player
Teams: *Louisville Falls Citys*
He was a player with the Louisville Falls Citys, one of eight teams that were charter members of the League of Colored Baseball Clubs in 1887. However, the league's existence was ephemeral, lasting only a week. His position is uncertain.

Garrett, Solomon
Career: 1950   Position: 2b
Team: New York Black Yankees
He played second base with the New York Black Yankees in 1950, when the Negro Leagues was struggling to survive the loss of players to organized baseball and the Black Yankees had dropped from league competition.

Garrett, William
Career: 1943   Position: officer
Team: New York Black Yankees
He served as an officer for the New York Black Yankees in 1943.

Garrido
Career: 1918   Position: player
Team: Cuban Stars
He appeared in one game with the Cuban Stars in 1918.

Garrido, Gil
Career: 1944–46   Positions: **2b**, ss, 3b
Team: New York Cubans
Bats: Right   Throws: Right
Height: 5'8"   Weight: 165
Born: 1922, Panama City, Panama
The light-hitting infielder played three seasons for the New York Cubans during the '40s,

beginning his career in 1944 as a reserve second baseman. In 1945 the slick fielding sensation earned a starting position, playing both second base and third base while batting leadoff and hitting .258 for the year. During his last season, 1946, he was a part-time starter, usually batting at the bottom of the order when in the lineup.

Garrison

Career: 1934   Position: 1b
Team: Bacharach Giants

He was a first baseman with the Bacharachs in 1934, when the team entered the Negro National League for the second half in their final effort to retain a major-league caliber of play.

Garrison, Robert

Career: 1909   Position: p
Team: St. Paul Gophers

He was a pitcher with the 1909 St. Paul Gophers, who won the western championship by defeating the Leland Giants in a playoff.

Garrison, Ross

Career: 1889–97   Positions: ss, 3b, of
Teams: New York Gorhams ('89), Cuban Giants ('90)

During his nine-year career (1889–97), the nineteenth-century infielder played shortstop and third base for the two top teams of the era, the Cuban Giants and the New York Gorhams. Each of these teams sometimes played as representatives of a host city in that city's regular league. In 1889 the New York Gorhams represented Philadelphia in the Middle States League in 1889, and in 1890 the Cuban Giants represented York, Pennsylvania, in the Eastern Interstate League.

Garry

Career: 1919   Position: cf
Team: *Pittsburgh Stars of Buffalo*

He was an outfielder with the 1919 Pittsburgh Stars of Buffalo, a marginal team during the end of the deadball era.

Garvin, Leedell

Career: 1942   Position: p
Team: Philadelphia Stars

He was a seldom-used pitcher with the Philadelphia Stars in 1942.

Gary, Charles

Career: 1948–50   Position: 3b
Team: Homestead Grays
Bats: Left   Throws: Right
Height: 5'9"   Weight: 170

An ordinary player afield, at bat, and on the bases, he broke in with the Homestead Grays in 1948, the last year of the Negro National League's existence. The left-handed hitter was the starting third baseman, contributing a .279 batting average to the Grays' pennant race as they captured the last Negro National League flag and defeated the Birmingham Black Barons in the World Series for the 1948 championship. After the demise of the Negro National League he continued for two more seasons with the Grays, as they played as an independent team until disbanding after the 1950 season.

Gaston

Career: 1921   Position: ss
Team: Hilldale Daisies

He appeared in one game at shortstop for Hilldale in 1921.

Gaston, Isaac

Career: 1949   Position: ut
Team: Kansas City Monarchs

He was an utility player with the Kansas City Monarchs when the Negro American League was struggling to survive the loss of players to organized baseball.

Gaston, Robert (**Rab Roy**)

Career: 1932–49   Position: c
Team: Homestead Grays ('32–'49), *Brooklyn Brown Dodgers ('46)*
Bats: Right   Throws: Right
Height: 6'1"   Weight: 185
Born: Mar. 19, 1913, Chattanooga, Tenn.

Considered an average catcher defensively, he was only a fair base runner and, although he had moderate power, he was a little lacking at the plate. After playing briefly in 1932, he became a part-time starter for the Homestead Grays in 1933, catching when Ted "Double Duty" Radcliffe moved from behind the plate to the mound. There is a paucity of statistics from the Depression era, and incomplete data for the years 1933–35 show a composite .155 batting average.

Josh Gibson joined the Grays in 1937, and most of Gaston's career was spent as a backup catcher behind the great slugger, with his only starting seasons behind the plate coming in 1940–41, when Gibson jumped to Mexico. Gaston hit .256 and .220 during his two years as a starter, and .250 and .267 for 1942–43 after he returned to a backup status.

After Gibson's death, Eudie Napier assumed the regular catching duties, with Gaston again in a reserve capacity. His skills had deteriorated somewhat, and his batting average in league play in 1947 was an abysmal .083. In 1948 the Grays won the last pennant in the history of the Negro National League, with Gaston on the roster as a third-string catcher. He continued with the Grays for another season while they played as an independent ballclub before ending his active baseball career.

During his playing days he lived in Homestead in the off-season and was considered an "evil" individual who was rumored to have killed a man. The tough, hard-living receiver was Jud Wilson's roommate and friend and was the only person on the team who could hold Wilson down when he had an epileptic seizure.

Gatewood, Bill (Big Bill)

Career: 1905–28   Positions: **p**, *1b, of,* manager

Teams: Leland Giants ('06–'09), Chicago Giants ('11–'12), Chicago American Giants ('12, '15), New York Lincoln Giants ('14), Cuban X-Giants ('06), Philadelphia Giants, Brooklyn Royal Giants, St. Louis Giants ('15–'17), Indianapolis ABCs ('17), Detroit Stars ('20–'21), St. Louis Stars ('22–'27), Toledo Tigers ('23), Milwaukee Bears ('23), Memphis Red Sox ('25), Bacharach Giants ('26), *Albany Giants ('26')*, Birmingham Black Barons ('27–'28)

Bats: Right   Throws: Right
Height: 6'7"   Weight: 240

Gatewood played with fifteen different teams during his twenty-four-year career, and in addition to his pitching prowess, he was a good hitter and a successful manager. The tall right-hander mastered the spitball and emery ball, and was not hesitant to knock a batter down as a matter of instruction directed at the offending hitter. He was a tremendous pitcher in the early years of black baseball.

Pitching with the Leland Giants in 1909, he started two games in the playoffs for the western championship against the St. Paul Colored Gophers, but lost his only decision. The next season Frank Leland and Rube Foster went their separate ways, with Foster's team becoming the Chicago American Giants in 1911, and Gatewood joined Foster's mound corps in 1912. Although statistical data are sparse, he is credited with winning his only recorded decision that season. Two years later he was with the New York Lincoln Giants, one of the top teams in the East, and posted a 6–8 pitching record and a .433 batting average while also playing in the outfield in his only season in New York. Leaving the Lincolns, he returned to the American Giants for a short stint before signing on with the St. Louis Giants. After an interval in St. Louis, he joined C. I. Taylor's Indianapolis ABCs in 1917, posting a 4–6 record. His next stop was with the Detroit Stars for two years, 1920–21. He posted a 6–9 record in the latter season, including a no-hitter in his win total.

In 1922, he returned to St. Louis to take the helm of the St. Louis Stars in their maiden season. At his new managerial post, Gatewood gave Cool Papa Bell his nickname. Bell was then a young left-handed pitching prospect and showed a remarkable amount of poise for a player of his youth in a game where he struck out Oscar Charleston in a clutch situation. Observing how "cool" the nineteen-year-old had been under pressure, Gatewood added the "Papa" to make the name sound better, and the nickname became a permanent part of Bell's persona. Gatewood made a much more important contribution to Bell's success when he changed him from a pitcher to an everyday player and switched him over to swing from the left side to utilize his speed.

In addition to his managerial duties, he continued his pitching duties as well, splitting two decisions in 1925. The next season, his travels took him South to Georgia, as the manager and ace pitcher for the Albany Giants of the Negro Southern League, and he pitched a no-hitter against the Birmingham Black Barons. The next year he was pitching with the Black Barons, and while posting only a 1–2 record, he helped to develop a young hard-throwing right-hander named Satchel Paige. Included in his instruction to the lanky youngster was how to throw a hesitation pitch. He also served as the Black Barons' manager during his stint in Birmingham.

During his long career he also played with the Chicago Giants, Cuban X-Giants, Philadelphia Giants, Brooklyn Royal Giants, Toledo Tigers, Memphis Red Sox, and Milwaukee Bears.

Gatewood, Ernest
Career: 1914–27   Positions: **c**, 1b, of, *2b*
Teams: New York Lincoln Giants ('14–'15, '22–'23), Mohawk Giants ('14–'15), **Brooklyn Royal Giants** ('14–'18, '20–'21), **Bacharach Giants** ('19–'21, '24–'27), Harrisburg Giants ('27)

He began his career as a backup catcher looking for a home with several New York teams in 1914, and in 1917, playing with the Brooklyn Royal Giants as a catcher-first baseman, he hit .231. As a veteran receiver in the '20s, he had an adequate arm and was a fair hitter but very slow afoot, but after a dozen years in black baseball he was a backup catcher

for the Bacharachs as they won consecutive Eastern Colored League pennants in 1926–27, batting .241 the first year.

Gavin
Career: 1935   Position: p
Team: Brooklyn Eagles

He was a seldom-used pitcher with the 1935 Brooklyn Eagles, in their last season before being consolidated into the Newark Eagles.

Gay, Herbert
Career: 1929–30   Positions: **p**, *of*
Teams: Chicago American Giants ('29), Birmingham Black Barons ('30), Baltimore Black Sox ('30)

As a pitcher, he registered seasons of 1–2 in 1929 with the Chicago American Giants and 1–1 in 1920 with the Birmingham Black Barons and the Baltimore Black Sox. During his two years in the Negro Leagues, he also garnered some playing time in the outfield. His brother W. Gay also pitched with the American Giants in 1929.

Gay, W.
Career: 1929   Position: p
Team: Chicago American Giants

He joined his brother Herbert on the Chicago American Giants' pitching staff in 1929, his only year with the ballclub.

Gearhart
Career: 1919   Position: player
Team: Brooklyn Royal Giants

He played in one game with the Brooklyn Royal Giants in 1919.

Gee, Richard (Rich)
Career: 1923–29   Positions: **c**, cf
Teams: *New Orleans Crescent Stars* ('22), New York Lincoln Giants ('23–'26), *Miami Giants* ('34)

As a youngster with fewer than three years' playing experience, he replaced Doc Wiley as the regular catcher for the New York Lincoln Giants in 1924 and hit .349 despite missing about a third of the season due to illness and injuries. He was a very reliable catcher, being a capable receiver with a good throwing arm, but was only a fair base runner. Although hitting in the lower part of the batting order and regarded by some as only a fair hitter, he hit .341 in 1925, making two straight years over .300. He also played in the outfield with both the Lincoln Giants and the New Orleans Crescent Stars, and was with the Miami Giants in 1934. His brother Tom was also a catcher with the Lincoln Giants for two years, 1925–26.

Gee, Sammy

Career: 1948   Positions: **ss**, of
Teams: *minor leagues ('47–'49, '53)*, New York Cubans ('48), *Detroit Stars ('55)*
Bats: Right   Throws: Right

In 1948, after being released by Olean in the Pony League while hitting .324, the shortstop was signed by the New York Cubans for the remainder of the season, where he batted in the eighth position in the lineup and shared playing time with Ballesteros. The next season he made another attempt at organized baseball with Sioux Falls in the Northern League but hit only .135 in a dozen games. Another effort with the same team in 1953 resulted in a .154 average in only 4 games. This was the end of his organized baseball career, which began in 1947 with Three Rivers in the CanAm League, where he hit a dismal .184 in 37 games.

Gee, Thomas (**Tom**)

Career: 1925–26   Positions: **c**, of
Teams: New York Lincoln Giants ('25–'26), Newark Stars ('26)

A catcher for two seasons in the Eastern Colored League, he hit .298 with the Lincoln Giants in 1925. The next season he was the starting catcher for the Newark Stars, but batting at the bottom of the order, until they disbanded at midseason, and then he returned to the Lincoln Giants. Baseball has produced several brother batteries, but during his stints with the Lincoln Giants, he and his brother Rich formed a unique combination of brothers who were both catchers on the same squad.

George, John

Career: 1921–25   Positions: ss, 3b
Teams: *New Orleans Crescent Stars ('21)*, Chicago American Giants ('22), Chicago Giants ('23), Harrisburg ('24), Bacharach Giants ('24–'25)

He was a reserve infielder with the Chicago American Giants in 1922, playing both shortstop and third base. In 1924 he had a shot at the starting shortstop position in the unsettled infield situation at Harrisburg, but his play failed to impress the management and he was released late in the season. The infielder finished the season as a third baseman with the Bacharachs and made a pretty good showing. He was a fair fielder with a good arm but a light hitter, batting a composite .231 for the season. His weak bat kept him out of the starting lineup in 1925, his last season with a quality team.

Gerrard, Alphonso (Al)

a.k.a. Gerald
Career: 1945–49   Positions: lf, rf
Teams: New York Black Yankees ('45–'47), Indianapolis Clowns ('47–'49), American Giants ('48), *minor leagues ('50), Canadian League ('51–'52)*
Bats: Right   Throws: Left
Height: 5'10"   Weight: 180

A mediocre contact hitter without appreciable power, he hit for averages of .258 and .128 in 1945 and 1947 with the New York Black Yankees and .262 in 1948 with the Chicago American Giants. During the 1947 season he was also with the Indianapolis Clowns as their starting right fielder, hitting .340 while batting seventh in the order. The outfielder was an average player defensively and could also fill in at an infield position. A fast base runner, he could steal a base when needed. He also developed a good eye at the plate.

He broke in as a right fielder with the New York Black Yankees in 1945 after manager George Scales discovered him in the winter league in Puerto Rico where, although he was from St. Thomas in the Virgin Islands, he played as a Puerto Rican with Santurce. He was projected as a deadly hitter and tabbed as a coming star of the league, but the failed to live up to his advance billing. He was usually placed in the lower part of the order with the Black Yankees and Clowns when he was in the lineup, but with the Chicago American Giants in 1948, he batted in the third slot.

Entering organized baseball in 1950, he split the season between Kingston of the Colonial League (.333) and Pittsfield of the CanAm League (.258). The next two seasons he played in the Canadian Provincial League, batting .337 and .303 with Three Rivers and Granby. Leaving Canada, he returned to Puerto Rico to play with Santurce, where he had been discovered by Scales, and hit .282 and .335 in the winters of 1953–55.

Gholston, Bert E.
Career: 1923–43   Position: umpire
Leagues: NNL, EWL

He was one of the top umpires in the Negro Leagues, arbitrating for twenty years in the Negro National League and the only season of the East-West League's existence.

Giavanni, Beale
Career: 1948   Position: p
Team: New York Black Yankees
Bats: Left   Throws: Left

A young southpaw from New York City and considered a brilliant prospect, he pitched with the New York Black Yankees in the early spring of 1948.

Gibbons
Career: 1923   Position: 3b
Team: Harrisburg Giants

He was a reserve third baseman with the Harrisburg Giants in 1923, his only appearance in the Negro Leagues.

Gibbons, Walter Lee
Career: 1941–49   Position: p
Team: Philadelphia Stars ('41), New York Black Yankees ('41), Indianapolis Clowns ('48–'49)

A seldom-used pitcher, he lost his only decision in 1941 while splitting the season between the Philadelphia Stars and the New York Black Yankees in the Negro National League. After World War II he signed with the Indianapolis Clowns in the Negro American League and pitched for two seasons, 1948–49.

Gibson
Career: 1918   Position: p
Team: *Dayton Marcos*

He was a pitcher with the Dayton Marcos in 1918, when they were an independent team of marginal quality.

Gibson, B.
Career: 1927   Position: p
Team: Cleveland Hornets

He was a pitcher with the 1927 Cleveland Hornets during their only season in the Negro Leagues.

Gibson, Jerry
Career: 1934–43   Positions: p, of
Teams: Homestead Grays ('34), Cincinnati Tigers ('36, *'40, '43*)
Bats: Right   Throws: Right
Height: 6'1"   Weight: 170

In 1934 he pitched briefly with the Homestead Grays while his brother Josh Gibson was playing with the rival Pittsburgh Crawfords on the other side of town. Later he made appearances with the Cincinnati Tigers, as an outfielder in 1936 and on the mound in the early '40s.

Gibson, Joshua (**Josh**)
Career: 1929–46   Positions: c, of, 3b, 1b
Teams: **Homestead Grays** ('29–'31, '37–'40, '42–'46), **Pittsburgh Crawfords** ('32–'36), *Santo Domingo ('37), Mexican League ('40–'41)*
Bats: Right   Throws: Right
Height: 6'1"   Weight: 210

Born: Dec. 21, 1911, Buena Vista, Ga.
Died: Jan. 20, 1947, Pittsburgh, Pa.

In black baseball, only Satchel Paige was a better known personality than Josh Gibson. A natural hitter, the right-handed slugger hit for both distance and average, and was the standard against whom other hitters were measured.

Gibson was aptly titled "the black Babe Ruth," and his indomitable presence in the batter's box personified power and electrified a crowd. The slugger's rolled-up left sleeve revealed the latent strength in his massive arm muscles, and his eyes riveted the pitcher from beneath a turned-up cap bill as he awaited the pitch with a casual confidence. Hitting from a semicrouched, flat-footed stance and without striding, he generated a compact swing that produced tape-measure home runs with such regularity that they came to be expected as the norm.

Gibson was idolized by black youngsters, and in every ballpark they would point to a spot in the remotest part of the field and say, "Josh hit one over there." He is even credited with hitting a fair ball out of Yankee Stadium, and his prodigious homers have taken their place in baseball lore.

An amusing, apocryphal anecdote alluding to Gibson's legendary power is told about a home run he hit in Pittsburgh. The ball jumped out of the park like it was shot out of a cannon, clearing the fence and sailing out of sight. The next day, in Philadelphia, a ball came down out of the sky and landed in an outfielder's glove, whereupon the umpire promptly declared to Josh, "You're out yesterday in Pittsburgh!"

Gibson was credited with 962 home runs in his seventeen-year career, although many of these were against nonleague teams. Many of the individual season marks that are accredited to him also are against all levels of opposition, including 75 home runs in 1931, 69 homers in 1934, and 84 homers in 1936 in 170 games. Regardless of the uneven competition, his power numbers are impressive. In Mexico he hit 44 homers in 450 at-bats with an .802 slug-

ging percentage and, in one winter season in Puerto Rico, he hit 13 home runs in 123 at-bats, smashing a home run every 9.5 at-bats and an extra-base hit per 4.2 at-bats.

He also hit for average, compiling a .354 lifetime batting average in the Negro Leagues, a .373 average for two seasons in Mexico, a .353 average for two winter seasons in Cuba, a .412 average in exhibition games against major-leaguers, and a .479 average while earning the Most Valuable Player Award in the Puerto Rican winter league.

In addition to his slugging prowess, Gibson possessed a rifle arm and, by hard work behind the plate, made himself into one of the best receivers in the league. His only shortcomings defensively was a weakness on pop-ups behind the plate. For a big man he was quick, both behind the plate and on the bases, and was a good base runner. Two of the greatest pitchers in baseball history, Walter Johnson and Carl Hubbell, placed him among the all-time great catchers, and Johnson assessed his major-league value at $200,000, twice the value he placed on Bill Dickey.

Always affable and easygoing, Gibson was well liked and respected by his peers. His popularity extended to the fans, and he was voted to start in nine East-West All-Star games, in which he compiled a sensational .483 batting average. He missed two other All-Star appearances when he spent a pair of prime seasons in Mexico, and on another occasion he was withheld by his ballclub after being selected for the 1938 game; the East squad lost the game without his services.

Born in Georgia, the eldest of three children, Josh completed five years of elementary school before moving North to Pittsburgh, where his father had secured employment as a laborer with Carnegie-Illinois Steel. After arriving in Pittsburgh, he enrolled at Allegheny Prevocational School to study to be an electrician. After the ninth grade he dropped out to become an apprentice in an air-brake factory. In 1927 he also began playing baseball with the Pleasant Valley Red Sox, a Pittsburgh sandlot team, before joining the Pittsburgh Crawfords (at that time a semipro boys' team) later in the season.

He was starring for the Crawfords when he first attracted the attention of the Homestead Grays. One account has him playing an isolated game with the Grays in July 1929, but the husky teenager was not signed for regular duty as a professional player with the Grays until after he was pressed into service behind the plate late in the 1930 season, when Buck Ewing split a finger. Immediately the big catcher transformed a good team into a great team, and the Grays defeated the New York Lincoln Giants in the playoffs for the eastern championship. He is credited with a .441 batting average for his first season with the Grays and .367 the following year when, playing amid one of the greatest aggregations of talent ever assembled, he was credited with 75 home runs to spearhead the Grays' drive to another championship.

Leaving the Grays to join Gus Greenlee's Pittsburgh Crawfords in 1932, Gibson combined 34 home runs with a .380 batting average in his initial season with the club. Thereafter he recorded batting averages of .464, .384, .440, and .457, and he slugged 69 home runs in 1934 to become a star among stars on the great Crawfords teams of the 1930s. Although their existence as a team was brief, the Pittsburgh Crawfords are considered the greatest team in the history of black baseball.

Shortly after rejoining the Grays in 1937, he jumped to Santo Domingo (along with Satchel Paige and several other black Americans) to play for the Trujillo All-Stars. In a short season fraught with political tension, Gibson led the league in batting with a .453 average (more than 100 points ahead of the runner-up) and in RBIs to lead his team to the championship.

Back in the United States for the remainder of the season, he teamed with Buck Leonard to form a power tandem that was the nucleus of a "murderers' row" that restored the Grays to a position of dominance in black baseball. The pennant that season was the first of nine consecutive Negro National League flags the

Grays would win. During the next two seasons, 1938–39, he is credited with batting averages of .433 and .440 and incredible slugging percentages of 1.389 and 1.190.

After these sensational seasons, Gibson succumbed to the lure of South America and the rustle of pesos and spent two summers in Latin American leagues. He split the first year between Venezuela and Mexico, leaving Venezuela when the league folded and joining Veracruz, where he promptly pounded the ball at a .467 clip and, although playing only a quarter of the season, finished only one short of the home-run title. The following year, with the luxury of playing the entire season, he hit .374 and led the league in home runs with 33 (almost double the total of the runner-up), and in RBIs to lead his team to the Mexican League pennant.

His salary in Mexico was $6,000, but when Posey filed a $10,000 suit against him and made plans to take his house, a settlement was reached and he agreed to return to the Grays. After arriving back in the United States in 1942, he lead the Grays to four more Negro National League flags, with batting averages of .344, .474, .345, and .398 for the seasons 1942–45.

Gibson's return coincided with the resumption of the Negro World Series after a fifteen-year hiatus, and in the first four Series played, the Grays broke even. Sandwiched between a pair of losses (Kansas City Monarchs in '42 and Cleveland Buckeyes in '45), the Grays earned back-to-back championships (1943–44) over the Birmingham Black Barons. In the latter Series victory, Gibson hit a cool .400, including one round-tripper.

In 1945, the premier slugger repeated as the league's home-run champion as the Grays won their ninth consecutive Negro National League title.

The exceptional success achieved by every team on which Josh played stands as further tribute to his extraordinary talent. While Gibson was enjoying continued success on the playing field, off the diamond, a dark side of his personal life had begun to manifest itself. Earlier in his career, he had avoided a lifestyle that would lead to dissipation. But by the end of the 1942 season, a decline in his physical and psychological well-being was in evidence, and in January 1943 he was committed to the hospital after having suffered a nervous breakdown. For the remainder of his life he was plagued with personal problems resulting from excessive drinking and possible substance abuse.

Players returning from the service after World War II noticed the marked deterioration in both his playing skills and his health. Although he could still hit, his power had diminished and his defensive skills had eroded. Once a superb physical specimen, Gibson could no longer get down in a catcher's squat and resorted to trying to catch by standing up and just stooping down. By the end of the 1946 season he was only a shadow of his former self but still demonstrated awesome power, smashing a 550-foot home run in St. Louis against the Buckeyes in a 12–2 victory in front of 20,000 fans. He finished the season with a batting average of .361, with a slugging percentage of .958. Even in the last year of his career, he maintained his graceful, fluid swing and was a marvel to watch swinging a bat.

When Gibson was in his prime, Washington Senators' owner Clark Griffith had once sent for Gibson and Buck Leonard to come to his office to discuss the possibility of the pair of slugging playing for the Senators. Years had passed but, as the beginning of 1947 approached, Jackie Robinson was slated for duty with the Brooklyn Dodgers in the spring and, despite his limitations, the fading star still clung to visions of playing major-league baseball.

When Gibson suffered a fatal stroke only a month after his thirty-fifth birthday and just a few months prior to Robinson's becoming the first black major-leaguer in more than half a century, romantics attributed his untimely death to a broken heart from disappointment at not getting the same opportunity. Regardless of the cause, the greater loss was suffered by the American sports world, who never were afforded the opportunity to witness Josh Gibson's greatness in the major leagues.

In 1972, preceded only by Satchel Paige, Gibson became the second player from the Negro League to be inducted into the Hall of Fame.

Gibson, Joshua, Jr. (Josh)

Career: 1949–50   Positions: 3b, 2b
Teams: *minor leagues ('48)*, Homestead Grays ('49–'50), *Canadian League ('51)*
Bats: Right   Throws: Right
Height: 5'10"   Weight: 170
Born: Aug. 11, 1930, Pittsburgh, Pa.

The son of the greatest slugger Josh Gibson, he played briefly in organized baseball in 1948 after being signed at age seventeen by the Youngstown (Ohio) Colts of the Class C Mid-Atlantic League, immediately after his graduation from Schenley High School in Pittsburgh. While with Youngstown, in addition to the pressure of living up to his name, the youngster had sociological stress relating to his presence on the previously all-white team. The team had to have a meeting to decide who would room with him, and he was told not to drink out of the water ladle. These factors contributed to a low batting average, and he did not hit well enough to stick with the team.

The next season he was given a chance with the Grays because of his father, and for two years (1949–50) he played with the Grays. His father's close friend Sam Bankhead was his manager and mentor. As a second baseman he had difficulty with the pivot on double plays, and Bankhead moved him to third base. Following the breakup of the Grays, he went with Bankhead to Farnham in the Canadian Provincial League, where he played third base and hit .230 with average power for the '51 season. He was very fast on the bases; Bankhead gave him the green light to run, and he pilfered 20 bases in 68 games before breaking his ankle sliding into second base. Despite the injury, he continued to play with the ankle deadened with

Novocain. But that was to be his last year in baseball, and at age twenty-one his career was ended.

As a youngster, he had been the Pittsburgh Crawfords' batboy when his father was with the team. His mother died giving birth to him and his twin sister, and he was reared by his grandmother, but in later years he developed a close relationship with his father. However, Bankhead served as a surrogate father and probably had a greater influence on him than his real father. After their baseball careers had ended, he and Bankhead worked together for the city of Pittsburgh's Sanitation Department. He later had to retire because of health conditions that eventually necessitated a kidney transplant.

Gibson, Paul
Career: 1934–35   Position: p
Teams: Homestead Grays ('34), Newark Dodgers ('35)

For two years during the depression, this pitcher made appearances with the Homestead Grays and the Newark Dodgers.

Gibson, Ted
a.k.a. Gipson
Career: 1941   Positions: p, 3b, lf
Teams: *Columbus Buckeyes ('40)*, Chicago American Giants ('41)

Primarily a pitcher with the Chicago American Giants in 1941, he also played at third base and in left field. The previous season he had played as an infielder with the Columbus Buckeyes, an independent team of lesser caliber.

Gibson, Welda
Career: 1949–50   Position: p
Teams: Houston Eagles ('49–'50), *minor leagues ('55–'57)*
Bats: Both   Throws: Right
Born: 1929

Pitching with the 1949–50 Houston Eagles, he compiled records of 3–4 and 4–12 with ERAs of 3.70 and 6.50. After entering organized baseball, he pitched with Yuma in the

Arizona-Mexico League and finished with a 6–5 record and a 5.22 ERA in 1955. He also pitched briefly, without a decision, with Oklahoma City, Victoria, Tucson, and Hobbs during the 1955–57 seasons. At the plate he was a woeful hitter, striking out almost 60 percent of the time he came to bat in 1950.

Gilbitee, Juan
Career: 1947   Position: p
Team: Indianapolis Clowns ('47)

He was a pitcher with the Indianapolis Clowns in 1947, his only season in the Negro Leagues.

Gilchrist, Dennis
a.k.a. Gilcrest
Career: 1931–35   Positions, c, 2b, *ss, 3b, of*
Teams: Indianapolis ABCs ('31), Columbus Blue Birds ('33), Cleveland Red Sox ('34), Homestead Grays ('34), Brooklyn Eagles ('35)

This catcher-infielder was an all-purpose player with the Columbus Blue Birds, who were entered in the Negro National League for the first half of the 1933 season before the franchise experienced difficulties and withdrew from league play. He played four different positions, and is credited with a .279 average while hitting sixth in the batting order. During the five Depression years in which he played, he was usually with franchises struggling to remain solvent and maintain quality baseball. In addition to Columbus (who folded after the 1933 season), these ballclubs included the Indianapolis ABCs (who folded after the 1932 season), the Cleveland Red Sox (who folded after the 1934 season), and the Brooklyn Eagles (who folded after the 1935 season).

Gilers
Career: 1928   Position: cf
Team: Birmingham Black Barons

The outfielder appeared with the Birmingham Black Barons in 1928.

Giles, George Franklin
Career: 1927–39   Positions: **1b**, of

Teams: *Kansas City Royal Giants ('25), Gilkerson Union Giants ('26, '29)*, Kansas City Monarchs ('27–'28, '32–'34, '39), St. Louis Stars ('30–'31), Philadelphia Stars ('32, '38), Detroit Wolves ('32), Homestead Grays ('32), Baltimore Black Sox ('33), Brooklyn Eagles ('35), New York Black Yankees ('36–'38), Pittsburgh Crawfords ('38), Satchel Paige's All-Stars ('39)

Bats: Left   Throws: Right
Height 6'1"   Weight: 180
Born: May 2, 1909, Junction City, Kan.
Died: Mar. 3, 1992, Manhattan, Kan.

He was an exceptionally skilled defensive first baseman whose speed allowed him to play a very deep first base and extended his defensive range into short right field. The hustling ballplayer was also a fast base runner, a good bunter, and an outstanding hit-and-run man. A good all-around hitter, he was basically a slash hitter who used a flat-footed open stance and went with the pitch, hitting line drives to all fields. Against Satchel Paige and other pitchers with exceptional speed, he adapted by choking up on the bat and punching the ball.

Giles started playing baseball at age twelve and had a tryout with the Kansas City Monarchs at age fifteen, but his inexperience was apparent to manager José Mendez, and he was farmed out for more seasoning. On his sixteenth birthday in 1925, he signed to play with the Kansas City Royal Giants, a team of lesser status, for $120 a month. The next year, in 1926, he went with Gilkerson's Union Giants, based in Spring Valley, Illinois, who were barnstorming through Minnesota, North Dakota, and Canada. With the additional playing experience, he signed with the Monarchs in 1927 at age seventeen and recorded batting averages of .292 and .302 in his first two years with the Monarchs.

In 1929 he became embroiled in a salary dispute and became the first player to hold out in the franchise's history, jumping back to Gilkerson's Union Giants for the 1929 season, then getting married in the off-season.

When Mule Suttles jumped the St. Louis Stars for the eastern habitat of the Baltimore Black Sox, Giles was signed by the Stars to fill the vacancy at first base. For the next two seasons he batted second in the lineup behind the fabulous Cool Papa Bell, hitting .320 and .239 in 1930–31 as the Stars captured consecutive NNL championships. When the St. Louis Stars clinched their first pennant in Indianapolis, emotions ran high and the players had to lie down in the bus to get out of town without a riot.

After the 1931 season, the NNL broke up, and Giles joined the Homestead Grays for the first part of the 1932 season but rejoined the Monarchs, along with Willie Wells and Newt Allen, after the team reorganized in June, and Giles finished the year with a composite .308 batting average. During this stint with the Monarchs, he played in the *Denver Post* Tournament in 1934 against Satchel Paige, who pitched with the House of David in the tournament.

Giles left Kansas City again after the 1934 season and traveled East to play with the Brooklyn Eagles. Ben Taylor was the Eagles' manager, and Giles was appointed captain of the team, but early in the season Taylor's conservative play led to his dismissal, and Giles, at age twenty-six, was elevated to manager and paid $450 a month, his top salary in the Negro Leagues. In recognition of George's sterling glovework and all-around ability, he was selected to the 1935 All-Star team, and he finished the season with a .365 batting average.

When the Eagles were consolidated with the Newark Eagles, Giles joined the New York Black Yankees for three seasons (1936–38) before going back with the Monarchs for a third time, in 1939. Incomplete statistics show averages of .277 and .372 in 1936–37 with the Black Yankees. He spent part of the 1938 season with the Philadelphia Stars and the Pittsburgh Crawfords before going back to Kansas City, ending with a combined .267 average for the year.

In 1939 he retired, allegedly because of racism, and is credited with a lifetime batting average of .309. During his career he played in the winter leagues of several Latin American countries, including with Cienfuegos, Cuba, in 1930, in Mexico on the Kansas City Monarchs' tour in 1932, and with San Juan, Puerto Rico, in 1936. Another highlight from his career was when he barnstormed against Dizzy Dean and Lefty Grove.

After retirement he took a civil service job at Fort Riley, Kansas, and later operated George's Motel and Tavern in Manhattan, Kansas, a dingy establishment accessible only via a back alley. Giles had four children. One of his sons played in the Cincinnati Reds' organization with Frank Robinson, and a grandson, Brian Giles, was signed by the Mets in 1978 and played in the major leagues for five years with the Mets, Brewers, and White Sox (1981–86).

Gilkerson, Robert (Bob)
Career: 1911   Positions: 1b; owner
Teams: Chicago Union Giants ('11); Gilkerson's Union Giants

As a player he only had one season with a team of even marginal quality, when he played first base for the Chicago Union Giants in 1911. Later in life he was the organizer and owner of Gilkerson's Union Giants during the '20s. With his light complexion he passed for white, but problems in his personal life eventually led to his suicide.

Gill, William
Career: 1931–37   Positions: 1b, 3b, of
Teams: Detroit Stars ('31, '33), Louisville Red Caps ('32), Homestead Grays ('33), Indianapolis Athletics ('37)
Bats: Right   Throws: Right

He finished his career as a part-time starter at first base with the Indianapolis Athletics in 1937. His last previous appearance in league play was with the Grays in 1933, where he is credited with a .368 batting average in limited play at third base and in right field. Prior to the Grays, he played on the corners and in the outfield with the Detroit Stars and the Louisville Red Caps.

Gillard, Albert (Hamp)
Career: 1910–14   Position: p
Teams: *Birmingham Giants ('09)*, West Baden Sprudels ('10), St. Louis Giants ('11–'12), Chicago American Giants ('14)

An 18–5 season with Birmingham in 1909 earned this hurler a chance with the top teams, and after a stint with the St. Louis Giants in 1911–12 he pitched with Rube Foster's 1914 Chicago American Giants powerhouse, posting a 2–1 record.

Gillard, Luther (Pen)
a.k.a. Gilliard
Career: 1934–40   Positions: of, 1b
Teams: Memphis Red Sox ('34–'37), Kansas City Monarchs ('38), Chicago American Giants ('38–'39), Indianapolis Crawfords ('40)

Although he had good speed, he was not a good hitter, and most of his seven-year career was spent as a reserve player or spot starter. He was one of several reserve players who saw spot duty in left field with the Memphis Red Sox in 1937, and after appearing briefly with Kansas City as a left fielder, he joined the Chicago American Giants where, as a reserve player, he split playing time between the outfield and first base. His last year was in 1940, with the Indianapolis Crawfords of the Negro American League.

Gillem, Frank
[see Gilliam, James]

Gillespie, A.
Career: 1931   Position: p
Team: Cleveland Cubs

He was a pitcher with the Cleveland Cubs in 1931, when the Nashville Elite Giants relocated to Cleveland and played under the Cubs' banner.

Gillespie, H.
Career: 1887   Position: player
Team: Louisville Falls Citys

He was a player with Louisville Falls Citys, one of eight teams that were charter members of the League of Colored Baseball Clubs in 1887. However, the league's existence was ephemeral, lasting only a week.

Gillespie, Henry
Career: 1917–34   Positions: **p**, of
Teams: Bacharach Giants ('17, '24–'25, '27, '33), *Pennsylvania Giants ('18), Madison Stars ('20–'21)*, Hilldale Daisies ('20–'22, '30), *Philadelphia Giants ('24)*, New York Lincoln Giants ('25), Harrisburg Giants ('26), Philadelphia Tigers ('28), *Quaker Giants ('29)*, New York Black Yankees ('31), Baltimore Black Sox ('31)

This pitcher, who was called "the iron man" while with the Philadelphia Giants in 1924, had a career that covered parts of three decades and was spent mostly with teams along the Philadelphia-New York City axis. With Hilldale in 1921, pitching against all levels of opposition, he won his only decision and had a 1.93 ERA. In 1925, with the Bacharachs, he posted a 2–4 record but was not used extensively afterward by either the Bacharachs or Hilldale in his stints with each team. Throughout his career he sometimes filled an outfield position when not on the mound, and in 1933 he shared the right-field position on manager Otto Briggs's independent Bacharach Giants team.

Gillespie, Murray (Lefty)
Career: 1930–32   Position: p
Teams: Memphis Red Sox ('30–'32), Nashville Elite Giants, Monroe Monarchs ('32)
Bats: Left   Throws: Left

A good left-handed pitcher playing primarily with the Memphis Red Sox during the first three years of the '30s, he had a 6–7 record for the 1930 season. He also pitched with the Nashville Elite Giants and the Monroe Monarchs.

Gillespie, Ward (Pinky)
[see Ward, Pinky]

Gilliam, James William (**Junior**)
a.k.a. Frank Gillem
Career: 1946–50   Position: 2b
Teams: *Nashville Black Vols ('45)*, **Baltimore Elite Giants** ('46–'51), *minor leagues ('51–'52), major leagues ('53–'66)*
Bats: Both   Throws: Right
Height: 5'10"   Weight: 170
Born: Oct. 17, 1928, Nashville, Tenn.
Died: Oct. 8, 1978, Inglewood, Calif.

Reared by his grandmother after his father died when he was only six months old, the youngster began playing softball at age seven and was playing on a sandlot baseball team named the Crawfords at age fourteen. He quit school in his last year of school to sign with Paul Jones's Nashville Black Vols for $150 per month.

After a year with the Nashville Black Vols in the Negro Southern League, Gilliam broke in with the black major leagues in 1946 at age seventeen, as a reserve infielder. He was given his nickname by manager George Scales in 1947, when he was trying out at Sulphur Dell in Nashville. Gilliam was having trouble hitting right-handers and Scales yelled, "Hey, Junior, get over on the other side of the plate," and both the advice and the nickname stuck. The youngster's arm was not considered strong enough for him to play third base, and he was moved to second base. Both changes paid dividends and, in 1947, he succeeded Sammy T. Hughes as the Baltimore Elite Giants' second baseman and formed an excellent double-play combination with Pee Wee Butts during the closing years of the existence of the Negro Leagues.

The youngster was still growing when he debuted in the Negro National League and, although small, he was quick and had good speed, making him an accomplished base stealer and a good fielder, albeit with only an average arm. The infielder was a smart player with great desire and had a good eye at the plate, hitting .253 in his first full season with the Elite Giants. The next year he improved to .302 before dropping back to .265 in 1950. His efforts ended him selection to the East All-Star squad during his last three years in the league, 1948–50.

After the inevitable breakup of the Negro Leagues, the young prospect signed with the Dodger organization and was assigned to Montreal, hitting .287 and .301 in 1951–52 before earning a promotion to the parent club in 1953, where the twenty-four-year-old led the league with 17 triples, received 100 bases on balls, batted .278, and was voted the National League's Rookie of the Year. Initially joining the Dodgers as a second baseman, he played the latter part of his fourteen-year major-league career at third base, finishing with a lifetime major-league batting average of .265.

During a career that spanned two great Dodger eras, Brooklyn's "Boys of Summer" of the '50s and Los Angeles's Koufax Dodgers of the '60s, the speedster stole more than 200 bases. The switch-hitter's best year at the plate in the major leagues was in 1956, when he hit an even .300. He had his best World Series in 1955, when he hit .292 as the Dodgers won their only world championship while based in Brooklyn. Altogether he played in seven World Series, batting .211 in Series action. After retiring as an active player, the popular longtime Dodger became a coach for the team, a position he held until his death in 1978, only one week short of his fiftieth birthday.

Gillard, Feniker
Career: 1938   Position: p
Team: Atlanta Black Crackers

This pitcher from New Orleans was on the roster of the Atlanta Black Crackers of the Negro American League in early spring of 1938, before the two factional Atlanta teams consolidated.

Gilliard, Luther
[see Gillard, Luther]

Gilmore, Quincy Jordan
Career: 1922–37   Positions: business
                          manager, secretary-
                          treasurer
Leagues: NNL, *TOL*

The business manager served as secretary-treasurer of the NNL and later was president of the Texas-Oklahoma League.

Gilmore, Speed
Career: 1926–28   Position: p
Team: New York Lincoln Giants

The big, rangy pitcher from Sanford, North Carolina, showed good speed when he joined the Lincoln Giants in 1926 and was called manager John Henry Lloyd's "busher."

Gilyard, Luther
Career: 1937–42   Positions: 1b, of
Teams: St. Louis Stars ('37), Chicago American Giants ('37–'39), Birmingham Black Barons ('42)
Bats: Right   Throws: Right
Height 5'11"   Weight: 180

This first baseman began his career in 1937 with the St. Louis Stars and was batting in the heart of the order when, at midseason, he left the Stars in the cellar to join the second-place Chicago American Giants. He was the American Giants' regular first baseman until he lost his starting position in 1939. Three years later he again gained a regular position, as the Birmingham Black Barons' first sacker. Not noted as a good hitter with both the Chicago American Giants and the Birmingham Black Barons, he batted in the bottom part of the lineup.

Gipson, Alvin (**Bubber**, Skeet)
Career: 1941–50   Position: p
Teams: *Cincinnati Buckeyes ('40)*, **Birmingham Black Barons** ('41–'47), Chicago American Giants ('41, '49–'50), *Detroit Senators ('47)*, Houston Eagles ('49)
Bats: Right   Throws: Right
Born: Shreveport, La.

This right-handed submariner had a good rising fastball complemented by his underhand curve and good control. A good-hitting pitcher, he joined the Birmingham Black Barons in 1941 but suffered through seasons of 0–7 and 1–4 before improving to a 3–4 record as the Black Barons won the 1943 Negro American

League pennant. In the ensuing World Series against the Homestead Grays, he pitched in 2 games without a decision. The following season he recorded a 10–6 work sheet with a 3.24 ERA as the Black Barons repeated as pennant winners but again lost the World Series to the Homestead Grays.

In the next two years he posted seasons of 2–2 and 5–6 with the Black Barons before leaving Birmingham during the 1947 season. After a stint with the Detroit Senators, a team of lesser quality, he played briefly with the Houston Eagles after the franchise had moved from Newark, and joined the Chicago American Giants for the 1949–50 seasons, registering marks of 6–6 and 2–4. Prior to joining the Birmingham Black Barons he had played with the Cincinnati Buckeyes when they had not yet attained major-league status.

Gipson, Ben
Career: 1948   Position: of
Team: Birmingham Black Barons

The aspiring ballplayer from Grambling College was vying for an outfield position with the Birmingham Black Barons in the spring of 1948.

Gisentaner, Willie (**Lefty**)
Career: 1921–36   Positions: **p,** of
Teams: Columbus Buckeyes ('21), Chicago American Giants ('21), Kansas City Monarchs ('22–'23), Washington Potomacs ('23), *Philadelphia Giants ('24, '26)*, Harrisburg Giants ('25), Newark Stars ('26), New York Lincoln Giants ('26–'27), Cuban Stars (East) ('29), Louisville White Sox ('30–'31), Louisville Black Caps ('32), Pittsburgh Crawfords ('32), Nashville Elite Giants ('33), Homestead Grays ('35–'36)
Bats: Left   Throws: Left
Height: 5'8"   Weight: 180

A ''three-fingered hurler'' due to his mangled throwing hand, he averaged almost one team per season during his sixteen-year career, never staying more than two years with any team. A good-hitting pitcher, throughout most

of his career he also played in the outfield, and his batting averages include marks of .333 in 1936 and .264 in 1932.

His travels included a stint with the 1932 Pittsburgh Crawfords, where he posted a 6–2 record. He began his career in 1921, posting a 1–4 record for the Columbus Buckeyes in their only year in the Negro National League. After stints with the Kansas City Monarchs and Ben Taylor's Washington Potomacs, he signed with Harrisburg in the Eastern Colored League, posting a 5–4 record for the 1925 season. The next year he joined the Lincoln Giants until the Eastern Colored League broke up, and in 1933 he split two games for the Nashville Elite Giants. In 1935 he joined the Homestead Grays for his last two seasons in black baseball, registering a 4–3 record in 1935.

Givens
Career: 1927   Position: ss
Team: Cleveland Hornets

He was a reserve shortstop with the 1927 Cleveland Hornets during the team's only season in the Negro National League.

Givens, Oscar
Career: 1946–48   Positions: ss, 2b
Team: Newark Eagles
Bats: Right   Throws: Right
Height: 6'2"   Weight: 187

Considered a good prospect when he joined the Newark Eagles, this speedy shortstop had good range and a good arm but proved only an average hitter, and was unable to land a starting position during his three seasons with the Eagles.

Gladney
Career: 1932   Position: ss
Team: Indianapolis ABCs

He was with the Indianapolis ABCs briefly as a reserve shortstop during the 1932 season, when the team was in the Negro Southern League, a recognized major league that season only.

Gladstone, Granville A.
Career: 1950   Position: of

Teams: Indianapolis Clowns ('50), *minor leagues ('51–'59), Mexican League ('58)*
Bats: Right   Throws: Right
Height: 5'11"   Weight: 170
Born: Jan. 26, 1925, Panama

The young outfielder hit .240 with the Indianapolis Clowns in 1950 in his only season in the Negro Leagues. The following year he played with Portland in the Pacific Coast League, where he hit .230. He split the next three seasons between Portland and Victoria of the Western International League. The free-swinger hit better with Victoria, posting a .349 average in 1953, but was unable to maintain that level with Portland. After a .219 season in 1954 he was assigned to Eugene of the Northwestern League, where he again topped the .300 mark (.301). The next two seasons he was with St. Paul in the American Association, where he hit .277 and .252. In 1958 he played with the Mexico City Reds of the Mexican League and hit .293, and in the ensuing winter hit .272 with Azucarreros in the Panamanian winter league. His final appearance in organized baseball was in 1959 with Amarillo in the Texas League, where he played in 3 games without a hit.

Glass, Carl Lee (Butch, Lefty)
Career: 1923–36   Positions: **p**, of, 1b
Teams: Birmingham Black Barons ('23), St. Louis Stars ('26), Kansas City ('27), **Memphis Red Sox** ('24, '27–'30), Louisville White Sox ('30), Chicago American Giants ('30), Cincinnati Tigers ('36)
Bats: Left   Throws: Left
Height: 5'10"   Weight: 180
Born: Feb. 26, 1898, Lexington, Ky.

This left-hander had a good curve, and despite a lack of control was regarded as the ace of the Memphis Red Sox during the late '20s, posting records of 7–13 and 6–10 in 1927 and 1929 for the second-division ballclub. The latter year, he tried his hand at managing, as one of three players who piloted the team in 1929. Sometimes he would also play in the outfield or at first base, and in 1929 he had one of his better years at the plate, batting .276. The next

year, after leaving the Red Sox, he was winless for the Chicago American Giants against 3 losses, and in 1926, before he joined the Red Sox, he split 8 decisions. During his fourteen-year career he also played for a short time with the Cincinnati Tigers, Birmingham Black Barons, and Louisville White Sox.

Glen, Hubert (Country)
Career: 1943–49   Position: p
Teams: Philadelphia Stars ('43–'47), New York Black Yankees ('48), *Brooklyn Brown Dodgers ('46)*, Indianapolis Clowns ('49)
Bats: Right   Throws: Right
Height: 6'6"   Weight: 230

The big, hard-throwing North Carolinian broke in with the Philadelphia Stars in 1943 and continued in black baseball for the last half of the decade. He was a good-hitting pitcher, and his career was spent primarily with the Stars, but he also played with the New York Black Yankees, the Brooklyn Brown Dodgers, and the Indianapolis Clowns. He was not related to Stanley Glenn, a catcher on the Philadelphia Stars during that same time frame.

Glenn, Oscar (Pap, Happy)
Career: 1937–38   Positions: **3b**, ss
Team: Atlanta Black Crackers
Bats: Right   Throws: Right
Height: 5'5"   Weight: 152

A little country boy from Stone Mountain, Georgia, he was a natural with the necessary tools for a ballplayer, but suffered from unfulfilled potential. He utilized his quickness, sure hands, and gifted arm to perform adequately at third base, but still had some problems afield, was weak at the plate, and at best a mediocre base runner. He began his career as a shortstop with the Atlanta Black Crackers in 1935 and was impressive through the 1936–37 seasons, but in 1938 he fell into aimless ways and was content to take it easy. The little infielder also disliked the traveling necessary when the team joined the Negro American League and developed a habit of "vanishing" when the ballclub left town on a road trip. Although he was with the Atlanta Black Crackers for most of their 1938 championship season, his actions in refusing to travel away from home eventually led to his being released by the Black Crackers, and by August he was playing semipro ball with the Atlanta Red Caps.

Glenn, Stanley Rudolf (Doc)
Career: 1944–50   Position: c
Teams: Philadelphia Stars ('44–'50), *minor leagues ('50–'53), Canadian League ('54–'55)*
Bats: Right   Throws: Right
Height: 6'3"   Weight: 200
Born: Sept. 19, 1926, Wachatreague, Va.

A big catcher with a strong arm, he broke in with the Philadelphia Stars during the war years while still a student at Philadelphia's John Bartram High School. Oscar Charleston, then a coach with the Stars, scouted the high-school standout and signed him after the end of the school year. After graduation in 1945, he continued with the Stars, and fared better defensively than offensively, with available stats showing batting averages of .211 (1945), .206 (1947), .205 (1949), and .222 (1950). In the winter between his last two years in the Negro Leagues, he was a member of the New York Stars' team that played in Caracas, Venezuela, in 1949.

After returning to the Stars for the first part of the 1950 season, he was signed by Honey Russell, the basketball coach at Seton Hall University and a scout for the Boston Braves' organization. The Braves assigned him to Hartford in the Eastern League, where he hit .259 and .216. After beginning the 1952 season in Hartford, he joined Quebec in the Provincial League for two seasons, where he hit .248 and .275 while also playing the outfield and first base. The next two years were spent with St. Thomas, an independent team in Ontario, Canada.

After leaving the baseball diamond he worked in the wholesale electric supply business until his retirement in 1986.

Glover, Thomas (Tom, **Lefty**)
Career: 1934–45   Position: p

Teams: Cleveland Red Sox ('34), Birmingham Black Barons, Cleveland Red Sox ('37), New Orleans Black Pelicans, Washington Elite Giants ('36–'37), **Baltimore Elite Giants** ('38–'39, '42–'45), *Mexican League ('40–'41)*
Bats: Right   Throws: Left

The tall, hard-throwing left-hander began his career in 1934 with the Cleveland Red Sox and pitched for a dozen seasons, but gained his most acclaim with the Baltimore Elite Giants. His records for the Elites were 4–2, 2–3, 4–3, and 5–5 for the years 1942–45. In his last season in the Negro Leagues, his smoking fastball earned him the starting assignment for the East in the 1945 All-Star game, but he was tagged with the loss when the West took an early lead that was never relinquished.

In 1940 he jumped the Elites to pitch in the Mexican League, registering an 8–13 mark with a 5.30 ERA while splitting his time between Santa Rosa and Nuevo Laredo. After changing teams for the 1941 season, he finished at 4–6 with a 4.27 ERA for Monterrey before returning to the Elites in 1942.

Godinez, Manuel
a.k.a. Guardinez
Career: 1946–49   Position: p
Teams: Indianapolis Clowns ('46–'49), *minor leagues ('50)*
Bats: Right   Throws: Right

Mixing a fastball and curve while pitching with the Indianapolis Clowns during the late '40s, he split a pair of decisions in each of the 1946 and 1948 seasons. After leaving the Clowns, he played with Minot in the Mandak League, posting a 4–2 mark in 1950.

Goines, Charles
Career: 1915–16   Positions: c, of
Teams: Indianapolis ABCs ('15), Bowser's ABCs ('16)

This reserve catcher appeared briefly with the Indianapolis ABCs in 1915, with available statistics showing a .250 batting average for his severely restricted playing time.

Goins

Career: 1932   Position: p
Team: Montgomery Grey Sox

He was a pitcher with the Negro Southern League Montgomery Grey Sox in 1932, the only season the Negro Southern League was considered a major league.

Golden, Clyde

Career: 1948–50   Position: p
Teams: Newark Eagles ('48), Houston Eagles ('49–'50), Cleveland Buckeyes ('50), *New Orleans Eagles ('51), Chicago American Giants ('52)*

This pitcher broke in with the Newark Eagles in 1948, posting a 3–2 record, and accompanied the team to Houston when the Manleys sold the franchise following the season. He split the 1950 season between the Eagles and the Cleveland Buckeyes, finishing with a combined 1–3 league ledger. Although the Negro American League had declined significantly in quality and was strictly a minor league, he returned to the Eagles, who had relocated in New Orleans, in 1951, for a season before joining the Chicago American Giants in 1952.

Golder

Career: 1932   Position: p
Team: Cuban Stars

He was a member of the Cuban Stars' pitching staff in 1932, his only season in the Negro Leagues.

Goldie

Career: 1919, 1926–28 Position: 1b
Teams: Indianapolis ABCs ('19–'26), Cleveland Elites ('26), Cleveland Hornets ('27), Cleveland Tigers ('28)

After making his first appearance in black baseball with the ABCs in 1919, it was seven years before he made his second appearance with a team of major-league caliber. During his three seasons in the Negro National League, he was a reserve first baseman with each of the Cleveland franchises entered in the league.

Goliath, Fred

Career: 1920   Position: of
Team: Chicago Giants

The inaugural Negro National League season, 1920, was the only season for this Chicago Giants reserve outfielder.

Gomez, David

Career: 1925–28   Positions: **p**, *of, 1b, 3b*
Team: Cuban Stars (West)

This right-handed pitcher was in the starting rotation during the latter half of the '20s for the Negro National League Cuban Stars (West), posting a 5–7 record in 1927, and occasionally filled in at first base and in the outfield, showing averages of .167 and .143.

Gomez, Domingo (**Harry**)

a.k.a. Gantz
Career: 1926–29   Position: c
Teams: Harrisburg Giants ('26–'27), Cuban Stars (East) ('27), Philadelphia Tigers ('28), Baltimore Black Sox ('29)

During his four-year career in the Negro Leagues he was a reserve catcher with four different teams in the Eastern Leagues, including the American Negro League champion Baltimore Black Sox in 1929. He began his career with Harrisburg in 1926 and batted .169 with the team in 1927 before moving to the Cuban Stars (East) and the Philadelphia Tigers prior to landing with the Black Sox.

Gomez, Joe

Career: 1932–33   Position: p
Team: Bacharach Giants

He was a pitcher with manager Otto Briggs's Bacharach Giants in the waning years of the ballclub's existence.

Gomez, W. (**Sijo**)

Career: 1929   Positions: p, c
Team: Cuban Stars (East)
Bats: Right   Throws: Right

Listed as both a pitcher and catcher with the American Negro League's Cuban Stars (East) in 1929, the seldom-used right-hander was 2–3 on the mound and had a minuscule .059 batting average in limited play. He was sometimes identified in box scores only as Sijo.

Gonzales

Career: 1918–19   Position: 3b
Teams: Dayton Marcos ('18), Cuban Stars of Havana ('19)

This third baseman played two seasons at the end of the deadball era with marginal teams.

Gonzales, A.

Career: 1910–12   Position: p
Team: Cuban Stars

He was a pitcher with the earlier Cuban Stars team that came to this country during the deadball era.

Gonzales, Gervacio (**Strike,** Strique)
a.k.a. Gonzalez, Gervasio

Career: 1910–17   Positions: **c,** 1b
Teams: Cuban Stars (West) ('10–'11, '14, '16–'17), Long Branch Cubans
Bats: Right   Throws: Right

He was the first great Cuban catcher, and, with José Mendez, formed Cuba's most famous battery. He was Mendez's personal favorite, and in the early years of Cuban baseball was unrivaled as the best receiver. He excelled in all defensive skills but was most noted for his strong and accurate throwing arm, which was seldom equaled. He was also a good base stealer and hit well in clutch situations, and although not considered a heavy hitter, he batted in the heart of the order with the Cuban Stars (West).

He had already been playing nine seasons before he came to the United States in 1910 to play with the Cuban Stars. Installed as the cleanup hitter for the Stars in his first season, he usually hit in the third slot in subsequent years. For eight years, with the Stars and the Long Branch Cubans, he played against the top black teams in this country. In his later years he also played first base and was regarded as a good fielder at that position with the Cuban

Stars in 1917. His entire career was played during the deadball era, both in the United States and in Cuba, where he played for 17 years (1902–19) and finished with a .249 lifetime batting average. Most of his Cuban career was spent with Almendares, and he only hit over .300 two years, in 1915–16 with a .330 average and in 1912 with a .309 average, playing with the Fe ballclub.

While playing with Almendares he twice faced major-league opposition, first against the Detroit Tigers in the winter of 1910, when he hit a disappointing .087, and again the following winter (1911–12), when he redeemed himself against the New York Giants with a .294 average. The high esteem in which he was held in his home country was evidenced in 1939, when he was among the first group elected to the Cuban Hall of Fame.

Gonzales, Hiram (**Rene**)

Career: 1950   Positions: 1b, of
Team: New York Cubans
Bats: Right   Throws: Right
Height: 6'2"   Weight: 206
Born: 1923, Cuba

In his only season in the Negro Leagues, this first baseman-outfielder hit .302 with the 1950 New York Cubans. Most of his career was spent in Mexico, where he was a consistent .300 hitter. Prior to joining the Cubans, he hit .316, .311, and .359 in 1947–49. After his single season with the Cubans, he returned to Mexico and posted averages of .324, .371, .336, .359, .334, and .257 for the next six seasons, 1951–56. During his career he also played winter ball in Cuba, Venezuela (where he led the league in homers, doubles, and RBIs in 1950–51) and Nicaragua (where he hit .340 in 1957–58, his last season). Wherever he played he displayed good power, had more than average success in pilfering bases, and accumulated a high ratio of walks and strikeouts.

Gonzales, Luis (Chicho)

Career: 1910   Position: p
Team: Cuban Stars

While he was not a power pitcher, he had good control and pitched effectively for the 1910 Cuban Stars. In the ensuing winter he pitched for Havana against the Detroit Stars, winning both of his decisions over the American Leaguers, including a 3–0 five-hitter in which he held Ty Cobb hitless. In 1907 he pitched with Fe in the Cuban winter league and was reported to be a white player, but this has not been substantiated.

Gonzales, Miguel (**Mike**)
Career: 1911–16   Positions: **c**, 1b, of
Teams: Cuban Stars ('11–'12, '14), Long Branch Cubans ('13), New York Lincoln Stars ('16)

This catcher also played first base with the Cuban Stars and played in the outfield with the Lincoln Stars.

Gonzales, Miguel (Mike)
Career: 1890   Position: of
Team: Cuban Giants

He was an outfielder with the Cuban Giants when they represented York, Pennsylvania, in the Eastern Interstate League in 1890.

Good
Career: 1890   Position: of
Team: York Cuban Giants

He was an outfielder with the Cuban Giants when they represented York, Pennsylvania, in the Eastern Interstate League in 1890.

Good
Career: 1916   Positions, c, rf
Team: New York Lincoln Stars

He was a seldom-used reserve player with the Lincoln Stars in 1916, playing as a catcher and outfielder.

Good, Cleveland
Career: 1937   Position: p
Team: Newark Eagles
Bats: Left   Throws: Left

This left-hander from Spartanburg, South Carolina, pitched briefly with the Newark Eagles in 1937.

Gooden, Ernest (Pud)
Career: 1922–23   Positions: 2b, 3b, ss
Teams: Pittsburgh Keystones ('21–'22), Cleveland Tate Stars ('22–'23), Detroit Stars ('23), Toledo Tigers ('23), Chicago American Giants ('23)

He was a reserve infielder for two seasons in the early '20s, playing second base and third base mostly with dying franchises. In his first season he played with the Pittsburgh Keystones, who were an independent ballclub. The next year, 1922, they entered the Negro National League and he split the year between the Keystones and the Cleveland Tate Stars, both of whom dropped out of the league at the end of the season. In his next season, he began with the Negro National League's Toledo Tigers, who disbanded in mid-July, before he landed with a good team, the Chicago American Giants, to finish the season.

Goodgame, John
Career: 1917   Position: p
Team: Chicago Giants

The man with the good name was a pitcher with the Chicago Giants in 1917, his only season with a team of major-league caliber.

Goodman
Career: 1928   Position: of
Team: Harrisburg Giants

He was an outfielder with the Harrisburg Giants in 1928, a year after they dropped out of the Eastern League.

Goodrich, Joe
Career: 1923–26   Positions: 3b, 2b, ss
Teams: *Philadelphia Giants,* Washington Potomacs ('23–'24), Wilmington Potomacs ('25), Harrisburg Giants ('26)

The peppy little infielder could play any spot in the infield, and he played for four teams during his four-year career. In 1923 he left Austin, Texas, to join the Washington Potomacs, a team being organized by Ben Taylor. The team played as an independent for a year and then joined the Eastern Colored League in 1924. Goodrich was a good fielder and won a spot at third base for the Potomacs in 1924, his first season in the black big time. But bad luck plagued him. First he hurt his arm in the spring of 1924 and never fully recovered. Then during the winter (1924–25) he was hit by a car, and the injury left his right eye partly paralyzed. But the gutty little guy never gave up. He stayed in condition, continued to give his best effort at all times, and played to win. Because of his attitude and desire to play, he was projected as the starting third baseman for the 1925 season if the Potomacs fielded a team. Unfortunately, after a move to Wilmington, Delaware, the franchise folded early in the spring.

Goodson, M. E.
Career: 1932   Position: officer
Team: New York Black Yankees
    He served as an officer with the New York Black Yankees in 1932, in the franchise's first season.

Goodwin, Alfred (Lon)
Career: 1920   Position: officer
Team: New York Lincoln Giants
    He served as an officer with the Lincoln Giants in 1920, before the franchise entered into league competition.

Gorden, Charlie
[see Gordon, Charles]

Gordon
Career: 1911–15   Positions: **of**, 2b, 1b
Teams: New York Lincoln Giants ('11), *Brooklyn Stars,* Indianapolis ABCs ('14–'15), *West Baden Sprudels ('15)*
    This outfielder joined the Indianapolis ABCs in 1914, the first year that the team was of major-league caliber, and the following year was an alternate starter in right field where, despite a .167 average, he proved to be a heavy

hitter and "fast as lightning" on the bases. Previously he had played with the Brooklyn Stars and, late in the 1915 season, he left the ABCs to play with the Sprudels of West Baden, Indiana.

Gordon
Career: 1923   Position: lf
Team: Baltimore Black Sox
    He was an occasional starter in left field with the Baltimore Black Sox in 1923, the inaugural season of the Eastern Colored League.

Gordon, Charles William (Charlie, Flash)
a.k.a. Gorden
Career: 1939–40   Position: of
Team: New York Black Yankees
    A reserve outfielder with the Black Yankees, he made appearances in both 1939 and 1940.

Gordon, Harold (BeeBop)
Career: 1950   Position: p
Teams: *Cincinnati Crescents ('48), San Francisco Sea Lions ('49),* Chicago American Giants ('50–'51), *minor leagues ('51–'53)*
    He was a pitcher with the Chicago American Giants in 1950, when the Negro Leagues were in rapid decline. He had played earlier with two black semipro teams, the Cincinnati Crescents (1948) and the San Francisco Sea Lions (1949), and began the 1951 season with the Chicago American Giants but left to enter organized baseball with the Paris Lakers of the Mississippi-Ohio Valley League for three seasons, 1951–53. His last appearance on a baseball diamond was with the semipro Detroit Stars in 1954.

Gordon, Herman
Career: 1920–24   Positions: **p**, of, 2b, 3b
Teams: Kansas City Monarchs ('20), Birmingham Black Barons ('24), St. Louis Stars ('23), Toledo Tigers ('23), Cleveland Browns ('24)
    A versatile player, he began his career as a second baseman with the Kansas City Monarchs during the Negro National League's inaugural season, but played primarily as a pitcher

for the remainder of his years in black baseball during the first half of the '20s. Playing mostly in the Midwest, he also served stints in the outfield and infield and averaged playing with a different team for each of his five seasons in the Negro Leagues.

Gordon, Sam

Career: 1905–11   Positions: 3b, ss
Teams: Genuine Cuban Giants ('05–'06, '11) Famous Cuban Giants, Chicago Union Giants

This infielder played with the two best-known teams of his era (1905–10), as a shortstop with the Genuine Cuban Giants and as a third baseman with the Famous Cuban Giants.

Gorham

Career: 1911   Position: rf
Team: Philadelphia Giants

He played right field with the 1911 Philadelphia Giants when the once-proud franchise was in decline.

Goshay, Samuel

Career: 1949   Position: of
Team: Kansas City Monarchs

He was an outfielder with the Kansas City Monarchs in 1949, when the Negro American League was struggling to survive the loss of players to organized baseball.

Goshen

Career: 1931   Position: of
Team: Cuban Stars (East)

He was listed as an outfielder with the Cuban Stars in 1931, his only season in black baseball.

Gottlieb, Eddie

Career: 1936–50   Positions: promoter, booking agent, owner, officer, secretary (NNL)
Team: Philadelphia Stars

For the last fifteen years (1936–50) of the Negro Leagues as a viable major league, this white entrepreneur operated as a promoter, booking agent, owner, and officer for the Philadelphia Stars. He also served a term as secretary of the Negro National League and was often at odds with Effa Manley, owner of the Newark Eagles.

Gould, John (Willie, Hal)

Career: 1947–48   Position: p
Team: Philadelphia Stars
Bats: Right   Throws: Right
Height: 6'0"   Weight: 205

This big, strong, hard-throwing youngster lacked experience and pitching "know-how" to be productive consistently, and his career with the Philadelphia Stars was brief. He hailed from Gouldtown, New Jersey, a town named after a member of his family.

Govantes, Manuel

Career: 1909–10   Positions: 3b, 2b, of
Teams: Cuban Stars ('09), Stars of Cuba ('10)

Beginning his career in the United States in 1909 with the Cuban Stars, he joined the Stars of Cuba the following season, playing third base and batting third in the order. Like most Cuban players of his era, he was proficient in several positions and could play in the infield or outfield. In his homeland, two years before joining the Stars, he played right field with the Fe ballclub.

Govens

Career: 1909   Position: of
Team: *Quaker Giants*

In 1909 he was an outfielder with the Quaker Giants, a marginal team.

Govern, S. K. (Cos, Siki)

Career: 1887–88, 1896 Position: manager
Teams: Cuban Giants ('87–'88), Cuban X-Giants ('96)

Best known as the manager of the Cuban Giants, this West Indian from St. Croix was a smart businessman with a shrewd baseball mind. His involvement with baseball dated back to the early 1880s, when he managed the Manhattans of Washington, D.C., for four years, 1881–84. In March 1887 he and Gilbert

Ball represented Philadelphia at a meeting of the Colored League owners held in Louisville, but he ended up with the Cuban Giants and set up residence at the Cuban House in New York. Following the 1888 season, he and Bright took the team on a southern tour all the way to Jacksonville and spent the winter months playing ball. He reentered the baseball arena with the Cuban X-Giants in 1896, his last involvement with a top team.

Grace, Ellsworth
Career: 1950   Position: 2b
Team: New York Black Yankees

He played second base with the New York Black Yankees in 1950, when the team was playing as an independent ballclub and struggling to survive the loss of players to organized baseball.

Grace, William (Willie)
Career: 1942–50   Position: **of**, *p*
Teams: Cincinnati Buckeyes ('42), **Cleveland Buckeyes** ('43–'48, '50), Louisville Buckeyes ('49), Houston Eagles ('50), *minor leagues ('51)*
Bats: Both   Throws: Left
Height: 6'0"   Weight: 170
Born: June 30, 1918, Memphis, Tenn.

A switch-hitting outfielder with good bat control but without appreciable power, he had only average speed and defensive skills but a pretty good arm. He played with the Negro American League champion Cleveland Buckeyes of 1945 and 1947, and after Ducky Davenport jumped the team late in the 1945 season, the burden fell on Grace, and he responded with some clutch hitting. In the 1945 World Series sweep of the Homestead Grays he batted .313 and contributed a rare home run. In the 1947 World Series the Buckeyes lost to the New York Cubans in five games. Sandwiched between the two Negro American League pennants was his All-Star season of 1946, when the Negro Leagues held two All-Star games and he started in both games, collecting 4 hits in 8 at-bats for an even .500 average.

Although not noted as a strong hitter, with averages of .237 and .232 in 1944–45, he strung together three consecutive .300 seasons (.305, .301, and .322) in 1946–48 before falling off in his production (.221, .273) the following two years. Originally signed in 1942 off the sandlots of Laurel, Mississippi, at age twenty-five, he joined the Buckeyes soon after a tragic automobile accident in which two players were killed. Not long after his arrival, the team had another accident, when the bus turned upside down, but fortunately there were no serious injuries. Grace remained with the franchise as the team relocated in Louisville in 1949, before finishing his career in the Negro Leagues with the Houston Eagles in 1950. The following year, the last in his baseball career and his first in organized baseball, he hit .293 with Erie in the Middle Atlantic League.

Grady
Career: 1924   Position: p
Team: Washington Potomacs

A pitcher from Washington, D. C., he was with the Washington Potomacs very briefly in 1924 but did not demonstrate sufficient baseball skills to remain with the team.

Graham, Dennis
Career: 1918–31   Position: rf
Teams: Washington Red Caps ('18), Bacharach Giants ('21–'22), St. Louis Stars ('22), Homestead Grays ('25–'30), Pittsburgh Crawfords ('31)

The speedy Homestead Grays' outfielder was one of the fastest players in the game before his untimely demise. He was the starting right fielder with the Grays for five seasons, 1925–29, hitting in the third, first, fifth, and second spots in the batting order during the last four seasons. Batting averages from each end of the decade of the '20s show averages over .300 with his hitting .310 in 1921 as a substitute with the Bacharachs and hitting .360 in 1929 as a regular with the Homestead Grays. He dropped out of the starting outfield with the Grays in 1930 but moved across town to the

Pittsburgh Crawfords in 1931, where he was batting in the leadoff spot.

Graham, Vasco
Career: 1895–99   Positions: c, of
Teams: *Colored Capital All-Americans*, Page Fence Giants ('95), *minor leagues ('94–'95), Cuban Giants ('99)*

In 1895 he played a single game as an outfielder with the Page Fence Giants, one of the best black teams of the nineteenth century, but was hitless in the contest. The remainder of the season the Denver native played with Adrian of the Michigan State League, batting .324, but injured his hand in mid-September and missed 7 games. The previous season he played with the Dubuque, Iowa, ballclub. The catcher-outfielder also played with the Cuban Giants in 1899 and appeared with the Colored Capital All-Americans and a Lansing, Michigan, team.

Gransbury, Bill
Career: 1929   Positions: of, 1b
Teams: Chicago American Giants, Chicago Giants

He played briefly as an outfielder-first baseman with the Chicago American Giants and the Chicago Giants in 1929, his only season with a Negro League club.

Grant, Art
Career: 1920   Position: c
Team: Baltimore Black Sox

He played as a backup catcher with the Baltimore Black Sox in 1920, when the team was still struggling to become a major-league-caliber ballclub.

Grant, Charles (Charlie, Chief Tokahoma)
Career: 1896–1916   Position: 2b
Teams: Page Fence Giants ('96), Columbia Giants ('99–'01), Cuban X-Giants ('03, '06), Philadelphia Giants ('04–'06, '13), New York Black Sox ('10), New York Lincoln Giants, Quaker Giants ('09), Cincinnati Stars ('14–'16)
Bats: Right   Throws: Right

Height: 5'8"   Weight: 160
Born: 1879, Cincinnati, O.
Died: July 1932, Cincinnati, O.

One of the first great black ballplayers, he was a good hitter and a smooth fielder, and starred for the outstanding Cuban X-Giants' teams around the turn of the century. Later he became a member of the 1906 champion Philadelphia Giants.

He was light-skinned with straight hair, and John McGraw, managing the American League's Baltimore Orioles at the time, tried to sign the slick-fielding infielder with the Orioles in 1901 by passing him off as an Indian named "Chief Tokahoma." Grant was working as a bellboy at the Eastland Hotel in Hot Springs, Arkansas, and playing on the hotel team for the entertainment of the winter guests when he was discovered by McGraw. Grant had played the 1900 season in Chicago with the Columbia Giants, and Charles Comiskey, president of the Chicago White Sox, alerted by the response of black fans, was instrumental in the exposure of McGraw's plan, and the attempt to bring a black player into the majors was aborted. Grant returned to the Columbia Giants for the 1901 season and also played with the Page Fence Giants, Lincoln Giants, and New York Black Sox during his career.

Grant's childhood was spent in Cincinnati, where his father was a horse trainer. After retiring from baseball, he returned to his hometown and worked as a janitor in an apartment building. In 1932, while sitting outside the building, a passing car blew a tire, jumped the curb, and hit Grant, inflicting fatal injuries.

Grant, Frank
[see Grant, Ulysses F. (Frank)]

Grant, Leroy
Career: 1911–25   Positions: **1b**, *3b*
Teams: **Chicago American Giants** ('11, '16–'25), New York Lincoln Giants ('12–'15), Mohawk Giants ('13), *military service ('18–'19)*, Indianapolis ABCs ('23), Cleveland Browns ('24)

Bats: Right   Throws: Right
Height: 6'4"   Weight: 215

A towering first baseman with a long stretch, he was a good fielder whose career spanned 15 years, including stays with the top teams of both the East and West during the deadball era. In the East he played with the great New York Lincoln Giants of 1912–13, batting .284 and .305 against all competition, and in the West he played with Rube Foster's powerful Chicago American Giants of 1917, where he hit .268. After Foster organized the Negro National League in 1920, Grant held down the first-base positions as the American Giants captured the first three league championships (1920–22).

He hit with good power but not for a high average, usually batting in about the sixth spot in the order. Playing against all levels of competition, he posted averages of .308 in 1914, .263 in 1916, and .290 in 1918, while in league play he batted .234 in 1921. He was very slow on the bases but managed a surprising number of successful stolen bases.

The hulking first sacker was susceptible to bonehead plays in the field and on the bases, and made some critical errors during the 1917 season. Evidently temperamental and moody, he was dropping throws at first base like he had hands of iron and exercised some dubious judgment while plodding around the bases. The press was unkind in their reporting of the incidents, but he apparently overcame the related stigma attached by the media.

In August of the following season, he was drafted into military service for the duration of World War I, but he was back with the Chicago American Giants before the end of the 1919 season but managed only a .198 batting average. After anchoring the infield for the three consecutive pennant winners under Foster's tutelage, in 1923 Grant was sent to the Indianapolis ABCs, whose ranks had been decimated by the raids of eastern teams. But he was back in Chicago before the end of 1924 and was unconditionally released by Foster, along with a large number of other veteran players, in the spring of 1925.

Grant, Ulysses F. (**Frank**)
Career: 1886–1905   Positions: **2b**, ss, p, of, 3b, c
Teams: *minor leagues ('86–'88, '90),* **Cuban Giants** ('89, '91–'97, '99), New York Gorhams, Colored Capital All-Americans, New York Big Gorhams ('91), Page Fence Giants ('91), Cuban X-Giants ('99), Philadelphia Giants ('02–'03), Genuine Cuban Giants
Bats: Right   Throws: Right
Height: 5'7½"   Weight: 155
Born: Aug. 1, 1865, Pittsfield, Mass.
Died: May 27, 1937, New York, N.Y.

This second baseman was one of the most outstanding black professional ballplayers of the nineteenth century. Exceptionally quick afield and with a strong arm, he was called the "black Dunlap" in comparison with Fred Dunlap, the best-fielding white second baseman of the 1880s. Most astute baseball observers felt he could have played in the major leagues if he had been provided the opportunity. During his ten-year career, the middle infielder played with the top black clubs of the era, including the Cuban Giants, New York Gorhams, and Philadelphia Giants. He also played with many teams in organized baseball, since the color line had not been officially drawn there. He was a consistent .300 hitter with power, a fast base runner, an outstanding fielder, and a popular player. He was sometimes referred to as a "Spaniard" to make his presence more acceptable, but he still periodically encountered racial prejudice.

The youngest of seven children, he was given the name "Ulysses F." at birth, but his parents began calling him Frank, probably because his father, Franklin, died when he was four months of age. He began playing baseball as a catcher with a Plattsburgh, New York, semipro team called "Nameless," but he soon advanced to the professional ranks in 1886 with Meriden, Connecticut, of the Eastern League as a combination second baseman-pitcher, and was the leading hitter with a .316 batting average when the team folded in midsummer and he joined Buffalo, where he hit

.344, third best in the International League. The next season he batted .353 and led the league with 11 home runs and 40 stolen bases in 105 games, and was called the best all-around player in Buffalo's baseball history. But despite his success, his stint in Buffalo was not welcomed by everyone and, most likely attributed to racial pressures, his hitting and fielding were adversely affected. In one game against Toronto, fans were yelling "Kill the nigger!" Despite such tribulations, he remained with Buffalo through the 1888 season and hit .346 (tied for fifth best in the league) and again hit 11 home runs, although injured and missing almost a month of playing time. However, the International League eliminated the use of black players within their league, and Grant signed with the Cuban Giants.

In 1889, to avoid future injuries, he began wearing wooden shinguards for protection from runners coming in with spikes high at second base, and on occasion he was moved to the outfield for his own protection. Grant barnstormed in the South with the Cuban Giants and stayed with the team when they came North to represent Trenton, New Jersey, in the Middle States League, batting .313 for the 1889 season while playing both second base and third base. The next year, he jumped to Harrisburg, Pennsylvania, in the Middle States League. Later in the season the team changed to the Atlantic Association and he hit a composite .333. In 1891 he played with the Big Gorhams of New York, who represented Ansonia in the Connecticut State League. But the league folded and the team barnstormed as an independent ballclub for the remainder of the year, finishing with a 100–4 record. But despite the team's success on the diamond, financial conditions forced it to fold and he returned to the Cuban Giants for the greater part of the decade. However, in 1898 he played with the Page Fence Giants in their last year before disbanding. After the turn of the century he played with the strong Philadelphia Giants' ballclub in 1902–03.

After finally leaving the baseball trail, the quiet, modest ex-ballplayer worked as a waiter for a catering service for the last thirty-six years of his life, and died in New York City in 1937 of arteriosclerosis.

Graves, Bob
Career: 1932, 37   Positions: **p**, of
Teams: Indianapolis ABCs ('32), Indianapolis Athletics ('37)

The pitcher began and ended his career in Indianapolis, breaking in with Jim Taylor's Indianapolis ABCs in 1932, when they were a member of the Negro Southern League, and bowing out with the Indianapolis Athletics, charter members of the Negro American League, in 1937. He also filled in as an outfielder with the A's.

Graves, John **Whitt**
Career: 1950   Position: p
Teams: Indianapolis Clowns ('50–'51), *minor leagues ('52–'55)*
Bats: Right   Throws: Right

This right-handed hurler fashioned a 7–8 record with a 3.62 ERA for the Indianapolis Clowns in 1950. For a pitcher he also swung a good stick, batting a respectable .259 and counting three round-trippers in his 54 at-bats that season. Two years later he was in organized baseball with Las Vegas of the Southwest International League and posted a 14–15 record with a 4.74 ERA. The next two seasons found him in the Piedmont League, where he had seasons of 6–12, 6.34 ERA with Richmond in 1953 and 9–6, 4.62 ERA with Petersburg in 1954. In the latter year he again showed his power, with 3 homers in only 45 at-bats. The next season was his last in baseball, as he managed only a 6–13 record with Sioux City in the Western League. That season he also pitched in 4 games with Minneapolis in the American Association, losing his only decision.

Graves, Lawrence
Career: 1923   Position: p
Team: Harrisburg Giants

He was a pitcher with the Harrisburg Giants

in 1923, the year before the ballclub entered the Eastern Colored League and were playing as an independent team.

Gray
Career: 1931   Position: 3b
Team: Nashville Elite Giants
He was a reserve third baseman for the Nashville Elite Giants in 1931, a year before the Negro Southern League was recognized as a major league.

Gray
Career: 1945   Position: p
Team: Newark Eagles
A wartime player, he pitched briefly with the Newark Eagles in 1945, his only appearance in the Negro Leagues.

Gray, Chesley (Chester)
Career: 1940–45   Positions: c, of
Teams: St. Louis Stars ('40), New York Black Yankees ('42), Harrisburg-St. Louis Stars ('43), Kansas City Monarchs ('45)
Bats: Right   Throws: Right
Height: 5'7"   Weight: 170
He began his career in 1940 as a reserve catcher with the St. Louis Stars and in 1943 shared duty as the club's regular catcher when the franchise reorganized with joint home cities in Harrisburg and St. Louis. Defensively he was a mediocre receiver with an average arm, and offensively he lacked speed on the bases and power at the plate, usually batting in the eighth spot. In his last year in the Negro American League he was a spot starter with the Kansas City Monarchs during the last year of World War II (1945), batting .292. In the interim he also was with the New York Black Yankees in 1942, where he hit .167 in a handful of games, and the Toledo Cubs of the U.S. League.

Gray, G. E. (Willie, Dolly)
a.k.a. Grey
Career: 1920–32   Positions: **cf**, 1b, p
Teams: Dayton Marcos ('20), Pittsburgh Keystones ('22), Cleveland Tate Stars ('22–'23),

Homestead Grays ('24–'27), New York Lincoln Giants ('28–'29), *Pennsylvania Red Caps of New York ('30–'34)*, Newark Browns ('32)
A fleet center fielder who excelled defensively, this ballhawk was especially adept at running down fly balls and nonchalantly making outstanding catches look routine. Best identified with the Homestead Grays of the '20s, he often batted in the first or second spot in the order. After leaving the Grays he joined the Lincoln Giants, playing center field and batting leadoff in 1928–29 and posting a .291 average the latter year. During his fifteen-year career he also played with several teams in the East and Midwest.

Gray, Roosevelt (Chappy)
Career: 1920–23   Positions: 1b, 2b, p
Teams: Cleveland Tate Stars, Dayton Marcos, Kansas City Monarchs, Toledo Tigers ('23)
Born: 1900
Died: June 4, 1972
A first baseman with struggling midwestern teams during the early '20s, he also did some mound duty during his short career (1920–23).

Gray, William
Career: 1884–87   Position: of
Teams: *Baltimore Atlantics ('84–'85, '87)*, Lord Baltimores ('87)
In the late 1880s he was an outfielder with teams in the Baltimore area. After playing with the semipro Baltimore Atlantics, the outfielder joined the Lord Baltimores, one of eight teams that were charter members of the League of Colored Baseball Clubs in 1887. However, the league's existence was ephemeral, lasting only a week.

Gray, Willie (Dolly)
[see Gray, G. E.]

Grayson
[see Greyer]

Greason, William (Willie, Bill)
Career: 1948–50   Position: p

Teams: *Nashville Black Vols ('47), Asheville Blues ('48),* Birmingham Black Barons ('48–'51), *Mexican League ('51–'52), minor leagues ('53–'58),* major leagues ('54)
Bats: Right   Throws: Right
Height: 5'10"   Weight: 170
Born: Sept. 3, 1924, Atlanta, Ga.

This right-handed hurler mixed a curve and a fastball effectively to fashion a 6–4 record with a 3.30 ERA to help pitch the Birmingham Black Barons to a Negro American League pennant in 1948. In the World Series he was the workhorse of the Black Barons, pitching in 3 games and gaining the team's only victory over the strong Homestead Grays. The following year he dropped to a 7–12 record but threw 3 shutout innings for the West in the All-Star game.

In 1950, his last year with Birmingham, he rebounded with a 9–6 record and a 2.41 ERA and continued his artistry with Jalapa in the Mexican League, where he was 10–1 with a 3.88 ERA. After slipping to a 1–4 mark in another season at Jalapa, he spent two years with Oklahoma City in the Texas League (9–1, 2.14 ERA and 16–13, 3.62 ERA).

In 1954, after a 10–13 season at Columbus in the American Association, the right-hander had a brief fling at the major leagues when the St. Louis Cardinals brought the thirty-year-old up to the parent club, where he pitched in 3 games and lost his only decision. The remainder of his career was spent with Houston in the Texas League, where he fashioned seasons of 17–11 and 10–6 in 1955–56, and Rochester in the International League, where he managed a composite 16–18 for the years 1956–59. During his career he also pitched winters in Cuba (2–2 in 1950–51) and Puerto Rico (12–6 in 1957–58).

He began his professional career with the Nashville Black Vols in 1947 and began the next season with the Asheville Blues in the Negro Southern League prior to joining the Birmingham Black Barons later in the 1948 season. While a successful pitcher, as a batter he was relatively ineffective and showed a high strikeout ratio. In addition to playing baseball, Greason pursued goals in higher education, and after retiring from baseball he became a minister.

Green
Career: 1920   Position: p
Team: Detroit Stars

He was a pitcher with the 1920 Detroit Stars during their initial season in the Negro National League.

Green
Career: 1931   Position: of
Team: Homestead Grays

He appeared briefly as a reserve outfielder with the Homestead Grays in 1931.

Green
Career: 1939–41   Position: p
Teams: Cleveland Bears ('39), Memphis Red Sox ('41)

He was an infrequently used pitcher during his three years (1939–41) in the Negro American League with the Cleveland Bears and the Memphis Red Sox.

Green, Alvin
Career: 1950   Position: if
Team: Baltimore Elite Giants

This infielder began his career in 1950 with the Elite Giants when the franchise had shifted to the Negro American League after the demise of the Negro National League in 1948, when the Negro Leagues were struggling to survive the loss of players to organized baseball. However, league statistics do not confirm his playing time.

Green, Charles (**Joe**, Greenie)
Career: 1902–31   Positions: **of**, c, **manager**, owner
Teams: Columbia Giants ('02), Chicago Union Giants ('03–'06, '08–'09), Leland Giants ('05–'07, '09), **Chicago Giants** ('10–'21), Chicago American Giants ('12)
Born: July 26, 1878, Chicago, Ill.

Beginning his baseball career in 1900 with a hometown team called the Clippers, this Chicago native left after two years to play with a top team, the Columbia Giants. In 1903 he joined the Union Giants, where he distinguished himself as a ballplayer. Two years later he switched to the Leland Giants in their first year of existence, and was the starting center fielder for two seasons before giving way to Pete Hill and moving to right field for his third season with the team. The next year he returned to the Union Giants to captain the 1908 squad. The following season, when the Leland Giants' outfielder Bobby Winston broke his ankle in midseason, Green was again summoned by owner Frank Leland. Playing in left field, he responded by leading the team in batting with a .330 average, had 7 stolen bases in 100 at-bats, and fielded at a .957 clip. In a postseason exhibition game against the Chicago Cubs, Green earned high praise for a superb effort he made as a base runner. After suffering a broken leg while sliding into third base, he got to his feet and tried to score on the overthrow on the play. While hobbling home on his broken leg, he was thrown out by a step.

The next season, owner Frank Leland and manager Rube Foster parted ways, and Green went with Leland and his newly formed team, the Chicago Giants, which was his home for many years. His batting dropped with the new team, hitting only .238 for the 1910 season, but he rebounded, batting .316 against all opposition in 1911. He retained his pep and remained with the team, usually hitting in the sixth slot of the order while playing aggressive but clean baseball. In the latter years of the decade the veteran outfielder assumed the added duty of coaching and kept the crowds ''alive with his antics.'' In 1921 he was given the managerial reins of the club and later assumed the ownership as well, and continued with the Chicago Giants in this capacity throughout the decade.

Green, Curtis
Career: 1923–25   Positions: 1b, of, p

Teams: Birmingham Black Barons ('23–'25), *Brooklyn Cuban Giants ('26), Ewing's All-Stars ('28)*

He began his career as a pitcher with the Birmingham Black Barons in 1923 but spent most of his playing time at first base or in the outfield, making his last appearance in 1928 at the initial sack with Ewing's All-Stars, a team of lesser caliber.

Green, Dave
Career: 1950   Position: rf
Team: Baltimore Elite Giants

He was listed as an outfielder with the Elites in 1950, when the Negro American League was struggling to survive the loss of players to organized baseball, but league statistics do not confirm him playing time.

Green, Henryene P.
Career: 1949–50   Position: owner
Team: Baltimore Elite Giants

After the death of her husband, Vernon Green, she became the official owner of the Baltimore Elite Giants. Realizing her limitations in administering the team's business matters, she gave power of attorney to Richard Powell, a close associate of her late husband, to oversee the team's operations. Following the demise of the Negro National League in 1948, the Elites entered the Negro American League and won the pennant in 1949. After the 1950 season, she sold the franchise to William Bridgeforth.

Green, James
Career: 1950   Position: 3b
Team: New York Black Yankees

He played third base with the New York Black Yankees in 1950, when the team was playing as an independent ballclub and struggling to survive the loss of players to organized baseball.

Green, Julius
Career: 1929–30   Positions: of, 1b, *p*

Teams: Memphis Red Sox ('29), Detroit Stars ('30)

Bats: Left   Throws: Left

In 1929 this little thin outfielder played for the Memphis Red Sox, batting .249 while also making a mound appearance and losing his only decision. The next season, his second and last in the Negro Leagues, he played with the Detroit Stars.

Green, Leslie, Sr. (**Chin**)

Career: 1939–46   Position: cf

Teams: St. Louis Stars ('39), New Orleans-St. Louis Stars ('40–'41), New York Black Yankees ('42), *Mexican League ('43–'45)*, Memphis Red Sox ('46)

Bats: Left   Throws: Right

Height: 5'11"   Weight: 190

Died: Mar. 2, 1985, St. Louis, Mo.

A hustling outfielder with exceptional speed and well-balanced defensive skills, he had a wide range and a good arm. Although only an average hitter, he batted in the leadoff spot, where he utilized his speed on the bases and basestealing capabilities. He began his career as a center fielder with the St. Louis Stars in 1939, and a year later, with the franchise playing as the New Orleans-St. Louis Stars, he played in the 1940 All-Star game, getting 1 of the West team's 5 hits. In 1942, as the New York Black Yankees' center fielder and leadoff hitter, he batted .237, and jumped to the Mexican League for the next three seasons. Returning to the United States, he finished his career as a substitute with the Memphis Red Sox in 1946, batting .227 for the season.

Before playing in his professional career, he excelled in sports at Sumner High School and continued his athletic pursuits while attending Bishop College, Tennessee State University, Le Moyne University, and the University of Michigan. After retiring from baseball, he worked in the postal service and as a salesman.

Green, Peter (Ed)

Career: 1916–20   Positions: of, p

Teams: *Brooklyn Colored Giants ('08–'09)*,

Pittsburgh Giants, New York Lincoln Stars ('16–'17), *Philadelphia Giants ('16, '20)*, Brooklyn Royal Giants ('19–'20)

A light-hitting outfielder, he was one of a trio of players who shared playing time in one outfield slot with the 1916 Lincoln Stars. Incomplete statistics while he was with the Brooklyn Royal Giants in 1919, show only two hits in 7 games while playing as a reserve outfielder. During his career he also played with several lesser teams, including the Philadelphia Giants.

Green, Vernon (**Fat**, Baby)

a.k.a Greene

Career: 1921; 1942–49 Positions: c, manager, officer, owner

Team: Baltimore Elite Giants

Died: 1949

He was a catcher with the Nashville Elites in 1921, their first year, when they were not playing a major-league caliber of baseball. Later he became an officer of the Elite Giants' franchise during most of the '40s, serving in a variety of positions, and, as owner Tom Wilson's right-hand man, was instrumental in the club's success. While Wilson remained in Nashville, Green traveled with the team and was in charge of its operations. Among his other duties he was responsible for organizing the winter league team. As Wilson's health worsened, Green's involvement increased. In 1946 he was the manager of the Elites, but the team was floundering under his on-field leadership, and he returned to the front office. After Tom Wilson's death, he bought the franchise from Wilson's son. After his death two years later, his wife gave power of attorney to Dick Powell and let him take charge of the team's operations.

Green, William

a.k.a Greene

Career: 1915–23   Positions: **3b**, *of*

Teams: **Chicago Giants** ('15–'21), Chicago Union Giants ('16)

He began his career in 1915 as a third baseman with the Chicago Giants and had been batting in the leadoff spot for four years when the Giants became a charter member of the Negro National League in 1920. Following a last-place finish in 1921, they dropped out of the league, and their quality of play lessened considerably thereafter. He also played with the Chicago Union Giants during his career.

Green, Willie (Will)

a.k.a. Greene
Career: 1910–12   Positions: c, p
Teams: St. Louis Giants ('10), *Pittsburgh Giants ('12)*

He was a catcher with the St. Louis Giants in 1910, and he appeared two years later with the Pittsburgh Giants as a pitcher.

Greene

Career: 1914   Position: rf
Team: Philadelphia Giants

He was a right fielder with the Philadelphia Giants in 1914, when the performance level of the once-proud team was in rapid decline.

Greene

Career: 1938   Position: p
Team: Eagles

He was a second-line pitcher with the 1938 Eagles, his only appearance in the Negro Leagues.

Greene, James Elbert (**Joe**, Pea, Pig)

a.k.a. Green
Career: 1932–48   Positions: **c**, 1b, of
Teams: Atlanta Black Crackers ('32–'38), Homestead Grays ('39), **Kansas City Monarchs** ('39–'43, '46–'47), *military service ('43–'45)*, Cleveland Buckeyes ('48), *minor leagues ('51)*
Bats: Right   Throws: Right
Height: 6'1"   Weight: 200
Born: Oct. 17, 1911, Stone Mountain, Ga.
Died: Stone Mountain, Ga.

The catcher who handled the great Kansas City Monarchs' pitching staffs of the 1940s, he was a good and durable receiver with a quick release and a powerful throwing arm. Complementing his defensive skills, he was a fastball-hitting pull hitter with good power, and batted fifth in the order behind Willard Brown. Playing against all levels of competition, he was credited with league highs of 33 and 38 home runs in 1940 and 1942, respectively. His primary shortcoming was a lack of speed on the bases. In the Monarchs' 1942 World Series victory over the Homestead Grays, he hit .444 and homered to key the Monarchs' offense. At that time he was considered the best catcher in the Negro American League and made his second appearance in the All-Star classic.

In 1943, following his three best years, he entered military service during World War II. While serving with the 92nd Division in Algiers and Italy and spending eight months on the front lines in a 57-millimeter antitank company, he was decorated for his combat experience. When his company entered Milan, they had to take down the bodies of Benito Mussolini and his mistress, Clara Petacci, who had been executed and were hanging upside down.

While in service he also played with the baseball team that won the championship of the Mediterranean Theater of Operations. After his discharge, he returned to his spot behind the plate for the Monarchs and caught for the 1946 pennant-winning Monarchs, and registered averages of .300, .324, and .257 in 1946–48, but he never fully regained his old form after the end of World War II.

This big catcher had two nicknames, earning his first early in his career when, with the Atlanta Black Crackers, he was called "Pig" because of the quantity of food he ate. Later in his career he earned his second nickname, "Pea," because he threw "peas" to second base.

He began his professional career with the Atlanta Black Crackers in 1932, when they were in the Negro Southern League, and continued with the ballclub until they finally joined the Negro American League in 1938. That season he was the starting catcher, and his bat provided the impetus for the team to win the second-half Negro American League title. With the 1938 Atlanta Black Crackers he improved his ability to hit a curveball. After leaving Atlanta he joined the Homestead Grays for a short time, but he still had some difficulty with a good curveball despite an extra-long thirty-seven-inch bat that the Grays brought specifically for him to reach curves on the outside part of the plate. Before the season was over he left the Grays for the Monarchs, where incomplete statistics show averages of .231 and .225 in 1941–42. A decade after joining the Monarchs, he was traded to the Buckeyes, where he finished out his Negro League career in 1948.

In 1951 he played with Elmwood in the Mandak League, batting .301 for his last year in professional baseball.

Greene, Vernon
[see Green, Vernon]

Greene, Walter
Career: 1928   Positions: 1b, of
Teams: *Brooklyn Cubans,* ('28) Atlantic City Bacharach Giants

In his only season in the Negro Leagues, he was a reserve first baseman with the Bacharach Giants and also played in the outfield for the Brooklyn Cubans, an independent team of lesser caliber.

Greene, Willie
[see Green, Willie]

Greenfield
Career: 1922   Position: c
Team: Baltimore Black Sox

The catcher was one of the new recruits for the Baltimore Black Sox in 1922, and appeared briefly in the spring before being dropped from the team.

Greenidge, Victor (Slicker)
a.k.a. Greenege; Panama Green
Career: 1941–45   Position: p

Teams: New York Cubans ('41–'45), Cuban Stars
Bats: Right   Throws: Right
Height: 5'11"   Weight: 185
Born: 1919, Panama

The right-handed Panamanian pitcher began his career in 1941 with a 3–0 record for the New York Cubans. After a 3–2 record in 1944, he was called one of the best pitchers in the Negro Leagues the following season, but 1945 proved to be his last season in black baseball. He was also a member of the Almendares team that won the Cuban championship, but he never attained the baseball status predicted by the press releases.

Greenlee, William Augustus (Gus, Big Red)
Career: 1931–45   Positions: owner, officer, founder (NNL, USL), president (NNL)
Team: Pittsburgh Crawfords
Height: 6'3"   Weight: 210
Born: 1897, Marion, N.C.
Died: July 10, 1952, Pittsburgh, Pa.

A businessman, politician, sportsman, and numbers banker, he owned a stable of boxers, including the first black light-heavyweight champion, John Henry Lewis, and ran a popular cabaret, the Crawford Grill, but he was best known as the owner of the Pittsburgh Crawfords. Political motivations caused him to buy the Crawfords in 1930 but, once involved, he wanted the best team possible and signed established stars, including Satchel Paige and Josh Gibson. The Crawfords reached the pinnacle of success during his ownership, and for five years (1932–36) his team was ranked with the best each season. In 1933, acting as the president of the Negro National League, he awarded his team a contested pennant, but in 1935 the Crawfords defeated the New York Cubans in a playoff for an undisputed championship. This team is considered by most historians to be the greatest black team of all time. The Crawfords won the second-half title the following year, but the playoffs were not completed and no 1936 champion was recognized.

That season was marred by a scandal when the Crawfords were unjustly accused of throwing a game against the Brooklyn Bushwicks.

A wealthy man who spent his money freely, he was generous with his players and in 1932 built Greenlee Field, the only black-owned ballpark in the East, to be the home field for his team. A combination of losing Paige and Gibson, and having to make a big payoff from a ''hit'' on a heavily played number, ultimately led to his divesting himself of the team and razing Greenlee Field after the 1938 season.

Although his association with the Negro Leagues was of relatively short duration, his impact was unmistakable. He was the primary force behind the formation of the new Negro National League in 1933 and served as the league's president for its first five years. While at the head of the league, he worked to end rowdyism and assaults on umpires, and opposed raids that decimated his playing personnel. That season he was also responsible for the creation of the East-West All-Star game, which became an annual event and which was the most popular and profitable venture in black baseball.

Greenlee was born in a log cabin in North Carolina, but left his home state in 1916 after a year of college to travel North to Pittsburgh, where he worked as a shoeshine boy, steel mill worker, and taxicab driver. After serving overseas in the 367th Army Division during World War I, he began establishing himself as a prominent man in Pittsburgh's black community. During the Prohibition era he operated nightclubs as a front for his numbers operations and bootlegging activities, and the Crawford Grill served as the center of activity for jazz, booze, gambling, and girls. In the '30s he became a power in Pittsburgh's political arena.

He tried to resume an active role in black baseball in 1945, when he formed the United States League, in conjunction with Branch Rickey's pursuit of a black candidate to integrate organized baseball. The league lasted only two seasons and was never of major-league caliber. After his second exit from the baseball scene, he continued to operate the Crawford Grill until it was destroyed by fire in 1951. For the last year of his life he was besieged by white racketeers encroaching on his numbers business, and by federal government agents harassing him over income taxes he owed.

Greer, J. B.
Career: 1939–41   Position: officer
Teams: Cleveland Bears ('39–'40), Jacksonville Red Caps ('41), *Knoxville Red Caps*

He served as an officer for the Jacksonville Red Caps when they were transplanted to Cleveland and played as the Bears during the 1939–40 season, continuing in that capacity for a season after they returned to Jacksonville.

Gregory
Career: 1940   Position: **p**
Team: Birmingham Black Barons

He was a pitcher with the Birmingham Black Barons in 1940, his only season in the Negro Leagues.

Grey
Career: 1899   Position: 2b
Team: Cuban Giants

He was a second baseman with the Cuban Giants in 1899, after the historic and once great team had declined in quality since they were first organized in 1885 as the first black professional team.

Grey, William
Career: 1920   Position: p
Team: Dayton Marcos

He was a pitcher with the 1920 Dayton Marcos when they were a member of the Negro National League in its inaugural season.

Greyer
a.k.a. Grayson
Career: 1916–22   Position: 1b
Team: Baltimore Black Sox

Beginning in 1916, he was the regular first

baseman for the Baltimore Black Sox during their formative years, when they were playing as an independent club and still struggling to become a major-league-caliber team. He hit third in the batting order until the end of the deadball era, then dropped to the bottom of the order as the Black Sox became more competitive, and was relegated to part-time status in 1922, his last year in black baseball.

Grier, Claude (**Red**)
Career: 1924–28   Position: p
Teams: Washington Potomacs ('24), Wilmington Potomacs ('25), Bacharach Giants ('25–'28)
Bats: Left   Throws: Left

In a packed five-year career, Grier gained lasting fame when he tossed a no-hitter in the 1926 Negro World Series. Pitching for the Eastern Colored League's pennant-winning Bacharach Giants against the Negro National League champion Chicago American Giants in Baltimore, he hurled the 10–0 gem in the third game of the Series. Altogether he started 4 games in the Series, winning 2 and recording a respectable 3.58 ERA. He had registered a 12–2 record during the regular season and, after the Series, he pitched in the Cuban winter league, where he logged a 5–3 record preparatory to helping the Bacharachs to another pennant in 1927.

Before signing with the Bacharachs, the youngster was secured from the Brooklyn All-Stars in 1924 by manager Ben Taylor of the Washington Potomacs. He had everything needed to be a successful starting pitcher in the Negro Leagues, bringing with him a repertory that included a fastball, an assortment of breaking pitches, a good change-up, and good control for a left-handed pitcher. However, his inexperience was evident in his weakness at holding runners and fielding his position, especially on bunts. A further shortcoming was his unwillingness to adhere to proper training procedures, and had he taken good care of himself, he would have had a long career and he could have been one of the best left-handers of all-

time. The next year the Potomacs moved their base of operation to Wilmington, where he had a 3–8 record for a weak team. The next year he joined the Bacharachs and had his brush with fame.

Griffin
Career: 1903   Position: p
Team: Philadelphia Giants

He pitched with the Philadelphia Giants in 1903, his only season with a top black team.

Griffin, C. B. (Clarence)
Career: 1933–35   Position: of
Teams: Columbus Blue Birds ('33), Cleveland Red Sox ('34), Brooklyn Eagles ('35)

The light-hitting outfielder began his Negro League career as the left fielder and eighth-place batter with the Columbus Blue Birds in 1933, moving in turn to the Cleveland Red Sox and Brooklyn Eagles in each of the next two seasons. Incomplete statistics show almost contradictory batting averages for his short career, crediting him with a .346 average in 1933 and a .056 average in 1935.

Griffin, James (Horse)
Career: 1917   Position: 2b
Teams: *Philadelphia Giants ('15),* Cuban Giants ('17), *Pittsburgh Giants, Nashville Elite Giants ('21)*

Beginning with the Philadelphia Giants in 1915, this Washington, D.C., player was a second baseman with several marginal teams, including the Cuban Giants, Pittsburgh Giants, and Nashville Elite Giants. Most of his five years in black baseball (1917–21) were spent during the deadball era.

Griffin, Robert
Career: 1931–37   Position: p
Teams: Chicago Columbia Giants ('31), Chicago American Giants, St. Louis Stars ('37)
Born: 1913
Died: June 14, 1940

He was a pitcher under David Malarcher with the Chicago Columbia Giants in 1931 and closed his playing career with the St. Louis Stars in 1937. Three years after his last season in the Negro Leagues he passed away at age twenty-seven.

Griffith, Robert Lee (**Bob,** Schoolboy, Big Bill)
a.k.a. Griffin
Career: 1933–49   Positions: **p,** *of*
Teams: Nashville Elite Giants ('33–'34), Columbus Elite Giants ('35), Washington Elite Giants ('36–'37), *Santo Domingo ('37),* **Baltimore Elite Giants** ('38, '41), *Mexican League* ('40), New York Black Yankees ('42–'43, '46–'48), *military service ('44–'45),* Kansas City Monarchs ('46), Philadelphia Stars ('49–'51), *Indianapolis Clowns ('52), Candian League ('51, '53)*
Bats: Right   Throws: Right
Height: 6'5"   Weight: 235
Born: Oct. 1, 1913, Liberty, Tenn.
Died: Nov. 8, 1977, Indianapolis, Ind.

The big, right-handed, hard-throwing spitballer could break a pitch up, down, in, or out. He pitched in the 1935 All-Star game, representing the Columbus Elite Giants, and, after a thirteen-year interim, made back-to-back appearances in 1948 and 1949, representing the New York Black Yankees and Philadelphia Stars. He was the winning pitcher in the latter contest.

As a young boy in his hometown during the late '20s and early '30s, he was a star pitcher for the Smithville Tigers and also played trombone in the town band that paraded before a game. He attended Tennessee State University in Nashville before signing with Tom Wilson's Nashville Elites in 1933, and remained with the franchise as the club relocated in Columbus, Washington, D. C., and Baltimore. In 1936 he was selected to the Negro National League All-Star squad that walked away with the *Denver Post* Tournament. Griffith struck out 29 batters in the 17 innings he pitched, allowed only two runs, and won both his decisions. During the 1936 regular season he was credited with a 21–9 record and was regarded as one of the

brightest prospects in black baseball, a distinction he retained throughout the late '30s and early '40s.

In 1937 the Dominican dictator Rafael Trujillo signed Griffith, Satchel Paige, and Leroy Matlock to pitch for the Ciudad Trujillo baseball club in Santo Domingo. The big fastballer threw smoke and won 2 of his 3 decisions in helping the team win the championship. At that time his services were also in demand in Cuba, and he spent two consecutive seasons (1937–39) in the Cuban winter league, fashioning a composite 16–11 record. Following the last winter in Cuba, he signed with the Mexican League's Nuevo Laredo club for the 1940 season, where he was 7–6 as a pitcher and hit .321. Always a decent hitter for a pitcher, he batted .340 in both the 1947 and 1949 seasons, and hit .347 for Brandon in the Mandak League in 1953, his last season in baseball.

During World War II he served in the European Theater as a corporal in the Army. After the war he played briefly with the Kansas City Monarchs, but soon rejoined the New York Black Yankees and toiled for them during most of the '40s. The team was the doormat of the Negro National League, and the poor support caused him back-to-back records of 2–3 and 2–9 in the postwar seasons of 1946–47. With the Philadelphia Stars in 1949 he rebounded with a 9–3 record and a 2.31 ERA.

In September 1948 he was the winning pitcher for the American All-Stars over the Cuban All-Stars in Havana. He also played winter ball in Puerto Rico and in Venezuela, where he pitched for the 1949–50 champion Megallanas ballclub. After the decline of the Negro Leagues, he signed with Granby in the Provincial League and had a 6–5 record with a 4.34 ERA, and finished his professional career with Brandon with a 8–5 ledger in 1953. However, he continued to pitch semipro ball while in his fifties.

After ending his career in professional baseball, he worked as a night watchman in city, county, and state governmental buildings in Indianapolis. He retired during the '70s and was still living in Indianapolis when he fell in the bathtub and sustained head injuries that took his life.

Griggs, Acie (Skeet)
Career: 1949–50   Positions: cf, 2b, ss
Team: Birmingham Black Barons
Born: Sept. 13, 1924, Birmingham, Ala.
Bats: Right   Throws: Right
Height: 6'0"   Weight: 200
He began playing in the City League of Birmingham, Alabama, as a teenager in 1938 and continued during the '40s, prior to joining the Birmingham Black Barons in 1949. His career with the Black Barons was brief and was during the years when the Negro Leagues had begun to decline.

Griggs, Wiley Lee (Willie, Diamond Jim, *Robert*)
Career: 1948–50   Positions: **3b**, 2b
Teams: Birmingham Black Barons ('48–'58), Cleveland Buckeyes ('50), Houston Eagles ('50), *New Orleans Eagles ('51)*
Bats: Right   Throws: Right
Height: 5'11"   Weight: 160
Born: Mar. 24, 1925, Birmingham, Ala.
Primarily a third baseman, this infielder joined the Birmingham Black Barons in 1948, batting .242 in limited play during their championship season. He first began playing baseball in Birmingham's City League when he was signed off the school grounds as a teenager, and continued in the City League during the '40s until joining the Black Barons. After being released by Birmingham after an injury, he played briefly with both the Cleveland Buckeyes and Houston Eagles in 1950, but returned to the Black Barons and remained with them on into the '50s, after the decline of the Negro Leagues. After ending his baseball career, he worked for the Birmingham Water Works for twenty-eight years, before retiring in 1987. In later years, he suffered the loss of both legs, but learned to cope with life as a double amputee.

Grimes
Career: 1943   Positions: p, of
Teams: Harrisburg-St.Louis Stars ('43), Cleveland Buckeyes ('43)
He pitched with the Harrisburg-St. Louis Stars early in the 1943 season, but after the team withdrew from the league, he finished the year with the Cleveland Buckeyes, appearing briefly as an outfielder.

Grimm
Career: 1921   Position: of
Team: Atlantic City Bacharach Giants
In his only appearance in black baseball, he was an outfielder with the 1921 Bacharachs.

Gross, Ben, Jr.
Career: 1887   Position: rf
Team: *Pittsburgh Keystones*
He was a rightfielder with the Pittsburgh Keystones, one of eight teams that were charter members of the League of Colored Baseball Clubs in 1887. However, the league's existence was ephemeral, lasting only a week.

Guerra, Juan
a.k.a. Marcelino
Career: 1910–24   Positions: 1b, of, c
Teams: Stars of Cuba ('10), New York Cuban Stars ('16), Cuban Stars (West) ('17–'24)
He started with the Stars of Cuba in 1910 as an alternate first baseman, and was the starting first baseman and cleanup hitter with owner Alejandro Pompez's New York Cuban Stars in 1916. The following season he joined Molina's Cuban Stars (West) and continued to hit cleanup most of the time, while splitting his playing time between first base and left field.

Guerra, Marcelino
[see Guerra, Juan]

Guilbe, Felix (Felo)
Career: 1946–47   Positions: rf, lf, cf
Team: Baltimore Elite Giants ('46–'47)
Bats: Right   Throws: Right
Height: 5'8"   Weight: 152
Born: Mar. 2, 1924, Ponce, Puerto Rico

The speedy young Puerto Rican outfielder batted leadoff for the Elite Giants in 1946–47 and was a spark plug on the team. Considered a pretty good hitter, he batted .220 and .284 in his only seasons in the Negro Leagues. In the field he got a good jump on the ball and had good range and a wonderful throwing arm. A brother, pitcher Juan Guilbe, also played in the Negro Leagues.

In the off-season he resided in his hometown, Ponce, and played ball with both the Ponce and Mayagüez teams in the Puerto Rican winter league, and is credited with being the first outfielder to use the basket catch in that league. After retiring from baseball, he worked for the U.S. Post Office in Puerto Rico.

Guilbe, Juan (Telo)

Career: 1940–47   Positions: **p**, *of*
Teams: New York Cubans ('40), Indianapolis Clowns ('47)
Bats: Right   Throws: Right
Height: 6'1"   Weight: 207
Born: June 26, 1914, Ponce, Puerto Rico

This right-handed pitcher broke in with the New York Cubans in 1940 but did not register a decision. He had a balanced repertory that included a fastball, curve, drop, and change-up, and pretty good control. In the winter season he played with his hometown team, Ponce, in the Puerto Rican League. He is the oldest of three brothers who played baseball. One brother, Felix, Guilbe, was an outfielder with the Indianapolis Clowns during the late '40s; the other brother did not play in the Negro Leagues. Guilbe was elected to the Puerto Rican Hall of Fame in 1993.

Guiterrez, Luis

Career: 1926–27   Position: rf
Teams: Cuban Stars (West) ('26)

He was a starting outfielder with the 1926 Negro National Cuban Stars (West), hitting .271 while batting sixth in the order and playing in both side pastures. The following season he was relegated to being a substitute, and played very sparingly while with the squad.

Guiwn, Jefferson

a.k.a. Guinn
Career: 1943–44   Position: c
Team: Cleveland Buckeyes

An infrequently used wartime reserve, he was listed as a catcher with the Cleveland Buckeyes in 1943–44.

Gulley, Napolean (**Nap**)

Career: 1941–49   Positions: **p**, of
Teams: Kansas City Monarchs ('41), Chicago American Giants ('41, '46, '49), Birmingham Black Barons ('41–'42), Cleveland Buckeyes ('43–'45), *Harlem Globetrotters ('45), Mexican League ('46–'49), Canadian League ('48),* Newark Eagles ('47–'48), *minor leagues ('50–'56)*
Bats: Left   Throws: Left
Height: 6'0"   Weight: 168
Born: Aug. 29, 1924, Huttig, Ark.

This left-handed hurler had a good fastball, but his "out pitch" was an overhand drop-curveball. However, he was bothered by lack of control during his nine-year pitching career in the Negro Leagues during the '40s, and was never a front-line pitcher. Some observers think that his performance may also have suffered from trying to live up to a "playboy" image off the field.

Gulley began playing ball almost from the time he began to walk, and as a youngster played sandlot ball. He developed a regional reputation and joined the Kansas City Monarchs in the spring of 1941, but was released early in the year. Before the year was over, he played with two other teams, joining Jim Taylor's Chicago American Giants and then Winfield Welch's Birmington Black Barons. In 1943, he joined the Cleveland Buckeyes, where he lost his only decision in each 1943 and 1945. He missed most of the 1944 season, because he was called for an Army physical and, although not inducted, he remained on the West Coast for the rest of the year. He left the Buckeyes near the end of their 1945 championship season and barnstormed with "Double Duty" Radcliffe's independent Harlem Globetrotters.

For the remainder of the '40s he pitched in several leagues, ranging from Mexico to Canada, and interspersed between his playing time in the Negro Leagues were appearances in the Mexican League. He began the 1946 season with the Chicago American Giants in the Negro American League, posting a 2–4 pitching record and a .385 batting average in limited play, before jumping to Tampico for the last part of the season. He began the next year with the San Luis in the Mexican League before returning to the United States to join the Newark Eagles in the Negro National League for the remainder of 1947 and the beginning of the 1948 season. He was back in Mexico in 1949 for most of the year, splitting his time between San Luis and the Mexico City Reds, before appearing briefly with the American Giants late in the season. During all of his travels before entering organized baseball, he also played with St. Jean's in the Canadian Provincial League in the last half of the 1948 season.

After signing with the Brooklyn Dodgers' organization in 1950, he appeared briefly with a Dodgers' farm team in California but was quickly disenchanted. He switched from the mound to the outfield, and played with Visalia in the California League in four of the next five seasons, demonstrating good power and a measure of speed on the bases while posting averages of .292, .288, .333, and .316 in 1950–54, exclusive of 1953. That season was spent with Victoria in the Western International League, where he batted .270. His last two seasons in baseball were spent with Spokane in the Northwest League, where he hit .361 and .316 in 1955–56 as an outfielder, but he broke his arm in the latter season, and that ended his baseball career.

After leaving baseball, he was employed in a variety of fields, including graphic art, marketing, and food processing in the restaurant business.

Gurley, James (Jim)
Career: 1922–32   Positions: lf, rf, p, *1b*
Teams: St. Louis Stars ('22–'23), Memphis Red Sox ('24, '28), Indianapolis ABCs ('25), Chicago American Giants ('25–'26), Nashville Elite Giants ('27–'28), Birmingham Black Barons ('27, '29), Harrisburg Giants ('27), Cleveland Hornets ('27), Montgomery Grey Sox ('32)

He began his career as a pitcher with the St. Louis Stars in 1922, but was with the Chicago American Giants as a reserve outfielder during 1925, Rube Foster's last year at the helm. The next season he was an outfielder-pitcher with the American Giants under new manager Dave Malarcher but did not receive substantial playing time at either position. In 1927 he split the season between Harrisburg and Birmingham, batting a composite .243 for the year. After a year with the Memphis Red Sox, he returned to the Black Barons in 1929 but was used sparingly, with partial statistics showing a .176 average in very limited play. He continued to split his time between pitching and the outfield until 1932, the last of his eleven seasons in the Negro Leagues, when he also spent some time at first base.

Gutierrez, Eustaquio
Career: 1913   Position: ut
Team: Long Branch Cubans

In 1913, his only year in black baseball, he was a utility player for the Long Branch Cubans.

Guy, Wesley
Career: 1927–29   Position: p
Team: *Chicago Giants*

He was a pitcher with the Chicago Giants 1927–29, at a time when the franchise was no longer of major-league caliber.

H

Hackett
Career: 1932   Position: p
Teams: Washington Pilots ('32), Atlantic City Bacharach Giants ('32)

His pitching career coincided with the existence of the 1932 Washington Pilots and the East-West League, each being of less than one year in duration.

Hackley, Albert (Al)
Career: 1887–96   Positions: lf, rf, cf, 3b, ss
Team: Chicago Unions

This nineteenth-century player performed both in the outfield and infield with the Chicago Unions for a decade beginning in 1887.

Haddad
Career: 1931   Positions: p, of
Team: Cuban House of David

He pitched and played with the Cuban House of David team in 1931.

Hadley, Henry (Bubba, Red)
Career: 1937–38   Positions: of, c
Team: Atlanta Black Crackers
Bats: Right   Throws: Right
Height: 5'6"   Weight: 160

A good defensive outfielder, he had very good speed, great range, and a rifle shot arm. Although he was short, the Waycross, Georgia, native was a strong little guy and a good line-drive hitter. He played center field and catcher for the Atlanta Black Crackers, winners of the second-half championship of the Negro American League in 1938. A college man, he attended Morris Brown University and was a former halfback on the football team. He made his home in Atlanta, and when the Black Crackers picked up Alex Crumbley as an outfielder for the 1938 playoffs against the Memphis Red Sox, winners of the first-half title, Hadley was left at home.

Haines
Career: 1920   Position: p
Team: Indianapolis ABCs

He was a pitcher with the Indianapolis ABCs in 1920, the first year of the Negro National League.

Hairston, Harold (Hal)
a.k.a. Harriston
Career: 1946–47   Position: p
Teams: Homestead Grays ('46–'47), *Birmingham Black Barons ('53)*
Bats: Right   Throws: Right

He pitched with the Grays for two years between the pennant-winning seasons of 1945 and 1948, registering a 1–2 record in 1946. His only appearance in the Negro Leagues was with the Birmingham Black Barons in 1953, after the leagues had declined to a very definite minor-league level.

Hairston, Napoleon
Career: 1938–40   Positions: lf, rf

Teams: Pittsburgh Crawfords ('38), Toledo Crawfords ('39), Indianapolis Crawfords ('40)

Beginning his Negro League career with the Crawfords in 1938, he played left field and was credited with a .246 batting average while hitting cleanup. He remained with the Crawfords for three years while the franchise played out of three different home locations, moving to Toledo and Indianapolis in the next two seasons.

Hairston, Rap

Career: 1934–35   Position: ut
Team: Newark Dodgers

He was a utility player with the Newark Dodgers during the two years of the franchise's existence.

Hairston, Sam

a.k.a Harriston
Career: 1944–50   Positions: c, 3b, 1b, of
Teams: Birmingham Black Barons ('44), Cincinnati-Indianapolis Clowns ('45), Indianapolis Clowns ('46–'50), major leagues ('51), *minor leagues ('50–'60)*
Bats: Right   Throws: Right
Height: 5'10½"   Weight: 187
Born: Jan. 28, 1920, Columbus, Miss.

A rough-and-tumble player who caught for the Indianapolis Clowns in the last half of the 1940s, he also performed at third base when the occasion demanded it. He began playing baseball in 1942 in Birmingham's Industrial League and joined the Birmingham Black Barons two years later, but was traded to the Clowns for Pepper Bassett. With the Clowns he was primarily a catcher but also played infield positions at the corners and occasionally in the outfield. He hit .285 and .279 in his first two seasons (1945–46) with the Clowns and soon was hitting over .300, registering averages of .361, .319, and .307 in three successive seasons (1947–49). In the middle season he was selected to the West squad for the All-Star game but did not appear in the game. In 1950 he won the Negro American League's Triple Crown (.424 batting average, 17 home runs, 71 RBI) averaging over one RBI per game in the 70-game season.

After compiling those numbers, he became the first black player signed by the Chicago White Sox and finished the season at Colorado Springs in the Western League, batting .286 in the last 38 games of the season. He spent the winter with Vargas in Venezuela and hit for a .380 average, returning to Colorado Springs again briefly in the spring before getting a chance with the parent White Sox, where he played four games and batted .400 in only 5 at-bats.

Although he played nine more years in organized baseball, he never had another major-league at-bat. His best years in the minors were with Colorado Springs, where he hit over .300 four times. He followed a .316-batting-average, 98-RBI season in 1952 by winning the MVP award in 1953 with a .310 batting average and 102 RBIs for the pennant-winning Sky Sox. Two years later he won the league batting title with a .350 average while driving in 91 runs. He also played with Sacramento in the Pacific Coast League, Indianapolis in the American Association, San Antonio in the Texas League, and Charleson of the Sally League. With Charleston he hit .330 in 1959 and finished his baseball career there the following season. The husky receiver also played one winter season (1956–57) in the Mexican League, batting .362 with Puebla, the second-highest mark in the league.

During his career he played four consecutive winters in Venezuela, 1949–53, and had a 26-game hitting streak during his stint there. After ending his career as a player, he continued in baseball as a scout for the White Sox, and signed his son Jerry to a contract. Another son, John, also played in the major leagues, with the Chicago Cubs.

Hairstone, J. Burke (Harry, J. B.)

Career: 1916–22   Positions: of, manager
Teams: **Baltimore Black Sox** ('18–'21), Atlantic City Bacharach Giants ('22)

During the formative years when the Baltimore Black Sox were in transition from a regional semipro team toward becoming a major-league-caliber team, he was a regular outfielder from 1916 until leaving the team during the 1922 season to join the Bacharachs. Hairstone had very good speed and began his professional baseball career with the Rochester Big Horns, a white ballclub, before joining the Black Sox. In 1916 he played right field and batted cleanup for the team, but moved to center field and the leadoff position the following season.

As the team moved into the '20s, preparatory to joining the Eastern Colored League, he remained in the starting outfield but dropped in the batting order. The veteran outfielder still registered a .445 batting average in 1921 against all levels of opposition.

A few years later he narrowly avoided tragedy when he suffered a bayonet wound at a late summer National Guard encampment, and an operation was required to save his hand from being amputated due to blood poisoning. In the latter stages of his active playing career Hairstone doubled as a manager, mostly with lesser teams.

Hale, E. **(Red)**
Career: 1937–39   Position: ss
Teams: Detroit Stars ('37), Chicago American Giants ('38–'39)

He began his career as the starting shortstop with the Detroit Stars in 1937, when the new Detroit franchise entered the Negro American League in its inaugural season. After the Stars dropped out of league competition, he closed out his three seasons in the Negro American League by sharing the shortstop position for the 1939 Chicago American Giants.

Haley
Career: 1923   Position: p
Team: Detroit Stars

He was a pitcher with the Detroit Stars in 1923, his only year in the Negro Leagues.

Haley, Red
Career: 1928–33   Positions: **2b**, 3b, 1b
Teams: Chicago American Giants ('28), Birmingham Black Barons ('28), Cuban Stars ('33), *Bismarck, North Dakota ('34–'35)*

Although primarily a second baseman, he could play any infield position, and in 1928 he was a utility infielder with the Chicago American Giants. After leaving the Negro National League, the long-ball hitter played with several barnstorming teams during the early '30s before being recruited by a strong semipro team in Bismarck, North Dakota, in 1934. Shortly after he arrived, owner Neil Churchill signed Satchel Paige to pitch with the team and they became a midwestern powerhouse. By 1935 the team also featured Hilton Smith, ''Double Duty'' Radcliffe, Quincy Trouppe, and Barney Morris and breezed through the season undefeated. Unconfirmed sources suggest the possibility that he is related to *Roots* author Alex Haley.

Hall
Career: 1934   Position: ss
Teams: *Washington Pilots*

He was a shortstop with the Washington Pilots in 1934, his only year in black baseball.

Hall, Bad News
Career: 1937–40   Positions: **3b**, 2b, of
Teams: Indianapolis Athletics ('37), Indianapolis Crawfords ('40)

He began his career as a third baseman with the Indianapolis Athletics in the Negro American League's inaugural season, 1937. With the A's he batted cleanup and also played some games in right field. After the A's folded, the Crawfords joined the Negro American League and relocated in Indianapolis for the 1940 season, and Hall found a spot in the lineup, splitting his time between third base and second base, while batting eighth in the order.

Hall, Blainey
Career: 1913–25   Positions: **lf**, cf, rf
Teams: Mohawk Giants ('13), **New York Lin-**

coln Giants ('14–'19), Philadelphia Giants ('18), Baltimore Black Sox ('20–'25)
Bats: Right   Throws: Right
Born: 1889

An excellent line-drive hitter with outstanding bat control, while he was not a home-run hitter, he had good extra-base power and good speed. He played left field and batted in the heart of the Lincoln Giants' lineup, usually hitting cleanup, for a half dozen years during the deadball era.

He was playing semipro ball in Harrisburg, Pennsylvania, when he was discovered by the Lincoln Giants' manager Spot Poles. Before reporting to the Lincolns he was almost killed in a runaway horse and wagon accident. Fortunately, he survived to enjoy a fruitful baseball career. Playing against all levels of competition, he batted .411 in 1914, and during his last three years (1917–19) with the Lincolns he hit .383, .337, and .351.

With the advent of the lively ball, the outfielder continued his hard hitting with the Baltimore Black Sox as their center fielder and cleanup hitter for four more years, registering averages of .366, .383, and .360 in 1921–23. During his last year in black baseball, 1925, he hit .319 in limited play, and is credited with a lifetime .397 batting average over a thirteen-year career.

Hall, Charley
Career: 1948   Position: ut
Team: Kansas City Monarchs

This utility player made his only appearance in the Negro Leagues with the Kansas City Monarchs in 1948.

Hall, Emory
Career: 1887   Position: 2b
Team: *Philadelphia Pythians*

He was a second baseman with the Philadelphia Pythians, one of eight teams that were charter members of the League of Colored Baseball Clubs in 1887. However, the league's existence was ephemeral, lasting only a week.

Hall, Horace G.
Career: 1933–42   Positions: officer; vice president (NAL)
Team: Chicago American Giants

He was an officer with the Chicago American Giants for a decade (1933–42) and served a term as vice president of the Negro American League.

Hall, Perry
Career: 1921–45   Positions: **3b**, 2b, of, p
Teams: St. Louis Giants ('21), Detroit Stars ('21–'22, '26), Milwaukee Bears ('23), Memphis Red Sox ('27), Cleveland Tigers ('28), Birmingham Black Barons ('28), Gilkerson's Union Giants ('30, '32, '35), Chicago Columbia Giants ('31), Indianapolis Athletics ('37), *Chicago Giants ('38–'45)*
Bats: Right   Throws: Right
Born: Apr. 18, 1901, Obidgeville, Ga.
Died: April 3, 1992, Chicago, Ill.

A good hitter with some power, he had very good speed and appreciable basestealing skills. Although third base was his favorite position, the infielder began his career as a pitcher with three different midwestern teams during the first three years of the Negro National League's existence. He credits Pete Hill and Bruce Petway as being instrumental in helping him make the transition from the mound to the infield.

Coming from a family of nineteen children, he ran away from home in 1915 and went to Atlanta to live with an older brother. Two years later he began playing baseball in a Sunday school league, and the youngster's performance warranted a tryout with Rube Foster's Chicago American Giants in the early '20s. Rube sent him to Milwaukee, where he played until the club dropped out of the league late in the season. At that time he was a pitcher, but a lack of success on the mound coupled with a desire to play every day soon resulted in a switch to the infield. The aspiring player was returned to Foster, who again shipped him out to strengthen another league team. In 1927 he hit .387 with the Memphis Red Sox, and the next year he played with both the Birmingham

Black Barons and the Cleveland Tigers until the team disbanded after the season.

Between stints with league teams, he toured with Gilkerson's Union Giants, an independent team that toured throughout the Midwest, Northwest, and Canada. In 1932, while playing in Tacoma, Washington, he stepped in a gopher hole and popped a knee, putting him out of commission for the remainder of the year. After recovering from the injury, he returned to baseball, playing with the Kansas City Monarchs in 1934, his favorite team of all that he played with.

In 1937, his last season in league play, he was with the Indianapolis ABCs. The following year, tired of traveling, he signed with Joe Green's Chicago Giants so he could play ball locally, while also driving a cab in the off-season and have a normal lifestyle. Before retiring in 1945, he also served as manager during the last five years with the team.

Hall, Sellers McKee (**Sell**)
Career: 1916–20   Position: p
Teams: **Homestead Grays** ('17–'20), Chicago American Giants ('17), *Pittsburgh Colored Giants* ('16)

He was a pitcher with the Grays in their early years before they became a major-league-caliber team, and was signed from the Grays by Rube Foster in the late summer of 1917 to play with the Chicago American Giants.

Hamilton
Career: 1886   Position: 2b
Team: *New York Gorhams*

In 1886 he was the second baseman for the New York Gorhams, one of the earliest black professional teams.

Hamilton
Career: 1921   Position: of
Team: Chicago Giants

He was a reserve outfielder with the Chicago Giants in 1921, their last year in league play.

Hamilton
Career: 1921–24   Position: p

Teams: Kansas City Monarchs ('21), Atlantic City Bacharach Giants ('23), Cleveland Browns ('24), St. Louis Stars ('24)

He was a pitcher with the Kansas City Monarchs, Cleveland Browns, and St. Louis Stars during the early '20s.

Hamilton, George
Career: 1923–32   Position: c
Teams: Memphis Red Sox ('23–'28), Birmingham Black Barons ('29), Washington Pilots ('32)

Beginning his career in 1923, the catcher played exclusively with southern teams for his first seven years in black baseball, primarily with the Memphis Red Sox. In 1927 he hit .281 in limited play with the Red Sox, and joined the Birmingham Black Barons two years later. His last appearance in the Negro Leagues was in 1932, with the Washington Pilots of the ill-fated East-West League.

Hamilton, J. C. (Gaitor, John, Ed)
Career: 1939–42   Position: p
Team: Homestead Grays
Bats: Left   Throws: Left
Height: 5'10"   Weight: 180

Utilizing a two-pitch repertory, the Homestead Grays' left-handed hurler mixed his fastball and curve effectively. After joining the Grays in 1939, he moved into the starting rotation the following year, fashioning a 5–4 ledger in league play to help the Grays annex the Negro National League pennant. In 1941 he finished with a 3–2 work sheet as the Grays repeated as champions. Although Hamilton dropped out of the regular pitching rotation and his contributions to the pennant drive were lessened, the Grays won their third straight Negro National League flag in 1942 but lost the World Series to the Kansas City Monarchs.

Like most Grays' hurlers, he was a pretty good hitter for a pitcher, but he reserved his power for the golf links, where the native Floridian (who often served as Dizzy Dean's caddie during his spring training) featured a tremendous drive in his golf game.

Hamilton, J. H. (John)

Career: 1924–27   Positions: 2b, ss, 3b

Teams: Washington Potomacs ('24), Wilmington Potomacs ('25), Indianapolis ABCs, ('25), Cleveland Elites ('26), Birmingham Black Barons ('27), Memphis Red Sox ('27)

Arriving from Dallas in 1924 with a label as the best shortstop in Texas, the youngster failed to develop a good arm and was moved by Washington Potomacs' manager Ben Taylor to second base, where he performed fairly well. Considered a very dangerous man with a bat, he batted in the second slot in the order, and was reserved by the Potomacs for the 1925 season, where he hit .277 after the club was transferred to Wilmington for the season. In 1926 he hit .309 with the Cleveland Elites and followed with a .262 average with the Memphis Red Sox in 1927. He also played third base during his four-year career, playing mostly with teams in the Midwest and South.

Hamilton, Jim

Career: 1946   Position: ss

Team: Kansas City Monarchs

The rookie shortstop with the 1946 Negro American League champion Kansas City Monarchs showed great promise despite a .204 batting average, but he suffered a career-ending broken leg when his inexperience prevented him from avoiding burly Bob Harvey's hard slide to break up a double play in the first game of the World Series. Ironically, his replacement, Chico Renfroe, led the team in batting for the Series.

Hamilton, L.

Career: 1923–25   Positions: 2b, 3b, lf

Teams: Memphis Red Sox, Indianapolis ABCs, Birmingham Black Barons ('25)

In 1924 he played as a second baseman with the Memphis Red Sox, Indianapolis ABCs, and Birmingham Black Barons.

Hamilton, Lewis

[see Hampton, Lewis]

Hamilton, Theron B.

Career: 1934   Position: officer

Team: Homestead Grays

In 1934, when the Homestead Grays were associate members of the Negro National League, he served as the ballclub's vice president.

Hamman, Ed

Career: 1945, 1946–50   Position: comedian, officer, owner

Teams: Cincinnati-Indianapolis Clowns ('45), Indianapolis Clowns ('46–'76)

Bats: Left   Throws: Right

Height: 5'5½"   Weight: 160

Born: March 2, 1907, Fostoria, Ohio.

Died: Jan. 9, 1989, Inverness, Fla.

A white baseball comedian who created, designed, and performed many of the comedy routines used by the Indianapolis Clowns' baseball team, he later became the owner of the team. In his earlier years, prior to joining the Clowns, he was a legitimate ballplayer and played in organized ball in the Michigan State League and the Middle Atlantic League. But he gravitated toward the touring teams that combined baseball and entertainment.

In 1933, he and Syd Pollock organized the Canadian Clowns, a white team, and the pair formed a lifelong friendship. Hamman also toured with the Canadian House of David and other barnstorming teams, and introduced a blend of fun and skill on ball diamonds all across America. As the years passed, he let the younger players play the baseball and became strictly a comedian, participating in the team's skits for the delight of the fans. In 1944 he joined the original House of David franchise, and the next year he joined his old friend Syd Pollock's Indianapolis Clowns as a comedian.

In 1952 Pollock offered Hamman a partnership with the Clowns. That was the year that the Clowns signed Hank Aaron to his first professional contract, at $200 a month. Aaron played about three months as the team's shortstop and cleanup hitter before his contract was purchased by the Braves' organization.

Later Hamman became sole owner of the Clowns, and long after the color line was obliterated, he continued to take the Clowns across the country. Over the years the Clowns began attracting white ballplayers and, although the golden age of barnstorming was past, the style was the same. In the 1970s he was still acting as the general manager of the Indianapolis Clowns and was a focal character in the 1974 book *Some Are Called Clowns*. He also served as an advisor on the movie *Bingo Long's Traveling All-Stars and Motor Kings* in 1976, and suffered a heart attack during the filming of the movie. After recovery, he finally retired from the game he loved. But baseball became big business and passed him by, leaving him in obscurity at the time of his death.

Hammond, Don
Career: 1923–24   Positions: 3b, ss, *p*
Teams: Toledo Tigers ('23), Cleveland Tate Stars ('23–'24), Cleveland Browns ('24)

This infielder played for two seasons during the '20s with struggling teams in Ohio, primarily with franchises in Cleveland.

Hampton, Eppie
Career: 1925–38   Positions: **c**, 1b, *p*
Teams: Birmingham Black Barons ('25–'26, '29), **Memphis Red Sox** ('27–'28, '36–'38), Cleveland Tigers ('28), Washington Pilots ('32), New Orleans Crescent Stars ('33)

Early in his career he did double duty as a catcher-pitcher combination, but in the latter stages of his career he tended toward catcher-first base duty. With the 1927 Memphis Red Sox he shared catching duties with Larry Brown, batted .205, and filled in on the mound on occasion. Two years later, catching with the Birmingham Black Barons, he hit .333 in limited play.

When the ill-fated East-West League was organized in 1932, he joined the league's Washington Pilots as the starting catcher. During this rare excursion outside the South, he also supplied additional duty at first base while batting in the lower part of the batting order. Follow-

ing the breakup of the league in midseason, he renewed his alignment with southern teams. After returning to Memphis in the waning years of his career, the veteran began playing more at first base in 1937, and closed out his career in a reserve role on manager "Double Duty" Radcliffe's 1938 Negro American League first-half champion Memphis Red Sox.

Hampton, Lewis (Lucius, Hamp)
a.k.a Lewis Hamilton
Career: 1921–28   Positions: p, *of*
Teams: Columbus Buckeyes ('21), Indianapolis ABCs ('22), Atlantic City Bacharach Giants ('23), Hilldale Daisies ('23), Washington Potomacs ('24), Wilmington Potomacs ('25), New York Lincoln Giants ('25), Detroit Stars ('25–'27)

He began his pitching career with the Columbus Buckeyes in 1921, posting a 4–2 record, but frequently changed teams during his career. He switched to the Indianapolis ABCs in 1922 and played with both the Bacharachs and Hilldale the next season, before finally joining the Washington Potomacs in 1924, where he was in the starting rotation. After defeating Hilldale several times that year, he earned recognition as a good pitcher. He was placed on the Potomacs' reserved list for 1925, and the franchise moved to Wilmington, where he endured a 1–6 performance before the Potomacs dropped out of league play. Returning to the Midwest, he pitched with the Detroit Stars through the 1927 season. In addition to his pitching ability, he was also a good hitter, batting .305, .269, and .295 in 1923, 1925, and 1926, respectively, and with sufficient power to be characterized as having a "hobby" of hitting home runs.

Hampton, Wade
Career: 1918–23   Position: p
Teams: *Pennsylvania Giants ('18)*, Hilldale Daisies ('22–'23)

This pitcher spent a half-dozen years with Hilldale and the Pennsylvania Giants, a team of lesser caliber.

Hancock, Art
Career: 1926–27   Positions: 1b, of, p
Teams: Cleveland Elites ('26), Cleveland Hornets ('27)

He was one of a multitude of players to wear the uniform of the two Cleveland entries in the Negro National League in 1926–27. He began as a pitcher in 1926 with the Elites, losing his only decision, and played with the Hornets as a first baseman-outfielder during the following season, but did not receive much playing time either year at any position.

Hancock, Charles Winston (Charlie)
Career: 1921   Position: c
Team: St. Louis Giants

He was a reserve catcher with the 1921 St. Louis Giants in his only year in the Negro National League.

Hancock, W.
Career: 1885   Position: player
Team: *Brooklyn Remsens*

He was a player with the 1885 Brooklyn Remsens, one of the earliest black baseball teams.

Handy, George
Career: 1946–49   Positions: **2b**, 3b
Teams: Memphis Red Sox ('46–'48), Houston Eagles ('49), *minor leagues ('49–'50, '52–'55), Canadian League ('50–'51)*
Bats: Left   Throws: Right
Height: 5'6"   Weight: 175
Born: 1924

This infielder began his career in 1947 by hitting .326 while batting third in the order with the Memphis Red Sox. His offensive production fell off the following season and he began the 1949 season with the Houston Eagles, but was shortly playing in organized baseball with Bridgeport of the Connecticut League, where he hit .346 with 22 home runs and 25 stolen bases in 126 games. He split the following year between Bridgeport (.272) and St. Hyacinthe (.352) of the Provincial League, while playing the entire 1951 season in the

Provincial League and batting .333 with 72 RBIs in 121 games.

Beginning the 1952 season with Keokuk in the Three-I League, his .303 average won him advancement to Miami Beach in the Florida International League, where his average slipped to .265. For the next three years, the last of his career, he hit over .300 each season while playing with a different team in a different league each year. From 1953 to 1955 he registered marks of .314 (94 RBIs) with Fort Lauderdale of the Florida International League, .306 with Montgomery of the Sally League, and .333 with Norfolk in the Piedmont League.

Handy, William Oscar (Bill)
Career: 1910–27   Positions: **2b**, ss, 3b, of
Teams: **Brooklyn Royal Giants** ('10–'17), St. Louis Giants ('12, '15), G.C.T. Red Caps ('18), Atlantic City Bacharach Giants ('17–'21, '27), New York Lincoln Giants ('18), *Philadelphia Giants, New York Black Sox*

The best second baseman in the East during the '10s, he was a good fielder who played airtight defense, was fast going to first base, and was a good man at the plate, usually batting in the fifth slot for the Brooklyn Royal Giants. In 1917 he hit for a .423 average against all levels of competition, and after joining the Bacharachs in 1919 he hit for a .286 average. He broke in with the Royal Giants as a shortstop and also played at third base and in the outfield, but his best position was at the keystone spot. Making the transition to the lively-ball era, he hit .234 with the Bacharachs in 1921 and was still regarded as an outstanding defensive player. The remainder of his career was spent primarily with teams of lesser quality.

Hanks
Career: 1908   Position: c
Team: *Brooklyn Colored Giants*

In 1908 he was a catcher with the Brooklyn Colored Giants, a team of marginal quality.

Hannibal
Career: 1914–17   Position: of

Teams: Indianapolis ABCs (*'13*–'14, '17), Bowser's ABCs ('16)

He began his career with the Indianapolis ABCs in 1914, the first season when they fielded a team of major-league caliber. When owner Thomas Bowser and manager C. I. Taylor went their separate ways in 1916, forming two ABCs teams, he was one of the outfielders used by Bowser in an effort to fill the center-field void left by the defection of Oscar Charleston early in the season. The following season Hannibal appeared briefly with C. I. Taylor's Indianapolis ABCs.

Hannibal, Leo Jack
Career: 1932–38   Position: p
Teams: Indianapolis ABCs ('32), Indianapolis Athletics ('37), Homestead Grays ('38)

He pitched with Indianapolis Athletics in 1937, the only year in which he played substantially. He made a brief pitching appearance with the Grays the following season and had appeared with the Indianapolis ABCs in 1932 when they were in the Negro Southern League.

Hannon
Career: 1908–13   Positions: c, of, 3b
Teams: *Pop Watkins's Stars ('08),* Philadelphia Giants ('09), St. Louis Giants ('10–'13)

After playing as a third baseman with Pop Watkins's Stars, a team of lesser caliber, he appeared briefly as a reserve outfielder with the Philadelphia Giants in 1909 before joining the St. Louis Giants the following season. In 1913 he was the Giants' starting catcher, batting seventh in the order.

Hanson
a.k.a. Hansen
Career: 1915   Position: ss
Team: Chicago American Giants

A reserve shortstop with the Chicago American Giants in 1915, his playing time was severely restricted.

Harden, James
Career: 1947   Position: p

Team: Homestead Grays

He pitched with the Homestead Grays in 1947, his only year in the Negro Leagues.

Harden, John H. (Johnny)
Career: 1938–48   Positions: officer, owner
Teams: Atlanta Black Crackers ('38), Indianapolis ABCs ('39), New York Black Yankees

This black businessman was granted a franchise in the Negro American League in 1938 and engaged in competition with Michael Schaine, owner of the Atlanta Black Crackers, for baseball dominance in Atlanta. After Schaine decided to step aside, Harden secured the best ballplayers from both franchises and appropriated the team name Atlanta Black Crackers as well. As the owner and president of the Atlanta Black Crackers in 1938, he made the necessary personnel changes and captured the second-half league championship. The service station impresario sometimes had difficulty meeting the payroll. In search of a larger baseball market, he moved the franchise to Indianapolis in 1939 and played as the ABCs. The relocation was not successful, and he returned to Atlanta for the next season, playing in the Negro Southern League, where he also served as the league treasurer.

Harden, Lovell (Big Pitch)
a.k.a. Hardin
Career: 1943–45   Position: p
Team: Cleveland Buckeyes
Bats: Right   Throws: Right
Height: 6'0"   Weight: 170
Born: 1918, St. Louis, Ms.

Signed off the sandlots of Laurel, Mississippi, by the Cleveland Buckeyes in 1943, this right-hander exhibited a modicum of speed and control. His second season, 1944, was his best, as he crafted a 5–3 work sheet with a 1.99 ERA. The next year he finished with a 3–2 league ledger with a 3.98 ERA as the Buckeyes won the Negro American League pennant and swept the Homestead Grays in the World Series to win the 1945 championship.

Hardiman
Career: 1937   Position: p
Team: St. Louis Stars

He was a pitcher with the St. Louis Stars in 1937, the inaugural season of the Negro American League.

Harding, A. Hallie
Career: 1926–31   Positions: ss, 2b, 3b, of, p
Teams: Indianapolis ABCs ('26), Detroit Stars ('27–'28), **Kansas City Monarchs** ('28–'31), Chicago Columbia Giants ('31), Atlantic City Bacharach Giants ('31), Baltimore Black Sox ('31)

A versatile infielder with good speed, he was the shortstop and leadoff batter for the 1929 Negro National League champion Kansas City Monarchs, hitting .327 for the year. Although his presence at the plate was not imposing, he was a good hitter, but dropped off to a .269 average the next season. Prior to joining the Monarchs, he began his career with the Indianapolis ABCs in 1926, batting .371, and joined the Detroit Stars the following season, hitting .285. Although he played different positions, he usually batted in the leadoff position, as he did with David Malarcher's 1931 Chicago Columbia Giants as their second baseman. In that year, his last in the Negro Leagues, he also played briefly with the Baltimore Black Sox, the Bacharachs, and the Kansas City Monarchs.

Harding, Roy
Career: 1937–38   Position: p
Teams: Philadelphia Stars ('37), New York Black Yankees ('38), Atlanta Black Crackers ('38)

This versatile curveball pitcher, formerly with the New York Black Yankees, was added to the Negro Americana League second-half champion Atlanta Black Crackers' squad in late June 1938.

Harding, Tom
Career: 1940   Position: of
Team: Indianapolis Crawfords

In 1940 he played with the Indianapolis Crawfords of the Negro American League as a reserve outfielder.

Hardy, Arthur Wesley (Art, Bill)
a.k.a. Shin Norman
Career: 1905–12   Position: p
Teams: *Topeka Giants ('05)*, Kansas City, Kansas, Giants ('05, '07–'12), Union Giants ('06), Leland Giants ('07–'09), Chicago Giants ('10)
Born: Mar. 3, 1886, Topeka, Kan.

Beginning his career in 1905 with the Topeka Giants and Kansas City, Kansas, Giants, the tall moundsman was a top pitcher in the state of Kansas. After one season he joined the Union Giants, for whom he hurled several shutout games and proved to be one of the best men on the team. He returned to the Kansas City aggregation, playing intermittently for half a dozen years, but playing with Chicago-based teams during the latter part of each season.

When he signed with the Chicago Leland Giants in 1907, he assumed the alias of Billy "Shin" Norman and retained that identity for the remainder of his career. The tough competitor proved his worth during the 1909 season, helping pitch the team to the City League pennant. In seven games on the mound he compiled a 3–2 ledger, including 31 strikeouts and 12 walks. Meanwhile, at the plate he was able to manage only a weak .176 batting average. During the ensuing winter he accompanied Rube Foster's team to Havana for the Cuban winter league.

The following season, after Foster split with owner Frank Leland, Hardy remained with Leland and was regarded as a star among the owner's celebrated pitchers on the new Chicago Giants' ballclub. Two years later, in the winter of 1912, he returned to Havana as a member of the Stars of Cuba. A college man, he earned degrees from Washburn University (B.S.) in Topeka and Ohio State University (M.A.).

Hardy, Doc

Career: 1950　　　　Position: 2b
Team: Cleveland Buckeyes

He was an infielder with the Cleveland Buckeyes in 1950, but league statistics do not confirm his playing time.

Hardy, Paul James

Career: 1932–47　　　Position: c
Teams: Montgomery Grey Sox (*'31*–'32), Detroit Stars ('33), Nashville Elite Giants ('34), Columbus Elite Giants ('35), Washington Elite Giants ('36), Chicago American Giants ('37–'38, '51–'52), Satchel Paige's All-Stars ('39), Kansas City Monarchs ('39, '42), **Birmingham Black Barons** ('40–'43), *military service ('43–'45)*, Memphis Red Sox ('47), *Harlem Globetrotters ('47)*
Bats: Right　　　Throws: Right
Height: 5'11"　　　Weight: 175

A very good receiver with a strong arm, this aggressive backstop was proficient at blocking the plate. He was only a fair hitter with some power, but his hustle and defensive skills kept him in the Negro Leagues for sixteen seasons despite a lack of offensive output.

During the '30s Hardy served stints with several teams, including the Chicago American Giants and Kansas City Monarchs, before landing with the Birmingham Black Barons as their first-string catcher when the team rejoined the Negro American League in 1940. He was still the starting catcher for the Black Barons when they captured the pennant in 1943, but was called into military service just before the start of the World Series. The Negro National League champion Homestead Grays granted permission for him to be replaced by the Chicago American Giants' star receiver "Double Duty" Radcliffe. Following World War II he returned to the Negro Leagues, batting .326 with the Memphis Red Sox in 1947, his last season.

Hardy, Walter

Career: 1945–50　　Positions: 2b, ss
Teams: New York Black Yankees ('45–'47), *Holdout ('48)*, New York Cubans ('49), Kansas City Monarchs ('50), *Canadian League ('50–'51, '55)*
Bats: Right　　　Throws: Right
Height: 5'10"　　　Weight: 160
Born: 1927

This flashy-fielding, weak-hitting middle infielder played for half a dozen seasons in the latter years of the Negro Leagues (1945–50). In his first season, the rookie displaced another sensational young fielder, shortstop Rufus Baker, by giving the fans a thrill on every play. After three years, despite a lack of power, low batting averages (.129, .215, and .160), and poor fielding in his third season, he was a holdout in 1948. The New York Black Yankees, who felt that he was not justified in his demands, failed to concede to them, and he played the 1949 season with the New York Cubans, where he boosted his average to .267. In 1950 the hustling infielder moved West to join the Kansas City Monarchs and hit .252 before leaving the last part of the season to play in the Provincial League with St. Jean, for whom he hit an even .200 to finish the season. Playing the entire 1951 season with the same team, he batted .251 and managed a .276 mark while back with St. Jean again in 1955.

Hareway

Career: 1931　　　　Position: p
Team: *Newark Browns*

He was a pitcher with the Newark Browns in 1931, a year before they entered the East-West League.

Hargett

Career: 1918　　　　Position: p
Team: Hilldale Daisies

He was a pitcher with Hilldale in 1918, winning his only recorded decision.

Hargett, York

Career: 1887　　　　Position: player
Team: *Philadelphia Pythians*

He was a player with the 1887 Philadelphia Pythians, one of eight teams that were charter members of the League of Colored Baseball

Clubs in 1887. However, the league's existence was ephemeral, lasting only a week.

Harland, Bill

Career: 1929   Position: p
Team: New York Lincoln Giants

He pitched briefly with the Lincoln Giants in 1929, his only year in the Negro Leagues.

Harmon, Charles Byron (**Chuck**)

a.k.a Charlie Fine
Career: 1947   Position: of
Teams: Indianapolis Clowns ('47), *minor leagues ('47, '49–'54, '56–'61), voluntarily retired ('48),* major leagues ('54–'57)
Bats: Right   Throws: Right
Height: 6'2"   Weight: 175
Born: Apr. 23, 1926, Washington, Ind.

While going to school at the University of Toledo, he played with the Indianapolis Clowns in 1947 under the alias Charlie Fine to protect his amateur standing. He was looking for a summer job and Hank Rigney, a white promoter in Toledo, asked him to play under the fictitious name. After five games, his college athletic director called and asked him to return to Toledo to work with the city's Recreation Department, so he left the team. About two months later, in July, he signed to play in organized baseball.

He played with Gloversville in the CanAm League in 1947 and hit .270, while demonstrating good speed, to earn a spot on their roster for the next season, but he voluntarily retired for a season, rejoining the team briefly in 1949 for 14 undistinguished games before moving to Olean in the Pony League, where he hit .351 with good power.

Back on track at Olean, the next two seasons he compiled batting averages of .374 and .375 and led the league in doubles and RBIs each year. In 1950 he also led the league in games played, at-bats, and hits while accumulating good stolen-base totals. While at Olean he played outfield and every infield position. With Burlington of the Three-I league in 1952, he played third base and center field and hit .319

while leading the league in stolen bases, hits, and games played. The next season, 1953, he moved up to Tulsa in the Texas League, and while alternating between third base and the outfield, he hit .311 with good power (14 home runs). That winter he played with Ponce in Puerto Rico and hit .331.

His performance convinced the Cincinnati Reds that he was ready for the major leagues, and he made his debut in the big show in 1954, hitting .238 while playing in 94 games and alternating between the infield corner positions. From 1954 to 1957 he was in the major leagues with Cincinnati, the St. Louis Cardinals, and the Philadelphia Phillies, and he compiled a lifetime major-league batting average of .238 while playing in the outfield and on the corners but never getting in as many as 100 games in any season.

In 1956 he spent most of the season in Omaha, where he hit .360, but after another year in the major leagues he was back in the minors for the remainder of his career. He spent the next four years with Miami in the International League, St. Paul and Charleston in the American Association, and Salt Lake City and Hawaii in the Pacific Coast League. After two productive seasons at Salt Lake City (.310 and .287), he finished his career in Hawaii in 1961, playing in only 7 games.

Harmon, (House Lady)

Career: 1938   Position: ss
Team: Atlanta Black Crackers
Bats: Right   Throws: Right
Height: 6'0"   Weight: 160

A shortstop from Chicago, he was quick and a good fielder, but his stay with the Atlanta Black Crackers in 1938 was very brief and he made a rapid departure. A linebacker on the football team at Morris Brown University, he was tall, wiry, and rough, but not as suitable for baseball.

Harness, Robert Marseilles (O.)

Career: 1927   Position: p
Team: *Chicago Giants*

In 1927 he was a pitcher with the Chicago

Giants, a team that had declined significantly in their level of play.

Harney, George
Career: 1923–31   Position: p
Teams: Chicago American Giants ('23–'30), Chicago Giants, Chicago Columbia Giants ('31)
Bats: Right   Throws: Right

A spitball star for the Chicago American Giants, he paired with Willie Foster during the '20s to form a formidable mound duo, pitching the team to consecutive Negro National League pennants in 1926–27 under manager David Malarcher's direction. In 1926 Harney fashioned a 12–4 record to help the American Giants in their first pennant drive, before dropping off to a 8–9 mark the latter season. Each year the American Giants faced the Eastern Colored League champion Bacharach Giants of Atlantic City in the World Series. The right-hander started two games and earned a victory in each Series, showing ERAs of 3.14 and 1.74, respectively. Prior to the pennant-winning seasons, Harney posted seasons of 9–2 and 7–4 in 1924–25. In addition to his spitter, he also employed a ''cut'' ball, but as he neared the end of his career his effectiveness declined, and in 1930 he split his only 2 decisions. The next season, his last in the Negro Leagues, was spent with Malarcher's Chicago Columbia Giants.

Harper
Career: 1909–16   Position: p
Teams: Leland Giants ('09–'10), Chicago Giants ('16)

Not much is known about Harper, not even his first name. He appeared with the Leland Giants in one game in 1909, spent the winter with the team in the Florida Hotel League, and came North with them in the spring, pitching briefly at the beginning of the season before dropping out of sight. He resurfaced briefly in 1916 with the Chicago Giants before melding into baseball obscurity.

Harper
Career: 1920   Position: ss
Teams: Hilldale Daisies ('20), *Norfolk Stars ('25)*

A reserve shortstop with Hilldale in 1920, he later also played with the Norfolk Stars, a team of lesser status.

Harper
Career: 1920   Position: of
Team: Kansas City Monarchs

He was a reserve outfielder with the Kansas City Monarchs during their first year in the Negro National League.

Harper, Chick (Chalky)
Career: 1920–25   Positions: p, of
Team: Detroit Stars ('20–'22, '25)

A pitcher with the Detroit Stars in the early '20s, he also played occasionally in the outfield.

Harper, David T. (Dave, Rough House)
Career: 1943–46   Positions: of, 1b, *ss*
Teams: Philadelphia Stars ('43), *Atlanta Black Crackers ('43)*, Cincinnati Clowns ('44), Kansas City Monarchs ('44–'45), Birmingham Black Barons ('46)
Bats: Right   Throws: Right
Height: 6'0"   Weight: 185

A very fast ball hawk with good range and a good throwing arm, this stocky outfielder was a wartime player with the Kansas City Monarchs in 1944–45. He started the 1944 season with the Cincinnati Clowns but soon joined the Monarchs, where he shared a starting spot in the outfield. With Kansas City he usually batted sixth or seventh in the order, but was reputed to pack a wallop at the plate despite his .211 batting average. In 1943 he signed and accepted money from the Philadelphia Stars and was claimed by the Stars but was playing center field with the Atlanta Black Crackers. He attended college at Atlanta's Clark University, where he was an All-Southern triple-threat halfback.

Harper, John
Career: 1923–26   Position: p
Teams: *Richmond Giants ('22),* Atlantic City Bacharach Giants ('23–'25), New York Lincoln Giants ('25–'26), Cuban Stars ('25)

After a year with the Richmond Giants, a team of lesser status, he pitched with the Bacharach Giants during the Eastern Colored League's first two years. In 1925 he was traded to the New York Lincoln Giants for third-base great Oliver Marcelle, but when Harper refused to report, the trade fell through. Later in the year another trade was successfully negotiated, and eventually he joined the Lincoln Giants and the Cuban Stars, but suffered through a winless season, losing all four league decisions.

Harper, Walter
Career: 1929–32   Positions: c, 1b
Teams: *Birmingham Black Barons ('23),* Chicago American Giants ('29–30), Chicago Columbia Giants ('31), Cole's American Giants ('32)

He shared the catching assignment with David Malarcher's 1931 Chicago Columbia Giants, batting seventh in the order. He also played first base during his irregular career with the Chicago American Giants during their last two years in the Negro National League and the year they spent in the Negro Southern League in 1932 under Robert Cole's ownership. Harper began his career in 1923 with the Birmingham Black Barons, who were still playing as an independent team and were a year away from joining the Negro National League.

Harris
Career: 1919   Position: of
Team: New York Lincoln Giants

In 1919 he appeared as a reserve outfielder with the Lincoln Giants.

Harris
Career: 1921   Position: p
Teams: Indianapolis ABCs ('21), Columbus Buckeyes ('21), Chicago American Giants ('21)

This pitcher served short stints with three midwestern Negro National League teams during the 1921 season but failed to figure in a decision with any of them.

Harris
Career: 1938   Position: of
Team: Atlanta Black Crackers

He was on the Atlanta Black Crackers' roster in late March 1938 as an outfielder but did not stick with the team.

Harris, Ananias
Career: 1921–23   Position: p
Teams: Brooklyn Royal Giants ('21), Hilldale ('22), Harrisburg Giants ('23)

During the early '20s, he was a pitcher for three years with teams in the eastern alignment: the Brooklyn Royal Giants, the Harrisburg Giants, and Hilldale.

Harris, Andy
Career: 1917–27   Positions: **3b**, 2b, 1b
Teams: Hilldale ('17), *Pennsylvania Giants ('18), Pittsburgh Stars of Buffalo ('19),* Pennsylvania Red Caps of New York ('19–'20, '25), Newark Stars ('26), New York Lincoln Giants ('27)

Beginning his career with Hilldale in 1917, this light-hitting third baseman played with teams along the New York-Philadelphia axis for a decade. Much of his playing experience was with lesser teams, including the Pennsylvania Giants and the Pittsburgh Stars of Buffalo. In 1919 he was in the starting lineup for the Pennsylvania Red Caps of New York, playing both second base and third base while hitting in the seventh slot in the batting order. His last two seasons before closing his career were with teams in the Eastern Colored League. In 1926 he batted in the heart of the order for the Newark Stars before they disbanded in midseason. The next season he played as an occasional starter at first base for the New York Lincoln Giants, batting at the bottom of the order when in the lineup.

Harris, Bill
Career: 1930–32   Positions: c, of

Teams: Memphis Red Sox ('30), Indianapolis ABCs ('31), Monroe Monarchs ('32)

Beginning in 1930 with the Memphis Red Sox, he spent three years with league teams, closing his career in 1932 with the Monroe Monarchs. During the middle season, when he was a backup catcher with the Indianapolis ABCs, he received more playing time than in any other year.

Harris, Charles (**Charlie**)
Career: 1943   Positions: 2b, ss
Teams: Cincinnati Clowns ('43), *Chicago Brown Bombers ('43)*

A light-hitting infielder, he was a wartime player, sharing duty at second base with the Negro American League's Cincinnati Clowns in 1943.

Harris, Chick (Moochie, Popsicle)
Career: 1931–36   Positions: 1b, lf, rf
Teams: Kansas City Monarchs ('31–'32, '34, '36), Detroit Wolves ('32), Cleveland Stars ('32), *New Orleans Crescent Stars ('33–'34)*

A first baseman, he played in the 1936 East-West All-Star game while with the Kansas City Monarchs. His first year with the Monarchs was in 1931, and he also played in the outfield for the next two years, usually batting in the lower part of the batting order. He also appeared with the New Orleans Crescent Stars, Cleveland Stars, and Detroit Wolves during his career. He seemed to collect sobriquets, earning two distinct nicknames during his six seasons with top ball clubs. He was called "Popsicle" in the East and "Moochie" in Texas.

Harris, Cornelius (**Neal,** Nate)
Career: 1931   Positions: of, 3b
Team: *Pittsburgh Crawfords*

In 1931 he played in the outfield and at third base with the Pittsburgh Crawfords, a year before they became one of the powers of black baseball.

Harris, Curtis (Popeye)
Career: 1931–40   Positions: 2b, 3b, of, 1b, ss, c

Teams: Pittsburgh Crawfords ('31, '34–'35), Kansas City Monarchs ('36), **Philadelphia Stars** ('37–'40)

An extremely versatile player who played every regular position, he was a valuable utility man for the outstanding Pittsburgh Crawford teams of the midthirties, with incomplete statistics showing a consolidated .325 average for his years with the Crawfords. After leaving the Crawfords, he played a season with the Kansas City Monarchs before moving back East to join the Philadelphia Stars as the regular second baseman in 1937, where he usually hit sixth in the batting order. The next year he retained his starting position, with partial statistics showing a .348 batting average. In 1939 he hit .295 after being relegated to a reserve role, and dropped off to a .192 average in limited play in 1940.

Harris, Dixon
Career: 1932   Position: player
Team: Homestead Grays

He was listed as a player with the Grays in 1932, when they were in the East-West League, but his position is not known.

Harris, Elander Victor (**Vic**)
Career: 1923–50   Positions: lf, rf, cf, 1b, manager, coach
Teams: Cleveland Tate Stars ('23), Toledo Tigers ('23), Cleveland Browns ('24), Chicago American Giants ('24–'25), **Homestead Grays** ('25–'33, '35–'48), Detroit Wolves ('32), Pittsburgh Crawfords ('34), *defense work ('43),* Baltimore Elite Giants ('49), Birmingham Black Barons ('50)
Bats: Left   Throws: Right
Height: 5'10"   Weight: 168
Born: June 10, 1905, Pensacola, Fla.
Died: Feb. 23, 1978, San Fernando, Calif.

Vic Harris spent almost his entire career with the Homestead Grays, logging twenty-three years with the organization as player and manager. His career spanned the three eras of the Grays' greatness, first as a player on the teams of the late 1920s and early 1930s, and then as a player-manager of the revitalized dynasty that captured nine consecutive Negro National League pennants from 1937 to 1945, and in his final year as a manager of the Grays, when, featuring a number of young ballplayers, Homestead captured the last Negro National League championship.

As a player, the left-handed batter was a consistent spray hitter with a short, compact swing; he slapped the ball to all fields. He was a smart hitter with good bat control, making him a good hit-and-run man. Although he had only moderate power and a bit of a weakness on high fast balls, he hit for a good average and finished his career with a lifetime .299 batting average. Defensively, he was a good fielder in each phase of the game and gave a little extra hustle on the playing field. Underrated, in his prime he was one of the best players in the game, and as he got older he was still valuable as an utility outfielder and pinch hitter. He appeared in six East-West All-Star games, ranging from a starting spot in left field in the inaugural game in 1933 to a pinch-running appearance in the 1947 contest.

A native Floridian, he moved to Pittsburgh in 1914 and began playing baseball with the YMCA. Owner Cum Posey wanted him for the Grays, but he began his professional career in 1923 as an infielder with the Cleveland Tate Stars, hitting .304 for the Negro National League team. The next season he began the year with the Cleveland Browns, who had replaced the Tate Stars in the Negro National League, but joined Rube Foster's Chicago American Giants later in the season, batting a combined .277. The next season he signed with Foster's team but jumped to Posey's Grays, who were playing as an independent team, and was installed as the regular left fielder, usually hitting in the second or third spot in the batting order. Posey continued to improve the team, and in 1929 he entered the American Negro League, with Harris batting leadoff and contributing a .333 average to the team's effort.

During the next two years the Grays fielded their strongest team since their inception, with

Josh Gibson, Oscar Charleston, and Smokey Joe Williams joining Harris on the team. In this great aggregation of talent, Harris moved down to the sixth slot in the batting order and was credited with averages of .324 and .237 as the Grays copped top honors in the East each season. After these two great seasons, Gus Greenlee began raiding Posey's ballclub. For two years Harris resisted the offers, remaining with the Grays and hitting .348 and .351 as the Gray's leadoff man, but in 1934 he succumbed to Greenlee's entreaties and signed with the Crawfords, hitting .360 in his only year away from the Grays.

In 1935, Posey lured Harris back with the offer of a position as player-manager of the Grays. In his first year back in Homestead he hit .370, but it was not until Josh Gibson rejoined the Grays in 1937 that the team began their "long Gray line" of nine straight pennants. Already a fifteen-year veteran, Harris continued as the regular left fielder as he guided the Grays to six straight pennants, with the last one culminating in the first World Series between the Negro American League and the Negro National League. Unfortunately, the Grays lost the World Series to the Kansas City Monarchs.

In 1938 the playing manager hit for a .380 batting average, slugged 10 home runs, and stole 17 bases to lead his team to what some observers feel was their best season during the dynasty years. That season the Grays won the first half with a .813 winning percentage, and captured the second half as well to avoid the necessity of a playoff.

Harris had good speed and was a capable base stealer and feared base runner who thought the basepaths belonged to him. A slashing scrapper, he played to win, and his zealous hustle and aggressiveness often went beyond the bounds of reckless abandon, earning him the sobriquet "Vicious Vic" and the reputation as one of the "four big bad men" of black baseball. He was good with his fists and quick to use them. Once when the team was traveling by automobile and a player in the car that he was driving engaged in verbal comments that Harris found offensive, he stopped the car, pulled the player from the car, and physically whipped him on the spot. Considered by many to be a dirty ballplayer, on another occasion, while engaged in an argument with an umpire, he spit in the arbiter's face.

In many ways his behavior toward umpires was in contrast to the generally quiet approach he used with his players, never saying too much and preferring to inspire them by example to give their maximum effort. Although he was not noted as a brilliant strategist, the players responded to the fiery manger by giving good performances on the baseball diamond.

After the five straight pennants, Harris interrupted his managerial career for two seasons, taking a leave of absence from the post to take a job in a defense plant in 1943–44. Although he continued to play with the Grays when his work schedule permitted, he did not return to the helm until he guided the club to another Negro National League flag in 1945. After two years without a pennant, he directed them to another championship in 1948, as they won the Negro National League playoff and defeated the Birmingham Black Barons in the World Series. He coached for the 1949 Baltimore Elite Giants, who won the Negro American League championship, and managed the Birmingham Black Barons in 1950.

During his career he also played and managed in the Caribbean, playing with Santa Clara in Cuba in 1937–39 and in San Juan, Puerto Rico, in 1935–36, while returning a decade later to manage the Santurce teams in the Puerto Rican league in the winters of 1947–50.

Harris, Frank
Career: 1885   Position: p
Team: *Argyle Hotel Athletics*

He was a pitcher with the Argyle Hotel team, organized in 1885 by Frank P. Thompson, the headwaiter at Long Island's Argyle Hotel in Babylon, New York, who recruited players from the Philadelphia Keystones to work at the hotel as waiters and form a base-

ball team to play for the entertainment of the summer guests. After the end of the tourist season, the team added some more players from the Philadelphia Orions and the Manhattens of Washington, D.C., to form the Cuban Giants, the first black professional team. Harris was one of the players displaced.

Harris, George
Career: 1932–33   Position: 2b
Teams: Louisville Black Caps ('32), *Louisville Red Caps ('33)*

He was a second baseman with the Louisville ball clubs for two seasons in the early Depression years: the Black Caps of the Negro Southern League during their only adventure into the major-league ranks ('32), and the Red Caps the following season.

Harris, H. B.
Career: 1919   Position: business manager
Team: Brooklyn Royal Giants

In 1919 he served as the business manager for Nat Strong's Brooklyn Royal Giants.

Harris, H. C.
Career: 1916   Position: manager
Team: Baltimore Red Sox

During the Baltimore Black Sox's formative years, he served as the manager during the 1916 season.

Harris, Henry
Career: 1928–34   Position: ss
Teams: Memphis Red Sox ('28–'29), Louisville White Sox ('30–'31), Louisville Black Caps ('32), Baltimore Black Sox ('34)

He was a light-hitting shortstop with the Memphis Red Sox, Louisville Black Caps, Louisville White Sox, and Baltimore Black Sox during his seven-year career. In 1929, in very limited play, he hit a paltry .080 with the Memphis Red Sox.

Harris, Isaiah
Career: 1949–50   Position: p
Team: Memphis Red Sox

In the years when the Negro American League was struggling to survive the loss of players to organized baseball, he was a pitcher with the 1949–50 Memphis Red Sox, fashioning a 9–4 record with a 3.13 ERA in 1950.

Harris, J. (Sonny)

Career: 1936–42   Positions: of, 2b
Teams: Cincinnati Tigers ('36–'37), Cincinnati Buckeyes ('42)

He could play either outfield or infield, and he hit .282 with the Cincinnati Tigers in 1936, when the team was still playing as an independent ballclub. The next season the Tigers joined the Negro American League in its inaugural season and Harris was a part-time starter, batting in the lower part of the order. He later played with the Buckeyes franchise in 1942, his last year in league play.

Harris, James

Career: 1884–87   Position: of
Teams: *Baltimore Atlantics ('84–'87), Baltimore Lord Baltimores ('87)*

Beginning his baseball career in 1884, playing amateur ball, he was an outfielder with the Baltimore Atlantics, one of the earliest black teams, and the Lord Baltimores, organized in 1887 as one of eight teams that were charter members of the League of Colored Baseball Clubs. However, the league's existence was very brief, lasting only a week.

Harris, Joe

Career: 1933   Position: p
Team: Atlantic City Bacharach Giants

He pitched briefly with the Bacharachs in 1933, when the franchise was in decline and of marginal quality.

Harris, Joseph

Career: 1887   Position: player
Team: *Boston Resolutes*

He was a player with the 1887 Boston Resolutes, one of eight teams that were charter members of the League of Colored Baseball Clubs in 1887. However, the league's existence was ephemeral, lasting only a week. His position is uncertain.

Harris, Lefty

Career: 1940–41   Positions: p, 1b
Teams: Philadelphia Stars ('40), New York Cubans ('41)
Bats: Left   Throws: Left

This left-hander pitched with the 1941 New York Cubans, and previously played first base for the Philadelphia Stars.

Harris, Mo

[see Harris, Raymond]

Harris, Moochie

[see Harris, Chick]

Harris, Nathan (Nate)

Career: 1903–11   Positions: 2b, ss, of
Teams: *Smoky City Giants ('00, '04), Columbia Giants ('01–'02),* Cuban Giants ('03), Leland Giants ('05, '07–'09), Philadelphia Giants ('06), Chicago Giants ('10–'11)
Bats: Right   Throws: Right
Born: 1880, Middleport, O.

He was born in Middleport, Ohio, in 1880, where he remained until he was fourteen years of age. His parents then moved to Columbus, Ohio, where he entered high school and played football and baseball on the school teams. In his second year, Harris pitched for the baseball team and also played third base in 1897, but missed most of the 1898 baseball season due to a football injury. His parents then moved to Pittsburgh, Pennsylvania, where he played third base for the Keystone team, the first colored team in organized baseball. Once again, football injuries knocked him out of another year of baseball, and he missed the entire 1899 season. But in 1900 he pitched and played third base for the Smoky City Giants, a team organized by Bud Fowler.

In June of 1901 he joined the Columbia Giants at Buffalo, New York, and in the absence of William Binga, the regular third baseman, was given a trial at third base. Given the opportunity, he made a favorable impression and was allowed to remain with the team as a utility man until the end of the season. In 1902 he rejoined the Columbia Giants, which represented Big Rapids, Michigan, and he played second base. Harris remained in Big Rapids that winter, where he coached the football team of Preparatory College.

In 1903 he signed with the Cuban Giants of New York, playing third base until he was again injured during a game at Portland, Maine, and confined himself to playing in the outfield and pitching for the remainder of the season. The following season, he organized a team known as the Smoky City Giants, which included Scotty Bowman and Jap Payne, future members of the Philadelphia Giants. In 1905, the Leland Giants' first year of existence, he was the starting second baseman.

After wintering in Palm Beach, Florida, he joined manager Sol White's Philadelphia Giants as their shortstop for the 1906 season. Returning to Chicago, he was reunited with owner Frank Leland's ballclub in 1907 under manager Rube Foster, and remained with the Giants until the close of the 1909 season. In 1909 he maintained a batting average of .255 and he led the team in runs scored and stolen bases, pilfering 17 in only 149 at-bats. An active player, Harris's fielding earned him designation as a "bright star."

After the season, Leland and Foster went their separate ways, with Leland forming a new ballclub, the Chicago Giants. Harris remained loyal to the owner and was appointed captain of the new team. His ability as a player, captain, and organizer was unquestioned, and he was considered a "natural-born baseball diplomat" of exemplary judgment. His playing skills aroused the fans' enthusiasm in the stands, and great results were expected of him as captain of Leland's team in 1910. He batted in the second slot in the lineup and played second base, left field, and center field. He was a good outfielder and, having returned to old-time form, was considered the peer of second basemen. Harris continued to provide solid leadership for the Chicago Giants until he closed out his career in 1911.

Harris, Popsicle
[see Harris, Chick]

Harris, Raymond M. (**Mo**)
Career: 1916–29; Positions: **2b**, 3b, of,
1930–43 umpire
Team: Homestead Grays ('23–'29)

A player with the Grays in the early years, he started in the field as a second baseman and as a third baseman in the late '20s, usually batting in the lower part of the order. In 1929, his last season with the Grays, he hit .248 and he also spent some playing time in the outfield during his long association with the team. After his playing career ended, he enjoyed a second baseball career as a longtime umpire in the Negro National League and in the East-West League.

Harris, Robert (**Bob**)
Career: 1935 Position: ph
Team: Pittsburgh Crawfords

He is credited with a pinch-hitting appearance with the Pittsburgh Crawfords in 1935.

Harris, Roger
Career: 1942 Position: player
Team: Birmingham Black Barons

He played briefly with the Birmingham Black Barons in 1942, but his position is uncertain.

Harris, Samuel (**Sam**)
Career: 1932–40 Positions: p, of
Teams: Monroe Monarchs ('32), Chicago American Giants ('40), Birmingham Black Barons ('40)

He made brief pitching appearances with the American Giants and the Birmingham Black Barons in 1940. His only other appearance in the Negro Leagues was as an outfielder with the Monroe Monarchs in 1932, when the Negro Southern League was recognized as a major league.

Harris, Tom (**Tommy**)
Career: 1946–49 Position: c

Teams: Cleveland Buckeyes ('46–'48), Louisville Buckeyes ('49)

A backup catcher for four seasons with the Buckeyes during the late '40s, including their Negro American League championship season of 1947. In his first two seasons he hit .311 and .300, but in his last two years his average dropped to .214 and .203.

Harris, Vic
[see Harris, Elander Victor (Vic)]

Harris, Virgil (Schoolboy)
Career: 1936–37   Positions: **2b**, of, p
Team: Cincinnati Tigers

Primarily a second baseman, this part-time starter also played in the outfield with the Cincinnati Tigers' ballclub during their last season as an independent and their only season in the Negro American League, 1937. Usually batting in the lower part of the order, he also made an occasional mound appearance during his short career.

Harris, William (**Bill**)
Career: 1928   Position: of
Teams: Homestead Grays ('28), Pittsburgh Crawfords ('*30*–'31)

A brother of Homestead Grays' star Vic Harris, he and Teenie Harris organized a group of Pittsburgh schoolboys to play in the city's recreation league as representatives of the Crawford bathhouse in 1926. The youngsters won the title in their first season and expanded their baseball horizons. In these formative years, Harris and Harry Beale booked games and ran the team. The team continued to improve and were called "the little Homestead Grays." In the fall of 1928 he signed with the Homestead Grays but later returned to the Pittsburgh Crawfords for two seasons (1930–31) as an outfielder. Late in the 1931 season, Gus Greenlee bought the team and brought in Satchel Paige, soon to be followed by other higher-quality ballplayers, which led to Harris's departure from the team.

Harris, Wilmer
Career: 1945–50   Position: p
Teams: Philadelphia Stars ('45–'50, '52), *Canadian League ('51)*
Bats: Right   Throws: Right
Height: 6'0"   Weight: 175
Born: Mar. 1, 1924

A product of the sandlots of Philadelphia, he pitched with the Passon Stars before signing with the Philadelphia Stars in 1945. He was regarded as an up-and-coming youngster trying to make the starting rotation, and for the next three years (1945–47) he posted marks of 2–3, 1–5, and 3–1. Continuing with the Stars through the 1950 season, he registered a 5–5 mark with a 2.78 ERA. The next year he played one year with the Elgin team in New Brunswick, Canada, but returned for a final appearance with the Stars in 1952.

He also played winter ball in Latin America, pitching in Panama (1945), Venezuela (1949), and Santo Domingo (1950). Off the mound, he was lacking as a hitter but was an average fielder and base runner.

Harris, Win
Career: 1922–28   Positions: 1b, ss
Team: Homestead Grays

This infielder played seven seasons (1922–28) with the Homestead Grays during the '20s as a first baseman and shortstop.

Harrisburg Giants
Duration: 1922–27   Honors: None
Affiliations: Independent ('22–'23), ECL ('24–'27)

Organized as an independent ballclub, this franchise entered the Eastern Colored League during its second year of existence and remained a member for four years. Oscar Charleston, the playing manager, was the featured performer, and the team usually was good at hitting and made a good swing. After finishing the second division with a losing record in their initial season, Charleston's charges bounced back in 1925 for their best season ever, finishing in second place (37–18,

.673 pct.) behind the great Hilldale ballclub. After a great start in 1926, they faded late in the season, to lose to the Bacharachs, repeating their second-place finish but with at lower winning percentage .595. The following year, the Eastern Colored League's first split season, was to be their last in the league. They finished fourth in the first half and second to the Bacharachs in the second half, finishing with a combined .562 winning percentage. They dropped out of the league at the end of the season, and the league broke up early in the 1928 season.

Harrisburg-St. Louis Stars

Duration: 1943   Honors: None
Affiliation: NNL

In 1943, Harrisburg served as one of two cities that was used as a home base for the old St. Louis Stars' franchise, which was entered as a seventh team in the Negro National League, but their presence in the league was short-lived as they withdrew to go on a barnstorming tour with Dizzy Dean's All-Stars.

Harrison

Career: 1910   Positions: 2b, cf
Team: St. Louis Giants

In 1910 he played with the St. Louis Giants, dividing his playing time between second base and center field.

Harrison

Career: 1946   Positions: 2b, 3b
Team: Newark Eagles

He played briefly as a reserve infielder with the Newark Eagles in 1946, playing both second base and third base.

Harrison

Career: 1916   Positions: of, 1b, 3b
Teams: *West Baden Sprudels ('14–'15)*, Bowser's ABCs ('16)

In 1916, when C. I. Taylor and Charles Bowser organized a split into two factional ABCs teams, he was a substitute outfielder with Bowser's aggregation. Previously he had played with the West Baden Sprudels, a team of lesser quality.

Harrison, Abram (Abe)

a.k.a. Harris
Career: 1885–97   Position: ss
Teams: *Philadelphia Orions, Argyle Hotel Athletics ('85)*, Cuban Giants ('86–'97)

Regarded as the top shortstop of the earliest years of black professional baseball, he was one of the players who enjoyed a long association with the Cuban Giants. Although he was from Philadelphia, he lived in Trenton, New Jersey, most of his life and worked for the city. He joined the Cuban Giants in June 1886 and was considered a "plucky shortstop and a lightning thrower." He remained with the team throughout the various leagues and hometowns that the Cubans represented for a dozen seasons, including Trenton in the Middle State League in 1887–89 and York, Pennsylvania, in the Eastern Interstate League in 1890. Before joining the Cubans, he was a member of the Argyle Hotel team of 1885, joining that ballclub from the strong Philadelphia Orions' team.

Harrison, Tomlin

Career: 1927–30   Position: p
Teams: St. Louis Stars ('27), Kansas City Monarchs ('30)

He began his mound career with the St. Louis Stars in 1927, registering a 5–3 mark, and closed out his four years in the Negro National League in 1930, appearing with the Kansas City Monarchs without a decision.

Harrison, Clyde

Career: 1944   Positions: c, if
Teams: Cincinnati–Indianapolis Clowns ('40), Birmingham Black Barons ('44)

A wartime player, in 1944 he was a reserve catcher and utility player with the Birmingham Black Barons. Prior to World War II he also appeared with the Cincinnati–Indianapolis Clowns.

Hart

Career: 1887   Position: c

Team: *Pittsburgh Keystones*

He was a catcher with the Pittsburgh Keystones, one of eight teams that were charter members of the League of Colored Baseball Clubs in 1887. However, the league's existence was ephemeral, lasting only a week.

Hartley, Hop

Career: 1925   Position: p

Team: Kansas City Monarchs

In 1925, when the Kansas City Monarchs won their second straight Negro National League pennant, he pitched briefly with the team.

Hartman, Garrel

Career: 1944   Positions: lf, 3b

Team: Philadelphia Stars

A wartime player utility player with the Philadelphia Stars in 1944, he received most of his playing time in left field and at third base.

Harvey

Career: 1937   Position: ss

Team: Philadelphia Stars

He was a reserve shortstop with the 1937 Philadelphia stars, playing behind Jake Dunn under manager Jud Wilson.

Harvey, Charles

Career: 1950   Position: ss

Team: Cleveland Buckeyes

In 1950, when the Negro American League was struggling to survive the loss of players to organized baseball, he was a shortstop with the Cleveland Buckeyes and hit .286.

Harvey, David William (**Bill**, Lefty, *Willie*)

Career: 1931–47   Positions: **p**, 1b

Teams; Memphis Red Sox ('31–'33), Cleveland Giants ('33), Pittsburgh Crawfords ('33–'38), Cleveland Red Sox ('34), Toledo Crawfords ('39), Indianapolis Crawfords ('40), *Mexican League ('40–'41)*, **Baltimore Elite Giants** ('42–'47), *minor leagues ('50)*

Bats: Left   Throws: Left

Height: 5'8½"   Weight: 176

Born: Mar. 23, 1908, Clarksdale, Miss.

Died: Mar. 5, 1989, Baltimore, Md.

After learning baseball on the sandlots of Mississippi and Memphis, he had his first taste of professional baseball with the Memphis Red Sox at age eighteen, when they were in the Negro Southern League. Later, when the team moved into the Negro National League, he moved into the black major leagues. He split his playing time in 1933–34 between the league's Cleveland entries and the Pittsburgh Crawfords. While a member of the great Crawfords' team of 1935, he pitched a brilliant one-hit 5–1 victory over the Newark Eagles. Although not a top-line hurler with that squad, the left-hander suffered only a single recorded loss for the season.

However, there were two other games that he considered more memorable than that one-hitter. One game was a 13-inning, 1–0 win over the champion Homestead Grays in Washington, D.C., and the other career highlight was beating Bob Feller, 5–3, in Los Angeles's Hollywood Stadium during the California's 1939 winter league. A good-hitting pitcher, Harvey also belted a triple off Feller in the contest, and once hit 3 home runs in a game in Yankee Stadium. Sometimes he was used as a first baseman or a pinch hitter, recording batting averages of .313, .212, and .233 in 1942–44.

In addition to playing in California's winter league, Harvey played five winters in Puerto Rico and three seasons in Mexico. After first joining the Crawfords in 1933, he stayed with the team after the franchise was sold by owner Gus Greenlee and relocated in Toledo and Indianapolis. But in 1940 he jumped the team for Mexico and, despite a sore arm, finished his first season with a 7–9 record and a 4.64 ERA while splitting his time between Monterrey and Tampico. With his arm ailing and unable to break a curve in the high altitude, he resorted to "tricky" pitching, cutting the ball to get movement, but still dropped to a 2–7 mark with an inflated 9.16 ERA for Tampico during the 1941 season. Meanwhile, with World War II in progress and the Army looking for him for two years, the FBI was sent to Mexico to escort him back to the United States.

However, once back home, he joined the Baltimore Elite Giants in 1942 and fashioned league records of 4–2, 2–5, 3–2, and 1–1 through 1945. Ironically, his only losing season during this time, 1943, was the year he was selected to pitch in the East-West All-Star game, and he responded with 3 shutout innings, allowing only 1 hit.

Early in his career he encountered control problems, and coupled with his wildness was a willingness to knock a batter down. He broke two of Vic Harris's ribs and Ted Page's arm with pitched balls. As he gained experience, he improved his control and his effectiveness. Numbered in the lefty's repertory of pitches was a "needleball," creating an "overload" that only he knew was there, and could use to his advantage.

After his career in the Negro Leagues ended, he tried his hand in organized baseball in 1950, at age forty-two, when he pitched for the Youngstown team of the Mid-Atlantic League, but managed only a 5–10 record with a 6.51 ERA. Off the field the hurler was a dapper dresser and an acknowledged "ladies' man" who was fined frequently for violating the club curfew.

Harvey, Frank

Career: 1912–21   Positions: **p**, of
Teams: St. Louis Giants ('12), Brooklyn Royal Giants ('13–'14, '16–'17), New York Lincoln Stars ('15–'16), New York Lincoln Giants ('14, '16–'17), G.C.T. Red Caps ('18), Atlantic City Bacharach Giants ('21), Philadelphia Giants ('13, '22–'24)
Bats: Left   Throws: Left

A left-handed curveballer, he was a good pitcher in the deadball era, beginning his career with the St. Louis Giants in 1912. However, most of his career was spent in the East, mostly with New York-based teams. His first team in the metropolis was the Brooklyn Royal Giants, who won the Eastern title in 1914 but lost to the Chicago American Giants in the championship playoffs. The next year he pitched against the Chicago American Giants in the playoffs again, this time with the New York Lincoln Stars.

After the Stars broke up, he played with both the Lincoln Giants and the Royal Giants, where he had Louis Santop as his batterymate. Although he was never the ace of the staff, he was in the starting rotation and had an 8-3 record in 1917. The next year he joined the Grand Central Terminal Red Caps, and during the early '20s he pitched with the Bacharach Giants and the Philadelphia Giants. But by this time the Philadelphia Giants were no longer a quality ballclub.

Harvey, Robert A. (**Bob**)

Career: 1943–50   Positions: **rf**, lf, cf
Teams: **Newark Eagles** ('44–'48), Houston Eagles ('49–'50), *minor leagues ('50–'51), New Orleans Eagles ('51)*
Bats: Left   Throws: Right
Height: 6'0"   Weight: 220
Born: May 28, 1918, St. Michaels, Md.
Died: June 27, 1992, Montclair, N.J.

The big, husky right fielder's hitting contributed significantly to the Newark Eagles' 1946 championship, as they won the Negro National League pennant, breaking the Homestead Grays' skein of nine straight pennants, and defeated the Kansas City Monarchs in the Negro World Series. In the first game of the Series, although not a basestealing threat and possessing only average speed, the hustling ex-grid star broke up a double play with a hard slide that put Monarchs' shortstop Jim Hamilton out of commission for the remainder of the Series.

Joining the Eagles in 1943, he recorded successive batting averages of .309, .307, .389, .284, .335, and .363 through the 1948 season. The left-handed slugger made his first of two East-West All-Star game appearances that year, representing the East squad. That year marked the demise of the Negro National League, and the Eagles were sold to a new owner and relocated in Houston to play in the Western Division of the Negro American League. Harvey responded to the new locale with a .295 mark in 1949. The next season he encored with a .367 batting average, with 8 home runs in 59 games, to earn his second All-Star appearance, representing the West squad this time.

As a youngster, Harvey starred in both baseball and football, and after graduating from St. Michael's, High School in Maryland, he starred in football at Bowie State College in Baltimore. His gridiron prowess earned him a spot in the college's football Hall of Fame.

After two years of college, Harvey first contacted Eagles' owner Abe Manley, requesting a tryout, but he missed connections with manager Dick Lundy and had to wait five years for another chance. While waiting for the opportunity, he honed his diamond skills by playing with the Denton Tigers, a semipro team. When time for the tryout finally materialized, he hammered 2 homers in the game to earn a place on the roster.

He was also a member of the 1945 All-Star squad that toured after the season, and he played winter ball with Aquadilla in Puerto Rico in 1946–47. The hard-hitting outfielder closed out his baseball career with the Elmwood Giants in the Mandak League in 1950–51, batting .306 with 9 home runs in 44 games during the latter year. Afterward he worked for a pharmaceutical manufacturer for thirty-two years, before his retirement. In June 1992 he died from a blood disorder.

Harvey, Willie
[see Harvey, David William (Bill)]

Haslett, Claude
a.k.a. Hazelet
Career: 1936–37   Position: p
Teams: Memphis Red Sox ('36), Indianapolis Athletics ('37)

After a year with the Memphis Red Sox, he pitched with the Indianapolis Athletics when the franchise joined the Negro American League in 1937.

Hastings
Career: 1928   Position: p
Team: St. Louis Stars

He was a pitcher with the St. Louis Stars in 1928, when they won the first-half championship of the Negro National League.

Hatcher, Gene
Career: 1948   Position: of
Team: New York Black Yankees

This aspiring ballplayer was among the players trying to win an outfield position with the New York Black Yankees in the early spring of 1948.

Hatchett
Career: 1913   Position: 2b
Teams: Brooklyn Royal Giants ('13), *Philadelphia Giants of New York ('20)*

He was a reserve second baseman with the Brooklyn Royal Giants in 1913, and later played with the Philadelphia Giants of New York, a lesser team.

Havana Red Sox
Duration: 1917   Honors: None
Affiliation: Independent

This was a marginal team that was generally a little below the major-league level and that did not compare favorably with either of the Cuban Stars' teams.

Havana Stars
Duration: 1917   Honors: None
Affiliation: Independent

In 1917 the New York-based Cuban Stars played as the Havana Stars.

Havis, Chester
Career: 1947   Position: p
Team: Memphis Red Sox

During the 1947 season he was one of many pitchers taking a turn on the mound for the Memphis Red Sox.

Hawk
Career: 1905   Position: c
Team: Brooklyn Royal Giants

He was a catcher with the Brooklyn Royal Giants in 1905, their first year of existence.

Hawkins
Career: 1940   Position: ss
Team: New York Black Yankees

In 1940, he was a light-hitting reserve shortstop for the New York Black Yankees, and his playing time was very limited.

Hawkins, Lemuel (**Lem**, Hawk)
Career: 1921–28   Positions: **1b**, of, *2b, 3b*
Teams: *military service ('18–'19), Los Angeles White Sox ('19–'21),* Chicago Giants ('21), **Kansas City Monarchs** ('21–'28), Chicago American Giants ('28)
Born: Georgia
Died: Aug 10, 1934, Chicago, Ill.

A good-fielding first baseman but a light hitter, he played on the great Kansas City Monarchs' teams of 1923–25, winners of three consecutive Negro National League pennants. In the latter two seasons the Monarchs played the Eastern Colored League champion Hilldale team in the first World Series played between the Negro National League and the Eastern Colored League. The Monarchs won the first Series but lost in the 1925 rematch.

Hawkins was appointed captain of the team in 1924 and hit for averages of .259, .276, .263, and .231 for the 1924–27 seasons. He served in the Army Infantry during World War I and was one of the players from the 25th Infantry team stationed at Fort Huachuca who were recommended to Monarchs' owner J. L. Wilkinson by Casey Stengel. He could also play the outfield, having started his professional career at those positions for the Los Angeles White Sox in 1919, and he moved to the outer garden when George Giles joined the Monarchs in 1928.

Off the field he was considered a "hard case," and not long after his baseball career ended, he was imprisoned for armed robbery. After his release he was involved in another robbery attempt, and was shot and killed by his partner while holding up a beer truck. He was mistaken for the truck driver's helper and was shot through the left ear, with the bullet entering his brain. His body remained in a morgue for a month before being identified.

Hawks
Career: 1913   Position: 3b
Team: Philadelphia Giants

In 1913 he played third base for the Philadelphia Giants, a team that was in decline.

Hawley
Career: 1932   Position: c
Team: Memphis Red Sox

He was a catcher with the Memphis Red Sox in 1932, his only year with a league team.

Hayes
Career: 1912–13   Positions: c, of, ss
Teams: *Pittsburgh Giants,* ('12) Havana Red Sox, ('12) Philadelphia Giants ('13)

A versatile player, he could play infield, outfield or catcher, but spent his two years in the early '10s with teams of marginal quality.

Hayes, Buddy
Career: 1916–24   Position: c
Teams: Chicago American Giants ('16), St. Louis Giants ('16), Indianapolis ABCs ('19), Pittsburgh Keystones ('21–'22), Milwaukee Bears ('23), Toledo Tigers ('23), Cleveland Browns ('24)

He began his career when he filled the catching vacancy with the Chicago American Giants after Bruce Petway was injured in September 1916, and the youngster's performance was described as "grand." Apparently this appraisal was for his defensive work, since incomplete statistics show a .111 batting average. A "crackerjack" little player, he caught for seven different teams during his nine-year career.

Hayes, Burnalle James (**Bun**)
a.k.a. Burnell
Career: 1928–35   Position: p
Teams: Baltimore Black Sox ('28–'30,

'33–'34), Chicago American Giants ('30), Washington Pilots ('32), Newark Dodgers ('35)

He pitched with the Baltimore Black Sox in 1928 and was on Baltimore Black Sox reserved list in 1929 but still in school in March when the spring training camps opened. He attended J. C. Smith University in Charlotte, North Carolina. In college he often hooked up in pitching duels with Laymon Yokely, who pitched for Livingstone College in Salisbury, North Carolina. Hayes usually got the better of their mound duels in college, but both hurlers were scouted and signed by the Baltimore Black Sox.

In 1929 Hayes fashioned a 4–0 work sheet for the Black Sox, but on a professional level his old adversary Yokely, outdid him. Hayes had a fastball but relied more on guile and deception. He was often outguessed by veteran hitters, and his success did not come easily. In October 1932, pitching with the Washington Pilots, he faced his old college adversary Yokely once more. Although neither pitcher finished the game, Washington won the game, and Hayes struck out 2 while allowing 6 hits in 5 innings with 5 walks. Without the decision, he finished the season winless against 3 losses.

The next season he returned to the Black Sox, who had joined the Negro National League, and won both of his decisions in league play. In 1934, a new Baltimore Black Sox franchise, based in Chester, Pennsylvania, entered the league as a second-half replacement, and Hayes joined the team for their last year as a ballclub. The next year he and the Newark Dodgers both finished their association with baseball together.

Hayes, Jimmy
Career: 1949   Position: c
Team: Kansas City Monarchs

He was a catcher with the Kansas City Monarchs in 1949, when the Negro American League was struggling to survive the loss of players to organized baseball.

Hayes, John W.
Career: 1940   Positions: ss, 2b
Teams: Philadelphia Stars ('40), St. Louis Stars ('40)
Bats: Right   Throws: Right
Height: 5'8"   Weight: 160

A mediocre player in the field and on the bases, this reserve middle infielder was a light hitter and split the 1940 season between subbing at shortstop with the St. Louis Stars and subbing at second base for the Philadelphia Stars. When he did get some playing time he batted at the bottom of the order, hitting only .179, and failed to impress either team sufficiently.

Hayes, Johnny William (John)
Career: 1934–50   Positions: c, of
Teams: Newark Dodgers ('34–'35), Newark Eagles ('36–'39), **New York Black Yankees** ('40–'48), *Pittsburgh Crawfords ('46), Boston Blues ('46),* Baltimore Elite Giants ('49–'51), *minor leagues ('52)*
Bats: Left   Throws: Right
Height: 5'9"   Weight: 178
Born: Apr. 27, 1910, Independence Mo.

A good catcher with average skills but a good head for pitch selection, John played for seventeen years in the Negro Leagues. Although slow afoot, he was noted for his quickness behind the plate. A left-handed slap hitter, he was a mediocre batter with only fair power and had trouble hitting the curveball, but he still managed an average of .295 for the Black Yankees in 1946 and made his only All-Star appearance the following season, despite a drop in his batting average to .257.

He began his career with the 1934 Newark Dodgers, where he shared the catching duties with McCoy because he was a better hitter and had fairly good power, batting .275 in 1935. The next year, Abe Manley consolidated the Dodgers with the Brooklyn Eagles to form the Newark Eagles, and Hayes registered batting averages of .179 and .205 in 1937 and 1939 while batting at the bottom of the order. The following season he joined the New York

Black Yankees and posted averages of .151, .254, and .296 for the 1940–42 seasons.

Hayes ended his Negro League career after three years with the Baltimore Elite Giants, in 1949–51, recording averages of .239 and .270 in the first two seasons. In 1952 he played 7 games with Hartford in the Eastern League and had a .357 average for his brief stint in organized baseball.

In the winter of 1938–39 he played winter ball in Cuba, batting a lowly .125 in only 32 at-bats. The next winter he opted for the Puerto Rican League, hitting .273 with Aquadilla, but when he returned to the same team in the winter of 1941–42, he was released.

Hayes, Thomas H., Jr. (Tom)
Career: 1939–50   Positions: owner, officer
Team: Birmingham Black Barons

For a dozen years he served as an officer with the Birmingham Black Barons and also served a stint as vice president of the Negro American League. As the owner of the Birmingham Black Barons during the '40s he formed a partnership with Abe Saperstein, allowing him to remain in the background while Saperstein handled the ballclub's business operations. When he sold Willie Mays for $15,000, he gave Mays $6,000 of the selling price.

Hayes, Wilbur
Career: 1942–50   Position: owner
Teams: Cincinnati Buckeyes ('42), Cleveland Buckeyes ('43–'48, '50), Louisville Buckeyes ('49)

He was the owner of the Buckeyes franchise that started in Cincinnati in 1942 and moved to Cleveland the following year. With the exception of 1949, when the team was located in Louisville, the ballclub remained in Cleveland through 1950. He also served as sergeant-at-arms for the Negro American League. In 1942, his first year with the team, he was injured in a car wreck but recovered.

Hayman, Charles (Bugs)
a.k.a. Heyman
Career: 1909–16   Positions: p, 1b
Team: Philadelphia Giants

He pitched and played first base for the Philadelphia Giants in 1909, when the team was still formidable, and remained with the team through 1916, when the team had declined in quality.

Haynes
Career: 1905   Position: of
Team: Brooklyn Royal Giants

He was an outfielder with the Brooklyn Royal Giants in 1905, the team's first season.

Haynes
Career: 1946   Position: p
Team: Homestead Grays

In 1946 he made his only appearance in the Negro Leagues, appearing as a pitcher with the Homestead Grays.

Haynes, Leroy (Roughhouse)
Career: 1936   Position: of
Team: Atlanta Black Crackers

A big, strong, fast outfielder with a great throwing arm called one of the best in the Negro American League, he played left field for the Atlanta Black Crackers. After his days on the baseball diamond were over, he turned into a restaurant entrepreneur and is credited with introducing chitterlings to the French cuisine.

Haynes, Sam (Sammie)
Career: 1943–45   Positions: c, 1b, manager
Teams: *Atlanta Black Crackers ('39–'42, '46–'47)*, Kansas City Monarchs ('43–'45)
Bats: Right   Throws: Right
Height: 6'1"   Weight: 195
Born: May 29, 1920, Atlanta, Ga.

Secured from the Atlanta Black Crackers by the Kansas City Monarchs to replace Joe Greene, who had been called to military duty, this big catcher became a key player on the club during three wartime seasons, 1943–45. He proved to be a workhorse who enjoyed the hard work and was a good, sound receiver who knew how to handle pitchers and offered them a good target. In his first season with the Monarchs, when not behind the plate he also helped the club by assuming the first-base duties when Buck O'Neill left for naval service. Although batting in the eighth slot in the order and managing averages of only .177 and .189, the big right-handed batter was considered by some to be a potent presence at the plate.

Before the Monarchs beckoned, he had played with the Atlanta Black Crackers of the Negro Southern League for four seasons, joining them after three years with the semipro Scripto Black Cats, where he began his baseball career in 1936. After World War II he returned to Atlanta and served a term as manager before ending his career following the 1947 season.

Haynes, Willie

Career: 1921–24   Position: p

Teams: *Dallas Giants ('21)*, Hilldale Daisies ('22), Baltimore Black Sox ('23), Atlantic City Bacharach Giants ('23), Harrisburg Giants ('24)

During his four-year career he was a pitcher with the Dallas Giants and most of the teams that comprised the Eastern Colored League, including Hilldale, the Harrisburg Giants, the Baltimore Black Sox, and the Bacharach Giants.

Haywood

Career: 1925   Position: p

Team: New York Lincoln Giants

In 1925 he lost both of his decisions while pitching for the New York Lincoln Giants in the Eastern Colored League.

Haywood, Albert (**Buster**, Tarzan, Wahoo)

Career: 1940–50   Positions: c, manager

Teams: Birmingham Black Barons ('40), Miami Ethiopian Clowns ('40–'41), New York Cubans ('42), Cincinnati Clowns ('43), Cincin-

nati-Indianapolis Clowns ('44–'45), Indianapolis Clowns ('46–'54), *Memphis Red Sox ('54)*

Bats: Right   Throws: Right

Height: 5'8"   Weight: 161

Born: 1910, Portsmouth, Va.

One of the smallest receivers in the league, he was also one of the best behind the plate. While he was good defensively and was a hustler, he had only average speed and was at best an average hitter. He began his career with the Birmingham Black Barons in 1940 as a backup catcher, but soon joined the Miami Ethiopian Clowns and, in 1941, he was voted the MVP in the *Denver Post* Tournament. The next year he shared the catching duties with the New York Cubans, showing a .211 batting average in limited play, then returned to the Clowns in 1943 and remained with them through their franchise shifts to Cincinnati and Indianapolis.

Offensively he usually batted near the bottom of the lineup, but although lacking power at the plate, he hit for averages of .270 in 1944 and .267 in 1948. He was selected to West and North All-Star squads in 1944 but did not appear in either of the games. Two years later, in 1946, two All-Star contests were held, and he played in the game at Griffith Stadium, going hitless in his only at-bat. In other seasons his batting average fluctuated, with marks of .152 in 1945, .223 in 1946, .300 in 1949, and .307 in 1950.

During the years when he was with the Clowns, he engaged in postseason play, touring with Jackie Robinson's All-Stars in Mexico City in 1947 and playing winter ball on the West Coast with the Kansas City Royals' All-Star team (1945–47), which also played against Bob Feller's All-Stars.

In the waning years of the Negro Leagues he managed the Clowns for seven seasons (1948–54), primarily after they were relegated to a minor-league level of play, and also managed the Memphis Red Sox in 1954. In his last two years with the Clowns (1952–53), he was selected to manage in the East-West All-Star game.

Hazelet
[see Haslett, Claude]

Hazely
Career: 1941   Position: p
Team: New York Black Yankees

In 1941 he gave up 5 hits in a single inning and was the losing pitcher in his only appearance with the New York Black Yankees.

Heard, Jehosie (Jay)
Career: 1945–50   Position: p
Teams: Birmingham Black Barons ('45–'49), Houston Eagles ('49–'50), *New Orleans Eagles ('51), minor leagues ('52–'57), major leagues ('54), Memphis Red Sox ('58)*
Bats: Right   Throws: Left
Height: 5'7"   Weight: 147
Born: Jan. 17, 1920, Atlanta, Ga.

The little left-hander's best pitch was his slider, but he had a varied repertory, further supplementing the basic pitches with a screwball. He had good control of his pitches, fashioning a 6–1 record for the 1948 pennant-winning Birmingham Black Barons and making a relief appearance in the World Series against the Homestead Grays. He followed with seasonal records of 10–6, 2.49 ERA with Birmingham and 8–9, 3.38 ERA with the Houston Eagles.

After the breakup of the Negro leagues, he shaved five years off his age to enhance his chances of getting into organized baseball. Successful in his ploy, he signed with the St. Louis Browns' organization and, in 1952–53, fashioned two successful seasons in the minor leagues. His records of 20–12 (2.94 ERA) with Victoria in the Western International League and 16–12 (3.19 ERA) with Portland of the Pacific Coast League were sandwiched around a good winter season in Caracas, Venezuela, where he posted a 3.03 ERA.

In 1954 the St. Louis Browns' franchise shifted to Baltimore and Heard became the first black player with the Baltimore Orioles, pitching two games without a decision. Following his brief stint with the parent club he played three more seasons with Seattle in the Pacific Coast League (5–7), Charleston in the American Association (1–3), Tulsa in the Texas League (10–15), and Havana in the International League (3–5). In the winter of 1956–57, pitching for Vanytor in the Colombian winter league, he had a record of 7–7 with a 2.09 ERA, but suffered an arm injury that impacted on his diamond capability. Although he tried to make a comeback, pitching with the Memphis Red Sox in 1958, he was not able to overcome the affects of the injury. After his baseball career ended, he worked in a cotton mill for four years and then joined the Postal Service.

Heat
Career: 1941   Position: p
Team: New York Cubans

In 1941 he pitched briefly, without a decision, for the New York Cubans.

Hefner, Arthur
Career: 1947–49   Positions: of, 3b
Teams: New York Black Yankees ('47–'48), Philadelphia Stars ('49)

In 1948 he was the starting center fielder and leadoff batter with the Black Yankees, but after the demise of the Negro National League at the end of the season, he signed with the Philadelphia Stars and hit .273 in 1949.

Heiskell
Career: 1902   Position: p
Team: Algona Brownies

In 1902 he was a pitcher with the Algona Brownies of Algona, Iowa, one of the top teams of the era.

Henderson
Career: 1921   Position: p
Teams: Detroit Stars ('21), Chicago Giants ('21)

In 1921 he pitched with the Detroit Stars and the Chicago Giants, accruing a 0–4 record for the season.

Henderson

Career: 1925   Position: c

Team: Birmingham Black Barons

He appeared briefly as a reserve catcher with the Birmingham Black Barons in 1925, while they were in the Negro National League.

Henderson, Armour

Career: 1915   Position: p

Team: Mohawk Giants

He was a pitcher with the Mohawk Giants in 1915.

Henderson, Arthur Chauncey (**Rats**)

Career: 1923–31   Position: p

Teams: *Richmond Giants ('22–'23),* **Atlantic City Bacharach Giants** ('23–'29), *Chappie Johnson's Stars ('24),* Detroit Stars ('31)

Bats: Right   Throws: Right

Height: 5'7"   Weight: 180

Born: Aug. 29, 1897, Richmond, Va.

Died: Wilmington, Del.

One of the finest curveball pitchers of the '20s, Henderson had a short but impressive career before it prematurely ended because of arm trouble. In addition to his sharp-breaking curve, the right-handed sidearm hurler had blinding speed, and both pitches looked alike to a batter until the last moment, when the bottom fell out of his curveball.

While growing up in a family of a dozen children, "Rats" acquired his peculiar nickname in his early teens, when someone hid a rat in his lunch box while he was working at a glass factory. From the time the unsuspecting youngster opened his lunch and a rat jumped out, he had a lifelong moniker that later in life would be despised by his wife for obvious reasons. In 1922, while pitching for the Richmond Giants, he defeated the Bacharach Giants in an exhibition game as they played their way North from spring training, and the Bacharachs signed the young hurler. His parents reluctantly approved of his leaving home, and the rookie fashioned a 16–5 performance for the independent ballclub.

In 1923, when the Eastern Colored League was organized, the Bacharachs were charter members, and Henderson fashioned league records of 8–6, 8–1, and 13–5 in his first three seasons of league play. In 1924 he was considered the best young pitcher in baseball and jumped briefly to Chappie Johnson's team in New York State. He recorded a 8–5 record in Cuba during the winter of 1924–25 while honing his pitching skills in the Caribbean. However, he was back with the Bacharachs for the 1925 season, and as an established ace pitcher had become one of the highest paid players in the East, at $375 a month.

In 1926 he registered a 15–5 mark to help carry the Bacharachs to the Eastern Colored League pennant. In the subsequent World Series, facing the Chicago American Giants, he pitched the first game, which ended in a 3–3 tie after 9 innings. He pitched in a total of 5 games, with 4 starts, 3 complete games, a shutout, and a 1.45 ERA, but split his 2 decisions, with his other 2 starting assignments ending in deadlocks. The Bacharachs lost the best-of-9 Series, 5 games to 3, with 2 ties. The next season he had an even better season, sporting a 19–7 record and leading the Bacharachs to another pennant and a repeat appearance against the American Giants in the World Series. Unfortunately, Henderson suffered a late-season injury and missed the Series rematch, but the result was the same, with the Bacharachs dropping the Series in 8 games.

Henderson was on his way to another outstanding year in 1928 with a 13–2 record at midseason when his arm went dead. The arm plagued him during the next year and he was further handicapped by carrying considerable extra weight, leading to a disappointing 6–10 ledger for the 1929 season. His last recorded statistics are from the 1931 season, when he was 0–2 for the Detroit Stars in his last year with a quality club in black baseball.

Afterward he sold rugs on the Atlantic City boardwalk for a decade while playing with John Henry Lloyd's Johnson Stars. Later Judy Johnson assisted him in gaining employment at the Continental Can Company, where he worked for eighteen years before retiring in 1965.

Henderson, Ben
Career: 1936–37   Position: p
Teams: St. Louis Stars ('36), Birmingham Black Barons ('37)

He began his career as a pitcher with the St. Louis Stars in 1936, when the team was playing as an independent team, and closed out his career with the Birmingham Black Barons in 1937, the first year of the Negro American League.

Henderson, Curtis (Curt, Dan)
Career: 1936–42   Positions: **ss**, 3b, 2b, of
Teams: Homestead Grays ('36), New York Black Yankees ('37, '42), Washington Black Senators ('38), Toledo Crawfords ('39), Indianapolis Crawfords ('40), Philadelphia Stars ('41), American Giants ('41)

During his seven seasons in the Negro Leagues, this light-hitting infielder usually found himself sharing a starting position with another ballplayer and generally batting in the lower part of the order. In 1936 he hit .212 for the Homestead Grays in limited play. In 1937 he shared the shortstop position with Jake Stevens for the Black Yankees, and the following season had another shared situation with the Washington Black Senators when the franchise entered the Negro National League as a seventh entry. The team had a horrible record and disbanded before the end of the season, and the infielder had to find another ballclub, landing with the Crawfords, who had relocated in Toledo and joined the Negro American League. The versatile player was a part-time starter for two seasons, remaining with the club when they moved to Indianapolis in an effort to salvage the once-proud Crawford ballclub, and played shortstop, third base, and center field. When the team dropped from the league, he substituted in left field with the Philadelphia Stars for part of the 1941 season, but spent the greater part of the year with the Chicago American Giants as a regular, playing shortstop and third base.

Henderson, George (Rube)
Career: 1921–23   Positions: **of**, 3b, ss

Teams: *Madison Stars ('20)*, Chicago Giants ('21), Cleveland Tate Stars ('22–'23), Toledo Tigers ('23)

His three-year career was spent with struggling Negro National League teams, none of which lasted more than two seasons in the league. Beginning with the Chicago Giants in 1921, their last year in the Negro National League, he left after only one year to play as the right fielder and leadoff batter for the Cleveland Tate Stars. In 1923 he also played with the Toledo Tigers until they disbanded in mid-July.

Henderson, H. (Long)
Career: 1932   Position: 1b
Team: Nashville Elite Giants

He was a first baseman with the Nashville Elite Giants in 1932, when the Negro Southern League was classified as a major league.

Henderson, Lenon
Career: 1930–33   Positions: 3b, ss, lf
Teams: Nashville Elite Giants ('30–'32), Indianapolis ABCs, ('31, '33) Birmingham Black Barons ('32), Louisville Black Caps ('32), Montgomery Grey Sox ('33)

For four seasons in the early '30s, the infielder played both third base and shortstop with several of the leading black ballclubs in the South. Beginning with the Nashville Elites in 1930, he played as a reserve until the 1932 season, when he was the regular third baseman, and hit in the seventh slot in the batting order. He also appeared as a reserve player with the Birmingham Black Barons, Louisville Black Caps, and Montgomery Grey Sox.

Henderson, Louis
Career: 1925   Positions: **p**, of
Team: Atlantic City Bacharach Giants

He was a pitcher-outfielder with the 1925 Bacharach Giants in his only year in the Negro Leagues. As a pitcher, he lost his only decision.

Henderson, Neal (Duke)
Career: 1949   Position: of
Team: Kansas City Monarchs ('49, *'52–'53*)

This outfielder played with the Kansas City Monarchs in 1949, his only season in the Negro American League before its marked decline in quality. He continued with the Monarchs after the league was strictly a minor league.

Hendricks
Career: 1918–22   Positions: **p**, of
Teams: New York Lincoln Giants ('18), Baltimore Black Sox ('22)

In 1918 he split six contests while a member of the Lincoln Giants' pitching staff also made appearances in center field. Four years later he appeared briefly as an outfielder with the Baltimore Black Sox before they entered the Eastern Colored League.

Henriquez
Career: 1913   Position: 1b
Team: Long Branch Cubans

In 1913 he was a first baseman with the Long Branch Cubans, one of the better Cuban teams of the era.

Hendrix, Stokes
Career: 1934   Position: p
Team: Nashville Elite Giants

He appeared briefly as a pitcher with the 1934 Nashville Elites.

Henry, Alfred
Career: 1950   Position: rf
Teams: Baltimore Elite Giants ('50), *Philadelphia Stars ('51)*

He was an outfielder with the Baltimore Elites and the Philadelphia Stars for two seasons after the decline in quality of the league.

In 1993 he was arrested for sending a series of threatening letters to baseball officials, including Bud Selig, the director of the major leagues' executive council.

Henry, Charles (**Charlie**)
Career: 1922–31;   Positions: **p**, manager
1941–42
Bats: Right   Throws: Right
Teams: Hilldale Daisies ('22–'23, '26), Harris-

burg Giants ('23–'25), Washington Potomacs ('24), Detroit Stars ('29), Atlantic City Bacharach Giants ('31); *Detroit Black Sox ('41), Louisville Black Colonels ('42), Zulu Cannibal Giants ('34–'37)*

In 1924 he became the focal point of a unique personnel situation. During the season he was released by the Harrisburg Giants because he failed to maintain himself in good playing condition, but the release was not put in writing. Without knowing the circumstances of his release and acting on the advice of Harrisburg manager Oscar Charleston, Washington manager Ben Taylor picked up Henry to pitch for his Potomacs. After making a good showing in one game, Henry was reclaimed by Harrisburg and became their most dependable pitcher for the remainder of the season. He was reserved for the 1925 season and finished with a 3–2 record, followed by a 1–3 record with Hilldale in 1926.

Three years later, pitching with the Detroit Stars, he forged a 9–7 record for the 1929 season. In 1931, pitching for the Bacharachs, he closed a decade in the Negro Leagues. But following the end of his active playing days, he began a second career as a manager, including a tour with the minor-league Detroit Black Sox in 1941. During the '30s he organized and managed the Zulu Cannibal Giants, a traveling team that combined baseball and show business. Altogether he logged a total of twenty-one years in black baseball.

Henry, Joe
Career: 1950   Position: 2b
Teams: Memphis Red Sox ('50–'52), *minor leagues ('52–'54), Detroit Stars ('58)*
Bats: Both   Throws: Right

A second baseman with the 1950 Memphis Red Sox, he hit .284 with slightly less than average power and was a pretty good base stealer, but he struck out more than average. Two years later, after the rapid decline of quality in the Negro Leagues, he entered organized baseball, batting .303 while playing third base with Canton, Ohio. The next two seasons were spent with Mt. Vernon in the Mississippi-Ohio Valley

League, where he proved consistent at the plate, with batting averages of .275 and .274.

Henry, Leo (**Preacher**)
Career: 1938–47   Position: p
Teams: Jacksonville Red Caps ('38, '41–'42), Cleveland Bears ('39–'40), Cincinnati Clowns ('43), *military service ('44–'45),* Indianapolis Clowns ('46–'47, *'51*)
Bats: Right   Throws: Right
Height: 5'4"   Weight: 135
Died: Jacksonville, Fla.

This little right-hander with the devastating drop broke in with the Jacksonville Redcaps in 1938 and quickly established himself as the ace of the staff. He went North with the franchise for two seasons, when they played as the Cleveland Bears. In 1940 he was a top pitcher with the Bears and registered a 7–2 ledger in preseason play, but dropped to a 2–4 mark in league play. When the team returned South to their original location in 1941, "Preacher" was selected to pitch in the 1941 East-West All-Star game, but yielded 3 hits while getting 4 outs in his appearance. Leaving the Red Caps after the dissolution of the franchise in 1942, he joined the Clowns, winning his only recorded decision in 1943 and showing a 3–6 league ledger in 1946. In between he spent two years in the Army during World War II. After extending his mound career against top-level competition to a full decade, he continued against the weakened opposition for a few more years before retiring from the diamond.

Henry, Otis
Career: 1931–37   Positions: 2b, 3b, of
Teams: Memphis Red Sox ('31–'32, '36), Monroe Monarchs ('34), Indianapolis Athletics ('37)

For seven seasons during the '30s he played both infield and outfield, mostly with teams in the South, including the Memphis Red Sox and the Monroe Monarchs. Early in his career, 1932, he was the regular third baseman for the Memphis Red Sox, batting second in the order. Five years later, 1937, his last year in the Negro Leagues, he played left field and usually batted leadoff for the Indianapolis Athletics during their only season in the Negro American League.

Hensley, Logan (**Eggie**, Slap)
a.k.a. Hemsley
Career: 1922–39   Position: p
Teams: **St. Louis Stars** ('22–'31), Toledo Tigers ('23), Cleveland Tate Stars ('23), Cleveland Browns ('24), Indianapolis ABCs ('32), Detroit Stars ('33), Cleveland Giants ('33), Chicago American Giants ('39)

A right-handed pitcher with a sharp-breaking curve that he kept down, and a good change of pace, he was the ace of the 1930 Negro National League champion St. Louis Stars' pitching staff, with a record of 17–6. He also pitched with the Stars when they won championships in 1928 and 1931, giving them three of the last four flags before the demise of the Negro National League. Other strong seasons for the Stars by Hensley included ledgers of 17–7 and 13–6 in 1926 and 1929.

A product of St. Louis's semipro Tandy Baseball League, he joined the St. Louis Stars directly from the sandlots. During his seventeen-year career in the Negro Leagues he also pitched with several other midwestern teams, including a 4–2 record with the Detroit Stars in 1933.

Heredia, Ramon (Napoleon)
Career: 1939–45   Positions: **3b**, ss, 2b, 1b, of
Teams: New York Cubans ('39–'41, '45), *Mexican League ('42–'45)*
Bats: Right   Throws: Right
Height: 6'0"   Weight: 205
Born: 1917, Matanzas, Cuba

Although he was versatile and could play any infield position, he lacked good speed and was better suited to a position with constricted range. He began his career in 1939 as a twenty-two-year-old third sacker with the New York Cubans, hitting .211 as a part-time starter. He moved into the starting lineup the following year, proving to be a classy expert at the hot corner while improving his average to .239. He was a good contact hitter and raised his average to .288 in 1941, but did not hit the long ball, having only mediocre power, with most of his extra-base hits being doubles. Although he was referred to as a .300 hitter and considered to be dangerous at the plate, he did not bat in the heart of the lineup, usually hitting second or sixth in the order.

After three seasons in the United States he opted to play in Mexico and did not return to the States for four years. With Monterrey in the Mexican League he hit .280 and .257 in his first two seasons, 1942–43. He also played with Marianao and Cienfuegos in Cuba, where he had a lifetime average of .240 for the eight winters he played on the island during the interval 1937–48, with his best year coming in the winter of 1941–42, when he hit .298 with Cienfuegos. Later in his career, during the mid-'50s, he coached in Cuba.

Herman
[see Andrews, Herman]

Hernandez
Career: 1941   Position: of
Team: New York Cuban Stars
An outfielder with good range and good defensive skills, he played with the New York Cubans in 1941.

Hernandez, Chico
Career: 1945   Positions: c
Team: Indianapolis Clowns
A wartime player, this catcher appeared with the Indianapolis Clowns in 1945.

Hernandez, José
Career: 1920–22   Positions: **p**, of
Team: Cuban Stars (West).
During the first three years of the '20s he was a pitcher with the Cuban Stars of the Negro National League and also played outfield. In 1920, playing with Almendares against the New York Giants in an exhibition series in Cuba, he

was 2–1 as a pitcher and had 3 hits in 8 at-bats for a .375 batting average for the series.

Hernandez, Ramon
Career: 1929–30   Position: 3b
Team: Cuban Stars (West)
In 1929–30 he was a third baseman with the Cuban Stars (West), batting .237 and .221 for his two seasons in the Negro National League.

Hernandez, Ricardo (Chico)
Career: 1909–16   Positions: 3b, 2b, lf, cf, rf
Teams: Cuban Stars ('09–'11, '14), All Cubans, All Nations ('16)
He was one of best Cuban infielders during the deadball era, playing both second base and third base for eight seasons, primarily with the Cuban Stars. In 1914 he was a regular player, batting in the seventh slot, but divided his playing time between the outfield and the infield. In 1910, playing with Havana against the Detroit Tigers in an exhibition series in Cuba, he played center field and batted fifth in the order but hit only .087.

Herndon
Career: 1931   Position: p
Team: *Newark Browns*
He was a pitcher with the Newark Browns in 1931, a year before they entered the East-West League.

Herrera, Ramon (Paito, **Mike**)
Career: 1916–28   Positions: **2b,** 3b, *ss*
Teams: Jersey City Cubans, ('16) Long Branch Cubans ('16), Cuban Stars (West) ('20–'21), major leagues ('25–'26)
Bats: Right   Throws: Right
Height: 5'6"   Weight: 147
Born: Dec. 19, 1897, Havana, Cuba
A white Cuban, during his career this infielder played with various Cuban teams in the Negro Leagues both before and after his two seasons in the major leagues. In 1920 he was the regular second baseman and leadoff batter for the Cuban Stars in the Negro National

League's inaugural season. During the ensuing winter, while playing for Almendares against the New York Giants in an exhibition series in Cuba, he hit .292. In 1925 he was in the major leagues with the Boston Red Sox, playing primarily at second base, and compiled a lifetime .275 major-league batting average for his stint as an utility infielder in the American League.

Herring
Career: 1920   Position: 3b
Team: St. Louis Giants

He was a third baseman with the St. Louis Giants in 1920, the inaugural season of the Negro National League.

Herron, Robert Lee (Big Daddy)
Career: 1950   Position: of
Teams: Houston Eagles ('50), *New Orleans Eagles ('51)*
Born: 1924
Died: Jan. 17, 1994, Wichita Falls, Tex.

He was an outfielder with the Eagles in 1950 after they moved to Houston, and relocated with them in New Orleans the following season.

Hewitt, Joe
Career: 1910–32   Positions: **ss**, 2b, 3b, of, p, manager
Teams: **St. Louis Giants** ('10–'13, '15, '17, '21), Brooklyn Royal Giants ('14–'18), New York Lincoln Giants ('13–'14, '18), New York Lincoln Stars ('14), G. C.T. Redcaps ('18), Philadelphia Giants ('18), Detroit Stars ('19–'20, '25–'26, '28), Chicago American Giants ('22–'24), St. Louis Stars ('22–'23), Milwaukee Bears ('23), Birmingham Black Barons ('24), Dayton Marcos ('26), Nashville Elite Giants ('27, '30, '32), Cleveland Cubs ('31)

Exceptionally fast on the bases, he was an outstanding base stealer and also utilized his speed to expand his range at shortstop. He began his career with the St. Louis Giants in 1910 and played for four years, before heading East in 1914 to play in New York City, the center of black baseball activity on the East Coast. Playing initially with the Lincoln

Giants, he soon joined the fledgling New York Lincoln Stars, who had splintered from the Giants during the season. With each of these teams he played second base, but upon joining the Brooklyn Royal Giants in 1916 he returned to shortstop, batting in the leadoff position to utilize his speed fully for three consecutive seasons. Incomplete statistics show a batting average of .282 with the Royal Giants in 1917.

Soon he was back in the Midwest, playing shortstop with Rube Foster's Chicago American Giants during the spring of 1922, while Bobby Williams remained in Chicago working in the post office. Two years later Hewitt was still with the American Giants, sharing playing time at second base behind Bingo De Moss. In 1926 Hewitt was with the Dayton Marcos entry in the Negro National League but left during the season to join the Detroit Stars, batting a composite .138. In the latter stages of his career, as his performance on the diamond diminished, Hewitt also tried his hand at managing, taking the helm at various times between 1921 and 1932.

Heyman
[see Hayman, Charles (Bugs)]

Heywood, Charlie (Dobie)
Career: 1925–26   Position: p
Team: New York Lincoln Giants

He was a pitcher with the Lincoln Giants for two seasons in the mid-'20s.

Hicks, James Eugene (Dobby, Jimmy)
Career: 1939–41   Position: p
Teams: Homestead Grays ('39–'40), New York Cuban Stars ('41)
Bats: Right   Throws: Right
Height: 6'1"   Weight: 195

After accepting terms and advance money from the Homestead Grays, this elongated right-hander pitched with the Grays in 1939 and 1940, splitting a pair of decisions the latter season. In 1941 he pitched with the New York Cubans but lost his only decision in his last year in the Negro Leagues.

Hicks, Wesley

Career: 1927–31   Positions: lf, rf, p
Teams: Chicago American Giants ('27), Memphis Red Sox ('27–'28), Kansas City Monarchs ('31)

He was an outfielder with a trio of Negro American League teams during his five years in the league, beginning as a part-time left fielder with the Memphis Red Sox in 1927, when he hit .291.

Hickson

Career: 1931   Position: 2b
Team: *Newark Browns*

He was a second baseman with the Newark Browns in 1931, a year before they entered the East-West League.

Hidalgo, Heliodoro

Career: 1905–13   Positions: **of**, 3b
Teams: All Cubans ('05), Stars of Cuba ('10), **Cuban Stars** ('11–'13)

This center fielder and cleanup batter for Cuban teams during the early '10s was small in stature but played like a giant. Outstanding defensively, he had very good speed afield and on the bases and, as an accomplished base stealer, was better known for his running than for his hitting.

In his homeland, the Cuban had a lifetime .231 average for his 16 years (1901–1916), spent mostly with Almendares. His best year batting (.303), was his last, the only time he was over .300. In 1913 he hit .282, which ranked second highest in the league, and he stole 12 bases in only 85 at-bats. In 1910 he played center field with Almenderos against the Detroit Tigers and hit .210 with a double and 3 stolen bases in 6 games.

He was a hard worker on the field and quiet and gentlemanly off the field. He was elected to the Cuban Hall of Fame in 1943.

Higdon, Barney

Career: 1943   Position: p
Team: Cincinnati Clowns

He pitched briefly with the Cincinnati Clowns in 1943, his only season in the Negro Leagues.

Higgins, Robert (**Bob**)

Career: 1896   Position: p
Teams: *minor leagues ('87–'88),* Cuban Giants ('96)

One of the talented black pitchers of the nineteenth century, he was a pitcher with the Syracuse International League team in 1887–88, posting records of 20–7 (2.91 ERA) and 17–7 (2.56 ERA), but racial preconceptions created problems during his short stay with the ballclub. In early June 1887 two players refused to sit for team pictures with him included in the group, and a year later he was released by Syracuse and returned to his Memphis barbershop. Years later, he returned to play with the Cuban Giants, the first and most successful black professional team of the era.

Hill

Career: 1910   Position: 3b
Team: St. Louis Giants

In his only appearance in black baseball, he was a third baseman with the St. Louis Giants in 1910, the second year of the club's existence.

Hill, Ben

Career: 1943   Position: p
Teams: Philadelphia Stars ('43), *Pittsburgh Crawfords ('46)*

He was a wartime pitcher with the 1943 Philadelphia Stars, and after World War II he pitched with the Pittsburgh Crawfords in the U.S. League.

Hill, Charley (**Lefty**)

Career: 1914–24   Positions: **of**, 1b, p
Teams: Chicago American Giants ('14), *Chicago Union Giants ('15),* Dayton Marcos ('18–'19), Detroit Stars ('20–'21), St. Louis Giants ('20, '23–'24), *Richmond Giants ('23)*

He played right field with the Detroit Stars in 1920–21, batting in the lower part of the order. Earlier in his career he pitched briefly with the Chicago American Giants, winning his only decision in 1914. He also played in the outfield at first base and batted seventh in the order with the Dayton marcos in 1919.

Hill, Fred
[see Hill, Johnson (Fred)]

Hill, Herb
Career: 1949   Positions: of, p
Team: Philadelphia Stars

An outfielder with the Philadelphia Stars in 1949, he also saw a little service on the mound. However, at this time the Negro American League was in decline and struggling to survive the loss of players to organized ball.

Hill, J. Preston (Pete)
Career: 1899–26   Positions: **cf, lf,** rf, 1b, 2b, manager, business manager
Teams: Pittsburgh Keystones ('99–'00), Cuban X-Giants ('01–'02), **Philadelphia Giants** ('03–'07), Leland Giants ('07–'10), **Chicago American Giants** ('11–'18), Detroit Stars ('19–'21), Milwaukee Bears ('23), Baltimore Black Sox ('24–'25)
Bats: Left   Throws: Right
Height: 6'1"   Weight: 215
Born: 1880
Died: 1951, Buffalo, N.Y.

A left-handed batter, Hill was a great hitter, both for average and power. An amazingly consistent line-drive hitter who used the entire field and excelled at bunting for base hits, he was a superior contact hitter with a near perfect eye for the strike zone and seldom struck out. In 1911 he was credited with hitting safely in 115 of 116 games. As the first great outfielder in black baseball history, he was compared to Ty Cobb, and rightfully so. If an all-star team had been picked from the deadball era, Cobb and Hill would have flanked Tris Speaker to form the outfield constellation.

Hill was a complete ballplayer and, although slightly bowlegged, could field and run the bases as well as hit. The star center fielder was one of the fastest outfielders in the game, fielded flawlessly, and had a deadly arm. On the bases he was a very fast, graceful runner and a good base stealer. But more than that, he was a nervy base runner who upset pitchers and infielders like Jackie Robinson was to do a quarter decade later. He was described as a "restless type, always in motion, jumping back and forth, trying to draw a throw from the pitcher."

Reported by one source to be part Indian, Hill started his career with the Pittsburgh Keystones in 1899, leaving after two seasons to join the Cuban X-Giants, the dominant team of that time. In 1903 the outfield star moved to the newly organized Philadelphia Giants, where he first joined forces with Rube Foster. After helping the team win consecutive championships in 1905–06, Hill accompanied Foster in a move to the Chicago Leland Giants. He also accompanied Foster, Home Run Johnson, and Bill Monroe to Cuba in 1907 to play with the Fe ballclub, and had little trouble making good, being described as having great range afield and being an excellent batter and a very fast runner. When Foster and owner Frank C. Leland split in 1910, Hill yielded to Foster's persuasion and signed with his club. The transition proved to be a good one, as Foster assembled a cast that comprised the greatest talent in black baseball at the time. The aggregation of stars finished the season with a record of 106–7, and manager Foster called it the greatest team, black or white, of all time. Hill, a smart ballplayer whose studied approach to the game made him Foster's choice as team captain, smashed the ball for a .428 average, outhitting teammate John Henry Lloyd. If an MVP award had been given that year, Hill would have been the choice for the honor.

The following season Foster's aggregation became known as the Chicago American Giants, and Hill remained with the team, providing solid hitting, outstanding fielding, superior baserunning, and responsible leadership to the ballclub for the next eight years. During this time he was the best hitter on the team, often hitting to the opposite field, and hitting left-handers equally well. Statistics extrapolated from existing box scores show averages of .400, .357, and .302 for the seasons 1911, 1912, and 1914.

In 1915, in a hotly contested game against the Indianapolis ABCs, with heavy betting on the outcome, he became engaged in an argument with the umpire, who pulled a gun and hit Hill in the nose. A riot ensued and the game was forfeited to the ABCs. The two teams were very evenly matched, but by the end of the season the American Giants won the playoff for the championship.

As captain of the American Giants, he continued to be a team leader and, being above draft age, remained a stabilizing presence when the team lost many younger players to military service during World War I. During his tenure with the organization, Foster often let Hill run the ballclub, and in 1919 the apprenticeship paid dividends when Hill assumed the reins of the Detroit Stars as playing manager. In late August he matched up with his mentor in a challenge series and connected with his 19th homer of the season as he led his team to victory over his ex-teammates.

Although entering the last phase of his career, the transition to the rabbit-ball era presented no problem for Pete as he rapped out a .391 average as the cleanup hitter in 1921, his last season with Detroit. Yielding the Stars' managerial reins to Bruce Petway, he made an interim stop with the Milwaukee Bears before moving East in 1924 to manage the Baltimore Black Sox.

As the year passed, Hill relegated himself to a role as part-time outfielder and pinch hitter but, even as he neared the end of his career, he remained a dangerous hitter. Ben Taylor, Hill's successor as manager of the Black Sox, said of the aging star, "The time was he was numbered among the greatest in the game, and will probably never have an equal as a hitter. I think he is the most dangerous man in a pinch in baseball."

In 1925 the popular, clutch-hitting "money player" closed out his brilliant 27-year career as one of black baseball's finest outfielders. Incomplete records indicate a lifetime .326 bat-

ting average in black baseball, and he proved his hitting ability in Cuba as well, compiling a .307 average for six winter seasons. Included was an unforgettable 1910–11 winter when he won the batting title with a .365 average while also leading the league in hits and triples. That same winter, Hill played with Havana against the Detroit Tigers and Philadelphia Athletics, who were touring the island after a successful baseball season, and batted a cool .333 in 11 games against the American League's finest. In one game against the Tigers, with Ed Summers on the mound, he had 2 hits and knocked in all 3 runs in the 3–2 win. Altogether he is credited with a .354 average against major-league opposition in his lifetime.

A hitting master, Hill could hit both left-handers and right-handers equally well and was the backbone of the great Chicago American Giants' teams for almost twenty years. After leaving the black major leagues, he formed the Buffalo Red Caps, a team of lesser distinction, and later worked for the Ford Motor Company in Detroit. In 1944 Cum Posey, in selecting Hill to his All-Time All-Star team, called him the "most consistent hitter of his lifetime" and, in 1952, he was picked on the *Pittsburgh Courier*'s second team All Time All-Star team, losing to Monte Irvin by one vote.

Hill, Jimmy (Lefty, Squab)
Career: 1938–50   Position: p
Teams: *Albany Black Sox ('37),* **Newark Eagles** *('38–'45), Raleigh Grays ('46), minor leagues ('46–'48),* Homestead Grays ('49–'50)
Bats: Left   Throws: Left
Height: 5'5"   Weight: 134
Born: June 6, 1918, Plant City, Fla.
Died: May 31, 1993, Sarasota, Fla.

A terrific little left-hander with a blazing fastball, a fine assortment of curves, and a slider, he was the ace of the Newark Eagles' pitching staff for a couple of seasons. While with the Eagles he loved to pitch against the Homestead Grays, once beating them in a doubleheader in 1945. But the highlight of the diminutive hurler's career came in 1941, when he pitched hitless relief in the midseason East-West All-Star classic and defeated Satchel Paige in the North-South All-Star game at the end of the season.

The Lakeland, Florida, native was discovered while pitching batting practice for the Detroit Tigers in spring training. Hank Greenberg and other Tigers labeled him a major-league pitcher, but before he signed with the Newark Eagles of the Negro National League in 1938, he played with the Albany Black Sox in the twilight League of Albany, New York, for a year.

After two years with Newark, in October 1939 both the Clowns and Grays sought his services. However, he remained with the Eagles, although he frequently wrote to owner Effa Manley asking for advances on his salary and intimating that he might sign elsewhere if the money was not made available. Mrs. Manley took a special interest in his well-being.

His best year came in 1940, when he registered an 8–2 record with a 3.15 ERA, but the early promise dissipated and he never experienced another winning season in the Negro Leagues. He dropped to identical 2–5 records during the next two seasons, and then posted marks of 4–5, 1–2, and 2–3 for 1943–45.

He left the Eagles when the doors to organized baseball opened, playing three seasons (1946–48) in the Florida State League. He pitched two years with the Lakeland Tigers sandwiched around one with the Palm Beach Rockets. After his tour of duty in the minor leagues, he returned to black baseball to close out his career, playing with the Homestead Grays in 1949–50, when they had dropped out of league play and were playing a lesser caliber of ball.

In his early years he played for Cienfuegos in the Cuban winter league of 1939. He was a fine fielder, and like most pitchers, he regarded himself as a pretty good man at the plate, hitting for averages of .257 and .250 in 1940–41, but without much power.

Hill, John
Career: 1900–1907   Positions: 3b, ss
Teams: Genuine Cuban Giants ('00–01), Philadelphia Giants ('02–'04–'07), Cuban X-Giants ('03)

Beginning at the turn of the twentieth century, he played on the left side of the infield for the best eastern teams of the era, including the Genuine Cuban Giants, the Cuban X-Giants, and the Philadelphia Giants. Although primarily a third baseman, he also played shortstop. With Philadelphia in 1907, his last year in black baseball, he was the backup for superstar shortstop John Henry Lloyd.

Hill, Johnson (John, Fred)
Career: 1920–27   Positions: **3b, 2b,** ss, of
Teams: St. Louis Giants ('20), New York Lincoln Giants ('20), Detroit Stars ('21), Milwaukee Bears ('23), Brooklyn Royal Giants ('22–'27), *Philadelphia Colored Giants of New York* ('28)

This native Texan played most of his career in the Lone Star State before leaving to join the midwestern teams of the Negro National League. Primarily a second baseman early in his career, he was also a fair third baseman and could play the outfield. With the St. Louis Giants in 1920, Hill played right field and second base while batting in the second slot.

He was considered a veteran by the time he arrived in the East as the regular third baseman for the Brooklyn Royal Giants in 1922. With the exception of part of 1923, when he was with the Milwaukee Bears, Hill spent the next half dozen years in the lineup for the Royals and registered averages of .304 and .244 for the 1924–25 seasons. Although he usually hit in the lower part of the batting order, he was inserted in the cleanup spot in 1925. His last year with a top ballclub was in 1927, although he continued to play with teams of lesser status.

Hill, Jonathan
Career: 1937   Positions: of, p
Teams: Atlanta Black Crackers ('37), St. Louis Stars ('37)

In 1937 he was an outfielder-pitcher with the Atlanta Black Crackers and the St. Louis Stars.

Hill, Lefty
[see Hill, Charley (Lefty)]

Hill, Samuel (**Sam**)
Career: 1946–48   Position: of
Teams: Chicago American Giants ('46–'48), *minor leagues ('50–'58), Memphis Red Sox ('52, '58)*
Bats: Left   Throws: Right
Height: 6'2"   Weight: 180
Born: 1929

The outfielder played with the Chicago American Giants for three years, 1946–48, batting .313 with good power in his last season to earn a trip to the 1948 East-West All-Star game as the right fielder for the West squad. A good contact hitter but with only average speed on the bases, he made the transition to organized baseball after the doors were opened to black players. After leaving the American Giants, he played three years (1950–52) in the Mandak League, with Winnipeg and Carman. His best season was the middle year, when he hit .290 with Winnipeg. In 1954 he played with Williamsport in the Eastern League and hit .272 with respectable power. His last years in baseball were with Duluth-Superior in 1957–58, when he hit .312 and .265, respectively.

Hill, Slim
Career: 1917   Position: rf
Team: Chicago Giants

In 1917 he played right field for the Chicago Giants.

Hill, W. R.
Career: 1885   Position: ss
Team: *Brooklyn Remsens*

He was a shortstop with the 1885 Brooklyn Remsens, one of the earliest black teams.

Hilldale Daisies
Duration: 1916–32   Honors: ECL pennants ('23–'25); World Series champions ('25)
Affiliations: Independent ('16–'22, '30–'31), ECL ('23–'28), ANL ('29), EWL ('32)

This ballclub began as a boys' team in 1910 but became a professional-level club in 1916. In 1917 they had Spot Poles and Bill Pettus in the lineup and posted a record of 23–15–1. For postseason exhibitions against major leaguers they added Smokey Joe Williams, Louis Santop, Dick Lundy, and other "ringers" to the lineup. The next year, 1918, they improved the quality of their team considerably and became competitive with any team in the East.

In 1923 they became a charter member of the Eastern Colored League, and won the first three pennants with records of 32–17, 47–13. The latter two years, they played in the first two Negro World Series between their league and the more established Negro National League. After losing the first Series to the Kansas City Monarchs in 1924, they defeated the Monarchs in a rematch between the same two teams in 1925, to claim the first (and only) World Series victory by an Eastern Colored League team. After the dissolution of the Eastern Colored League early in the 1928 season, the ballclub joined the American Negro League in 1929, which was essentially the same league with a new name. That league also folded, after only one season, and Hilldale played as an independent team for the next two seasons.

The franchise was sold to John Drew, who owned a bus line from Darby to Philadelphia, in 1929 and he called the team the Darby Daisies, but to the public, the team remained Hilldale. Under Drew's direction the club faltered, and in 1932 Ed Bolden resumed control. He and manager Judy Johnson tried one more effort for financial stability by joining the East-West League, but both the league and the franchise folded in the throes of the Depression.

Hines, John
Career: 1924–34   Positions: **c, of,** *1b, 2b*
Teams: Chicago American Giants ('24–'30), Columbia American Giants ('31), Cole's American Giants ('32–'34)
Bats: Right   Throws: Right
Height: 6'0"   Weight: 190

A big, light-complected catcher with a good arm, he was a "straight out" player who also played in the outfield. During his years with the Chicago American Giants, the franchise twice won back-to-back pennants, in 1926–27 and 1932–33. He began the 1924 season with the Wiley College baseball team in the spring, but signed with Rube Foster's American Giants and was soon playing right field and also pulling occasional duty as an alternate catcher. In 1926 he hit .328 during the regular season while gaining considerable playing time as a center fielder and backup catcher as the American Giants won the Negro National League pennant and defeated the Eastern Colored League Bacharachs in the World Series. The following season he dropped to a .242 average while batting fifth in the order until suffering a broken leg and the American Giants repeated as both the Negro National League champions and World Series victors over the Bacharachs.

After Rube Foster's death in 1930, when the franchise experienced instability and financial difficulties, Dave Malarcher kept the club alive, fielding the Columbia American Giants in 1931. After the year with Malarcher's team, he hit .319 as the regular catcher with Robert A. Cole's American Giants in 1932 as they copped the Negro Southern League championship under new ownership. The next season the American Giants joined the new Negro National League and, while playing out of Indianapolis during the latter part of the season, won the league's first pennant. Hines was relegated to a substitute basis for the season and never regained his starting position.

He was a hard case who was hard to get along with in the clubhouse. He was also a heavy drinker and, while drinking with teammate James Bray, a fight erupted between the two, resulting in Bray being killed and Hines being sentenced to life imprisonment at the Illinois state penitentiary at Joliet.

Hinson
Career: 1932   Position: p
Team: Newark Browns

He was a pitcher with the Newark Browns in 1932, when the team was a member of the East-West League.

Hinson, Frank
Career: 1896   Position: p
Team: Cuban Giants

In 1896 he was a pitcher with the Cuban Giants, the first black professional team when founded in 1885 and considered the top ballclub of the early era. However, by the late '90s the ballclub was in decline.

Hinton, Roland (Archie, Charlie)
Career: 1945–46   Positions: p, if
Team: Baltimore Elite Giants
Bats: Right   Throws: Right
Height: 5'9"   Weight: 170
Born: Raleigh, N.C.

This former UCLA student pitched briefly with the Baltimore Elite Giants for two seasons in the '40s, winning his only decision in 1945. He could also fill in an infield position, and he hit .333 in limited play in 1945.

Hitchman
Career: 1925   Position: 3b
Team: Indianapolis ABCs

In 1925 he was a reserve third baseman with the Indianapolis ABCs during the period of turbulence following the death of longtime owner and manager C. I. Taylor.

Hoard
Career: 1921   Position: p
Team: Kansas City Monarchs

He was a pitcher with the Kansas City Monarchs in 1921, his only year in the Negro Leagues.

Hobgood, Freddie (Fred, Lefty, John)
a.k.a. Hopgood
Career: 1941–46   Position: p
Teams: Newark Eagles ('41–'43), Philadelphia Stars ('44), New York Black Yankees ('46)
Bats: Left   Throws: Left
Height: 5'9"   Weight: 160
Born: Oct. 1, 1921, Kingston, N.C.

He was a left-handed pitcher with a good fastball, screwball, and change, an assortment of curves, and average control. He pitched with the Newark Eagles for three seasons in the early '40s, registering marks of 4–3, 3–3, and 1–3. He was a good-fielding pitcher but did not have much power as a hitter.

Hobson, Charles (Johnny)
a.k.a. Hopson
Career: 1923–25   Positions: p, ss, of, 2b, 3b, 1b
Teams: *Richmond Giants ('22–'23),* New York Lincoln Giants ('23), Atlantic City Bacharach Giants ('23–'24), *Chappie Johnson's Stars ('26–'27)*

During the '20s this multifaceted player performed at an array of positions. Beginning as an infielder with the Richmond Giants, he joined the big time with the Lincoln Giants in 1923 as a reserve shortstop and had a short stint on the mound with the Bacharach Giants in 1924 before closing his career back in the infield with Chappie Johnson's team.

Hocker
Career: 1915   Position: p
Team: *Louisville White Sox*

A brother of Bruce Hocker, he was a pitcher for Louisville, a marginal team, in 1915 under manager "Steel Arm" Johnny Taylor.

Hocker, Bruce
a.k.a. Hooker; Becker
Career: 1914–20   Positions: **1b**, of
Teams: *West Baden Sprudels ('13),* Chicago American Giants ('14), Louisville White Sox ('15), Bowser's ABCs ('16), New York Lincoln Stars ('16), Pennsylvania Red Caps of New York ('17), Hilldale Daisies ('18), Dayton Marcos ('20)

This big first baseman was a good hitter and played with the Chicago American Giants in the 1914 championship playoff against the Brooklyn Royal Giants. He also played in the outfield and frequently split his playing time between the two positions. In 1915 he and his brother both played under manager "Steel Arm" Johnny Taylor at Louisville. The following year, when ABC's owner Thomas Bowser and manager C. I. Taylor split, forming two rival teams, Hocker began the year with Bowser's team, but left during the season to play in the East with the Lincoln Stars, who won the Eastern Championship. When the team dissolved after the season, Hocker was among the ex-Stars who joined the Pennsylvania Red Caps of New York in 1917. The next season he was the regular first baseman for Hilldale and usually hit in the fifth slot in the batting order, as he did throughout much of his career. In 1920 he returned to the Midwest to close out his seven seasons in black baseball, with the Dayton Marcos, a charter member of Rube Foster's Negro National League.

Hockett
Career: 1913–18   Position: 2b
Team: Brooklyn Royal Giants

During the '10s he was a reserve second baseman with the Brooklyn Royal Giants.

Hodges, William
Career: 1920–25   Position: p
Teams: Baltimore Black Sox ('18–'22), New York Lincoln Giants ('25)

He was a pitcher with the Lincoln Giants and the Baltimore Black Sox during the first half of the '20s (1920–25).

Hogan, Julius
Career: 1932   Positions: c, of
Team: Atlantic City Bacharach Giants

He appeared briefly as a reserve catcher with the Bacharachs in 1932, when the team was in its waning years.

Holcher
Career: 1918   Position: 1b
Team: New York Lincoln Giants

He played one game at first base for the Lincoln Giants in 1918.

Holcomb
Career: 1923   Position: p
Team: Detroit Stars

In 1923 he appeared briefly as a pitcher with the Detroit Stars.

Holden
Career: 1910   Position: rf
Team: St. Louis Giants

He was a right fielder with the St. Louis Giants in 1910, the second year of the club's existence, in his only appearance in black baseball.

Holiday
[see Holliday, Charles (Flit)]

Holland
Career: 1921   Position: 1b
Team: Hilldale Daisies

He played briefly as a first baseman with Hilldale in 1921.

Holland, Elvis William (Bill)
Career: 1920–41   Positions: **p**, manager
Teams: Detroit Stars ('20–'22), Chicago American Giants ('21), New York Lincoln Giants ('23–'24, '27–'30), Brooklyn Royal Giants ('25–'27), Hilldale Daisies ('27), Harlem Stars ('31), **New York Black Yankees** ('32–'41), Philadelphia Stars ('41)
Bats: Both   Throws: Right
Height: 5'9"   Weight: 180
Born: Feb. 2, 1901, Indianapolis, Ind.
Died: New York, N.Y.

A fastball pitcher, this right-hander's repertory also included a curve, drop, change-up, and emery ball. He is credited with a 29–2 record in 1930 with the New York Lincoln Giants, and on July 10 of that year he became the first black pitcher ever to pitch in Yankee Stadium.

He began his twenty-two year career with a 17–2 record in 1920, followed by seasons of 13–12 and 16–13 before joining the Lincoln Giants. In New York his fortunes turned and he had only a 2–5 league ledger in his first season with the Lincolns, but that winter (1923–24), pitching with the great Santa Clara ballclub, he led the Cuban League in wins with 10. The following season, with the Lincoln Giants, he was expected to be a mainstay on the pitching staff and forged an 8–5 record, but was released around midseason for an unspecified reason. After his release he went to Cuba and worked himself back into form. He often pitched in the Latin American winter leagues, including four years in Cuba, where he logged a 27–22 lifetime record.

Upon his return, he signed with the Brooklyn Royal Giants for four seasons (1925–28) and experienced a notable lack of success in league play, with records showing a composite 7–13 ledger without a winning season. He returned to New York for the 1929 season and enjoyed a resurgent 13–7 season for the Lincoln Giants. After the record-setting 1930 season, the last in the Lincoln Giants' history, he played with John Henry Lloyd's Harlem Stars, which was an interim team between the Lincolns and the New York Black Yankees, who were organized in 1932. Holland had a record of 6–1 in his first year with the Black Yankees, but available statistics show an aggregate record of only 8–13 for the next 8 seasons.

However, during much of his long association with the New York Black Yankees he was considered the ace of the staff, and he was selected to pitch in the 1939 East-West All-Star game but did not figure in the decision. Aside from his work on the mound, he was at best a mediocre player in other phases of the game, being an average fielder and below average in batting and baserunning.

Holland, William (Billy)
Career: 1894–1908   Positions: **p**, of, 3b
Teams: Chicago Unions ('94, '97–'00), Page Fence Giants ('95–'97), Algona Brownies ('03), Leland Giants ('05), Brooklyn Royal Giants ('06), *Pop Watkins Stars*('07–'08)

In a career that bridged two centuries, he was one of the top pitchers of the era and played with many of the best black teams of the era, including the famed Page Fence Giants of Adrian, Michigan; the Algona Brownies, champions of the Northwest in 1903; and the famed Leland Giants in 1905, their first year of existence. A native of Aurora, Illinois, while with the Page Giants in 1895 he won 2 games against 3 losses and batted .197 while also playing outfield and third base. After his active baseball days were over he became an umpire in the Negro National League during the '20s.

Holliday, Charles Dourcher (Flit)
a.k.a. Holiday
Career: 1938   Position: of
Team: Atlanta Black Crackers
Bats: Left   Throws: Right

A skinny little "dude" who wore spats on his shoes, this Texan shared some playing time in left field for the 1938 Negro American League second-half champion Atlanta Black Crackers. When the speedster from Texas joined the Black Crackers in April 1938, he proved to have an eager spirit and a will to win. However, he was not a very good player and was dropped from the squad near the end of the first half, but was reinstated in a short time and was back with the team in August. A left-handed batter with a wide stance at the plate, he was a patient batter and a capable leadoff hitter but lacked real punch at the plate. He proved to be an adequate fielder.

Hollingsworh, Curtis
Career: 1946–50   Position: p
Team: Birmingham Black Barons
Bats: Right   Throws: Left

This left-handed pitcher had stints with the Black Barons during the post-World War II years, beginning with a brief appearance in 1946. The next season he had a 4–0 record, but in his last year, 1950, he pitched only one third of an inning.

Hollins
Career: 1936   Position: p
Team: Birmingham Black Barons

He was a pitcher with the Birmingham Black Barons in 1936, a year before they joined the Negro American League.

Holloway
Career: 1932   Position: p
Team: Newark Browns

While pitching with the East-West League's Newark Browns in 1932, he had a 1–2 record in league play when the league folded.

Holloway, Christopher Columbus (Crush)
Career: 1921–39   Positions: rf, cf
Teams: Indianapolis ABCs ('21–'23), **Baltimore Black Sox** ('24–'28, '31–'33), Hilldale Daisies ('29, '32), Detroit Stars ('30), New York Black Yankees ('32), Atlantic City Bacharach Giants ('34), Brooklyn Eagles ('35), Baltimore Elite Giants ('39)
Bats: Both   Throws: Right
Height: 5'11½"   Weight: 180
Born: Sept. 16, 1896, Hillsboro, Tex.
Died: June 1972, Baltimore, Md.

A fast, aggressive base runner, he would slide hard into a base with spikes high to try to intimidate opposing infielders. The big, light-complected, green-eyed outfielder kept his spikes sharpened and considered the basepaths to be his own domain. A tough man to tangle with, he once stopped Jud Wilson from doing bodily harm to an umpire in the locker room by picking up a bat and threatening to "bust" Wilson's head if he didn't let the ump go.

Holloway began his career with C. I. Taylor's Indianapolis ABCs in 1921, and in addition to being one of the best base stealers on the ABCs, he perfected the drag bunt to further take advantage of his exceptional speed. He was also a good defensive outfielder and a good hitter, and hit .330 in his last season with the team.

Joining manager Pete Hill's Baltimore Black Sox in 1924, Crush, usually batting leadoff, hit for averages of .331, .289 and .284 for the next three seasons. In 1929 he was traded to Hilldale, along with Jackson, for Warfield and Ryan, and promptly batted .296 and led the league in stolen bases. In each of the next two seasons he hit .250 for the Detroit Stars and the Baltimore Black Sox. In 1932 he split his playing time among three teams, beginning with the Black Sox but joining Hilldale before ending up with the New York Black Yankees when the Hilldale franchise folded. His batting patterns from the Negro Leagues were consistent with his performance in two Cuban winter seasons, where he hit for a .290 average. He also played with the Philadelphia Royal Giants in the winter of 1925.

Holmes, Benjamin F. (**Ben**)
Career: 1885–89   Position: 3b
Teams: *Argyle Hotel Athletics ('85),* Cuban Giants ('86–'89), *minor leagues ('94)*
Bats: Right   Throws: Right
Born: April 3, 1858, King and Queen County, Va.

After holding down the hot corner for the 1885 Argyle Hotel team, he helped organize the original Cuban Giants in 1886, also playing third base with the team. He remained with the Cuban Giants for four years, during which the team represented Trenton, New Jersey, in the Middle States League in 1887 and 1889. Later, in 1894, he played in the Nebraska State League.

Holmes began playing baseball in 1876 at age eighteen with the famous colored Douglas Club of Washington, D. C., and throughout his lifetime he retained his pride at being a member of the original Cuban Giants. In 1942, while living in Orange, New Jersey, he wrote a letter to Effa Manley, owner of the Newark Eagles, asking for tickets to the Eagles' games and signed himself as an "original Cuban Giants' player."

Holmes, Eddie
Career: 1932   Position: p
Team: Baltimore Black Sox

He was a pitcher with the 1932 Baltimore Black Sox when they were in the East-West League, posting a 4–2 record for the season.

Holmes, Frank (Sonny)
Career: 1929–38   Position: p

Teams: New York Lincoln Giants ('29), Atlantic City Bacharach Giants ('31), Philadelphia Stars ('34–'35, '37), Washington Elite Giants ('36), Baltimore Elite Giants ('38), Washington Black Senators ('38)

He was a pitcher for a decade with several eastern teams, beginning with the Lincoln Giants in 1929. After a brief stop with the Bacharachs, he landed with the Philadelphia Stars in 1934, their championship season. Although he contributed only a 2–3 ledger to the Stars' successful drive to the Negro National League pennant, he provided pitching depth for the team. The next year was less successful for both Holmes and the Stars, as they were unable to repeat in their run for the pennant and he dropped to a 2–6 record for the 1935 season. After leaving the Stars he played briefly with the Elites in both Washington and Baltimore, and with the Washington Black Senators. In May 1938 the veteran hurler was sought by the Atlanta Black Crackers, but he chose to remain in the East.

Holmes, Leroy Thomas (**Phillie**)
Career: 1938–45   Positions: ss, 2b
Teams; Jacksonville Red Caps (*34,* '38), Atlanta Black Crackers ('39), Cleveland Bears ('39), Kansas City Monarchs, New York Black Yankees   ('45),   Cincinnati-Indianapolis Clowns ('45)
Bats: Left   Throws: Right
Height: 5'10"   Weight: 170

This slick-fielding middle infielder was very deadly on ground balls and was good making the pivot on double plays. He was a smart ballplayer and always alert in the field. Although primarily a shortstop, he knew his way around the keystone sack and also could play second base. The hustling speedster was an outstanding base stealer and, although only a mediocre hitter without substantial power, he was a superb bunter.

The shortstop began as a professional with the Jacksonville Redcaps in 1934, when they were in the Negro Southern League, and most of his career was spent in the South. He signed with top teams in 1938 and was the leadoff batter for the Atlanta Black Crackers in 1939. Leaving the South, he closed out his Negro League career hitting .238 as a newcomer with the New York Black Yankees in 1945. After his playing career was over, he scouted for the St. Louis Browns.

Holsey, Robert J. (**Frog**)
Career: 1928–32   Position: p
Teams: Chicago American Giants ('28–'30), Chicago Columbia Giants ('31), Cleveland Cubs ('31), Nashville Elite Giants ('32)

Most of his five-year career was spent with the Chicago American Giants' franchise, registering marks of 11–11 and 8–10 in 1929–30. He split the next season between Dave Malarcher's Columbia Giants and the Cleveland Cubs, and closed out his career with Tom Wilson's Nashville Elite Giants in 1932.

Holt
Career: 1934   Position: p
Team: Philadelphia Stars

He appeared briefly with the Philadelphia Stars in 1934, their championship season.

Holt
Career: 1922–27   Position: 2b
Team: Chicago American Giants

A second baseman, this youngster was given a good trial with the Chicago American Giants by Rube Foster in spring training of 1922. In 1927, when the American Giants won the pennant, he was injured in Birmingham late in the season when he ran into a fence, and he missed the playoffs and World Series.

Holt, Johnny
Career: 1922–23   Position: lf
Teams: Pittsburgh Keystones ('22), Toledo Tigers ('23)

In his first year he was a reserve outfielder with the Pittsburgh Keystones, but the next season he earned a starting position in left field with the Toledo Tigers until the team disbanded in mid-July.

Holt, Joseph
Career: 1928   Position: of
Team: *Brooklyn Cuban Giants*

In 1928 he was an outfielder with the Brooklyn Cuban Giants, a team of lesser status.

Holtz, Eddie
a.k.a. Holt
Career: 1919–24   Positions: **2b**, ss
Teams: St. Louis Giants ('19–'21), Chicago American Giants ('22), St. Louis Stars ('22–'24), Ne York Lincoln Giants ('23)

This little middle infielder played both shortstop and second base with the St. Louis Giants beginning in 1919. After the franchise was sold in 1922, he was considered to be a "fast coming" infielder and played second base in the team's first game ever as the St. Louis Stars. Although most of his career was spent in St. Louis, he also played briefly with the Chicago American Giants and the New York Lincoln Giants.

Homestead Grays
Duration: 1912–50   Honors: Eastern championship ('30–'31), NNL pennant ('37–'45, '48)
Affiliations: Independent ('12–'28, '30–'33, '49–'50), ANL ('29), NNL ('34–'48)

One of the best-known black baseball teams, the Homestead Grays' ballclub was organized in 1910, and Cum Posey, who would become the owner of the team, joined it as a player in 1912. Homestead was a steel mill town, and the workers at the U.S. Steel mill formed a baseball team for weekend recreation. Posey, a former football player and basketball star at Penn State University, was a railway mail worker and joined the steelworkers to play for the team. Playing on West Field in Homestead, the team began also playing twilight games during the week in addition to weekends. New players kept joining the team, and their reputation increased to the point of their becoming the leading attraction in the tristate area. At first they added a little comedy to the game to enhance their appeal as a good gate attraction.

Soon after Posey started handling the team, it became a full-time job. He booked all the leading teams around the Pittsburgh area and, with the Grays playing as an independent team, made a good profit every year from 1912 to 1929. They joined the American Negro League in 1929, but the league lasted only one year. The next two seasons the Grays fielded its strongest teams since the franchise's inception, winning eastern championships both seasons. The 1931 club is called by many the greatest black team of all time.

But when the Depression hit in the thirties, there were some lean years for the Grays, and Gus Greenlee took advantage of Posey's economic situation to lure some of his best players to the Crawfords. With no league in the East and the collapse of the Negro National League in the West, in 1932 Cum Posey organized the East-West League, but it didn't even last the year and folded in June.

In 1933 the Negro National league reorganized, and a year later, with Posey forming a partnership with Rufus "Sonnyman" Jackson to bring some money back to the organization, the Grays entered the Negro National League as associate members and became full members the following year, fielding a team each year until the league folded after the 1948 season.

During this time the Grays dominated the league, building a dynasty around the power tandem of Josh Gibson and Buck Leonard, dubbed the "thunder twins" and also called the black Babe Ruth and Lou Gehrig by the media. The Grays won nine consecutive Negro National League pennants, 1939–45, and also annexed the last flag in 1948. During this time they also played in five of the seven World Series played between the Negro National League and the Negro American League, including the first and the last of these Series. They lost the first Series to the Kansas City Monarchs in 1942 and lost to the Cleveland Buckeyes in 1945, but defeated the Bir-

mingham Black Barons in each of the other three Series, in 1943–44 and 1948. After the league broke up the Grays continued to play for two more years as an independent team, playing against lesser opposition, but disbanded after the 1950 season.

Hood, Dozier Charles
Career: 1945   Position: c
Team: Kansas City Monarchs

This wartime player was a reserve catcher and pinch hitter with the Kansas City Monarchs in 1945.

Hoods, William
Career: 1887   Position: player
Team: *Philadelphia Pythians*

He was a player with the Philadelphia Pythians, one of eight teams that were charter members of the League of Colored Baseball Clubs in 1887. However, the league's existence was ephemeral, lasting only a week.

Hooker
[see Hocker, Bruce]

Hooker, Lenial Charlie (**Lennie**, Len, Elbow)
Career: 1940–49   Position: p
Teams: Newark Eagles ('40–'48), Houston Eagles ('49), *Canadian League ('50–'51), Mexican League ('45)*
Bats: Right   Throws: Right
Height: 6'0"   Weight: 169
Born: June 28, 1919, Sanford, N.C.

This Newark Eagles right-hander's specialty was the knuckleball, but he also had a pretty good fastball and an assortment of off-speed breaking pitches. He joined the Eagles in 1940 and posted marks of 2–5, 2–2, and 3–0 during his first three seasons. His ability to control the knuckler enabled him to register a 7–1 record during the second half of the 1943 season, his best year. The next two years he had records of 8–9 and 5–7, preparatory to the Eagles' 1946 championship campaign. In the Eagle's surge to the Negro National League pennant, he split 10 decisions during the regular season and split another pair in the ensuing World Series against the Kansas City Monarchs. The hard-luck pitcher spent his entire career with the Eagles and lost many 1-run games, falling off to a 3–7 record in 1947. He was an excellent fielder and a fair hitter for a pitcher but did not generate much power.

When the Eagles' franchise was sold and relocated in Houston, he played for a year under the new ownership. After leaving the Negro Leagues he pitched two seasons (1950–51) with Drummondville in the Provincial League, where he enjoyed seasons of 11–6 (2.52 ERA) and 10–9 (3.78 ERA). He also played in the Mexican League, with Vera Cruz in 1945 and in the Cuban winter league of 1946–47.

Hopgood

[see Hobgood, Freddie]

Hopkins

Career: 1945   Position: p
Team: Newark Eagles

A wartime player, he pitched briefly with the Newark Eagles in 1945.

Hopkins, George

Career: 1890–1902   Positions: p, 2b, of
Teams: Chicago Unions ('90–'99), Adrian Page Fence Giants ('95), Algona Brownies ('02)

For the first half of the decade of the 1890s he was a pitcher with the Chicago Unions, but after 1895 he became an everyday player as a second baseman and occasional outfielder. He also played with two championship teams separated by the turn of the century, the Adrian Page Fence Giants and the Algona Brownies. Each ballclub was of short duration but was a top team during its existence. With the Page Fence Giants in 1895 he played outfield but batted only .100 for the duration.

Hopson, John

Career: 1924   Position: p
Team: Atlantic City Bacharach Giants

He was the number three pitcher in the starting rotation with the 1924 Bacharach Giants.

Hopwood

Career: 1928   Position: lf
Team: Kansas City Monarchs

He appeared briefly as a reserve outfielder with the Kansas City Monarchs in 1928.

Hordy, J. H.

Career: 1887   Position: player
Team: *Baltimore Lord Baltimores*

He was a player with the Baltimore Lord Baltimores, one of eight teams that were charter members of the League of Colored Baseball Clubs in 1887. However, the league's existence was ephemeral, lasting only a week. His position is uncertain.

Horn

Career: 1925   Position: 2b
Team: Birmingham Black Barons

He was a second baseman with the 1925 Birmingham Black Barons.

Horn, Herman (Doc)

Career: 1949–50   Positions: of, 3b
Teams: Kansas City Monarchs ('49–'54)
Born: Mar. 3, 1927

He is listed as having played with Kansas City Monarchs in 1949–54 and with Monterrey in the Mexican winter league of 1953.

Horn, William (Will)

Career: 1896–1905   Position: p
Teams: Chicago Unions ('96–'00), Algona Brownies ('02–'03), Philadelphia Giants ('04), Leland Giants ('05)

He was one of the top three pitchers with the Chicago Unions in 1899–1900 and also pitched with the Philadelphia Giants before joining the Leland Giants in their first year of existence, 1905, to close out his decade in black baseball.

Horne, William (Billy)

Career: 1938–46   Positions: 2b, ss, 3b
Teams: American Giants ('38–'41), Cincinnati

Buckeyes ('42), Harrisburg–St. Louis Stars ('43), Cleveland Buckeyes ('43–'46), *military service ('45), minor leagues ('51)*
Bats: Right   Throws: Right
Height: 5'10"   Weight: 165
Born: New Orleans, La.

The hustling little middle infielder was at home at both shortstop and second base, and was equally adept at turning the double play at either keystone spot. The pepperpot played both positions with the Chicago American Giants and the Cleveland Buckeyes. He also made appearances at each position in East-West All-Star games. His first All-Star appearance was in 1939, and he contributed a hit and an RBI to the West's 4–2 victory, but he went hitless in his second All-Star game, two years later.

The following season he signed with the Buckeyes as a second baseman, proving to be an ace at turning double plays, and was rated among the best at it in the league. While with the American Giants he had batted in the lower part of the order, but with the Buckeyes he was a consistent hitter and, while not a distance hitter, was good in the clutch and batted in the first two slots, hitting .286 in 1942. After two seasons on the right side of the keystone sack, he moved back to shortstop in 1944, hitting .235, and was appointed to the All-Star team as a reserve. In 1945, when the Buckeyes signed Avelino Canizares to play shortstop, he moved back to second base, his best natural position. However, early in the season he went into military service for the duration of World War II, returning to the Buckeyes in 1946. After leaving the Negro Leagues he played in the Mandak League in 1951 but batted only .207.

Horns, James J.

Career: 1887   Position: player
Team: *Boston Resolutes*

He was a player with the 1887 Boston Resolutes, one of eight teams that were charter members of the League of Colored Baseball Clubs in 1887. However, the league's existence was ephemeral, lasting only a week. His position is uncertain.

Hoskin, Buddy

Career: 1938   Position: p
Team: Atlanta Black Crackers

A pitcher from Canton, Mississippi, he was on the Atlanta Black Crackers' early-season roster in 1938 but didn't stick with the team.

Hoskins, David Taylor (Dave)

Career: 1942–49   Positions: of, p
Teams: Indianapolis Clowns ('42), Chicago American Giants ('43), Homestead Grays ('44–'47), *minor leagues ('48, '50–'52, '55–'60),* Louisville Buckeyes ('49), major leagues ('53–'54), *Mexican League ('60)*
Bats: Left   Throws: Right
Height: 6'1"   Weight: 180
Born: Aug. 4, 1925, Greenwood, Miss.
Died: Apr. 2, 1970, Flint, Mich.

A pitcher-outfielder for eight years in the Negro Leagues, Hoskins was part of the Homestead Grays' "murderers' row" in the mid-1940s. He joined the Grays as a pitcher in 1944, with a fastball, curve, and control, but his bat and speed necessitated his switch to an everyday player. He hit a resounding .355 with good power to help the Grays to the Negro National League pennant and a World Series victory over the Birmingham Black Barons in 1944. The next year he was 2–0 as a pitcher, but was utilized primarily as an outfielder and hit .278 while batting in the third slot of the Grays' powerful lineup. The Grays won another flag, but lost the World Series to the Cleveland Buckeyes. In 1946 his average dropped to .260, but he was still dividing his time between the outfield and the mound.

Hoskins made his first foray into organized baseball with Grand Rapids and batted a robust .393 in 1948. The next year he returned to the Negro Leagues for a last season and hit .305 with the Louisville Buckeyes in the Negro American League, earning his only appearance in the East-West All-Star game.

Although known primarily for his hitting in

the Negro Leagues, he made it to the major leagues as a fireballing pitcher in 1953–54 for the Cleveland Indians, for whom he compiled a composite 9–4 record and 3.79 ERA. The Indians' management had some difficulty deciding which role he should play in their organization, as an outfielder or as a pitcher.

The progression from outfielder to pitcher is evident in his minor-league career. In 1950, with Dayton in the Central League, he was 0–2 as a pitcher but hit .318, with a slugging percentage of .530. The next year, with Wilkes-Barre in the Eastern League, he was 5–1 on the mound and batted .286. In 1952, with Dallas in the Texas League he was 22–10 with a 2.12 ERA and also batted .328.

After his brief stay in the American League with the Indians, he played for half a dozen more seasons. His best year was back with Dallas in 1958, when he was 17–8 with a 3.18 ERA. He also played with Indianapolis (9–13), San Diego (7–11) and Louisville (9–11) before splitting his last year, 1960, between Montreal (0–2) and Poza Rica in the Mexican League (7–5). He also pitched two winters with Gavilanes in the Occidental League, where he hit .323 and had seasons of 14–5, 1.68 ERA and 12–7, 2.28 ERA during the years 1956–57 and 1958–59.

Hoskins, William (**Bill**)
a.k.a. Erskine Hoskins
Career: 1937–46   Position: of
Teams: Memphis Red Sox ('37), Detroit Stars ('37), St. Louis Stars ('37), Washington Black Senators ('38), **Baltimore Elite Giants** ('38–'46), Kansas City Monarchs ('43), New York Black Yankees ('46)
Bats: Right   Throws: Right
Height: 6'3"   Weight: 210
Born: c. 1915, Charleston, Miss

A good hitter with long-distance power, this hefty hitter demonstrated consistency at the plate, with batting averages of .330, .361, .377, .293, .288, .318, and .315 for the years 1939–45. Although only an average fielder, the Elite Giants' outfielder was fast on the bases.

He made his only East-West All-Star appearance in 1941, batting third in the East lineup, ahead of Hall of Famers Buck Leonard, Monte Irvin, and Roy Campanella. That season Hoskins compiled team highs in batting average (.377) and homers (11) and also rapped 6 triples. He first joined the Elites in the fall of 1938 after short stints with several other teams, and batted in the heart of the order for the next eight seasons. Although best identified with the Elites, he also played briefly with several other teams during his career.

House, Charles (**Red**)
Career: 1937–42   Positions: 3b, 2b, ss, of
Teams: Detroit Stars ('37, '41), Homestead Grays ('42), *Detroit Black Sox* ('41)

He shared the third-base position, while batting sixth in the order, with the Negro American League Detroit Stars in 1937, during their last attempt at playing league ball. In 1942, in his last appearance in the Negro Leagues, he played briefly as a shortstop with the Homestead Grays. He also played with the Detroit Black Sox, a team of lesser quality.

Houston
Career: 1919–20   Positions: **p**, 2b
Teams: Indianapolis ABCs ('19–'20), Kansas City Monarchs ('20)

In 1920 he pitched with the Indianapolis ABCs and made an appearance at second base with the Kansas City Monarchs in the inaugural season of the Negro National League.

Houston, Bill
Career: 1941–42   Position: p
Team: Homestead Grays
Bats: Right   Throws: Right
Height: 5'11"   Weight: 185

This right-hander was a second-line pitcher with the Homestead Grays in 1941–42, splitting two decisions in 1941.

Houston Eagles
Duration: 1949–50   Honors: None
Affiliation: Negro American League

After the Manleys sold the Newark Eagles, the new owner moved them to Houston to play in the Negro American League's Western Division during the 1949 and 1950 seasons.

Houston, Nathanial (Jess)
Career: 1930–39   Positions: **p**, ss
Teams: Memphis Red Sox, ('30) Cincinnati Tigers ('36–'37), Chicago American Giants ('38–'39)

His career encompassed the entire decade of the '30s, and while primarily a pitcher, he also made an occasional appearance in the infield in the waning years of his career with the American Giants. Earlier in his career he was with the Memphis Red Sox and the Cincinnati Tigers.

Houston, William
Career: 1910   Positions: c, ss
Team: West Baden Sprudels

In 1910, with the West Baden Sprudels, he split his playing time between two positions, catcher and shortstop.

Hovley
Career: 1932   Position: p
Team: Nashville Elite Giants

He was a pitcher with the Nashville Elite Giants in 1932, when the Negro Southern League was accorded major-league status.

Howard
Career: 1897–99   Positions: p, 2b, of
Teams: Cuban Giants, Cuban X-Giants

He was a utility man with the 1897–99 Cuban Giants and Cuban X-Giants, playing in the infield and outfield and also pitching.

Howard
Career: 1921–27   Positions: p, 3b
Teams: Detroit Stars ('21), Cleveland Tate Stars ('22), Indianapolis ABCs, Memphis Red Sox ('23, '27), New York Lincoln Giants ('26, '29), Cleveland Hornets ('27)

He was a pitcher and also played at third

Howard
Career: 1921–22   Position: ss
Teams: *Madison Stars ('20), Norfolk Giants ('20–'21),* Harrisburg ('22)

During the early '20s he played shortstop with the Madison Stars and the Norfolk Giants, two teams of lesser status, before signing for a season with the Harrisburg Giants in 1922.

Howard
Career: 1922–29   Position: p
Teams: Baltimore Black Sox ('22), New York Lincoln Giants ('29)

He had two seasons during the '20s when he pitched with top teams, appearing with the Baltimore Black Sox in 1922 and winning his only decision with the Lincoln Giants in 1929.

Howard, Carl
Career: 1935–36   Position: of
Teams: Pittsburgh Crawfords ('35), Birmingham Black Barons ('36)

This outfielder appeared briefly with the Pittsburgh Crawfords and the Birmingham Black Barons during the mid-'30s.

Howard, Carranza (Schoolboy)
Career: 1940–50   Position: p
Teams: New York Cubans ('41–46), Indianapolis Clowns ('47), New York Black Yankees ('49–'50)
Bats: Right   Throws: Right
Height: 6'2"   Weight: 210
Born: 1920

This big right-hander was a consistent winner for the New York Cubans in 1944, credited with a 24–4 record against all opposition, and pitched in the season's East-West All-Star game. In his first two years with the Cubans his league ledger shows marks of 0–1 and 2–1, but most of the Cubans' games were with nonleague opponents. Howard was a native of Daytona Beach, Florida, and was a three-letter man at Shaw University. His college training earned him the nickname "Schoolboy."

Howard, Charles

Career: 1897–99   Position: Player
Team: Cuban X-Giants ('97–'99)

One of the original Cuban X-Giants, he was shot and killed by a woman after an argument in East Liverpool, Ohio. Nothing else is known about this obscure player.

Howard, Elston (Gene, Ellie)

Career: 1948–50   Positions: c, of, 1b
Teams: Kansas City Monarchs ('48–'50), *minor leagues ('50–'53), military service ('51–'52),* major leagues ('55–'68)
Bats: Right   Throws: Right
Height: 6'2"   Weight: 196
Born: Feb, 23, 1929, St. Louis, Mo.
Died: Dec. 14, 1980, New York, N.Y.

Beginning in 1948, at age nineteen, the future New York Yankees' star played three seasons in the Negro Leagues with the Kansas City Monarchs as an outfielder-catcher. He posted batting averages of .283, .270, and .319 while hitting with good power. In 1950 he also played in organized baseball with Muskegon in the Central League and hit .283 for the last half of the season. After two years of military service he joined Kansas City in the American Association, where he hit .286. In 1954, with Toronto in the International League, he hit .330 with 22 homers, 21 doubles, and a league-leading 16 triples. The next season he went up to the Yankees, and for the next 13 years he was one of their most indispensable players. His best years were 1961, when he hit .248 with 21 homers, and 1963, when he hit .287 with 28 homers and 85 RBIs. Although an all-time Yankees favorite, he ended his major-league career in 1968 with the Boston Red Sox, finishing with a .274 lifetime major-league batting average.

Howard, Herb

Career: 1948–49   Positions: p, of
Team: Kansas City Monarchs

A reserve pitcher-outfielder, he pulled double duty while playing with Kansas City Monarchs in 1948–49, batting .283 and .270 in his only seasons in the Negro Leagues.

Howard, Herman (Roy, **Red**, Lefty)

Career: 1936–46   Position: p
Teams: *Little Rock Black Travelers ('32)* Atlanta Black Crackers ('32, '38), Memphis Red Sox ('36), Indianapolis Athletics ('37), Birmingham Black Barons ('37–'40), Jacksonville Red Caps ('38), Washington Elite Giants, Indianapolis ABCs ('39), Cleveland Bears ('39), Kansas City Monarchs, American Giants ('46)
Bats: Left   Throws: Left
Height: 5'10"   Weight: 195

Pitching mostly in the South, this southpaw had a fastball that he called "dead red." He was a pitcher with the 1938 Negro American League second-half champion Atlanta Black Crackers. He pitched with the Birmingham Black Barons in 1937 and made his home there. At the beginning of the 1938 season he pitched with the Atlanta Black Crackers but was dropped and picked up by Jacksonville shortly after the end of the first half. He relied strictly on a fastball and could throw hard but was "wild as a jackrabbit." He had a very stocky build and was a fair hitter.

Howard, Telosh

a.k.a. Twelosh; Tweloshes
Career: 1938   Position: p
Team: Atlanta Black Crackers
Bats: Right   Throws: Right
Height: 6'2"   Weight: 185

This big, veteran hurler had a sidearm delivery and a graceful, easy motion, and cleverly mixed his pitches and speeds. He had a good curve, good control, and, as one of the top pitchers with the 1938 Negro American League second-half champion Atlanta Black Crackers, was named to the SNS Negro American League All-Star team at the end of the season. He got his baseball start with a semipro team, the Macon Peaches, in his hometown. Later he made his home in Atlanta and became the manager of the Atlanta Black Crackers.

Howard, William (Bill)
Career: 1931–33   Position: 1b, 3b
Team: Birmingham Black Barons ('31)

A first baseman with the Birmingham Black Barons in 1931, this infielder played on both corners during his three seasons with the ballclub.

Howell
Career: 1908   Position: of
Team: Brooklyn Royal Giants

He was an outfielder with John Connors' Brooklyn Royal Giants in 1908.

Howell, Henry
Career: 1918–21   Position: p
Teams: *Pennsylvania Giants ('18),* Atlantic City Bacharach Giants ('18), Pennsylvania Red Caps of New York, Brooklyn Royal Giants ('21)

In his four-year career he pitched with four different eastern teams along the New York-Philadelphia axis during the years before an eastern league was formed, with incomplete statistics showing a 2–0 mark with the Bacharachs in 1918.

Hubbard, DeHart
Career: 1934–42   Position: officer
Teams: Cincinnati Tigers ('34–'37), Cincinnati Buckeyes ('42)

He served as secretary for the Cincinnati Tigers and the Cincinnati Buckeyes of the Negro American League.

Hubbard, Jess James (Mountain)
Career: 1917–34   Positions: **p, rf,** lf, cf, 1b
Teams: **Brooklyn Royal Giants** ('17–'26), *military service ('18),* Hilldale Daisies ('19, '30), New York Lincoln Giants ('23), Atlantic City Bacharach Giants ('27–''28, '34), Baltimore Black Sox ('28–'29, '33–'35), Homestead Grays, *minor leagues ('31),* New York Black Yankees ('32–'33)
Bats: Left   Throws: Right
Height: 6'2"   Weight: 200
Born: July 18, 1895, Bering, Tex.

This big, light-complexioned Texan, who was nicknamed "Mountain," was part Indian and almost passed for white to make it to the major leagues, but destiny dictated that his career would be spent entirely in the Negro Leagues. The New York Giants sent him to their farm team in Massena, New York, and tried to pass him as white, and the Detroit Tigers were among several teams that expressed an interest, but none took the risk to sign him.

After attending public schools through the fifth grade, he dropped out and, at age sixteen, began working in a sawmill in Elizabeth, Texas, and playing baseball. From there he progressed to a semipro team in Beaumont before joining the Houston Black Oilers in 1915. After one year there, he played in Alexandria, Louisiana, for a year before his first contact with the Brooklyn Royal Giants, in 1917. In 1918 he was inducted into the Army and pitched for the baseball team at Fort Dix, New Jersey.

In 1919, after his Army service, he rejoined the Brooklyn Royal Giants, whose pitching staff spotlighted two of the greatest pitchers of all time, Smokey Joe Williams and Dick Redding. However, this duo did not entirely overshadow Hubbard, who had an opportunity to demonstrate his abilities when he pitched 2 shutouts against the New York Giants.

He remained with the Royal Giants as they entered the Eastern Colored League in 1923, but in 1925 he suffered from a bad arm. Fortunately, the arm responded to treatment and he played that winter in California with the Philadelphia Royal Giants. The big hurler had begun his career as an overhand pitcher, but as he gained more experience he developed both sidearm and underhand deliveries to give batters a variety of looks. He also was mostly a "junkball" pitcher, but could hum a fastball when necessary and sometimes, in critical situations, he would utilize a "cutball" to pitch out of a jam. Although he started as a pitcher, and enjoyed moderate success on the mound, throughout his career he was oft used in the outfield or as a pinch hitter. A respectable hitter with good power, incomplete statistics show a .316 lifetime batting average and a high of .409 in 1930.

Although Jesse spent most of his career with the Royal Giants, he joined the Bacharach Giants in 1927 at age thirty-two and posted an 8–3 ledger to help pitch them to the Eastern Colored League pennant. In the ensuing World Series against the Chicago American Giants, the giant right-hander won one of his three starts, but in a losing cause. The next season the league folded and he joined the Baltimore Black Sox under Ben Taylor. In 1929 Frank Warfield replaced Taylor, and Hubbard pitched for another pennant winner as the Black Sox captured the American Negro League flag in the league's only year of existence. Unfortunately he was not able to complete the season, being released by the Black Sox in late July after suffering side injuries.

After his release he opened a restaurant, and after recuperating returned for the 1930 season with Hilldale. The next year he played for Providence, Rhode Island, the only black team in the New England League. In 1932 he returned to New York City and joined the New York Black Yankees. In his earlier years with the Royals he pitched batting practice to Lou Gehrig in the spring, when he was still a student at Columbia University. Handsome and a sharp dresser, Hubbard was a ladies' man and had a lasting preference for big cigars and bigger Cadillacs. He continued playing baseball until 1938, appearing with half a dozen teams, and always maintained his popularity with the fans.

Hubbard, Larry

Career: 1946   Position: of
Team: Kansas City Monarchs

Although primarily an outfielder, he appeared briefly as a utility player with the Kan-

sas City Monarchs during the 1946 season but was not on their World Series roster.

Huber

Career: 1930–31   Position: c, of, *3b*
Teams: Memphis Red Sox ('30), Nashville Elite Giants ('31), Birmingham Black Barons ('31)

His career, spent with three different southern teams, coincided with the last two seasons before the first Negro National League collapsed (1930–31). He began as a catcher in 1930 with the Memphis Red Sox and played in the outfield the following season with the Nashville Elite Giants and the Birmingham Black Barons.

Huber, John Marshall (Bubber)
a.k.a. Hubert
Career: 1941–50   Positions: **p**, c
Teams: Ethiopian Clowns ('39), Chicago American Giants ('42, '50), Cincinnati Clowns ('43), Birmingham Black Barons ('43–'45), Memphis Red Sox ('46–'47)
Bats: Right   Throws: Right

This right-hander gained his biggest fame as a member of the mound corps of the Negro American League pennant-winning Birmingham Black Barons in 1943 and 1944. Although the Black Barons lost the World Series years to the Homestead Grays, he pitched in each Series, winning his only decision (a shutout) in 1944. His regular-season records show marks of 3–0, 2–3 (2.83 ERA), and 5–6 (3.41 ERA) in 1943–45. The next year he played with the Memphis Red Sox, posting a 5–8 record for the season.

He began his career with the Ethiopian Clowns in 1939 and appeared with the Chicago American Giants before landing with the Black Barons. A native of Chicago, he joined the American Giants for a second stint in 1950, suffering through a winless season against 6 losses and a 5.14 ERA. Huber also went behind the plate on occasion, and he hit for averages of .232, .280, and .186 in 1944–46.

Hubert, Willie (**Bubber,** Hank)
Career: 1935–46   Position: p
Teams: Miami Giants ('34), Newark Dodgers
('35), Ethiopian Clowns ('38) Newark Eagles
('39), Baltimore Elite Giants ('39–'40), Homestead Grays ('40), Philadelphia Stars ('41),
Cincinnati Buckeyes ('42), Pittsburgh Crawfords, Baltimore Grays, *Brooklyn Brown
Dodgers ('46)*, New York Black Yankees
Bats: Right   Throws: Right
Height: 5'11"   Weight: 175
    He played with the Miami Giants in 1934
and was considered a bright prospect. Before
he joined the Newark Eagles in 1939, he
pitched with the Clowns. He was a "hard
case" and had a bad temperament both on and
off the field, running with Fred Wilson, a notorius "bad actor." Using a good fastball and a
mediocre curve and control, he "cut" the ball
and used the pitch effectively to compensate
for his lack of other, legitimate pitches. After
leaving the Eagles he signed with the Baltimore Elite Giants and posted a 5–2 record in
1940. After a stint with the Philadelphia Stars,
he landed with the Cincinnati Buckeyes in
1942, where he split 4 decisions.

Hudson, **Charles** (Keen Legs)
Career: 1923–30   Position: p
Teams: Milwaukee Bears ('23), Louisville
White Sox ('30)
    This pitcher made two appearances with
marginal ballclubs struggling to maintain
league quality of play, the Milwaukee Bears in
1923 and the Louisville White Sox in 1930.

Hudson, **William**
a.k.a. Henry
Career: 1937–42   Positions: **p,** of, 1b
Teams: Cincinnati Tigers ('37), Chicago American Giants ('40–'41)
    This Chicago American Giants' hurler won
both of his recorded decisions in 1940, and a
year later was selected to the West Squad for
the East-West All-Star game and was used as
a pinch hitter.

Hudspeth, Robert (Bob, **Highpockets**)
Career: 1920–33   Positions: **1b,** *p, of*
Teams: *San Antonio Black Aces ('20)*, Indianapolis ABCs ('20–'21), Columbus Buckeyes
('21), Atlantic City Bacharach Giants
('22–'25), New York Lincoln Giants ('23–'26,
'29), Brooklyn Royal Giants ('27–'30, '33),
Hilldale Daisies ('29), New York Black Yankees ('32)
Bats: Left   Throws: Left
Height: 6'6"   Weight: 235
Died: 1933
    In 1924 with the Lincoln Giants, he was the
tallest man in black baseball, and his stretch
and long reach made him one of the best-fielding first basemen, but he was a little weak
on handling low throws. A fancy fielder when
playing with some teams, he also provided
clever comedic antics for the enjoyment of the
fans. He also had a good arm, was a fair base
runner, and, as expected with his size, had
good power at the plate, hitting 7 home runs
in each of three consecutive seasons, 1924–26,
in a limited number of league games. During
these same years he recorded batting averages
of .362, .268, and .365.
    In the latter season, John Henry Lloyd managed the team and batted fourth, with Hudspeth
hitting behind him in the lineup. In his first
year with the Lincolns he hit .336, but after
leaving the team in 1927 to join the Brooklyn
Royal Giants, his averages dropped to a mediocre level, with marks of .264 and .272 in 1927
and 1929. The big first sacker began his professional career in Texas with the San Antonio
Black Aces in 1920, but joined the ABCs during the season. He played with the Columbus
Buckeyes and the Bacharach Giants during the
next two years, hitting .277 and .302, respectively. Later he played with the Philadelphia
Royal Giants in the California winter league,
and was a part-time starter with the New York
Black Yankees in 1932. In 1933 he appeared
briefly with the Brooklyn Royal Giants, but
contracted TB and died shortly after leaving
the team.

Hueston, William C.
Career: 1926–31   Position: officer.
League: Negro National League
He served as president of the Negro National League for six years.

Huff, Eddie
Career: 1923–32   Positions: c, of, p, manager
Teams: Atlantic City Bacharach Giants ('23), Dayton Marcos ('26)
Beginning his career in 1923 as a third-string catcher with the Bacharachs, he next emerged as the playing manager with the Negro National League's 1926 Dayton Marcos. The skipper ensconced himself in the cleanup spot and hit .246 while sharing the catching duties and also playing in the outfield. A smart baseball man, he forged a decade-long career on the diamonds of black baseball.

Hughes, A.
Career: 1927   Position: of
Team: Kansas City Monarchs
He appeared as a reserve outfielder with the Kansas City Monarchs in 1927.

Hughes, Charlie
Career: 1931–38   Positions: 2b, ss
Teams: Pittsburgh Crawfords ('31), Columbus Blue Birds ('33), Homestead Grays ('33), Cleveland Red Sox ('34), Washington Black Senators ('38)
During the '30s, this light-hitting second sacker played with five teams, including the Pittsburgh Crawfords. He was one of only three players from the original semipro Crawfords who was still with the team on June 20, 1931. That memorable date is when, behind the pitching of Satchel Paige, the Crawfords won their first game ever against the Homestead Grays. During most of Hughes's career he was with teams struggling to maintain a caliber of play commensurate with league membership.

Hughes, Frank
Career: 1937   Position: p
Team: Indianapolis Athletics
He was a pitcher with the Indianapolis Athletics in 1937, their only year in the Negro Leagues.

Hughes, Lee
Career: 1950   Position: p
Team: Kansas City Monarchs
He was listed as a pitcher with the Kansas City Monarchs in 1950, when the Negro National League was struggling to survive the loss of players to organized baseball, but league statistics do not confirm his playing time.

Hughes, Robert
Career: 1931   Position: p
Team: Louisville White Sox
He was a pitcher with the 1931 Louisville White Sox in their only season in the Negro National League.

Hughes, Samuel Thomas (**Sammy T.**)
Career: 1931–46   Positions: **2b**, ss, *1b*
Teams: Louisville White Sox ('29–'31), Washington Pilots ('32), Nashville Elite Giants ('33–'34), Columbus Elite Giants ('35), Washington Elite Giants ('36–'37), **Baltimore Elite Giants** ('38–'40, '42, '46), *Mexican League ('41), military service ('43–'46)*
Bats: Right   Throws: Right
Height: 6'3"   Weight: 190
Born: Oct. 20, 1910, Louisville, Ky.
Died: Aug. 9, 1981, Los Angeles, Calif.
Tall and graceful, he was a complete ballplayer and was considered the premier second baseman of the Negro National League. A magnificent fielder with a wide range and a strong arm who excelled on the double play, the agile keystoner could do it all. A well-rounded ballplayer, he had no weakness. In addition to his picture-perfect work afield, he was also a good base runner and a solid hitter. A thinking man's player, Hughes was a consistent contact hitter who excelled on the hit-and-run play and was a good bunter, which made him an excellent number-two batter in the lineup.
A tough competitor, the rangy right-handed batter hit with good extra-base power, but

mostly doubles. Although he could reach the fences, his home-run production was not sufficiently consistent for him to be considered a home-run threat. Playing with the Elite Giants in the Negro National League, he recorded batting averages of .355, .353, .319, .302, .345, and .254 for the seasons 1935–40. The following season, the smooth second sacker was lured south of the border to Mexico, where he batted .324 with Torreon.

During his sixteen-year career Sammy was selected to the East-West All-Star team more than any other second baseman. The flashy fielder compiled a respectable .263 batting average during the five years that he faced All-Star pitching. Representing the Elite Giants when they were in Nashville, Columbus, Washington, and Baltimore, he was on the West squad twice (1934–35) and on the East Squad three times (1936–39).

In 1936 he was also selected to the Negro National League All-Star team that entered the *Denver Post* Tournament and breezed through the competition so easily that they were told not to come back. Hughes hit a cool .379 for the tournament.

In 1942 the star keystoner hit a heavy .301 and fielded brilliantly to spark the Elites in a fierce pennant battle with the Homestead Grays that went down to the wire. During this time, a reporter for the *Peoples Voice* newspaper wired him that a tryout with the Pittsburgh Pirates had been tentatively arranged for Hughes, Roy Campanella, and Dave Barnhill. The three players jumped at the chance and left the Elites to showcase in a game against the Toledo Mudhens. However, the two players from the Elites did not get permission from their owner beforehand and were fined and benched temporarily. Hughes was quickly reinstated, but Campanella jumped to Mexico, and the Elites lost out in the final week of the pennant race after losing the services of their young catcher.

Not long afterward, Hughes's baseball career was interrupted by World War II. He served in the Army with the 196th Support Battalion during the invasion of New Guinea. He was discharged early in 1946 but, after returning from three years in the service, he held out for more money, asking for an additional $1,500 per month. He remained at home in Los Angeles, while the Elites were floundering in early June, but eventually signed with the club. However, the super second sacker played only a short time, hitting .277 in his last year to close out a career as the best second baseman in black baseball during the 1930s and early 1940s. He finished with a lifetime batting average of .296 in the Negro Leagues and also is credited with an average of .353 in exhibitions against major leaguers. During his last season he tutored Junior Gilliam as his replacement at second base for the Elites.

As a youngster Hughes attended school in Louisville, completing the eighth grade before dropping out, and learned to play baseball in that city, making his professional debut with the Louisville White Sox in 1929. After two seasons of independent play, the White Sox entered the Negro National League for the 1931 season. The following season the tall infielder signed with the East-West League's Washington Pilots as a first baseman, but when manager Frank Warfield died suddenly, he was moved to the vacated second-base position. After the Pilots encountered financial difficulty and the franchise folded, Hughes signed with Tom Wilson's Elites and remained with the organization for the remainder of his Negro League career. After leaving baseball he worked for the Pillsbury Company and the Hughes Aircraft Company in Los Angeles.

Humber, Thomas William (**Tom**, Charlie)
Career: 1945, 1950   Positions: 2b, of
Teams: Newark Eagles ('45), *Asheville Blues ('49),* Baltimore Elite Giants ('50), *minor leagues ('55–'61)*
Bats: Right   Throws: Right
Height: 5'9"   Weight: 168

He was a good-fielding reserve second baseman with the Newark Eagles in 1945, batting .267 with only a modicum of power. In 1950 the speedy ballplayer was with the Elites as

THE BIOGRAPHICAL ENCYCLOPEDIA OF

an outfielder and hit .286. In 1955 he was in organized baseball with Clinton as an outfielder-second baseman and hit .303 and .345 in his two seasons with the team. He also lead the league each year in stolen bases, swiping 36 and 67, respectively.

The next two seasons were spent with Reno in the California League, where he hit .323 and .378. In his first year there, the speedster continued his base-stealing honors as he topped the league with 75 successful thefts. He was headed toward another theft title during his second season, with a total of 38 after 81 games, before being moved to other teams. His first stop was with Green Bay in the Three-I League, and then he joined Des Moines in the Western League to finish the 1958 season. In 1959 he started with Montreal in the International League, but was hitting only .257 when he was farmed to Macon. Playing the remainder of the season there, he raised his average to .275, but the following year he was with Macon for the entire season, and his average dropped to .248, with 22 stolen bases. In 1961 he closed out his baseball career, batting .255 in 77 games with Salem in the Northwestern League.

Humes, John (**Johnny**)
Career: 1937   Position: p
Team: Newark Eagles
This left-hander from Whipple, West Virginia, pitched briefly with the Newark Eagles in 1937, his only year in the league.

Humphries
a.k.a. Humphrey
Career: 1936–38   Position: of
Teams: Memphis Red Sox ('36), Atlanta Black Crackers ('37–'38)
This outfielder began his career with the Memphis Red Sox. He joined the Atlanta Black Crackers in 1937 and had a couple of stints with the team again in 1938, their championship season. He was on the roster in late March, was cut in early May, but was back for

another shot in late June before being released again.

Hundley, Johnny Lee
Career: 1943   Positions: **of**, c
Team: Cleveland Buckeyes
A wartime player, he was the right fielder for the 1943 Cleveland Buckeyes, batting sixth in the order. In the field he had "iron hands" and lacked appreciable defensive skills.

Hungo, Fidelio
Career: 1916   Position: 1b
Team: Long Branch Cubans
In 1916 he was a first baseman with the Long Branch Cubans. In 1920, playing for Havana in an exhibition series against the New York Giants, he hit .320.

Hunt, Grover
Career: 1946   Position: c
Team: American Giants
He appeared briefly as a reserve catcher with the American Giants in 1946.

Hunt, Leonard (**Len**)
Career: 1949–50   Position: of
Teams: Kansas City Monarchs ('49–'51), *minor leagues ('50–'57)*
Bats: Left   Throws: Left
Height: 5'9"   Weight: 170
Born: 1929
An average-fielding outfielder but with only a fair arm, he was a good bunter and, although not regarded as more than a moderately good hitter, he hit for a .347 average during his first season with the Kansas City Monarchs in 1949. After beginning the next season with the Monarchs, he signed with Springfield in the Mississippi-Ohio Valley League, batting .332 and demonstrating some power, pretty good speed, and a good eye at the plate. In 1953 he hit .313 with Texarkana in the Big State League, and began the next season in the same league, with Tyler. After getting off to a good start with a .389 average, he spent most of the campaign with Augusta of the Sally League, bat-

ting .325 for the remainder of the season. He closed out his baseball career with Aberdeen in the Northern League, batting .317 in 1956 and .255 in only 15 games the following season.

Hunter, Bertrum (**Bert**, Nate, Buffalo)
Career: 1931–36   Position: p
Teams: St. Louis Stars ('31), Detroit Wolves ('32), Homestead Grays ('32), Kansas City Monarchs ('32, '34), Pittsburgh Crawfords ('33–'36), Philadelphia Stars ('36–'37), *Santo Domingo ('37), Mexican League ('40–'44)*
Bats: Right   Throws: Right
Height: 5'9"   Weight: 175

In his rookie year he pitched for the Negro National League champion St. Louis Stars of 1931. The next season was a year of chaos as leagues and teams fell victim to the Depression. The young right-hander was in demand and split the season with three teams, beginning with the Detroit Wolves (and posting a 4–3 record until they were assimilated by the Homestead Grays) and ending with the Kansas City Monarchs, who had folded and reorganized in midseason.

In 1933, as a member of the great Pittsburgh Crawfords, the curveballer framed a 7–1 record and pitched in the first East-West All-Star game ever played. During the next two years he posted marks of 3–3 and 5–4. The 1935 Crawfords are considered by many to be the greatest black team of all time, and Hunter was a key member of their mound staff. However, he and manager Oscar Charleston did not enjoy a cordial relationship, and related difficulties made Hunter expendable.

Philadelphia Stars' manager Webster McDonald signed Hunter without having to give any compensation to the Crawfords. During Hunter's second season with the Stars, he "disappeared" in mid-June. His absence from the team was the result of a jump to Santo Domingo, where he had a record of 4–5 and, more importantly, was married and decided to remain in the country. Later he continued his career in Mexico, posting marks of 2–3, 9–11,

8–13, 3–4, and 0–1 for the 1940–44 seasons, playing with a different team each season. He finished with a composite 4.79 Mexican ERA, but he never again pitched in the United States.

Hunter, Eugene
Career: 1924   Position: p
Teams: Memphis Red Sox ('24), Cleveland Browns ('24)

He was a pitcher in 1924, splitting his playing time between the Memphis Red Sox and the Cleveland Browns.

Hunter, Willie
Career: 1933   Position: p
Team: Akron Tyrites

In 1933 he was a pitcher with the Akron Tyrites, who combined with the Columbus Blue Birds to form the Cleveland Giants' team that entered the Negro National League during the second half as a replacement for Columbus.

Hutchinson, Fred (Hutch, Pug, Puggey)
Career: 1910–25   Positions: ss, 2b, 3b,
                                          of, p
Teams: Leland Giants ('10), Chicago American Giants ('11–'13, '15), Indianapolis ABCs ('14–'15, '25), Bowser's ABCs ('16), Jewell's ABCs ('17), Atlantic City Bacharach Giants ('19)

Playing in the Palm Beach Hotel League in the 1909–10 winter, Hutchinson demonstrated fast fielding and a great arm. Impressed with the little infielder's performance, Rube Foster signed him for the Leland Giants in 1910. A versatile player, he could play any position in the infield or outfield and, with John Henry Lloyd established at shortstop, served as a utility man in his first season with the Lelands, batting .276. He was predicted to be a coming star, and the press stated that "more will be expected of him later." Opportunity came sooner than expected when, with Lloyd's departure to the Lincoln Giants the following season, Hutchinson moved into the vacated shortstop position. A light hitter, he was locked into the eighth slot in the batting order, but his good glovework kept him in the lineup until Lloyd returned three years later, making Hutchinson expendable.

With Lloyd's return, he joined the ABCs as the starting shortstop, batting .219 for the season. A year later, Lloyd was back in New York and Hutch was back in the starting lineup in Chicago. But later in the season Lloyd returned, and Hutch again left to join the ABCs. When third baseman Todd Allen was injured, Hutchinson stepped right into the lineup as a replacement. In 1916, when the ABCs' owner Thomas Bowser and manager C. I. Taylor split, creating two ABCs teams, he joined Bowser's ABCs as the regular shortstop. The following year found him with Jewell's ABCs, a team of lesser quality, where he played shortstop and batted fifth in the order.

In 1919 he ventured East to join the Bacharachs and continued in black baseball for half of the new decade with the lively ball. During his career the little man with the good glove picked up the nicknames "Hutch," "Pug," and "Puggey."

Hutchinson, Willie (Ace)
Career: 1939–50   Positions: **p**, *of*
Teams: Kansas City Monarchs ('39–41), **Memphis Red Sox** ('40–'50), *Mexican League ('45), minor leagues ('51–'53)*
Bats: Right   Throws: Right
Height: 5'10"   Weight: 165

The right-handed pitcher began his career with the Kansas City Monarchs in 1939, losing all three of his decisions, but spent most of his dozen Negro League seasons with the Memphis Red Sox. He was a mediocre pitcher with average control but, without effective off-speed and breaking balls, was forced to rely mostly on his fastball.

In 1942 he split a half-dozen decisions and the next season fell to a 1–6 record. He rebounded in 1944 with a 6–10 record with a 3.19 ERA for the second-division Red Sox, and after a season in Mexico with Tampico (6–11, 3.88 ERA) he returned to the Sox with a 6–8 record in 1946. In his last two years in Memphis he posted marks of 8–8 (3.81 ERA) in 1949 and 1–2 (2.70 ERA) in 1950.

The next three seasons were spent with Carman in the Mandak League, where he had a 5–8 record in 1951 and a 3–6 record for 1953 before he left the team to play with Danville in the Mississippi-Ohio Valley League, where he fashioned a 4–2 record with a 3.71 ERA.

Hutt
Career: 1920–24   Positions: 1b, of
Teams: St. Louis Giants ('20), Dayton Marcos, ('21) Toledo Tigers ('23), St. Louis Stars ('24)

A combination first baseman-outfielder, he began and ended his career as a reserve player in St. Louis, beginning with the Giants in 1920 and closing with the Stars in 1924. During the interim he played with the Dayton Marcos and Toledo Tigers, two marginal teams in Ohio.

Hyatt
Career: 1940   Position: If
Team: Philadelphia Stars

In 1940 this outfielder appeared briefly with the Philadelphia Stars.

Hyde, Cowan F. (**Bubba**)
Career: 1927–50   Positions: lf, cf, rf, 2b
Teams: Memphis Red Sox ('24, '27), Birmingham Black Barons ('30), Indianapolis Athletics ('37), Cincinnati Tigers ('37), **Memphis Red Sox** ('38–'50), *Mexican League ('40). Palmer House All-Stars ('40), minor leagues ('49–'54),* Chicago American Giants ('50–'51), *Canadian League ('51)*
Bats: Right   Throws: Right
Height: 5'8"   Weight: 150
Born: Apr. 10, 1908, Pontotoc, MS

With exceptional speed on the bases, this Memphis Red Sox outfielder could run as fast looking back as anyone in baseball, and he was a good base stealer. In 1937 with the Cincinnati Tigers, manager "Double Duty" Radcliffe gave him a green light to run when he could get a good jump. When Radcliffe managed a team, he always wanted Hyde on it, so the pair went to Memphis together the next year, and

Hyde was the left fielder on the 1938 Negro American League first-half champion Memphis Red Sox.

A good hitter and a fast runner, he usually batted leadoff, but he had a low walk ratio and sometimes also hit in the second or third slots. A right-handed hitter, Bubba hit for averages of .313 in 1942 and .278, .275, and .298 in 1944–46, with slightly better than average power. In 1948 he hit .274 for the Red Sox and then hit .292 with the Chicago American Giants in 1950. During his career he played on two West All-Star squads in 1943 and 1946, getting a composite 2 hits in 3 times at bat.

Hyde had his first trial with the Memphis Red Sox when he was only fourteen years old, but he got homesick and did not stay with the team, choosing instead to return home and prepare for college. He attended Morris Brown College and, despite his slight stature, played football. After attending college he returned to the Red Sox and stayed this time, although his success was not immediate. In 1927 he is credited with a .190 average with the Red Sox. Three years later he was playing with the Birmingham Black Barons, and he hit .237 for the 1930 season. During his career he also played second base when circumstances required his services in the infield. Most of his career was spent with the Memphis Red Sox, but he jumped the team once to play in Mexico, batting .306 with Santa Rosa in 1940. Returning to the United States in August, he finished the year with the Palmer House All-Stars, a Chicago-based independent team.

In 1949 he played in organized baseball with Bridgeport, Connecticut, under manager Jimmy Foxx and hit .327. He also played in the Mandak League for five years, beginning with the Elmwood Giants (1950–51), hitting .315 and .348, and then spending a season with Winnipeg (1952) before playing two years with Brandon (1953–54), hitting .292 the former year. In 1951 he also played part of the season with Farnham in the Canadian Provincial League. Earlier in his career he played winter ball with the Baltimore Giants (1943) and the Kansas City Royals (1946), batting against the top major-league pitchers in exhibition games, including Bob Feller, Bob Lemon, and Johnny Sain.

Hyde, Harry

Career: 1896–1904   Positions: **3b**, 1b

Teams: Chicago Unions ('96–'00), Chicago Union Giants ('02–'04)

He joined manager W. S. Peters's Chicago Unions in 1896 and was the regular third baseman for the next five years until 1901, when Frank Leland combined the team with the Columbia Giants to form the Chicago Union Giants. In 1902 Hyde was the starting first baseman for the consolidated Union Giants under Leland's managership, but then moved back to the hot corner in 1903–04, his last two seasons in black baseball.

I

Indianapolis ABCs

Duration: 1913–26, 1931–33, 1938–39   Honors: Western championship ('16)

Affiliations: Independent ('13–'19), NNL ('20–'26, '31, '33), NSL ('32), NAL ('38–'39)

This was previously a franchise of lesser distinction, but owner Thomas Bowser and manager C. I. Taylor stocked the team with players of major-league caliber in 1914, and it immediately became one of the best teams in black baseball. An intense rivalry developed between Taylor and Rube Foster, the two managers acknowledged as the best in black baseball. After losing a hard-fought championship series to Foster's Chicago American Giants in 1915, the ABCs overcame a division within the management between Bowser and Taylor to defeat the Chicago American Giants for the western championship in 1916.

A schism had developed between Bowser and Taylor following the 1915 season, and at the beginning of the 1916 season there were two ABC teams, with Bowser leading one and Taylor the other. Eventually Taylor's aggregation retained the quality players who formed the nucleus of his championship squad, and Bowser's team melded into obscurity. Under Taylor's leadership the ABCs became charter members of the Negro National League and fielded a team each year from 1920 to 1926. After Taylor's death in 1922, his wife tried to run the team with C. I.'s brother Ben at the helm, but wholesale defection of players to the new Eastern Colored League and a misunderstanding that led Ben also to take a managerial position in the East led to financial difficulties for Mrs. Taylor, and the team was disbanded.

In later years, a different franchise under new ownership but bearing the same name entered into league play in 1931–33, and again in 1938–39 in the Negro American League. Each of the teams from the Depression years of the '30s who bore the once-proud ABCs name were characterized by instability and confusion. About the only commonality between the 1931 and 1932 teams was the manager, Candy Jim Taylor (another of the famous Taylor brothers). The players were different and they played in different leagues, with the former team in the Negro National League and the latter in the Negro Southern League. In 1933 the team started in Indianapolis but very early in the spring moved to Detroit and played as the Stars. In the last effort to bring an ABCs team back to Indianapolis, the 1938 ABCs franchise shifted operations to the Midwest and played as the St. Louis Stars in 1939–40, while the Atlanta Black Crackers of 1938 moved into Indianapolis and played under the ABCs banner for a short time in 1939.

Indianapolis Athletics

Duration: 1937   Honors: None
Affiliation: NAL

When the Negro American League organized in 1937, Indianapolis became a charter member and fielded a team called the Athletics, with star Ted Strong as the playing manager. The team lasted only for the first season, with the franchise folding and being replaced in 1938 with a new team called the Indianapolis ABCs.

Indianapolis-Cincinnati Clowns

Duration: 1944   Honors: None
Affiliation: NAL

For financial reasons, the franchise that began as the Miami Clowns and evolved into the Ethiopian Clowns shared two cities as their hometown for the 1944 season before finally locating exclusively in Indianapolis.

Indianapolis Clowns

Duration: 1943–50   Honors: NAL Eastern
                              Division title ('50)
Affiliation: NAL

The franchise that began as the Miami Giants and evolved into the Ethiopian Clowns found a home in Indianapolis in 1946–50 while playing in the Negro American League. For financial reasons the city of Indianapolis shared the Clowns' franchise with Cincinnati in other years. In 1950, when the Negro American League was in decline in player quality and organization, the Clowns won the first-half title of the Eastern Division and were awarded the second-half title, despite a third-place finish among four teams, due to a ruling that teams must play at least 30 games in a half. There was no playoff with the Kansas City Monarchs, Western Division winners, for the league pennant. The Clowns' franchise continued on into the '50s and '60s but was not a high-quality ballclub during these later years after the major league's color line had been eradicated. Their continued history is beyond the scope of this volume.

Indianapolis Crawfords

Duration: 1940   Honors: None
Affiliation: NAL

After Gus Greenlee divested himself of the franchise, the Crawfords moved to Indianapolis for one season, 1940, and played in the Negro American League.

Ingersoll

Career: 1905   Position: 2b
Team: Brooklyn Royal Giants

He was a second baseman in 1905 with the Brooklyn Royal Giants, one of the top teams in the East of that era.

Ingram, Alfred

Career: 1942   Position: p
Teams: Jacksonville Red Caps ('42), *Atlanta Black Crackers ('47–'51)*

Prior to the dissolution of the Jacksonville Red Caps during the 1942 season, he was a pitcher with the ballclub. During the post–World War II years he played with the Atlanta Black Crackers of the Negro Southern League for five additional seasons, 1947–51.

Ipeña

(See Peña)

Irvin, Irwin (Bill)

Career: 1906, 1919   Positions: 3b, of,
                                    manager
Teams: Leland Giants ('06), Cleveland Tate Stars ('19)

He had one-year careers as both a player and a manager, playing as a third baseman and outfielder with the Leland Giants in 1906 and managing the Cleveland Tate Stars in 1919.

Irvin, Monford Merrill (Monte)

a.k.a. Jimmy Nelson
Career: 1937–48   Positions: cf, ss, 3b
Teams: **Newark Eagles** ('37–42, '45–'48), *military service ('43–'45), Mexican League ('42), minor leagues ('49–'50, '57), major leagues ('49–'56)*
Bats: Right   Throws: Right

Height: 6'1"   Weight: 190
Born: Feb. 25, 1919, Halesburg, Ala.

Irvin was one of the few fortunate players whose age and ability allowed them to bridge the divide between the two once-separate worlds of baseball. A power hitter who also hit for high average, the right-handed slugger won two batting titles in the Negro National League. He captured the first in 1941 with a .395 average and, after returning from service during World War II, he hit .404 in 1946 to lead the Newark Eagles to the pennant. Irvin's post-season encore produced 3 home runs and a batting average of .462 to spearhead the Eagles' hard-fought victory over the Negro American League champion Kansas City Monarchs in the Negro World Series.

As a teenager Irvin overcame a near-fatal illness to preserve his career as an all-around high-school athlete, earning a combined sixteen letters in four different sports (football, basketball, baseball, and track), while setting the New Jersey state record for the javelin. After graduation he earned a scholarship offer to the University of Michigan but had to decline the opportunity because he lacked the money for train fare. Instead he accepted a scholarship at Lincoln College in Oxford, Pennsylvania, and attended for two years until opting for a professional baseball career with the Newark Eagles. Irvin had already begun his baseball career with the Eagles, playing under the name Jimmy Nelson on weekends to protect his amateur standing, while in high school and college.

A versatile baseball player, he played both infield and outfield with the Eagles, often starting at third base or shortstop but eventually finding his niche in center field. In 1939 he hit .403 with good power, and followed with strong seasons of .377 and .400. The latter performance earned him his first trip to the East-West All-Star game, where he contributed a double and a single to the East's 8–3 victory. The young slugger had really come into his own going into the 1942 season, and the Eagles fielded their strongest team ever. Newly married and coming off of a super season in 1941,

the Eagles' favorite expected a modest raise, but dead-end negotiations with Effa Manley resulted in Irvin leaving the team early in the season to play in Mexico.

Irvin was hitting at a .531 clip with the Eagles when he jumped to Vera Cruz in the Mexican League and, although he missed almost a third of the Mexican season before he made the transition, he led the league in both batting (.397) and home runs (20), finished second in RBIs (79) in only 63 games, and won the MVP award. Then, during his baseball prime, his career was interrupted when he was drafted into the Army, spending three years in military service with the Army Engineers in Europe during World War II. After his discharge he returned to the Eagles at the end of the 1945 season, batting .222 in only 5 games. Then he had seasons of .404, .317, and .319 and appeared in 4 more East-West All-Star games (2 games were played in 1946) in his last three years with the Eagles before entering organized baseball after the 1948 season.

After his three-year hiatus from baseball, Irvin felt a need for additional winter ball to work back into his prewar condition, and resumed play in the Latin American winter leagues. In Puerto Rico he had hit for averages of .245 and .297 before the war (1940–42), averaging a home run every 39.5 at-bats and an extra-base hit every 5.9 at-bats during the latter season. After the war he hit for averages of .368 and .387 for the winter seasons for 1945–47, and then played two seasons in the Cuban winter league, 1947–49. Irvin played on championship teams in both countries, winning the title with the San Juan Senadores in Puerto Rico (1945–46) and during his last year in Cuba (1948–49). He posted a lifetime .355 batting average in Puerto Rico, and while playing two years in Cuba he registered a .265 lifetime average.

Before the war Irvin had been the Negro League owner's choice to be the player to break the color line, but while he was in the Army, Branch Rickey selected and signed Jackie Robinson. After his discharge, Irvin was still originally signed by the Dodgers, but Eagles' owner Effa Manley demanded compensation, and the Dodgers withdrew their claim, allowing the New York Giants to seize the opportunity to sign the star outfielder. Employing Alex Pompez, owner of the Negro Leagues' New York Cubans, as a scout, the Giants signed Irvin. The hard-hitting outfielder was assigned to Jersey City in the International League in 1949 and hit .373 until he was brought up to the Giants near the end of the season. Beginning the 1950 season at Jersey City, he quickly asserted his hitting capabilities, ripping the ball for a .510 average in only 18 games before he was sent to the parent club to stay, hitting .299 in his first full season and going on to a successful career in the major leagues.

His best season was in 1951, when he hit .312 with 24 home runs and a league-high 121 RBIs. After breaking an ankle the following spring and missing most of the season, he rebounded in 1953 with a .329 average, 21 home runs, and 97 RBIs. An integral factor in the Giants' pennant-winning years of 1951 and 1954, Monte tied a World Series record in 1951 with 11 hits, producing a Series-high .458 batting average, but his biggest thrill in baseball occurred in the first game, when he stole home against the Yankees' Allie Reynolds.

After seasons of .262 and .253 with the Giants in 1954–55, he was farmed to Minneapolis late in the 1955 season, batting .352 for the remainder of the year. Promptly drafted by the Chicago Cubs, the hard-hitting outfielder played his last major-league season for the Cubs, hitting a respectable .271 and leaving a .293 lifetime batting average to show for eight years in the major leagues. This came after most of his prime years were spent in the Negro Leagues, where his lifetime average was .346. Irvin's accomplishments during his eleven-year career in black baseball, combined with his major-league record, were sufficient to merit his selection to the National Baseball Hall of Fame in 1973.

In 1957 he played 4 games with the Los Angeles Angels in the Pacific Coast League, batting .300, but physical problems dictated that retirement was a more viable alternative to continuing as an active player. After ending his diamond career, Irvin scouted for the New York Mets and continued his work as the community relations director with Rheingold Brewery that he had begun in 1951, until 1968, when he was appointed assistant to the baseball commissioner, where he served until 1984. Irvin was chairman of the Hall of Fame's Special Committee on the Negro Leagues until it dissolved, and he now serves on the Hall of Fame's Veterans' Committee.

Israel, Clarence Charles (Pint)
Career: 1940–47   Positions: **3b**, 2b
Teams: Newark Eagles ('40–'42, '46), Homestead Grays ('43–'45, '47)
Bats: Right   Throws: Right
Height: 5'7"   Weight: 160
Born: Feb. 15, 1918, Marietta, Ga.
Died: Apr. 12, 1987, Rockville, Md.

An infielder noted as being a hustler, he was good fielder and a mediocre hitter without power but with good speed. He broke in with the Newark Eagles in 1940 and hit .250 despite suffering a leg injury that put him out of the lineup for about two weeks. The next season he continued as the Eagles' regular second baseman and, hitting second in the batting order, finished with a .226 average. After the 1942 season he signed with the Homestead Grays to help fill the vacancy at third base after Howard Easterling entered military service during World War II, but his own career was also interrupted by the war.

Israel did not play regularly again until he returned to the Eagles for the 1946 season, when they won the Negro National League pennant, snapping the Homestead Grays' nine-year skein. In the World Series victory over the Kansas City Monarchs, he played third base in 3 games when Pat Patterson was out with an injury, hitting .250, and had a pinch-hit single off Satchel Paige to help win the Series. The next season, his last in the Negro Leagues, he signed with the Grays, hitting .213 while batting at the bottom of the order and playing primarily at third base.

Israel, Elbert
Career: 1950   Position: if
Team: Philadelphia Stars
He was listed as an infielder with the Philadelphia Stars in 1950 after the club had joined the Negro American League, but league statistics do not confirm his playing time.

Ivory
Career: 1936   Positions: p, 1b
Team: Chicago American Giants
He appeared in a few games with the Chicago American Giants in 1936, making occasional starts as both a pitcher and a first baseman, and hit .455 in his limited playing time.

J

Jackman, Will (Bill, Earl, Cannonball)
Career: 1925–36   Position: p
Teams: New York Lincoln Giants ('25), *Philadelphia Giants ('25–'27), Quaker City Giants ('28),* Philadelphia Tigers ('28), Brooklyn Eagles ('35), Newark Eagles ('36), *Boston Royal Giants ('42)*
Bats: Right   Throws: Right
Height: 6'3"   Weight: 225
Born: Oct. 7, 1897, Carta, Tex.
Died: Sept. 9, 1972, Marion, Mass.

A tall, husky, strong right-handed submariner with exceptional control, Cannonball fashioned an eighteen-year career in black baseball. He changed his style of delivery from overhand after recovering from an arm injury incurred while barnstorming with the Philadelphia Giants, and subsequently enjoyed his prime years in the late 1920s and early 1930s. During this time he was credited with a 52–2 mark for one season with the Giants and bested Satchel Paige twice in two outings. Jackman's fastball was described as being faster than either Paige's or Bib Feller's, and Will had big hands that completely wrapped around the ball, making his fastball seemingly explode out of nowhere.

The Texan was very dark and had a gap-toothed, boyish smile to complement his easy-going temperament. Most of his career was spent with independent teams of lesser status, including Danny McClellan's Quaker City Giants, with his only record in league play showing a 5–6 ledger with the Brooklyn Eagles in 1935. The next season he appeared briefly with the Newark Eagles, and in 1942 he played with the Boston Royal Giants, a black professional team of lesser quality.

During his prime he earned $175 a game with a bonus of $10 for each strike out, and he continued pitching for semipro teams past age fifty. Aside from baseball, during his life he was employed at a variety of jobs that included driving trucks, digging ditches, and working in oil fields.

Jackson
Career: 1921   Position: p
Team: Indianapolis ABCs

In 1921, making his only appearance in the Negro Leagues, he pitched briefly with the Indianapolis ABCs.

Jackson
Career: 1931   Position: p
Team: Brooklyn Royal Giants

In 1931 he pitched with the Brooklyn Royal Giants, a team that was in decline after having dropped out of league play to pursue an independent continuance.

Jackson
Career: 1932   Positions: **of**, c
Team: Indianapolis ABCs

He was a reserve center fielder and sometime catcher with the Indianapolis ABCs when they were in the Negro Southern League in 1932.

Jackson
Career: 1931–33   Positions: p, 2b
Team: Detroit Stars

During the early '30s he spent three seasons with the Detroit Stars, losing his only decision as a pitcher in 1931 and playing as a reserve second baseman in 1933.

Jackson, A. Matthew
Career: 1932–34   Positions: 3b, ss, 1b
Teams: Montgomery Grey Sox ('32), Birmingham Black Barons ('34), Cincinnati Tigers ('34)

For three seasons the infielder played as a third baseman and shortstop with the Montgomery Grey Sox and Birmingham Black Barons, and as a first baseman with the Cincinnati Tigers.

Jackson, Andrew (Andy)
Career: 1888–96   Position: 3b
Teams: New York Gorhams ('87–'89), Cuban Giants ('90, '93–'94, '96, '99), *Colored Capital All-Americans,* Cuban X-Giants, New York Big Gorhams ('91)

A nineteenth-century third baseman for almost a decade, he played with the leading black teams of the era, including the New York Gorhams, the Cuban Giants, and the Cuban X-Giants. During the time that he was with the Cuban Giants and the New York Gorhams, the teams played as representatives of a host city in the Middle States League. In 1889 the New York Gorhams represented Philadelphia in the league, and in 1890 the Cuban Giants played in the league as representatives of York, Pennsylvania. He also played with the Colored Capital All-Americans of Lansing, Michigan.

Jackson, B. (Bozo)
Career: 1938–45   Positions: 3b, ss
Teams: Atlanta Black Crackers ('38, *'43–'44*), Philadelphia Stars ('43), Homestead Grays ('45)

Bats: Right   Throws: Right
Height: 5'6"   Weight: 160

A light hitter, he provided infield insurance for the Homestead Grays during their run for a ninth straight pennant in 1945, the last year of wartime baseball. Earlier in his career he played briefly at shortstop for a few games in late May with the 1938 Atlanta Black Crackers, as an interim replacement for Dick Lundy, who had suffered a broken arm, until Pee Wee Butts was signed. In 1943 Jackson was claimed by the Philadelphia Stars when he signed a contract and collected money from the club, but decided to play instead with Atlanta.

Jackson, Big Train
[see Jackson, W. (Big Train)]

Jackson, Bob
Career: 1887–96   Positions: c, 1b, of
Teams: New York Gorhams ('87–'89), Cuban Giants ('91), Cuban X-Giants ('96)

A nineteenth-century player for a decade, beginning in 1887, he was a catcher but also often played both first base and in the outfield. He began his career with the New York Gorhams, one of eight teams that were charter members of the League of Colored Baseball Clubs in 1887. However, the league's existence was ephemeral, lasting only a week, and he continued his career playing for a decade with the top independent black teams of the era, including the Cuban Giants and the Cuban X-Giants. During the time that he was with the New York Gorhams and the Cuban Giants, the teams played as representatives of a host city in an otherwise white league. In 1889 the New York Gorhams represented Philadelphia in the Middle States League, and in 1891 the Cuban Giants played in the Connecticut State League as representatives of Ansonia.

Jackson, C.
Career: 1929   Position: 3b
Team: Homestead Grays

As a reserve player with the 1929 Homestead Grays, this third baseman's playing time was limited.

Jackson, Carlton
Career: 1928   Position: officer
Team: Harrisburg Giants

He served as an officer with the Harrisburg team in 1928 after the franchise had dropped out of league competition.

Jackson, Dallas
Career: 1950   Positions: 2b, ss
Team: Cleveland Buckeyes

Primarily a second baseman, in 1950 he was also listed as a shortstop with the Cleveland Buckeyes, but his playing time was restricted.

Jackson, Daniel M. (**Dan**, Hatchet)
Career: 1949   Positions: 2b, lf
Team: Homestead Grays

A year after the demise of the Negro National League, he played with the Homestead Grays as a second baseman and outfielder while they played as an independent team against a lesser caliber of opposition.

Jackson, Edgar S.
Career: 1937   Position: c
Teams: Memphis Red Sox ('37), Kansas City Monarchs ('37)

He was with the 1937 Memphis Red Sox for a short time as a third-string catcher, and also appeared with the Kansas City Monarchs.

Jackson, F.
Career: 1887   Position: officer
Team: *Brooklyn Remsens*

In 1887 he was an officer with the Brooklyn Remsens, one of the earliest black teams.

Jackson, Gen
Career: 1947   Positions: of, p
Team: Baltimore Elite Giants

He appeared briefly with the 1947 Baltimore Elite Giants as an outfielder and pitcher.

Jackson, George
Career: 1886–87   Position: p
Teams: Cuban Giants ('86–'87), *Philadelphia Pythians ('87)*

A native of Philadelphia, he played his first game with the Cuban Giants in July 1886 as a pitcher, and was with the Giants the next season when they represented Trenton, New Jersey, in the Middle States League. That season he was also a pitcher with the Philadelphia Pythians, one of eight teams that were charter members of the League of Colored Baseball Clubs in 1887. However, the league's existence was ephemeral, lasting only a week.

Jackson, George
Career: 1950   Position: if
Team: New York Black Yankees

In 1950, when the Negro American League was struggling to survive the loss of players to organized baseball, he played infield with the New York Black Yankees, who had dropped out of league play and were pursuing an independent schedule.

Jackson, Guy
Career: 1911–15   Positions: ss, 3b
Teams: Chicago Union Giants ('11–'13), New York Lincoln Stars ('14), Chicago Giants ('15)

After beginning his professional career with the Chicago Union Giants, this infielder played third base and batted cleanup for the New York Lincoln Stars in 1914, but returned to the "Windy City" the following season to play shortstop with the Chicago Giants.

Jackson, Jack
Career: 1927–28   Position: of
Teams: Atlantic City Bacharach Giants ('27), Baltimore Black Sox ('28)

This reserve outfielder was briefly with the Bacharach Giants and the Baltimore Black Sox in the last two years of the Eastern Colored League.

Jackson, Jackie
Career: 1950   Position: of
Team: Homestead Grays

He was an outfielder with the Homestead Grays in 1950, after the team had dropped out of league play and was playing as an independent ballclub against opposition of lesser quality.

Jackson, John

[see Fowler, Bud]

Jackson, John (Stony)

Career: 1950   Position: p
Teams: Houston Eagles ('50), *Kansas City Monarchs ('51–'53)*

He was a pitcher with the 1950 Houston Eagles, appearing in 3 league games and losing his only decision. In the early '50s, when the Negro American League was strictly a minor league, he pitched for the Kansas City Monarchs for three more seasons.

Jackson, Lester E.

Career: 1938–41   Positions: p, of
Teams: Newark Eagles ('38), New York Black Yankees ('40–'41)

He appeared briefly with the Newark Eagles and the New York Black Yankees as a pitcher and outfielder during the last four seasons before World War II.

Jackson, Lincoln

Career: 1933   Position: 1b
Teams: Cuban Stars ('33), *Washington Pilots ('34)*

A reserve first baseman with the Cuban Stars in 1933, he also played with the Washington Pilots after they had dropped out of league play.

Jackson, Matthew

[see Jackson, A. Matthew]

Jackson, Norman (Jelly)

Career: 1934–45   Positions: ss, 2b
Teams: Cleveland Red Sox ('34), **Homestead Grays** ('35–'42, '44–'45), Washington Elite Giants ('37) *military defense work ('41–'43)*

Bats: Right   Throws: Right
Height: 5'10"   Weight: 165
Born: 1912, Washington, D.C.
Died: Feb. 13, 1980, Washington, D.C.

This hustling infielder began his career with the Homestead Grays in 1935, after a season with the Cleveland Red Sox, and was the regular shortstop for the next six seasons, including the Grays' first four Negro National League championship teams, 1937–40. A weak hitter, he batted in the eighth slot in the lineup and his averages were frequently below .200, with marks of .183, .185, .197, and .184 in 1935, 1936, 1938, and 1940, respectively. His best average was in 1939, when he registered a .265 batting average. With the batting strength of the Grays' murderers' row, the team could afford to carry his light bat, and he supplied needed speed and defense to the team effort. He was a fast base runner, skilled base stealer, and a fine defensive player with a good arm, and he was considered one of the best players on the team at getting a run when it was needed.

During World War II he worked in a defense plant and, while able to play occasional games, accumulated some athletic rust. When he returned to the Grays, although moving to second base in 1944–45, he hit only .133 in 1944 and had slowed down afield to the extent that he was unable to regain his prewar playing form. A native of Washington, D.C., he was popular with the fans when the Grays used Griffith Stadium as a home field.

Jackson, Oscar (Oss)

Career: 1887–96   Positions: of, 1b
Teams: New York Gorhams ('87–'89), Cuban Giants ('88, '90, '93–'94, '96), Big Gorhams ('91), Cuban X-Giants ('06)

A nineteenth-century player for a decade (1887–96), he began his career as an outfielder and first baseman with the New York Gorhams, one of eight teams that were charter members of the League of Colored Baseball Clubs in 1887. However, the league lasted only a week, and he continued his career for a decade playing with independent black teams of the era, including the Cuban Giants and the Cuban X-Giants. During the time that he was with the New York Gorhams and the Cuban Giants, the teams played as representatives of a host city in an otherwise white league. In 1889 the New York Gorhams represented Philadelphia in the Middle States League, and in 1890 the Cuban Giants played in the Eastern Interstate League as representatives of York, Pennsylvania.

Jackson, R. B.
Career: 1931–50   Positions: owner, officer; president (NSL), vice president (NSL)
Teams: *Nashville Black Vols, Nashville Cubs*

For twenty years he was a club officer and owner of Nashville teams, operating almost exclusively in the Negro Southern League. Except for the 1932 season, the league was recognized as a minor loop, and Jackson served a term each as president and vice president of the league.

Jackson, R. R. (Major)
Career: 1889   Position: manager
Team: Chicago Unions

He managed the Chicago Unions for a single season, 1889, succeeding Abe Jones, who had managed the team during its first two years of operation. He in turn was followed by W. S. Peters, who managed the team into the new century.

Jackson, R. T.
Career: 1928–31   Positions: officer; president (NSL)
Team: Birmingham Black Barons

For four years he was a club officer for the Birmingham Black Barons and also served as president of the Negro Southern League.

Jackson, Richard (Dick)
Career: 1921–31   Positions: **2b**, ss, 3b, of
Teams: Atlantic City Bacharach Giants ('21), New York Bacharach Giants ('22), Brooklyn Royal Giants ('22), Harrisburg Giants ('23–'26), Baltimore Black Sox ('26–'28, '31), Hilldale Daisies ('29–'30)

A capable little player, he was only a fair fielder and base runner but was a better-than-average hitter. Although primarily an infielder, he could also play in the outfield. He began his career with the Bacharachs, playing in both Atlantic City and New York, and also spent a short time with the Brooklyn Royal Giants before joining the Harrisburg Giants. With Harrisburg he played second base and hit .269 and .302 in 1924–25 while batting in the lower part of the order.

During the 1926 season he moved over to the Baltimore Black Sox under manager Ben Taylor. In his first full season he batted in the third spot in the order and contributed a .327 average, even though he lost playing time in August after he suffered cuts in an automobile accident. The next year the second sacker was their leadoff batter, but in 1929 he was traded to Hilldale along with Crush Holloway for Frank Warfield and Red Ryan. With his new team in the American Negro League, he hit .263 for the season. The league broke up after only one year, but he remained for a second season with Hilldale, who returned to play as an independent ballclub. He returned to the Baltimore Black Sox in 1931 to close out his career, hitting in the third slot in the batting order in his final season.

Jackson, Robert (Boob)
Career: 1897–1900   Position: c
Team: Chicago Unions

A catcher with the Chicago Unions during the last years of the nineteenth century, he was also a pugilist, and was regarded as the middleweight champion of New Jersey in 1888.

Jackson, Robert R.
Career: 1939–42   Position: executive
League: Negro American League

He served as the commissioner of the Negro American League for four years, 1939–42.

Jackson, Rufus (Sonnyman)

Career: 1934–49 Positions: officer, owner
Team: Homestead Grays
Born: 1900
Died: Mar. 6, 1949, Pittsburgh, Pa.

When Homestead Grays' owner Cum Posey had financial difficulties during the Depression years, he turned to Jackson for assistance, taking him in as co-owner. Posey handled the responsibilities of general manager, while Jackson served as the president and treasurer for the team. Jackson's money came from two primary sources: the piccolo business and the numbers racket. He supplied the money and Posey supplied the organizational skills during the Grays' glory years. When Mexican officials began raiding the Negro League teams, Jackson was almost arrested because of an altercation when they tried to lure away some of his players. After Posey's death, Jackson ran the team himself, winning the last pennant in Negro National League history in 1948. The following season, the Grays toured as an independent team, but the attrition of players had reduced the team's quality, and their years of greatness were gone, never to return.

Jackson, Sam

Career: 1887 Position: c
Team: *Pittsburgh Keystones*

He was a catcher with the Pittsburgh Keystones, one of eight teams that were charter members of the League of Colored Baseball Clubs in 1887. However, the league's existence was ephemeral, lasting only a week.

Jackson, Sam

Career: 1916–26 Positions: **c**, of, 1b
Teams: New York Lincoln Giants ('16), New York Lincoln Stars ('16), *Pennsylvania Giants ('22),* Pennsylvania Red Caps of New York ('16–'19), Newark Stars ('26), Cleveland Elites ('26)

A reserve catcher whose career spanned more than a decade, he appeared mostly with teams in the vicinity of New York City. He began his career in 1916 and played with three different teams during the season, progressing from the Lincoln Giants to the Lincoln Stars and then finishing with the Pennsylvania Red Caps of New York in the fall. With the Red Caps he consistently demonstrated good defensive work, but at the onset of the lively-ball era he played primarily with lesser teams. In his last year with a league team he began as a backup catcher with the Newark Stars, and after they disbanded at midseason he finished the year with the Cleveland Elites.

Jackson, Samuel (Sam)

Career: 1942–47 Positions: **p**, 1b
Team: Chicago American Giants

He was a wartime player with the Chicago American Giants, and his playing time was divided between pitching and playing first base during his career. Although he hit .301 in 1944 as a reserve first baseman, he was never a regular player.

Jackson, Stanford (Jambo)

Career: 1923–31 Positions: **cf, ss,** lf, 3b, 2b
Teams: Birmingham Black Barons ('23), Memphis Red Sox ('23–'27), **Chicago American Giants** ('26–'30), Homestead Grays ('29), Chicago Columbia Giants ('31)
Bats: Right Throws: Right
Height: 5'0" Weight: 140–150

This speedy little punch hitter could play either outfield or infield. After beginning his career in 1923 in the South, he signed with manager David Malarcher's Chicago American Giants in 1926, and the club won back-to-back Negro National League pennants and World Series championships in his first two seasons with the team. In both years their opponent was the Eastern Colored League champion Bacharachs, and the Series were closely contested. The diminutive Jackson played shortstop the first year, batting .192, and center field the latter season, when he hit .275.

In 1926 the team surged to the second-half title and defeated the Kansas City Monarchs in the playoffs by winning a doubleheader the final day to give them a 5–4 edge in the best-of-9 Series. After claiming the Negro National League pennant, the American Giants defeated the Eastern Colored League champion Bacharach Giants in a closely contested World Series that took 10 games (including two ties) before victory could be claimed. In 1927 the American Giants won the first-half title and swept the Birmingham Black Barons in 4 straight games in the playoffs to win their second straight flag. In the World Series rematch with the Bacharachs, they won by the same margin, 5 games to 3, but in only 9 games. Jackson expected to be traded the next season, but the deal did not materialize and he remained in Chicago.

Throughout his career he usually batted near the top of the order, either first or second, to utilize his speed and ability as a "place-setter." In July 1929 he and Buck Miller were suspended by the new Chicago American Giants' manager, Jim Brown, and they were signed by the Homestead Grays, for whom he hit .270. The next season he was back in Chicago, hitting .245 for the 1930 season. He closed out his career in 1931 while reunited with manager David Malarcher and the old American Giants franchise, playing as the Chicago Columbia Giants.

Jackson, Stony
[see Jackson, John]

Jackson, Thomas **(Tom)**
Career: 1916–28   Positions: manager, officer, owner
Team: Atlantic City Bacharach Giants

One of the two businessmen responsible for the Duval Giants leaving Jacksonville, Florida, in 1916 to relocate in Atlantic City as the Bacharach Giants, he remained as an officer into the '20s as the team became members of the Eastern Colored League. He managed the Bacharachs in 1923.

Jackson, Tom
Career: 1924–31   Position: p
Teams: St. Louis Stars ('24–'27), Memphis Red Sox ('27–'28), Cleveland Tigers ('28), Nashville Elite Giants ('28–'29), Louisville White Sox ('31)

During the '20s this second-line hurler survived for eight years pitching for Negro National League teams in the Midwest and the South. Beginning with the St. Louis Stars in 1926, when he won his only decision, he posted a 1–3 ledger while splitting the 1927 season between the Stars and the Memphis Red Sox. After dividing the 1928 season between the Cleveland Tigers and the Nashville Elite Giants, he lost both of his decisions with the Elites in 1929 before closing out his career in 1931 with the Louisville White Sox.

Jackson, Verdell
Career: 1950   Position: p
Team: Memphis Red Sox

He was listed as a pitcher with the Memphis Red Sox in 1950, when the Negro American League was struggling to survive the loss of players to organized baseball, but league statistics do not confirm his playing time.

Jackson, W. (Big Train)
Career: 1938–40   Position: p
Teams: Kansas City Monarchs ('38–'39), Satchel Paige All-Stars ('39), Memphis Red Sox ('40)
Bats: Left   Throws: Left
Height: 5'11"   Weight: 195

As his nickname would imply, this left-handed pitcher had a good fastball. However, the remainder of his pitches were only mediocre, and he had some problems with his control. He began his career in 1938 with the Kansas City Monarchs under manager Andy Cooper, an ex-left-handed pitcher. In his second year with the club, the Monarchs won the Negro American League pennant. That proved to be his last year with the Monarchs, and in 1940 he sported a 3–0 record with the Memphis Red Sox to close out his career.

Jackson, William
Career: 1890–1906   Positions: of, c, 2b, 1b
Teams: Cuban Giants ('90–'93, '99–'00, '03–'04, '06), Cuban X-Giants ('03)

Playing primarily as an outfielder and catcher, his seventeen-year career began in 1890 and spanned the turn of the century. Most of his playing years were spent with the two top black teams of the time, the Cuban Giants and the Cuban X-Giants. During his time with the Cuban Giants, the team represented York, Pennsylvania, in the Interstate League in 1890 and Ansonia in the Connecticut State League in 1891.

Jackson, William (Ashes)
Career: 1910   Position: 3b
Teams: Kansas City, Kansas, Giants ('10), *Kansas City Royal Giants, Kansas City Colored Giants* ('17)

He was a third baseman with the 1910 Kansas City, Kansas, Giants, one of the earliest black teams in the Plains states. He also played with other Kansas City teams of lesser status.

Jacksonville Red Caps
Duration: 1938,   Honors: None
1941–42
Affiliation: Negro American League

Normally a member of the Negro Southern League, a black minor league, the franchise attained major-league status in 1938 when they joined the Negro American League. After their initial season in the more prestigious league, the franchise moved to Cleveland and played in the league as the Cleveland Bears for two seasons, 1939–40, before returning to Jacksonville. The club remained in the Negro American League until July 1942, when they dropped out of league play. Alonzo Mitchell, who had skippered the team in their first season in the league, was on hand to watch the end of their flirtation with the Negro American League.

Jamerson, Londell (Tincy)
Career: 1950   Position: p
Teams: Kansas City Monarchs ('50–'51)
Born: 1931
Died: Jan. 1976

He pitched with the Kansas City Monarchs in 1950, when the Negro American League was struggling to survive the loss of players to organized baseball, but league statistics do not confirm his playing time.

James
Career: 1896   Position: p
Team: Cuban X-Giants

In 1896 he was a pitcher with the Cuban X-Giants, the dominant team of the era.

James
Career: 1923   Position: p
Teams: Baltimore Black Sox ('23), Cuban Stars (East) ('25)

A nondescript pitcher, he appeared briefly with the Baltimore Black Sox and the Cuban Stars (East) in the mid-'20s.

James, Gus
[see James, Nux]

James, J.
Career: 1912   Position: 1b
Team: Smart Set

He was a first baseman for the Smart Set in 1912, when they fielded one of their strongest teams.

James, Livingston (Winky, Tice, Tarzan)
a.k.a. Livingstone
Career: 1939–42   Position: ss
Teams: *Memphis Red Sox ('36)*, Ethiopian Clowns ('39–'40, '42), Chicago American Giants ('41), Cincinnati Buckeyes ('42)

The light-hitting shortstop from Miami was a regular with the Ethiopian Clowns in 1939. After leaving the Clowns, he was the leadoff batter with the Chicago American Giants in 1941 and was a reserve shortstop with the Cincinnati Buckeyes in 1942.

James, Tice
[see James, Livingston)]

James, W. (Nux, Gus)
a.k.a. Nucks
Career: 1905–20   Positions: **2b,** of, c, p
Teams: Brooklyn Royal Giants ('05–'12, '17–'18), Philadelphia Giants ('07–'10), *Pop Watkins Stars ('08),* Smart Set ('12), Mohawk Giants ('13–'14), New York Lincoln Giants ('14–'15, '17, '20), New York Lincoln Stars ('15), Atlantic City Bacharach Giants ('16), *Pittsburgh Stars of Buffalo ('16–'17)*
Bats: Right   Throws: Right

Already regarded as a star infielder by the middle of the first decade of the modern era, he played second base with the Philadelphia Giants, batting clean-up in 1910. A good fielder, he also played with several teams in the New York area during the '10s, including the Smart Set, the Mohawk Giants, the Lincoln Giants, the New York Lincoln Stars, and the Brooklyn Royal Giants. Apparently he moved freely among the teams, with his club associations sometimes overlapping.

His affiliation with the Royals began in 1905 and continued for most of the deadball era, with James usually batting in the fifth spot in the order. He left the Royals in 1912, playing with the Smart Set and the Mohawk Giants, before signing with the Lincoln Giants. In 1914, after joining the Lincolns, he batted .237 while batting in the seventh spot in the lineup. In the latter years of the decade, incomplete statistics show a composite .286 batting average for 1917–18. In 1920 he made an attempt to hang on as a player by taking the mound as a reserve pitcher for the Lincoln Giants, but his efforts did not meet with a high degree of success, and he was soon relegated to duties as a coach.

James, William
Career: 1887   Position: player
Team: *Philadelphia Pythians*

He was a player with the Philadelphia Pythians, one of eight teams that were charter members of the League of Colored Baseball Clubs in 1887. However, the league's existence was ephemeral, lasting only a week.

Jameson
[see Jamison]

Jamison
a.k.a. Jameson
Career: 1932–35   Position: p
Teams: Homestead Grays ('32–'34), Newark Dodgers ('35)

He was a pitcher with the Newark Dodgers and the Homestead Grays for four years during the Depression years.

Jamison, Caesar
Career: 1923–32   Position: umpire
Leagues: Negro National League, East-West League

He was an umpire for a decade (1923–32), working in the Negro National League for nine seasons before closing out with a year in the East-West League.

Jamison, Eddie
Career: 1950   Position: c
Team: Cleveland Buckeyes

He was listed as a catcher with the Cleveland Buckeyes in 1950, when the Negro American League was struggling to survive the loss of players to organized baseball, but league statistics do not confirm his playing time.

Jarmon, Don
Career: 1933   Position: p
Team: Columbus Blue Birds

In 1933 he was a pitcher with the Columbus Blue Birds, losing his only decision before the team disbanded at midseason.

Jarnigan
Career: 1934   Position: rf
Team: Homestead Grays

He was an outfielder with 1934 Homestead Grays in his only year in the Negro Leagues.

Jasper
Career: 1932–33   Position: p
Teams: Birmingham Black Barons ('32), Memphis Red Sox ('33)

He was a pitcher with the 1932 Birmingham

Black Barons, when the Negro Southern League was recognized as a major league, and with the Memphis Red Sox in 1933, when the Negro Southern League was not considered a major league.

Jauron
Career: 1928   Position: p
Team: Cleveland Tigers

He appeared as a pitcher with the Cleveland Tigers, a 1928 entry in the Eastern Colored League, when the team was struggling to survive after the league folded early in the season.

Jefferson
Career: 1931   Position: p
Team: Atlantic City Bacharach Giants

He appeared briefly as a pitcher with the Bacharachs in 1931, when they were playing as an independent team.

Jefferson, Edward L. (Eddie)
Career: 1945–47   Position: p
Team: Philadelphia Stars
Born: 1922
Died: Feb. 26, 1987, Clinton, Md.

Beginning in 1945, he was a pitcher with the Philadelphia Stars during the latter years of the Negro National League's existence. Later he played with the Motor City Giants, a semi-pro team in Detroit.

Jefferson, George Leo (Jeff)
Career: 1942–50   Position: p, of
Teams: Jacksonville Red Caps ('42–'43), **Cleveland Buckeyes** ('44–'48, '50), Louisville Buckeyes ('49), *minor leagues*
Bats: Right   Throws: Right
Height: 6'2"   Weight: 185
Born: Aug. 8, 1923, Boley, Okla.

Beginning his career with the Jacksonville Redcaps in 1942 as an eighteen-year-old, the tall, right-handed fastballer sparkled in the 1945 season as he led the Cleveland Buckeyes to the Negro American League pennant. His 11–1 record and 1.75 ERA followed on the heels of a 9–6, 1.99 ERA the preceding year.

In both years he finished second behind his brother and teammate Willie Jefferson. His only loss in 1945 was a 13-inning contest with the Memphis Red Sox. To cap his sensational season that year, he shut out the powerful Homestead Grays, champions of the Negro National League, in his only start as the Buckeyes swept the World Series.

In addition to his fastball, he had a curve, overhand drop, and change-up. He also had a good move to first base and liked to hit, sometimes playing outfield or first base. He first gained attention when he pitched in the *Denver Post* Tournament as a youngster. The Oklahoman started his career as a teenager with the Oklahoma City Black Indians in 1937–38, then pitched with the Stillwater Tigers for three years. Following high-school graduation, he made the jump to the Jacksonville Red Caps at age eighteen. Reportedly he fashioned a 15–8 mark against all opposition, but the Red Caps dropped out of the Negro American League before the season ended.

He was also reported with a 6–3 mark in 1943, although he remained out of baseball for most of the year. After signing with the Buckeyes in 1944, he was credited with marks of 16–5 and 20–1 against all opposition for the next two seasons. After his sterling 1945 season, he remained with the Buckeyes through the 1950 season, but never regained the same level of performance on the mound. He pitched infrequently during the next three seasons and, when the franchise moved to Louisville in 1949, he finished with a 3–7 record. In 1950, pitching for a terribly weak team, he had a 1–2 record in 5 pitching appearances, but played most of the season in the outfield, where he posted a .298 batting average.

Jefferson was born in the all-black town of Boley, Oklahoma, and had a reputation of having a mean streak. Earlier in his life, before he started pitching with the Buckeyes, he was reputed to have killed a white man in Kansas. In the winter of 1945–46, while a member of the All-Star team that toured Venezuela, he was involved in an altercation after an argument over money and was choking the promoter before he was restrained.

After leaving the Negro Leagues he played in organized baseball with the Olean and Youngstown ballclubs. When he finally left the baseball diamond, he worked in a paper company until his retirement.

Jefferson, Ralph
Career: 1918–32   Positions: lf, rf
Teams: *Peter's Chicago Union Giants ('18),* Indianapolis ABCs ('20–'21), Atlantic City Bacharach Giants ('21, '32), *Philadelphia Royal Stars,* Washington Potomacs ('23), *Philadelphia Giants ('24–'27)*
Bats: Right   Throws: Right

He was an outfielder with Ben Taylor's Washington Potomacs in 1923, playing in the side pastures and batting in the second spot in the batting order. He also played with the Indianapolis ABCs, the Bacharach Giants, and several lesser teams during his career in black baseball.

Jefferson, Robert (Bob)
Career: 1939   Positions: 3b, p
Team: Indianapolis ABCs

When the Atlanta Black Cracker's franchise relocated to Indianapolis in 1939 and played as the Indianapolis ABCs, he was a reserve third baseman and also did some mound work for the team.

Jefferson, Willie (Bill)
Career: 1937–46   Position: p
Teams: *Claybrook Tigers ('36),* Cincinnati Tigers ('37), Memphis Red Sox ('38–'39), *Mexican League ('40–'41),* Cincinnati Buckeyes ('42), *military service ('42–'43),* Cleveland Buckeyes ('43–'46), *minor leagues ('51)*
Bats: Right   Throws: Right
Height: 5'9"   Weight: 165
Born: July 16, 1904, Clearview, Okla.
Died: 1976, Shreveport, La.

A smart pitcher with good breaking pitches, the wily forty-one-year-old veteran right-hander was the older half of the 1945 Negro American League champion Cleveland Buckeyes' brother combination on the mound. His 1.57 ERA was tops in the league, and he lost but a single game while recording 10 victories. Continuing his superlative pitching in postseason play, he defeated the Homestead Grays in the opening game of the World Series.

He started his career with the Arkansas City Oilers in 1928, and, after stints with the A. C. Beavers in 1929–30, Sioux City, Iowa, in 1931–34, and the Omaha Packers in 1935, he signed with manager "Double Duty" Radcliffe's Claybrook Tigers in 1936. After a season he went with Radcliffe to the Cincinnati Tigers in the Negro American League's inaugural season of 1937. After the Tigers made a strong showing in league play, Jefferson moved again with Radcliffe, making the change to Memphis, where he helped pitch the Red Sox to the first-half title. After two years with the Memphis Red Sox, he cast his lot south of the border, in Mexico. In 1940 with Monterrey, he led the Mexican League in wins with a 22–4 record and a 2.65 ERA. The next season he fell to a 9–16 ledger with a 4.32 ERA and signed with the Cleveland Buckeyes for the 1942 season.

Back in the United States he hurled the first victory in the franchise's history and fashioned a 7–2 record before leaving the team for military service. However, his hitch in the Army was short and he was discharged in time for the Buckeyes' next spring training session in 1943 and posted records of 3–5 and 6–11 for the 1943–44 seasons. After the latter season, he returned to Mexico for the 1944 winter season, but was back with the Buckeyes in 1945 to help pitch them to the championship. After one more season with the Buckeyes, he closed out his career in the Negro Leagues, but later pitched in the Mandak League, posting a 4–7 mark in 1951.

Jeffery
Career: 1931   Position: lf
Team: Birmingham Black Barons

He was an outfielder with the Birmingham

Black Barons in 1931, a year after they had dropped out of the Negro National League.

Jeffreys, Frank
a.k.a. Jeffries
Career: 1917–20   Positions: ss, 2b, of
Team: Chicago Giants

He played four seasons with the Chicago Giants, beginning in 1917 as a reserve second baseman, but soon earned a spot in the starting lineup. In 1919 he started in right field, and the following season, when the team joined the Negro National League, he was the starting shortstop. A light hitter, he was usually placed in the lower part of the batting order when in the lineup.

Jeffries, E.
Career: 1922   Position: c
Team: Chicago Giants

He was a catcher with the Chicago Giants in 1922, a year after they had dropped out of the Negro National League.

Jeffries, Harry
a.k.a. J. Jeffries
Career: 1920–34   Positions: **3b**, c, ss, 1b, of, manager
Teams: Chicago Giants ('20–'21), Chicago American Giants ('22, '29–'30), Detroit Stars ('23–'24, '26–'27), Cleveland Tate Stars ('23), Washington Potomacs ('23), Cleveland Browns ('24), Baltimore Black Sox ('24–'25, '32), Cleveland Tigers ('28), Harrisburg Giants ('28), Chicago Columbia Giants ('31), Newark Browns ('32), Hilldale Daisies ('32), Newark Dodgers ('33), Atlantic City Bacharach Giants ('33–'34), *Knoxville Giants, Baltimore Panthers*

Although primarily a third baseman, he could play almost any position, but spent fifteen seasons as an active player looking for a home. He played mostly with teams in precarious situations and never stayed with any team more than two successive years.

The youngster was given a good trial with the Chicago American Giants by Rube Foster

in spring training of 1922 but was not able to win a spot at the hot corner. However, the next season he did earn a starting spot at third base with the Detroit Stars and was often utilized as the leadoff batter. In 1924, After bouncing around with several other clubs, the little third baseman was secured by the Baltimore Black Sox to replace Henry Blackman when he passed away suddenly in 1924. He was a fair third baseman, but "too light for a championship club." Throughout his career he usually batted in the lower part of the order but sometimes was placed in one of the two top spots in the lineup.

In 1928 he was among the throng of players who wore the uniform of the Cleveland Tigers. In addition to playing as a regular at third base, he also handled the managerial chores for the latter part of the season. When the team folded following the season, Jeffries landed back in Chicago in 1929. While playing at the hot corner and also sharing catching duties with the American Giants, he usually batted in the sixth slot in the lineup, but hit only .199 in 1930. The next season he shared the catching duties with David Malarcher's Columbia Giants, which was basically only an extension of the American Giants' franchise.

In 1932 he was back in the East, appearing at the hot corner with Newark Browns in the East-West League until the league folded in midsummer, and then filling the same role with Hilldale for the remainder of the year. Most of the next two seasons were spent with the Bacharachs in a reserve role, substituting at both third base and catcher during the club's last season in the Negro National League.

Jeffries, James C. (Jim)
Career: 1914–31   Positions: **p**, of
Teams: **Indianapolis ABCs** ('13–'24), Chicago American Giants ('22), Harrisburg Giants ('24), Baltimore Black Sox ('24–'25), Birmingham Black Barons ('26–'28, '31)
Bats: Left   Throws: Left

A fleet outfielder and a solid pitcher, he began his career with the Indianapolis ABCs in 1913, a year before they achieved a major-league level of play. In 1915 the ABCs challenged Rube Foster's Chicago American Giants for the western championship but lost a closely contested playoff. The following season the ABCs reversed the playoff results, defeating the Chicago American Giants for the 1916 western championship. Jeffries, George Shively, and Oscar Charleston formed a trio that was considered one of the fastest outfields in baseball.

Incomplete statistics show a composite batting average of .260 for the 1915–16 seasons. On the mound, the left-hander fashioned records of 2–3, 5–5, 4–0, and 3–0 for four seasons (1915–18) with the ABCs. He played with the Colored All-Stars in the winter of 1921 and, while still playing in the outfield on occasion, he began gravitating more toward the mound in the '20s. In 1921–22 he had records of 14–11 and 7–9.

As part of the exodus from the ABCs to the East after C. I. Taylor's death and the inception of the Eastern Colored League, the veteran underhand hurler joined Harrisburg for a short time in 1924, before being sold to the Baltimore Black Sox in the latter part of the season. His sore arm resulted in a substandard pitching performance, but the Sox, counting on the arm coming back, reserved him for the 1925 season. Unfortunately, their optimism was not rewarded, as he lost his only decision in 1925 and did not return to the team for the next season. Leaving the East, he signed with the Birmingham Black Barons, pitching with them during the 1927 season, when they won the second-half title.

Jeffries, James C. (Jim, **Jeff**)
Career: 1940   Position: p
Teams: Brooklyn Royal Giants ('40), Homestead Grays ('40)
Bats: Right   Throws: Right

A right-handed pitcher, he split his playing time in 1940 between the Brooklyn Royal Giants and the Homestead Grays, winning his only decision for the Grays.

Jeffries, M.
[see, Jeffries, Harry]

Jenkins
Career: 1924   Position: p
Team: Washington Potomacs

A pitcher from Dayton, Ohio, he pitched very briefly with the Potomacs in 1924 but was ineffective and quickly released.

Jenkins, Clarence (**Barney**)
Career: 1929   Position: c
Teams: *Philadelphia Giants ('25–'26)*, Detroit Stars ('29)

He was a catcher with the Philadelphia Giants for two seasons before eventually landing with the Detroit Stars in 1929 for a season.

Jenkins, Clarence (**Fats**)
Career: 1920–40   Positions: of, manager
Teams: New York Lincoln Giants ('20, '28, '30), Atlantic City Bacharach Giants ('22, '28–'29), Harrisburg Giants ('23–'27), Hilldale Daisies ('28), Baltimore Black Sox ('30), New York Harlem Stars ('31), Pittsburgh Crawfords ('32, '38), **New York Black Yankees** ('32–'34, '36–'38, '40), Brooklyn Eagles ('35), Brooklyn Royal Giants ('39–'40), Toledo Crawfords ('39), Philadelphia Stars ('40)
Bats: Left   Throws: Left
Height: 5'7"   Weight: 180
Born: Jan. 19, 1898, New York, N.Y.
Died: Dec. 6, 1968, Philadelphia, Pa

A left-hander all the way, Jenkins had exceptional quickness and was a very fast man in the field and on the bases, especially from the batter's box to first base. A very smart player, he studied the art of baserunning and was an exceptional base stealer. At the plate he was a slap hitter with only average power but was a good contact hitter. He was a good fielder with a wide range and an average arm. A hustling, gifted, versatile athlete, in the off-season he was a member of the great Renaissance basketball team. Jenkins joined the team in 1924 and, although the smallest man on the team, he captained the squad for over a decade

(1932–42), with the team winning 88 straight games during the 1934–35 season. Excelling in both sports, he was an asset to any team that was fortunate enough to acquire his services.

He began his professional baseball career with the 1920 New York Lincoln Giants. His skills and success on the diamond led him to manager Oscar Charleston's Harrisburg Giants in 1923, where he was the right fielder and leadoff hitter for the next five years, recording batting averages of .317, .315, .283, and .398 for the 1924–27 seasons, until they dropped out of the Eastern Colored League. While at Harrisburg, he and George Fiall (another basketball star) were dubbed the "heavenly twins" by the press, but Fiall never enjoyed the measure of success on the diamond that Jenkins achieved.

After leaving Harrisburg, Jenkins settled with the Bacharach Giants for two years, where he continued his hot hitting, with averages of .379 and .365, the latter coming during the American Negro League's only year of existence, 1929. In the absence of a league in the East, in 1930 Jenkins rejoined the Lincoln Giants, who were playing as an independent ballclub in their last year of existence. With Jenkins contributing a .329 batting average, the Lincolns proved to be one of the top teams in the East, dominating play most of the season before losing a late-season playoff for the eastern championship to the Homestead Grays. In 1931 he joined manager John Henry Lloyd's New York Harlem Stars, a team that replaced the Lincolns and in turn was replaced by the New York Black Yankees the following season. With each of the New York-based teams he was the left fielder and leadoff batter and is credited with averages of .256 and .288.

In 1933 he was selected to the East squad for the inaugural East-West All-Star game and earned his second appearance in the midseason classic in 1935, when he hit .321 during the regular season with the Brooklyn Eagles. He was back with the New York Black Yankees in 1936–38 but had slowed a half step and moved from the leadoff spot to the heart of

the order; although batting statistics from this period are incomplete, he is credited with a composite average of .266 for these years. He played for two more seasons with four teams before retiring from the diamond. Much of his twenty-one-year career was played in New York. He finished with a .334 lifetime batting average in black baseball.

Off the field, Jenkins enjoyed music, playing the piano and singing as a member of his team's quartet. A very frugal man, after his baseball career he was a successful businessman, opening a package store in the Bronx while also becoming a boxing referee in New York City.

Jenkins, Horace
Career: 1914–25   Positions: **of**, p
Teams: *Chicago Union Giants ('11, '17)* Chicago American Giants ('14–'15), **Chicago Giants** ('16–'21)

He began his career with top clubs in 1914 as a pitcher with Rube Foster's Chicago American Giants, contributing a 5–1 mark to the team's 112–14 record for the season. The next year, due to an injury to left fielder Frank Duncan, he moved into the lineup as an everyday player, and batting third in the order, compiled a .245 batting mark. In 1916 he left Foster's team and joined the Chicago Giants, where he pitched, played center field, and batted cleanup. The following season he resumed the dual role, but during the season jumped to the Chicago Union Giants, a team of lesser caliber, where he played left field and batted in the cleanup spot. He was back in center field with the Chicago Giants for their entry into the Negro National League during the inaugural season of 1920. He continued with lesser ballclubs through 1925, giving him a dozen years with black teams in Chicago as an outfielder and pitcher.

Jenkins, James Edward (**Pee Wee**)
Career: 1944–50   Positions: **p**, *of*
Teams: Cincinnati-Indianapolis Clowns ('44), New York Cubans ('46–'50), *Birmingham*

Black Barons ('52), Indianapolis Clowns ('52), Canadian League ('51), minor leagues ('51–'53)

Bats: Right Throws: Right
Height: 5'8" Weight: 160

He began his pitching career with the 1944 Cincinnati-Indianapolis Clowns but spent most of his playing time with the New York Cubans. He had an ample variety of pitches and good control, and was 2–2 during the New York Cuban's championship season of 1947 as they took the Negro National League pennant and defeated the Cleveland Buckeyes in the World Series. Three years later he was 0–2 in his last season in the Negro Leagues. He began the 1951 season with Three Rivers in the Provincial League as a pitcher-outfielder but hit only .170 during his stay there, before joining the Mandak League, where he recorded a 7–5 slate with Winnipeg. The next two seasons were spent with Brandon in the same league, and he had a 5–2 record in his last year, 1953. Aside from his pitching, he was a good hustler but was at best a mediocre player in any other phase of the game.

Jenkins, Tom
Career: 1916 Positions: player, secretary
Team: Hilldale Daisies

He was a player with Hilldale in 1916, when the team was in its formative stages, and later became secretary of the ballclub in 1928.

Jennings, Thurman (Jack)
Career: 1914–27 Positions: **2b**, ss, of
Team: Chicago Giants ('14–'27)

This little middle infielder was called a "sensational infielder" when he was a rookie second baseman with the Chicago Giants in 1915. The next season he switched to shortstop, batting in the leadoff spot both seasons. In 1917 he moved back to his original position and started batting third in the order, and was still there when the Giants became charter members of the Negro National League in 1920. After the team dropped out of the Negro

National League, they quickly became a team of lesser quality, and he remained with the ballclub through the 1927 season.

Jessie, W.
Career: 1887 Position: player
Team: *Louisville Falls Citys*

He was a player with the Louisville Falls Citys, one of eight teams that were charter members of the League of Colored Baseball Clubs in 1887. However, the league's existence was ephemeral, lasting only a week.

Jessup
Career: 1911 Position: p
Team: *Chicago Union Giants*

In 1911 he appeared as a pitcher with the Chicago Union Giants, a team of lesser status.

Jessup, Gentry (Jeep)
Career: 1940–49 Position: p
Teams: Birmingham Black Barons ('40), **Chicago American Giants** ('41–'49), *minor leagues ('50–'52)*
Bats: Right Throws: Right
Height: 6'0" Weight: 180

This hard-throwing right-hander was a stalwart of the Chicago American Giants' mound corps during the late 1940s, fashioning records of 8–7, 14–9 (2.32 ERA), 15–10 (2.95 ERA), and 7–8 in 1943–46. A great competitor, Jessup made four appearances in the All-Star game (1944–45, 1947–48) without a decision. He spent his entire career in the Negro Leagues with only two teams, beginning his career with the Birmingham Black Barons in 1940 before joining the American Giants. While on loan, he started a game in the 1943 World Series for the Black Barons against the Homestead Grays.

In the late '40s he was highly regarded for his pitching skills, and in 1946 he was selected to be a member of Satchel Paige's All-Stars who barnstormed against Bob Feller's All-Stars in postseason exhibitions. Earlier in the season, Jessup, who had exceptional stamina, pitched a 20-inning game in Comiskey Park against the Indianapolis Clowns that ended in a 3–3 tie.

The lanky hurler had some control problems, and batters knew not to dig in at the plate when he was on the mound. In 1948 he posted a 6–9 ledger with a 3.10 ERA. Also a good hitter, Jessup hit .300 that season and was thought to have a better shot at the majors based on his hitting skills. After leaving the Negro Leagues he entered organized baseball, playing with Carman in the Mandak League in 1950–52, hitting .278 and .298 in the first two seasons while posting pitching marks of 10–4 and 9–6.

Jethroe, Samuel (**Sam**, Sambo, The Jet)
a.k.a. Jethrow
Career: 1938–48   Position: **cf**, lf, c
Teams: Indianapolis ABCs ('38), Cincinnati Buckeyes ('42), **Cleveland Buckeyes** ('43–'48), *minor leagues ('48–'49, '53–'58),* major leagues ('50–'52, '54)
Bats: Both   Throws: Right
Height: 6'1"   Weight: 178
Born: Jan. 20, 1922, East St. Louis, Ill.

He was nicknamed "The Jet" because of his acceleration and speed, which was described by one player by saying that Jethroe could "outrun the word of God." During his seven years in the Negro American League, prior to signing with the major leagues, the quick outfielder established himself as the premier base stealer in the league. One opponent noticed that the speedster had a habit of pulling his pants leg up when he was going to run, but was still not able to stop him from successfully pilfering a base. In 1944–45 the switch-hitter led the league in both batting, with averages of .353 and .393, and stolen bases, with 18 and 21. In the latter year the Cleveland Buckeyes won the Negro American League pennant and swept the Homestead Grays 4 straight in the World Series, with Jethroe contributing a .333 batting average. In 1945 Jethroe, Jackie Robinson, and Marvin Williams had a tryout with the Boston Red Sox in Fenway Park, but despite their ability, they were not signed.

Jethroe was an all-around athlete. His father

taught him to play baseball, and at Lincoln High School, he played football, basketball, and boxed. After high school he began playing semipro ball with the East St. Louis Colts and the St. Louis Giants. Jethroe began his career as a catcher, appearing briefly with the Indianapolis ABCs in 1938, but it was not until he joined the Cincinnati Buckeyes as an outfielder in 1942 that his baseball talents began to shine, and he made his first All-Star appearance that season. Offensively his only shortcoming was a tendency toward too many strikeouts. Defensively he had great range in the outfield but had difficulty on ground balls and had only an average arm. After signing with the Buckeyes, owner Ernie Wright gave him a job tending bar at the Pope Hotel, and he also worked for General Electric in the off-season.

Incomplete statistics show batting averages of .487 and .286 in 1942–43, and he was runner-up for the Negro American League MVP the latter season. In an exhibition game that year he hit a grand slam off Dizzy Dean, and three years later Jethroe faced Bob Feller when he played on Satchel Paige's All-Stars, who toured with Feller's All-Stars in postseason exhibitions.

Paige's All-Star team was not the first he had played with, as he was a member of the American All-Star team that went to Caracas, Venezuela, in the winter of 1945, with the fleet-outfielder taking the honor as the top base stealer. The excursion to Venezuela was not his only season in Latin America, as he had played the previous winter (1944–45) with San Juan in the Puerto Rican League, and he played three winters with Almendares in Cuba. His best season on the island was 1947–48, when he posted a .308 average, and he followed with a .273 average the next winter. After an absence of seven years he finished his Cuban career with a .276 average in 1954–55, giving him a .274 lifetime average in the Cuban League.

With Jackie Robinson playing with the Brooklyn Dodgers in 1947, Jethroe was being sought by the major leagues. In 1946 he had batted .310 and played in both All-Star games played that season. In 1947 he was again selected to play in the East-West All-Star game, bringing his total All-Star appearances to five. At the All-star break he was hitting .321 and leading the league with 21 stolen bases. He finished with 90 runs, 52 stolen bases, 35 doubles, 10 triples, 7 home runs, a .353 batting average, and a .601 slugging percentage. The next season, his last year in the Negro Leagues, the outfield flash again led the league in stolen bases with 29 while batting .296, to close his Negro League career with a lifetime average of .347.

His last year in the Negro Leagues was also his first in organized baseball, and he took a pay cut to play in organized baseball, from $700 to $400 a month. After being signed by the Dodgers, he was assigned to the Montreal Royals, where he hit .322 for the remainder of the season. In the spring he was timed in the sprints, and his time was close to a world record. Later, in a running exhibition, he defeated Olympic champion Barney Ewell, and in 1949, his first full season at Montreal, he hit .326 and led the league in stolen bases with 89.

The Boston Braves' organization acquired his contract, and he joined the team in 1950. As a major-league rookie with them he hit .273 and led the league in stolen bases with 35, to earn Rookie of the Year honors. He followed this with a near-duplicate season, hitting .280 and again leading the league in stolen bases with 35.

After an off-season with the Braves, he was assigned to Toledo in the International League in 1953, and hit .309 to get another chance in the majors, and he closed out his abbreviated major-league career in 1954 with the Pittsburgh Pirates. After being sent down to the minors by the Pirates, he spent five seasons (1954–58) with Toronto in the International League where he hit .305, .262, .287, .277, and .234 to end his professional baseball career. He returned to Erie, Pennsylvania, opened a tavern, and played semipro ball.

Jewell, Warner
Career: 1917–25   Position: owner
Teams: Jewell's ABCs, Indianapolis ABCs

During the '10s there were three teams playing out of Indianapolis who were called the ABCs. In 1917, he was the owner of the team that bore his name, Jewell's ABCs, one of the lesser teams. Later, after the death of C. I. Taylor, he became owner of the Indianapolis ABCs until shortly before the franchise's demise.

Jimenez, Bienvenido (**Hooks**)
a.k.a. Jiminez
Career: 1914–29   Positions: **2b**, 3b
Teams: Cuban Stars (West) ('14–'21, '28–'29), Cuban Stars (East) ('22–'24)

An outstanding infielder, he was known as the king of Cuban second basemen. The big infielder was a hard-nosed player and was regarded as second only to Bingo DeMoss at his position. He earned the nickname "Hooks" from his bowlegs, but he was very fast and a great base runner who was very adept at stealing bases. He also had great range afield, a good throwing arm, and was a good hitter with better than average power.

The youngster began his career with the Cuban Stars in 1914, when they were still an independent team, and was batting ninth in the order a year later. But in 1916 he moved to the top of the order, where he stayed until 1920, when the team joined the Negro National League. After two seasons of league play, he jumped owner Augustin Molina's team to join Alexander Pompez' Cuban Stars, who were based in the East. During his second year with the team, Pompez entered his club in the Eastern Colored League in the loop's inaugural season. The veteran infielder was late reporting to the team in 1924, and hit only .215 for the season. For the next three years he was not with either of the Cuban Stars aggegations, but in 1928 he rejoined Molina's Cuban Stars and was installed as the leadoff batter. The next season was his last year in the Negro Leagues and, although he was dropped in the batting order, he hit .302 to wrap up his career.

In his own country he had a lifetime batting average of .266 for a dozen winters of play (1913–29) and was elected to the Cuban Hall of Fame in 1951. His best year in Cuba was the winter of 1918–19, when he hit .321 and had 30 stolen bases in only 140 at-bats. After the turn of the decade he put together two good seasons, with batting averages of .291 (1920–21) and .300 (1922–23). Sandwiched between these marks was a league-leading .619 batting average with San Francisco, but this mark is misleading, as it represented only 21 at-bats with 13 hits.

In the United States Jimenez had been teammates with the Cuban great Estaban Monatavlo, and during Jimenez's Cuban career they were also teammates one year at Yara, a team in the southern part of the island.

Jimenez, E.
Career: 1920–21   Position: of
Teams: Cuban Stars (East) ('20), *Philadelphia Giants of New York ('20)*, Cuban Stars (West) ('21)

He was an outfielder for both of the Cuban Stars ballclubs, appearing with each team for a year. In 1920 he was the regular right fielder for the eastern-based Stars but batted at the bottom of the order. The next year he was a reserve outfielder with the Negro National League club that was playing out of Cincinnati. Between playing for these two teams was a stint with the Philadelphia Giants of New York, a team of lesser quality.

Johnson
Career: 1886   Position: cf
Team: *New York Gorhams*

In 1886 he was a center fielder with the New York Gorhams, one of the earliest black professional teams.

Johnson
Career: 1938   Position: player
Team: Memphis Red Sox

He was briefly with the 1939 Memphis Red Sox in his only appearance in the Negro Leagues, but his position is not known.

Johnson
Career: 1922   Position: of

Teams: Detroit Stars ('22), *Chappie Johnson's Stars ('25)*

This outfielder appeared briefly as a reserve with the Detroit Stars in 1922, and was a center fielder with Chappie Johnson's Stars in 1925.

Johnson
Career: 1923–24   Position: c
Teams: Homstead Grays ('23), *Philadelphia Giants ('24)*, Washington Potomacs ('24)

After an appearance with the Grays, this big, strapping youngster started the 1924 season with Dan McClellan's Philadelphia Giants, but was secured by the Washington Potomacs as an understudy to Mac Eggleston. Johnson was not reserved for the 1925 season.

Johnson
Career: 1926   Position: if
Teams: Chicago American Giants

An infielder from Dallas, Texas, he appeared briefly with the 1926 Chicago American Giants.

Johnson
Career: 1928   Position: of
Team: Birmingham Black Barons

In 1928 he appeared briefly as an outfielder with the Birmingham Black Barons.

Johnson
Career: 1931   Position: 3b
Team: Newark Browns

He was a reserve third baseman with the Newark Browns in 1931, a year before they entered the East-West League.

Johnson, A.
Career: 1914–16   Positions: 2b, 3b
Teams: New York Lincoln Giants ('14), New York Lincoln Stars ('16)

A reserve infielder, he appeared briefly with both New York-based teams, the Lincoln Giants and the Lincoln Stars, playing second base and third base.

Johnson, A.
Career: 1885   Positions: c, lf
Team: Cuban Giants
This Washington, D.C., resident was a left fielder and a catcher for the Cuban Giants.

Johnson, A. (Sampson)
Career: 1913–22   Position: c
Teams: Philadelphia Giants ('13), Atlantic City Bacharach Giants ('16), *Pennsylvania Giants ('18)*, Homestead Grays ('22)
He was a catcher during the deadball era with teams that were phasing down, struggling to get started, or of lesser quality. His last season was with the Homestead Grays in 1922, when they were still playing independent ball.

Johnson, Al
Career: 1938–40   Position: p
Teams: Washington Black Senators ('38), Baltimore Elite Giants ('39–'40)
He began his career as a pitcher with the Washington Black Senators during their only season in the Negro National League and then joined the Baltimore Elite Giants for two additional seasons.

Johnson, B.
Career: 1940   Position: ss
Team: Brooklyn Royal Giants
He was a shortstop with the Brooklyn Royal Giants in 1940, when the team was playing as an independent ballclub.

Johnson, B. (**Monk**)
Career: 1917–26   Positions: **p**, of, 1b, *2b*
Teams: G.C.T. Red Caps ('18), New York Lincoln Giants ('18, '25), Pennsylvania Red Caps of New York ('17, '19, '26)
He was a pitcher and all-purpose player with New York-based teams for a decade; mostly with clubs of marginal quality.

Johnson, Ben
Career: 1916–23   Position: p
Teams: Atlantic City Bacharach Giants
A pitcher with the Bacharach Giants during

their formative years, he joined the team in 1916, and his last year coincided with their entry into the Eastern Colored League, 1923.

Johnson, Bert (**Bucky**)
[see Johnston, Bert (Bucky)]

Johnson, Bill
Career: 1933   Position: 3b
Team: Akron Tyrites
In 1933 he was a third baseman with the Akron Tyrites, a team that was sometimes also called the Grays.

Johnson, Bill (Willie)
Career: 1938–39   Position: c
Teams: Chicago American Giants ('38), New York Black Yankees ('39)
He was briefly a reserve catcher with the New York Black Yankees and the Chicago American Giants in the late '30s.

Johnson, Byron (Mex, Jew Baby)
Career: 1937–40   Position: ss
Teams: Kansas City Monarchs ('38–'39), Satchel Paige's All Stars ('39–'40)
Bats: Right   Throws: Right
Height: 5'8"   Weight: 160
Born: Sept. 16, 1911, Little Rock, Ark.
An outstanding fielder with great range, sure hands, and a strong arm, his quickness afield was matched by his speed on the bases. He was a good base stealer and, although a light hitter, was a good bunter. He played with the Kansas City Monarchs in 1937 and 1938, earning a spot on the West squad in the 1938 All-Star game. In that game Johnson asked to use one of Turkey Stearnes's bats. Stearnes, who usually was very protective of his bats, agreed and promised to give him the bat if he hit safely in the game. Byron smacked a hit and collected his bat after the game.
At a time when he was generally conceded to be the best shortstop in the West, the hustling little shortstop left league play to join Satchel Paige on the Monarchs' traveling All-Star team for the next two years. When he

began playing professional baseball, he also began a second career in the off-season, as a teacher and coach. He continued his employment in education for seven years until he entered military service in 1943. He served in the Quartermaster Corps and spent thirteen months in England, living in the field, and preparing for the D-Day invasion. His unit landed five days after the initial assault, and he was in combat for eighteen days. After his discharge he never again played in the Negro Leagues.

As a youngster he liked cowboys, and when his father bought him a sombrero, he acquired the nickname "Mex." A good all-around athlete, after finishing high school he played quarterback in the same backfield with Pat Patterson on the Wiley College football team. When school was not in session, he was also playing baseball on the sandlots of Little Rock, Arkansas. Johnson played with two different teams, the DuBisson Tigers and the Little Rock Stars, before being discovered by the Monarchs in 1936.

Johnson, C.
[Johnson,
see G. Claude (Hooks)]

Johnson, Cecil (Sess)
Career: 1917–31   Positions: p, of, ss, 1b, 3b
Teams: Hilldale Daisies ('17–'18, '20), Atlantic City Bacharach Giants ('19), *Norfolk All-Stars ('20)*, Baltimore Black Sox ('22), Newark Stars ('26), Philadelphia Tigers ('28), Newark Browns ('31)

He was a pitcher with Hilldale in their early years and turned to other positions later in his career. In 1922 he played third base with the Baltimore Black Sox, and in 1928 he played both first base and outfield with the Philadelphia Tigers. When in the lineup with the Tigers, he sometimes batted cleanup. He also continued to take a turn on the mound, as he did with the Newark Stars in 1926. His last appearance with a league club was in 1931 with another Newark club, the Browns.

Johnson, Charles
Career: 1949–50   Positions: **3b**, 2b
Teams: Memphis Red Sox ('49), Cleveland Buckeyes ('50)

He was a third baseman with the Memphis Red Sox in 1949, batting .333 in limited playing time. The following year he split his playing time between third base and second base with the Cleveland Buckeyes, batting .256 for the season.

Johnson, Claude (Hooks)
[Johnson, see G. Claude (Hooks)]

Johnson, Clifford Jr. (Cliff, **Connie**)
Career: 1940–50   Positions: **p**, *1b*
Teams: Indianapolis **Crawfords** ('40), **Kansas City Monarchs** ('41–'42, '46–'50), *military service ('43–'45), Canadian League ('51), minor leagues ('52–'54, '59–'60),* major leagues ('53, '55–'58,) *Mexican League ('61)*
Bats: Right   Throws: Right
Height: 6'4"   Weight: 200
Born: Dec. 27, 1922, Stone Mountain, Ga.

Primarily a fastball pitcher early in his career, after arm trouble he developed a good breaking pitch. In his prime, the big right-hander had good control and an assorted repertory, including an outstanding fastball and curve, a good slider, and an average change-up. He made two appearances, a decade apart, in the East-West All-Star game. He pitched in the 1940 contest while with the Indianapolis Crawfords, and after achieving greater recognition as a member of the superb Kansas City Monarchs' mound corps of the '40s, he notched the victory in the 1950 game.

Before signing with the Crawfords in 1940, he played baseball in high school at Stone Mountain, Georgia. After a year with the Crawfords, he joined the Kansas City Monarchs and played a key role in the 1941 and 1942 Negro American League championships, posting league ledgers of 2–2 and 3–0 before entering military service during World War II for three years. Returning from the Army in 1946, he registered a 9–3 record as the Mon-

Satchel Paige was a master showman and the nearest thing to a legend produced by black baseball. The elongated hurler earned his greatest fame with the Kansas City Monarchs, and was the first player from the Negro Leagues elected to the Hall of Fame. *(Author collection)*

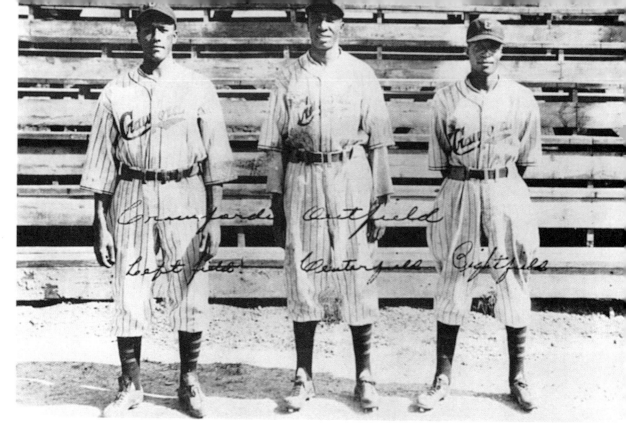

The Pittsburgh Crawfords fielded one of the greatest outfields of all-time, featuring Sam Bankhead, Cool Papa Bell and Jimmy Crutchfield (left-to-right). Satchel Paige said that when it rained, this trio of racehorses could catch every raindrop before they hit the ground. Bell is acknowledged as the fastest player to ever play baseball. Also an exceptional hitter and fielder, he starred for over twenty years with the top teams in the Negro Leagues. *(National Baseball Hall of Fame)*

Three sluggers (Jud ''Boojum'' Wilson, Heavy Johnson and John Beckwith) pose with their bats. Wilson, one of the greatest hitters of all time, was a pure hitter and at his best in the clutch. *(National Baseball Hall of Fame)*

Featured in the Kansas City Monarchs sweep of the 1942 Negro World Series, was the play of Willard Brown, Ted Strong and Newt Allen (left-to-right). Brown was the premier homerun hitter of the Negro American League, and possessed almost unlimited potential. Strong, a versatile athlete, played with basketball's Harlem Globetrotters in the off-season. In his prime, Allen was a slick-fielding secondbase-man, who sparkled while turning double plays. (National Baseball Hall of Fame)

Three ex-Negro Leaguers, Ray Dandridge, Dave Barnhill and Willie Mays (left-to-right), wer
teammates with the Minneapolis Millers in 1951. Dandridge and Barnhill starred with th
Newark Eagles and New York Cubans, respectively, while Mays began his career with th
Birmingham Black Barons. *(Author collection)*

The Homestead Grays' "murderers row" in 1946 consisted of Sam Bankhead, Josh Gibsor
Buck Leonard, Dave Hoskins and Jerry Benjamin (left-to-right). They are shown at Griffitl
Stadium in Washington, D.C. *(Author collection)*

Five sluggers from baseball's golden age, Jess Hubbard, Biz Mackey, John Beckwith, Rap
Dixon, and Clint Thomas (left-to-right), pose before a ballgame. Mackey was a superlative
receiver with unsurpassed defensive skills and was also a good hitter. Beckwith was knowr
for his powerful and consistent hitting. Dixon and Thomas were complete ballplayers, excel
ling in every phase of the game. *(Author collection)*

BANKHEAD   GIBSON   LEONARD   HOSKINS   BENJAMIN
S.S.   C.   1st   R.F.   C.F.

1946 WASHINGTON, D.C.

The legendary Satchel Paige with his teammate Jackie Robinson, Kansas City Monarchs, 1945.

Fort Riley, Kansas in 1943 with Roscoe Devore.

When he appeared in a Brooklyn Dodgers uniform in 1947, Jackie Robinson, shown here with teammate Satchel Paige, became the first black player in the major leagues in modern times. Two years earlier, he played with the Kansas City Monarchs in the Negro American League. *(Lawrence D. Hogan)*

Turkey Stearnes was a lefthanded homerun hitter, who also hit for high averages during his
years with the Detroit Stars and Chicago American Giants. *(Author collection)*

The two greatest pitchers of the deadball era (Smokey Joe Williams and Cannonball Dick Redding) shake hands. During the first half of its existence, Williams was to black baseball what Satchel Paige was to the latter half. Those who saw the big, hard-throwing righthander regard him as Satchel's equal, if not his superior. Redding's overpowering speed earned him his nickname and made him one of black baseball's greatest pitchers. *(National Baseball Hall of Fame)*

archs copped another pennant, but he did not pitch in the World Series. The next two seasons he was a .500 pitcher with the Monarchs, but in 1950 he was 11–2 with a 2.17 ERA.

In 1951 he played with St. Hyacinthe in the Canadian Provincial League and was 15–14 with a 3.24 ERA and a league-high 172 strikeouts. In 1952 his contract was purchased by the Chicago White Sox organization and he was sent to Colorado Springs in the Western League, where he posted an 18–9 mark with a 3.38 ERA and led the league with 233 strikeouts.

In 1953, at age thirty, Johnson's fastball and picture-book curve earned him a shot at the major leagues, and he split the season with Charleston (6–6, 3.62 ERA) of the American Association and the parent White Sox (4–4, 3.54 ERA) of the American League. After two fine seasons with Toronto of the International League (17–8, 3.72 ERA and 12–2, 3.05 ERA) in 1954–55, he was back with Chicago before the end of the latter season and was 7–4 with a 3.45 ERA.

During the winter (1954–55) sandwiched between these two seasons with Toronto, he played with Marianao in Cuba and was 12–11 with a 3.29 ERA. He also toured with Roy Campanella's All-Stars in 1954.

Traded to Baltimore in 1956, he fashioned the best season of his five-year major-league career with the Orioles in 1957, when he posted a 14–11 record with a 3.20 ERA. He remained in the majors through 1958, with a composite recod of 29–31 for the three seasons, before being sent back to the minors. Pitching with Vancouver in the Pacific Coast League, he registered an 8–4 mark in 1959 but lost his only game in 1960. In 1961 he finished his baseball career with a 1–0 record with Puebla in the Mexican League.

Johnson, Curtis
Career: 1950   Position: p
Team: Kansas City Monarchs

He was a pitcher with the Kansas City Monarchs in 1950, when the Negro American League was struggling to survive the loss of players to organized baseball, but league statistics do not confirm his playing time.

Johnson, D. (Dud)
Career: 1914–15, 19   Positions: ss, 3b, 2b, of
Teams: *Philadelphia Giants ('14–'15)*, Brooklyn Royal Giants ('19), *Madison Stars ('20)*

This infielder played shortstop and third base for the Brooklyn Giants in 1919, and also played with the once-proud Philadelphia Giants after they had declined in their level of play.

Johnson, Dan (Shang)
Career: 1916–21   Positions: p, c
Teams: Atlantic City Bacharach Giants ('16–17), Brooklyn Royal Giants ('18), Hilldale Daisies ('18), Pennsylvania Red Caps of New York ('18), New York Lincoln Giants ('21)
Born: 1899

Breaking in as a seventeeen-year-old pitcher with the Bacharach Giants in 1916, this young pitcher had good speed and a sharp-breaking curve. He stayed with the team for two years and demonstrated good stamina, seeming to thrive on hard work instead of tiring. He joined the Brooklyn Royal Giants in 1918, on a pitching staff that included Smoky Joe Williams, Cannonball Dick Redding, and John Donaldson. He also pitched with Hilldale and made his last appearance with the Lincoln Giants in 1921.

Johnson, Dick
Career: 1931   Position: player
Team: Baltimore Black Sox

He appeared briefly with the Baltimore Black Sox in 1931, but his position is not known.

Johnson, Ernest (Schoolboy)
Career: 1949–50   Positions: p, of
Teams: Kansas City Monarchs ('49–'53), *Canadian League ('54), minor leagues ('55–'59)*
Bats: Left   Throws: Right

Height: 6'3"   Weight: 180
Born: 1931

With the Kansas City Monarchs in 1949, he was only a mediocre pitcher with average control. His possessed a three-pitch repertory, consisting of an average fastball and curve and a fair change-up. As a batter he was a free-swinger with some extra-base power, and in 1950 he was used in the outfield. He continued with the Monarchs through 1953, although the Negro American League was no longer of major-league caliber, and when he went into organized baseball, it was as an outfielder.

With the Thetford Mines in the Provincial League in 1954 he hit .288. The next year he split the season between two leagues and turned in a consistent batting performance, hitting .292 with Magic Valley in the Pioneer League and .291 with Macon in the Sally League. In three seasons in the Western League (with Des Moines the first two years and Sioux City the latter year), he hit .320, .300, and .308. He finished his career by hitting .265 with Charleston in the Sally League in 1959.

Johnson, Frank
Career: 1932–37   Positions: of, manager
Teams: Monroe Monarchs ('32), Memphis Red Sox ('37)

In 1932, when the Negro Southern League was considered a major league, he played in the outfield with the Monroe Monarchs. Later in the '30s he served as a manager.

Johnson, G. Claude (**Hooks**)
Career: 1921–30   Positions: **2b**, 3b, ss, p, of, 1b, manager
Teams: Baltimore Black Sox, Cleveland Tate Stars ('22–'23), Harrisburg Giants ('23–'24), Detroit Stars ('27–'29), Birmingham Black Barons ('29–'30), Memphis Red Sox ('30)

In 1922 he was the regular second baseman with the Cleveland Tate Stars, batted third in the order, and was appointed playing manager the next season. After leaving Cleveland he hit .211 as a reserve second baseman with Harris-

burg in 1924. With Bingo DeMoss's Detroit Stars in 1927, he played second base and sometimes third base while batting second in the order. Three years later he hit .257 for the 1930 season while playing third base for the Birmingham Black Barons.

Johnson, George (**Chappie,** *Rat*)
Career: 1896–1919   Positions: **c, 1b**,
                                            manager
Teams: Page Fence Giants ('96–'98), Chicago Columbia Giants ('99–'00), Chicago Union Giants ('01–'02), Cuban X-Giants ('03), Algona, Iowa, Brownies ('03–'04), Philadelphia Giants ('04, '06), *Renville, Minnesota ('05)*, St. Paul Gophers ('07–'09), Leland Giants ('09), Chicago Giants ('10), St. Louis Giants ('11–'12), Brooklyn Royal Giants ('12), Mohawk Giants ('13–'14), *Dayton Chappies ('17), Custer's Baseball Club of Columbus,* Atlantic City Bacharach Giants ('19), *Philadelphia Royal Stars, Norfolk Stars ('19–'21), Pennsylvania Red Caps of New York, Chappie Johnson's Stars ('25–'27)*
Bats: Right   Throws: Right
Height: 5'9"   Weight: 160
Born: 1876, Bellaire, O.
Died: Aug. 17, 1949, Clemson, S. C.

A skilled handler of pitchers, Chappie Johnson was one of the best catchers in black baseball during the first two decades of the century. A smooth receiver, he was a member of the well-known Leland Giants' team of 1909 and the Mohawk Giants of 1914. During his twenty-three-year career he also played first base and was an outstanding manager in his latter years.

As a youngster Johnson attended elementary and high school in Bellaire, Ohio, and also learned his diamond skills then. In 1896, at age twenty, he signed to play with the Page Fence Giants, and during his first two seasons played left field and first base, respectively, before being offered the catching position for his third season. In 1899 the Page Frence Giants' franchise was facing dissolution, and a new team, the Columbia Giants, was organizing in Chicago. Johnson joined Charlie Grant and Home Run Johnson on the team and was the starting first baseman and alternate receiver for the next two seasons as the team immediately became a midwestern power. As Johnson assumed more of the catching responsibilities, he and Lefty Wilson, one of the top black pitchers of the era, were regarded as one of the greatest batteries in baseball.

In 1901 the Columbia Giants consolidated with the Union Giants to form the Chicago Union Giants. After the 1902 season he left the Union Giants and became associated with the Algona, Iowa, Brownies, who gained immediate fame in 1903 and 1904. Johnson left Algona during the latter season to join the Philadelphia Giants, batting .352 in the championship playoffs against the Cuban X-Giants. In 1905 he again paired with Wilson when they joined the Renville, Minnesota, team, where they formed a famous black battery that gave Renville the state championship.

The next season, Johnson traveled back East to catch for the Philadelphia Giants, whose star pitcher was Rube Foster. During the winter he traveled to Cuba to play with the Fe ballclub and was credited with being the reason for the team doing so well, as he led the team in fielding and was described as a "heady" player. This recognition of his baseball acumen led to his return to the Midwest to take charge of the St. Paul Colored Gophers in 1907.

His ability to work with young players led to a well-deserved reputation as a teacher and a coach that crossed racial boundaries. While at his new post, Johnson was also engaged by the management of the white St. Paul team of the American Association to take the team to Little Rock, Arkansas, for spring training, and he was in charge of them until the season opened. He remained in this capacity through 1912. This was not a new experience for Johnson, who had been in demand as a trainer and coach during the spring training months for several years, and he had worked in this capacity under some of the leading managers of the era, including his service as the head trainer

for the National League's Boston team during spring training in 1906 at Palm Beach, Florida.

After leading the St. Paul Gophers to victory over the Leland Giants in a series to determine the western championship, he was signed by owner Frank Leland for his team. During the ensuing winter (1909–10) he played first base with the Leland Giants in the Florida Hotel League in Palm Beach, and entertained the crowd with his "humorous catching." Off the field he displayed a jovial, pleasant personality, wore tailored suits, and was regarded as one of the "swellest" dressers. After returning North for the 1910 season, owner Leland and manager Rube Foster went their separate ways, each with their own team, and Johnson cast his lot with Leland's Chicago Giants. Still an innovative defensive player, he was the only player in the league to wear shinguards that season. But he was a light hitter, usually batting in the lower part of the order, and managed only a .186 average for the season.

In 1911 he signed with the St. Louis Giants, where he caught the Taylor brothers, Ben (who later became a great first baseman but was still pitching at that time) and "Steel Arm" Johnny. Although increasing his reputation as a skillful handler of pitchers, he was still hitting at the bottom of the batting order. The next year, still in St. Louis, he was catching Dizzy Dismukes before leaving during the season to join the Brooklyn Royal Giants, where he caught Frank Wickware, a premier pitcher of the era.

As the years passed and his playing skills faded, he began leaning more toward managing. In 1917 he was co-owner and manager of the Dayton Chappies. Johnson was quiet, calm, and dignified, and always showed class and maintained a gentlemanly demeanor, even in his protests with umpires. He insisted on being addressed as "Mr. Johnson." Off the field he was a sharp, stylish dresser who wore spats, carried a walking cane, and had a valet who carried his bags to the ballpark.

Most of his later years were spent with lesser teams, but incomplete statistics for the 1919 season show a .214 batting average with the Bacharachs. Although his active career as a player ended in 1921, when he was a playing manager with the Norfolk Stars, he continued as a manager through the 1939 season. While with Norfolk, he developed Nip Winters and Scrip Lee, and in later years at Saratoga he polished Dick Seay and Ted Page.

Johnson, George Washington (Dibo)
Career: 1912–31   Positions: **cf, rf,** lf
Teams: *Fort Worth Wonders ('09),* Kansas City, Kansas, Giants ('12), Brooklyn Royal Giants ('18–'19), **Hilldale Daisies** ('18–'25, '27), New York Lincoln Giants ('26–'27), Philadelphia Tigers ('28), Atlantic City Bacharach Giants ('31)
Bats: Right   Throws: Right
Born: 1890, San Marcos, Tex.
Died: Aug. 13, 1940, Philadelphia, Pa.

A complete ballplayer, this fast outfielder demonstrated a strong throwing arm, good base-running ability, and power at the plate. Playing with Hilldale in 1921 he hit .336, with 16 home runs and a .607 slugging percentage, and in 1922 the right-handed slugger hit 31 home runs to go with a .384 batting average. He followed this effort with a .376 batting average and 50 stolen bases in 1923 as the team won their first of three consecutive Eastern Colored League pennants. The next two seasons he hit .283 and .327 as Hilldale added two more flags, and opposed the Kansas City Monarchs in the first two World Series between the Eastern Colored League and the Negro National League. Hilldale lost the first Series in 1924. But their last flag season culminated in a World Series victory over the Monarchs in 1925 as Johnson contributed a solid .286 batting average.

The Texan began his career as a pitcher with southern ballclubs and a served a "stiff apprenticeship" with those clubs, including the Fort Worth Wonders. He was a "much sought-after player" and joined Hilldale in 1918. Misfortune struck in midsummer when he broke his left leg sliding into third base. The following season he had recovered from the injury and moved into the cleanup slot, batting .337 and providing power in the heart of the Hilldale lineup through the 1925 season. During the eight years that he played with the club, he was one of the most popular players on the team. After leaving the Darby clan, he played with the New York Lincoln Giants and the Philadelphia Tigers, where he patroled center field in 1928.

After retiring from baseball he made his home in Philadelphia, rooming with former teammate and ex-spitball pitcher Phil Cockrell. When Johnson died in 1940, Cockrell was a pallbearer at his funeral, and his former teammates conducted a fund raiser to erect a bronze memorial tablet over his grave.

Johnson, Grant (**Home Run**)
Career: 1895–1916   Positions: **ss,** 2b, p, manager
Teams: *minor leagues ('94),* **Page Fence Giants** ('95–'98), Chicago Columbia Giants ('99), Chicago Unions ('00), Cuban X-Giants ('03–'04), Philadelphia Giants ('05–'06), **Brooklyn Royal Giants** ('06–'09, '12), Leland Giants ('10), Chicago Giants ('11), **New York Lincoln Giants** ('11–'13), Mohawk Giants ('13), New York Lincoln Stars ('16), *Pittsburgh Colored Stars of Buffalo ('16–'17, '19–'21), Buffalo Giants ('23)*
Bats: Right   Throws: Right
Height: 5'10"   Weight: 170
Born: 1874, Findlay, O.
Died: 1964, Buffalo, N.Y.

In a career that started before the turn of the century, Johnson was a right-handed slugger in the deadball era. The most famous shortstop before John Henry Lloyd came on the scene, he starred with some of the most outstanding clubs of the era, including the 1903 Cuban X-Giants, the 1905 Philadelphia Giants, and the 1909 Brooklyn Royal Giants before joining Lloyd on Rube Foster's Leland Giants in 1910. After leaving Foster's team he again joined Lloyd on the Lincoln Giants in 1913. Although shortstop was his best position, in deference to

Lloyd's outstanding ability, Johnson used his versatility to shift across to the keystone sack. He formed a superior middle infield combination with the legendary Lloyd when they played together.

He attended Public School 9 in his hometown of Findlay, Ohio, and is credited by one source as being a college man. Regardless of his educational status, at age twenty, he began playing shortstop for the strong semipro Findlay Sluggers in 1894. That season he is credited with 60 home runs and, according to one source, earned his nickname "Home Run" at that time. Later in the season he was reportedly playing professional baseball with Dubuque, Iowa, for a short stint.

In 1895 he and Bud Fowler formed the Page Fence Giants in Adrian, Michigan, and Johnson was the captain and shortstop. He batted .471 as the team ended a successful season with a 118–36 record for a .766 winning percentage. After the 1898 season the Page Fence Giants were not able to continue financially, so Johnson took most of the players with him to Chicago, and they played as the Chicago Columbia Giants in 1899. After a season as their regular shortstop, he played a year with the Chicago Unions before moving East to play after the turn of the century.

He joined the Cuban X-Giants, who were the eastern champions in 1903 but lost to the Philadelphia Giants in a playoff the following season. In 1905 he joined the Philadelphia Giants, and they won championships for the next two seasons.

He was captain of the Brooklyn Royal Giants for several years and helped guide them to a championship in 1909. But the next season he left the team in April when owner John W. Connor refused to give him an interest in the team. Subsequently a rift developed between the two men and Connor accused Johnson of attempting to influence other players to leave the Royals and go with him to the Leland Giants. Johnson did sign with Rube Foster's Lelands but did not take any other players with him.

By the beginning of the second decade of the century, he was an established veteran, and according to the press he was "a high-class ballplayer and not showing his age." At this stage in his career he was called "Dad" by other players, was a favorite with the crowds, and "his witty sayings, good playing, and good conduct won him many friends."

The star infielder was also a winner in Cuba, captaining the Havana Reds to a winter league championship, and became the first American to win a batting title on the island. During his five years there he averaged .319, with his best effort being a .424 average. Johnson hit .309 for the 1908–09 winter season but gained his greatest notoriety when he hit .412 in exhibition games there in 1910 against the Detroit Tigers, outhitting Ty Cobb and Sam Crawford. Altogether, in 19 exhibition games against major leaguers his average was .293.

Johnson was a natural hitter, and his confidence, patient pitch selection, and superior batting eye enabled him to hit all kinds of pitching. A smart batter, he was cool under pressure, and after hitting .397 while batting in the third slot for the 1910 Lelands, he recorded batting averages in New York of .374, .413, and .371 in 1911–13, playing against all levels of competition. In the latter season he batted cleanup behind John Henry Lloyd as the Lincoln Giants won the eastern title and outclassed Rube Foster's Chicago American Giants in the 1913 championship playoff, Owner Jess McMahon proudly proclaimed that the Lincolns could beat any major-league team. A line-drive hitter, Johnson placed an emphasis on making contact rather than swinging for the fences and, playing in the deadball era, his power was comparable to that of the Athletics' Frank Baker. And like Baker, his home runs, while not numerous, came at opportune times and reinforced the sobriquet "Home Run" for the duration of his playing career.

During the latter years of the deadball era, he played with the Pittsburgh Colored Stars of Buffalo, and managd the Buffalo Giants in 1923. He was a good instructor for young ballplayers, sharing valuable advice with the prospects under his management. In addition to hitting, he also liked to sing and had a good baritone voice. The sturdy, raw-boned infielder refrained from vices, maintained good physical condition, and continued playing with lesser teams until finally retiring in 1932 at age fifty-eight. After leaving the baseball diamond he remained in Buffalo and worked with the New York Central Railroad Company. Late in life he lost his eyesight and passed away at age ninety.

Johnson, H. (Hamp)
Career: 1933–34, 1946 Position: of
Team: Birmingham Black Barons

He began his career in 1933–34 as an outfielder with Birmingham Black Barons, and returned to the diamond for the Black Barons in 1946.

Johnson, Harry
Career: 1886–89   Positions: **2b**, c, of
Teams: Cuban Giants ('86–'89)
Born: May 1, 1860, Burlington, Vt.

He was a utility player when he began his professional career with the Cuban Giants, the first professional black ballclub. During the four years he was with the club, he played second base, catcher, and in the outfield. He was with the club for two seasons when they represented Trenton, New Jersey, in the Middle States League (1887 and 1889). Prior to joining the Cuban Giants he played second base for the Post Office ballclub and for the Department League of Washington, D.C., in 1883.

Johnson, J.
Career: 1916   Positions: 3b, of
Team: *Baltimore Black Sox*

He played with the Baltimore Black Sox in 1916, when they were in their formative years and had not yet attained a major-league level of play. He played both third base and in the outfield, and usually batted in the lower part of the order.

Johnson, J. (Lefty)
Career: 1929–33   Positions: p, 1b, of
Team: Memphis Red Sox
Bats: Left   Throws: Left

This Memphis Red Sox player began his career in 1929 as a left-handed pitcher, losing his only decision his first year before posting a 1–4 record in 1930. But as the years passed, he played more as a first baseman.

Johnson, Jack
Career: 1903–04   Position: 1b
Team: Philadelphia Giants
Born: 1878, Galveston, Tex.
Died: 1946

The famous heavyweight boxing champion played first base for the Philadelphia Giants in 1903–04, when he held the Negro heavyweight title. With the Giants he was a teammate of Rube Foster, and the two great athletes remained fast friends throughout their lives. In July 1912, shortly after he retained his heavyweight title with a KO over Jim Flynn in Las Vegas, New Mexico, he made application for the first-base position on the Chicago American Giants. Foster agreed to give him a chance and asked him to report for morning practice for a couple of weeks to rekindle his batting skills. Johnson was confident that he could come back, but there is no record to indicate that he ever made the attempt.

He earned fame in the world of boxing as the first black heavyweight champion. He defeated Tommy Burns for the championship in 1908 and held the title until being knocked out by Jess Willard in a controversial bout in 1915. During his reign as champion he was often at odds with society and the law. He began his boxing career in 1899 and continued his pugilistic pursuits until 1926. After retiring from the ring he operated a nightclub and remained in the limelight until his death in 1946.

Johnson, Jack
Career: 1938–39   Position: 3b
Teams: Homestead Grays ('38–'39), Toledo Crawfords ('39), *Cincinnati Buckeyes ('40)*

Bats: Right   Throws: Right
Height: 6'0"   Weight: 190

He was a local Pittsburgh boy who was picked up by the Homestead Grays to play third base in 1938. Although he got off to a good start, hitting .381 at the end of the first half, he faded fast and was released before the end of the season, when the Grays signed Henry Spearman to play third base. Johnson also played with the Toledo Crawfords in 1939 and with the Cincinnati Buckeyes, who were still two years away from major-league status, in 1940.

Johnson, Jack (Topeka Jack)
Career: 1909–10   Positions: ss, of
                                         manager
Teams: Kansas City, Missouri, Royal Giants ('09–'10), Kansas City, Giants ('10)

He was a shortstop, outfielder, and manager for the 1910 Kansas City Royal Giants. Because he was a boxer and had the same name as the heavyweight champion of that era, unconfirmed oral sources maintain that it was the heavyweight champion who played with the 1909 Kansas City Royal Giants.

Johnson, James
Career: 1898   Positions: of, c
Team: Page Fence Giants

He was an outfielder-catcher with the Page Fence Giants of Adrian, Michigan, one of the top black teams before the turn of the century.

Johnson, James
Career: 1922   Position: ss
Team: Baltimore Black Sox

He was a reserve shortstop with the Baltimore Black Sox in 1922, when they were still playing as an independent team.

Johnson, James (J. D.)
Career: 1950   Position: p
Teams: Philadelphia Stars ('50), *Birmingham Black Barons ('52), Kanas City Monarchs ('52)*

He was a pitcher with the 1950 Philadelphia

Stars during the time when the Negro Leagues were struggling to survive the loss of players to organized baseball. He continued to pitch on into the early '50s, when the Negro American League was strictly a minor league.

Johnson, Jim (Jimmy)
Career: 1932–34   Positions: **ss**, 3b, of
Teams: Hilldale Daisies ('32), Atlantic City Bacharach Giants ('33), Newark Dodgers ('33)

His three years in black baseball were spent with three teams, including the two teams that once had dominated the Eastern Colored League but were now in decline and on the verge of collapse. Hilldale, in 1932, was in their last year of existence, and the Bacharachs, in 1933, were of dubious quality and only a year away from their last attempt at being a major-league team. He was the regular shortstop and batted third in the order with Hilldale, and when the franchise folded he joined the Bacharachs as their shortstop, batting in the second or third slot in the lineup.

Johnson, Jimmy (**Jeep**)
Career: 1947   Position: ss
Team: *Pittsburgh Crawfords ('46),* Homestead Grays ('47)

This infielder played briefly at shortstop with the Homestead Grays in 1947 after playing with the U.S. League Pittsburgh Crawfords the previous year.

Johnson, Jimmy (Slim)
Career: 1939–43   Positions: **p**, 1b
Teams: Toledo Crawfords ('39), Indianapolis Crawfords ('40), Philadelphia Stars ('43)

He pitched with the Crawfords in 1939–40, and, after the franchise faltered, with the Philadelphia Stars.

Johnson, John
Career: 1950   Positions: ss, 3b, 2b
Team: New York Cubans

He was listed as a utility player with the 1950 New York Cubans, but league statistics do not confirm his playing time.

Johnson, John (Johnny)
Career: 1938–46   Position: p
Teams: New York Black Yankees ('38, '45–'46), Newark Eagles ('38), Baltimore Elite Giants ('39), Birmingham Black Barons ('41–'42), Homestead Grays ('44)

He served short stints with several teams in the Negro National League, primarily the New York Black Yankees, but without notable success. In 1945–46 with the Black Yankees he posted unimpressive marks of 1–3 and 0–7.

Johnson, John H., Rev.
Career: 1947–48   Position: officer
League: NNL

A minister with limited baseball acumen, he was selected to serve as president of the Negro National League for the last two years of its existence, 1947–48.

Johnson, John Wesley (Smokey)
Career: 1922–28   Position: p
Teams: Cleveland Tate Stars ('22), Cleveland Browns ('24), New York Lincoln Giants ('25), Cleveland Elites ('26–'28)

During the '20s he was a pitcher with the Negro National League's assorted Cleveland teams, posting a 2–8 record in 1926 with the Elites.

Johnson, Johnny
Career: 1943   Positions: p, *of*
Team: Cleveland Buckeyes

He was a wartime pitcher, winning his only recorded decision with the Cleveland Buckeyes in 1943, his only season in the Negro American League.

Johnson, Johnny (Pee Wee)
Career: 1939   Position: 2b
Team: Newark Eagles
Bats: Right   Throws: Right
Height: 5'7"   Weight: 155

Biz Mackey brought the little second baseman from California in 1939 to play with the Newark Eagles, but although his speed was sufficient, his hitting was weak and his fielding

not adequate to play at that level of ball. Consequently his playing time was restricted and his stay with the team was short.

Johnson, Joseph
Career: 1937   Position: officer
Team: Indianapolis Athletics

He was an officer with the Indianapolis Athletics in 1937, when they participated in the Negro American League's inaugural season and then disbanded.

Johnson, Joshua (Josh, Brute)
Career: 1934–42   Positions: c, of, *p*
Teams: Homestead Grays ('34–'35, '38–'42), New York Black Yankees ('38, '42), Cincinnati Tigers ('35–'37), Brooklyn Royal Giants ('39), *military service ('42–'45)*
Bats: Right   Throws: Right
Height: 6'1"   Weight: 195
Born: Jan. 24, 1913, Evergreen, Ala.

A catcher with a strong arm, but limited mobility behind the plate, he spent a portion of his career with the Homestead Grays in the shadow of Josh Gibson. In 1940, however, Gibson opted to play in Mexico, allowing Johnson a bigger share of the playing time as catcher. He responded with a .429 batting average in league games as a part-time starter. A long-ball hitter, the big, strong, right-handed batter was a former Cheyney College football star, and first played with the Grays in 1934, after three seasons with good semipro teams, the Coraopolis Greys (1931–32) and the Pittsburgh Giants (1933).

Following his first stint with the Grays, he rejoined the Giants for the first part of 1935, but left in about midseason to play briefly with the New Kensington Elks preparatory to joining the Cincinnati Tigers, a strong independent professional team. He hit a respectable .287 in 1936, and the following season the club entered the Negro American League under the managership of "Double Duty" Radcliffe. For the next five seasons Johnson shuttled between the Grays and two teams based in New York

THE NEGRO BASEBALL LEAGUES

City, the Black Yankees and the Brooklyn Royal Giants.

In 1942 he was playing ball and working in the Philadelphia Naval Yard when he was drafted into the Army. After getting his commission as a second lieutenant, he spent the next four years assigned to an antiaircraft unit and as a truck commander in the Red Ball Express. Later he advanced to the rank of major in the Army Reserve but never again played in the black major leagues. However, his involvement with baseball never ended, as he managed the St. Louis Metro All-Stars for five years (1949–54), and, having earned his B.S. and M.Ed. degrees by attending college in the off-season, he entered education as a teacher and coach. Eventually he became an administrator, attaining the level of assistant state superintendent of education.

Johnson, Judy
[see Johnson, William Julius (Judy)]

Johnson, Junior
Career: 1899–1906   Positions: 1b, c
Teams: Columbia Giants ('99–'00), Philadelphia Giants, ('02–'06), Quaker Giants, Brooklyn Royal Giants

A combination first baseman-catcher, he played primarily with eastern teams during the early years of the twentieth century.

Johnson, L.
Career: 1948   Position: p
Team: Kansas City Monarchs
Bats: Right   Throws: Right
Height: 5'11"   Weight: 170

This right-hander's fastball was lacking somewhat, and his control and off-speed and breaking pitches were only average, but he mixed his pitches and changed speeds to achieve a measure of effectiveness, posting a 1–2 record with the Kansas City Monarchs in 1948.

Johnson, Leaman
Career: 1941–45   Position: ss

Teams: Newark Eagles ('41), Birmingham Black Barons ('43), Memphis Red Sox ('45)

This light-hitting infielder played shortstop for the Newark Eagles in 1941, batting only .214, and finished his career in the Negro American League with southern teams, including the Negro American League pennant-winning Birmingham Black Barons in 1943. In his last season in the Negro Leagues he hit .181 as a reserve shortstop with the Memphis Red Sox.

Johnson, Lee
Career: 1941   Position: c
Team: Birmingham Black Barons

He appeared briefly as a reserve catcher in 1941 with the Birmingham Black Barons.

Johnson, Lefty
[see Johnson, J. (Lefty)]

Johnson, Leonard
Career: 1947–48   Position: p
Team: Chicago American Giants

He was a pitcher with the Chicago American Giants in 1947–48, winning his only recorded decision the latter year.

Johnson, Leroy
Career: 1950   Position: p
Team: Birmingham Black Barons ('50–'51)

He broke in with the Birmingham Black Barons in 1950, when the Negro American League was struggling to survive the loss of players to organized baseball, but league statistics do not confirm his playing time.

Johnson, Louis (Dicta)
Career: 1911–25   Position: p, manager, coach
Teams: *Twin City Gophers (11)*, Chicago American Giants ('12–'14, '23), Indianapolis ABCs ('15–'22), Bowser's ABCs ('16), Detroit Stars ('20), Pittsburgh Keystones ('22), Toledo Tigers ('23), Milwaukee Bears ('23)
Bats: Right   Throws: Right

This spitballer pitched a no-hit game for

Rube Foster's Chicago American Giants in 1913 but joined the Indianapolis ABCs in 1915, registering a 20–4 record as the ABCs challenged the American Giants for the western title. The next year, owner Thomas Bowser and manager C. I. Taylor went separate ways, with each fielding an ABCs team. Johnson went with Bowser's ABCs at the beginning of the season, but by July, was back with C. I. Taylor's team, where he posted a 15–10 ledger. After the internal management problems, the Indianapolis ABCs regrouped and defeated Foster's American Giants to claim the 1916 western championship.

He continued with the ABCs into the lively ball era, posting a 13–10 record in 1921 before leaving the team during the 1922 season. After short stints with two shaky franchises, the Toledo Tigers and the Milwaukee Bears, he was signed again by Foster in 1923. During his career Johnson also worked as a coach and manager.

Johnson, M.
Career: 1920   Position: lf
Team: New York Lincoln Giants

In 1920 he played left field with the New York Lincoln Giants and was a dependable hitter.

Johnson, Mamie (Peanut)
Career: 1954   Positions: p, ut
Team: *Indianapolis Clowns*
Bats: Right   Throws: Right
Height: 5'4"   Weight: 120
Born: Sept. 27, 1932, Long Branch, N.J.

Another of the Indianapolis Clowns' female players, she was used as a pitcher and utility player. Nicknamed "Peanut" because of her size, the little right-hander threw as hard as many male pitchers. She attended Long Branch High School, where she played boys' sports, including football. She also attended New York University, where she studied medicine and engineering, before signing with the Clowns at age twenty-two.

Johnson, Monk
[see Johnson, B.]

Johnson, Nat
a.k.a. Nate
Career: 1922–24   Position: p
Teams: Atlantic City Bacharach Giants ('22–'23), Brooklyn Royal Giants ('23), Harrisburg Giants ('23), Cleveland Browns ('24)

After beginning his career with the Bacharachs in 1922, he pitched with four different teams during a three-year career in the Eastern Colored League, ending his career with the struggling Cleveland Browns in 1924.

Johnson, O.
Career: 1919   Position: p
Team: Atlantic City Bacharach Giants

He was a pitcher with the Bacharach Giants in 1919, while they were still developing into a top ballclub.

Johnson, Oscar (Heavy)
Career: 1922–33   Positions: of, c, 2b
Teams: Kansas City Monarchs ('22–'24), Baltimore Black Sox ('25–'26), Harrisburg Giants ('27), Cleveland Tigers ('28), Memphis Red Sox ('28–'33)
Bats: Right   Throws: Right
Height: 6'0"   Weight: 250
Born: 1896, Atchison, Kan.
Died: 1966, Cleveland, O.

A heavy player with an equally heavy bat, he was one of the league's power hitters during the '20s. The big slugger was fat, carrying 250 pounds on his frame, which he used to good advantage in generating power at the plate. Jocko Conlon, who barnstormed against Johnson, said that he could hit a ball out of any park. He played with the 25th Infantry baseball team as a catcher, but moved to the outfield when he, Bullet Rogan, and Dobie Moore signed with the Kansas City Monarchs.

Breaking in with the Monarchs in 1922, the youngster posted a .389 batting average, and continued his offensive production for Santa Clara in the Cuban winter league with a .345 average. He was back in the United States for the 1923 season, and his heavy hitting helped the Monarchs to the Negro National League pennant as he had his best season with a .380 average and 18 home runs in 46 games. In 1924 he was credited with more than 60 home runs against all opposition, and he hit .411 in league play to help the Monarchs capture another pennant. In the subsequent showdown with Eastern Colored League champion Hilldale in the first World Series, he contributed a .296 average to the Monarchs' victory.

Johnson was an unpolished fielder and not noted for performance afield. However, in the 1924 World Series he turned in a defensive gem when he snared Hilldale's George Johnson's long drive at the wall, robbing him of an extra-base hit, and then whirled and pegged the ball to the plate to double up base runner George Carr, who had tagged at third base and was trying to score.

The next season he made the jump east to the Baltimore Black Sox, hitting .345 and .337 for his two seasons with them, batting fifth in the order behind Jud Wilson and John Beckwith. In 1927 he signed with Harrisburg, where he hit .316 while teaming with Beckwith and Oscar Charleston to provide the offensive power for the Eastern Colored League team. In 1928 he was back in the Negro National League, splitting the season between the Cleveland Tigers and the Memphis Red Sox. With each team he hit in the heart of the batting order when in the lineup and finished with a combined .315 average.

The burly outfielder's bat was what kept him in the lineup, and he could hit under any circumstances, once blasting a pinch-hit home run with a fungo bat after being rousted from his sleep on the bench. The slugger closed out his career in 1933, after twelve years in the Negro Leagues, compiling a lifetime .337 batting average.

Johnson, Othello
Career: 1916–22   Positions: **of**, c, *1b*
Teams: Philadelphia Giants *('16)*, Brooklyn Royal Giants ('16), Atlantic City Bacharach Giants ('19), New York Lincoln Giants ('20–'22)

A reserve right fielder with the Brooklyn Royal Giants in 1916, he later played with the Bacharach Giants and the New York Lincoln Giants.

Johnson, P.
Career: 1933   Position: p
Team: Memphis Red Sox
He pitched with the Memphis Red Sox in 1933, a year after the Negro Southern League's only season as a recognized major league.

Johnson, Peter (Perly, Pearley, Tubby)
Career: 1920–27   Positions: of, 2b, ss, p
Team: Baltimore Black Sox
He was an all-purpose player with the Baltimore Black Sox during the '20s. In 1926 he was a utility player, appearing as a middle infielder and outfielder. In 1927 he was the starting right fielder and hit .254 as the leadoff batter. Earlier in his career he had also appeared as a pitcher.

Johnson, R.
Career: 1932   Position: of
Team: Washington Pilots
He was an outfielder with the 1932 Washington Pilots in his only year in black baseball.

Johnson, Ralph
Career: 1940–45   Positions: p, lf
Team: Philadelphia Stars
He was a pitcher with the Philadelphia Stars in the years before World War II, losing his only recorded decision in 1940. He also played in left field for the Stars in 1941 but did not hit adequately, posting a meager .167 batting average, and did not field the position very well, committing several errors during his temporary assignment at that position. He made a final appearance during the 1945 season.

Johnson, Ralph
Career: 1950   Positions: ss, 3b, of
Teams: Birmingham Black Barons ('50), Indianapolis Clowns ('50–'52), *Kansas City Monarchs ('52–'54)*

441

Bats: Right   Throws: Right
Born: 1924, Lakeland, Fla.

The beginning of this infielder's career coincided with the years when the Negro American League was struggling to survive the loss of players to organized baseball. He was primarily a shortstop, and most of his career in the Negro Leagues was after they were no longer of major-league quality. He also played third base and in the outfield. He began playing semipro baseball for the Lakeland Tigers at age eighteen, and also played with semipro clubs in Tampa, Miami, and Santo Domingo prior to joining the Birmingham Black Barons in 1950, where he played with Willie Mays.

After leaving Birmingham, he played with the Indianapolis Clowns in the early '50s, when they were no longer of major-league quality but featured Hank Aaron and female second baseman Toni Stone. He also played with the New Orleans Creoles and the Kansas City Monarchs, where he hit .296 in 1954, his last season in the Negro American League. Afterward he returned to Florida, played semipro ball, and drove a truck. After retiring in 1983, he moved to Atlanta and managed a poolroom.

Johnson, Rat
[see Johnson, George (Chappie)]

Johnson, Ray
Career: 1923   Position: of
Team: St. Louis Stars

He was a reserve outfielder with the St. Louis Stars in 1923, in his only year in the Negro Leagues.

Johnson, Robert
Career: 1944   Position: p
Team: Kansas City Monarchs

A wartime player, he was a pitcher with the Kansas City Monarchs in 1944.

Johnson, Robert
Career: 1939–40   Position: of
Team: New York Black Yankees

He was a reserve outfielder with the New York Black Yankees for two seasons, 1939–40.

Johnson, Robert (Bob)
Career: 1928   Position: 3b
Teams: Philadelphia Tigers *Brooklyn Cuban Giants*

This infielder was a third baseman with the Philadelphia Tigers in 1928, their only year in league play, and also played part of that year with the Brooklyn Cuban Giants, a team of lesser status.

Johnson, Roy (Bubbles)
Career: 1920–22   Positions: 1b, 2b
Teams: St. Louis Giants ('20), Kansas City Monarchs ('20–'22)

A marginal player during the early '20s, he appeared briefly as a first baseman with the St. Louis Giants before joining the Kansas City Monarchs as a reserve second baseman.

Johnson, Rudolph (Rudy)
Career: 1950   Position: of
Team: Buckeyes

He was listed as an outfielder with the Buckeyes in 1950, when the Negro American League was struggling to survive the loss of players to organized baseball, but league statistics do not confirm his playing time.

Johnson, S.
Career: 1922–26   Positions: 3b, ss
Teams: *Philadelphia Royal Stars ('22)*, Baltimore Black Sox ('22), Harrisburg Giants ('26)

This infielder played third base with the 1922 Baltimore Black Sox and shortstop with the 1926 Harrisburg Giants. He also played with lesser teams, including the Philadelphia Royal Stars.

Johnson, Thomas (Tom, Tommy, Schoolboy)
Career: 1914–25   Positions: p, umpire
Teams: Mohawk Giants ('14), Indianapolis ABCs ('14–'15), **Chicago American Giants** ('15–'21, '23), *military service ('18–'19)*, Pittsburgh Keystones ('22)
Bats: Right   Throws: Right

This right hander was a smart pitcher with good control and began his career in 1914. In 1915, his second season with the team, he had a 3–4 record for the Indianapolis ABCs before joining Rube Foster's Chicago American Giants. He gained his most acclaim with Foster's club during the years immediately preceding World War I. Although Dick Redding was showcased by the American Giants in the first game of the 1917 season, Johnson entered the season as the ace of the staff and was credited with a 15–1 record as the American Giants fielded one of the best teams in the franchise's history.

Having attended Morris Brown College, he was called "Schoolboy" while playing with the American Giants that season. In 1918, at the peak of his pitching career, he was drafted into the Army for service in World War I and served in France as an officer in the 365th Infantry. In May 1918, before shipping overseas, he pitched for the Camp Grant baseball team. After his discharge, Lieutenant Tom Johnson rejoined the American Giants during the 1919 season, splitting half a dozen decisions.

In 1921 he had a 7–7 record as the American Giants annexed the Negro National League pennant. However, he spent most of the 1922 season in the hospital and was never able to recapture the form he had prior to the war. After ending his playing career he became an umpire in the Negro National League.

Johnson, Tom (**Tommy**)
Career: 1937–42   Position: p
Teams: St. Louis Stars ('37), Chicago American Giants ('38–'42)

A pitcher during the first six seasons of the Negro American League after it was founded, he began with the St. Louis Stars in 1937 but pitched primarily with the Chicago American Giants, where he split a pair of decisions in 1940.

Johnson, Tommy F.
Career: 1950   Position: p
Team: Indianapolis Clowns

He was a pitcher with the Indianapolis Clowns in 1950, when the Negro American League was struggling to survive the loss of players to organized baseball, but league statistics do not confirm his playing time.

Johnson, U.
Career: 1905   Position: 3b
Team: Brooklyn Royal Giants

He was a third baseman with the Brooklyn Royal Giants in 1905, their first year of existence.

Johnson, W.
Career: 1944–45   Position: p
Team: Memphis Red Sox

A wartime pitcher with the Memphis Red Sox, he pitched infrequently during the last two seasons before the end of World War II.

Johnson, W.
Career: 1919   Positions: **lf**, 2b
Team: Brooklyn Royal Giants

In 1919 he was the regular left fielder and leadoff batter for the Brooklyn Royal Giants, with incomplete statistics showing a .255 batting average for the season.

Johnson, William H. (**Bill**, Wise, Big C)
Career: 1923–29   Positions: **c**, of, 1b, manager
Teams: Dayton Marcos ('20–'21), *Washington Braves ('21)*, Homestead Grays ('22–'23), *Philadelphia Giants ('24)*, Washington Potomacs ('24), Wilmington Potomacs ('25), Harrisburg Giants ('25–'26), *Pennsylvania Red Caps of New York ('27, 30–'35)*, Hilldale Daisies ('27–'28), Philadelphia Tigers ('28), Brooklyn Royal Giants ('28–'29)
Bats: Both   Throws: Right
Height: 6'0"   Weight: 185
Born: Nov. 21, 1895, Sparta, Ga.

After serving in the U.S. Army for four years (1915–19), during which he was stationed at Schofield Army Barracks in Hawaii, he bought his way out of the Army for $150 and began his baseball career with the Dayton

Marcos in 1920. The big receiver spent two years with Dayton and another pair of seasons with the Homestead Grays before joining Ben Taylor's Washington Potomacs as a backup catcher. After the Potomacs disbanded he signed with Harrisburg, where he was the starting catcher, batting sixth in the order, and also playing in right field when not behind the plate. After two seasons in Harrisburg he joined Hilldale to fill a vacancy created when Biz Mackey left the team to tour the Orient with an All-Star squad. With Hilldale in 1927 he hit .293 as a part-time starter while batting eighth in the lineup. Afterward he played with other Eastern Colored League teams, including the Philadelphia Tigers, where he hit in the heart of the order when in the lineup, and the Brooklyn Royal Giants, where he won a starting spot in the lineup and batted in the sixth slot in the order. He spent his last years in black baseball with lesser teams, ending with the Pennsylvania Red Caps of New York in 1935.

Johnson, William Julius (**Judy,** Jing)
Career: 1918–37 Positions: **3b**, ss, manager
Teams: Bacharach Giants ('18), *Madison Stars ('19–'21),* **Hilldale Daisies** ('21–'29, '31–'32), Homestead Grays ('30, '37), **Pittsburgh Crawfords** ('32–'36)
Bats: Right Throws: Right
Height: 5'11" Weight: 150
Born: Oct. 26, 1900, Snow Hill, Md.
Died: June 15, 1989, Wilmington, Del.

A cool, patient, sure-handed infielder with good range and a strong, accurate arm, he was an all-around great third baseman. Johnson was a good instinctive base runner, which offset his lack of outstanding speed. A right-handed line-drive hitter with an excellent batting eye, he hit for good average but not with exceptional power.

As a youngster he played football and baseball on the sandlots of Wilmington, Delaware, after his seaman father settled in the city and took a job as the athletic director of the Negro Settlement House. His father wanted him to become a pugilist and taught both him and his older sister the art of boxing, but Johnson preferred baseball. He attended school in his adopted hometown and, after completing one year at Howard High School, he terminated his formal education to take a job on the loading docks as a stevedore at Deep Water Point, New Jersey. In 1918 he joined the Bacharach Giants, having previously begun his semipro career with the Chester Stars of Chester, Pennsylvania. After the end of World War I he had a tryout with Hilldale and signed with the Madison Stars, a team that served as an unofficial farm team for Hilldale. After he had two years of seasoning, Hilldale, in need of an infielder, bought his contract back from the Stars for $100. In 1922 he signed his first contract for $135 per month; previously he had been playing for $5 a game.

As a rookie with Hilldale in 1921, he was moved to shortstop by manager Billy Francis, who played third base himself, but his range was a little limited for that position. Later switching to his natural position, he played with the great Hilldale clubs of the 1920s, posting batting averages of .391, .369, and .392 in 1923–25 to help them win pennants in the Eastern Colored League's first three years of existence. In the first World Series against the Kansas City Monarchs in 1924, he led the team with a .341 batting average in a losing cause. The following year, as Hilldale capped their third consecutive pennant with a World Series victory over the Monarchs, he recorded a .250 average and contributed crucial hits to the team effort. The next season Johnson moved into the cleanup spot in the batting order and hit .327 for the season. He continued as a key player with Hilldale for three more years, hitting .390 in 1929 while batting fifth.

He was always a smart baseball player, and after the 1929 season he left Hilldale for a season as playing manager of the Homestead Grays. Already an outstanding collection of talent, the team was transformed into the best team in black baseball by the end of the season, when Johnson inserted the youthful Josh Gibson into the lineup as the regular catcher.

After only one season in Homestead, he returned to Hilldale to take the managerial reins for his old ballclub for the last two years before the franchise's demise. During this period, the slick-fielding infielder played in the Cuban winter league and finished with a .334 batting average. In 1932 the slender third sacker left Hilldale again, joining the third superteam of his career as captain of Gus Greenlee's Pittsburgh Crawfords. Usually batting fifth, he continued his steady hitting with averages of .332, .333, .367, and .306. The Crawfords of 1935 are considered by most authorities to be the best black team of all time, while some argue that the team of 1936, Johnson's last season with the Crawfords, was even better.

In the spring of 1937 he and Josh Gibson were traded to the Homestead Grays for a small amount of cash and token players, but he retired shortly afterward and did not play substantially in the regular season. After leaving the baseball diamond he returned to Wilmington, worked as a supervisor for the Continental Can Company, and operated a general store with his brother. Later he scouted for the Philadelphia Athletics, Philadelphia Phillies, and Milwaukee Braves. One of the Braves' players, Bill Bruton, later became Johnson's son-in-law. Always a gentleman, when he retired in 1972 he had earned the respect of baseball players, executives, and fans.

The superb fielder's .309 lifetime batting average over a seventeen-year career in the Negro Leagues qualified him for induction into the National Baseball Hall of Fame in 1974. Fourteen years later, he died of a stroke at age eighty-eight.

Johnson, Willie
Career: 1945   Position: c
Team: Philadelphia Stars

A wartime player, he was a reserve catcher with the Philadelphia Stars in 1945.

Johnston
Career: 1911   Position: ss
Team: Chicago Giants

He was a shortstop with the Chicago Giants in 1911, his only season in black baseball.

Johnston, Bert (Bucky)
a.k.a. Johnson
Career: 1933–38   Position: of
Teams: Newark Dodgers ('34–'35), Baltimore Black Sox ('33), Birmingham Black Barons ('38), Newark Eagles ('38)
Bats: Right   Throws: Right

He began his career with the Baltimore Black Sox in 1933 and joined the Newark Dodgers the following season. A big, awkward fellow and only a mediocre player, he played right field for the Dodgers without distinction, and his tenure in the league was short.

Johnston, C.
Career: 1916   Positions: 2b, 3b
Team: New York Lincoln Stars

A reserve infielder, he played both second base and third base for a short time in 1916 with the New York Lincoln Stars.

Johnston, Tom
Career: 1923   Position: umpire
League: Negro National League

In 1923 he was an umpire in the Negro National League.

Johnston, Wade
a.k.a. Johnson
Career: 1920–33   Positions: lf, cf, rf, p
Teams: *Pennsylvania Red Caps of New York* *('20)*, Cleveland Tate Stars ('22), Kansas City Monarchs ('23–'27), Baltimore Black Sox ('24), Detroit Stars ('28–'31, '33)
Bats: Left   Throws: Left

A very underrated ballplayer, he was a complete player who began his career as a pitcher but excelled as an outfielder. He was very fast, a good base runner, a fine hitter, was adept at the drag bunt, had good range afield, and had a fair arm. Throughout his career he usually batted in the leadoff spot with each of his teams.

He joined the Kansas City Monarchs in

1923, when they won their first Negro National League pennant. The next season he began with the Monarchs but jumped East to play with the Baltimore Black Sox for most of the 1924 season, hitting .264 from the leadoff spot. The next year he was back with the Monarchs, beginning three years as the leadoff batter, with averages of .313, .288, and .322. In 1925, the Monarchs won their third straight pennant and faced Hilldale in the World Series. In 1926 the Monarchs narrowly missed winning a fourth title as they lost a hotly contested playoff to the Chicago American Giants.

In 1928 he left the Monarchs for the Detroit Stars and was inserted into his customary leadoff spot in the lineup. The left fielder hit .357 and .322 in 1929–30 for the Stars. When the Negro National League folded following the 1931 season, the team disbanded, but when the new Negro National League was organized in 1933, the Stars fielded a new team and Johnston was a part-time starter, batting third in the order when in the lineup, in his last year in the Negro Leagues.

Johnstone
Career: 1913   Position: c
Team: Philadelphia Giants

He was a catcher with the Philadelphia Giants in 1913, his only year in black baseball.

Jones
Career: 1920–21   Position: ss
Team: Indianapolis ABCs

He appeared briefly as a reserve shortstop with the Indianapolis ABCs in 1920–21, the first two years of the Negro National League's existence.

Jones
Career: 1915   Position: c
Team: Louisville White Sox

He was a catcher with the Louisville White Sox in 1915, his only year in black baseball.

Jones
Career: 1931   Position: cf

Team: Homstead Grays
Bats: Right   Throws: Right
Height: 5'10"   Weight: 175

This young outfielder joined the Homestead Grays for the last half of the 1931 season, and held down a regular outfield position for a team often called the greatest in the history of black baseball.

Jones
Career: 1943   Position: ss
Team: Harrisburg-St. Louis Stars

In 1943, the Harrisburg-St. Louis Stars fielded a team in the Negro National League for a short time, and Jones was a shortstop with the club until they withdrew from the league to barnstorm.

Jones
Career: 1910–14   Positions: p, lf
Teams: St. Louis Giants ('10, '13), Cuban Giants ('12), West Baden Sprudels ('14)

In 1910, the second year of the St. Louis Giants' existence, Jones's first appearance in black baseball was as a left fielder with the emerging ballclub. Two years later he appeared as a pitcher with the Cuban Giants, and the following season he returned to St. Louis as a member of the Giants' mound staff to help them repeat as champions of the City League. His last appearance was in 1914 with the West Baden Sprudels, a team of lesser status, where he pitched and played in the outfield.

Jones
Career: 1938   Position: player
Team: Memphis Red Sox

A player named Jones appeared briefly with the Memphis Red Sox in 1938, but his first name and position are not known.

Jones, Abe
Career: 1887–94   Positions: c, manager
Teams: Unions ('87), Chicago Unions ('88–'94)

He was the regular catcher and manager for the Unions when they were organized in 1887.

After their initial season they became known as the Chicago Unions, and he continued in the same capacity for another season under the new team designation. After the 1888 season he relinquished the managerial duties while continuing as the regular catcher for the 1889 season. Beginning in 1890 the team was under the management of W. S. Peters, and for the last five years of his career, Jones shared the catching assignments until his retirement from the game.

Jones, Albert Alonzo (**Al**)
Career: 1944–46   Position: p
Teams: Chicago American Giants ('44), Memphis Red Sox ('44–'46), *Harlem Globetrotters ('47)*

He began his career as a wartime pitcher in the Negro American League suffering through seasons of 0–11 (4.82 ERA) and 2–10 (5.81 ERA) in 1944–45 before leaving the league after the 1946 season to join the barnstorming Harlem Globetrotters, a team of lesser quality.

Jones, Alvin
Career: 1928   Position: officer
Team: Harrisburg Giants

He served as an officer with the Harrisburg Giants in 1928, a year after they dropped out of the Eastern Colored League.

Jones, Archie
Career: 1939   Position: p
Team: New York Cubans

He was a pitcher with the New York Cubans in 1939, his only year in the Negro Leagues.

Jones, Arthur Brown (Mutt, Dump)
Career: 1921–25, 1935 Positions: **ss**, p
Teams: Indianapolis ABCs ('21, '25), Birmingham Black Barons ('25, '34)

He began his career as a shortstop with the Indianapolis ABCs and the Birmingham Black Barons in the '20s, and made a return to the Black Barons as a pitcher in 1934.

Jones, Ben
Career: 1950   Position: ss
Team: New York Black Yankees

He was a shortstop with the New York Black Yankees in 1950, when black baseball was struggling to survive the loss of players to organized baseball.

Jones, Benny (Hoghead)
Career: 1932–35   Positions: of, c, if
Teams: Pittsburgh Crawfords ('32), Newark Dodgers ('33), Cleveland Red Sox ('34), Hilldale Daisies ('34), Brooklyn Eagles ('35)

He was a marginal player who played as an outfielder, infielder, and catcher, and who used his versatility to remain with independent and league teams during his four years on the fringes of black baseball during the mid-'30s.

Jones, Bert
Career: 1896–1903   Position: p
Teams: *Atchison (Kansas State League),* ('96–'98), Chicago Unions ('98–'01), Algona Brownies ('02–'03)
Bats: Left   Throws: Left

During the early years of the century he was considered to be one of the best left-handed pitchers in the history of black baseball. After starring on the mound with the Chicago Unions, he joined the Algona Brownies and, as a right fielder, helped them win the western championship in 1903.

Jones, Charles
Career: 1950   Position: 3b
Team: Cleveland Buckeyes

He was listed as a third baseman with the Cleveland Buckeyes in 1950, when the Negro American League was struggling to survive the loss of players to organized baseball, but league statistics do not confirm his playing time.

Jones, Clinton (**Casey**)
Career: 1940–50   Position: c
Team: Memphis Red Sox ('40–'55)
Bats: Right   Throws: Right

Height: 6'2"   Weight: 195
Born: July 19, 1918, Mississippi

This tall, slender catcher broke into black baseball as a backup for Memphis Red Sox playing-manager Larry Brown, but by 1945 had taken over the backstopping chores on a regular basis. Possessing a fine arm, he learned his trade under Brown, who was one of the best receivers in the league. Playing on a regular basis improved his batting average from .194 in 1944 to .237 in 1945, and by 1948 he was up to .265. Big and strong with good power at the plate, he was a pull hitter and also was noted as hitting many foul home runs every year. In 1950 he hit 11 home runs between the lines, good for a .635 slugging percentage despite a mediocre .267 batting average, and was selected to play in the 1950 All-Star game for the West squad.

Originally from Mississippi, he moved to Memphis as a youngster and played with the city teams prior to beginning his professional career.

Jones, Collins (Collis)
Career: 1943–44   Positions: 2b, 3b, of
Teams: Cincinnati Clowns ('43), Black Barons ('44), *Harlem Globetrotters ('47)*

This wartime player could play either infield or outfield and earned a spot on the Cincinnati Clowns' roster as a utility player, filling the same role the following season with the Birmingham Black Barons. After leaving the league he joined the Harlem Globetrotters, a team of lesser quality.

Jones, Country
Career: 1932–33   Positions: c, 2b
Team: Brooklyn Royal Giants

He began his career as a catcher in 1932 and also gained some playing time at second base during his two seasons with the ballclub.

Jones, Curtis
Career: 1946   Position: p
Team: Cleveland Buckeyes

He posted a 2–1 record as a pitcher with the Cleveland Buckeyes in 1946, when the Negro American League was struggling to survive the loss of players to organized baseball.

Jones, Edward
Career: 1915–29   Position: c
Teams: Chicago American Giants ('15), Chicago Giants, Chicago Union Giants, ('16), Bowser's ABCs, ('16), Harrisburg Giants ('25), **Atlantic City Bacharach Giants** ('27–'29)

A catcher with a quick arm, he began his career in the West, with Chicago-based teams, but moved East to play with teams in the Eastern Colored League, including the 1927 Eastern Colored League champion Bacharach Giants.

Jones, Ernest (Mint)
Career: 1937–41   Position: 1b
Teams: Jacksonville Red Caps (*'34, '38*), Philadelphia Stars ('37–'38), Cleveland Bears ('39–'40)

This first baseman played with Jacksonville in the Negro Southern League in 1934 and was noted for his long stretch on close plays and for errant throws. When the Red Caps joined the Negro American League in 1938, he batted in the leadoff spot, and he remained with the franchise when the team was relocated in Cleveland to play as the Cleveland Bears in 1939–40.

Jones, Eugene (Lefty)
Career: 1943   Position: p
Teams: Philadelphia Stars ('43), Homestead Grays ('43), *Atlanta Black Crackers ('43)*, Baltimore Elite Giants ('43)
Bats: Left   Throws: Left
Born: 1922

In 1943 he signed with and accepted money from the Philadelphia Stars but was claimed by both the Stars and the Homestead Grays. The Stars protested his use by any other team, and he was ordered back to Atlanta, where he had been playing.

Jones, Fate
Career: 1950   Position: of
Team: Birmingham Black Barons

He was an outfielder with the Birmingham Black Barons in 1950, when the Negro American League was struggling to survive the loss of players to organized baseball, but league statistics do not confirm his playing time.

Jones, Hurley
Career: 1931   Position: p
Team: Birmingham Black Barons

He was a pitcher with the Birmingham Black Barons in 1931, a year after they dropped out of the Negro National League.

Jones, James
Career: 1949–50   Positions: of, 1b
Team: Philadelphia Stars ('49–'52)

After the demise of the Negro National League in 1948, the Philadelphia Stars joined the Negro American League, and he was an outfielder-first baseman with the Stars when the league was struggling to survive the loss of players to organized baseball. He batted .309 and .313 in his first two years, 1949–50, and continued through the 1952 season.

Jones, John
Career: 1922–34   Positions: **of**, 1b, 2b, 3b
Teams: Detroit Stars ('22–'29), Indianapolis ABCs ('26), Memphis Red Sox ('31–'32), Washington Pilots ('32), Atlantic City Bacharach Giants ('32)
Bats: Right   Throws: Right

An outfielder who could also play in the infield, he is best identified with the Detroit Stars. He began his career in 1922, playing in the side pastures, and moved to second base in 1923. During the next two seasons he became the regular left fielder and moved from the lower part of the batting order to the leadoff spot. He spent most of the 1926 season in left field with the Indianapolis ABCs, hitting .337 for the year. Back in the Detroit fold in 1927, playing as a part-time starter in left field, he resumed full-time duty in 1929 and, while batting in the leadoff position, he hit .341 with 11 home runs in the 70-game season. After leaving the Stars he played with the Memphis Red Sox, the Washington Pilots, and the Bacharach Giants, with whom he played center field in 1932.

Jones, Lee
Career: 1912–22   Position: of
Teams: *Dallas Giants, Brooklyn Colored Giants ('08–'11),* Brooklyn Royal Giants ('12–'22)

The outfielder began playing ball in Texas with the Dallas Giants, joining the Brooklyn Colored Giants in 1908 for four seasons before signing with the Brooklyn Royal Giants in 1912 playing irregularly in right field but being unable to break into the starting lineup.

Jones, Ollie
Career: 1919   Position: 3b
Team: St. Louis Giants

He was a part-time starter at third base with the St. Louis Giants in 1919, batting leadoff when in the lineup.

Jones, Paul H.
Career: 1949–50   Position: p
Teams: Louisville Buckeyes ('49), Cleveland Buckeyes ('50, '58), *minor leagues ('50–'52, '54)*
Bats: Right   Throws: Right
Height: 6'3"   Weight: 223
Born: 1929

He had an unimpressive beginning as a pitcher with the 1949 Buckeyes, posting a 2–11 mark with a 6.11 ERA. The next season he was winless, showing a 0–5 mark with an 8.10 ERA, when he left the Buckeyes to join the Elmwood team of the Mandak League, where he improved his record with a 9–10 ledger. He was equally unimpressive in three more seasons in organized baseball, with Flint in 1951 (3–19, 6.84 ERA), Vancouver in 1952 (4–6, 3.45 ERA), and Winston-Salem in 1954 (5–10, 6.02 ERA). He returned to the Buckeyes in

1958, but by then the team was no longer of major league quality.

Jones, Reuben

Career: 1918–34   Positions: lf, rf, manager

Teams: *Dallas Giants ('18),* Birmingham Black Barons ('23–'25, '27–'28), Indianapolis ABCs ('26), Memphis Red Sox ('27), Chicago American Giants ('28), *Little Rock Black Travelers ('32),* Cleveland Red Sox ('34), Houston Eagles ('49)

Bats: Left   Throws: Right

A left-handed batter, this hard-hitting outfielder had good power, sufficient speed on the bases, and was a good fielder. He is best identified with the Birmingham Black Barons, and was their playing manager in 1927. As the left fielder and cleanup hitter, Jones hit .295 and guided the team to the second-half title in the Negro National League, but they lost the play-off to the Chicago American Giants. The next year he again played on the second-half title winner, when he joined the American Giants during the season, stepped into the regular right-field position, and helped them win this distinction. This marked the second time in three years that he had left the Birmingham fold, having left the Black Barons temporarily in 1926 to play with the Indianapolis ABCs in the original franchise's last season, playing right field and hitting .341 while batting in the heart of the order. In 1934 he batted leadoff and played center field for the Cleveland Red Sox.

Before joining the Black Barons he began his career in Texas with the Dallas Giants and closed his career with the Little Rock Black Travelers, both teams being of lesser quality. He extended his baseball career by entering the managerial ranks during the later stages of his career, taking the helm of the Houston Eagles in 1949.

Jones, Robert Leo (Fox)

Career: 1933–34   Position: lf

Team: Memphis Red Sox

He was an outfielder with the Memphis Red Sox in 1933–34, as a part-time starter in the former year and as a reserve during the latter season.

Jones, Samuel (Red, Sad Sam, Toothpick)

Career: 1946–48   Position: p

Teams: Homestead Grays ('46), Cleveland Buckeyes ('47–'48), *minor leagues ('50–'55),* major leagues ('51–'52, '55–'64)

Bats: Right   Throws: Right

Height: 6'4"   Weight: 192

Born: Dec. 14, 1925, Stewartsville O.

Died: Nov. 5, 1971, Morgantown, W.Va.

As a twenty-one-year-old Sam posted a 4–2 ledger with the 1947 pennant-wining Cleveland Buckeyes, but lost his only World Series decision as the Buckeyes were defeated in the Series by the New York Cubans. The next year he finished with a 9–8 record with a 4.91 ERA while leading the league in both strikeouts and walks. Two years later, with the color line removed, the big right-hander made the transition to organized baseball. Known as "Red" in the Negro Leagues, the fireballer's nicknames in the major leagues were "Toothpick" and "Sad Sam."

After entering organized baseball, he played with Wilkes-Barre in 1950 and posted a 17–8 record. He began the next season with San Diego but got his first taste of the major leagues when he appeared in two games with Cleveland at the end of the season. In 1952 he played with Indianapolis in the American Association most of the season but had another short stint in the American League with Cleveland. After his 2–3 record with the Indians, he spent the next two years with Indianapolis, and finally made it to the majors to stay with the Chicago Cubs in 1955. In his first full season he established himself as the ace of the staff, hurled a no-hitter, and finished with a 14–20 record. Two years later he was traded to the St. Louis Cardinals, and after two winning seasons there, had his best season in 1959 with the San Francisco Giants, fashioning a 21–15 work sheet with a league-leading 2.83 ERA. The next season he won 18 games but never had another big season. In 1964 he finished his highly successful twelve-year major league career, during which he won 102 games and compiled a lifetime 3.59 ERA.

After leaving the majors, he pitched with Columbus of the International League, where he had seasons of 7–6, 12–4, 7–3, and 7–8. He also played winter ball with Aquilas in the Dominican Republic (1963–64), where he was 4–1 with a 1.55 ERA, and in Nicaragua in 1964–65, where he was 2–0 for the winter.

Jones, Squab (Professor)
Career: 1938   Position: manager
Team: Atlanta Black Crackers

He was manager of the 1937 Atlanta Black Crackers for a few weeks and was replaced by Ormond Sampson.

Jones, Stuart (**Slim**)
Career: 1932–38   Position: p
Teams: Baltimore Black Sox ('32–'33), **Philadelphia Stars** ('34–'38)
Bats: Left   Throws: Left
Height: 6'6"   Weight: 185
Born: May 6, 1913, Baltimore, Md.
Died: December 1938, Baltimore, Md.

During the mid-'30 this towering, hard-throwing left-hander dominated black baseball with his overpowering speed. His low "running" fastball was difficult for catchers to handle and even more difficult for batters to hit. With a good snaky curve to complement his fastball, he was always among the leaders in strikeouts. In 1933 he struck out 210 men in the Puerto Rican winter league. The following year the fastballer had a season like Lefty Grove's 1931 season, earning an enviable 32–4 record, including a 22–3 league slate, as he virtually pitched the Philadelphia Stars to the Negro National League championship single-handedly. After his regular-season heroics he hurled a 2–0 shutout over the Chicago American Giants in the deciding playoff game to nail down the Star's championship. His last victory in the 1934 season was in a postseason exhibi-tion contest against Dizzy Dean, a 30-game winner for the world champion St. Louis Cardinals.

In 1935, the temperamental left-hander had problems. He wanted more money even though he had not won a game at the East-West break, and he left the team shortly afterward, not returning until a promise of a pay increase. However, despite the pay reconciliation, his production suffered and he finished with a 4–10 record for the season.

He was selected as the starting pitcher for the East squad in both the 1934 and 1935 East-West All-Star games, and he pitched 6 innings of scoreless ball against the West's best hitters. Buck Leonard, who faced both pitchers, said that Jones was faster than Lefty Grove. Many other observers assert that Jones threw harder than Satchel Paige, and matchups between the two superstar black pitchers in Yankee Stadium were the featured attraction during the 1930s. One encounter in 1934, a 10-inning, 1–1 tie ended by darkness, is referenced as the best black baseball game of all time. Jones pitched a perfect game for 6 innings, yielding only 3 hits while registering 9 strikeouts. Paige gave up 6 hits and struck out a dozen batters in the contest.

Before switching to baseball, Jones played softball, but made the transition easily and earned a tryout with manager Dick Lundy's Baltimore Black Sox in 1932, but failed to stick with the team in his first try. The next season, the elongated hurler stuck with the Black Sox, logging a 4–2 record. After his sensational 1934 season, he never again regained the same form he had previously enjoyed, posting a composite mark of 6–4 for the last three years of his career. Part of the reason for this decline was his inability to control his drinking. In the winter of 1938, after his arm had gone bad, he sought an advance on his salary, and when his request was refused, he sold his overcoat to buy a bottle of whiskey and subsequently contracted pneumonia and died shortly afterward.

Jones, Tom (Pete)
Career: 1946   Position: c
Team: Philadelphia Stars

He was a backup catcher with the 1946 Philadelphia Stars, and entered the opening day game against the Newark Eagles when starter Bill Cash was ejected from the game. That contest turned out to be a historic game as Eagles hurler Leon Day pitched a no-hitter.

Jones, W.
Career: 1934   Position: of
Team: *Birmingham Black Barons*

He was an outfielder with the Birmingham Black Barons in 1934, when the team was in the Negro Southern League.

Jones, William (Fox)
Career: 1915–30   Positions: c, p
Teams: Chicago American Giants ('15–'17), Chicago Giants, Chicago Union Giants, Atlantic City Bacharach Giants ('22–'29), Hilldale Daisies ('30)

Beginning with the Chicago American Giants in 1915, he spent sixteen seasons in black baseball, including a season with the 1926 Eastern Colored League champion Bacharachs. He was one of the smallest catchers in baseball but was a fairly good man, with a good arm, and was a fair hitter. After joining the Bacharachs in 1922 as a young catcher, he showed improvement each year and shared the regular catching duties through the 1929 season, usually hitting the lower part of the batting order and posting averages of .291 and .254 in 1924–25. The little receiver added a .287 average in 1929, his last year with the Bacharachs, and in 1930 he closed out his career hitting .337 while sharing the catching responsibilities for Hilldale.

Jones, Willis (Will)
Career: 1895–1911   Positions: of, ss
Teams: Chicago Unions ('95–'00), Chicago Union Giants ('01–'02), Algona Brownies ('03), Leland Giants

Beginning in 1895 he was the starting right fielder for the Chicago Unions franchise for eight consecutive seasons. The following season he played on the Champion Algona Brownies team.

Jordan, Henry (Hen)
Career: 1922–25   Positions: c, of
Teams; Harrisburg Giants ('22–'25), Baltimore Black Sox ('23), *Pittsburgh Stars of Buffalo*

A veteran player, he was the regular catcher for the Harrisburg Giants for three seasons (1922–24), batting .292 while managing the ballclub for part of the 1924 season. He was a good receiver with a fair throwing arm and proved very dependable, always remaining in the thick of battle despite often being badly injured. He was a good hitter, contributing a .318 average as a part-time starter in 1925, and also playing in the outfield on occasion during his career.

Jordan, Larnie
a.k.a. Lonnie
Career: 1936–42   Position: ss
Teams: Bacharach Giants ('36), Brooklyn Royal Giants ('39), Philadelphia Stars ('40–'41), New York Black Yankees ('42)
Bats: Right   Throws: Right

Basically this infielder was an ordinary player both offensively and defensively. He was not a good bunter but was average in most other categories, including hitting, fielding, throwing, and running. He played shortstop for the Philadelphia Stars in 1940–41, usually batting third in the order until he injured his leg in 1941. He hit .324 in 1940 but dropped off to .200 in 1941, perhaps due to the injury. The next season he was a part-time starter with the New York Black Yankees, batting at the bottom of the order when in the lineup but posting a .348 batting average in what proved to be his last season in the Negro Leagues. He learned his diamond skills on the sandlots of Philadelphia, and before signing with the Stars he played with the Bacharachs.

Jordan, Maynard
Career: 1950   Position: of
Team: Houston Eagles

He hit .239 as an outfielder with the Houston Eagles in 1950, when the Negro American League was struggling to survive the loss of players to organized baseball.

Jordan, Robert
Career; 1896–1906   Positions: c, 1b
Teams: Cuban Giants ('96, '97, '99–'00, '03–'04), Cuban X–Giants, ('98–'00, '03–'04), Philadelphia Giants ('06)

For over a decade he was a catcher and first baseman with three of the top black teams of his era, the Cuban Giants, the Cuban X-Giants, and the Philadelphia Giants.

Jordan, Willie
Career: 1933   Position: p
Team: Chicago American Giants ('33), *Louisville Black Colonels* ('38)

He pitched briefly with the Chicago American Giants in 1933, his only appearance with a top team. In 1938 he played with the Louisville Black Colonels, a team of lesser quality.

Joseph, Walter Newton (**Newt,** Pep)
Career: 1922–39   Positions: **3b**,   2b,
                                      manager
Teams: **Kansas City Monarchs** ('22–'35), Satchel Paige's All-Stars ('39)
Bats: Right   Throws: Right
Height: 5'6"   Weight: 185
Born: Oct. 27, 1899, Montgomery, Ala.
Died: Jan. 19, 1953, Kansas City, Mo.

A gutty hustler, always full of pep and chatter, this husky little third baseman was "chesty" and made the most of his modest natural talents. He was the Kansas City Monarchs' third baseman during the 1920s and early 1930s, when he and second baseman Newt Allen were roommates and were almost inseparable. On the field he was hotheaded and sometimes even mean, and off the field he was mischievous, sometimes shooting rabbits out of the bus window. He had a good arm but not good hands. Although weak on sharply hit balls, he excelled on slowly hit balls and bunts, scooping up the ball and making the throw to first base without raising up.

The strong-wristed batter hit a clutch home run to clinch the 1923 Negro National League pennant, the first of three consecutive flags the Monarchs captured. He had his best years in 1924–25, when he hit .334 and .326 as the Monarchs copped back-to-back pennants and faced the Eastern Colored League champion Hilldale club in the World Series each year. The Monarchs won the first encounter but lost the rematch in 1925. Joseph followed with a .296 batting average as the Monarchs barely missed their third consecutive flag in 1926. For the next four seasons, usually batting in the lower half of the batting order, he posted averages of .290, .264, .283, and .269 before the Monarchs dropped out of the Negro National League. During most of the '30s the Monarchs played as an independent barnstorming team, but later in the decade they joined the Negro American League while maintaining a second Monarchs team which continued barnstorming.

Reared in Muskogee, Oklahoma, he began his career as a catcher and pitcher, and hitchhiked to Kansas City, where he demanded a uniform and was given one as a joke. He soon abandoned the idea of being a batteryman and switched to third base, where he found a home. A smart player, he was an expert at stealing signals, and later in his career he became the manager of the Monarch's traveling team that featured Satchel Paige and was sometimes billed as Satchel Paige's All-Stars.

After retiring from baseball he owned a taxi stand in Kansas City that served as a center for sports discussions until shortly before his death from tuberculosis in 1953.

Josephs, William
Career: 1924–25   Position: ss
Teams: Indianapolis ABCs ('24), Cleveland Browns ('24), Birmingham Black Barons ('25)

This light-hitting shortstop played two years during the mid-'20s with the Cleveland Browns and the Birmingham Black Barons. After breaking in with Cleveland in 1924, he played as a regular with the Black Barons the next season, batting at the bottom of the order.

Josh
Career: 1917   Position: p
Teams: New York Lincoln Giants

A player identified only with this single name pitched in one game with the New York Lincoln Giants in 1917.

Joyner, William
Career: 1893–1902   Positions: ss, of
Teams: Chicago Unions ('93–'00), Chicago Union Giants ('01–'02)

In 1893 he began a five-year tenure as the starting shortstop for the Chicago Unions before becoming a center fielder and utility player for three seasons. In 1901 Frank Leland combined the Chicago Unions and the Columbia Giants to form the Chicago Union Giants, and Joyner closed out his career as a regular outfielder for two years with the consolidated team.

Juanello
[See Mirabal, Juanello]

Juillo
a.k.a. Julio
Career: 1940   Positions: p, rf
Team: New York Cubans

He was a pitcher and reserve outfielder with the New York Cubans in 1940.

Junco, José
a.k.a. Juncos
Career: 1912–22   Positions: p, of
Teams: Cuban Stars (West) ('12–'18), Cuban Stars (East ('20–'22)

Their right-handed pitcher played for both Cuban Stars teams during his career. After beginning his career in 1912, he was one of the top pitchers with Augustin Molina's Cuban Stars during the last decade of the deadball era, with incomplete statistics showing marks of 4–2 and 0–5 for the 1917–18 seasons. With the advent of the lively ball, he switched for Molina's Stars to Alex Pompez's Cuban Stars in the East, closing out his career after the 1922 season.

Jupiter
Career: 1887   Position: p
Team: Cuban Giants

He pitched with the 1887 Colored champions, the Cuban Giants, who had been organized in 1885 as the first black professional team.

Juran, B.
Career: 1923   Position: p
Team: Birmingham Black Barons

He was a pitcher with the Birmingham Black Barons in 1923.

Juran, Eli
Career: 1923–26   Position: p
Teams: Birmingham Black Barons ('23–'24), Newark Stars ('26)

After pitching with the Birmingham Black Barons for two seasons, 1923–24, he made his final league appearance with the Newark Stars in 1926.

Justice, Charles P. (Charley)
Career: 1933–37   Positions: p, of
Teams: Akron Tyrites ('33), Detroit Stars ('37)
Born: 1913
Died: Nov, 9, 1974, Ann Arbor, Mich.

He was a pitcher with the Akron Tyrites in 1933 and with the Detroit Stars in 1937, also playing in the outfield the latter year.

K

Kaiser, Cecil (*Aspirin Tablet Man, Minute Man*)

Career: 1945–49   Positions: **p** *of, 1b*
Teams: Homstead Grays ('45, '47–'49), *Pittsburgh Crawfords ('46), Mexican League ('46), Canadian League ('51), minor leagues ('52)*
Bats: Left   Throws: Left
Height: 5'6"   Weight: 165
Born: June 27, 1916 New York, N.Y.

Mixing a fastball with an assortment of off-speed breaking pitches, this little Homestead Grays' hurler used control and know-how effectively. His best salary year with the Grays was in 1947, when he earned $700 per month. He also pitched with the Pittsburgh Crawfords in the U.S. League and played in Latin American leagues, including those in Puerto Rico, Cuba, Mexico, Panama, and the Dominican Republic.

His best showing in the winter leagues was in 1949–50, pitching with Caguas in the Puerto Rican League, where he sported a league-leading 1.68 ERA. His earlier outings in the Latin climate were not as productive, showing a 2–2 record in 15 games while pitching with Havana in the Cuban League in 1944–45 and a 6–12 record with a 5.00 ERA in 1946 while pitching with San Luis in the Mexican League.

In 1951 he ventured to the northern side of the United States to pitch with Farnham in the Canadian Provincial League, where he had a 14–13 record with a 3.96 ERA and a .260 batting average with 4 homers in 69 games while also playing in the outfield when not on the mound. The following season, 1952, he ended his professional career pitching with Tampa in the Florida International League, appearing in 20 games with no record listed.

After the demise of the Negro National League, a drawing was held to determine the dispersal of players among the remaining teams. When Kaiser was assigned to the Clowns, he refused to report and returned to Puerto Rico.

As a youngster during the early '30s, he was an outfielder with sandlot teams that played down through West Virginia. These teams included the Bishop Street Liners, the Gary (West Virginia) Grays, and the Kimbrell Red Sox. In 1938 he played as an outfielder with the world champion softball Pontiac Big Six, and reportedly appeared with the Crawfords as an outfielder, but when the mound staff was depleted due to injuries, manager Candy Jim Taylor converted him into a pitcher. A reluctant Kaiser hurled a complete-game victory over the Cincinnati Clowns.

He spent most of his career with teams of lesser status, including the new Detroit Stars in 1939–40, the Motor City Giants in 1941–44 and the new Pittsburgh Crawfords in the U.S. League in 1946. When Gus Greenlee died, the U.S. League teams folded. After Kaiser's arm went dead, he left professional ball and played another five years in the Detroit Industrial League with the Ford Motor Company team.

Kansas City, Kansas, Giants

Duration: 1909–15   Honors: None
Affiliation: Independent

Owner Tobe Smith's team briefly rose to some prominence during the early years of the century but was generally of marginal major-league caliber at best. In 1909 the team, managed by Topeka Jack Johnson and playing against all levels of opposition, won 54 straight games. Originally the team was organized to defeat the Kansas City Monarchs, and consisted primarily of members of the Topeka Giants' ballclub.

Kansas City Monarchs

Duration: 1920–50   Honors: World Series champions ('24, '42), Pennants ('23–'25, '29, '37, '39–'42, '46), first-half title ('26, '49), second-half title ('48), division title ('50)
Affiliations: NNL ('20–'31), independent ('32–'36), NAL ('37–'59)

Owned by J. L. Wilkinson, a white businessman, the Monarchs were one of the best known and most successful black teams. The Monarchs captured a total of ten pennants, tying the Homestead Grays for the most flags by any Negro League team, and suffered only one losing season during their entire association with the Negro Leagues. And that season was during World War II, when the roster was decimated by the loss of players to military service. The Monarchs also hold the distinction of having won the first World Series ever played between opposing leagues, both in the initial World Series in 1924 between the Negro National League and the Eastern Colored League, and again in the reinstated World Series in 1942 between the Negro National League and the Negro American League.

A charter member of the Negro National League, they played through the 1930 season, winning pennants in 1923–25 and 1929 while never experiencing a losing season. They narrowly missed a fourth straight pennant in 1926, when they won the first-half title but lost a bitter nine-game playoff to the Chicago American Giants by dropping a doubleheader on the last day. The Monarchs played in the first two World Series ever played, facing the Hilldale team on both occasions.

After dropping out of the league they played independent ball until joining the Negro American League as a charter member in 1937 and remaining even after the league lost its major status. During the first six seasons (1937–1942) they won five pennants, missing only in 1938. After the return of many of their best players, who had been called to service during World War II, they annexed another flag in 1946. In 1942, the first World Series since 1927 was played between the Monarchs and the Homestead Grays, with the Monarchs sweeping the Grays in four straight games. In 1946 the Monarchs lost a tough seven-game Series to the Newark Eagles.

In 1948 the Monarchs won the second half of the split season but lost a seven-game playoff to the Birmingham Black Barons for the pennant and thereby missed a chance to appear in the last Negro World Series ever played. Following that World Series, the Negro National League folded and the Negro American League absorbed some of the franchises and expanded into division play. The Monarchs won the first-half title in 1949 and annexed a division title in 1950.

Wilkinson had sold the franchise after the 1948 season to Tom Baird, who continued to operate the Monarchs through the '50s, but by then the league was strictly a minor-league operation.

Kearney

Career: 1932   Position: p
Team: Newark Browns

He was a pitcher with the Newark Browns in 1932, when the team was in the East-West League.

Keaton, Eugene

a.k.a. Keeton

Career: 1921–26   Position: p
Teams: *Madison Stars ('20),* Dayton Marcos ('21), Cleveland Tate Stars ('22), Indianapolis ABCs ('25)

After beginning his career in 1920 with a lesser team named the Madison Stars, he joined major clubs and during the early '20s pitched for half a dozen seasons (1921–26) with teams in the Midwest, including the Dayton Marcos, the Cleveland Tate Stars, and the Indianapolis ABCs.

Keeler

Career: 1931   Position: of
Team: Bacharach Giants

He was a reserve outfielder with the Bacharachs in 1931, when the team was playing as an independent team.

Keenan, James J. (Jim, Orator)

Career: 1919–30   Positions: owner, officer
Team: New York Lincoln Giants
Height: 6'2"   Weight: 200

An Irishman, he served as both a club and league officer for a dozen years, acting as business manager for the New York Lincoln Giants and as secretary-treasurer of the Eastern Colored League. He ran the Lincoln Giants and paid his players well, but as the owner in 1930, he had to dissolve the franchise. He also owned the famous Renaissance basketball team at that time.

Keene

Career: 1915   Position: 3b
Teams: *West Baden Sprudels ('15), Bowser's ABCs ('15)*

In 1915 he was a third baseman with two Indiana teams of marginal caliber, the West Baden Sprudels and Bowser's ABCs.

Keigeri

Career: 1887   Position: player
Team: *Louisville Falls Citys*

He was a player with the Louisville Falls Citys ballclub, one of eight teams that were charter members of the League of Colored Baseball Clubs in 1887. However, the league's existence was ephemeral, lasting only a week.

Kelley, Palmer

[see Kelly, Palmer]

Kellman, Edric **Leon**

Career: 1946–50   Positions: **3b**, 2b, c, of, *p*
Teams: **Cleveland Buckeyes** ('46–'48), Louisville Buckeyes ('49), Memphis Red Sox ('50, '52–'53), *Mexican League ('51, '54–'58), Indianapolis Clowns ('52)*
Bats: Right   Throws: Right
Height: 5'11"   Weight: 160
Born: 1927, Panama

This Panamanian was a good hitter with power and had a good arm, but although versatile, was only an average fielder and base runner with mediocre speed. Joining the Cleveland Buckeyes in 1946, the hard-hitting third baseman registered batting averages of .297, .306, and .307 in his first three years in the Negro American League and batted in the heart of the order during his tenure with the ballclub. In 1947 the Buckeyes won the Negro American League pennant but lost to the New York Cubans in the World Series. He remained with the franchise when they relocated in Louisville for the 1949 season, but slumped at bat to .254. The following season he signed with the Memphis Red Sox and rebounded with a .329 average.

After a season with Vera Cruz, where he hit .292 with ten homers, he returned to the United States for two more seasons in the decimated Negro American League, now a minor league. In 1954 he returned to Mexico, where he remained for the next five seasons, playing primarily as a catcher with the Nuevo Laredo and Yucatán ballclubs. His best season in Mexico was in 1955, when he hit .336, followed by averages of .297, .309, and .279 for the next three seasons to close out a fifteen-year career that had begun in the Venezuelan winter league of 1944–45.

Throughout his career he played winters in

his homeland, Panama, beginning in the 1945–46 season, when he hit a carreer-high .370 playing with the General Electric team. As in Mexico, he was utilized primarily as a catcher, with most of his years being spent with the Spur Cola team, where he enjoyed seasons of .357 (1948–49), .343 (1950–51), and .304 (1952–53) before ending his decade in Panamanian ball with a lifetime .297 average.

Kelly

Career: 1900–'08 Positions: ss, lf, cf, 3b
Teams: Genuine Cuban Giants ('00), Cuban Giants ('01–'04), Famous Cuban Giants ('05–'06), New York Colored Giants ('07–'08)

During the first decade of this century he played three different positions with three different teams but is most identified with the Cuban Giants. He began his professional career as a shortstop with the Genuine Cuban Giants in 1900, then switched to the outfield with the Cuban Giants for six seasons before ending his career as a third baseman with the New York Colored Giants for two seasons.

Kelly

Career: 1918 Position: 1b
Team: *Philadelphia Giants*

In 1918 he was a first baseman for the Philadelphia Giants, who had become a marginal team at best.

Kelly

Career: 1931 Position: p
Team: Detroit Stars

He pitched with the Detroit Stars in 1931, losing his only recorded decision in his only year in the Negro Leagues.

Kelly

Career: 1941 Position: p
Team: Jacksonville Red Caps

He pitched with the 1941 Red Caps after they returned to Jacksonville after playing two seasons as the Cleveland Bears. That was his only year in the Negro Leagues.

Kelly, Palmer

a.k.a. Kelley
Career: 1916–18 Position: p
Teams: Chicago Giants ('16–'18), Chicago Union Giants ('17–'18)

This spitballer is best identified with the Chicago Giants, for whom he pitched in the latter part of the deadball era, but he also pitched briefly with the Chicago Union Giants.

Kelly, William

Career: *1898* Position: 3b
Team: *Celeron Acme Colored Giants*

He was a third baseman with the Celeron Acme Colored Giants, an all-black team formed in 1898 by a white man, Harry Curtis, to play in the Iron and Oil League as representatives of Celeron, New York. Both the team and the league folded in July, and it was to be the last time a black team played in a white league.

Kelly, William

Career: 1944–47 Position: c
Teams: New York Black Yankees ('44–'46), Homestead Grays ('47)

A product of the sandlots of New York City, he was a reliable worker slated for a backup role behind the plate with the Black Yankees, but won a starting position during the war years ('44–'45). After the war he served as a capable understudy, and in 1947 was one of many catchers tried by the Homestead Grays in an effort to fill the vacancy left by the death of Josh Gibson.

Kemp

Career: 1943 Position: c
Team: New York Black Yankees

A light hitter, this wartime player shared catching duties and batted eighth in the order with th Black Yankees in 1943, his only season in the Negro Leagues.

Kemp, Ed

Career: 1914–28 Positions: cf, lf, rf
Teams: *Norfolk Stars* ('20–'21), *Philadelphia*

Royal Stars ('22), Baltimore Black Sox ('23), New York Lincoln Giants ('24), *Chappie Johnson's Stars ('24–'28), Ewing's All-Stars ('28)*

He was a part-time starter in center field with the Baltimore Black Sox in 1923 and joined the New York Lincoln Giants in 1924 in the same capacity while batting .206 for the season. In each instance the swift outfielder usually batted leadoff when in the starting lineup, but sometimes also batted at the bottom of the order. With the exception of these two seasons, he played most of his career with teams of lesser status.

Kemp George

Career: 1917   Position: rf
Team: Hilldale ('15–'17)

He was an outfielder with Hilldale in their formative years in the latter part of the '10s, when the team was developing as a team of major-league caliber.

Kemp, James Allen (**Gabby**, Mouth, Ripper, *John*)

Career: 1937–39   Positions: **2b**, ss
Teams: Atlanta Black Crackers ('35–'38, '40–'47), Jacksonville Red Caps ('38), Indianapolis ABCs ('39)
Bats: Both   Throws: Right
Height: 5'5"   Weight: 145
Born: 1919

This hustling, scrappy little middle infielder had a good glove and an excellent arm, was fast afoot, and was a daring base runner and good base stealer. He had a good eye at the plate and was good at drawing walks. A switch-hitter, he was frequently hit by inside pitches when batting left-handed. He hit whatever was thrown but was only a fair hitter, lacked power, and initially was not a good bunter, but after many years of practice, he almost perfected the art of drag bunting from the left side.

Although primarily a second baseman, he originally joined the Atlanta Black Crackers in 1935 as a shortstop. The team was in the Negro Southern League at that time, and he remained

with the club until he signed with Jacksonville in the spring of 1938. He made his home in Atlanta and wanted to play in the city but, although he still was on the Black Crackers' roster, he signed with Jacksonville because of doubts about the Black Crackers for the upcoming season. After considerable maneuvering, he was released to Jacksonville at about the end of May and played good ball with them. He especially had a big day in his first game against his old teammates when the Red Caps returned to play the Black Crackers.

When the Black Crackers joined the Negro American League in 1938, Kemp was recalled from Jacksonville for the second half and, at age nineteen, was appointed manager. He proved to be a young, eager, peppery, spirited, impulsive player who sparked the team to the Negro American League second-half championship. He loved to play and had both the desire to play and devotion to the game but, although he was a popular player with some local fans, he was often second-guessed about his managerial decisions. The following season, when the franchise was relocated in Indianapolis to play as the ABCs, he went along as the manager, second baseman, and eighth-place hitter with the ballclub and remained manager through the 1940 season.

In high school he made the All-Star team three years, was an All-American at Morris Brown College, and, proving he was an all-around athlete, earned varsity letters in baseball, track, football, basketball, and debate to become the only person in school history to receive five letters in one year. In addition to his excelling in sports, he earned both a B.S. (1940) and an M.A. (1941) degree from the college.

In professional baseball he played for thirteen seasons (1935–47); all except one year was with the Black Crackers' franchise. In 1949, after having ended his career with the Black Crackers, he toured with Jackie Robinson's All-Stars. Kemp enjoyed a full life in baseball but suffered from partial paralysis in the latter years of his life.

Kemp, John
Career: 1923–28   Position: of
Teams: Birmingham Black Barons ('23), Memphis Red Sox ('24–'25, '28)

After beginning his career with the Birmingham Black Barons in 1923, this outfielder joined the Memphis Red Sox the following season and remained with them during most of the '20s.

Kendall
Career: 1918–25   Positions: **2b**, ss
Team: New York Lincoln Giants

He was a substitute with the New York Lincoln Giants, as a shortstop in 1918 and as a second baseman in 1920 while playing both middle infield positions in 1925.

Kennard, Dan
a.k.a. Kinnard
Career: 1915–25   Positions: **c**, 1b, of
Teams: Indianapolis ABCs ('15–'16), *West Baden Sprudels ('14–'15)*, Bowser's ABCs ('16), Chicago American Giants, **St. Louis Giants** ('16–'21), New York Lincoln Giants ('17), St. Louis Stars ('22–'24), Detroit Stars ('25)
Bats: Right   Throws: Right
Died: June 18, 1946, St. Louis, Mo.

He had good power at the plate and was a solid catcher for over a decade in black baseball. He began with the West Baden Sprudels in 1914 and moved up in competition in 1915, when he joined the Indianapolis ABCs as a backup for Russell Powell. In the fall Kennard rejoined the Sprudels as their top receiver. When a schism developed within the ABCs management, he split the next season between the Indianapolis ABCs and Bowser's ABCs. His batting average, in limited play with the ABCs, in his first two seasons was only .111, but in 1917, after moving East to play with the New York Lincoln Giants, he hit for a .317 average.

He was the regular catcher with the St. Louis Giants, batting fifth in the order, when they became charter members of the Negro National League in 1920. Two years later, in 1922, after the team was reconstituted as the St. Louis Stars, he was their catcher in their first game ever played, and was credited with winning the league batting championship that season with a .372 average. He closed out his career with the Detroit Stars in 1925.

Kennedy
Career: 1916   Position: cf
Teams: All Nations

He was an outfielder with the All Nations team in 1916, when the ballclub was at its peak of popularity.

Kennedy
Career: 1926   Positions: ss, 3b
Team: New York Lincoln Giants

This infielder made appearances on the left side of the infield with manager John Henry Lloyd's New York Lincoln Giants in 1926.

Kennedy, Dave
Career: 1917   Position: player
Team: Havana Red Sox

A native of Helena, Montana, he played with the 1917 Havana Red Sox, a team of marginal quality.

Kennedy, Ernest D.
Career: 1950   Position: if
Team: Memphis Red Sox

This reserve infielder appeared briefly with the Memphis Red Sox in 1960, during the decline of the Negro Leagues.

Kennedy, Walter
Career: 1950   Position: rf
Team: Chicago American Giants

This reserve outfielder appeared briefly with the Chicago American Giants in 1950, during the decline of the Negro Leagues.

Kenner
Career: 1921   Positions: **ss**, 2b
Team: Hilldale ('21), *Madison Stars ('21),*

Washington Braves ('21), Washington Grays ('28)

This middle infielder appeared in two games with Hilldale in 1921, batting .374 in his abbreviated career with a top ballclub. He split the remainder of the season between two lesser teams, the Madison Stars and Washington Braves. In later years (1928) he also played with the Washington Grays and other teams of lesser caliber.

Kent

Career: 1919   Position: player

Team: Brooklyn Royal Giants

He appeared in two games with the Brooklyn Royal Giants in 1919, his only year in black baseball.

Kent, Richard W. (**Dick**)

Career: 1922–31   Positions: owner, officer

Team: St. Louis Stars

A businessman who owned a fleet of funeral cars, he was the owner of the St. Louis Stars when they won three Negro National League pennants in 1928, 1930, and 1931. His association with the team began in 1922, when he and Dr. George Keys purchased the St. Louis Giants' franchise from Charlie Mills. Kent retained most of the playing personnel, but moved the club to the ballpark on Compton Avenue and Market Street for their home games, and renamed the team the St. Louis Stars. Subsequently the Stars fielded a team in the Negro National League every season until the demise of the league following the 1931 season.

Kenwood

Career: 1927   Position: p

Team: Hilldale

He pitched briefly with the Hilldale ballclub in 1927.

Kenyon, Harry C.

Career: 1919–29   Positions: **p, of,** 2b 1b, 3b, manager

Teams: Brooklyn Royal Giants ('19–'20), Indianapolis ABCs ('21), Hilldale ('22), Chicago American Giants ('23), Detroit Stars ('23, '25–'27), New York Lincoln Giants ('24), Kansas City Monarchs ('28), Memphis Red Sox ('28–'29)

He played extensively as both an outfielder and a pitcher for more than a decade. He began his career with the Brooklyn Royal Giants in 1919, batting sixth in the lineup while splitting his diamond time among center field, second base, and the pitcher's mound. The following season he tended more toward mound duty but still saw frequent action in the outfield. In 1921 he moved West to play center field with C. I. Taylor's Indianapolis ABCs, hitting .277 while batting third in the order, and also registering a 6–12 record as a pitcher.

The next two seasons found him jumping twice more between the East and West, playing with two of the greatest ballclubs of the era, Hilldale and the Chicago American Giants, batting .256 with Hilldale in 1922. He made two more latitudinal jumps, center field and pitching with the New York Lincoln Giants in 1924, and batting .259, before finding a home in Detroit with the Stars, where he hit .314 in 1926.

He also continued to split his playing time between the mound and the outfield, but gravitated more toward pitching. As an outfielder he was a pretty good fielder and a fair hitter, who also filled in occasionally at an infield position. As a pitcher he fared well but suffered from a lack of specialization. Later he also managed at the end of his career, and in 1929 he was the last of three managers who guided the Memphis Red Sox during the season.

Kerner, J.

Career: 1931–33   Position: rf

Teams: Indianapolis ABCs ('31–'32), Columbus Blue Birds ('33), Detroit Stars ('33)

He was a reserve outfielder in the early '30s with a trio of midwestern teams, including the

Columbus Blue Birds, the Detroit Stars, and the Indianapolis ABCs.

Keyes
Career: 1918   Position: p
Team: Chicago American Giants

Although not in the regular rotation, he won his only two decisions with the Chicago American Giants in 1918.

Keyes, Garvin
Career: 1943   Position: if
Team: Philadelphia Stars

A wartime player, he was an infielder with the 1943 Philadelphia Stars.

Keyes, Robert (Spike)
Career: 1941–46   Position: p
Team: Memphis Red Sox
Bats: Right   Throws: Right

For half a dozen seasons during the '40s he pitched with the Memphis Red Sox. His records for three wartime seasons (1943–45) show ledgers of 1–2, 3–5 (4.03 ERA), and 0–6.

Keyes, Steve (Youngie, Zeke, Ezekial)
a.k.a. Khora
Career: 1940–48   Position: p
Height: 5'6"   Weight: 136
Teams: Indianapolis Crawfords ('40), **Memphis Red Sox** ('41–'42, '48), Ethiopian Clowns ('42), Philadelphia Stars ('43)

Best identified with the Memphis Red Sox, he began his career with the Indianapolis Crawfords in 1940 and also pitched with the Philadelphia Stars and the Ethiopian Clowns, where his "Clown name" was "Khora." In 1948 he won his only decision in league play. A small, hard-throwing pitcher, he threw his fastball overhand and made it rise. Playing with Satchel Paige's All-Stars in October 1941 in California against Bob Feller's All-Stars, he used his fastball, which was described as "just like a streak of white lightning," to strike out Johnny Mize twice.

Keys
Career: 1950   Position: p
Team: Houston Eagles

He pitched one game with the Houston Eagles in 1950, yielding 5 runs in 4 innings and taking the loss in the only decision of his career.

Keys, Dr. George B.
Career: 1922–32   Position: officer
Team: St. Louis Stars

This doctor was the principal associate who helped Dick Kent buy the St. Louis Giants' franchise from Charlie Mills in 1922. Other of his business associates who invested in ownership included Dr. J. W. McClelland and Dr. Samuel Shepard. The team was renamed the St. Louis Stars and, for a decade, Dr. Keys served as both a club officer and as a league officer with the Negro National League.

Kimbro, Arthur (Jess, Ted)
Career: 1915–18   Positions: **3b**, 2b
Teams: *West Baden Sprudels ('14)*, New York Lincoln Giants ('15–'18), Louisville Sox ('15), Bowser's ABCs ('16), Hilldale ('17), St. Louis Giants ('17), G.C.T. Red Caps ('18)
Bats: Uncertain   Throws: Right
Died: 1918

A good hitter, he was one of the top third basemen during the '10s, playing primarily with the New York Lincoln Giants. After hitting .373 with the Lincolns during the season, in the fall of 1917 he was picked up by Hilldale to play against Joe Bush and a major-league all-star team. Inducted into service during World War I, he played on the Camp Dix baseball team before receiving his Army discharge. Tragically, soon afterward his career was prematurely ended in 1918 when he died from influenza contracted while in the service.

Kimbro, Henry Allen (Kimmie, Jimbo, *Scooter Motoneta*)
Career: 1937–50   Positions: **cf**, lf, manager
Teams: Washington Elite Giants ('37), **Balti-**

more Elite Giants ('38–'40, '42–'51), New York Black Yankees ('41), *Birmingham Black Barons* ('52–'53)
Bats: Left   Throws: Right
Height: 5'8"   Weight: 175
Born: Feb. 19, 1912, Nashville, Tenn.

A compact blend of speed and power, Kimbro starred in the Negro Leagues for fourteen years, all except one season with the Elite Giants. In 1941 he was traded to the New York Black Yankees for Charley Biot, but returned with the Elites the following year. An all-around ballplayer, Kimbro excelled in the field, at bat, and on the bases. A good defensive center fielder with great range and a good arm, he was regarded as the best center fielder in the Negro National League in his prime. He was especially adept at going into the alleys on flys but was a little weak on fielding ground balls in the outfield. Equally dangerous offensively, he was an outstanding line-drive hitter for both average and power and was a constant basestealing threat. His sharp eye and superior speed made him an ideal leadoff batter and, hitting from the left side but to left field, he utilized his speed to get leg hits on ground balls to the infield, and to augment his normal power by stretching would-be singles into extra-base hits.

One of the teams' sluggers, Kimbro had strong arms and shoulders and was consistently among the league leaders in a variety of major offensive categories. In 1944 he hit .329, led the league in stolen bases, and finished only one home run behind league leaders Josh Gibson and Buck Leonard; in 1945 he hit .291 and tied with Cool Papa Bell for the league lead in at-bats; in 1946 he hit .371 and led the league in runs scored; in 1947 he hit .353, led the league in runs scored, and tied for the lead in doubles. In three of these seasons he finished in the top ten hitters in batting average as well, and he appeared in six All-Star games.

Before and after these peak seasons he was also a very productive hitter. In his first year in the Negro National League he hit .276, one of the few times that he failed to hit .300 during his career. The next year two seasons he was credited with averages of .318 and .310, but after dropping to .269 in 1940, he was traded to the Black Yankees, where he hit .247 in his only season before returning to the Elites for seasons of .288 and .333 in 1942–43. In 1948, the last year before the Negro National League folded, he hit .314, and after the Elites joined the Eastern Division of the Negro American League, he hit .352 and .370 in 1949–50, with the latter effort being fourth-best in the league. Although the quality of play in the Negro American League dropped to a minor-league level during the early '50s, Kimbro continued to play for three more years, moving to the Birmingham Black Barons in 1952–53.

He was also a star in the Caribbean winter leagues, leading the Cuban League with a .346 batting average with Havana in 1947–48, and leading the league with 18 stolen bases while hitting .294 with Almendares in 1939–40. When the color bar was removed, the Nashville native was thirty-three years of age and, by major-league standards, too old to make the transition. A loner described as intense, aloof, and "evil," he played with a fierce determination. Baseball to him was just another job, but he was a smart player and served a brief stint as manager at one point in his career. After retiring from baseball he channeled his efforts into building a business and now operates a successful service station and cab dispatch.

Kimbroe
Career: 1936   Position: c
Team: Birmingham Black Barons

He was a catcher with the Birmingham Black Barons in 1936, a year before they entered the Negro American League in its inaugural season.

Kimbrough, Jim
[see Kimbrough, Larry]

Kimbrough, Larry Nathaniel (Schoolboy)
a.k.a. Jim
Career: 1941–50   Positions: p, of, if

Teams: Philadelphia Stars ('41–'43, '45–'48), *military service ('44–'45)*, Homestead Grays ('49–'50)
Bats: Both   Throws: Both
Height: 5'10"   Weight: 195
Born: Sept. 23, 1923, Philadelphia, Pa.

An ambidextrous player, batting and pitching from both sides, he was more effective as a right-handed hurler, but recalled that he once pitched both ways in the same Negro League contest. He was discovered by the Philadelphia Stars when he pitched a no-hitter as a high-school phenom, and in midsummer of 1942, as a nineteen-year-old youngster only recently graduated from Ben Franklin High, he pitched a 6-hit, 4–0 shutout over the Newark Eagles at Niagara Falls. But after this auspicious beginning his career was delayed by World War II, and he spent two years in military service.

In 1946, after his discharge, he was regarded by the Philly Stars as an up-and-coming youngster trying to make the starting rotation, and during the late '40s he was a member of the Stars' pitching staff. He also gained playing time at infield and outfield positions, but his hitting was not sufficient to allow him to break into the lineup as an everyday player.

After being released by the Stars, during the late '40s and early '50s he spent his last playing days pitching with the Richmond Giants and the Homestead Grays, who had already dropped out of league play. Later, in 1958, he pitched with a team in the minor Eastern League, that bore the same name as one of the greatest teams of all time, the Pittsburgh Crawfords. After wrapping up his baseball career he worked with the post office as a letter carrier and retired in January 1981 after thirty-three years of service.

Kinard, Roosevelt
Career: 1932   Positions: 3b, 2b
Team: Washington Pilots

He was a third baseman with the East-West League's Washington Pilots during their only season in a major league.

Kincannon, Harry (Tin Can)
Career: 1930–39   Position: p
Teams: **Pittsburgh Crawfords** ('30–'36), New York Black Yankees ('37), Homestead Grays ('37), Washington Black Senators ('38), Toledo Crawfords ('39), Philadelphia Stars
Bats: Right   Throws: Right
Height: 5'10"   Weight: 190

A pitcher with a wide-breaking curveball, he was a member of the great Pittsburgh Crawfords of the '30s, beginning as a member of the original Crawfords before they became famous. In the summer of 1930, when the youthful Crawfords met the established and powerful Homestead Grays for the first time, he suffered the loss for the Crawfords. By late summer of the next season, after owner Gus Greenlee began stocking the team with veteran stars, he was one of only three players who remained on the Crawfords' squad. In 1932 he compiled a 15–8 record as the Crawfords began their reign of supremacy, and in the East-West All-Star game of 1934 he combined with Satchel Paige and Slim Jones to shut out the powerful West squad.

In 1937 he was traded by the Crawfords to the Black Yankees but somehow ended up with the Grays. The next season he pitched with the Washington Black Senators during their brief entrance into the Negro National League. In 1939 he closed a career that spanned the entire decade of the '30s with the same franchise where he started, returning to the relocated Crawfords in Toledo.

Off the field, the light-complexioned dandy, who carried both a pistol and the nickname "Tin Can," earned a reputation as an excellent dancer. Once, on a road trip, he bought a bag of fried chicken and put it on the bus rack, brandishing his pistol and threatening his teammates if they dared touch his food. He then dropped off to sleep and the pistol fell out of his pocket. The players emptied the gun, ate his chicken, and made a necklace of chicken bones, which they put around his neck. When he woke up and saw what happened, everyone laughed, including Kincannon.

Kindle, William **(Bill)**
Career: 1911–25   Positions: **2b,** ss, *3b, of*
Born: 1924
Died: Sept. 11, 1993, Bessemer, Ala.
Teams: West Baden Sprudels, Indianapolis ABCs, Chicago American Giants, Brooklyn Royal Giants ('11–'14, '16–'17, '19), New York Lincoln Stars ('14–'15), New York Lincoln Giants ('18, '20, '25), *military service ('18), Brooklyn All-Stars, ('14), New York Stars ('14)*

A good-fielding infielder, he was "quick as a cat" and had a good arm. Although he began his career in the Midwest with the West Baden Sprudels, Indianapolis ABCs, and Chicago American Giants, he is best identified with New York-based teams, especially the Brooklyn Royal Giants. As a regular with the Royal Giants in 1911–12, he frequently hit in the second slot in the batting order while playing second base and shortstop. After joining the New York Lincoln Stars late in the 1914 season, he was the youngest player on the 1915 ballclub, batting second in the order between Spot Poles and John Henry Lloyd. In 1916 he returned to the Royals and, during the next season, he was serving as the director of the Wabash YMCA when he left to rejoin the Royal Giants. Incomplete statistics show an average of .238 for the 1917 season.

In 1918 his career was interrupted by World War I, and after induction into the Army, he played on the Camp Dix baseball team. After his discharge he played with the Royals and the Lincoln Giants but never regained his prewar performance level. A graduate of Fiske University, where he played both football and baseball, he later joined the faculty of Talladega College.

King, Brendan
Career: 1943   Position: p
Team: Cincinnati Clowns

In 1943 he was a member of the pitching staff for the Cincinnati Clowns in their first year in the Negro American League.

King, Clarence (Charley, Pijo)
Career: 1947–50   Position: of

Teams: Birmingham Black Barons ('47'–'50, '52, '54), Detroit Stars ('58)

He was an outfielder with the Birmingham Black Barons during the late '40s and early '50s, continuing to play in the Negro American League after the league's decline to minor-league status.

King, Leonard
Career: 1921   Position: of
Team: Kansas City Monarchs

He was a reserve outfielder with the 1921 Kansas City Monarchs.

King, Richard
a.k.a. King Tut
Career: 1937–50   Position: 1b
Teams: *Miami Clowns,* ('34–'36), Ethiopian Clowns, ('37–'42) Cincinnati Clowns ('43), Cincinnati-Indianapolis Clowns ('44–'45), Indianapolis Clowns ('46–'59)
Born: 1905
Died: Dec. 29, 1966, Philadelphia, Pa.

The tall, thin first baseman was with the Clowns from their beginning and was a main attraction for three decades. With the Indianapolis Clowns King Tut combined comedy and athletic talent to hold center stage during the Clowns' exhibition baseball tours. Famous for his pantomine ability and oversized first baseman's mitt, as he got older he confined himself to the comedy routines, leaving the serious playing to younger, more talented players. He and the Clowns' midget, Spec Bebop, were well known for their classic rowboat routine, an act that always "brought the house down." The man known as King Tut retired in 1959.

King Tut
[see King, Richard]

King, Wilbur (Dolly)
Career: 1944–47   Positions: ss, 2b, rf
Teams: Memphis Red Sox ('44), Cleveland Buckeyes ('44), Chicago American Giants ('45), Homestead Grays ('47)

This middle infielder played both keystone positions for a trio of Negro American League teams during the last two war years and played briefly as a utility man, playing both infield and outfield with the Homestead Grays in 1947. In 1944, although his playing time was very limited, he hit .500, but with his playing time increased in 1945, his average was halved to .250, a more accurate indication of his batting ability.

King, William
Career: 1890–92   Position: ss
Team: Chicago Unions

For three years, 1890–92, he was a shortstop with the Chicago Unions, one of the strongest teams of the era.

Kinkeide, John
Career: 1887   Position: player
Team: *Louisville Falls Citys*

He was a player with the Louisville Falls Citys ballclub, one of eight teams that were charter members of the League of Colored Baseball Clubs in 1887. However, the league's existence was ephemeral, lasting only a week.

Kinnon
Career: 1917   Position: lf
Team: All Nations

He was an outfielder with the All Nations team in 1917.

Kirby
Career: 1928   Position: p
Team: Cleveland Tigers

He was a pitcher with the Cleveland Tigers in 1928, the team's only season in the Negro National League.

Kirksey
a.k.a. Kirksley
Career: 1926   Positions: c, 2b, lf
Team: Dayton Marcos

This catcher was a part-time starter with the 1926 Dayton Marcos, batting in the fifth spot in the order when in the lineup and hitting .250 for the season.

Klepp, Eddie
Career: 1946   Position: p
Team: Cleveland Buckeyes

A white player signed by the Cleveland Buckeyes in 1946, after the signing of Jackie Robinson by the Brooklyn Dodgers, his ability was overprojected and he lacked the basic playing skills to capitalize on the opportunity afforded. During spring practice, in most localities he was forced to be segregated from his teammates and was not allowed to play on the same field or even sit in the same dugout wearing a Buckeyes uniform, and was required to sit in the stands in civilian attire. Although it was hoped that he would be a ''reverse Jackie Robinson,'' he met with little success and his playing career was brief and undistinguished.

Klondyke
Career: 1914   Position: c
Team: Chicago American Giants

He appeared briefly as a reserve catcher with the Chicago American Giants in 1914.

Knight
Career: 1910   Position: cf
Team: St. Louis Giants

He was a center fielder with the St. Louis Giants in 1910, the team's second year of existence.

Knight, Dave (Mule)
Career: 1921–30   Positions: 1b, of, p
Teams: Detroit Stars ('21), Baltimore Black Sox ('22), Chicago American Giants ('30)

In an irregular career he made his first appearance as an outfielder with the Detroit Stars in 1921, followed by a brief stint as a reserve with the Baltimore Black Sox before reappearing as a pitcher with the 1930 Chicago American Giants, where he split two decisions. When not able to hold on to a spot on a Negro Leagues team roster, he sometimes played in a semipro league in Grand Rapids, Michigan, during the '20s.

Knox, Elwood C.
Career: 1920   Position: codrafter of
                                  NNL Constitution
League: Negro National League

He was the codrafter of Negro National League Constitution.

Kramer
Career: 1916   Position: 3b
Team: All Nations

He was a third baseman for the All Nations team in 1916, when the ballclub was at its peak of popularity.

Kranson, Floyd Arthur
a.k.a. Kranston
Career: 1935–41   Position: p
Teams: **Kansas City Monarchs** ('35–'40), Chicago American Giants ('36), Memphis Red Sox ('37)
Bats: Right   Throws: Right
Height: 6'1"   Weight: 180

An average pitcher in every aspect of the game, he had average control and a standard three-pitch repertory without an exceptional pitch. The Kansas City Monarchs' hurler pitched for the West squad in the 1936 East-West All-Star game but yielded 4 hits and 4 runs in 2 innings as the West lost decisively, 10–2. In 1939–40 the Monarchs won back-to-back Negro American League pennants, with Kranson contributing 2–1 and 3–1 league ledgers to the Monarchs' success. The light-complexioned hurler came from racially mixed parentage.

Krider, J. Monroe
Career: 1890   Position: manager
Team: York Cuban Giants

He served as manager of the Cuban Giants when they represented York, Pennsylvania, in the Eastern Interstate League in 1890, playing under the name of the Colored Monarchs.

Kyle, Andy
Career: 1922   Positions: of, p
Teams: Baltimore Black Sox ('22), Bacharach Giants ('22)

He was an outfielder and pitcher with the Baltimore Black Sox in 1922, batting .379 in limited play while winning 2 of his 3 pitching decisions.

L

Lackey, Obie

Career: 1929–43   Positions: ss, 2b, 3b

Teams: *Philadelphia Giants ('27)*, Homestead Grays ('29, '38), Hilldale Daisies ('29–'32), Atlantic City Bacharach Giants ('31–'34, '36), Pittsburgh Crawfords ('33), Baltimore Black Sox ('33), Philadelphia Stars ('35–'37), Brooklyn Royal Giants ('39), New York Black Yankees ('43)

Bats: Right   Throws: Right
Height: 5'8"   Weight: 160

This infielder's career spanned parts of three decades, beginning as a backup shortstop in 1929 with Hilldale, where he hit .278, and ending in 1943 with the New York Black Yankees. In 1930 he earned a starting berth with Hilldale, splitting his playing time between shortstop and second base and hitting .331 despite batting in the lower part of the lineup. In 1932 he began the season playing second base with Hilldale but finished playing shortstop with the Bacharachs. In 1933 he again split the season between two teams, sharing the playing time at shortstop with Chester Williams for the Pittsburgh Crawfords, and sharing playing time at second base with Dick Seay for the Baltimore Black Sox. By 1937 he was a substitute infielder with the Philadelphia Stars, playing both second base and third base under new manager Jud Wilson. During his career he also played with the Homestead Grays and the Brooklyn Royal Giants.

Lacy, Raymond

Career: 1949–50   Position: of
Team: Houston Eagles

This outfielder joined the Eagles after the franchise moved from Newark to Houston in 1949, batting .299 for the season. During this time the Negro American League was struggling to survive the loss of players to organized baseball, and although he was listed with the Eagles in 1950, league statistics do not confirm his playing time.

Laflora, Louis

Career: 1925   Position: of
Team: Kansas City Monarchs

He appeared briefly as a reserve outfielder with the Kansas City Monarchs in 1925, his only season in the Negro Leagues.

Lain, William

a.k.a. Lane
Career: 1911   Positions: 3b, ss
Teams: Chicago Giants ('11), Chicago American Giants ('11)

In 1911 he appeared briefly as a shortstop with the Chicago American Giants and was a part-time starter at third base for the Chicago Giants.

Lamar, Clarence (Horacio, Lemon)

Career: 1937–42   Positions: ss, 2b, 3b
Teams: St. Louis Stars ('37), Birmingham

Black Barons ('37, '42), **Jacksonville Red Caps** ('38, '41–'42), Cleveland Bears ('39–'40), Atlanta Black Crackers ('39), Indianapolis ABCs ('39)

This light-hitting middle infielder began his six seasons in the Negro American League as the regular shortstop with the St. Louis Stars in 1937. When the team folded after the Negro American League's maiden season, he played with the Jacksonville Red Caps as a reserve second baseman in 1938, but began playing more at shortstop when the franchise moved to Cleveland (playing as the Bears). He earned the starting position in 1940, a spot he kept when the ballclub returned to Jacksonville in 1941 and until the club dropped out of the Negro American League in July 1942. He finished out the season with the Birmingham Black Barons, getting some playing time at third base. Throughout his career he usually batted eighth in the lineup.

The infielder was from Augusta, Georgia, and attended Morehouse College. He was a reserve second baseman for the Atlanta Black Crackers when they moved to Indianapolis in 1939 and played as the Indianapolis ABCs.

Lamar, E. B., Jr. (Ed)
Career: 1895–1926   Positions: manager, owner, officer
Teams: Cuban X-Giants, Cuban Stars, Atlantic City Bacharach Giants, Harrisburg Giants, *Brooklyn Cuban Giants*

He began as the manager of the Cuban X-Giants in 1895 and later acquired ownership of the Philadelphia-based ballclub. In addition to being a club officer, he served as a booking agent through the mid-'20s.

LaMarque, James Harding (**Lefty**, Jim)
Career: 1942–50   Position: p
Teams: Kansas City Monarchs ('41–'51), *Mexican League ('50)*
Bats: Left   Throws: Left
Height: 6'1"   Weight: 180
Born: July 29, 1921, Potosi, Mo.
The Kansas City Monarchs' top left-handed

pitcher, he was a hardworking, cagey hurler who was tough in the clutch. His sharp-breaking curve was his best pitch, but he had an assortment of effective pitches, including a blazing fast ball, a good drop, a screwball, and good control. After splitting 2 league decisions while breaking in with the pennant-winning Monarchs in 1942, he pitched with Kansas City for a decade. Before joining the Monarchs, the Missourian was pitching for the Potosi Tigers in his hometown when he was discovered by Dizzy Dismukes.

In 1943 he missed most of the season after breaking his pitching arm in an off-season accident. Back in the rotation a year later, he posted a 2–3 league ledger and really came into his own in 1945, proving invaluable to the ballclub. That season he measured up to manager Frank Duncan's expectations for a member of the strong Kansas City Monarchs' staff when he registered an 8–2 record with a 3.04 ERA.

A year later, the left-hander fashioned a 7–3 record as the Monarchs won the 1946 Negro American League pennant, and he pitched 2 games in the ensuing World Series, winning his only decision. Although the Monarchs failed to repeat as Negro American League titlists in 1947, he improved his personal performance by finishing with a 12–2 record, good for an .857 winning percentage. In 1948 his league-leading 1.96 ERA and impressive 15–5 record earned him the first of two back-to-back All-Star game appearances.

However, even after establishing these solid credentials, he was still overlooked by the major leagues, who considered him to be in need of more seasoning. In 1950 his record dropped to 6–7 but he maintained a respectable 3.25 ERA. In addition to his superb pitching with the Monarchs, he played winter ball in Cuba (1946–47) and Puerto Rico (1948–49). He also played with the Mexico City Red Devils in the Mexican League in 1950, and toured Japan as a member of the Fort Wayne, Indiana, ballclub, winners of the 1950 National Baseball Congress Tournament in Wichita, Kansas.

After the tour he pitched with the Fort Wayne team until 1958.

Lamberto

Career: 1929   Position: of
Team: Cuban Stars (East)

He was an outfielder with the Cuban Stars in 1929, when they were members of the American Negro League.

Land

a.k.a. Lang
Career: 1908–14   Positions: of, 1b
Teams: New York Colored Giants ('08), Brooklyn Royal Giants ('10), Cuban Giants, Smart Set ('12) Mohawk Giants ('13–'14)

He began his career as a first baseman with the New York Colored Giants in 1908 and ended as an outfielder with the Mohawk Giants in 1913.

Landers, John

Career: 1917   Position: p
Team: Indianapolis ABCs

In the Indianapolis ABC's injury-plagued 1917 season, he was one of the few pitchers who remained healthy throughout the season.

Landers, Robert Henry

Career: 1949   Position: p
Team: Kansas City Monarchs ('49–'52)

He was a pitcher with the Kansas City Monarchs when the Negro American League was struggling to survive the loss of players to organized baseball.

Lane, Alto

Career: 1929–34   Position: p
Teams: Memphis Red Sox ('29), Indianapolis ABCs ('31), Kansas City Monarchs ('31), Louisville White Sox ('32), Cincinnati Tigers ('34)

Beginning with the Memphis Red Sox in 1929, where he pitched briefly without a decision, he was a pitcher with several teams for half a dozen seasons during the early years of the Depression.

Lane, Isaac S.

Career: 1917–24   Positions: p, 3b, *of*
Teams: Dayton Giants ('17), Dayton Marcos ('20), Columbus Buckeyes ('21), and Detroit Stars ('21–'24)

He began his career as a pitcher and ended as a third baseman, combining the two roles for four seasons with the Detroit Stars. In 1921, pitching with the Columbus Buckeyes, he split 2 league decisions.

Lang, John F.

Career: 1885–86   Position: manager
Teams: *Argyle Hotel Athletics ('85)*, Cuban Giants ('86)

A white man from Philadelphia, according to Sol White he was the owner and manager of the Argyle Hotel Athletics in 1885. The team evolved into the Cuban Giants, baseball's first black professional team, and the following year he sold the team to Walter Cook prior to the 1886 season.

Langford, Ad

Career: 1912–20   Positions: **p**, of
Teams: St. Louis Giants ('12), Mohawk Giants ('13), New York Lincoln Stars ('14, '16), New York Lincoln Giants ('15–'16, '18), Pennsylvania Red Caps of New York ('16–'20), Brooklyn Royal Giants ('17), Philadelphia Giants ('17)

Playing primarily with New York-based ballclubs, he pitched with the leading teams during the deadball era, including the Lincoln Giants and the Lincoln Stars. In 1914, when the McMahon brothers organized the Lincoln Stars, he signed with the ballclub, but jumped to the rival Lincoln Giants in 1915 before returning to help pitch the Stars to the eastern championship in 1916. In the play-off series against Rube Foster's western champion Chicago American Giants, he won 2 games, but the Stars lost the Series in 7 games.

The challenge series was played in August, and Langford joined the Pennsylvania Red Caps in the fall, but was with the Philadelphia Giants in midsummer of the following season and played with the Brooklyn Royal Giants before returning to the Red Caps. In 1918 he split the season between the Red Caps and the Lincoln Giants, with incomplete statistics showing him with a 2–2 record. Langford also sometimes played in the outfield when not pitching, with incomplete statistics showing a .200 batting average in 1917.

Langram
Career: 1939   Positions: 2b, of
Team: Kansas City Monarchs

This reserve second baseman could also play in the outfield. He made his only Negro League appearance with the 1939 Kansas City Monarchs.

Langrum, Dr. E. L.
Career: 1934   Position: officer
Team: Cleveland Red Sox

He was an officer with the Cleveland Red Sox in 1934, their only season in the Negro National League.

Lanier, A. S.
Career: 1921   Position: officer
Team: Cuban Stars (West)

In 1921 he was an officer with the Negro National League's Cuban Stars when they were playing as a representative of Cincinnati.

Lansing, Wilbur
Career: 1948–50   Position: p
Teams: Newark Eagles ('48), Houston Eagles ('49–'50)

He was a pitcher with the Eagles during their last season in Newark and both years in Houston.

Lantiqua, Enrique
Career: 1935   Position: c
Team: New York Cubans
Bats: Right   Throws: Right

He was a catcher with the 1935 New York Cubans, winners of the second-half Negro National League title.

Lanuza, Pedro
a.k.a. Lantuza, Pedro
Career: 1931–32   Position: c
Teams: Cuban Stars ('31), Cuban House of David ('32)
Bats: Right   Throws: Right

He was the regular catcher, usually batting in the lower part of the batting order, for the 1931–32 Cuban Stars, who also played as the Cuban House of David.

Larrinago, Perez
Career: 1946   Positions: 2b, ss
Team: Cleveland Buckeyes

A reserve middle infielder with the 1946 Cleveland Buckeyes, he could play either shortstop or second base.

Latimer
Career: 1921   Position: **p**
Team: Indianapolis ABCs

This pitcher posted a 2–3 record while with the Indianapolis ABCs in 1921, his only season in the Negro Leagues.

Lattimore, Alphonso
Career: 1929–33   Position: c
Teams: Baltimore Black Sox ('29), Brooklyn Royal Giants, Columbus Blue Birds ('33)

A backup catcher for five seasons, he broke in with the Baltimore Black Sox in 1929, batting .250 in limited play, and closed out his career under manager Dizzy Dismukes with the Columbus Blue Birds, a team that folded after the first half of the 1933 season.

Lau
Career: 1927   Position: p
Team: Cubans (East)

He was a pitcher with the Eastern Colored League Cubans in 1927.

Laurent, Milfred Stephen (Milt, **Milton**, *Rick*)
a.k.a. Larent
Career: 1929–35   Positions: 3b, 1b of, 2b, c, *ss, p*
Teams: Memphis Red Sox ('29–30), Cleveland

Cubs ('31), Birmingham Black Barons ('29, '32), Nashville Elite Giants ('32), New Orleans Crescent Stars ('33)
Born: Dec. 26 1901, New Orleans, La.

A versatile player who played every position, he spent seven seasons with southern ballclubs. In his first two season, 1929–30, he hit .206 and .250 for the Memphis Red Sox.

Lavelle
Career: 1908–12   Positions: c, 1b
Teams: Genuine Cuban Giants ('08), Cuban Giants, Cuban Stars ('12)

He began his career as a catcher with the Genuine Cuban Giants in 1908 and finished four years later as a first baseman with the Cuban Stars.

Lavera
Career: 1919   Position: c
Team: Cuban Stars

In 1919, his only year in black baseball, he was a catcher with the Cuban Stars when they were playing as an independent team.

Lawson, L. B. (Flash, Chick)
Career: 1940   Position; p
Teams: *Washington Pilots ('34),* Philadelphia Stars ('40)

He pitched briefly with the 1940 Philadelphia Stars, without a decision, but had pitched for lesser teams earlier in his career, including with the Washington Pilots in 1934, after they had dropped out of league play.

Lawyer, Floyd
Career: 1913   Position: rf
Team: Mohawk Giants

He played as an outfielder with the Mohawk Giants of Schenectady, New York, in 1913.

Layton, Obie
Career: 1931   Position:p
Teams: Hilldale Daisies ('31), *Detroit Black Sox ('41)*

He appeared briefly as a pitcher with Hill-

dale in 1931 but otherwise spent the remainder of his career with lesser teams.

Lazaga, Agipito
Career: 1916–22   Positions: rf, lf, 1b, p
Teams: New York Cuban Stars ('16), Cuban Stars (East) ('18, '22)

He began his career as a a first baseman-outfielder with owner Alejandro Pompez's 1916 New York Cuban Stars, batting fifth in the order. Two years later he was batting in the second slot for the Cuban Stars, and hit .218 while dividing his playing time between left field and right field. Remaining with the franchise, he also pitched during his seven seasons with the Cubans.

Leach
Career: 1914   Position: c
Team: Indianapolis ABCs

He was with the Indianapolis ABCs briefly in 1914 as a third-string catcher.

Leak, Curtis A
Career: 1940–48   Positions: officer; secretary (NNL)
Team: New York Black Yankees

During the '40s he was an officer for the New York Black Yankees and also served as secretary for the Negro National League.

Leary
Career: 1920   Position: 3b
Team: Dayton Marcos

He was a reserve third baseman with the Dayton Marcos in 1920, as they joined the Negro National League in the league's first year of existence. He later played shortstop with the Pennsylvania Red Caps of New York, a team of lesser status.

Leary
Career: 1934   Position: if
Team: Philadelphia Stars

He was a reserve player with the 1934 Negro National League champion Philadelphia Stars, appearing in 2 games.

LeBeaux

Career: 1936   Positions: ss, 2b
Team: Chicago American Giants

In 1936 this reserve middle infielder played both shortstop and second base with the Chicago American Giants, who were playing as an independent team.

LeBlanc

Career: 1915   Position: ss
Team: New York Lincoln Giants

He was a reserve shortstop with the 1915 Lincoln Giants.

LeBlanc, Julio (José)

a.k.a. Leblan
Career: 1919–21   Position: p, of
Teams: Cuban Stars (West) ('19–'21)
Height: 6'3"   Weight: 190

Beginning with the Cuban Stars during the last season of the deadball era, this versatile player began to flourish as a pitcher when the Cubans entered the Negro National League the following season. In 1921 he fashioned a 13–7 record in the Negro National League and after the season pitched with Havana in the Cuban winter league, where he led the league in wins. However, his promising career was abruptly ended when he became embroiled in an argument and was hit with a bat and killed by another ballplayer, Antonio Susini.

Lee, Dick

Career: 1917–18   Position: of
Team: Chicago Union Giants

In 1917–18 he was an outfielder with the Chicago Union Giants, a team of marginal quality.

Lee, Ed

Career: 1916   Position: ss
Teams; Philadelphia Giants ('16), Chicago Union Giants ('16)

This shortstop split his playing time in 1916 with two teams of marginal quality, the Philadelphia Giants and the Chicago Union Giants.

Lee, Fred

Career: 1915   Position: of
Team: Kansas City, Kansas, Giants

He was an outfielder with the 1915 Kansas City, Kansas, Giants.

Lee, Holsey Scranton Scriptus (**Scrip**, Script)

Career: 1922–34   Positions: **p**, 1b, of,
                                                 umpire (NNL)
Teams: *Norfolk Stars ('20–'21)*, Baltimore Black Sox ('22, '29–'33), **Hilldale Daisies** ('23–'27, '30), *Richmond Giants*, Atlantic City Bacharach Giants ('33–'34), *Philadelphia Giants ('26)*, Cleveland Red Sox ('34), Philadelphia Stars
Bats: Right   Throws: Right
Height: 6'0"   Weight; 185
Born: Jan. 29, 1899, Washington, D.C.
Died: Feb. 13, 1974, Washington, D.C.

A submariner with a variety of curves, this right-hander pitched for the Eastern Colored League champion Hilldale teams of 1923–25, registering a 24–8 record in 1923. He continued his superb pitching in the 1924 and 1925 World Series against the Kansas City Monarchs, recording a composite ERA of 2.30 in a total of 4 games. After losing to the Monarchs in 1924, Hilldale reigned victorious in 1925, and during the 1925 regular season Lee posted a 4–2 league ledger. In 1926, although Hilldale failed to retain their Eastern Colored League title, he posted an 18–5 record against all competition. In 1928 he left Hilldale in a dispute over money and signed with the Baltimore Black Sox.

Although best known for his curves, he also had a wide assortment of pitches, including a drop, screwball, knuckler, fastball, and change-up. His underhand delivery made his curve break up and his fastball break down, enhancing his effectiveness. In 1929 he played with another championship team, posting a 4–1 league record for the American Negro League champion Baltimore Black Sox while being credited with a 27–4 mark against all levels of competition. He spent several seasons with the Black Sox dating from 1922, when he recorded a 5–1 ledger while the Sox were still playing as an independent ballclub. In 1931, with the Sox once again playing as an independent, he posted a 7–11 record for the season.

He started playing baseball with broomsticks in a vacant lot as a youngster, went to school with Duke Ellington, and was a good football player. Lee was especially adept as a kicker, once drop-kicking a ball 100 yards. He played both football and baseball with an amateur team called the Georgetown Athletics, which also featured future Negro National League slugger Jud Wilson. In 1916 the teenager joined the National Guard and was sent to the Mexican border with General Pershing during Pancho Villa's uprising. When World War I started, he was with the 372nd Infantry attached to the 157th French Brigade. While serving in France he earned two Battle Stars and a Purple Heart, and he was discharged at Fort Dix, New Jersey, in 1919.

Nip Winters, a future star with Hilldale, was pitching with Chappy Johnson's Norfolk Stars and encouraged Lee to try out for the team. Johnson liked what he saw, and Lee began his professional career with the Stars in 1920 for $175 a month. In his second year in Norfolk he was ready to move up in competition and again joined Winters with Hilldale. In addition to his pitching skills, Lee was an outstanding bunter and excelled at squeeze plays. After his playing career ended he became a successful umpire in the Negro National League, continuing in this capacity through the 1943 season. Afterward he drove a taxi in Washington, D.C., and worked for the Veterans Administration for thirty-one years.

Lee, Lown
Career: 1909   Position: p
Team: Kansas City Royal Giants
He was a pitcher with the Royal Giants of Kansas City, Missouri, in 1909.

Lee, William
Career: 1888   Position: ss
Team: Chicago Unions

He was a reserve shortstop with manager W. S. Peters's Chicago Unions in 1888.

Leftwich, John (*Hymie*)
Career: 1945   Position: p
Team: Homestead Grays
Bats: Right   Throws: Right
Height: 5'10"   Weight: 190
A youngster from Duquesne, Pennsylvania, with only sandlot experience, during the last spring of wartime baseball he was given a thorough tryout with the Homestead Grays and showed enough promise to pitch briefly with the Grays that season, logging a 2–1 record.

Legrove
Career: 1937   Position: of
Team: Indianapolis Athletics
He was an outfielder with the Indianapolis Athletics in 1937, the first year of the Negro American League.

Leland, Frank C.
Career: 1887–1912   Positions; of, manager
Teams: Washington Capital Citys ('87), Unions ('87), Chicago Unions ('88–'00), Chicago Union Giants ('01–'04), Leland Giants ('05–'09), Chicago Giants ('10–'12)
Best known as a pioneering organizer, manager, and owner, Leland played outfield for three seasons with the ballclub that was called the Unions in 1887 and the Chicago Unions in 1888–89. In 1901 he combined the team with the Columbia Giants to form the Chicago Union Giants. In 1905 he formed the team that carried his name, the Leland Giants, and managed the team until 1907, when he lured pitching superstar Rube Foster to Chicago to take the reins of his team.

This combination proved a good one until 1910, when the two black baseball pioneers parted company and he formed the Chicago Giants. He and Foster both claimed the pennant from 1909 and the name "Leland Giants," and the dispute required legal rulings before accord was reached. Leland's team, because he had a numerical majority of players from the previous season, won the right to fly the pennant. On the other hand, Foster's team won the right to retain and use the name Leland Giants, which caused much confusion, with Foster's team being called the Chicago Leland Giants and Leland's team being referred to as Leland's Chicago Giants.

Leland, a graduate of Fisk University in Nashville, Tennessee, moved to Chicago and was instrumental in organizing and developing five successful baseball teams in that city, with the Chicago Giants being his last. The sportsman and businessman remained active in black baseball through 1912.

Leland Giants

Duration: 1905–10   Honors: Western champions ('10)

Affiliation: Independent

In 1901 Frank Leland combined the Chicago Unions, a well-established franchise dating back to 1887, and the Columbia Giants, a team of recent origin but a strong ballclub, to form the Chicago Union Giants (1901–04). In 1905 they became the Leland Giants and, under Leland's managerial command, fashioned a 48-game winning streak during the season. In 1907 Rube Foster joined the team and was their mound ace and manager for three years. In 1909 the Lelands lost a challenge series for the western championship to the St. Paul Colored Gophers. However, Foster had broken his leg in midseason and missed the playoffs, with his absence possibly determining the outcome of the series. After recovery, Foster culminated the 1909 season by arranging a postseason series against the Chicago Cubs. Although the Lelands lost the 3-game series, the games were closely contested, proving that black teams could be competitive with the best white teams.

The next season Foster and Leland separated and formed two distinct teams, with Foster's group winning the legal right to retain the name of Leland Giants for the 1910 season, although he chose to change it to the American Giants in 1911. Leland's new team was called the Chicago Giants and continued through the

deadball era to become a charter member of the Negro National League in 1920.

Lemon

[see Lamar, Clarence]

Lenox

Career: 1943   Position: 1b
Team: New York Black Yankees

He appeared briefly as a wartime first baseman with the New York Black Yankees in 1943.

Leon

Career: 1917–18   Positions: of, p, c
Team: Cuban Stars (East)

In 1917–18 he was an outfielder with the Cuban Stars (East) and also pitched on occasion.

Leon, Isididoro

a.k.a Isidore
Career; 1948   Positions: of, p
Team: New York Cubans

An outfielder with the New York Cubans in 1948, the last year of the Negro National League, he had pitched with the All Cubans squad of 1945–46.

Leonard, James (Bobo)

a.k.a. James Bobo
Career: 1919–32   Positions: **of**, 1b, *p*
Teams: Cleveland Tate Stars ('22–'23), Toledo Tigers ('23), Cleveland Browns ('24), Chicago American Giants ('24), Indianapolis ABCs ('24), New York Lincoln Giants ('24), Atlantic City Bacharach Giants ('24–'25), Baltimore Black Sox ('24–25), Cleveland Elite Giants ('26), Cleveland Hornets ('27), Cleveland Tigers ('28), Homestead Grays ('28), *Pennsylvania Red Caps of New York ('28–'32)*
Bats: Left   Throws: Uncertain

A good hitter, fast on the bases and in the field, and with a fair arm, he joined the Baltimore Black Sox in the latter part of the 1924 season after bouncing around with several other teams, and formed a good outfield with

Crush Holloway and Wade Johnston. He was cast in the same mold as the two veteran outer gardeners except that he was younger and not quite able to match their ability. However, he was considered a good young player and expected to come into his own with a little more seasoning.

Leonard was credited with averages of .358 and .247 in 1924–25 with the Black Sox, and .289 with Cleveland after joining the Elites in 1926. The Elites had a big turnover in personnel that season, and Leonard was sometimes used in center field and batted third when in the lineup. He also played as a substitute center fielder with the Negro National League's other Cleveland teams in 1927–28. The left-handed batter spent most of his career with struggling league teams but was unable to earn a permanent spot with an established team.

Leonard, Walter Fenner (**Buck**)
Career: 1933–50   Positions; **1b**, *of*
Teams: Brooklyn Royal Giants ('33), **Homestead Grays** ('34–50), *Mexican League ('51, '55), minor leagues ('53)*
Bats: Left   Throws: Left
Height: 5'10"   Weight: 185
Born: Sept. 8, 1907, Rocky Mount, N.C.

The left-handed half of the Homestead Grays' power tandem, Buck Leonard paired with Josh Gibson to lead Cum Posey's Grays to nine consecutive Negro National League championships during their halcyon years, 1937–45. While Gibson was slugging tape-measure home runs, Leonard was hitting screaming line drives both off the walls and over the walls. Trying to sneak a fastball past him was like trying to sneak a sunrise past a rooster. Batting fourth in the lineup of the Grays' "murderers' row," the muscular pull hitter displayed a powerful stroke, recording first-half averages of .500 and .480 in 1937–38 and seasonal averages of .363, .372, .275, .265, .327, .290, and .375 for the years 1939–45. Following the 1943 season Leonard was credited with averaging 34 home runs per year for the past eight years. Two years later he was

selected by Cum Posey as the first baseman on his All-Time All-American team chosen for a national magazine. Posey stated that Leonard was in a class by himself as a fielder and consistently hit over .320.

Possessing a smooth swing at the plate, he was equally smooth in the field. In 1941 one media source described four or five sensational stops that "were way beyond the reach of 99 percent of major-league first basemen." Sure-handed, with a strong and accurate arm and acknowledged as a smart ballplayer who always made the right play, Buck was a team man all the way. Respected by his teammates, he was even-tempered and professional, and his consistency and dependability were a steadying influence on the Grays. A class guy, he was the best-liked player in the game.

So great were his contributions to the team's success that even in the years when Gibson was in Mexico, the Grays continued to win pennants. In 1942, with Josh rejoining Buck in the Grays' lineup, the Grays won their sixth consecutive Negro National League pennant and faced Satchel Paige's Kansas City Monarchs in the first Negro World Series between the Negro American League and the Negro National League. The Monarchs had won five of the first six Negro American League flags, and the World Series was a showdown between the two dark dynasties. Leonard was suffering from a broken hand but taped the hand and played in the series. But despite his heroic effort, the Grays lost to the Monarchs in 4 straight games.

After the disappointing Series loss, the Grays rebounded to win back-to-back World Series in 1943–44 over the Birmingham Black Barons, featuring Leonard's torrid .500 batting average in the latter series. The home-run duo had finished the regular season tied for the league lead in home runs and followed in 1945 with another one-two finish in that category, with Leonard pounding out a .375 batting average as well, to lead the Grays to another flag.

After a two-year absence from the Negro World Series, the Grays, under Leonard's inspirational leadership, defeated the Baltimore Elites in the playoffs to cop the final Negro National League flag, then defeated the Black Barons, now featuring a youngster named Willie Mays, in the 1948 World Series to again become champions of black baseball. That year, following batting averages of .322 and .410 the previous two years, Leonard won his third batting title with a .395 average and tied for the league lead in home runs as well. Over a seventeen-year career in the Negro National League, his lifetime stats show a .341 average in league play and a .382 average in exhibition games against major leaguers.

Leonard was born in Rocky Mount, North Carolina, the oldest son in a family of six children. His father, John Leonard, was a railroad fireman, and his mother, Emma, was a housewife. His parents called him "Buddy," but when his younger brother Charlie was small, his efforts to pronounce the name resulted in "Buck," hence the nickname by which he is known. He enrolled in Lincoln Elementary School in 1913 and attended through the eighth grade. When his father died from the influenza epidemic in 1919, he had to help support the family by working after school in a hosiery mill and shining shoes at the railway station. When he turned sixteen, he began working full-time at the Atlantic Coastline Railroad Shop, putting brake cylinders on boxcars.

His first interest in baseball came from watching the white Rocky Mount minor-league ballclub, whose ballpark was near his home. Later he became batboy for the local black semipro team. Later, while working at the railroad shop, he began playing semipro baseball, and for seven years he worked a full-time job and was a star on his hometown baseball team. But in 1933 the Depression required a cutback at the railroad shop and Leonard was forced by the Depression to leave home to pursue a professional baseball career.

That season he played successively for the Portsmouth Firefighters, the Baltimore Stars, and the Brooklyn Royal Giants, where he played in the outfield. Smokey Joe Williams

saw him playing with the Royals and connected him with the Homestead Grays for the 1934 season, and Leonard remained with the Grays through the 1950 season.

During his tenure in the Grays' flannels, he quickly gained the respect and appreciation of inside baseball men. He was also a favorite of the fans, and became a fixture in the annual East-West All-Star classic. As usual, in 1948 Leonard was selected to the East squad's starting lineup, marking his eleventh year, an All-Star record. His first appearance came in 1935, in the middle of a .338 season, when he entered the game as a pinch hitter. His first starting assignment in an All-Star game was two years later, when he batted cleanup and counted a homer in his pair of hits as he powered the East to a 7–3 victory over the West squad. That began a skein of five straight starting assignments in the East-West classic, culminating in another homer among his pair of hits in the 8–3 victory in the 1941 contest. After missing the 1942 game due to an injury, he banged out another homer in the 1943 classic to establish an All-Star record while also compiling a lifetime .317 average in this star-studded competition.

When he was in his prime, he and Josh Gibson were called into Clark Griffith's office and asked if they were interested in playing in the major leagues. Although they responded affirmatively, nothing came of the meeting, and it was eight years before Jackie Robinson was signed and the door finally opened for blacks in the major leagues. In 1952, when Bill Veeck offered him a chance to play with the St. Louis Browns, the veteran slugger's age was against him, and he knew the opportunity had come too late. After the demise of the Negro National League following the 1948 season, he continued with the Grays for another two years, playing against a lesser caliber of competition, until the Grays folded following the 1950 season.

Being accustomed to Latin American climates from when he had played in Cuba (Marianao in 1948–49), Puerto Rico (Mayaquez in

1940–41), and Venezuela (Caracas in 1945–46 on an American All-Star team), he signed to play in the Mexican League, registering averages of .325 and .328 for the 1951–52 seasons with Torreon. The respect that his powerful bat commanded is apparent in the number of free passes he was issued, averaging more than a walk per game and almost one fourth of his plate appearances. His winters in Cuba yielded a lifetime .284 batting average. During his winter in Puerto Rico he had compiled some impressive credentials, including a .389 batting average with 8 homers in only 118 at-bats, yielding 1 homer per 14.8 at-bats and one extra-base hit per 4.7 at-bats.

In 1953 he returned to his home in Rocky Mount, North Carolina, but was prevailed upon to finish the season with the Portsmouth team in the Piedmont League, where he hit .333 in 10 games. Two years later, at age forty-eight, he slammed 13 home runs in 62 games while hitting .312 with Durango in the Central Mexican League to close out a twenty-three-year career in baseball.

After retiring from baseball he worked as a truant officer with the Rocky Mount school system, operated his own realty agency, and was an officer with the Rocky Mountain baseball team in the Carolina League.

Fortunately, although national recognition of his great talent also came late, Buck Leonard was still able to smell the roses when he was inducted into the National Baseball Hall of Fame along with Josh Gibson in 1972. Called the Black Lou Gehrig, he showed the same skill on the diamond and the same strength of character off the field.

LeRue
Career: 1921   Position: c
Team: Detroit Stars

He appeared briefly as a third-string catcher with the Detroit Stars in 1921, his only year in the Negro Leagues.

Lester
Career: 1932   Position: p
Team: Nashville Elite Giants

He was a pitcher with the Nashville Elites in 1932, when the Negro Southern League was recognized as a major league.

Lett, Roger
Career: 1943   Position: p
Team: Cincinnati Clowns

He pitched briefly with the Cincinnati Clowns in 1943, the franchise's first year in league play after touring as an independent team for many years.

Lettlers, George
Career: 1887   Position: player
Team: Washington Capital Citys

He was a player with the Washington Capital Citys, one of eight teams that were charter members of the League of Colored Baseball Clubs in 1887. However, the league's existence was ephemeral, lasting only a week.

Leuschner, W. A., Jr. (Bill)
Career: 1940–43   Position: officer
Team: New York Black Yankees

After Nat Strong's death, he was Strong's successor as the booking agent for the New York area, and also served as an officer for the New York Black Yankees in the early '40s.

Levis, Oscar (Oscal)
a.k.a. Oscar; Oscal
Career: 1921–32   Positions; p, of
Teams: Cuban Stars (East) ('21–'29, '31–32, '34), Baltimore Black Sox, Hilldale Daisies ('30–'31), All Cubans ('21)
Bats: Left   Throws: Left

This spitball ace's two best pitches were his spitter and his fake spitter. He was a leading pitcher with the Cuban Stars during the 1920s, and was their ace in 1924, but the Cubans had the worst team in the Eastern Colored League that season. The next year the team fielded another weak lineup, and Levis had a 4–7 league ledger. By 1927 the team had improved, and the change was reflected in Levis's 8–4 record. After the collapse of the Eastern Colored League, the Cuban hurler joined the independent Hilldale ballclub and as their ace was credited with records of 2–7 and 12–10 for the 1930–31 seasons.

While he was with the Cubans, the box scores often listed him simply as ''Oscar'' or ''Oscal'' instead of using his last name, and he often played in the outfield, posting batting averages of .285, .281, and .239 for the Cubans in 1924–25 and 1927, while batting a robust .426 in 1930 with Hilldale.

In his homeland, his prime years coincided with those in the Negro Leagues, and in the winter of 1924–25 he played with Havana in the Cuban League and tied for the league lead in wins with 9. Three years later he again topped the league in victories while posting a 7–2 mark.

Lewis
Career: 1887   Position: player
Team: Boston Resolutes

He was a player with the Boston Resolutes, one of eight teams that were charter members of the League of Colored Baseball Clubs in 1887. However, the league's existence was ephemeral, lasting only a week.

Lewis
Career: 1923   Position: p
Team: Indianapolis ABCs

He was a pitcher with the 1923 Indianapolis ABCs.

Lewis
Career: 1935   Position: ss
Team: Brooklyn Eagles

He was a reserve shortstop with the Brooklyn Eagles in 1935.

Lewis
Career: 1937   Position: 1b
Team: Birmingham Black Barons

He was with the Birmingham Black Barons briefly in 1937 as a reserve first baseman.

Lewis, Cary B.
Career: 1920   Position: secretary
League: Negro National League

In 1920 he was a codrafter of the Constitution of the Negro National League, and served as the first league secretary under Rube Foster's presidency.

Lewis, Charles (Babe)
Career: 1926   Positions: ss, 2b
Teams: *Philadelphia Giants ('25)*, New York Lincoln Giants ('26)

After a season playing second base with the Philadelphia Giants in 1925, this young infielder was signed to replace the retiring Bill Lindsay as shortstop with the 1926 New York Lincoln Giants.

Lewis, Clarence (Foots)
Career: 1931–37   Positions: ss, 2b, 1b
Teams: Birmingham Black Barons ('31–'32), Memphis Red Sox ('31–'33, '37), Pittsburgh Crawfords ('33), Akron Tyrites ('33), Cleveland Giants ('33), Cleveland Red Sox ('34), Nashville Elite Giants ('34)
Bats: Right   Throws: Right

In 1932, after he had not received pay from the Birmingham Black Barons for 1931, he was signed by the Memphis Red Sox, who argued that he was a free agent and refused to abide by league president Dr. R.B. Jackson's order to release him. Tom Wilson, owner of both the Birmingham Black Barons and the Nashville Elites, disagreed, and wanted to sign Lewis for the Elites. The quarrel lasted through the first half of the Negro Southern League season. He remained with the Red Sox and was the starting shortstop in 1932–33, batting sixth in the order in 1932 and in the second slot in 1933. In 1933 he also played with the Akron Tyrites, a team that combined with the Columbus Blue Birds to form the Cleveland Giants, a replacement team for the second half of the Negro National League season. With both these teams, Lewis played second base, as he did in 1937 after returning to the Memphis Red Sox.

Lewis, F.
Career: 1932   Position: of
Team: Montgomery Grey Sox

He was an outfielder with the Montgomery Grey Sox in 1932, when the Negro Southern League was recognized as a major league.

Lewis, George (Peaches)

Career: 1917   Position: p

Teams: New York Lincoln Giants ('17), Atlantic City Bacharach Giants ('22)

This pitcher served two short stints with top teams, making an appearance with the Lincoln Giants in 1917 and winning his only recorded decision, and with the Bacharachs in 1922.

Lewis, Grover

Career: 1928   Positions: **3b**, rf

Team: Homestead Grays

A reserve third baseman with the Homestead Grays in 1928, he could also play in the outfield when needed.

Lewis, Ira F.

Career: 1922   Position: officer

Team: Pittsburgh Keystones

He served as secretary for the Pittsburgh Keystones in 1922, their only season in the Negro National League.

Lewis, Jerome

Career: 1910–13   Position: 1b

Team: West Baden Sprudels ('10–*13*)

In 1910 he was a backup first baseman with the Sprudels of West Baden, Indiana, playing when Ben Taylor left the initial sack to take his turn on the mound. After the Taylor brothers and most of the top players left the team after the 1910 season, Lewis benefited by receiving more playing time.

Lewis, Jim (Slim)

Career: 1947   Positions: p, 2b

Teams: *Chicago Brown Bombers ('43)*, New York Black Yankees ('47), *Indianapolis Clowns ('53)*

In 1947 he was a pitcher with the New York Black Yankees and earlier, in 1943, he pitched with the Chicago Brown Bombers, a team of lesser status. After the Negro Leagues were in decline and no longer of major-league quality, he played second base with the Indianapolis Clowns in 1953.

Lewis, Joseph Herman (Joe, Sleepy)

Career: 1918–34   Positions: c, 3b

Teams: Baltimore Black Sox ('18–'23, '33), Washington Potomacs ('23), Homestead Grays ('23), Hilldale Daisies ('24–'25, '27—'32), New York Lincoln Giants ('26), Quaker Giants, Atlantic City Bacharach Giants ('26, '33–'34), *Norfolk-Newport News Royals*

Bats: Right   Throws: Right

Born: 1899, Sparrows Point, Md.

A catcher who was a pretty good hitter, he spent most of his seventeen seasons as a backup or part-time starter with good eastern ballclubs. He began his career at age nineteen with George Rossiter's Baltimore Black Sox in 1918, while they were in their formative years. Within two years he had earned a starting position while often hitting third in the batting order, but by 1922, when the Sox strengthened their roster preparatory to becoming a member in the Eastern Colored League, he was sharing the catching position and batting near the bottom of the order. He left the team in 1923 to play with the newly organized Washington Potomacs, but finished the season with the Homestead Grays.

The following season, 1924, he joined Hilldale, the winners of the first Eastern Colored League pennant, where he served as the backup receiver for Louis Santop and hit .347. The next season, with Santop fading, Biz Mackey stepped into the starting catcher's role, with Lewis remaining as a backup. During each of his first two seasons with the Hilldale club, the team annexed Eastern Colored League flags to make three consecutive pennants. Both seasons, Hilldale played the Kansas City Monarchs in the Negro World Series, losing the inaugural matchup but defeating the Monarchs in 1925 to claim the Negro championship.

After a year split between the Bacharachs and the Lincoln Giants, where he was a part-time starter with both clubs, he returned to Hilldale for an additional six seasons, serving primarily as a backup, except for two seasons when circumstances permitted him to move into the regular lineup. He hit .283 and .205 for the 1927–28 seasons, and then in 1930, when Mackey played shortstop for most of the season to fill a team need, Lewis hit .302 while handling the backstopping chores. In 1932 the star catcher absented himself from the team, leaving a vacancy. During his time as a starter, he usually batted in the lower part of the order. The 1932 season was Hilldale's final year, and after the club folded, he played two seasons with the Bacharachs, another once-grand team now in decline. Although he was the regular catcher on the team, the club was now a marginal ballclub. During his career, he also played third base, and he tried his hand as a manager in 1946.

Lewis, Milton
Career: 1922–28   Positions: **2b**, 1b, of, 3b, ss

Teams: *Madison Stars ('20), Norfolk Stars ('21),* Harrisburg Giants ('22), Atlantic City Bacharach Giants ('22, '24–'25, '27–'28), *Richmond Giants ('23),* Wilmington Potomacs ('25), *Philadelphia Giants ('26–'27)*

A big man who was a good power hitter and could play any nonbattery position, he was a very good utility man. However, he lacked the skill to excel at each position, as did some other players. Although he was primarily a second baseman, he played both infield and outfield with a variety of clubs during the '20s, but is best identified with the Bacharachs.

Lewis, Robert S. (**Bubber**, Bubbles)
Career: 1923–28   Positions: owner, executive

Team: Memphis Red Sox

He was the owner of the Memphis Red Sox and an officer for half a dozen seasons during the '20s, also serving as the vice president of the Negro National League.

Lewis, Rufus (Lew)
Career: 1936–50   Position: p
Teams: Pittsburgh Crawfords ('36–'37), *mili-*

tary service ('43–'45), **Newark Eagles** ('46–'48), Houston Eagles ('49–'50), *Mexican League ('50–'52), minor leagues ('52)*
Bats: Right   Throws: Right
Height: 6'1"   Weight; 189
Born: Dec. 13, 1919, Hattiesburg, Miss

After playing baseball during three years of service in the U.S. Army Air Corps during World War II, Lewis signed with the Newark Eagles. With good control, a knuckler, a good fastball and curve, the big right-hander starred for the Eagles in the 1940s. As a rookie he finished the 1946 season with an 18–3 record (6–1 in league play) and won the decisive seventh game in the World Series, giving him a 2–1 record and 1.64 ERA for the Series. The next season he fashioned a 11–6 record, and in 1948, showing a 38–15 record over three years (1946–48), he was selected as the starting pitcher for the East in the East-West game, making his only All-Star game appearance. He struck out 4 batters while yielding only 3 hits in his 3 innings, but was pinned with the loss in the 3–0 contest. That season proved to be the last for the Negro National League, as the league folded following the 1948 season. The Eagles, under new ownership, joined the Negro American League's West Division after relocating in Houston, and the fireballer dropped to a 10–11 record in 1949.

While with the Eagles he spent two seasons (1947–49) in the Cuban winter league, honing his craft. In his first year, playing for the Havana Reds under Mike Gonzales, he tied with Lefty LaMarque for the league high in wins with a record of 11–6 (2.40 ERA), and continued with an 8–5 record the following winter.

The hard-throwing right-hander was highly coveted, and in 1950, after pitching in only 3 games for the Eagles without a decision, he was contacted by the Dodgers organization to play with St. Paul of the American Association, and was invited to spring training. Unable to reach agreement with the club relating to a salary and bonus, Lewis opted to play in Mexico.

His years in the Mexican League were uneven, with records of 5–8 (4.05 ERA) with Mexico City in 1950 and 10–9 (3.40 ERA) in

1951. During the latter year he was involved in an incident with Chiquitin Cabrera, who charged the mound and hit Lewis with a bat, knocking him down, and attempted to hit him again while he was lying on the ground unconscious. Only swift action by Lewis's teammate Bill Wright, who rushed from the dugout with a bat to intervene, saved Lewis's life. After starting the next season (1952) with Mexico City, he completed the season with Chihuahua in the Arizona-Texas League, finishing with an 8–15, 4.92 ERA ledger to show for his last year in baseball.

An all-around athlete, he played football for four years at Lanier High School in Hattiesburg, Mississippi, before graduating in 1939, and began his Negro Leagues career with the Pittsburgh Crawfords prior to joining the Eagles, where he was a good-fielding pitcher, a hustling base runner with respectable speed, and a pretty-good-hitting pitcher with average power. His biggest thrill in baseball came in 1946, when he pitched a two-hitter against the Kansas City Monarchs.

Lewis, Tuck
Career: 1916–17   Positions: 2b, 3b
Team: Chicago Giants

He was a reserve infielder with the Chicago Giants, playing second base in 1916 and third base in 1917.

Liggons, James
Career: 1932–34   Positions: p, of
Teams: Monroe Monarchs ('32) Memphis Red Sox, ('34) *Little Rock Black Travelers ('32)*

During the early '30s he was a pitcher and outfielder with the Monroe Monarchs, the Memphis Red Sox, and the Little Rock Black Travelers

Lightner
a.k.a. Linder
Career: 1920–22, 1932 Position: p
Teams: Kansas City Monarchs ('20–'22), Cole's American Giants ('32)

He made appearances with top ballclubs, as a pitcher with the Kansas City Monarchs in 1920 and again with the Cole's American Giants in 1932, the year they won the Negro Southern League pennant. It is uncertain where he was in the intervening decade.

Ligon, Rufus C.
a.k.a. Ligons
Career: 1944–46   Position: p
Team: Memphis Red Sox
Bats: Right   Throws: Right

This wartime pitcher began his career in 1944 with the Memphis Red Sox and lost his only three decisions in 1945 before closing his career after a postwar appearance in 1946.

Lillard, Joe
Career: 1932–37, 1944 Positions: p, of, c
Teams: Cole's American Giants ('32), Chicago American Giants ('33–'34, '37), Cincinnati Tigers ('36), Birmingham Black Barons ('44)
Bats: Right   Throws: Right
Height: 6'0"   Weight: 185

A good power hitter and a hard-throwing right-hander, he pitched, played outfield, and even took a few turns behind the plate on special occasions for the American Giants. During his first two seasons with the team they copped pennants, winning the Negro Southern League flag in 1932 and the Negro National League flag in 1933, with Lillard contributing 4–5 and 6–0 mound records and batting averages of .280 and .393.

An all-around athlete, he balanced two professional sports careers, also playing professional football with the Chicago Cardinals as a running back.

Lillie
Career: 1925   Position: ut
Team: Birmingham Black Barons

He was a utility player with the 1925 Birmingham Black Barons.

Linares, Abel
Career: 1911–12   Positions: owner, officer
Team: Cuban Stars

He was the owner and president of the Cuban Stars and also the owner of the Almendares baseball park.

Linares, Rogelio (Ice Cream)

Career: 1940–46   Positions: **1b**, cf, lf, rf
Teams: Cuban Stars ('40), New York Cubans ('40, '43–'46)
Bats: Left   Throws: Left
Height: 5'10"   Weight: 175
Born: 1916, Havana, Cuba

This New York Cubans' outfielder was selected to the East All-star squad in 1945, and followed with a .287 batting average for the Cubans the next year. He was fast on the bases and in the field, had a strong and accurate throwing arm, and at the plate was an extremely dangerous distance hitter who also hit consistently for average. A fleet-footed, hard-driving player, his speed and skill earned him the admiration of teammates and fans alike.

He broke in with the Cubans in 1940 as a first baseman and finished with a .276 batting average, but did not play in the United States again until 1943, with partial statistics showing a .349 batting average. Beginning in 1944 he played more in the outfield than at first base and hit .263 and .266 in 1944–45, batting cleanup in 1945 but usually batting in the sixth spot in the order during the other seasons with the Cubans.

He was one of the best Cuban players during the '40s, and during his five seasons in his home country he became the idol of Havana's sports world and was on the 1945–46 All Cubans team. The outfielder also could play first base, and he handled the task with aplomb, pleasing the crowd with his flashy showmanship.

Lincoln, James

Career: 1895   Positions: 3b, ss
Teams: *Lincoln, Nebraska Giants ('90)*, Page Fence Giants ('95)

He was a third baseman with the 1895 Adrian Page Fence Giants, batting .471 for the season. He previously played shortstop with the Lincoln, Nebraska, Giants, in 1890.

Lincoln Giants

Duration: 1911–30   Honors: Eastern championship ('11–'13)
Affiliations: Independent ('11–'22, '27, '30), ECL ('23–'26, '28), ANL ('29)

Founded by Jess McMahon, a white businessman and sports promoter, in 1911 and based in New York, for a decade they were usually the best team in the East. With a team featuring John Henry Lloyd, Smokey Joe Williams, Cannonball Dick Redding, Spot Poles, and Louis Santop, the Lincoln Giants began as the class of the eastern teams, finishing with a 108–12 record in their first season to win the first of three straight eastern championships. In 1913 the Lincoln Giants easily defeated Rube Foster's western titlists, the Chicago American Giants, in a playoff for the championship. In their early years the Lincolns added a shadow ball routine to their pregame warm-ups for the entertainment of the fans, but abandoned the practice before they began league play. The next season the McMahons formed a rival team, the Lincoln Stars, and Jim Keenan took over the operation of the Lincoln Giants' franchise, which continued for twenty years.

When the Eastern Colored League was formed in 1923, the Lincoln Giants became charter members and fielded a team every year except 1927, but their only winning team was in 1924, when they finished in third place with a 31–25 record. They also were a member of the American Negro League in 1929, finishing with the second-best mark for the season, with a combined 40–22 record for a .606 winning percentage. Upon the league's demise after a single season, the Lincolns returned to independent play and in 1930 fielded one of the strongest teams in the East but lost a playoff to the Homestead Grays for the eastern championship. That was the last year for the Lincoln Giants, but eventually the ballclub evolved into the New York Black Yankees.

Lincoln Stars

Duration: 1914–16   Honors: Eastern championship ('15–16)

Affiliation: Independent

The ballclub was formed as a rival splinter group from the Lincoln Giants by Jess and Rod McMahon, who had formed the Lincoln Giants in 1911, and also was based in New York. During the midteens they were a good ballclub, but their notoriety was short-lived, lasting only three years. In 1915 they played Rube Foster's Chicago American Giants in a championship series, with the playoff ending in a standoff amid controversy. Each team won 5 games, but with the Stars leading the deciding game by a run, the game was called in the fourth inning. The following year, their last season, they won the eastern championship, but lost a challenge playoff to Foster's western champion American Giants in a hard-fought 7-game series. The championship series was held in August, and Oscar Charleston, who was their center fielder, jumped the team to return to the Indianapolis ABCs shortly before the showdown. Despite the loss the Stars took a 3–2 lead, needing only to win one of their last two games to take the championship, but lost both games. The team disbanded following the season, with many of the players going to the Pennsylvania Red Caps.

Linder

[see Lightner]

Lindsay, Bill (the Kansas Cyclone)

Career: 1910–14   Position: p

Teams: Kansas City, Kansas, Giants ('10), Leland Giants ('10), Chicago American Giants ('11–'14)

Bats: Right   Throws: Right

Died: Sept. 1, 1914, Chicago, Ill.

Beginning his career during the 1910 season with the Giants of Kansas City, Kansas, he earned the nickname "the Kansas Cyclone," but after pitching against Rube Foster's Leland Giants in late June and striking out 7 batters in a losing effort, the big, hard-throwing right-

hander found favor in the manager's appraising eye and later in the year was signed to pitch with the Lelands for the remainder of the season, with a commitment for 1911 as well. Foster noted that he was a good pitcher and needed only a good team behind him to win, and the American Giants' skipper was determined to provide that ingredient for success.

Foster's new acquisition traveled with the team to Cuba for the winter season and, after returning to the States in the spring, became a star pitcher with the American Giants. During his brief career Lindsay was considered to be, mechanically, the best right-handed pitcher on the staff, and was sometimes referred to as the best all-around pitcher in the franchise's history. Sketchy statistics show a composite 6–0 record during his short tenure with the American Giants.

Tragically, four short years after joining Foster's club, the star pitcher's career was ended prematurely when he died only a few days prior to the Giants' championship playoff against the eastern champion Brooklyn Royal Giants. While in mourning for Lindsay, the Giants won 4 straight games to sweep the Series and claim the title.

Lindsay, Charles Clarence (Bill)

a.k.a. Lindsey

Career: 1920–34   Positions: ss, 2b, 3b, of

Teams: *Philadelphia Giants of New York ('20)*, New York Lincoln Giants ('20, '25–'26), *Richmond Giants ('22–'23)*, Baltimore Black Sox ('23–'24), Washington Potomacs ('24), Wilmington Potomacs ('25), Dayton Marcos ('26), *Pennsylvania Red Caps of New York ('26–'27, '30, '32)*, Hilldale Daisies ('28), Atlantic City Bacharach Giants ('29, '31, '34), Washington Pilots ('32)

One of the shortstops competing for the starting slot at a weak position in the Baltimore Black Sox' lineup in 1924, he batted .260 and was a fair player but short on experience. He was expected to make a bid for the starting position in 1925 but was on the Wilmington Potomacs' reserved list for that season. When the Potomacs' franchise folded, he landed with the New York Lincoln Giants and hit .282 for the season. However, in midsummer of 1926 the star shortstop for the Lincoln Giants quit the team for a year-round job. His defection from the baseball scene was not permanent, and he played with Dayton that same season, batting .226 in limited play. Subsequently he played with other teams but without particular distinction.

Lindsay, James
Career: 1943   Position: if
Team: Birmingham Black Barons
He was an infielder with the 1943 Birmingham Black Barons.

Lindsay, Leonard **(Sloppy)**
a.k.a. Yahodi
Career: 1942–46   Positions: 1b, p, 3b
Teams: Ethiopian Clowns ('42), Birmingham Black Barons ('43), Cincinnati Clowns ('43), Indianapolis Clowns ('46)
Bats: Right   Throws: Right
Playing with the Clowns during the '40s, he performed under the Clown name of "Yahodi" before the franchise entered the Negro American League and the players began using their correct names. He also played later for the Havana La Palomas ballclub in 1947.

Lindsay, Merf
Career: 1910   Position: cf
Team: Kansas City Giants
He was an outfielder with the 1910 Kansas City, Kansas, Giants.

Lindsay, P.
Career: 1910   Positions: 1b, of
Team: Kansas City Giants
He was a first baseman-outfielder with the 1910 Kansas City, Kansas, Giants.

Lindsay, Robert (Frog)
Career: 1910–15   Position: ss
Team: Kansas City, Kansas, Giants
A shortstop with the Kansas City, Kansas,

Giants in 1910, he was regarded as a good fielder and hitter. He made his home in Lexington, Missouri, and was the brother of Bill Lindsay, who later pitched with Rube Foster's Chicago American Giants.

Lindsey
Career: 1912–14   Position: of
Teams: New York Lincoln Giants ('12), *West Baden Sprudels ('14)*
He was an outfielder with the 1912 Lincoln Giants. Two years later he played with the Sprudels of West Baden, Indiana, a team of lesser status.

Lindsey, Ben
Career: 1929   Positions: **ss**, *p*
Teams: Baltimore Black Sox ('28), Atlantic City Bacharach Giants ('29)
He was the regular shortstop with the 1929 Atlantic City Bacharach Giants, batting second in the order and hitting .275 for the season.

Lindsey, Bill
[see Lindsay, Charles Clarence (Bill)]

Lindsey, James
Career: 1887   Position: of
Team: *Pittsburgh Keystones*
He was an outfielder with the Pittsburgh Keystones, one of eight teams that were charter members of the League of Colored Baseball Clubs in 1887. However, the league's existence was ephemeral, lasting only a week.

Lindsey, Robert
Career: 1931   Positions: **p**, of, 1b
Team: Indianapolis ABCs
He was a pitcher under manager Candy Jim Taylor with the Indianapolis ABCs in 1931, their last season in the Negro National League. He also had played in the outfield and at first base.

Lipsey
Career: 1942   Position: p
Team: Memphis Red Sox

He was a pitcher with the Memphis Red Sox in 1942.

Lisby

Career: 1934   Position: p

Teams: Newark Dodgers ('34), Atlantic City Bacharach Giants ('34)

He was a pitcher with the Newark Dodgers and the Bacharach Giants in 1934.

Listach, Nora

Career: 1941   Position: of

Teams: *Cincinnati Buckeyes ('40)*, Birmingham Black Barons ('41)

He was an outfielder with the 1941 Black Barons after having played the previous year with the Cincinnati Buckeyes, a lesser team at that time.

Little, William

Career: 1937–50   Position: officer

Team: Chicago American Giants

He was an officer with the Chicago American Giants during their years in the Negro American League, beginning when the league was organized in 1937.

Littles, Ben

a.k.a. Little

Career: 1947–50   Position: of

Teams: Homestead Grays ('48), Black Yanks ('48), Philadelphia Stars ('49–*'51*)

This outfielder was a part-time starter with the New York Black Yankees in 1948, batting in the lower part of the batting order when in the lineup. The next year he began a three-year stint with the Philadelphia stars, batting .204 for the 1949 season.

Livingston, Curtis

Career: 1950   Position: of

Team: Cleveland Buckeyes

He was listed as an outfielder with the Cleveland Buckeyes in 1950, when the Negro American League was struggling to survive the loss of players to organized baseball, but league statistics do not confirm his playing time.

Livingston, L. D. (Lee, Leo, Goo Goo)

Career: 1928–32   Position: of

Teams: Kansas City Monarchs ('28–'31), New York Black Yankees ('31), Pittsburgh Crawfords ('32), *Pennsylvania Red Caps of New York ('32)*

He was an outfielder for four seasons with the Monarchs, batting .284 and .300 in 1929–30, and also played briefly with the 1932 Pittsburgh Crawfords.

Lloyd, John Henry (Pop, El Cuchara)

Career: 1906–32   Positions: ss, 2b, 1b, c, manager

Teams: *Macon Acmes ('05)*, Cuban X-Giants ('06), Philadelphia Giants ('07–'09), Leland Giants ('10), New York Lincoln Giants ('11–'15, '26–'30), Chicago American Giants ('14–17), New York Lincoln Stars ('15), Brooklyn Royal Giants ('18–'20), New York Bacharach Giants ('19), Atlantic City Bacharach Giants ('22, '24–'25, '31–'32), Columbus Buckeyes ('21), Hilldale Daisies ('23), Harlem Stars ('31)

Bats: Left   Throws: Right

Height: 5'11"   Weight; 180

Born: April 25, 1884, Palatka, Fla.

Died: Mar. 19, 1965, Atlantic City, N.J.

Essential to any team's success during the deadball era was the presence of John Henry Lloyd, the greatest black baseball player during the first two decades of the century. The tall, rangy superstar was the greatest shortstop of his day, black or white, and with the exception of Honus Wagner in his prime, no major leaguer could compare with him. Wagner is reported to have said that he considered it a privilege to be compared to Lloyd.

He was a complete ballplayer who could hit, run, field, throw, and hit with power, especially in the clutch. A superior hitter and a dangerous base runner, his knowledge and application of inside baseball as defined in the era allowed him to generate runs with a variety of skills.

In the field he was a superlative fielder who studied batters and positioned himself wisely, got a good jump on the ball, and possessed exceptional range and sure hands with which he dug balls out of the dirt like a shovel. Lloyd's play afield earned him the nickname in Cuba of ''El Cuchara,'' Spanish for ''The Tablespoon.''

Left fatherless as an infant, Lloyd left school at an early age to work as a delivery boy to help meet the family's financial needs. The youngster gravitated toward baseball and played in Jacksonville with a team called the ''Old Receivers'' and earned the nickname ''just in time'' because he would field the ball and time his throws so he would get the players out ''just in time'' and stand at his shortstop position and laugh at them. He was discovered in 1905 on the sandlots of Jacksonville, Florida, by Rube Foster, Harry Buckner, and Sol White, who were traveling south with the Cuban X-Giants. A year later, when the team's owner, Ed LeMarc, decided to let several of his best players go and replace them with talented youngsters, he sent for Lloyd, who was playing second base with the Macon Acmes, a semipro team in Georgia. Lloyd, who had joined the impoverished team as a catcher and had to resort to using a wire basket for a catcher's mask, was glad to get a chance with a top team. From the time he joined the Cuban X-Giants in 1906 until he became player-manager of the Brooklyn Royal Giants in 1918, the presence of his all-around ability assured a team of being a big winner. The teams on which he played during this period was a roll call of the great teams of the era.

Leaving the X-Giants, who were ending a decade of dominance, the superstar shortstop played for Sol White's champion Philadelphia Giants in 1907–09. In his first year with Philadelphia he is credited with a modest .250 batting average. After three years he left Philly to join former teammate Rube Foster's Chicago Leland Giants. Always one to go where the most money was available, after finishing the 1910 season with a .417 batting average, Lloyd returned East to play with the newly organized New York Lincoln Giants. At midseason he assumed the managerial reins, replacing Sol White at the helm for the McMahon brothers' team. During his three-year tenure he recorded batting averages of .475, .376, and .363, and under his leadership the Lincoln Giants became champions of the East. In 1912 he and Spot Poles had a disagreement, and Poles left the team and joined the Brooklyn Royal Giants, but returned later in the season. In 1913 his team compiled a phenomenal 101–6 record and soundly defeated Rube Foster's Chicago American Giants in the playoffs. The Series victory resulted in Foster pirating Lloyd back to the American Giants for the 1914 season.

Lloyd was a smart player who easily fit into the Foster style of play. In the deadball era, when pitching dominated and teams played for a single run, Lloyd excelled at getting the run. He was an exceptional bunter and base stealer and, with good bat control and an excellent eye at the plate, he was expert at playing hit-and-run. Indicative of Lloyd's batting ability is that with all the talent on Foster's team, he batted in the fourth spot in the lineup. With Lloyd starring, the American Giants reigned as western champions three times during his four-year tenure with the team, and defeated the eastern champions in playoffs in 1914 and 1917.

Lloyd had returned East to the Lincoln Giants at the beginning of the 1915 season, but played most of the year with the Lincoln Stars. In a summer series billed as being for the championship, Lloyd batted .390 as the Stars and American Giants deadlocked at 5 games apiece. With the American Giants engaged in a hot battle with the Indianapolis ABCs for the West title, he was induced to rejoin Foster's club in late August. After making the jump, the star shortstop's presence made the difference, and he was there in time to lead Chicago to the title over the ABCs.

In 1917 Lloyd missed a little playing time when Frank Warfield's spikes opened a gash (requiring two stitches to close) on Lloyd's knee after the shortstop had applied the tag in a successful pickoff play at second base. The setback was temporary and the Chicago American Giants easily won the western title and defeated the Lincoln Giants in the playoff. But after the 1917 playoffs he jumped again and became the playing manager of Nat C. Strong's Brooklyn Royal Giants for two years, sandwiched around a season with the New York-based Bacharach Giants in 1919. During World War I he worked in the Army Quartermaster Depot in Chicago in 1918.

In 1921 Lloyd left the New York City baseball scene to become playing manager of the Negro National League Columbus Buckeyes and hit .336, but stayed only a single season when owner Connors brought him back to New York to replace Dick Redding as manager of the New York Bacharachs. Before the season started the Bacharachs decided to return to Atlantic City as their home base for the season, and although he hit .387, his stay there was only a season as he left when Hilldale beckoned. Later in life Lloyd was to say, "Wherever the money was, that's where I was."

When the Eastern Colored League was organized in 1923, Lloyd, serving as playing manager, hit .418 to lead Hilldale to the inaugural pennant. Despite their winning the pennant, Lloyd was not in good graces with the owner and was fired because of alleged dissension on the team. Joining the Bacharach Giants the following year as manager, he left Dick Lundy at shortstop and placed himself at second base, his first year at the position after twenty years at shortstop, and responded to his new position by continuing his hitting heroics, winning the batting title with a .444 average. The next season he hit a solid .330, but after two years with the Bacharachs, Lloyd again returned to New York in 1926 to take the reins of the Lincoln Giants, recording batting averages of .349 and .375 in his first two seasons while continuing to play at second base until 1928, when he made a further concession to age and moved himself to first base. The change must have been a good one, as he led the league in both batting (.564) and home runs (11.) While that

season was a good one for Lloyd personally, it was disastrous for the Eastern Colored League, which collapsed early in the season despite the individual teams trying to complete the schedules.

After the collapse of the Eastern Colored League, Lloyd entered his hard-hitting Lincoln Giants in the replacement American Negro League in 1929 and hit for a .362 average while forming a formidable slugging triad with John Beckwith and Chino Smith. Unfortunately, the American Negro League survived only one season, and in 1930, Lloyd's last season at the helm, the Lincolns played as an independent team and fielded their strongest team since Lloyd's 1913 powerhouse. Lloyd batted .312 during the regular season, but the Lincolns lost a hard-fought series for the eastern championship to a strong Homestead Grays' team, who had strengthened themselves with the late-season acquisition of a young catcher named Josh Gibson. During the 1930 season, his Lincolns were the host team for the first game ever played by black teams in Yankee Stadium.

The last two years of his playing career were spent with the Bacharach Giants, and following the 1932 seasons, his last year as an active player, he settled in Atlantic City after his retirement from the game. A rugged competitor as a player, his aggressive play on the field contrasted with his easygoing nature off the field. He neither drank nor smoked and seldom used coarse language.

In his managerial capacity Lloyd was a master at instilling confidence in younger players. In these latter years he became known affectionately as "Pop" and was considered the elder statesman of black baseball even after he retired as an active player. Newspapers of 1910 referred to Lloyd's good nature by saying that he was "one comical man off the diamond," and indicated that when he quit baseball he could make good on the stage as a comedian. However, after closing out his professional baseball career, he continued as manager and first baseman of sandlot teams, the Johnson Stars and the Farley Stars, until age sixty. Residing in Atlantic City, he worked as a custodian for the post office and school system. In addition to his work he served as the city's Little League commissioner, and in recognition of his involvement with youngsters, in 1949 the John Henry Lloyd Park for baseball was dedicated in his honor.

The left-handed place hitter who batted out of a slightly closed stance had an easy, powerful swing that produced a lifetime .368 average over a phenomenal twenty-seven-year career in black baseball. Twelve winter seasons in Cuba, interspersed between the years 1908 and 1930, show a .321 lifetime average. During his prime, island records of the 1912 and 1913 seasons show a composite .361 batting average, and in one reknowned series in 1910, against Ty Cobb's Detroit Tigers, he hit .500 to lead all hitters. John McGraw assessed the country's sociological climate while appraising his ability: "If we could bleach this Lloyd boy, we would show the National League a new phenomenon." Some historians say that he was born too soon. But in 1949 at the dedication of the Atlantic City ballpark in his honor, Lloyd expressed his thoughts. "I do not consider that I was born at the wrong time. I felt it was the right time, for I had a chance to prove the ability of our race in this sport . . . and . . we have given the Negro a greater opportunity now to be accepted into the major leagues with other Americans."

Baseball historians concur that Lloyd was one of the greatest black players ever, but Babe Ruth, in response to a question by announcer Graham McNamee, eliminated the color distinction when he stated that Lloyd was his choice as the greatest baseball player of all time. In 1977 John Henry Lloyd was voted into the National Baseball Hall of Fame.

Locke, Clarence Virgil (Dad)
Career: 1945–48   Positions: **p**, 1b
Team: Chicago American Giants

He began his pitching career with the Chicago American Giants in 1945 with a 2–1 league ledger and followed with postwar marks

of 3–7 and 2–4 (4.96 ERA) in 1946 and 1948. During the 1945 season he played more at first base than he did as a pitcher. After the war he concentrated almost exclusively on his pitching career, but he still hit .235 in 1948.

Locke, Eddie
Career: 1943–'50   Positions: **p**, 3b, of
Teams: Cincinnati Clowns ('43), Kansas City Monarchs ('44–'45, '48–'49, *'51*), New York Black Yankees ('49–'50), *minor leagues ('50–'56), Mexican League ('56–'59)*
Bats: Left   Throws: Right
Height: 5'11"   Weight: 178
Born: 1923

An average pitcher with a standard three-pitch repertory and a modicum of control, he began his career during the war years, playing a season with the Cincinnati Clowns before joining the Kansas City Monarchs in 1944, where he had a 3.80 ERA while splitting six decisions. He batted .297 that season and occasionally played third base or outfield during his baseball career.

After the color line was eliminated, he remained in the Negro Leagues for a few years with the Monarchs, Chicago American Giants, and New York Black Yankees before entering organized baseball with Springfield in the Mississippi-Ohio Valley League in 1950, where he was 10–8 (3.17 ERA) on the mound and hit .291 as a pitcher-outfielder. After a season back with the Monarchs in 1951, he played in the Western International League with Vancouver, where he had an 11–13 record with a 3.44 ERA. After starting the next season in the same league with Yakima and meeting little success (1–5 record), he moved to Amarillo in the West Texas–New Mexico League. His two complete seasons there were very productive, both pitching (21–7 and 24–15) and hitting (.368 and .311). He began the 1955 season there also but moved to Artesia, where he fashioned a 20–7 pitching record and hit .355.

The next season he launched his Mexican career, joining Monterrey after beginning with Victoria in the Big State League. With Monterrey he registered consecutive seasons of 18–12 (3.20 ERA), 19–16 (3.37 ERA), and 21–14 (3.56 ERA) for the seasons 1957–59. For two winter seasons spent with Cordoba he had records of 18–6 and 19–7.

Lockett, Lester (Buck, *Lou*)
Career: 1938–50   Positions: **of, 3b**, 2b, *ss*
Teams: Birmingham Black Barons ('38, '41–46), Cincinnati Buckeyes ('40), Chicago American Giants ('42, '50), Cincinnati-Indianapolis Clowns ('46), Baltimore Elite Giants ('47–'49), *Canadian League ('51), minor leagues ('52–'53), Mexican League ('53)*
Bats: Right   Throws: Right
Height: 6'0"   Weight: 195
Born: Mar. 26, 1912, Princeton, Ind.

A good-hitting outfielder for the pennant-winning Birmingham Black Barons of 1943–44 and later for the Baltimore Elite Giants in the latter part of the decade, Lockett made All-star appearances in 1943, 1945, and 1948. Usually batting in the heart of the order with both Birmingham and Baltimore, he hit for averages of .328, .315, .408, .249, and .300 with the Birmingham Black Barons for the years 1941–1945, and .313 and .386 with the Elites in 1947–48. Whenever the game situation dictated, Lockett could hit with power or steal a base, and his versatility was also utilized in the field throughout his career, when he frequently played in the infield, especially at third base.

In 1950, his last year in the Negro Leagues, he hit .301 with the Chicago American Giants before signing with Farnham in the provincial League, where he batted a disappointing .217 for the 1951 season. The next two years were spent in the Mandak League with Winnipeg and Carman, batting .332 the latter season.

He also played winter ball in Venezuela in 1947 and in Panama in 1948, and played with the Fort Wayne Capeharts, winners of the Wichita Tourney. Off the field Lockett was known as a "ladies' man," but his pursuits that earned him this reputation never interfered with his play on the field.

Lockett, Monroe
Career: 1938   Position: p
Team: Indianapolis ABCs

He pitched briefly with the Indianapolis ABCs in 1938.

Lockett, Willie
Career: 1937–38   Position: of
Teams: St. Louis Stars ('37), Indianapolis ABCs ('38)

He appeared as a reserve outfielder with the St. Louis Stars in 1937 and with the Indianapolis ABCs in 1938.

Lockhart, A. J. *(Joe)*
Career: 1925–26   Positions: 3b, p
Teams: Washington Potomacs ('24), Wilmington Potomacs ('25), *Philadelphia Giants ('24–'26)*

This former Morris Brown University star was a pitcher with the Potomacs and also played at third base with the franchise. He was placed on the Potomacs' reserve list for 1925, and when the club moved to Wilmington, he moved with them until they disbanded. Then he played as a third baseman with the Philadelphia Giants.

Lockhart, Hubert
a.k.a. Herbert, Hulbert
Career: 1923–29   Position: p
Teams: Atlantic City Bacharach Giants ('23–'28), Chicago American Giants ('29)

He pitched with the Bacharach Giants and was their second-best pitcher, regarded only slightly below ace Rats Henderson. While attending Talladega College he was one of the best college pitchers of the early '20s, pitching a no-hitter against Morris Brown College in 1922. The following season he joined the Bacharachs but continued his formal education while playing professional baseball. In 1925 he lost all 4 of his decisions, but in 1926 he was in the starting rotation and split 6 decisions as the Bacharachs captured the first of two consecutive Eastern Colored League pennants, in 1926–27. Each season, however, the Bacharachs lost to the Negro National League champion Chicago American Giants in the World Series. Lockhart pitched in 7 games in the two Series, starting 4 games but losing all 3 of his decisions.

Lockhart was preparing an alternate career apart from the life of a professional baseball player, and during the 1927 season he served as the athletic director at Talladega College. The next two seasons he was a teacher and coach at Alabama State Normal College in Montgomery, Alabama, where he was still coaching in June 1929 when the Chicago American Giants signed him. He registered a 2–1 record with the American Giants for the remainder of the season to close out his active playing career so he could concentrate on his coaching career. The gifted athlete was also a gentleman and a talented writer, singer, and cartoonist.

Loftin, Louis Santop
[see Santop, Louis]

Logan, Carl
Career: 1934–40   Position: ss
Teams: Atlantic City Bacharach Giants ('34), Philadelphia Stars ('40)

He was a shortstop for the Bacharachs in 1934 when the ballclub entered the Negro National League as a second-half replacement team. His only other appearance was with the Philadelphia Stars, in 1940.

Logan, Fred
Career: 1950   Position: of
Team: New York Black Yankees

He was an outfielder with the New York Black Yankees when black baseball was struggling to survive the loss of players to organized baseball.

Logan, J.
Career: 1922   Position: p
Team: Baltimore Black Sox

The brother of Nick Logan, he was among the new pitching recruits who appeared with the Baltimore Black Sox in 1922.

Logan, Nick
Career: 1920–25   Position: p
Team: Baltimore Black Sox

A pitcher with the Baltimore Black Sox for half a dozen seasons in the early '20s, he had his best season in 1921, when he registered an 18–7 record, but he dropped to a 6–5 ledger the next season.

Lomax
Career: 1942   Position: player
Team: Newark Eagles

He appeared in a game with the Newark Eagles in 1942, but his regular position is uncertain.

London, Julius
a.k.a. Londo
Career: 1940   Position: p
Team: St. Paul Colored Gophers

As a pitcher for the 1909 St. Paul Colored Gophers, he started 2 games in the playoffs against the Leland Giants and won his only decision.

Long
Career: 1940   Position: player
Teams: Baltimore Elite Giants ('40), Palmer House All-Stars ('40)

He was an ex-Baltimore Elite Giants player who appeared with the Palmer House All-Stars, an independent team based in Chicago and of near-major-league caliber, in August 1940.

Long
Career: 1920–26   Position: of
Teams: Detroit Stars ('20–'21, '26), Indianapolis ABCs ('25)

With the exception of the 1925 season, which he spent with the Indianapolis ABCs, this outfielder played his entire Negro National League career with the Detroit Stars, beginning in 1920 and closing his career in 1926, after hitting .186 for the season in limited play.

Long Branch Cubans

Duration: 1915–16   Honors: None
Affiliation: Independent

Based in Long Branch, New Jersey, this ballclub fielded a good team for a couple of years before the advent of World War I. Some sources indicate that this was an all-white team, but this has not been confirmed.

Long, Buck

Career: 1950   Position: c
Team: Memphis Red Sox

He was a catcher with the Memphis Red Sox in 1950, when the Negro American League was struggling to survive the loss of players to organized baseball, but league statistics do not confirm his playing time.

Long, Emory (Bang)

Career: 1936–45   Positions: 3b, 2b, of
Teams: *Atlanta Black Crackers ('32)*, Chicago American Giants ('36), Indianapolis Athletics ('37), Washington Black Senators ('38), Philadelphia Stars ('40), Kansas City Monarchs ('45)

He began his career in his hometown, with the Atlanta Black Crackers in the Negro Southern League, but joined the Chicago American Giants in 1936 when they were playing as an independent team. The next season, 1937, was the first year of the Negro American League, and he was the starting third baseman, batting sixth in the order, for the Indianapolis Athletics in their only year in the league. When the A's disbanded, he joined the Washington Potomacs in their only season in the Negro National League, 1938, where he assumed the role of regular third baseman when Henry Spearman was grabbed by the Homestead Grays to fill a weak spot in their lineup.

In 1940 Long was a reserve infielder with the Philadelphia Stars, and he next appeared in 1945 when he joined the war-weakened Kansas City Monarchs as an outfielder. He hit consistently for them and was described as "swinging a mean club," earning the respect of the pitchers. He also demonstrated a powerful throwing arm and made some sensational catches in the field. However, he was unable to maintain a grasp on a starting position, and after the war ended he never played in the major black leagues again.

Long, Ernest S. (The Kid)

Career: 1948–50   Positions: p, *of, 1b*
Teams: *Chattanooga Choo Choos ('45–'47)*, Cleveland Buckeyes ('48, '50), Louisville Buckeyes ('49)
Bats: Right   Throws: Right
Born: 1927, Chattanooga, Tenn.

After a three-year apprenticeship with the Chattanooga Choo Choos beginning in 1945, he joined the Cleveland Buckeyes for another three years of baseball, this time with a Negro American League franchise (1948–50). In his first season, 1948, he registeed a 7–3 mark with a 3.60 ERA. The next season the Buckeyes moved to Louisville and fielded a weak aggregation, finishing in the cellar with a dismal .216 winning percentage. Long's 3–14 record reflected the lack of support, but he was selected to the West squad for the East-West All-Star game and, although not utilized in the contest, he considered this the highlight of his career.

The Buckeyes moved back to Cleveland for the 1950 season, but although he was listed on the roster, he never pitched in a league contest. An arm injury suffered from playing winter ball in South America curtailed his pitching career, and although he also played at first base and in the outfield, he never hit enough to earn a spot in the regular lineup and never was able to recapture his early success. After leaving baseball he moved to Rome, Georgia, and retired in 1988.

Long, Tom

Career: 1926   Position: c
Team: Kansas City Monarchs

He was a reserve catcher with the Kansas City Monarchs in 1926, and his playing time was limited.

Longest, Bernell (Chick)
Career: 1942–47   Positions: 2b, 3b, of
Teams: Chicago American Giants ('42,'46), *Chicago Brown Bombers ('46–'47), minor leagues ('52–'55)*
Bats: Left   Throws: Right

This infielder was among the many players who wore an American Giants uniform in 1942 and was their starting second baseman and leadoff batter in 1946, batting .259 for the season. That year he also played with the Chicago Brown Bombers, an independent team of lesser status. After leaving the Negro Leagues he played two seasons (1952–53) with Carman in the Mandak League, batting .321 with 6 home runs the latter season. In 1955 he played in the outfield with Burlington of the Provincial League, batting .276 but without appreciable power.

Longest, Jimmy
Career: 1942   Position: 1b
Team: *Chicago Brown Bombers*

In 1942 he played first base with the Chicago Brown Bombers, an independent team of lesser status.

Longley, Wyman (Red, Ray)
a.k.a. Wayman
Career: 1932–50   Positions; of, 2b, c, 3b, ss, 1b
Teams: *Little Rock Black Travelers ('32)*, Memphis Red Sox ('37–'49), Chicago American Giants ('50), *New Orleans Eagles ('51)*
Bats: Right   Throws: Right

A versatile player who could play infield, outfield, or catcher and field the position adequately, he was also a strong hitter who could deliver the long ball, usually batting fifth or sixth in the order. In 1944–46 he hit for averages of .205, .203, and .273. During his years with the Memphis Red Sox he played every position except pitcher, and was stationed at second base in 1938 when the Sox won the second-half title in the Negro American League's split season. Longley continued playing in the Negro American League even after

its decline, finishing his career in black baseball in 1951 with the New Orleans Eagles.

Longware
Career: 1920   Positions: 2b, 3b, of, ss
Team: Detroit Stars

This infielder played with the Detroit Stars in 1920, his only season in the Negro National League.

Looney, Charley
Career: 1933, 1938   Position: 2b
Teams: Akron Tyrites ('33), *Louisville Black Colonels ('38)*

He was a second baseman with the 1933 Akron Tyrites, a team that consolidated with the Columbus Buckeyes to form the Cleveland Giants, a replacement team in the Negro National League.

Lopez, Candor (**Cando**, Police Car)
Career: 1920–35   Positions: **cf**, lf, 2b, 3b, *ss*
Teams: **Cuban Stars (West)** ('20, '26–'34), New York Cubans ('35), *Santo Domingo ('37)*
Bats: Right   Throws: Right
Born: Cuba

An all-around ballplayer, he could hit, field, and run, earning the nickname "Police Car" because of his speed. He excelled defensively and was regarded as the best center fielder in Cuba. While not as well known for his hitting as his fielding, he played for sixteen seasons in black baseball, primarily with the Cuban Stars in the first Negro National League, where he batted second in the order, and hit .362, .291, .236, and .205 in 1926–27 and 1929–30, respectively.

Later, with the New York Cubans in the new Negro National League, he hit .267 in 1935 to help them win the second-half Negro National League title before losing a hard-fought playoff to the Pittsburgh Crawfords. In 1937 he played in Santo Domingo with Martin Dihigo's Aguilas Cabaenas team and hit .283 with moderate extra-base power. Playing in his homeland during his prime, he led the league with 15 stolen bases in the 1926–27 winter season.

Lopez, Justo
Career: 1939   Position: 1b
Team: Cuban Stars
   He was with the 1939 Cuban Stars as a first baseman.

Lopez, Lorenzo
Career: 1944   Position: p
Team: Homestead Grays
   As an eighteen-year old he was the winning pitcher for the Homestead Grays over the Black Yankees in a 13–11 slugfest in 1944. A wartime player, his stay with the Grays was short.

Lopez, Pedro
Career: 1938–39   Positions: cf, lf
Team: Cuban Stars
   He was with the 1938–39 Cuban Stars as an outfielder, batting .297 in 1939 while batting leadoff.

Lopez, Raul
Career: 1948–50   Position: p
Team: New York Cubans
Bats: Left   Throws: Left
Height: 5'11"   Weight: 154
Born: 1923, Cuba
   A left-handed pitcher, he broke in with the New York Cubans in 1948, the last season before the demise of the Negro National League. The Cubans joined the Negro American League the following year and he fashioned a 5–3 record with a 3.36 ERA. The next year, after losing his only start with the Cubans, he signed with Jersey City in the International League but had difficulty, finishing with an unimpressive 2–7 record with a 6.57 ERA. His career continued to slide downhill in 1951, during stints with Ottawa (2–8, 4.96 ERA) and Oakland (0–2) before finishing his career with two appearances without a decision at Sioux City in 1952 and a 2–4 record with Havana in the Florida International League in 1953 to close

his career. Earlier in his career he had spent two seasons in the Cuban winter league with a combined 13–16 record, and a year with Monterrey in the Mexican League.

Lopez, Vidal
Career: 1923–39   Position: p
Teams: Cuban Stars (East) ('23–'24,'28), Cuban Stars (West ('29)
Bats: Right   Throws: Right
Died: Mar. 1972, Caracas, Venezuela
   This right-handed pitcher broke in with the Alejandro Pompez's Cuban Stars (East) in 1923, but also played with Tinti Molina's Cuban Stars (West). In 1929, with the Cubans in the Negro National League, he was winless against 4 losses in league play. As a veteran playing with Cienfuegos in the Cuban winter league of 1940–41, he led the league in wins with 12.

Lorenzo, Jesus
Career: 1928–30   Positions: **p**, 1b, rf
Team: Cuban Stars (West)
   He was a pitcher with the Cuban Stars of the Negro National League in 1928–30 but also played first base and in the outfield, batting .324 in 1930.

Lott, Hugh Benjamin (Benny, **Honey**)
Career: 1949–50   Positions: **3b**, ss, 2b, *of*
Teams; New York Black Yankees ('49–'50), Indianapolis Clowns ('50–*'51), minor leagues ('51–'55)*
Bats: Right   Throws: Right
Height: 5'11"   Weight:167
Born: 1927
   This infielder was a free-swinger with good power, who played with the New York Black Yankees and Indianapolis Clowns in the waning years of the Negro American League, batting .304 the latter year with 9 homers in 237 at-bats. Entering organized ball in 1951, he played in five leagues, hitting over .300 every year except the last one (1955), when he hit .274 and 16 home runs with San Angelo in the Longhorn League. In 1951 he split the season

between Colorado Springs (.345) and Waterloo (.304), and in 1953 he split the season between Tulsa (.303) and Carman (.301).

Lott, Raymond (Ray)
Career: 1950   Position: of
Team: Philadelphia Stars

He was a reserve outfielder, batting .160 in limited play, with the Philadelphia Stars in 1950, when the Negro American League was struggling to survive the loss of players to organized baseball.

Louden, Louis Oliver (Lou, Tommy)
Career: 1942–50   Positions: c, of, manager
Teams: **New York Cubans** ('42–'50), Cuban Stars, *minor leagues ('52–'53, '57)*
Bats: Right   Throws: Right
Height: 5'10"   Weight: 172
Born: Aug. 19, 1919, West Point, Va.
Died: Aug. 31, 1989, Newark, N.J.

This strong-armed catcher was a pull hitter who hit with consistency and good power, batting .290 for the 1947 Negro National League champion New York Cubans. He was a superb receiver whose hustle and pep kept the players on their toes and the fans pleased with his antics. He had a bit of a drinking problem and would sometimes show up so inebriated he couldn't snap his own shinguards, yet still he could catch a flawless game.

A product of New York playgrounds, he was discovered on the sandlots by Alex Pompez and came directly to the New York Cubans. He hit for averages of .229, .265, .247, and .250 in 1943–46. After the passing of Josh Gibson he played in three of the next four East-West All-Star games, making appearances in 1947, 1948, and 1950. He also played on Willie Mays's All-Star team in 1948–49. the only member of the squad who was not playing in the major leagues. In addition he played with Jackie Robinson's All-Stars in 1946–47, and during the early '50s with Roy Campanella's All-Stars.

In 1948 he served briefly as a manager with the Cubans' ballclub and hit .315, .245, and .311 in the next three seasons, his last in the Negro Leagues. He played winter ball in both Puerto Rico (1947–48), hitting .304 with Ponce, and in Cuba (1950–51), hitting .222 with Cienfuegos in limited play. After leaving the Cubans he played with Winnipeg in the Mandak League for two years (1952–53), batting .252 the latter season. His last appearance in organized baseball was in 1957, when he hit .194 with El Paso in the Southwest League. Earlier in his career, before being discovered by Pompez, he played with teams of lesser status, including the Tidewater Giants from Newport News.

Louisville Black Caps
Duration: 1932   Honors: None
Affiliation: NSL

Louisville fielded a team in the Negro Southern League in 1932, the only year it was designated a major league. They finished the first half only half a game out of the cellar, with a 13–17 record for a .433 winning percentage. During the second half they were replaced by the Columbus (Ohio) Turfs.

Louisville Buckeyes
Duration: 1949   Honors: None
Affiliation: NAL

The Cleveland Buckeyes moved to Louisville for the 1949 season but returned to Cleveland the following year. During the one season in Louisville the franchise finished the first half in the cellar with an abysmal 8–29 record, for a .216 winning percentage. No final second-half standings were published, but reconstructed results show a 7–22 record for the Buckeyes.

Louisville White Sox
Duration: 1931   Honors: None
Affiliation: NNL

Louisville fielded a team in the Negro National League in 1931, their only year in the league.

Love, William (**Andy**)
Career: 1930–31   Positions: 1b, of, c, 2b, *p*
Teams: Memphis Red Sox ('30), Detroit Stars ('30–'31), *Toledo Cubs ('46)*

An all-purpose player (catcher-infielder-outfielder) with two Negro National League clubs during the last two seasons before the league's demise, he hit .279 in 1930. For the remainder of his career he played with teams of lesser quality, including the Toledo Cubs of the U.S. League.

Loving, J. G.
Career: 1887   Position: player
Team: Washington Capital Citys

He was a player with the Washington Capital Citys, one of eight teams that were charter members of the League of Colored Baseball Clubs in 1887. However, the league's existence was ephemeral, lasting only a week.

Lowe, William M. (*Count*)
Career: 1921–33   Positions: 3b, ss, 2b, of, manager
Teams: Indianapolis ABCs ('21), Detroit Stars ('24), **Memphis Red Sox** ('25–'33), *Chattanooga Black Lookouts*, Nashville Elite Giants ('30–'31)

He was an all-purpose player who could play either infield or outfield and who played mostly with southern teams during his eleven years in black baseball. Most of his career was spent with the Memphis Red Sox: He hit .269 and .304 in 1927 and 1929, respectively, and closed out his career with them in 1933. He broke in with the Indianapolis ABCs in 1921 and played with the Detroit Stars and Nashville Elite Giants, batting .222 in limited play during the Elites' first year in the Negro National League, 1930.

Lowell
Career: 1924   Position: p
Team: Atlantic City Bacharach Giants

He was a pitcher with the Bacharachs in 1924, his only season in the Eastern Colored League.

Lucas, Miles
Career: 1919–20,   Positions: p, rf, lf
1925–27
Teams: Cuban Stars of Havana ('19), Cuban Stars (East) ('19–'20), *New Orleans Crescent Stars ('22)*, Harrisburg Giants ('25–'27)

During his first two seasons (1919–20), he was in the starting lineup of the Cuban Stars (East), playing as an outfielder and pitcher while batting in the lower part of the order. In 1925, after a stint with lesser teams, he pitched with the Harrisburg Giants of the Eastern Colored League for parts of three seasons.

Lucas, Scotty
Career: 1928   Position: officer
Team: Philadelphia Tigers

He served as an officer with the Philadelphia Tigers in 1928, their only season in the Negro National League.

Lugo, Levingelo (**Leo**)
Career: 1944–46   Position: of
Teams: Cincinnati-Indianapolis Clowns ('44), Indianapolis Clowns ('46)

This outfielder began his short career with the Clowns in 1944, batting .327. He closed out with a .214 average in 1946.

Lumpkins, Lefty
Career: 1931–32   Position: p
Team: Newark Browns

He was a pitcher with the Newark Browns when they were in the East-West League in 1932.

Lundy, Richard (**Dick**, King Richard)
Career: 1916–39,   Positions: **ss**, 3b, 2b, 1940–48   c, manager
Teams: *Duval Giants ('15)*, **Atlantic City Bacharach Giants** ('16–'18,'20–'28), Havana Red Sox ('17), Hilldale Daisies ('17–'19), New York Lincoln Giants, Baltimore Black Sox

('29–'32), Philadelphia Stars ('33), Newark Dodgers ('34–'35), New York Cubans ('35), Newark Eagles ('36–'39), Atlanta Black Crackers ('38), Brooklyn Royal Giants, *Jacksonville Eagles*

Bats: Both   Throws: Right
Height: 5'11"   Weight: 180
Born: July 10, 1898, Jacksonville, Fla.
Died: Jan. 5, 1965, Jacksonville, Fla.

The best shortstop during the 1920s, Lundy bridged the time gap between John Henry Lloyd and Willie Wells. Lundy is generally categorized with them as the three greatest shortstops in black baseball history. A superb fielder with a wide range and an exceptionally strong arm that allowed him to play a deep shortstop, the graceful Lundy polished his skills with quiet professionalism. A great showman who thrived on pressure and performed his most amazing feats with ease in front of large crowds, the big, husky shortstop's sterling play made him one of the greatest gate attractions of his day. A switch-hitter who hit for average and with power, he was a smart base runner who posed a threat on the bases and led the Cuban winter league in stolen bases in 1924.

Lundy attended Florida Baptist Academy in St. Augustine, Florida, and later played ball while attending Cookman Institute for two years, 1914–15. He began his professional career in 1915 as a third baseman with his hometown team, the Duval Giants, of Jacksonville, Florida. With the team he also served as an utility man and played almost every position, including catcher. He came North with the team the following year when they moved to Atlantic City and became the Bacharach Giants. His outstanding ability was immediately recognized and Hilldale, another emerging team, picked him up in the fall of 1917 to play against Joe Bush and other barnstorming major-league all-stars. He was lured away again by Hilldale in the latter part of the 1918 season and remained with the club in 1919, hitting in the third slot. In 1920 his services were so much in demand that he had to go to

court because he had signed contracts with three clubs at the same time. In accordance with the court's ruling, he went back to the original Bacharachs' franchise, and for a decade he was a fixture at shortstop and in the heart of the batting order.

When he returned to the Bacharachs, Lundy was on a par with John Henry Lloyd, and when Lloyd joined the team as manager in 1924, he placed himself at second base, acknowledging Lundy's defensive superiority at that time. Lundy, a Lloyd-style player who could do everything (hit, field, run, and throw), was the best shortstop in the East. The Bacharachs' owner, John W. Connors, temporarily based the team in New York in 1921, but the franchise returned to Atlantic City for the duration of the '20s.

With the Bacharachs he compiled batting averages of .484, .335, .310, .363, .273, .347, .341, .409 and .336 for the years 1921–1929. Defensively he was paired with third baseman Oliver Marcelle to form an almost impregnable left side of the infield, and Lundy earned the sobriquet "King Richard" for his superlative play. A natural leader respected by teammates and opponents alike, Lundy served as team captain in 1923–25. Still comparatively young after ten seasons, his leadership qualities were recognized and he was appointed playing manager from 1926 to 1928, during which time he directed the team to two Eastern Colored League pennants, in 1926 and 1927. Playing in the 1926 World Series against the Negro National League's Chicago American Giants, the classy shortstop hit for a .325 average and stole 6 bases. He batted .250 in the next season's Series, but all in a losing cause as the Bacharachs lost both World Series to the strong Chicago American Giants' team.

After being traded to the Baltimore Black Sox for Ben Taylor, Mac Eggleston, and cash in February 1929 in an exchange of managers, Lundy managed the Black Sox to the American Negro League pennant. During the drive to the pennant, despite being spiked by Lloyd and put out of action for a period of time, Lundy contributed a .336 batting average and 16 stolen bases. That season the Sox boasted of an infield consisting of Lundy, Marcelle, Frank Warfield, and Jud Wilson that was called the "million-dollar infield." The dapper shortstop followed with averages of .321, .307, and .341 while leading the Black Sox to the top spot in the East-West League the latter year. The next two years were spent with the Philadelphia Stars and the Newark Dodgers, and although he was past his prime, he was selected to start the first two East-West All Star games at short-stop for the East. In 1935 he hit .310 to help the New York Cubans to the second-half title and a losing showdown with the great Pitts-burgh Crawfords, winners of the first half, in the Negro National League playoffs.

His last years as an active player were spent in Newark, where he still managed to hit .293 in 1937 in a reserve role. While associated with the Newark franchise, he was instrumental in helping two other great infielders, Ray Dandridge and Willie Wells. As manager of the Newark Dodgers in 1934, he signed Dandridge and played him at the hot corner, and later with the Newark Eagles he coached both Dandridge and Wells, who were part of the new "million-dollar infield" of whom the Eagles boasted.

While making his home in Daytona Beach in 1938, he was steadfastly sought by the Atlanta Black Crackers. He sent several telegrams promising to play with the team before finally reporting. He had been friends with Nish Williams (acting manager at that time) for fifteen years and based his decision to play in Atlanta on their friendship (among other factors). In mid-April, while playing in one of his first games with Atlanta, he was hit on the right arm by a pitch from Mute Banks that fractured his arm, knocking him out of action for several weeks. While waiting for the arm to heal, the thirty-six-year-old infielder did road work to keep his legs in shape. He was still considered one of the best shortstops and best baseball minds in the game, acting as manager after Nish Williams was relieved of that position in the early part of the season until being released

to assume the managerial reins of the Newark Eagles for the second half of the season.

He was a natural hitter and a perfect fielder. John McGraw watched him play and said, "I wish I could paint that Lundy white," and, excepting Honus Wagner, labeled him "the greatest shortstop to ever live." He finished his career in the Negro Leagues with a lifetime .330 average. He also had a .341 average to show for eight seasons in the Cuban winter league, and a .344 average in exhibitions against major-league opposition.

After ending his career as an active player, he continued as a coach and manager during the '40s. After leaving baseball he returned to his hometown and worked in the Jacksonville Terminal Station as a redcap for many years, until his retirement. He died in 1965 after a lingering illness.

Luque, Adolfo (Dolf, The Pride of Havana)
Career: 1912–13   Positions: p, of, 3b
Teams: Cuban Stars ('12), Long Branch Cubans ('13), major leagues (1914–15, 1918–35)
Bats: Right   Throws: Right
Height: 5'7"   Weight: 160
Born: Aug. 4, 1890, Havana, Cuba
Died: July 3, 1957, Havana, Cuba

This fiery-tempered white Cuban played two seasons with Cuban teams in the Negro Leagues and pitched in the major leagues for twenty years, finishing with a 193–179 lifetime record and a 3.24 ERA. Major-league highlights include two World Series appearances (in 1919 with the Cincinnati Reds and in 1933 with the New York Giants) without yielding a run, and leading the league with 27 wins in 1923. Nicknamed "The Pride of Havana," he was a respected player and manager in his own country, and he managed many black Americans who played winter ball in the Cuban League.

Luther
[see Farrell, Luther]

Lyda
Career: 1932   Position: p
Team: Cole's American Giants

He pitched briefly with Cole's American Giants in 1932, when they won the Negro Southern League pennant.

Lyles
Career: 1916   Position: p
Team: All Nations

He pitched with the All Nations team in 1916, one of the ballclub's peak seasons.

Lyles, John
Career: 1932–43   Positions: of, ss, 2b, 3b, c
Teams: Indianapolis ABCs ('32, '38), Homestead Grays ('34), Cleveland Bears ('39), St. Louis Stars ('39), New Orleans-St. Louis Stars ('40–'41), Chicago American Giants ('41), Cincinnati Buckeyes ('42), Cleveland Buckeyes ('43), Indianapolis Clowns
Bats: Both   Throws: Right
Height: 5'9"   Weight: 190

He was an average ballplayer in most aspects of the game, including hitting, fielding, and baserunning. However, this hustling ballplayer had a good arm and stayed in the game for a dozen seasons, mostly in the Negro American League. With the Indianapolis ABCs in 1938, he was the regular third baseman, batting third in the order, while also seeing some duty in centerfield. When the franchise moved to St. Louis for the 1939 season, Lyles signed with the Cleveland Bears (who were the transplanted Jacksonville Red Caps), playing shortstop while batting in the third slot.

After a season with the Bears, who were having financial problems and would soon move back to Jacksonville, he joined the St. Louis Stars as a middle infielder, starting at shortstop in 1940 and at second base in 1941 while hitting in the number two slot both seasons. When the Stars disbanded for a season, the versatile player, who could play both outfield and infield, joined the Cincinnati Buckeyes in 1942 and won a starting position in right field, batting variously in the leadoff and cleanup spots. When the franchise moved to Cleveland in 1943, Lyles lost his starting position and was a substitute third baseman during

what proved to be his last season in the Negro Leagues.

Lynch, Thomas (Jim)
Career: 1917–18   Positions: **of**, 3b, 2b, p
Teams: *West Baden Sprudels ('14), Gilkerson's Union Giants ('14),* Indianapolis ABCs ('17, '19), Dayton Marcos ('18)

An outfielder with the Indianapolis ABCs and Dayton Marcos during the World War I deadball era, he was a very good defensive player, making sensational catches in center field for the ABCs in 1917. He also was a good power hitter who liked high pitches, and gave evidence of his power while performing with the Union Giants in 1914. Although the club was of lesser quality and playing against all levels of competition while touring the Midwest, the pitcher-outfielder batting third in the lineup and swatted his 33rd home run of the season in July. He also played third base with the West Baden, Indiana, Sprudels for part of the season. During the '20s he continued to play with the Union Giants.

Lynn
Career: 1917   Position: p
Team: Jewells' ABCs

In 1917 he was a pitcher with Jewell's ABCs, a team of lesser status.

Lyons
Career: 1950   Position: p
Team: Cleveland Buckeyes

This pitcher appeared in a league game without a decision for the Cleveland Buckeyes in 1950, at a time when the Negro American League was struggling to survive the loss of players to organized baseball.

Lyons, Bennie
Career: 1917–18   Positions: 1b, of, c
Teams: *Indianapolis ABCs ('13),* Bowser's ABCs ('16), Jewell's ABCs ('17), Dayton Marcos ('18)

He was a first baseman with three different ABCs teams (Indianapolis, Bowser's, Jewell's) and the Dayton Marcos, all marginal teams during the deadball era before and during the World War I era.

Lyons, Chase
Career: 1899–1905   Position: p
Teams: Cuban Giants, Genuine Cuban Giants ('99), Famous Cuban Giants ('05)

During the early years of the century he was a pitcher with an assortment of teams, each trying to capitalize on the popularity of the Cuban Giants by appropriating a variation of the Cuban Giants' name as their own, and playing a quality of baseball close to that of the original team.

Lyons, Granville
Career: 1931–42   Positions: **1b**, *p, of*
Teams: Nashville Elite Giants ('31–'32, '34), Louisville Black Caps ('32), Detroit Stars, ('33), *Louisville Red Caps,* Philadelphia Stars ('35), Memphis Red Sox ('37), Baltimore Black Sox, Baltimore Elite Giants ('38, '42)
Bats: Left   Throws: Left

This first baseman broke in with the Nashville Elites in 1931, batting in the second slot in the lineup, and remained with the team as the franchise moved into the Negro National League in 1932. In 1933 he was the regular first baseman with the Detroit Stars, again batting second in the order, but two years later he was a seldom-used reserve for the Philadelphia Stars. In 1937 he was back in the lineup as a regular, hitting in the sixth slot, but returned to his reserve status the following year, with the Baltimore Elites. In 1942, still a reserve for the Elites, he closed out his career, with sketchy statistics showing a composite .148 batting average.

Lyons, James (**Jimmie**)
Career: 1910–25, 1932 Positions: **lf**, cf, rf *p,*
                                    manager
Teams: St. Louis Giants ('10–12, '15–'17, '19), New York Lincoln Giants ('11), Brooklyn Royal Giants ('14), Indianapolis ABCs ('15–'18), Bowser's ABCs ('16), *Jewell's ABCs ('17),* Chicago Giants ('17), *military ser-*

vice ('18–'19), Detroit Stars ('20), Atlantic City Bacharach Giants ('20), **Chicago American Giants** ('21–'25), Washington Potomacs ('24), Cleveland Browns ('24), Louisville Black Caps ('32)
Bats: Left   Throws: Right
Height: 5'8"   Weight: 175
Born: Chicago, Ill.

One of the fastest men ever to wear a baseball uniform, Jimmie Lyons fit precisely into Rube Foster's style of play. A good hitter and an expert drag bunter, he utilized his speed at the plate as well as in the field and on the bases. He took an exceptionally long lead and, with speed comparable to that of Cool Papa Bell, he was rarely picked off or thrown out at second on attempted steals.

Finding his niche with the Chicago American Giants during the early 1920s, when the Giants were dominating black baseball, his all-around ability contributed heavily to their successive pennants in the first three years of the old Negro National League's existence. In 1920, the first year of the league, he hit .386 and stole a league-high 22 bases in 44 games. The next year he stole 28 bases, but his batting average dropped to .289, and in 1922, although he continued to bat in the third slot, his average dropped again, to .249. In 1923 the American Giants lost the title to the Kansas City Monarchs, with Lyons batting .251 for the season.

Prior to joining the American Giants, he played amateur ball in Chicago's Church League as a youngster, but began his professional career in 1910 with the St. Louis Giants. A year later he was playing left field and batting in the third slot while also taking an occasional turn on the mound. Late in the season he joined the top eastern club, the New York Lincoln Giants, and batted .452 in limited play. While with the Lincolns, he and Spot Poles formed the fastest outfield duo in the history of black baseball, and in one exhibition game against a major-league all-star team Lyons collected a pair of hits off Walter Johnson. During the ensuing winter, the youngster played in the Cuban League and hit for a .288 average, returning afterward to the St. Louis Giants for the 1912 season. The St. Louis franchise was not the most stable ballclub, and during his tenure with the team he would leave intermittently for stints with other ballclubs before finally leaving the team for good when he joined the American Giants.

In 1914 he joined the eastern champion Brooklyn Royal Giants and hit .375 in limited play. Returning to the St. Louis Giants in 1916, he was their center fielder and leadoff hitter, but when the team broke up in May of the following year, he joined the Indianapolis ABCs but encountered physical problems that curtailed his playing time. He had first joined the ABCs in the late fall of 1915, but his time with them was during a difficult time for the franchise. His tenure with the ABCs was a bit troubled, as he played with a splinter team for parts of two season (Bowser's ABCs in the early part of 1916 and Jewell's ABCs in late July 1917) before returning to manager C.I. Taylor's fold. In 1918 Lyons teamed with Oscar Charleston and George Shively to form one of the greatest outfields of all time.

Along with teammate Dave Malarcher, Lyons was drafted into the Army during World War I. He played baseball in the Allied Expeditionary Force League in Le Mans, France, against a team that included Ty Cobb's brother, who claimed that Lyons played better than the Tiger superstar. After his tour of duty was over, the outfield star remained in the East for a while before rejoining the St. Louis Giants in 1919 as their right fielder and leadoff batter.

When the Negro National League was formed in 1920, Lyons was assigned by Rube Foster to the Detroit Stars to provide better balance for the newly formed league. However, Lyons's stay with the Stars was short, and he left them during the season to join the Bacharachs in the East. A hard competitor and an aggressive base runner, Lyons always kept his spikes sharpened and would cut a fielder without compunction. After being added to the Bacharachs' roster in late August, he added John Beckwith to his list of victims when, on a steal attempt, he cut the big infielder.

After the end of the season, Rube Foster traded for him, and his talent and Rube's style of play proved to be a perfect marriage as the speedy outfielder's presence and performance helped the American Giants win Negro National League flags in 1921 and 1922. His stay with the team was not uneventful, however, as he suffered injuries in late July 1921 when he fell twenty-five feet down an open elevator shaft in Cincinnati. Lyons was among a large number of other veteran players who were unconditionally released by Foster in the spring of 1925 in a youth movement. After ending his active playing career, Lyons tried his hand with the managerial reins, managing the Louisville Black Caps in 1932.

Lyttle, Clarence
Career: 1901–06   Position: p
Teams: Chicago Union Giants ('01–'02), Leland Giants ('06)

He was a pitcher with Frank Leland's teams, first with the Chicago Union Giants and then with the recently formed Leland Giants.

M

Mack, John H.
Career: 1945   Position: p
Team: Kansas City Monarchs

A wartime pitcher for the Kansas City Monarchs in 1945, he was infrequently utilized in league contests.

Mack, Paul
Career: 1916–17   Positions: 3b, of, p
Teams: Atlantic City Bacharach Giants ('16–'17), *Jersey City Colored Giants ('17)*

In 1916, during the Bacharach Giants' formative years, he was the team captain and leadoff batter. In the field he guarded the hot corner and also on occasion took the mound for the Bacharachs. As the Bacharachs began stocking their roster with more quality players, he was displaced and played with the Jersey City Colored Giants, a lesser team.

Mack, Robert
Career: 1945   Position: p
Team: New York Black Yankees

A wartime player, he pitched for the New York Black Yankees in 1945, compiling a record of 3–5 in his only season in the Negro Leagues.

Mackey, Raleigh (Biz)
Career: 1920–47, 1950 Positions: **c**, ss, 3b, *2b, 1b, of, p,* manager
Teams: *San Antonio Black Aces ('18),* Indianapolis ABCs ('20–'22), New York Lincoln Giants ('20), *Colored All-Stars ('21),* **Hilldale Daisies** ('23–'31), Philadelphia Royal Giants ('25), Washington Elite Giants ('36–'37), **Baltimore Elite Giants** ('38–'39), Philadelphia Stars ('33–'35), Newark Dodgers ('35), **Newark Eagles** ('39–'41, '45–47, '50)
Bats: Both   Throws: Right
Height: 6'0"   Weight: 200
Born: July 27, 1897, Eagle Pass, Tex.
Died: 1959, Los Angeles, Calif.

Biz Mackey was an incredibly talented receiver who remained cool under pressure, and his defensive skills were unsurpassed in the history of black baseball. Considered the master of defense, he possessed all the tools necessary behind the plate, but gained the most acclaim for his powerful and deadly accurate throwing arm. He could snap a throw to second from a squatting position and get it there harder, quicker, and with more accuracy than most catchers can standing up. Mackey delighted in throwing out the best basestealers, and his pegs to the keystone sack were frozen ropes passing the mound belt high and arriving on the bag feather soft.

Although he was barely literate, Mackey was intelligent, had a good baseball mind, and employed a studious approach to the game. The ballpark was his classroom, and inside baseball was his subject of expertise. He relied on meticulous observation and a retentive memory to match weaknesses of opposing hitters with the strengths of his pitching staff. An expert handler of pitchers, he also studied people and could direct the temperaments of his hurlers as well as he did their repertoires.

He was also a jokester, and utilized good-natured banter and irrelevant conversation to try to distract a hitter and break his concentration at the plate, and was a master at "stealing" strikes from umpires by framing and funneling pitches. Pitchers recognized his generalship and liked to pitch to the big, husky receiver who, for his size, was surprisingly agile behind the plate. This unexpected quickness, coupled with soft hands, enabled the versatile athlete to play often at shortstop, third base, or in the outfield, and although lacking noteworthy range, he proved adept at any position. He was also a smart base runner and, although not fast, pilfered his share of bases.

In his prime, the switch-hitting Mackey was one of most dangerous hitters in baseball, with power from both sides of the plate, as evidenced by a .423 batting average, 20 home runs, and a .698 slugging percentage for Hilldale in the Eastern Colored League's inaugural season, 1923. Biz followed this campaign with averages of .337, .350, .327, .315, .327, .337, .400, and .376 for the years 1924–31.

His competitive spirit led the Hilldale club to three successive pennants, capped by a victory over the Kansas City Monarchs in the 1925 Negro World Series. In that Series, in addition to his superior defensive talent, he further displayed his batting skills, leading the team with a .375 average.

The big Texan learned the rudiments of baseball in the Lone Star State and, at age eighteen, began playing with his two brothers on a Prairie League baseball team in his hometown of Luling, Texas. After two years he began playing professionally with the San Antonio Black Aces in 1918. Financial problems plagued the ownership, and the team folded in 1920, but Mackey and several of the other top players were ready for the big time and were sold to the Indianapolis ABCs in time for the Negro League's inaugural season. Initially he served as a utility man, playing a variety of positions while learning the craft of baseball under manager C.I. Taylor, a master teacher. In his three seasons with the ABCs he batted .306, .296, and .361 and had slugging percentages of .558 and .630 the latter two seasons. When the Eastern Colored League was organized in 1923, the owners raided the Negro National League for players, and Mackey was one of the plums picked by Hilldale owner Ed Bolden.

In his first two seasons with the club, he split his playing time between catching and shortstop, sharing duties behind the plate with aging superstar Louis Santop. But for the championship 1925 season he won the position full time, and for the next decade retained recognition as the premier receiver in black baseball.

Mackey was in demand for postseason exhibitions and played against major-league all-star squads in Baltimore (including a 1926 series when Hilldale won 5 of 6 games from the Philadelphia Athletics with Lefty Grove) until the weather dictated a halt to the contests, after which he would travel to the West Coast for the California winter league. Playing with the Philadelphia Royal Giants in 1921–22, he hit for a lusty .382 average, and against a team headed by the Meusel brothers, Bob and Irish, rapped the ball at a .341 clip as the black stars annexed 7 victories in the 11-game series.

His barnstorming almost led to his banishment from the Negro Leagues, when in the early spring of 1927, despite warnings of a possible lifetime expulsion from angry league owners, he signed with an all-star team embarking on a baseball tour to Japan. Although he missed most of the season, the peerless receiver was welcomed upon his return, and stepped right back into the clean-up slot for Hilldale. After the regular season ended, he played with the Homestead Grays in postseason games.

In the Orient, the black Americans were immensely successful, both as diamond favorites and as diplomats. They lost only a single ball game, and their shadow ball routines and exhibitions of baseball skills delighted the fans and are credited as the catalyst for the organization of the Japanese professional leagues a decade later. Mackey, who was especially popular with the Japanese, made two more trips to the Land of the Rising Sun, in 1934–35, after he had joined Ed Bolden's new team, the Philadelphia stars.

Mackey teamed with the Stars' young left-handed fireballer, Slim Jones to form a superb battery, and together they provided the impetus for the Stars' 1934 drive to win the Negro National League pennant with a come-from-behind victory over the Chicago American Giants in the 7-game league championship series.

In balloting for the inaugural East-West All-Star game in 1933, Mackey's all-around skills were preferred over the slugging ability of young Josh Gibson. Mackey was then thirty-six years old and past his prime, while Gibson was just beginning to hit his full stride. However, Mackey's defensive skills were still so far above those of other catchers that he played in four of the first six midsummer classics.

Even as late as 1937, when he was managing the Baltimore Elite Giants, he was still considered the best all-around receiver in the Negro Leagues. One of his protégés with the Elites was Roy Campanella, who credits Mackey with teaching him the finer points of catching. Observers say that watching Campanella was like seeing Mackey behind the plate again.

In 1939 Mackey relinquished the managerial reins to George scales and joined the Newark Eagles, where he continued his work grooming young players. Monte Irvin, Larry Doby, and Don Newcombe were all beneficiaries of the Mackey touch during his stint as player-manager at Newark. Toward the end of his thirty-year career he directed the Eagles to the 1946 Negro world championship with a victory over the Kansas City Monarchs in the World Series.

Even then, Mackey was a formidable player, showing a .307 batting average for 1945 and receiving a free pass in a pinch-hitting appearance in the 1947 All-Star game at age fifty. Mackey, a nonsmoker and nondrinker, was an exemplary role model for young players and was still managing the Eagles in 1950, after a change in ownership had resulted in the franchise being moved to Houston, in his native state.

After retiring from baseball, he lived in Los Angeles and ran a forklift. On a special day for Roy Campanella at the Los Angeles Coliseum in 1959, Campy introduced Mackey for a final bow in baseball. Shortly after he heard the applause of the crowd for a last time, the great catcher passed away.

The smooth-operating receiver finished his career with a lifetime average of .335 in league play and an average of .326 against major-league competition in exhibition games. Biz's tremendous hitting, coupled with his sterling defensive skills, leave no doubt that he was one of the the true greats at his position.

Macklin
Career: 1924–29   Positions: 3b, of
Team: Chicago Giants

He played both infield and outfield with the Chicago Giants during the latter half of the '20s, after they had dropped out of the Negro National League and were playing as an independent ballclub.

Maddix, Raydell (Ray, Bo)
Career: 1949–50   Positions: **p**, *of*
Team: Indianapolis Clowns

A power pitcher with control problems, he pitched with the Clowns during the 1949–50 seasons, when the Negro American League was struggling to survive the loss of players to organized baseball. In the latter year he contributed a 5–5 record (3.73 ERA) as the Clowns won the Eastern Division title. He continued with the Clowns into the '50s, after the Negro American League had declined to a minor-league status.

Maddox, Arthur
Career: 1935–36   Position: p
Teams: *Cincinnati Tigers*

He pitched two seasons with the Cincinnati Tigers in 1935–36, when they were playing as an independent team.

Maddox, (One-wing)
Career: 1923   Positions: p, of
Team: Birmingham Black Barons

Carrying an unusual nickname, this little-known player was a pitcher-outfielder with the 1923 Birmingham Black Barons, who were accorded associate membership in the Negro National League that season.

Madert
Career: 1917   Positions: 2b, ss
Team: Chicago Giants

This reserve middle infielder played both keystone positions with the Chicago Giants in 1917, his only season in black baseball.

Madison, Robert
Career: 1935–42   Positions: **p** lf, 2b, ss, 3b, c
Teams: Kansas City Monarchs ('35–36), Indianapolis Athletics ('37), Memphis Red Sox ('37–'38), Birmingham Black Barons ('42)
Bats: Right   Throws: Right
Height: 6'0"   Weight: 170

Although primarily a pitcher, he was employed as an all-purpose player during his career in the Negro American League, also playing as an outfielder and infielder. As a pitcher he was at best a mediocre pitcher, with average control and fastball but only a fair curveball. As a position player he was adequate afield but lacking offensively, with subpar average and power. He broke in with the Kansas City Monarchs in 1935 as a pitcher-shortstop and appeared briefly with the Indianapolis Athletics before joining the Memphis Red Sox. In 1938 he played in left field and at second base for the Red Sox as they won the first-half championhiship of the Negro American League. After four more years he ended his career with the Birmingham Black Barons in 1942.

Maginet
[see Magrinat, Hector]

Magrinat, Hector
a.k.a Maginet
Career: 1909–16   Position: lf
Teams; Cuban Stars ('09–'16), All Cubans

Playing with the Cuban stars during the deadball era, he is regarded as one of best Cuban outfielders of the first quarter century of modern baseball.

Mahan
[see Mahoney, Ulysses]

Mahoney, Anthony (**Tony**)
Career: 1921–23   Position: p
Teams: *military service ('18–'19), Norfolk Giants ('20),* Brooklyn Royal Giants ('21), Indianapolis ABCs ('21–'22), Baltimore Black Sox ('23)
Bats: Left   Throws: Left
Born: Washington, D.C.
Died: Sept. 25, 1924, Washington, D.C.

This left-handed curveball artist was a star with the Norfolk Giants before breaking into the big time in 1921 with the Indianapolis ABCs, where he split 10 decisions. He had a good baseball mind and served as captain of the Baltimore Black Sox in 1923 while fashioning a 3–0 work sheet. A year later, the Washington, D.C., native died at Walter Reed Army Hospital after an illness of several months. The World War I veteran had been gassed during the war and never fully regained his health.

Mahoney, Ulysses
a.k.a. Mahan
Career: 1944   Position: p
Team: Philadelphia Stars
Bats: Right   Throws: Right

This wartime player pitched with the Philadelphia Stars in 1944 and was only a mediocre performer. Although he was regarded as an average player in all aspects of the game, in his limited playing time (only 10 at-bats) he recorded a .500 batting average during his only year in the Negro Leagues.

Mainor, Hank
Career: 1950   Position: p
Teams: Baltimore Elite Giants, *Philadelphia Stars ('51)*

In the declining years of the Negro Leagues, he pitched briefly with the Baltimore Elite Giants in 1950, but did not have a decision and was not listed in the official Negro American League statistics. The following year he pitched for the Philadelphia Stars, but the league was then definitely of minor-league caliber.

Maison, J.
Career: 1887   Position: player
Team: *Pittsburgh Keystones*

He played with the Pittsburgh Keystones, one of eight teams that were charter members of the League of Colored Baseball Clubs in 1887. However, the league's existence was ephemeral, lasting only a week. His position is uncertain.

Makell, Frank
a.k.a. Makel; Mackell
Career: 1944, 1949   Positions: c, p
Teams: Newark Eagles ('44), Baltimore Elite Giants ('49)
Bats: Right   Throws: Right
Height: 5'10"   Weight: 170

Beginning his career as a wartime reserve catcher with severely restricted playing time for the Newark Eagles in 1944, he was a hustling player with good hands, but only mediocre at best in any other facet of the game, batting only .111 during his brief stint with the Eagles. His next and last appearance with a Negro League team was in the declining years of the Negro American League, as a pitcher with the Baltimore Elite Giants.

Malarcher, David Julius (**Dave**, Gentleman Dave, Cap, Preacher)

Career: 1916–34   Positions: **3b**, 2b, ss, rf, c, p, manager
Teams: Indianapolis ABCs ('16–18), *military service ('18–'19),* Detroit Stars ('19), **Chicago American Giants** ('20–'28), Chicago Columbia Giants ('30–'31), Cole's American Giants ('32–'34)
Bats: Both   Throws: Right
Height: 5'7"   Weight: 148
Born: Oct. 18, 1894, Whitehall, La.
Died: May 11, 1982, Chicago, Ill.

A smooth-fielding third baseman who did his best hitting in the clutch, Malarcher was a speedy switch-hitter who could bunt and run the bases in the Rube Foster style of baseball. He was also adept at fouling off pitches and working the pitcher for a free pass to first base. Breaking in as a rookie with the champion Indianapolis ABCs in 1916, he hit .309 and learned baseball under one of the greatest managers in black baseball, C. I. Taylor. After utility service in 1916, he moved into the starting lineup in 1917, batting .240 as the regular right fielder while also logging playing time at third base. During his tenure with the ABCs he also played at second base and was once even pressed into emergency service behind the plate when Cobb, the regular catcher, was injured, and Malarcher caught two exhibition games against the American Association champion Indianapolis team. In 1918 he moved to the third-base position that was to become his home, with partial statistics showing a .227 batting mark for him before entering military service in World War I, when he was drafted into the Army. Along with teammate Jimmie Lyons, he played baseball in the allied Expeditionary Force League in Le Mans, France.

After returning from overseas service, he joined the Chicago American Giants and was afforded the opportunity to learn under the great tactician Rube Foster. This union was to be a lasting one, enduring for a decade and a half. Intelligent and observant, Malarcher learned from Rube and developed into a brilliant baseball strategist when he took over the managerial reins after Foster's mental breakdown.

When Malarcher joined the American Giants in 1920, the inaugural year of the Negro National League, he was called the best third baseman in black baseball and began his career with the American Giants by hitting .344. The first three years, the American Giants won the league championship, with Malarcher's winning spirit making him a key cog in Foster's machine, usually batting in one of the top two spots in the lineup. During the middle season of the three consecutive pennants, Malarcher suffered physical setbacks and missed considerable playing time. He was ordered not to play in 1922 because of torn ligaments around his heart, but was undeterred. He injured his leg in May but, determined to play, was back in lineup in July. Despite the handicaps, he managed a batting average of .235 for the 1921 season.

Back to full strength in 1923, he hit .295, and in 1924 Foster moved him to the third slot in the batting order for a season, and he responded with another solid season, hitting .293. In 1925 he succeeded Bingo DeMoss as team captain after DeMoss was shipped to the ABCs by Foster to maintain league balance. Leading by example, Malarcher was a model of consistency, hitting for a .330 average during the season, his last under Foster. The following year, after assuming the position of player-manager, Malarcher was credited with batting averages of .256 and .250 for the 1926–27 seasons while directing the Giants to consecutive World Series victories over the Eastern colored League champion Bacharach Giants in 1926 and 1927. In each of these two Series he led the team in stolen bases. Malarcher was a rough base runner, but considered "sneaky" by some opponents because he would always apologize after spiking an infielder.

In 1928, his third season as manager, he fractured a bone in his shoulder and was out action for about ten days, but steered his team to the second-half title before losing the playoff

to the St. Louis Stars. Although highly successful on the diamond, he left the American Giants after the season because of a money dispute with owner William E. Trinkle, and formed the Columbia Giants, an independent team. After three seasons with his new aggregation, he returned to the American Giants, who were now in the new Negro National League, and won his last championship in 1933. After one more final run for the flag, winning the first-half championship before bowing to the Philadelphia Stars in the 1934 playoff, "Gentleman Dave" retired from baseball after a full and rewarding career.

Malarcher overcame many obstacles in life to experience his diamond accomplishments. He was born the youngest of ten children to parents struggling to escape the underside of society. His father was a farm laborer on a sugar plantation and his mother was a former slave, but they instilled positive values in their son that he retained throughout his life.

At a very young age he began playing baseball as a catcher with the Baby T's, a team for little boys. He was a clean-living, intelligent, and able youngster, and as he grew older he attended Dillard University in New Orleans and Xavier University. During his school days, 1912–16, he played baseball during the summers with the New Orleans Black Eagles. The team traveled around East Texas and North Louisiana and was owned by a man named Palambo, but the manager was Charlie Stevens, who converted Malarcher from a cross-handed batter into a switch-hitter. After two years of college he signed with the ABCs and began a long and distinguished career in baseball. After his baseball days were over he utilized his education when he established a real-estate business and became an accomplished poet.

Malloy
Career: 1918–21   Position: of
Teams: Pennsylvania Red Caps of New York ('18), Nashville Elite Giants ('21)

He began his career in 1918 as a part-time starter in right field, batting in the lower part of the order, for the Pennsylvania Red Caps of New York. He also played with the Nashville Elite Giants, an independent team at that time.

Malone, William H.
Career: 1887–97   Positions: **3**, of, 1b, 3b, *ss*

Teams: *Philadelphia Pythians ('87), Pittsburgh Keystones ('87),* **Cuban Giants** *('88–'90, '97),* New York Gorhams ('91), Page Fence Giants ('95)

Died: May 10, 1917

For more than a decade in black baseball, this Detroit native played with many of the best teams of the nineteenth century. He began his career as a pitcher with the Philadelphia Pythians and the Pittsburgh Keystones, two of the teams that were charter members of the League of Colored Baseball Clubs in 1887. He joined the Cuban Giants in 1888 and played with them for the next three seasons, including the years when they represented Trenton, New Jersey, in the Middle States League (18189) and York Pennsylvania, in the Eastern Interstate League (1890). The next season, 1891, he signed with the New York Gorhams, who played in the Middle States League. Four years later he was an original member of the famous Page Fence Giants of Adrian, Michigan, batting .257 while posting a 2–1 record on the mound. A versatile player, when not in the pitching box he played in the outfield or infield and closed out his career as an outfielder with the Cuban Giants, the team with whom he gained the most identification.

Manella
[see Marcello]

Manese, E.
Career: 1923–26   Position: 2b

Teams: Detroit Stars ('23), Kansas City Monarchs ('24), Indianapolis ABCs ('26)

For four seasons during the '20s he played second base with the Detroit Stars, Kansas City Monarchs, and Indianapolis ABCs.

Mangrum
Career: 1948   Position: lf

Team: New York Cubans

He was a reserve outfielder for the New York Cubans in 1948, in the last year of the Negro National League's existence.

Manley, Abraham (**Abe**)
Career: 1935–46   Positions: owner, officer

Teams: Brooklyn Eagles ('35), Newark Eagles ('36–'46)

A colorful sportsman and numbers banker, he loved baseball and bought two ailing franchises (the Brooklyn Eagles and the Newark Dodgers) and consolidated them into the Newark Eagles for the 1936 season. His team was always competitive, and in 1946 the Eagles won the Negro National League championship, snapping the Homestead Grays nine-year skein of pennants, and defeated the Kansas City Monarchs in the World Series.

He liked to associate with his players to get a personal feel for the atmosphere of the game, and frequently rode on the bus with the team and played cards with the players in the clubhouse. In addition to overseeing his own ballclub's affairs, he was active in the operations of the Negro National League, serving terms as both vice president and treasurer of the league.

He and his wife, Effa, first met at Yankee Stadium, and after their marriage, Abe allowed her to take an active role in the team's operations, as business manager. He was a positive influence in black baseball and loved the game until his death. Afterward, Effa, a woman ahead of her time, continued to operate the team through the 1948 season.

Manley, Effa
Career: 1935–48   Positions: owner, officer

Teams: Brooklyn Eagles ('35), Newark Eagles ('36–'48)

An attractive and visable personage with a good business head, she was a woman ahead of her time. Although she was actually white, having been born from an illicit affair between her white mother and a white man who was not her husband, Effa was accepted as a fair-complexioned Negro because she was reared in a home with a black father.

After marrying Abe Manley, she shared both his love of baseball and operated as the business manager of their baseball team, the Newark Eagles. She had a proclivity for younger players and was involved in amorous relationships was several of her favorites. She liked to show off her players to the members of her ladies' club and sometimes told the manager to pitch a particular player for this purpose. Pitcher Terris McDuffie was a particular favorite, and when Abe found out about their amorous involvment, he traded McDuffie to the New York Black Yankees for two old bats and a pair of used sliding pads. Managers and players sometimes resented her intrusion into the affairs of the ballclub, but after her husband's death she took over total operation of the team through the 1948 season.

When Branch Rickey and other owners began signing her players, she fought for just compensation, and Bill Veeck paid her when he signed Larry Doby. Other players she lost to organized baseball were Don Newcombe and Monte Irvin.

Manning

Career: 1932   Position: 1b
Team: Montgomery Grey Sox

He was a first baseman with the Montgomery Grey Sox in 1932, when the Negro Southern League was considered a major league.

Manning, John

Career: 1902–03   Position: of
Team: Philadelphia Giants

In his only two seasons with a top team, he played as a centerfielder for the Philadelphia Giants.

Manning, *Maxwell* (**Max,** Emilio, *Dr. Cyclops*)

Career: 1938–49   Position: p

Teams: Newark Eagles ('38–'42, '46–'48), *military service ('42–'45),* Houston Eagles ('49), *Mexican League ('51), Canadian League ('51)*
Bats: Left   Throws: Right
Height: 6'4"   Weight: 185
Born: Nov. 18, 1918, Rome, Ga.

This tall, bespectacled sidearmer was a power pitcher with a good but not overpowering fastball and a complementing curve and slider. Nicknamed "Dr. Cyclops" because of his thick glasses, he had some control problems but managed to keep everything low and had less trouble with power hitters than with punch hitters. A member of the 1946 Negro National League champion Newark Eagles' pitching staff, he finished the regular season with an 11–1 league record and compiled the league's second-highest strikeout total, surpassed only by teammate Leon Day. At one stretch during the year he was credited with 15 straight wins against all opposition, losing only his first game of the season. Manning pitched in 3 games in the ensuing World Series against the Negro American League Kansas City Monarchs, splitting 2 decisions and registering a 3.64 ERA.

After the Series he pitched with Satchel Paige's All-Stars against Bob Feller's All-Stars in a postseason barnstorming exhibition and, in one game at Dayton, Ohio, he struck out 14 batters, including Charlie Keller three times, but lost the game, 2–1. In Cuba the following spring he learned the straight change from Carl Erskine, which completed his repertory of pitches and filled a need, allowing him to change speeds more effectively. The following year he had a 15–6 record and appeared in the East-West All-Star game.

In 1948 New York Cubans' owner Alex Pompez, who doubled as a New York Giants' scout, approached Manning about playing with the Giants. When Manning insisted that since he was part of the Eagles' organization, protocol necessitated that negotiations include the Manleys, Pompez never pursued the suggestion. The following spring, Manning was a holdout and missed spring training until the final week. Shortly after joining the team, he was called in to relieve early in a ball game without being sufficiently warmed up and, although he pitched 8 shutout innings, he suffered a shoulder separation that never completely healed and that robbed him of his speed. He undersent an operation and rehabilitation at Temple University but never fully recovered, and pitched with pain and without the same velocity as previously. Despite pitching in pain, he fashioned records of 10–4 and 8–4 in 1948 and 1949.

In his youth, the big right-hander starred with the Johnson Stars in Atlantic City and in high school in Pleasantville, New Jersey. After graduating in 1937, he was contacted by a Detroit Tiger scout about a tryout with the Tigers, but the offer was rescinded upon learning that Manning was black. Instead, he pitched with the semipro Camden Giants and attended Lincoln University in the fall before being signed, along with Monte Irvin, by Eagles' owner Abe Manley in 1938. In his first game as an Eagle, he faced the defending champion Homestead Grays in Winston-Salem, North Carolina, in the spring and struck out the first five batters he faced. After that auspicious beginning, he posted season records of 11–6, 5–4, and 6–4 in 1940–41. Then his baseball career was interrupted when he entered military service during World War II.

Drafted in 1942, he was sent first to Fort Dix and then to Richland Air Force Base with the 316th Air Squadron, serving in the Quartermaster Corps, an assignment that shattered his dreams. Later he was shipped overseas to England and then to France, where he spent over two years as a truck driver on the Red Ball Express, supplying gasoline and supplies for General Patton's Third Army. During this time he helped supply the 101st Airborne Division, which was involved in the breakthrough at Bastogne. However, his military experience was not generally positive. Once, in an incident resulting from the existing racial climate, he served fifteen days in the stockade for insubordination. At another time Manning suffered a back injury in a truck accident, and he was glad when his Army service was over. After his discharge he resumed his baseball career with the Eagles, helping pitch them to the 1946 championship.

During his career he also played in most Latin American leagues, pitching with Ponce in Puerto Rico in 1938; the Dominican Republic in 1940; Guadalajara and Jalixco, Mexico, in 1941, Cienfuegos, Cuba, in 1946–49 (where he won a shutout over Max Lanier and posted a combined 27–33 record); Maracaibo, Venezuela, in 1950; and again in Mexico with Torreon in 1951, where he played with Buck Leonard. He also played in Canada, pitching with Sherbrooke and Branford in the provincial League, but still troubled with a bad arm from the shoulder separation three years earlier, that was his last year in baseball.

After ending his active baseball career, he utilized the GI Bill to complete his education, graduating from Glassboro State College and teaching in the Pleasantville, New Jersey, school system for twenty-eight years before retiring.

Manolo
[see Monolo]

Manuel, (Clown)
Career: 1940   Position: lf
Teams: *Louisville Black Colonels ('38),* Cleveland Bears ('40)
He was a reserve outfielder with the Cleveland Bears in 1940, with spot duty in left field. Earlier he had played left field with the Louisville Black Colonels, in 1938.

Mara, Candido
Career: 1948–49   Position: 3b
Team: Memphis Red Sox
This Cuban infielder was the regular third baseman, hitting .271 while batting sixth in the order, for the Memphis Red Sox in 1948.

Marbury, Jimmy
Career: 1948   Position: of
Team: Birmingham Black Barons

An outfielder from Saginaw, Alabama, he vied for a place on the roster with the Birmingham Black Barons in the spring of 1948.

Marcel, Everett (Ziggy, Sam)
a.k.a. Marcell; Marcelle
Career: 1939–48   Positions: c, *of, p*
Teams: Satchel Paige's All-Stars ('39), Kansas City Monarchs ('39), Homestead Grays ('40), New York Black Yankees ('39, '41), Chicago American Giants ('42), Baltimore Elite Giants ('39, '47), Newark Eagles ('48), *Canadian League ('50)*
Bats: Right   Throws: Right
Height: 6'3"   Weight: 185
Born: Sept. 1, 1916, New Orleans, La.
Died: 1990, Los Angeles, Calif.

Although he generally spelled his surname differently, he is the son of the great third baseman Oliver Marcelle. He lacked his father's ability on the diamond, and much of his career was spent in a utility role or as a backup catcher. Other than his name, his only favorable attribute was a strong throwing arm, and he began his career as a combination catcher-pitcher with the Kansas City Monarchs in 1939. The following year he was one of the many catchers tried by the Homestead Grays in a futile effort to replace Josh Gibson, who had jumped to Mexico. He was lacking defensive skills, speed on the bases, and, as a batter, failed to demonstrate either a high percentage or good power. His batting average, in very limited play, was .273 and .158 for 1940–41.

As a youngster he asked manager Biz Mackey for a tryout as a catcher with the Baltimore Elite Giants, but after watching another youngster named Campanella make some sensational plays during a game, he approached Mackey and informed the manager that he could play other positions, too. Playing with the Elite Giants in a reserve capacity, he hit a weak .229 in 1947, and the following season, his last in the Negro Leagues, he was among four catchers who shared the receiving chores for the Newark Eagles. In 1950 he played with Farnham in the Canadian Provincial League

and hit a respectable .272 with moderate power.

Marcelle, Oliver H. (Ghost)
a.k.a. Marcell; Marcel
Career: 1918–34   Positions: **3b**, ss
Teams: Brooklyn Royal Giants ('18–'19, '30), Detroit Stars ('19), **Atlantic City Bacharach Giants** ('20–'22, '25–'28), New York Lincoln Giants ('23–'25), Baltimore Black Sox ('29), Miami Giants ('34)
Bats: Right   Throws: Right
Height: 5'9"   Weight: 160
Born: June 24, 1897, Thibedeaux, La.
Died: June 12, 1949, Denver, Colo.

Oliver Marcelle was a superior defensive third baseman, and his skillful play and faultless style earned him distinction as the peer of black third baseman in the '20s. In a 1952 *Pittsburgh Courier* poll he was selected over Hall of Famers Ray Dandridge and Judy Johnson as the all-time greatest player at the hot corner, and was also picked by John Henry Lloyd in 1953 for his All-Time All-Star team. A rare gem afield, he could do everything. He was very fast, covered lots of territory, and possessed a quick and snappy arm. He had no equal in knocking down hard-hit balls and getting his man at first. Whether making spectacular plays to his left or to his right, or fielding bunts like a master, he delighted the fans.

While idolized by the fans, he was also respected by the media and players. The press considered him to have "the ability of Frisch" and to be "as brainy as Herzog." In 1924, although still young, he was classed as a veteran and appointed captain of the New York Lincoln Giants. He and Frank Wickware were with teammate Dave Brown the night Brown killed a man in a barroom fight. Although not involved in the incident, the next day at the ballpark he and Wickware were picked up but later released.

The following year, after an effort by the Bachrarach Giants to secure him earlier in the season had fallen through, he was traded in midseason to Atlantic City, where he teamed with Dick Lundy to form an almost impregnable left side of the infield, and was an integral part of the team's success in the pennant years of 1926–27. In the 1926 World Series against the Chicago American Giants, he hit a solid .293 in a losing effort.

Moving with Lundy to the Baltimore Black Sox after the Eastern Colored League's breakup, he still had enough hits left in his bat to hit a respectable .288 in 1929 as the Black Sox won the American Negro League pennant. A good hitter (.305, .364, .295, .343, .308, .255, .306, and .296 for the years 1921–28), he was most dangerous in the clutch, registering a .305 lifetime average in Negro League competition. During eight winter seasons in Cuba, "Ghost" also had a .305 average, including a league-leading .393 in 1923–24 with the league champion Santa Clara team. He is also credited with an average of .333 in exhibitions against major-leaguers.

After finishing eight years at Tomey Lafon Elementary School and attending high school at New Orleans University, the New Orleans native began playing semipro baseball in 1914. After playing with the New Orleans Black Eagles, he began his professional career in 1918 with the Brooklyn Royal Giants. He hit .229 in 1919, playing primarily with the Royals, but also appeared briefly with the Detroit Stars. In 1920 he began his first stint with the Bacharachs, leaving to join the Lincoln Giants in the middle of the decade, but returning to the Bacharachs in 1925 for his second tour of duty in Atlantic City. Although he batted in the second slot most of his career, when he returned to the Bacharachs he hit in the third spot as they won their first Eastern Colored League pennant.

Marcelle was a good base runner and a fierce competitor who was always in the thick of battle. He had lots of pep and fight but was too temperamental on the field. The competitive Creole's quick and fiery temper frequently caused him trouble with umpires, opponents, and teammates. Once, on the field, in a flash of temper he hit Oscar Charleston over the head with a bat. In 1930, in an off-the-field incident, his temperment led to a dice-game quarrel with Frank Warfield, resulting in a fight in which Warfield literally bit off part of his nose. Afterward Marcelle continued to play ball, but wore a patch over the hole left when the nostril portion was ripped off in the fight. Oral accounts indicate that this incident was indirectly responsible for his withdrawal from league play because Marcelle, a vain man, could not endure the "ragging" from fans and opposing players about his appearance. Although his league playing career was prematurely ended, he continued with independent teams for sometime afterward, attempting a comeback with the Miami Giants in 1934. Eventually he faded from the sports scene and into obscurity.

After retiring from baseball in 1934, he became a house painter in Denver, Colorado. That year he arranged for the Kansas City Monarchs to play in the *Denver Post* tournament, marking the first time a black team was permitted to participate. When he died of arteriosclerosis in 1949, he was living in abject poverty, but he left behind a legacy of greatness over a seventeen-year career in black baseball. One of his sons, Everett "Ziggy" Marcel, also played in the Negro Leagues, and entered organized baseball after the color line was eradicated.

Marcello
a.k.a. Manella
Career: 1921   Position: p
Team: Cuban Stars (West)

He pitched with the Cuban Stars (West) in 1921, when the team represented Cincinnati in the Negro National League, and posted a 2–6 record.

Markham, John *Matthew (Johnny)*
a.k.a. Marcum
Career: 1930–45   Position: p
Teams: Kansas City Monarchs ('30, '37–'40), *Shreveport Acme Giants ('36), Monroe Monarchs,* Satchel Paige's All-Stars ('39), *Palmer*

House All-Stars ('40), **Birmingham Black Barons** *('41–'45), Detroit Senators ('47)*
Bats: Right   Throws: Right
Height: 5'11"   Weight: 170
Born: Oct. 1, 1908, Shreveport, La

A control artist with an average fastball, curve, and knuckler, he pitched for five of the first eight Negro American League pennant-winners. In his first trial with the Kansas City Monarchs, he finished with an unimpressive 2–7 record and was not retained by them for the following season. For the next six years he played with lesser teams, including the Shreveport Acme Giants in 1936, before returning to Kansas City for the first of three pennant-winning seasons (1937, 1939, and 1940).

Leaving the pitching-prosperous Monarchs, he played briefly with the Palmer House All-stars, a strong, independent, Chicago-based team, prior to signing with the Birmingham Black Barons in 1941. Incomplete statistics show marks of 2–1 and 3–1 in his first two seasons with the team. The next two seasons, with Markham in the starting rotation and posting marks of 7–2 and 4–2 (3.39 ERA), the Black Barons won back-to-back Negro American League flags in 1943 and 1944 and faced the Homestead Grays in a losing cause in each of the ensuing World Series. In the 1943 Series, after losing an earlier decision, he outpitched Roy Partlow in the sixth game, winning a 1–0 decision to force the Series to a final seventh game. After pitching in 3 games in the first Series showdown, he suffered a loss in his only appearance in the second Series, in 1944. He followed with a 2.94 ERA for the 1945 regular season, his last season in the Negro Leagues.

Markham, Melvin

Career: 1935–36   Position: p
Teams: Brooklyn Eagles ('35), Newark Eagles ('36)

A pitcher with the Brooklyn Eagles in 1935, he was one of the players who remained with the club when it was consolidated with the Newark Dodgers in 1936 to form the Newark Eagles.

Marlotica

Career: 1911   Position: rf
Team: All Cubans

In 1911 he played right field with the all Cubans, one of the best Cuban teams of the era.

Marquez, Luis *Angel (Canena)*

a.k.a. Sanchez
Career: 1945–48   Positions: cf, 2b, ss, 3b
Teams: New York Black Yankees ('45), Baltimore Elite Giants ('46), Homestead Grays ('46–'48), *minor leagues ('49–'61),* major leagues ('51, '54), *Mexican League ('62–'63)*
Bats: Right   Throws: Right
Height: 5'11"   Weight: 174
Born: Oct. 28, 1925, Aguadilla, Puerto Rico
Died: Mar. 1, 1988, Aguadilla, Puerto Rico

A versatile player who could play either infield or outfield, this Puerto Rican had a powerful arm, excellent speed, and was a good hitter. After joining the Homestead Grays in 1946 with a .309 performance, Marquez followed with his best year. In 1947 he led the Negro National League in hitting with a .417 batting average and in stolen bases with 29, warranting a starting assignment in the annual East-West All-Star game. After two years as the starting second baseman, he switched to centerfield and assumed the leadoff spot in the batting order, hitting .274 and playing an integral role as the Grays captured the final Negro National League pennant in 1948. That year marked his second consecutive appearance in All-Star competition and his last year in the Negro Leagues. He ended his four-year Negro Leagues career with a lifetime .371 batting average.

After the color barrier was lifted, he played with the Boston Braves in 1951 and had a second chance with the Chicago Cubs and the Pittsburgh Pirates in 1954, but managed only a .182 lifetime average for the major leagues. However, he enjoyed a long career in organized ball, playing from 1949 through 1961, and then an additional two years in the Mexican League with Poza Rica, where he hit .357 and .314.

His entry into organized baseball was marked with controversy. Marquez had signed a two-year contract to play with the Homestead Grays for the 1947–48 seasons, and when the league broke up after the 1948 season, the Negro American League consolidated, absorbing some of the Negro National League teams and assigning the players of the New York Black Yankees and Homestead Grays to various league teams. Dr. J. B. Martin, president of the Negro American League, assigned Marquez to the Baltimore Elite Giants, and Vernon Green, owner of the Baltimore ballclub, agreed in January 1949 to sell Marquez's contract to Larry McPhail of the New York Yankees contingent on his signing and reporting to the Newark Bears of the International League. However, during the previous November, Posey of the Grays had given Cleveland Indians' owner Bill Veeck a 120-day option to purchase his contract. Under these conflicting conditions, the rights to Marquez's contract were disputed, being claimed by both the Cleveland Indians and the New York Yankees, and Baseball Commissioner Happy Chandler ruled in favor of the Indians.

Before the Yankees' contract was ruled null and void, Marquez played 18 games in 1949 for Newark, International League, batting .246, before going to Portland in the Pacific Coast League for most of the season. With Portland he had seasons of .294 (32 stolen bases) and .311 (38 stolen bases), in 1949–50, earning his first trip to the major leagues. Although he failed to hit in the majors, after he was sent down he continued to hit at the AAA level, batting .345 and .292 in the American Association in 1952–53, with Milwaukee and Toledo, respectively. After his second unproductive opportunity in the majors, he returned to Toledo for two partial years and then back to Portland for four years (1955–58), where he hit .312, .344, .277, and .266. His last three seasons

were spent with Dallas-Fort Worth, where he hit .345 and .264 in two full seasons, and .209 in only 18 games before moving to Williamsport in the Eastern League to finish the 1961 season, while hitting .259 with his new team.

During his baseball career he played in the winter leagues of his native Puerto Rico, primarily with the Mayaguez Indios (1944–46, 1953–56, 1957–64), but also playing five years with Aguadilla (1946–51) and a year each with San Juan (1952–53) and Ponce (1956–57). As a twenty-year-old rookie in 1944–45 he batted .361, and followed the next winter by leading the league with 10 triples in only a 40-game season, a mark he duplicated in the 1949–50 season. During his third season he led the league in doubles with an all-time league high of 27, adding 14 homers in only 60 games for an impressive .664 slugging percentage, the highest ever for a Puerto Rican player. In 1948–49 he became the only Puerto Rican to get more than 100 hits in a season, with 108. With Aquadilla he led the league in stolen bases in consecutive seasons (1947–49) with 20 and 29, adding a third stolen-base title in 1953–54 with Mayagüez, when he had 32 to go with his .333 batting average. With Ponce he hit .273, .311, and .309 in 1956–59, with 38 successful base thefts in the winter of 1956–57.

Altogether, during his twenty-year Puerto Rican career he led the league in a major category fifteen times, and his versatility is indicated by the fact that these totals were accumulated in ten different categories (batting average, runs, hits, RBIs, doubles, triples, home runs, stolen bases, slugging percentage, and MVP awards).

After ending his baseball career as an active player, he worked in the Department of Sports in Aquadilla and coached both amateur and professional baseball. Preceded in death by his wife, he died tragically when he was shot twice and killed by his son-in-law during an argument in his home in Puerto Rico.

Marsans, Armando
Career: 1905, 1923   Positions: **of**, 1b

Teams: All Cubans ('05), major leagues ('11–'18), Cuban Stars ('23)
Bats: Right   Throws: Right
Height: 5'10"   Weight: 157
Born: Oct. 3, 1887, Matanzas, Cuba

A white player, he signed with the Cincinnati Reds in 1911, batting .317 as a regular the following season, and enjoyed an eight-year career in the major leagues, where he compiled a .269 lifetime batting average with four different teams. The Cuban had begun playing baseball in his homeland in the first decade of the century, and he played with Almendares in 1907 as a first baseman. He made two appearances in black baseball, first as a youngster with the All Cubans in 1905, and again as an aging veteran nearing the end of his playing career with the Cuban Stars in the Negro Leagues in 1923.

Marsellas, David, Jr.
Career: 1941   Position: c
Team: New York Black Yankees

He was briefly a reserve catcher with the Black Yankees in 1941, his only season in the Negro Leagues.

Marsh, Charles
Career: 1937   Position: p
Team: Newark Eagles

This pitcher's career in the Negro Leagues was abbreviated; he appeared with the Newark Eagles in the spring of 1937.

Marsh, Lorenzo
Career: 1950   Position: c
Team: Cleveland Buckeyes

He was a reserve catcher with the Cleveland Buckeyes in 1950, appearing in fewer than 10 games.

Marshall
Career: 1934   Position: c
Team: Atlantic City Bacharach Giants

A reserve catcher with the Bacharachs in 1934, he played during their last year in league play, when the club was a replacement team

in the Negro National League for the second half of the season.

Marshall, Jack
Career: 1920–29   Position: p
Teams: **Chicago American Giants** ('20–'21, '23, '25, '29), Detroit Stars ('22, '28), Kansas City Monarchs ('24)
Bats: Right   Throws: Right

He is best identified with the Chicago American Giants, where he was on the pitching staff who pitched the team to the first two Negro National League championships, forging a 7–3 record in the latter season. After leaving the American Giants for a season apiece with the Detroit Stars and the Kansas City Monarchs, he was among a large number of veteran players unconditionally released by Rube Foster in the spring of 1925. Returning to the American Giants in 1929, he finished with a 4–7 record to close out his career. He enjoyed the money that he made playing baseball, as opposed to having to resort to other endeavors to earn a living.

Marshall, Robert W. (Bob, **Bobby**)
Career: 1909–11   Positions: 1b, manager.
Teams: St. Paul Gophers (09), Leland Giants ('09), Chicago Giants ('10, *Twin City Gophers ('11)*

An ex-University of Minnesota football and baseball star, he joined "Daddy" Reid's St. Paul Gophers in 1909, The big, strong first sacker hit a home run as the Gophers defeated Rube Foster's Leland Giants in the playoff for the western title. Later in the fall, the Lelands picked him up to play first base in a heralded postseason exhibition series against the Chicago Cubs, and he made two crucial errors in the first game that contributed to the Cubs' victory. He was removed from the game and did not appear in the remainder of the contests. The following season he was one of four players from the Gophers to jump to Leland's Chicago Giants. After leaving the Leland Giants, he managed the Twin City Gophers in 1911.

Before joining the professional ranks, he had

played high-school, college, and semipro ball. He began playing baseball in 1899 as a first baseman with the Minneapolis Central High School team, and during his next two years (1900 and 1901) the school won the Twin Cities' high-school championship. After graduation he played at the University of Minnesota, and was the starting first baseman during his last two seasons (1904 and 1905), with the team winning the Western Conference championship the latter year.

Marshall then played semipro ball, playing third base for the Lund Lands of Minneapolis in 1906. The next season he played third base with LaMoure, North Dakota, and his team finished third in a league of eight teams. In 1908 he joined the Minneapolis Keystones as an utility player, but won the starting first-base position during the latter part of the season.

Marshall, William James (**Jack**, Boisy)
Career: 1926–44   Positions: **2b**, 3b, 1b, ss, rf, c
Teams: Dayton Marcos ('26–27), Michigan City Wonders ('27), Gilkerson's Union Giants ('28), Texas Giants ('29–'30), Chicago Columbia Giants ('31), Cole's American Giants ('32–'35), Philadelphia Stars ('36), Chicago American Giants ('37), Kansas City Monarchs ('38), semipro ball ('38), Palmer House all-stars ('39–'40), Satchel Paige's All-Stars ('41), Cincinnati-Indianapolis Clowns ('44)
Bats: Right   Throws: Right
Height: 5'11"   Weight: 182
Born: Aug. 8, 1907, Montgomery, Ala.

A team man all the way, this pepper-pot infielder was sure-handed and considered an expert second baseman but was adept at any position on the diamond. He was not a heavy hitter, usually batting in the lower part of the order, but was a good bunter with a special flair for the drag bunt. He began his career as a reserve player with the Dayton Marcos in 1926 and played most of his nineteen-year career in the Midwest.

At Dayton his manager was a friend, Eddie Huff. After leaving the Marcos after two years,

Marshall traveled for a year with Gilkerson's Union Giants. In 1929 he organized a minstel show, a band, and two baseball teams, the Texas Giants and the New York Stars, to tour in Canada for a white Canadian, Rod Whitman, from Saskatchewan. Following two years with this combination of baseball and show business, Marshall was ready to move on.

A gusty competitor, he was signed by manager Dave Malaracher for the Chicago Columbia Giants' team that was formed in 1931, and then earned a starting position on owner Robert A. Coles's American Giants team that won pennants in two different leagues the next two seasons. In 1932 they won the Negro Southern League title and then annexed the first pennant in the new Negro National League in 1933. In the latter year, Marshal teamed with Willie Wells to form a smooth double-play combination.

After the American Giants dropped out of league play for a season, he joined the Philadelphia Stars in 1936 and was selected as the utility man on the Negro National League All-Star team that easily won the Denver Post Tournament. Due to an injury to Felton Snow, Marshall played most of the tournament at third base.

When the American Giants entered the Negro American League in 1937, he returned to Chicago for another season. However, 1938 proved an unsettled season, with Marshall being sought by the Negro American League's unnamed Atlanta entrant, which tried to lure him away from his home in Germantown, Pennsylvania. Although his name was on their roster in March, he chose to play with a white semipro team in Elgin, Illinois, for the season, while also appearing briefly with the Kansas City Monarchs.

The next two seasons were spent with the Palmer House All-Stars, a Chicago-based independent team of less that major-league caliber that was booked by Abe Saperstein. In 1941 he traveled with Satchel Paige's All-Star team, and his last year in the Negro Leagues was in 1944, when he hit .311 as a reserve second baseman with the Clowns. After retiring from baseball, he operated a chain of bowling alleys in Chicago and was an outstanding tourney bowler.

Martin
Career: 1913   Position: p
Team: Chicago Giants

He pitched with the Chicago Giants in 1913, his only year in black baseball.

Martin
Career: 1921   Position: p
Team: *Pittsburgh Keystones*

He was a pitcher with the Pittsburgh Keystones in 1921, a year before they joined the Negro National League.

Martin, A. T., Dr.
Career: 1923–50   Position: officer
Team: Memphis Red Sox

A member of the prominent Martin family, well known because of their social and sporting endeavors, he served as an officer of the Memphis Red Sox for twenty-eight years.

Martin, B. B., Dr.
Career: 1933–50   Positions: owner,
                                        officer
Team: Memphis Red Sox

A member of the prominent Martin family, well known because of their social and sporting endeavors, this dentist was a co-owner of the Memphis Red Sox ballclub and also served as an officer of the Negro Southern League.

Martin, Jim (Pepper, Beany)
Career: 1935   Position: if
Team: Brooklyn Eagles

A reserve infielder, he played briefly with the Brooklyn Eagles in 1935.

Martin, John B., Dr.
Career: 1929–50   Position: officer
Teams: Memphis Red Sox, Chicago American Giants

A member of the prominent Martin family, well known because of their social and sporting endeavors, this dentist was a co-owner and a club officer for the Memphis Red Sox and the Chicago American Giants. He also operated a drugstore and a funeral home and had investments in real estate. In Memphis he built his own ballpark for the team, owned a hotel next to the park, and operated the concession stands, where he served chitterlings in addition to the standard ballpark cuisine. During his association with the Red Sox and the American Giants he also served as the president of three different leagues: the Negro Southern League, the Negro American League, and the Negro Dixie League.

Martin, R.
Career: 1885   Position: p
Team: *Argyle Hotel Athletics*

He was a pitcher with the Argyle Hotel Athletics, a team organized in 1885 by Frank P. Thompson, the headwaiter at the hotel in Babylon, New York, who recruited players from the Philadelphia Keystones to work at the Hotel as waiters and to form a baseball team to play for the entertainment of the summer guests. After the end of the tourist season the team added more players from the Philadelphia Orions and the Manhattens of Washington, D.C., to form the Cuban Giants, the first black professional team.

Martin, William (Stack)
Career: 1925–28   Positions: of, 1b, c,
                                        3b, *p*
Teams: Wilmington Potomacs ('25), Indianapolis ABCs ('25–'26), Dayton Marcos ('26), Detroit Stars ('27–'28)

He was an all-purpose player, and his versatility gained him additional playing time during his four seasons in the Negro Leagues. He pitched part of the 1926 season with the Dayton Marcos but was winless against 4 losses. For the remainder of the year he was an everyday player for the Indianapolis ABCs in their last season before disbanding, and he hit .341 while usually batting in the lower half of the order. The next season he was a regular for the Detroit Stars, splitting his playing time between left field and first base. In 1928 he made appearances as an outfielder, pitcher, and catcher while closing out his career.

Martin, William S., Dr.
Career: 1927–50   Position: officer
Team: Memphis Red Sox

A member of the prominent Martin family, well known because of their social and sporting endeavors, he served as an officer of the Memphis Red Sox ballclub and also served as the president of the Negro Southern League and as an officer of the Negro American League.

Martinez, C.
Career: 1928   Position: c
Team: Cuban Stars (West)

During his only season in the Negro National League, he was a catcher with the Cuban Stars (West).

Martinez, Francisco
Career: 1939   Position: p
Team: New York Cubans

He was a pitcher with Alexander Pompez's New York Cubans in 1939, his only season in the Negro National League.

Martinez, Horacio (Rabbit)
a.k.a. Millito Martinez
Career: 1935–47   Positions: ss, 2b, 3b
Teams: **New York Cubans** ('35–'36, '39–'47), Cuban Stars ('37–'38)
Bats: Right   Throws: Right
Born: 1915, Santo Domingo
Died: 1992

A star shortstop for the New York Cubans during the 1940s, Martinez was selected to the East-West All-Star squad every year between 1940 and 1945, except 1942. In All-Star competition he averaged a rousing .545. In 1945 his sterling glovework and the skill and ease with which he executed his position earned him a description as "the perfect shortstop" and the distinction of being the best shortstop in the league. He had outstanding range, a strong and accurate arm, and exceptional fielding mechanics.

He was only an average hitter, batting .222, .240, and .171 in 1940–42, but was a good bunter, fast on the bases, and good on either end of the hit-and-run play. Always a hustler, he broke in with the New York Cubans in 1935, registering batting averages of .244 and .216. A product of Santo Domingo, he played in the winter leagues of Cuba, Puerto Rico, and Mexico, and managed Caracas to the Venezuelan League championship in the playoffs of 1945–46. In his latter years he suffered from Parkinson's disease before passing away in 1992.

Martinez, Pasquel
Career: 1918–28   Position: p
Teams: Cuban Stars (West) ('18'–'22), Cuban Stars (East) ('23–'28)

Pitching with the Cuban Stars (West) in 1918, he lost his only recorded decision and, although not a first-line pitcher, continued to play with the Cuban Stars in both leagues for another decade.

Martini, José
Career: 1928   Position: p
Team: Cuban Stars (West)

He pitched for the Negro National Cuban Stars (West) in 1928, his only season in the Negro Leagues.

Marvin, Alfred
Career: 1938   Position: p
Team: Kansas City Monarchs

He pitched briefly with the Kansas City Monarchs in 1938, his only season in the Negro Leagues.

Marvray, Charles
Career: 1949–50   Positions: of, 1b
Teams: Louisville Buckeyes ('49), Cleveland Buckeyes ('50)

This outfielder batted .278 and .288 for the Buckeyes during the 1949–50 seasons, when the Negro American League was struggling to survive the loss of players to organized baseball.

Mason
Career: 1927   Position: 3b
Team: Baltimore Black Sox

This third baseman was a reserve player for manager Ben Taylor's Baltimore Black Sox in 1927.

Mason, Charles (Corporal)
Career: 1922–29   Positions: **lf, rf**, *p*
Teams: Richmond Giants ('22), Atlantic City Bacharach Giants ('22–'25), New York Lincoln Giants ('25–'28), Newark Stars ('26), Homestead Grays ('29)

This power hitter was one of biggest men in baseball and, in his prime, was often compared to Babe Ruth. In addition to being a good hitter, the outfielder had one of the best arms in the league. His rapid development after joining the Bacharachs earned him the designation as one of the best outfielders and hitters in the Negro Leagues in 1924. While playing right field and batting cleanup with the Bacharachs that season, he broke his hand in midseason, putting him out of commission for a time, but he still managed a .326 batting average for the year. In 1925 the Bacharachs were determined to secure star third baseman Oliver Marcelle from the New York Lincoln Giants and, after their first effort to effect a trade fell through, near midseason they traded Mason and third baseman Tom Finley to the Lincolns for Marcelle. The big outfielder finished the season with the Lincolns, batting a collective .261 for the year. At the beginning of the next season, he joined Newark's entry in the Eastern Colored League until they broke up in midsummer. Following the breakup, Mason returned to the Lincolns. He and George Scales, who also signed with the Lincoln Giants after the Newark team's dissolution, supplied power in the heart of the batting order for manager John Henry Lloyd's club through the 1928 season. In 1929 Mason joined the Homestead Grays,

who had joined the American Negro League, and batted fifth in the order during his final season in the Negro Leagues.

Mason, Dolly
Career: 1929   Position: lf
Teams: New York Lincoln Giants ('29), Baltimore Black Sox ('29)

Formerly with the New York Lincoln Giants, he appeared briefly with the Baltimore Black Sox in 1929.

Mason, James
Career: 1938   Position: p
Team: Atlanta Black Crackers

This pitcher, who made his home in Cross City, Florida, was on the roster of the Atlanta Black Crackers in March 1938.

Mason, Jim
Career: 1931–34   Positions: 1b, of
Teams: Cuban House of David ('31), Cuban Stars ('32), Washington Pilots ('32), Memphis Red Sox ('33–'34)

An outfielder-first baseman, he batted in the power positions for several teams during the early years of the Depression, hitting cleanup and playing right field with the Memphis Red Sox in 1933.

Massey
Career: 1930   Position: of
Team: *Louisville White Sox*

He was an outfielder with the Louisville White Sox in 1930, a year before they joined the Negro National League.

Massip, Armando
Career: 1920–34   Positions: 1b, of
Teams: Memphis Red Sox, Cuban Stars (West), Cuban Stars (East) ('25–'29), Cuban Stars ('30–'34), Washington Pilots ('32)

He was a first baseman for the Cuban Stars, playing with the team when they were independent and in three different leagues: the Negro National League, the Eastern Colored League, and the East–West League. In 1925 he hit .208

in limited play for the Cubans, and he also played with the Memphis Red Sox and the Washington Pilots.

Matchett, Jack
Career: 1940–45   Position: p
Team: Kansas City Monarchs
Bats: Right   Throws: Right
Height: 6'1"   Weight: 170

A member of the Kansas City Monarchs' great pitching corps, this right-hander had a free, easy motion and good control of a variety of pitches, including a fastball, screwball, quick-breaking curve, and a very good change of pace. When on the mound nothing seemed to bother him, and his even temperament, hearty determination, and bountiful stamina enabled him to fashion some well-pitched games for the Monarchs.

In 1940, his first season, he is credited with 6 wins without a loss as the Monarchs captured the Negro American League pennant. In 1942 he had an 8–2 record as the Monarchs won their third straight pennant and faced the Homestead Grays in the first World Series between the Negro American League and the Negro National League. Matchett combined with Satchel Paige to pitch an opening day shutout in the 1942 World Series against the Grays. Altogether Matchett pitched in three games, scoring 2 victories without a defeat as the Monarchs won an exciting Series. In the last game, he was forced into a starting role when Paige, who was scheduled to start, failed to show up by game time. The Monarchs fell behind, 5–2, before Paige finally arrived at the ballpark, after having been detained by police and issued a traffic ticket. Matchett gave way to Paige, who was credited with the victory when the Monarchs rallied.

In 1943, with the team weakened by World War II, Matchett dropped to a 2–4 record in league play. But he rebounded in 1944 with a 5–3 mark and a 2.40 ERA in league play before closing out his career in 1945.

Mathew
[see Mathis, Verdell]

Mathews
Career: 1938   Position: 3b
Team: Memphis Red Sox

In 1938 he gained some playing time at third base for the Negro American League first-half champion Memphis Red Sox.

Mathews
a.k.a. Mathews
Career: 1916   Position: 2b
Team: *Baltimore Black Sox*

Playing with the Baltimore Black Sox in their formative years, he played second base and batted leadoff in 1916

Mathews, Dell
Career: 1904–05   Positions: p, of
Teams: Chicago Union Giants ('04–'05), Leland Giants ('05)

He began his career as a pitcher with the Chicago Union Giants but joined the Leland Giants in their first year of existence and was the starting right fielder.

Mathews, Dick
Career: 1932–33   Position: p
Teams: Monroe Monarchs ('32), *New Orleans Crescent Stars ('33)*

He pitched with the Monroe Monarchs in 1932 when the Negro Southern League was recognized as a major league, and with the New Orleans Crescent Stars the following year after many of the top players in the league had returned to the new Negro National League.

Mathews, Francis Oliver (**Fran**)
Career: 1938–45   Positions: **1b**, of
Teams: **Newark Eagles** ('38, '40–'42, '45), Baltimore Elite Giants ('39), *Boston Royal Giants ('42), military service ('42–'44)*
Bats: Left   Throws: Left
Height: 5'9"   Weight: 170

A good all-around college athlete, he had good speed, was a good hitter with power, and although he had a scatter arm, this first sacker could field his position. When he joined the Newark Eagles he was considered a bright prospect but never demonstrated sufficient improvement to realize his early promise fully. In 1940–41 he hit .323 and .252, and suffered an arm injury in the former season when struck by a rifle throw from third baseman Monte Irvin. In 1942, Mathews entered military service during World War II and, after his discharge, batted .309 in 1945, his last year in the Negro Leagues.

Mathews, Jack
Career: 1923   Position: 3b
Team: Toledo Tigers

He was a third baseman with the Toledo Tigers in 1923, before they dropped out of the Negro National League and disbanded in mid-July.

Mathews, Jesse
Career: 1942   Position: player
Team: Birmingham Black Barons

In 1942 he was among the multitude of players who appeared briefly in a Birmingham Black Barons' uniform.

Mathews, John (Johnny, Big)
a.k.a. Mathews
Career: 1919–33   Positions: owner,
                                          officer
Team: Dayton Marcos

He was the owner of the Dayton Marcos' ballclub for fifteen years, including their two unsuccessful excursions into the Negro National League, first in 1920 and again in 1926.

Mathis, Verdell (Lefty)
Career: 1940–50   Positions: p, of, 1b
Teams: Memphis Red Sox ('40–'50), Philadelphia Stars ('43)
Bats: Left   Throws: Left
Height; 5'11"   Weight: 150
Born: Nov. 18, 1914, Crawfordsville, Ark.

This slender hurler had a terrific curve, a good fastball, screwball, change of pace, and a great pickoff move, which made this quiet competitor the best left-hander in the Negro American League during the '40s. He copied his pickoff move from Luis Tiant, Sr. (later successfully using the move to pick Jackie Robinson off base several times), but listened to advice on pitching from Satchel Paige, his boyhood hero. After making it to the black big leagues, he matched up with Paige several times, defeating him on three occasions, winning 1–0 in 11 innings in New Orleans, 2–1 in Kansas City and 2–1 again in Chicago on "Satchel Paige Day" in front of thirty thousand fans.

Although he pitched with a losing ballclub, Mathis's regular-season records of 9–9 and 8–10, with corresponding ERAs of 3.46 and 2.79, earned him back-to-back starts for the West squad in the 1944 and 1945 All-Star games. The Memphis Red Sox ace capitalized on the opportunity, holding the East scoreless each time, thereby joining Satchel Paige as the only pitchers to win two East-West games. Although slight physically, he had a lot of heart and was an "overpowering pitcher," winning almost half of the last-place Red Sox victories in 1945. However, the workload took its toll, and after the season, he needed surgery to remove bone chips from his left elbow. After the operation, he was never the same pitcher and, although he posted marks of 2–6, 5–5, 7–11 (4.75 ERA), and 9–11 in 1946–49, his career was cut short as a result of the arm injury.

He spent almost his entire ten-year career in Memphis and, like many outstanding players on southern teams, never received the publicity accorded to players on other teams. Mathis, who had attended Booker T. Washington High School, had only one year of semipro experience when he joined the Memphis Red Sox in 1940 and was rejected by the Memphis management when first recommended by his coach, William Lowe, in 1939. Reuben Jones, who had played against Mathis in semipro ball, interceded on his behalf, personally taking Mathis to Red Sox owner Dr. B. B. Martin's office and negotiating terms for him with the Red Sox. Joining the team as an outfielder and pitcher, Mathis loved to play baseball and preferred to play center field so he could play every day. But he was credited with a 3–1 mound mark in his initial season, and soon afterward, despite records of 1–2, 6–5, and 6–5 for 1941–43, he was considered the top left-handed pitcher in the Negro American League.

In addition to his East-West appearances, he pitched in two North-South All-Star games. He also played winter ball, with Vargas in the winter of 1947–48 and with Tampico in Mexico, where he once defeated Mexico City in a doubleheader. He also toured with Satchel Paige's All-Stars against Bob Feller's All-Star team in 1946.

A good-hitting pitcher with average power, Mathis often played first base or the outfield when not performing on the mound, and posted batting averages of .310, .261, .200, .276, and .263 for the years 1944–48. He had a good throwing arm and good speed in the field and on the bases. In 1949 he was earning the highest salary of his career, $700 a month, and he closed out his career in 1950. After leaving the baseball diamond, he worked with the Colonial Country Club in Memphis for fifteen years before retiring.

Matlock, Leroy

Career: 1929–42   Position: p
Teams: St. Louis Stars ('29–'31), Detroit Wolves ('32), Homestead Grays ('32), Washington Pilots ('32), Pittsburgh Crawfords ('33–'38), *Santo Domingo ('37), Venezuelan League ('39), Mexican League ('40–'41),* New York Cubans ('42)
Bats: Left   Throws: Left
Height: 5'9"   Weight: 175
Born: Mar. 12, 1907, Moberly, Mo.
Died: Feb. 6, 1968, St. Paul, Minn.

A top left-handed pitcher during the '30s, he had a good fastball and a variety of good breaking pitches, including a curve, drop, screwball, and slider. He was a smart pitcher and also mixed in a good change-up with his other pitches and had excellent control.

Breaking in with the St. Louis Stars in 1929, he fashioned a 5–2 record and improved to an 11–3 mark in 1930 to help pitch the team to

consecutive pennants in the last two years of the first Negro National League's existence ('30–'31). After the demise of the league, he played with several teams during the chaotic 1932 season, with incomplete statistics showing a 2–4 combined ledger.

The following season he joined the Pittsburgh Crawfords, where he posted records of 7–3 and 5–2 in 1933–34. Quickly establishing himself as one of the star pitchers on the great Crawfords teams, the tough left-hander took over as the ace of the staff in 1935, when Satchel Paige jumped to Bismarck, North Dakota; Matlock was undefeated, finishing with a 18–0 ledger. In 1936 he posted a 19–9 record and appeared in back-to-back East-West All-Star games in 1935 and 1936, starting and winning the 1936 game. When the Negro National League took an All-Star game to the *Denver Post* Tournament, Matlock was on the squad and turned in a commanding performance as the team won handily.

After a successful winter in Puerto Rico, he was reluctant to sign with the Crawfords in 1937, and joined Satchel Paige and other Crawfords defecting to Santo Domingo, where he fashioned a 4–1 record for the champion Ciudad Trujillo team. Rejoining the Crawfords in 1938, he dropped to a 2–4 mark, and in 1939 he jumped again, this time to Venezuela. The next season he joined Mexico City in the Mexican League and posted marks of 15–10 (3.26 ERA) and 15–9 (3.94 ERA) in 1940–41.

In addition to his pitching skills, Matlock was a good-hitting pitcher with average power and speed on the bases, and was a good fielder and hustler who refrained from dissipating influences.

Maxwell

Career: 1914   Position: of
Team: Chicago American Giants

A reserve outfielder, he played briefly as a right fielder with the Chicago American Giants in 1914.

Maxwell, Zearlee (Jiggs)

Career: 1931–38   Positions: **3b**, 2b

Teams: *Monroe Monarchs ('31)*, Memphis Red Sox ('38)

He played at third base for the Negro American League first-half champion Memphis Red Sox in 1938. He had played earlier in the decade with the Monroe Monarchs in the Negro Southern League.

Mayari
Career: 1923   Position: 1b
Team: Cuban Stars (East)

He was a reserve first baseman with the Eastern Colored League's Cuban Stars in 1923.

Mayers, George
[see Meyers, George]

Mayfield, Fred
Career: 1887   Position: player
Team: *Louisville Falls Citys*

He was a player with the Louisville Falls Citys, one of eight teams that were charter members of the League of Colored Baseball Clubs in 1887. However, the league's existence was ephemeral, lasting only a week. His position is uncertain.

Mayo
Career: 1906   Position: p
Team: Cuban X-Giants

He was a pitcher in 1906 with the Cuban X-Giants, one of the leading teams of the era.

Mayo, George (Hot Stuff)
Career: 1912–18; 1928 Positions: **1b**, of
Teams: *Pittsburgh Giants ('11)*, Hilldale Daisies ('12–'18, '28), *Pittsburgh Colored Stars of Buffalo ('16)*

He was a star first baseman for Hilldale during their formative years and, after his playing days were ended, served as an officer with the ballclub in 1928. During his active career he also played with two lesser teams, the Pittsburgh Giants and the Pittsburgh Colored Stars of Buffalo.

Mays
Career: 1937–38   Position: p
Teams: St. Louis Stars ('37), Memphis Red Sox ('37–'38)

This pitcher appeared in the Negro American League for two years, playing primarily with the Memphis Red Sox.

Mays, Dave (Tom)
Career: 1937   Position: of
Team: Kansas City Monarchs
Bats: Right   Throws: Right
Height: 5'11"   Weight: 170

He was generally an average player afield, on the bases, and at the plate, except for an inability to pull the ball and a lack of power. In 1937 he played as a reserve outfielder for the Kansas City Monarchs.

Mays, Willie Howard, Jr. (Buck)
Career: 1948–50   Position: cf
Teams: Birmingham Black Barons ('48–'50), *minor leagues ('50–'51)*, major leagues ('51–'52, '54–'73), *military service ('52–'53)*
Bats: Right   Throws: Right
Height: 5'11"   Weight: 175
Born: May 6, 1931, Westfield, Ala.

Mays started his baseball career as a teenager with the Negro American League champion Birmingham Black Barons in 1948. When manager Piper Davis penciled in his name on his lineup card as the left fielder and seventh-place batter for the Black Barons, the future superstar was a seventeen-year-old high-school student. During his tenure with the team, Davis became Mays's mentor and was like a second father to the youngster.

Mays began playing sandlot ball as a shortstop with a team called the Fairfield Stars but quickly advanced to a semipro team, the Chattanooga Choo Choos, when Davis recruited him for the Black Barons. As a minor, Mays had to secure permission from his father, "Cat" Mays, who had been a center fielder in the industrial leagues around Birmingham, and who was reported to have played with the Black Barons for a short time.

At the time Willie began his professional career with the Black Barons, he was called "Buck" by his friends, and it was not until years later that he became the "Say Hey Kid." When he joined the team it was obvious that he could run and throw, but Davis saw beyond the basic raw skills. On his fist day in a Black Barons' uniform, the team was playing a Sunday doubleheader at Rickwood Field in Birmingham. Mays sat out the first game but was inserted into the starting lineup for the second game, causing some grumbling among many of the veteran players. But Davis's support and Mays's performance dispelled any concerns about his ability. Although Mays had 2 hits in the game off a tough veteran pitcher, he was still the fourth-best outfielder on the team. Conveniently, Fate stepped in, and by the first of June he was the regular center fielder, taking over when starter Norman Robinson broke his leg. Neither of the fielders in the side pastures was noted for his range, and when a ball was hit to the outfield they would yell, "Come on, Willie!"

In 1948, his first year with the Black Barons, he hit .262 with only 1 home run and 1 stolen base, but played well in the field during the regular season and in the ensuing Negro World Series in a losing cause. The youngster had difficulty hitting a curveball, but with Piper Davis's help, he began maturing as a hitter, and in 1949 he elevated his batting average to .311 and continued to raise his average in 1950, hitting .330 with good power (.547 slugging percentage) before being signed by the Giants and shipped to Trenton for the remainder of the season. There he continued to blister the ball, hitting .353 and slugging .510. That performance earned a promotion to Minneapolis in the AAA American Association, where he stayed for about a month, hitting .477 and slugging .799 before being called up to the New York Giants in 1951 at age twenty.

Leo Durocher inserted him into center field and he hit .274 with 20 home runs as a rookie, and the Giants won the National League pennant. That was his last full season until 1954

when, after two years in the Army, he returned to lead the Giants to another National League flag and to a World Series victory over the Cleveland Indians in a Series most remembered for "the catch." He also led the league in batting with a .345 average and in triples with 13, while slugging 41 home runs and collecting 110 RBIs.

The rest of his career is well chronicled, finishing his twenty-two-year assault on major-league baseball with a .302 lifetime average, 660 home runs, 1903 RBIs, 2062 runs, and 338 stolen bases. Along the way he won a batting title, three home-run titles (with a personal high of 52 in 1965), four stolen-base titles, and assorted titles in triples, hits, and runs.

In a career that started as a teenager in the Negro Leagues, he finished with election to the National Baseball Hall of Fame in his first year of eligibility.

Mayweather, Eldridge (Chili, Ed)
a.k.a. Mayweathers
Career: 1935–46   Positions: **1b**, of, *3b*
Teams: *Monroe Monarchs ('34),* Kansas City Monarchs ('35–'38), St. Louis Stars ('39), New Orleans-St. Louis Stars ('40–'41), New York Black Yankees ('42), *Boston Blues ('46)*
Bats: Left   Throws: Left
Height: 5'10"   Weight: 180
Born: 1910, Shreveport, La.

A dead pull hitter with plenty of power, this left-handed batter also made good contact but was a poor bunter. He was only an average-fielding first baseman with an average arm, but he could also play capably in the outfield. Although he was slow on the bases, he compensated with his hustle.

A product of Shreveport Louisiana, he began playing with the Monroe Monarchs in 1934 and quickly attracted the attention of the Kansas City Monarchs. During his four years with Kansas City he hit in a power slot in the batting order and was selected for the West squad in the 1937 East-West All-Star game, although he was limited to a pinch-hitting appearance in the contest.

In 1939 he moved to the St. Louis Stars and assumed a power position in the batting order. The following season the franchise was shared by two cities and Mayweather, as a member of the New Orleans-St. Louis Stars, was voted to a starting position as the first baseman for the 1940 All-Star classic. Batting third in the lineup, he had a hit in three trips to the plate. In 1941, as the captain and cleanup hitter with the Stars, he lead the team in home runs while maintaining a .342 batting average. When the Stars disbanded after the season, he was among the ex-Stars who traveled East to play with the New York Black Yankees for the 1942 season, his last with a major league team.

Mayweather, Elliot
Career: 1928–29   Position: p
Team: Memphis Red Sox
He pitched with the Memphis Red Sox for two seasons in the late '20s, losing both of his decisions in 1929.

Maywood
Career: 1917–19   Position: p
Team: New York Lincoln Giants
During the last years of the deadball era, he pitched without distinction for the New York Lincoln Giants.

McAdoo, Dudley **(Tully)**
Career: 1908–24   Position: 1b
Teams: *Topeka Giants ('07),* Kansas City Monarchs ('08), Kansas City, Kansas, Giants ('08),**St. Louis Giants** ('11–'17, '19–'21), Chicago American Giants ('16), Chicago Giants ('14), Chicago Union Giants ('16), *Topeka Giants ('18),* St. Louis Stars ('22–'23), Cleveland Browns ('24)
Bats: Uncertain   Throws: Right
A premier first baseman of the latter years of the '10s and early '20s, he is best identified with the St. Louis Giants. He joined the St. Louis team when it was organized in 1911 and was the regular first baseman for half a dozen seasons, usually batting sixth in the order, until the club broke up in the spring of 1917. He

played the 1918 season with his hometown team, the Topeka Giants. That marked the second time that McAdoo had left the St. Louis aggregation. The first was when Rube Foster, a shrewd judge of talent, signed him to play first base with the Chicago American Giants during the winter of 1915–16, but he returned to the St. Louis Giants after a short stint with Foster.

The youngster from Topeka began his baseball career in 1907 playing with the Jenkins Sons team of Kansas City, Missouri, a semipro team backed by a local music store. The team played an exhibition against the Kansas City Blues of the American Association, losing, 16–2. The following season the youngster became a member of the original Kansas City Monarchs.

McAllister, Frank (Chip, Bud)
Career: 1938–46   Positions: **p**, of
Teams: Indianapolis ABCs ('38), St. Louis Stars ('39), New Orleans-St. Louis Stars ('40–'41), New York Black Yankees ('42), Harrisburg-St. Louis Stars ('43), *Brooklyn Brown Dodgers ('45), Cleveland Clippers ('46)*
Bats: Right   Throws: Right
Height: 6'3"   Weight: 210
Born: April 29, 1918, Forest City, Ark.
Died: May 5, 1987, Cairo, Ill.
This big right-hander began his career with the Indianapolis ABCs in 1938 but joined the St. Louis Stars the following year and was with the Stars throughout the years of franchise relocations. In 1941 he was one of the Big Four pitchers of the Stars' staff. A power pitcher with good stamina and average control, his best pitch was his slider and he also utilized a fastball and change, but his curve was subpar.

When the Stars failed to field a team in 1942, he moved East to join the New York Black Yankees, returning the following year when the Stars had dual hometowns, Harrisburg and St. Louis. Throughout his career he sometimes played in the outfield, where he was an average fielder and had a modicum of power at the plate, but he did not hit for sufficient average and had little speed on the bases. His last fling in baseball came during the fledgling U.S. League's unsuccessful attempt to play on a major-league level.

McAllister, George

Career: 1923–34   Positions: 1b, of
Teams: **Birmingham Black Barons** ('23–'24, '26–'29, '31–'32), Indianapolis ABCs ('25), Detroit Stars ('25), Memphis Red Sox ('30, '33), Chicago American Giants ('30), Cuban Stars ('32), Homestead Grays ('33), Cleveland Red Sox ('34)
Bats: Left   Throws: Left

A speedy first baseman with lots of pep, he was the leadoff batter for the Negro American League second-half champion Birmingham Black Barons in 1927, hitting .305 for the season. The left-hander was smooth afield and played a dozen seasons in the Negro Leagues, mostly with Birmingham in both the Negro National League and the Negro Southern League. In 1929 he hit .287, but afterward left the Black Barons for a season, playing with the Memphis Red Sox in 1930 and posting a .277 average as their leadoff batter. During the next four seasons he played with five different teams, counting another stint with both the Black Barons and the Red Sox. In 1932 he played with the Cuban Stars and Memphis before landing with the Homestead Grays in 1933 as their regular first baseman, with partial stats showing a .316 batting average. The next year he closed out his career with the Cleveland Red Sox, hitting second in the batting order, as he had for the Grays.

McAllister, Mike

Career: 1921   Positions: 1b, of
Team: Kansas City Monarchs

He was a reserve player with the Kansas City Monarchs in 1921, appearing at first base and in the outfield.

McBride, Fred

Career: 1931–40   Positions: **1b**, 3b, of
Teams: Indianapolis ABCs ('31), Chicago

American Giants ('40), Birmingham Black Barons ('40)

This first baseman began his career in 1931 with the ABCs in the Negro National League, hitting sixth in the batting order, and closed his career with the Birmingham Black Barons in 1940 as a reserve first baseman, but batting cleanup when in the starting lineup.

McCabb

Career: 1923   Position: p
Team: St. Louis Stars

He was pitcher with the St. Louis Stars in 1923, his only year in the Negro Leagues.

McCall, Henry (Mac, Muff)

Career: 1936–45   Positions: **1b**, of
Teams: Chicago American Giants ('36–'37, '45), Indianapolis Athletics ('37), Birmingham Black Barons ('38–'39), *Voluntarily retired ('40–'44)*
Bats: Left   Throws: Left
Height: 6' 0"   Weight: 190
Born: Nov. 6, 1907, Hattiesburg, Miss.

A left-handed power hitter, he played first base with a trio of Negro American League clubs during the late '30s. He began his career with the Chicago American Giants in 1936 when they played as an independent team, hitting .383 against all levels of competition. The following year, when they became charter members of the Negro American League, he continued as a part-time starter, hitting fifth in the batting order, but left later during the season to finish out the season with the Indianapolis Athletics. In 1938 he joined the Birmingham Black Barons for two seasons as the regular first baseman before quitting the diamond for a regular job in industry. After five years away from the game he returned to the Chicago American Giants in 1945 as a reserve first baseman-outfielder to bolster a war-depleted team, batting fifth in the order when in the lineup.

McCall, William L. (**Bill**)

Career: 1922–31   Position: p

Teams: Pittsburgh Keystones ('22), Toledo Tigers ('23), Cleveland Tate Stars ('23), Birmingham Black Barons ('24), Kansas City Monarchs ('24), Chicago American Giants ('25), Indianapolis ABCs ('26), Cleveland Tigers ('28), Detroit Stars ('31)
Bats: Left   Throws: Left
Height: 6' 0"   Weight: 185

A journeyman pitcher, he pitched for several midwestern teams during the '20s. In 1924 he joined the Negro National League champion Kansas City Monarchs late in the season and was credited with winning both of his league decisions down the stretch. In his last season, 1931, he posted a 3–7 record with the Detroit Stars. The lefthander had good speed but experienced some control problems during his career.

McCampbell, Ernest
Career: 1915   Position: player
Team: Kansas City Giants

A player on the original Kansas City Monarchs in 1908, he later was with the Kansas City, Kansas, Giants in 1915. His position is uncertain.

McCampbell, Thomas (Tom)
Career: 1908, 1915   Position: player
Teams: Kansas City Monarchs ('08), Kansas City, Kansas, Giants ('15)

A player on the original Kansas City Monarchs in 1908, he later was with the Kansas City, Kansas, Giants, in 1915. His position is uncertain.

McCarey, Willie
Career: 1944–45   Position: p
Team: Cleveland Buckeyes

A wartime player, he appeared briefly with the Cleveland Buckeyes, but his playing time was severely restricted.

McCauley
Career: 1930   Position: p
Team: Nashville Elite Giants

The Nashville Elite Giants' first year in the Negro National League was the pitcher's only year in the league, as he suffered through an 1–8 season in 1930.

McClain, Bill
a.k.a. McLain
Career: 1933   Position: p
Team: Columbus Blue Birds

He was a pitcher on the Columbus Blue Birds, a team that dropped out of the Negro National League after the first half of their only season in the league.

McClain, Edward (Boots)
a.k.a. McLain
Career: 1920–26   Positions: ss, 2b, 3b, cf, p
Teams: Dayton Marcos ('20, '26), Indianapolis ABCs ('20), Columbus Buckeyes ('21), Cleveland Tate Stars ('22), Detroit Stars ('23), Toledo Tigers ('23), Cleveland Browns ('24)
Bats: Right   Throws: Right
Height: 5' 2"   Weight: 137

One of the smallest players ever to make an appearance in the Negro Leagues, this diminutive infielder played for several midwestern teams during the '20s, beginning and ending his career with the Dayton Marcos, with incomplete statistics showing a .200 batting average in his last season.

McClain, Eugene Walter (Jeep)
Career: 1945–47   Positions: 3b, c, of
Teams: Darby Daisies ('41), Philadelphia Meteors ('42–'43), Washington Potomacs ('44), Philadelphia Stars ('45–'46), New York Black Yankees ('47), Boston Giants ('48–'49)
Bats: Right   Throws: Right
Height: 6'1"   Weight: 205
Born: Mar. 25, 1922, Boston, Mass.

An infielder during the '40s, mostly with semi-pro teams, he also played with the Philadelphia Stars for two seasons followed by one season with the New York Black Yankees in 1947. The highlight of his baseball career was hitting 4 homers in a doubleheader. After retiring from his brief baseball career, he became a cabinetmaker.

McClellan, Dan (Danny)
Career: 1903–23;
1924–30   Positions: **p**, 1b, cf, rf,
                    manager
Teams: Cuban X-Giants ('03–'04), **Philadelphia Giants** ('04–'10, '23–'24), Brooklyn
Royal Giants ('10), New York Lincoln Giants
('11), Smart Set ('12), Quaker Giants, Washington Potomacs ('24), Wilmington Potomacs
('25)
Bats: Left   Throws: Left
Died: 1931

One of the best pitchers during the first decade of the century, McClellan pitched the first
perfect game in black baseball history in 1903
while hurling for the Cuban X-Giants, the most
dominant team of that time, against York,
Pennsylvania, of the Tri-State League, facing
only 27 batters.

After the completion of the season, the X-
Giants made their second tour of Cuba, regis-
tering a 9–2 record against the island's best
players. Three years earlier, in 1900, the X-
Giants had made the first tour of Cuba by a
black team and finished with a 15–3 record.
Later McClellan pitched with Havana in the
Cuban winter league of 1907.

Leaving the Cuban X-Giants team the year
after his perfect outing, he teamed with Rube
Foster to pitch the Philadelphia Giants to
three straight championships, with the team
registering seasons of 81–43–2 and
134–21–3 the first two years (1904–05 before
copping their third straight title in 1906 with
a ballclub that is considered their best team
of the period.

He was a smart pitcher, mixing an assortment of off-speed curves effectively to offset
his lack of a substantial fastball. Along with
Foster, Ball, and Buckner, he was considered
"head and shoulders above" other pitchers of
the first decade of the century. An all-around
ballplayer, he was a good hitter and usually
played first base or in the outfield when not on
the mound and batted in the heart of the batting
order. After Foster, John Henry Lloyd, and

several other players went West to play with
the Leland Giants, McClellan remained with
the Philadelphia Giants in 1909–10, playing
center field and batting cleanup.

He returned to New York City in 1911 for
a couple of seasons with the Lincoln Giants
and the Smart Set, with incomplete statistics
showing a 1–3 record in 1911 and a batting
average of .311. As his playing days shortened,
he extended his career in baseball by becoming
a highly respected manager, eventually organizing the new Philadelphia Giants in 1923
and touring New England and Canada, as a
playing manager while playing semipro teams
and compiling a record of 71–30–3. The following season he became a bench manager
with the club and also managed the Wilmington Potomacs in 1925. In 1931 he became ill
and was taken to the hospital, but died while
waiting to see a doctor.

McClelland, Dr. **J. W.**
Career: 1922   Position: officer
Team: St. Louis Stars

He served as an officer with the St. Louis
Stars in 1922, their first year of existence,
under owner Charlie Mills.

McClinnic, Nathaniel (**Nat**)
a.k.a. McClinic
Career: 1946–48   Position: of
Team: Cleveland Buckeyes ('46–'48), Birmingham Black Barons ('48)

A light-hitting reserve outfielder, he appeared briefly with the postwar Cleveland
Buckeyes for three seasons, including the
Negro American League championship team
of 1947. However, his playing time was severely constrained, and the only available
statistics show a .086 batting average for the
1948 season. He also played with the Atlanta
Black Crackers in the Negro Southern
League and was vying for an outfield position with the Birmingham Black Barons in
the spring of 1948 but did not land a spot in
their outfield.

McClure, Robert (**Bob,** Big Boy)
Career: 1920–30   Position: p
Teams: *San Antonio Black Aces ('20),* Indian-apolis ABCs ('20–'22), Cleveland Tate Stars ('22–'23), Toledo Tigers ('23), Baltimore Black Sox ('24–'27), Atlantic City Bacharach Giants ('28–'29), Brooklyn Royal Giants ('30)
Bats: Right   Throws: Right
Height: 6'0"   Weight: 190
Born: 1903, San Antonio, Tex.
Died: Sept. 6, 1931, Baltimore, Md.

A right-handed pitcher with a good fastball, good slowball, and fast-breaking curve, he was a consistent winner for the Baltimore Black Sox in 1924, but lacked heart. He began his career with the ABCs in 1920, coming up from Texas with Hudspeth, Blackman, Mackey, Williams, Washington, and Hol-loway and posting a 3–2 record in 1921. He pitched the next two seasons with the Cleve-land Tate Stars and the Toledo Tigers before joining the Baltimore Black Sox in 1924. he had a phenomenal debut with the Black Sox but experienced a decline as sudden as was his rise to prominence.

However, the Texan was still young and ex-pected to improve. While pitching for the Royal Poinciana team in Florida's Hotel League in the winter of 1924–25, he was only one out away from a no-hitter but yielded 2 hits and 2 runs and had to hang on to win, 3–2. His winter success carried over to the next season, with McClure posting a 12–4 mark in 1925 and a 15–8 mark in 1927. The next sea-son he left the Black Sox and joined the Bach-arach Giants, but dropped to a 6–7 record in 1929, and played with the Brooklyn Royal Giants in 1930.

He was set to rejoin the Bacharachs for the 1931 season but became ill and died of pneu-monia before the end of the year. He had been complaining of illness for five months, but did not "take to his bed" until about a week be-fore his death. He collapsed before getting to Provident Hospital and was dead on arrival

there. His Baltimore Black Sox teammates served as his pallbearers.

McCord, Clinton Hill, Jr. (**Butch**)
Career: 1947–50   Positions: **1b,** of, 2b
Teams: *military service ('44–'45), Nashville Cubs ('46), Nashville Black Vols ('47),* Balti-more Elite Giants ('48–'50), Chicago Ameri-can Giants ('50), *minor leagues (51–'61)*
Bats: Left   Throws: Left
Height: 5'10"   Weight: 161
Born: Nov. 2, 1925, Nashville, Tenn.

A first baseman-outfielder, he started his professional career in 1946, after he completed his military service. While still attending Ten-nessee State University, he signed to play in the Negro Southern League with manager Fel-ton Snow's Nashville Black Vols in 1947. The next year he joined the Baltimore Elite Giants under Hoss Walker's managership, batting .269 in 1949, and stayed there until leaving during the 1950 season to join "Double Duty" Rad-cliffe's Chicago American Giants, where he raised his average to .349 for the 1950 season.

He entered organized baseball in 1951, and during his eleven seasons he won two batting titles, two silver gloves, three pennants, and three playoffs. He was also voted the most popular player and was given a special night, with Bill Veeck in attendance.

He enjoyed outstanding success in his first two years while showing great defensive skills at first base with Paris in the Mississippi-Ohio Valley League. He hit for average (.363 and .392), with power (16 and 15 home runs) and timeliness (118 and 109 RBIs) while demon-strating good speed (22 and 20 stolen bases) and scoring often (132 and 123 runs). In the first season there he also collected 102 walks. Afterward, as he moved up to higher classifi-cations, he never enjoyed the same degree of success.

In two years at Denver he hit .281 and .358 and then, in 1955–56, he spent two years in the International League, batting .258 with Richmond and .275 with Columbus. In Louisville in the American Association he hit .267 in 1957. The next three seasons were productive at their levels, as he hit .305 with Macon in the South Atlantic League and .298 and .300 with Victoria in the Texas League in 1959–60. After another brief trial with St. Paul in the American Association he finished his career back in the Texas League, where he hit. 285 in 1961.

After closing out his baseball career he worked with the YMCA before embarking upon a twenty-four-year career as a postal clerk, retiring from the post office in 1988.

McCoy, Frank (Chink)
Career: 1931–43   Position: c
Teams: Newark Browns ('31–'32), Atlantic City Bacharach Giants ('32), Newark Dodgers ('33–'34), Harrisburg-St. Louis Stars ('43)
Bats: Right   Throws: Right
Height: 5'6"   Weight: 150

A small guy from New Jersey, he was an average receiver and a fairly good hitter with about average power. He was the regular catcher with both the Newark Browns of the East-West League in 1932 and the Newark Dodgers when they organized late in the 1933 season. With each team he batted in the lower part of the order. He closed out his career as a backup catcher with the Harrisburg-St. Louis Stars in 1943.

McCoy, Roy
Career: 1932   Position: officer
Team: Washington Pilots

He was an officer with the Washington Pilots in 1932, the only year of the East-West League's existence.

McCoy, Walter
Career: 1945–48   Position: p
Teams: Chicago American Giants ('45–'48), *minor leagues ('49–'53), Mexican League ('55)*
Bats: Left   Throws: Left
Height: 5'9"   Weight: 170
Born: 1925

This left-hander pitched with the Chicago

American Giants in the late '40s, posting a record of 9–6 (3.45 ERA) in his first season, 1945, but dropping to a 6–13 mark the following year. He closed his Negro League career in 1948 and moved into organized baseball, but without significant success. After splitting four decisions with Visalia in the California League, he was winless with 4 losses and a 6.23 ERA in a short stint with Sacramento in the Pacific Coast League in 1950. The next two seasons he pitched with Tijuana in the Southwest International League, with records of 1–5 and 5–2. The latter year he also pitched in the Mandak League with Winnipeg and in 1953 with Carman, where he was 10–8. His last foray into professional baseball was in 1955 with Nuevo Laredo in the Mexican League, where he pitched in 2 games without a decision.

McCrary, George
a.k.a. McCreary
Career: 1943   Position: p
Team: New York Black Yankees

A wartime player, he pitched with the New York Black Yankees in 1943, his only season in the Negro Leagues.

McCreary, Fred
Career: 1938–49   Position: umpire
Leagues: NNL, NAL

He was an umpire for a dozen seasons, all except the last one in the Negro National League.

McCune
Career: 1913   Position: 3b
Team: Chicago Giants

He was a third baseman with the Chicago Giants in 1913.

McCurrine, James (Big Jim)
Career: 1946–49   Positions: rf, 1f, 3b
Team: Chicago American Giants

This big outfielder was a part-time starter with the Chicago American Giants for four seasons during the late '40s, batting .296 and .257 in 1946 and 1948, respectively.

McDaniels, Booker Taliaferro (Cannonball, Balazos)
a.k.a. McDaniel
Career: 1940–49   Positions: **p**, *of*
Teams: **Kansas City Monarchs** ('40–'45, '49), *Mexican League ('49–'48), minor leagues ('49)*
Bats: Right   Throws: Right
Height: 6'2"   Weight: 195
Born: 1912
Died: Dec. 12, 1974, Kansas City, Mo.

A big, strong, hard-throwing right-handed power pitcher with some control problems, his entire Negro League career was spent with the Kansas City Monarchs. After joining the Monarchs in 1940, he had records of 3–0, 7–0, and 10–1 in 1941–43. The next two seasons he posted marks of 2–5 and 6–3 in league play while maintaining respectable ERAs of 3.33 and 3.03 for 1944–45. Acknowledged as one of the Monarchs' Big Four on the pitching staff, he was a clutch player who liked pitching under tough conditions, and the more difficult the circumstances, the harder he pitched. Although he did not have a good curve, his drop and change-up were adequate, and he utilized them as off-speed pitches. He already had several one-hit games to his credit through the first half of his career, when he made his only All-Star appearance in the 1945 East-West game.

Although the veteran hurler liked pitching for the Monarchs, in 1946 he jumped to the Mexican League along with teammates Jesse Williams and Barney Serrell. With San Luis, Vera Cruz, and Mexico City, he had records of 14–18 (3.01 ERA), 14–14 (3.41 ERA), and 12–11 (4.81 ERA) for the next three seasons, and registered 171 strikeouts in 254 innings in 1946. Returning to the Monarchs in 1949, he was 4–2 with a 2.62 ERA when he was signed by the Los Angeles Angels in June and, at age thirty-eight, became the first black player in the Pacific Coast League. In his first game with Los Angeles, he won an 8–3 decision with a 5-hitter over Portland.

McDaniels was popular, enthusiastic, aggressive, and had some success on the Coast (8–9, 4.22 ERA in 1949; 3–4, 6.49 ERA in 1950), but was considered by the parent Cubs to be a little short on pitching skills for the major leagues, and he was not given a chance in Chicago. Some observers contend that he ruined his arm by throwing so hard.

For a pitcher, he was a pretty good hitter with power, and sometimes was called on to make an appearance as a pinch hitter. During his prime he also played winter baseball in California, Cuba, and Puerto Rico. In the winter of 1943 he played with the Baltimore Giants in California, and a year later split eight decisions with Marianao, Cuba, and was 2–5 with Ponce, Puerto Rico, five winters later. He finally closed out his career with a weak 1–2 effort in a dozen games during the 1951 summer season with Mexico City.

As a youngster he was reared in Morrilton, Arkansas, with three brothers, who were forced to raise themselves when their mother died. The responsibilities he learned from doing his chores around the house stayed with him throughout his life. After leaving baseball he settled in Kansas City but developed a drinking problem and later died of throat cancer.

McDaniels, Fred
a.k.a. McDaniel
Career: 1939–50   Positions: **of**, 3b, *2b, c*
Teams: Satchel Paige's All-Stars ('39), **Memphis Red Sox** ('40–'46, '50), Kansas City Monarchs ('44), *New Orleans Eagles ('51), Canadian League ('52–'53)*
Bats: Left   Throws: Right
Height: 5'11"   Weight: 135
Born: Jan, 21, 1912, Henderson, Tex.

A slender outfielder with an adequate arm and pretty good range despite a lack of speed, he was a fair hitter, batting .280, .161, and .235 in 1944–46. He joined the Memphis Red Sox in 1940 but did not land a starting position until 1942, when he hit .220 while batting in the heart of the order. The next season he played third base, but moved back to his usual left-field position in 1944 while also moving into the leadoff spot in the batting order.

Most of his career was with the Memphis Red Sox, but he began his career in the late '30s, touring with Satchel Paige's All-Stars against all levels of opposition, including Dizzy Dean's All-Stars. During the late '40s and early '50s McDaniels also barnstormed with all-star teams headed by Willie Mays, Jackie Robinson, and Joe Black. After the 1948 season he faced the Cleveland Indians' World Series star Gene Bearden and broke up Bearden's no-hitter with a ninth-inning two-out double.

His biggest thrill in baseball came from a defensive play he made in Comiskey Park, playing against the Chicago American Giants. McDaniels was in left field and a ball was hit down the left-field line that looked like a certain home run, but he jumped in the stands and made the catch. The game was held up for a long time while appreciative fans threw money out on the field. He had both back pockets full of money that he picked up. After the inning ended, he gave the money to owner B. B. Martin to count, and Martin generously added some more bills to the take.

McDaniels almost lost his baseball career before it really began. In 1940 he was drafted for Army duty, but he did not pass the induction physical examination because of a bad stomach and was deferred. After leaving the Negro Leagues, McDaniels played two years in Canada, finishing his career in 1953.

McDevitt, John J.
Career: 1922   Position: officer
Team: Baltimore Black Sox
He served as an officer for the Baltimore Black Sox in 1922, before they entered the Eastern Colored League.

McDonald
[see McDonnell]

McDonald
Career: 1913   Position: rf
Team: Philadelphia Giants

In 1913 he played as an outfielder with the Philadelphia Giants, who were in decline as a quality ballclub.

McDonald
Career: 1922   Position: p
Team: Baltimore Black Sox
He pitched with the Baltimore Black Sox in 1922, when they were still playing as an independent ballclub.

McDonald, Earl
Career: 1938   Position: officer
Team: Washington Black Senators
He served as an officer with the Washington Black Senators in 1938, their only season in the Negro National League.

McDonald, G.
Career: 1910–18   Position: p
Teams: Philadelphia Giants ('10–'13), Atlantic City Bacharach Giants ('17), New York Lincoln Giants ('17–'18)
He pitched with the New York Lincoln Giants during the latter years of the deadball era, and incomplete statistics show a combined record of 4–2. Earlier in his career he pitched with the Philadelphia Giants and the Bacharach Giants.

McDonald, Luther (Vet, Old Soul)
Career: 1927–37   Position: p
Teams: St. Louis Stars ('27–'29), Detroit Stars ('31), Chicago Columbia Giants ('31), Cole's American Giants ('32), Chicago American Giants ('35), Memphis Red Sox ('37)
Bats: Right   Throws: Right
He began his career in 1927 with the St. Louis Stars and posted marks of 7–3 and 6–2 in 1927 and 1929. After leaving St. Louis he fashioned a 2–3 ledger in 1931 with the Detroit Stars before joining the American Giants in 1932, when Robert Coles bought the franchise. However, he was seldom used and was not an integral part of the team's success that season. In 1935, with Coles's team, he was credited with losses in both of his league decisions, and

he closed his career in 1937, pitching with the Memphis Red Sox.

McDonald, Webster (Mac)
Career: 1920–40   Positions: **p**, manager
Teams: *Madison Stars ('19, 21), Norfolk Stars ('20),* Detroit Stars ('20), *Chappie Johnson's All-Stars (22),* New York Lincoln Giants ('22), *Richmond Giants ('22, Philadelphia Giants ('18, '22–'24),* Wilmington Potomacs (25), Chicago American Giants ('25–27, '29–'30), Homestead Grays ('28), *Little Falls (Minn.) Independents (Northwestern League) ('28–'31),* Hilldale Daisies ('30–'31), Baltimore Black Sox ('30), Washington Pilots ('32), **Philadelphia Stars** ('33–'40), Washington Black Senators ('38)
Bats: Left   Throws: Right
Height: 6'0"   Weight: 190
Born: Jan. 1, 1900, Wilmington, Del.
Died: June 12, 1982, Philadelphia, Pa.

This submariner used an effortless motion, good control, a sinking fastball, a rising curveball, and a good change of speed to fashion a successful career in the Negro Leagues. He pitched to a batter's weakness, and his ability to mix pitches earned him the moniker "56 Varieties." He posted league ledgers of 14–9 and 10–5 in 1926–27 while pitching for the Negro National League champion Chicago American Giants. Facing the Eastern Colored League champion Bacharach Giants, he pitched in 2 games in each World Series, starting 2 games in the latter Series, recording an ERA of 2.07, and winning his only decision.

His best single game with Chicago was in 1927, when he struck out 16 batters in a 2-hit, 3–1 win over the Kansas City Monarchs. Leaving the American Giants after three years with a winning percentage of .652, he pitched briefly with the Homestead Grays, winning 2 decisions without a loss, before joining an independent white semipro team in Little Falls, Minnesota, of the Northwestern League; there was the star pitcher for four seasons, 1928–31. In 1932 he was with the Washington Pilots of

the East-West League and became the manager when Frank Warfield died suddenly.

The next season he joined forces with owner Ed Bolden, who organized the Philadelphia Stars, and posted a modest 3–2 mark. In 1934 he was named manager, replacing Dick Lundy, and guided the Stars to the Negro National League championship. The skipper contributed an 8–2 record during the regular season and won a crucial game against Willie Foster in the championship playoffs to wrest the title from the defending Chicago American Giants.

After the championship season, McDonald secured a government job in Philadelphia and considered retiring from baseball, but returned for the 1935 season and finished with a 10–6 record. In 1936, his last year as manager, he fashioned a 7–2 record for the Stars. Although pitching less often, he continued to pitch through the 1940 season, posting marks of 4–4, 4–5, 2–5, and 0–1. McDonald was quiet, dignified, and a complete gentleman at all times, with impeccable manners. Throughout his career he was respected by both fans and players.

He had a measure of difficulty breaking in with league teams, and spent three years playing in New England before finally catching on with a league ballclub. He had some difficulty fielding bunts, and some teams attempted to exploit this weakness. In 1919 he was with Danny McClellan's Madison Stars, a team of lesser quality that served as a farm team for Hilldale and other teams. Along with McDonald, the team included future stars Judy Johnson, Chance Cummings, and Eggie Dallard. In 1922 McDonald joined Chappie Johnson's All-Stars but was soon traded to the New York Lincoln Giants for a brief stint before being sent to Zack Pettus's Richmond Giants in July to finish the season. In 1923–24 he was again under McClellan's tutelege, playing with the Philadelphia Giants in New England and enjoying much success at that level of play. During his first year with the team he pitched three no-hitters, and strikeout strings of 18 and 24 were commonplace. He signed with George Robinson's Wilmington Potomacs in 1925, but the club folded in July and he signed with Rube Foster's Chicago American Giants, posting a 6–2 record for the year.

During his career the underhand hurler was especially tough on major leaguers in exhibition games, compiling a 14–4 lifetime record against them. Counted among the wins were four wins over Dizzy Dean during his prime, defeating the St. Louis Cardinals' ace by scores of 7–1 and 1–0 in 1934 and 7–1 and 11–1 in 1935.

McDonald, lived in Philadelphia since age three and was reared by his Aunt Sally Clayter. As a youngster he learned to play baseball on the playgrounds of South Philadelphia and often sneaked away on Sundays, without his aunt's permission, to take the ferry to Camden for games. In 1931 he ended his nomadic baseball career, and he and his wife established a permanent home in Philadelphia. After closing out his baseball career in 1942, he worked in Philadelphia at the U.S. Mint and with the U.S. Postal Service until his retirement. In his latter years, while living alone in a drab North Philadelphia housing project after his wife's death, he was robbed twice and remained vulnerable to being victimized again until the day he died in quiet obscurity.

McDonnel

[see McDonnell]

McDonnell

a.k.a. McDonald; McDonnel
Career: 1921　　　　Position: p
Teams: *Madison Stars ('20),* Atlantic City Bacharach Giants ('21)

He pitched briefly with the Bacharach Giants in 1921, after a season with the Madison Stars, a team of lesser quality

McDougal, Lemuel (Lem)

Career: 1917–20　　　Position: p
Teams: Indianapolis ABCs ('17), Chicago Giants ('20), Chicago American Giants ('19–20)

In 1917 this former Chicago high-school youngster left his position as the swimming director of the Wabash YMCA for a better salary, and pitched with the Indianapolis ABCs, winning both of his recorded decisions.

McDougall

Career: 1909　　　　Position: ss
Team: St. Paul Colored Gophers

He played shortstop for the 1909 western champion St. Paul Colored Gophers, his only participation in black baseball.

McDuffie, Terris (Speed, Elmer the Great, Terris the Terrible)

Career: 1930–45　　　Positions: p. *of*
Teams: Birmingham Black Barons ('30–'31), Baltimore Black Sox ('31–'34), Atlantic City Bacharach Giants ('32), *minor leagues ('54),* Pennsylvania Red Caps of New York ('34), Newark Dodgers ('35), Brooklyn Eagles ('35), New York Black Yankees ('35, '38–'39), Newark Eagles ('36–'38, '44–'45), *Mexican League ('40–'41, '43, '45–46),* Philadelphia Stars ('40, '42), Homestead Grays ('41), Hilldale Daisies ('32), Cuban Stars (West) ('32)
Bats: Right　　　　Throws: Right
Height: 6'1"　　　　Weight: 200
Born: July 22, 1910, Mobile, Ala.
Died: New York, N. Y.

A flamboyant, strong-armed, right-handed hurler with a sinker, slider, curve, fastball, change-up, and moderate control, he was not a power pitcher but was called "Elmer the Great" by the press. In 1936, his first year with the Newark Eagles, he suffered stomach ailments and did not perform on a regular basis, but was credited with a record of 19–8 in league games. Among his triumphs were 2 victories over Satchel Paige in 3 matchups. With the Eagles in 1937 and 1938, the workhorse had league ledgers of 10–5 and 11–3 and, playing against all levels of competition, he finished all 27 games that he started the latter season.

After joining the Homestead Grays in 1941, he registered a 27–5 record as the Grays won the 1941 pennant. At midseason McDuffie was the starting and winning pitcher for the East in the All-Star game. Like most Grays' hurlers, he was a pretty good hitter for a pitcher, with a little above average power, and the previous year, 1940, he hit .400 in Mexico. He began his career as an outfielder but didn't hit enough to remain an everyday player, so he turned to pitching. He was also a good fielder and had good speed on the bases and was a good base stealer in his youth, leading the league in 1930.

His year with the Grays was sandwiched around two years with the Philadelphia Stars, when he registered identical records of 5–3. In 1940 he had begun the season with the Stars but jumped to Mexico with Santa Rosa and was hit hard and failed to win a game, finishing with a 0–4 record. That winter he played in Cuba and wrote to the Manleys from the island in February 1941, asking to come back to United States to play with the Eagles. Abe Manley demurred, and McDuffie signed with the Grays.

After the 1942 season he jumped the Stars a second time for the Mexican League. His second foray into Mexico was in 1943, when he joined Torreon and compiled a 9–11 record with a 3.14 ERA. During one of his respites from Mexico because of his draft status, he rejoined the Newark Eagles in 1944 and, despite a 5–6 league ledger, started his second All-Star game that year. He was back in Mexico in 1945 for half a dozen games with Nuevo Laredo, but, hampered by an appendix operation, he pitched ineffectively (1–4, 6.08 ERA). In 1946 he was 4–4 for Torreon in Mexico when he underwent a major stomach operation to remove an internal growth, and was released from St. Phillips Hospital in mid-July.

In addition to his exploits in Mexico, he was also a favorite in Cuba and spent eight winter seasons on the island with five teams, pitching 135 games and getting 37 victories, a number exceeded only by Raymond Brown, but losing a total of 43 to finish with a lifetime losing record. He had only three winning seasons in Cuba, with his best years coming in 1944–45, when he was 7–6 with a 2.35 ERA, 1940–41

with 7–6, and 1950–51 with a 5–2 ledger and a 3.00 ERA.

McDuffie's approach to the game sometimes caused him problems. Once, in Cuba, his manager, Dolph Luque told him to start a ball game, but McDuffie didn't want to pitch that day and let Luque know in no uncertain terms. Luque, a fiery-tempered Latin, pulled the gun that he carried in his hip pocket and inquired indelicately if McDuffie didn't want to reconsider his position immediately. McDuffie looked at the pistol pointed at him and made a smart decision. "Give me the ball," he said, taking the game ball, and pitched a two-hitter that day.

McDuffie also played in other Latin American leagues, playing and managing for Ponce during winters in the mid-'30s. In 1951, at age forty, he was voted the MVP for Caracas in the Venezuelan League and in 1952 he was the MVP in the Dominican Republic.

Early in his career, McDuffie played with the 24th Infantry while in the U.S. Army (1924–29) and began his professional career in 1930 as an outfielder with the Birmingham Black Barons, batting .297 and leading the league in stolen bases with 18. He joined the Baltimore Black Sox the following year as an outfielder and also played as an infielder prior to becoming a pitcher in 1932. In 1934, with the Pennsylvania Red Caps, he pitched and won an 18-inning game against the Jacksonville Red Caps, 3–1. At the beginning of 1935 he made his first appearance in the "Big Apple" with the New York Black Yankees and the Brooklyn Eagles, and later in the season pitched a no-hitter against the House of David. The next season owner Abe Manley consolidated the Newark Dodgers and the Brooklyn Eagles to form the Newark Eagles, and McDuffie became part of the consolidated team. This set the stage for a tempestuous relationship between the cocky, colorful pitcher and the owner's wife, Effa Manley.

McDuffie was a flashy dresser and took pride in how he looked. Sporting diamond rings and gold watches, he was a "pretty boy" and fancied himself a lover. Effa Manley liked young ballplayers, and he quickly became her favorite paramour. At the ballpark she would show him off for her ladies' club friends, sometimes ordering the manager to pitch him in a particular game for this purpose. In early August 1938, after a lover's quarrel at Pennsylvania Station, where McDuffie reportedly knocked her down and kicked her, Abe Manley became aware of the relationship and traded McDuffie to the Black Yankees for two broken bats and an old pair of sliding pads.

McDuffie was a crowd-pleaser and wore a jacket that had the words "The Great McDuffie" emblazoned on the back in large letters. Sometimes, when he struck out a batter, he would "boogie" on the mound, and the crowd loved it. When he came back to Newark to pitch his first game after being traded, he rubbed it in with his "shenanigans" on the mound. On another occasion, after striking out Josh Gibson, he "boogied" all the way from the mound to home plate. His behavior attracted attention, which translated into more money. During the post-World War II years he was the highest-salaried player in the East, making $6,000 a year, including bonuses.

The hurler was functionally illiterate but successfully hid it for a long time, employing an "easy come, easy go" philosophy. Once when barnstorming with the Homestead Grays, when a low turnout produced only $10 per player, he wagered it all on one roll of the dice and lost. When a game was rained out the players did not get paid, so McDuffie, shrugging off his loss, said, "Today we got rained out."

Before joining the Grays he was property of the New York Black Yankees and posted a mark of 5–3 in 1939, but pitched for the Elite Giants in the ensuing California winter league, helping pitch the team to the title and earning the nickname "Speed."

In the spring of 1945, with McDuffie well past his prime, he and Showboat Thomas had an unauthorized but highly publicized tryout with the Brooklyn Dodgers when *People's Voice* sportswriter Joe Bostic took them to the Dodgers' camp. Although they were uninvited, they were permitted to work out in uniform, but Branch Rickey was not impressed. "He has good control but doesn't follow through on any delivery," opined the Mahatma. "It may take time to break that habit."

Although he never got a chance in the major leagues, McDuffie did get to organized baseball, and closed his baseball career with Dallas in the Texas League in 1954, with a 3–4 record and a 3.04 ERA. The forty-four-year-old hurler injured his leg, and the injury combined with his age convinced him to retire.

McErvin
Career: 1948   Position: of
Team: Chicago American Giants
Bats: Right   Throws: Right

He played as a reserve outfielder with the Chicago American Giants in 1948, but his playing time was very restricted.

McFarland, John
Career: 1944–47   Position: p
Team: New York Black Yankees

Pitching with the New York Black Yankees during the mid-'40s, he began his career with a 2–4 record in 1944, and closed his career with a brief appearance in 1947. Earlier in his career, while making his home in Atlanta in the spring of 1938, he was listed as a first baseman on the roster of the unnamed Negro American League team that became the Atlanta Black Crackers.

McGee, Horace
Career: 1887   Position: manager
Team: *Cincinnati Browns*

He was the manager of the Cincinnati Browns, one of eight teams that were charter members of the League of Colored Baseball Clubs in 1887. However, the league's existence was ephemeral, lasting only a week.

McGowan, Curtis
Career: 1950   Position: p
Team: Memphis Red Sox

He was a pitcher with the Memphis Red Sox in 1950, when the Negro American League was struggling to survive the loss of players to organized baseball, but league statistics do not confirm his playing time.

McHaskell, J. C.
Career: 1927–29   Position: 1b
Team: Memphis Red Sox
Bats: Left   Throws: Left

A college man, he had a three-year career with the Memphis Red Sox. Beginning his career in 1927, he had a .203 batting average as the Sox leadoff batter, and posted a .246 mark during his last year. Regarded as a fine fellow who would not cause trouble for anyone, his career was tragically ended when he was shot by an intoxicated teammate, Robert Poindexter, and lost both legs when the wounds required amputation.

McHenry, Henry (Cream)
Career: 1930–50   Position: p
Teams: Kansas City Monarchs ('30–31, '37), New York Harlem Stars ('31), Newark Browns ('32), Pennsylvania Red Caps of New York ('32), New York Black Yankees ('35–'37), **Philadelphia Stars** ('38–'48, '50), Indianapolis Clowns ('50)
Bats: Right   Throws: Right
Height: 6'0"   Weight: 200

The Philadelphia Stars' ace of the early 1940s had a good curve and good control and also threw a fastball, screwball, and knuckler. The high-strung right-hander was cocky and eccentric but appeared in the 1940 and 1941 East-West All-Star games, starting and winning the 1940 game. That season he fashioned an 11–5 record, and in 1941 he posted a 7–11 mark with a 4.42 ERA. By 1946 he was being referred to as the Philadelphia Stars' veteran ace, and he posted marks of 6–5 and 6–7 in 1946–47.

Before joining the Stars he pitched with the New York Black Yankees and the Kansas City Monarchs, including the 1937 season, when the Monarchs captured the first Negro American League pennant. A good-hitting pitcher with a better-than-average power, he batted .333 in 1940 and was credited with 6 home runs against all opposition. Sometimes he was used as a pinch hitter, but he usually hit for a lesser average, as shown by his .130 and .125 batting averages in 1946–47. In the field he was adequate but with limited range, and he did not have much speed on the bases. He was called "Cream" by other players because of his light complexion.

McInnis, Gready
[see McKinnis, Gready]

McIntosh, Jimmy
Career: 1937   Position: c
Team: Detroit Stars

A reserve catcher with the Detroit Stars in 1937, he was one of five players who appeared on the Stars' roster in an effort to shore up a weak position.

McIntyre, B.
Career: 1924   Position: p
Team: Memphis Red Sox

He pitched with the Memphis Red Sox in 1924, his only season in the Negro Leagues.

McKamey
a.k.a. McKinney
Career: 1946   Position: ss
Team: Kansas City Monarchs

A reserve shortstop fro the Kansas City Monarchs in 1946, his playing time was very limited.

McKeg
Career: 1897   Position: ss
Team: Cuban Giants

He was a shortstop with the Cuban Giants, the first professional black team, organized in 1885, but still considered one of the top ballclubs in 1897.

McKellan, Fred
[see McKelvin, Fred]

McKellum
[see McKelvin, Fred]

McKelvin, Fred
a.k.a. McKellan; McKellum
Career: 1942   Position: p
Teams: Cincinnati Buckeyes ('42), Jacksonville Red Caps ('42)
In 1942 this pitcher played with both the Buckeyes and the Red Caps but did not gain appreciable playing time with either team.

McKenzie, Herbert
Career: 1950   Position: c
Team: New York Black Yankees
He was a reserve catcher with the New York Black Yankees in 1950, when the club had suffered a loss in their quality of play and were playing as an independent team. His playing time was severely restricted.

McKinley
Career: 1940   Position: p
Team: Chicago American Giants
He was a pitcher with the Chicago American Giants in 1940, his only season in the Negro Leagues.

McKinney
[see McKamey]

McKinnis, Gready (Gread, Lefty)
a.k.a. McInnis, Selassie
Career: 1941–49   Position: p
Teams: Birmingham Black Barons ('41–'43), Ethiopian Clowns ('42), Kansas City Monarchs ('42), Chicago American Giants ('44–'45, '49), *Pittsburgh Crawfords, ('46) minor leagues ('50–'55)*
Bats: Right   Throws: Left
Height: 6'2"   Weight: 170
Born: Oct. 11, 1913, Bullock County, Ala.
After joining the Birmingham Black Barons in 1941, he posted successive seasonal marks of 4–1 and 3–5. During the latter year he left the Black Barons to tour with the Ethiopian Clowns, playing under the "Clown name" of

Selassie. During the 1942 World Series the Kansas City Monarchs picked him up to pitch against the Homestead Grays in a game in Yankee Stadium that was designated as an exhibition, and he hurled a 3-hit shutout.
The next season, the big left-hander was back with the Black Barons and posted a 6–4 record to help them capture the 1943 Negro American League pennant. He started two games in the World Series against the Grays, who had repeated as Negro National League champions, but was charged with the loss in both contests. He also pitched in the East-West All-Star game that year, making the first of three appearances in the annual classic. His other All-Star games came in 1944 and 1949, after joining the Chicago American Giants. McKinnis was 6–6 in 1944 with a 3.23 ERA and 6–5 in 1945 with an even better 2.56 ERA. In 1949 his 12–7 record and 3.21 ERA paced manager Winfield Welch's Chicago American Giants to the Negro American League Western Division title, before losing 4 straight to the Eastern Division champion Baltimore Elites in the playoffs.
During the '50s he pitched for six years in organized baseball, playing with Brandon in the Mandak League (11–6 in 1951 and 7–5 in 1953) and with Tampa and St. Petersburgh the Florida International League. With Tampa he posted a composite 4–9 for two partial seasons, and with St. Petersburg he finished the 1955 season with a 5–8 mark and a 4.58 ERA.

McLain
[see McClain, Edward]

McLaughlin
a.k.a. McLoughlin
Career: 1917–19   Positions: **p**, 1b, of
Teams: Jewell's ABCs ('17), New York Lincoln Giants ('17–'19), *military service ('17–18)*
In 1917 he was pitching with the New York Lincoln Giants when he was drafted in late August. At the time he was drafted, he was he was credited with having "allowed only 1 hit

and no runs this season'' and was called the ''greatest living spitball pitcher'' and the ''idol of Harlem.'' After he rejoined the Lincolns in 1918, incomplete statistics show a 4–2 record.

McLaurin, Felix

Career: 1942–49   Positions: **cf**, rf, lf
Teams: Jacksonville Red Caps ('42), Birmingham Black Barons ('42–'45), New York Black Yankees ('45–'48), Chicago American Giants ('49–52)
Bats: Left   Throws: Right
Height: 5'9"   Weight: 185
Born: Jacksonville, Fla.

One of best ball hawks in the Negro Leagues during the '40s, he had a wide range in the outfield and was a pretty good hitter, beginning his Negro Leagues career in 1942 with a .382 batting average. During the next two seasons he was the Birmingham Black Barons' leadoff batter and star center fielder as they captured consecutive Negro American League pennants in 1943–44, with McLaurin batting .236 the latter year.

During the winter he was traded to the New York Black Yankees in exchange for an aging Jim Williams. With the Black Yankees he assumed the leadoff spot in the batting order and hit .343 and .295 in 1945–46. Following the 1948 season he moved to the Chicago American Giants, batting .301 in 1949. After the color line fell, the quality of the Negro American League was reduced to a minor-league status, but he remained with the American Giants through the 1952 season.

McLawn

a.k.a. McLaurin
Career: 1948   Position: c
Team: Newark Eagles

He was one of five catchers who shared playing time behind the plate for the Newark Eagles in 1948.

McMahon, Ed (Eddie)

Career: 1911–16   Positions: owner, officer
Team: New York Lincoln Giants

The brother of Jess McMahon, he and his brother organized two black ballclubs in New York during the '10s, and each team immediately became a top team in the East and won a championship. The Lincoln Giants, formed in 1911, easily defeated Rube Foster's Chicago American Giants in a playoff for the 1913 title. The next season, the McMahon brothers formed a rival team, the Lincoln Stars, and in 1915 they played Foster's American Giants in another championship series, with the playoff ending in a standoff, with each team winning 5 games; the final and deciding contest was called in the fourth inning with the Stars leading by a run.

Once McMahon, who ''liked his liquor,'' missed a payday and lost the services of Louis Santop and Doc Sykes, who jumped to the Brooklyn Royal Giants. The Lincoln Stars disbanded after only three seasons, but the Lincoln Giants' franchise continued for twenty years.

McMahon, Jesse Rod (Jess)

Career: 1911–16   Positions: owner, officer
Teams: New York Lincoln Giants ('11–13), New York Lincoln Stars ('14–'16)
Height: 6'3½"
Weight: 210
Born: May 26, 1880, Manhattanville, N.Y.

A white businessman and sports promoter, he and his brother organized two black ballclubs in New York City during the '10s, and both teams immediately became a top ballclub in the East, with each club winning at least one championship. In 1911 he formed the New York Lincoln Giants, adding a ''shadow ball'' routine to their pregame warm-ups as an added gate attraction, and for three years fielded a team featuring John Henry Lloyd, Smokey Joe Williams, Cannonball Dick Redding, Spot Poles, and Louis Santop, that was the class of the eastern teams. In 1913 the Lincoln Giants easily defeated Rube Foster's Chicago American Giants in a playoff for the championship. The next season, McMahon formed a rival team, the Lincoln Stars, and in 1915 they played Foster's American Giants in another championship series, with the playoff ending in a standoff amid controversy. Each team won 5 games, but with the Stars leading the deciding game by a run, the game was called in the fourth inning. The Lincoln Stars disbanded after only three seasons, but the Lincoln Giants' franchise continued for twenty years.

McMahon, a big, broad-shouldered, Harlem-born Irishman with curly, iron-gray hair, also promoted other sports in the New York area, including boxing, wrestling, football, and basketball. He organized the first black professional basketball team, the Commonwealth Five, which later became the Renaissance Five. He had been orphaned at age five and attended City College, finishing his studies at sixteen and embarking on a career in sports promotion. In 1902 he circumvented the Sunday blue laws to promote semipro football successfully, and three years later he formed the Olympic Athletic Club and built Olympic Field as a home park for the ballclub. One of his players was Rube Oldring, who later signed with Connie Mack's Philadelphia A's.

When blacks began moving into Harlem, he capitalized on the new ethnic influx by organizing the Lincoln Giants' baseball team. He attracted the top players by offering them higher salaries than were available elsewhere, enabling him to field teams comparable to those in the white major leagues. New York Giants' manager John McGraw was a frequent observer at his club's ball games and acknowledged the abilities of the black players as being equal to those of the best white players of the era.

McMeans, Willie
Career: 1945   Position: p
Team: Chicago American Giants

A wartime player, he pitched with the Chicago American Giants in 1945 and was winless against 3 losses.

McMillan, Earl
Career: 1923   Position: of
Team: Toledo Tigers

He was an outfielder with the Negro National League's Toledo Tigers in 1923, until the team broke up in midseason.

McMullin, Clarence
a.k.a. McCullin
Career: 1945–49   Position: of
Teams: Kansas City Monarchs ('45–'46), Houston Eagles ('49)

This outfielder made two appearances in the Negro Leagues, first with the Kansas City Monarchs in 1945–46 and again with the Houston Eagles in 1949.

McMurray, William
Career: 1909–11   Positions: c, 1b
Teams: St. Paul Colored Gophers ('09), St. Louis Giants ('10–'11), *West Baden Sprudels ('12–'13)*

A catcher for the St. Paul Colored Gophers in 1909, when they won the Western title, he also played with the St. Louis Giants for two years, 1910–11, as a first baseman. After leaving St. Louis he played two more seasons with a lesser team, the Sprudels of West Baden, Indiana.

McNair, Hurley Allen (Mac, Bugger)
Career: 1911–37; 1946   Positions: rf, lf, cf, p.
                                                    umpire
Teams: Chicago Giants ('11–'12), Chicago Union Giants ('14, '16), Chicago American Giants ('15–'16), All Nations ('17), Detroit Stars ('19, '28), **Kansas City Monarchs** ('20–27,'34), *Gilkerson's Union Giants ('30–'31)*, Cincinnati Tigers ('37)
Bats: Both   Throws: Right
Height: 5'6"   Weight: 150
Born: Oct. 28, 1888, Marshall, Tex.
Died: Dec. 2, 1948, Kansas City, Mo.

A solid hitter batting in the heart of the Kansas City Monarchs' batting order, he recorded averages of .312, .306, .375, 354, .311, .360, .280, and .278 for his eight seasons in Kansas City. He demonstrated his power with consecutive seasons of 11 home runs in 1922–23, and was also a good base runner. During his stint with the Monarchs, the team won three straight pennants, 1923–25, and won the first World Series played between the Negro National League and the Eastern Colored League. In the second World Series, in 1925, he posted a respectable .273 batting average, but in a losing cause.

He had a good batting eye and supreme confidence in his hitting. He would take two pitches and then calmly hit the third one. Pressure situations failed to shake him. Once he was getting a drink of water when his turn came to bat and he grabbed a fungo bat and hit a grand-slam home run.

The veteran outfielder played most of his 27-year career with the Monarchs, but early in his career he was also a pitcher. He played with the Chicago Union Giants in 1914, touring throughout the Midwest, playing center field, and batting cleanup. He caught the eye of Rube Foster, and in 1915 he stepped into the cleanup spot for Foster's American Giants as the regular right fielder and hit .288 for the season. McNair returned to the Union Giants for most of the 1916 season, playing left field and batting third in the lineup, but joined the All Nations team the following season. In 1919 he played with the Detroit Stars for a season before signing with the Monarchs. In 1928 he returned to the Stars for a season and hit .274.

Earlier in his life McNair played with the 25th Infantry Wreckers baseball team at Fort Huachuca. He was a little man with a big head, and hit with the power of a big man. At times he was moody and self-centered, insisting on doing things his way and not playing if something was not to his liking. He also played with winter-league teams, including the Los Angeles White Sox in 1920 and the Colored All-Stars in 1921. He was always available to help young players learn the game. A few years later in California, he taught Willie Wells to hit a curveball by tying his leg to home plate so he could not back away from the curve.

After his playing career ended he extended his career in baseball as an umpire in the Negro American League. For his services in this ca-pacity, he was paid the princely sum of $140 per month. Once, when his decision as an arbiter inflamed passions, a group of players chased him around the field with bats, but he turned on those who were chasing him and pulled a knife, quickly dispelling their disagreement.

McNeal, Clyde (Junior)
a.k.a. McNeil
Career: 1944–50   Positions: **ss**, 2b, 3b
Teams: Chicago American Giants ('44–'50), *minor leagues ('53–'55, '57), Mexican League ('55–'56)*
Bats: Right   Throws: Right
Height: 6'0"   Weight: 185
Born: Dec. 15, 1928, San Antonio, Tex.

This infielder was playing with Lonnie Greer's All-Stars in San Antonio, Texas, when he was signed by Chicago American Giants' manager Candy Jim Taylor in 1944. He won the starting shortstop position in 1946 and remained with the American Giants through 1950. He was a mediocre hitter with good power, but had a relatively high strikeout ratio and usually batted in the lower part of the order. In 1946 he batted only .189, but he improved his hitting with averages of .251, .266, and .286, in 1948–50.

In the field he had good range and a strong arm. Shortstop was his best position, but in 1948 he was moved to second base for a season before returning to shortstop the following year. "Double Duty" Radcliffe, who managed him during his last year in the Negro Leagues, was high in his praise for the infielder, and McNeal was selected for the West squad in the 1950 East-West All-Star game.

After that season, the Dodgers purchased his contract and, after entering organized ball, he hit .275 with Elmira in 1953 while playing third base and shortstop. With Newport News in the Piedmont League during the next two years, he hit .309 and .269, but the latter season he also played with Pueblo in the Western League and Monterrey in the Mexican League. In 1956 he hit .303 with 27 home runs and 89

RBIs in 116 games. The next season he dropped off dramatically, finishing at .185 for his second tour with Pueblo, in 1957.

McNealy
Career: 1946   Position: of
Team: Birmingham Black Barons

This reserve outfielder appeared briefly with the Birmingham Black Barons in 1946.

McNeil
Career: 1918–20   Positions: 1b, c
Team: Dayton Marcos ('18–20)

A reserve player with the Dayton Marcos beginning in 1918, when they were playing as an independent team, and continuing through the 1920 season, when they entered the Negro National League, he played both first base and catcher.

McNeil
Career: 1930   Position: of
Team: Baltimore Black Sox

He appeared briefly as a reserve outfielder with the Baltimore Black Sox in 1930.

McNeil, William (Red)
Career: 1930–33   Positions: of, p
Teams: Nashville Elite Giants ('33), Louisville White Sox ('30-'31), Louisville Black Caps ('32), Louisville Red Caps ('33)

An outfielder during the early years of the '30s, he was the leadoff batter and center fielder with the Louisville White Sox in 1931, when the White Sox were in the Negro National League.

McQueen, Pete
Career: 1937–45   Position: of
Teams: Little Rock Black Travelers ('32), Memphis Red Sox ('37), New York Black Yankees ('38–'45)

A light-hitting outfielder, he began his career in 1937 as a reserve left fielder with the Memphis Red Sox and closed his career in the same capacity with the New York Black Yankees in 1945, batting .176 in very limited play.

McReynolds
Career: 1916   Positions: of, p
Teams: Indianapolis ABCs ('16), Bowser's ABCs ('16)

In 1916 a schism developed between ABC's owner Charles Bowser and manager C. I. Taylor, and consequently two ABC teams were fielded that year. The Indianapolis ABCs were headed by Taylor, and Bowser's ABCs were headed by the owner. At times during the season, McReynolds appeared with each squad.

Meade, Fred (Chick)
Career: 1916–22   Positions: **3b**, of, 2b, ss, business manager
Teams: *Brooklyn All-Stars, New York Stars,* Indianapolis ABCs ('16), *Pittsburgh Stars of Buffalo ('16–'19),* Hilldale Daisies ('19), Atlantic City Bacharach Giants ('20), Baltimore Black Sox ('21), Harrisburg Giants ('22)
Bats: Right   Throws: Right

A white man who passed for black to play in the Negro Leagues, his full identity did not come to light until years after his playing career was ended, when he was arrested for passing bad checks and his prison record showed his true race. In 1916 he was a reserve second baseman for the Indianapolis ABCs, with incomplete statistics showing only a .143 batting average for the year. Moving East, he joined the Pittsburgh Stars of Buffalo, a marginal team, for three full seasons before beginning a four-year period where he played as a regular with a new team each year. In 1919 he joined Hilldale to begin the cycle, moving in turn to the Bacharach Giants in Atlantic City, the Baltimore Black Sox, and finally, in 1922, the Harrisburg Giants. With each team he was the starting third baseman except with the Bacharachs, where he started at second base. He also usually hit sixth in the batting order, except in his last season, when he hit in the third slot while with the Harrisburg Giants. Three years later, Meade held the position of business manager for the Harrisburg team.

Meagher
Career: 1932   Position: of
Team: Washington Pilots

In 1932 he was a reserve outfielder during his brief stint with the Washington Pilots in the East-West League.

Means, Lewis
Career: 1920–28   Positions: **2b**, c, 1b
Teams: Atlantic City Bacharach Giants ('20–22, '27), Birmingham Black Barons ('23–'24, 28)

He began his career as a second baseman but ended his career as a catcher, combining playing time at both positions in between. With the Bacharachs in 1927 he played both positions, batting. 192 in very limited play.

Means, Thomas
Career: 1900–1904   Position: p
Team: Chicago Unions ('00), Chicago Union Giants ('04)

He pitched for the Chicago Unions in 1900, their last season before uniting with the Columbia Giants to form the Chicago Union Giants. Then he pitched for the Chicago Union Giants in 1904, their last season before they became the Leland Giants. Research has not uncovered any other season that he played in black baseball.

Meckling, S.
Career: 1909   Position: c
Team: Kansas City Royal Giants

He was a catcher with the Kansas City, Missouri, Royal Giants, one of the better black teams in the Midwest during the latter years of the century's first decade.

Mederos, Frank (Lico, Luis)
a.k.a. Medero; Medros
Career: 1910–20   Positions: **p**, of

Teams: Cuban Stars ('10), All Cubans ('11), Atlantic City Bacharach Giants ('20)

During the '10s he was a reasonably effective pitcher who threw "wide curves" and had moderately good control but was not a power pitcher. He began his career in black baseball with the Cuban Stars in 1910, and returned to the United States again in 1911 with the All Cubans team. During the intervening winter season he played with Havana against the Detroit Tigers in exhibitions in Cuba. During the 6-game series he pitched in half of the contests and sported a 1–2 ledger while hitting .250. That same winter, pitching against Connie Mack's American League champion Philadelphia A's, he beat Eddie Plank while pitching 5 innings of relief. A decade later the Cuban hurler made his last appearance in the United States, with the Bacharach Giants in Atlantic City.

Medina, Lazarus (Lazaro, Leonardo)
a.k.a. Leonardo Medina Chapman
Career: 1944–46   Position: p
Teams: Cincinnati-Indianapolis Clowns ('44–45), Indianapolis Clowns ('46)
Bats: Left   Throws: Left
Height: 5'7"   Weight: 160
Born: 1922, Havana, Cuba

This young bachelor began his pitching career in the Negro Leagues with the Clowns in 1944 at age twenty-two and posted marks of 4–3 (3.06 ERA) and 7–6 (3.10 ERA) in 1944–45. He began playing professionally a year earlier, in the Panama Republic Professional League, and also played with Ponce, the champions of the Puerto Rican winter league, under manager George Scales, and in the championship series in Venezuela.

Medina, Pedro
Career: 1905   Position: c
Team: Cuban Stars of Santiago

In 1905 he was a catcher with the Cuban Stars of Santiago, one of the top Cuban teams of that era.

Medley, Calvin
Career: 1946   Position: p
Team: New York Black Yankees

He pitched briefly with the New York Black Yankees in 1946, his only year in the Negro Leagues.

Mellico
[see Mellix, George]

Mellito
[see Navarro, Emilio (Mellito)]

Mellix, Felix
[see Mellix, George]

Mellix, George Ralph (Felix, **Lefty**)
a.k.a. Mellico
Career: 1922–34   Positions: **p**, 1b,
                         manager
Teams: Cuban X-Giants, Homestead Grays, Newark Dodgers ('34), *Pitt. Giants ('24)*
Bats: Left   Throws: Left
Height: 5'10"   Weight: 170
Died: 1985

An almost legendary pitcher in the semipro baseball leagues around the Pittsburgh area, he was credited with pitching in more than 1,500 games and pitching nine no-hitters among his more than 600 victories against semipro opposition. The lanky, left-handed pitcher was noted for his style as much as his ability, employing comedic antics on the mound, faking throwing spitters, and using a windmill windup. He was a finesse pitcher who mixed a curve, drop, and sneaky fastball and delivered them all with good control. He was considered the stopper on the semipro circuit and also played firstbase on occasion.

While he was an outstanding pitcher in the semipro league, on those occasions when he was coaxed to play with a league team, indications are that he did not fare as well. However, he is alleged to have compiled a 25–1 mark while pitching one unspecified season for the Homestead Grays. Earlier in his career he played with the Cuban X-Giants under the name Mellico. After his active career was over, he served as manager for the Brooklyn Brown Dodgers in the U.S. League in 1946.

Mello, Harry
[see Millon, Herald]

Melton
Career: 1916   Position: p
Team: St. Louis Giants

In his only season in black baseball, he was a member of the St. Louis Giants' pitching staff in 1916.

Melton, Elbert (Babe)
a.k.a. Milton
Career: 1928–29   Position: of
Teams: *Brooklyn Cuban Giants ('28)*, New York Lincoln Giants ('29), Baltimore Black Sox ('29)

A reserve outfielder with the New York Lincoln Giants and Baltimore Black Sox in 1929, he batted a combined .329 for the season.

Memphis Red Sox
Duration: 1923–50   Honors: First-half
                          champions ('38)
Affiliations: *Independent ('23)*, NNL ('24–30), NSL ('26, '32), NAL ('37–50)

The Memphis Red Sox franchise was owned by two brothers, Dr. J. B. Martin and Dr. B. B. Martin, members of a prominent family in Memphis. Both men were dentists, and J.B. also operated a drugstore and a funeral home and had investments in real estate. He built his own ballpark for the team, owned a hotel next to the park, and operated the concession stand where he served chitterlings in addition to the standard ballpark cuisine. The franchise fielded a team in the Negro National League each year between 1924 and 1930, except for 1926, when they joined the Negro Southern League in its inaugural season. The Red Sox also fielded a team in the Negro Southern League in 1932, the only season when it was designated as a major league.

In 1937 Memphis became a charter member

in the Negro American League and won the first-half championship in 1938 with a 21–4 record. In the playoff with the second-half winner, the Atlanta Black Crackers, the Red Sox won the first 2 games but the Series was canceled because of discord between the managements of the two ballclubs. The Red Sox remained in the league through 1950 but never again contended for the title.

Mendez, José (Joe, The Black Diamond)
a.k.a. José Mendez Baez (his real name)
Career: 1908–26   Positions: **p**, ss, 3b, 2b, of, manager
Teams: Brooklyn Royal Giants ('08), **Cuban Stars** ('09–'12), Stars of Cuba ('10), All Nations ('12–'17), Chicago American Giants ('18), Detroit Stars ('19), **Kansas City Monarchs** ('20–26)
Bats: Right   Throws: Right
Height: 5' 8"   Weight: 160
Born: Mar. 19, 1887, Cardenas, Matanzas, Cuba
Died: Oct. 31, 1928, Havana, Cuba

A lean and rangy right-hander with a smooth delivery, this wiry Cuban had tremendous speed that was deceptive. A smart pitcher who changed speeds, his rising fastball, coupled with a sharp-breaking curve, made him one of the greatest black pitchers of his time. Mendez had long arms and exceptionally long fingers, enabling him to get more spin on a ball. Some observers considered him to be faster than Smokey Joe Williams, and the graceful hurler threw with a deceptively easy motion that created havoc with batters' timing. He also utilized a quick release that was legal during the time he played but that is now ruled an illegal delivery.

Born in Cuba in 1888, he made his baseball debut in 1903 at age sixteen. Five years later he was pitching with Havana, the top team in Cuba, and that same year, 1908, he made his debut in the United States, recording a 3–0 ledger with the Brooklyn Royal Giants. The next season he was credited with a 44–2 record with the Cuban Stars, including a pitching gem

on July 24, 1909, when he hurled a perfect game for 10 innings. In 1910 he pitched in Cuba, posting an 18–2 mark.

During this same approximate time frame he posted records in the Cuban League of 7–0, 15–6, 7–0, 11–2 and 9–5 for 1908–1912 and 10–0 in the winter of 1913–14. His win totals were tops in the Cuban League for three consecutive years, 1908–11, with 15, 7, and 11, respectively. During his prime years, the Cuban hurler faced America's best teams and best pitchers, black and white. In his native country he outpitched Hall of Famers Christy Mathewson and Eddie Plank in exhibition games.

In 1910, he engaged in a classic pitcher's duel with Rube Foster that ended in an 11-inning 4–4 deadlock. In general Mendez had some hard luck pitching against Rube Foster's Leland Giants, easily the best black team of the era, winning only 3 games while losing 6. That winter in his homeland, pitching with Almendares against Ty Cobb's Detroit Tigers, he wielded a potent bat, hitting an even .300, but was unlucky on the mound, posting a 0–2–1 mark in 3 games as a pitcher, despite yielding only 21 hits in 28 innings pitched and striking out 10 batters in the series. When Connie Mack's world champion Philadelphia A's came to town, he fared better, winning both decisions, including a victory over Eddie Plank. Altogether, pitching against major-leaguers over a six-season span (1908–13), he fashioned a 9–11 record.

In 1911, pitching for Almendares, he faced Smokey Joe Williams of the New York Lincoln Giants at New York's Highlanders Park for the colored championship of the world. The game matched the United States' best against Cuba's best. Williams was superb, allowing no hits for 9 innings, but Mendez allowed only 2 hits, and the game remained scoreless after regulation play. Mendez won the game in the tenth inning, 1–0, when the Cubans bunched three hits off Williams to push across a run.

The following year, pitching against John McGraw's New York Giants, fortified with some Dodgers added to the roster, Mendez defeated both Christy Mathewson (4–3 in 10 innings) and Nap Rucker (2–1) over a three-day span, with only a day of rest between games. McGraw proclaimed Mendez to be "sort of Walter Johnson and Grover Alexander rolled into one" and, appraising his value to a club to be worth $30,000 a year if he were white, would have welcomed his presence on the Giants' pitching staff alongside Mathewson.

Going into the 1914 winter season, Mendez had logged a seven-year 62–15 record when, after developing arm trouble, he dropped out of regular pitching rotation. Returning to the States, he joined J. L. Wilkinson's All Nations club as a shortstop, playing with the team in 1916–17. The next season he joined his old nemesis Rube Foster's Chicago American Giants, but failed to experience a large measure of success as he split 2 pitching decisions while hitting only .189. The next season he was among several veteran players who signed with the Detroit Stars. Frank Wickware, John Donaldson, Peter Hill, and Bruce Petway were all on the team, and Mendez played shortstop, in the outfield, and pitched while batting in the sixth slot. The Stars proved to be a top ballclub, beating Foster's American Giants in a showdown series. He was still hanging on as an everyday player and taking an occasional turn on the mound, which he did in the winter of 1921, when he played with the Los Angeles White Sox.

But the event that shaped his future was when he was signed by J. L. Wilkinson as playing manager of the Kansas City Monarchs, Wilkinson's entry in the new Negro National League in 1920. He played shortstop and still pitched occasionally, and under his leadership the Monarchs won pennants in 1923, 1924, and 1925. In the first of these three campaigns Mendez fashioned an 8–2 pitching record, followed by league ledgers of 4–0, 2–0, and 3–1 for the next three seasons. In the latter two seasons Mendez led the Monarchs into the World Series against the Eastern Colored League champion Hilldale ballclub. In the 1924 World Series victory over Hilldale, Men-

dez rediscovered his old-time magic as he pitched in 4 games, including a shutout in his only start, and picked up 2 victories without a loss to go with an impressive 1.42 ERA. In his last season, 1926, the Monarchs lost a hard-fought playoff league championship series to the Chicago American Giants.

The great John Henry Lloyd, who had faced most of the greats, said that he had never seen a pitcher superior to Mendez. The quiet, unassuming hurler compiled a composite mark of 20–4 with 7 saves during his years with the Monarchs, 1920–26. In the winter of 1923 he pitched with Santa Clara in the Cuban winter league and fashioned a 3–1 work sheet, and in 1924 he was classed with Pedrosa and Padrone to form a triad of the greatest Cuban pitchers ever to come out of Cuba. His lifetime Cuban stats show a 74–25 ledger, good for a .747 winning percentage, with 40 percent of his losses coming after 1913. He was a power pitcher, with a deadly fastball having such velocity that he accidently killed a teammate when Mendez hit him in the chest with a fastball in batting practice. His lifetime totals also indicate impressive strikeout and walk ratios, striking out 5.17 batters per game while walking only 2.67 batters a game. As impressive as his pitching stats are, he batting totals are equally unimpressive, with only a .186 batting average to show for fourteen years interspersed between 1908 and 1927.

Mendez died from broncopneumonia in the autumn of 1928, at forty-one, barely two years after his last game with the Monarchs. In 1939 he was in the first group of players elected to the Cuban Hall of Fame.

Mendieta, Inocente
Career: 1912–13   Positions: **2b**, of
Teams: Cuban Stars ('12), Long Branch Cubans ('13)
He played second base with the Cuban Stars in 1912 and joined the Long Branch Cubans in 1913.

Merchant, Henry L. (Frank, Speed)
Career: 1940–50   Positions: **cf, lf**, 1b, p

Teams: Chicago American Giants (40–'42), Cincinnati Clowns ('43), Cincinnati-Indianapolis Clowns ('44–'45), Indianapolis Clowns ('46–'54)

Bats: Left　　　　　Throws: Left
Height: 6' 0"　　　　Weight: 170
Born: 1918, Birmingham, Ala.

As his nickname implies, this Clowns' outfielder was truly a "speed merchant" and acknowledged as one of the fastest men in Negro American League. After spending the first two years of his career with the Chicago American Giants, he joined the Clowns in 1943 and remained with them for a dozen years. During this time the franchise changed their home location form Cincinnati to Indianapolis, with the two cities jointly sharing the team for a couple of seasons during the interim. During his stint with the Clowns he hit for averages of .196, .255, .259, .283, .223, and .256 for the years 1944–49. In 1950 he hit .306 and stole 45 bases in 80 games, a total that was more than double that of the runner-up. His play earned him a trip to the East-West All-Star game, where he played left field and batted leadoff, but went hitless in the 5–3 loss to the West. An all-around athlete, he was a four-sport letter man at Henderson Institute prior to playing baseball professionally.

Meredith, Buford (Geetchie)

Career: 1923–31　　　Positions: ss, 2b
Teams: **Birmingham Black Barons** ('23–'29, '31), Memphis Red Sox ('27), Nashville Elite Giants ('30)
Bats: Right　　　　　Throws: Right

Sometimes listed in the box scores by only his nickname "Geetchie," this light-hitting shortstop was fast afield and on the bases. Playing exclusively with southern teams, primarily the Birmingham Black Barons, during the 1920s, he was the starting second baseman on the 1927 team that won the Negro National League second-half title but lost the championship playoff to the Chicago American Giants. He hit .240 for the season, raised his average to .273 in 1929, and, after playing with the

Nashville Elite Giants in 1930, returned to the Black Barons in 1931 for a final season before his untimely death in an off-season mining accident.

Merritt, B.

Career: 1905–17　　　Positions: **p**, of
Teams: Brooklyn Royal Giants ('05–'07), New York Lincoln Giants ('17)

A pitcher during the deadball era, he made his first appearance with the Brooklyn Royal Giants in the first decade of the century and made his last appearance in 1917, appearing in a game without a decision for the New York Lincoln Giants.

Merritt, Schute

Career: 1934–35　　　Position: ut
Team: Newark Dodgers

A utility player with the Newark Dodgers during their two years of existence, 1934–35, he was not selected to make the transition to the Newark Eagles in 1936.

Mesa, Andres (Anares)

Career: 1948　　　　Position: of
Teams: Indianapolis Clowns ('48)
Bats: Left　　　　　Throws: Left
Height: 5' 8"　　　　Weight: 160

Regarded as a good hitter and fielder, after a stint with the La Palomas club in 1947 he joined the Indianapolis Clowns in 1948, playing left field and batting leadoff while hitting for a .267 average.

Mesa, Pablo (Champion)

Career: 1921–27　　　Position: of
Team: Cuban Stars (East)
Bats: Left　　　　　Throws: Left
Height: 6' 0"　　　　Weight: 175
Born: 1902, Caibarien, Las Villas, Cuba

A complete ballplayer, he was an excellent hitter with good power, a good bunter, a very fast base runner, and an outstanding fielder with good range and an adequate arm. The light-complexioned Cuban was a brother of Cuban sportsman J. M. Mesa and was a colorful player, although he was the least known member of the Cuban Stars' great outfield trio that he formed with Martin Dihigo and Alejandro Oms during the 1920s. During the years when the Cubans fielded a team in the Eastern Colored League, 1923–27, he hit for averages of .258, .296, .311, .277, and .217.

While playing in the winter league in his homeland in 1926–27, the veteran outfielder led the league in batting with an average of .409. He began his Negro League career in 1921 when the team was still playing as an independent team, and was the regular left fielder and leadoff batter when they entered the league in 1923, but batted in the fifth and sixth slots most other years. Before Dihigo moved to the outfield, his mates in the outer garden were Bernardo Baro and Oms, and this trio formed another great outfield for the Cuban Stars in 1923–24. During the intervening winter in his homeland, playing with the champion Santa Clara team that is considered the greatest Cuban team of all time, he teamed with Oscar Charleston and Oms to form a third great outfield that he anchored.

Metz
Career: 1939   Position: unknown
Team: Kansas City Monarchs

He was listed as a player with the 1939 Kansas City Monarchs, but his playing time was severely restricted.

Meyers, George (Deacon)
Career: 1921–26   Positions: **p**, 1b, *2b, ss*
Teams: St. Louis Giants ('21), St. Louis Stars ('22–'25), Toledo Tigers ('23), Dayton Marcos ('26)

Beginning his career in 1921 with the St. Louis Giants, he posted an unimpressive 1–2 mark but remained with the franchise when new ownership transformed the team into the St. Louis Stars, and was the starting pitcher in the first game ever played by the St. Louis Stars. After leaving the Stars, in his last year in the Negro Leagues, 1926, his mound record with the Dayton Marcos was 1–7, but he also

received some playing time at shortstop, batting. 167 in limited action.

Miarka, Stanley V.
a.k.a. Miraka
Career: 1950   Positions: 2b, p
Team: Chicago American Giants

He was one of the white players signed by manager "Double Duty" Radcliffe for the Chicago American Giants in 1950, but he was not able to perform satisfactorily at this level of play.

Mickey, James
Career: 1940   Positions: ss, 3b
Teams: Birmingham Black Barons ('40), Chicago American Giants ('40)

In 1940, his only season in the Negro Leagues, he was a utility infielder with the Birmingham Black Barons, playing third base and shortstop and batting in the second slot when getting an occasional starting assignment.

Mickey, John
Career: 1898   Position: p
Team: *Celeron Acme Colored Giants*

In 1898 he was a pitcher with an all-black team dubbed the Acme Colored Giants that played in the Iron and Oil League as representatives of Celeron, New York. Both the team and the league folded in July, and it was to be the last time a black team played in a white league.

Miles, Jack
Career: 1937–40   Positions: of, p
Teams: Chicago American Giants ('37–'40), *Cincinnati Buckeyes ('40)*

Beginning his career as an outfielder with the Chicago American Giants in 1937, he also pitched with the American Giants, losing his only decision in 1940.

Miles, John (Mule, Sonnyboy)
Career: 1946–48   Positions: **of**, 3b
Team: Chicago American Giants
Bats: Right   Throws: Right

Height: 6' 3"   Weight: 228
Born: Aug. 11, 1922, San Antonio, Tex.

A power hitter, he was given his nickname by manager Candy Jim Taylor after crushing two home runs in a game. Taylor told the young slugger, "You hit that ball like a mule kicks," and the name stuck. Previously, in San Antonio, where he played basketball in high school and at Sam Phillips Junior College, he had been called "Sonnyboy." Although he was better known locally for his basketball exploits, he also played semipro baseball and, encouraged by Clyde McNeil, tried out with the Chicago American Giants and was signed in 1946. He played all three outfield positions and, although not possessing good speed, had pretty good range and a strong arm. In 1947, while batting .250, he was credited with 26 homers against all competition but, despite his power, usually batted in the lower half of the batting order for his duration with the Chicago American Giants.

Miles, Tom
Career: 1934   Positions: of, 1b, p
Team: Philadelphia Stars

He was a reserve player with the 1934 Negro National League champion Philadelphia Stars, with his limited playing time being split among the outfield, first base, and pitcher.

Miles, Willie
Career: 1923–27   Positions: **of**, 1b, 3b
Teams: Toledo Tigers ('23), Cleveland Tate Stars ('23), Homestead Grays ('24), Cleveland Browns ('24), Cleveland Elites ('26), Cleveland Hornets ('27), Memphis Red Sox ('27)

During his five-year Negro League career, this speedy outfielder played for four different Cleveland Negro National League entries, most notably as the center fielder and leadoff batter for the Cleveland Elites in 1926, when he hit .230. The next season he closed out his career by posting a .226 batting average with the Cleveland Hornets.

Miles, Zell
Career: 1946–49   Positions: **of**, 3b

Teams: Chicago American Giants ('46, '48–'49, '51), *Harlem Globetrotters ('47)*

During the post-World War II era he played all three outfield positions while batting in the lower half of the order with the Chicago American Giants. In 1947 he left the American Giants to play with the Harlem Globetrotters, a team of lesser status.

Miller
Career: 1906   Position: p
Team: Brooklyn Royal Giants

He was a pitcher with the 1906 Brooklyn Royal Giants, one of the top teams of the era.

Miller
Career: 1913–14   Positions: 3b, ss
Team: Philadelphia Giants

He was an infielder with the Philadelphia Giants for two seasons, 1913–14, after the ballclub had begun a decline in quality.

Miller
Career: 1920   Position: c
Team: *Pittsburgh Giants ('20),* Dayton Marcos ('20)

A marginal player, he is listed as a reserve catcher with the Dayton Marcos in 1920, but he played primarily with teams of lesser quality.

Miller
Career: 1937   Position: p
Team: St. Louis Stars

In 1937, the first year of the Negro American League, he was a member of the pitching staff of the St. Louis Stars.

Miller, A.
Career: 1927–28   Position: of
Teams: Memphis Red Sox ('27), Birmingham Black Barons ('28)

A reserve outfielder for two seasons with southern teams, he batted .250 in limited play with the Memphis Red Sox in 1927, and played with the Birmingham Black Barons in 1928 to close out his Negro League career.

Miller, Bob (Ruby)
Career: 1923–28   Positions: 2b, 3b, ss
Teams: Birmingham Black Barons ('23, '27), Memphis Red Sox ('24–'28)

This infielder spent most of his career with the Memphis Red Sox, and was the regular second baseman from 1924 through 1927, hitting progressively higher in the batting order until reaching the fifth slot in 1927. He closed out his career the following year.

Miller, Buck
[see Miller, Eddie (Buck)]

Miller, Dempsey (Dimps)
Career: 1926–37, 1945 Positions: **p**, *of*,
                        manager
Teams: Kansas City Monarchs ('26), Cleveland Elites ('26), Cleveland Hornets ('27), Cleveland Tigers ('28), Nashville Elite Giants ('30–'31), Cleveland Cubs ('31), Birmingham Black Barons ('31), Newark Browns (*'31*–'32), Memphis Red Sox, Detroit Stars ('37), *Detroit Giants ('45)*
Bats: Left   Throws: Left

Beginning his pitching career with the Kansas City Monarchs in 1926, this left-hander missed the 1926 postseason championship series because he was shot in the pitching arm by his wife in late September. He split 6 decisions in 1927 but was winless in 1930, losing all 3 decisions. With the Newark Browns in the East-West League in 1932, he again was winless, losing all 4 of his decisions. In 1937 he was the playing manager of the Detroit Stars and later managed the Detroit Giants, a team of lesser status.

Miller, Eddie (Ed, **Buck**)
Career: 1924–31   Positions: **p**, ss, 3b,
                        of, 1b
Teams: Chicago American Giants ('24–'30), Indianapolis ABCs ('26), Homestead Grays ('29), Chicago Columbia Giants ('31)
Bats: Right   Throws: Right
Born: 1902, Calvert, Tex.

A right-handed control pitcher with a good

memory for batters' weaknesses, he pitched for a dozen seasons with top black ballclubs. His best year was in 1926, when he logged a 16–3 record with the Indianapolis ABCs. He began his baseball career with the Fort Worth semipro ballclub, earning $72 a month because he wanted something better in life than his father, who earned $1 a day for ten hours of hard labor digging ditches. In 1920 he moved up a notch in competition and began his professional career with Shreveport.

The Texan pitched for the Chicago American Giants in 1926–27, splitting 4 decisions the latter season. He signed with the American Giants again in 1928 but was suspended in July 1929, along with Stanford Jackson, by manager Jim Brown, and they were signed by the Homestead Grays. Miller finished with a 1–2 mark for the year. he sometimes played infield or outfield, batting .161 in 1927 and .253 and .223 in 1929–30 as a shortstop.

During his prime he played against Babe Ruth in Cuba, but fell victim to the Depression, ending his career with the Chicago Columbia Giants following the 1931 season. After the demise of the Negro National League he remained in Waxahachie, Texas, and took a job loading trucks until his eyesight began to fail. He retired in Dallas, Texas, in 1986, eventually losing 90 percent of his sight.

Miller, Eugene
Career: 1909   Position: of
Team: St. Paul Gophers

The outfielder played with the 1909 western champion St. Paul Gophers, who defeated the Leland Giants in playoff for the title.

Miller, Frank
Career: 1887–97   Positions: p. of
Teams: Pittsburgh Keystones ('87), Cuban Giants ('87), New York Gorhams ('89), Cuban X-Giants ('96–'97), Philadelphia Giants

In 1887 he was a pitcher with the Pittsburgh Keystones, one of eight teams that were charter members of the League of Colored Baseball Clubs. However, the league collapsed after only a week and he joined the Cuban Giants. In March of that year the team played a series with the Metropolitans, a white major-league team. A Cleveland sportswriter indicated that Miller had no equal among colored pitchers of the day. Two years later, in 1889, he pitched with the New York Gorhams when they represented Philadelphia in the Middle States League. Later in his career, with the Cuban X-Giants, he also played in the outfield.

Miller, Henry Joseph (Hank)
Career: 1938–50   Position: p
Teams: Philadelphia Stars ('38–'50), *minor leagues ('51–'53)*
Bats: Right   Throws: Right
Height: 6' 1"   Weight: 180
Born: July 17, 1917, Glenolden, Pa.
Died: Aug. 30, 1972, Philadelphia, Pa.

This Philadelphia Stars' hurler began his career in 1938, posting unimpressive marks of 1–2 and 0–1 in limited playing time for the years 1940–41. Three years later, in 1944–45, he had records of 5–3 and 2–4, but in 1946 he was still regarded as an up-and-coming youngster trying to make the starting rotation. In 1947 he fulfilled his promise, forging a 9–3 record and earning a spot on the East roster for the All-Star game, where he pitched 2 scoreless innings in a losing cause. He continued in the Stars' starting rotation for three more seasons, including a 6–4, 3.00 ERA record in 1949.

In 1951 he pitched in half a dozen games without a decision for San Diego in the Pacific Coast League. His final appearance in organized ball was with Hutchinson in the Western Association in 1953, where he was 5–13 with a 4.85 ERA. A pretty fair hitter for a pitcher, with average power when he made contact, he hit for a .298 average with Hutchinson.

Miller, James (Jim, Bo, Bub)
Career: 1938   Position: 3b
Teams: Homestead Grays ('38), Atlanta Black Crackers ('38)
Bats: Left   Throws: Right
This infielder from New Orleans was a steady fielder and a fair left-handed hitter. In 1938 the Homestead Grays played the Atlanta Black Crackers a 3-game exhibition series in late April, and Miller played with the Homestead Grays. After the series, Miller was secured from the Grays by the Black Crackers to fill a vacancy at the hot corner created when Ormond Sampson decided to play with the Chicago American Giants. Miller filled in capably at third base for a time but was eventually released.

Miller, Jasper
Career: 1939–40   Positions: **p**, of
Team: Memphis Red Sox
He appeared briefly as a pitcher with the Memphis Red Sox for two seasons, 1939–40.

Miller, Joseph (Joe, Kid)
Career: 1895–1903   Position: **p**, of
Teams: *Lincoln, Nebraska, Giants ('90)*, Page Fence Giants ('95–'98), Columbia Giants ('99–'00), Chicago Union Giants ('01–'03)
With a pitching career that spanned the turn of the century, he began with the Page Fence Giants, one of the top teams of the nineteenth century, in 1895, posting a 7–4 record and a .231 batting average. When the team disbanded in 1898, he was among the ex-Page Fence players who signed with the Columbia Giants. After two seasons Frank Leland combined the giants with the Chicago Unions to form the Chicago Union Giants, and Miller was one of the team's leading hurlers for three years, finishing his career in 1903. He also played with the Adrian team in the Michigan State League and the Lincoln Giants from Lincoln, Nebraska.

Miller, Lee (Red)
Career: 1911–23   Position: 3b, 2b, ss, of
Teams: **Brooklyn Royal Giants** ('11, '16–'17, '20–'21), Smart Set ('12), New York Lincoln Giants ('15), New York Lincoln Stars ('15–'16), Atlantic City Bacharach Giants ('17, '19), *Norfolk Stars ('20)*, Baltimore Black Sox ('22–'23)

Beginning his career with an appearance for the Brooklyn Royal Giants in 1911, he joined the Smart Set in 1912 and played with the top teams in the East during the remainder of the deadball era, frequently moving from one team to another. After splitting the 1915 season between the Lincoln Giants and the Lincoln Stars as a reserve infielder, he filled the starting spot at third base with the Stars in 1916 until moving to the Brooklyn Royal Giants in September. In 1917 he again split the season between two teams, but continued his role as a regular third baseman with both the Brooklyn Royal Giants and the Bacharachs, with incomplete statistics showing a combined batting average of .294.

Usually hitting in the lower part of the batting order previously, with the demise of the deadball era in 1920, Miller moved into the leadoff position for the Royals. However, after joining the Baltimore Black Sox in 1922 for his last two years in black baseball, he dropped back down to his customary spot near the bottom of the batting order, hitting .240 in 1922 and closing out his career in 1923 as the Black Sox entered the Eastern Colored League in its inaugural season.

The infielder had a drinking problem, and he was killed when someone pounded his head on a concrete sidewalk while he was intoxicated.

Miller, Leroy (Flash)
Career: 1935–44   Positions: **2b**, ss, *3b*
Teams: Newark Dodgers ('35), New York Black Yankees ('38–'44)

This light-hitting, quick middle infielder began his career in 1935 with the Newark Dodgers, but played most of his career with the New York Black Yankees. He was a regular player with the Black Yankees in 1939–40, hitting .175 and batting in the eighth spot in the lineup as the starting shortstop in 1939, and moving to second base and into the second slot in the batting order during the latter year. His only other season as a regular was in 1943, when he again was the regular at the keystone

position. He closed out his decade in the Negro Leagues the following season as a reserve infielder.

Miller, Ned
Career: 1937   Position: 1b
Team: Indianapolis Athletics

In 1937, the Indianapolis Athletics' only year in the Negro American League, he was the regular first baseman and hit fifth in the batting order.

Miller, Percy
Career: 1921–34   Positions: **p**, of
Teams: Chicago Giants ('21), St. Louis Giants ('21), St. Louis Stars ('22–'26), Kansas City Monarchs ('22, '34), Nashville Elite Giants ('30–34)

Beginning his career with the Chicago Giants in 1921, he was winless against 4 losses, but enjoyed more success after joining the St. Louis Stars, reversing those numbers with a 4–0 mark in 1926, his last season with the Stars. He was with the Nashville Elite Giants in 1930, their first year in the Negro National League, and is credited with a 6–2 mark with them in 1933.

Miller, Pleas (**Hub**)
Career: 1913–16   Positions: **p**, of
Teams: *West Baden Sprudels ('12–'15),* St. Louis Giants ('13, '16)

This pitcher made his first appearance with the St. Louis Giants in 1913 and his last in 1916. During this same period he also played with the West Baden Sprudels, a team of lesser status.

Miller, W.
Career: 1940   Position: p
Team: Chicago American Giants

He pitched with the Chicago American Giants in 1940, posting a 2–4 record for his only year in the Negro Leagues.

Milliner, Eugene (Gene, Eddie)
a.k.a. Millner

Career: 1903–10   Positions: lf, cf
Teams: Chicago Giants ('03), St. Paul Gophers ('09), Kansas City Royal Giants ('09–'10)

Exceptionally fast in the field and on the bases, he was the fastest man in baseball during his time, giving up that designation only upon the arrival of Jimmy Lyons. He played left field with the St. Paul Gophers' team that defeated Rube Foster's Leland Giants for the western championship in 1909. The following season he played center field with the Kansas City, Missouri, Royal Giants.

Millner
[see Milliner, Eugene]

Millon, Herald (Harry)
a.k.a. Mello
Career: 1946–47   Positions: **ss**, 3b, 2b
Team: Chicago American Giants

An utility infielder with the Chicago American Giants for two post-World War II seasons, he was primarily a shortstop but also played third base and second base.

Mills, Charles A. (**Charlie**)
Career: 1911–24   Positions: owner, officer
Teams: St. Louis Giants, ('11–'21) *St. Louis Black Sox ('24)*

A white businessman, he was the owner of the St. Louis Giants, a team formed in 1909, but he sold the franchise after the 1921 season, with the team becoming the St. Louis Stars.

Milton, C.
Career: 1933–34   Position: if
Teams: Columbus Blue Birds ('33), Cleveland Giants ('33), Cleveland Red Sox ('34)

This infielder played two seasons with marginal teams, beginning with the Negro National League Columbus Blue Birds in 1933, until the team dropped out of the league after the first half and disbanded. Some of the players joined the Cleveland Giants, the second-half replacement team, and continued with the Red Sox, Cleveland's 1934 entry.

Milton, Edward
Career: 1926–28   Positions: **of**, 2b, *1b, c, p*
Teams: Cleveland Elites ('26), Cleveland Hornets ('27), Cleveland Tigers ('28)

A reserve outfielder with the Cleveland entries in the Negro National League for three successive seasons, 1926–28, he hit .256 in 1926.

Milton, Henry (Streak)
Career: 1932–43   Positions: **rf, lf**, 2b, ss
Teams: *Chicago Giants,* Indianapolis ABCs ('32), Chicago American Giants, Brooklyn Royal Giants, Brooklyn Eagles ('35), **Kansas City Monarchs** ('35–'40), New York Black Yankees ('43)
Bats: Left   Throws: Left
Height: 5' 9"   Weight: 155

As leadoff batter for the Kansas City Monarchs during their dominant years, this small, speedy outfielder seemed to always be on base. A good base stealer, he was very fast and was nicknamed "Streak" in 1937. He was a good bunter, a contact hitter without appreciable power, and was regarded as an average batter and fielder, batting .256 in 1939. During his eight-year career he was selected to the West All-Star squad five consecutive years, 1936–40. The latter season was his last as a regular player, and soon afterward he was out of baseball. He died at a young age from spinal meningitis.

While a member of his college football team at Wiley College, he played in the same backfield into two other players from the Negro Leagues, Pat Patterson and Byron Johnson.

Milwaukee Bears
Duration: 1923   Honors: None
Affiliation: NNL

This Milwaukee franchise fielded a team in the Negro National League in 1923 but failed to finish the year, dropping out of the league late in the season with a 14–32 record for a winning percentage of .304.

Mimin

[see Minin]

Mimms

Career: 1932   Position: p
Team: Columbus Turfs

He was a pitcher with the Columbus Turfs, a second-half replacement team in the Negro Southern League in 1932.

Mims

Career: 1910   Position: cf
Team: St. Louis Giants

In 1910, the second year of the team's existence, he played center field for the St. Louis Giants.

Mincy, Lefty

a.k.a. Mency; Mencey; Mincey
Career: 1930–40   Position: p
Teams: Philadelphia Stars ('39), New York Black Yankees ('40), Newark Eagles ('40)
Bats: Left   Throws: Left
Height: 6'3"   Weight: 200

This left-hander pitched briefly and without distinction for a trio of Negro National League teams, finishing the 1940 season winless against 3 combined losses while splitting his playing time between the Newark Eagles and the New York Black Yankees. After retiring from baseball he worked as a cabbie in New York City.

Minin

a.k.a. Nimin; Mimin
Career: 1931   Position: 1b
Team: Cuban Stars

In 1931 he played first base and batted in the cleanup spot for the Cuban Stars, who had dropped out of the Negro National League and were playing part of the season as the Cuban House of David.

Minor

Career: 1920   Position: lf
Team: Baltimore Black Sox

He was a reserve left fielder with the Balti-more Black Sox in 1920, while they were still playing as an independent team and still improving toward the league level of play.

Minor, George

Career: 1944–49   Position: of
Teams: Chicago American Giants ('44), Cleveland Buckeyes ('44–'48), Louisville Buckeyes ('49)

Beginning his career in 1944 as a reserve right fielder with the Chicago American Giants, he joined the Cleveland Buckeyes during the season and batted a combined .234. The outfielder played for the Buckeyes during the remainder of the '40s, batting .314 and .339 in 1946–47 in a reserve role. The next season he earned the starting center-field position and batted in the leadoff spot, posting a .278 batting average. He stayed with the franchise when the ballclub relocated in Louisville in 1949, his last year in the Negro Leagues.

Minoso, Saturnino Orestes Arrieta Armas (Minnie)

Career: 1945–48   Position: 3b
Teams: New York Cubans ('45–'48), *minor leagues ('48–'50, '64)*, major leagues ('49, '51–'64, '76, '80), *Mexican League ('65–'73)*
Bats: Right   Throws: Right
Height: 5' 10"   Weight: 175
Born: Nov. 29, 1922, Perico, Cuba

This young Cuban third baseman broke in with a .309 average for the New York Cubans in 1946 and continued his hot hitting into the next season. He was the top hitter on the team with a torrid .336 average going into August, before cooling off and finishing at .294. Minoso's offensive production from his leadoff spot in the batting order aided the Cubans as they captured the Negro National League pennant and won World Series from the Negro American League's Cleveland Buckeyes. He was the starting third baseman in both the 1947 and 1948 East-West All-Star games before entering the major leagues with the Cleveland Indians in 1949.

Moved to the outfield and traded to the Chicago White Sox, the speedster promptly led the league in stolen bases his first three full major-league seasons, 1951–53. Minoso spent the most productive of his fifteen true major-league seasons with the "Go–Go" White Sox of the 1950s. He consistently maintained a batting average of about .300, and finished his major-league career with a lifetime .298 batting average, 186 home runs, 205 stolen bases, and was hit by a pitch 189 times. During his major-league career he also played a season apiece with the St. Louis Cardinals and the Washington Senators. A legitimate three-decade player, Minoso was brought back to the White Sox for special pinch-hitting appearances in 1976 and 1980 so he could qualify as a five-decade player.

Minoso also had a short career in the minor leagues, beginning with a brief stint at Dayton (.525 batting average) between the New York Cubans and his first appearance in a Cleveland Indians' uniform. After that first "cup of coffee" in the big leagues, he was sent to San Diego in the Pacific Coast League, where he spent two seasons (1949–50) proving that he was ready for the major leagues. In addition to batting averages of .297 and .339, he had 30 stolen bases and 115 RBIs the latter year.

Fourteen years later he was back in the minor leagues, with Indianapolis of the International League, prior to beginning a second career, in the Mexican League. Although past his prime, he spent nine more seasons in Mexico, beginning with averages of .360 and .348 in his first two years with Jalisco. While in Mexico he played much of his time at first base to accommodate his aging legs. His last year was in 1973, when he hit .265 at age fifty.

He also enjoyed a good career in his native country, leaving a lifetime Cuban batting average of .289 for eight winter seasons. He began his baseball career in his homeland a year before he joined the New York Cubans, and was selected to the All Cubans team of 1945–46 at third base. He continued his Cuban career with averages of .294, .249, .285, .263, .321, .271,
.327, and .295 for the years 1945–54, except for the winter of 1949–50, when he did not play winter ball.

Mirabal, Autorio

a.k.a. Mirable; Mirabel
Career: 1939–40   Positions: 2b, c, rf
Team: New York Cubans

A reserve player, he could catch or play infield or outfield, and was with the New York Cubans for two seasons, 1939–40, batting .200 the latter year.

Mirabal, Juanelo

a.k.a. Mirabel; Miraval; Juanello
Career: 1921–34;   Positions: **p**, officer
1949–50
Teams: *Atlanta Black Crackers ('18–'21), Birmingham Black Barons ('19–'21)*, Cubans Stars (East) ('21–'34), New York Cubans ('49–'50)
Bats: Right   Throws: Right
Height: 5' 8"   Weight: 150
Born: Apr. 22, 1901, Tampa, Fla.

A formidable pitcher for fourteen years in the Negro Leagues, this rifle-armed right-hander used a three-quarters overhand delivery, excellent control, a sinking fastball, and a baffling curve to anchor the Cuban Stars' mound corps.

When he first joined the Stars, they were playing as an independent team, but in 1923 they joined the Eastern Colored League in its inaugural season and remained a member until the league's demise in 1928. In 1925 he suffered through a 2–9 season, but in 1928 he held Hilldale hitless until, with one out in the ninth, a pinch hit broke up his no-hitter. Throughout his career, Mirabal was always effective against the Hilldale ballclubs. The Cuban Stars, with Juanelo doing the bulk of the pitching, were having their best season ever, sporting a league-leading 93–22 record at the time the Eastern Colored League broke up.

The Cuban Stars' hurler used a quick delivery to good advantage until 1929, when the practice was abolished in the Negro Leagues.

That season, Pompez's Cuban Stars played in the American Negro League in its only year of existence, and Mirabel, suffering from an arm injury, finished with a 1–2 record. Three seasons later, when the Cubans were members in the ill-fated East-West League, he was still a member of their pitching staff.

During the winters, Juanelo pitched in the Cuban League, posting a 9–2 record as the ace of Dolph Luque's Havana team. Playing there was like playing in his own backyard, since Havana was considered to be his hometown. Although born in Tampa of Cuban parentage, his childhood was spent primarily in Havana, and that is where he learned to play baseball. Mirabal was young when his father died, and Alejandro Pompez was his godfather and mentor.

The youngster first attracted attention when, as a sixteen-year-old, he shut-out Pompez's Cuban Stars in both ends of a doubleheader in New Orleans. Although he did not sign at that time, three years later, after tours with the Atlanta Black Crackers and the Birmingham Black Barons, the young hurler joined Pompez's Cuban Stars. With the Cubans he was always in the starting rotation but was usually listed in box scores by his first name only, Juanelo.

After completing his career on the diamond, he became Pompez's right-hand man and moved into the front office, serving as president of both the Cuban Stars and Pompez's New York Cubans after they were organized.

Miraka, Stanley
[see Miarka, Stanley V.]

Miranda, P.
Career: 1916   Position: player
Team: Cuban Stars
He played with owner Alejandro Pompez's 1916 Cuban Stars, but his position is uncertain.

Miraval, J.
[see Mirabal, Juanelo]

Miro, Pedro
Career: 1945–48   Position: 2b
Team: New York Cubans
A second baseman with the New York Cubans during the late '40s, he closed out a four-year career in 1948, when the Negro National League folded.

Missouri, Jim
Career: 1937–41   Position: p
Team: Philadelphia Stars
This pitcher fashioned a five-year career with the Philadelphia Stars during the late '30s and early '40s, finishing winless against 3 losses in 1940.

Mitchell
Career: 1901   Position: c
Team: Chicago Union Giants
He was the regular catcher for the Chicago Union Giants in 1901, his only season in black baseball.

Mitchell
Career: 1926   Positions: p, rf
Team: Newark Stars
A pitcher with the Eastern Colored League's Newark Stars in 1926, he also appeared in the outfield during his stint with the Stars, before the team folded in midseason.

Mitchell, Alonzo (Bo, **Fluke, Hooks**)
Career: 1923–41   Position: p, 1b, of,
                                     manager, officer
Teams: Baltimore Black Sox ('23, '26), Atlantic City Bacharach Giants ('24–'26, '28), Harrisburg Giants ('26), Akron Tyrites ('33), Jacksonville Red Caps ('34–'38, '41), Birmingham Black Barons ('37–'38), Atlanta Black Crackers ('38), Indianapolis ABCs ('39), Cleveland Bears ('39–'40)
Bats: Right   Throws: Right
Height: 5' 10"   Weight: 160
A sidearm curveballer, the slight, bowlegged right-hander could also throw hard, even in later years, when he was a veteran. During the '30s and early '40s he was a pitcher and man-

ager with ballclubs based in the South, primarily with the Jacksonville Red Caps. He was appointed manager of the Jacksonville Red Caps when they were playing independent ball, 1934–37, but left the team for stints with the Birmingham Black Barons and the Atlanta Black Crackers.

Classified as an "old-timer" in 1938, he was pitching with the Black Crackers in April but was released in the latter part of July in an acrimonious termination. His pitching effectiveness was not questioned, as he was described as being a "wonderful pitcher," but he was at odds with the manager and players and was called "a troublemaker of the rankest sort." When released he cut up a $10 lumberjacket provided for the players by the owners, an act that essentially destroyed any chance of his return to the ballclub. Leaving the Black Crackers, he returned to the Red Caps and, when the team relocated in Cleveland, he served as manager of the Cleveland Bears in 1939–40 and continued at the helm when the franchise returned to Jacksonville in 1941.

In earlier years, during the '20s, he pitched with the Bacharachs, posting marks of 1–5 and 4–2 in 1925–26. He also pitched with the Baltimore Black Sox and Harrisburg Giants, and sometimes also played in the outfield and at first base. He played at the initial sack with the Akron Tyrites in 1933 before joining the Red Caps in 1934.

Mitchell, Arthur Harold
Career: 1939   Position: if
Team: New York Black Yankees

He appeared briefly as a reserve infielder with the New York Black Yankees in 1939.

Mitchell, Bob
Career: 1950   Position: p
Team: Cleveland Buckeyes

This Cleveland Buckeyes' hurler was the losing pitcher in the only game he pitched in 1950, when the Negro American League was struggling to survive the loss of players to organized baseball.

Mitchell, Bud
Career: 1929–34   Positions: of, p, c, 1b, 3b
Teams: Atlantic City Bacharach Giants ('29), Hilldale Daisies ('29–32), Washington Pilots ('32), Philadelphia Stars ('33)

Although he began his career as a pitcher with the Bacharachs, he moved over to Hilldale as a first baseman-catcher. He batted .263 in 1930, his first of three full seasons with Hilldale. In his last season with the ballclub he moved to the outfield, a position he also played with the Philadelphia Stars in 1933.

Mitchell, George (Big)
Career: 1924–43, 1949 Positions: p, of, 1b, 2b, manager, business manager
Teams: *Mounds City Blues ('24)*, St. Louis Stars ('24, '39), Indianapolis ABCs ('25–'26, '31, '38), Chicago American Giants ('25–'26, '30), Kansas City Monarchs ('27), Detroit Stars ('28–'29, '33), Cleveland Cubs ('31), Cleveland Stars ('32), *Montgomery Grey Sox ('33)*, New Orleans-St. Louis Stars ('41), New York Black Yankees ('42), Harrisburg-St. Louis Stars ('43), Houston Eagles ('49)
Bats: Right   Throws: Right
Height: 6' 4"   Weight: 200
Born: Sparta, Ill.

A right-handed pitcher with a big roundhouse curve and an average fastball, he and his twin brother, Robert, a catcher, formed an unique battery with the St. Louis Stars in 1924. George's first stint with the Stars was short, and he soon had joined the pitching staffs of both the Chicago American Giants and the Indianapolis ABCs, playing for the two top managers of black baseball, Rube Foster and C. I. Taylor. He bounced around quite a bit during his career, never staying with the same team for more than two consecutive years, but posted seasons of 8–6 with the Kansas City Monarchs in 1927, 4–7 with the Detroit Stars in 1929, and 11–8 with the Chicago American Giants in 1930.

As he neared the end of his playing career,

his pitching production dipped as he showed records of 0–2 and 1–2 in 1932–33 with the Cleveland Stars and the Detroit Stars. His extensive travels provided him with enough experience to warrant a chance at managing, and he became a player-manager for the St. Louis Stars in 1939, and held this position for several seasons. In 1941 he was selected to the East-West All-Star squad and appeared in the contest as a pinch hitter in the ninth inning.

Mitchell, Hooks

[see Mitchell, Alonzo (Hooks)]

Mitchell, John

Career: 1932   Positions: c, of
Team: Montgomery Grey Sox

A catcher who also played the outfield, he played with the Montgomery Grey Sox in 1932, when the Negro Southern League was recognized as a major league.

Mitchell, Leonard Otto

Career: 1930–31   Position: 2b
Teams: Birmingham Black Barons ('30), Louisville White Sox ('31, '38)

He was a second baseman for the Birmingham Black Barons in 1930, hitting .303, and joined the Louisville White Sox the following season, in their only season in the Negro National League. In 1938 he assumed the managerial reins for the Louisville ballclub.

Mitchell, Robert

Career: 1923–24   Positions: c, of
Teams: Birmingham Black Barons ('23), St. Louis Stars ('24)

This catcher began his career with the Birmingham Black Barons in 1923, and the following season he and his twin brother, George, formed a twin battery for the St. Louis Stars.

Moade

Career: 1914   Position: rf
Team: Philadelphia Giants

A player listed by that name appeared in right field with the Philadelphia Giants in 1914, when the team was in decline.

Mochello

Career: 1931   Position: 3b
Team: Newark Browns

He was a reserve third baseman with the Newark Browns in 1931, a year before the team joined the East-West League.

Mohawk Giants

Duration: 1913–15   Honors: None
Affiliation: Independent

This was a team based in Schenectady, New York, that was a first-class independent ballclub during the midteens when Frank Wickware and Chappie Johnson formed their favorite battery. Subsequently the team returned to a semipro category, playing good ball at that level on into the forties.

Moles, Lefty

Career: 1935   Position: p
Team: Philadelphia Stars
Bats: Left   Throws: Left

A left-handed pitcher, he appeared briefly with the Philadelphia Stars in 1935, when the Stars were the defending Negro National League champions.

Molina

Career: 1929–30   Position: p
Team: Cuban Stars (West)

A pitcher with the Negro National League's Cuban Stars for two seasons, he posted records of 1–4 and 2–4 in 1929–30.

Molina, Augustin (Tinti)

Career: 1907–10,
1911–31   Positions: 1b, of, c, p,
                       manager, officer
Teams: Cuban Stars (West)
Height: 6' 4"   Weight: 185
Born: Cuba

As a player he was a fair fielder, playing as a combination first baseman-outfielder with the Cuban Stars in 1910. The tall, thin Cuban played for a dozen years in his homeland, interspersed between the years 1894 and 1909, finishing with a minuscule .162 lifetime batting average. Playing mostly with Havana, he also failed to demonstrate any power at the plate, but he did top the league in most games played in 1904. However, it is not as a player that he is best remembered.

A veteran of the Spanish-American War, he was the owner and manager of the Negro National League Cuban Stars from 1921 until the league broke up after the 1931 season, but he never wore a uniform. In Cuba he was the right-hand man of Linares and managed the 1923–24 Santa Clara championship team, who recorded a .766 winning percentage and are called the greatest Cuban team ever. In recognition of his achievements in his native country, he was elected to the Cuban Hall of Fame in 1942.

Mollett

Career: 1913–16   Positions: 2b, ss
Teams: Mohawk Giants ('13), New York, Lincoln Stars ('16)

This middle infielder played shortstop for the Mohawk Giants in 1913 and second base with the Lincoln Stars in 1916.

Molloy

Career: 1922   Position: p
Team: Atlantic City Bacharach Giants

He was a pitcher with the Bacharach Giants in 1922, their last year as an independent team before entering the Eastern Colored League.

Monceville

[see Monchile]

Monchile

a.k.a. Monchille; Monceville
Career: 1930–32   Position: of, 3b
Teams: Cuban Stars ('30–'31), Newark Browns ('32), *Quaker Giants*

This outfielder spent two season with the Cuban Stars before appearing with the Newark Browns in the East-West League in 1932. He also played third base and was with the Quaker Giants, a team of lesser status.

Monchille

[see Monchile]

Mongin, Sam

a.k.a. Mungin, Mungen
Career: 1908–22   Positions: **3b**, 2b, of, *p*
Teams: Philadelphia Giants ('07–'08), Brooklyn Royal Giants ('09–'10, '22), St. Louis Giants ('11–'13, '21). Chicago Giants ('14), New York Lincoln Stars ('15–'16), New York Lincoln Giants ('16–'22), Atlantic City Bacharach Giants ('21)
Bats: Right   Throws: Right
Born: Jan. 17, 1884, Savannah, Ga.

One of the top third baseman in the East during the '10s, he played with the top teams of the era. He began his career in 1908 with the Philadelphia Giants, and he joined the Brooklyn Royal Giants as the regular third baseman, batting in the eighth slot, as the Royals won the eastern championship in 1909–10. The next season he moved West to join the St. Louis Giants and earned a starting position at third base in 1913. After his stint in St. Louis, he was the leadoff batter with the Chicago Giants for a season while playing the hot corner in the "Windy City."

In 1915 he moved back East as the regular third baseman for the eastern champion Lincoln Stars. The next year he joined the Lincoln Giants, maintaining a starting position through 1920. The first and last years were at the hot corner, but in the three middle seasons (1917–19) he held down the keystone position while batting .270, .333, and .216. In 1918 he batted in the leadoff spot, and in 1919 he batted in the second slot, but otherwise he batted in the lower part of the batting order with each team he was with. In 1920 he was still a dependable hitter for the Lincoln Giants, but in 1921 he joined the Bacharachs as a substitute second baseman, and closed out his career with top teams in 1922, with the Lincolns and the Royals.

Monolo

a.k.a. Manolo; Manno; Manzano
Career: 1916–22   Positions: 1b, 3b, p
Teams: Cuban Stars (East) ('16–'19, '22), Cuban Stars (West) ('20–'22)

He began his career as a first baseman with the Cuban Stars in 1916, when they were based in New York, and remained with the team until 1920, when he joined the other Cuban Stars team that joined the Negro National League. In 1921 the league's Cuban Stars used Cincinnati as a home site and were sometimes called the Cincinnati Cubans. In later years, in addition to playing on the corners, he pitched for the Stars.

Monroe, Al

Career: 1937   Position: officer
League: NAL

In 1937, the Negro American League's inaugural year, he served as secretary of the league.

Monroe, Bill

Career: 1927   Positions: 3b, 2b, ss
Teams: *Pittsburgh Starts of Buffalo ('20)*, Baltimore Black Sox ('27)

An utility infielder with the Baltimore Black Sox in 1927, he played second base, third base, and shortstop during the season. Earlier in his career he played with the Pittsburgh Stars of Buffalo, a team of lesser status.

Monroe Monarchs

Duration: 1932   Honors: None
Affiliation: NSL

Based in Monroe, Louisiana, this ballclub was generally a member of a high minor league, but following the demise of the Negro National League, the Negro Southern League was considered a major league in 1932, and the Monroe Franchise finished the first half of the season only half a game behind the champion Chicago American Giants. With the exception of this one season, the team played primarily as an unofficial farm club for the Kansas City Monarchs.

Monroe, William (Bill)

Career: 1896–1914   Positions: 2b, 3b, ss, 1b
Teams: Chicago Unions ('90–'00), Cuban X-Giants ('00), Philadelphia Giants ('03–'06), Brooklyn Royal Giants ('07–'10), Quaker Giants of New York ('08), Chicago American Giants ('11–'14), Chicago Giants ('13)
Bats: Right   Throws: Right
Born: 1876
Died: Mar. 16, 1915, Chicago, Ill.

One of the first great black ballplayers, he began his career before the turn of the century, and was already an established star during the first decade of the deadball era. A versatile and exceptionally adept fielder, he had good hands, great speed, and played all infield positions with grace. When playing at the hot corner, he excelled at fielding bunts and was considered to be a better fielder and hitter than his white contemporary at third base, Jimmy Collins. But it was as a second baseman that he won the most acclaim. A crowd favorite throughout his career, he entertained the fans with his showmanship as well as his baseball skills. He would catch "Texas Leaguers" behind his back, kick ground balls with his toe and make them bounce into his hand, and yell to batters that if they hit the ball to him they might as well just go back to the dugout and sit down and not bother running to first base.

Once Hall of Famer Joe McGinnity was paid $500 to pitch for a semipro team against Monroe's Philadelphia Giants, and he bet the entire sum that he would win the game. After seven innings the game was still scoreless, and when Monroe came to bat, he aimed the bat at McGinnity, sighting down the bat like a rifle. McGinnity naturally took exception to this behavior and promptly knocked Monroe down with the next pitch. Monroe dusted himself off and again repeated his charade, with the same response from McGinnity. After the second knockdown pitch the two exchanged some words that ended with Monroe challenging,

"I'll bet you $500 that I hit a home run." The pitcher quickly called, "It's a bet." Behind in the count, McGinnity fired his fastball to the plate and Monroe smacked his offering for a home run that proved to be the game-winning hit. To cap off his performance for the pleasure of the crowd and the agitation of McGinnity, he ran the bases backward.

Monroe began his career in 1896, and for two years, 1899–90, he played with the Chicago Unions under manager W. S. Peters, starting at shortstop the former year and at second base the latter season. After leaving the Unions, he joined the Cuban X-Giants, the top team of the era, and hit in the third slot in the batting order. His next stop was with the Sol White's Philadelphia Giants in 1903, where he again batted third in the order, as the Giants challenged his former mates, the Cuban X-Giants, for the title but lost in the championship playoffs. However, Philadelphia prevailed during the next three seasons, winning championships each year (1904–06), with Monroe playing an integral part in the Giants' success while starting at three different infield positions (shortstop, third base, and second base) in consecutive years.

Signing with the Brooklyn Royal Giants in 1907, he quickly established himself as one of the top players. During this period of time the infield star's public acceptance extended to Cuba, where he accompanied Rube Foster, Peter Hill, and Home Run Johnson to the island to play ball in the 1907–08 winter season. Playing shortstop with Fe, he fielded well and posted a .333 batting average for the winter. Back in the United States, he played briefly with the Quaker Giants of New York before signing back on with the Brooklyn Royal Giants, quickly establishing himself as one of the top players and batting in the leadoff spot. Monroe helped the Royals capture two eastern championships in 1909–10 before leaving New York to journey westward.

Joining Rube Foster's great Chicago American Giants' ballclub in 1911, he batted in the cleanup spot behind Peter Hill. Monroe spent four years in Chicago, all with the American Giants except for part of the 1913 season, when he was with the Chicago Giants. By 1914 Foster had assembled what is considered to be one of the greatest black teams of all time, adding John Henry Lloyd to the already formidable lineup. Despite the talent-laden lineup, Monroe batted .348 and was called the "king of second basemen," "idol of all the ladies," and "the most sensational player on the American Giants' team." Foster's juggernaut easily won the western title and, with Monroe hitting fifth and Lloyd in front of him, swept the eastern champion Brooklyn Royal Giants in four straight games. Monroe's best game was in the third contest, when he had 4 hits to pace the offensive attack.

Monroe's untimely death the following season, 1915, brought a productive nineteen-year career to an abrupt end. Former managers Sol White, Rube Foster, and Dan McClellan were high in their praise for the star infielder, and New York Giants' manager John McGraw stated that Monroe was the greatest player of all time and would have been a star in the major leagues if he had been given the opportunity to play at that level. Reports persisted that McGraw wanted to sign the handsome, light-complexioned infielder and pass him as a Cuban.

Montalvo, Estaban
Career: 1923–28   Positions: rf, 1b, lf, p
Teams: Cuban Stars (West) ('23–'25, '27–'28),
New York Lincoln Giants ('27)
Died: 1930

The big, strong Cuban was a powerful hitter and, as the home-run king, was a major attraction during the '20s and batted in the cleanup spot for Tinti Molina's Cuban Stars. He once hit three homers against Rube Foster's Chicago American Giants, and also hit for a high average, posting batting averages of .337, .308, and .346 in 1923–25.

After starring for the Negro National League's Cuban Stars, he was enticed away by the New York Lincoln Giants in 1927, precipitating a big "war" between the East and West when he was signed. The Lincoln Giants even threatened to drop out of the Eastern Colored League rather than give up their slugging superstar and were suspended by the league. He played both in the outfield and at first base, and also took a few turns on the mound (with a 2–4 mark in 1925), but was not the sensation with the Lincolns that was expected. After a year in New York he returned to the Cuban Stars, but two years after his jumping caused such a furor, he was dead from tuberculosis.

Montgomery Grey Sox

Duration: 1932   Honors: None
Affiliation: NSL

The Grey Sox played primarily in the Negro Southern League, which was organized in 1926 and was considered a high minor league, except in 1932, the year after the demise of the Negro National League. That season, when the league served as a refuge for players from the Negro National League teams that had disbanded rather than pursue an independent schedule, the Negro Southern League was considered a major league and the Montgomery franchise fielded a major league team in 1932, finishing the first half of the season in the middle of the pack with a .564 winning percentage.

Montgomery, Lou

Career: 1942   Positions: p, of, if
Team: Ethiopian Clowns

A former college football star, this versatile athlete signed with the Ethiopian Clowns in 1942, playing as an outfielder, infielder, and pitcher.

Moody

Career: 1931   Position: ss
Team: Memphis Red Sox

In 1931 he was a shortstop with the Memphis Red Sox, when the team was between seasons as a recognized major-league team. Sandwiched around this year were two major-league seasons, one each in the Negro National League and the Negro Southern League.

Moody, Frank

Career: 1940   Position: p
Team: Birmingham Black Barons

He pitched with the Birmingham Black Barons in 1940, when the team reentered the Negro American League.

Moody, Lee

Career: 1944–47   Positions: 1b, of, 3b, ss
Teams: Kansas City Monarchs ('44–'47), Birmingham Black Barons ('46–'47), *minor leagues ('50), Canadian League ('51)*
Bats: Right   Throws: Right
Height: 6'0"   Weight: 190

He broke in with the Kansas City Monarchs as a wartime player, playing as an outfielder in 1944 but moving to first base the following season to plug a hole left when Buck O'Neill was called to military service. He adapted quickly, adding polish, and worked brilliantly with the infield unit. At the plate he was a steady batter, hitting .251 in his first year and raising his average to .325 in 1945, with a little power, before dropping back to .226 in 1946. But his strength was in his defensive play. He played two seasons in organized ball, batting .279 with Cairo in the Kitty League in 1950 and hitting a soft .242 with Three Rivers in the Provincial League in 1951.

Moody, Willis

Career: 1921–29   Position: of
Teams: *Pittsburgh Keystones ('21)*, Homestead Grays ('22–'26

After a season with the Pittsburgh Keystones he signed with the Homestead Grays, playing as a reserve outfielder.

Moore, Boots

Career: 1948   Position: p
Team: Birmingham Black Barons

A former football player from Grambling College, he vied for a position on the pitching staff with the Birmingham Black Barons in the spring of 1948.

Moore, Charles

Career: 1943   Position: umpire
League: NNL

In 1943 this arbiter was among the umpires working ball games in the Negro National League.

Moore, Excell

Career: 1950   Position: p

Teams: Cleveland Buckeyes ('50), *New Orleans Eagles ('51), Indianapolis Clowns ('52)*

A pitcher with the 1950 Cleveland Buckeyes, losing the 3 games he pitched while yielding a 10.13 ERA, he continued on into the fifties when the Negro American League was in decline and struggling to survive the loss of players to organized baseball.

Moore, Harry W. (Mike)

Career: 1894–1913   Positions: **of**, 1b, 3b, *2b, ss, p*

Teams: Chicago Unions ('94–'00), Chicago Union Giants ('01), Algona Brownies ('02–'03), Cuban X-Giants ('03–'04) Philadelphia Giants ('05–'06), Leland Giants ('06–'09), Chicago Giants ('10–'11, '13), St. Louis Giants ('11), New York Lincoln Giants ('12)

Bats: Right   Throws: Right

Born: Oct. 9, 1875, Detroit, Mich.

Died: July 1917, Chicago, Ill.

One of the top outfielders of his era, he began his baseball career with the Chicago Unions in 1894, five years after his parents moved to Chicago. Beginning as a left fielder, he remained with the Unions through the beginning of the new century, also playing at firstbase and trying his skills on the pitching mound for a couple of seasons before returning to the outfield for his last three seasons with the club. In 1901 owner Frank Leland consolidated the Unions and the Columbia Giants to form a single team called the Chicago Union Giants, with Moore playing second base. In 1902 he joined an exodus of ex-Chicago Union Giants who left Chicago for Iowa to play as the Algona Brownies. During his second season with the team (1903), with Moore splitting his time between center field and first base, the

Brownies won the western championship, but disbanded soon afterward.

New York City was the next stop for the star outfielder on his tour of the top teams of the era, as he journeyed East to play center field and bat cleanup for the Cuban X-Giants, who lost the playoff for the eastern title to the upstart Philadelphia Giants, with Rube Foster hurling for Philly. The next season, Moore took his glove and bat to the winning side, playing center field and batting in the fifth slot for the Philadelphia Giants as they successfully defended their title by taking the next two championships (1905–06).

In 1907, accompanying Giants' ace Rube Foster, Moore returned home to Chicago and was reunited with Frank Leland as the first baseman on the Leland Giants for three seasons. In the last of these years he hit .316, sixth-best in the Chicago City League, as the Lelands copped the 1909 pennant. The next season, Leland and Foster went their separate ways, each fielding their own team in 1910. Moore, considered to be in a class by himself as an outfielder, was described as "invincible and unequaled" and "one of the coveted prizes of the baseball flock." Remaining loyal to Leland, he signed with the Chicago Giants and, in addition to his superior fielding, he batted in the heart of the order, and at season's end, he was involved in a disputed batting title with Ben Taylor. That marked Moore's fifteenth consecutive year over the .300 mark. In 1911 Moore led the City League with a .341 batting average while also playing with the St. Louis Giants during the season. In 1912 he batted .315 with Rod and Jess McMahon's great aggregation of talent, the New York Lincoln Giants. He closed out his career in 1913 with the Chicago Giants.

A gentlemanly ballplayer, Moore's reputation was impeccable and he was widely respected and a highly popular player. In July 1917, within four years of his last ball game, he was in the last stages of consumption, and a charity baseball game between the Chicago American Giants and a combination of Chicago

Giants and Chicago Union Giants was arranged with all proceeds to go to him. Rube Foster and Pat Dougherty sold tickets for the contest and John Henry Lloyd and Pete Hill were the managers for the two squads. There was an overflow crowd. Shortly afterward the great ball hawk and all-around ballplayer was dead.

Moore, Henry L.

Career: 1937–38   Position: officer
Teams: St. Louis Stars, Birmingham Black Barons

During the late '30s he served as an officer with two Negro American League ballclubs, the St. Louis Stars and the Birmingham Black Barons.

Moore, James (Red)

Career: 1936–40   Position: 1b
Teams: *Chattanooga Choo Choos ('35), Mohawk Giants ('36)*, Atlanta Black Crackers ('35, '38), Newark Eagles ('36–'37, '40), Indianapolis ABCs ('39), Baltimore Elite Giants ('39–'40), *military service ('41–'45)*
Bats: Left   Throws: Left
Height: 5' 10"   Weight: 165
Born: Nov. 18, 1916, Atlanta, Ga.

A superb, fancy-fielding first baseman who added finesse to a team, he was expert at handling ground balls, a master at catching bad throws and making it look easy, and he excelled at making a 3–6–3 double play. Described as the "most perfect" first baseman ever, the slick fielder was quiet, unassuming, and practical. But the peerless fielder also liked to showboat at times and was a crowd favorite, frequently taking throws behind his back in pregame infield practice and making other trick catches to provide entertainment for the fans.

While outstanding in all defensive categories and regarded as one of the greatest defensive first basemen in the league during his short career, he was only mediocre in the offensive categories. At the plate he demonstrated only average consistency and power with the bat, and had difficulty hitting a sinker, although he homered off one of Ted Trent's super sinkers.

In contrast to his active footwork around first base, he was a heavy-footed base runner and, although he did not present a consistent base-stealing threat, he could pilfer a base when the game situation dictated it.

One of four children born to James Moore II, he developed an interest in baseball as a youngster, and he played ball at Booker T. Washington High School in Atlanta. In 1934 he began playing semipro ball with the Macon Peaches, and he started his professional career in 1935, playing with both the Negro Southern League's Chattanooga Choos Choos and the Atlanta Black Crackers. The following season he played with the Mohawk Giants of Schenectady, New York, before being grabbed by the Newark Eagles for the remainder of the 1936 season. In 1937 he was an adjunct member of the "million-dollar infield," often sending slugger Mule Suttles to an outfield position as he teamed with second baseman Dick Seay, shortstop Willie Wells, third baseman Ray Dandridge, and catcher Leon Ruffin to give the Eagles a gold glove man at each infield position. He also held his own at the plate, posting a .280 batting average for the season.

In 1938, when the Atlanta Black Crackers joined the Negro American League, he returned to his hometown as the regular first baseman for the Black Crackers and helped lead them to the second-half league championship. His contribution to the team's success did not go unnoticed, and the fans had a special day for him at Ponce de Leon Park, presenting the star first sacker with $350 worth of gifts and merchandise. Early in the spring he had been locked in a battle with Jim Canada for the starting first-base position, but Moore's superior fielding and improved hitting won the spot for him. Throughout his career Moore was injury-prone, and 1938 proved no exception as he injured his ankle sliding into second base in mid-June. Back in the lineup after a short loss of playing time, he was one of the earliest players to wear a batting glove, and by the end of July he was batting .331. At the end of the season he was selected to the Southern News

Service's Negro American League All-Star team.

In 1939 the Black Crackers relocated in Indianapolis and played as the ABCs, but Moore soon signed with the Baltimore Elite Giants. During his two years with the Elites he roomed with Roy Campanella, while batting .238 in 1940. In 1941 he entered military service for the duration of World War II, serving in England, Belgium, and France in a combat engineer battalion attached to General George Patton's Third Army.

After his discharge he never again played with a top ballclub. A quiet, retiring man who loved chicken dinners and had a minimum of words to say, he was well liked by fellow players. A smart ballplayer, his top salary was $650 a month, and he wanted to enter business after his baseball career was over. Leaving baseball in 1948, he returned to Atlanta and took a job with Colonial Warehouse, until retiring in 1981.

Moore, John (Johnny)
Career: 1928–29   Position: ss
Teams: *Pittsburgh Crawfords ('28),* Homestead Grays ('28), Birmingham Black Barons ('29)

This shortstop played with the Pittsburgh Crawfords when they were only a semipro team, years before they became a major-league-caliber ballclub, and was signed by the Homestead Grays in the fall of 1928, but moved to the Birmingham Black Barons in 1929.

Moore, L.
Career: 1910–20   Positions: rf. lf
Teams: West Baden Sprudels ('10), New York Lincoln Giants ('14), Louisville Sox ('15), Bowser's ABCs ('16), St. Louis Giants ('20)

He began his career as the regular left fielder for the Sprudels of West Baden, Indiana, in 1910 and was the regular right fielder and lead-off hitter for the St. Louis Giants in 1920, his last year with a quality team, but between these

years he spent most of his career as a reserve outfielder.

Moore, N.
Career: 1920–24   Position: of
Team: Detroit Stars

Beginning with the Detroit Stars in 1920, he shared a starting outfield position, playing center field and hitting in the sixth spot when in the lineup. He closed out his five-year career, spent entirely in Detroit, in 1924.

Moore, P. D.
Career: 1932   Position: c
Team: Monroe Monarchs

He was a catcher with the Monroe Monarchs in 1932, when the Negro Southern League was considered a major league.

Moore, Ralph (Roy, Squire, Square)
Career: 1921–28   Positions: p, of, 1b
Teams: Chicago American Giants ('20), Cleveland Tate Stars ('21–'22), Birmingham Black Barons ('23, '25), Memphis Red Sox ('23–'25), Kansas City Monarchs ('26), Cleveland Elites ('26), Cleveland Hornets ('27), Cleveland Tigers ('28)

He played with eight teams in an equal number of years, and most of his time was spent with the various Cleveland entries in the Negro National League during the '20s. While pitching with the Cleveland Elites in 1926, he lost both of his decisions, and with the Cleveland Hornets the next season he posted a mark of 1–3. He began his career in 1920 with the Chicago American Giants and also played with the Birmingham Black Barons, Memphis Red Sox, and Kansas City Monarchs, occasionally playing outfield and first base.

Moore, Roy
[see Moore, Ralph]

Moore, Shirley
Career: 1914–16   Position: p
Teams: Louisville White Sox ('14–'15), Bowser's ABCs ('16)

A steady pitcher with an assortment of good curves, beginning in 1914 he pitched for three seasons during the deadball era with the Louisville White Sox and Bowser's ABCs, both marginal teams.

Moore, Squire (Square)
[see Moore, Ralph]

Moore, Walter (Dobie)
Career: 1920–26 Positions: ss, of
Team: Kansas City Monarchs
Bats: Right Throws: Right
Height: 5' 11" Weight: 230
Born: 1893, Ga.
Died: Detroit, Mich.

A great shortstop, Dobie Moore was a superb fielder with outstanding range and a terrific arm. He could go in the hole, make a diving, backhand stab, stand up, and, flat-footed, throw the man out at first. An outstanding hitter, he hit for average and could also hit the long ball, with his best season coming in 1924, when he hit .453, led the league in doubles, and had 10 home runs and a .694 slugging percentage. The outspoken shortstop was not hesitant to offer criticism of teammates, and sometimes this practice caused resentment.

Moore was one of the players from the 25th Infantry team stationed at Fort Huachuca who were recommended to Monarchs' owner J. L. Wilkinson by Casey Stengel. After joining the Monarchs for the first Negro National League season, he stepped into the cleanup spot and posted respectable marks of .274 and .264 in their first two seasons. In 1922 he really came into his own, slapping the ball for a .385 batting average. During the next three years he led the Kansas City Monarchs to three consecutive pennants, with batting averages of .365, .453, and .325. In the 1924 World Series victory over Hilldale, he hit an even .300, second-best on the team, and in the following Series he led the team at the plate with a .364 average while leading the team in hits, runs batted in, and slugging percentage.

In 1926 he continued his hot hitting, getting off to a .381 start, but his brilliant career was cut short early in the season due to a shooting incident that disabled him while still in his prime. The incident was cloaked in an ''air of mystery'' as the parties involved told conflicting stories. The night began when Moore and three other ballplayers started out for a cabaret party in their honor, but he changed his mind and went to see Elsie Brown, who allegedly mistook him for a prowler in the alley and shot him. Later she claimed that Moore had hit her in the face three times before she shot him, but Moore responded that if he had hit her three times, she would not have been able to go get a gun. Other accounts indicated that Ms. Brown was his girlfriend and that she shot him in the brothel she owned following a lovers' quarrel. In an effort to escape, Moore jumped off a terrace and shattered the bones in his already wounded leg. Whatever the details regarding the cause of the shooting, Moore was shot in the leg, with the bullet breaking two bones into six pieces, which ended his baseball days.

With his career prematurely terminated, he left behind a lifetime .365 average for his seven seasons in the Negro Leagues. During the winters of 1920 and 1921 he played with the Los Angeles White Sox and the Colored All-Stars, respectively. In other winters he plied his trade in Cuba, where he smacked the ball for a .356 lifetime average.

Moorhead, Albert
Career: 1932 Position: c
Teams: *Chicago Giants ('25)*, Cleveland Cubs ('32), *Chicago Brown Bombers ('43)*

A reserve catcher, he appeared sporadically on the rosters of marginal teams for three decades, beginning in 1925 and concluding in 1943.

Morales
Career: 1932 Position: of
Team: Cuban Stars (East)

A reserve outfielder, he played briefly with the Cuban Stars in 1932.

Moran, Carlos (Chino)
Career: 1911   Position: of
Team: All Cubans ('11)
Bats: Left   Throws: Left
Born: Cuba

A great hitter and a fine base stealer, he was a center fielder with the All Cubans in 1911, his only season in the United States. He was a good contact hitter with a reputation for not striking out very much, but did not have much power, finishing his long Cuban career without a home run. But he was a star in his homeland, playing with Havana and Fe for 15 years (1900–1916) and registering a lifetime Cuban League batting average of .283. His best season averages were .394 in 1913, .336 in 1912, .308 in 1910–11, .304 in 1910, .301 in 1903, .318 in 1901, and .297 in 1906. He led the league in doubles in 1903, in runs scored (32) in 1912, and in games played in 1900, 1907, and 1910–11.

In the winter of 1910 he played right field for Havana against the Detroit Tigers, batting leadoff and hitting .333. On the down side, he was suspended from the league in 1902, but that did not detract from his career achievements, and he was elected to the Cuban Hall of Fame in 1945.

Moran, Francisco
Career: 1911–14   Positions: of, 3b
Teams: All Cubans ('11), Cuban Stars ('13–'14)

A steady player, this outfielder played with the All Cubans in 1911 and the Cuban Stars in 1913–14, and also played center field with Fe in Cuba in 1907.

Morehead, Albert
Career: 1943   Position: c
Teams: Birmingham Black Barons ('43), *Chicago Brown Bombers ('43)*

A wartime player, he was a catcher with the Birmingham Black Barons in 1943, also appearing with the Chicago Brown Bombers, a team of lesser status.

Moreland, Nathaniel (**Nate**)
Career: 1940–45   Position: p
Teams: Baltimore Elite Giants ('40–'45), Kansas City Monarchs ('45), Mexican League ('46), minor leagues *('47–'56)*
Bats: Right   Throws: Right

He began his Negro League career in 1940 with the Baltimore Elite Giants, logging a 2–4 record, and closed out his years in the league by splitting his playing time between the Elite Giants and the Kansas City Monarchs in 1945, losing his only decision. Between these two seasons, in the spring of 1943, the Elite Giants' right-hander, along with Chet Brewer and Howard Easterling, was promised a tryout with the Los Angeles Angels of the Pacific Coast League by the club president, Clarence "Pants" Rowland. However, the offer was revoked under pressure from officials of other ballclubs.

In 1946 he pitched with Monterrey in the Mexican League but managed only a 2–6 record despite a respectable 3.29 ERA. The next year Moreland began a decade in organized ball, pitching four years (1947–50) with El Centro in the Sunset League and recording seasons of 20–12, 17–15, 13–10, and 13–3. This was followed by five years (1951–55) with Mexicali, recording seasons of 14–13, 5–10, 20–13, 22–11, and 11–9. Mexicali was in the Southwest International League the first two years and in the Arizona-Texas League the last three years. His final season was in the same league, with Cananea in 1956, where he fashioned a 17–8 record and batted .326.

Throughout his career Moreland had been a good hitter, often playing outfield, first base, or pinch hitting. His other seasons above .300 were in 1950 (.325) and 1954 (.347)

Morgan
Career: 1928   Position: of
Team: Birmingham Black Barons

This outfielder played with the Birmingham Black Barons in 1928, his only season in black baseball.

Morgan, Connie
Career: 1954–55   Position: 2b
Team: *Indianapolis Clowns*
Bats: Right   Throws: Right
Height: 5' 4"   Weight: 140
Born: Oct. 17, 1935, Philadelphia, Pa.

A female player primarily utilized as a gate attraction, she played second base with the Clowns in 1954, replacing Toni Stone, another female player. At this time the Negro League was no longer a quality organization. Before signing with the Clowns at age nineteen, she played five years with the North Philadelphia Honey Drippers, an all-girl baseball team, and finished with a .368 batting average to show for her tenure with the team. An all-around athlete, she played basketball in the off-season. Prior to signing with the Clowns, she attended John Bartrum High School and William Penn Business School in her hometown.

Morgan, John L. (J. L.)
Career: 1937   Position: of
Teams: Memphis Red Sox ('37), Indianapolis Athletics ('37)

He was an outfielder with two teams, the Memphis Red Sox and the Indianapolis Athletics, in the Negro American League during the league's first year of existence.

Morgan, Slack
a.k.a. Sack
Career: 1938   Position: p
Team: Atlanta Black Crackers
Bats: Left   Throws: Left

A gangling left-handed fastball artist, he was added to the 1938 Atlanta Black Crackers' squad in late June but received very limited playing time. During World War II he was pitching with the Atlanta Black Crackers in 1943, but at that time the Black Crackers were not of major-league quality.

Morgan, William (Wild **Bill**, Slack, Sack)
Career: 1938–49   Position: p
Teams: Atlanta Black Crackers ('38–*'43*), Bal-

timore Elite Giants ('45), Memphis Red Sox ('48–'49), Birmingham Black Barons ('48)
Bats: Left   Throws: Left

A gangling left-handed fastball artist, he was added to the 1938 Atlanta Black Crackers' squad in late June but received very limited playing time. He pitched with the Black Crackers in 1943, but at that time they were not of major-league quality. He moved North to join the Baltimore Elite Giants in 1945 but lost his only decision. But in 1948, with the Memphis Red Sox, he split 4 decisions despite showing a 6.40 ERA. The following season was his last in the Negro Leagues.

Morin, Eugenio
a.k.a. Moran
Career: 1910–23   Positions: 3b, 2b, ss, c, 1b
Teams: Cuban Stars (West) ('10–'14, '21–'23)

One of the greatest infielders to come out of Cuba in the first two decades of the century, he played with the Cuban Stars (West) both when they were an independent team and after they joined the Negro National League. Beginning his career in black baseball in 1910, for five straight seasons he was the regular third baseman and hit in the second slot in the batting order for the Cuban Stars. After the Stars joined the Negro National League, he played for three more seasons, 1921–23, but most of his playing time was behind the plate.

Morney, Leroy
Career: 1931–44   Positions: **ss**, 3b, 2b, 1b, of, c
Teams: Monroe Monarchs (*'31*–'32), Homestead Grays ('33), Columbus Blue Birds ('33), Cleveland Giants ('33), Pittsburgh Crawfords ('34), Columbus Elites ('35), Washington Elite Giants ('36–'37), New York Black Yankees ('38), Philadelphia Stars ('39), Toledo Crawfords ('39), Chicago American Giants ('40), *Mexican League ('41)*, Birmingham Black Barons ('42–'44), Cincinnati Clowns ('43)
Bats: Both   Throws: Right

This bowlegged, versatile infielder was a

master at shortstop and could play second base and third base as well. In 1933 he played with three different teams during the course of the season and batted a combined .419, earning a trip to the inaugural East-West All-Star game. With superstar Willie Wells entrenched at shortstop, he was selected as the starting second baseman, and the duo turned the first All-Star double-play. He also cracked a base hit for the victorious West squad in the first of three All-Star appearances he would make during a 14-year career spent with almost as many teams. He represented the Cleveland Giants in 1933, and in his other two All-Star appearances he represented the Pittsburgh Crawfords and the Chicago American Giants in 1939 and 1940, respectively. In the last contest, the only losing All-Star game in which he appeared, he was the starting shortstop for the West squad.

After his first All-Star season he signed with the Pittsburgh Crawfords and was their regular shortstop, but his batting average dropped to .219. Leaving the Crawfords after one season, he joined the Columbus Elites in 1935, with incomplete statistics showing a .326 batting average, and relocated with the franchise in Washington in 1936–37, playing as a part-time starter. In 1938 he moved to the New York Black Yankees for a season as the regular shortstop, batting in the sixth slot.

The next year, Morney returned for his second stint with the Crawfords, who had moved to Toledo and changed leagues, playing in the Negro American League for the second half of the season. With the Crawfords he hit in the second slot in the batting order and split his playing time between shortstop and second base, as he did after moving to the Chicago American Giants the following year, while batting in the third slot.

In 1941 he jumped to the Mexican League, batting .236 with Monterrey. After only one season he returned to the United States, for the next stop in his baseball travels, Birmingham, where he batted cleanup, hitting .296, while playing third base and second base for the Black Barons in 1942. He spent most of the

next season as the regular shortstop with the Cincinnati Clowns, before returning to the Black Barons to close out his career in a reserve role, playing center field, first base, and second base while batting .237 in 1944.

Morris
Career: 1914　　　　　Position: 2b
Teams: *Indianapolis ABCs ('11)*, Mohawk Giants ('14)

He began his career with the Indianapolis ABCs in 1911, before they were a major-league-quality ballclub, and played one year with the Mohawk Giants in 1914, one of their top seasons.

Morris
Career: 1936　　　　　Position: p
Team: Newark Eagles
Bats: Right　　　　　Throws: Right

A light-complected right-handed pitcher, he pitched briefly with the Newark Eagles in 1936.

Morris
Career: 1938　　　　　Position: p
Team: Memphis Red Sox

He appeared as a pitcher with the champion 1938 Memphis Red Sox but did not pitch frequently.

Morris, Al
Career: 1930　　　　　Positions: of, 2b
Teams: Nashville Elite Giants ('27–'30), *Louisville White Sox ('30)*

This outfielder batted .250 in very limited play with the Nashville Elites Giants in 1930, the franchise's first year in the Negro National League. That marked his fourth season with the Elites, beginning in 1927, when the team was still playing in the Negro Southern League. He also played part of the 1930 season with the Louisville White Sox, who entered the Negro National League a year later. During his career he occasionally receiving playing time at second base.

Morris, Barney (Big Ad)
Career: 1932–48　　　　　Position: p
Teams: Monroe Monarchs ('32), New Orleans

Stars ('33), Cuban Stars, Pittsburgh Crawfords ('37–'38), Toledo Crawfords ('39), *Mexican League ('41)*, **New York Cubans** ('42–'48)
Bats: Right   Throws: Right
Height: 6'   Weight: 170
Born: 1915

Regarded as the best knuckleballer in the league, this veteran moundsman threw his knuckler as hard as a fastball. Unlike most pitchers who throw the butterfly ball, he could control the unruly pitch. He also had an excellent drop and a good curve and change-up. A strong pitcher, he was good in the clutch, and pitched in two East-West All-Star games. His first appearance was as a member of the Pittsburgh Crawfords in 1937, when he was the winning pitcher. Following a 7–3 season for the New York Cubans in 1944, he made his second All-Star appearance but dropped to a 1–3 ledger in 1945. Over the next two seasons he improved somewhat, with marks of 4–5 and 4–6 in 1946–47. The latter year he helped pitch the Cubans to the pennant and threw a shutout in his only start in the 1947 World Series as the Cubans defeated the Negro American League's Cleveland Buckeyes for the championship.

Earlier in his career he was credited with a 2–3 record in 1942, and also pitched in the Latin American Leagues, leading the Cuban winter league in wins with 13 in 1939–40 while with Cienfuegos. In 1941, with Monterrey in the Mexican League, he finished with an 11–16 ledger, a 4.86 ERA, and 105 strikeouts (fifth-highest in the league).

In 1934–35 he pitched with Neil Churchill's predominantly white ballclub in Bismarck, North Dakota and often doubled as a catcher for teammate Satchel Paige. Apart from his pitching accomplishments, he fielded his position adequately and was not a bad hitter for a pitcher, having a modicum of power, but he was not a very able base runner.

Morris, Harold (**Yellowhorse**)
Career: 1924–36   Positions: p, c
Teams: Kansas City Monarchs ('24, 36), De-

troit Stars ('25–'28), Chicago American Giants ('29–'30), Monroe Monarchs ('32)

He began and ended his Negro League career with the Kansas City Monarchs, posting a 6–5 regular-season mark in 1924, when the Monarchs captured the Negro National League pennant and won the first World Series over the Eastern Colored League's Hilldale ballclub. After leaving Kansas City he joined the Detroit Stars, where he enjoyed his best season in 1927, with a 14–8 record. With the Chicago American Giants in 1929–30 he fashioned records of 11–6 and 5–5.

Morrison, Jimmy
Career: 1930   Position: of
Team: Memphis Red Sox

He appeared briefly as a reserve outfielder in 1930 with the Memphis Red Sox, when they were in the Negro National League.

Morse
Career: 1917   Position: p
Team: Brooklyn Royal Giants

Pitching briefly with the Brooklyn Royal Giants in 1917, he lost his only decision.

Mortin, R.
Career: 1885   Position: p
Team: *Argyle Athletics*

A pitcher on the Argyle Hotel team in Babylon, New York, he was recruited by Frank P. Thompson to work at the hotel as a waiter and to play baseball for the entertainment of the summer guests in 1885. After the end of the tourist season the team added players and formed the Cuban Giants, the first black professional team.

Morton
Career: 1917   Position: 2b
Team: Havana Red Sox

In 1917 he played second base with the Havana Red Sox, a team of marginal quality.

Morton, Ferdinand Q.
Career: 1935–38   Position: executive
League: NNL

He served four years during the latter '30s as commissioner of the second Negro National League, spanning the last two years when it was the only league and the first two years after the formation of the rival Negro American League.

Morton, Sydney Douglas (**Sy, Cy**)
Career: 1940–48   Positions: 2b, ss, 3b
Teams: Philadelphia Stars ('40–'43), Newark Eagles ('44), Pittsburgh Crawfords ('46), Chicago American Giants ('47), *Canadian League ('51)*
Bats: Right   Throws: Right
Height: 5' 9"   Weight: 165
Born: 1920
Died: 1993, Philadelphia, Pa.

An infielder who could play any infield position, he was a shortstop for the Philadelphia Stars during the mid forties and was an average ballplayer in most facets of the game. A pretty good fielder with average speed, range, and arm, he was selected to play on the Negro National League All-Star team against the champion Homestead Grays in a 1943 postseason exhibition series between the two squads. That season he hit .202 as the regular second baseman, and the next year he changed teams and positions, starting at shortstop with the Newark Eagles. With both teams he batted in the eighth slot in the lineup, and was a light hitter with only average power. After leaving the Negro Leagues he played with Elmwood in the Provincial League in 1951.

Mosely, Beauregard F.
Career: 1910–11   Position: officer
Teams: Leland Giants ('10), Chicago American Giants ('11)

He was an officer with the Leland Giants in 1910, the first season that Rube Foster was in charge of the team, and the last season before changing the name of the team to the American Giants.

Mosely, C. D. (Gatewood)
a.k.a. Mosley

Career: 1935   Position: p
Teams: *New Orleans Crescent Stars ('34),* Homestead Grays ('35)

Joining the Homestead Grays in 1935 after a stint with the New Orleans Crescent Stars, he pitched briefly and without distinction.

Moses, Lefty
Career: 1938–40   Position: p
Team: Kansas City Monarchs
Bats: Left   Throws: Left:
Height: 5' 10"   Weight: 155

This lean left-hander had an adequate curve and change-up but lacked good velocity and control. He fashioned a 3–1 record in 1939, and the Monarchs won two pennants in the three seasons that he was on their pitching staff.

Mosley, C. D.
[see Mosely, C. D.]

Mosley, Lou
Career: 1932   Position: p
Teams: Atlantic City Bacharach Giants ('32), Cuban Stars ('32)

This pitcher appeared briefly with both the Bacharach Giants and the Cuban Stars in 1932.

Mosley, William
Career: 1928–33   Position: officer
Team: Detroit Stars

He was an officer with the Detroit Stars over a six-season span, ending with the Stars' last effort to maintain a team in the Negro National League.

Moss
Career: 1918   Position: p
Team: Chicago American Giants

He pitched briefly without a decision for the Chicago American Giants, who were weakened somewhat in 1918 by the World War I draft.

Moss, Porter
Career: 1936–44   Position: p

Teams: Cincinnati Tigers (*'34*–'37), **Memphis Red Sox** ('38–'44)
Bats: Right   Throws: Right
Height: 5' 11"   Weight: 185
Died: 1944

The Memphis Red Sox ace pitched in three East-West All-Star games without a decision. In 1936 the right-handed submariner fashioned a sterling 35–8 record for the Cincinnati Tigers preceding his first All-Star game appearance in 1937. The following year he was a pitcher with the 1938 Negro American League first-half champion Memphis Red Sox. After joining the Red Sox he also pitched in the 1942 and 1943 All-Star games and had seasonal records of 4–5 and 5–3. Still in his prime, Porter was fashioning another good season (8–6, 2.34 ERA) in 1944 when his career was tragically ended as he was fatally wounded in a shooting accident. After an argument over a dice game, a man fired a shot that hit Moss, who was an innocent bystander. The pitcher did not die immediately, but a doctor refused to treat him because he was black, and by the time he was taken to another town, it was too late to save him.

Mothel, Carroll Ray (**Dink**, Deke)
Career: 1920–34   Positions: of, 2b, 1b, 3b, ss, *c, p,* manager
Teams: *Topeka Giants ('18),* **Kansas City Monarchs** ('20, '23–'34), Chicago American Giants ('20), *semipro teams ('21–'22),* All Nations ('23), Cleveland Stars ('32)
Bats: Both   Throws: Right
Height: 6' 0"   Weight: 175
Born: Aug. 16, 1897, Topeka, Kan.

A versatile player of remarkable ability, he could play every position. In the outfield he had good range, deft hands, and a strong arm. At second base he also had a wide range and could go to his left or right with ease and was especially proficient at charging slowly hit balls and making a quick flip to first base to nip the runner, but he had much difficulty executing the pivot on double plays. An outstanding utility man, most of his fifteen-year career was spent with the Kansas City Monarchs, where he hit .268 batting in the sixth spot, while playing center field with the 1924 Negro National League pennant-winning team. Mothel played both outfield and first base as the Monarchs defeated Hilldale in the first world Series between the Negro National League and the Eastern Colored League. The next season he hit .294 while sharing the starting assignments at first base as the Monarchs repeated as Negro National League champions but lost the World Series to Hilldale in a repeat matchup.

In 1926 Mothel's versatility continued to manifest itself as he assumed the duties at second base, enabling Newt Allen to move to shortstop to fill the void left when Dobie Moore's career was ended in a shooting incident early in the spring. Not only did he handle the defensive requirements of the new position, but he also recorded a .301 batting average as the Monarchs won the first-half championship before losing to the Chicago American Giants in the playoff for the pennant. In 1927 he stepped into the cleanup spot left vacant by the loss of Moore and Christobal Torriente, and maintained a solid offensive performance with a .288 batting average, but the Monarchs failed to make the playoffs for the first time since 1922. Two years later he was back at first base and batting in the second slot, and registered averages of .247 and .266 in 1929–30.

Following the 1930 season the Monarchs disbanded for half a season, but when they reorganized at midseason of 1931 Mothel was their second sacker and leadoff batter. In 1932 he left the Monarchs for part of the season, playing first base and hitting in the third spot while serving as manager of the Cleveland Stars in the East-West League. When the league folded during the season, the ultimate utility man returned to Kansas City, where he added another starting position to his list, as the regular third baseman.

As a youngster he had been a cross-handed batter, and he joined Topeka Jack Johnson's Topeka Giants in 1914. In 1920 he had a tryout with the Kansas City Monarchs as a catcher, but he quit the Monarchs because he could make more money doing construction work. Later in the summer he signed with the Chicago American Giants, but as the third catcher on the squad, his playing time was very limited. After the 1920 season he played semipro ball for the next two seasons while working in a full-time job with the Santa Fe Railroad and did not play professionally again until 1923.

He began the year with the Monarchs but was sent to Wilkinson's All Nations team, which was serving as a farm team for the Monarchs. He was a good base runner and a hard competitor and was sometimes called a dirty ballplayer because of his aggressive baserunning. On one occasion, he spiked David Malarcher, putting him out of action for close to a month. He did almost anything to win, and he assisted Chet Brewer when he pitched by scuffing the ball with an emory board.

Throughout his career Mothel often played against major-leaguers, both in the California winter league and while barnstorming in the Midwest, where the opposition sometimes featured Joe Jackson, Buck Weaver, and other members of the infamous Chicago "Black Sox." In 1934 Mothel was still with the Monarchs when he closed out his career in the Negro Leagues.

Mouna
Career: 1930   Position: player
Team: Cuban Stars

In 1930 he was listed as a player with the Cuban Stars, but his position is uncertain.

Mullen, A.
Career: 1928   Position: of
Team: Birmingham Black Barons

He played outfield with the Birmingham Black Barons in 1928, his only year in the Negro Leagues.

Mullets
Career: 1914   Position: ss
Team: Mohawk Giants

A shortstop for the Mohawk Giants in 1914,

one of the team's stronger seasons, he lost some playing time due to injury.

Mungin, Sam
[see Mongin, Sam]

Mungin, J.
Career: 1925–27   Position: p
Teams: Baltimore Black Sox ('25–'26), Harrisburg Giants ('27)

During the '20s he pitched for three seasons, splitting a pair of decisions with the Baltimore Black Sox in his first season, 1925, and posting a 6–2 mark with Harrisburg in his last season, 1927.

Mungin, Sam
[see Mongin, Sam]

Muñoz, José (Joe, Joseito)
Career: 1904–16   Positions: **p**, lf, cf
Teams: All Cubans ('04–'05), Cuban Stars ('07–'10), Stars of Cuba ('10), Jersey City Cubans ('16), Long Branch Cubans ('16)
Bats: Right   Throws: Right
Born: Cuba

In his prime he was called "the premier pitcher of Cuba," and in 1910, while on the same pitching staff as José Mendez with the Stars of Cuba, he was regarded more highly than Mendez. He had a good fastball, a fierce screwball, and almost perfect control. When not on the mound he played outfield and batted in the second and fifth spots in the batting order for the Stars. With the Long Branch Cubans in 1916 he combined with Luis Padron to form a pair of aces for the New Jersey-based ballclub.

In his homeland he was the ace pitcher with Almendares and, except for one year with Havana, was with the same club throughout his Cuban baseball career. He tied for the Cuban League lead in wins in 1905 with 10 and finished on top alone in 1908, his best year, when he finished with a 13–1 record. In the winter of 1910–11 he posted a 5–1 ledger and, still pitching with Almendares, defeated Eddie

Plank and the Champion Philadelphia A's, 2–1. But the same winter, facing George Mullin, he lost his only start against the Detroit Tigers, 4–0, with Ty Cobb getting 3 hits, including a home run. Altogether he finished with a lifetime 81–57 record, giving him a .601 winning percentage for his fourteen years in the Cuban League. In recognition of his great career in baseball he was elected to the Cuban Hall of Fame in 1940.

Munro
Career: 1920   Position: 2b
Team: New York Lincoln Giants
He played briefly with the New York Lincoln Giants in 1920 but was not dependable defensively.

Murdock
Career: 1924   Position: p
Team: Indianapolis ABCs
In 1924, his only season in the Negro Leagues, he pitched briefly with the Indianapolis ABCs.

Murphy
Career: 1915   Positions: cf, lf
Team: Chicago American Giants
A reserve outfielder with the Chicago American Giants in 1915, he appeared in a few games in his only season under Rube Foster's management.

Murphy
Career: 1916–17   Position: p
Teams: Philadelphia Giants ('16), New York Lincoln Stars ('16), New York Lincoln Giants ('17)
After a year split between the Philadelphia Giants, a team in decline, and the Lincoln Stars, he lost all 3 decisions with the New York Lincoln Giants in 1917.

Murphy
Career: 1922   Position: p
Team: Kansas City Monarchs

He was a member of the Kansas City Monarchs' pitching staff in 1922.

Murphy
Career: 1930   Position: player
Team: Birmingham Black Barons
In 1930 he pinch hit in a game with the Birmingham Black Barons. His position is uncertain.

Murphy, Al
Career: 1936–37   Position: p
Teams: Cincinnati Tigers ('36), Indianapolis Athletics ('37), Birmingham Black Barons ('37)
A marginal pitcher, he played with the Cincinnati Tigers in 1936 and made appearances with two teams, the Indianapolis Athletics and the Birmingham Black Barons, in the Negro American League in 1937.

Murray
Career: 1943   Position: p
Team: Baltimore Elite Giants
A wartime player, this pitcher lost his only decision with the Baltimore Elite Giants in 1943.

Murray, Charles
Career: 1949–50   Position: c
Teams: Louisville Buckeyes ('49), Cleveland Buckeyes ('50)
He is listed with the Buckeyes 1949–50, when the Negro American League was struggling to survive the loss of players to organized baseball, but league statistics do not confirm his playing time.

Murray, Mitchell (Mitch)
Career: 1920–32   Position: c
Teams: Dayton Marcos (*'19*–'20), Indianapolis ABCs ('20, '31–'32), Cleveland Tate Stars ('22), Toledo Tigers ('23), **St. Louis Stars** ('23–'28), Chicago American Giants ('28–'30)
Bats: Right   Throws: Right
Height: 5' 9"   Weight: 170
A smart receiver, he was a good defensive

catcher with a fair arm and, although not a power hitter, he was dangerous in the clutch, batting cleanup in 1925 for the St. Louis Stars and hitting .317 and .284 in 1926–27, although being dropped to the lower half of the batting order. After leaving the Stars in 1928 he was a backup catcher with the Chicago American Giants until returning to the Indianapolis ABCs to close out his career where he had started his league play a dozen years earlier. Although his hitting had fallen off and he batted last in the order, he finished his career in 1931–32 as the regular catcher for the Indianapolis ABCs. Prior to joining the St. Louis Stars for the second half of the 1923 season, he had played as a backup catcher with the ABCs in 1920, and also played a reserve role with some struggling teams of marginal quality, including the Dayton Marcos, the Cleveland Tate Stars, and the Toledo Tigers.

Muse, B.

Career: 1922   Positions: **p**, ss, 2b
Teams: Hilldale Daisies ('22), *New Orleans Crescent Stars ('33), Monroe Monarchs ('34)*

Early in his career he was a pitcher with Hilldale, but a decade later, nearing the end of his career, he was a middle infielder with two southern teams of lesser quality, the New Orleans Crescent Stars and the Monroe Monarchs.

Myers, Lefty

Career: 1908–10   Positions: c, ss
Teams: *Pop Watkins Stars ('08)* Brooklyn Royals Giants, ('10)

Dating from the first decade of the century, as a left-handed catcher with the Brooklyn Royal Giants in 1908, he was a rarity.

N

Nance
Career: 1929   Position: ss
Team: Chicago American Giants

He appeared briefly as a reserve shortstop with the Chicago American Giants in 1929.

Napier, Euthumn (Eudie)
Career: 1941–50   Position: c
Teams: **Homestead Grays** ('46–'50), Pittsburgh Crawfords, *Canadian League ('51)*
Bats: Left   Throws: Right
Height: 5' 9"   Weight: 190
Born: Jan. 3, 1915, Baldwin County, Ga.

In 1946 he was Josh Gibson's backup during the great catcher's last season with the Homestead Grays, and assumed the starting role the following season, batting .286, and still shared the position when the Grays won the Negro National League's last pennant in 1948, batting .467 while alternating behind the plate. The stocky left-handed batter had long-ball capability, but his power production was nowhere near that of his predecessor, and Luke Easter was moved into Gibson's slot in the batting order, with Napier usually batting in the seventh spot. When the Grays disbanded at the end of the 1950 season he went to Canada for the 1951 season, batting .285 with Farnham in the Provincial League.

Napoleon, Lawrence (Larry, Lefty)
Career: 1946–47   Position: p
Team: Kansas City Monarchs

He was a pitcher with the Kansas City Monarchs for two post-World War II seasons, including their pennant-winning year of 1946.

Naranjo, Pedro
Career: 1950   Position: p
Teams: Indianapolis Clowns ('50–'51, *minor leagues ('50–'54)*
Bats: Left   Throws: Left
Height: 5' 10½"   Weight: 180
Born: 1932

This lefthander pitched with the Indianapolis Clowns briefly in 1950, appearing in only 3 games and losing his only decision. Both that season and the next were split between the Clowns and Brandon in the Mandak League, where he posted a composite 7–3 record. In 1952 he had his best season in organized ball, with a 13–10 record and a 2.33 ERA at Decatur in the Mississippi-Ohio Valley League. His last two seasons were each split between two teams in different leagues, with composite records of 5–14 in 1953 and 2–3 in 1954.

Nash, William
Career: 1928–34   Positions: p, of
Teams: Birmingham Black Barons ('28, '32), Memphis Red Sox ('29), Nashville Elite Giants ('32)

Over a seven year period he pitched without distinction for three southern teams.

Nashville Elite Giants

Duration: 1921–34   Honors: Second-half
champions ('32)
Affiliations: *Independent* *('21–'25)*, NSL
('26–'29, '32), NNL ('30, '33–'34)

Tom Wilson's team was organized in 1921 and played as an independent team until 1926, when the Negro Southern League was formed. In 1930 the Elites joined the Negro National League for the first of four seasons in the major leagues. The team fared poorly, finishing in last place for the first half and, although improving slightly in the second half, still managed only an aggregate .299 winning percentage for the season. In 1931 Wilson moved the club to Cleveland for part of the season, with the team playing in the Negro National League as the Cleveland Cubs.

The Negro National League folded after the season, and in 1932 the franchise was back in Nashville and back in the Negro Southern League, which was recognized as a major league that season. After a solid third-place first-half finish, the Elites won the second-half title and faced the Chicago American Giants in the league championship playoff, losing a seven-game Series, 4 games to 3. In 1933 Wilson helped organize the new Negro National League, and the Elites were members for the first two seasons, finishing in the middle of the pack. Their home field was Wilson Park, built by Tom Wilson and one of the two black-owned parks in the Negro Leagues. After the 1934 season Wilson moved his franchise to Columbus, Ohio, and subsequently to Washington and Baltimore, where the Elites played through the 1950 season.

Navarrete, Ramundo

Career: 1950   Position: p
Team: New York Cubans

In 1950 he posted a 1–2 record with a 3.52 ERA as a pitcher with the New York Cubans, at a time when the Negro American League was struggling to survive the loss of players to organized ball.

Navarro, Emilio (Millito)

a.k.a. Millito
Career: 1928–29   Positions: **ss**, 2b, 3b
Teams: Cuban Stars (East)
Bats: Right   Throws: Right
Height: 5' 5"   Weight: 160
Born: Sept. 26, 1905, Patillas, Puerto Rico

This little infielder had good hands and was considered an excellent hitter. In 1928 he was the regular shortstop and leadoff batter for the Cuban Stars in the Eastern Colored League, and the following season posted a .337 batting average but was suspended for part of the season, along with Ramon Bragana and Alejandro Oms, for not reporting to the ballclub as scheduled by the management. Ofttimes he was listed in the box scores only by his nickname, Millito. A star in his homeland, he was elected to the Puerto Rican Hall of Fame in 1992.

Navarro, Raymond **Raul**

Career: 1945–46   Positions: of, if, c
Teams: Cincinnati-Indianapolis Clowns ('45), Indianapolis Clowns ('46)
Bats: Right   Throws: Right
Height: 6' 2"   Weight: 178
Born: 1920, Havana, Cuba

A twenty-five-year-old Cuban bachelor when he joined the Clowns in 1945 after a season's professional experience in the Cuban winter league with the Havana Reds, he played as a catcher and outfielder in his first year, batting .212. In his second season with the Clowns he also played in the infield.

Neal

Career: 1938   Position: player
Team: Memphis Red Sox

He was with the Memphis Red Sox in 1938, when the team won the first-half Negro American League title.

Neal

Career: 1940   Position: p
Team: Homestead Grays

This pitcher appeared in a game without a decision for the Homestead Grays in 1940.

Neal, George
Career: 1910–11   Position: 2b
Teams: Kansas City, Kansas, Giants ('10), Chicago Giants ('11)

During the deadball era, this second baseman began his career in 1910 with the Kansas City, Kansas, Giants. The following season he played as a reserve for the Chicago Giants.

Nears, Red
Career: 1940   Positions: c, of
Team: Memphis Red Sox

A reserve catcher with the Memphis Red Sox in 1940, he could also play in the outfield.

Neely
Career: 1932–33   Position: p
Teams: Louisville Black Caps ('32), Cuban Stars (West) ('32–'33)

He pitched briefly in two seasons in the early '30s, beginning with the Louisville Black Caps in 1932 and closing with the Cuban Stars (West) a year later.

Neely, R. J.
Career: 1926   Position: c
Team: Chicago American Giants

A new backup catcher for the Chicago American Giants in 1926, he was their third-string receiver.

Nehf
Career: 1926   Position: ph
Team: Cleveland Elites

He singled as a pinch hitter for the Cleveland Elites in his only recorded appearance in the Negro Leagues.

Neil, Raymond (**Ray**)
a.k.a. Aussa
Career: 1942–50   Position: 2b, ss
Teams: Ethiopian Clowns ('42), Cincinnati Clowns ('43), **Indianapolis Clowns** ('46–'*54*)
Bats: Right   Throws: Right
Height: 5' 9"   Weight: 165

A strong-armed second baseman with the Clowns during the '40s, he had good power

and batted in the third slot. He hit for averages of .241, .272, .369, and .291 in 1946–50, exclusive of 1947. During his last seasons with the ballclub he became very good friends with Mamie Johnson, a female pitcher with the Clowns. He also played winter ball with the Kansas City Royals in 1946.

Nelson
Career: 1908   Position: 2b
Team: Genuine Cuban Giants

In 1908 he was a second baseman with the Genuine Cuban Giants, one of the various Cuban Giants ballclubs that flourished during the early years of the century. Several of these ballclubs, copying the success of the Cuban Giants (the first and most successful black professional team), appropriated a variation of the Cuban Giants name as their own and played a quality of baseball close to that of the original team.

Nelson
Career: 1924   Position: 2b
Team: St. Louis Stars

He was a reserve second baseman with the St. Louis Stars in 1924, his only year in black baseball.

Nelson, Clyde
Career: 1939–49   Positions: 3b, 2b, 1b, of
Teams: Indianapolis ABCs (1939), *Chicago Brown Bombers ('43)*, **Chicago American Giants** ('44–'46), Cleveland Buckeyes ('47–'48), Indianapolis Clowns ('49)
Bats: Right   Throws: Right
Born: 1921
Died: July 25, 1949, Philadelphia, Pa.

For three years, 1944–46, he was in the starting lineup for the Chicago American Giants, usually batting in the fifth slot. The first season he split his playing time between the infield corners before finding a home at the hot corner in the latter two seasons. The first two seasons with the Chicago American Giants he hit .231 and .273, but in 1946 he led the Negro American League in hits with 88 while hitting .327, third-highest in the league.

The next year he was the regular left fielder and cleanup hitter, batting .333, for the Negro American League champion Cleveland Buckeyes. However, in the ensuing World Series the Buckeyes lost to the New York Cubans. In 1948 Nelson moved back to the infield, playing both third base and second base, while hitting .310 for the Buckeyes. The following season he closed his career, with the Indianapolis Clowns. In 1946 he played winter ball with the Kansas City Royals.

Nelson, Everett (Ace)
Career: 1922, 1931–33 Position: p
Teams: Montgomery Grey Sox ('32), Detroit Stars ('22, '33)

He was a pitcher with the Detroit Stars and the Montgomery Grey Sox during the early '30s, losing his only recorded decision in 1933, his last year in the Negro Leagues.

Nelson, John
Career: 1887–1903   Positions: p, of, *ss*
Teams: New York Gorhams ('87–'89), Cuban Giants ('89–94), Adrian Page Fence Giants ('95), **Cuban X-Giants** ('96–02), Philadelphia Giants ('02–'03)

He was one of the first black professional ballplayers, playing both as a pitcher and outfielder for seventeen years, mostly with the Cuban Giants and Cuban X-Giants, for whom he pitched for seven years (1896–1902). Several years of his career was spent playing in predominantly white leagues, as the Cuban Giants often played as representatives of a host city in that city's regular league. They represented Trenton, New Jersey (in 1889), and York, Pennsylvania (in 1890), in the Middle States League, and Ansonia in the Connecticut State League (in 1891). The New York Gorhams did the same, representing Philadelphia in the Middle States League in 1889 while Nelson was with the team.

Sandwiched between his years with the Cuban Giants and the Cuban X-Giants was the 1895 season with the Page Fence Giants of Adrian, Michigan, where records show a batting average of .125 in only 2 games played. After leaving the X-Giants he played with Sol White's Philadelphia Giants for two years to close out his career, in 1903.

Nesbit, E. E., Dr.
Career: 1929   Position: officer
Team: Memphis Red Sox

He served as an officer for Dr. J. B. Martin's Memphis Red Sox in 1929.

Nestor, S. (Jace)
Career: 1926   Position: of
Team: New York Lincoln Giants

He appeared briefly as an outfielder with the 1926 Lincoln Giants.

New Orleans–St. Louis Stars
Duration: 1940–41   Honors: None
Affiliations: Independent ('40), NAL ('41)

In 1939 the Indianapolis franchise moved to St. Louis in an effort to revitalize black baseball in the city, but financial difficulties necessitated a change, and New Orleans and St. Louis served as cohome cities for the franchise that had previously been playing out of St. Louis exclusively. In 1941 the team joined the Negro American League, but after a season the franchise folded.

New York Black Yankees
Duration: 1932–50   Honors: None
Affiliations: Independent ('32–'35, '49–'50), NNL ('36–48)

The New York Black Yankees' franchise was basically an extension of the New York Lincoln Giants, filling a void created when the Lincoln Giants folded operations after the 1930 season. In 1931 John Henry Lloyd managed an interim New York team, the Harlem Stars, which served as a bridge between the two long-time franchises. In 1932 the New York Black Yankees began operation, with George Scales installed as manager. In 1936 the Black Yankees entered the Negro National League for the second half, finishing with an 8–7 league ledger, and for the next dozen seasons (1937–48) the Black Yankees fielded a team in the Negro National League. But rather than dominating their league, as did their white counterparts (the New York Yankees), they were the doormats of the Negro National League, usually finishing in the cellar and never higher than fifth in a six-team league.

New York Cubans

Duration: 1935–50   Honors: Second-half champions ('35, '41), World Series champions ('47)

Affiliations: NNL ('35–'36, '39–'48), NAL ('49–'50)

A resurrection of owner Alex Pompez's Cuban Stars from earlier years, the Cubans played in the Negro National League from 1935 to 1950 except for two seasons (1937–38). Playing their home games in the Polo Grounds, they fielded a strong ballclub in 1935, winning the second-half title, but lost the league championship playoffs to the powerful Pittsburgh Crawfords, 4 games to 3. After a losing season in 1936, the Cubans did not field a team for two seasons, but rejoined the Negro National League in 1939, and two years later again captured the second-half title, but lost to the Homestead Grays in the league championship playoffs, 3 games to 1. Finally, in 1947, the Cubans copped a pennant, and then captured the championship by defeating the Negro American League's Cleveland Buckeyes in the ensuing World Series. After the Negro National League folded following the 1948 season, the Cubans joined the Eastern Division of the Negro American League.

New York Gorhams

Duration: 1887–91   Honors: Eastern champions ('87, '89)

Affiliation: Independent

One of the earliest professional black teams, for a brief spell the New York Gorhams were one of the leading teams in the East during the late 1880s, and the team was recruited to represent Philadelphia in the Middle States League in 1889.

New York Lincoln Giants

[see Lincoln Giants]

New York Lincoln Stars

[see Lincoln Stars]

Newark Browns

Duration: 1932   Honors: None

Affiliation: EWL ('32)

In 1932 the franchise fielded a team, under the management of John Beckwith, in the East-West League.

Newark Dodgers

Duration: 1933–35   Honors: None

Affiliation: Independent ('33), NNL ('34–'35)

The team was organized in the fall of 1933 and entered the Negro National League for two losing seasons, 1934 and 1935, ending in the cellar the latter year. After that inauspicious finish, Abe Manley bought the franchise and consolidated it with the Brooklyn Eagles to produce the Newark Eagles.

Newark Eagles

Duration: 1936–48   Honors: World Series champions ('46), NNL first-half champions ('47)

Affiliation: NNL

Abe Manley acquired ownership of two floundering teams, the Brooklyn Eagles and the Newark Dodgers, and consolidated the two franchises into the Newark Eagles. The Eagles joined the Negro National League in 1936 and remained a highly competitive team until the league's demise in 1948. The highlight of the franchise's history was in 1946, when they won the Negro National League pennant and defeated the Kansas City Monarchs in a hard-fought 7-game World Series. The next season they again started strong, winning the first-half title, but lost Larry Doby to organized baseball and slumped in the second half, losing the pennant to the New York Cubans without a play-off. After the league folded in 1948, the Eagles were sold and moved to Houston.

Newark Stars

Duration: 1926   Honors: None
Affiliation: ECL ('26)

In 1926 the Newark Stars fielded a team in the Eastern Colored League but did not finish the season, disbanding in midyear with only a single victory.

Newberry, Henry

Career: 1947   Position: p
Team: Chicago American Giants

He pitched with the Chicago American Giants in 1947, his only season in the Negro Leagues.

Newberry, James (**Jimmy**)

Career: 1942–50   Position: p
Teams: Birmingham Black Barons ('42–'50), *minor leagues ('50–'51, '53–'56), Japanese League ('52)*
Bats: Both   Throws: Right
Height: 5'7"   Weight: 170
Born: 1922 Birmingham, Ala.

This rubber-armed curveball artist's favorite pitch was a straight overhand drop that he called his "dipsy doodle." He also had a good but not exceptional fastball, which was utilized primarily to keep batters off balance and set up his curve. The Birmingham Black Barons' ace notched a 14–5 record for the 1948 Negro American League champions, and led the league in victories, was tied with Sam Jones for the lead in strikeouts, and compiled a 2.18 ERA. In the World Series loss to the Homestead Grays, he pitched in 3 games, losing his only decision.

Although he really came into his own in 1948, he was also a member of the Black Barons' pitching staff in 1943–44, when they won their earlier pennants. Newberry was a favorite of Abe Saperstein, who handled the business affairs of the Black Barons, and could always

count on an advance from Saperstein when he needed money. Throughout his career he was a top-notch pitcher when not encumbered by residual influences from his late-night drinking, a condition that prompted manager Piper Davis to keep him apart from young Willie Mays after ball games.

The right-hander learned his craft on the sandlots of his hometown, beginning his career with the L&N Stars of Birmingham prior to joining the Black Barons. Records from early in his career show league marks of 1–3, 4–5 (3.22 ERA), 5–3 (3.06 ERA), and 11–6 for the 1943–46 seasons. He began the 1950 season with Birmingham and had a 4–1 record before leaving for Winnipeg, Canada, in the Mandak League, where he split 14 decisions.

In 1952 he shifted his base of operations from Canada to Japan, where he pitched for the Hankyu Braves, fashioning an 11–10 record with a 3.22 ERA. Exiting the Orient after a single season, he returned to the Mandak League with Carman but dropped to a 5–10 record. The next three seasons were spent with five different teams in the Soutwest in four different leagues: Abilene (2–6), Amarillo (0–3), Big Springs (1–4), Port Arthur (6–4, and El Paso (0–1), but without significant success at any of his stops.

Newberry, Richard

Career: 1947   Positions: ss, 2b
Teams: Chicago American Giants ('47), *minor leagues ('51–'54)*
Bats: Right   Throws: Right
Height: 5'8"   Weight: 165
Born: 1926

This infielder began his career as a shortstop with the Chicago American Giants in 1947, the same year that Jackie Robinson broke the major-league color barrier. When the doors of organized baseball were opened, Newberry played four seasons, 1951–54, as a second baseman with Duluth in the Northern League, where he demonstrated good speed and power while batting .289, .307, .326, and .330.

Newcombe, Donald (**Don**, Newk)
Career: 1944–45   Position: p
Teams: Newark Eagles ('44–'45), *minor leagues ('46–'49, '61),* **major leagues** ('49–'51, '54–'60), *military service ('52–'53), Japanese League ('62)*
Bats: Left   Throws: Right
Height: 6'4"   Weight: 220
Born: June 14, 1926, Madison, N.J.

As a nineteen-year-old fastball pitcher for the Newark Eagles, Don registered an 8–3 record in 1945. A left-handed swinger, the big youngster was often used as a pinch hitter. The previous year, in his first season in the Negro Leagues, he was winless against 3 losses, but his progress and raw talent were noted by the Brooklyn Dodger organization.

Later signed by Brooklyn, he enjoyed a great ten-year major-league career, including pennants with the Dodgers in 1949, 1955, and 1956. After registering seasons of exactly 20 wins in 1951 and 1955, his best year was 1956, when his 27–7 record earned him both the Cy Young Award and the National League's MVP honor. The big right-hander finished his major-league career with a 149–90 record and a 3.56 ERA.

After first signing with the Dodger organization, he played two seasons in the New England League with Nashua, and fashioned seasons of 14–4 and 19–6, batting .311 with power in his first season and leading the league in victories his second season. After a 17–6 record at Montreal in the International League sandwiched between two winters in Vargas, Venezuela (10–3) and Maranao, Cuba (1–6), he earned his first trip to the parent club, registering a 17–8 season after joining the Dodgers in 1949. Two more outstanding seasons (19–11 and 20–9) preceded his loss of two prime seasons to military service, after which he returned to form, with a 20–5 record in 1955 preparatory to his sensational MVP season in 1956.

In the aftermath of his career season, his effectiveness dissipated as he pitched successively with the transplanted Dodgers in Los Angeles, the Cincinnati Reds, and the Cleveland Indians before dropping out of the major leagues after the 1960 season. In 1961 he pitched with Spokane in the Pacific Coast League, barely breaking .500 with a 9–8 record. In 1962 he closed out his professional baseball career as an outfielder-first baseman, hammering 12 home runs and batting .262 with the Chunichi Dragons in Japan.

Newkirk, Alexander (**Alex**)
Career: 1946–49   Position: p
Teams: New York Black Yankees ('46–'49), New York Cubans ('49), *Canadian League ('50–'51)*
Bats: Left   Throws: Right
Height: 5'10"   Weight: 175

A pitcher of moderate skills and effectiveness, he included a fastball, curve, slider, change, and drop in his repertoire, but none of his pitches was exceptional. He was not a power pitcher and had only average control. The right-hander began his career with the New York Black Yankees in 1946, logging 4–8 and 2–9 records with this weak ballclub. After moving to the New York Cubans he improved his record to 5–2 in 1949.

The next two seasons were spent in the Provincial League, where he had records of 3–2 with St. Jean and 7–12 with St. Jean and Granby. Although not considered a good hitter, he batted .313 and .290 with the Black Yankees and .318 and .356 in the Provincial League, but with little power.

Newman
Career: 1909   Position: p
Team: Leland Giants

He was listed as a pitcher with the Leland Giants during the last season before Rube Foster and Frank Leland split up.

Newman
Career: 1940   Position: p
Team: Memphis Red Sox

He was a pitcher with the Memphis Red Sox

in 1940, his only appearance in the Negro Leagues.

Newman
Career: 1926   Position: ss
Team: Cleveland Elites

He was a shortstop for the 1926 Cleveland Elites and batted sixth in the batting order.

Newsome, Omer
Career: 1923–29   Positions: **p**, 1b
Teams: Indianapolis ABCs ('23–'25), Washington Potomacs ('24), Wilmington Potomacs ('25), Detroit Stars ('25–'26), Dayton Marcos ('26), *Philadelphia Colored Giants of New York ('28)*, Memphis Red Sox ('29)
Bats: Right   Throws: Right

He was a hard thrower but did not change speeds effectively, so the batters could time his pitches and consequently his pitching ability was compromised. He was with the 1924 Washington Potomacs but was released after about a month for more seasoning. He split the 1926 season between the Detroit Stars and the Dayton Marcos, with a 1–2 mound record while also making an appearance at first base for the Marcos, batting .364 in only 11 recorded at-bats. However, this average may be deceptive, as he hit only .100 with the Potomacs in 1924. He began his pitching career in 1923 with the Indianapolis ABCs; prior to that time he had been incarcerated in a penitentiary. Seven seasons later he closed out his career with the Memphis Red Sox, losing his only decision.

Newson
Career: 1940   Position: of
Team: Newark Eagles

This reserve outfielder appeared in a game with the Newark Eagles in 1940.

Nicholas, William
[see Nichols, William]

Nichols, Charles
Career: 1885   Position: of
Team: *Argyle Hotel Athletics*

He was an outfielder with the Argyle Hotel ballclub that evolved into the Cuban Giants, the first black professional team.

Nichols, William
a.k.a. Nicholson; Nicholas
Career: 1936   Position: p
Team: Newark Eagles

Appearing as a pitcher with the Newark Eagles in 1936, the first year of the franchise's existence, he did not figure in a decision.

Nicholson, William
[see Nichols, William]

Nirsa
Career: Position: of
Team: Cuban Stars (West)

He was a reserve outfielder with the Cuban Stars (West) in 1923.

Nix, Nathaniel (Tank)
Career: 1939   Position: p
Team: Brooklyn Royal Giants

He was a pitcher with the Brooklyn Royal Giants in 1939, when the team was playing as an independent ballclub.

Nixon
Career: 1940–41   Position: of
Team: Birmingham Black Barons

In 1940 he was the starting right fielder with the Birmingham Black Barons, batting fifth, but in 1941 he was relegated to part-time status.

Noble, Carlos
Career: 1950   Position: p
Team: New York Cubans
Bats: Right   Throws: Right

He was a right-handed pitcher with the New York Cubans in 1950, when the Negro American League was struggling to survive the loss of players to organized baseball. He fashioned a 2–3 record with a 4.62 ERA.

Noble, Juan (John, Gyp)
Career: 1949–50   Position: p

Team: New York Cubans

He was a pitcher with the New York Cubans for two seasons, 1949–50, when the Negro American League was struggling to survive the loss of players to organized baseball.

Noble, Rafael Miguel (Ray)
a.k.a. Sam Nobles
Career: 1945–50   Position: c
Teams: New York Cubans ('45–'50), *minor leagues ('49–'50, '52–'61)*, major leagues ('51–'53)
Bats: Right   Throws: Right
Height: 5'10"   Weight: 215
Born: Mar. 19, 1920, Contramaestre, Cuba

He came to the United States in 1945, at the age of twenty-five, beginning his career with the New York Cubans as a catcher. He was a good receiver and had a rifle arm. A solid hitter with power, he batted .325 with the Cubans in 1947, their championship season, as they won the World Series after capturing the Negro National League flag.

Before joining the Cubans he played with the Santiago Cuba Mines, where he hit over .300 every year, and he came to the Cubans highly recommended by the team. His contract was sold to the New York Giants' organization, and after stays at Jersey City in the International League (.259 batting average in 1949) and Oakland in the Pacific Coast League (.316 and 15 home runs in 1950), he joined the New York Giants in 1951 and was with them for part of the next two seasons (1952–53), ending with a .218 lifetime average for his three years with them. He split each of the last two seasons with AAA teams, hitting .298 with Oakland in 1952 and .306 with Minneapolis of the American Association in 1953. He played the last eight years of his baseball playing career at the AAA level, with Havana (.286 and .253), Columbus (.230), Buffalo (.251 and .269), and Houston (.294, .274, and .250), ending his career in 1961 with only 4 at-bats for the year. His best power seasons were with Buffalo, when he hit 21 and 20 home runs in the 1957–58 seasons.

In Cuba he forged a lifetime batting average of .258 for ten years. With the exception of his first year, when he played 3 games with Havana in the 1942–43 winter, he played with Cienfuegos and hit .267, .292, .254, .233, .269, .321, .258, .281, and .255 for the winter seasons of 1946–55. His highest batting average was in the winter of 1951–52, when he hit .321, and his best power season was 1953–54, when he hit 10 in 203 at-bats.

Nobles, Sam
[see Noble, Rafael Miguel (Ray)]

Noel, Eddie
Career: 1921   Position: p
Team: *Nashville Elite Giants*

He was a pitcher with the Nashville Elite Giants in 1921, the first year in the franchise's history, when the Elites were still playing as an independent team.

Nolan
Career: 1916–20   Positions: c, 1b
Teams: St. Louis Giants ('16), Kansas City Colored Giants ('17), Kansas City Monarchs ('20)

He was one of three reserve catchers who appeared as a backup to regular receiver Dan Kennard with the St. Louis Giants in 1916. Nolan played with the Kansas City Colored Giants the following season, while the St. Louis aggregation disbanded in the spring of 1917. In 1920 he appeared briefly with the Kansas City Monarchs as a first baseman.

Norman, Alton
Career: 1920–26   Position: ss
Teams: New York Lincoln Giants ('20), Cleveland Elites ('26)

He was a shortstop for the 1920 New York Lincoln Giants and was erratic afield, mixing showboating with shoddy fielding. In addition to his "wobbly" defensive work he was also weak at the plate, as evidenced by his .067 average in very restricted play for the Dayton Marcos in 1926.

Norman, Bud (Ace)
Career: 1940   Position: p
Team: Indianapolis Crawfords

He was a pitcher with the Indianapolis Crawfords in 1940, the last season for the Crawfords' franchise.

Norman, Garrett
Career: 1923–24, 1933 Position: of
Teams: Memphis Red Sox ('23–'24), Kansas City Monarchs ('33)

This outfielder began his career in 1923, and he remained with the club when they joined the Negro National League the following year. He appeared again in 1933, with the Kansas City Monarchs, when they were playing as an independent team.

Norman, Jim
Career: 1909   Positions: 3b, 2b
Team: Kansas City, Kansas, Giants

A good hitter, he was an infielder with the Kansas City, Kansas, Giants in 1909, his only year with a team above a marginal level of play. Originally a second baseman, he moved to third base when Bingo DeMoss joined the team.

Norman, William (**Billy,** Shin)
[see Hardy, Arthur (Bill)]

Norris, Slim
Career: 1930   Position: 3b
Team: *Louisville White Sox*

He was a third baseman with the Louisville White Sox in 1930, a year before the Sox entered league play.

North, L.
Career: 1922–23   Position: of
Team: *Richmond Giants*

He was an outfielder with the Richmond Giants, a team of lesser status.

Norton
Career: 1942   Position: player
Team: New York Cubans

He appeared in a game, without an at-bat, with the New York Cubans in 1942. His position is uncertain.

Norwood, C. H.
Career: 1887   Position: player
Team: *Philadelphia Pythians*

He was a player with the Philadelphia Pythians, one of eight teams that were charter members of the League of Colored Baseball Clubs in 1887. However, the league's existence was ephemeral, lasting only a week.

Norwood, Walter
Career: 1933   Position: officer
Team: Detroit Stars

He was an officer with the Detroit Stars in 1933, the last year for the franchise in the Negro National League.

Nunley, Beauford
Career: 1934   Position: 1b
Team: *Memphis Red Sox*

He was a first baseman with the Memphis Red Sox in 1934, when the Red Sox were not in the major leagues.

Nuttall, H. (Bill)
Career: 1924–26   Position: p
Teams: Bacharach Giants ('24–'25), New York Lincoln Giants ('25–'26)

This youngster was a fairly good pitcher with the 1924 Bacharachs in his first year in the Eastern Colored League, and registered a 2–5 ledger in 1925, but was not a very good hitter, batting only .118.

Nutter, Isaac H.
Career: 1927–28   Position: officer
Team: Bacharach Giants

He was president of the Bacharach Giants during their last two years in the Eastern Colored League, including their pennant-winning 1927 season, and also served as the league president.

O

Obie
[see Layton, Obie]

O'Bryan, Willie
a.k.a. O'Bryant
Career: 1932   Positions: ss, of
Team: Washington Pilots
While sharing playing time in left field, he often batted in the leadoff spot with Washington manager Frank Warfield's East-West League entry.

O'Dell, John Wesley
Career: 1950   Position: p
Team: Houston Eagles
He pitched one season with the Eagles after they had relocated in Houston and entered the Negro American League.

Oden, Johnny Webb
a.k.a. Odom; Odum
Career: 1927–32   Positions: **3b**, ss, of
Teams: Birmingham Black Barons ('27–'29), Memphis Red Sox ('27, '29, *Knoxville Giants, Louisville Black Caps ('32)
A light-hitting infielder, he batted in the eighth slot when in the lineup at third base for the 1927 Birmingham Black Barons, winners of the second-half Negro National League title. While splitting the season between the Black Barons and the Memphis Red Sox, he batted .193, and in 1929, again splitting the season between the same two teams, he hit .213.

O'Farrell, Orlando
Career: 1949   Positions: of, ss
Teams: Indianapolis Clowns ('49), Philadelphia Stars ('49), *Baltimore Elite Giants ('51)*
A versatile player but light hitter, he split his first season in the Negro Leagues between the Clowns and the Philadelphia Stars, and later played with the Baltimore Elite when the league was in decline.

Offert, Mose
Career: 1925–26   Position: p
Team: Indianapolis ABCs
He pitched with the Indianapolis ABCs during the franchise's last two years of existence.

O'Kelley, Willie James (Stretch)
Career: 1949   Position: 1b
Team: Cleveland Buckeyes
Born: Mar. 25, 1920, Atlanta, Ga.
Died: June 9, 1991, Atlanta, Ga.
A very speedy, slick-fielding first baseman with an abundance of confidence, this Atlanta native played most of his career with the Atlanta Black Crackers, but spent one season in the Negro American League, in 1949 with the Cleveland Buckeyes. He quit school after seventh grade and played sandlot ball around Atlanta before signing with the Black Crackers

in 1946. After his season with the Buckeyes, he played the Cleveland Barons, a lesser team, in 1951–52. Ironically, his only son died of a heart attack only a few days before O'Kelley passed away in 1991.

Oldham, Jimmy
Career: 1920–23　　Position: p
Teams: St. Louis Giants ('20–'21), St. Louis Stars ('22–'23)

Beginning his career as a pitcher with the St. Louis Giants in the first year of the Negro National League, he fashioned an 11–3 record in 1921, and he remained with the team when they became the St. Louis Stars in 1922.

Oliver, James (Pee Wee)
a.k.a. Selassie
Career: 1943–46　　Position: ss
Teams: Birmingham Black Barons, Cincinnati Clowns ('43), Cincinnati-Indianapolis Clowns ('44), Indianapolis Clowns ('45–'46)

Regarded as both a good fielder and good hitter, he was a reserve shortstop for the Clowns in 1943 and was known as Selassie at that time. A player using the same name, Selassie, was the regular shortstop with the Ethiopian Clowns for the preceding five years, but since sometimes different players used the same "Clown name," it is not certain that this was Oliver. The remainder of his career was as a substitute infielder. His son, Nate Oliver, later played in the major leagues with the Los Angeles Dodgers.

Oliver, John
Career: 1885　　Position: 3b
Team: *Brooklyn Remsens*

In 1885 he was a third baseman with the Brooklyn Remsens, one of the first black teams.

Oliver, John Henry
Career: 1945–46　　Positions: ss, 2b
Teams: Memphis Red Sox ('45), Cleveland Buckeyes ('46)

This middle infielder was a reserve player for two years in the Negro American League, beginning his career during the last season of World War II, when he hit .261 with the Memphis Red Sox, playing primarily at second base, and closing it in 1946 as a reserve shortstop with the Cleveland Buckeyes.

Oliver, Leonard
Career: 1913　　Position: ss
Team: Philadelphia Giants

He was a shortstop with the Philadelphia Giants when this once-proud team was in decline.

Oliver, Martin
Career: 1930–34　　Positions: c, of, 2b
Teams: Memphis Red Sox ('30), Birmingham Black Barons ('32–'34), Louisville Black Caps ('32)

A versatile player, he spent five seasons with southern teams during the early years of the Depression, beginning with the Memphis Red Sox in 1930.

O'May
Career: 1917　　Position: 1b
Team: Havana Red Sox

He played first base with the Havana Red Sox, generally a team of lesser quality, but a marginal club in 1917.

Omeada
Career: 1932　　Position: if
Team: Cuban Stars (West)

He was a reserve infielder with the Cuban Stars (West) in 1932.

Oms, Alejandro (El Caballero, Walla Walla, Papa)
Career: 1917–35　　Position: **cf,** lf, rf, *p*
Teams: **Cuban Stars (East)** ('17, '22–'32), All Cubans ('21), New York Cubans ('35)
Bats: Left　　　　Throws: Left
Height: 5'9"　　　Weight: 190
Born: Mar. 13, 1895, Santa Clara, Cuba
Died: Nov. 9, 1946

Flanked by Bernardo Baro and Pablo Mesa,

Oms was the centerfielder of the great outfield of the Eastern Colored League's Cuban Stars of the 1920s. He had exceptional range and an accurate but not strong arm. A colorful player, if a game was not close he would give the crowd a show by catching fly balls behind his back. He also was a very fast base runner and a skilled base stealer but was best known for his batting ability. A left-handed batter, he was a great hitter, hit to all fields with power, and was credited with setting a record of 40 home runs in the early '20s. During the six-year history of the Eastern-Colored League (1923–28) he batted third except for two years when he hit cleanup behind Martin Dihigo, and hit for averages of .400, .326, .318, .342, .348, and .308.

In 1929 he and two other players were suspended by the ballclub for not reporting. After a year's absence he returned to the team, and four years later the slugging outfielder batted cleanup and hit .381 to help the New York Cubans win the second-half title before losing to the Pittsburgh Crawfords in the 1935 Negro National League championship playoff series. That season, his last year in the Negro Leagues, Oms was selected to play in the East-West All-Star game and went 2-for-4 in his only All-Star game appearance. He began his Negro Leagues career in 1921 and finished with a .332 batting average for the years he spent with the Cuban teams in the United States.

He was a gentleman and controlled his temper, never arguing with an umpire. However, he did devise an unusual ploy to filter out anything that he chose not to hear, pretending not to speak or understand English until one day when he blew his cover after being hit in the head by a pitch and asking teammates to "give me some water" when they gathered around as he lay on the ground after being revived.

During the latter years of his baseball career, during the '40s, after he had stopped playing in the Negro Leagues, he played in Venezuela and was the league's top defensive outfielder in 1943. In Cuba, earlier in his career, playing primarily in his hometown of Santa Clara, he earned the nickname "El Caballero" and set records for hitting over .300 eleven times, eight of those times consecutively. His lifetime Cuban batting average was .351 for fifteen years during the interval 1922–46, with five intermittent winter seasons when he did not play in Cuba.

He led the league three times in batting with averages of .393, .432, and .380. Including these marks, his yearly batting averages from 1922 to 1930 were .436, .381, .393, .324, .366, .328, .432, and .380. His last three seasons were not in succession, but his marks were .389 (1931–32), .311 (1935–36), and .315 (1937–38). He displayed his speed in 1931–32 when he led the league with 14 stolen bases. His power performance is illustrated by his back-to-back slugging percentages of .619 and .572 in 1928–30. A proven winner, he played on four championship teams. For his remarkable diamond feats in his homeland, he was elected to the Cuban Hall of Fame in 1944. His skills and playing style were considered to be similar to those of Paul Waner.

O'Neill
Career: 1910   Positions: p, c
Teams: West Baden Sprudels ('10–'14)

In 1910 he pitched for a single season with the West Baden, Indiana, Sprudels, who served as the forerunners of the Indianapolis ABCs. Four years later, after most of the top players had left, he appeared as a catcher with the Sprudels.

O'Neill, Charles
Career: 1921–23   Position: c
Teams: Columbus Buckeyes ('21), Atlantic City Bacharach Giants ('21–'22), Toledo Tigers('23), Chicago American Giants ('23)

He was a catcher with struggling franchises in the early '20s before landing with the Chicago American Giants in a reserve role for a brief time in 1923, his last season.

O'Neill, John Jordan (**Buck**, Foots, *Nancy*)
Career: 1937–55   Positions: **1b**, *of*, manager

Teams: *Miami Giants ('34), New York Tigers ('35), Shreveport Acme Giants ('36),* Memphis Red Sox ('37), *Zulu Cannibal Giants ('37),* **Kansas City Monarchs** ('38–'43, '46–'55), *military service ('43–'45)*
Bats: Right   Throws: Right
Height. 6'2"   Weight: 190
Born: Nov. 13, 1911, Carabelle, Fla.

A smooth-fielding first baseman for the Kansas City Monarchs as they won four consecutive Negro American League pennants (1939–42), O'Neill hit .353 as the Monarchs swept the Homestead Grays in the first World Series played between the Negro American League and the more established Negro National League. That year, 1942, also marked the first of his three appearances for the West squad in the All-Star game.

The Monarchs' dynasty was temporarily derailed by World War II, as O'Neill and several other Kansas City regulars were inducted into military service. O'Neill served in the U.S. Navy in a construction battalion. He left the Monarchs in mid-August to travel to Norfolk, Virginia, preparatory to entering the Navy. After three years he returned to the Monarchs and resumed his position at first base.

A steady hitter, O'Neill won the 1946 Negro American League batting title with an average of .353 to lead the Monarchs to another pennant. Although not known as a power hitter, the steady right-hander hit 2 home runs to go along with his .333 batting average in the ensuing World Series against the Newark Eagles. In the sixth game, centerfielder Leon Day made an outstanding catch to rob O'Neill of a triple and save the game and the Series, as the Eagles won the final game in the hard-fought 7-game series, despite O'Neill's heroics.

Before embarking on a professional baseball career, O'Neill first had to escape the celery fields of Florida, where he worked as a youngster. He moved to Sarasota when he was twelve years of age and began working in the fields soon afterward. One day during a break from work he voiced his desire to play baseball, and his father, overhearing his conversation, encouraged him to pursue his dream. Working toward this end, O'Neill attended Edward Waters College in Jacksonville, Florida, where he played baseball for six years and picked up the nickname "Foots" because he had big hands and feet. After graduating from college in 1930, he began his professional baseball career touring with the Miami Giants in 1934 and got his nickname "Buck" from one of the team's owners, Buck O'Neal. The other owner was Johnny Pierce, but booking agent Syd Pollock soon took over the ballclub and renamed them the Ethiopian Clowns in 1935.

O'Neill also toured with the New York Tigers and the Shreveport Acme Giants in 1936 before signing with the Memphis Red Sox of the Negro American League in 1937. The Red Sox came through Shreveport and, after watching him play, signed him for the black big leagues. With the Red Sox he was an outfielder, but his stay in Memphis was not long, and he jumped to owner Charlie Henry's Zulu Giants for more money.

The next season he became a Monarch and stayed with the franchise until 1955, managing the last eight years, after Tom Baird bought out Wilkinson in 1948. A consistent hitter with good extra-base power to right-center field, he hit .258, .257, .345, .250, .247, and .222 from the time he joined the team in 1938 until he joined the Navy during the 1943 season. He usually batted in the sixth slot, although he preferred hitting in the second slot, which he did for a couple of seasons. After his batting title in 1946, he followed with seasons of .358, .253, .330, and .253 for the years 1947–50. On the bases he had only average speed but was a smart base runner, and in the field he was a graceful fielder but with only an average arm.

A knowledgeable player, he became a successful manager for the Monarchs, winning the second-half title in 1948 but losing a seven-game playoff to the Birmingham Black Barons for the NAL flag. Then in 1949, with the advent of divisional play, he guided the Monarchs to the first-half title in the Western

Division, but due to the loss of so many players to organized baseball, he declined to meet the second-half titlists, the Chicago American Giants. Finally, winning both halves of the Western Division in 1950, the Monarchs claimed the western championship. He continued to manage the Monarchs through 1955, winning a total of five pennants and serving as skipper of the West squad in four straight All-Star games, 1951–54.

Throughout his career he played in winter leagues and on barnstorming teams. In 1946 he was a member of the Satchel Paige All-Stars, who toured with Bob Feller's All-Stars. After the fall exhibitions O'Neill played winter ball with Almendares in the Cuban League in 1946–47 and played with Obregon in the Mexican winter league in 1951.

Although denied a chance to play in the major leagues, O'Neill did get to the "big time" when he joined the Chicago Cubs as a scout in 1956, and he became the first black coach in major-league history in 1962, with the Cubs. As a Cub scout he signed Ernie Banks and Lou Brock and later was also a special scout for the Kansas City Royals. He serves as a member of the Hall of Fame's Veterans' Committee and also is chairman of the board of the Negro Leagues Museum in Kansas City.

Ora, Clarence
Career: 1932   Position: of
Team: Cleveland Stars
He was an outfielder with the Cleveland Stars in 1932, their only year in the Negro National League.

Orange, Grady
Career: 1925–31   Positions: 2b, ss, 3b, 1b, of
Teams: Birmingham Black Barons ('25), Kansas City Monarchs ('26–'27, '31), Cleveland Tigers ('28), Detroit Stars ('28–'31)
Bats: Right   Throws: Right
Rube Foster sought to sign the shortstop known as the "Texas flash" for the 1926 Chicago American Giants, but Orange signed with

the Kansas City Monarchs. He was with the team as a part-time player, batting only .167 and .202, during the 1926–27 seasons, and playing mostly at second base, since Newt Allen shifted to shortstop for those years. The next season he left the Kansas City fold to play with the Detroit Stars, batting .278 in 1929, his first full season with the Stars. When the Monarchs reorganized in midseason of 1931, he rejoined the Monarchs in a utility role. A teacher in the off-season, he played every infield position during his career, which was hindered at times by having to report late or to leave the team before the end of the season due to an overlapping with his career in education.

Ormes, A. W.
Career: 1911   Position: player
Team: Chicago Giants
In 1911 he was listed as a player with the Chicago Giant's team.

Ortiz, Julio Arango (Ortie, **Bill**)
Career: 1944–45   Positions: of, ss
Teams: Kansas City Monarchs ('44), Cincinnati-Indianapolis Clowns ('45)
A wartime player, he was a reserve infielder with the Clowns in 1945, batting .212. He also played in the outfield and spent a short stint with the Kansas City Monarchs during his two seasons in the Negro Leagues.

Ortiz, Rafaelito
Career: 1948   Position: p
Team: Chicago American Giants
Bats: Right   Throws: Right
This right-handed pitcher's only season in the Negro Leagues was in 1948, with the Chicago American Giants, when he fashioned a 4–6 record.

Osborne
Career: 1905   Position: p
Team: Philadelphia Giants
He pitched with the 1905 Philadelphia Giants, the best black team in the East at that time.

Oscar
a.k.a. Oscal
[see Levis, Oscar]

Osley
Career: 1938   Position: p
Team: Birmingham Black Barons

He pitched with the Birmingham Black Barons in 1938, his only year in the Negro American League.

Osorio, Alberto
Career: 1949   Position: p
Teams: Louisville Buckeyes ('49), *minor leagues ('50–'59), Mexican League ('58–'72)*
Bats: Right   Throws: Right
Height: 6'0"   Weight: 165
Born: Nov. 21, 1929, Panama

He pitched with the Buckeyes in 1949, logging a 3–7 record with a 4.31 ERA, in his only year in the Negro American League. The next season he embarked on a twenty-three-year professional career that encompassed a decade in the minor leagues of the United States and fifteen seasons in Mexico. He also played six winter seasons in Venezuela, with an aggregate 27–15 ledger. His best year in organized ball was in 1952 with Denver in the Western League, where he had his only 20-win season (20–6, 3.25 ERA). In the Mexican League his best year was in 1964 (15–5, 2.56 ERA), the first of eight consecutive seasons with double-digit wins. He ended his career with 222 career victories, exclusive of his winter league wins.

Otis, Amos
Career: 1921   Position: of
Team: *Nashville Elite Giants*

He was an outfielder with the Nashville Elite Giants in 1921, their first year of existence, when they were playing as an independent team and were not of major-league caliber.

Ousley, Guy C.
Career: 1931–32   Positions: **ss,** 2b, 3b
Teams: Chicago Columbia Giants ('31), Cleveland Cubs ('31), Memphis Red Sox ('32)

The Chicago American Giants, under the management of David Malarcher, were playing under the name of the Chicago Columbia Giants in 1931, and this light-hitting infielder was their regular shortstop, batting eighth.

Overton, Albert
Career: 1937–44   Position: p
Teams: Philadelphia Stars ('38), Cincinnati-Indianapolis Clowns ('44)

He pitched with the Philadelphia Stars in 1937 and Cincinnati-Indianapolis Clowns in 1944.

Overton, John
Career: 1925   Position: officer
Team: Indianapolis ABCs

In 1925 he served as an officer with the Indianapolis ABCs.

Owens
Career: 1943   Position: 2b
Team: Baltimore Elite Giants

A wartime player, he was a reserve second baseman with the Baltimore Elite Giants in 1943, his only season in the Negro Leagues.

Owens
Career: 1934, 1937   Position: p
Teams: Newark Dodgers ('34), Newark Eagles ('37)

This pitcher made two appearances in the Negro Leagues, both with Newark teams, first with the Newark Dodgers in 1934, and later with the Newark Eagles in 1937, when he was winless against 2 losses.

Owens, A.
Career: 1928   Position: ss
Team: Cleveland Tigers

He was shortstop with the Cleveland Tigers in 1928, their only year in existence.

Owens, Albert
Career: 1930   Position: p
Team: Nashville Elite Giants ('30–*'31*)

He pitched with the Elite Giants for two seasons, posting a 1–2 ledger in 1930 when they were in the Negro National League, before the team dropped to the lesser Negro Southern League in 1931.

Owens, Aubrey
Career: 1920–26   Positions: p, *ss*
Teams: Indianapolis ABCs ('20), New Orleans Caulfield Ads, ('21) **Chicago American Giants** ('22–'26), Chicago Giants

He pitched with Rube Foster's Chicago American Giants during the '20s, including 1922, when they won their third consecutive Negro National League pennant. In addition to being a professional baseball player, he attended Alcorn College and Meharry Medical College while playing ball, and after graduation he practiced dentistry.

Owens, DeWitt
Career: 1936–39   Positions: **of,** 2b, ss, 3b, *p*
Teams: Birmingham Black Barons ('36–'38), Indianapolis ABCs ('39)

This outfielder began his career with the Birmingham Black Barons in 1936, spitting his time between left field and center field in his three seasons with the club and usually batting fifth. In 1939 he played with the transplanted Atlanta Black Crackers' franchise that relocated in Indianapolis under the banner of the ABCs.

Owens, Jackson
Career: 1950   Position: p
Teams: Chicago American Giants ('50–'52), *Detroit Stars ('54)*

His first year in the Negro Leagues was in 1950, when the league was struggling to survive the loss of players to organized baseball. He pitched with the Chicago American Giants for three seasons.

Owens, Jesse
Career: 1940   Position: officer
Team: Pittsburgh Crawfords

The Olympic great was the business man-ager of the Crawfords in 1940 and sometimes staged races against those players who were reputed to be the fastest on their team, or even against Thoroughbred horses as a gate attraction to bring in a big crowd for a game.

Owens, Judge (Dusty)
Career: 1941–43   Positions: of, if
Team: Philadelphia Stars
Bats: Left   Throws: Right

This left-handed batter was described as a natural hitter, but while sharing the center-field position in 1941 with the Philadelphia Stars, he batted in the seventh slot when in the lineup and finished with a lowly .086 average. A versatile player, he could play in the outfield or the infield, and in 1943 he signed with the Stars and accepted advance money from the club, but joined the Atlanta Black Crackers as an utility man despite claims on his services by the Stars.

Owens, Raymond (**Smoky**)
a.k.a. Kankol
Career: 1939–42   Positions: **p**, of
Teams: Jacksonville Red Caps ('38), Cleveland Bears ('39–'40), New Orleans-St. Louis Stars ('41), Ethiopian Clowns ('42), Cincinnati Buckeyes ('42)
Bats: Left   Throws: Left
Died: Sept. 7, 1942, Geneva, O.

A native of Jacksonville, Florida, he played with the Jacksonville Red Caps, who moved their franchise to Cleveland in 1939 and played as the Bears. During the last year of his two-year stint in Cleveland he was one of the top three pitchers with the team. Before signing with Ernie Wright's Cincinnati Buckeyes, he played with the New Orleans-St. Louis Stars and the Clowns. With the Buckeyes he was one of the best relief pitchers for the team, fashioning a 7–5 record in 1942 before his untimely demise in an automobile accident.

On September 7, 1942, a car he was driving, with five Cincinnati Buckeyes teammates as passengers, was struck from behind by a truck, and Owens and Ulysses "Buster" Brown were killed instantly. Four others were injured, with Eugene Bremmer and Herman Watts being hospitalized, and Alonzo Boone and owner Wilbur Hayes escaping with minimal injuries. The accident occurred at 3:00 A.M. just west of Geneva, Ohio, on a return trip from a series against the New York Black Yankees. The collision occurred when Owens was reentering a highway after having stopped to change a flat tire.

Owens, W. E.
Career: 1887   Position: player
Team: *Cincinnati Browns*

He was a player with the Cincinnati Browns, one of eight teams that were charter members of the League of Colored Baseball Clubs in 1887. However, the league's existence was ephemeral, lasting only a week.

Owens, W. Oscar
Career: 1913–31   Positions: **p**, 1b, of
Teams: Indianapolis ABCs ('13), Pittsburgh Keystones ('22), **Homestead Grays** ('23–'31)
Bats: Right   Throws: Right
Height: 5'6"   Weight: 165

In a long career he gained his most notoriety with Cum Posey's Homestead Grays during the late '20s. Although a top pitcher, he was a good hitter, and his versatility allowed him frequently to play at first base or in the outfield. In 1929 he hit .360 while splitting a pair of mound decisions, and was the winning pitcher for Homestead in 1930 in the first game ever between the Grays and the Pittsburgh Crawfords. The next year, his last season in black baseball, he returned to Homestead, and the 1931 Grays are often called the greatest black team ever. The right-hander and Lefty Williams were the same size and similar in appearance and frequently were confused by the fans, leading to stories that the Grays had a pitcher who could pitch with both arms.

Owens, William John (**Bill**, Willie)
Career: 1923–33   Positions: **ss**, 2b, 3b, p
Teams: Washington Potomacs ('23–'24), Wilmington Potomacs ('25), Chicago American Giants, Indianapolis ABCs ('25, '32), Dayton Marcos ('26), Cleveland Elites ('26), Cleveland Hornets ('27), Harrisburg Giants ('27), Brooklyn Royal Giants ('27), Birmingham Black Barons ('28, '30), Memphis Red Sox ('27, '29), Detroit Stars ('31, '33)
Bats: Right   Throws: Right

This middle infielder had a good glove and a strong arm that kept him active in the Negro Leagues for over a decade despite a lack of offensive punch. A native of Indianapolis, as a youngster he joined Ben Taylor on the Washington Potomacs in 1923 as a shortstop, but in 1924 his hitting was too light for the black big leagues and he was sent to Providence, Rhode Island, for seasoning. Later in the year after the Providence club folded, and he returned to the Potomacs and earned a starting position. It wasn't until later in his career that Owens learned to hit adequately.

Playing with the Memphis Red Sox, he hit .293 and .220 for the 1927 and 1929 seasons and followed in 1930 with a .243 average with the Birmingham Black Barons. In 1931, the last season before the Negro National League folded, he spent a year in Detroit as a part-time starter at shortstop, batting in the eighth slot when in the lineup.

The next season he joined the Indianapolis ABCs, but in 1933 manager Candy Jim Taylor took the team South and told Owens to stay home in Indianapolis. The weather was bad and Owens didn't get to work out, and when the team came back North, he was put in at shortstop and made a couple of errors; when Taylor criticized him in front of the hometown fans, he was embarrassed and quit the team. While only an average player, in his latter years he gained a measure of notoriety as the last living player from the Eastern Colored League.

P

Pace
Career: 1930   Position: of
Team: Nashville Elite Giants

An outfielder with the 1930 Nashville Elite Giants, he hit .223 in limited play during his only season in the Negro Leagues.

Pace, Benjamin (Brother)
Career: 1921–22   Position: c
Teams: Pittsburgh Keystones ('21–'22), Homestead Grays ('22)

He was a catcher for a couple of seasons during the early '20s with the Pittsburgh Keystones and the Homestead Grays.

Padron, Juan Luis (José, El Mulo)
a.k.a. Padrone
Career: 1909–26   Positions: **p**, 2b, of, 3b
Teams: Cuban Stars ('09–'10, '15–'19), Smart Set, Long Branch Cubans ('13), New York Lincoln Stars ('15), Chicago American Giants ('17, '22, '24–'25), New York Lincoln Giants, All Cubans ('21–'22), Birmingham Black Barons ('23), Cuban Stars (East) ('18–'20, '23), Brooklyn Royal Giants ('25), Indianapolis ABCs ('26), Cuban Stars (West) ('26), Cuban Stars of Havana ('16, '19)
Bats: Left   Throws: Left
Born: Cuba

Pitching for Havana in the 1908 Cuban winter league, this clever hurler outpitched his teammate the great Rube Foster. Years later, the light-complexioned left-hander taught Rube's half brother, Willie Foster, to throw a change-up. Padron's own change of pace was exceptional, and he threw it at two different speeds—slow and slower. He also had a good fastball and curve, and would employ an illegal pitch if necessary to win. In addition to his superlative work on the mound, when not taking his regular turn in the pitching rotation Padron played second base, third base, or in the outfield, and was regarded as a terrific hitter with average power and as a fast and clever base runner.

The following year, "El Mulo" came to the States, joining the Cuban Stars for the first of his eighteen years in the Negro Leagues. In August 1910 he left the Cuban Stars temporarily to join Eddie Hahn's Red Sox of the Chicago League, and he hit 2 home runs soon after his arrival. In the winter of 1917 he pitched for the Royal Poinciana team in the Florida Hotel League, posting a 3–1 record. During the regular season of 1917, despite a mediocre 6–8 record, he was regarded as the best Cuban pitcher in "many moons," and in 1922 he was favored over Chicago American Giants' ace Dave Brown. In 1924 Padron was classed with José Mendez and Eustaquio Pedroso as the three greatest Cuban pitchers, while simultaneously being considered one of the greatest Cuban outfielders. He posted seasonal records of 10–5 and 9–5 in 1924–25, but in the early winter of 1926 he was scheduled to be traded by the Chicago American Giants, and that was to be his last year in the Negro Leagues.

Playing in his homeland, Padron played exhibitions against major-league ballclubs. In an exhibition series against the Detroit Tigers in 1910, he played right field for Havana, batting eighth in the order and hitting .200 for the series. The next winter, again with Havana, he hit .333 against the New York Giants.

Padron played nineteen seasons (1900–1919) in Cuba, posting a lifetime batting average of .251. During this span he pitched for 11 years, carving a lifetime 39–23 record for a .629 winning percentage. Although he was best known for his pitching skills, he began his career as both a pitcher and an everyday player, hitting .313 in 1900, his first season as a professional. Two years later he led the league in batting with an average of .463, his best year as a hitter. In 1907 he was the regular left fielder on the Havana ballclub, and in 1908 he hit .270, led the league in home runs, and had 21 stolen bases in only 159 at-bats. While he played primarily with Havana, in 1913 he hit .280 with the Fe ballclub. Back with Havana in the winter of 1918–19, he hit .297 for the season.

His first season, 1900, was a good one for Padron, because in addition to leading the league in batting, he also topped the league in wins as he fashioned a 13–4 mark. Two of his other best years as a pitcher were back-to-back seasons of 9–2 and 7–3 in 1907–09. For his baseball achievements as both a pitcher and a hitter, he was elected to Cuban Hall of Fame in 1943.

After closing out his professional baseball career he pitched with semipro teams, including the Fineis Oils ballclub in Grand Rapids, Michigan, in 1931. In postseason exhibitions, pitching with the Interstate Tournament All-Stars in 1931, he defeated both major-league pennant-winners of that year, winning 4–3 over the American League champion Philadelphia A's and 2–1 over the National League cham-

pion St. Louis Cardinals. Both games were 10-inning contests, with Padron pitching the first 5 frames against the A's and hurling the complete game against the Cardinals, yielding only 6 hits while fanning 7 batters. He pitched and managed the Grand Rapids team for seven years, 1932–38, before going to Flint, Michigan, and working at a Ford garage. He is reported to have died in 1939, while still a relatively young man.

Padrone, Juan Luis
[see Padron, Juan Luis]

Page Fence Giants
Duration: 1894–98   Honors: Champions
                                  ('96)
Affiliation: Independent

Founded by Bud Fowler and Grant "Home Run" Johnson, the team was based in Adrian, Michigan, with Fowler as playing manager and Johnson as captain. For one season, 1896, they were the best team in black baseball, defeating the Cuban Giants, the top team in the East, in a 15-game challenge Series for the championship, winning 9 games to 6.

The Page Fence Giants were organized on September 20, 1894, and Fowler selected his first players based on both ability and character. Among his original dozen players, he maintained that none used alcohol and only two used tobacco, while five were college graduates.

J. Wallace Page, a Civil War veteran and founder of the Page Woven Wire Fence Company of Adrian, Michigan, sponsored the all-black ballclub as a promotional stunt, with the team traveling throughout the United States and Canada by railroad in a special coach with the identifying words "Page Woven Wire Fence Co., Adrian, Michigan" painted on the side. The coach was parked on a railroad side track in each town, while the team paraded from the coach to the ballpark, usually on bicycles, dressed in uniforms and fire hats. The parade was only one part of the show business approach to the game, and during the contest, players often provided an assortment of antics for the entertainment of the fans. One aspect of this routine, the team's "noisy coaching," was considered objectionable to some fans, but the distaste was probably due to preconceived prejudices of the offended spectators.

The team played their first game on April 9, 1895, losing their first four games and posting a 5–13–1 record for the entire month of April, but played at an .831 clip for the remainder of the year, finishing the season on October 10 with a 118–36–2 record. Augustus S. "Gus" Parsons was appointed manager on May 15, and his presence at the helm contributed to the team's reversal of fortune. By the end of the season the team had played games in 112 towns in 7 states. In games against teams in the Michigan State League in 1895, the team registered 8 wins against 7 losses while compiling a team batting average of .310.

In 1896 they strengthened their team and fashioned a record of 80–19 through the first of August, including a streak of thirty-two consecutive wins, and went on to claim the colored championship. Despite their success on the diamond, the team suffered financial difficulties created from rained-out games. In 1897 they had a 125–12 record, with 82 straight victories, but again suffered from bad weather, and in 1898 it was apathy rather than bad weather that hurt the team. That was to be the last full season for the Page Fence Giants, as the franchise dissolved, and most of the players moved to the Chicago Columbia Giants in 1899.

Page, Pedro
[see Pages, Pedro]

Page, R.
Career: 1925   Position: officer
Team: Indianapolis ABCs
He was an officer with the Indianapolis ABCs in 1925.

Page, Theodore Roosevelt (**Ted,** Terrible Ted)
Career: 1923–37   Positions: rf, 1b
Teams: Toledo Tigers ('23), *Buffalo Giants*

('24–'25), Newark Stars ('26), *Chappie Johnson's Stars ('27–'28), Mohawk Giants ('28),* Brooklyn Royal Giants ('29–'30), Baltimore Black Sox ('29–'30), Homestead Grays ('30–'31), New York Black Yankees ('32), **Pittsburgh Crawfords** ('32–'34), Newark Eagles ('35), Philadelphia Stars ('35–'37)
Bats: Left   Throws: Right
Height: 5'11"   Weight: 175
Born: 1903, Glasgow, Ky.
Died: Dec. 1, 1984, Pittsburgh, Pa.

A tough competitor, Ted Page could beat you at the plate, on the bases, or in the field. A good bunter and a slashing base runner, he used his speed to his greatest advantage. Bullheaded and aggressive, he played to win and would intimidate a player with his spikes or with rough language. The hard-playing outfielder had the distinction of playing on two of the greatest teams in black baseball history, the 1931 Homestead Grays and the 1932 Pittsburgh Crawfords.

With the Crawfords Ted was a teammate of Satchel Page, but when on opposing teams, it was a different story. With a bat in Ted's hand, Satchel became his "cousin." He also hit other pitchers, as evidenced by his averages of .352 and .362 for the 1932–33 Pittsburgh Crawfords, his lifetime .335 average in black baseball, and his .429 average in exhibitions against major-leaguers.

Page was reared in Youngstown, Ohio, and as a youngster was an all-around athlete, earning an offer of a football scholarship to Ohio State as a halfback. But he declined the opportunity, choosing to concentrate on baseball. After leaving high school he signed with the Toledo Tigers in 1923 but was quickly released and played with semipro teams around Ohio before spending two years with the Buffalo Giants, managed by Home Run Johnson. Each winter Johnson took the aspiring outfielder to Palm Beach, Florida, to play with the Breakers Hotel team in the hotel league, where his ability was eventually noticed, and he was recruited by both the Homestead Grays and the New York Lincoln Giants but signed with the

Newark Stars, a new Eastern Colored League team, in 1926.

He was the regular center fielder, batting in the sixth slot, but unfortunately the team disbanded in mid-July. After stops with Chappie Johnson's All-Stars and the Brooklyn Royal Giants, He joined the Grays in 1931, where he batted second and hit .315 as the regular right fielder. He had joined the Grays a year earlier in the spring but left after only a few weeks to return to the Royals.

While with the Grays, he and roommate George Scales were involved in an argument, and the exchange of words led to an incensed Page knocking out two of Scales's teeth and Scales responded by cutting Page with a knife. George "Chippy" Britt, one of baseball's "big bad men," separated the two antagonists, but they were still distrustful of each other when they retired that night. Both players spent a sleepless night in bed, each turned facing the other, Scales with a knife under his pillow and Page with a gun in his hand.

The next day the players resolved their differences, and by the following season both players were with new teams. Page began the year as the left fielder for the New York Black Yankees in their first year of existence, hitting in the third spot in the lineup, until he jumped to Gus Greenlee's Pittsburgh Crawfords during the season. During his three-year stint in Pittsburgh, Page worked in the off-seasons at the Crawford Grill as a lookout for Greenlee's numbers racket.

In 1934 Page injured his knee sliding into a base while playing a game in Jackson, Mississippi, and the injury robbed him of his speed. In 1935 he was released by the Crawfords and signed with the Newark Eagles, but he was released again in mid-May and was signed this time by Webster McDonald to play with the Philadelphia Stars. Even with the loss of his speed, he could still hit, as evidenced by his .329 batting average in 1935. A line-drive hitter, he usually batted either second or sixth, but in 1937, when Jud Wilson took over the Stars' managerial reins, he installed Page as

his leadoff batter, and the right fielder responded with a .351 batting average in his last season in the Negro Leagues.

Shortly after leaving baseball, he began working at a bowling alley owned by former Stars teammate Jack Marshall, and within a few years Page owned the business himself. He became a prominent person in bowling circles and even wrote a regular bowling column for a newspaper for many years. After living in retirement for several years, he was beaten to death with a ball bat in an attempted burglary.

Pages, Pedro
a.k.a. Page
Career: 1939, 1947   Positions: **of**, 1b
Teams: New York Cubans ('39, '47), *Mexican League ('40–'46), Canadian League ('51)*
Bats: Both   Throws: Right
Born: Cuba

This Cuban was one of the starting outfielders for the New York Cubans in 1947, when they won the Negro National League pennant and defeated the Negro American League Cleveland Buckeyes in the World Series. Pages (pronounced "Pah-hez") had good speed, was a good base runner, had a good eye at the plate, and batted second in the order while batting .237 during the regular season.

He first joined the New York Cubans in 1939, playing in the outfield and first base, but after only one season he jumped to the Mexican League, batting .299 for the Mexico City ballclub. In 1942 he joined Puebla, and for the next five seasons he hit .365, .353, .347, .269, and .296 before rejoining the Cubans in their pennant-winning season.

He also played in the winter league in his home country, and after a .239 season with Cienfuegos, he played with Sherbrooke in the Canadian Provincial League, hitting .244 in 1951.

Paige, Robert LeRoy (**Satchel**)
Career: 1926–50   Position: **p**
Teams: *Chattanooga Black Lookouts*

('26–'27), Birmingham Black Barons ('27–'30), Baltimore Black Sox ('30), Cleveland Cubs ('31), **Pittsburgh Crawfords** ('31–'37), **Kansas City Monarchs** ('35–'36, '39–'48, *'50, '55*), *Santo Domingo ('37),* Santo Domingo All-Stars ('37), Newark Eagles ('38), *Mexican League ('38),* Satchel Paige's All-Stars ('39), New York Black Yankees ('43), Memphis Red Sox ('43), Philadelphia Stars ('46, '50), major leagues ('48–'49, '51–'53, '65), *Chicago American Giants ('51), minor leagues ('56–'58, '61, '65–'66), Indianapolis Clowns ('67)*

Bats: Right   Throws: Right
Height: 6'4"   Weight: 180
Born: July 7, 1906, Mobile, Ala.
Died: June 8, 1982, Kansas City, Mo.

Regarded as the nearest thing to a legend that ever came out of the Negro Leagues, this tall, lanky right-hander parlayed a pea-sized fastball, nimble wit, and a colorful personality into a household name that is recognized by people who know little about baseball itself and even less about the players who performed in the Jim Crow era of organized baseball. His name has become synonymous with the barnstorming exhibitions played between traveling black teams and their white counterparts.

A mixture of fact and embellishment, Satchel's stories are legion and form a rich array of often-repeated folklore. On many occasions he would pull in the outfielders to sit behind the mound while he proceeded to strike out the side with the tying run on base. Once he intentionally walked Howard Easterling and Buck Leonard to load the bases so he could pitch to Josh Gibson, the most dangerous hitter in black baseball, and then struck him out. He was advertised as guaranteed to strike out the first nine batters he faced in exhibition games, and he almost invariably fulfilled his billing. Satchel frequently warmed up by throwing twenty straight pitches across a chewing gum wrapper that was being used for home plate. His "small" fastball was described by some hitters as looking like a half dollar. Others said that he wound up with a pumpkin and threw a

pea. But Biz Mackey had the best story about how small his fastball looked. He said that once Satchel threw the ball so hard that the ball disappeared before it reached the catcher's mitt. The stories are endless. But the facts are also impressive.

His generally accepted birth date is July 7, 1906, in Mobile, Alabama, but no one really knows the true date, and Satchel maintained an air of mystery about his age throughout his career. The only certainty about his birth is that it was sometime in this century. As one of a dozen children, he learned early to fend for himself. He rarely attended school and frequently got into mischief.

When he was a youngster he carried suitcases at the train station for tips. Once he attempted to steal a man's satchel but the owner ran him down and cuffed him about the head while recovering his property. A friend who witnessed the incident gave him the nickname "Satchel," which young LeRoy hated. In later years he concocted various versions of the origin of his nickname that were more socially acceptable.

Later he was caught stealing costume jewelry and was sent to Mount Meigs reform school, where he converted his natural ability into a measure of pitching polish. After leaving Mount Meigs he pitched for the Mobile Tigers and other local semipro teams for a couple of years before embarking on his professional career in 1926 with Chattanooga in the Negro Southern League. After arriving in Chattanooga he was described as "just a big ol' tall boy" who had extraordinary speed but was lacking the fine control that he developed later in his career. He joined the Birmingham Black Barons of the Negro National League in 1927, where he fashioned an 8–3 record, and soon thereafter established himself as a gate attraction and began playing year-round. While with the Black Barons he finished seasons of 10–11 and 10–4 in 1929–30.

In 1931 he joined Tom Wilson's Nashville Elite Giants when they moved to Cleveland to play as the Cleveland Cubs, but before the season was over he had been persuaded by Gus Greenlee to sign with his newly acquired ballclub, the Pittsburgh Crawfords. In the latter part of June he pitched the first victory for the Crawfords over the Homestead Grays, winning a close 6–5 contest. Paige's greatest popularity came through this association with the Pittsburgh Crawfords during the early 1930s. He compiled marks of 32–7 and 31–4 in 1932–33. In 1934 he was credited with a league record of 10–1. That season he and Slim Jones matched up in Yankee Stadium in what is considered the greatest game ever played in Negro Leagues history. The game, ended by darkness after 10 innings, was a 1–1 tie. As a result of Paige's relationship with Greenlee, his stay with the Crawfords was interrupted with frequent salary disputes leading to intervals when Satchel pitched in Bismarck, North Dakota, with a white semipro team. He is credited with winning 134 of 150 games pitched with Bismarck and, while in the Midwest, he pitched on occasions with the Kansas City Monarchs, including an October exhibition game victory over Detroit Tiger ace Schoolboy Rowe and a team of major-leaguers. After returning to the Pittsburgh Crawfords in 1936, he is credited with a 24–3 record.

In the spring of 1937 he jumped to the Dominican Republic, where he pitched the Ciudad Trujillo team to a championship. He topped the league in wins, with a 8–2 record in the 31-game season. When he returned to the United States, he was banned by the Negro National League, so he formed his own team and toured across the country for the remainder of the season, outdrawing the league teams. In 1938 his contract was sold to the Newark Eagles, but although he was on the roster, he never actually participated in a game with them. Unable to reach accord in his negotiations with Effa Manley, he went to Mexico, but developed a sore arm, and the experts predicted that he was washed up. Needing a job, Satchel signed with J. L. Wilkinson to play on the Kansas City Monarchs' traveling team as a gate attraction, but unexpectedly, his arm "came back," and

he also developed a curve and his famous hesitation pitch to add to his "bee ball," "jump ball," "trouble ball," "long ball," and the other pitches in his repertory.

He joined the Monarchs' league team during the latter part of the 1939 season, and for the next decade he pitched for them, pitching them to four consecutive Negro American League pennants (1939–42), culminating in a clean sweep of the powerful Homestead Grays in the 1942 World Series, with Satchel himself winning 3 of the games. During the regular season of 1942 he posted a 9–5 record, after having finished undefeated in league play with a 6–0 ledger the previous year. After many key players were drafted, the Monarchs' baseball fortunes fell on leaner times, and Paige dropped to an 8–10 record in 1943. During the next two seasons he pitched more exhibition games than league contests, often with other teams. In 1944 he pitched in only 8 league games, posting a 4–2 record with a 0.75 ERA, and the following season he was still an effective worker on the mound and knew "all the tricks of his trade" but was "on loan" most of the year and infrequently pitched in league games.

In 1946, with the key starters back in the Kansas City fold, he helped pitch the Monarchs to their fifth pennant during his tenure with the team, but during the ensuing World Series against the Newark Eagles he missed the last 3 games, reportedly to make arrangements to play in a Caribbean winter league, and the Monarchs lost the Series in 7 games. In addition to the 2 Negro World Series, during his career in the Negro Leagues Paige also pitched in 5 East-West All-Star games, being credited with 2 victories in the midseason classic.

Like most pitchers, Paige thought he was a good hitter, but he was really a relatively weak hitter and only an average fielder. However, sometimes in the Caribbean winter leagues he would play at first base, and he acquitted himself there adequately. In the 1939–40 Puerto Rican winter league with Guayama, he led the team to the pennant with a performance that produced statistics that included a 19–3 record for a .864 winning percentage, and a 1.93 ERA with 208 strikeouts in 205 innings pitched and 6 shutouts in 24 games. His only other year in Puerto Rico was in 1947–48. Other winters he pitched in the California winter league with teams including the Royal Giants and the Baltimore Giants. Joe DiMaggio and Babe Herman, who played against him on the West Coast, said Satchel was the toughest pitcher they ever faced. Paige estimated that in his career he pitched 2,600 games, 300 shutouts, and 55 no-hitters.

Finally, with Satchel at an undetermined age, Bill Veeck brought him to the major leagues in 1948, and the rest is history. As the oldest rookie ever to play major-league baseball, he registered a 6–1 record and a 2.48 ERA down the stretch to help pitch the Indians to the pennant and World Series victory that year.

Reunited with the consummate showman Veeck on the St. Louis Browns in 1951, Satchel relaxed in his own personal rocking chair in the bullpen when not in action and kept the legend going. Twelve years after making appearances in the major-league All-Star games of 1952–53, Satch, at the dubious age of fifty-nine, pitched 3 innings for the Kansas City A's in 1965 to become the oldest man to pitch in a major-league game, contributing still another chapter to the ever-expanding collection of "Satchel stories."

In 1971, on the proudest day of his life, Satchel was elected to the National Baseball Hall of Fame, becoming the first player elected from the Negro Leagues. In the years after his induction, Satch was continuing to follow his own rare advice, "Don't look back, something might be gaining on you," when, indeed, something finally did catch up with him. On June 8, 1982, death stilled the baseball immortal.

Paine, Henry
Career: 1885   Position: of
Team: *Brooklyn Remsens*

He was an outfielder with the 1885 Brooklyn Remsens, one of the earliest black teams.

Paine, John
Career: 1887   Position: of
Team: *Philadelphia Pythians*

He was a player with the Philadelphia Pythians, one of eight teams that were charter members of the League of Colored Baseball Clubs in 1887. However, the league's existence was ephemeral, lasting only a week.

Paize, Pedro
[see Pages, Pedro]

Palm, Robert Clarence (**Spoony**)
Career: 1927–46   Position: c
Teams: Birmingham Black Barons ('27), St. Louis Stars ('28–'29, '36), Detroit Stars ('30–31, '33), Homestead Grays ('32, '41), Cole's American Giants ('32), Cleveland Giants ('33), Akron Tyrites ('33), Pittsburgh Crawfords ('34), Brooklyn Eagles ('35), New York Black Yankees ('36, '38–'39, '43, '46), *Santo Domingo ('37)*, Philadelphia Stars ('39–'42, '45)
Bats: Right   Throws: Right
Height: 5'8"   Weight: 180

He began his career in 1927 with the Birmingham Black Barons, batting .299 for the season before joining the St. Louis Stars in 1928 to share the catching duties. A mediocre catcher defensively, with an average arm, he was just learning to catch when he was with St. Louis, but the free-swinger had pretty good power and wielded a potent bat, as evidenced by his .349 batting average in 1929. He joined the Detroit Stars in 1930 and continued his solid hitting with a .315 average, batting in the heart of the order again in 1931 and 1933. Like most catchers, he lacked speed on the bases, but as an adequate receiver who could contribute to the team offense with his bat, he was an asset to a ballclub. Moving frequently from one team to another during his career, he played with the American Giants and the Pittsburgh Crawfords during the early '30s and joined the New York Black Yankees in 1936, playing sporadically as a backup and part-time starter for the next decade with intermittent interruptions.

The first came when he jumped the Black Yankees in 1937 to play in Santo Domingo, where he hit .254 with Martin Dihigo's ballclub. Another came in 1941, when he hit .240 as one of the catchers the Homestead Grays used in trying to replace Josh Gibson. Sandwiched around the partial season with the Grays were seasons with the Philadelphia Stars, where he was used as a backup receiver.

For the remainder of his career he played primarily as a backup, with the Stars and Black Yankees, with his last starting assignment coming in 1943, a war year. Before closing out his career with the Black Yankees in 1946, he also played on selected winters in the Latin leagues, including in the first season of the Puerto Rican League in 1939.

Palma
Career: 1930   Position: p
Team: Cuban Stars (West)

In 1930 he pitched with the Cuban Stars in the Negro National League, but was winless against 4 losses.

Palmer, Curtis
Career: 1949–50   Position: of
Team: New York Black Yankees

He was a reserve outfielder with the New York Black Yankees in 1949–50, after the team had dropped out of league play and was struggling to survive the loss of players to organized baseball.

Palmer, Earl
Career: 1918–19   Position: of
Teams: Chicago Union Giants ('18), New York Lincoln Giants ('19), *Madison ('21)*

He was an outfielder during the World War I years, but his playing time was severely restricted with top-level ballclubs.

Palmer, Leon
Career: 1926   Positions: of, 2b

Teams: Dayton Marcos ('26), *Louisville White Sox ('30)*

He made two appearances with teams of marginal major-league caliber. He began his career in 1926 as a seldom-used reserve second baseman with the Dayton Marcos, a ballclub making a final effort to be competitive in the Negro National League. He also played as an outfielder with the Louisville White Sox in 1930, a year before they entered the Negro National League.

Palomino, Emilio
a.k.a. Pulamino
Career: 1904–05   Position: of
Teams: All Cubans
Bats: Left   Throws: Left
Born: Cuba

A white Cuban, he played only two seasons in the United States (1904–05), with the All Cubans team, but was a start in his own country, where opposing pitchers' respect for his hitting ability was reflected in his relatively high ratio of free passes. In 1908, playing in his homeland with the champion Almendares team, he led the Cuban League in batting with a .350 average while playing right field and hitting third in the order, and also tied with Pete Hill for the league lead in runs scored. Two years later, in a 1910 winter exhibition series against the Detroit Tigers, he was the cleanup batter for Almendares but hit only .182 for the short series.

Panier
Career: 1917   Position: p
Teams: Cuban Giants ('17), *Philadelphia Giants of New York ('20)*

He was a pitcher with the Cuban Giants in 1917, his only year with a top ballclub. He also played with the Philadelphia Giants of New York, a lesser team.

Pannell, (Handsome)
Career: 1914   Position: c
Teams: *Cuban Giants*

An experienced player with good power, he

was a catcher with Cuban Giants, a team of lesser quality, in 1914.

Parago, George A.
[see Parego, George A.]

Pardee
Career: 1925   Position: c
Team: Birmingham Black Barons

In 1925, his only year in the Negro Leagues, he was a catcher with the Birmingham Black Barons.

Pareda, H. (Pastor, **Monk**)
a.k.a. Parera
Career: 1910–21   Positions: **p**, 1b
Teams: Stars of Cuba ('10), Cuban Stars ('14–'15), Cuban Stars (West) ('21)

Possessing average control and not considered a power pitcher, he fashioned a career that extended over a dozen seasons with the Cuban teams in black baseball. He began his career in 1910 with the Stars of Cuba. The following winter, in Cuba, he pitched in half of the 6 games between his Havana club and the Detroit Tigers but lost his only decision. Following close on the heels of the Tigers was Connie Mack's Philadelphia Athletics, and he enjoyed more success against the A's, as he pitched a 6-inning, 1-hit victory over Chief Bender. Three years later, pitching with the Fe ballclub, he topped the Cuban winter league with 11 victories.

Parego, George A.
a.k.a. Parago; Perego; Perago
Career: 1885–88   Positions: p, of, 1b, *c, ss*
Teams: *Argyle Hotel ('85)*, Cuban Giants ('85–'88)
Born: Aug. 20, 1861, Charlottesville, Va.

In 1884 he played first base and catcher for the Keystone Athletics of Philadelphia, a top amateur ballclub, and accompanied the top players to Long Island in the summer of 1885 to form a team at the Argyle Hotel to play for the entertainment of the guests. After the sum-

mer season the team acquired some additional players and a new team name, the Cuban Giants, and began touring as the first black professional team. He played with the new team for four seasons, the first two as the team's right fielder, but soon began taking his turns on the mound. In 1887 the Cuban Giants entered the Middle States League as representatives of Trenton, New Jersey.

Parera, H.
[see Pareda, H.]

Parker
Career: 1890–1900   Position: of
Teams: Chicago Unions ('90–'91), Genuine Cuban Giants ('00), *New York Colored Giants (1908)*

Beginning his career in 1890 with the Chicago Unions, under the management of W. S. Peters, he was a regular outfielder for two years, playing center field the first season and moving to left field in 1891. After leaving the Unions, he played in the outfield with Genuine Cuban Giants, one of the ballclubs appropriating a variation of the Cuban Giants' name as their own and playing a quality of baseball close to that of the original team.

Parker
Career: 1921–23   Positions: 1b, of
Teams: *Pittsburgh Stars of Buffalo ('21)*, Baltimore Black Sox ('22), Memphis Red Sox ('23)

He played with two teams that were still one year away from league competition. He was an outfielder with the Baltimore Black Sox in 1922, while they were still playing as an independent team but were building a team of major-league caliber preparatory to joining the Eastern Colored League the next season. He also played as a combination first baseman-outfielder with the Memphis Red Sox in 1923, a season before they entered the Negro National League.

Parker, Jack
Career: 1938   Position: if
Team: Pittsburgh Crawfords

During the Pittsburgh Crawfords' last season in Pittsburgh, 1938, he appeared briefly as a reserve infielder.

Parker, Sonny
Career: 1942–43   Position: p
Teams: *Chicago Brown Bombers ('42)*, Harrisburg-St. Louis Stars ('43), Kansas City Monarchs ('43)

A wartime player, he played with the Chicago Brown Bombers, a team of lesser status, for a year before joining the Negro National League's Harrisburg-St. Louis Stars at the beginning of the 1943 season. Early in the spring the Stars withdrew from the league to barnstorm with Dizzy Dean's All-Star team and were suspended from the league, but Parker returned to league play with the Monarchs later in the season.

Parker, Thomas (**Tom**, Big Train)
Career: 1929–49   Positions: **p**,   rf,
                              manager
Teams: Memphis Red Sox ('29), Indianapolis ABCs ('31), Monroe Monarchs, Nashville Elite Giants ('34), **Homestead Grays** ('35–'39, '48), Indianapolis Athletics ('37), Toledo Crawfords ('39), New Orleans-St. Louis Stars ('41), New York Black Yankees ('41–'42), Harrisburg-St. Louis Stars ('43), *military service ('44)*, New York Cubans ('45), Birmingham Black Barons ('45), *Boston Blues ('46), Detroit Senators ('47), minor leagues ('51–'53)*
Bats: Right   Throws: Right
Height: 6'1"   Weight: 230
Born: 1911; Alexandria, La.

A big, robust fastball pitcher with a good curve, he also threw a slider, knuckler, and change-up with a modicum of success and had a fair drop with average control of his pitches. Joining the Homestead Grays in 1935, he won only 1 game while enduring 6 losses, but he remained with the Grays during the first part of their dynasty period, helping them win the first three pennants, 1937–39.

He returned to add his support as they captured the final Negro National League flag in 1948, contributing a 7–4 record. Like most players in the Grays' pitching rotation, he was a good hitter, and the dynamite in his bat was apt to explode at any time. With his big bat and powerful throwing arm he was often pressed into regular outfield duty when not on the mound, and was considered a classy outfielder. Beginning in 1939 and going through 1948 at three-year intervals, he hit .264, .200, .286, and .235. On the bases he had adequate speed but was not a threat to steal very many bases.

Leaving the Grays, he pitched with the St. Louis Stars and the New York Black Yankees before being called into military service during World War II. After serving ten months in the armed forces, he was discharged and within three months signed with the New York Cubans for the 1945 season, returning to the diamond where he had gained his national fame while with the Black Yankees.

Beginning the next season, he played with lesser black teams until opting to play in the Mandak League for three years in the early '50s. In 1951 he posted a 5–2 record as a pitcher, and in 1953 he batted .286. Off the field the big, hard-throwing, hard-hitting player was considered a true gentleman throughout his twenty-one seasons in the Negro Leagues.

Parker, Willie
Career: 1918–21   Position: p
Teams: Baltimore Black Sox ('18, '20–'21), New York Lincoln Giants ('19)

He pitched with the Baltimore Black Sox during their formative years before they entered league play, and he hurled for a season with the Lincoln Giants in 1919.

Parkinson, Parky
Career: 1950   Position: p
Team: Houston Eagles

He was a pitcher with the 1950 Houston Eagles when the Negro American League was struggling to survive the loss of players to organized baseball, but league statistics do not confirm his playing time.

Parks
Career: 1916   Position: p
Team: New York Lincoln Stars
In 1916 he pitched with the Eastern champion Lincoln Stars.

Parks, Charles Edison (**Charlie**, Hunkie, John)
Career: 1939–47,   Positions: **c**, 3b, of
Teams: New York Black Yankees ('39), Newark Eagles ('41–'42, '46–'47), Military Service ('43–'45)
Bats: Right   Throws: Right
Height: 5'11"   Weight: 193
Born: June 19, 1917, Chester, S.C.
Died: Sept. 13, 1987, Salisbury, N.C.

A hustling catcher with good hands and a strong throwing arm, he was considered a good hitter with respectable power and, although he usually batted in the lower part of the order, he could deliver the long ball at times. Parks was a little bit on the chubby side and, at best, possessed only mediocre speed on the bases and was not a basestealing threat.

He joined the Newark Eagles in 1940, and after a season with a .190 batting average as Biz Mackey's understudy, he worked his way into the starting lineup. As a regular he batted .206 and .231 in 1941–42, but was sidetracked by World War II. After being drafted, he served three years in the Army, winning three Bronze Stars and being discharged with the rank of sergeant.

Returning to the Eagles in 1946, he caught Leon Day's opening-day no-hitter, and ended the season with a .250 batting average. The following season he ended his career with the Eagles as he had started, by sharing the catching duties with Biz Mackey, while batting .227 in his final year.

After his playing days he tried his hand as manager of the Asheville Blues, a minor-league team. Having spent his formative years in Charlotte, North Carolina, when he finally retired from baseball, he returned to the area and worked as a machine operator for a construction company until retiring in 1980.

Parks, G.
Career: 1917   Position: rf
Team: Pennsylvania Red Caps of New York ('17)
A reserve outfielder, he was one of three players named Parks who played with the Pennsylvania Red Caps in 1917.

Parks, Joseph B.
Career: 1909–19   Positions: **of**, c, 1b, ss, 2b
Teams: Cuban Giants ('09), Philadelphia Giants ('10–'13), Pennsylvania Red Caps of New York ('17–'19), Brooklyn Royal Giants ('18), New York Bacharach Giants ('19)

An all-purpose player during the '10s, he played a variety of positions with several teams, mostly in a reserve role. In 1910 he was a starting catcher with the Philadelphia Giants, batting fifth in the order, but in the next few seasons the Giants began a rapid decline. In 1917 he began a three-year stint with the Pennsylvania Red Caps, and after a year as a reserve first baseman, he shared a starting position each of the next two seasons, splitting his playing time between the outfield and the infield.

Parks, William (*Bubber*)
Career: 1910–20   Positions: ss, 2b, of
Teams: Philadelphia Giants ('10), Chicago Giants ('11), *Chicago Union Giants ('11),* New York Lincoln Giants ('14, '18), Chicago American Giants ('11, '15), New York Lincoln Stars ('14–'16), *Pennsylvania Red Caps of New York ('17–'20)*

A middle infielder during the last decade of the deadball era, most of his time was spent in New York City. Joining the Lincoln Stars when they were organized by the McMahon brothers in 1914, he was the starting second baseman in 1914 and 1916, hitting in the second slot each season. In 1915 he split the year between the Lincolns and Rube Foster's Chicago American Giants, as did John Henry Lloyd, but while with the American Giants, neither he nor Lloyd accompanied the ballclub on their spring training tour. After the Stars disbanded, he was among the ex-Stars who joined the Pennsylvania Red Caps in 1917, and he was the regular second sacker for three seasons. After batting leadoff the first season, he moved to the third slot for the next two years. In 1920, his last year in black baseball, the team had suffered a rapid decline in quality.

Parnell

Career: 1934   Position: p
Team: Atlantic City Bacharach Giants

In 1934 the Bacharachs entered the Negro National League as a second-half replacement team, and he was a member of the pitching staff in their last year as they struggled to maintain a quality ballclub.

Parnell, Roy (Red)

Career: 1926–43   Positions: **lf**, rf, cf, 1b,
                                            p, manager
Teams: Birmingham Black Barons ('26–'28), *Houston Black Buffaloes ('32),* Monroe Monarchs ('32), *New Orleans Crescent Stars ('33–'34),* Nashville Elite Giants ('34), Columbus Elite Giants ('35), **Philadelphia Stars** ('36–'43), *Santo Domingo ('37),* New York Black Yankees ('37), Pittsburgh Crawfords ('46), New York Cuban Stars, Houston Eagles ('50)
Bats: Right   Throws: Right
Height: 5'10"   Weight: 180

Underpublicized because he spent much of his career in the South, he was a good, all-around ballplayer who could do everything. A right-handed hitter who hit for average and with occasional power, he also had a good eye at the plate and was a good bunter. Although not gifted with exceptional speed, he was a good base runner. He was a dependable fielder with good hands and range but with only an average arm. A valuable and well-traveled player, he appeared twice in the East-West All-Star game, in 1934 with the West squad and in 1939 with the East squad. In each contest he played left field but failed to hit safely in either contest.

A native of Austin, Texas, he began his professional career in the Lone Star State but joined the Birmingham Black Barons in 1927, where he played right field and hit third in the batting order. He contributed a .426 average as the Black Barons won the second-half title before being swept by the Chicago American Giants in the Negro National League championship playoffs.

In 1928 he followed with a .326 batting average, and by 1932 he was the playing manager for the Houston Black Buffaloes in the Texas-Oklahoma League. He also played with the New Orleans Crescent Stars for a season before rejoining the Negro National League. In 1934 he joined Tom Wilson's Nashville Elites, earning his first trip to the All-Star game for his performance. When the franchise moved to Columbus in 1935, he is credited with a .257 batting average after the relocation.

He joined the Philadelphia Stars in 1936, batting .310 in his first year with the team. But in 1937 he jumped the Stars in mid-June to play in Santo Domingo with the Aquilas Cibaenas ballclub in an effort to overtake Satchel Paige's Ciudad Trujillo team. But despite Parnell's .283 batting average, they finished second to the Trujillo club. In 1938 he returned to the Stars and hit .324 and .304, successively, and earned his second All-Star appearance the latter year.

Parnell was a smart ballplayer and started the 1940 season as manager, but was replaced by Jake Dunn in June. He remained with the Stars as a player, usually hitting second in the batting order, and posted marks of .273, .248, .278, and .311 for the seasons 1940–43. He played for eighteen years despite an excessive drinking problem, and after leaving the Stars he eventually returned to Houston, at the helm of the Houston Eagles, in 1950.

Parpetti, Augustin

Career: 1909–23   Positions: **1b**, of
Teams: **Cuban Stars (West)** ('09–'10, '13, '15), Cuban Stars (East) ('17), Kansas City

Monarchs ('21), Atlantic City Bacharach Giants ('23)

This big Cuban first baseman was the best of his countrymen at his position during the first two decades of the century. He was a clever batter with good power and was considered one of the best Cuban hitters of all time. Beginning with Tinti Molina's Cuban Stars in 1909, he usually batted fifth in the order, but in his last year with the team, 1915, he hit in the third slot. Moving over to the New York-based Cubans in 1917, he stepped into the cleanup spot in the batting order.

Parpetti left the Cuban teams to play in both the Negro National League, with the Kansas City Monarchs in 1921, and the Eastern Colored League, with the Bacharachs in 1923 in a backup role, to close out his career in black baseball. In his homeland, playing for Havana against major-league teams during winter exhibitions, he hit .217 against the Detroit Tigers in 1910 and .288 against the New York Giants in 1911–12.

Parris, Jonathan **Clyde** (The Dude)
Career: 1946–49   Positions: 3b, 2b, of, ss, 1b
Teams: Baltimore Elite Giants ('46), New York Black Yankees ('46–'48), Louisville Buckeyes ('49), *Canadian League ('51), minor leagues ('52–'59), Mexican League ('60)*
Bats: Right   Throws: Right
Height: 5'8"   Weight 170
Born: Sept. 11, 1926, Panama

This Panamanian youngster was picked up from his country's winter league by Baltimore and was playing second base for the Elite Giants in 1946, but was released to make room for Willie Wells and Sammy T. Hughes, who were signed in early June. He was picked up immediately by the New York Black Yankees, where he hit .214 while playing both second base and third base. In 1947 his average improved to .246 and he remained with the Black Yankees until the Negro National League folded following the 1948 season. The next year he moved to the Negro American League

with the Cleveland Buckeyes for a final season in black baseball.

In 1951 he joined St. Jean in the Provincial League, batting .294 with 16 home runs, and then embarked on a long career in the minor leagues. In 1954, with Elmira, he hit .313 and led the league in doubles (40) and RBIs (90), earning him a promotion to AAA ball with Montreal in the International League. In his five years (1955–59) with Montreal, he hit .289 (16 home runs), .321 (17 home runs), .238 (7 home runs), .300 (10 home runs), and .299 (23 home runs). He closed out his career in 1960, playing with three different teams, and finishing with Monterrey in the Mexican League, where he hit .305.

He began his career in Venezuela but played most of his winter career in his home country. When he signed with the Elite Giants, he had only recently completed the winter season in Panama, with a .267 batting average. The following winter, 1947–48, again with the General Electric team in Panama, he hit .355 with good power. For the next thirteen winter seasons he continued to play in Panama, hitting .353 (1948–49), .328 (1952–53), .344 (1953–54), .331 (1954–55), and .434 in his last winter (1959–60).

Parson
Career: 1908   Position: p
Team: Genuine Cuban Giants

He was a pitcher with the Genuine Cuban Giants in 1908, one of the various Cuban Giants ballclubs that flourished during the early years of the century. Several of these clubs, copying the success of the first black professional team and appropriating a variation of the Cuban Giants' name as their own, played a quality of baseball close to that of the original team.

Parsons, Augustus S. (**Gus**)
Career: 1895–98   Position: manager
Team: Page Fence Giants

Parsons was appointed manager of the newly organized Page Fence Giants on May 15, 1895, after the team had a poor first month, and his presence at the helm contributed to the team's reversal of fortune. By the end of the season the team had compiled a 118–36–2 record. In 1896 he strengthened the team by adding some new players, and the Giants forged a record of 80–19 through the first of August, including a streak of 32 consecutive wins. Parsons' charges continued their winning ways and went on to claim the colored championship, defeating the eastern champion Cuban Giants, 9 games to 6, in a 15-game challenge series. In 1897 they were 125–12 with 82 straight victories, but despite their success on the diamond, the team began to suffer financial difficulties created by bad weather and apathetic fans. Parsons remained at the helm until the end, but 1897 proved to be the last full season for the Page Fence Giants.

Partlow, Roy

Career: 1934–50   Positions: p, of
Teams: Memphis Red Sox ('34) Cincinnati Tigers ('37), **Homestead Grays** ('38–'43, '49–'50), Philadelphia Stars ('45, '47–'48), *minor leagues ('46), Canadian League ('51–'52)*
Bats: Left   Throws: Left
Height: 6'0"   Weight: 180
Born: 1912
Died: Apr. 19, 1987, Cherry Hill, N.J.

A hard-throwing left-hander with excellent control, he possessed a natural talent for pitching, with a whistling fastball, a great curve, and a good drop, but he was never taught *how* to pitch. He was temperamental and headstrong, on the field and off. When he was pitching he would sometimes lose his poise and concentration if something went wrong.

Partlow pitched for the Homestead Grays during the greater part of their dynasty period of the late '30s and early '40s. In 1938, his first year with the Grays, he posted a 6–4 record as they forged a .813 for the first half and won the second half as well. The next season he pitched in the 1939 East-West All-Star game and suffered the loss. That winter, he pitched

in Cuba and compiled a 7–4 record. After he returned to the United States the Grays continued their dominance, winning the next four pennants. The left-hander posted marks of 3–1 and 9–1 in league play for the 1941–42 seasons. In the pennant-winning years of 1942 and 1943, he pitched for the Grays in the World Series, starting 2 games each year. After leaving the Grays he joined the Philadelphia Stars, and in 1945 he compiled a 9–4 record and led the league in strikeouts.

While with Homestead he was one of the Grays' stable of hard-hitting pitchers, and sometimes played in the outfield, hitting a composite .295 for the 1941–43 seasons. He also batted .366 and .441 in consecutive winters (1939–41) with San Juan in the Puerto Rican winter league while establishing pitching credentials that included consecutive ERAs of 1.40 and 1.49 and an 11–4 ledger at the front end of this pair of seasons. His batting credentials include marks of .260 and .222 for the Philadelphia Stars in 1945 and 1947. He was also a good fielder and a fast base runner.

After the color barrier was lifted, Roy played AAA ball, but had problems unrelated to his performance on the diamond. He was selected to replace Johnny Wright, who had paired with Jackie Robinson as the Dodgers' second black signee. When Wright was unable top maintain the finer control he had demonstrated in the Negro Leagues, Partlow was given a chance with Montreal in the International League. He was 2–0 with Montreal but inexplicably left the team. The root of the problem has never been definitely identified, but Robinson and Partlow were different type personalities, were not friends, and did not socialize. Robinson distanced himself from Partlow, and their wives never even met. Reassigned to Three Rivers in the CanAm League for the remainder of the 1946 season, Partlow registered a 10–1 record with a 3.22 ERA while hitting .404.

After leaving organized ball, he returned to the Negro Leagues, playing with the Philadelphia Stars in 1947, where he had an uncharacteristic 4–7 record. He rebounded to reverse the record in 1948 with a 7–4 mark. After another two-year stint with the Grays, he spent two years with Granby in the Provincial League, posting marks of 7–2 and 8–3 with accompanying ERAs of 1.90 and 3.46.

Throughout his career, when off the field he tended to be arrogant and hard to handle, especially when he was drinking. On those occasions he wanted to fight, and his propensity for alcohol led to problems later in his life.

Passon, Harry
Career: 1934   Position: officer
Team: Atlantic City Bacharach Giants

He was an officer for the Bacharachs in 1934, when they were second-half additions to the Negro National League in their last season as a quality ballclub.

Pastoria
Career: 1924   Position: p
Team: Cuban Stars (West)

He pitched with the Negro National League's Cuban Stars in 1924, his only year in the Negro Leagues.

Pate, Archie
Career: 1909, 1917   Positions: of, c
Teams: St. Paul Gophers ('09), Chicago Giants ('13, '17), New York Stars ('14), Bowser's ABCs ('16)

He was an outfielder with the champion St. Paul Gophers in 1909, but was a marginal player for most of his career. In 1914 he appeared briefly with the New York Stars in their first year, and two years later he returned to the midwest, playing with Thomas Bowser's ABCs, when the owner fielded a second ABCs ballclub in 1916. The next year he closed out his career as a reserve right fielder with the Chicago Giants.

Patterson
Career: 1886   Position: lf
Team: *New York Gorhams*

In 1886 he played left field with the New York Gorhams, one of the earliest black teams of professional quality.

Patterson, Andrew L. (Pat)
Career: 1934–49   Positions: **3b**, 2b, ss, of
Teams: *Pennsylvania Red Caps,* Cleveland Red Sox ('34), Homestead Grays ('34), Pittsburgh Crawfords ('35, '37), Kansas City Monarchs ('36, '41), **Philadelphia Stars** ('38–'39, '41–'42), *Mexican League ('40), military service ('42–'45),* Newark Eagles ('46–'47), Houston Eagles ('49)
Bats: Both   Throws: Right
Height: 5'11"   Weight: 185
Born: Dec. 19, 1911, Chicago, Ill.

A switch-hitter, he was a good contact hitter with moderate power and could also bunt and execute the hit-and-run play. He had good speed on the bases and was a fine fielder who gave a little extra hustle. Patterson was a smart and versatile ballplayer and could play any position, exclusive of the battery, and became one of the best third basemen during the late '30s and early '40s. However, early in a career that spanned sixteen years, he was the regular second baseman with the great Pittsburgh Crawfords team of 1935, considered to be the greatest team in the history of the Negro Leagues. The young infielder batted .346 for the season as the Crawfords defeated the New York Cubans in the Negro National League playoff for the championship.

The steady infielder is also identified with the Philadelphia Stars and Newark Eagles, playing on the Eagles' 1946 championship team. He was selected to participate in four East-West All-Star games, two with the West and two with the East, recording an All-Star batting average of an even .300.

Patterson's stint with the Crawfords was in his second year in the Negro National League, after playing with the Cleveland Red Sox and the Homestead Grays in 1934 and earning a spot on the All-Star team in his rookie year. After his first year with the Crawfords, he signed with the Kansas City Monarchs in 1936 and earned his second trip to the All-Star game. Back with the Crawfords in 1937, he was hitting in the third slot when he jumped to Santo Domingo to play with the Aguilas Cibaenas team that was trying to catch the Ciudad Trujillo team that had been fortified by former Crawford teammates Satchel Paige, Josh Gibson, and Cool Papa Bell. Patterson contributed a .319 batting average to the stretch drive, but his team was unable to overtake the Trujillo stars.

After returning to the United States he signed with the Philadelphia Stars and posted averages of .349 and .404 for the 1938–39 seasons, playing second base and batting third in the order the latter year to earn his third trip to the All-Star game. The next season he interrupted his tenure with the Stars' organization to play ''south of the border.'' Playing with Mexico City in 1940, he hit .341 with good power (a .554 slugging percentage) and good speed, finishing the year close behind Cool Papa Bell's stolen-base frequency. After returning from Mexico, Patterson hit .293 and .264 while batting in the heart of the order for the 1941–42 seasons and earning his fourth All-Star appearance the former year.

Late in 1942 he entered military service for three years during World War II. After being discharged he joined the Newark Eagles as the starting third baseman and hit .321 to help them to the 1946 Negro National League pennant and a World Series victory over the Kansas City Monarchs. A consistent hitter, he followed with a .320 average in 1947. When the Eagles' franchise moved to Houston, he played one year after the relocation, closing out his career in 1949 with a .217 average for the season.

A graduate of Wiley College, where he was an all-around athlete, starring in both football and baseball, after the end of his professional baseball career he pursued a second career in education, as a successful teacher, coach, athletic director, and eventually superintendent of schools in Houston, Texas.

Patterson, Gabriel (Gabe)
Career: 1941–50   Positions: rf, c

Teams: New York Black Yankees ('41, '47–'48), *Pittsburgh Crawfords ('46)*, Philadelphia Stars ('47), Homestead Grays ('47, '50), *minor leagues ('51)*
Bats: Right   Throws: Right

He began his career in 1941 as a reserve right fielder with the New York Black Yankees, but his next appearance had to wait until after World War II. After a year in the U.S. League, a league of lesser quality, he was back with the New York Black Yankees, hitting .296 with average power and posing a basestealing threat from the leadoff spot, while sharing the starting assignment in center field. After leaving the Black Yankees, in 1950 he toured with the Homestead Grays, who were playing a lesser independent schedule since the Negro National League folded two years earlier. In 1951 he played with Butler in the Middle Atlantic League and hit .327 with average power, but posting good stolen-base numbers and high walk and strikeout ratios.

Patterson, George
Career: 1895   Position: 3b
Team: Page Fence Giants

A good hitter with power, he left his home in Starkville, Mississippi, to play third base with the Page Fence Giants in 1895, with a batting average of an even .500 in 11 games against Michigan State League teams.

Patterson, John W. (Pat)
Career: 1893–1907   Positions: lf, 2b, ss, manager

Teams: *Lincoln, Nebraska, Giants ('90), Plattsmouth, Neb. ('92)* Cuban Giants ('93–'94), Page Fence Giants ('97–'98), Columbia Giants ('99–'00), Chicago Union Giants ('02), Philadelphia Giants ('03), Cuban X-Giants ('04), Quaker Giants of New York, Brooklyn Royal Giants ('07),

He joined the Cuban Giants in 1893 as a substitute second baseman, playing behind Sol White, but won a starting position in left field in 1894. The Cuban Giants had been the first black professional team but were now being challenged for supremacy by other clubs. After leaving the Cubans he played with the Page Fence Giants, who had quickly become a top team in the West and who had defeated the Cuban Giants for the championship in 1896.

When the team disbanded after the 1898 season, many of the players joined the Columbia Giants. Patterson was the regular left fielder for two seasons until Frank Leland combined the Giants with the Chicago Unions to form the Chicago Union Giants in 1901. After a year's absence, Patterson joined the team for a season as the starting left fielder before joining the Philadelphia Giants in 1903 and the Cuban X-Giants in 1904. In each of these seasons his team was the losing team in the playoff for the eastern championship.

In 1907 he played left field for the Brooklyn Royal Giants, usually batting in the second slot, to close out an active career that began in 1890 with the Lincoln Giants from Lincoln, Nebraska, and included a stint with the Plattsmouth ballclub in the Nebraska State League.

Patterson, Roy (Willie, Pat)
Career: 1950   Position: c
Teams: New York Cubans ('50), *Birmingham Black Barons ('51), Chicago American Giants ('52), Philadelphia Stars ('52), Memphis Red Sox ('53)*

He was a reserve catcher with the New York Cubans in 1950, when the Negro American League was struggling to survive the loss of players to organized baseball, but his playing time was severely restricted. He continued in the Negro American League for three more years with four different teams before closing out his career in 1953.

Patterson, William B.
Career: 1914–25   Position: manager
Teams: *Houston Black Buffaloes, Austin Senators,* Birmingham Black Barons

A manager for a dozen seasons, primarily with teams of lesser status, he began his managerial career in Texas with the Houston Black Buffaloes and the Austin Senators before managing the Birmingham Black Barons.

Patton
Career: 1909   Position: rf
Team: Philadelphia Giants

A light-hitting outfielder, he was a part-time starter in right field for the 1909 Philadelphia Giants, batting ninth when in the lineup.

Patton
Career: 1926   Position: p
Team: St. Louis Stars

He pitched with the St. Louis Stars in 1926, winning his only recorded decision in his only season in the Negro Leagues.

Payne
Career: 1916   Position: p
Team: New York Lincoln Giants

In 1916 he was a member of the pitching staff for the Lincoln Giants, along with Smokey Joe Williams and Cannonball Dick Redding.

Payne
Career: 1928   Position: of
Team: Birmingham Black Barons

He was an outfielder with the Birmingham Black Barons in 1928, his only season in the Negro Leagues.

Payne
Career: 1926–31   Positions: 2b, p
Teams: Newark Stars ('26), *Philadelphia Colored Giants of New York ('28),* Brooklyn Royal Giants ('31)

He began his career as a pitcher with the Newark Stars in 1926, but his next appearance with a quality ballclub was as a second baseman with the Brooklyn Royal Giants in 1931.

Payne, Andrew H. (**Jap**)
Career: 1902–19   Positions: rf, lf, cf, 3b, 2b, ss
Teams: Philadelphia Giants ('02–'04), Cuban X-Giants ('03), Brooklyn Royal Giants ('06,

'14), Leland Giants ('07–'10), Chicago American Giants ('11–'13), Chicago Giants ('13), New York Lincoln Stars ('14), Chicago Union Giants ('17), Grand Central Terminal Red Caps ('18–'19), Pennsylvania Red Caps of New York ('19), *Philadelphia Giants of New York ('20–'22)*

A smart player and one of the better outfielders during the first two decades of the century, he was the right fielder on the great Leland Giants of 1910 and, in his fourth year with the team, was already an established veteran who could help a team in many ways. A complete ballplayer, he was a good, consistent hitter with above-average power, an excellent base stealer, and a proven fielder with a good arm. The media reported that there were "few better [at] cutting runners off at the plate."

He began his career with the Philadelphia Giants in 1902 and was with them in 1904 when they won their first championship. Sandwiched between these two years he played with the Cuban X-Giants, the dominant team of the century prior to losing their title to the Philadelphia Giants in the 1904 playoffs. In 1906 he was the left fielder and leadoff hitter for the Brooklyn Royal Giants before moving West to join the Leland Giants in 1907. After seven years in Chicago with Rube Foster's teams, he returned to New York in 1914 to play left field and bat lead off for the Lincoln Stars in their first season. With the Grand Central Terminal Red Caps of New York in 1918–19, he played left field, batting cleanup the latter season. For the next three seasons he played with the Philadelphia Giants, the same name of the team that he started with twenty years earlier, but the team was now of much lesser quality.

In 1953 a former teammate on the Leland Giants, John Henry Lloyd, selected him as the right fielder on his all-time team.

Payne, Ernest (Rusty)
Career: 1937, 1940   Position: of
Teams: Cincinnati Tigers ('37), Indianapolis Crawfords ('40)

This youngster was with the Cincinnati Ti-

gers in 1937 and, after being discovered by Oscar Charleston during spring training in Dallas, became part of the 1940 Indianapolis Crawfords' youthful outfield. Charleston let him play to gain experience; however, by late June he was still having problems with the bat.

Payne, James
Career: 1887–88   Position: of
Teams: *Baltimore Lord Baltimores* ('87), Cuban Giants ('88)

He was an outfielder with the Lord Baltimores, one of eight teams that were charter members of the League of Colored Baseball Clubs in 1887. However, the league's existence was ephemeral, lasting only a week. The next season he played with the Cuban Giants, who were the champions in 1888.

Payne, Tom
Career: 1933   Position: of
Teams: Homestead Grays ('33), Baltimore Black Sox ('33), Pittsburgh Crawfords ('33)

A reserve outfielder, he appeared briefly with a trio of teams in 1933, but garnered most of his playing time with the Homestead Grays, where he played all three outfield positions and batted a lowly .150 in very limited play.

Payne, William (Doc)
Career: 1898   Position: cf
Team: *Celeron Acme Colored Giants*

He played center field for the Acme Colored Giants, an all-black team formed in 1898 to play in the Iron and Oil League as representatives of Celeron, New York. Both the team and the league folded in July, and it was to be the last time a black team played in a white league.

Peace, Warren
Career: 1945–48   Position: p
Teams: Newark Eagles
Bats: Right   Throws: Right
Height: 5'9"   Weight: 160

A pitcher who came with Biz Mackey from California, he was a two-pitch pitcher with a fair fastball and curve but lacking control and was never able to pitch effectively for the Newark Eagles, finishing with an aggregate 6–3 record, while pitching primarily against weaker opposition.

Peacock
Career: 1933   Positions: 3b, 2b
Team: Homestead Grays

An infrequently used utility infielder with the Homestead Grays in 1933, he hit .250 in very limited play, split between third base and second base.

Peak, Rufus
Career: 1931   Position: officer
Team: Detroit Stars

In the last season of the Negro National League, he was an officer with the Detroit Stars.

Pearson, Frank (Wahoo, *Jimmy, Ivy*)
Career: 1945–50   Position: p
Teams: Memphis Red Sox ('45–'47), New York Black Yankees ('48), New York Cubans ('49), Chicago American Giants('50)
Bats: Right   Throws: Right
Height: 5'6"   Weight: 145
Born: Sept. 10, 1919, Memphis, Tenn.

After learning baseball on the sandlots of Memphis, he joined with the Little Rock Black Travelers in the Negro Southern League, but when the Memphis Red Sox' ace moundsman Porter Moss was killed in a shooting incident, the Sox signed the hometown hurler to fill the vacancy in the pitching rotation. His best pitch was a curveball, but he also employed a fastball and change-up to mix speeds. After joining Memphis in the Negro American League he posted a 2–5 record with a 3.69 ERA for the balance of the 1945 season.

The following season he lost both of his league decisions, and in 1948 he moved to the Negro National League with the New York Black Yankees. When the league folded following the season, he joined the New York Cubans for a year and then joined the Chicago American Giants, where he split 4 decisions while carrying a 6.00 ERA in 1950.

After leaving Chicago he joined the Ligon All-Stars, a traveling team out of Hondo, Texas, and barnstormed through the Midwest and into Canada. The next year he accompanied former Memphis teammate Verdell Mathis to Leseur, Minnesota, to play with an otherwise all-white team. After a season with the Leseur Giants, he gave up baseball.

During his early years in baseball, a teammate gave him the nickname "Wahoo" because of an imagined resemblance to an Indian. After leaving baseball he returned to Memphis and worked at an assortment of jobs, including twenty years in a machine shop, before retiring in 1985.

Pearson, Leonard Curtis (**Lennie**, Hoss)
a.k.a. Pierson
Career: 1937–50   Positions: **1b**, of, 3b,
                      ss, manager
Teams: **Newark Eagles** ('37–'48), Baltimore Elite Giants ('49), *minor leagues* ('50–'51), *Canadian League* ('53)
Bats: Right   Throws: Right
Height: 6'2"   Weight: 200
Born: May 23, 1918, Akron, O.
Died: 1984, Newark, N.J.

A hard-hitting first baseman, Lennie Pearson was one of the "Big Four" sluggers in the lineup for the 1946 Negro National League champion Newark Eagles, batting .276 with good power. In the ensuing World Series victory over the Negro American League champion Kansas City Monarchs, he hit a torrid .393.

He was a dangerous, consistent hitter and a steady fielder at first base, noted for his ability to handle bad throws. As an outfielder his only liability was a weak arm, resulting from a high-school football injury. On the bases Pearson could get a good jump on the pitchers, and he could steal a base when needed. But it was his confidence and productivity with a bat that earned him the most acclaim, as he recorded season batting averages of .253, .296, .191,

.385, .279, .269, .314, .326, .309, .299, and .291 for the seasons 1937–1947 with the Newark Eagles. When the Eagles moved to Houston in 1949, Pearson chose to stay closer to home and became the playing manager of the Baltimore Elite Giants, batting .332 in his last year in the Negro Leagues while guiding the team to the 1949 championship.

The solid first sacker was selected to five East-West All-Star games for the East squad. In 1944, the only year during the interval 1941–45 that he did not play in the All-Star game, their versatile athlete, who was an outstanding basketball player, played for the Renaissance basketball team.

After the color barrier was lifted, he played in organized baseball with the Milwaukee Brewers in the American Association in 1950, batting .305. After beginning the next season with the Brewers, he moved to Hartford in the Eastern League, where he batted .272. Two years later he played with Drummondville in the Provincial League and hit .290 with 16 home runs.

Pearson, handsome and broad-shouldered, was one of owner Effa Manley's favorites, and she wanted to keep her paramour close to Newark during the off-season. Taking advantage of the relationship, he frequently borrowed money from the Eagles as an advance on his salary. In the winter of 1940, Mrs. Manley wanted him to stay in Newark and play basketball, but he chose to play baseball with Caguas in the Puerto Rican winter league. The next season, with Newark, he suffered a severe ankle injury in late June that caused him to lose substantial playing time.

He also played in the Cuban winter league, compiling a lifetime .262 batting average for five winter seasons. He hit .257, .284, .256, .271, and .200 for the years 1946–51, all except the last one with Havana. Counted among his honors on the island were three RBI titles, while his best home-run season was the winter of 1949–50, with 11 homers in 280 at-bats. Usually he had twice as many doubles as hom-

ers in Cuba, and he led the league in 1949 with 19 two-baggers.

Pearson came from a family with ten children, and as a youngster he was an all-around athlete, excelling at football, basketball, and baseball. In high school in East Orange, New Jersey, he and Monte Irvin played together, and both had very strong arms and took turns pitching and catching each other. But after Pearson hurt his arm playing football in high school, it was never the same, necessitating his move to first base. He dropped out of school in 1937 to work and to play semipro baseball with the Orange Triangles.

After joining the Eagles he had some difficulty hitting a curveball until manager Mule Suttles helped him develop into a good curveball hitter. After establishing himself with the Eagles, the gregarious outfielder was a hustler and a team player. Following his retirement from baseball he opened a tavern with the financial assistance of Effa Manley, and he operated the establishment for a number of years.

Peatross, Maurice (Baby Face)
a.k.a. Peatros
Career: 1947   Position: 1b
Teams: *Pittsburgh Crawfords ('45)*, Homestead Grays ('47), *minor leagues ('49–'52)*, *Canadian League ('53)*
Bats: Left   Throws: Left
Height 5'11"   Weight: 210
Born: 1930

An aspiring first baseman when he joined the Homestead Grays in 1947, he failed to show enough to stick with the team for the duration of the season. In 1949 he began his career in organized ball, appearing briefly as an outfielder with Geneva in the Border League but batting only .208 in 16 games. Back at first base for the next three years, he hit .316, .299, and .288, respectively, for Fargo in the Northern League, Erie in the Mid-Atlantic League, and Magic Valley in the Pioneer League. He displayed only an average amount of power and speed but had a high walk ratio. In 1953 he played with Drummondville in the Provincial

League, batting .290 while dividing his time between first base and the outfield.

Pedemonte

Career: 1926   Positions: p, 3b, of
Team: Cuban Stars (West)

A pitcher with the Negro National League's Cuban Stars in 1926, he also appeared at third base and in the outfield, batting .267 in limited play.

Pedrero

Career: 1931   Positions: 2b, c
Team: *Newark Browns*

He was an infielder with the Newark Browns in 1931, a year before they entered the East-West League.

Pedroso, Eustaquio (Bombin)

a.k.a. Pedrosa

Career: 1910–30   Positions: **p**, rf, 1b, c,
                                     ss
Teams: **Cuban Stars (West)** ('10–'20, '22–'30), All Cubans ('21), Cuban Stars (East) ('26)
Bats: Right   Throws: Right
Born: Cuba

A great all-around player, this native Cuban had a sterling twenty-one-year career in the Negro Leagues from 1910 to 1930, playing primarily for the Cuban Stars. In his prime, his outstanding fastball and good control made him one of the top pitchers in the league. But when not pitching, the versatile "Bombin" was playing first base, in the outfield, or catching, while usually batting in the sixth slot. The right-handed hurler was described as being a "big brute" and having an "awkward body," and in 1917, while coaching with the Cuban Stars, he "amused fans with his antics and his gibberish in his native tongue."

In 1924 he was classed with José Mendez and Luis Padron as the three greatest Cuban pitchers of all time, but was past his prime, posting a 5–8 record for the season. In the late '20s he began gravitating more toward playing first base and even catching, but his batting

skills were also eroding and his averages are not impressive, with statistics showing marks of .175, .256, and .182 for 1924 and 1926–27, respectively. Earlier in his career he had been a good hitter, and he led the Cuban league in batting in the 1915–16 winter season with a .413 average while also showing good power.

Pitching with Almendares in his homeland, he led the Cuban League in wins in 1913 and 1914–15 with 11 and 10, respectively. In winter exhibitions against major-leaguers in Cuba, he pitched impressively against both the Detroit Tigers and the New York Giants. Facing the Tigers in 1909, he pitched a no-hitter, and in 1910 he split 2 decisions against Ty Cobb's team while yielding only 15 hits in 22 innings pitched. His victory was a superlative 2–1, 11-inning 5-hitter. The next winter, 1911–12, he posted a 2–1 record against John McGraw's National League champion New York Giants.

Pedroso, Fernando Diaz (Bicho)

a.k.a. Fernando Diaz

Career: 1945–50   Positions: 2b, ss, of, 3b
Team: New York Cubans
Bats: Right   Throws: Right
Height: 5'11"   Weight: 180
Born: May 30, 1924, Marianao, Cuba

An exceptionally fast infielder, he broke in with the New York Cubans in 1945 and was regarded as an outstanding prospect with a brilliant and sensational future. With veterans Silvio Garcia and Horacio Martinez on the Cubans' squad, competition for a starting position was stiff, but the youngster earned his playing time. In 1945 he batted in the third slot, hitting .291, while playing second base, third base, and all three outfield positions. The next year he was a part-time starter at shortstop, usually batting in the leadoff spot. He dropped to a .210 average, but stole 10 bases in only 39 league games.

In his third season he was the regular second baseman, batting sixth in the order and hitting .247, as the Cubans captured the 1947 Negro National League pennant and defeated the Cleveland Buckeyes in the Negro World Series. In the aftermath of the championship season he lost his starting position the next year and did not play as a regular with the Cubans again.

While he had good speed, he had only average power at the plate, and his early promise was never completely fulfilled. In the winter of 1945–46 he was the second baseman on the All Cubans team, but for two years after the Cubans' 1947 pennant he did not play in his homeland. Most of his nine years in the Cuban League was spent with Marianao, and he compiled a lifetime batting average of .244. His highest average was in 1949–50, when he hit .292 in only 13 games, and his highest as a regular was .265 in 1951–52.

Peebles, A. J.
Career: 1933   Position: officer
Team: Columbus Blue Birds

He was an officer with the Columbus Blue Birds in 1933, during their venture into the Negro National League.

Peeples, Nathaniel (**Nat,** Nate)
Career: 1949–50   Positions: c, of
Teams: Kansas City Monarchs ('49–'50), Indianapolis Clowns ('50, *minor leagues ('51–'59), Mexican League ('60)*
Bats: Right   Throws: Right
Height: 6'2"   Weight: 180
Born: June 29, 1926, Memphis, Tenn.

Splitting the 1950 season between the Kansas City Monarchs and the Indianapolis Clowns, and his duties between catching and the outfield, this right-handed batter still hit for a .302 average for the year while demonstrating uncharacteristically good speed for a catcher.

After only one full season in the Negro Leagues, he began a decade-long career in organized baseball, covering ten teams and nine leagues, beginning as an outfielder with Elmira in the Eastern League, where he batted .252 for the 1951 season. Leaving Elmira the next season after only 12 games, he had a good year with Santa Barbara in the California League,

batting .327 with 14 home runs and 52 stolen bases. For the remainder of the '50s his best years were in the Three-I League with Keokuk in 1953 (.331) and Evansville in 1955 (.325). He also had a good summer with Corpus Christi in the Big State League, where he hit .314 with 25 homers, 99 RBIs, and 31 stolen bases.

After two years in the Texas League with Austin, and playing with Louisville in the American Association for a dozen games at the end of 1959, he made his last baseball appearance in the Mexican League, playing two games with the Mexico City Reds in 1960.

Peete, Charles (**Charlie,** Mule)
a.k.a. Peet
Career: 1950   Position: of
Teams: Indianapolis Clowns ('50), *minor leagues ('50–'51), military service ('52),* major leagues ('56)
Bats: Left   Throws: Right
Height: 5'10"   Weight: 190
Born: Feb. 22, 1929, Franklin, Va.
Died: Nov. 27, 1956, Caracas, Venezuela

His Negro Leagues career consisted of only a partial season after the quality of play there was in decline. Playing in 31 games with the Indianapolis Clowns in 1950, the youngster batted only .214, with a high percentage of strikeouts, before jumping to Brandon in the Mandak League, where he fared little better, with a .220 batting average.

After his discharge from the Army, he played with Portsmouth in the Piedmont League and hit .275 and .311 in 1953–54. The former year he was a teammate with Buck Leonard, and in the latter year he hit 17 homers, earning a promotion within the Cardinals' chain. The next season was split between Rochester in the International League (.280) and Omaha in the American Association (.317).

In 1956 he came into his own, hitting .350 with Omaha and earning a trip to the major leagues with the St. Louis Cardinals. Although he hit only .192 at the end of the season, with his minor-league lifetime average of .311, and coming off the big season, his future was promising. However, the promise was tragically denied when, flying to Venezuela to play in the winter league, he was killed in a plane crash.

Pelham, *William* **(Don)**
Career: 1933–38   Positions: **of**,   ss, manager
Teams: Atlantic City Bacharach Giants ('33), Atlanta Black Crackers ('37–'38)
Bats: Left   Throws: Right
Height: 6'3"   Weight: 177

A big, strong line-drive hitter with an "easy, graceful, rhythmic follow-through," this left-handed batter used a split grip on the bat and was a natural hitter, with a good eye at the plate, usually hitting about .300 with considerable power. In 1937 the long-ball hitter hit 11 home runs and 7 triples against league competition. The next season he batted in a power slot with the Negro American League second-half champion Atlanta Black Crackers. A pull hitter, he swung for the fences, and in an Easter game against the Columbus Wildcats, he hit four balls over the fence in four at-bats, but due to ground rules they were counted as doubles. An all-around ballplayer, the center fielder had both good range and a strong arm, and was called a "circus ball hawk" because of his defensive ability.

A native Floridian, he made his home in Atlanta and was popular around town. In March 1938, while Colonel Michael "Mike " Schaine was still the owner of the Black Crackers, Pelham was appointed manager of the ball club. After the franchise was sold to the competing Negro American League Atlanta ball-club, the new team assumed the Black Crackers' name and Nish Williams was retained as the manager. Pelham remained with the team as a player and, later in the year, assisted two subsequent managers. First he helped Dick Lundy, who took the helm when Williams was fired, and then he assisted Gabby Kemp when he first assumed the managerial

reins at the beginning of the second half. Pelham's managerial assistance and contributions on the playing field were both major factors in the team's success in 1938.

Pellas
Career: 1923   Position: p
Team: Cuban Stars (West)

He was a second-line pitcher with the Cuban Stars in the Negro National League in 1923.

Peña
Career: 1929   Positions: c, 1b
Team: Cuban Stars (West)

A catcher with the Negro National League's Cuban Stars in 1929, he hit .246 and also could play first base.

Pendleton, James **(Jim)**
Career: 1948   Positions: **ss**, of
Teams: Chicago American Giants ('48), *minor leagues ('49–'52, '55–'56, '58–'61, '63),* major leagues ('53–'59, '62)
Bats: Right   Throws: Right
Height: 6'0"   Weight: 190
Born: Jan. 7, 1924, St. Charles, Mo.

He played shortstop with the Chicago American Giants in 1948, batting .301 with good power, and later played in the major leagues as an outfielder with the Braves. He jumped from the Negro American League straight to St. Paul of the American Association in 1949 with a respectable .274 average and 27 stolen bases. After two more good years with St. Paul (.299 and .301) and another at Montreal (.291), he made the jump to the major leagues. Joining Milwaukee in 1953, he made the transition from shortstop to the outfield and had his best major-league season, hitting .299 while playing in 120 games. After four seasons with the Braves' franchise he played two years with Pittsburgh and another with Cincinnati. After two good seasons with Jersey City in the International League (.302 and .304), he bounced back for a final major-league season in 1962, with the Houston Astros. He split the next year between San Antonio and Oklahoma City, his last season in baseball.

Early in his career he played winter ball in Venezuela for four years (1948–52) and demonstrated his versatility, banging 8 homers in his first year, winning a batting title (.387) in his second year, leading the league in both doubles (18) and triples (5) in his third year, and leading the league in stolen bases (12) in his last year. The next winter (1952–53) he played in the Cuban winter league, batting .291 and slugging .436.

Pennington
Career: 1929   Position: p
Team: Nashville Elite Giants

In 1929 he pitched briefly with the Nashville Elite Giants, without a decision.

Pennington, Arthur David (**Art**, Superman)
Career: 1940–50   Positions: **of**, 1b, *2b, 3b, ss, p*
Teams: **Chicago American Giants** ('40–'46, '50), Pittsburgh Crawfords ('46), *Mexican League ('46–'50), minor leagues ('51–'59)*
Bats: Both   Throws: Right
Height: 5'11"   Weight: 195
Born: May 18, 1923, Memphis, Tenn.

Playing for the Chicago American Giants, "Superman" compiled batting averages of .299 in 1944 and .359 in 1945 while finishing second to Sam Jethroe in stolen bases with 18. In 1950 he hit .370 with good power and started the 1950 East-West All-Star game, getting a hit in three at-bats. That marked the second All-Star appearance for the switch-hitter, having pinch hit in the 1942 game. Pennington had a lifetime batting average of .336 in his eight years in the Negro Leagues. The last of these came after a three-year Mexican League hiatus, beginning in 1946 with Monterrey, where he hit .314, and continuing with marks of .291 and .294 with Puebla.

Although playing mostly in the outfield or at first base, Pennington was a versatile player and also could play any infield position, and because he had a strong arm and could throw so hard, he sometimes was utilized as a relief pitcher for a 2-inning stint.

In addition to his summers in Mexico, he played winter ball there, playing in three seasons (1948–51) in Culiacan. He also played winters in Caracas, Venezuela, and in Cuba, where he hit .234 in 1947–48. Highlights of his performance in each of the last two leagues include grand-slam homers, with the last one netting him a $500 prize. During his career he also homered off Dizzy Dean in an exhibition contest.

After the breakup of the Negro Leagues, the outfielder-first baseman played in organized ball for an additional nine years but never made it to the majors. A partial season with Portland in the Pacific Coast League in 1949 is the closest he came to the top rung, and he managed only a .208 batting average in the 20 games he played. His greatest success in organized baseball came in the Three-I League in 1952–54. With Keokuk the first year he won the batting title with a .349 average and slugged 20 home runs. The next two seasons he batted .329 and .345, the last year with Cedar Rapids. His last two years were with St. Petersburg in the Florida State League (.339) and with Modesto in the California League (.256). He retired following the 1959 season.

After leaving baseball, he worked at Rockwell Collins for twenty-three years, and two years on the railroad in Cedar Rapids, Iowa, before retiring in 1985.

Penno, Dan
Career: 1893–96   Positions: of, 2b, p
Teams: Cuban Giants ('93, '96), Cuban X-Giants

A nineteenth-century player with the two top teams in the East during the era, the Cuban Giants and the Cuban X-Giants, he was an outfielder, infielder, and pitcher. The Cuban Giants, organized in 1885, were the first black professional team, but by the 1890s they were being challenged by the Cuban X-Giants, who replaced them as the dominant team in the East.

Pennsylvania Red Caps of New York
Duration: 1917–19   Honors: None
Affiliation: Independent

A team playing as Red Caps from New York's Pennsylvania Station, they were at their best in the late '10s. After the demise of the Lincoln Stars, many of the ex-Stars' players joined the Red Caps, and for three years they fielded a marginal major-league team. Although they continued to operate into the '20s and early '30s, their play at that time was below major-league standards.

Peoples
Career: 1933   Position: p
Team: Memphis Red Sox

He pitched briefly with the Memphis Red Sox in 1933, his only season in the Negro Leagues.

Perago, George A.
[see Parego, George A.]

Perdue, Frank M.
Career: 1920–24   Positions: officer; president (NSL)
Team: Birmingham Black Barons

For five years during the early '20s he served as a club officer with the Birmingham Black Barons and also as president of the Negro Southern League.

Perego, George A.
[see Parego, George A.]

Pereira, José
Career: 1947   Position: p
Team: Baltimore Elite Giants

In 1947 he split four decisions while pitching with the Baltimore Elite Giants.

Perez
Career: 1906   Position: p
Team: Cuban X-Giants

He was a pitcher with the Cuban X-Giants in 1906, when the ballclub was still one of the top teams in the East.

Perez, Blue
[see Perez, Javier (Blue)]

Perez, Javier (Blue)
Career: 1933–45   Positions: 3b, 2b, of, 1b
Teams: Atlantic City Bacharach Giants ('33–'34), New York Cubans ('35, '42–'45), Brooklyn Eagles ('35), Newark Eagles ('36) Homestead Grays ('37)
Bats: Right   Throws: Right
Height: 5'10"   Weight: 165
Born: 1905, Cuba

A good defensive infielder with a good arm, he was versatile but best at the hot corner. At the plate he was a contact hitter with good power, but not above the norm for batting average. He had average speed but seldom stole a base. During the war years the veteran infielder played with the New York Cubans as the regular second baseman in 1943–44 and as a reserve at the hot corner in 1945, at age forty. His averages for those years were .291, .244, and .224, but he was still considered a "dangerous" man at bat and "a pillar of strength" in the infield. He was a popular player, but sometimes took exception to beanball tactics, once precipitating a brawl in a game against the Newark Eagles, when he threw his bat at the pitcher after being knocked down.

Prior to joining the New York Cubans, he had starred with the Homestead Grays, playing third base and hitting sixth on the Grays' first Negro National League pennant-winner, in 1937. Earlier in his career he shared the starting assignment at second base for the Bacharachs in 1933, hitting eighth. After two years with the Bacharachs he made his first appearance with the New York Cubans under manager Martin Dihigo but was released in the spring and joined the Brooklyn Eagles for the remainder of the 1935 season, posting a .327 average for the year. He also played in the Philippines, Japan, and other foreign countries.

Perez, José (Pepin)
Career: 1911–34   Positions: **1b**, 2b, ss, 3b, c, *p*

Teams: *Madison Stars ('20)*, Cuban Stars (West) ('24–'25), Cuban Stars (East) ('18–'25, '27–'29), Harrisburg Giants ('26–'27), Cuban Stars ('30–'34)

With the Cuban Stars in the Eastern Colored League in 1923, he shared a starting position, playing first base when Martin Dihigo pitched or played second base. He left the Cubans temporarily to play with another Eastern Colored League team, the Harrisburg Giants, where he was the regular first baseman in 1926–27, batting .227 in the latter year. After two years with Harrisburg, he returned to his regular status with Tinti Molina's Cuban Stars for the next two years, hitting .232 in 1929, he batted near the bottom of the order for both teams. After playing through the last season of the Eastern Colored League and the only season of the American Negro League, he joined the Cuban Stars, who were playing as an independent ballclub. In 1933–34, his last years, he played first base and hit in the second slot. Earlier in his career he had pitched with the Cubans, but he lost both pitching decisions in 1918.

Perez, Luis
[see Caballero, Luis Perez]

Perkins
Career: 1944   Position: 1b
Term: Kansas City Monarchs

A wartime player, he was a reserve first baseman with the Kansas City Monarchs in 1944, his only season in the Negro Leagues.

Perkins, William Gamiel (**Bill**, George, Cy)
Career: 1928–48   Positions: c,   lf,
                                          manager
Teams: Birmingham Black Barons ('28–'30), Cleveland Cubs ('31), Pittsburgh Crawfords ('31–'36), Cleveland Stars ('32), Homestead Grays ('32), *Santo Domingo ('37)*, Philadelphia Stars ('38–'39, '46–'47), Baltimore Elite Giants ('40, '47–'48), New York Black Yankees ('45–'46)
Bats: Right   Throws: Right

Height: 5'11"   Weight: 195
Born: Georgia

Perkins was Satchel Paige's favorite catcher, beginning as a batter with the Birmingham Black Barons and continuing together with the Cleveland Cubs, Pittsburgh Crawfords, and in the Dominican Republic. While not a mobile catcher, he was a good receiver with a strong arm and wore a chest protector with the words "Thou shalt not steal" printed on front. On the bases he was slow and infrequently stole a base. At the plate he was not a good bunter but had good power and hit with appreciable consistency, batting .244 and .313 with the Black Barons in 1928 and 1930, respectively. Going with Paige to the Cleveland Cubs and then to the Pittsburgh Crawfords when the team was organized, the hard-hitting catcher-outfielder hit .335, .360, .291, and .265 in 1932–33 and 1935–36, and appeared in the 1934 and 1940 East-West All-Star games. Always a good hitter, he maintained a .288 average while playing five winters in Cuba.

With the Crawfords he had the misfortune of playing behind Josh Gibson, but owner Gus Greenlee would not trade him, using him instead as a backup catcher and part-time outfielder. In the spring of 1937 he jumped to Santo Domingo with Paige, catching and playing the outfield while hitting .253 to help the Ciudad Trujillo team win the championship. Perkins, Paige, and most of the other "jumpers" were suspended by the league and, upon returning to the United States, formed their own team, touring the country for the remainder of the season. The suspensions were soon lifted, and beginning in 1938, Perkins joined the Philadelphia Stars, with incomplete statistics showing averages of .313 and .299 for his first two years with them.

In 1940 he joined the Baltimore Elite Giants and hit .279, earning a trip to the All-Star game. Later in the '40s, he hit .214 (1945) and .139 (1947) in limited play, closing out his career the following season. He was killed in a restaurant, but the circumstances surrounding the incident are uncertain.

Perry
Career: 1943   Position: p
Team: Baltimore Elite Giants

A wartime pitcher with the Baltimore Elite Giants in 1943, he failed to post a decision during his stint with them.

Perry, Alonzo Thomas
Career: 1946–50   Positions: **1b, p**
Teams: *Atlanta Black Crackers ('45),* Homestead Grays ('46), **Birmingham Black Barons** ('46–'50), *minor leagues ('49, '51), Mexican League ('55–'59, '62–'63)*
Bats: Both   Throws: Right
Height: 6'3"   Weight: 190
Born: Apr. 14, 1923, Birmingham, Ala.

He was originally a pitcher, but Perry's strong hitting resulted in his becoming an everyday player. As a pitcher for the 1948 Negro American League champion Birmingham Black Barons, the curveballer compiled a 10–2 (4.73 ERA) regular-season record, was the number one pinch hitter, and served as manager Piper Davis's lieutenant, becoming very adept at stealing signs. He also hit .325 in 1948. The next year he was 12–4, with a 3.45 ERA. In 1950, as a first baseman, he posted a .313 batting average with balanced power (14 homers, 7 triples, 14 doubles) and started at first base for the West squad in the 1950 All-Star game, getting a couple of hits from his coiled crouch in three at-bats.

After a season with the Atlanta Black Crackers, he joined the Homestead Grays as a pitcher in 1946 and fashioned a 4–0 record before leaving the team after a disagreement with the owner over money he had won gambling. During his brief stint with the Grays, he often kept his teammates awake on bus trips by "spinning stories." After joining the Black Barons that same season, the lanky hurler continued on the mound, but began playing more at first base, became adept at making the stretch to catch throws from infielders, and was a natural showboat on the field. He was also a good base runner, but was best known for his hitting ability.

The power hitter was indirectly responsible for the discovery of Willie Mays. Scouts sent to see Perry recognized the super talent of his younger teammate and signed both of them, assigning Perry to AAA ball. He never played an entire season at this level, and his two short stints with top-level minor-league clubs were too brief to be conclusive. In 1949, with Oakland in the Pacific Coast League, he hit .200 in a dozen games, and two years later, with Syracuse in the International League, he hit .278 in only 9 games. He played the balance of the 1951 season with Brandon in the Mandak League.

Perry compiled outstanding statistics while playing in Mexico, where he is almost a legend. With Mexico City he hit for averages of .375, .392, .352, .365, and .333 for the years 1955–59, and with Monterrey in 1962–63 he posted averages of .318 and .353. In 1956 he had a career season as he led the league in hits (177), doubles (33), triples (13), home runs (28), runs (103), and RBIs (118) while batting .392 in 123 games. During his Mexican career he led the league twice each in hits, doubles, triples, and runs, and he led in RBIs four times.

He also excelled in the Caribbean leagues, including in Cuba, where he was called "His Majesty," and in the Dominican Republic, where he played winters during the years 1951–59, all except the last season with Licey. His batting marks were .400, .327, .293, .336, .325, .252, .332, and .270, earning him the batting title in 1954 and 1957. He also led the league in home runs twice (1952–53), in stolen bases once (1954), and he established a record by hitting safely in 32 consecutive games in 1951.

Despite his success in the Latin American leagues, Perry never had a chance to play in the major leagues. Some scouts indicated that he lacked "style," but his temperament and off-field activities might have been the real reason he was not signed by a major-league ballclub. He was often in trouble with the law, both while he was playing ball and after he retired from the diamond, and may have spent some "hard time" as a result of his illegal activities.

Perry, Carlisle (Carl)
Career: 1921–26   Positions: **2b**, 3b, ss
Teams: *Norfolk Stars ('20), Madison Stars ('20)*, Hilldale Daisies ('20, '26), New York Lincoln Giants ('20, '22–'23), Detroit Stars ('21), Indianapolis ABCs ('21), Atlantic City Bacharach Giants, Cleveland Tate Stars ('22), *Richmond Giants ('22–'23)*, Washington Potomacs ('23), Baltimore Black Sox ('23), Cleveland Browns ('24)

While best at second base, he was a versatile infielder and usually was able to find a place on a roster. He averaged two teams for each year he played in the Negro Leagues, beginning in 1920, when he played with four different teams while batting .257. A marginal player, he was often with struggling teams or teams of lesser status, but he played with the Lincoln Giants for parts of three seasons and closed out his career in 1926 with Hilldale.

Perry, Don
Career: 1922   Position: 1b
Teams: *Madison Stars ('21), Washington Braves ('21)*, Harrisburg Giants ('22), *Chappie Johnson's Stars ('25–'27)*

A fringe player, this first baseman spent most of his career with marginal teams, with his only stint with a top team coming in 1922, when he played with the Harrisburg Giants.

Perry, Ed
Career: 1887   Position: player
Team: *Washington Capital Citys*

He was a player with the Washington Capital Citys, one of eight teams that were charter members of the League of Colored Baseball Clubs in 1887. However, the league's existence was ephemeral, lasting only a week.

Perry, Hank
Career: 1926–34   Position: p
Teams: Hilldale Daisies ('26), Newark Dodgers ('34)

This pitcher made two appearances in the Negro Leagues, first in 1926 with Hilldale, and in 1934 with the Newark Dodgers.

Perry, Walter
Career: 1940   Position: c
Team: Homestead Grays

He was one of half a dozen catchers trying to fill the void left in the Homestead Grays' lineup when Josh Gibson jumped to Mexico in 1940.

Pervis
Career: 1932–37   Position: p
Teams: Monroe Monarchs ('32), Birmingham Black Barons ('37)

Pitching with the Monroe Monarchs, he made his first of two appearances in the Negro Leagues, in 1932, when the Negro Southern League was considered a major league. In 1937, in the Negro American League's inaugural season, he made his second and last appearance, as a member of the Birmingham Black Barons' pitching staff.

Peters, Frank
Career: 1916–23   Position: ss
Teams: Chicago Union Giants ('16–'18), Peters Union Giants ('19–'23)

Beginning his career in 1916 as a shortstop with the Chicago Union Giants, he hit second in the batting order in his first year with the team but moved into the third slot for the next two years.

Peters, *William S. (W. S.)*
Career: 1887–1923   Positions: 1b, manager, owner
Teams: Unions ('87), Chicago Unions ('88–'00), Peters Union Giants

He began as a first baseman with the Unions in 1887, under manager Abe Jones. The next season the team changed their name to the Chicago Unions, and he remained anchored at the initial sack through the 1894 season. In 1890 he had taken the managerial reins, and after he terminated himself as an active player, he continued as the manager for the duration of the team's existence, through the 1900 season. When owner Frank Leland consolidated the team with the Columbia Giants in 1901, Peters organized his own ballclub, the Peters Union Giants, and retained his ownership through 1923.

Peterson

Career: 1914   Position: p
Team: Chicago American Giants

He appeared briefly as a pitcher with the Chicago American Giants in 1914, but the depth of the pitching staff limited his participation.

Peterson, Harvey (Pete)

Career: 1931–37   Positions: of, p, 2b, 3b
Teams: *Montgomery Grey Sox ('31),* Birmingham Black Barons ('32), Memphis Red Sox ('32–'33), Cincinnati Tigers ('36–'37), *Cleveland Clippers ('46)*

A marginal player but with varied abilities, he could pitch and play both in the outfield and the infield. He pitched with the Memphis Red Sox in 1932 but spent the majority of his career as a reserve player at other positions, with the Birmingham Black Barons, the Cincinnati Tigers, and teams of lesser status.

Peterson, L.

Career: 1885   Position: 1b
Team: *Brooklyn Remsens*

He was a first baseman with the Brooklyn Remsens, one of the earliest black teams.

Petricola

Career: 1924   Position: p
Team: Cuban Stars (West)

He was a pitcher with the Cuban Stars in the Negro National League in 1924, his only season in the Negro Leagues.

Pettiford

Career: 1918   Position: p
Team: *Dayton Marcos*

He was a pitcher with the Dayton Marcos

in 1918, before they joined the Negro National League and when they were still playing a lesser caliber of baseball.

Pettus, William Thomas (Bill, Zack)

Career: 1909–23   Positions: **1b, c,** 2b, 3b, ss, of, manager
Teams: Kansas City Giants ('09), Chicago Giants ('10–'11, '17), New York Lincoln Giants ('12, '16–'20), Brooklyn Royal Giants ('13), New York Lincoln Stars ('14–'16), Philadelphia Giants ('16–'17), St. Louis Giants ('17), Atlantic City Bacharach Giants ('17, '21), Hilldale Daisies ('17–'20), G.C.T. Red Caps ('18), Richmond Giants ('22), Harrisburg Giants ('23)
Bats: Left   Throws: Right
Born: Aug. 13, 1884, Goliah County, Tex.
Died: Aug. 25, 1924, New York, N.Y.

This big, left-handed power hitter was one of the best batsmen of the deadball era and is one of the most underrated players from black baseball. Playing with many of the top teams, he was always hitting in the heart of the batting order, yet he demonstrated an ability to steal bases when the game situation dictated a need. A versatile player afield, he could play any position and was a catcher early in his career, but played more at first base as the years passed.

The Texan began playing baseball in 1902 in Albuquerque, New Mexico, and remained on the same ballclub until 1904, when he ventured to California to play for teams in otherwise all-white leagues in San Francisco and Oakland. After only one year on the West Coast, he returned to Albuquerque in 1905 to manage a team composed of ten Mexicans and two black players. At the end of the season the team had defeated every ballclub in that section of the country, finishing with a 48–1 record. This experience proved useful, as he became fluent in Spanish; in later years, when he played against the Cuban Stars, he would always know when they were going to steal.

In 1906 Pettus was the catcher, and the only black player, for Albuquerque's team in the white league, and then spent two years behind the plate for a team in Santa Fe, New Mexico. While playing with Albuquerque he established a reputation for being an outstanding hitter with very good power. He had two big series that demonstrated his batting capabilities. In one home series he had 15 hits in 18 at-bats, including 8 triples; in another series, at Las Vegas, New Mexico, he had 15 hits in 20 at-bats, including 3 home runs.

In 1909 he caught and played first base for the Kansas City Giants, a team of higher quality than those in the Southwest. At the close of the season Pettus joined the Occidental ballclub, a "crack" black team in Los Angeles, California, for the winter baseball season.

When the 1910 summer season started, Pettus joined Frank Leland's Chicago Giants. At the time he was considered one of the best catchers in the country, and was an excellent hitter with very good power. The free-swinger, expected to be the premier hitter on the team, was placed in the cleanup spot and fulfilled expectations with a .385 batting average for the season. After two seasons with Leland's team he jumped East to New York, playing first base and catching with Jess McMahon's Lincoln Giants. Batting fifth in the order behind John Henry Lloyd, Pettus hit .357 for the season.

In 1913 he jumped to the Brooklyn Royals as their first baseman and cleanup hitter, leaving after a year to reunite with the McMahon brothers, who formed the New York Lincoln Stars. He remained with the Stars for three seasons, hitting in the heart of the order and playing primarily at first base as the Stars captured the eastern championship in 1916.

In the fall of that season he began a series of moves that requires a road map to trace. In September, when the franchise began dissolving, he jumped back to the Lincoln Giants for the remainder of the season. Then in 1917, he played with half a dozen teams, beginning as the first baseman with the Chicago Giants. He was first sought by Jewell's ABCs in June, before serving brief stints with a trio of teams

in July (the Philadelphia Giants, Hilldale, and the Bacharachs), and ending the season again with the Lincoln Giants. In 1918 the jumping between teams within the season continued, but on a lesser scale, and he left the Lincolns in August to join Hilldale, where he was called "old reliable." Returning to the Lincolns again for most of the seasons of 1919–20, he was dropped in the batting order, usually batting in the sixth slot, but was still considered a dangerous hitter, even in the latter year, and is credited with a .434 batting average in 1920. In 1921 he played with the Bacharachs but managed only a .219 average.

Throughout his career Pettus was a clever ballplayer who used "good headwork," and as his remaining years as an active, full-time player diminished, he tried his hand as the playing manager of the Richmond Giants in 1922. Early in his career he had been a pugilist and could handle even the roughest ballplayers, but after only a year, he left the helm of the team. In 1923 he shared the first-base duties at Harrisburg, again batting in the cleanup spot when in the lineup.

But that was his last season, as he contracted tuberculosis and was confined to Sea View Hospital on Staten Island. Fans contributed $230.50, including a $25 donation by New York Lincoln Giants' owner James Keenan, to send Pettus to Phoenix to benefit from the desert climate, but the effort was too late. Before another season was over, and fewer than two weeks past his fortieth birthday, Pettus passed away.

Petway
Career: 1931–32   Positions: **ss**, 2b, lf, c
Teams: Nashville Elite Giants ('31–'32), Birmingham Black Barons ('32), Louisville Black Caps ('32)

A middle infielder for southern teams for two seasons, he could also play outfield or catch when needed.

Petway, Bruce (Buddy)
Career: 1906–25   Positions: **c**, 1b, of, manager

Teams: Cuban X-Giants ('06), Leland Giants ('06–'10), Brooklyn Royal Giants, Philadelphia Giants ('08–'09), **Chicago American Giants** ('11–'18), Detroit Stars ('19–'25)
Bats: Both   Throws: Right
Height: 5'11"   Weight: 170
Born: 1883, Nashville, Tenn.
Died: July 4, 1941, Chicago, Ill.

An outstanding receiver with a strong and accurate arm that is regarded as one of the best ever and that few base runners challenged, he intimidated base runners and, according to the press, had them "hugging the bases." Although his pegs to second base were almost invariably on the money, he threw a "light" ball. He caught much of the game on his knees, but threw to second base without standing up, and was exceptionally quick fielding bunts.

In 1910 he was the best catcher in baseball, and gained notoriety in Cuba when, in exhibition games against the Tigers, he threw out the immortal Ty Cobb three times in three attempts. As a base runner himself, Petway was a good base stealer. The lean, speedy athlete was better known as a basestealing threat than as a slugger. His prowess on the bases was demonstrated when he led the 1912 Cuban winter league with 20 stolen bases. Also an excellent bunter, he fit right into Rube Foster's racehorse style of baseball and was often used in the leadoff position. He was also a respectable hitter, batting .390 in the exhibitions against the Tigers.

The premier catcher of the day and the first great receiver in black baseball history, Petway was always in demand by the best teams. He first caught for the Leland Giants in 1906 but, abandoning his studies at Nashville's Meharry Medical College, he left after the season to serve stints with the Brooklyn Royal Giants and the Philadelphia Giants before returning to Chicago, accompanied by John Henry Lloyd and Frank Duncan, for the 1910 season. That year he registered a .397 average as a member of an aggregation that Rube Foster considered to be the greatest team of all time, black or white.

Petway continued as the backstop for Foster's superb Chicago American Giants, at a time (1910–18) when they were virtually perennial champions. During his tenure with Foster's team he was disabled twice by strained ligaments in his throwing arm and once by a leg injury, losing substantial playing time for three consecutive seasons, 1914–16.

Also a relatively good hitter, he hit .393 for the Lelands in 1910 but, although he was referred to as "Home Run" Petway early in his career, he was not a genuine power hitter, as attested by his averages of .253, .208, and .200 in 1916–18. In 1916, on his last trip to Cuba, he hit .333, but managed only a .210 lifetime average for his Cuban career, interspersed during the years 1908–16. He is credited with averages of .182 in 1918 and .171 against major-leaguers in exhibitions.

A smart ballplayer, the scrappy receiver was a student of the game and learned much from his years with Rube Foster, enabling him to end his baseball career as a playing-manager with the Detroit Stars. As a manager he was slightly hotheaded but was good with young players. His batting averages in Detroit were .313, .268, .337, and .341 in 1921–24, before slumping to .156 in 1925, his last season. Altogether he spent seven seasons with the Stars. After his retirement he lived in Chicago, where he managed an apartment complex.

Petway, Howard
Career: 1906   Position: p, c
Teams: Leland Giants ('06), *Nashville Athletics* ('15)

A sidearm pitcher with a good change of pace and effective "mudball," he won 12 straight games during the late summer and early fall of 1915 with the Nashville Athletics. He was the brother of the great catcher Bruce Petway, and also performed some catching chores himself when not on the mound for the Nashville team. Earlier in his career, in 1906, he had pitched with the Leland Giants, a team for whom his famous brother later starred.

Petway, Shirley (Charlie)

Career: 1937–44   Position: c

Teams: Detroit Stars ('37), *Chicago Brown Bombers ('42)*, Cleveland Buckeyes ('44)

A light hitter, he was a backup catcher during his appearances with top teams, beginning with the Detroit Stars in 1937, when he hit in the eighth spot when in the starting lineup, and ending in 1944, when he was a seldom-used reserve, with partial statistics showing a .273 average in very limited play.

Pfiffer

Career: 1937   Position: 3b

Team: St. Louis Stars

He was a substitute third baseman with the St. Louis Stars in 1937, the first year of the Negro American League.

Philadelphia Giants

Duration: 1902–16   Honors: Eastern champions ('04–'07, '09)

Affiliation: Independent

Organized in 1902 by Sol White, a former star baseball player, and H. Walter Schlichter, a white sportswriter, the team finished with a 81–43–2 record the first year. The following season the Giants improved to a 89–37–4 mark, but lost the championship play-off to the Cuban X-Giants. The next season, White lured Rube Foster away from the X-Giants, and after fashioning a 95–41–6 work sheet, Philadelphia reversed the previous season's playoff results, defeating the X-Giants for their first eastern championship. In 1905 the Giants had their highest winning percentage (.848), with a 134–21–3 mark. In 1906 their record was 108–31–6, and in 1907 they won their fourth straight championship.

In 1909 they captured another title, but Schlichter and White had a disagreement, and in 1910 White left to form his own team. Rube Foster had already left the team in 1907, and after the end of the decade many of Philadelphia's remaining star players defected to other teams. The Giants' caliber of play dropped significantly as they rapidly became a minor team.

Although a club continued on into the '20s with the same name, that team cannot be equated with the original franchise.

Philadelphia Stars

Duration: 1933–50   Honors: Negro National League pennant ('34)

Affiliations: Independent ('33), NNL ('34–'48), NAL ('49–'50)

Organized by Ed Bolden in 1933, the Stars won a Negro National League flag in 1934, their first season in the league. After copping the second-half title, the Stars defeated the Chicago American Giants in a bitterly contested 7-game championship series. One of the games in the playoff was protested by the Chicago American Giants, but the Stars' victory was upheld, and Philadelphia claimed the pennant. Unfortunately, this was to be their last flag, even though they remained in the league until its demise in 1948. The nearest they came to another title were strong second-half finishes in 1938 and 1944, with their front office claiming they were cheated out of the latter pennant. After the Negro National League folded, the Stars entered the Eastern Division of the Negro American League but without any appreciable success.

Philadelphia Tigers

Duration: 1928   Honors: None

Affiliation: Eastern Colored League ('28)

In 1928, the final year of the Eastern Colored League, Philadelphia fielded a team called the Tigers, but the league broke up during the season and the franchise struggled unsuccessfully to finish the schedule.

Phillips

Career: 1921–23   Positions: ss, 2b

Teams: Nashville Elite Giants ('21), Detroit Stars ('23)

A reserve middle infielder during the early '20s, he played without distinction for the Nashville Elite Giants and the Detroit Stars.

Phillips
Career: 1927   Position: p
Team: Birmingham Black Barons

Pitching with the Birmingham Black Barons in 1927, he lost his only decision during the season.

Phillips, John (Lefty)
Career: 1938–40   Position: p
Team: Baltimore Elite Giants
Bats: Left   Throws: Left

A left-handed pitcher for the Baltimore Elite Giants, he appeared in three seasons, failing to register a decision in 1940, his last season in the Negro Leagues.

Phillips, Norris (Richard)
Career: 1942–43   Position: p
Teams: Kansas City Monarchs ('42–'43), Memphis Red Sox ('42)
Bats: Left   Throws: Left
Height: 5'11"   Weight: 180

This left-hander had excellent control and a good curve and change-up but only an average fastball. He pitched with the Kansas City Monarchs for part of the 1942 season, when they won their fourth straight Negro American League pennant, but was not on their World Series roster. In each of his two seasons with the Monarchs, 1942–43, he won his only league decision.

Pierce, Herbert
Career: 1925–26   Position: c
Teams: Homestead Grays ('25–'26), *Ewing's All-Stars ('28)*

After two seasons with the Homestead Grays during the mid-'20s, this catcher joined Chappie Johnson's Stars, a lesser team, to finish out his active career.

Pierce, Leonard
Career: 1924   Positions: p, of
Teams: Washington Potomacs ('24), *Philadelphia Giants ('25–'27)*

A pitcher with the Washington Potomacs in the Eastern Colored League in 1924, he subsequently pitched three years with the Philadelphia Giants, a team of lesser quality.

Pierce, Steve
Career: 1925–28   Position: officer
Team: Detroit Stars

He was an officer with the Negro National League's Detroit Stars for four seasons during the latter half of the '20s.

Pierce, William H. (Bill)
Career: 1910–26   Positions: **c, 1b**, of, umpire
Teams: Philadelphia Giants ('10, '26), Chicago American Giants ('11–'12), Mohawk Giants ('13), New York Lincoln Stars ('14–'16), Pennsylvania Red Caps of New York ('17–'19), New York Lincoln Giants ('16–'18,, '21–'23), Atlantic City Bacharach Giants ('20–'21), *Norfolk Stars ('21),* Baltimore Black Sox ('22), Detroit Stars ('24)

While best known as a catcher, he also played first base and outfield for the Chicago American Giants, the New York Lincoln Giants, and other teams during the '10s. He began his career in 1910 with the Philadelphia Giants and proved to be a good hitter with apparent power. Joining Rube Foster's Chicago American Giants in 1911, he shared the catching duties with Bruce Petway the first season, but in 1912 he and Petway were both in the lineup, alternately filling the catcher and first-base positions.

In 1913 he left the Midwest for New York, playing for a season with the Mohawk Giants before joining the Lincoln Stars when they were organized in 1914. After two years with the Stars and two years with the Lincoln Giants, he joined the Pennsylvania Red Caps for three seasons, 1917–19. While with the American Giants, Lincoln Stars, and Lincoln Giants, he usually batted in the lower half of the order, but with the Red Caps he was the cleanup hitter, and sometimes in later years he was referred to as "Home run" Pierce.

By the late '10s he was beginning to play more at first base, and in 1920 he joined the

Bacharach Giants, but suffered an early-season slump and, at that time, was considered the weakest hitter in the Bacharachs' lineup. But later in the year he regained his hitting eye, walloping 3 homers in a game against the Baltimore Black Sox while they were still striving to be a league-level team. The next season he switched to the New York Lincoln Giants and played first base with lots of pep and also batted in the cleanup spot, while splitting his playing time between first base and catcher through the 1923 season.

After his playing days ended, he was an umpire in the East-West League during its single season of existence in 1932.

Pierre, Joseph

Career: 1950   Position: if
Team: Kansas City Monarchs ('50–'51)

In 1950 he was a reserve infielder with the Kansas City Monarchs, when the Negro American League was struggling to survive the loss of players to organized baseball, but his playing time was severely restricted and is unconfirmed by league statistics.

Pierre, Rogers (Shape)

a.k.a. Pierre Rogers; Pierre Rodgers; Askari
Career: 1939–41   Position: p
Teams: Chicago American Giants ('39), Ethiopian Clowns ('39–'41), *Harlem Globetrotters ('47)*

He began his career with the Chicago American Giants in 1939, but gained most of his notoriety with the Ethiopian Clowns, where he pitched under the "clown name" of Askari. A few years later he continued his clowning identity with the baseball Harlem Globetrotters, a team of lesser quality of play.

Pierson

Career: 1933   Positions: 3b, 2b
Team: Homestead Grays

He appeared briefly as a reserve infielder with the Homestead Grays in 1933, playing both third base and second base.

Pierson

[see Pearson, Lennie]

Pigg, Leonard (Fatty)

Career: 1947–50   Positions: c, 1b
Teams: *military service ('40–'45),* Indianapolis Clowns ('47–'49, '51), Cleveland Buckeyes ('50), *Canadian League ('50, '52–54)*
Bats: Right   Throws: Right
Height: 5'9"   Weight: 230
Born: Sept. 18, 1919, Grant, Okla.

A good-hitting catcher with a fair arm, he lacked mobility behind the plate and was slow on the bases. He played baseball on the sandlots of Lawton, Oklahoma, until he joined the Army in 1940. While stationed in the Quartermaster Corps at Fort Sill, he played on the base baseball team, who were champions for five years. During World War II he spent nine months in the Philippines but was not engaged in combat. After he returned to the United States, he played with the Havana La Palomas ballclub in 1947, but joined the Indianapolis Clowns during the season. In his two full seasons with the Clowns, 1948–49, he hit .345 and .386. In 1950 he signed with the Cleveland Buckeyes, but chose instead to play in Canada with the Brandon ballclub. In 1951 the Chicago White Sox tried to sign him, but were going to send him to Hot Springs, and Pigg opted to return to the Clowns. His weight had ballooned and, due to his late start in professional baseball, his age was also against him. He returned to Canada and played through the 1954 season, primarily with lesser teams. After leaving baseball, he located in Seattle, Washington, and worked in construction until his retirement.

Pillot, Guillermo Luis (Guido, Guillo, Victor)

a.k.a. Pillot
Career: 1941–43   Position: p
Teams: New York Black Yankees ('41), Cincinnati Clowns ('43)
Bats: Right   Throws: Right

This right-hander pitched for the New York Black Yankees in 1941 without a decision, and after joining the Cincinnati Clowns he registered only a single victory against 5 losses in 1943.

Piloto, José (Potato)
a.k.a. Polotto
Career: 1948–50   Position: p
Team: Memphis Red Sox
Born: Cuba

This youngster was pitching barefoot in the Cuban sandlots when he was discovered. He began in the Negro Leagues in 1948 with the Memphis Red Sox. The following winter he played his only season in the Cuban winter league. He was back with Memphis in 1949, but in 1950 he pitched in only 2 games and did not register a decision. After having one bad year in baseball, he went to Mexico, where he became embroiled in an argument and was killed.

Pinder, Eddie
Career: 1916   Position: of
Team: Hilldale Daises

An outfielder for Hilldale during the team's formative years, he is the brother of shortstop Fred Pinder, who also played with Hilldale.

Pinder, Fred
Career: 1916–18   Position: ss
Team: Hilldale Daisies ('17)

A shortstop with Hilldale during the team's formative years, he was the starting shortstop for the ballclub in 1917, until Dick Lundy was recruited to play against the major-leaguers in the fall. When in the lineup Pinder often batted in the third slot, but he was benched in favor of Lundy in 1918. He is the brother of outfielder Eddie Pinder, who also played with Hilldale.

Ping
Career: 1914   Position: 1b
Team: Philadelphia Giants

He was a first baseman with the Philadelphia Giants in 1914, after the team had begun to decline in quality.

Pinkston, Alfred Charles (**Al**)
a.k.a. Pinkison; Pinkiston
Career: 1948   Position: 1b, of, c
Teams: *St. Louis Stars ('36),* Cleveland Buckeyes ('48), *Canadian League ('51–'52), minor leagues ('53–'58), Mexican League ('59–'65)*
Bats: Left   Throws: Right
Height: 6'5"   Weight: 225
Born: October 22, 1917, Newbern, Ala.
Died: March, 1981, New Orleans, La.

A hard-hitting first baseman-outfielder, he had a sterling career in organized baseball but only a token appearance in the Negro Leagues. After belting 23 home runs in 1947 with a New Orleans team, he was the sensation of the Cleveland Buckeyes' training camp in the spring of 1948. However, his stay with the Buckeyes was brief, and he moved on to a career in organized baseball, including stays in the Mexican League and the Canadian League.

He played in the Provincial League in 1951–52, batting .301 and .360 while leading the league with 30 homers and 121 RBIs to win the Triple Crown the latter season. However, the following year, with Ottawa in the International League, he hit only .198 with 1 home run in 45 games. He continued his good hitting in the lower minors, hitting .331, .369, .300, .293, .372, and .337 through 1958. His last two seasons were with Amarillo in the Western League, and he led the league in RBIs each year.

In 1959 he began his career in the Mexican League, winning batting titles his first four years in the league, with averages of .369, .397, .374, and .381. The first two titles were while he was with the Mexico City Reds, and the last two were with the Vera Cruz ballclub. He played three more seasons with Vera Cruz, hitting .368, .364, and .345, and ending his fifteen-year minor-league career after the 1965 season, with a lifetime batting average of .352. In 1975 he became the first American to be elected to the Mexican Hall of Fame.

Pipkin, Robert (Lefty, Black Diamond)
a.k.a. Pipkins; Pipkens

Career: 1928–33, 1942 Position: p
Teams: Birmingham Black Barons ('28–'29, '42), Cleveland Cubs ('31), *New Orleans Crescent Stars ('33), Detroit Senators ('47)*

Often called the Black Diamond in 1928, when he began his career with the Birmingham Black Barons, he fashioned a 3–5 work sheet in 1929, and pitched with the Cleveland Cubs in 1931 until the team disbanded. He returned to the Birmingham Black Barons in 1942, and is credited with a 5–2 mark for the season.

Pitts, Curtis
Career: 1950   Positions: c, *ss*
Teams: Cleveland Buckeyes ('50), Chicago American Giants ('50–*'51)*

In 1950, when the Negro American League was struggling to survive the loss of players to organized baseball, he was a regular catcher, splitting the season between the Buckeyes and the Chicago American Giants, but batting a composite .175 for the year. He returned to the American Giants for the 1951 season before closing out his short Negro League career.

Pitts, Ed
Career: 1940   Position: c
Team: Philadelphia Stars

He was listed as a reserve catcher with the Philadelphia Stars in 1940, but the Stars had three other catchers who figured prominently in their plans for the season, and his time with the team was brief.

Pittsburgh Crawfords
Duration: 1931–38   Honors: NNL pennant ('35–'36)
Affiliations: Independent ('31–'32), NNL ('33–'38)

Formed by Gus Greenlee from a youth team in 1931, the new owner loaded the team with outstanding talent, including Satchel Paige and Josh Gibson, and the Crawfords became a powerhouse for the following five years (1932–36). The Crawfords played as an independent in 1932, finishing with a 99–36 record for the season. In 1933 they joined the new

Negro National League and were a coclaimant to the league's first pennant. The Crawfords finished the first half with a 20–8 league record, only half a game behind the Chicago American Giants. The second half of the season was not completed, and the Chicago American Giants claimed the title, but Greenlee, as president of the league, declared the Crawfords to be the champions, and the matter was never resolved. In 1934 the Crawfords fielded another outstanding team, finishing with a combined 29–17 record for a .630 winning percentage in league play. However, they failed to win either half of the split season, and missed the playoffs.

But in each of the next two seasons, 1935–36, the Crawfords won Negro National League pennants, and the 1935 club is generally regarded as the greatest black baseball team of all time. The 1935 squad won the first half with a 26–6 mark, for a .785 winning percentage, then defeated the second-half titlists, the New York Cubans, in a closely contested 7-game championship series. In 1936, after a third-place first-half finish, the Crawfords copped the second-half title with a 20–9 mark and finished with the best overall record, 36–24, for a .600 winning percentage, while the first-half titlists, the Washington Elites, finished under .500 for the entire season. A playoff was not completed, and again Greenlee declared the Crawfords champions. Unfortunately, the team was falsely accused of throwing a game to the Bushwicks, and despite the denial and retraction, the team's reputation was tarnished.

The following spring Satchel Paige, Josh Gibson, Cool Papa Bell, and several other Crawfords players departed for Santo Domingo to play for the country's dictator, Trujillo, and the franchise never again reclaimed the glory from the five preceding seasons. After two second-division finishes and a business reversal, Greenlee sold the team, and the franchise moved to Toledo in 1939 and then to Indianapolis in 1940, playing in the Negro American League each of these seasons, and eventually disbanded. In the mid-'40s another team using the same Pittsburgh Crawfords' name was formed, but it was not related to the original franchise.

Pittsburgh Keystones
Duration: 1887   Honors: None
Affiliation: *League of Colored Baseball Clubs*

In 1887 the Pittsburgh Keystones were one of eight teams that were charter members of the League of Colored Baseball Clubs. However, the league's existence was ephemeral, lasting only a week.

Pittsburgh Keystones
Duration: 1922   Honors: None
Affiliation: NNL ('22)

Thirty-five years earlier, a team with the same name had operated briefly, but only the name was the same. This franchise fielded a team in the Negro National League in 1922, their only season in the league, and, as did their namesake predecessor, met with ill fortune.

Pla
Career: 1933   Position: p
Team: Cuban Stars

He was a pitcher with the Cuban Stars in 1933, when they were playing as an independent team.

Pluno
Career: 1887   Position: player
Team: *Boston Resolutes*

He played with the Boston Resolutes, one of eight teams that were charter members of the League of Colored Baseball Clubs, in 1887. However, the league's existence was ephemeral, lasting only a week.

Poindexter, Robert (Albert)
Career: 1924–29   Positions: **p**, 1b
Teams: **Birmingham Black Barons** ('24–'25, '27–'28), Chicago American Giants ('26, '29), Memphis Red Sox ('29), *Gilkerson's Union Giants ('29)*

Bats: Right   Throws: Right
Height: 5'11"   Weight: 175

This right-hander had a good curve and spitball and was a fairly effective pitcher during the '20s. Beginning his career with the Birmingham Black Barons in 1924, he left the team after two years to join Rube Foster's Chicago American Giants, and forged a 6–2 mark for the pennant-winning American Giants. The next season he was back with the Birmingham Black Barons for another two-year stint, posting a 10–12 mark in 1927. Poindexter sometimes played first base and was a decent hitter, batting .246 in league games in 1927.

However, in 1929 his fortunes turned against him. He returned to Chicago, playing for a short time with the Chicago American Giants and Gilkerson's Union Giants, but spent most of the season with the Memphis Red Sox, finishing with a 4–2 composite ledger for the 1929 season. Off the field he had a drinking problem and was somewhat on the wild side, once spending time in jail for shooting a teammate, first baseman J. C. McHaskell. Depressed over his troubles on and off the field, he tried to commit suicide by taking bichloride of mercury. Although his attempt to take his life failed, he never again played baseball in the Negro Leagues.

Poinsette
Career: 1939   Position: p
Team: Toledo Crawfords

He was a pitcher with the Toledo Crawfords in 1939, after the franchise had moved from Pittsburgh and joined the Negro American League.

Poinsette, Robert
Career: 1939   Position: of
Team: New York Black Yankees

He was an outfielder with the New York Black Yankees in 1939, his only season in the Negro Leagues.

Pointer, Robert Lee
Career: 1950   Position: p
Team: Kansas City Monarchs

He was a pitcher with the Kansas City Monarchs in 1950, when the Negro American League was struggling to survive the loss of players to organized baseball, but league statistics do not confirm his playing time.

Polanco, Rafael (Ralph)
Career: 1942   Position: p
Team: Philadelphia Stars

He was a pitcher with the Philadelphia Stars in 1942, his only season in the Negro Leagues.

Poles, E. (Possum, **Googles**)
Career: 1922–28   Positions: ss, 3b, 2b, of
Teams: Baltimore Black Sox ('22–'24), Harrisburg Giants ('24)
Bats: Right   Throws: Right

Poles was one of several players who played shortstop for the 1924 Baltimore Black Sox in an effort to fill a weak position on the team. He was a fair player but was "green," and after being benched, he and Lefty Smith quit the Baltimore Black Sox in the latter part of June. He played with Harrisburg for the remainder of the season, but afterward played with teams of lesser status.

Poles, Spottswood (**Spot**)
Career: 1909–23   Position: cf
Teams: *Harrisburg Colored Giants ('06–'08)*, Philadelphia Giants ('09–'10), **New York Lincoln Giants** ('11–'14, '17, '19–'23), Brooklyn Royal Giants ('12), New York Lincoln Stars ('14–'16), Hilldale Daisies ('17, '20), *military service ('18),* New York Bacharach Giants ('19), *Richmond Giants ('23)*
Bats: Both   Throws: Right
Height: 5'7"   Weight: 165
Born: Nov. 7, 1889, Winchester, Va.
Died: Sept. 12, 1962, Harrisburg, Pa.

A fleet-footed, slightly bowlegged, sharp-hitting center fielder during the deadball era, Spot Poles usually batted in the leadoff position to utilize his incredible speed, which was comparable to that of Cool Papa Bell. Once in spring training he was clocked under 10 seconds for a 100-yard dash. A left-handed batter, he watched the ball all the way to his bat and consistently hit for a high average. He was also a good bunter but, despite a stocky build and arms described as "massive" for his size, he had only moderate power. In the field he had excellent range, good hands, and an accurate arm. An intense competitor, he was confident but not cocky in his baseball ability, and was called the black Ty Cobb.

Born to Matilda and French Poles, a laborer, he began playing baseball at age six, using a broomstick for a bat, and advanced progressively through a boys' league called the Hello Bill Club in 1897; the Springdale Athletic Club in Harrisburg, Pennsylvania, in 1902; and the Harrisburg Colored Giants in 1906. Then, at age nineteen, he began his professional career in 1909 as the center fielder for Sol White's eastern champion Philadelphia Giants. Poles soon settled in as the leadoff batter, playing two years with White's charges, before following his skipper to the New York Lincoln Giants when the team was organized in 1911 by Jess and Rod McMahon, and Sol White was appointed manager. During his initial season with the squad, Poles demonstrated his incredible speed by stealing 41 bases in only 60 games. He also demonstrated his proficiency with a bat, and over the first four seasons with the Lincolns, Poles hit for averages of .440, .398, .414, and .487 against all levels of competition, which included a 1913 game when he faced Grover Cleveland Alexander and rapped three straight hits off the Hall of Famer. That season the Lincolns soundly defeated Rube Foster's Chicago American Giants in the championship playoffs, and owner Jess McMahon boasted that the Lincolns could beat any team, including the best major-league ballclubs.

In 1915 the speedburner jumped to the rival New York Lincoln Stars for a season, but returned to the Lincoln Giants the following year. Twice previously, Poles had left the Lincoln Giants briefly, but each time he returned during the same season. The first time was in 1912, when Poles and John Henry Lloyd, who had succeeded Sol White as manager, had a dispute, and Poles jumped to the Brooklyn Royal Giants but returned later in the season. The second temporary break in his service with the Lincoln Giants came in 1914, when the Lincoln Stars were first organized by the McMahon brothers, and he played with the Stars in the Early spring but was back in the Giants' fold in May.

Each of these defections were to other teams in New York City, but during his seventh campaign with New York-based teams, he returned to Philadelphia to join Ed Bolden's fledgling Hilldale club. His Hilldale tenure was interrupted by World War I, and Poles joined the Army infantry and served his country with distinction, earning decorations (five battle stars and a Purple Heart) for his combat experience in France as a sergeant in the 369th Infantry, attached to the French Army.

While overseas he wrote Ed Bolden, expressing his desire to resume his baseball career with Hilldale upon his discharge from military service. When he did return Stateside, however, Poles played with four different teams in 1919. Initially he was with his old team the Lincoln Giants in the spring, but returned to the Hilldale fold when the regular season started. He left the Darby clan in turn to assume the role of player manager with the Hellfighters, a team of black servicemen. His stay there was brief, and he finished the season at Atlantic City with the Bacharach Giants. By the close of the season, the Bacharachs were the best team in black baseball. Rejoining the Lincoln Giants in 1920, he batted leadoff and was still a dangerous hitter, playing until 1923.

When he retired from baseball after 15 years, he was credited with a lifetime batting average of over .400 against all competition, and an average of .319 for four winters in Cuba, including the 1913 Cuban winter season, when he recorded a .355 average. While in Cuba he often played exhibitions against the Phillies, Athletics, and other major-league teams, and is credited with a .594 average against major-league competition.

Regardless of the paucity of complete statis-tics, eyewitesses corroborate his greatness. New York Giants' manager John McGraw listed Poles, John Henry Lloyd, Cannonball Dick Redding, and Smokey Joe Williams as the four black players he would pick for the major leagues if the color line were not so firmly entrenched. Paul Robeson, a reknowned athlete and actor, was more emphatic in his praise, and once grouped Poles with Jesse Owens, Joe Louis, and Jack Johnson as the greatest black athletes of all time.

After Poles retired following the 1923 season, he bought five taxis and went into business for himself. He and his wife later worked at Olmsted Air Force Base in Middletown, Pennsylvania, and when they retired were "fairly well to do," enabling Poles to endulge in some of his favorite luxuries. He loved Studebakers and bought a new one every other year. In later years he loved to play the horses and made an annual trip to the Kentucky Derby.

Most importantly, he was able to continue in baseball as a coach, managing an integrated semipro team called the Harrisburg Giants. He was an enthusiastic teacher, counting future major-leaguer Brooks Lawrence among his protégés. In one game, when he was in the vicinity of sixty years of age, he proved he could still hit, when he entered a game as a pinch hitter and lined a base hit through the right side of the infield. After reaching first base he removed himself for a pinch runner, but his team won the game. To the end, he loved the game of baseball and was never bitter about the social conditions that prevented him from playing in the major leagues. He and his wife are buried in Arlington National Cemetery.

Pollard, Nathaniel Hawthorne **(Nat)**
Career: 1943–50　　　Position: p
Teams: Birmingham Black Barons ('43, '46–'50), *military service* ('44–'45)
Bats: Right　　　Throws: Right
Height: 5'9"　　　Weight: 209
Born: Jan. 1915, Alabama City, Ala.

After joining the Birmingham Black Barons briefly in 1943, he entered the Navy during World War II, but returned to the ballclub after his discharge. Primarily a curveball pitcher with a good change-up, he also mixed in a fastball and had fine control. Pitching with the Black Barons during the late '40s, he posted marks of 5–2 and 2–3 in 1946 and 1948, respectively, and closed out his Negro League career in 1950 with a 7–3 ledger.

As a youngster he went to school in Piper, Alabama, and worked in the mines of that area before leaving to play semipro baseball in Birmingham. He played with the Acipico team in the Birmingham Industrial League and with the Stockham Bears before being discovered by the Black Barons. After leaving baseball he entered the ministry and spent more than thirty years as a pastor.

Pollock, Syd

Career: 1926–50 Position: officer
Teams: Havana Red Sox ('26–'30), Cuban Stars ('33), Cuban House of David ('31–'32), Ethiopian Clowns ('37–'42), Cincinnati Clowns ('43), Indianapolis Clowns ('44–'65)
Born: March 20, 1901, North Tarrytown, NY.
Died: Nov. 22, 1968, Hollywood, Fla.

He is best identified with the Indianapolis Clowns' ballclub, becoming partners with Hunter Campbell when they were still based in Miami. After assuming control of the franchise, he was instrumental in promoting and popularizing the team and developed them into a nationally known combination of show business and baseball that earned them the designation as the Harlem Globetrotters of baseball.

His first involvement with black baseball was in 1926, when he became associated with the Havana Red Sox. In 1929 the Red Sox won their 100th game of the season by mid-August, but their opposition was primarily teams of lesser quality. In 1933 he helped Ed Hamman organize the Canadian Indians, a white comedy team, and became a successful promoter and booking agent.

In 1941, Pollock's Clowns won the Denver Post Tournament. Two years later, he joined the Negro American League, beginning a 12-year membership in the League before withdrawing following the 1954 season.

In 1955 Pollock sold his longtime friend Ed Hamman a partnership in the Clowns and then the remainder of his interest in 1965. In 1952, Pollock signed Hank Aaron to his first professional contract, at $200 a month. Aaron played about three months as the team's shortstop and cleanup hitter before his contract was purchased by the Braves' organization. Pollard stalled the New York Giants, who were seeking Aaron, and when Aaron made it to the major leagues, Pollard received the last installment on the $10,000 contract price.

Pollock was twice awarded the National Baseball Congress Placque for Outstanding Contribution to Baseball based upon the Clowns' contribution to the sports popularity created by their comedy and appearances in cities and towns in all states in the Continental U.S.

Pompez, Alejandro (Alessandro, Alex)

Career: 1916–50 Positions: manager, officer, owner; vice president (NNL)
Teams: Cuban Stars (East) ('22–'29), New York Cubans ('35–50)
Height: 5'11"
Born: May 3, 1890, Havana, Cuba
Died: Mar. 15, 1974, New York, N.Y.

A sports promoter and numbers banker, he owned the New York Cubans for their duration in the Negro National League. He also served as the vice president of the Negro National League. Earlier in his career, he owned, managed, and promoted the Cuban Stars' team that began in the deadball era and was based in the East during the '20s. An influential owner, after the Eastern Colored League was established he helped negotiate the first Negro World Series, in 1924.

When the Cuban Stars disbanded temporarily during the early '30s, he organized the New York Cubans in 1935 and won the second-half title behind the play of Martin Dihigo. By this time Pompez was an important member of Dutch Schultz's mob and was one of the wealthiest men in Harlem. When Thomas E. Dewey, district attorney of New York County, began a crackdown on New York racketeers, he selected Pompez as one of his targets, and in 1936, Pompez was indicted by a grand jury for his involvement in policy rackets. Tipped off by an elevator operator while on his way into Dewey's trap, Pompez disappeared, giving rise to rumors that he had been kidnapped or was in hiding to avoid the grand jury's jurisdiction. Actually he escaped to Mexico, where he resumed his flamboyant lifestyle until arrested by Mexican authorities as he was stepping into a bulletproof sedan with Chicago license plates. Mexican officials refused Dewey's request for extradition, but Pompez decided to return to the United States to turn state's evidence. He is considered to be the only man who informed on another racketeer and lived.

Pompez was no stranger to either this element of societal concerns or unusual occurrences. Once, when a number was heavily played, he shared a part of the "business" with an Italian banker, and when the number hit, Pompez could not cover the payoff and tried to leave town with a substantial sum of money, but the train was stopped by the Mafia and he was taken off the train. Needless to say, the payoff was covered.

The New York Cubans dropped out of competition for a season following Pompez's indictment, but were back in the Negro National League in 1938 when Pompez returned to the baseball scene. His New York Cubans were in a Negro National League championship playoff in 1941 and won the Negro National League flag and World Series in 1947. The next season the Cuban Giants became a New York Giants' farm club, with Pompez doubling as a scout for the New York Giants. In this capacity he was responsible for many black players being signed by the major leagues. Later in life he was a member of the Hall of Fame's special committee for the Negro Leagues.

Pontello
Career: 1927   Position: p
Team: Cuban Stars (East)

He was a pitcher with the Eastern Colored League's Cuban Stars in 1927.

Poole, Claude
Career: 1945–46   Position: p
Team: New York Black Yankees

This pitcher began his two-year career as a wartime player, winning only a single game against 5 losses in 1945 with the Negro National League doormat New York Black Yankees. He closed out his career the following year.

Pope, David (**Dave**)
Career: 1946   Position: of
Teams: Homestead Grays ('46), *Canadian League ('48–'49), minor leagues ('50–'53, '56–'61), major leagues ('52, '54–'56)*
Bats: Left   Throws: Right
Height: 5'10"   Weight: 170
Born: June 17, 1925, Talladega, Ala.

Beginning with the Homestead Grays in 1946, this speedy outfielder eventually played in the major leagues with the Cleveland Indians and the Baltimore Orioles, and had a lifetime major-league batting average of .265. After leaving the Negro Leagues, he batted .361 and .306 with Farnham in the Provincial League in 1948–49, followed by two years at Wilkes-Barre, where he led the league in triples each year, batting .268 and .309. In 1952, with Indianapolis, he won the American Association batting title with a .352 average to get his first trip to the majors, batting .294 in a dozen games. Back with Indianapolis for the entire 1953 season, he dropped to a .287 average, but led the Venezuelan winter league with a .345 batting average in 1953–54 to earn another chance in the major leagues.

In 1954 he was with the pennant-winning Cleveland Indians, batting .294, and also spent the entire 1955 season in the majors, batting .264 for the year. After beginning the 1956 season in the major leagues, he was sent down to Indianapolis again and hit .302. The next two seasons, 1957–58, he was with San Diego in the Pacific Coast League and hit .313 and .316, but didn't get another shot at the bigs. His last three years were spent with Toronto and Houston, finishing his baseball career in 1961.

Pope, Edgar (James)
Career: 1938   Positions: **of,** if
Teams: Atlanta Black Crackers
Bats: Right   Throws: Right
Height: 5'8"   Weight: 165

As a freshman at Morris Brown College, he played in left field for the Atlanta Black Crackers in 1938. He also participated in track and football in college, and was strong, muscular, very fast, and had an excellent throwing arm. Originally from Pennsylvania, he made his home in Atlanta while playing with the Black Crackers.

Pope, James
Career: 1931–32   Position: p
Teams: Louisville White Sox ('31), Montgromery Grey Sox ('32), Columbus Blue Birds ('32)

A marginal player, he pitched two seasons in the early '30s, with three teams during their only season in a major league.

Pope, William (**Willie,** Bill)
Career: 1947–48   Positions: **p,** of
Teams: *Pittsburgh Crawfords ('46),* Homestead Grays ('47–'48), *Canadian League ('49–'51), minor leagues ('52–'55)*
Bats: Left   Throws: Right
Height: 6'4"   Weight: 240
Born: December 24, 1918, Birmingham, Ala.

This big right-hander began his career with the Homestead Grays in 1947, notching a 6–7 record, and the next year was a member of the Grays' pitching staff as they captured the last Negro National League pennant. He had a key triple in the ensuing World Series that helped the Grays defeat the Birmingham Black Barons for the championship. His brother Dave was an outfielder on the team. Willie was a good-hitting pitcher and occasionally also played in the outfield.

Leaving the Grays after the 1948 season, he spent the next three years in the Provincial League, where he registered ledgers of 3–5 (2.37 ERA) with Farnham in 1950 and 12–11 (3.82 ERA) with St. Hyacinthe in 1951. He spent three of the next four years with Colorado Springs in the Western League, registering seasons of 12–5, 16–12, and 13–8. In 1954 he was with Charleston in the American Association, where he managed only a 4–11 record with a 5.27 ERA.

Porsee
Career: 1921   Position: p
Team: St. Louis Giants

He was a pitcher with the St. Louis Giants in 1921, his only season in the Negro Leagues.

Porter, Andrew (**Andy,** Pullman)
Career: 1932–50   Position: p
Teams: Louisville Black Caps ('32), Cleveland Cubs ('32), Nashville Elite Giants ('32–'34), Columbus Elite Giants ('35), Washington Elite Giants ('36–'37), **Baltimore Elite Giants** ('38–'39, '42–'46), *Mexican League ('39–'43),* Newark Eagles ('47), Indianapolis Clowns ('48–'50), *minor leagues ('52)*
Bats: Right   Throws: Right
Height: 6'4"   Weight: 190
Born: Mar. 7, 1911, Little Rock, Ark.

This big right-handed power pitcher threw smoke and had a good slider, and along with Bill Byrd and Jonas Gaines formed the Big Three on the Baltimore Elite Giants' pitching staff. He began his pro career with the Louisville Black Caps in 1932, but joined the Elites, then based in Nashville, in the fall and stayed with the ballclub as the franchise moved to Columbus, Washington, and finally to Baltimore. After one full season in the Elites' final location, Porter jumped to Mexico for five years.

During his first two seasons (1939–40), pitching with Tampico (10–7, 2.38 ERA) and

Nuevo Laredo (21–14, 3.35 ERA), he led the league in strikeouts, averaging 6.8 and 7.1 per game, respectively. During this time he also pitched two seasons (1939–41) in the Cuban winter league, splitting 18 decisions on the island. Back in Mexico for the 1941 summer, he experienced his first losing season (11–16, 4.48 ERA), pitching with the Mexico City Reds. In 1942 he had a 7–1 record with the Elites, but after joining Vera Cruz he experienced control problems and dropped to a 5–8 record and a 5.66 ERA. The following season he appeared in only 3 games without a decision, before returning to Baltimore.

Upon his return to the Elites, "Pullman" won 3 of his 4 decisions in 1944, and followed in 1945 with a perfect 7–0 record, including 2 shutouts. In 1946, his last year with the Elites, he dropped to a 2–4 mark. Following a brief stint with the Newark Eagles, he signed with the Indianapolis Clowns in the Negro American League, where he posted a 4–5 mark with a 4.68 ERA in 1948. In 1949 he improved to a 10–6 record with a 3.64 ERA, and made his only appearance in the All-Star game. In 1950 he appeared in only 3 games, winning his only 2 decisions.

Two years later he entered organized ball briefly, pitching with Porterville in the Southwest International League in 1952 and posting a 3–5 record to close out his playing days. During his baseball career Porter always wore tailor-made suits, and after ending that career, he worked for twenty-three years with a rubber company before retiring in Los Angeles.

Portuondo, Bartolo

a.k.a. Portuando, Portounda
Career: 1916–27   Positions: **3b**, 1b, 2b, lf, c
Teams: Cuban Stars (East) ('16, '23–'27), Cuban Stars (West) ('17–'18), All Nations ('19), Kansas City Monarchs ('20–'22)
Bats: Right   Throws: Right
Born: Cuba

A veteran third baseman for Alejandro Pompez's Eastern Colored League Cuban Stars, he

hit .209 and .247 in 1924–25 while batting in the second slot in the lineup. He also played with Tinti Molina's Cuban Stars and J.L. Wilkinson's two teams, the All Nations club and the Kansas City Monarchs.

The Cuban infielder had very good speed and was an excellent base runner and an above-average batter. He began his career as the regular third baseman for owner Alejandro Pompez's 1916 New York Cuban Stars. In his first season he also played part-time in left field and hit second in the batting order, as he did in his prime, but by the end of his career he was batting near the bottom of the batting order. However, he still managed a .286 average in 1927.

Playing with Almendares in the 1919–20 Cuban winter league, he tied for the league lead with 10 stolen bases. The following winter, in a series against the New York Giants, he hit .250 while batting lead off for Almendares.

Posey, Cumberland Willis, Jr. (**Cum**)

Career: 1911–46   Positions: of, manager, officer, **owner**; secretary (NNL)
Teams: **Homestead Grays** ('11–'46), Detroit Wolves ('32)
Height: 5'9"   Weight: 145
Bats: Right   Throws: Right
Born: June 20, 1880, Homestead, Pa.
Died: Mar. 28, 1946, Pittsburgh, Pa.

The man who could properly be called the father of the Homestead Grays, his association with the ballclub had roots reaching virtually to the team's inception, and his genius made the Grays a successful franchise. Beginning as a player, he rose through the ranks, progressing to manager, booking agent, business manager, and owner of the ballclub. A fair baseball player, he joined the Grays in their early years as a player, but gained his baseball fame after his playing days were ended, as their owner, as an officer of the Negro National League, and as the founder of the East-West League.

Born in Homestead, the son of Cumberland W. and Anna Stevens Posey, he was fortunate to have parents who served as good role models for his achievements. His father worked as a riverboat engineer on the Ohio River and later became general manager of the Delta Coal Company while also pursuing interests in banking and real estate. His mother was the first black graduate of Ohio State University also to hold a teaching position at that institution.

After starring as an all-around athlete at Homestead High School, he went to Pennsylvania State College in 1909–10, the University of Pittsburgh in 1913, and Holy Ghost College (which later became Duquesne University) in 1915. He studied chemistry and pharmacy and was an outstanding basketball player. While at the latter school he was enrolled under a fictitious name, Charles W. Cumbert, led the basketball team in scoring, and was captain of the golf team.

He later played professional basketball with the Monticello-Delaneys before organizing and starring with the famed Leondi teams, which for years dominated the scene as national champions. His last year with the Leondi team was 1925, and two years later he formed a Grays' basketball team that defeated the New York Celtics. The seemingly ubiquitous Posey also coached the Homestead High cage team.

After having starred as a basketball player, baseball became his second sport. Posey was a railway mail clerk when the Homestead Grays were first organized in 1910 as a team of steelworkers playing as weekend diversion. He joined the Grays as an outfielder in 1911, when they were a true semipro team, playing only on Saturday and Sunday at Homestead Park. But as their ability and reputation increased, the club was in demand for games, and in 1912 Posey took charge and began booking enough games to permit the players to devote all their time to playing baseball.

Within the next decade the Homestead Grays were the biggest attraction in independent baseball and quickly broadened their scope of competition. As more teams appeared, they patterned their operations after Posey's Grays. Posey's dynamic leadership kept the Grays near the top of the talent pool, and under his guidance they became a team of major-league quality and a dominant dynasty in the Negro Leagues.

In the early years Posey split his time between playing and managing, and the Homestead Grays had been moneymakers from 1912 to 1929 under his guidance and leadership. As manager, Posey maintained pretty strict clubhouse rules, and while allowing players to play cards, he did not allow gambling. In 1929 he ended his career as an active player and became a bench manager until turning the team over to Vic Harris in 1937 and concentrating on the business end of the Grays.

In 1922, when the Grays first encountered difficulty by the raiding tactics of the Pittsburgh Keystones, Posey countered by bringing in Charlie Walker as a partner to establish the ballclub on sound financial foundations by putting the players on salary, and gaining permission to use Forbes Field for home games when the Pittsburgh Pirates were out of town. This broke the Keystones' challenge to the Grays' supremacy in Pittsburgh.

The following season, 1923, when the Eastern Colored League was organized, he remained independent and raided league ballclubs to improve his own team. By 1926 he had a powerful team that recorded a 140–13 ledger for the season, while winning 43 straight games at one point in the season. Clearly the Grays outclassed all opponents at that level of competition, but they also defeated a team of major-leaguers behind the hurling of Lefty Grove, winning 3 of the 4 games played.

He continued to improve his team and entered the American Negro League in 1929, but when the league folded, he returned to independent play in 1930, picking up some more stars, including Oscar Charleston, Josh Gibson, and Judy Johnson. The team defeated the New York Lincoln Stars for the eastern championship and improved in 1931, with a record of 163–23, to claim a second consecutive championship.

He who lives by the sword dies by the

sword, and Posey, who had built a powerhouse by signing players from other teams, became the target for Gus Greenlee's similar raiding tactics. Posey lost Charleston, Gibson, and Johnson among other players to Greenlee's Pittsburgh Crawfords because he could not top Greenlee's salaries.

As Posey did the first time he encountered financial difficulties, the Depression necessitated him seeking additional funds by taking in a co-owner, Rufus "Sonnyman" Jackson. Under the ballclub's new structure, Jackson was president, Posey was secretary, his brother Seward "See" Posey was booking agent and business manager, and Vic Harris was the field manager. Harris remained at the helm except for the 1943–44 seasons, when Jim Taylor was manager due to Harris's wartime employment.

Posey was an innovative owner, initiating night ball years before the major leagues explored the possibility of playing night games. He also served as the executive secretary of the Negro National League, and wrote a regular column, *Posey's Points,* for the *Pittsburgh Courier.* Off the field he was reputed to be a ladies' man, with a woman in each city, but his activities apart from baseball failed to deter him from building a baseball dynasty.

The new money again rescued Posey, and he lured Josh Gibson back into the fold to form a dynamic power duo with Buck Leonard. Under his leadership, beginning in 1937, when the Grays had a record of 152–24 against all opposition, the Grays won nine consecutive Negro National League pennants. In 1940 Posey secured the use of Griffith Stadium for some home games.

Posey continued to corral top players, keeping the Grays the class of the league, but during the last year of the "long Gray line," his health began failing. After ailing for more than a year, and being confined to a bed for three weeks due to his illness, he died of lung cancer at Mercy Hospital in Pittsburgh in the spring of 1946.

Posey, Seward Hayes (**See**)
Career: 1911–48   Positions: officer, business manager

Team: Homestead Grays
Born: 1886
Died: Aug. 25, 1951, Homestead, Pa.

A longtime associate and confidant of his brother and owner of the Homestead Grays, Cum Posey, he was instrumental in handling the business affairs for the Grays, leaving his brother free to handle other administrative responsibilities. When Cum restructured the Grays in 1936, bringing in Rufus "Sonnyman" Jackson as a co-owner, See became the booking agent and business manager, and his responsibilities were more clearly delineated. Even after his brother's death he continued working with Jackson, until the Negro National League folded in 1948.

Post
Career: 1916   Position: player
Team: New York Lincoln Stars

He appeared briefly with the Lincoln Stars in 1916. His position is uncertain.

Potter
Career: 1921   Position: c
Team: Kansas City Monarchs

He appeared briefly as a reserve catcher with the Kansas City Monarchs in 1921, his only season in the Negro Leagues.

Powell
Career: 1914–15   Position: p
Team: New York Lincoln Giants

He pitched briefly with the New York Lincoln Giants in 1914 but enjoyed more playing time the following season.

Powell
Career: 1931   Position: 2b
Team: Memphis Red Sox

A middle infielder with the Memphis Red Sox in 1931, his best position was second base.

Powell, Edward D. (**Eddie,** Big Red, Boche)
Career: 1936–38   Position: c
Teams: New York Cubans ('36, '38), New York Black Yankees ('37), Washington Black Senators ('38)

A catcher for three seasons in the late '30s, he was with the New York Cubans and the New York Black Yankees, and was listed on the spring roster as a reserve catcher for the Washington Black Senators in 1938.

Powell, Melvin **(Put)**
Career: 1930–43   Positions: **p**, of, *1b*
Teams: **Chicago American Giants** ('30, '36–'43), Chicago Columbia Giants ('31), Cole's American Giants ('32–'35), *Palmer House All-Stars ('40), Chicago Brown Bombers ('42)*
Bats: Right   Throws: Right
Height: 5'5"   Weight: 145

His entire career was spent with Chicago-based teams, beginning in 1930 with the Chicago American Giants, where he posted a 2–1 mark. The next season he pitched with Dave Malarcher's Columbia Giants, but returned to the American Giants in 1932, when Robert A. Cole purchased the team, and posted a 13–4 record as Cole's American Giants captured the Negro Southern League title. He remained with the franchise through 1943, except for two ventures with teams of lesser status (the Palmer House All-Stars and the Chicago Brown Bombers) in the early '40s. In addition to his pitching, he sometimes played in the outfield, and although small in stature, he used a long bat and could hit with pretty good power. After his playing days he owned and operated a restaurant in Chicago.

Powell, Richard D. **(Dick)**
Career: 1938–52   Position: officer
Team: Baltimore Elite Giants
Born: Nov. 29, 1911, Baltimore, Md.

As a youngster in Baltimore, he was a sandlot ballplayer and a fan of the Baltimore Black Sox. As an adult he was instrumental in bringing the Elite Giants' franchise to Baltimore. When the team began playing in Baltimore in the latter part of 1937 on a promotional basis, he recognized the opportunity to bring baseball back to Baltimore full-time. After securing press support from Leon Hardwick, sports editor of the *Baltimore Afro-American,* he began

traveling with the team as a correspondent. He and general manager Vernon Greene formed a good team, and Powell was appointed director of publications for the team.

After returning from military service during World War II, he served as traveling secretary and troubleshooter for the Elites. After Greene bought the team before the 1947 season, he took Powell off the road and placed him in charge of the team's operations. After Greene's death in 1949, Powell continued to operate the team under power of attorney from Greene's widow. As general manager he oversaw the demise of the Elite Giants in Baltimore. In the spring of 1951 he sold the team to William Bridgeforth for $11,000.

After selling the team, Powell tried unsuccessfully to obtain a job as a major-league scout, and secured employment with the Social Security Department.

Powell, Russell
Career: 1914–21   Positions: **c**, 2b, of
Team: Indianapolis ABCs

Beginning in 1914, he spent his entire eight-year career as the regular catcher for the Indianapolis ABCs, usually hitting no higher than sixth in the batting order. During the ABCs' best seasons, 1915–16, he hit for averages of .260 and .246. The latter season, the ABCs defeated the American Giants in the championship series but were unable to defend their title successfully in 1917. Powell injured his shoulder in August, and his absence from the lineup contributed to their disastrous performance for the season. His average dropped to .200 and .206 in 1917–18, and by the beginning of the new decade, young Biz Mackey began sharing the catching assignments during the last two years of Powell's career.

Powell, William H. **(Bill)**
Career: 1946–50   Position: p
Teams: Birmingham Black Barons ('46–'50, '52), *minor leagues ('50–'61), Mexican League ('57)*
Bats: left   Throws: Right

Height: 6'2½"   Weight: 195
Born: 1926, West Birmingham, Ala.

Following 4–5 and 5–0 marks in his first two seasons, this Birmingham Black Barons' right-hander posted an 11–3 record with a 3.81 ERA to help the Barons to the 1948 Negro American League pennant, and started 2 games in the World Series against the Homestead Grays. Powell also started and won the All-Star game that year for the West squad, yielding only a hit in 3 shutout innings. After a mediocre season (11–11, 3.61 ERA) in 1949, he bounced back with a 15–4 record and a 3.00 ERA the following season to earn another trip to the All-Star game, where he pitched the last 3 innings in the West's 5–3 victory. A pretty good hitting pitcher, he contributed a .286 batting average to the Black Barons' cause in his last season with the team.

Entering organized baseball the next year, he posted a 15–15, 4.75 ERA ledger with Colorado Springs in the Western League, but lost his only decision with Sacramento in the Pacific Coast League. Two uneven years (5–15, 5.09 ERA and 14–9, 3.06 ERA) in the American Association followed, in 1952–53. A respectable 10–8, 4.23 ERA season, split between Toronto and Havana, in the International League in 1954 was his last quality year, although he pitched for seven more years in the minor leagues before finishing his career with Charlotte in the South Atlantic League in 1961.

His best year during this time was with Savannah in the Sally League in 1956, when he fashioned an 8–12 record with a 3.12 ERA. The next season, after winning his first two decisions with Savannah, he jumped to the Mexican League, where he had a 3–7 record with a 3.96 ERA for Nuevo Laredo and batted .286. The next season he was back in the Sally League, with Knoxville.

Although his entrance into baseball was delayed by military service during World War II, he still pitched for fifteen years, including some winters in Latin American leagues. He played with Ponce (7–6, 2.83 ERA) in the 1949–50 Puerto Rican League and had a combined 4–6 record for two seasons in the Cuban League.

Powell, Willie Ernest (Piggy, Pigmeat, Pee Wee, Wee Ernest, Wee Willie)
a.k.a. Ernest A. Powell
Career: 1925–35   Positions: p, of
Teams: *Chicago Giants ('22)*, **Chicago American Giants** ('25–'29), Detroit Stars ('30–'31), Cole's American Giants ('32–'33), Akron Tyrites ('33), Cleveland Red Sox ('34)
Bats: Left   Throws: Right
Height: 5'8"   Weight 158
Born: Oct. 30, 1903, Eutaw, Ala.
Died: May 16, 1987, Three Rivers, Mich.

He was a right-handed pitcher with a wide repertory of pitches, including a darting curveball, a sneaky hopping fastball, a change-up curve, a screwball, and a drop. In addition to his legal pitches, he also knew how to use a cut ball. The little hurler began his career as a boy wonder with the Chicago American Giants in 1925, earning the nickname "Piggy" because he was so young. He was very confident about his ability and helped pitch the Chicago American Giants to the Negro National League pennant in his first two full years (1926–27) in Chicago, posting marks of 10–4 and 15–6, including a no-hitter in the latter season. In each of the World Series, the American Giants defeated the Bacharach Giants, with Powell starting a combined 5 games, winning 2 of 3 decisions (including a shutout) while notching ERAs of 2.66 and 1.12, respectively.

In 1928 he improved to a 19–3 mark as the American Giants copped the second-half title, and he won his only start, a 3–0 shutout over the St. Louis Stars. Powell was beginning his baseball prime, but misfortune stalked him in the off-season, when he was shot in the face by his father-in-law in a shotgun accident. His misfortune was compounded in the ensuing season when, plagued by a sore arm, he was unable to pitch in the regular rotation, and on those occasions when he did pitch, his effectiveness was extremely limited. After losing both of his decisions during the season, he was sold to the Detroit Stars.

At Detroit he rebounded with seasons of 17–7 and 16–3 in 1930–31, and returned to the American Giants in 1932–33 as the club won two more pennants. In 1932 the American Giants played in the Negro Southern League, considered to be a major league that season, and finished with a 14–7 record. In postseason play he won 2 of 3 decisions, including 1–0 shutout, as the American Giants won the championship series over New Orleans. The following season the franchise was in the new Negro National League, winning the first pennant, with Powell posting a 19–3 mark.

He first had a look with the American Giants in 1922, but he played with semipro teams, including the Progressives for the next two years before getting a second look in 1925. Rube Foster liked his willingness to follow instructions, and this time he stayed with the team. During his career he also played exhibition games against major-leaguers, defeating both Babe Ruth's All-Stars and Leo Durocher's All-Stars. When he retired from black baseball, Powell had a lifetime 111–37 record to show for nine years in the Negro National League.

Like most pitchers, he considered himself to be a complete ballplayer, and was a fast base runner, a capable fielder, and claimed a .412 batting average while playing with Havana in the 1927 Cuban winter league.

After closing out his baseball career, he worked at a leather tannery, but in the later years of his life he encountered severe physical difficulties. He had circulatory problems and had both legs amputated, and had a stroke that cost him the use of his left arm. The last years of his life were spent as a resident of Three Rivers Manor in Three Rivers, Michigan.

Powers
Careers: 1942   Position: player
Team: New York Black Yankees

He appeared as a substitute in one game with the New York Black Yankees in 1942. His position is uncertain.

Presswood, Henry
Career: 1948–50   Positions: ss, 3b
Teams: Cleveland Buckeyes ('48–'50), *Kansas City ('52)*

Beginning his career as the Negro Leagues began their decline, he was a shortstop with the Buckeyes for three years, batting only .198 for the 1948 season. Two years after leaving the Buckeyes, he played with the Kansas City Monarchs as a third baseman, but the Negro American League was strictly a minor league at that time.

Preston, Albert Webber (Al)
Career: 1943, 1946–49 Position: p
Teams: New York Black Yankees ('43, '46–'49), *minor leagues ('47, '50–'51)*, Baltimore Elite Giants ('50), *Chicago American Giants ('52)*
Bats: Right   Throws: Right
Height: 6'1"   Weight: 170
Born: June 26, 1926, New York, NY
Died: Sept. 21, 1979, New York, NY

This right-hander pitched in the Negro Leagues during the late '40s and early '50s, when black baseball was in the latter years of quality existence, but left for intermittent stints with ballclubs in organized baseball. After beginning the 1947 season with the Black Yankees, he played most of the year with Stamford in the Colonial League, registering a 2–3 record and 4.59 ERA in 11 games. Following a similar pattern three years later, he pitched in 2 games with the Elites before joining Elmwood in the Mandak League, where he split 4 decisions. Back in the same league again the next year, he finished with a 4–5 record for Carman in his last year in baseball.

Preston, Robert
Career: 1950   Position: p
Team: Baltimore Elite Giants

He is listed as a pitcher with the Baltimore Elites in 1950, when the Negro American League was struggling to survive the loss of players to organized baseball, but his participation in league games is uncertain.

Price

Career: 1922   Position: of
Team: Pittsburgh Keystones

He was an outfielder with the Pittsburgh Keystones in 1922, their only year in the Negro National League.

Price, Marvin

Career: 1950   Position: 1b
Teams: Chicago American Giants ('50, '52), Cleveland Buckeyes ('50), *New Orleans Eagles ('51)*

This first baseman began his career in 1950, splitting his playing time between the Chicago American Giants and the Cleveland Buckeyes, while hitting .296. He continued in the Negro American League with the New Orleans Eagles and the Chicago American Giants for two more years, when the Negro American League was struggling to survive the loss of players to organized baseball and were no longer of major-league quality.

Prichett, W.

[see Pritchett, Wilbur]

Pride, Charlie

Career: 1953–58   Position: p
Teams: *Memphis Red Sox ('53, '58), Birmingham Black Barons ('54)*

Before embarking on a highly successful career as a country music singer, Charlie Pride was a pitcher with a "pretty good little curve" for the Memphis Red Sox and the Birmingham Black Barons during the early '50s. He was first discovered when he pitched for a sandlot team against the the Memphis Red Sox. In his first tryout with the Red Sox, he failed to stick with the club, but he was more successful in his second effort. At that time the Negro American League was struggling to survive the loss of players to organized baseball and had declined to a strictly minor-league status. A measure of the financial status of the league at that time is indicated by an unconfirmed story that Pride and the right fielder were traded for a team bus.

Prim, Randolph

a.k.a. Primm
Career: 1926   Position: p
Team: Kansas City Monarchs

While pitching with the Kansas City Monarchs in 1926, he won his only decision.

Prim, William

a.k.a. Primm; Primer
Career: 1905–10   Position: c
Teams: Leland Giants ('05), St. Louis Giants ('10), *Indianapolis ABCs ('11)*

Prim joined the Leland Giants in 1905, their first year of existence, and was one of the two catchers on the team. In 1910 the catcher was with another emerging team, the St. Louis Giants, in only their second year of existence. The following year he joined the Indianapolis ABCs, but the team was not yet playing major-league-caliber baseball.

Primer

[see Prim, William]

Primm

[see Prim, Randolph]

Primm

[see Prim, William]

Prince

Career: 1936   Position: 3b
Team: Chicago American Giants

As the regular third baseman for the Chicago American Giants in 1936, he hit in the lower part of the batting order and finished the season with a .250 batting average against all levels of competition.

Pritchett, Wilbur

a.k.a. Prichett
Career: 1921–32   Position: p
Teams: Hilldale Daisies ('21, '24, '29–'30), Harrisburg Giants ('25–'26), Baltimore Black Sox ('26–'27), Brooklyn Royal Giants ('31), Atlantic City Bacharach Giants ('32)
Bats: Left   Throws: Left

This left-handed pitcher appeared briefly without a decision for Hilldale in 1921, when they were an independent team, and rejoined the team in 1924 as a young college player. After stints with Harrisburg and the Baltimore Black Sox, he returned to Hilldale to close out his career. In 1929 he split 4 decisions, but he was winless against 2 losses in 1930, his last season.

Proctor, James (Cub)
Career: 1887   Positions: **p**, c
Teams: *Baltimore Atlantics ('84–'87), Baltimore Lord Baltimores ('87)*

He was a pitcher for teams in the Baltimore area, including the Lord Baltimores, one of eight teams that were charter Members of the League of Colored Baseball Clubs. However, the league's existence was brief, lasting only a week, and he returned to the semipro Baltimore Atlantics.

Prophet, Willie
Career: 1934   Position: of
Team: Atlantic City Bacharach Giants

He appeared briefly as a reserve outfielder with the Bacharach Giants in 1934.

Pryor
Career: 1916–17   Position: p
Teams: St. Louis Giants ('16), Bowser's ABCs ('16), Indianapolis ABCs ('16), Jewell's ABCs ('17)
Bats: Left   Throws: Left

For two years during the deadball era, this big left-hander pitched with the St. Louis Giants and three different ABCs teams, including the Indianapolis ABCs under manager C. I. Taylor.

Pryor, Anderson
Career: 1923–33   Positions: **2**b, ss, 3b
Teams: *New Orleans Crescent Stars ('22),* Milwaukee Bears ('23), Detroit Stars ('23–'31, '33), Memphis Red Sox ('33)

This second baseman could play any infield position, but he was the regular keystoner for the Detroit Stars during much of the '20s. He batted in the seventh slot during 1924–25, but moved up to the second spot in the batting order in 1926, recording a .252 average. But he lost his starting position in 1927, and played as a backup at third base. In 1931, the last season of the first Negro National League, and again in 1933, the first season of the new Negro National League, he shared the starting assignments at second base for the Stars. In the latter season he also shared playing time at shortstop in closing out his eleven seasons in the Negro Leagues.

Pryor, Bill (Big Boy)
Career: 1927–31   Positions: **p**, of
Teams: Memphis Red Sox ('27), Detroit Stars ('31)
Height: 7'0"

After joining the Memphis Red Sox in May 1927, this towering seven-footer was 3–13 in his first season, and closed his career in 1931 with the Detroit Stars, without a decision. The large hurler also had big feet and always had difficulty finding spikes to fit him. In addition to pitching, he sometimes played in the outfield, but batted only .176 in 1927, the year he played most extensively.

Pryor, Edward
Career: 1925   Position: 2b
Teams: New York Lincoln Giants ('25), *Pennsylvania Red Caps of New York ('25–'34)*

In his only appearance with a quality team, this light-hitting second baseman hit only .179 in 1925 with the New York Lincoln Giants. The remainder of his career was with the Pennsylvania Red Caps of New York, a team of lesser status.

Pryor, Wes (Whip)
a.k.a. Prior
Career: 1910–14   Position: 3b
Teams: Leland Giants ('10), Chicago American Giants ('11), St. Louis Giants ('12), Brooklyn Royal Giants ('13), Chicago Giants, ('11) Mo-

hawk Giants ('14), Lincoln Giants ('14), Louisville White Sox ('14)

Signed by Rube Foster from the Chicago Unions, he was the starting third baseman on the 1910 Leland Giants' squad. Pryor was hitting .297 in mid-June, and the media reported that he was in major-league form. By late August he was reported to be "developing into a star player" and was being compared to the New York Giants' Art Devlin. However, he finished the season with a mediocre .256 batting average, and did not sustain his early promise over the course of his career. The next two seasons he was the regular third baseman with the St. Louis Giants and the Brooklyn Royal Giants, batting in the fifth and sixth spots in the batting order, respectively. In 1914 he was considered to have the "best arm in the game" and was called the "Whip," but he played with three different teams (Lincoln Stars, Mohawk Giants, and Louisville White Sox) during the season, which proved to be his last with quality ballclubs.

Puch, Jimmy
[see Pugh, Johnny]

Pugh, Johnny
a.k.a Punch, Jimmy
Career: 1912–22   Positions: **3b, lf,** 2b, rf, cf
Teams: **Brooklyn Royal Giants** ('12, '14, '16–'19), Mohawk Giants ('12–'13), New York Lincoln Giants ('14), New York Lincoln Stars ('16), Philadelphia Giants ('18), New York Bacharach Giants ('19), Atlantic City Bacharach Giants ('20–'21), Harrisburg Giants ('22)

A third baseman playing primarily with New York based teams during the '10s, he had good speed, especially from the batter's box to first base. Best identified with the Brooklyn Royal Giants, he began his career in 1912 as a third baseman, usually hitting in the sixth slot in the batting order. He also played with the Mowhawk Giants in 1912–13, when the Schenectady team was at its peak. He left after two

years to join the New York Lincoln Giants for a season, hitting .265 while batting last in the lineup. In 1916 he split the season between the Lincoln Stars and the Royal Giants, but suffered a broken arm when hit by a pitch by Cannonball Dick Redding. For the next two years, 1917–18, he moved to the outfield for the Royals, batting .296 in 1917. Leaving the team in 1919 to play with the Bacharachs for three years, he was still an outfielder, starting in left field in 1919 when the Bacharachs were based in New York. Incomplete statistics show a composite batting average of .213 for the seasons of 1918–19. In 1920 the franchise moved back to Atlantic City, and although he was nearing the end of his career, Pugh batted in the leadoff spot to utilize his speed. However, the following season he was relegated to service as a substitute.

Pulamino
[see Palomino, Emilio]

Pullen, O'Neal (**Neal,** Neil)
Career: 1920–27   Position: c
Teams: *military service ('18–'19),* Brooklyn Royal Giants ('20), Hilldale Daisies ('20), Kansas City Monarchs, Baltimore Black Sox ('24–'25), New York Lincoln Giants ('20, '27)
Bats: Right   Throws: Right
Height: 6'0"   Weight: 230
Born: 1910 Beaumont, Tex.

He got his start in baseball with a team in his hometown of Beaumont, Texas, in 1917. But with the advent of World War I he enrolled in the Army and was shipped overseas to France in 1918 for eighteen months. After his discharge he played with three teams (the Brooklyn Royal Giants, the New York Lincoln Giants, and Hilldale) in 1920, batting only .167. After the season, he accompanied Bill Pettus to the West Coast to play in the California winter league with the Colored All-Stars. When spring came he stayed in California to manage the local ballclub and remained at that post until joining the Baltimore Black Sox in 1924. With the Black Sox he alternated with

Rojo behind the plate. His arm was not as strong as Rojo's but he was a better receiver and compensated for his weak arm by a quick release. He was a fair hitter, batting .305 with apparent power, but was very slow on the bases. A weight problem, causing him to balloon from 190 to 230 pounds, and a lack of ambition inhibited his development, and the following season he was relegated to a backup role. During the ensuing winter he continued playing ball on the West Coast, and he was with the Philadelphia Royal Giants in 1925.

Pulliam, Arthur (Chick)
a.k.a. Pullam
Career: 1909–15   Position: c
Team: Kansas City Royal Giants
For seven seasons he was a catcher with the Royal Giants of Kansas City, Missouri.

Punch
Career: 1922–23   Position: p
Teams: Baltimore Black Sox ('22), *Richmond Giants ('23)*

A marginal player, he pitched with the Baltimore Black Sox before they entered league competition and with the Richmond Giants, a team of lesser status.

Purcell, Harman
Career: 1944–47   Positions: p, 3b
Teams: Cleveland Buckeyes ('44), Memphis Red Sox ('47)
In a varied career, he was a third baseman with the Cleveland Buckeyes in 1944 and a pitcher with the Memphis Red Sox in 1947.

Purgen
Career: 1921   Positions: ss, 2b
Teams: *Madison Stars ('20–'21),* Hilldale Daisies ('21)
Beginning his baseball career with the Madison Stars, a lesser team that served as an unofficial farm team for Hilldale, this middle infielder joined the big club in 1921 and hit .224 for Hilldale against all competition.

Q

Quickley
Career: 1937   Position: lf
Team: Birmingham Black Barons

He was a left fielder with the Birmingham Black Barons in 1937, the inaugural season of the Negro American League.

Quinones, Tomas Planchardon (Thomas)
Career: 1946–47   Position: p
Team: Indianapolis Clowns
Bats: Right   Throws: Right
Born: Puerto Rico
Died: New York, NY

He was a successful and very popular right-handed pitcher in Puerto Rico and played with the Clowns in the late '40s. He died in New York and his friends raised the money to send him back to Puerto Rico for interrment.

Quintana, Busta
Career: 1928–34   Positions: 2b, 3b, ss
Teams: Cuban Stars (West) ('28), Cuban Stars (East) ('32), Newark Dodgers ('34)
Bats: Right   Throws: Right

This utility infielder began his career in 1928 with the Cuban Stars of the original Negro National League, and after the league's demise, appeared briefly with another Cuban Stars franchise that was playing as an independent team during the Depression's early years. He closed out his career in 1934 with the Newark Dodgers of the new Negro National League.

R

Radcliffe, Alexander (Alex, **Alec**)
Career: 1932–46   Positions: **3b**, ss, of, *p*
Teams: *Chicago Giants ('27),* Cole's American Giants ('32–'35), New York Cubans ('36), **Chicago American Giants** ('36–'39, '41–'44, '49), *Palmer House All-Stars ('40),* Birmingham Black Barons ('42), Cincinnati-Indianapolis Clowns ('44–'45), Memphis Red Sox ('46), *Detroit Senators ('47)*
Bats: Right   Throws: Right
Height: 6'0"   Weight: 205
Born: July 26, 1905, Mobile, Ala.
Died: July 18, 1983, Chicago, Ill.

The hard-hitting third baseman of the Chicago American Giants for most of his fifteen-year career, Radcliffe was virtually a perennial All-Star, making eleven All-Star appearances during his career. He played in every All-Star game from its inception in 1933 through 1946, except for the 1940–42 seasons, registering a .341 average in All-Star competition. He is the lifetime All-Star leader in at-bats and hits, and is second to Buck Leonard in games played, runs batted in, and runs scored.

A good clutch hitter, this right-handed slugger used a 40-ounce bat and had power to all fields. Noted as being a good curveball hitter with the ability to execute the hit-and-run, Radcliffe earned his acclaim with his bat, but he did everything well. He was an adequate fielder with a strong arm, and although not fast, he was a little better than average as a base runner for his size. He was a "Sunday player" and at his best in front of a big crowd, but he was not known for his hustle and was considered a bit lazy, a quality that prompted his manager in Cuba, Mike Gonzales, to discontinue his team's association with Radcliffe despite a solid batting performance.

He began playing baseball as a youngster in Mobile, Alabama, but moved in 1917 to Chicago, where he served a stint as the batboy for the Chicago American Giants. After honing his baseball craft on the sandlots of the city, he began his professional career in 1927 with the Chicago Giants, a team of lesser status than the league teams. He joined Robert A. Cole's American Giants in 1932, when they were playing in the Negro Southern League, and contributed a .283 average to their successful pennant race while holding down third base and hitting in the second slot in the batting order. At the end of the season he played in the California winter league, where he compiled a .381 batting average.

In 1933 the new Negro National League was formed, and the American Giants captured the league's first pennant, making two consecutive championships in Radcliffe's first two seasons with a top ballclub. Hitting fifth in the order, he enjoyed a superlative season, batting .431 and delivering key hits in the clutch. In 1934, with Radcliffe hitting .309, the American Giants almost made it three straight pennants. But after winning the league's first-half title, they lost a seven-game championship playoff to the Philadelphia Stars, winners of the second half.

In 1935 Radcliffe hit for an average of .354 as the American Giants played their last season in the Negro National League. In 1936 the ballclub played as an independent team, and Radcliffe signed with the New York Cubans, but returned to the American Giants in midseason, batting a combined .352 for the year.

In 1937 the Negro American League was formed, and the American Giants joined the new league in its inaugural season, playing their way into the playoffs but losing to the Kansas City Monarchs. Radcliffe hit third in the batting order for both the 1937 and 1938 seasons and moved into the second slot in 1939, with incomplete statistics showing averages of .231, .219, and .292. After a winter in Havana, where he batted .266 in the Cuban league, he returned to United States but left the American Giants to join the Palmer House All-Stars, a Chicago-based independent club, as the player-manager. In addition to holding down the job at the hot corner, he took an occasional turn on the mound, and was credited with topping all batters with a .404 average for 1940.

In the next two seasons he was a bit unsettled but rejoined the Chicago American Giants in 1941 and, while hitting in the cleanup spot much of the 1942 season, he is credited with an average of .211 for the year. In 1943 he was back to his usual batting level, hitting .354 in his last full season as a regular with the American Giants.

He joined the Cincinnati-Indianapolis Clowns in 1944, and played with them for two years near the end of his career. Each season, he led the Negro American League in home runs, with accompanying batting averages of .281 and .325. A 1945 press release credited him with never hitting under .320 in fourteen years, but in view of available statistics, this apparently included nonleague games or was simply media hype. In 1946 he played with the Memphis Red Sox, hitting .272 and, after playing with lesser teams, he closed out his career.

Even considering all his accomplishments, Alex had to play in the shadow of his older and more colorful brother, Ted "Double Duty" Radcliffe, for most of his career, thus detracting from the full recognition that was his due as the best third baseman in the history of the Negro American League. In the 1944 All-Star game, with his mother in the stands, he slammed a two-run triple, but "Double Duty" hit a two-run homer to overshadow his performance. After retiring from baseball he worked as a bouncer in his brother's bar in Chicago.

Radcliffe, Red

Career: 1926   Position: ss
Teams: Dayton Marcos

He was listed as a shortstop for the Dayton Marcos in 1926, during their second and last entry in the Negro National League.

Radcliffe, Theodore Roosevelt (Ted, **Double Duty**)

Career: 1928–50   Positions: **c, p,** manager

Teams: Detroit Stars ('28–'29, '31), St. Louis Stars ('30), Homestead Grays ('31, '33, '36, '46), Pittsburgh Crawfords ('32), Columbus Blue Birds ('33), Cleveland Giants ('33), New York Black Yankees ('33), *Bismarck, North Dakota ('34–'35)* Chicago American Giants ('34, '41–'43, '49–'50), Brooklyn Eagles ('35), Cincinnati Tigers ('36–'37), Memphis Red Sox ('38–'39, '41), *Mexican League ('40)*, Birmingham Black Barons ('42–'46), Kansas City Monarchs ('45), *Harlem Globetrotters ('47)*, Louisville Buckeyes ('49)

Bats: Right   Throws: Right
Height: 5'10"   Weight: 190
Born: July 7, 1902, Mobile, Ala.

Nicknamed "Double Duty" because he would pitch the first game of a double header and catch the second game, Radcliffe was one of the most colorful players in black baseball. He was truly unique and never received the full credit due him for his contributions to baseball. In three consecutive years he played on three of the greatest teams in black baseball history, first with the St. Louis Stars of 1930, then with the Homestead Grays of 1931, and finally with the Pittsburgh Crawfords of 1932. His "double duty" produced impressive numbers for those seasons, including batting averages of .283, .298, and .325 and corresponding pitching records of 10–2, 9–5, and 19–8.

With the Stars he was the regular catcher for the first half of the season, but when the pitching staff wore thin, he stepped in and proved to be one of the top two hurlers on their championship squad. The 1931 Grays, featuring Josh Gibson, Oscar Charleston, Jud Wilson, and Smokey Joe Williams, is the team that Radcliffe selects as the all-time best. After the 1931 season he was one of several stars (along with Gibson, Charleston, and Ted Page) who formed the nucleus of Cum Posey's ballclub and who were lured away when Gus Greenlee raided the Grays to stock his Pittsburgh Crawfords and turn the franchise into an immediate powerhouse for the 1932 season.

Before joining the St. Louis Stars, he had played two years with the Detroit Stars as a catcher, hitting .266 and .310 in 1928–29. The nomadic Radcliffe played with four teams during the 1933 season, and followed his instincts to the Midwest in 1934, where he played with a predominantly white semipro team in Bismarck, North Dakota. He was one of several black stars who were signed by Neil Churchill to build a superior ballclub that dominated the baseball scene in the Midwest. In 1935 Bismarck won the Wichita Tournament, with Radcliffe, Satchel Paige, Hilton Smith, Chet Brewer, and Quincey Trouppe among the players on the team.

Always quick to jump a team if more money was offered, he played with the Brooklyn Eagles in 1935, hitting .268 and posting a 4–6 record on the mound, and landed with the Cincinnati Tigers in 1936, where the right-hander hit a solid .333. The next season he contributed a .356 batting average and managed the team

to a first-division finish during their only season in the Negro American League.

In 1938 he signed with the Memphis Red Sox as playing manager, guiding them to the first-half title and ensuring a spot in the ensuing playoffs against the second-half winners, the Atlanta Black Crackers, for the Negro American League championship. In the opening game Radcliffe took the mound against Atlanta's ace hurler, Chin Evans, and won the first game. After the Red Sox won the second game, the management of the respective clubs became embroiled in a dispute that resulted in the Series being canceled without a final determination of an uncontested champion. He returned to the Red Sox in 1939, with incomplete statistics showing aggregate marks of .263 batting and 7–5 pitching for the two seasons.

Meanwhile, he continued his nomadic ways, traveling for the 1939–40 winter to Cuba, where he pitched for Almendares and bested Martin Dihigo with a 5–hit shutout in a head-to-head matchup. In the summer of 1940 he journeyed to Mexico, playing with Vera Cruz, batting .247, and posting a 5–6 pitching ledger, with a 5.93 ERA. Back in the United States, he oscillated between Birmingham and Chicago for a couple of years before settling with the American Giants, and was selected as the Negro American League's MVP in 1943.

When the Negro American League champion Birmingham Black Barons lost the services of their regular catcher to the military draft shortly before the impending World Series, Radcliffe was loaned to the Black Barons, with the permission of the Homestead Grays, to play in the World Series against the Grays. After a winter playing with the Baltimore Giants, Radcliffe returned to Birmingham for the entire 1944 season, contributing a heavy .215 batting average and invaluable leadership as the Black Barons repeated as Negro American League champions and faced the Grays in a losing World Series rematch.

In 1945 he was traded to the Kansas City Monarchs, who were desperate for catching help, to share the workload behind the plate.

A dangerous hitter in the clutch, his knowledge of the batters, skill at calling a game, and ability to handle pitchers made him a valuable asset to the team. As a bonus he won 3 victories as a pitcher without a loss. After the end of World War II the players who were in the service returned to crowd the rosters, and Radcliffe signed with the Homestead Grays, primarily as a pitcher, posting a 7–4 record while also batting .222 and providing some catching relief for a fast fading Josh Gibson in his last season before his death.

He appeared in six East-West All-Star games, dividing them equally as a catcher and pitcher, batting .308, and winning his only decision in All-Star competition. In the 1944 game, with his mother in the stands, he contributed a crucial home run to the West squad's 7–4 victory. As a smart, strong-armed catcher he was a good hitter, and as a pitcher he mastered the emery ball and utilized other pitches of dubious legality. When catching he was able to work well with other pitchers because, as a pitcher himself, he "thought along with them."

Frequently in his career he became "triple duty," adding the title "manager" to complete the triad. As manager of the Chicago American Giants in 1950 he signed three white players in an effort to find a "reverse" Jackie Robinson, but the players lacked the requisite skills to perform at a major-league level. That season, "Duty" rounded out a colorful twenty-three-year career spent with more than a dozen different teams in the Negro Leagues.

There have been better pitchers, better catchers, and better hitters, and there may have been a more colorful player, but there has never been another single player embued with the diverse talents he manifested during his baseball career. "Double Duty" was unique in baseball annals.

Raggs, Harry
[see Roberts, Harry]

Ragland, Hurland Earl
a.k.a. Herlin Raglan

Career: 1920–21   Position: p
Teams: Indianapolis ABCs ('20), Dayton Marcos ('20), Kansas City Monarchs ('21), Columbus Buckeyes ('21)

A marginal player who enjoyed his most success as a pitcher with the Dayton Marcos in the first season of the Negro National League, he was unable to stick with a top team, appearing only briefly in the Negro Leagues for two years without completing a season with any team.

Ramirez, Ramiro (Rome)
a.k.a. Ramires, Romo
Career: 1916–48   Positions: cf, lf, rf, *2b*,
                                        manager
Teams: Cuban Stars (East) ('16–'20), Havana Cuban Stars ('17), Brooklyn Royal Giants ('20), All Cubans ('21), Atlantic City Bacharach Giants ('22, '24), Baltimore Black Sox ('23), Richmond Giants ('23), Havana Red Sox ('29–'30) Cuban Stars (West) ('31, '32, '34), New York Black Yankees ('36), Indianapolis Clowns ('48)
Bats: Right   Throws: Right
Born: Cuba

He was the regular center fielder on owner Alejandro Pompez's Cuban Stars in 1916 and played on a variety of teams representing the island country during the latter years of the deadball era and the early years of the lively ball era. In his first season he hit in the seventh spot in the batting order, but beginning the next year, he usually batted either first or third in the order for the remainder of his stay with the club. In 1917 the Cuban Stars were based in New York and were sometimes referred to as the New York Cuban Stars or the Havana Cuban Stars.

Ramirez was considered an above-average hitter, but statistics show batting averages of .246 in 1918 with the Cuban Stars and .252 with the Bacharachs in 1924. The Cuban started in left field for the Bacharachs that season and was a good outfielder but suffered from bad legs, which significantly impaired his baserunning. He was the playing manager of Syd Pollock's Havana Red Sox in 1929 and 1930, and continued this relationship with Pollock's Cuban Stars the following season. During the early years of the Depression the Cuban Stars alternately played as the Cuban House of David for a pair of seasons (1931–32), and Ramirez was a reserve outfielder and manager, piloting the team during their entry in the ill-fated East-West League in 1932. Later in his career he became a bench manager, taking the helm of the New York Black Yankees in 1936, the Havana La Palomas in 1947, and the Indianapolis Clowns in 1948.

Ramos
Career: 1912–13   Positions: p, 1b, of
Teams: Cuban Stars ('12), Long Branch Cubans ('13)

He appeared briefly for a couple of years with Cuban teams playing in the United States during the deadball era.

Ramos, José (Cheo)
Career: 1921–29   Positions: of, 3b
Teams: All Cubans ('21), Cuban Stars (East) ('29)

Playing with the Cuban teams during the '20s, his first year in black baseball was in 1921, with the All Cubans ballclub. In 1929, his last season, he played left field and hit .306 while batting third in the order with the Cuban Stars in the American Negro League during the league's only year of existence. The following winter (1929–30) he played on the Cienfuegos team that won the Cuban championship.

Ramsay, William
Career: 1889   Position: rf
Team: Chicago Unions

In 1889 he played right field with the Chicago Unions under the management of W. S. Peters, who was at the helm of the ballclub from 1890 through the 1900 season.

Randall
Career: 1943   Position: cf
Team: Homestead Grays

A wartime player, he was a reserve center fielder with the Homestead Grays in 1943, his only year in the Negro Leagues.

Randolph
Career: 1938   Position: p
Team: Atlanta Black Crackers

A fringe player, he pitched with the Atlanta Black Crackers briefly in early August as they sustained their second-half spurt toward the championship, but his tenure with the club was very limited.

Randolph, Andrew G.
Career: 1885–88   Positions: 1b, of
Teams: *Argyle Athletics* ('85), Cuban Giants ('86, '88)
Born: Nov. 14, 1861, Philadelphia, Pa.

He was a member of the Argyle Athletics, a team formed in 1885 by Frank P. Thompson, the headwaiter at Long Island's Argyle Hotel in Babylon, New York, to play for the entertainment of the summer guests. After the end of the tourist season, the team added some more players to form the Cuban Giants, the first black professional team.

Randolph was a member or this historic team, and he traveled through the South with the Cuban Giants in the 1885–86 winter. He was released by the Cuban Giants in 1886 and replaced by Forbes, but later rejoined the club and, although primarily a first baseman, he also played in the outfield during the 1888 season, his last with the team.

Before becoming a professional ballplayer, he began his amateur career in 1882–83 with the Active ballclub of Philadelphia, and played in 1884–85 with the Resolutes of Boston. He was a member of the Progressive Association of the U.S.A., formed in St. Augustine, Florida.

Rankin, Bill
Career: 1923   Positions: **p,** *c*
Teams: Washington Potomacs ('23), *Richmond Giants ('23), Philadelphia Giants ('26–'27)*

A fringe player who played on teams of lesser status, he never really played with a top team. The closest he came to playing with a major-league-caliber team was when he pitched with manager Ben Taylor's Washington Potomacs in 1923, the year before they joined the Eastern Colored League.

Rankin, George
Career: 1887   Position: player
Team: *Cincinnati Browns*

He was a player with the Cincinnati Browns, one of eight teams that were charter members of the League of Colored Baseball Clubs in 1887. However, the league's existence was ephemeral, lasting only a week. His position is uncertain.

Ranson, Joe
Career: 1926   Position: c
Team: Cleveland Elites

A fringe player, he batted .154 as one of six catchers who appeared briefly with the Cleveland Elites in 1926, their only season in the Negro National League.

Rawlins
Career: 1905   Position: of
Team: Famous Cuban Giants

He played in the outfield with one of the various Cuban Giants' ballclubs that flourished during the early years of the century. Several of these ballclubs, copying the success of the Cuban Giants (the first and most successful black professional team) and appropriating a variation of the Cuban Giants' name as their own, played a quality of baseball close to that of the original team.

Ray, John (Johnny)
Career: 1932–45   Positions: **cf**, lf, 2b, 3b, c
Teams: Montgomery Grey Sox ('31–'33), Pittsburgh Crawfords ('32), *Claybrook Tigers ('34–'36),* Birmingham Black Barons ('37–'38, '45), Chicago American Giants, Cleveland Bears ('39–'40), Jacksonville Red Caps ('41–'42), Cincinnati Clowns ('43), Cincinnati-Indianapolis Clowns ('44–'45), Kansas City Monarchs ('45)

Bats: Left   Throws: Right
Height: 5'8"   Weight: 170
Born: 1907, Nashville, Tenn.

A hustling ballplayer who never spent more than three years with any ballclub, he had good speed, was proficient at stealing bases, and was an average defensive player with an ordinary throwing arm. At the plate he had good bat control, was a good bunter and a contact hitter, but lacked consistency and power.

He began his career with the Montgomery Grey Sox and was with them in 1932 when the Negro Southern League was considered a major league. He spent most of his career with teams in the South, playing with the Black Barons in 1937 as their regular center fielder and batting second in the order. For four years he played with the Jacksonville Red Caps' franchise (including the two years they played in Cleveland as the Bears). He batted in the leadoff spot while playing centerfield most of the time, but also filled a void in the infield when the need arose. After the Red Caps dropped out of the Negro American League in July 1942, Ray caught on with the Cincinnati-Indianapolis Clowns for the latter part of his career, batting .212 and .245 in 1944–45. His ability as an expert pepper-ball artist served him well with the Clowns.

Ray, Otto C. (Jaybird)
Career: 1920–24   Positions: c, of, 1b, p
Teams: Kansas City Monarchs ('20–'22, '24), Chicago Giants ('21), St. Louis Stars ('22–'23), Cleveland Tate Stars ('23), Toledo Tigers ('23), Cleveland Browns ('24)
Born: 1894
Died: Jan. 24, 1976, Leavenworth, Kan.

Primarily noted as a catcher, he was a versatile player but a light hitter. He began his career with the Kansas City Monarchs during the inaugural season of the Negro National League, and spent most of his career as a reserve catcher with that ballclub. He played with the Los Angeles White Sox in the winter of 1920, and during his five-year career he tried to break into the starting lineup with several teams in the Midwest. After his baseball career he worked as a deputy sheriff in Kansas City until retiring to Liberty, Missouri.

Ray, Thomas
Career: 1887   Position: player
Team: *New York Gorhams*

He was a player with the New York Gorhams, one of eight teams that were charter members of the League of Colored Baseball Clubs in 1887. However, the league's existence was ephemeral, lasting only a week. His position is uncertain.

Rayond
Career: 1922   Position: p
Team: Harrisburg Giants

A marginal player, he pitched with the Harrisburg Giants two years before they entered the Eastern Colored League.

Reavis, W.
Career: 1920–32   Positions: **p,** *of*
Teams: New York Lincoln Giants ('20–'21), *Pennsylvania Red Caps of New York ('25–'28, '32)*

He was in the starting rotation for the New York Lincoln Giants in 1920–21, but played most of his career with the Pennsylvania Red Caps of New York, a team of lesser status.

Rector, Cornelius (**Connie,** Broadway)
Career: 1920–44   Positions: **p,** of, 1b
Teams: Hilldale Daisies ('20–'23), **Brooklyn Royal Giants** ('22–'26), **New York Lincoln Giants** ('27–'30), Harlem Stars ('31), **New York Black Yankees** ('32–'41, '44), New York Cubans ('39)
Bats: Right   Throws: Right
Height: 5'8"   Weight: 165
Born: Texas

This slender right-hander spent most of his twenty-five-year career with New York-based teams and is most frequently identified with the Brooklyn Royal Giants, the New York Lincoln Giants, and the New York Black Yankees. A good control pitcher with a great change-up

and a variety of good breaking pitches, including a curve, slider, and knuckler, he was a heady hurler who knew how to pitch and keep batters guessing. But he was not a power pitcher, having only an average fastball. With the Lincoln Giants in 1929 he fashioned a 20–3 record, tops in the American Negro League that year. A dapper ladies' man, the Texan readily adapted to the New York nightlife, earning the nickname "Broadway."

He began his professional career in the East with Hilldale in 1920, and posted a 17–4 record with a 2.89 ERA in 1921. After his last season with Hilldale, he spent the winter of 1923 playing in Cuba, and upon his return to the United States, he joined the Brooklyn Royal Giants, where he was considered a "top-notcher" and assumed the role as the third starter behind Smokey Joe Williams and Cannonball Dick Redding on the 1924 team. In 1925 he fashioned a 5–2 record in Eastern Colored League play. He joined the Lincoln Giants in 1927 and fashioned records of 5–7 and 6–2 in 1928 and 1930.

In addition to his pitching skills, he was a good hitter with good power and was sometimes used at first base, in the outfield, or as a pinch hitter, batting .343 and .419 with Hilldale in 1921–22, .219 and .265 with the Brooklyn Royal Giants in 1924–25, and .237 and .261 with the Lincoln Giants in 1929–30. He was also a good fielder but a little slow on the bases.

In 1931 the Lincoln Giants' franchise folded and was replaced by the Harlem Stars, with John Henry Lloyd continuing at the helm. Rector dropped to a 2–6 mark with the Stars. But the next year the franchise became the New York Black Yankees, and Rector remained with the team for another dozen seasons. His marks with the Black Yankees included 2–5 and 1–3 in 1941 and 1944.

Redd, Eugene (**Gene**)
Career: 1922–23   Positions: 3b, ss
Teams: Kansas City Monarchs ('22), Pittsburgh Keystones ('22), Cleveland Tate Stars

('22), Milwaukee Bears ('23), *New Orleans Crescent Stars ('23)*

He began his career in his hometown of Kansas City in 1922 as a third baseman, but his stay was brief and he spent most of the season as a reserve infielder, playing both third base and shortstop, with the Cleveland Tate Stars during their only entry into the Negro National League. The next season he played a similar role with the Milwaukee Bears in their only year in the league, spending most of his limited playing time at third base.

Redd, Ulysses A.
Career: 1940–41   Positions: **ss**, 2b, 3b
Teams: Birmingham Black Barons ('40–'41), *Harlem Globetrotters ('47), Chicago American Giants ('51)*

He was the regular shortstop for the Birmingham Black Barons in 1940–41, usually hitting sixth or seventh. Although shortstop was his best position, he could play any infield position, and after World War II he played with the Harlem Globetrotter's baseball team, although they played a lesser quality of ball. He later returned to the Negro American League, playing with the Chicago American Giants after the league had gone into decline.

Redding, Richard (**Cannonball Dick**)
Career: 1911–38   Positions: **p**, of, 1b, manager
Teams: Philadelphia Giants ('11), **New York Lincoln Giants** ('11–'16), New York Lincoln Stars ('15), Indianapolis ABCs ('15), **Brooklyn Royal Giants** ('16, '18, '23–'32, '38), Chicago American Giants ('17–'18), *military service ('18–'19),* Atlantic City Bacharachs ('19–'21), New York Bacharachs ('22)
Bats: Right   Throws: Right
Height: 6'4"   Weight: 210
Born: 1891, Atlanta, Ga.
Died: 1948, Islip, N.Y.

One of the great pitchers of black baseball, Dick Redding's overpowering speed earned the big, tall right-hander the nickname "Cannonball Dick." During his prime years in the de-cade of the 1910s, he maintained a position among the top pitchers in black baseball. Along with his speed, Dick utilized a no-windup deliver and developed a "hesitation pitch" long before Satchel Paige appeared on the baseball scene. Redding was credited with 30 no-hitters against all levels of opposition during a career that began with top teams in 1911, at age twenty.

That season he was with the Philadelphia Giants until July, when he moved to the New York Lincoln Giants for the remainder of the year. After joining the Lincoln Giants, the rookie won 17 straight games, relying almost exclusively on his blinding speed and good control, since he had not yet developed a curve. The following year, when he was paired with Smokey Joe Williams on the pitching staff, he recorded a 43–12 season, punctuated with several no-hitters, including one against the Cuban Stars. In another game that season, he struck out 25 men and faced only 27 batters.

In 1914 Redding's ledger showed a 12–3 record and 101 strikeouts in 18 games pitched. The next season, 1915, after moving over to the Lincoln Stars, he won 20 straight games before finally losing, and was 23–2 through the first week in August, earning him the description "the Demon pitcher" from the press. In early September he left the Lincoln Stars and rejoined the Lincoln Giants. In the playoffs against the Chicago American Giants he fashioned a 3–1 record, including a shutout, and hit .385 in the Series.

A hard worker with exceptional stamina, in his prime years he often pitched doubleheaders two or three days in succession. Redding usually finished what he started, and it was rare for him not to finish a game. Although generally calm and collected on the mound, especially when protecting a lead, he sometimes lost his composure when opponents jumped off to a quick start from errors by his teammates.

While pitching in the East for the first half dozen seasons, he was coveted by the two leading managers in the West, C.I. Taylor and Rube Foster. After a brief stint with Tayor's

Indianapolis ABCs two years earlier, Redding joined Foster's Chicago American Giants in 1917, with incomplete statistics showing a 13–3 record as the ace of the staff. That season the press called him "Smiling Dick" and declared the big, hard-throwing hurler to be another Walter Johnson.

The advent of World War I interrupted Redding's career while still at its peak. After combat duty in France, he returned to the United States, joining the Bacharach Giants and assuming the role of player-manager in midsummer of 1919. He continued in that capacity through the 1922 season. The Eastern Colored League was formed the next season, and the big Georgian signed with the Brooklyn Royal Giants. A feud developed between him and Smokey Joe Williams, with the pair of fastball artists refusing to shake hands and be photographed together. However, in 1924 the two aces were again paired on the same staff when Williams joined the Royal Giants, and Redding was regarded as the number two pitcher. He probably had more speed than anyone, but he still relied almost exclusively on his fastball and would not hesitate to use it to knock a batter down to assert his dominion.

Redding left the Royals to manage the 1921 New York Bacharachs and compiled a 17–12 personal ledger. The next year he was replaced at the helm by John Henry Lloyd, and signed with Atlantic City to play for the "original Bacharachs" under manager Dick Lundy. After one season there, he returned to the Brooklyn Royal Giants, but his skills were fading and in 1925 his league ledger showed a 3–4 mark. However, Redding was still a presence in black baseball, and he was appointed manager, holding the Royals' reins for a half dozen seasons, 1927–32. Redding was a functional illiterate, but although lacking formal education, he had extensive experience in baseball, and as a manager he was clean-living, good-natured, easygoing, and well liked by his players.

Before beginning his professional career, he played with the Atlanta Depins, a semipro team

in his hometown. During his career he also pitched in the Cuban winter league, accumulating a total of 18 victories while playing in five winter seasons. He retired from the baseball scene in 1938. He became ill with a "strange malady" in late July 1948 that led to his death in a mental hospital.

Redding, Sam
Career: 1929   Position: of
Team: Brooklyn Royal Giants

A brother of Dick Redding, he played left field with the Brooklyn Royal Giants when they were playing as an independent team.

Reddon, Bob
Career: 1919   Position: p
Team: *Cleveland Tate Stars*

A marginal player, he pitched with the Cleveland Tate Stars in 1919, three years before they joined the Negro National League.

Redmon, Tom
Career: 1911   Position: player
Team: Chicago Giants

He was listed as being with the Chicago Giants in 1911, but his position is uncertain.

Redus, Wilson (**Frog**)
Career: 1924–40   Positions: **lf**, rf, cf, manager, coach
Teams: Cleveland Browns ('24), Indianapolis ABCs ('24), **St. Louis Stars** ('24–'31), Kansas City Monarchs ('30), Cleveland Stars ('32), Cleveland Giants ('33), Columbus Blue Birds ('33), Cleveland Red Sox ('34), Chicago American Giants ('34–'40)
Bats: Right   Throws: Right
Height: 5'7"   Weight: 160
Born: Jan. 29, 1905, Muskogee, Okla.
Died: 1986, Oklahoma

A good contact hitter with better than average power, he could either bunt or execute a hit-and-run when the occasion required a run. Although lacking good speed and having only average defensive capabilities, the outfielder compensated with hustle in the field and on the bases, and was a successful base stealer.

"Frog" was a member of the champion 1930–31 St. Louis Stars and especially enjoyed hitting in the St. Louis ballpark with the car barn in left field, batting .384, .326, .344, .338, .321, and .281 for the years 1925–30. With the Stars he usually batted in about the sixth spot, but he was not a regular in the Stars' pennant-winning seasons of 1930–31.

After leaving St. Louis he played with the Cleveland Stars, Cleveland Giants, Columbus Blue Birds, and Cleveland Red Sox before joining the Chicago American Giants. Despite the multiple transitions, he hit .319 in 1933, but after joining Chicago, he got off to a bad start in 1935, with partial statistics showing only a .170 average in his first full season with the American Giants. But the outfielder got back on track, batting .327 in 1936 and making consecutive All-Star appearances in 1936 and 1937. Redus remained with the American Giants, as a part-time starter the last two years, and closed out his career in 1940.

Much later in life, as an octogenarian returning from a friend's funeral in Texas, he was killed in an automobile accident.

Redwine
Career: 1926   Position: p
Team: Cleveland Elites

A marginal player, he was one of the four-teen pitchers who were among the throng passing through Cleveland's Hooper Field in 1926 wearing an Elites' baseball uniform, but he did not figure in a league decision.

Reed, Andrew
Career: 1917–21   Positions: 3b, of
Teams: Chicago Union Giants ('18), Chicago Giants ('17), Detroit Stars ('19, '21)

In 1917 he was a substitute third baseman with the Chicago Giants, who were struggling to maintain a major-league level of play. He was with the Detroit Stars briefly as a fringe player but was never able to secure a starting position on any quality team.

Reed, Curtis
Career: 1937   Positions: lf, cf
Team: St. Louis Stars

In his only year with a league team, this outfielder was the cleanup hitter for the St. Louis Stars during the Negro American League's inaugural season. This new franchise was an extremely weak entry (.185 winning percentage for the first half) and had no connection with the earlier team of the same name.

Reed, Fleming
[see Reedy, Fleming]

Reed, John D.
Career: 1934–42   Position: p
Teams: Cole's American Giants ('34), Indianapolis Athletics ('37), St. Louis Stars ('37), **Chicago American Giants** ('38), Indianapolis ABCs ('38), Atlanta Black Crackers ('38), *Palmer House All-Stars ('40), Chicago Brown Bombers ('42)*

A pitcher of marginal ability, he played briefly with several teams during the '30s without receiving substantial playing time with any ballclub. In 1940 he pitched with the Palmer House All-stars, a Chicago-based independent team.

Reedy, Fleming (Buddy)
a.k.a. Fleming Reed
Career: 1950   Positions: 3b, of, 2b
Teams: Baltimore Elite Giants ('50–'51), *minor leagues ('52–'61)*
Bats: Left   Throws: Right
Height: 5'11"   Weight: 165
Born: 1929

An infielder-outfielder with good speed, he began his career with the Elites when the Negro American League was in decline, hitting .299 with some power in 1950. After two years with the Elites, he began playing in organized baseball with Lincoln in the Western League, batting .281. A decade later he wrapped up his career by splitting the season between Daytona Beach in the Florida State League and Minot in the Northern League. In between, his best years were with Lancaster in the Piedmont League (.311 and .323 in 1954–55), Albany in the Eastern League (.305 and .314 in 1958–59), and Sarasota in the Florida State League (.314 in 1961).

Reel, Jimmy
Career: 1923   Position: of
Team: Toledo Tigers

Most of his baseball career was spent with teams of lesser quality. In his only appearance with a top team in the Negro Leagues, he was an outfielder with the Toledo Tigers in 1923, before they folded in mid-July in their only season in the Negro National League. Before he began playing baseball, he was a professional singer with a beautiful voice and style that were similar to those of Billy Eckstine. Grant "Home Run" Johnson, in his latter years, liked to ride in the same touring car with Reel just to hear him sing while they were traveling between games.

Reese, Charles
Career: 1910–11   Position: p
Teams: Cuban Giants ('10), Chicago Union Giants ('11)

He was a pitcher with the Cuban Giants, a once-proud team now in the declining stages of their existence.

Reese, James (Lefty, Jimmy, Big Jim, Slim)
a.k.a. Reece
Career: 1937–40   Positions: p
Teams: Atlanta Black Crackers ('37–'38), Indianapolis ABCs ('39), Baltimore Elite Giants ('40)
Bats: Left   Throws: Left
Height: 6'0"   Weight: 170

As the mainstay for the 1937 Atlanta Black Crackers' pitching staff, the big, elongated left-hander had a fastball and pretty good control and won more than 20 games. While playing baseball he continued his educational pursuits, and he graduated from Morris Brown College in June 1938. At the beginning of the season the Black Crackers encountered some difficulty

getting him to sign. He was working as a high-school teacher and had to iron out a "technicality" involving his contractural obligations to the Jacksonville Red Caps, with whom he had signed after the Black Crackers' franchise was sold to the Negro American League owners.

But he had continued playing with the Atlanta Black Crackers and was officially purchased near the end of May. He made his home in Atlanta, and the Black Crackers also had to work out arrangements permitting him to report late without interrupting his career as an educator, which eventually led to him becoming a school principal later in life.

In 1939 the Black Crackers' franchise moved North, playing out of Indianapolis as the ABCs, but when financial conditions forced the team to disband, Reese signed with the Baltimore Elites for a season but failed to register a league decision.

Reese, John E. (Johnny, *Speed Boy, Sparkplug*)
Career: 1918–31   Positions: of, manager
Teams: Atlantic City Bacharach Giants ('18), Hilldale Daisies ('18–'19), Chicago American Giants ('20–'22), Detroit Stars ('21), Toledo Tigers ('23), St. Louis Stars ('23–'31)
Born: Florida

Very fast on the bases and in the field, he was a defensive standout. The Morris College product had good range in the outfield, and with Hilldale in 1918 he was described as making "spectacular catches in the field." In 1919, his last year with Hilldale, he batted .281. The next season he joined Rube Foster's American Giants, and remained with the club as they won the Negro National League's first three pennants, 1920–22. During his first year with the team, he shared a starting outfield spot but, unable to break into a starting outfield that featured Cristobal Torriente, Jimmy Lyons, and Jelly Gardner, he was relegated to bench service for the remainder of his time with the American Giants.

However, he joined the St. Louis Stars in

1923, hitting .261 in 1926. The lessons he learned under Foster helped him in later years when he was appointed manager of the Stars, and he guided them to a Negro National League pennant in 1931.

Reeves
Career: 1929   Position: c
Teams: Hilldale Daisies

In his only season in the Negro Leagues, he was with Hilldale briefly in 1929 as a third-string catcher.

Reeves, Donald (Soup, *Andy Gump*)
Career: 1937–41   Positions: **rf**, lf, 1b
Teams: Atlanta Black Crackers ('37–'38), Indianapolis ABCs ('39), Chicago American Giants ('39–'41)
Bats: Left   Throws: Left
Height: 6'2"   Weight: 188

In 1940 this Chicago American Giants' outfielder was credited with 36 home runs by the end of July and 50 by the end of the season, earning him a spot in the 1940 East-West All-Star game. However, he went hitless in the contest.

A big, strong, left-handed batter, he was a good hitter, batting in the heart of the order for the American Giants and also for the 1938 Atlanta Black Crackers, winners of the second-half Negro American League title. He had a keen natural batting eye and, although he did not hit for a high average, he was the heaviest hitter on the team. Despite his power production, he was a straightaway hitter and did not pull the ball. A first-ball hitter, he had difficulty hitting a change-up because of his lack of patience.

Reeves had a sullen, sulky attitude, but a competitive spirit and was the fastest man on the team. He usually played right field, but was below average defensively. He also played first base and occasionally pitched in 1938, but mostly against lesser teams.

He was a Clark University graduate, and was an All-American athlete in three sports, playing end in football and also starring in basketball

and baseball. He was sometimes called "Andy Gump," after the comic strip character, because of a recessive chin. After leaving baseball he made his home in Atlanta and was a teacher in the city's school system.

Reggie
Career: 1921   Position: p
Teams: Indianapolis ABCs

He pitched briefly with the Indianapolis ABCs in 1921, his only year in the Negro Leagues.

Reid, Ambrose
a.k.a. Reed
Career: 1922–32   Positions: **of**, 2b, 1b, 3b, ss, c
Teams: **Atlantic City Bacharach Giants** ('22–'29), Hilldale Daisies ('30), Pittsburgh Crawfords ('31), Homestead Grays ('31), *Atlanta Black Crackers ('32)*

A good hitter with good speed, he was versatile and could play either outfield or infield. He began his career in 1922 with the Bacharachs and spent most of his career with the Atlantic City ballclub. Playing as the regular center fielder in 1923, he hit fifth in the batting order. The following season he shifted to third base to fill a team need, but had difficulty adjusting defensively and left a big hole in the infield. However, he was productive at the plate, batting .297 for the season. Moved back to the outfield, he played in the middle garden in 1925, batting .255 for the year. He was the left fielder and leadoff batter for the Bacharachs' two consecutive Eastern Colored League pennant winners in 1926–27, although his average dropped to .204 and .219. Each season the Bacharachs faced the Chicago American Giants in the World Series in a losing cause, with Reid's Series contributions including batting averages of .387 and .269.

With the collapse of the Eastern Colored League, the 1928 season was somewhat chaotic, and Reid again changed positions for the welfare of the team. Playing primarily at second base, he also garnered playing time in the outfield and at third base. While his personal situation afield was about as unsettled as the eastern organizational structure, he gained some stability by being retained in the leadoff position in the lineup. The following season, the teams restructured, and the Bacharachs joined the replacement American Negro League, with Reid playing a utility role in his last year with the Bacharachs.

In 1930 he joined Hilldale, splitting his playing time between second base and right field while batting second in the order and hitting .214. The next year he began the season with the Homestead Grays but moved to the Pittsburgh Crawfords during the season as Gus Greenlee began his efforts to build a strong ballclub. With the Crawfords Reid batted in the third slot in the lineup while playing in the outfield and on the corners. When Greenlee raided the Grays for the 1932 season, Reid was among the players displaced. After his release he found a spot on the Atlanta Black Crackers, a team of lesser quality at that time, and never again played with a top ballclub.

Reña
[see Peña]

Rendez, Cuban
Career: 1938   Position: p
Team: Atlanta Black Crackers

This pitcher was on the spring roster of the 1938 Atlanta Black Crackers, but his previous experience was limited to a semipro Florida team (Coca-Cola Company), and he did not stick with the Black Crackers.

Renfroe, Othello Nelson (**Chico,** Chappy)
Career: 1945–50   Positions: **ss,** of, c, 2b
Teams: Kansas City Monarchs ('45–'47, '53), Cleveland Buckeyes ('48–'49), Indianapolis Clowns ('49–'50) *Mexican League ('50–'52)* *Minor Leagues ('54)*
Bats: Right   Throws: Right
Height: 5'11"   Weight: 175
Born: Mar. 1, 1923, Newark, N.J.
Died: Sept. 3, 1991, Atlanta, Ga.

A scrappy, versatile player, in 1946 he represented the Kansas City Monarchs in the 1946 East-West All-Star game and had the highest batting average in the World Series against the Newark Eagles, hitting .414 while playing at shortstop in all 7 games. After the Series he was a member of Satchel Paige's All-Star team that barnstormed across the country with Bob Feller's All-Stars.

The hustling infielder had only average defensive skills and speed, but was a good base stealer and was adequate afield at several positions. He hit for averages of .232, .245, .296, and .231 for the years 1945–49 (exclusive of 1947) and, although not a strong hitter, he was a good bunter and hit-and-run man.

His passion for baseball developed from his days as a youngster in Jacksonville, Florida, hanging around the spring training camps of black teams and running errands for the players. He moved to Atlanta during his junior year in high school and enrolled at Clark College after graduation. While continuing his education he also played semipro ball until signing with the Kansas City Monarchs in 1945. At that time he was twenty-two years of age, skinny, and fast. The starting shortstop for the Monarchs at that time was Jackie Robinson, but after he signed with the Brooklyn Dodgers' organization, Renfroe became the regular shortstop, batting second in the order.

The next season he shared the second-base position but was dropped to the bottom of the batting order. After being traded to the Cleveland Buckeyes, he moved back to shortstop but continued to bat in the lower part of the order. During the 1949 season he moved to the Indianapolis Clowns until heeding a call from "south of the border" to play with Torreon in the Mexican League in 1950. Before ending his professional career with Minot, North Dakota, in 1954, he also played several winter seasons in various locales. He was a member of Chet Brewer's Kansas City Royals in the California winter league in 1945 and 1947, and toured Venezuela in 1950 with the New York

Stars (a team that featured Buck Leonard), and in the Dominican Republic in 1951–52.

After retiring from baseball in 1954, he returned to Atlanta and worked for the U.S. Post Office. Later he became a sportscaster and sports director for Atlanta radio station WIGO and sports editor for the *Atlanta Daily World*. He was also a scout for the Montreal Expos and was the first official scorer for the Atlanta Braves.

Reveria, Charlie
[see Rivero, Charles (Charlie)]

Reynolds
Career: 1946   Position: of, 1b
Team: Birmingham Black Barons

A light hitter, he was a substitute outfielder and occasional first baseman with the Birmingham Black Barons in 1946, batting .198 for the season.

Reynolds, Jimmy (Johnny)
Career: 1940, 1946   Position: 3b
Teams: Indianapolis Crawfords ('40), Cleveland Buckeyes ('46)

He was a marginal player who appeared briefly as a reserve infielder with a couple of midwestern teams.

Reynolds, Joe (Little Joe)
Career: 1935   Position: p
Team: Philadelphia Stars

He was a second-line pitcher who appeared briefly with the Philadelphia Stars in 1935, losing his only decision.

Reynolds, Louis Thomas (**Lou**)
Career: 1897–99   Positions: of, 1b
Teams: Chicago Unions ('97–'98), Chicago Columbia Giants ('99)

After two years as the starting first baseman for W. S. Peters's Chicago Unions in 1897–98, he joined the Chicago Columbia Giants as the regular right fielder when they organized in 1899. Featuring players such as Grant "Home Run" Johnson, Chappie Johnson, and Charlie

Grant, the Giants were one of the top black teams during their two years of existence.

Reynolds, William Ernest (**Bill**)
Career: 1948–50   Positions: **2b**, ss, 3b
Teams: Cleveland Buckeyes ('48, '50), Louisville Buckeyes ('49)

This light-hitting infielder joined the Buckeyes as the regular second baseman in 1948, hitting .226 while batting eighth. The next year, the fanchise moved to Louisville, and he hit .209 for the 1949 season. His playing time in 1950 was severly restricted, as his career coincided with the onset of the Negro American League's decline.

Rhoades, Cornelius (**Neal**)
Career: 1916–18   Positions: **c**, of
Teams: Bowser's ABCs ('16–'17), Hilldale Daises ('18), *Madison Stars ('21), Washington Braves ('21)*

A marginal player who played almost exclusively with teams of lesser quality, he appeared briefly as a reserve catcher with Hilldale in 1918.

Rhodes, Claude (**Dusty**)
Career: 1931–33   Position: p
Teams: *Chattanooga Black Lookouts,* Louisville Black Caps ('32), Columbus Blue Birds ('33)

During this pitcher's short career in the Negro Leagues in the early '30s, he appeared with second-division ballclubs, first with the Louisville in the Negro Southern League in 1932, when it was designated as a major league, and the following season with the Columbus Blue Birds during their only year in the Negro National League.

Rhodes, Harry (Lefty)
a.k.a Rhoades
Career: 1942–50   Positions: **p**, 1b, of
Team: Chicago American Giants ('42, '46–'50)
Bats: Left   Throws: Left

He appeared briefly with the Chicago American Giants before World War II, and pitched in the regular rotation during the postwar years, registering marks of 3–6, 5–6, and 5–6 for the years 1946, 1948, and 1949. With the American Giants he occasionally played at first base and in the outfield, batting .286 and .210 for the seasons 1946 and 1948, respectively. In 1947 he played with the Havana La Palomas.

Rice, Miller
Career: 1934–37   Position: of
Team: Cincinnati Tigers ('34–'37)

He began playing with the Cincinnati Tigers while they were an independent team, and he continued as a reserve outfielder when they entered the Negro American League in 1937.

Rich
Career: 1924   Position: 3b
Team: St. Louis Stars

He appeared briefly in 1924 with the St. Louis Stars as a reserve third baseman.

Richardson
Career: 1903   Position: 2b
Team: Algona Brownies

He played second base with the 1903 Algona Brownies, the top team in the West that season.

Richardson
Career: 1924   Position: of
Teams: *Philadelphia Giants ('18, '24)*, Washington Potomacs ('24)

Most of his career was spent with lesser teams, but he played briefly as a right fielder with the Washington Potomacs in 1924, their only year in the Eastern Colored League.

Richardson, Bob
[see Richardson, Johnny Bob]

Richardson, Dewey
Career: 1922   Position: c
Team: Hilldale Daisies

He was a backup catcher for Louis Santop with the Hilldale team in 1922, and was credited with a .472 batting average in his only year with a top team.

Richardson, Earl
Career: 1943   Positions: ss, 2b
Team: Newark Eagles
Bats: Right   Throws: Right
Height: 5'9"   Weight: 150

A high-school star, he was taken from the Montclair High School team in 1943, and although this was a big jump for a schoolboy, his defensive ability as a middle-infielder allowed him to make the team during the war-depleted season.

Richardson, Eugene (Gene)
Career: 1947–50   Position: p
Teams: Kansas City Monarchs ('47–'53), *Baltimore Elite Giants ('51)*
Bats: Left   Throws: Left
Height: 5'10"   Weight: 160

A left-handed pitcher with a good curve and change-up, an average fastball, and good control, he began pitching with the Kansas City Monarchs in 1947 and posted a 5–6 record the following season. In 1949, his third year in Kansas City, he was scouted by the the Boston Braves, who were interested in signing him, but he remained with the Monarchs, and fashioned a 4–2 work sheet in 1950. As the Negro American League was struggling to survive the loss of players to organized baseball, he pitched with the Baltimore Elites in 1951 for a season, but returned to the Monarchs, playing through 1953; but the league was strictly a minor league at that time.

Richardson, George
Career: 1901–03   Positions: ss, 2b
Teams: Chicago Union Giants ('01), Algona Brownies ('02–'03)

With the Algona (Iowa) Brownies, he played second base the first year and shortstop the second season, 1903, when they won the championship.

Richardson, George
Career: 1925   Position: officer
Team: Detroit Stars

He was an officer with the Detroit Stars in 1925.

Richardson, Glenby (**Glenn**)
Career: 1946–49   Positions: **2b**, p
Team: New York Black Yankees
A light-hitting reserve second baseman for the Black Yankees, he hit only .182 in 1947; on occasions when he drew a starting assignment, he was placed at the bottom of the batting order.

Richardson, Henry (Long Tom)
Career: 1921–38   Positions: **p**, of, 2b
Teams: Atlantic City Bacharach Giants ('21), Richmond Giants ('22), **Baltimore Black Sox** ('22–'23, '33), Cuban Stars (West) ('31), Washington Pilots ('32), Black Senators ('38), Pittsburgh Crawfords ('38)
With the Baltimore Black Sox in 1922, he played as a substitute at second base and in the outfield, batting .284 while also posting a 3–2 work sheet as a pitcher. Beginning the next season, he gravitated more toward pitching, with most of his playing time being on the mound, although he still occasionally played in the outfield. However, his numbers were less impressive: He lost his only decision in 1923 before recording seasons of 4–3 and 4–1 in 1932–33 with the Washington Pilots and the Black Sox, respectively.
Although his career spanned 18 years, beginning with the Bacharachs in 1921, he was not with a quality ballclub throughout his career. His last appearance in the Negro Leagues came after an absence of five seasons, when he gained playing time with both the Washington Potomacs and the Pittsburgh Crawfords in 1938.

Richardson, Jim
Career: 1934–39   Position: p
Teams: Philadelphia Stars ('34), New York Black Yankees ('39)
He made two appearances in the Negro Leagues during the '30s, first with Ed Bolden's Philadelphia Stars during their 1934 championship season, and again in 1939, when he was fifth on the pitching depth chart for owner James Semler's New York Black Yankees.

Richardson, John
Career: 1924–25   Positions: p, 2b, 3b, rf
Team: Birmingham Black Barons
He was an all-purpose player for the Birmingham Black Barons during the '20s, when the Black Barons were in the Negro National League.

Richardson, Johnny Bob
Career: 1949–50   Position: ss
Team: Homestead Grays
The infielder played as a shortstop with the Homestead Grays after they had dropped out of league competition and were playing a much less demanding schedule as an independent team.

Richardson, Vicial
Career: 1946   Position: ss
Team: Cleveland Buckeyes
A fringe player, this shortstop appeared briefly as a reserve with the Cleveland Buckeyes in 1946.

Richbourg, Lefty
Career: 1938   Position: p
Teams: Atlanta Black Crackers
This left-handed pitcher appeared briefly with the 1938 Atlanta Black Crackers.

Ricks, Curtiss
Career: 1921–26   Positions: 1b, of, p
Teams: Dayton Marcos ('21), Cleveland Tate Stars ('22), Chicago American Giants ('23), Cleveland Browns ('24), Indianapolis ABCs ('24), Harrisburg Giants ('26)
A marginal player, during his short career with Negro National League teams in the early '20s he was a pitcher in 1922–23 but played as a first baseman in 1924.

Ricks, Napoleon
Career: 1887   Position: player
Team: *Louisville Falls Citys*
He played with the Louisville Falls Citys, one of eight teams that were charter members of the League of Colored Baseball Clubs in

1887. However, the league's existence was ephemeral, lasting only a week. His position is uncertain.

Ricks, Pender

Career: 1928   Positions: 1b, 3b
Teams: *Philadelphia Giants ('23–'24),* Harrisburg Giants ('28)

This first baseman played two years with the Philadelphia Giants (1923–24) and captained the squad each year, before appearing with Harrisburg in 1928.

Ricks, William (**Bill**)

Career: 1944–50   Position: p
Team: Philadelphia Stars
Bats: Right   Throws: Right
Height: 6'1"   Weight: 190

The Philadelphia Stars' right-handed speedballer had everything necessary for pitching success, including good control, a good fastball, and one of the best spitballs in the league. Beginning his career in 1944, he posted a 10–4 record and led the league in strikeouts. Continuing his superb pitching in 1945, despite a 1–4 mark he earned a spot on the East squad for the East-West All-Star game, relieving starter Tommy Glover. In 1946 Ricks was still considered a strikeout marvel, but dropped to a 1–3 record in league play. Although he remained in the Stars' rotation, he never reclaimed his early promise, showing records of 5–2 and 4–8 (3.94 ERA) for 1948–49 and splitting two decisions in 1950.

In 1951 he pitched with Granby in the Provincial League, posting an 8–8 record with a 4.21 ERA. In addition to his pitching, Ricks displayed a modicum of fielding and baserunning skills, and was a fair hitter with average power, batting .417 with the Stars in 1945 and .255 with Granby in 1951.

Riddick, Vernon

Career: 1939–41   Position: ss
Team: Newark Eagles
Bats: Right   Throws: Right
Height: 5'9"   Weight: 165

This infielder from Morgan State College had good speed and power, but his difficulty hitting the curveball limited his playing time during his three seasons with the Newark Eagles after joining the ballclub in 1939.

Riddle, Marshall Lewis (Jit)

Career: 1937–43   Positions: 2b, ss
Teams: St. Louis Stars ('37, '39, 41), Indianapolis ABCs ('38), New Orleans-St. Louis Stars ('40), Jacksonville Red Caps ('42), Cleveland Buckeyes ('43), *Canadian League ('51)*
Bats: Right   Throws: Right
Height: 5'8"   Weight: 115
Born: 1917, St. Louis, Mo.

A classy fielder with the St. Louis Stars, he played in the East-West All-Star game of 1940, substituting for Tommy Sampson. The following season Riddle hit .290 and was considered by many experts to be one of the best second baseman in the Negro Leagues. The middle infielder broke in with the Stars in 1937, at age twenty, and could also play shortstop. He lacked power at the plate and was not a basestealing threat, but his glovework more than compensated for these deficiencies. After playing the 1943 season with the Cleveland Buckeyes, he never reappeared in the Negro Leagues. The next record of the infielder was in 1951, when he played with Three Rivers in the Provincial League, batting .238 without any appreciable power.

Ridgely, Buck

a.k.a. Risley
Career: 1920–23   Positions: **ss, 2b,** 3b, of
Teams: Baltimore Black Sox ('16–'22), New York Lincoln Giants ('20), Harrisburg Giants ('23), Washington Potomacs ('23), *Chappie Johnson's Stars ('25–'28)*

This middle infielder began his career as a shortstop with the Baltimore Black Sox in 1916, before they were a major-league-caliber ballclub. He was an integral part of the team for the next seven seasons, usually batting at one of the top two spots in the batting order. In 1920 he played part of the season with the

Lincoln Giants at shortstop, but returned to the Black Sox, where he switched to second base for the remainder of his years with them. In 1921–22 he hit .375 and .353 against all levels of competition. After leaving the Sox he joined Harrisburg for part of the 1923 season, playing second base and batting cleanup in those games he started. He closed out his career playing with Chappie Johnson's Stars, a touring, independent team of lesser quality.

Ridley, Jack
Career: 1927–34   Positions: cf, 1b
Teams: Nashville Elite Giants ('27–'34), Cleveland Cubs ('31), Louisville Red Caps ('32)

Beginning his career in 1927 with the Nashville Elites, he hit .233 in 1929 in limited play and .277 in 1930. He played center field and batting leadoff with the Elites in 1931, when they relocated in Cleveland, and played in the Negro National League as the Cleveland Cubs. The franchise returned to Nashville, and he rejoined the Elites during the 1933 season, again playing center field and batting leadoff when in the lineup. The next season, when the Elites entered the Negro National League, he was again in center field when a tragic accident terminated his career and almost cost him his life. While a passenger in an automobile, he had his arm hanging out an open window when the driver passed a truck and cut back in the lane too soon, ripping off Ridley's arm when the vehicles meshed.

Rigal
Career: 1922–27   Positions: ss, 3b
Team: Cuban Stars (West)

This infielder began his career with the Negro National League Cuban Stars as a shortstop in 1922 and finished as a third baseman in 1927, batting .245 for the season.

Riggins, Orville (**Bill,** Bo, Junior)
Career: 1920–36   Positions: **ss**, 3b, 2b, 1b, manager
Teams: Chicago American Giants ('20), **Detroit Stars** ('20–'26), Cleveland Hornets ('27),

Homestead Grays ('27), New York Lincoln Giants ('28–'30), Harlem Stars ('31), New York Black Yankees ('32), Brooklyn Royal Giants ('32–'33), Miami Giants ('34–'36)
Bats: Both   Throws: Right

This fast infielder had quick hands and could play all infield positions, but was best known as a shortstop. A switch-hitter, he swung a good stick, hitting for average and with power while also demonstrating proficiency on the hit-and-run play. Unfortunately, he had a drinking problem that sometimes interfered with his performance.

For a decade he batted in the heart of the order as a shortstop with the Detroit Stars during the early '20s and as a third baseman with the Lincoln Giants in 1928–30. With the Stars he hit .294, .260, .287, .301, .278, and .302 for the years 1921–26. Then after an interim season with the Cleveland Hornets and the Homestead Grays, where he hit .327, he recorded batting averages of .331 and .357 in 1929–30. In the latter year the Lincoln Giants had their best team since 1913, but lost a playoff for the eastern championship to the Homestead Grays in what was to be the Lincoln Giants' final season. In 1931 Riggins joined John Henry Lloyd's Harlem Stars, with incomplete statistics showing an uncharacteristic .137 batting average. After stints with the New York Black Yankees and the Brooklyn Royal Giants, he finished his career with the Miami Giants in 1934–36.

Following the 1925 season, Riggins was selected to play with the Philadelphia Royals, an all-star squad that played in the California winter league. In a game early in the winter, he broke his leg, and his misfortune opened the door for a young Willie Wells, who was signed as Riggins's replacement. The broken leg subsequently impaired his running somewhat, but his hitting was not affected. Generally a strong hitter, he averaged .301 for three winters in Cuba during the 1920s.

Rigney, H. G. (**Hank**)
Career: 1939–45   Position: officer.
Teams: Toledo Crawfords ('39), Indianapolis Crawfords ('40), *Toledo Cubs (USL) ('45)*

Born: 1888
Died: Feb. 12, 1958, Sayro, Pa.

This white sportsman was owner of the Toledo Crawfords and promoted black games in Sportsman's Park in St. Louis. Black entrepreneurs employed pressure tactics in an unsuccessful effort to have his booking privileges taken away and given to a black promoter.

Rile, Edward (Ed, **Huck**)
Career: 1920–36   Positions: **p, 1b**, 2b
Teams: *Dayton Marcos ('19),* Indianapolis ABCs ('20, '25–'26, '31), New York Lincoln Giants ('20–'21, '23), Columbus Buckeyes ('21), Kansas City Monarchs ('21), Chicago American Giants ('22–'24), Homestead Grays ('24), Detroit Stars ('27–'30), Brooklyn Royal Giants ('31–'36), Cole's American Giants
Bats: Both   Throws: Right
Height: 6'6"   Weight: 230
Died: Columbus, Oh.

One of the biggest men in the Negro Leagues, he broke in as a pitcher and, in the early years of his career (1920–25), was most noted for his pitching, posting marks of 2–1, 3–0, 4–5, 14–8, 5–1, and 2–5 in league play. But because of his hitting ability, for the next four seasons (1926–29) he began combining pitching and playing first base, and posted marks of 4–1 and 14–6 in 1926–27. He was primarily a first baseman from 1930 until he closed out his baseball career.

In 1920 he was pitching for the New York Lincoln Giants and was described as "a Westerner with a rare combination of pitching and hitting power." When he was signed by Rube Foster in 1922, he was expected to be a great player for the Chicago American Giants, but in February 1923 he and Dave Brown jumped to eastern clubs. However, Rile was soon back with the Chicago American Giants, but was released by Foster to the Indianapolis ABCs in the spring of 1925 to help bolster their team.

The ABCs had suffered from a high attrition rate due to raids from eastern ballclubs. In 1926 he hit .322 with the ABCs, but joined the Detroit Stars the following season, where he hit .401 and 10 home runs in 68 games. In 1929 he again hit 10 home runs but his average dropped to .299, and in 1930 he hit .323 and registered a slugging percentage of .584.

He was a good hitter, and as a pitcher he could throw hard but enjoyed getting a batter out on a change of pace, and would laugh at the batters when he fooled them.

Riley, Jim (Jack)
Career: 1945   Position: 2b
Team: Birmingham Black Barons

This second baseman left his hometown of Birmingham to play with the Pensacola Pepsi-Colas, and returned in 1945 to play with the Birmingham Black Barons, but lacked the skills to play at a major-league level and was not with the team very long.

Rims
Career: 1920   Position: p
Team: Atlantic City Bacharach Giants

A marginal player, he pitched briefly with the Bacharachs in 1920, when the club was still an independent team.

Rios, Herman
Career: 1915–24   Positions: 3b, ss
Teams: Cuban Stars (West) ('15–'24), Havana Stars
Born: 1897, Cuba
Died: 1925

This diminutive infielder for the Cuban Stars played both positions on the left side of the infield and had exceptional range, an accurate arm, good hands, and demonstrated "lightning-fast fielding." A light hitter, he usually batted in the lower part of the order, but sometimes hit in the second slot. An orphan when he first joined the Cubans, he played for a decade, but in June 1924 he suffered from bad health and was sent home for a rest. The following month, at age twenty-eight, Rios died.

Risley
[see Ridgely, Buck]

Ritchey, John T.
Career: 1947   Position: c
Teams: Chicago American Giants ('47), *minor leagues ('48–'56)*
Bats: Left   Throws: Right
Height: 5'10"   Weight: 170
Born: Aug. 5, 1924, San Diego, Calif.

In 1947, his only season in the Negro American League, he won the batting title with a .378 average. By this time, the decline in the Negro Leagues had already begun, and the pitching was uneven, allowing him to fatten his average. Although he was not fast, he got a good jump on pitchers and managed to steal 27 bases.

The next year, with the doors to organized baseball open, he signed with the San Diego Padres in the Pacific coast League, confident that he could hit .300. Ritchey's confidence paid off, as he hit .323 in his first season there, but racial pressures were difficult for him to handle. He had a good bat and good attitude and his competitive spirit made him a better ballplayer. Although he was not big and husky, he had a thick chest, broad shoulders, a size 18 neck, big hands, and thick wrists, and was rugged enough to withstand the physical demands of playing behind the plate. Manager Bucky Harris, who had managed the New York Yankees, touted Ritchey in the spring as better than anything the Yankees had the previous season, and predicted that he would be the "number one" catcher within two years. But although he was a very good hitter, he did not have a major-league-caliber arm and could not gun the base runners out. Observers agreed that this shortcoming kept him out of the major leagues.

Altogether, he played nine years in the minor leagues, mostly in the Pacific Coast League. In 1950 he batted .270 with Portland, but after only one game the next year, he was shipped to Vancouver in the Western International League. In his first year he copped the batting title with a .346 average, and followed with a .343 average in 1952. The next three years he was back in the Pacific Coast League

with Sacramento (.291 and .272) and San Francisco (.285). His last year came in 1956, with Syracuse in the International League, where he hit .185 in only 19 games. During his career he also played winters in Mexico, Venezuela, and Puerto Rico.

Before World War II he played semipro ball with Jackie Robinson all across the South. Reserved and serious-mined, he attended San Diego State College for two years in prelaw, but when Air Corps recruiters visited the campus, they did not talk to him because he was black. Eventually he joined the Army and spent 27 months in an Army engineering outfit in Europe (serving at Normandy, St.-Lo, and in the Battle of the Bulge) and seven months in the South Pacific. After retiring from baseball he worked as a salesman with the Continental Baking Company.

Rivas
Career: 1917–18   Positions: 3b, 2b
Team: Cuban Stars (East)

This infielder was the starting third baseman for the Cuban Stars (East) in 1917 and batted eighth in the order when in the lineup. The Cubans were based in New York that season and sometimes played under the name Havana Cuban Stars.

Rivell
Career: 1934   Position: umpire
League: Negro National League

In 1934 he was an umpire in the Negro National League.

Rivera, Nenene Aniceto
Career: 1933   Positions: p, if
Team: Cuban Stars
Bats: Right   Throws: Right

He was a right-handed pitcher with the Cuban Stars for a season when they were playing as an independent team during the Depression. He also gained some playing time in the infield as a utility man.

Rivera, Snooker
[see Rivero, Carlos (Charlie Snooker)

Rivero, Carlos (**Charlie,** Snooker)
a.k.a. Rivera; Reveria; Reviera
Career: 1933–44   Positions: ss, 2b, 3b
Teams: Cuban Stars ('33), Baltimore Elite
Giants ('39), Ethiopian Clowns ('41), New
York Cubans ('43–'44), New York Black Yankees ('44)
Bats: Right   Throws: Right
    This light-hitting but versatile Cuban in-
fielder's first appearance in the Negro Leagues
was in 1933 with the Cuban Stars, but six seasons passed before he joined the Baltimore
Elite Giants in July 1939 as a substitute third
baseman. Baltimore manager and resident third
baseman Felton Snow elected not to retain Rivero's services for the Elites, and Rivero joined
the Ethiopian Clowns, playing shortstop while
hitting eighth in the batting order. Joining the
New York Cubans in 1943, he was a part-time
starter, hitting .297 while alternating between
shortstop and second base. In 1944 he split his
playing time between the New York Cubans
and New York Black Yankees, where he was
their regular third baseman, batting .227 for the
season, his last year in the Negro Leagues.

Rivers, Bill
a.k.a. Rivera
Career: 1944   Position: of
Team: Kansas City Monarchs
    A wartime player, he was a reserve center
fielder with the Kansas City Monarchs for a
brief time in 1944.

Rivers, Dewey
Career: 1926–33   Position: of
Teams: Hilldale Daisies ('26), *Chappie Johnson's Stars ('27),* Baltimore Black Sox ('33)
    He began his career with an appearance with
the Hilldale club in 1926, joining Chappie
Johnson's Stars the following year as their center fielder. After gaining more experience, he
had another shot with a top ballclub, appearing
with the Baltimore Black Sox in 1933.

Roberson, Charley
Career: 1934   Positions: ss
Team: Nashville Elite Giants

He was a shortstop with the Elite Giants in
1934, when they played in the Negro National League.

Roberts
Career: 1920   Position:ss
Team: Chicago Giants
    He was a reserve shortstop for the Chicago
Giants in 1920, when they were members of
the Negro National League in its inaugural
season.

Roberts
Career: 1931   Position: c
Team: Chicago Columbia Giants
    He was one of seven catchers who played
with David Malarcher's Chicago Columbia
Giants, a team that was basically the Chicago
American Giants' franchise playing for a sea-
son under a different name.

Roberts, Charley
Career: 1938   Position: p
Team: Washington Black Senators
    He was in the pitching rotation with the
Washington Black Senators during their only
season in the Negro National League.

Roberts, Curtis Benjamin (**Curt**)
Career: 1947–50   Positions: **2b**, 3b, ss, lf
Teams: Kansas City Monarchs ('47–'50),
minor leagues ('51–'53, '55–'63), major
leagues ('54–'56)
Bats: Right   Throws: Right
Height: 5'8"   Weight: 155
Born: Aug. 16, 1929, Pineland, Tex.
Died: Nov. 14, 1969, Oakland, Calif.
    A good-fielding infielder with the Kansas
City Monarchs for four years before entering
organized baseball, he began his career in 1947
and batted .265, .276, and .299 during his last
three seasons in the Negro Leagues, 1948–50.
He had good speed and could steal when the
occasion dictated. At the plate he was moderately successful, but hitting better for average
than with power.
    After leaving the Monarchs he spent three

years with Denver in the Western League, hitting with consistency (.280, .280, .291) and earning a shot at the big leagues with the Pittsburgh Pirates. In 1954, his only full season in the major leagues, Roberts batted .232 as the Pirates' regular second baseman. He was with the Pirates for short stints in each of the next two seasons, but spent most of the time with Hollywood of the Pacific Coast League and Columbus of the American Association, hitting .321 and .320, respectively.

In 1957–58, it was back to Denver for the second sacker, where he responded with averages of .324 and .298. But there was not to be another chance at the major leagues, and the remainder of his career was spent primarily in AAA ball, where he continued to hit with consistency, posting marks of .296, .290, and .307 in 1959–61. The latter two years were with Spokane in the Pacific Coast League, and he spent the next two years with Omaha in 1962 and with Lynchburg of the South Atlantic League in 1963, where he closed out his career with a .284 average. During his career he played winter ball in Cuba, compiling a lifetime batting average of .255. He also played in Panama, Nicaragua and the Dominican Republic.

Roberts, Elihu
Career: 1916–20   Positions: of, 2b
Teams: Atlantic City Bacharach Giants ('16–'19), Hilldale Daisies ('19–'20)

In 1917, when the Bacharachs were in their formative years, he was the regular left fielder and third-place hitter. In 1919–20, when Hilldale was still playing as an independent ballclub, he shared the starting left-field position, batting leadoff the former year and in the seventh slot during the latter season. He also had some playing time at second base for the 1919 team, and hit .250 for the season.

Roberts, Harry (Rags)
a.k.a. Harry Raggs
Career: 1922–32   Positions: c, of
Teams: *Norfolk Stars ('20–'21),* Baltimore

Black Sox ('22–'23), Harrisburg Giants, Homestead Grays ('23–'26), Chicago Columbia Giants ('31), Pittsburgh Crawfords ('32)

A backup catcher with Cum Posey's Homestead Grays in 1926 and Dave Malarcher's Chicago Columbia Giants in 1931, he began his career with top teams in 1922 with the Baltimore Black Sox, after two seasons with the Norfolk Stars, a team of lesser status. He is credited with a .323 batting average for the season, and he joined the Grays the following season. Five years later he was a reserve catcher with the Baltimore Black Sox before closing out his career with a brief appearance for the Pittsburgh Crawfords in 1932.

Roberts, J. D.
Career: 1918–19   Positions: ss, 2b, 3b, lf
Teams: *Pennsylvania Giants ('18),* Atlantic City Bacharach Giants ('18), Hilldale Daisies ('19), *Madison Stars ('21), Richmond Giants ('23)*

In the latter years of the deadball era and early years of the lively ball era, this infielder played mostly with teams of lesser quality, but made appearances as a substitute second baseman for the 1918 Bacharachs and also as a reserve for Hilldale in 1919.

Roberts, Leroy (**Roy,** Everready)
Career: 1916–34   Positions: **p, c**
Teams: **Atlantic City Bacharach Giants** ('16–'19, '22–'27), Hilldale Daisies ('18–'19, '30), *Madison Stars ('20),* Brooklyn Royal Giants ('20), Columbus Buckeyes ('21), New York Lincoln Giants ('25), Cleveland Giants ('33), Cleveland Red Sox ('34)

Beginning his career in 1917, he pitched for the Bacharach Giants prior to military service during World War I. While in service he played on the Camp Dix team, and after his discharge pitched with Hilldale in 1918–19, winning his only decision in his first campaign. After a stint with the Brooklyn Royal Giants he pitched for the Columbus Buckeyes in 1921, posting a 7–15 record. Returning to the Bacharachs the following year, the veteran was still a fairly good pitcher in 1924. After losing both league decisions in 1925, he fashioned a good season in 1926, finishing with a 5–1 mark for the first of two consecutive Eastern Colored League championship seasons. His last appearance in league play was with the Cleveland entries in the Negro National League in 1933–34.

Roberts, P.
Career: 1903   Position: 2b
Team: Chicago Union Giants

He was the regular second baseman for the Chicago Union Giants in 1903, one of the last years of the team's existence.

Roberts, Rags
[see Roberts, Harry (Rags)]

Roberts, Sarah (Mutt)
Career: 1937–39   Position: p
Teams: Philadelphia Stars ('37–'38), Baltimore Elite Giants ('39)

He pitched briefly without distinction for the Philadelphia Stars and the Baltimore Elite Giants during the late '30s.

Roberts, Tom (Specs, Speck)
Career: 1937–45   Position: p
Teams: Washington Black Senators ('38), Homestead Grays ('39–'40), *Mexican League ('40)*, New York Black Yankees ('41–'43), Philadelphia Stars ('44), Newark Eagles ('45)
Bats: Right   Throws: Right
Height: 5'10"   Weight: 175

He had an outstanding season with the Homestead Grays in 1939 as they captured the Negro National League pennant with one of their strongest teams. While in demand he opted to play in the Mexican League the following season, where he was 6–3 with a 5.70 ERA for Mexico City. After returning to the United States, he signed with the New York Black Yankees, but never recaptured the success he enjoyed with the Grays. He closed out his Negro League career in 1945, winning two of three decisions for the Newark Eagles. His

repertory included a fastball, curve, drop, and change-up, but none of his pitches was above the norm for major-league competition, and his effectiveness resulted from being a good control pitcher. Unlike most Grays' pitchers, he was not a good hitter, but he fielded his position adequately.

Robertson, Bobbie
[see Robinson, William (Bobbie)]

Robertson, Charles
a.k.a. Charles Robinson
Career: 1923–25   Position: p
Teams: Birmingham Black Barons ('23, '25), St. Louis Stars ('24)

During the '20s he pitched without distinction for three seasons with the Birmingham Black Barons and the St. Louis Stars.

Robinson
Career: 1903   Position: 1b
Team: Algona Brownies

He played first base for the Algona, Iowa, Brownies, the top team in the West during the 1903 season.

Robinson
Career: 1943   Positions: 3b, ss
Team: New York Black Yankees

He shared a starting infield position and batted in the leadoff spot when in the lineup for the New York Black Yankees in 1943.

Robinson, Al
Career: 1905–12   Positions: 1b, p
Teams: Brooklyn Royal Giants ('05–'12), *New York Black Sox ('12)*

Considered one of the top first baseman in the East, he was one of the early players (along with Scotty Bowman and Grant Johnson) who helped make the Brooklyn Royal Giants a top team during the first decade of the century. Playing in the Florida winter league in 1909–10, he entertained the crowd with ''humorous catching'' at the initial sack.

Robinson, Babe
Career: 1933   Position: p
Team: Atlantic City Bacharach Giants

He pitched with the Bacharachs in 1933, when the Franchise was of marginal quality.

Robinson, Bill (Bojangles)
Career: 1931–50   Positions: owner, officer
Teams: New York Harlem Stars ('31), New York Black Yankees ('32–'50)

This great dancer and show business personality was a true sportsman as well as an entertainer. He had quick feet and was gifted with an ability to run backward faster than most people could run forward. He loved baseball and would sometimes run exhibitions at the ballpark against a team's fastest player, with Robinson running backward. After the Lincoln Stars folded following the 1930 season, he took over the franchise and renamed the club the Harlem Stars, combining show biz and baseball for the 1931 season. In 1932 the team changed its name to the Black Yankees, and Robinson eventually became a part owner and officer with them.

Robinson, Bob
Career: 1905   Position: c
Team: Leland Giants

He joined the Leland Giants in 1905, their first year of existence, and was one of the two catchers on the team in his only year of experience with a top ballclub.

Robinson, Bobbie
[see Robinson, William (Bobbie)]

Robinson, Bobby (Robby)
Career: 1945   Positions: 3b, ss, 2b
Teams: Atlanta Black Crackers ('44), Homestead Grays ('45)
Bats: Both   Throws: Right

This infielder could play an infield position, but in the 1945 he was battling with Ray Battles for the regular third-base job with the Homestead Grays. Although the switch-hitter had a slight edge on Battles when batting from the left side, he lost the starting position at the hot corner. He made his home in New York City, but played in 1944 with the Atlanta Black Crackers prior to joining the Grays. He also played shortstop and second base during his baseball career.

Robinson, Charles
[see Robertson, Charles]

Robinson, Charles
Career: 1939   Position: rf
Team: Chicago American Giants

He played as a reserve outfielder with the American Giants in 1939, his only year in the Negro Leagues.

Robinson, Cornelius Randall (Neil, Shadow)
Career: 1934–50   Positions: cf, lf, rf, ss, 3b
Teams: Homestead Grays ('34), Cincinnati Tigers ('36–'37), Memphis Red Sox ('38–'52)
Bats: Right   Throws: Right
Height: 5'11"   Weight: 182
Born: July 7, 1908, Grand Rapids, Mich.

Over an eleven-year period, 1938–48, this Memphis Red Sox outfielder played in every East-West All-Star game except three, 1942, 1946, and 1947. In the midseason classic he compiled a sensational .476 batting average and a superb .810 slugging percentage, which included two home runs, an All-Star total exceeded only by Hall of Famer Buck Leonard.

Robinson was credited with 54 home runs in 1939 against all levels of competition. The following season he had accumulated 35 homers by the end of July, with his final total not being recorded, but he won the second of his back-to-back Negro American League home-run titles. While consistently generating power, the big, strong right-handed slugger was a free-swinger and also frequently struck out. Although best known for his hitting prowess, he was a respectable fielder with a strong but erratic arm, and had good speed on the bases but was not a daring baserunner.

Oscar Charleston (center) is flanked by Pablo Mesa (left) and Alejandro Oms (right). This trio formed the greatest outfield in the history of Cuban baseball. A blend of speed and power, Charleston could run, field, throw, hit and hit with power. He is considered by many to be the greatest all-around ballplayer in black baseball history. *(National Baseball Hall of Fame)*

Fastball artist Leon Day was the ace of the Newark Eagles pitching staff. He holds the Negro National League record for strikeouts in a single game and the career record for strikeouts in All-Star competition. (Author collection)

(facing page, top) Buck Leonard teamed with Josh Gibson to form the Homestead Grays' power tandem that were given the appelation, "The Thunder Twins." A lefthanded slugging firstbaseman, he was called the black Lou Gehrig. (Author collection)

(facing page, bottom) Before going on to stardom in the major leagues as outfielders, Monte Irvin (left) and Larry Doby (right), were a double-play duo for the 1946 Negro World Series Champion Newark Eagles. (Author collection)

Mule Suttles was a big, strong power hitter, whose homeruns were features of the East-West All-Star games. *(Lawrence D. Hogan)*

The most versatile athlete to ever play the game of baseball, Martin Dihigo excelled at every position. He has the unique distinction of being a member of the baseball Hall of Fame in three countries—Cuba, Mexico and the U.S. *(Lawrence D. Hogan)*

(facing page, top) Four members of the West squad (Verdell Mathis, Artie Wilson, Piper Davis and Bill Powell) await the beginning of the 1948 Negro All-Star game. *(Author collection)*

(facing page, bottom, left) Willie Wells was one of the greatest shortstops of all time, black or white. Nicknamed ''El Diablo'' in Mexico, he was outstanding both in the field and at the plate. *(Author collection)*

(facing page, bottom, right) A masterful performer at the hot corner, Hall of Famer Ray Dandridge was a consistent .300 hitter and starred in both the Negro Leagues and the Mexican League. *(Author collection)*

(above) Hilton Smith was an excellent pitcher with a masterful curveball among his repertory. The Kansas City Monarchs hurler was considered ''Satchel's shadow'' because he frequently relieved his more flamboyant teammate. *(National Baseball Hall of Fame)*

Superstar shortstop John Henry Lloyd was the greatest player in black baseball during the deadball era, and was comparable to Honus Wagner as an all-around ballplayer. *(Atlantic City Public Library)*

Hank Aaron, the major leagues' lifetime homerun leader, began his professional career as an infielder with the Indianapolis Clowns in 1952. *(Syd Pollock family)*

After a short stint with the Homestead Grays that was aborted due to a severe drinking problem, he signed with the Cincinnati Tigers in 1936 and launched his career with a robust .367 batting average. In 1938 he joined the Memphis Red Sox and was the regular shortstop as they copped the Negro American League first-half championship in 1938. That season marked his first trip to the East-West All-Star game, and he celebrated the occasion with an inside-the-part three-run homer to trigger the West's 5–4 victory. The next year heavyweight boxing great Joe Louis threw out the first ball at the All-Star game and was photographed before the game congratulating Robinson for his hitting from the previous contest. Robinson responded with another home run to key the West's 4–2 victory. In each of his first two All-Star games, his crucial home run was one of a trio of hits he collected.

In the winter of 1940–41 he played in Puerto Rico, but upon his return to Memphis for the regular season, he was moved to the outfield, and he stayed with the Red Sox for the remainder of his career. In 1942 he hit .314, and in 1944 and 1945 he had averages of .319 and .303, respectively. In the former year Robinson also demonstrated both his speed and his power by finishing second in the league in stolen bases and home runs. In 1949–50 he hit .272 and .283, with 10 home runs the latter season. Although the Negro American League had declined to a minor-league status, he continued for two more seasons with the Memphis Red Sox before retiring after the 1952 season.

Robinson, Edward

Career: 1931   Position: of
Team: Louisville White Sox

He was an outfielder with the Louisville White Sox during the 1931 season, their only year in the Negro National League.

Robinson, George

Career: 1924   Position: officer
Team: Washington Potomacs

He was an officer with the Washington Potomacs during their only season in the Eastern Colored League.

Robinson, George (Sis)

Career: 1918–23   Position: p
Team: Atlantic City Bacharach Giants ('18–'23)

Called the "Southern Bearcat," this Bacharach Giants hurler defeated Smokey Joe Williams, 2–1, in a 1918 pitching duel.

Robinson, Henry Frazier (Pep, Sloe, Hank)

Career: 1942–50   Position: c
Teams: Satchel Paige's All-Stars ('39), Kansas City Monarchs ('42–'43), New York Black Yankees ('43), **Baltimore Elite Giants** ('43, '46–'50), *military service ('43–'45), Baltimore Greys ('42)*
Bats: Right   Throws: Right
Height: 5'11"   Weight: 178
Born: Mary 30, 1916, Birmingham, Ala.

Late in the 1942 season, when Kansas City catcher Joe Greene split a finger and was out of action, the Monarchs picked him up in Baltimore to catch until Greene was able again. The Monarchs held on to win the Negro American League pennant, earning the right to play the Negro National League Champion Homestead Grays, and Robinson was listed on the World Series roster but never actually participated. With Greene well again, Robinson moved to the New York Black Yankees in 1943, making a brief appearance as a reserve catcher. But he had three other receivers ahead of him on the ballclub and joined the Baltimore Elite Giants early in the same season before joining the Navy. He serving for the duration of World War II. After his discharge in 1946 he returned to the Elites as a backup catcher. Although reporting for spring training in top condition, he was released in early June to make room for veterans Willie Wells and Sammy T. Hughes, who had been signed.

A slap hitter with a weakness on curveballs, he did not hit consistently but could hit the ball hard at times. He was a subpar base runner, lacking sufficient speed to steal or take an extra base. In the field he was a hustler and had a good arm, but otherwise he had only average defensive skills.

He moved to Oklahoma as a boy and began playing professional baseball with Satchel Paige's All-Stars in 1939. He and his brother, Norman "Bobby" Robinson, formed a brother combination on the Elites in 1946, and the receiver continued with the Elites through 1950, batting .225 in his last season.

Robinson, J.
Career: 1905–10   Position: of
Teams: Brooklyn Royal Giants ('06), Kansas City, Kansas, Giants ('10)

He was an outfielder during the deadball era, appearing with the Brooklyn Royal Giants in 1906 and the Kansas City, Kansas, Giants in 1910.

Robinson, J.
[see Robinson, Bobby]

Robinson, Jack Roosevelt (**Jackie**)
Career: 1945   Position: ss
Team: Kansas City Monarchs
Bats: Right   Throws: Right
Height: 5'11 ½"   Weight: 190
Born: Jan. 31, 1919, Cairo, Ga.
Died: Oct. 24, 1972, Stamford, Conn.

The man who would be selected by Branch Rickey to break the color barrier in modern baseball began his career in the Negro Leagues. In 1945 Robinson played his only season in black baseball as a shortstop with the Kansas City Monarchs. A former UCLA football All-American, had played college and semipro baseball but was lacking professional experience. He strengthened the Monarchs' war-depleted infield and displayed the right attitude and winning spirit, typical of a college athlete. He proved to be an outstanding hitter for both average (.345) and power. On the bases he was an outstanding base stealer and an aggressive base runner who also utilized his speed with the bunt and the hit-and-run play.

The hustling ex-college man was one of best

infielders in the Negro Leagues that season and was expected to improve with more experience, but it was felt that shortstop was not his best position. He had some difficulty going into the hole and making the play. After being signed by the Dodgers, he was shifted to second base, a more suitable position, at Montreal, and during his ten-year major league career he also played on both corners and in the outfield. Robinson's role as the first black ballplayer in the majors during modern times has been well chronicled.

After signing with Rickey in the winter of 1945, he accompanied a black All-Star team to Venezuela. The other players saw Rickey talking to Robinson at the airport before they left, but when they asked about the conversation, Robinson told them it pertained to a new black league that Rickey was organizing. Later, when Rickey made the announcement about the true topic of discussion, Robinson was in Venezuela. During the intervening winter, Robinson expressed doubts to roommate Gene Benson about his ability to make it with the Dodgers. Benson reassured him that if he could hit the pitching in the Negro Leagues, he could hit major-league pitching.

The records bear out Benson's prediction. After a year of adjustment with Montreal, where Robinson hit .349, he joined the Dodgers and hit .297 while stealing a league-high 29 bases, and was voted Rookie of the Year while the Dodgers won the National League pennant. Two years later he had his best year, winning the batting title with a .342 average, leading the league in stolen bases with 37, hitting 16 homers, and knocking in 124 runs while leading the Dodgers to another pennant.

For the next five seasons he was the catalyst for the Dodgers, with his exciting baserunning and clutch hitting (.328, .338, .308, .329, and .311), and the Dodgers won two more pennants, in 1952–53, but lost the World Series to the Yankees each time. But in 1955, although Robinson had his worst major-league season, the Dodgers finally beat the Yankees in the

Series. The next year he hit .275 and the Dodgers won another pennant, their fourth in five years. But when the Dodgers traded him during the off-season, he retired from baseball with a .311 lifetime average. Five years later he was voted into the Hall of Fame in his first year of eligibility.

Robinson, Jacob (Red)
Career: 1946–47   Positions: 3b
Team: Chicago American Giants
He was a reserve third baseman for the Chicago American Giants for two seasons after World War II.

Robinson, James (Black Rusie)
Career: 1893–1906   Positions: p, cf
Teams: Cuban Giants ('93, '97, '00, '03–'04), Cuban X-Giants ('04), Brooklyn Royal Giants ('06), *Colored Capital All-Americans, Pawtucket (New England League) (94)*
This Cuban Giants' hurler was one of the top pitchers of the 1890s and was compared to Amos Rusie. After beginning with the Cuban Giants, he played for the Cuban X-Giants and ended his career in black baseball as a center fielder with the Brooklyn Royal Giants. During his career he also played with lesser teams, including the Colored Capital All-Americans of Lansing, Michigan, and the Pawtucket team of the New England League.

Robinson, John H.
Career: 1948   Position: of
Team: Birmingham Black Barons
An outfielder from St. Louis, he vied for a roster position with the Birmingham Black Barons in the spring of 1948.

Robinson, Johnny
Career: 1930–42   Positions: of, if
Teams: Memphis Red Sox ('30), *Detroit Black Sox ('42)*
He was a left fielder with the Memphis Red Sox in 1930 when they were in the Negro National League, batting .309 for the season, and

for a decade afterward he played with lesser teams, including the Detroit Black Sox.

Robinson, Joshua
Career: 1939   Position: of
Team: New York Black Yankees
He was with the New York Black Yankees briefly as a reserve outfielder in 1939.

Robinson, Kenneth (**Ken**)
Career: 1931–39   Positions: 2b, 3b, lf
Teams: *Newark Browns ('31), Jacksonville Red Caps ('34),* Brooklyn Royal Giants('39)
He was a marginal player during the '30s, primarily playing with lesser teams. He played with the Newark Browns a year before they entered the Negro National League, and was the regular second baseman with the Jacksonville Red Caps in 1934 before they were in the Negro American League. In 1939 he was the regular second baseman, batting seventh in the order, for the Brooklyn Royal Giants, an independent team of approximate major-league caliber.

Robinson, Neil
[see Robinson, Cornelius Randall]

Robinson, Norman Wayne (Bobby, Norm)
Career: 1939–50   Positions: **cf**, lf, ss, 3b
Teams: Satchel Paige's All-Stars ('39), Baltimore Elite Giants ('40, '43–'47), Birmingham Black Barons ('47–'52)
Bats: Right   Throws: Right
Born: Apr. 1, 1918, Oklahoma City, Okla.
An outfielder with exceptional speed and good range in the field, he was the center fielder for the Birmingham Black Barons before Willie Mays joined the team. Robinson suffered a leg injury, allowing Mays the opportunity to play on a regular basis. After recovering, Robinson played left field upon his return to the lineup. Always one of the fastest men on his team, he was a good base runner. Although a light hitter, he was considered at his best in the clutch.
The Oklahoman got his start with the San

Angelo Black Sheepherders, and after playing center field with Satchel Paige's All-Stars for a year, he joined the Baltimore Elite Giants in 1940 as a substitute outfielder. For the next two seasons he played with lesser teams in the Baltimore area until he caught on with the Elites again during World War II, in 1943. After two years as a substitute, he earned a spot in the starting lineup, playing as the regular right fielder and batting in the seventh slot during 1945–46. During these three seasons he hit for averages of .361, .321, and .206. In the latter year his brother, Frazier Robinson, joined the Elites as a catcher, forming a brother combination.

During the 1947 season he joined the Black Barons as the regular center fielder and batted in the leadoff position under manager Tommy Sampson. The next season he was again the center fielder with the Birmingham Black Barons under manager Piper Davis and hit .299 as the Black Barons won the 1948 Negro American League pennant and faced the Homestead Grays in the last World Series played between the Negro American League and the Negro National League. Robinson remained with the Black Barons for four more seasons, batting .323 and .309 in 1949–50 and retiring after the 1952 season.

Robinson, Ray
Career: 1938–47   Position: p
Teams: Newark Eagles ('38, '41), Cincinnati Buckeyes ('42), Philadelphia Stars ('47), *Canadian League ('55), minor leagues ('55–'56)*
Bats: Right   Throws: Right
Height: 6'2"   Weight: 208
Although he was sometimes called a "crack" hurler, he was used mostly against lesser teams when he began his career with the Newark Eagles in 1938. He dropped out of top competition after his first exposure to the Negro National League and, while making his home in Richmond, Virginia, next appeared in 1942 with the Negro American League Buckeyes, where he split 4 decisions. His third and

last appearance in the Negro Leagues was in 1947, with the Philadelphia Stars.

After the color line was eliminated, despite his inauspicious Negro League career he pitched in organized baseball during the mid-'50s. In 1955 he pitched briefly with the Thetford Mines team in Canada's Provincial League, losing his only decision, before joining Aberdeen in the Northern League for the remainder of the season and posting a 5–3 record with a 3.44 ERA. The next season , his last year in baseball, he pitched with Texas City in the Big State League, exiting with an 8–18 ledger and a 4.30 ERA.

Robinson, Richmond (Black Diamond)
Career: 1886   Positions: 1b, of
Team: *New York Gorhams*
Born: April 1, 1856, Washington, D.C.
In 1886 he was a first baseman with the New York Gorhams, one of the earliest black teams. Previously he had played center field with most of the top black teams of the era, including the famous St. Louis Black Stockings in 1883 and with the Altoonas in 1884–85.

Robinson, Walter (Skindown)
Career: 1938–42   Positions: **2b**, 3b, 1b
Teams: Atlanta Black Crackers ('38), Jacksonville Red Caps ('38, '41–'42), Cleveland Bears ('39–'40)
Although he was listed on the Atlanta Black Crackers' roster in March 1938, his home was in Jacksonville, and he played for the hometown Jacksonville Red Caps. When the franchise moved to Cleveland and played as the Bears, he was a part-time starter in 1940. Back in Jacksonville the following season, he resumed his regular spot at second base and hit second in the batting order.

Robinson, Walter William (Newt, Bill)
Career: 1925–42   Positions: **ss**, 2b, 3b
Teams: Hilldale Daisies ('25–'27), New York Lincoln Giants ('27), Harrisburg Giants ('27), New York Harlem Stars ('31), Atlantic City Bacharach Giants ('32)

A good-fielding but light-hitting infielder, he began his career as a substitute shortstop with the championship Hilldale team of 1925. Often playing in place of the light-hitting Jake Stevens, Robinson's role helped the team win the Eastern Colored League pennant, but in the World Series his playing time was severely restricted. After leaving Hilldale in 1927, he was a reserve shortstop with Harrisburg before landing with the Lincoln Giants as the regular shortstop. With the Lincolns he batted in the lower part of the order, as he did in 1931, when he shared the shortstop position for manager John Henry Lloyd's New York Harlem Stars. He closed out his career with the Bacharachs in 1932.

Robinson, William (Bobbie)
Career: 1925–42   Positions: 3b, ss
Teams: Indianapolis ABCs ('25–'26, '38), Cleveland Elites ('26), Chicago American Giants ('27), Birmingham Black Barons ('27), Memphis Red Sox ('27–'28), Detroit Stars ('29–'31), Baltimore Black Sox ('32), Cleveland Stars ('32), Cleveland Giants ('33), Cleveland Red Sox ('34), St. Louis Stars ('34–'37, '39–'41)
Bats: Right   Throws: Right
Height: 6'0"   Weight: 170

Noted for his good glove at third base, he was called "the human vacuum cleaner" by some observers. He developed his baseball skills as a youngster in Mobile, Alabama, and was playing semipro ball in Pensacola, Florida, in 1924 when he was recommended to the Indianapolis ABCs. After coming up with them in 1925, he split the 1926 season between them and the Cleveland Elites while batting only .129 for the year. In 1927 he continued his fine fielding and raised his batting average to .251 while again splitting the season between two teams, the Memphis Red Sox and the Birmingham Black Barons. The Black Barons captured the second-half title in the Negro National League's split season, only to lose the championship playoff to the Chicago American Giants.

In 1929 he joined the Detroit Stars, batting .309 and .260 in his first two years with the team. In 1930 Robinson played in his second league championship series, when the Detroit Stars went on a tear, winning 23 games in succession to capture the league's second-half title, only to lose to the St. Louis Stars in the playoff. That season provided Robinson with his most memorable defensive play, in a late-season game against the St. Louis Stars, when he made a one-handed stab of a line drive and fired to second base, from where the ball was relayed to first base to complete a lightning-fast triple play. The next season, his last with the Detroit Stars, he again held down the hot corner while usually hitting in the sixth slot.

At the plate he was a mediocre hitter with only fair power. He was an average base runner and not an active base stealer. After the original St. Louis Stars' franchise folded, he played with the new St. Louis Stars' ballclub that was organized, but the team fielded a league team in only one season, 1937. In 1938 he played with the new ABCs as a part-time starter, batting seventh in the order. The next season the franchise relocated to St. Louis, playing as the St. Louis Stars and marking the third franchise of the same name in the city's history. He became the regular third baseman, batting second in the order, and in 1940 he was still with the Stars but lost his starting position.

After closing out his baseball career in 1942, he worked as a brickmason for thirty years and eventually settled in Chicago.

Rochelle, Clarence
Career: 1944   Position: p
Team: Kansas City Monarchs

A wartime player, this pitcher appeared briefly with the Kansas City Monarchs in 1944.

Rodgers
a.k.a. Rogers
Career: 1923–24   Positions: 3b, 1b, c
Teams: Brooklyn Royal Giants ('23), Harrisburg Giants ('24)

A light-hitting infielder, during his two seasons in the Eastern Colored League he was a part-time starter at third base for both the Brooklyn Royal Giants and the Harrisburg Giants, batting in the eighth spot with each team.

Rodgers, Pierre
[see Pierre, Rogers]

Rodgers, Sylvestor Clifford (Speedie)
a.k.a. Silvestor
Career: 1949–50   Position: p
Team: Baltimore Elite Giants

After the demise of the Negro National League, he began his career as a pitcher with the Baltimore Elite Giants during their first two seasons in the Negro American League, when the league was struggling to survive the loss of players to organized baseball. In 1950, his last year in black baseball, he appeared in 2 games without a decision.

Rodoud
Career: 1921   Position: c
Team: Cuban Stars (East)

He was a reserve catcher with the Cuban Stars (East) in 1921, his only year in black baseball.

Rodriguez, Antonio
Career: 1939   Position: p
Team: New York Cubans

In 1939, his only season in the Negro Leagues, he pitched briefly with the New York Cubans.

Rodriguez, Antonio **Hector** (Hec, Herrado)
Career: 1939, 1944   Positions: 3b, ss
Teams: New York Cubans ('39, '44), *Mexican League ('45–'46, '62–'63), minor leagues ('48–'51, '53–'61),* major leagues ('52)
Bats: Right   Throws: Right
Height: 5'8"   Weight: 165
Born: June 13, 1920, Villa Alquizar, Cuba

In 1939 this infielder played a season with the New York Cubans as the regular shortstop and usually batted sixth in the order. Partial

statistics show a .361 batting average in 16 games played. Five years later, in 1944, he made his second appearance with the Cubans, as the starting third baseman, hitting .238 while batting in the leadoff spot and showing a good batting eye and good speed on the bases. The next two seasons were spent with Tampico in the Mexican League, where the contact hitter batted .326 and .327. After the doors to organized baseball were opened, he began a long career that would include a season with the Chicago White Sox in the major leagues in 1952.

His first season in organized ball was with Miami in the Florida State League in 1948, where he hit .286. After a .302 season with Montreal in 1951, he got the chance with the White Sox in 1952 and hit .265 in 124 games as their third baseman. However, that was to be his only chance in the big leagues, and he spent the next seven seasons in the International League. In his first year there, with Syracuse, he batted .302, followed by six seasons with Toronto, where he had averages of .307, .289, .273, .288, .228, and .256 while playing both third base and shortstop.

In 1960–61 he played with San Diego in the Pacific Coast League (.262, .293) before returning to the Mexican League, with Mexico City for two years (.277, .293). In 1966 he played with Tabasco in a lesser Mexican league and still batted .316 in 30 games. Throughout his career he played winter ball in Cuba, with his best year coming in 1950–51 with Almendares, when he hit .301.

Rodriguez, B.
Career: 1922–29   Positions: p, of, 2b, 3b
Teams: Cuban Stars (West) ('22), Cuban Stars (East) ('27–'29)

He was a pitcher with the Cuban Stars in the Eastern Colored League in 1927 but also was an all-purpose player.

Rodriguez, José
Career: 1913–29   Positions: c, 1b, 2b, ss
Teams: Cuban Stars (West) ('13–'18, '21–'23),

Detroit Stars ('19), Kansas City Monarchs ('20), All Cubans ('21)
Bats: Right   Throws: Right
Born: June 25, 1894, Havana, Cuba

An outstanding receiver, he began his career in black baseball in 1913 with the Cuban Stars when they were an independent team, hitting in the lower part of the batting order, until joining the Detroit Stars in 1919. In 1920 he was the regular catcher for the Kansas City Monarchs during the Negro National League's inaugural season, batting in the eighth spot. His value to a team was primarily in his defensive skills, while at the plate he lacked consistency and demonstrated only average power. On the bases he showed a modicum of speed but was not a skilled base stealer.

In his own country he was one of the best Cuban catchers in their baseball history and hit for a higher average there than in the United States, with his best averages being .326 (1926–27), .312 (1918–19), and .303 (1922–23). He began his Cuban career with Fe in 1913 but played most of his years with Almendares, guiding them to three pennants as a manager. He retired from Cuban baseball in 1939 after twenty-two years as an active player with a lifetime batting average of .250. He was elected to the Cuban Hall of Fame in 1951.

Rodriquez
Career: 1915   Position: p
Team: Cuban Stars

He was listed as a pitcher with the Cuban Stars in 1915, his only year in black baseball.

Rodriquez, Benvienido
Career: 1948   Positions: of, c
Team: Chicago American Giants
Bats: Right   Throws: Right

In 1948, his only season in the Negro Leagues, he was a part-time starter with the Chicago American Giants, splitting his playing time between left field and catcher and hitting .241 while batting at the bottom of the order when in the lineup.

Rodriquez, Conrado
Career: 1922, 1928–29 Positions: p, of
Team: Cuban Stars

He played briefly with the Cuban Stars in 1922, but it was five more seasons before he made another appearance in the United States, and although he was with the team for three seasons, his playing time was not extensive.

Roesink, John
Career: 1925–30   Position: officer
Team: Detroit Stars

He served as an officer with the Negro National League's Detroit Stars for the last half of the '20s.

Rogan, Wilbur (Bullet)
a.k.a. Bullet Joe
Career: 1917–38;
1939–46   Positions: p, of, 1b, 2b,
          3b, ss, manager, umpire
Teams: *Kansas City Colored Giants ('17),* All Nations ('17), **Kansas City Monarchs** ('20–'38)
League: Negro American League
Bats: Right   Throws: Right
Height: 5'7"   Weight: 180
Born: July 28, 1889, Oklahoma City, Okla.
Died: Mar. 4, 1967, Kansas City, Mo.

An outstanding pitcher with a tremendous fastball, a fine curve, and good control, "Bullet" Rogan was a star for the Kansas City Monarchs for almost twenty years. The right-hander was a smart pitcher who used a no-windup delivery, a sidearm motion, and always kept the ball down. In addition to his basic pitches, he included a forkball, palmball, and spitter in his repertory. A durable workhorse averaging thirty starting assignments per year for a decade and rarely being relieved, this versatile player's value to the team was inestimable. He also was a superb fielder and a dangerous hitter with good power.

He had strong wrists and used a heavy bat, an when not performing on the mound, he played in the outfield to keep his big bat in the lineup. A good curveball hitter with a smooth swing, he often batted in the cleanup position, and was credited with a league-high 16 homers in 1922. He consistently hit over .300, compiling averages of .351, .416, .412, .366, .314, .330, .353, .341, and .311 for the years 1922–1930. On the mound he registered seasons of 13–6, 12–8, 16–5, 15–2, 12–4, 15–6, and 9–3 for the first seven of those years.

He showcased his stamina and versatility when he gained 2 victories with a single loss in the 1924 Negro World Series against the great Hilldale club, pitching 3 complete games and relieving in another while compiling a 2.57 ERA and batting .325 while playing in the outfield in the other 6 games. That winter, in his only trip to Cuba, the hard worker continued his winning pace with Almendares, recording a 9–4 work sheet, tying him for the league lead in victories.

The following year, without Rogan on the mound in the World Series due to an injury incurred while playing with his young son, the Monarchs lost to the same Hilldale club. However, in the playoffs for the league championship against the St. Louis Stars, he hit. 500. In 1926 he assumed the team's managerial reins, and with his leadership and performance at bat and on the mound, the Monarchs won the first-half championship before losing a heartbreaking 5–out–of–9 playoff to the second–half champions, the Chicago American Giants. Rogan batted .583 and, in a valiant effort to stave off defeat, started both ends of a doubleheader on the last day of the playoff, but to no avail as he dropped both contests to Willie Foster, who also pitched both games.

The Monarchs captured another Negro National League pennant in 1929, but the next year Rogan was seriously ill and, at the end of the season, the club disbanded. In August 1931 the team was reorganized and, having regained his health, Rogan resumed his role as manager, and most of the ex-Kansas City players signed again with the Monarchs. A knowledgeable manager, he provide capable leadership and continued as manager of the Monarchs during his twilight years, until his retirement in 1938.

During this time he was variously described as easygoing, jolly, quiet, and gentlemanly by some observers, but characterized by others as arrogant, uncooperative, and demanding of his players.

An Oklahoman by birth, he was reared in Kansas City, Kansas, and began his baseball career as a catcher with Fred Palace's Colts in 1908. The next season he played with the Kansas City Giants, and was credited with 54 consecutive wins at that level of competition before joining the Army in the fall of 1911. He remained in the Army through 1919, captaining the camp baseball teams while stationed in the Philippines, Hawaii, and Arizona. While playing baseball with the infantry baseball team at Fort Huachua, he was recommended by Casey Stengel to J. L. Wilkinson, owner of the All Nations baseball team. Rogan was signed and played as a shortstop-left fielder-pitcher with the 1917 All Nations team. Wilkinson also owned the Kansas City Monarchs, and when he entered the Monarchs in the first Negro National League, he moved Rogan to the league club. The hard-throwing right-hander also played in the California winter league with the Los Angeles White Sox in 1917 and again in 1920, as a pitcher hitting fifth in the batting order. He had slim legs and hips, but a solid upper torso with square shoulders and a trim, military bearing that made him appear bigger than his actual size.

In exhibitions against major-leaguers, Rogan is credited with a .329 batting average, making his last appearance at age forty-eight, when he collected 3 hits against Bob Feller's All-Stars. Jocko Conlan, who often played against black teams before beginning his career as an umpire, regarded Rogan as one of the greats of the Negro Leagues, describing his motion as "a nice, easy delivery" and declaring him to be faster than Satchel Paige. After closing out his managerial career, Rogan followed Conlan's progression from player to arbiter, and umpired in the Negro American League through the 1946 season. After retiring from his second baseball career he worked in the post office in Kansas City.

Rogers

Career: 1900   Position: p
Team: Genuine Cuban Giants

He pitched with one of the various Cuban Giants' ballclubs that flourished during the early years of the century. Several of these ballclubs, copying the success of the Cuban Giants (the first and most successful black professional team) and appropriating a variation of the Cuban Giants' name as their own, played a quality of baseball close to that of the original team.

Rogers, Pierre

[see Pierre, Rogers]

Rogers, Sid

Career: 1887   Position: player
Team: *Cincinnati Browns*

He was a player with the Cincinnati Browns, one of eight teams that were charter members of the League of Colored Baseball Clubs in 1887. However, the league's existence was ephemeral, lasting only a week. His position is uncertain.

Rogers, William Nathaniel (**Nat**)
a.k.a. Rodgers
Career: 1923–46   Positions: **rf, lf**, 1b,
            3b, c
Teams: Brooklyn Royal Giants ('23), Philadelphia Giants ('24), Harrisburg Giants ('24–'25), Chicago American Giants ('27–'28, '44), **Memphis Red Sox** ('24–'30, '36–'46), Birmingham Black Barons ('30), Kansas City Monarchs ('31), Chicago Columbia Giants ('31), Cole's American Giants ('32–'34), Brooklyn Eagles ('35)
Bats: Left   Throws: Right
Height: 5'11"   Weight: 160
Born: June 7, 1893, Spartanburg, S.C.

This veteran outfielder joined the Chicago American Giants from the Memphis Red Sox in August 1927 and promptly hit in 31 consec-utive games to provide the impetus for the Giants to capture the pennant, finishing the season with a composite .284 average. In the subsequent World Series victory over the Bacharach Giants he hit a team-leading .400.

After the World Series he and Larry Brown were ruled by Negro National League President Hueston to be the property of Memphis, but he was back with Chicago American Giants in 1928 despite the decree. However, he did return to the Memphis Red Sox in 1929–30, hitting .287 and .366. When the Chicago American Giants' franchise collapsed soon after Rube Foster's death in 1930, David Malarcher organized the Chicago Columbia Giants in 1931, and Rogers played right field and batted third in the order for Malarcher, his manager from the 1927 season.

After Robert Cole bought the franchise in 1932, Rogers again found himself playing right field on the American Giants' championship teams of 1932 and 1933, batting in the cleanup spot both seasons, hitting .328 and .373 as the Giants won the 1932 Negro Southern League pennant and the 1933 Negro National League pennant.

He eventually did return to the Red Sox in 1936 and batted in the heart of the order for the next six season, including the 1938 season, when he was the regular right fielder for the Memphis Red Sox as they won the first-half Negro American League championship, and the 1939 season, when he won the league batting title.

He was one of nine baseball-playing brothers, but he was the only one who played professionally. A natural hitter, he began when he was fourteen years old, playing with teams while working at an assortment of jobs. In 1911 he played with a team in Norcross, Georgia, while working in Atlanta with the railroad as a water boy. The next year he played with the Cincinnati Colored Browns while working in a tannery, and in 1913 he played in Kentucky, where he was laying tracks for the railroad and developing his strong arms and shoulders by driving spikes. The next season he joined a team located near Covington, Kentucky, called the Williams Giants, progressing to teams in Johnstown, Pennsylvania, and Middletown, Ohio, in 1916. After playing with the Detroit Creamery ballclub in 1918, he went to Chicago for the following season. In 1920 he played with the Hugely Playground Stars and was given the nickname "Nat." In 1921 he played with the Illinois Giants in Spring Valley, and toured the Midwest playing a wide variety of ballclubs, including a team comprised of Joe Jackson and the other banned Chicago "Black Sox."

In 1925 he went to Grand Rapids, Michigan, to work in a furniture factory, after having played with three different ballclubs (the Brooklyn Royal Giants, the Philadelphia Giants, and the Harrisburg Giants) during the interim. He was secured from Memphis by the Harrisburg Giants in midseason of 1924 to play third base after two other players had failed at the position. He was also unimpressive at the hot corner, but hit .273 in limited play, and also caught a few games to provide relief for an overburdened receiving corps. After returning to Memphis in May 1927, under manager Charles "Two Sides" Wilson, he was traded with Larry Brown to the Chicago American Giants.

Off the field the poker-faced player was characterized as "evil," and on the field he was a hard-nosed ballplayer. While an adequate fielder with a good arm and a good base runner, he was best known for his batting prowess. A dangerous line-drive hitter who sprayed shots to all fields, the eagle-eyed batter preferred fastballs to curves, and hit with a downward swing to generate good power despite a slender physique. He could also execute the hit-and-run and the drag bunt, and would slide his hands up or down the bat, depending on whether he was going for a single or the long ball.

His hitting dropped in the latter years of his career, as shown by his .174 and .229 batting averages for 1944–45, and he closed out his career in 1946 after 24 years in the Negro Leagues. During the last several seasons with the Red Sox, he assumed a part-time role, but if his accepted birth date is correct, he continued to play until he was 53 years old. After retiring from baseball he worked as an elevator operator at a Memphis Hotel.

Rojo, Julio
a.k.a. Renshaw

Career: 1916–30   Positions: **c**, 1b, 3b, of, **p**

Teams: New York Cuban Stars ('16), Havana Stars ('17), Cuban Stars (East) ('18–'19), Atlantic City Bacharach Giants ('20–'22), Baltimore Black Sox ('23–'26), New York Lincoln Giants ('27–'30)

Bats: Both   Throws: Right

This wiry Cuban began his career as the regular catcher on owner Alejandro Pompez's 1916 Cuban Stars, and was generally conceded to be one of the best Cuban catchers ever to play in the Negro Leagues. He was an outstanding receiver with a very accurate throwing arm. At the plate, although he usually batted in the lower part of the order, he was a little better than average batter, with averages of .224, .333, .316, .309, and .250 in 1921–25, and .317 and .296 in 1929–30. Rojo also hit .320 in the Cuban winter league of 1926–27.

He was fast and, when so inclined, showed his speed on the bases, once stealing second, third, and home in succession. But he was not highly motivated, and his play was inconsistent. He would slide hard and jump at an infielder to cut him, and was considered a "dirty" ballplayer by some teams, who watched for an opportunity to retaliate. In addition to his backstop duties, he sometimes played third base or first base, where he used a catcher's mitt. Like most receivers, he knew the game well, and he managed in the Cuban League.

Most of his fifteen-year career was spent with teams in the East, including the Bacharach Giants, Baltimore Black Sox, and Lincoln Giants. He spent the entire decade of the '20s as a regular catcher, almost equally divided among these three teams.

He first joined the Bacharachs in 1920, and after three seasons he joined the Baltimore Black Sox. He was voted their most popular player in 1925, but the following year he asked for his release from the Black Sox because discipline on the team was too lax, especially relating to players drinking. In his request for a release, he indicated that fans were bringing alcoholic drinks into the ballpark and giving them to players on the field.

Leaving the Sox, he joined the Lincoln Giants until the franchise dissolved after the 1930 season. The last two seasons of the franchise were two of the best for the Lincoln Giants since they first entered league play. In 1929 the Lincolns finished in second place in the American Negro League, and improved in 1930 to earn a spot in the playoffs for the eastern championship, albeit losing to the Homestead Grays.

Rollins

Career: 1920   Position: of
Team: St. Louis Giants

He pitched briefly with the St. Louis Giants in 1920, the inaugural season of the Negro National League.

Rolls, Charles

Career: 1911   Position: player.
Team: Chicago Giants

He is listed as a player with Frank Leland's Chicago Giants in 1911, but his position is uncertain.

Romanach, Tomas

Career: 1916–20   Position: ss
Teams: Long Branch Cubans ('16), Cuban Stars (East) ('20)
Bats: Right   Throws: Right

He was the shortstop and leadoff batter for the 1916 Long Branch Cubans in his first season in black baseball, and in 1920 he appeared in a reserve role with Alejandro Pompez's Cuban Stars. He had very good speed and was

proficient at stealing bases, but he did not have much power at the plate.

Although it is not definite, indications suggest that he was a white Cuban. In his own country he played with Almendares for four years and with Havana for three years, but not consecutively. During his eight years (1910–19) in the Cuban league, his lifetime batting average was .224, with his best years coming in 1913 (.281) and 1915–16 (.280). He was elected to the Cuban Hall of Fame in 1948.

Romby, Robert L. (Bob)

Career: 1946–50   Positions: p, 1b
Teams: military service ('43–'45), Baltimore Elite Giants ('46–50)
Bats: Left   Throws: Left
Height: 5'11"   Weight: 180
Born: Dec. 15, 1918, Shreveport, La.

This left-hander was a sidearm pitcher with a fast ball, curve, and change, with his best pitch being his curveball. After being discharged from military service, he pitched for the Baltimore Elite Giants for five years, posting marks of 8–8, 8–5, and 12–6 in 1947–49. In 1947 he earned a trip to the East-West All-Star game but appeared only as a pinch hitter. As a batter he was a fair slap hitter with a weakness against curves, but better than most pitchers, although hitting only .161 in 1947. In 1950 he turned more toward play as an everyday player, dropping all four decisions as a pitcher but hitting a solid .381 as a first baseman. He had decent speed and was an average base runner, and could field his position.

Ronsell

a.k.a. Russell
Career: 1928–31   Position: of
Teams: Nashville Elite Giants ('28, '31), Birmingham Black Barons ('29), Memphis Red Sox ('30)

An outfielder with three different southern teams over a period of four years, he began and ended his career with the Nashville Elites, but in between he hit .274 with the Birmingham Black Barons in 1929 and .322 with the Memphis Red Sox in 1930.

Roque, Jacinto
Career: 1928–29   Positions: of, p
Team: Cuban Stars (West)

He played with the Cuban Stars (West) for two years when they were in the Negro National League.

Rose, Cecil
Career: 1924   Position: p
Team: St. Louis Stars

He was a pitcher with the St. Louis Stars in 1924, his only season in the Negro Leagues.

Rose, Haywood
a.k.a. Heywood
Career: 1907   Position: c
Teams: Leland Giants ('07), *Louisville Cubs ('10)*

This catcher had a good arm, was called the "backstop king," and was compared to Johnny Kling. Rose played with the Leland Giants in 1907 and three years later with the Louisville Cubs, one of the best teams in the South but probably of less than major-league caliber.

Rose, (Kissing Bug)
Career: 1901   Position: 1b
Team: *Algona Brownies*

This player with the colorful nickname was a first baseman for the 1901 Algona Brownies before they added quality players to become a major-league-level ballclub.

Roselle
[see Rosselle, Basilio (Brujo)]

Ross
Career: 1918   Position: p
Team: Indianapolis ABCs

He pitched with C. I. Taylor's Indianapolis ABCs in 1918, his only year in black baseball.

Ross, Arthur
Career: 1903–05   Position: p

Teams: Chicago Union Giants ('03–'05), Leland Giants ('05)

After two years as one of the top three pitchers for Frank Leland's Chicago Union Giants, he joined the Leland Giants in their first year of existence in 1905.

Ross, Dick
Career: 1925   Position: of
Team: St. Louis Stars

He appeared as a reserve outfielder with the St. Louis Stars in 1925.

Ross, E.
Career: 1919   Position: of
Team: Hilldale Daisies

He played briefly as a reserve outfielder with Hilldale in 1919, his only year in black baseball.

Ross, Harold
Career: 1922–28   Position: p
Teams: Indianapolis ABCs ('22, '25), Washington Potomacs ('23–'24), Chicago American Giants ('24–'25), Cleveland Browns ('24), Cleveland Elites ('26), Cleveland Hornets ('27), Cleveland Tigers ('28)

This pitcher began his career in 1922 with the ABCs and played with the Washington Potomacs and the Cleveland entries in the Negro National League. He was winless against 4 aggregate losses in 1926–27 before closing out his career in 1928.

Ross, Sam
Career: 1923   Position: p
Teams: Hilldale Daisies ('23), Harrisburg Giants ('23)

In 1923 he was on the pitching staff for Hilldale when they won the first Eastern Colored League pennant.

Ross, William
Career: 1923–30   Position: p
Teams: Washington Potomacs ('23), St. Louis Stars ('24–'27), Chicago American Giants

('25), Detroit Stars ('27), Homestead Grays ('28–'30)

Pitching in the starting rotation for the St. Louis Stars for four seasons, his best season was 1926, when he posted a 9–6 record. He closed out his career with a three-year stint with the Homestead Grays, where he had a 3–2 work sheet against league teams.

Rosselle, Basilio (Brujo)
a.k.a. Rosello; Roselle; Rosell
Career: 1926–29   Positions: **p**, 1b
Teams: Cuban Stars (West) ('26–'28), Cuban Stars (East) ('29), *Mexican League ('37–'47)*
Bats: Right   Throws: Right

This right-hander pitched with the Cuban Stars during the late '20s, in both the Negro National League and American Negro League, posting marks of 4–12 in 1927 and 3–6 in 1929. Sometimes he also played first base, batting .284 in 1926 and .300 in limited play for the 1929 season. The Cuban hurler played in Mexico beginning in 1937, and his first year was his best, as he posted an 11–2 record with a 2.06 ERA and led the league in strikeouts. The next two seasons produced marks of 4–0 and 4–2, and he appeared in one game each in three seasons during the '40s (1941, 1946–47), producing a lifetime 19–4 record and a 3.00 ERA.

Rossiter, George
Career: 1922–31   Positions: officer, owner
Team: Baltimore Black Sox

As a co-owner and officer of the Baltimore Black Sox during their years in the Eastern Colored League, this Irishman was honest and a man of his word. After taking over the team, he paid his players well and hired Pete Hill to manage the club and build a top-level team. After the collapse of the Eastern Colored League, he entered the Black Sox in the replacement American Negro League and won the league's only pennant. During the years when he was in control of the ballclub, he challenged Jake Dunn, owner of the International League's Baltimore Orioles, to a series, but his challenge was not accepted. Instead he arranged a postseason exhibition series against major-leaguers every year. He financed the team's operations from his ownership in a seafood restaurant in Baltimore that specialized in crabcakes. In the early years of the Depression he sold the franchise to Joe Cambria.

Roth, Herman Joseph (Bobby)
Career: 1923–25   Position: c
Teams: *New Orleans Crescent Stars ('21),* Milwaukee Bears ('23), Chicago American Giants ('23–25, Detroit Stars ('24), Birmingham Black Barons ('25)

After two seasons as the third catcher on the Chicago American Giants' roster, he was released by Rube Foster in the spring of 1925 and signed by the Birmingham Black Barons.

Rotoret
Career: 1950   Position:p
Team: New York Cubans

This pitcher appeared in a single game without a decision for the New York Cubans in 1950, when the Negro American League was struggling to survive the loss of players to organized baseball.

Rovira, Jaime
Career: 1911   Position: 3b
Team: All Cubans

He played third base on the All Cubans team in 1911, his only season in black baseball.

Rowe
Career: 1925   Position: player
Team: Indianapolis ABCs

He was listed with the Indianapolis ABCs, but his position is uncertain.

Rowe
Career: 1932   Position: p
Team: Nashville Elite Giants

He pitched with the Nashville Elite Giants in 1932, when the Negro Southern League was considered a major league.

Rowe, William (Schoolboy)
Career: 1944   Position: p
Teams: *Chicago Brown Bombers ('43),* Cleveland Buckeyes ('44), *Pittsburgh Crawfords ('45)*

A wartime player, he pitched with the Cleveland Buckeyes in 1944 between seasons with teams of lesser quality, the Chicago Brown Bombers and the new Pittsburgh Crawfords.

Royal, Joseph John (**Joe**)
a.k.a. Royall
Career: 1937–42   Positions: of, p, inf, c
Teams: Indianapolis Athletics ('37), Jacksonville Red Caps ('37–'38, '42), New York Black Yankees ('39), Cleveland Bears ('39)
Bats: Right   Throws: Right
Height: 5'11"   Weight: 178
Born: Apr. 9, 1912, Atlanta, Ga.

He began his career with the Florida Stars of St. Petersberg, Florida, in 1930 and later played with the Mohawk Giants of Schenectady, New York. Leaving the Mohawks, he joined the Jacksonville Red Caps in 1937. When the Red Caps relocated to Cleveland to play as the Bears, he accompanied the franchise, but left for a stint with the New York Black Yankees before rejoining the Red Caps when the franchise returned to Jacksonville. A hard hitter and a good, fast fielder with a strong arm, he usually played in the outfield but also could pitch, catch, or play in the infield.

Royall, Joseph John
[see Royal, Joseph John (**Joe**)]

Rudolph
[See Ash, Rudolph]

Ruffin, Charles **Leon** (Lassas)
Career: 1935–50   Positions: **c,** *manager*
Teams: Brooklyn Eagles ('35), **Newark Eagles** ('36, '39, '42–'43, '46), Pittsburgh Crawfords ('37–'38), Toledo Crawfords ('39), Philadelphia Stars ('39–'40), *Mexican League ('40–'41, '47–'48), military service ('43–'45),* Houston Eagles ('49–'50)

Bats: Right   Throws: Right
Height: 5'10"   Weight: 170

A superior defensive catcher, he was noted for his ability to detect a batter's weakness. His throwing arm was like a cannon and was reputed to be the best in the game. As a batter, he was a light hitter without any real power, but could help move runners around with a bunt or a hit-and-run play. On the bases he had only average speed, with little basestealing ability.

Pitchers liked to pitch to him, and despite his weak stick, he was the regular catcher for the Negro National League champion Newark Eagles in 1946 and was a member of the East squad in the All-Star game. And he hit a respectable .280 in the World Series against the strong Kansas City Monarchs' pitching staff. Ruffin's association with the Eagles began in 1935 in Brooklyn, but after two seasons, with incomplete statistics showing a composite .171 batting average, he landed with the Pittsburgh Crawfords. Although his hitting improved, he was dissatisfied with Gus Greenlee's team, and when the club moved to Toledo in 1939, he sought to avoid the transition. He wrote to Newark owner Abe Manley, requesting that the Eagles acquire him, and offered to play for $140 a month. Manley accommodated his request, and in May 1939 traded pitcher Bob Evans to the Crawfords for Ruffin.

He and Leon Day were both batterymates and friends. They went to Mexico together twice, once each before and after World War II. The first time was in 1940–41, when Ruffin hit .222 and .259 with Torreon, and the second time was in March 1947. The two Leons also went into military service at the same time, but into different branches, with Ruffin going into the Navy and Day into the Army. At the time of Ruffin's induction in 1943, he was hitting .303 after having batted only .175 in 1942. After being discharged, he hit .250 in the Eagles' 1946 championship season, but when the team relocated to Houston, he returned to his usual batting level, recording averages of .174 and .194 for the 1949–50 seasons.

Ruiz, Antonio (Perez)
Career: 1944   Position: p
Team: Cincinnati-Indianapolis Clowns
Bats: Right   Throws: Right

In his only season in the Negro Leagues, he registered a 10–4 record with a 2.76 ERA with the Clowns in 1944. Most of his professional career was spent with Juarez in the Arizona-Texas League, with his best season coming in 1947, when he posted an 11–7 record with a 5.94 ERA. During his four years with Juarez he was also used as a pinch hitter, and he batted .290 and .317 for the 1947–48 seasons. In 1951 he had a 10–9 record with Tucson in the Southwest International League, and he closed out his career the following year, splitting his playing time between Juarez and Odessa, but failed to win a game with either team.

Ruiz, Silvino (Poppa)
Career: 1928–42   Position: p
Teams: Cuban Stars (East) ('28–'29), New York Cubans ('38–'42)

This diminutive, jug-shaped Cuban hurler had one of the best screwballs in the game, and fashioned a 7–2 record with a 3.31 ERA in 1940 to earn a trip to the East-West All-Star game. That season the forty-one-year-old veteran, whose nickname was ''Poppa,'' teamed with New York Cubans manager-catcher José Fernandez to form the ''century battery.'' The veteran hurler began his career in 1928 with Alejandro Pompez's Cuban Stars and closed his career fifteen years later, with the New York Cubans in 1942.

Rush, Joe
Career: 1923–26   Positions: owner; secretary (NNL); president (NSL)
Team: Birmingham Black Barons

As owner of the Birmingham Black Barons during the '20s, he was selected as an officer for both leagues in which the Black Barons were members, serving variously as secretary of the Negro National League and president of the Negro Southern League.

Ruson
Career: 1931   Position: ss
Team: Brooklyn Royal Giants

He was a shortstop for the Brooklyn Royal Giants in 1931, when they were playing as an independent team.

Russ, Pythias
Career: 1925–29   Positions: c, ss
Teams: Memphis Red Sox ('25), Chicago American Giants ('26–'29)
Bats: Right   Throws: Right
Height: 5'11"   Weight: 195

A natural ballplayer, he was a good hitter with power, had an outstanding arm and quick release, and possessed outstanding speed and was very good at stealing bases. He was a heady ballplayer, always alert to find a way to trick the opposition to get an edge. He would tip the hitter's bat or do anything else that might help win a ball game. Off the field he was a ladies' man. He was sometimes difficult to get along with in the clubhouse.

An all-around athlete, he starred in football and baseball at Sam Houston College in Texas. He began his professional baseball career with the Memphis Red Sox in 1925. After the season, he continued his education, attending Meharry Medical School in the winter of 1925–26, and joined the Chicago American Giants at the close of the school year. When he arrived he took over the catching chores, with Jim Brown moving to first base, and stepped into the cleanup spot in the batting order, hitting .266. His bat and defensive play proved catalysts for the Chicago American Giants as they won the second-half Negro National League title, but he missed the playoffs and World Series in 1926.

While in Chicago, he held a job at the post office and played baseball at the same time, but still maintained a high level of productivity. The next season he moved to shortstop and hit .336 to help the American Giants repeat as league champions and again defeat the Eastern Colored League's Bacharach Giants in the World Series. He continued in his role as the cleanup batter, hitting .401 in 1928 to win the league's second-half title, and .407 in the season's play-offs against the St. Louis Stars. Still an integral part of the team's success, he was batting .386 in 1929 when his untimely death from tuberculosis prematurely ended his career.

Russell
[see Awkard, Russell]

Russell
[see Ronsell]

Russell
Career: 1933   Position: p
Team: Brooklyn Royal Giants
In 1933 he was a pitcher with the Brooklyn Royal Giants, who were playing as an independent team.

Russell, Aaron A.
Career: 1913–20   Position: 3b
Team: Homestead Grays
He was a third baseman with the Homestead Grays during their formative years, playing from 1913 through 1920.

Russell, Branch L.
Career: 1922–23   Positions: **rf**, 3b
Teams: Kansas City Monarchs ('22), **St. Louis Stars** ('23–'31), Cleveland Cubs ('31), Cleveland Stars ('32)
Bats: Left   Throws: Right
Height: 5'10"   Weight: 170
Born: Oct. 9, 1895, South Boston, Va.
Died: May 1, 1959, St. Louis, Mo.
The right fielder for the Negro National League champion St. Louis Stars of 1928, 1930, and 1931, he had a good arm and was a good hitter, recording batting averages of .291, .331, .334, and .331 for the years 1926–30, exclusive of 1928. He also batted .307 during the 1928–29 Cuban winter season. Most of his career he hit in the second slot, but during the 1930 season he was moved to the third spot. Most of his career was spent with the St. Louis Stars, and he served as captain during part of

his time with them. After retiring from baseball, he worked as a supervisor with the Parks and Recreation Department of St. Louis.

Russell, E.
Career: 1924–26   Positions: 3b, of
Teams: Harrisburg Giants ('24–'26), Dayton Marcos ('26)
A youngster secured in midseason of 1924 from a southern club to help Harrisburg at the beleaguered hot corner, he "looked pretty good" in limited action but failed to produce at the plate. Two years later he closed out his career, splitting the season between Harrisburg and the Dayton Marcos while hitting .233.

Russell, Ewing
Career: 1936   Position: c
Team: Cincinnati Tigers
In 1936, the Cincinnati Tigers' last season as an independent ballclub before entering the Negro American League, he was a reserve catcher with the team.

Russell, Frank (Junior)
Career: 1943–49   Position: **2b**, of
Team: Baltimore Elite Giants
Bats: Right   Throws: Right
Height: 5'8"   Weight: 188
He began his career during World War II, when he came off the sandlots of Nashville, Tennessee, to join the Baltimore Elite Giants in 1943. He was able to hang on with the team through the end of the following season, batting .240 and .268, before being farmed out to the Giants' Nashville Southern League team for the 1945 season. A determined effort in the Elites' spring training camp earned him another trial, in 1946, and he made the most of the opportunity.
A clever fielder who held down the keystone spot in a satisfactory manner, he had a fine throwing arm but was otherwise undistinguished afield or on the bases. At the plate he was a slap hitter and had difficulty hitting the curve, but was considered a dangerous batter

at times and was credited with a batting average of .335 in 1948.

Russell, John Henry (Pistol)
Career: 1923–34   Positions: **2b**, 3b, ss, 1b
Teams: Memphis Red Sox ('23–'25), **St. Louis Stars** ('26–'30), Indianapolis ABCs ('31), **Pittsburgh Crawfords** ('31–'33), Detroit Wolves ('32), Cleveland Red Sox ('34)
Bats: Right   Throws: Right
Height: 5'10"   Weight: 150–55
Born: Feb. 24, 1898, Dolcito, Ala.
Died: Dec. 4, 1972, Cleveland, O.

A standout gloveman for the St. Louis Stars, he had excellent range, a good arm, and was a superb pivot man, excelling on the double play. He had good speed and could pilfer more than his share of bases. At the plate he was described as a "foot-in-the-grave hitter" and was just an ordinary batter with average power, but a good clutch hitter. He posted averages of .331 and .250 in 1926–27 and .266 and .304 in 1929–30 while helping spark the Stars to Negro National League pennants in 1928 and 1930.

The flashy infielder was a member of the outstanding Pittsburgh Crawfords of 1932–33, hitting .332 and .297 while being selected as the second baseman for the East in the first East-West All-Star game the latter year. Before joining the Crawfords for the 1932 season, he and Cool Papa Bell were with the Detroit Wolves who were leading the East-West League before it was disbanded. He began his career in 1923 with the Memphis Red Sox, hitting .333 in his first year and .308 in 1925, his last year before joining the St. Louis Stars.

Russell, Thomas
Career: 1950   Position: p
Team: Cleveland Buckeyes

He pitched a single game without a decision for the Cleveland Buckeyes in 1950, when the Negro American League was struggling to survive the loss of players to organized baseball and the league's rapid decline was beginning.

Rutledge
Career: 1921   Position: p
Team: Dayton Marcos

He was a pitcher with the Dayton Marcos a year after they dropped out of the Negro National League.

Ryan, Merven J. (**Red**)
a.k.a. Mervyn
Career: 1915–32   Positions: **p**, *of*
Teams: Pittsburgh Stars of Buffalo ('15), New York Lincoln Stars ('16), Brooklyn Royal Giants ('19), Atlantic City Bacharach Giants ('20–'21), Harrisburg Giants ('22), **Hilldale Daisies** ('22–'29, '31), Homestead Grays ('27), Baltimore Black Sox ('29), New York Lincoln Giants ('28, '30), Harlem Stars ('31), Newark Browns ('32)
Bats: Right   Throws: Right
Height: 5'8"   Weight: 158
Born: 1898, Brooklyn, N.Y.

A veteran pitcher for Hilldale's Eastern Colored League pennant winners of 1923–25, Ryan maintained his composure on the mound and did not get rattled when an error was made behind him. Consequently, fielders played their best for him. The little right-hander was a speedball artist who threw hard for his size, but utilized a knuckleball and a forkball to earn a regular-season record of 20–11 in 1923. In postseason play he started 2 games in the 1924 World Series and relieved in a game the following year as Hilldale defeated the Kansas City Monarchs for the championship of black baseball. That season he fashioned a 5–1 league record, and followed with a 13–13 mark in 1926. He also pitched five winter seasons in Cuba during the 1920s, posting a composite 12–10 record.

Ryan, who earned the nickname "Red" because of his light complexion and dark red hair, began his baseball career in 1915 with the Pittsburgh Stars of Buffalo and played with the Lincoln Stars, Bacharach Giants and Harrisburg before joining Hilldale in 1922. In the fall of 1927 he was set to jump to the Grays, who were considered an outlaw club because they were an independent team and did not respect the contractual rights of league clubs.

The following spring he was with the New York Lincoln Giants but was traded with Rev. Cannady to Hilldale in exchange for Nip Winters and George Carr. In 1929 Hilldale in turn traded him and Frank Warfield to the Baltimore Black Sox for Crush Holloway and Richard Jackson, and Ryan finished the season with a 7–4 mark. Back with the Lincoln Giants in 1930, he was 5–2, and in 1931 he began the season with the Harlem Stars but joined Hilldale for most of the season, finishing with a 7–2 mark. In 1932 he closed out his career, with the Newark Browns.

As a fielder he not proficient at defensing bunts, but as a hitter he was better than most pitchers and sometimes played in the outfield. During his career he posted batting averages of .278, .300, .220, .282, and .308 interspersed between 1923 and 1930.

Ryle
Career: 1919   Position: ss
Team: Indianapolis ABCs

For one season, 1919, during the deadball era, he was a reserve shortstop for the Indianapolis ABCs.

S

Saabin

Career: 1927   Position: p
Team: Cuban Stars (East)

In 1927, his only season with a top team, he pitched with the Eastern Colored League's Cuban Stars.

Sadler, William A. (**Bill**, Bubby)

Career: 1934–38   Position: ss
Teams: Atlantic City Bacharach Giants ('34), Brooklyn Eagles ('35), Washington Black Senators ('38)

He was the regular shortstop with the Brooklyn Eagles in 1935 and accompanied the team to Puerto Rico in the ensuing winter for an exhibition series. When the Brooklyn franchise was acquired by Abe Manley and consolidated with the Newark Dodgers, Sadler became expendable. He next appeared with a top team as a part-time starter, batting second in the order, with the Washington Black Senators in 1938 during their brief tenure in the Negro National League.

Salas, Wilfredo

Career: 1948   Position: p
Teams: *Mexican League ('46–'47, '49–'56)*, New York Cubans ('48), *Canadian League ('48)*
Bats: Right   Throws: Right
Born: Cuba

A right-handed pitcher, he spent a partial season with the New York Cubans in 1948 in his only venture into the Negro Leagues, playing the remainder of the season with Sherbrook in the Canadian Provincial League. The balance of his career was spent in the Mexican League, where he pitched for a decade. Beginning in 1946 with Torreon, he compiled seasons of 7–7 and 5–13 prior to his stint with the New York Cubans. In 1949 he returned to Torreon for an 11–13 season with a 4.14 ERA. He spent four years with Monterrey (1951–54), with his best year coming in 1951 (14–7, 2.81 ERA). His composite record for the other three years showed a 21–24 mark. His last two years were spent with Vera Cruz, where he posted marks of 5–2 and 9–8 in 1955–56. With Ponce in the Puerto Rican League he had an unimpressive 1–4 record during his only winter there, and in two winter seasons with Marianao in the Cuban League, he had a combined 2–3 ledger.

Salazar, Lazaro

Career: 1924–36   Positions: **of**, p, 1b
Teams: **Cuban Stars (West)** ('24, '30, '32–'34), New York Cubans ('35–'36), *Santo Domingo ('37)*, **Mexican League** *('38–'39, '41–'52)*
Bats: Left   Throws: Left
Height: 5'9"   Weight: 177
Born: Feb. 4, 1912, Havana, Cuba
Died: Apr. 25, 1957

An all-around player in the mold of Martin Dihigo but much more restricted in his versatility and overall ability, this Cuban was both a good hitter and a good pitcher, playing in the outfield or at first base when not performing on the mound. The left-hander was an outstanding hitter with good power, and a good fielder with a strong arm, but possessed only average speed. Off the field he was a sharp dresser, and during the '40s he was instrumental in recruiting black Americans to play in Mexico.

He began his Negro League career in 1924 with a 3–5 pitching ledger, adding marks of 1–2 and 2–1 in 1930 and 1932 while hitting .355. Playing with the Cuban Stars during the Depression years of the early '30s, he joined Alejandro Pompez's New York Cubans in 1935, hitting .356 as the club won the Negro National League's second-half title and faced the strong Pittsburgh Crawfords in the playoffs. After another season with Pompez's ballclub, where he hit .367, he jumped to Santo Domingo to play with Trujillo's championship team. While contributing a .292 batting average, he led the league in runs (averaging a run per game in the 31-game season), tied Josh Gibson for the top spot in triples, and finished second in hits. With the strong pitching staff available he did little pitching (0–2), letting Satchel Paige do most of the mound work.

Afterward, rather than return to the United States, he took the helm of the Santa Clara ballclub in Cuba, actively recruited and signed American players for his team, and won to back-to-back pennants in the winter seasons of 1937–38 and 1938–39. Earlier in his Cuban career, during the winter of 1934–35, he led the league in batting with a .407 average and tied for the lead in wins as a pitcher with 6 victories. He won a second league batting title in 1940–41, playing for Almendares, with a .316 average. He finished in his homeland with a lifetime 35–24 pitching record and was called the "Cuban Peach."

While playing winters in Cuba, he had begun a summer career in the Mexican League in 1938 that lasted fourteen years (excluding the 1940 season) and ended in 1952. Beginning with Cordoba, he posted marks of 4–3 and 16–5 with ERAs of 1.89 and 2.20 in the first two seasons. He next played with the championship Veracruz team in 1941, where he contributed a 7–3 record to their pennant drive. He spent the rest of his career with Monterrey, with his best years coming in 1942 (14–12), 1944 (14–8), and 1949 (15–7). His lifetime totals show a 113–77 record with a corresponding 3.48 ERA and a .333 batting average, earning him selection to the Mexican Hall of Fame in 1954.

Salazar, Santos (Santiago)
Career: 1945–46   Positions: 2b, ss
Team: New York Cubans
Bats: Right   Throws: Right
Height: 6'0"   Weight: 195
Born: 1922, Santiago, Cuba

A product of Santiago, Cuba, this big, strong, husky player showed much promise as a first-class utility man when he joined the New York Cubans in 1945, on his first trip to the United States. He played with Alejandro Pompez's team for the next two seasons, splitting his time between the keystone positions in his second year.

Salmon, Harry (Beans)
Career: 1923–35   Positions: **p**, of
Teams: Birmingham Black Barons ('20–'32), Pittsburgh Keystones ('21–'22), Memphis Red Sox ('24, '30), Detroit Wolves ('32), Homestead Grays ('33–'35)
Bats: Right   Throws: Right
Height: 5'10"   Weight: 180
Born: May 30, 1895, Warrior, Ala.
Died: July 1983, Pittsburgh, Pa.

A lanky sidearm fastballer with a crossfire delivery and velocity comparable to Satchel Paige, this right-hander was the ace of the Birmingham Black Barons' staff when Paige first broke in with the team. Also incorporating a spitball into his repertory, he began pitching professionally in the summers while still working in the coal mines in the wintertime. He had begun shoveling coal at age eight, and learned to play baseball while working at the Edgewater Mine at Kimberly, Alabama.

He began his professional career in 1920, when the Black Barons signed the best players from the mining camps. He left during 1921 and pitched with manager Dizzy Dismukes's Pittsburgh Keystones for most of the next two years, before returning to the Black Barons when they were strong enough to join the Negro National League. During his first four seasons in the league he fashioned work sheets of 7–3, 8–3, 7–6, and 14–3, including a no-hitter in the latter year. In 1927 the thirty-two-year-old hurler registered a 14–6 record and pitched the Black Barons into the playoffs against the Chicago American Giants, but lost both his decisions to Chicago's Willie Foster as the American Giants took the pennant. Following his seasons of 11–10, 10–15 and 11–11 in 1928–30, the Negro National League folded, and he joined the Detroit Wolves of the East-West League for the 1932 season.

However, with the Wolves leading the league, the franchise faltered and was assimilated by Cum Posey's Homestead Grays, who retained the Wolves' best players and finished both schedules. Salmon posted marks of 2–2 and 0–2 in contests against league teams for the 1932–33 seasons. He remained with the Homestead Grays until he closed out his career in 1935. Some observers questioned his fortitude on the mound and his ability to overcome adversity, but the numbers speak for themselves. In addition to his superlative slabwork, Salmon was regarded as a good-hitting pitcher, with averages of .259 and .182 in 1927 and 1929, respectively, and sometimes was utilized in the outfield or as a pinch hitter.

Before pitching professionally, he served in the Army and played with the Fort Benning baseball team. Early in his development as a pitcher, his inexperience was apparent, but by the time the Black Barons entered league play, he had developed into a quality pitcher. During the '20s he played two winters with Cienfuegos in the Cuban League and spent the 1933–34 winter season in Puerto Rico. He quit his off-season job in the coal mines in 1929 to make his second trip to Cuba and never returned to the mines. After retiring from baseball he drove a taxi in Pittsburgh.

Salters, Edward
Career: 1937   Position: of
Team: Detroit Stars

When the Detroit Stars joined the Negro American League for its inaugural season in 1937, this outfielder was expected to pair up with Turkey Stearnes to provide a one-two power-hitting combo. However, those expectations were never fulfilled, and that season proved to be his only year in black baseball.

Salvat
Career: 1924–25   Position: p
Team: Cuban Stars (East)

He pitched with the Cuban Stars (East) in the Eastern Colored League for two years, but without notable success.

Sama, Pablo
Career: 1950   Positions: 3b, ss
Team: Indianapolis Clowns

The beginning of this infielder's career coincided with the decline of the Negro Leagues, when the franchise was struggling to survive the loss of players to organized baseball, and in his first and only season he hit .283 for the Indianapolis Clowns in 1950.

Sampson
Career: 1899–1905   Positions: **p**, of
Teams: Cuban Giants ('99), Genuine Cuban Giants ('05)

He was a pitcher and occasional outfielder with the Cuban Giants in 1899, and later was with one of the various ballclubs that flourished during the early years of the century copying the success of the Cuban Giants and appropriating a variation of the Cuban Giants' name for gate appeal.

Sampson, Emanual (**Eddie**, Leo)
Career: 1940–46   Position: of

Teams: Cleveland Bears ('40), Birmingham Black Barons ('41–'43)

After a short stint as a substitute outfielder with the Cleveland Bears in 1940, he was a part-time starter in right field for the Birmingham Black Barons in 1941, hitting seventh in the batting order when he was in the lineup, but he never again regained a regular position with the team.

Sampson, John
Career: 1942   Position: of
Team: New York Cubans

He appeared briefly as a reserve outfielder with the New York Cubans in 1942, his only year in the Negro Leagues.

Sampson, Ormand Leonard (Flash, George)
Career: 1932–38   Positions: ss, 3b, c, *p*
Teams: Atlanta Black Crackers (*'32, '37–'38*), Newark Dodgers ('34), Brooklyn Royal Giants ('33), Homestead Grays ('37), Chicago American Giants ('38), *Mexican League ('38–'39)*
Bats: Right   Throws: Right
Height: 5'11"   Weight: 190

A good hitter, a versatile fielder with a strong arm, and a smart base runner, he began his career with the Atlanta Black Crackers in 1932 and was their manager in 1937, leading this independent team to a highly successful season. A college man, he made his home in Gainesville, Florida, and spent the following off-season deep-sea fishing while several teams vied for his services for the coming year. He signed with the Homestead Grays in the spring, but despite being obligated to the Grays, he was expected to return to the Black Crackers to play third base alongside Dick Lundy at shortstop to form a solid left side of the infield.

However, the "old master" Candy Jim Taylor offered Sampson more money to play with the Chicago American Giants. Although still unsigned in mid-April, Sampson was working out at third base with Taylor's team and had 3 hits (a home run, a triple, and a single) to pace the American Giants over the Jacksonville Red Caps. Even after he signed with Chicago,

the Black Crackers continuously sought his return to Atlanta. Several times it appeared that he would relent and return, but he remained with the American Giants and moved behind the plate to fill a need at that position.

While Atlanta still expected him to join them for the second half of the 1938 season, he opted for Mexico instead, batting .345 with Agrario for the remainder of the season. He also moved from behind the plate to the other end of the battery, where he employed a knuckleball to split 4 decisions while posting a 5.40 ERA. The next year he remained in Mexico but switched to the Anahuach ballclub, where he batted .293 but lost his only pitching decision. He never returned to the Negro Leagues.

Sampson, T. (Sam)
Career: 1940–41   Positions: 2b, of
Teams: Cleveland Bears ('40), Jacksonville Red Caps ('41)

He played as a semi-regular at second base with the Bears in 1940, batting sixth in the order, when the Jacksonville Red Caps' franchise moved to Cleveland and played as the Bears. He remained with the team after their return to Jacksonville in 1941, playing as a substitute in right field, and batting fifth when in the lineup. In the winter of 1943 he played with the Baltimore Elite Giants in California.

Sampson, Thomas (Tommy, Toots)
Career: 1940–49   Positions: **2b**, 1b, of, manager
Teams: **Birmingham Black Barons** ('40–'47), Chicago American Giants ('48), New York Cubans ('49)
Bats: Right   Throws: Right
Height: 6'1"   Weight: 180
Born: Aug. 31, 1914, Calhoun, Ala.

A slick-fielding second baseman for the Birmingham Black Barons, Sampson was selected to play in four consecutive East-West All-Star games in his first four seasons (1940–43) in the Negro American League. In the last of these games Sampson got the first hit and knocked in the first run in the West's 2–1 victory.

As a youngster in Raleigh, West Virginia, he played sandlot ball, and quit school at age seventeen to work as a coal miner, while playing semipro baseball on weekends. He worked eight years in the mines, mostly as a brakeman, and suffered the loss of his right index finger in an accident while trying to jack a coal car back on the tracks after it had jumped the rails. In later years the missing digit caused his throws to first base to break unnaturally, presenting a bit of a problem for some first basemen.

From his beginnings, playing weekend ball at Raleigh, he moved to Portsmouth, Virginia, playing on a faster semipro team that played every day. They formed a league comprised of teams from Virginia and North Carolina, and also did some traveling outside those limits. While touring through the South with the team, he was discovered and signed by the Black Barons after a game in Atlanta in 1940. Birmingham's manager, Candy Jim Taylor, taught Sampson the intricacies of baseball. Originally a third baseman, Sampson hurt his arm earlier in his career and moved over to second base for the shorter throw, and, through hard work, taught himself to play the keystone position. After his arm healed, it was stronger than ever, and after fielding a ball, he made all of his throws underhanded, without raising up to throw.

A good right-field hitter, he was a good hit-and-run man and usually hit second in the batting order, maintaining an average close to .300, with respectable power. In 1942 he hit .354, and the next season the Black Barons fielded the strongest team in their history and won their first Negro American League pennant. In 1944, as the Black Barons were repeating as pennant winners, the speedy Sampson, an ideal second-place batter, hit .272 and stole 16 bases, only 2 thefts behind league leader Sam Jethroe.

During the World Series that year, Sampson's playing career was tragically altered when his right leg was broken in a car accident while traveling between cities. Four players were in the car, with Sampson driving, when a drunk driver hit them head-on. John Britton, Pepper Bassett, and Leandy Young were also in the car, but no one else was hurt as badly as Sampson. Britt hurt his thumb, Young had a chipped bone in his hip, and Bassett was just bruised and shaken. Sampson was in critical condition for about a week and missed the remainder of the World Series. His absence from the lineup was a contributing factor in the Black Barons' loss to the Grays.

After the accident, Tommy served a two-year stint as playing manager of the Black Barons, succeeding Winfield Welch. His play dropped off, with his batting average dipping to .205 and .272 for the 1946–47 seasons. Following an unspecified disagreement with owner Tom Hayes, he resigned as manager in October 1947 and was replaced by Piper Davis. During the 1948 season Sampson discovered Willie Mays and recommended him to Davis, who signed him for the Black Barons.

After leaving Birmingham, he played a year each with the Chicago American Giants (.252 batting average) and the New York Cubans, ending his career after the 1949 season, to round out the decade. After retiring from baseball, he worked at a variety of jobs, including operating a service station.

Samuels
Career: 1940   Position: p
Team: Philadelphia Stars

A second-line pitcher with the Philadelphia Stars in 1940, he did not figure in a league decision during his only season in the Negro National League.

San, Pedro Alejandro (Eli)
Career: 1926–28   Position: p
Team: Cuban Stars (East)
Bats: Right   Throws: Right

A right-handed, underhand pitcher with good control, he pitched for the Cuban Stars (East) during the last three years of the Eastern Colored League. His best year was 1927, when he posted a 12–9 record and batted .227. He also pitched in Cuba, Puerto Rico, Venezuela, Colombia, and the Dominican Republic.

Sanchez
Career: 1904–05   Position: c
Team: All Cubans

For two years, beginning in 1904, he was a catcher with the All Cubans ballclub, the most prominent Cuban team of the era.

Sanchez
Career: 1913   Positions: of, 1b
Team: *Philadelphia Giants*

He was an outfielder-first baseman with the Philadelphia Giants in 1913, after the team's quality of play had declined.

Sanchez, Amando
Career: 1948   Position: p
Team: Memphis Red Sox

He pitched with the Memphis Red Sox in 1948, losing both of his decisions in his only season in the Negro Leagues.

Sanchez, José
Career: 1916   Position: player
Team: Cuban Stars

He played with owner Alejandro Pompez's 1916 Cuban Stars, but his position is uncertain.

Sanders, Bob
[see Saunders, Bob]

Sanders, Willie
Career: 1936   Position: p
Team: Memphis Red Sox

He pitched briefly with the Memphis Red Sox in 1936, his only season in the Negro Leagues.

Sanderson, Johnny
Career: 1947   Position: ss
Team: Kansas City Monarchs

He was a reserve shortstop with the Kansas City Monarchs, playing behind Hank Thomp-

son in 1947, his only season in the Negro Leagues.

Sands, Sam (**Piggy**)
Career: 1950   Positions: ss, c
Teams: Indianapolis Clowns ('50–'53), Memphis Red Sox ('50), *Kansas City Monarchs* ('54)

He began as a shortstop in 1950, but his game experience was severely restricted that season, and he added catching chores to his shortstop duties later in the '50s. His entire career was while the Negro American League was in decline and struggling to survive the loss of players to organized baseball.

Santa Cruz, Eugenio (Santa)
Career: 1908–10   Position: cf
Team: Cuban Stars

A speedy outfielder with great range and outstanding glovework but lacking power at the plate, he usually batted either leadoff or at the bottom of the order.

Santaella, Anastacio (**Juan**, Tacho)
a.k.a. Santella
Career: 1935–36   Positions: 2b, ss, 3b, of
Team: New York Cubans

This Cuban infielder could play any infield position, but was the starting second baseman, hitting in the sixth slot and batting .267, with the New York Cubans in 1935. The Cubans won the Negro National League's second-half title but lost a hard-fought championship playoff to the Pittsburgh Crawfords. The next season he followed with a .333 average as a part-time starter, but never again played in the Negro Leagues.

Playing in the Cuban winter league, he hit between .268 and .277 each year between 1935 and 1938. In 1940 he began his Mexican career, batting .250 with Chihuahua and improved each of the next two seasons, batting .279 with Mexico City in 1941 and .305 with Monterrey in 1942. In each of the next two seasons his playing time was severely restricted, as he played in fewer than 10 games each season, ending his career in 1944.

Santiago

Career: 1935   Position: 2b
Team: New York Cubans

In 1935 he was a reserve second baseman with the New York Cubans, who won the Negro National League's second-half title but lost a hard-fought championship playoff to the Pittsburgh Crawfords.

Santiago, Carlos Manuel

Career: 1946   Positions: 2b, ss
Bats: Right   Throws: Right
Height: 5'11"   Weight: 170
Born: 1928, Puerto Rico
Teams: New York Cubans ('46) *minor leagues ('47–'49), Canadian League ('50), Mexican League ('55)*

After a season with the New York Cubans as a reserve middle infielder, playing both second base and shortstop, he entered organized baseball with Stamford in 1947–49, and also played with Farnham in Canada's Provincial League and with the Mexico City Reds in 1955. He was elected to the Puerto Rican Hall of Fame in 1993.

Santiago, José Guillermo (Pants)

Career: 1947–48   Position: p
Teams: New York Cubans ('47–'48), *minor leagues ('49–'59),* major leagues ('54–'56)
Bats: Right   Throws: Right
Height: 5'10"   Weight: 175
Born: Sept. 4, 1928, Coamo, Puerto Rico

This Puerto Rican right-hander pitched two years with the New York Cubans prior to embarking on an eleven-year career in organized baseball that carried him to the major leagues for three partial seasons. He pitched with the Cleveland Indians in 1954–55, with a combined 2–0 record, but was 1–2 with the Kansas City Athletics in 1956, giving him a lifetime 3–2 major-league ledger.

While working his way up to the major leagues, he spent seasons with Dayton (16–12,

2.60 ERA in 1949), Wilkes-Barre (12–7, 3.26 ERA and 21–5, 1.59 ERA in 1950–51), and Dallas (14–7, 2.83 ERA and 13–11, 3.47 ERA in 1952–53). The remainder of his career was spent with half a dozen minor-league teams without any significant success, finishing with aggregate 36–39 totals. His last season, with San Antonio in the Texas League in 1959, where he posted a 14–9 record with a 3.10 ERA, was the only time that he had double-digit wins during his last six seasons. He spent two winters with Mayagüez in Puerto Rico, 1956–58, with a combined 13–15 record.

He was elected to the Puerto Rican Hall of Fame in 1993.

Santop, Louis (Top, Big Bertha)

a.k.a. Louis Santop Loftin (his real name)
Career: 1909–26   Positions: c, lf, rf, 1b,   3b, manager
Teams: *Fort Worth Wonders ('09), Oklahoma Monarchs ('09),* Philadelphia Giants ('09–'10), **New York Lincoln Giants** ('11–'14, '18), **Brooklyn Royal Giants** ('14–'19), Chicago American Giants ('15), New York Lincoln Stars ('15–'16), **Hilldale Daisies** ('17–'26), *military service ('18–'19), Santop Bronchos ('27–'31)*
Bats: Left   Throws: Right
Height: 6'4"   Weight: 240
Born: Jan. 17, 1890, Tyler, Tex.
Died: Jan. 6, 1942, Philadelphia, Pa.

One of the earliest superstars and a crowd favorite, Santop was a solid, strong-armed catcher who excelled at blocking the plate, but was better known as a power hitter. He could stand at home plate and throw a ball over the center-field fence, but could hit a ball even farther. The big Texan used a big, heavy bat and was noted for his tape-measure home runs during baseball's deadball era, which earned him the nickname "Big Bertha" after the Germans' World War I long-range artillery piece. A left-handed hitter, he especially liked pitches out over the plate where he could get good arm extension in his swing, and is credited with one gargantuan drive that traveled more than 500 feet.

Also credited with being a lifetime .406 hitter, Santop starred with several great teams during his career, spending most of his playing time before World War I with New York-based teams, including the Lincoln Giants, the Lincoln Stars, and the Brooklyn Royal Giants. Playing against all levels of competition with the McMahon brothers' newly formed New York Lincoln Giants (1911–14), the big slugger registered batting averages of .470, .422, .429, and .455 while catching the era's two hardest throwers, Smokey Joe Williams and Cannonball Dick Redding.

Prior to coming to New York, Santop and Redding, as a pair of impressive youngsters, had formed a "kid battery" for manager Sol White's Philadelphia Giants in 1910. Santop had started his baseball career the previous year with the Fort Worth Wonders and Oklahoma Monarchs of Guthrie, Oklahoma. When he left the Lone Star State, Santop took the Texas custom of rolling his own cigarettes with him wherever he went.

In 1915 he returned West to play briefly with Rube Foster's Chicago American Giants, but soon returned to the familiar confines of the East Coast, where he joined Dick Redding, John Henry Lloyd, and Spot Poles on the Lincoln Stars. Ironically, it was Foster's American Giants whom the Stars met for the championship at the end of the season, with the Series ending in a deadlock. After 10 games, and the teams tied with 5 wins apiece, the eleventh game was called in the fourth inning with the Stars one run ahead and never resumed or replayed because of contention between the two teams.

Two years later, after returning to the New York Lincoln Giants, Santop found his team again facing Foster's club for the championship and, despite the double and 2 triples counted among his 7 hits, the Lincolns dropped a hard-fought 7-game series.

When playing exhibitions against white teams, he would perform a pregame throwing demonstration that was unbelievable. For fifteen minutes he would stay in a catcher's crouch and throw the ball around the infield randomly to every base, sometimes including the shortstop, with unerring accuracy. The crowds loved it and he liked to "play to the crowds."

In his prime, as the biggest drawing card, in black baseball, Santop was paid accordingly (receiving up to $500 a month) and lived up to his star image. In this role, Santop was sometimes called the "black Babe Ruth" and once had a chance to play on the same diamond with the Bambino. In the 1920 postseason exhibition against Casey Stengel's All-Stars, Santop cracked 3 hits, including a double, while the Babe went hitless and fanned twice.

Years later, in the reknowned 1932 World Series, Ruth would "call his shot," but claims are made that Santop often made home-run predictions and delivered on the promise. Once, in Atlantic City, when Santop was in the on-deck circle, an avid lady fan sitting in the grandstand taunted him, saying he was going to strike out. Santop shook his head and pointed to the right-field fence. The woman yelled, "Bet you a buck!" Santop went to the dugout, secured a dollar, and walked over and stuck it through the screen in front of the grandstand. When his turn came to bat, he delivered on his promise by smashing a homer far over the designated fence. After circling the bases and crossing home plate, he went over to the lady in the grandstand to collect his money.

The big, light-complected, gruff-voiced superstar enjoyed a good time, and this type of banter endeared him to the fans. Sometimes the good-natured verbal exchanges extended to the opposition. Santop and former New York Giants' hurler Jeff Tesreau were from the same hometown, Tyler, Texas, and the two faced each other in New York in an exhibition contest between Hilldale and Tesreau's Bears. When Santop came to the plate, Tesreau, who was almost as big as Santop, aimed a purpose pitch under his chin. Santop yelled out to the mound, "Jeff, you wouldn't throw at a hometown boy, would you?" Tesreau responded, "All niggers look alike to me!"

With different players and under different circumstances, the exchange could have provoked an ugly incident. Santop was amiable, but he could get riled on occasion. Once, after an exchange of words, he grabbed Oscar Charleston in a bear hug and, in a demonstration of strength, broke three of his ribs. He also evinced a toughness on the field, sometimes ignoring injuries to play hurt when the team depended on him. Once he caught a doubleheader with a broken thumb and won both games with crucial extra-base hits, a triple in the first game and a home run in the second game.

In 1917 Hilldale recruited the gritty competitor to play a 3-game series against a major-league all-star team largely comprised of Philadelphia Athletics, and Santop raked Chief Bender and Bullet Joe Bush for 6 hits as Hilldale won 2 of the 3 games. Santop proved that he could hit in the clutch regardless of the opposition, and compiled a .316 lifetime batting average against major-league pitching.

Santop missed most of the next two seasons (1918–19) due to Navy service during World War I, but after the Armistice he stayed with Ed Bolden's Hilldale club for the remainder of his career, including the pennant-winning teams of 1923–25. Santop hit for averages of .373, .358, .364, and .389 for the 1921–24 seasons, and .333 in the 1924 Negro World Series against the Kansas City Monarchs.

Unfortunately, Santop made an error that led to a Kansas City victory in the Series, and that miscue contributed to the demise of his career. With his team holding a tenuous 2–1 lead, the bases loaded, and 2 outs in the bottom of the ninth inning, Frank Duncan lifted an easy pop fly behind the plate and Santop muffed it, giving Duncan new life. Duncan made the most of the reprieve and, on the next pitch, drove in two runners to win the game. Santop was devastated, and a profane tongue-lashing by manager Frank Warfield after the game reduced him to tears.

The following year, the thirty-five-year-old receiver's playing time was severely restricted as Biz Mackey assumed the full-time catching duties, and by midsummer of 1926 Santop was released. Restricted primarily to pinch-hitting duties the latter two seasons, he had a composite batting average of .268 for 1925–26. Although he formed his own semipro team, the Santop Bronchos, and played with this club for a few years, he never again played for a top team and soon faded from the baseball scene.

During those years when he was hanging on in baseball, he worked as a broadcaster on radio station WELK in Philadelphia, did some charity work, and became involved in local politics. After drifting out of baseball, he settled in the "City of Brotherly Love" and tended bar. As the years passed he developed severe arthritis and other debilitating illnesses, and eventually died in a Philadelphia naval hospital a month after the Japanese attack on Pearl Harbor. But the saga didn't end, and black baseball's first legitimate home-run slugger is still remembered for his colorful exploits and his powerful bat.

Saperstein, A. M. (Abe)
Career: 1932–50   Position: officer
Teams: Cleveland Cubs, Cincinnati Clowns, Chicago American Giants

Best known for his association with basketball's Harlem Globetrotters, this roly-poly white promoter was also involved in black baseball. He was a partner with Tom Hayes and the Birmingham Black Barons during the '40s. Hayes owned the team but Saperstein ran the club. In addition to being a booking agent for several black teams, he was an officer with the Cincinnati Clowns, the Harlem Globetrotters of baseball, and served as the president of the Negro Midwestern League and the West Coast Negro Baseball Association.

Sarvis, Andrew (Smoky)
Career: 1939–42   Position: p

Teams: Cleveland Bears ('39–'40), Jacksonville Red Caps ('41–'42)

When the Jacksonville Red Caps' franchise moved to Cleveland for two seasons, playing as the Cleveland Bears, he held the distinction of being one of the top three pitchers for the 1940 ballclub, despite a 0–2 league record from incomplete statistics. Returning with the franchise to Jacksonville the following season, he continued as a member of the pitching staff until the team dropped out of the Negro American League in 1942 and disbanded.

Satterfield
Career: 1905–11   Positions: 2b, ss
Teams: Famous Cuban Giants ('05–'06), Genuine Cuban Giants ('08), Brooklyn Royal Giants ('11), *Indianapolis ABCs ('13)*

This middle infielder began his career with the Famous Cuban Giants, one of the various ballclubs that flourished during the early years of the century, copying the success of the Cuban Giants and appropriating a variation of the Cuban Giants' name as their own for gate appeal. His last year with a quality ballclub was in 1911, playing with the Brooklyn Royal Giants as a substitute second baseman. Two years later he played with the Indianapolis ABCs, who were still a year away from major-league status.

Saunders, Bob
a.k.a. Sanders
Career: 1926–32   Positions: **2b**, ss, 3b, p
Teams: Kansas City Monarchs ('26), Detroit Stars ('26, '31), Cleveland Hornets ('27), Atlantic City Bacharach Giants ('31), Monroe Monarchs ('32), Louisville Red Caps ('32)

He began his career as a pitcher with the Kansas City Monarchs in 1926, winning both of his decisions, but played most of his years in the Negro Leagues as an infielder. In 1926, in his limited play with both the Monarchs and the Detroit Stars, incomplete statistics show a meager .100 batting average. The following season he played with the Cleveland Hornets during their only season in the Negro National

League. He next appeared in 1931 with the Bacharachs, and closed his career in the Negro Southern League in 1932, while batting sixth in the order as the regular second baseman for the Monroe Monarchs.

Saunders, Leo
Career: 1937–40   Positions: ss, p
Teams: Memphis Red Sox ('37), Birmingham Black Barons ('40), Chicago American Giants ('40)

This light-hitting infielder was the regular shortstop for the Memphis Red Sox in 1937, batting at the bottom of the order, and was a reserve at that position with the Birmingham Black Barons in 1940.

Saunders, William
Career: 1887   Position: of
Team: *Pittsburgh Keystones*

He was an outfielder with the Pittsburgh Keystones, one of eight teams that were charter members of the League of Colored Baseball Clubs in 1887. However, the league's existence was ephemeral, lasting only a week.

Saunders, William
Career: 1950   Position: c
Team: Baltimore Elite Giants

The beginning of his career with the Baltimore Elite Giants in 1950 coincided with the decline of the Negro American League, when teams were struggling to survive the loss of players to organized baseball, but league statistics for the season do not confirm his playing time.

Savage
Career: 1925   Position: p
Teams: Atlantic City Bacharach Giants ('25), Wilmington Potomacs ('25)

A marginal player, he pitched briefly, without a decision, with two teams in the Eastern Colored League in 1925, joining the Bacharachs after the Potomacs' franchise folded.

Savage, Artie
Career: 1932   Position: officer
Team: Cleveland Stars
He was an officer with the Cleveland Stars in 1932, during their membership in the East-West League.

Savage, Bill (Junior)
Career: 1940   Position: p
Team: Memphis Red Sox
Pitching with the Memphis Red Sox, he won his only recorded decision in 1940, his only year in the Negro American League.

Sawyer, Carl
Career: 1924   Position: 2b
Team: Detroit Stars
A second baseman with the Detroit Stars in 1924, he had previously played with the Colored All-Stars in the 1921 winter season.

Saxon, Thomas (Lefty)
Career: 1942   Position: p
Team: New York Cubans
Bats: Left   Throws: Left
He pitched with the New York Cubans in 1942, but without being involved in a league decision.

Saylor, Alfred (Greyhound)
Career: 1941–45   Positions: **p**, 1b, c
Teams: *Cincinnati Buckeyes ('40)*, **Birmingham Black Barons** ('41–'45), Cincinnati Clowns ('43)
Bats: Right   Throws: Right
Born: Cleveland, Ohio.
A pitcher on the Birmingham Black Barons' back-to-back Negro American League pennant winners of 1943–44, he compiled a 14–5 record with a 2.74 ERA in 1944. In postseason play he started 2 games and relieved in another in the 1943 Series, registering 2 wins against a single loss. The next year he again started 2 games in the Series but lost both decisions as the Homestead Grays repeated as champions.
A native of Cleveland, he began his career as a first baseman with the Cincinnati Buck-

eyes, a team of lesser status, in 1940. The following season he began his stint with the Birmingham Black Barons and began his pitching career. The right-hander would do anything to give him an advantage over the batter, including throwing a "cut ball" and a spitball, and he had good control of all his pitches, legal or illegal. In 1945 he fashioned a 4–3 work sheet in his last season in the Negro Leagues.

Scales, George Walter (Tubby)
Career: 1921–48   Positions: **2b**, 3b, 1b, ss
                                              of, manager
Teams: *Montgomery Grey Sox ('19–'20)*, Pittsburgh Keystones ('21), St. Louis Giants ('21), St. Louis Stars ('22), **New York Lincoln Giants** ('23–'29), Homestead Grays ('25–'26, '29–'31, '35), Newark Stars ('26), **Baltimore Elite Giants** ('38, '40–'44, '46–'48), New York Black Yankees ('32–'34, '36, '39–'40, '45), Philadelphia Stars ('40), *Birmingham Black Barons ('52)*
Bats: Right   Throws: Right
Height: 5'11"   Weight: 195
Born: Aug. 16, 1900, Talladega, Ala.
Died: Apr. 1976, Los Angeles, Calif.
A good right-handed hitter for both average and power, he feasted on curveballs. Scales was a versatile fielder who could play third base, first base, shortstop, or the outfield, but who was at his best at second base. He was a fast big man but a little portly, and lacking the speed necessary for a wide range afield, he compensated by studying the hitters, positioning himself accordingly, and throwing runners out with his rifle arm. He also had a fast arm for double plays.
He attended Talladega College in his hometown, playing shortstop on the school team before signing with the Montgomery Grey Sox in 1919. After two years with the Grey Sox, he moved up to a quality team in 1921 with the St. Louis Giants. The following year he played third base with the St. Louis Stars in their first game ever, but later in the season he

suffered a broken leg sliding into second base and hit only .208 for the year.

The next season he traveled East to join the new Eastern Colored League and spent most of his prime years with the New York Lincoln Giants (1923–29), where he batted in the heart of the order and recorded batting averages of .429, .367, .361, .222, .446, .338, and .387 while starting at three different infield positions. He was lured away to join the great Homestead Grays of 1930–31, where he batted fifth in the order, hitting behind Judy Johnson the first year and Josh Gibson the latter year, while recording averages of .303 and .393. This aggregation of talent was one of the best of all time and featured Josh Gibson, Oscar Charleston, Jud Wilson, and Smokey Joe Williams.

While Scales was with the Grays, he and Ted Page engaged in an argument over Page's poor performance in a loss. Words were exchanged and Page hit him and knocked out two of his teeth. George "Chippy" Britt, one of baseball's "big bad men," got between them with one in each arm and broke up the fight. But their anger didn't subside, and the two players were roommates. That night they slept facing each other, each with a weapon in his hand.

Always a team man and a smart player, he was responsible for the New York Black Yankees being organized in 1932, and became the franchise's first manager. The team operated on a percentage basis, backed by two "shady" characters, with James Semler acting as the road secretary only because Scales wanted him in that capacity. Semler took control of the team in 1933, and Scales remained with the ballclub for the next five years, with the exception of 1935, when he returned to the Grays for a season, batting .263. His relationship with Semler soured and eventually led to his removal as manager. In 1937 he left the Black Yankees to play in Santo Domingo with the Estrellas Orientales ballclub, where he hit .295 for the season.

In 1938 he succeeded Biz Mackey as the Baltimore Elite Giants' manager, leaving in 1939 to take the reins of the New York Black Yankees for another season, but returning to Baltimore in 1940 as a player. Scales continued with the Elites through most of the '40s, playing both infield and outfield and posting averages of .304, .255, .244, .253, .300, and .309 in 1940–45. In 1942, with Scales hitting third in the order, the Elites challenged the Grays for the Negro National League pennant before losing out in the last days of the stretch drive. The next season, although nearing the end of his career, he appeared as a pinch hitter in the All-Star game. A line-drive hitter with a good eye at the plate, Scales compiled a lifetime .313 batting average over a twenty-five year career as an active player in the Negro Leagues.

In his latter years he became a playing manager and often was an overbearing, tough taskmaster who sometimes showed his temper or verbally assailed a player. But he knew baseball and groomed many young ballplayers for stardom, including Junior Gilliam. The veteran was familiar with the league's players, and in 1945 he was again obtained from the Elites to take the helm of the New York Black Yankees for a third time. Although he was still on the active roster, his best years were behind him, and he was reserved for pinch-hitting duties. After the demise of the Negro National League, he served as the traveling secretary for the Elites after they were assimilated into the Negro American League and won the 1949 championship. He continued in the Negro American League, managing the Birmingham Black Barons in 1952.

He also managed in Puerto Rico for a dozen winters (ten with the Ponce ballclub) and won six pennants, including four in succession (1941–45), which still stands as a record. He added a fifth flag while at the helm of the Ponce team in 1947–48 and a final one with Santurce in 1950–51, when he also guided the team to a victory in the Caribbean Series. He returned to Ponce to close out his baseball career in 1958. After retiring from baseball he became a stockbroker.

Scantlebury, Patricio Athelstan (**Pat**)
Career: 1944–50   Positions: p, 1b
Teams: New York Cubans ('44–'50), *minor leagues ('53–'61),* major leagues ('56)
Bats: Left   Throws: Left
Height: 6'0"   Weight: 178
Born: Nov. 11, 1917, Colón, Panama Canal Zone
Died: May 24, 1991, Montclair, NJ

This twenty-nine-year-old left-handed Panamanian compiled a 10–5 ledger for the 1947 Negro National League champion New York Cubans and pitched in 2 games in the subsequent World Series against the Negro American League Cleveland Buckeyes, winning his only decision. He had an outstanding fastball, an assortment of good breaking pitches (curve, slider, and screwball), and an adequate change-up. He also threw a spitball that was described by Bob Feller as looking "like a pigeon coming out of a barn." Although not a power pitcher, he was tough in the clutch, had good control, and had an effective move to first base. Regarded as an outstanding mound artist and a careful student of baseball, he utilized deception in his deliveries that often baffled the batter. With successive seasons of 7-5, 3.52 ERA and 5-3, 3.94 ERA in 1949–50, he earned selection to the East-West All-Star game in each of those seasons, closing out both by pitching scoreless ball. He began his career with the Cubans in 1944. He had records of 1-4 and 1-2 in 1944–45, but improved to a 5-2 ledger in 1946.

While pitching with the Cubans in the summers, he played winters in the Latin American leagues, splitting 4 decisions with Ponce in the Puerto Rican League in 1946–47 and posting a 10–6 mark with a 1.86 ERA with Almendares in the Cuban League the following winter.

Entering organized baseball after the color line had been eradicated, he shaved eight years off his true age to get the opportunity. Good performances with Texarkana (24–11, 3.37

ERA), Dallas (18–13, 4.12 ERA), and Havana (13–9, 1.90 ERA) in 1953–55 paid dividends, and in 1956, at age thirty-eight, Scantlebury pitched briefly in the major leagues with the Cincinnati Reds, rooming with Frank Robinson and posting a 0–1 ledger in 6 games. After his brush with the major leagues, he pitched with Seattle in the Pacific Coast League and with Havana and Toronto in the International League. In his final four seasons in baseball he recorded seasons of 15–9, 12–5, 7–5, and 2–4, closing out his career in 1961 barely short of his forty-fourth birthday.

Before coming to the United States, he learned to play baseball in Panama, and upon his arrival the Cubans' management had high expectations for him. A complete ballplayer, the hustling Panamanian was a fast base runner, a good fielder, and a dependable hitter. Available statistics from the Negro Leagues show averages of .500, .306, .366, .333, and .448 for intermittent seasons from 1945 to 1950. In organized ball he was often utilized as a pinch hitter, registering averages of .301 with Dallas in 1954, .379 with Seattle in the Pacific Coast League in 1956, .325 with Toronto in 1959, and .286 with Toronto in his last year in baseball.

In the latter years of his life he suffered from Parkinson's disease.

Schiff
Career: 1908   Position: lf
Team: Genuine Cuban Giants

He played in the outfield with one of the various Cuban Giants' ballclubs that flourished during the early years of the century. Several of these ballclubs, copying the success of the Cuban Giants and appropriating a variation of the Cuban Giants' name as their own for gate appeal, played a quality of baseball close to that of the original team.

Schlichter, H. Walter
Career: 1902–10   Positions: owner, officer
Team: Philadelphia Giants

A white sportswriter for the *Philadelphia Item,* he and Sol White were cofounders of the Philadelphia Giants in 1902, and under his ownership the Giants became the dominant black team in the country, winning four straight titles from 1904 to 1907. After suffering the defection of Rube Foster and other key players to the Leland Giants, there was a loss in quality. In 1910 Schlicter and White had a disagreement, and when White left to form his own team, the decline of the franchise was rapid. Schlichter also served as president of the National Association of Colored Baseball Clubs of the United States and Cuba.

Schmidt
Career: 1933   Position: p
Team: Philadelphia Stars

He pitched briefly with the Philadelphia Stars in 1933, the first year of the team's existence.

Schorling, John M.
Career: 1911–27   Positions: owner, officer.
Team: Chicago American Giants

Rube Foster's business partner with the Chicago American Giants, this very wealthy white man was a tavern owner who was active in the operation of sandlot clubs in Chicago for several years before entering into an agreement with Foster. Schorling leased the grounds of the old White Sox Park, built a new grandstand and bleachers seating nine thousand, and sought out Foster as a partner, agreeing to split the gates equally. Without benefit of a formal contract, their partnership lasted for seventeen years, 1910–26, without ever encountering any serious financial problems. Schorling served as an officer of the Chicago American Giants, and after Foster's illness he assumed control of the team until he was pressured out by a coalition of the other owners who conspired to keep the best clubs out of Chicago, thus diminishing the gate receipts. In the spring of 1928 he sold the club to William E. Trimble, a white florist, ending his association with the American Giants. However, he continued as a successful businessman and maintained a palatial mansion in Detroit.

Scotland, Joe (Old Forty-five)
Career: 1914–19   Position: cf
Teams: Indianapolis ABCs ('14), Louisville Sox ('15), Chicago Union Giants ('16), Bowser's ABCs ('16), Jewell's ABCs ('17)

A speedy outfielder, he was an excellent defensive center fielder but a light hitter, and his lack of offensive punch kept him out of the lineups of the top clubs. Playing in the Midwest, he played much of his career with an ABCs club, beginning in 1914 with C. I. Taylor's ABCs in their first season as a major ballclub, and also playing with Bowser's ABCs and Jewell's ABCs, teams of lesser status.

Scott
Career: 1914–16   Positions: p, of
Team: Chicago Giants

A pitcher with the Chicago Giants during the latter decade of the deadball era, he sometimes played in right field for the struggling Chicago club during his three seasons with the team.

Scott
Career: 1920   Position: c
Teams: *Madison Stars ('20),* Detroit Stars ('20)

The catcher played briefly with the Detroit Stars in 1920, his only association with a quality ballclub.

Scott
Career: 1932   Position: c
Team: Washington Pilots

He was a catcher with the Washington Pilots in 1932, when they were in the East-West League.

Scott
Career: 1934   Position: 2b
Team: Nashville Elite Giants

This infielder played as a reserve second baseman with the Nashville Elites in 1934.

Scott
Career: 1936   Position: of
Team: Philadelphia Stars

A marginal player, he appeared briefly as a reserve outfielder with the Philadelphia Stars in 1936, his only Negro League season.

Scott
Career: 1937   Position: p
Team: Birmingham Black Barons

This marginal player was on the pitching staff of the Birmingham Black Barons in 1937, the first year of the Negro American League.

Scott, C. L.
Career: 1915   Position: player
Team: Mohawk Giants

He was a player with the Mohawk Giants in 1915, but his position is uncertain.

Scott, Charles
Career: 1919–20   Position: lf
Team: St. Louis Giants

He was a part-time starter in left field for the St. Louis Giants for two years, hitting in the third slot when in the lineup.

Scott, Elisha
Career: 1920   Position: executive
League: Negro National League

Recruited by Rube Foster for the responsibility, he was a codrafter of the Negro National League constitution in 1920.

Scott, Frank
Career: 1887–94   Positions: 2b, ss
Teams: Unions ('87), Chicago Unions ('88–'94)

In 1887 he was the regular shortstop on the Unions, a team playing out of Chicago under the management of Abe Jones. After their initial season they became known as the Chicago Unions, and he moved across to the other side of the keystone sack as the team's regular second baseman. The next time he appears in the starting lineup is in 1894, at second base and under the management of W. S. Peters.

Scott, Jimmy
Career: 1950   Position: p
Team: Memphis Red Sox

A marginal player, he pitched in 3 games without a decision for the Memphis Red Sox in 1950 when the Negro American League was in decline and teams were struggling to survive the loss of players to organized baseball.

Scott, Joe
Career: 1933   Position: 1b
Teams: Columbus Blue Birds ('33), Homestead Grays ('33)

This big, husky player hit .304 with the Columbus Blue Birds in 1933. He was playing with a brewery team the next spring and was slated to take the starting first-base position with the Homestead Grays in 1934, but when Buck Leonard arrived, Scott was released.

Scott, John
Career: 1944–50   Positions: **of**, 1b, c
Teams: Birmingham Black Barons ('44), **Kansas City Monarchs** ('45–'48), Louisville Buckeyes ('49), Philadelphia Stars ('50), *Canadian League ('50–'51)*
Bats: Left   Throws: Left
Height: 5'11"   Weight: 170

He began his career as a catcher, but switched to the outfield when he joined the Birmingham Black Barons in 1944 and hit .327. Traded to the Kansas City Monarchs the following year, he had a powerful throwing arm, was a smart base runner, and strengthened the war-depleted outfield. Although his batting average dropped to .214, he still provided needed punch at the plate with his hard hitting.

In 1946 he hit .306 for the Monarchs as they won the Negro American League pennant before losing a hard-fought World Series to the Newark Eagles. In 1948 he continued his strong hitting with a .311 batting average, but in each of the next two seasons he was traded, first to the Louisville Buckeyes in 1949, where he batted .265, and then to the Philadelphia Stars, where he hit .258 in 1950.

But he played most of 1950 with Farnham in the Canadian Provincial League, batting .312 and drawing 124 walks in 106 games. He also spent the 1951 season in the same league, splitting the time between Farnham and St. Hycinthe, while batting .264 with 111 walks in 113 games.

Scott, Joseph (**Joe**)
Career: 1948–50   Position: **1b**, of
Teams: *military service ('41–'45), Detroit Senators ('46),* Birmingham Black Barons ('47–'49), Chicago American Giants ('50)
Bats: Left   Throws: Left
Height: 5'11"   Weight: 175
Born: June 15, 1918, Shreveport, La.

After a season with the Detroit Senators, a team of lesser quality, this first baseman was encouraged by Pepper Bassett to join the Birmingham Black Barons in the Negro American League, and played three years in Birmingham during the late '40s. He had good speed and a modicum of power but was not a good hitter for average and did not have a long career.

In 1948, with a season already under his belt, he competed for an outfield position with the Birmingham Black Barons and gained some playing time despite batting a lowly .196 batting average with a high strikeout total. The Black Barons won the 1948 Negro American League pennant but lost the World Series to the Homestead Grays. Scott showed some improvement the next season as he boosted his batting average to .249. During both seasons the Army veteran roomed with a young outfielder named Willie Mays.

In 1950 the Black Barons changed ownership, and manager Ted "Double Duty" Radcliffe recruited him for the Chicago American Giants, where he batted .226 and cut down on his strikeouts. But that was his last season in baseball, and he returned to Los Angeles, securing regular employment with the Santa Fe Railroad. Later he switched to Amtrak and

worked with their organization for twenty-eight years, until retiring in 1979.

He first began playing semipro baseball after graduating from Central High School in Shreveport, Louisiana. After playing with the Shreveport Black Sports in 1938, he left the next year to tour with the Texas Black Spiders, but they encountered financial difficulties and disbanded in Wichita, Kansas. For the remainder of the year he joined the Dunsiath Giants, a semipro team from North Dakota that was touring the Midwest and on into Canada. Returning home after the season, he spent 1940 back with the Shreveport ballclub.

In 1941 he entered the Army during World War II, serving with the 350th Field Artillery attached to the 46th Brigade. Crossing the English Channel six days after the Normandy invasion, the unit moved through France and on into Belgium until the end of the war. Discharged in November 1945 with the rank of staff sergeant, he returned to Los Angeles, where he played in the winter league on the Coast until joining the Detroit Senators in 1946.

Scott, Joseph Burt (**Joe**)
Career: 1945–49   Position: of
Team: Memphis Red Sox

A hustling outfielder for the Memphis Red Sox during the postwar 1940s, this spirited competitor had a brief but undistinguished career in black baseball, beginning as a reserve outfielder in 1945. In 1947 he was a part-time starter, batting leadoff when in the lineup. In 1948 he was again relegated to a reserve role, and batted .261, following with a .289 average in his last season in the Negro Leagues. Unconfirmed reports indicate that he later played briefly and without appreciable success in the low minors.

Scott, Robert
Career: 1920–27   Positions: **lf**, rf
Teams: **Brooklyn Royal Giants** ('20–'26), New York Lincoln Giants ('20, '26), Hilldale Daisies ('20, '27), Harrisburg Giants ('27)

This Texan was a very good fielder and hitter, had excellent speed on the bases, and was one of the smallest players on his ballclub. His small stature and patience in pitch selection made him a good leadoff batter. As a right fielder with Hilldale in 1920 he hit .340, but spent most of his career as the Brooklyn Royal Giants' left fielder, where the veteran batted .341 and .220 in 1924–25. After leaving the Royal Giants he played with the Lincoln Giants, the Hilldale Daisies, and the Harrisburg Giants.

Scott, Robert
Career: 1950   Position: p
Team: New York Black Yankees

He was a pitcher with the New York Black Yankees during the 1950 season, when the franchise was struggling to survive the loss of players to organized baseball.

Scott, William
Career: 1932   Position: officer
Team: Louisville Black Caps

He was an officer of the Louisville Black Caps during the 1932 season, when the Negro Southern League was considered a major league.

Scott, William, Jr. (Bill)
Career: 1950   Position: of
Team: Philadelphia Stars ('50–'51)

This outfielder began his career in 1950 when the Negro American League was in decline and struggling to survive the loss of players to organized baseball.

Scott, Willie Lee
Career: 1927–38   Position: 1b
Teams: Memphis Red Sox ('27), Louisville White Sox ('30–'31), Indianapolis ABCs ('32, '38), Chicago American Giants ('34)

He began his career in 1927 with the Memphis Red Sox, batting in only 5 games. During the early '30s he also played with the Louisville White Sox and the Chicago American

Giants before closing his career with the Indianapolis ABCs in 1938.

Scragg, Jesse
Career: 1915   Position: p
Team: *Philadelphia Giants*

He was a pitcher in 1915 with the Philadelphia Giants, when this once-proud team was in decline and of dubious quality.

Scroggins, John
Career: 1947   Positions: p, *of*
Team: Kansas City Monarchs

A fringe player, he pitched briefly with the Kansas City Monarchs in 1947 and also appeared as an outfielder.

Scruggs, Robert
Career: 1950   Position: p
Team: Cleveland Buckeyes

He was listed as a pitcher with the Cleveland Buckeyes in 1950, when the Negro American League was struggling to survive the loss of players to organized baseball, but league statistics do not confirm his playing time.

Scruggs, William C. (Willie)
Career: 1949–50   Position: p
Teams: Birmingham Black Barons ('49, '52, '58), Louisville Buckeyes ('49), Cleveland Buckeyes ('50), Houston Eagles ('50), *New Orleans Eagles ('51)*

He began his career in 1949 with the Birmingham Black Barons and pitched with a trio of franchises in the Negro American League in its declining years, when it was struggling to survive the loss of players to organized baseball. In 1950 he suffered through a 1–15 season, pitching primarily with the Cleveland Buckeyes but also appearing with the Houston Eagles. The next year the Eagles relocated in New Orleans, and after a season there he returned to Birmingham, playing on into the '50s, when the league was strictly a minor league operation.

Scudder

Career: 1887   Position: c
Team: *Philadelphia Pythians*

He was a catcher with the Philadelphia Pythians, one of eight teams that were charter members of the League of Colored Baseball Clubs in 1887. However, the league's existence was ephemeral, lasting only a week.

Seagraves

Career: 1937   Position: of
Team: Indianapolis Athletics

He was an outfielder with the Indianapolis Athletics in 1937, their only season in the Negro American League.

Seagraves, Samuel

Career: 1946   Position: c
Team: Chicago American Giants

A fringe player, he appeared briefly among the six catchers who were employed by the Chicago American Giants in the first post-World War II season.

Seagres

Career: 1942   Position: player
Team: Jacksonville Red Caps

He appeared briefly with the Jacksonville Red Caps in 1942, playing without distinction.

Searcy, Kelly (**Lefty**)

Career: 1950   Position: p
Teams: Baltimore Elite Giants ('50–*'51*), Memphis Red Sox ('50), Birmingham Black Barons ('50, *'53–'55*)
Bats: Left   Throws: Left

This left-handed hurler began his career in 1950, appearing with three different teams, including the Baltimore Elite Giants, when the franchise was a part of the Negro American League, and continued on into the '50s as the league was struggling to survive the loss of players to organized baseball. He also played with the Memphis Red Sox, and his last appearance was with the Birmingham Black Barons in 1955, after the Negro American League was strictly a minor league operation.

Seay, Richard William (**Dick**)

Career: 1925–47   Positions: **2b**, ss, *3b, of, p*
Teams: *Philadelphia Giants ('24), Pennsylvania Red Caps of New York ('25),* Brooklyn Royal Giants ('25, '27–'31), Newark Stars ('26), Baltimore Black Sox ('26, '32–'33), *Chappie Johnson's All-Stars ('28),* Newark Browns ('31), Philadelphia Stars ('34–'36), Pittsburgh Crawfords ('35–'36), **New York Black Yankees** ('36, '41–'42, '46–'47), **Newark Eagles** ('37–'40), *military service ('43–'45)*
Bats: Right   Throws: Right
Height: 5'8"   Weight: 156
Born: Nov. 30, 1904, West New York, N.J.
Died: Apr. 6, 1981, Jersey City, N.J.

Considered the best defensive second baseman in black baseball during the '30s, this hustling little infielder had a splendid throwing arm and adequate speed. Consistently playing an integral role on great teams, the superior gloveman played for three straight Negro National League championship teams, the Philadelphia Stars of 1934 and the Pittsburgh Crawfords of 1935–36. The next season he was part of the famous "million-dollar infield" of the Newark Eagles. Wherever he was, he put on a show for the fans when he took his glove to the field.

He left the Newark Eagles in midsummer of 1940, joining the New York Black Yankees until entering military service in 1943. After being discharged, he returned to the Black Yankees for two more seasons before closing out his Negro Leagues career. Outstanding in the field, especially on the double play, he was selected to the East All-Star squad three times. The first appearance was as a representative of the Philadelphia Stars in 1935, and the other appearances were as a Black Yankee in 1940–41.

While his defensive contributions to his team's success were immeasurable, his offensive contributions were generally lacking, but he produced some good seasons at the bat, including averages of .308 and .303 with the Baltimore Black Sox in 1932–33, and .281 and .302 with the Newark Eagles in 1938 and 1940. Other years, however, showed more representative batting marks from early in his career through the latter seasons, and are not impressive. Included are averages of .121 and .184 (in 1926–27), .137 and .215 (with the Philadelphia Stars in 1934–35), .211 and .179 (with the Eagles in 1937 and 1939), and .171, .238, and .192 (with the Black Yankees in 1941–42 and 1947).

The light-hitting Seay offset his lack of power and consistency at the plate by contributing in other ways. An excellent bunter who honed this oft-neglected offensive tool to perfection, he was also an excellent practitioner of the hit-and-run play. The amiable and popular player was always in demand by ballclubs in the Negro Leagues and in Latin America, especially in Puerto Rico, where he is still a national hero. Seay was an acceptable role model for youngsters, as he generally refrained from strong drink and profane language.

Seay was born into the only black family in West New York, New Jersey. The midwife who delivered him mistakenly listed him as "white" on his birth certificate. More interested in baseball than education, he dropped out of school after one year of high school. At about age twelve, the youngster was the batboy for local teams that played fall exhibitions against a team that included a few major-leaguers.

As he got older, he continued to play in the sandlots of the town until he was discovered by the Pennsylvania Red Caps of New York. The team signed him as a shortstop, and he formed a double-play combination with Chino Smith, who was the second baseman. Later the Brooklyn Royal Giants tried him as a shortstop, but released him because of his erratic throwing arm. Seay was picked up by Chappie Johnson, whose All-Stars ballclub played as an independent team. Johnson taught the young infielder how to play second base, and soon the Royals resigned him, along with outfielder Ted Page. However, owner Nat Strong was not

generous with his money, and Seay's pay was only $150 a month. After much dickering, the slick-fielding prospect finally got a $25 raise, but after one year, he and Page both left, with Seay signing with the Baltimore Black Sox. After a year with the Black Sox, he returned to the Royals until 1932, when he again landed with the Black Sox for two years, batting second in the order. In 1934 he signed with the Philadelphia Stars and started his skein of playing for three straight pennant winners.

See
Career: 1934   Positions: of, p
Team: Cleveland Red Sox

He appeared as both an outfielder and a pitcher with the Cleveland Red Sox in 1934, the team's only season in the Negro National League.

Segula, Percy
Career: 1921–23   Position: p
Teams: Kansas City Monarchs ('21), Milwaukee Bears ('23)

In his first year in the Negro Leagues, he pitched briefly with the Kansas City Monarchs in 1921, and appeared again with the Milwaukee Bears in 1923, their only year in the Negro National League.

Selden
a.k.a. Seldon; Seldom
Career: 1910–14   Positions: ss, 2b
Teams: Chicago Giants ('10), Indianapolis ABCs ('14), Mohawk Giants ('14)

In 1910 this youngster hit an even .200, but made good as a part-time starter at shortstop with the Chicago Giants despite a weak stick. Four years later the fringe player appeared briefly as a reserve middle infielder with the Indianapolis ABCs in their first season as a major-league-caliber team, and with the Mohawk Giants of Schenectady, New York.

Selden, William H.
Career: 1887–99   Positions: p, of
Teams: *Boston Resolutes ('87)*, **Cuban Giants**

('88–'90, '94, '96, '99), New York Gorhams ('91), Cuban X-Giants ('95–'99), *Colored Capital All-Americans*

He was a pitcher with the Boston Resolutes, one of eight teams that were charter members of the League of Colored Baseball Clubs in 1887. However, the league's existence was brief, lasting only a week. During his stint with the Resolutes he defeated the Fall River ballclub, champions of the New England League. In 1888 he joined the Cuban Giants and is best identified with that team. His stay with the ballclub included seasons when they represented Trenton in the Middle States League (1889) and York, Pennsylvania, in the Eastern Interstate League (1890). Following those two seasons, he played with the New York Gorhams when they represented Philadelphia in the Middle States League (1891), and with the Cuban X-Giants, the successor of the Cuban Giants as the top black team in the East. He also appeared with the Colored Capital All-Americans of Lansing, Michigan.

Seller
[see Suttles, George (Mule)]

Semler, James (Jim, Soldier Boy, Sarge, Sep)
Career: 1932–48   Positions: owner,
                                            officer
Team: New York Black Yankees

He was the owner of the New York Black Yankees and, as were most Negro National League owners, was a numbers banker. He was a charming, smooth-talking "con artist" who was sometimes excitable and disliked by some who had business dealings with him. When the Black Yankees were organized, they operated on a percentage basis, bankrolled by two "shady" characters, with Semler functioning as a road secretary. The players did not even want him in that capacity, but George Scales sided with him. The next season, 1933, he "stole" the team by incorporating the franchise with his wife as president and himself as vice president and took over operation of the

ballclub. Some veteran players left the team when he assumed control of the franchise. A few years later, in a business squabble with racial overtones, the Yankee Stadium promotions were taken away from Eddie Gottlieb, a white promoter and booking agent, due to black pressure, and given to Semler. However, he was unable to handle the job adequately and ended up in debt and out of baseball.

Serrell, William C. (**Bonnie**, Barney, El Grillo, The Vacuum Cleaner)
Career: 1942–50   Positions: **2b**, 3b, 1b,
                                            of
Teams: **Kansas City Monarchs** ('42–'44, '49–'51), *Mexican League ('45–'48, '52–'58), minor leagues ('51, '56–'57)*
Bats: Left   Throws: Right
Height: 5'11"   Weight: 160
Born: Mar. 9, 1922, Dallas, Tex.

This small, slender keystone man had a good, accurate arm and great range afield, earning him the nickname "The Vacuum Cleaner," and was one of the premier second basemen of black baseball during the 1940s. He had good speed on the bases, could bunt or execute the hit-and-run play, and was a good contact hitter with respectable power. Serrell anchored the 1942 champion Kansas City Monarchs' infield, batting .376 for the season. The left-handed swinger hit .556 in the 1942 World Series sweep of the Homestead Grays. The next year he was inducted into military service, but was exempted because of a rash and returned to the Monarchs. During the last year of World War II he was called again, but was then in Mexico and did not receive the induction notice. Upon his return to the United States, he was fined for failing to appear for another physical examination.

In 1944, his last season with the Monarchs before going to Mexico, he hit .321 and was selected to the East-West All-Star game, cracking 2 hits in 3 at-bats in his only All-Star appearance. The next season he left the Monarchs to play with Tampico in the Mexican League, and the Monarchs signed Jackie Robinson as an infield replacement. Serrell was considered to be the better of the two players, and at the end of the season, when Robinson was signed by the Brooklyn Dodgers, Serrell was greatly disappointed.

He remained in Mexico, where he posted batting marks of .313, .272, .264, and .289 for the years 1945–48, earning a spot as the starting second baseman for the North squad in the All-Star game during the first two years. After four years in Mexico he returned to the Monarchs, hitting .282 and .319 in 1949–50.

After starting the next year with the Monarchs, he entered organized ball with Yakima in the Western International League, batting .302 for half a season before moving up to the Pacific Coast League and hitting .243 with San Francisco for the remainder of the 1951 season. In 1952 he returned to Mexico, beginning his second tour with an average of .380, and continuing with Nuevo Laredo for six seasons. In 1953–54 he led the league in both hits and triples wile hitting .323 and .350, and then followed with averages of .333, .326, and .299 in his last three years. In 1958 he played with Nogales-Juarez in the Arizona-Mexican League and hit .376 to close out his career.

The previous two winters before his retirement he also played winter ball in Mexico, batting .330 and .265. Winter ball was nothing new to him, as earlier in his career he played two winters in Cuba with a composite .269 average, and with Ponce in the Puerto Rican winter league, where he hit .289 in 1949–50. Married to a Mexican woman, he settled in Mexico after he retired from baseball.

Seruby

Career: 1888   Position: of
Team: Cuban Giants

In 1888, his only year in black baseball, he was an outfielder with the Cuban Giants, the first black professional team, formed only three years earlier.

Seto

Career: 1929   Position: of
Team: Cuban Stars (East)

He was an outfielder with the Cuban Stars (East) in 1929, the American Negro League's only year of existence.

Shackleford, John G.

Career: 1924–30;   Positions: 2b, 3b, manager, officer
1945–46

Teams: Cleveland Browns ('24), Harrisburg Giants ('25), Chicago American Giants ('26), Birmingham Black Barons ('30), *Cleveland Clippers ('46)*

Bats: Left   Throws: Right
Height: 5'10"   Weight: 165

Beginning his career in 1924 with the Negro National League's Cleveland Browns, he jumped to Harrisburg in the Eastern Colored League the next year, hitting .294 for the season. In January 1926 he signed with the Chicago American Giants and, entering his third season with major-league teams, the skinny third baseman was regarded as a promising young infielder. Attending Wiley College at the time, he was to report when school was out for the summer. However, he showed more promise than ability, hitting only .154 and, although he was a fair fielder, he lacked the raw talent to become a solid ballplayer. In 1930, during his last year as an active player, he hit .286 with Birmingham.

While having shortcomings as a ballplayer, he utilized his college education to serve baseball capably in management and executive positions later in life. He was the manager of the Cleveland Clippers' ballclub, and he became the president of the U.S. League when it was organized in 1945.

Shamburg

Career: 1938   Position: 3b
Team: Atlanta Black Crackers

A fringe player, he appeared in a few games at third base in late June for the Atlanta Black

Crackers in 1938, their only year in the Negro American League.

Shanks, Hank

Career: 1927   Position: 1b
Team: Birmingham Black Barons

This first baseman batted .261 in limited play with the Birmingham Black Barons in 1927, his only year in the Negro National League.

Shannon

Career: 1932   Position: of
Team: Pittsburgh Crawfords

In 1932 he appeared briefly as an outfielder with the Pittsburgh Crawfords, their first full season as a quality team.

Sharpe

Career: 1923   Position: ss
Team: St. Louis Stars

He was a shortstop with the St Louis Stars in 1923, his only year in the Negro National League.

Sharpe, Robert (Pepper)

a.k.a. Sharp
Career: 1940–49   Positions; p, of
Teams: Chicago American Giants ('41), *Chicago Brown Bombers ('43)*, **Memphis Red Sox** ('44, '47–'48), *military service ('45–'46)*
Bats: Right   Throws: Right

He appeared briefly with the Chicago American Giants in 1941, but played most of his career with the Memphis Red Sox. He batted .245 as a reserve outfielder and fashioned a 2–4 record as a part-time pitcher with the Red Sox in 1944 but entered military service the next year. After being discharged from the Army, he concentrated more on his pitching in 1947–48, registering seasons of 8–3 and 3–7, but continued to be a fairly good hitter, batting .209 for the latter season.

Shartz

Career: 1911   Position: c

Teams: *Quaker Giants ('09)*, Philadelphia Giants ('11)

He was a catcher with the Philadelphia Giants in 1911, after having served an apprenticeship with the Quaker Giants, a team of lesser quality.

Shaw

Career: 1920   Position: rf
Team: St. Louis Giants

He was an outfielder with the St. Louis Giants in 1920, his only year in the Negro National League.

Shaw, R.

Career: 1897   Position: p
Teams: Page Fence Giants ('97), Chicago Unions ('97)

In 1897, his only season with quality black teams, this pitcher split the year with the Page Fence Giants and the Chicago Unions.

Shaw, Theodore (Ted)

Career: 1927–31   Position: p
Teams: Chicago American Giants ('27), Detroit Stars ('28–'30), Memphis Red Sox ('31)
Bats: Left   Throws: Left

As a curveball pitcher for five seasons in the Negro League, he had all the necessary tools for pitching success and also was a good hitter. His first year he was on the Negro National League champion Chicago American Giants, but most of his career was spent with the Detroit Stars, where he fashioned marks of 8–8 and 11–5 while batting .246 and .316 in 1929–30. In 1931 the Californian went to Honolulu, was married, quit baseball, and worked for the telephone company until his death.

Shawler

Career: 1909   Position: of
Teams: Leland Giants ('09), *Indianapolis ABCs ('13)*

He pitched with the Leland Giants in 1909 and later played with the Indianapolis ABCs in 1913, a year before the team was of major-league quality.

Shelby, Hiawatha

Career: 1946   Position: of
Team: Indianapolis Clowns

An outfielder for one season in the Negro Leagues, he appeared with the Indianapolis Clowns in 1946.

Shelton

Career: 1920   Position: c
Team: Dayton Marcos

He was a catcher with the Dayton Marcos in 1920, their first year in the Negro National League.

Shelton

Career: 1943   Position: of
Team: Harrisburg-St. Louis Stars

He was a member of the Harrisburg-St. Louis Stars in 1943, before they withdrew from the Negro National League to barnstorm.

Shepard, Sam

[see Sheppard, Samuel, Dr. (Sam)]

Shepherd, Fred

[see Sheppard, Frederick (Fred, Tommy)]

Sheppard, Frederick (**Fred**, Tommy)

a.k.a. Shepherd
Career: 1945–48   Positions: **p**, of
Teams: *Atlanta Black Crackers ('43)*, Birmingham Black Barons ('45–'46), *minor leagues ('47–'50)*, Chicago American Giants ('48)
Bats: Right   Throws: Right

This right-hander from Morris Brown College was a pitcher-outfielder with the Atlanta Black Crackers in 1943 when they were in the Negro Southern League. Two years later he played with the Birmingham Black Barons in the same capacity. Sandwiched between two stints with Stamford in the Colonial League, was brief playing time with the Chicago American Giants in 1948; he lost both of his Negro League decisions and posted a 1–2 mark with Stamford that same season. In 1950, his last

appearance on the baseball scene, he played with Minot in the Mandak League.

Sheppard, Ray

Career: 1924–32   Positions: **ss, 3b**, 2b, 1b, of, *p*
Teams: Indianapolis ABCs ('24), Birmingham Black Barons ('24, '28–'29), Detroit Stars ('25–'26), Kansas City Monarchs ('31), Monroe Monarchs ('32), Detroit Wolves ('32), Homestead Grays ('32)

An all-purpose player, he began his career with the Indianapolis ABCs in 1924 and was a utility infielder with the Detroit Stars for the next two years, batting .210 in 1926. In 1929, with the Birmingham Black Barons, he hit .310 in limited play, and in 1931, the last season before the Negro National League folded, he was an outfielder for the Kansas City Monarchs. In his last season, 1932, he played with the Detroit Wolves and the Homestead Grays and even pitched briefly with the Monroe Monarchs.

Sheppard, Samuel, Dr. (**Sam**)

a.k.a. Shepard
Career: 1887, 1922   Positions: player, owner
Teams: New York Gorhams ('87), St. Louis Stars ('22)

He was a player with the New York Gorhams, one of eight teams that were charter members of the League of Colored Baseball Clubs in 1887. However, the league's existence and his playing career were brief. Later he became a doctor and, along with Richard Kent and two other medical men, he bought the St. Louis Giants in 1922 and reorganized the franchise as the St. Louis Stars, with him as the business manager.

Sheppard, William

Career: 1922–25   Position: p
Teams: Kansas City Monarchs ('22–'23), Memphis Red Sox ('24–'25)

A native of Oklahoma City, this pitcher began his career with the Kansas City Monarchs in 1922 and closed it out with the Memphis Red Sox three years later.

Sherkliff, Roy (Ed)
Career: 1931   Position: p
Teams: Hilldale Daisies ('31), *Washington Pilots ('34)*

In 1931, his only year with a top club, he was a member of the Hilldale pitching staff; he later played with the Washington Pilots.

Shields
Career: 1916   Position: p
Team: New York Lincoln Giants

He pitched briefly with the New York Lincoln Giants in 1916, his only year in black baseball.

Shields, Charlie (**Lefty**)
Career: 1941–45   Position: p
Teams: Chicago American Giants ('41–'43, '45), Homestead Grays ('43), New York Cubans ('43), Birmingham Black Barons ('43)
Bats: Left   Throws: Left

He began his career in 1941 with the Chicago American Giants, under manager Candy Jim Taylor. When Taylor assumed the reins of the Homestead Grays in 1943, he brought Shields with him. But later league officials required that Shields be returned to the Chicago American Giants. He also pitched with the Birmingham Black Barons that season, finishing with a combined 3–1 ledger against league competition.

Shields, Jimmy
Career: 1928–29   Position: p
Team: Atlantic City Bacharach Giants

A pitcher with the Bacharachs for two seasons at the end of the decade of the '20s, he posted a mark of 1–2 in 1929.

Shipp, Jesse
Career: 1910–12   Positions: **p**, rf
Teams: *New York Colored Giants ('08–'10),* Brooklyn Royal Giants ('10–'12)

He began his career playing with the New York Colored Giants in 1908, and after two years with the lesser team, joined the Eastern champion Brooklyn Royal Giants in 1910 as a pitcher, also playing occasionally in right field during his stint with the Royals.

Shirley
Career: 1914   Position: of
Team: Brooklyn Royal Giants

In his only year in black baseball, he pitched with the 1914 Eastern championship team, the Brooklyn Royal Giants.

Shively, George (Rabbit)
Career: 1910–25   Position: of
Teams: West Baden Sprudels ('10–'13), **Indianapolis ABCs** ('14–'18, '20–'21, '23), Bowser's ABCs ('16), Atlantic City Bacharach Giants ('19–'22, '24–'25), Brooklyn Royal Giants ('24), Washington Potomacs ('24)
Bats: Left   Throws: Left

One the fastest men in baseball, he was regarded as a "desperate" base runner who commanded everyone's respect. His outstanding speed made him a great leadoff man and gave him wide range in the outfield. A solid defensive outfielder, one of the best bunters in black baseball, and an exceptional hitter with moderate power, he was superstitious about his hitting and would not let a right-handed batter use one of his bats.

Shively spent most of his career with the Indianapolis ABCs, including the 1916 championship season. He began his career in 1910 at West Baden, Indiana, under the management of C. I. Taylor, and followed Taylor to the ABCs in 1914, their first year as a major-league-level ballclub. Oscar Charleston joined the team a year later, and in 1918, when Jimmy Lyons joined the ABCs, the trio was called the greatest outfield in baseball. During Shively's years with the ABCs (1915–18) he hit .317, .352, .214, and .350.

The veteran left the ABCs to play with the Bacharachs in 1919, but vacillated between the East and the Midwest for half a dozen years before settling in the East, where he posted batting averages of .319 in 1921 and .305 in 1924. He began the latter season in center field with the Washington Potomacs, but was released in the early summer and secured by the Bacharachs for the remainder of the year. Even at that stage in his career, the short, stocky outfielder still retained sufficient speed to be called "Rabbit." He closed out his career with the Bacharachs the next season.

Shropshine
[see Shropshire]

Shropshire
a.k.a. Shropshine
Career: 1937   Position: c
Team: St. Louis Stars
   In 1937, the first year of the Negro American League, he shared the regular catching duties with the St. Louis Stars, hitting fifth in the order when he was in the lineup.

Sibley
Career: 1911–13   Positions: p, *c*
Team: *Indianapolis ABCs*
   A pitcher with the Indianapolis ABCs for three seasons during the early '10s, before the ballclub attained major-league status, he also took an infrequent turn at the other end of the battery.

Siebert
a.k.a. Sierbert
Career: 1937   Position: lf
Team: St. Louis Stars
   In 1937, the first year of the Negro American League, he was a substitute outfielder with the St. Louis Stars.

Sierbert
[see Siebert]

Sierra, Felipe
Career: 1921–32   Positions: **2b**, ss, 3b, 1b, of
Teams: All Cubans ('21), Cuban Stars (West) ('22–'32)

He played a dozen years with the Cubans and, although he could play either infield or outfield, his best position was second base. During the late '20s he was the regular second baseman and leadoff batter for the Cuban Stars (West) of the Negro National League, recording averages of .263, .191, .267, and .279 for the seasons 1926–30, exclusive of 1928

Sigenero
Career: 1940   Position: p
Team: New York Cubans
   He pitched with the New York Cubans in 1940, his only year in the Negro National League.

Sijo
[see Gomez, W. (Sijo)]

Siki
[see Sykes, Joe]

Siki, Roque
Career: 1931–32   Positions: **lf**, c
Teams: Cuban Stars ('31–'32)
   A good hitter, during his two seasons in black baseball he played left field and batted in the heart of the order for the Cuban Stars, who sometimes played under the name the Cuban House of David.

Silva, Pedro
Career: 1921–22   Positions: p, of, 1b
Teams: All Cubans ('21), Cuban Stars (West) ('22)
   During his two years playing with Cuban teams in the Negro Leagues, he was primarily a pitcher but also played first base and in the outfield.

Silvers
Career: 1933   Position: ss
Teams: Brooklyn Royal Giants ('33), Philadelphia Stars ('33)
   An infielder, he appeared very briefly with the Philadelphia Stars in 1933, the first year

of the franchise's existence, and also played shortstop with the Brooklyn Royal Giants.

Simmons
Career: 1914   Position: of
Team: Indianapolis ABCs

He was a reserve outfielder with the Indianapolis ABCs in 1914, the team's first season as a major-league-quality team.

Simmons, Hubert
Career: 1950   Position: p
Team: Baltimore Elite Giants

In 1950 he pitched 3 games and won his only decision with the Baltimore Elite Giants, when the franchise had joined the Negro American League and was struggling to survive the loss of players to organized baseball.

Simmons, J. R.
Career: 1887   Position: player
Team: *Baltimore Lord Baltimores*

He was a player with the Baltimore Lord Baltimores, one of eight teams that were charter members of the League of Colored Baseball Clubs in 1887. However, the league's existence was ephemeral, lasting only a week. His position is uncertain.

Simmons, R. S.
Career: 1943–49   Position: officer
Team: Chicago American Giants
League: Negro American League
Born: 1896
Died: Aug. 28, 1951, Chicago, Ill.

He was an officer with the Chicago American Giants during most of the '40s and served as secretary of the Negro American League.

Simmons, Si
Career: 1926   Position: p
Team: New York Lincoln Giants

He pitched briefly with the Lincoln Giants in 1926, his only year in the Eastern Colored League.

Simms, Leo
[see Sims, Leo]

Simms, Willie (Bill)
a.k.a. Sims
Career: 1936–43   Positions: of, *2b*
Teams: *Monroe Monarchs ('34),* Cincinnati Tigers ('35–'36), **Kansas City Monarchs** ('37–'38, '41–'43), Chicago American Giants ('38–'40)
Bats: Left   Throws: Right
Height: 6'0"   Weight: 170
Born: Dec. 23, 1908, Shreveport, La.

An underpublicized outfielder for the 1942 champion Kansas City Monarchs, this leadoff batter was a solid, all-around player. He was very fast on the bases, had appreciable range in the field, and a good throwing arm. Although his batting average was not high and he did not hit with power, he was an adequate batter and was a good bunter and a pretty good hit-and-run man. He began his career with the Monroe Monarchs and advanced to the Kansas City Monarchs during their Negro American League dynasty period, playing on three of their five pennant winners, leaving for three seasons (1938–40) to play with the Chicago American Giants before returning for two more pennant seasons, posting batting averages of .182 and .206 for 1941–42. The next season his playing status was reduced to that of a part-time starter; this was his last year in the Negro Leagues.

Simpson
Career: 1930   Position: c
Team: Memphis Red Sox

He was a catcher with the Memphis Red Sox in 1930, his only season in black baseball.

Simpson
Career: 1933   Positions: of, 1b
Teams: Cleveland Giants ('33), Baltimore Black Sox ('33), Akron Tyrites ('33)

Appearing with a trio of teams in 1933, his only year in black baseball, he played both in the outfield and at first base during the season.

At the beginning of the season he shared the starting assignment in left-field and hit fifth in the batting order with the Akron Tyrites, until the team combined with players from the disbanding Columbus Buckeyes to form the second-half replacement team, the Cleveland Giants, where he played as a substitute center fielder. Later in the season he found a spot with the Baltimore Black Sox as a reserve first baseman.

Simpson

Career: 1942   Position: of
Teams: Birmingham Black Barons ('42), *Harlem Globetrotters ('47), Chicago American Giants ('51)*

He was an outfielder with the Birmingham Black Barons in 1942, and after World War II he played left field with the Harlem Globetrotters and later pitched with the Chicago American Giants in 1951, when the Negro American League was in rapid decline.

Simpson, Harry Leon (Suitcase)

Career: 1946–48   Positions: **of**, p
Teams: Philadelphia Stars ('46–'48), *minor leagues ('49–'50, '54, '60–'63),* major leagues ('51–'53, '55–'59), *Mexican League ('63–'64)*
Bats: Left   Throws: Right
Height: 6'1"   Weight: 175
Born: Dec. 3, 1925, Atlanta, Ga.
Died: Apr. 3, 1979, Akron, O.

This left-handed power hitter spent eight years in the major leagues during the '50s, but began his baseball career as a young outfielder with the Philadelphia Stars in 1946, hitting .333 in limited action, with 3 homers in only 51 at-bats. The next year, while gaining more playing time, his average dropped to .244, but he showed good speed and proved to be a capable fielder.

After another year with the Stars, he entered organized baseball with Wilkes-Barre in the Eastern League, where he hit .305 and led the league in homers (31), runs (125), and RBIs (120). This offensive production earned him a promotion to San Diego in the Pacific Coast League, where he enjoyed another excellent offensive output that included a .323 batting average, and league highs in triples (19) and RBIs (156).

The next year, 1951, marked his rookie year in the major leagues with the Cleveland Indians, but proved a little disappointing as he hit only .229. In 1952, playing as a regular, he rebounded with a respectable offensive output that included a .266 batting average, 21 doubles, 10 triples, and 10 home runs. But after a drop in production the following season, he found himself with Indianapolis in the American Association for the 1954 season.

After a winter in Cuba, where he managed only a .212 average with Marianao, he was back in the majors again in 1955 and, despite being traded to the Kansas City Athletics during the season, still hit an even .300 for the year. In 1956 he had his best power season, hitting 21 homers and leading the league with 11 triples while batting .293. He led the league in triples again in 1957 and batted .270, and was part of the Kansas City-New York Yankees dealing that saw him with the Yankees part of each 1957 and 1958 season. In 1959 he played with three different major-league teams but could not find a home, ending up with San Diego in the Pacific Coast League for the 1960 season.

The next year he hit .303 with 24 homers and 105 RBIs, and in 1962 he hit .279 with 19 homers for Indianapolis of the American Association, but when he started the 1963 season still in the minors, he traveled below the border to close out his career in the Mexican League. In 1963–64 he hit .334 and .306 with 21 and 14 homers for Mexico City.

Simpson, James

Career: 1887   Position: player
Team: *Philadelphia Pythians*

He was a player with the Philadelphia Pythians, one of eight teams that were charter members of the League of Colored Baseball Clubs in 1887. However, the league's existence was ephemeral, lasting only a week. His position is uncertain.

Simpson, Lawrence (Slick)
Career: 1910–20   Positions: p, of
Teams: West Baden Sprudels ('10), *Indianapolis ABCs ('13),* Mohawk Giants ('14), Bowser's ABCs ('16), Chicago Union Giants ('16), Chicago Giants ('20)

Beginning his career with the Sprudels of West Baden, Indiana, under the tutelage of manager C. I. Taylor, he subsequently played with the Indianapolis ABCs, the Mohawk Giants, and Bowser's ABCs prior to joining the Chicago Union Giants as a pitcher in 1916, but ofttimes played in the outfield when not on the mound. Later he played with the Chicago Giants in the first year of the Negro National League.

Simpson, W. E.
Career: 1886   Position: owner
Team: Cuban Giants

He was a Trenton businessman who, backed by several sportsmen, brought the Cuban Giants to Trenton for the 1886 season. He leased Chambersburg Grounds from J. Henry Klein and signed the Cuban Giants for "the novelty of a professional colored team." He intended for it to play as an independent for a year and then join a league. He originally called his team the Trenton Browns, but because he had signed so many Cuban Giants, they became known as the latter. He sold the team to Walter Cook on May 12, 1886.

Sims, Leo
a.k.a. Simms
Career: 1938   Positions: ss, 2b
Team: Atlanta Black Crackers
Bats: Left   Throws: Right

This middle infielder played shortstop and second base for the Atlanta Black Crackers in 1938, and held a starting position for a while in June, but was lacking defensively and was dropped by mid-July.

Sims, Willie
[see Simms, Willie (Bill)]

Sinclair
a.k.a. Sinelan
Career: 1932–33   Position: 3b
Teams: Atlantic City Bacharach Giants ('32), Newark Dodgers ('33)

He was with the Bacharachs briefly as a reserve third baseman in 1932, when they were playing as an independent team and were of marginal major-league quality. He joined the Newark Dodgers as a reserve when they were formed late in the 1933 season.

Sinclair, Harry
Career: 1931   Position: secretary
League: Negro National League

He served as the secretary of the first Negro National League during the last year of its existence.

Sinelean
[see Sinclair]

Singer, Orville (**Red**)
Career: 1921–32   Positions: lf, cf, rf, 2b
Teams: **New York Lincoln Giants** ('22–'26), Cleveland Browns ('24), Cleveland, Tigers ('28), Cleveland Cubs ('31), Cleveland Stars ('32)

One of the fastest men in baseball, he was a fair hitter and also played infield during his dozen years in the Negro Leagues. In 1923 he played second base with the New York Lincoln Giants, often batting fourth in the lineup, and the following year he alternated in left field after rejoining the club in midseason. In 1925 he hit .335, and a year later he was sharing the right-field position and batting in the leadoff spot when in the lineup. His last two years in black baseball were spent in Cleveland, with the Cubs in the Negro National League in 1931 and the Stars in the East-West League in 1932. Each season he was the regular left fielder and hit in the sixth slot.

Singleton
Career: 1896   Position: c
Team: Cuban X-Giants

He was a catcher with the Cuban X-Giants in 1896. When the Cuban Giants, baseball's first black professional team, had financial success, other clubs were organized to capitalize on their name. One of these teams stocked the roster with so many ex-Cuban Giants' players that they took the name X-Giants. During the late nineteenth century and the early twentieth century the X-Giants was generally the dominant black ballclub.

Singleton
Career: 1946   Position: p
Team: Cleveland Buckeyes

He pitched with the Cleveland Buckeyes in 1946, his only year in the Negro American League.

Singlong
Career: 1929   Positions: 2b, of
Team: Nashville Elite Giants

This reserve player appeared briefly at second base and in the outfield with the Nashville Elite Giants in 1929, a year before they joined the Negro National League.

Sisco
Career: 1913   Position: lf
Team: Philadelphia Giants

In his only year in black baseball, he played left field with the Philadelphia Giants in 1913, during the declining years of the franchise.

Skinner
Career: 1948   Position: c
Team: Newark Eagles

He was a catcher with the Newark Eagles very briefly in 1948, in the last year before the Negro National League folded.

Skinner, A.
Career: 1910   Positions: c, 1b, ut
Team: Chicago Giants ('10)

He made his appearance in black baseball in 1910 as a catcher, first baseman, and utility player with the Chicago Giants.

Skinner, Floyd
Career: 1917   Position: c
Team: Kansas City Colored Giants

In 1917 he was a catcher with the Kansas City Colored Giants.

Slawson
Career: 1916   Positions: 3b, 2b
Team: Lincoln Stars

He was a reserve infielder with the Lincoln Stars in 1916, his only year in black baseball.

Sloan, Robert
Career: 1919–21   Position: of
Team: Brooklyn Royal Giants

In 1919, his first year with the Brooklyn Royal Giants, he was the regular center fielder and hit third in the batting order, but he lost his starting position the next season.

Smallwood, Louis
Career: 1923   Positions: 2b, of
Teams: Milwaukee Bears ('23), *Chicago Giants ('29)*

This infielder played with the Milwaukee Bears in 1923, when they were in the Negro National League. But the team failed to finish the season, folding in late summer, and he played with the declining Chicago Giants, at that time a team of lesser status.

Smart
Career: 1932   Positions: p, lf
Team: Indianapolis ABCs

He pitched for manager Jim Taylor's Indianapolis ABCs in 1932, when the team was in the Negro Southern League. He also played in left field on occasion during the season.

Smaulding, Owen Bazz
Career: 1927–28   Position: p
Teams: Monarchs ('27), Cleveland Tigers

('28), Chicago American Giants ('28), Birmingham Black Barons ('28)

During his two seasons in the Negro National League he pitched with four different teams, beginning in 1927 with the Kansas City Monarchs, where he posted a 2–1 mark.

Smith
Career: 1909   Position: 3b
Team: Kansas City, Missouri, Royal Giants

In 1909, his only season in black baseball, he was a third baseman with the Royal Giants of Kansas City, Missouri.

Smith
Career: 1918   Position: 3b
Team: Bacharachs

He was the regular third baseman with the Bacharachs in 1918, batting seventh in the order, in his only season in black baseball.

Smith
Career: 1921   Position: cf
Team: Detroit Stars

He played center field with the Detroit Stars in 1921, his only year in the Negro National League.

Smith
Career: 1930   Position: p
Team: Chicago American Giants

He pitched briefly, without a decision, for the Chicago American Giants in 1930.

Smith
Career: 1939   Positions: p, of
Team: Indianapolis ABCs

He was in the starting rotation in 1939 when the Atlanta Black Crackers relocated to Indianapolis and played in the Negro American League as the ABCs.

Smith
Career: 1938   Positions: 3b, c
Team: Memphis Red Sox

Playing with the Memphis Red Sox, winners of the first-half 1938 Negro American League title, this reserve split his limited playing time between third base and catcher.

Smith
Career: 1942   Positions: of, 1b
Team: Birmingham Black Barons

He was a regular player, alternating between the outfield and first base, while hitting sixth in the batting order for the Birmingham Black Barons in 1942.

Smith
Career: 1897–1900   Position: 1b
Teams: Cuban Giants ('97), Cuban X-Giants ('00)

A big man possessing good baserunning skills, he played with the Cuban Giants and the Cuban X-Giants, the dominant team of the early years of the century and comprised mostly of former Cuban Giants' players.

Smith
Career: 1924   Position: p
Team: Washington Potomacs

A pitcher with the Potomacs in 1924, he was released in the first month for more seasoning and never returned to team play.

Smith
Career: 1925   Position: c
Team: St. Louis Stars

He was a reserve catcher with the St. Louis Stars in 1925, his only year in the Negro National League.

Smith
Career: 1927   Position: of
Team: Memphis Red Sox

He appeared briefly as a reserve outfielder with the Memphis Red Sox in 1927.

Smith, Alphonse Eugene (**Al,** Fuzzy)
Career: 1946–48   Positions: ss, 3b, lf
Teams: Buckeyes ('46–'48), *minor leagues ('50–'52),* major leagues ('53–'64)
Bats: Right   Throws: Right

Height: 6'1"   Weight: 196
Born: Feb. 7, 1928, Kirkwood, Mo.

Prior to playing a dozen years in the major leagues, he began his career as a third baseman with the Negro American League's Cleveland Buckeyes, who signed him after he graduated from a St. Louis high school in 1946. In his first full season, 1947, he moved to shortstop and hit .285 as the Buckeyes took the Negro American League pennant. The next season he moved to the outfield and hit an even .300. Cleveland Indians' scouts evaluating Buckeyes' hurler Sam Jones during a July game at League Park discovered Smith and signed him also.

Assigned to the Class A Wilkes-Barre club in the Eastern League, he hit .316 for the remainder of the year, and after batting .311 with good power in a full season with the club in 1949, he was promoted to San Diego in the Pacific Coast League. After seasons of .248 and .281 on the Coast, he joined Indianapolis in the American Association for the 1952 season. After another good season and a half in Indianapolis, he earned a trip to the majors, taking a partial-season .332 average with him to Cleveland to finish the 1953 season.

In his first full year in the major leagues, he was a regular on their record-setting American League pennant winners in 1954, and contributed a .281 batting average to the team's success. His best season with the Indians was in 1955, when he hit .306 and slugged 22 home runs. After being traded, he enjoyed two more good years (1960–61) with the Chicago White Sox, when he posted marks of .315 with 12 home runs and .278 with 28 home runs. His last year in the major leagues, 1964, was also his last in baseball. During the early '50s he played winter ball in Ponce, Puerto Rico, with his best season coming in the winter of 1951–52, when he hit .294 and led the league with 9 homers.

Smith, B.B.H. (Babe)
Career: 1887   Position: p
Team: *New York Gorhams*

He was a pitcher with the New York Gorhams, one of eight teams that were charter members of the League of Colored Baseball Clubs in 1887. However, the league's existence was ephemeral, lasting only a week.

Smith, Buster
Career: 1932–33   Positions: p, 1b
Team: Birmingham Barons

A player with the Birmingham Black Barons in 1932 when the Negro Southern League was considered a major league, he pitched and also played first base. His career continued into the following season, when many of the better players returned North to the teams of the new Negro National League. That year Smith played first base and batted fifth in the order for the Birmingham Black Barons, who remained in the Negro Southern League.

Smith, C.
[see Smith, Marshall (Darknight)]

Smith, C.
Career: 1933–38   Position: c
Team: Birmingham Black Barons

He was a catcher with the Birmingham Black Barons, beginning in 1933 when the team was in the Negro Southern League, with his career extending to when the Black Barons were members of the Negro American League. In 1938, his last season, he shared the receiving responsibilities while batting in the lower part of the order.

Smith, Charles (Charlie, Chino)
Career: 1925–31   Positions: **of**, 2b
Teams: *Philadelphia Giants ('24), Pennsylvania Red Caps of New York ('25),* Brooklyn Royal Giants ('25–'27, '31), New York Lincoln Giants ('29–'30)
Bats: Left   Throws: Right
Height: 5'6"   Weight: 168
Born: 1903, Greenwood, S.C.
Died: Jan. 16, 1932

This compact dynamo who, according to Satchel Paige, was one of the two greatest hitters in the Negro Leagues, was a scrapper, arousing the fans and intimidating pitchers as he shot through the world of black baseball like a meteor, with a career as brief as it was bright.

Given the nickname ''Chino'' because of a slant across his eyes that lent him a bit of an Oriental appearance, he was also a good defensive outfielder and a fine base runner. However, it was as a hitter that he gained his greatest notoriety. A line-drive hitter whose line shots to all parts of the ballpark looked like frozen ropes, he had a good eye at the plate and rarely struck out. Going with the pitch to all fields, he hit everything thrown to him and respected no pitcher. Sometimes he would spit at a pitcher's best offerings as it came across the plate, taking two strikes, before lining a base hit back through the middle. Supremely confident at the plate, the little slugger had no weakness.

Batting third in the powerful New York Lincoln Giants' lineup, his records substantiate his reputation as a superior hitter. In an abbreviated seven-year career, Smith hit for a lifetime average of .423 in regular-season play, an identical average in exhibitions against major-leaguers, and .335 in the Cuban winter leagues. In 1930, in the first game ever played in Yankee Stadium by two black teams, he hit 2 home runs and a triple.

As a young man he worked as a redcap in New York's Pennsylvania Station, and played second base on their baseball team. Later that season he began his career with a top team, the Brooklyn Royal Giants. He is credited with averages of .341 in 1925 and .439 in 1927 before joining the New York Lincoln Giants in 1929. That season, he batted .464 and hit 23 home runs to lead the American Negro League in both categories, during the league's only year of existence. After the demise of the league, the Lincolns played as an independent ballclub, fighting the Homestead Grays for the eastern title before losing out at the end of the season.

This was the last season before his premature death, and he hit .468, his highest batting average ever. Not yet having reached his thirtieth birthday and still in his prime, many outstanding years lay ahead but he fell victim to an illness, thought to have been yellow fever. Baseball historians can only speculate about what Chino might have accomplished if he had enjoyed the luxury of a long career.

Smith, Charlie
Career: 1938   Position: lf
Team: Black Senators

He was a reserve left fielder with the Black Senators in 1938, their only year in the Negro National League.

Smith, Clarence
Career: 1921–33   Positions: **rf**, lf, 2b,
                              1b, manager
Teams: Columbus Buckeyes ('21), Detroit Stars ('22–'25, '33), Atlantic City Bacharach Giants ('27), Birmingham Black Barons ('29–'30), Baltimore Black Sox ('30), Columbia American Giants ('31), Cleveland Cubs ('31)
Bats: Right   Throws: Right
Height: 5'10"   Weight: 185

In 1927 he was the regular right fielder with the Eastern Colored League champion Bacharach Giants, hitting .353 from the fifth slot. Before coming to the Bacharachs he spent four seasons with the Detroit Stars, where he hit .286 and .340 in 1924–25, while also batting in the fifth slot.

A smart ballplayer, after leaving the Bacharachs the outfielder took the helm of the Birmingham Black Barons, hitting .390 in 1929, and often filling in at other positions when needed. Leaving Birmingham, he played briefly as an outfielder with the Baltimore Black Sox and the Cleveland Cubs before joining David Malarcher's Columbia American Giants as a first baseman. Most of his earlier years had been spent with the Detroit Stars, and he returned to Detroit to finish his career as a part-time starter in right field for the Stars in 1933. This was their last year in the Negro National League, and the team struggled to stay solvent but was unable to maintain a functioning franchise.

Smith, Cleveland (Cleo)
Career: 1922–31   Positions; 3b, ss, 2b, of
Teams: Baltimore Black Sox ('22–'24), Harrisburg Giants ('24), New York Lincoln Giants ('24–'25), *Chappie Johnson's Stars ('25),* Newark Stars ('26), Homestead Grays ('26–'27), Philadelphia Tigers ('28), Cuban House of David ('31)
Bats: Right   Throws: Right

Breaking in with a .319 batting average for the Baltimore Black Sox in 1922, he shared the starting second base position with the Black Sox in 1923, batting second in the order. In 1924 he began with the Sox, spent most of the season at Harrisburg as a substitute second baseman-outfielder, and finished the year with the New York Lincoln Giants as an alternate left fielder and utility man. In 1926 he was a regular at third base with the Homestead Grays, batting fifth in the order, and shared the starting assignment again the next season. His last year with a quality team was in 1931, when he played with the Cuban House of David.

Smith, Clyde (Carl, Boots)
Career: 1938   Position: 3b
Team: Pittsburgh Crawfords

This infielder played with the Pittsburgh Crawfords in 1938, his only year in the Negro Leagues.

Smith, Darknight
[see Smith, Marshall (Darknight)]

Smith, Dode
Career: 1942   Position: p
Team: Cincinnati Buckeyes

He pitched briefly with the Cincinnati Buckeyes in 1942, his only year in the Negro American League.

Smith, Douglas
Career: 1943   Position: officer
Team: Baltimore Elite Giants

He served as an official with the Baltimore Elite Giants in 1943.

Smith, Ed
Career: 1887   Position: player
Team: *Boston Resolutes*

He was a player with the Boston Resolutes, one of eight teams that were charter members of the League of Colored Baseball Clubs in 1887. However, the league's existence was ephemeral, lasting only a week. His position is uncertain.

Smith, Ernest
Career: 1934–40   Positions: c, of
Teams: *Monroe Monarchs,* **Chicago American Giants** ('39–'40)

He was a regular player for two years with the Chicago American Giants, playing primarily as an outfielder in 1939, but sharing the catching duties while batting sixth in the order in 1940.

Smith, Eugene (Gene, Genie)
Career: 1939–50   Position: p
Teams: Atlanta Black Crackers ('38), *Mexican League ('39),* Ethiopian Clowns ('39), St. Louis Stars ('39), New Orleans-St. Louis Stars ('40–'41), Kansas City Monarchs ('41), New York Black Yankees ('42), *military service ('43–'45), Pittsburgh Crawfords ('46),* Homestead Grays ('46–'47), Cleveland Buckeyes ('47–'48, '50), Louisville Buckeyes ('49), Chicago American Giants ('49–'51)
Bats: Both   Throws: Right
Height: 6'1"   Weight: 185

Regarded as a power pitcher, he had a good fastball and slider, which he used as his primary breaking pitch, since his curveball was somewhat lacking. He could change speeds, but his change-up and control were only average. After appearing in only 5 games and pitching ineffectively without a decision for Monterrey in the Mexican League in 1939, he joined the St. Louis Stars and two years later was one of the "Big Four" on the Stars' pitching staff. During his career he was credited with 3 no-hitters, and in 1941 he recorded one of his gems when he hurled a no-hitter against the New York Black Yankees. Ironically, when the Stars' franchise folded during the off-season, he signed with the Black Yankees for the 1942 season and was 3–5 for the year in league competition.

He entered military service after the season, spending three years in the Army. After his discharge in 1946, he joined the Homestead Grays and posted a 4–5 record for the year. After a 1–4 start with the Grays in 1947, he finished the season with the Cleveland Buckeyes, reversing his record with a 4–1 ledger for the Buckeyes as they captured the Negro American League pennant. In 1948 he dropped to a 2–6 pitching record, and when the franchise moved to Louisville in 1949, he signed with the Chicago American Giants. A strong performance in the "Windy City" resulted in a fine 9–3 record. In 1950 he pitched in only a single league game, but returned to the American Giants for the 1951 season before closing his career. In addition to his season in Mexico, he pitched in Puerto Rico and Canada. He was regarded as a good-hitting pitcher, as demonstrated by his .375 batting average in 1948, and he was a capable base runner and a good fielder. He was the brother of Quincy Smith, who was an outfielder in the Negro Leagues.

Smith, Eugene (Gene)
Career: 1942–46   Positions: **3b**, ss
Teams: Jacksonville Red Caps ('42), Cincinnati Buckeyes ('42), Indianapolis Clowns ('46)

Beginning as a third baseman with the Jacksonville Red Caps in 1942, his playing time was limited, and the team dropped out of league play during the season. Moving North, he landed with the Cincinnati Buckeyes as a reserve infielder for the remainder of the season. In the first post-World War II season he shared the starting shortstop position with the Indianapolis Clowns, hitting in the second slot.

Smith, F. (Lefty)
Career: 1920–24   Position: p

Teams: Baltimore Black Sox ('20–'24), *Richmond Giants ('24)*
Bats: Left   Throws: Left

This left-handed pitcher was one of the many Smiths who played with the Baltimore Black Sox during the early '20s. After leaving the Sox in 1924, he played with the Richmond Giants, a team of lesser quality.

Smith, Fred
Career: 1946   Position: c
Team: Kansas City Monarchs

In his only year in the Negro Leagues, he was with the Kansas City Monarchs briefly in 1946 as a fourth catcher.

Smith, Gunboat
Career: 1917   Position: of
Team: Pennsylvania Red Caps of New York

He was an outfielder with the Pennsylvania Red Caps of New York in 1917, his only year in black baseball.

Smith, H.
Career: 1922–29   Positions: **p**, of
Teams: Atlantic City Bacharach Giants ('22), Harrisburg Giants ('23), Washington Potomacs ('23–'24), Homestead Grays ('24), Baltimore Black Sox ('25, '29), *Ewing's All-Stars ('28)*

During the '20s he pitched with several eastern Colored League teams, but never as a top-line pitcher. Beginning his career with the Bacharachs in 1922, he received the most playing time with the Washington Potomacs before posting a 3–1 record with the Baltimore Black Sox in 1929, his last year.

Smith, Harry
Career: 1902–10   Positions: **1b**, of
Teams: Philadelphia Giants ('02–'05), Genuine Cuban Giants ('08), Brooklyn Royal Giants ('10)

A first baseman-outfielder, he was with the Philadelphia Giants during their formative years, including the year of their first championship, 1905, but not as a regular player. He later played with the Genuine Cuban Giants, one of the various ballclubs that flourished during the early years of the century, copying the success of the Cuban Giants and appropriating a variation of the Cuban Giants' name as their own. In 1910 he played as a substitute first-baseman with the eastern champion Brooklyn Royal Giants.

Smith, Harvey
Career: 1937–38   Position: p
Teams: Washington Elite Giants ('37), Pittsburgh Crawfords ('38)

This pitcher appeared briefly with the Washington Elite Giants and the Pittsburgh Crawfords during the late '30s.

Smith, Henry
Career: 1942–47   Positions: **2b**, ss, of, c
Teams: Jacksonville Red Caps ('41–'42), Chicago American Giants ('42–'43), Cincinnati Clowns ('43), Cincinnati-Indianapolis Clowns ('44–'45), Indianapolis Clowns ('46)
Bats: Right   Throws: Right
Height: 5'9"   Weight: 161
Born: 1914, Houston, Tex.

This infielder gained his first professional experience in the old Texas Negro Leagues before joining the Jacksonville Red Caps in 1941. When the Red Caps broke up during the 1942 season, he joined the Chicago American Giants for a short stint, batting a composite .227 for the year, although he continued to make his residence in Jacksonville. In 1943 he joined the Clowns, batting .241, .259, and .252 in 1944–46.

Smith, Herb
Career: 1930–33   Positions: **p**, of, 1b
Teams: Hilldale Daisies ('30), Baltimore Black Sox ('32), Philadelphia Stars ('33)

During his four years in black baseball, he pitched briefly with Hilldale in 1930, when they were playing as an independent team. Later he pitched under two well-known managers, posting a mark of 4–0 for Dick Lundy's 1932 Baltimore Black Sox in the East-West League, followed by a 2–1 work sheet for

Webster McDonald's 1933 Philadelphia Stars during their first year of existence when they were playing as an independent team.

Smith, Hilton Lee
Career: 1932–48   Positions: **p**, of, 1b
Teams: Monroe Monarchs ('32–'35), New Orleans Black Creoles ('33), New Orleans Crescent Stars ('33), **Kansas City Monarchs** ('36–'48)
Bats: Right   Throws: Right
Height: 6'2"   Weight: 180
Born: Feb. 27, 1912, Giddings, Tex.
Died: Nov. 18, 1983, Kansas City, Mo.

A teammate of Satchel Paige's on the Kansas City Monarchs, he was best known for being "Satchel's relief." After Satchel pitched 3 innings, Smith would come in and pitch the last 6 innings, with no appreciable difference in effectiveness. In October 1941, Bob Feller regarded him as even better than Paige. Yet because Smith's quietness contrasted with Satchel's flamboyance, Smith never received the publicity that Satchel attracted in abundance.

Possessing the best curveball in black baseball, many thought that Smith was the best all-around pitcher in the game. In addition to his superlative curves, he had a high, hard fastball that "took off," a sinker, a slider, and a change of pace, all of which he threw both sidearm or overhand, maintaining good control with both styles of delivery.

Smith began playing town ball with his father, a teacher by profession, in 1927, and continued his baseball when he attended Prairie View A&M College in Texas for two years. During his last season there, he began pitching, and afterward played semipro ball with the Austin Senators in 1931. The next season, as a 20-year old, he joined the Monarchs of Monroe, Louisiana, who were members of the Negro Southern League. In 1932 the league was recognized as a major league because of the influx of players from the defunct Negro National League.

For the next three years he played with

teams of lesser quality, including the New Orleans Crescent Stars, and pitched in the National Baseball Congress in Wichita in 1935–36, registering a perfect 5–0 slate, indicating that he was ready to step up to the black major leagues. In the fall of 1936 he began barnstorming with the Kansas City Monarchs, who became charter members of the Negro American League in 1937, and he became a mainstay with the franchise until his retirement after the 1948 season.

During his twelve years with the Monarchs, playing against all competition, the right-handed hurler won 20 or more games each year, pitched a no-hitter in 1937, and reportedly did not lose a league game in 1938. Over a six-year period he compiled a 129–28 ledger, with his best years coming in 1939–42, when he was credited with records of 25–2, 21–3, 25–1, and 22–5 against all opposition. In 1941 he is credited with a perfect 10–0 league ledger, suffering his loss in a nonleague contest. Also pitching two winters in Cuba during the late '30s, the native Texan compiled a 10–5 record on the island. A good hitter, Hilton often pinch hit and played first base or in the outfield.

The Monarchs' ace pitched in six consecutive All-Star games, 1937–42, striking out 13 batters, tying with Satchel Paige for second place on the all-time All-Star list, only one strikeout behind Leon Day. Smith was the winning pitcher in the 1938 contest, and his All-Star years coincided with the years of the Monarchs' domination in the Negro American League, a period during which they won five pennants in the first six years of the league's existence.

The last of these, 1942, was the year that the first Negro World Series was played between the Negro American League and the more established Negro National League. Smith pitched in this Series and again in the 1946 World Series, starting once in 1942 and twice in 1946 and winning a game in each Series for a composite 2–0 World Series record with a 1.29 ERA.

In 1943 Smith suffered an injury to his pitching arm, dropping to a .500 mark and splitting 8 league decisions for the war-weakened Monarchs, but the keen competitor bounced back in 1944 with a 2.74 ERA while turning in several one-hit gems and being credited with 8 strikeouts per game but managing only a 2–5 record in league contests. The next season the dependable hurler registered a 5–3 league ledger with a 2.31 ERA and, with many regulars lost to military service, the Monarchs sometimes utilized him as an outfielder, first baseman, or pinch hitter to take advantage of his batting skills.

His averages validate his ability with a bat, as he registered marks of .360 in 1942 and .333, .243, and .431 in 1944–46. In his assignments as an everyday player, his overall play was adequate, as he demonstrated an outstanding throwing arm and his hustle afield compensated for a lack of speed and other defensive deficiencies. In 1946, with the regulars back in the lineup after the War, he fashioned an 8–2 record to help pitch the Monarchs to the 1946 pennant.

That winter he pitched in Venezuela and fashioned an 8–5 record for the champion Vargas ballclub. In March, after the end of the winter season, he pitched for Vargas against the New York Yankees in Venezuela, and allowed the Yankees only 1 hit in 5 innings to earn the win in a 4–3 victory. With Jackie Robinson beginning his first spring with the Brooklyn Dodgers, the door to the major leagues was ajar, but Smith declined an offer from the Brooklyn organization, knowing that the invitation was a decade late. With a record of 6–1 in exhibition games against major-leaguers, once the color barrier was removed, his age was all that kept Smith from starring in the major leagues.

Back in the United States for the regular season, he forged a 7–3 mark for the 1947 season. But in 1948, at age thirty-six, after winning only a single league game against 2 losses, Smith decided to retire, leaving a lifetime ledger showing 161 wins against 32 losses in league play. After leaving the Monarchs he pitched two years in semipro ball in Fulda, New Mexico, before wrapping up his active baseball career. He entered the field of education as a teacher and coach, and afterward worked at Armco Steel until retiring in 1978. At the time of his death in 1983, he was an associate scout for the Chicago Cubs.

Smith, J.
Career: 1924–30   Positions: **ss**, 3b, 2b
Teams: Brooklyn Royal Giants ('24–'28), Detroit Stars ('25–'30)

This infielder played in the Eastern Colored League during the late '20s and also appeared with the Detroit Stars in the Negro National League.

Smith, J.
Career: 1925   Position: of
Team: Atlantic City Bacharach Giants

He was an outfielder with the Bacharachs in 1925, his only year in the Negro Leagues.

Smith, James
Career: 1903–06   Positions: ss, 3b, of
Teams: Chicago Union Giants ('03), Cuban X-Giants ('04), Leland Giants ('05–'06)

He had a year as the third baseman with the Cuban X-Giants in 1904 sandwiched between stints as shortstop with the Chicago Union Giants in his first season, and as the regular shortstop after joining the Leland Giants in their first year of existence, 1905.

Smith, John (Johnny, Lefty, Bill)
Career: 1940–48   Positions: of, 1b, p
Teams: Indianapolis Crawfords ('40), Chicago American Giants ('43–'45), New York Black Yankees ('46–'50)
Bats: Left   Throws: Left

After joining the Chicago American Giants in 1944–45, he hit .378 and .303 as the regular right fielder. In the latter season he batted in the third slot and also took a turn on the mound, but lost his only decision. The follow-

ing season he joined the New York Black Yankees and shared a starting outfield spot in 1947, usually hitting third in the batting order. As one of only eight holdovers in 1948, he was the starting right fielder and batted sixth in the order.

Smith, John Ford (Teniente, Geronimo)
Career: 1939–48   Positions: **p**, of, 1b
Teams: Chicago American Giants ('39), Indianapolis Crawfords ('40), **Kansas City Monarchs** ('41, '46–'48), *military service ('42–'45), minor leagues ('49–'50, '52–'54), Canadian League ('51)*
Bats: Both   Throws: Right
Height: 6'1"   Weight: 200
Born: Jan. 9, 1919, Phoenix, Ariz.
Died: Feb. 26, 1983, Phoenix, Ariz.

This hard-throwing right-hander had a good fastball, a moderately effective curve and change-up, and average control. He was one of the leading pitchers for the 1946 Negro American League pennant-winning Kansas City Monarchs, posting a 4–0 league ledger, and started 2 games in the World Series against the hard-hitting Newark Eagles, losing his only decision. During the seventh game he was pressed into service in the outfield due to the absence of Ted Strong, and played creditably.

He was a good-hitting pitcher (.288 batting average in 1948), and, when utilized as an outfielder, was an adequate fielder. The following year he had a 7–2 record with the Monarchs, and in 1948 he posted a 10–5 record with a 2.64 ERA in league play and was considered the top hurler in the Negro American League.

New York Giants' scouts watching the Monarchs expressed an interest in him and Hank Thompson. After a winter season with the Santurce Congrejeros, where he led the Puerto Rican League in victories, he signed with the Giants and was assigned to Jersey City, their AAA farm club in the International League. At Jersey City he was a teammate of Monte Irvin and fashioned a 10–8 record with a 4.15 ERA for the 1949 season. After another winter in the Caribbean, this time in Cuba, where he recorded an 8–6 work sheet, he was back with Jersey City in 1950, but had a disappointing 2–3 record despite a respectable 3.40 ERA.

In 1951 he pitched with Drummondville in the Provincial League and posted a 16–8, 2.97 ERA record. The next three years were spent near his home, in the Arizona-Texas League, where he had seasons of 13–4, 3.91 ERA and 11–14, 5.65 ERA with Phoenix and a 9–3, 3.54 season with El Paso in 1954, his final season. During his career he also pitched in the Dominican Republic.

His professional career was interrupted by military service in World War II, where he earned the rank of lieutenant in the Air Corps. After wrapping up his baseball career, he worked in the Phoenix Union High School system, was the executive director of the Arizona State Civil Rights Commission, and was vice president of the Civil Rights Department with the Arizona Bank.

Smith, L.
Career: 1942   Position: c
Team: Jacksonville Red Caps

He was a catcher with the Jacksonville Red Caps in 1942, before the team dropped out of league play later in the season.

Smith, Lefty
Career: 1920–21   Positions: p, of
Team: Kansas City Monarchs

He was a pitcher with the Kansas City Monarchs during the first two seasons of the Negro National League.

Smith, Lefty
[see Smith, John (Johnny, Lefty, Bill)]

Smith, Lefty
[see Smith, Wyman (Lefty)]

Smith, Marshall (Darknight)
a.k.a. C. Smith
Career: 1921–24   Position: p
Teams: *Madison Stars ('20)*, Baltimore Black Sox ('21–'23), *Richmond Giants ('23)*, Home-

stead Grays ('24), *Chappie Johnson's Stars ('25–'27)*
Bats: Left   Throws: Left

This left-handed pitcher played with the Baltimore Black Sox for three years, posting a 10–4 mark as a new recruit in 1921 and following with a 5–2 mark in 1922. He was one of three Smiths who were with the Black Sox in that season. While still the property of the Black Sox, he went to the Homestead Grays in the summer of 1924, but was released by the Grays later in the year. He then joined Chappie Johnson's Stars, a team of lesser quality, for three additional seasons.

Smith, Milton (Milt)
Career: 1949–50   Positions: **2b**, ss, 3b
Teams: Philadelphia Stars ('49–'51), *minor leagues ('52–'61)*, major leagues ('55)
Bats: Right   Throws: Right
Height: 5'10"   Weight: 165
Born: Mar. 27, 1929, Columbus, Ga.

In 1949–50, his first two seasons with the Philadelphia Stars, he hit for averages of .205 and .224. The Stars were playing in the Negro American League after the Negro National League folded following the 1948 season. After playing with the Stars in 1951, he entered organized baseball, hitting .318 with good power and 42 stolen bases for Lewiston in the Western International League. He began the next season in the same league with Salem and was hitting .391 at midseason when he moved up to the Pacific Coast League, finishing the year with San Diego.

In 1955 he was hitting .338 when he was called up to the major leagues with the Cincinnati Reds. Playing at both third base and second base, he hit only .196 for the remainder of the season. He played for six more years in the high minors (Pacific Coast League, International League, American Association) but never got another chance at the majors. During this time he also played winter ball in Cuba (.268), Panama (.279), and in the Dominican Republic (.287). His final year in baseball was 1961.

Smith, Monroe **Mance**
Career: 1944   Position: of
Team: Kansas City Monarchs
Bats: Right   Throws: Right
Height: 5'10"   Weight: 160

He was a wartime player, playing right field and hitting .225 while batting sixth in the order, with the Kansas City Monarchs in 1944, his only year in the Negro Leagues.

Smith, Oliver (**Ollie**)
Career: 1945   Position: p
Teams: Cincinnati-Indianapolis Clowns
Bats: Right   Throws: Right
Height: 6'1"   Weight: 202
Born: c. 1918, Edison, Ga.

A wartime player with raw potential, this big right-hander was viewed as being capable of becoming an outstanding hurler and, after a year with the Fort Lauderdale Giants, he had a trial with the Cincinnati-Indianapolis Clowns in 1945, but was winless in league play while suffering 3 losses. Although showing glimpses of promise, his lack of polish was apparent, and he was farmed out to the Mobile Black Shippers for more experience.

Smith, P.
Career: 1939   Position: p
Team: St. Louis Stars

He pitched with the St. Louis Stars in 1939, in his only year in the Negro Leagues.

Smith, Pete
Career: 1937   Position: of
Team: Pittsburgh Crawfords

When Satchel Paige and several other Crawford players jumped the team in 1937 to play in Santo Domingo, a large number of potential replacements were given a chance to earn a place on the roster with the Crawfords. This outfielder was among those appearing briefly during this time.

Smith, Quincy
Career: 1943–46   Position: of
Teams: Cleveland Buckeyes ('43), Bir-
mingham Black Barons ('45), *Mexican League ('45), Pittsburgh Crawfords ('46), minor leagues ('49–'54)*
Bats: Both   Throws: Right
Height: 5'10½"   Weight: 171
Born: 1921

This switch-hitting outfielder had a wartime career in the Negro American League before playing in Mexico, and in the minor leagues after the doors opened to organized baseball. He began his career with the Cleveland Buckeyes in 1943 and played the first half of 1945 with the Birmingham Black Barons before jumping to the Mexico City Reds. His averages in each league were about the same, hitting .284 with Birmingham and .287 in the Mexican League. His entire minor-league career was spent in the Mississippi-Ohio Valley League, mostly with the Paris ballclub, where he hit .279, .313, .306, .317, .314, and .292, while demonstrating good power and basestealing ability, during his six seasons (1949–54) in the league. He was the brother of Gene Smith, who pitched in the Negro Leagues.

Smith, R.
Career: 1912–17   Positions: p, of
Teams: New York Lincoln Giants ('12), New York Lincoln Stars ('16), Atlantic City Bacharach Giants ('17)

During the '10s he appeared as a pitcher and outfielder with the New York Lincoln Giants, the New York Lincoln Stars, and the Atlantic City Bacharach Giants.

Smith, Raymond D.
Career: 1945–46   Position: p
Team: Philadelphia Stars ('45–'46)

He pitched with the Philadelphia Stars for two years, 1945–46, without appreciable success.

Smith, Robert (**Bob,** Jake, Turkey)
Career: 1930–44   Positions: **c,** of, 3b, 1b
Teams: Birmingham Black Barons ('30), Cleveland Cubs ('31), Nashville Elite Giants ('32–'33), Memphis Red Sox ('33, '36–'38,

'42), Cincinnati Tigers ('35–'37), Chicago American Giants ('38, '42, '44), St. Louis Stars ('39), New Orleans-St. Louis Stars ('40–'41), Pittsburgh Crawfords

Bats: Right　　　　Throws: Right
Height: 5'10"　　　Weight: 170
Born: 1908

A good receiver, this Memphis native had a good throwing arm and was one of smartest catchers in the Negro American League. He was a fair hitter but regarded as dangerous in the clutch, and was a fast base runner. In 1930, his first season, he hit .269, but in his last season, fourteen years later, he batted only .129 with the Chicago American Giants.

Smith, Taylor

Career: 1948–49　　　Position: p
Teams: Chicago American Giants ('48–'49), *Birmingham Black Barons ('52, '58)*

Beginning his career in 1948, this pitcher posted a 4-5 record in 1949 with the Chicago American Giants. In the '50s, when the Negro American League had declined to a minor-league status, he continued pitching, with the Birmingham Black Barons.

Smith, Theolic (Fireball, Theo)

Career: 1936–43, 1949 Positions: **p**, of
Teams: Pittsburgh Crawfords ('36–'38), Toledo Crawfords ('39), St. Louis Stars ('39), New Orleans-St. Louis Stars ('40), Cleveland Buckeyes ('43), Kansas City Monarchs ('45, '49,) Chicago American Giants ('48–'49, *'51), Mexican League ('44–'48), minor leagues ('52–'55)*

Bats: Both　　　　Throws: Right
Height: 6'0"　　　Weight: 175
Born: May 19, 1914, St. Louis, Mo.

A fastball pitcher who earned the nickname "Fireball," this right-hander also had a good knuckler and a pretty good curve and change-up, but experienced some control problems. Smith broke in with the Pittsburgh Crawfords in 1936, with an unimpressive 1–2 record, but three years later, representing the St. Louis Stars, he made his first All-Star appearance.

After a 7–5 record with the Cleveland Buckeyes, he appeared in his second All-Star game, without a decision in either game.

In 1940 he jumped to Mexico and, except for the 1943 season, played with Mexico City through 1948. His first season in the Mexican League was one of his best, posting a 19–9 mark with a 3.49 ERA. He never failed to reach double-digit victories until his last season in the league, posting seasons of 16–8, 13–11, 16–15, 15–16, and 11–10 through 1946. The next year was his best as he fashioned a 22–10 work sheet with a 2.77 ERA for the 1947 season. He was an established star in Mexico, recording 48 victories over the course of three years (1940–42) prior to returning to the United States due to the war effort. Pitching with the Buckeyes in 1943, he managed only a 6–6 record, but had a string of 23 consecutive scoreless innings early in the year and was selected for the All-Star game.

The next year, during the height of World War II, eighty thousand Mexican workers were exchanged so he and Quincy Trouppe could leave their defense jobs and play in Mexico. Although he was listed on the Kansas City Monarchs' roster in 1945, there is no evidence that he actually played with the team, and deferred from military service, he stayed in Mexico through 1948.

A good hitter with moderate power, he sometimes played in the outfield, and while only an average player in the field and on the bases, he was a good hustler. After a losing season in 1948 (9–11), he returned to the United States, splitting two decisions for the Chicago American Giants for the last part of the year. In 1949 he spent the entire season with Chicago, posting a 4–5 mark with a 5.07 ERA.

Beginning in 1952, at age thirty-eight, he pitched for four years with San Diego in the Pacific Coast League, where he had an aggregate 27–29 ledger, closing out his career in 1955 at age forty-one. During his career he spent two winter seasons in Cuba, spread ten years apart, and had a composite 5–9 record on the island.

Smith, W.
Career: 1921, 1925   Positions: **ss**, p, 3b
Teams: Hilldale Daisies ('21), New York Lincoln Giants ('25)

He made two appearances in black baseball, in 1921 with Hilldale, and four years later with the Lincoln Giants. In his season with Hilldale he batted only .174 but registered a 3–0 mark as a pitcher.

Smith, Wardell
Career: 1946   Position: p
Team: Chicago American Giants

He pitched with the Chicago American Giants in 1946, his only year in the Negro Leagues.

Smith, William
Career: 1938   Positions: 2b, ss
Team: Newark Eagles

This middle infielder played briefly with the Newark Eagles in 1938, his only year in the Negro National League.

Smith, William T. (Big Bill)
Career: 1888–1913;   Positions: of, c, p, manager, 3b, 2b, 1b
1914
Teams: Chicago Unions ('89–'98), Cuban Giants ('97, '99–'00; '14), Genuine Cuban Giants ('00), Cuban X-Giants ('00, '03–'04), Philadelphia Giants ('09), Brooklyn Royal Giants ('05–'06, '11), Mohawk Giants ('13), *Memphis Giants ('16)*

An all-purpose player, he started as a pitcher with the Chicago Unions in 1889 and was an outfielder, infielder, and part-time pitcher until about the turn of the century and was a catcher after the turn of the century. In his last appearance in black baseball, in 1916, he managed the Memphis Giants.

Smith, William D. (**Willie**)
Career: 1948   Position: p

Team: Homestead Grays
Bats: Right   Throws: Right
Height: 6'2"   Weight: 173
Born: Apr. 19, 1915, Boswell, Ala.

He pitched with the Homestead Grays as a rookie in 1948 after a year with the L & N ballclub in 1947.

Smith, Wyman (Lefty)
Career: 1920–25   Position: of
Teams: Baltimore Black Sox ('20–'25), Homestead Grays ('24)
Bats: Left   Throws: Left

A good fielder and considered one of the best hitters in the league, batting .352 and .332 in 1921–22, he had become a fixture with the Baltimore Black Sox when he quit the team in the summer of 1924 and joined the Homestead Grays, apparently while he was still the property of the Baltimore club, who placed him on their reserved roster for 1925. He usually batted in the third or fifth slot in the lineup with the Black Sox and was one of three Smiths on the Baltimore roster in 1922.

Smoot
Career: 1886   Position: ss
Team: *New York Gorhams*

In 1886 he was shortstop with the New York Gorhams, one of the earliest black ballclubs. A year later the Gorhams became one of eight teams that were charter members of the abortive League of Colored Baseball Clubs.

Snaer, Lucien
Career: 1923   Position: umpire
League: Negro National League

He was an umpire in the Negro National League for the 1923 season.

Snead
Career: 1938   Position: 3b
Team: Homestead Grays

He was one of the players tried by the Homestead Grays in 1938 in an effort to fill a hole at third base. He played briefly in the early spring.

Snead, Sylvestor
a.k.a. Sneed
Career: 1939–46   Positions: of, 2b, ss
Teams: Ethiopian Clowns ('39–'40), Kansas City Monarchs ('41), Cincinnati Clowns ('43), New York Black Yankees ('46), *minor leagues ('50), Canadian League ('51)*
Bats: Right   Throws: Right
Height: 5'10"   Weight:170

One of the leading characters in the Ethiopian Clowns' comedy routines, he continued to entertain the crowds with his antics after the team entered the Negro American League and began playing under the name of the Indianapolis Clowns. In his prime, in addition to his clowning routines, he was also a legitimate performer on the baseball diamond. He was a fair hitter and average fielder, but had good speed, plenty of hustle, and could bunt, steal bases, and execute the hit-and-run play. In 1946 he played with the New York Black Yankees and hit .253. He also played in the Mandak League, hitting .253 with Elmwood in 1950, and in the Provincial League, hitting .174 as a catcher-first baseman in 1951.

Sneed Eddie (Lefty)
Career: 1940–42   Position: p
Team: Birmingham Black Barons
Bats: Left   Throws: Left

He was a pitcher with the Birmingham Black Barons in the early '40s, losing his only decision in 1941.

Sneed, Sylvestor
[see Snead, Sylvestor]

Sneeden
Career: 1894   Position: cf
Team: Cuban Giants

This center fielder was a member of the Cuban Giants in 1894, when they were the only professional black team in baseball.

Snow, Felton (Mammy, Skipper)
Career: 1931–47   Positions: **3b**, 2b, ss, of, p, manager
Teams: Louisville Black Caps ('29–'30, '32), Louisville White Sox ('31), Nashville Elite Giants ('33–'34), Cleveland Red Sox ('34), Columbus Elite Giants ('35), Washington Elite Giants ('36–'37), **Baltimore Elite Giants** ('38–'46), *Nashville Cubs ('48–'49), New Orleans Crescent Stars ('50)*
Bats: Right   Throws: Right
Height: 5'10"   Weight: 158
Born: Oct. 23, 1905, Oxford, Ala.

Though not a showman afield, he handled himself well and could make all the plays. Snow had a rifle arm, was a solid hitter with moderate power and, although not a basestealing threat, was a smart base runner. The Elite Giants' standout third baseman was on the West squad in the East-West All-Star games of 1935 and 1936, rapping 2 hits in 3 at-bats in the midseason classic. During this time he hit .322 in the 1933–34 California winter league, played with the Royal Giants in the winter of 1935, and was on the Negro National League All-Star team that completely dominated opposition in the *Denver Post* Tournament in 1936.

As a ten-year-old youngster he moved from Alabama to Louisville and learned to play baseball on the sandlots of that city. He began his professional career in 1929, playing for the Louisville ballclubs in the Negro Southern League before the White Sox entered the Negro National League in 1931. After four years in Louisville, he and teammate Sammy T. Hughes joined Tom Wilson's Elites in the spring of 1933, when the team was based in Nashville, and batted .247 for the season. He spent most of his career with the franchise, moving with the team to Columbus, Washington, and Baltimore. In 1939 he hit .301 for the season, and the Elites won a postseason four-team playoff over the Homestead Grays.

Snow was appointed playing manager in 1940, guiding the ballclub for seven straight seasons while playing third base and contributing batting averages of .333, .227, .269, .200, .270, .245, and .306. He usually penciled himself in the lower part of the batting order but sometimes hit in the second slot. He was a shrewd strategist, guiding the team to strong finishes every year while at the helm, with his best team coming in 1942, when they led the league for most of the year before losing to the Homestead Grays in the last week of the season. He was replaced in 1947, and managed lesser teams for another three seasons.

Snowden
Career: 1933   Position: p
Team: Detroit Stars

In 1933, his only year with a league team, he pitched with the Detroit Stars, posting a 1–4 mark in their last season in the Negro National League.

Snyder
Career: 1943   Position: of
Team: New York Cubans

He was an outfielder with the New York Cubans in 1943, his only year in the Negro National League.

Sockard
[see Stockard, Theodore (Licks)]

Soldero
Career: 1932   Position: p
Team: Cuban Stars (West)

He pitched briefly with the Cuban Stars in 1932, when they were in the East-West League.

Solis, Miguel L.
Career: 1928–34   Position: **3b**, 2b
Team: Cuban Stars (East)

He began his career with the Cuban Stars in the Eastern Colored League in 1928, playing third base and usually hitting in the heart of the batting order. After the collapse of the Eastern Colored League, the Cubans played in the American Negro League in 1929 and Solis was the regular third baseman, batting fifth in the order, but that league folded after only a season. With the exception of a partial season in the ill-fated East-West League in 1932, the Cubans played as an independent team for the remainder of Solis's tenure with the team. His last season in the Negro Leagues was in 1934.

Sosa, Ramon
a.k.a. Soss
Career: 1948   Position: c
Team: Homestead Grays
Bats: Right   Throws: Right
Height: 5'8"   Weight: 170
Born: Dec. 23, 1918, Cuba

This Cuban catcher was a reserve with the Homestead Grays in 1948, during their last pennant-winning season. He earned a chance with the Grays after making a good showing in his home country. He won the Cuban batting title in 1946 and played with Marianao in the Cuban League in 1947 before joining the Grays.

Soss, Ramon
[see Sosa, Ramon]

Sostro, Francisco
a.k.a. Sostre
Career: 1947   Position: p
Teams: New York Black Yankees, New York Cubans
Bats: Right   Throws: Right

This right-hander pitched briefly with the New York Black Yankees and the New York Cubans in 1947, his only year in the Negro Leagues.

Souell, Herbert (**Herb**, Baldy)
a.k.a. Herb Cyrus
Career: 1940–50   Positions: **3b**, of
Teams: Satchel Paige's All-Stars ('39), Kansas City Monarchs ('40–'51), *minor leagues ('52–'54)*
Bats: Both   Throws: Right
Height: 5'10"   Weight: 170
Born: Feb. 5, 1913, West Monroe, La.

A solid, dependable third baseman with

good hustle and an average throwing arm, he had good speed and was a good base runner. At the plate he was a respected hitter, with modest power, and at his best with men on base. He was also a good bunter and hit-and-run man, who usually batted in the second slot.

He was the Kansas City Monarchs' regular third baseman during most of the 1940s, but when he first joined the team, he was listed by the last name of Cyrus, and played under this name while sharing third-base duties with Newt Allen during the 1942 season. The Monarchs copped the Negro American League pennant and swept the Negro National League champion Homestead Grays in the ensuing World Series, the first ever between the two leagues. In 1943 he began playing under the name Souell, hit in the third slot, and took over the third-base chores exclusively. The next two years, 1944–45, he recorded batting averages of .244 and .277, moving to the second slot in the latter season. In 1946, when the Monarchs again won the Negro American League pennant and faced the Newark Eagles in the World Series, Souell hit .316 for the regular season and .344 in the Series, albeit a losing one.

In three of the next four seasons, Souell was the West squad's third baseman in the East-West game, getting the starting nod in the 1947, 1948, and 1950 All-Star games, batting second in the order in each contest. He earned his berth during the middle year with a .302 batting average in league play, and hit for averages of .269 and .301 in 1949–50.

Leaving the Monarchs in 1951, he played with Carman in the Mandak League for three years, hitting .306 (with 7 homers in 212 at-bats) in his first season and .302 (with 5 homers in 318 at-bats) in his last season. In the middle year he played with two other teams in addition to Carman, primarily with Tucson in the Arizona-Texas League (.297) but also with Spokane in the Western International League (.264).

Southall, John
Career: 1898   Position: c
Team: *Celeron Acme Colored Giants*

In 1898 Harry Curtis, a white man, formed an all-black team dubbed the Acme Colored Giants to play in the Iron and Oil League as representatives of Celeron, New York. Both the team and the league folded in July, and it was to be the last time a black team played in a white league.

Southy
Career: 1921   Position: ss
Team: New York Lincoln Giants

In his only year with a top ballclub, he was the regular shortstop with the New York Lincoln Giants in 1921, hitting seventh in the batting order while filling a problem spot in the lineup. Not until Bill Yancey joined the team at the end of the decade did the Lincoln Giants finally solve their shortstop problem.

Sowell, Clyde
Career: 1948   Position: p
Team: Baltimore Elite Giants

He pitched with the Baltimore Elite Giants in 1948, the last year of the Negro National League's existence.

Sowen
Career: 1933   Position: ss
Team: Cuban Stars

In 1933 he was a reserve shortstop with the Cuban Stars.

Sparks, Joe
Career: 1937–40   Positions: **2b**, ss, 3b, lf
Teams: St. Louis Stars ('37), Chicago American Giants ('37–'40)
Bats: Left   Throws: Right
Height: 5'8"   Weight: 160

This middle infielder from Oklahoma was a part-time starter at second base with the Chicago American Giants in 1937, and after Ormand Sampson moved behind the plate in 1938, Sparks moved into the vacated shortstop position and continued to share the starting assignments through the next season. In 1940, his last year in the Negro Leagues, he was a regular but split his playing time between second base and third base. During his four seasons with the Chicago American Giants, he was usually placed in the lower part of the batting order.

Sparrow, Roy W.
Career: 1938   Position: officer
Team: Washington Black Senators

He was an officer with the Washington Black Senators during their half season in the Negro National League in 1938. The franchise folded at the end of the first half in their only year in the league.

Spearman, Alvin
Career: 1950   Position: p
Teams: Chicago American Giants ('50–'51), *minor leagues ('52–'59)*
Bats: Right   Throws: Right

This right-hander's career in the Negro Leagues was brief; he went winless (0–3) in 5 games with the Chicago American Giants in 1950 during the Negro American League's declining years. After a second season with the Chicago American Giants, he entered organized ball, with Lewiston in the Western International League in 1952. The next season he pitched in three games without a decision with Decatur in the Mississippi-Ohio Valley League. After encountering no appreciable success until 1956, he strung together three successive winning seasons with Stockton in the California League, with records of 18–3 (2.62 ERA), 14–4 (2.73 ERA), and 20–9 (2.60 ERA). In 1959, his last season, he managed only a 3–9 record with Houston in the Texas League.

Spearman, Charles
Career: 1919–31   Positions: c, of, 2b, 3b, ss
Teams: **Brooklyn Royal Giants** ('19–'26), Cleveland Elites ('26), Homestead Grays ('27), New York Lincoln Giants ('28–'29), *Pennsylvania Red Caps of New York ('30–'31)*

A good-hitting catcher, he hit in the fifth slot for most of his career, but sometimes was dropped lower in the batting order. He was the regular catcher with the Royal Giants in 1923 and shared the catching duties until leaving the team during the 1926 season. His batting averages during this time include .200, .345, and .333 for the 1924–26 seasons. After joining the Cleveland Elites' ballclub, he played at third base, second base, and in the outfield. But the next season, he was back behind the plate with the Homestead Grays, leaving after a season to join the New York Lincoln Giants, where he shared the catching assignments for two seasons before moving to a lesser team.

Spearman, Clyde (Big Splo)
Career: 1932–46   Positions: **rf**, lf, cf, *3b*
Teams: Pittsburgh Crawfords ('32), New York Black Yankees ('34–'36, '46), New York Cubans ('35), *Santo Domingo ('37)*, Philadelphia Stars ('38–'39, '44–'45), Newark Eagles, Chicago American Giants ('41–'42), Birmingham Black Barons ('43)
Bats: Left   Throws: Right
Height: 5'9"   Weight: 175
Born: Arkadelphia, Ark.

One of five baseball-playing brothers, he was the older half of the brother combination known as "Big Splo" and "Little Splo." Although smaller than his brother Henry, he was called "Big Splo" because he was older. An outfielder, he was a good hitter with good power, was an overall good defensive player with an average arm, and had a little above average speed.

He began his career with the Pittsburgh Crawfords in 1932, hitting .247, but after a brief stint with Gus Greenlee's team he joined the New York Black Yankees. His next stop was with the New York Cubans, winners of the second-half Negro National League title in 1935 before losing the ensuing championship playoff to the Pittsburgh Crawfords. Spearman contributed averages of .300 and .359 for the Cubans in 1935–36, but in 1937 he jumped to Santo Domingo and, playing for the Aguilas

Cibaenas team, hit for a .352 average, second in the league to Josh Gibson.

The next season he was back in the Negro National League, playing right field with the Philadelphia Stars and batting in the leadoff spot, and in 1939 he hit .306. In 1941 he jumped to the Negro American League, playing right field with the Chicago American Giants and hitting second in the batting order. After a winter playing with the Baltimore Giants on the West Coast, he changed teams again, playing the 1943 season in right field for the Birmingham Black Barons and batting third in the order.

Spearman, Henry (Little Splo, Jake)
Career: 1936–46   Positions: **3b**, 1b
Teams: Newark Eagles ('36), Homestead Grays ('36–'39), Pittsburgh Crawfords ('37), Washington Black Senators ('38), New York Black Yankees ('40), Baltimore Elite Giants ('41–'42), Philadelphia Stars ('42–'45)
Bats: Right   Throws: Right
Height: 6'   Weight: 185
Born: 1911, Arkadelphia, Ark.

One of five baseball-playing brothers, he was the younger half of the brother combination known as "Big Splo" and "Little Splo." Although bigger than his brother Clyde, he was called "Little Splo" because he was younger. Perhaps not quite as proficient at the plate as his older brother, he was still a good hitter with good power, batting .392 with the Homestead Grays in 1936 and, with the Philadelphia Stars in mid-July of 1942, was hitting .370, tops on the club, but was called "swingtime" because of his high strikeout ratio.

In 1938 he played third base with the Washington Black Senators, batting fifth in the order, but when the team faltered and failed to field a team for the second half, he was again secured by the Homestead Grays to fill a need at third base. With Spearman added to their lineup they fielded their strongest team during their dynasty period. Hitting third in the order, he batted .344 for the season and followed with

a .415 batting average the next season, although dropped to sixth in the lineup.

In 1940 he played thirdbase with the New York Black Yankees, hitting .342 while batting cleanup. But after a year he left to join the Baltimore Elite Giants, where he found himself in the lower part of the batting order, and his average dropping to .254 for the 1941 season. In 1942 he joined the Philadelphia Stars, usually batting fifth in the order and hitting .299 and .292 in 1943–44, before dropping to .192 after losing his starting position in 1945. After only one more season, he was out of baseball.

Spearman, William (Bill)
Career: 1923–29   Positions: **p**, *of*
Teams: Memphis Red Sox ('23–'25), Cleveland Elites ('26–'27), Cleveland Hornets ('27), *Nashville Elite Giants ('27–'29)*, St. Louis Stars ('29)

A pitcher with several teams during the '20s, he began his career with the Memphis Red Sox in 1923 and closed out with the St. Louis Stars in 1929. In between, he pitched with the Cleveland entries in the Negro National League, the Elites in 1926 and the Hornets in 1927, fashioning identical 1–3 marks each season. He also sometimes played in the outfield, batting .214 in 1926.

Spedden, Charles P.
Career: 1922–31   Positions: officer, owner
Team: Baltimore Black Sox

A white businessman, he was owner and officer with the Baltimore Black Sox for a decade and oversaw their entry into the Eastern Colored League, remaining until the league collapsed early in the 1928 season. The next year he entered the team in the replacement league, and his team won the American Negro League's only championship.

Speedy, Walter
Career: 1914   Position: if
Team: Chicago American Giants

He appeared briefly in 1914 as an infielder with the Chicago American Giants.

Spencer

Career: 1921–22   Position: of
Team: Pittsburgh Keystones.

He was an outfielder with the Pittsburgh Keystones in 1922, their only season in the Negro National League.

Spencer, Joseph B. (Joe, J. B., J. C.)

Career: 1942–48   Positions: 2b, 3b, ss, of, c
Teams: Newark Eagles ('43), Baltimore Elite Giants ('43, '47), Homestead Grays ('43–'44), Birmingham Black Barons ('45), New York Cubans ('46), New York Black Yankees ('46–'48), *Pittsburgh Crawfords, minor leagues ('51)*
Bats: Right   Throws: Right
Height: 5'9"   Weight: 150

An average fielder and base runner, but weak at the plate with neither consistency nor power, this infielder began his career as a wartime player. Landing with the Homestead Grays in 1943, he became a part-time starter in 1944 while batting in the lower part of the order as the Homestead Grays won pennants both years and defeated the Birmingham Black Barons in the World Series each year.

In 1945 he switched to the Black Barons for a season, batting only .191 during his stint in Birmingham, then returning to the Negro National League in 1946 as a substitute with the New York Cubans. Leaving the Cubans to join the Black Yankees, he was a reserve in 1947, batting only .179 in limited play, but worked in as a part-time starter at third base in 1948, batting in the eighth slot when in the lineup.

After the breakup of the Negro National League in 1948, he eventually found his way into organized baseball, where he played with Elmwood in the Mandak League in 1951, batting .239 with 3 home runs in 201 at-bats, and with Sweetwater in the Longhorn League, where he hit .288.

Spencer, Willie (Pee Wee)

Career: 1933–41   Positions: rf, 3b, c
Teams: Chicago American Giants ('33), To-ledo Crawfords ('39), Indianapolis Crawfords ('40), Birmingham Black Barons ('41), *Toledo Cubs ('45)*

Hitting in the lower half of the batting order as the regular right fielder for the Crawfords in 1939–40, he also split his playing time at third base when the ballclub was in Toledo and as a catcher when the team was in Indianapolis. After the Crawfords franchise folded, he played with the Birmingham Black Barons as a substitute outfielder in 1941. Afterward he played with lesser teams, including the Toledo Cubs in the United States League.

Spencer, Zack

Career: 1931–33   Position: p
Teams: Chicago Columbia Giants ('31), Cleveland Cubs ('31), Detroit Stars ('31), Columbus Blue Birds ('33)

A marginal player, in 1931 he pitched with three teams—the Detroit Stars, the Cleveland Cubs, and David Malarcher's Chicago Columbia Giants—without a recorded decision. In 1933 he pitched with the Columbus Blue Birds during their brief membership in the Negro National League to close out his career.

Spike

Career: 1923   Positions: p, of
Team: Washington Potomacs

He played with the Washington Potomacs in 1923, their only year in the Negro National League.

Spottsville, Roy (Bill)

Career: 1950   Position: p
Teams: Houston Eagles ('50), *New Orleans Eagles ('51)*

He began his pitching career with the Houston Eagles, recording a 3–4 mark in 1950, when the Negro American League was struggling to survive the loss of players to organized baseball. When the Eagles moved to New Orleans in 1951, he relocated with the team, but the ballclub was strictly a minor-league franchise at that time.

St. Louis Giants

Duration: 1909–21   Honors: City League championship ('12–'13)

Affiliations: Independent ('09–'19), Negro National League ('20–'21)

Originally organized in 1909 by a white businessman, Charlie Mills, in partnership with Dr. Key, in 1910 the team played at the old Athletic Park until 1914, when they moved to Kuebler's Park. They won the City League championship in 1912–13 but subsequently had some troubled years and broke up temporarily in the spring of 1917. After reorganizing shortly afterward, the team became a charter member of the Negro National League in 1920. The next year the Giants finished in third place with a 33–23 record for a .589 winning percentage. After two seasons in the league, the franchise changed ownership and acquired a new nickname, the Stars.

St. Louis Stars

Duration: 1922–31   Honors: NNL pennant ('28, '30, '31), NNL second-half title ('25)

Affiliation: Negro National League ('22–'31)

The Stars were a continuation of a franchise originally organized as the St. Louis Giants in 1909 by a white businessman, Charlie Mills. The Giants were a charter member of the Negro National League in 1920, and after two seasons in the league, Mills sold the franchise to Dick Kemp and Dr. Sam Sheppard. Under the new ownership, the name was changed and the ballclub became the St. Louis Stars.

In their first year as the Stars, the team finished at an even .500 for the season. In 1923 the Stars experienced a losing season for the only time in their history, while remaining in the Negro National League until its demise following the 1931 season. In 1925 they won the second-half title of the split season but lost a seven-game series to the Kansas City Monarchs, winners of the first half, 4 games to 3. After this initial setback, the Stars won three pennants, in 1928, 1930, and 1931, winning

playoffs the first two seasons against the Chicago American Giants and the Detroit Stars, respectively. Their third flag was the last one in the history of the league that Rube Foster founded and, following the lead of the league itself, the Stars disbanded following the 1931 season.

Six years later, a new franchise bearing the same name became a charter member of the Negro American League, fielding teams in 1937 and 1939. Trying to survive, the franchise shifted to a cohometown status, pairing St. Louis with other cities—New Orleans in 1940–41 and Harrisburg in 1943.

St. Louis Stars

Duration: 1937–43   Honors: Negro American League second-half title ('39)

Affiliation: Negro American League ('37, '39, '41), independent ('40), Negro National League ('43)

In 1937, six years after the original St. Louis Stars disbanded, a new franchise bearing the same name became a charter member of the Negro American League in 1937. Two years later the Indianapolis ABCs shifted their franchise to St. Louis and became the St. Louis Stars. In 1939 they won the second-half title in the split season but lost the playoff to the Kansas City Monarchs, 3 games to 2. Struggling for financial survival, the franchise shifted to a cohometown status, pairing St. Louis with other cities—New Orleans in 1940–41 and Harrisburg in 1943. In 1940 the team played as an independent but returned to the Negro American League the following year. After disbanding for a year, they made a final effort to organize in 1943, when they were entered in the Negro National League, but withdrew early in the spring to barnstorm against a team headlining Dizzy Dean, and were promptly suspended by the league.

St. Paul Gophers

Duration: 1909   Honors: West championship ('09)

Affiliation: Independent ('09)

In 1909, the team based in St. Paul, Minnesota, won the championship of the West from the Leland Giants in a playoff. After their season in the sun, the team disbanded the following year.

St. Thomas, Larry

Career: 1943–47   Position: c
Teams: Newark Eagles ('43), New York Black Yankees ('47)

This catcher made two very brief appearances in the Negro Leagues, first as a wartime reserve player with the Newark Eagles, and four years later in the same capacity, with the New York Black Yankees in 1947.

Stafford, P. I.

Career: 1938   Position: p
Team: Atlanta Black Crackers

In 1938 he was a pitcher on the early spring roster of his hometown Atlanta's Negro American League team that shortly afterward acquired the name Atlanta Black Crackers.

Stallard

Career: 1914   Position: p
Team: Indianapolis ABCs

He pitched briefly with the Indianapolis ABCs in 1914, their first year of major-league caliber.

Stamps, Hulan (Lefty)

Career: 1924–33   Position: p
Teams: Indianapolis ABCs ('24), Memphis Red Sox ('24–'28), Detroit Stars ('33)
Bats: Left   Throws: Left

This left-hander pitched most of his career with the Memphis Red Sox during the '20s, posting a 1–6 mark in 1927, and closed out his career with the Detroit Stars in 1933 without a decision.

Stanford

Career: 1910   Position: player
Team: West Baden Sprudels

He was briefly a player with the West Baden Sprudels in 1910, but his position is uncertain.

Stanley, John Wesley (Neck)

Career: 1928–49   Position: p
Teams: Atlantic City Bacharach Giants ('28), Hilldale Daisies ('28–'29), New York Lincoln Giants ('29), *Wilmington Quaker Giants ('30)*, Brooklyn Royal Giants ('30), Baltimore Black Sox ('31), **New York Black Yankees** ('32–'34, '37–'49), New York Cubans, ('35–'36), Philadelphia Stars
Bats: Left   Throws: Left
Height: 5'11"   Weight: 215
Born: Kings County, Md.

A left-handed spitballer best identified with the New York Black Yankees, he also pitched for the New York Lincoln Stars, Baltimore Black Sox, and several other teams during a twenty-two-year career that started in the 1920s and encompassed the 1930s and 1940s. In addition to the spitter, Stanley had an excellent slider, a good screwball, drop, and change-up, an average curve, fastball, sinker, and knuckler, and he was also highly proficient with a ''cut ball.'' The hefty southpaw mixed a wide assortment of off-speed breaking pitches to keep batters off stride, and excelled at holding runners on first base, but acknowledged that an emery board and good control were key ingredients to his mound success.

He was a member of Satchel Paige's All-Star team that barnstormed against Bob Feller's All-Stars in 1946, but was dropped from the tour because of his use of illegal pitches. With 27,000 fans in attendance he shut out Feller's team at Yankee Stadium in the second game of the series by a score of 4–0, and Feller's All-Stars refused to continue the tour unless he was dropped from the squad.

A mainstay on the Black Yankees staff for eighteen years, during his career, while pitching against all levels of opposition, he was credited with five no-hitters and was a consistent 20-game winner for more than a decade. He once beat Babe Ruth's All-Stars, 8–0, and Dizzy Dean's All-Stars, 6–0. But in league play the competition was tougher and his records much less impressive, posting marks of 0–7, 3–6, 0–0, 0–3, 1–11, 2–5, 1–4, and 2–3 for the years 1940–47. However, the Black Yankees were the doormat of the league, and his support was lacking considerably.

He began his career with the Hilldale ballclub in 1928, but the Eastern Colored League folded early in the season, and the next year he joined the Lincoln Giants in the American Negro League, posting a 3–4 record for 1929. During the next two seasons he pitched with the Brooklyn Royal Giants and the Baltimore Black Sox, posting a 6–8 record in 1931 before joining the Black Yankees in 1932. He had the playing potential, but his poor attitude was credited as the factor preventing him from becoming a top pitcher.

Off the mound he was a poor hitter and a below-average fielder and was not a hustler. As with many baseball nicknames, he acquired his moniker because of a physical characteristic; in his case it was a long neck.

Stark, L.
Career: 1887   Position: player
Team: *Cincinnati Browns*

He played with the Cincinnati Browns, one of eight teams that were charter members of the League of Colored Baseball Clubs in 1887. However, the league's existence was ephemeral, lasting only a week. His position is uncertain.

Stark, Otis (Lefty) [see Starks, Otis (Lefty)]

Starks, James (Jim)
Career: 1938–46   Positions: **1b**, of
Teams: **New York Black Yankees** ('38–'42, '44–'45), Harrisburg-St. Louis Stars ('43)
Bats: Right   Throws: Right
Height: 6'2"   Weight: 225

A big, strong hitter with good power, he was otherwise only an ordinary player, being adequate in the field with an average arm, and slow on the bases with few successful steals. Although he hit .300 in 1941 while batting in the cleanup spot for the New York Black Yankees, he usually managed only a mediocre batting average and was a poor bunter. In 1942 he was dropped to the seventh spot in the

lineup as a part-time starter and then to a reserve status for the remainder of his career with the Black Yankees, as his batting average plummeted to anemic levels of .132 and .179 in 1942 and 1945, respectively. In 1943 he left the Black Yankees for a season to play with the St. Louis-Harrisburg Stars, but the Stars dropped out of league play early in the season to barnstorm against Dizzy Dean's All-Stars, and Starks returned to the Black Yankees the following season.

Starks, Leslie
Career: 1927–35   Positions: lf, cf, 1b
Teams: Memphis Red Sox ('27), Kansas City Monarchs ('27), Newark Dodgers ('33–'35)
Bats: Right   Throws: Right
Height: 6'4"   Weight: 220

He was a fair hitter with power, and played with the Newark Dodgers during their two years of existence, splitting his time between the outfield and first base. A big, strong, chunky man, he served as an "enforcer" whom teammates would hide behind for protection when "ragging" opposing players. When he left the Dodgers, he disappeared from the baseball scene. The only other trace of his diamond exploits was in 1927, when he split his playing time as a reserve outfielder between two teams, the Memphis Red Sox and the Kansas City Monarchs, while batting a composite .286.

Starks, Otis (Lefty)
a.k.a. Stark
Career: 1919–35   Position: p
Teams: Hilldale Daisies ('19–'20), Chicago American Giants ('21), St. Louis Giants ('21), Brooklyn Royal Giants ('22–'23, '27–'28, '30–'32), New York Lincoln Giants ('24), Atlantic City Bacharach Giants ('24, '29), Newark Stars ('26), Brooklyn Eagles ('35)

This left-handed hurler began his career with Hilldale in 1919 and stepped into the regular rotation during his two seasons with the ballclub. In an exhibition game against a major-league All-Star team in the fall of 1920, he struck out Babe Ruth three times. Most pitchers would not throw at Ruth, but Starks was an exception. The next year he compiled a combined 4–4 record while splitting the season between the St. Louis Giants and Rube Foster's Chicago American Giants, who annexed their second straight Negro National League pennant. In 1922 he returned to the East, joining the Brooklyn Royal Giants, where he played for most of the remainder of his career, closing out his career in 1935 with the Brooklyn Eagles and losing his only recorded decision.

Starmand
Career: 1887   Position: of
Team: *Pittsburgh Keystones*

He played in the outfield with the Pittsburgh Keystones, one of eight teams that were charter members of the League of Colored Baseball Clubs in 1887. However, the league's existence was ephemeral, lasting only a week.

Stars of Cuba
Duration: 1910   Honors: None
Affiliation: Independent ('10)

In 1910 this was a Cuban team of major-league caliber, but the following season most of the players joined Tinti Molina's Cuban Stars' ballclub, which played primarily in the Midwest.

Stearnes, Norman Thomas (**Turkey**)
a.k.a. Stearns
Career: 1923–42   Positions: **cf**, lf, 1b
Teams: *Nashville Elite Giants ('20), Montgomery Grey Sox ('21), Memphis Red Sox ('22),* **Detroit Stars** *('23–'31, '33, '37),* New York Lincoln Giants ('30), Kansas City Monarchs ('31, '34, '38–'41), Cole's American Giants ('32–'35), Philadelphia Stars ('36), Chicago American Giants ('38), *Detroit Black Sox, ('42) Toledo Cubs ('45)*
Bats: Left   Throws: Left
Height: 6'0"   Weight: 175
Born: May 8, 1901, Nashville, Tenn.
Died: Sept. 4, 1979, Detroit, Mich.

A left-handed power threat, Turkey Stearnes played "long ball" for twenty years in the black major leagues. After three seasons with teams in the Negro Southern League, Stearnes joined the Detroit Stars in 1923 and was credited with swatting 35 home runs in his Negro National League debut, followed by 50 home runs in 1924. These totals were for achieved against all levels of opposition, as were his 35 homers in 1937. In addition to hitting the long ball, Turkey was a great outfielder, with good speed and range. He also utilized his speed on the bases, leading the league in both triples and stolen bases at least once each during his career, while earning a reputation for his willingness to slide hard into an infielder trying to apply the tag.

Stearnes had an unique stance, with his front foot turned heel down and toe pointed straight up, but although not a heavy man, he was a natural hitter with powerful shoulders. Playing in Mack Park, a hitter's park, was an asset to the gifted slugger. During his first three seasons with the Detroit Stars, he led the Negro National League in homers against league competition, with 17, 10, and 18, respectively. In 1928 he again topped the league, with 24 homers in 88 games. In addition to hitting tape-measure home runs, he raked Negro National League pitching for averages of .365, .358, .369, .375, .346, .326, .378, .340, and .350 during his nine years with Detroit, 1923–31.

In 1931 the Stars encountered financial difficulties and could not pay his salary, and Stearnes left the team, eventually landing with the Chicago American Giants, where his presence helped them annex a pennant in two different leagues during his first two seasons with the team. In 1932 they won the Negro Southern League pennant, and the following year, with Stearnes batting in the leadoff spot to utilize his speed and contributing a .387 batting average, Chicago captured the new Negro National League's first flag. His sterling play made him the top vote-getter among outfielders and warranted a starting position in the first East-West All-Star game, held in Comiskey Park that season. He played center field, batted leadoff, and collected 2 hits in the West's victory in that first contest. After this initial All-Star appearance, the veteran outfielder played in three additional games, 1934–5 and 1937.

In 1935 he is credited with a league-high .430 batting average while with the American Giants. After playing with the Royal Giants in the 1935 winter, he left Chicago for a season to play with the Philadelphia Stars but returned in 1937, when the American Giants lost a playoff to the Kansas City Monarchs for the Negro American League title. The next season he shifted to the Monarchs and helped them to consecutive pennants in 1940–41.

Before he became a slugging outfielder, he was a schoolboy pitcher as a student at Pearl High School in his hometown, Nashville, Tennessee. At age fifteen, the budding ballplayer left school for the workplace after his father died. However, he continued his baseball pursuits, playing with the southern teams, including the Nashville Elite Giants and the Montgomery Grey Sox, before being discovered by Detroit Stars' manager Bruce Petway in 1923. Stearnes went to Detroit, working for the Briggs Manufacturing Company and playing for the Stars. Many years later, after he retired from baseball, he returned to Detroit and worked in the rolling mills of the city until 1964.

During his career he also played winter ball in Cuba and California, but the slugger never learned to bunt until Dave Malarcher taught him the art after Stearnes joined the American Giants. He closed out his career as one of the most prolific long-ball hitters in the Negro Leagues, with 185 home runs in league play, 7 home-run titles, and a .359 league batting average. As another indicator of his hitting prowess, he was credited with a .351 batting average in exhibitions against major-leaguers.

Stearnes, Norman Thomas (**Turkey**) [see Stearnes, Norman Thomas (Turkey)]

Stedgrass
Career: 1937   Position: p
Team: Memphis Red Sox

He pitched with the Memphis Red Sox in 1937, his only year in the Negro Leagues.

Steel, Harry
Career: 1938   Position: p
Team: Indianapolis ABCs

He pitched with the Indianapolis ABCs in 1938, his only year in the Negro Leagues.

Steele, Edward (**Ed**, Stainless)
Career: 1941–50   Positions: **rf**, lf, cf,
                                     manager
Teams: Birmingham Black Barons ('42–'51), *minor leagues ('52), Canadian League ('53–'54), Detroit Stars ('55–'58)*
Bats: Left   Throws: Right
Height: 5'10"   Weight: 195
Born: Aug. 78, 1915, Selma, Ala.

A flat-footed, left-handed, line-drive hitter who generated good power without striding, this Birmingham Black Barons' outfielder also had respectable speed, a good throwing arm, and had the dubious distinction of always being among the leaders in times hit by a pitch. He, "Double Duty" Radcliffe, and Gentry Jessup were added to the Black Barons' roster for the 1943 World Series against the Homestead Grays. Although the Black Barons lost the Series, they gained a right fielder. In 1944 he was the regular at that position as the Black Barons repeated as Negro American League champions, but again lost to the Grays in the World Series, despite his team-high .368 batting average for the Series.

During the regular season he hit for a .303 average with a .491 slugging percentage and proved proficient at pilfering bases. The following season was a duplication of the power and speed but with a higher batting average, .352, while hitting in his comfortable fifth slot. In 1946 he sustained an injury and a loss of playing time, with his average dropping to .277. But in 1948 he moved into the third slot, hitting an even .300 with a slugging percentage of .488 and continued his reliable basestealing as the Black Barons won their third Negro American League pennant in six seasons and for the third time lost to the Homestead Grays in the World Series. In 1949–50, he hit .316 and .306, while making his only All-Star game appearance in the latter year and cracking out 2 hits in the West's 5–3 victory.

The hard-hitting outfielder began his baseball career in his hometown, playing with the Acipco Company of Birmingham's Industrial League prior to joining the Black Barons in 1942 as a reserve outfielder. He played with the Black Barons for a dozen seasons, and during three post-World War II years, 1946–48, he barnstormed with Satchel Paige's All-Stars against Bob Feller's All-Stars.

After leaving Birmingham, he entered organized ball with Hollywood in the Pacific Coast League in 1952, but after batting only .213, he was farmed out to Denver in the Western League, where he improved to a .254 average but was injured in July and released. After two seasons in Canada with the Guelph ballclub, he closed out his career after a three-year stint as manager of the new Detroit Stars, a team of lesser status.

Stephens, Albert
Career: 1948   Position: p
Team: New York Black Yankees

This pitcher from Cleveland was among the many hurlers with the New York Black Yankees in the early spring of 1948, but his playing time was restricted and he did not finish the season with the team.

Stephens, Joe (Junior)
Career: 1949–50   Position: p
Team: New York Black Yankees

He began his pitching career with the New York Black Yankees at a time when the Negro American League was struggling to survive the loss of players to organized baseball, but league statistics do not confirm his playing time.

Stephens, Paul Eugene (Country Jake)
a.k.a. Stevens
Career: 1921–37   Positions: **ss, 2b**

Teams: **Hilldale Daisies** ('21–'29), *Philadelphia Giants ('24)*, Homestead Grays ('29–'32), Pittsburgh Crawfords ('32), Philadelphia Stars ('33–'35), New York Black Yankees ('36–'37)
Bats: Right   Throws: Right
Height: 5'7"   Weight: 150
Born: Feb. 10, 1900, Pleasureville, Pa.
Died: Feb. 5, 1981, York, Pa.

Small, fast, aggressive, argumentative, temperamental, and controversial, Jake was cat-quick and used this attribute to make acrobatic plays that pleased the crowd. The peppery shortstop had a wide range and a good arm and was also smart, excelling in decoying runners off the bag to set up a pickoff play to second base. Playing on championship teams with four different franchises, he was the hub of the infield and the backbone of the defense. In addition to his fielding prowess, he utilized his speed and quickness on the basepaths as well during his seventeen-year career.

The scrappy shortstop broke in with Hilldale in 1921 after sending a fake telegram to Hilldale owner Ed Bolden, with a glowing report about the great young prospect in York, Pennsylvania. Without knowing that Stephens sent the telegram himself, Bolden gave him a tryout. When he joined the team, manager Bill Francis, a third baseman, moved another young prospect, Judy Johnson, to shortstop to compete with Stephens. Although Stephens could outfield anybody at the position, he had great difficulty hitting a curveball, batting .263 against all levels of competition for the independent team. In anticipation of being dropped from the team, he jumped to a New England semipro league for more seasoning. He learned to compensate for the breaking pitch by using a heavy, large-barreled bat and hitting to right field, but curveballs continued to plague him throughout his career, and twice while playing winter ball (once each in Cuba and California), he sent fake telegrams to himself declaring that his father had died, so he could leave to avoid the steady diet of curves he was facing.

Hilldale, still searching for a shortstop, requested that he return to their team after a stint in semipro ball, and he responded with a .290 batting average against all levels of competition while playing as a part-time starter. His comparatively light hitting against top teams mandated that he continue as only a part-time starter when Hilldale joined the the Eastern Colored League in 1923, and he provided good defense up the middle but batted only .209 and .190 in league play as Hilldale won the first two league pennants in 1923–24. The latter season marked the first World Series, and the youngster was nervous against the Negro National League champion Kansas City Monarchs, and Biz Mackey was used at shortstop through much of the Series.

When Frank Warfield took over the managerial reins in 1924, he began working more with a set infield, and in 1925 he made Johnson a full-time third baseman and installed Stephens at shortstop, frequently placing him in the second slot in the batting order to utilize his superior bunting ability. The strong-willed little infielder responded with a .229 batting average as Hilldale won their third consecutive pennant and defeated the Kansas City Monarchs in their World Series rematch. The pair remained intact as the left side of Hilldale's infield through the 1928 season, with Stephens hitting .240, .278, and .168 in 1926–28. In 1929 Stephens was traded to the Homestead Grays with Rev Cannady for George Britt and Martin Dihigo, but Stephens jumped the Grays and rejoined Hilldale, jumping them in turn in August.

With the Grays in 1930, Stephens, who usually batted at the bottom of the order, was used as the leadoff batter, and responded with a .373 average against all opposition. Since the Grays played an independent schedule, their opposition was generally weaker than league teams, accounting for his higher average. In three of the next four seasons he played on great teams, including the 1931 Grays, who are generally conceded to be one of the greatest black teams of all time; the 1932 Pittsburgh Crawfords, where he hit .277; and the 1934 Negro National League champion Philadelphia Stars, where he hit .273 and teamed with Dick Seay

to form the best double-play combination in baseball. After the season he was selected by Cum Posey for his annual All-Star team, and in 1935, Stephens hit .219 with the Stars and garnered 2 hits as the leadoff batter for the East squad in the 1935 East-West All-Star classic.

In 1936 he joined the New York Black Yankees and played for them for two seasons before retiring from baseball after seventeen years. In the spring of 1938 he was sought by the Atlanta Black Crackers to play on their first league team, but he remained in New York City.

He was considered a fine gentleman and eventually ran a taproom for two years, worked for the state of Pennsylvania in the Bureau of Motor Vehicles (1939–55), operated a registry for auto tags and drivers' licenses, and was a part-time deputy sheriff. During the 1970s he was voted a member of both the Pittsburgh (1972) and York (1977) area Halls of Fame.

Off the field he was joking and good-spirited, and was nicknamed "Country Jake." He roomed with Jud Wilson on the Grays, Crawfords, and Stars, and they become very good friends. When Wilson was in the last days of his life and unable to recognize anyone else, he recognized Jake by name.

Stephens's quick temper sometimes caused Wilson problems. Once, when Stephens was arguing with an umpire about a close call, Wilson intervened by positioning himself between the two parties as a buffer, keeping the angry little shortstop behind him and away from the ump. Stephens reached around Wilson and hit the ump in the face, but the ump thought it was Wilson who struck the blow and tossed him out of the game. This infuriated Wilson and he had to be subdued by the police, who came out onto the field and beat Wilson with blackjacks, put him in a patrol wagon, and took him to jail.

On another occasion, at the East-West game in Chicago, when Stephens came in at 2:00 A.M. after a night of carousing and awakened Wilson, the angry Wilson held him out of the sixteenth-story window by a leg. While the inebriated Stephens kicked him with his free foot, Wilson just changed hands, like a gunfighter's "border shift." The next morning Wilson's arms were bruised from the kicks, but he never lost his grip, or Stephens would have plunged to his death.

Sterman, Tom [see Stirman, Thomas]

Stevens
a.k.a. Stevenson
Career: 1927–29   Position: c
Team: Detroit Stars
He was a reserve catcher with the Detroit Stars for three years during the late '20s, batting .322 in 1929.

Stevens
Career: 1950   Position: p
Team: Houston Eagles
He began his pitching career with the Eagles with a 1–3 record in 1950, a year after the franchise was moved to Houston and joined the Western Division of the Negro American League as it struggled to survive the loss of players to organized baseball.

Stevens, Frank
Career: 1921–29   Positions: **p** of, 1b
Teams; Indianapolis ABCs ('21, '26), Toledo Tigers ('23), Chicago American Giants ('25–'26), Cleveland Hornets ('27), St. Louis Stars ('27), Cleveland Tigers ('28), Atlantic City Bacharach Giants ('29)
A pitcher during the '20s, he played with seven teams in nine years during his career. He also sometimes played as an outfielder throughout his years in the Negro Leagues. Beginning his career with the Indianapolis ABCs in 1921 with a 4–0 slate, he returned after stints with the Toledo Tigers and Chicago American Giants to pitch for the ABCs in 1926, their last season in the Negro National League. The next season he split his playing time between the Cleveland Hornets and the St. Louis Stars, with a combined 6–8 ledger and a composite .289 batting average.

Stevens, Paul Eugene (Country Jake)
[see Stephens, Paul Eugene (Country Jake)]

Stevens, Robert
Career: 1948   Position: p
Team: New York Black Yankees
This pitcher from Joplin, Missouri, was among the moundsmen with the New York Black Yankees in the early spring of 1948.

Stevenson
Career: 1910   Position: p
Team: St. Louis Giants
He pitched with the St. Louis Giants in 1910, his only year in the Negro Leagues.

Stevenson
Career: 1921   Position: p
Team: Baltimore Black Sox
He pitched briefly with the Baltimore Black Sox in 1921, losing his only recorded decision.

Stevenson, Lefty
Career: 1925–28   Positions: p, of
Teams: Indianapolis ABC's, ('25), Birmingham Black Barons, ('25), Cleveland Tigers ('28)
Bats: Left   Throws: Left
This left-handed pitcher began his career in 1925 and ended his four seasons in the Negro Leagues with the Cleveland Tigers in 1928.

Stevenson [see Stevens]

Stevenson, Carl (Willie)
Career: 1940–43   Position: p
Team: Homestead Grays
Bats: Right   Throws: Right
He was a second-line pitcher with the Homestead Grays in the early '40s, splitting two decisions in 1940 and making another appearance with the Grays in 1943.

Stewart
Career: 1920–23   Positions: **p**, ss

Teams: St. Louis Giants ('20), St. Louis Stars ('23)

Bats: Right   Throws: Right

He pitched with the St. Louis teams in the Negro National League during the league's first three years of existence.

Stewart, Artis

Career: 1950   Position: p

Team: Cleveland Buckeyes

He pitched with the Buckeyes during the 1950 season when the Negro American League was struggling to survive the loss of players to organized baseball.

Stewart, Frank

Career: 1936–40   Position: p

Teams: Baltimore Elite Giants ('36), Indianapolis ABC's ('38), Memphis Red Sox ('40)

He pitched for three different teams during his short career in the Negro Leagues, beginning with the Baltimore Elite Giants in the Negro National League in 1936 and closing out his career with the Memphis Red Sox in the Negro American League five years later.

Stewart, Leon

Career: 1940, 1942   Positions: p, of

Teams: Newark Eagles ('40), Birmingham Black Barons ('42)

Bats: Right   Throws: Right

Height: 5'11"   Weight: 170

He made appearances in each league for one season, as a pitcher with the Negro National League Newark Eagles in 1940 without a decision, and as an outfielder with the Negro American League Birmingham Black Barons in 1942.

Stewart, Manuel

Career: 1943, 1946–47 Positions: p, 3b, ss

Teams: Baltimore Elite Giants ('43, '46)

He began with the Elite Giants as a wartime pitcher, losing his only decision, and played as an infielder during the postwar period.

Stewart, Riley

Career: 1946–50   Position: p

Team: Chicago American Giants ('46–'49), New York Cubans ('50)

He was a pitcher with the Chicago American Giants during the late '40s, posting a 2–8 mark in 1948, before moving to the East to pitch for the New York Cubans in 1950, where he had a 3–4 record in his last year in the Negro Leagues. A fair hitter for a pitcher, he hit .343 in 1948 for the American Giants.

Stewart, W.

Career: 1946   Position: p

Team: Memphis Red Sox

He pitched with the Memphis Red Sox in 1946, his only year in the Negro Leagues, and posted a 4–8 record.

Stiles, Norris

Career: 1950   Position: p

Team: Cleveland Buckeyes

He began his pitching career with the Cleveland Buckeyes in 1950, when the Negro American League was struggling to survive the loss of players to organized baseball, but league statistics do not confirm his playing time.

Still, Bobby

Career: 1887   Position: player

Team: *Philadelphia Pythians*

He played with the Philadelphia Pythians, one of eight teams that were charter members of the League of Colored Baseball Clubs in 1887. However, the league's existence was ephemeral, lasting only a week. His playing position and familial relationship with teammate Joe Still are uncertain.

Still, Joe

Career: 1887   Position: player

Team: *Philadelphia Pythians*

He played with the Philadelphia Pythians, one of eight teams that were charter members of the League of Colored Baseball Clubs in 1887. However, the league's existence was ephemeral, lasting only a week. His playing position and familial relationship with team-mate Bobby Still are uncertain.

Stinson, C. P.
Career: 1887   Position: player
Team: *Philadelphia Pythians*

He played with the Philadelphia Pythians, one of eight teams that were charter members of the League of Colored Baseball Clubs in 1887. However, the league's existence was ephemeral, lasting only a week. His position is uncertain.

Stirman, Thomas
a.k.a. Sterman; Stearman
Career: 1909–1915   Position: of
Team: Kansas City Royal Giants ('09–'10)

This left-fielder with the Kansas City, Kansas, Royal Giants in 1909 was considered the largest and fastest man in black baseball. That season the Royal Giants beat manager Rube Foster's Leland Giants in a challenge series billed as the colored championship of the West. He was the regular left fielder with the Kansas City Royal Giants again in 1910.

Stitler
Career: 1922   Position: p
Team: Atlantic City Bacharach Giants

He pitched with the Bacharachs in 1922, the year before entering the Eastern Colored League.

Stockard, Theodore (Licks)
a.k.a. Sockard
Career: 1927–28   Positions: ss, 3b
Teams: Cleveland Hornets ('27), Cleveland Tigers ('28)

He was a reserve infielder for two Cleveland Negro National League entries, the Hornets and the Tigers, but his playing time was limited and neither franchise survived for more than a season.

Stockley, Lawrence
Career: 1950   Position: lf
Team: New York Black Yankees

This outfielder began his career in 1950, when the New York Black Yankees were playing as an independent team and struggling to survive the loss of players to organized baseball.

Stokes
Career: 1933   Position: p
Team: Detroit Stars

He pitched with the Detroit Stars in 1933, their last year in the Negro National League, but was not involved in a decision during his only season in the Negro Leagues.

Stone, Ed
Career: 1931–50   Positions: **rf** lf, cf
Teams: *Wilmington Hornets*, ('30) Atlantic City Bacharach Giants ('31, '33–'34), Brooklyn Eagles ('35). **Newark Eagles** ('36–'40, '42–'43), Philadelphia Stars ('37, '44–'45), *Mexican League ('41)*, New York Black Yankees ('43, '50), *Pittsburgh Crawfords ('46)*
Bats: Left   Throws: Right
Height: 6'0"   Weight: 195
Born: Aug. 21, 1909, Black Cat, Del.
Died: Mar. 20, 1983, New York, N.Y.

A classy ballplayer, this left-handed batter was a good hitter with respectable power and could pull the ball. Pitchers showed their respect by issuing more than a normal share of free passes to him. He also was a good all-around outfielder, but his throwing arm was his best attribute. On the bases he had good speed but only an average number of steals. Off the field he was a loner. Although educated and intelligent, he was a hard case and, in the vernacular of the time, was considered to be "evil."

He began his career in 1931 with the Bacharach Giants, playing left field and batting cleanup in 1934, but he really blossomed as a hitter in 1935 with the Brooklyn Eagles, where he hit .323 and earned his first trip to the East-West All-Star game, making an appearance as a pinch hitter. The next year owner Abe Manley consolidated the Brooklyn Eagles and the Newark Dodgers into a single team called the

Newark Eagles. Stone was the starting right fielder and hit in the heart of the batting order, finishing the season with a .317 average. The Eagles had one of their best teams in 1937, and Stone contributed a .334 batting average and a .590 slugging percentage to their second-place finish. The hard-hitting outfielder moved into the cleanup spot in 1938–39, batting behind Willie Wells and in front of Mule Suttles, and helped the Eagles to another strong second-place finish the latter year with a .363 batting average.

In 1940, despite a drop in his batting average to .274, the Eagles' outfielder made his second All-Star appearance, starting in right field and hitting third in the batting order. The next year he went to Mexico and, during his year with Aquila in the Mexican League, he hit .336 with 12 home runs, fourth highest in the league. But when he returned to the Eagles in 1942, he batted only .229, and after another season with the Eagles, he joined the Philadelphia Stars, rebounding with averages of .300 and .298 in 1944–45. Playing with the New York Black Yankees in 1950, he ended a career that began in 1931 with the Bacharach Giants. In 1983, Stone died from cancer.

Stone, Toni
Career: 1953–54   Position: 2b
Teams: *Indianapolis Clowns ('53), Kansas City Monarchs ('54)*
Bats: Right   Throws: Right
Height: 5'7½"   Weight: 146
Born: 1931, St. Paul. Minn.

She was second baseman for the Indianapolis Clowns in 1953. Although signed primarily as a gate attraction, she holds the distinction of being the first female to play in the Negro American League. During the early '50s the league had become strictly a minor-league operation and was struggling to survive financially. Her appearance on the diamond reflected the extent of the exodus of players to organized baseball but, despite the circumstances, she played in 50 games and hit a respectable .243. During the winter she was traded to the Kansas City Monarchs for the 1954 season and was replaced on the Clowns by another female second baseman, Connie Morgan.

She began her diamond career as a softball player with the Girls Highlex Softball Club in St. Paul, Minnesota. At age fifteen, she began playing with a men's team, and after graduating from Roosevelt High School, she switched to baseball. In 1953, at age twenty-two, she signed with the Clowns and began her two-year stint in the Negro Leagues.

While playing in the Negro Leagues, she was knocked down by pitchers, taken out on double plays by baserunners, and generally treated the same as other ballplayers while on the ballfield. In September of 1993, she was inducted into the Women's Sports Hall of Fame on Long Island.

Stopughers
Career: 1909   Position: ss
Team: Kansas City Royal Giants

He played shortstop with the Royal Giants from Kansas City, Missouri, in 1909.

Stovall
Career: 1924   Position: p
Team: Cleveland Browns

He pitched with the Cleveland Browns in 1924, his only year in the Negro Leagues.

Stovall, Fred
Career: 1930–35   Position: officer
Team: Monroe Monarchs

He was an officer with the Negro Southern League's Monroe Monarchs for six seasons, including the 1932 season, when the Negro Southern League was recognized as a major league.

Stovey, George Washington
Career: 1886–96   Positions: **p**, of
Teams: Cuban Giants ('86, '88–'91, '93) *minor leagues ('86–'87),* New York Gorhams ('91),

Cuban X-Giants, ('96), Brooklyn Colored Giants ('96)

Bats: Left   Throws: Left

This phenomenal left-handed pitcher was a light-complexioned Canadian and was the best black pitcher of his era. Manager Govern of the Trenton-based Cuban Giants secured Stovey to pitch for his team in 1886. On June 21, in his only game for the Cuban Giants, he lost a 4–3 decision to Bridgeport, despite good pitching on his part. He struck out 11, walked 3, and yielded only 4 hits, and the winning run reached base after the catcher dropped the third strike, and scored after a stolen base and 2 errors. During the game he demonstrated "an effective delivery" and catchers had to "adjust to his movements." He was also good at holding runners close to the base, intimidating the runners with his good pickoff move.

Soon afterward, Stovey was "kidnapped" from the Cuban Giants by the Jersey City team and became the first black professional player in New Jersey. Although they had him signed to a contract, Trenton was pressured to refrain from contesting the change when the Eastern League threatened to prohibit future exhibition games in Trenton if they did not acquiesce. Later in the summer, Stovey defeated his former mates twice, 8–4 (with 11 strikeouts) and 4–2. By season's end he had won 30 games with Jersey City and held the opposition to a .167 batting average, prompting New York Giants' owner Walter Appleton to display an interest in signing him to pitch against Cap Anson's Chicago White Stockings.

But Anson's racial feelings were well known, and the new season found Stovey playing with Newark in the same league, but with the name changed to the International League. At Newark he and Fleet Walker formed the first black battery on an integrated team. On July 16, 1887, the Chicago White Stockings were scheduled to play an exhibition game against Newark, but Cap Anson refused to play if the two black players were allowed on the field, and they were withheld from competition. The same day the International League directors met in secret and decided not to approve future contracts for black players.

Afterward, Stovey continued with the Newark team, fashioning a 34–15 work sheet for the season while also playing in the outfield and batting .255, but he was released at the end of September. He returned to the Cuban Giants and continued to play for another nine years, sometimes with the Cuban Giants against black teams and sometimes in predominantly white leagues, where he registered a lifetime record of 60–40 with a 2.17 ERA for his six seasons in organized baseball.

Among the leagues that the Cuban Giants represented were Trenton, New Jersey, in the Middle States League in 1889; York, Pennsylvania, in the Eastern Interstate League in 1890; and Ansonia in the Connecticut State League in 1891. The New York Gorhams played in the Middle States League, and Stovey also played with Worcester in the Northeastern League and Troy in the New York State League.

Stratton, Felton

Career: 1930   Position: c

Team: Hilldale Daisies

He was a reserve catcher with Hilldale in 1930, his only year in black baseball.

Stratton, Leroy

a.k.a. Straiton

Career: 1920–33   Positions: **3b, ss**, 2b, of, *p*, manager

Teams: Milwaukee Bears ('23), Birmingham Black Barons ('23–'25, '31), Chicago American Giants ('25–'26), **Nashville Elite Giants** ('27–'33)

He played third base with the Birmingham Black Barons in 1923 and for the Chicago American Giants in 1926, but he could play any infield position and in the outfield. Most identified with the Elite Giants when they were based in Nashville, he registered batting averages of .217, .247, and .185 in 1929–30 and 1933, respectively.

Streeter, Samuel (**Sam**, Lefty)
Career: 1920–36   Position: p
Teams: *Montgomery Grey Sox ('20), Atlanta Black Crackers*, Chicago American Giants ('21), Atlantic City Bacharach Giants ('22), New York Lincoln Giants ('23), **Birmingham Black Barons** ('24–'28, '30), Homestead Grays ('26, '28–'30), Baltimore Black Sox ('30), Cleveland Cubs ('31), Pittsburgh Crawfords ('31–'36)
Bats: Right   Throws: Left
Height: 5'7"   Weight: 170
Born: Sept. 17, 1900, New Market, Ala.
Died: Aug. 9, 1985, Pittsburgh, Pa.

A star left-handed spitballer for the Pittsburgh Crawfords, he chalked up an 11–3 record in 1932. The following year he was the starting pitcher for the East squad in the first annual East-West All-Star game, but was knocked out in the sixth inning and suffered the loss in the inaugural classic. Remaining with the Crawfords through their halcyon years, he is credited with an aggregate 10–4 league ledger for the seasons 1933–36. He joined the Crawfords in 1931 after being signed from the Cleveland Cubs by Bobby Williams. Satchel Paige joined the Crawfords later that year and took over as the ace of the staff.

Streeter's stint with the Crawfords came near the end of his career. His best season was in 1924, when he sported a 14–7 mark for the Birmingham Black Barons and led the league in strikeouts. Three years later he and Harry Salmon were the two top pitchers for the 1927 Black Barons, when Paige was a rookie in his first full season. Streeter posted a 14–12 record as the Black Barons won the second-half Negro National League title but lost a tough playoff to the Chicago American Giants.

After leaving Birmingham during the next season, he began his second tour with the Homestead Grays, where he reclaimed his place among the clubhouse "hearts" card players, and joined a pitching staff that featured Smokey Joe Williams. Streeter finished the 1928 season and spent all of 1929 with the

Grays, before going back to Birmingham in 1930. He also played part of that season with the Baltimore Black Sox and posted marks of 4–3, 9–5, and 14–12 for the 1928–30 seasons. The chunky hurler had good control of his spitter and was an effective pitcher throughout most of his seventeen years in the Negro Leagues.

He began his professional career in 1920 with the Montgomery Grey Sox, champions of the Negro Southern League, and pitched a perfect game against the Atlanta Black Crackers. During the next three seasons he moved up in competition, playing with teams of higher caliber, and he joined the Birmingham Black Barons in 1924. Streeter was a pretty good hitter for a pitcher, posting intermittent batting marks of .370, .347, .344, .409, ad .304 during the 1927–33 period.

Streets, Albert
Career: 1925   Position: lf
Team: Chicago American Giants

He was a reserve infielder with the Chicago American Giants in 1925, his only year in the Negro Leagues.

Stricker
Career: 1920   Position: p
Teams: Baltimore Black Sox ('20), *Norfolk All-Stars ('20)*

This pitcher's only year in black baseball was with the Baltimore Black Sox in 1920, when the team was still progressing toward entrance into the Eastern Colored League.

Strickland
Career: 1924   Position: p
Team: Indianapolis ABCs

He pitched with the Indianapolis ABCs in 1924, his only year in the Negro Leagues.

Strong
Career: 1913   Position: p
Team: Chicago American Giants

He pitched with the Chicago American

Giants in 1913, his only year in the Negro Leagues.

Strong, Fulton
Career: 1922–23   Position: p
Teams: Cleveland Tate Stars ('22), Chicago American Giants ('23), New Orleans Crescent Stars, Milwaukee Bears ('23)

He pitched for two seasons with Negro National League teams in the Midwest, including Rube Foster's Chicago American Giants.

Strong, Henry
Career: 1936   Position: ss
Team: Chicago American Giants

He was a shortstop with the Chicago American Giants in 1936, his only year in black baseball.

Strong, Joseph Tarleton (Joe, J.T., Babyface)
Career: 1924–37   Positions: p, of
Teams: Baltimore Black Sox ('24–'27), Hilldale Daisies ('28–'29), St. Louis Stars ('30–'31), Homestead Grays ('32–'37)
Bats: Left   Throws: Right
Height: 5'9"   Weight: 190

A right-handed pitcher for the 1924 Baltimore Black Sox, he was the kid on the club and was expected to get better with age and experience. In 1925 he fulfilled the promise and posted an 11–6 record. During his early years with the team, discipline was lax, and fans brought alcoholic beverages to the ballpark and openly made them available to players. Strong and Eggie Dallard were dropped from the Baltimore Black Sox in mid-August of 1926 because of their drinking problems. However, Strong was reinstated and, a year later, he suffered a sprained left arm when he and other Black Sox players were involved in an automobile accident. He finished the year with a 6–5 record, but that was his last year with the Sox.

After two seasons with Hilldale, including an 8–3 ledger in 1929, he joined the St. Louis Stars for the 1930–31 seasons, when they won back-to-back Negro National League pennants.

Strong was in the regular rotation with the Stars and proved to be a workhorse, posting a 9–4 league record in 1930. Both the league and the Stars broke up after the 1931 season, and he returned East to pitch with the Homestead Grays, posting a 4–1 mark in 1932.

With the Grays he sometimes played in the outfield, as he had done throughout his career. As an everyday player he was an adequate fielder and base runner but was below average as a hitter, registering averages of .261, .283, .225, .231, and .229 for seasons ranging from 1924 through 1933. His last season was the Grays' first of nine consecutive Negro National League pennants.

Strong, Nathaniel Calvin (Nat)
Career: 1908–34   Positions: owner, officer
Teams: Brooklyn Royal Giants, New York Black Yankees
Born: Manhattan, N.Y.

Best known as a booking agent for the East Coast, this New York-based sportsman served as an officer with the Brooklyn Royal Giants and the New York Black Yankees, the two leading black ballclubs in New York City, and wielded considerable power in black baseball. The white-haired, blue-eyed promoter was strong-willed and dictatorial, and once forced the Lincoln Giants out of the league. Teams could not get booked in New York unless they went through him, and he was not liked by other owners because he demanded 10 percent of their part of the gate in addition to his usual share.

In addition to his booking activities, he owned the Brooklyn Royal Giants and provided financial support for the Black Yankees. In his younger years he attended City College, but bought the Royals from John Connors before World War I. He owned two cars—a seven-passenger Pierce-Arrow and a Cadillac—for the team to use in their travels. He also invested in strong white semipro teams in the area, and was a part owner of the Brooklyn Bushwicks, the Bay Parkways, and the Cuban

Stars. Aside from baseball, he was a salesman for the Spalding Sporting Goods Company and owned the World Building in New York City, but lived in New Rochelle. The freewheeling sports entrepreneur died of a heart attack at age sixty-one.

Strong, Othello L.

Career: 1949–40   Position: p
Teams: Chicago American Giants ('49–'52), *minor leagues ('51–'53)*
Bats: Both   Throws: Right

This right-handed pitcher began his career with the Chicago American Giants in 1949, when the Negro American League was struggling to survive the loss of players to organized baseball. After breaking in with the Chicago American Giants in 1949, he had a 5–8 season in 1950, and continued with the American Giants through 1952, except for spending two partial years with Winnipeg in the Mandak League. In 1951 he had a 2–1 record in 12 games, but he spent most of the next season back with the American Giants. In 1953, his last year in baseball, he had a 3–2 record with a 1.98 ERA in only 13 games with Danville in the Mississippi-Ohio Valley League.

Strong, T. R. (Ted)

Career: 1937–48   Positions: **rf**, 1b, lf, ss, cf, 3b
Teams: Indianapolis Athletics ('37), Indianapolis ABCs ('38), **Kansas City Monarchs** ('37–'42, '46–'47), *Mexican League ('40), military service ('43–'45)*, Indianapolis Clowns ('48), *minor leagues ('50), Chicago American Giants ('51)*
Bats: Both   Throws: Right
Height: 6'6"   Weight: 210
Born: Jan. 2, 1917, South Bend, Ind.
Died: 1951, Chicago, Ill.

A versatile athlete, in addition to starring in baseball he was a member of basketball's original Globetrotters, serving as captain of the western unit of the reknowned basketball club. In baseball he was an ideal player with all the tools required for stardom, and was outstanding in all phases of the game. He was an accomplished fielder with a good glove and range, and possessed an exceptionally strong arm. Although he possessed only average speed, he was a good base stealer. A switch-hitter with good power from both sides of the plate, the pull hitter led the league in both home runs (7) and RBIs (45) in 1946, while batting .287. However, he was a free-swinger and an inefficient bunter.

The talented player was selected to five East-West All-Star teams during a six-year interval, 1935–42, missing only the 1940 season, when he was in Mexico. His versatility was evident as he started at three different positions (shortstop, first base, and outfield), and he compiled a career All-Star batting average of .313. He made his first two All-Star appearances representing Indianapolis teams, but his other appearances came while playing with the Kansas City Monarchs.

In the last two All-Star seasons, 1941–42, Strong batted .319 and .345, with good power, while hitting third in the lineup in front of Willard Brown. The latter year marked the Monarchs' fourth consecutive pennant since Strong joined the team and was the year when World Series play was initiated between the Negro American League and the Negro National League. Strong hit .316 with a home run to pace the Monarchs' Series sweep of the Negro National League's Homestead Grays.

Following the 1942 World Series, he entered military service for three years, returning to help the team to the 1946 pennant under manager Frank Duncan. In the World Series that season against the Newark Eagles, he and Satchel Paige missed the last two games, ostensibly due to negotiations involving contracts for the impending winter season. The big slugger was easily influenced by others, sometimes for the better and sometimes for the worse, and this may have been true in this situation, as another version of his absence involves women and drinking.

Strong's first skipper in his Negro League career was his father, who was at the helm of the Indianapolis Athletics in 1937, the first year of the Negro American League. After he had two all-star seasons in Indianapolis, where he hit in the heart of the batting order, the Atlanta Black Crackers' franchise moved into town to play under the ABCs' banner, and Strong moved to Kansas City. In his first complete season with the Monarchs, 1939, he hit .273 and won a spot in the All-Star game.

The next year he made an excursion to Nuevo Laredo, Mexico, where he posted a .332 batting average and a .603 slugging percentage, which included 14 triples and 11 home runs, each only one behind the Mexican League leader. After only one season in the Mexican League, he returned to the Monarchs, leaving eight years later to play with the Indianapolis Clowns for the 1948 season, where he hit .242. In 1950 he played with Minot in the Mandak League, batting .236.

Strothers, C. W. (**Colonel,** Chief)
Career: 1924–27   Positions: owner,
                                                 officer
Teams: Harrisburg Giants
Height: Weight: 300

The corpulent Colonel was the owner of a billiard parlor, which served as a front for his numbers operation. The affluent numbers banker acquired control of the Harrisburg Giants in 1918, when they were an amateur team, and served as an officer with the ballclub while building them into a professional power. Under his leadership the team entered the Eastern Colored League but were never able to win a pennant.

Strothers, Tim Samuel (**Sam**)
Career: 1907–18   Positions: c, 1b. *2b*
Teams: Leland Giants ('07–'10), West Baden Sprudels ('10), Chicago American Giants ('12, '15–'16, '18), Chicago Giants ('13–'16), Chicago Union Giants ('17)

His career was spent almost entirely with Chicago-based teams. He was the backup catcher for the Leland Giants for three years (1908–10) and also served as an utility player,

filling in at first base or in the outfield when needed. In the early winter of 1910, owner Frank C. Leland and manager Rube Foster parted company, with each establishing his own team, and for the next eight years Strothers rotated between Foster's Chicago American Giants and Leland's Chicago Giants. In 1910, Strothers hit .201 in limited play as a substitute for Foster's team.

With the American Giants, a perennial powerhouse, he was a backup behind the plate for Bruce Petway, but with the Chicago Giants he was a regular for four seasons (1913–16), as a catcher the first two years and at first base the latter two seasons. In 1917 he moved to the Chicago Union Giants, a lesser team, as the regular firstbaseman, batting fifth in the order. His last season with a top club was in 1918, when he played briefly with the American Giants, who had been weakened by the loss of players to military service during World War I.

Stuart
Career: 1900   Position: ss
Team: Cuban X-Giants

He was a shortstop with the Cuban X-Giants in 1900, his only year with a top black team.

Stubblefield, Mickey
Career: 1948   Position: p
Team: Kansas City Monarchs

He pitched with the Kansas City Monarchs in 1948, his only year in the Negro Leagues.

Sturdeven, Mark
Career: 1916, 1928   Positions: player,
                                                 officer
Team: Hilldale Daisies

He was a player with Hilldale in 1916, during the team's formative years before attaining professional status, and later served as treasurer with the ballclub in 1928.

Sturm
Career: 1926   Position: unknown
Team: Indianapolis ABCs

A fringe player, he appeared in a single

game with the Indianapolis ABCs in 1926, the last season of the franchise.

Suarez
Career: 1916–21   Positions: p, *rf*
Team: Cuban Stars

This pitcher performed over a six-season stretch for the Cuban Stars' ballclub, posting a 5–9 record in 1921. In 1916, his first year, the team was billed as the Havana Cuban Stars, and the next year they were called the New York Cuban Stars. He also occasionally appeared in the outfield for the Cubans.

Sullivan
Career: 1918   Position: of
Team: *Chicago Union Giants*

In 1918 he was an outfielder with the Chicago Union Giants, a team of lesser quality.

Sullivan
Career: 1937   Position: p
Team: Birmingham Black Barons

He pitched with the Birmingham Black Barons in 1937, his only year in the Negro Leagues.

Summerall, William (Big, Red)
Career: 1940   Position: p
Teams: *St. Louis Stars ('36),* Memphis Red Sox ('40)

After gaining some mound experience with the St. Louis Stars in 1936, a year before they entered the Negro American League, he pitched with the Memphis Red Sox in 1940.

Summers, Lonnie (Carl)
Career: 1938–49   Positions: c, of, 1b, 3b, p
Teams: Baltimore Elite Giants ('38), *semipro ball ('39–'41), military service ('42–'45), Mexican League ('46–'47, '49),* Chicago American Giants ('48–'49, '51), *Venezuelan League ('50), minor leagues ('52–'56)*
Bats: Right   Throws: Right
Height: 6'0"   Weight: 202
Born: Aug. 2, 1915, Davis, Okla.

A big, strong player who hit powerful line drives, he could catch or play in the outfield. Earlier in his career he played in the infield as well, and did not start catching until he was with Tampico in the Mexican League. He had a strong arm but was not fast afoot. While adequate defensively, he was best known for his hitting.

In 1938, the young prospect joined the Elite Giants during their first year in Baltimore, and played as a reserve in the outfield and at third-base. Unable to break into the Elites' starting outfield of Henry Kimbro, Bill Wright, and Bill Hoskins, he returned to Los Angeles after the season and, for the next three years, he played semipro ball in California. In 1942 he joined the Army and was assigned to the 614th Tank Battalion, serving in the European Theater. Before going overseas he played service baseball against Jackie Robinson and Hank Thompson.

After his discharge he joined Tampico in the Mexican League, batting .306 with good power in 1946. With fewer than two full seasons below the border, he signed with the Negro American League's Chicago American Giants in 1948. Usually batting in the fifth slot, he hit .304 in 1949 and was selected for the East-West All-Star game as a catcher. In the game he and Piper Davis had the only 2 hits for the West squad. Late in the season, in a brief second stint south of the border, with the Mexico City Reds, he hit .370 with 3 homers and 3 doubles in only 27 at-bats. During his Mexican career he once had 11 RBIs in one game, and on other occasions he took the mound in a few games.

In 1950 he played with Caracas in the Venezuelan League, and following his last year in Mexico he played with Ponce in the Puerto Rican winter league, batting a modest .254. After returning to the United States he played with San Diego in the Pacific Coast League in 1952–53, batting only .241 and .165, but showing some power the first year with the team. The latter season was spent with three other teams, primarily with Boise in the Pioneer League, where he hit .255. His last full season was in 1954 with Yakima, where he hit .312, and two years later in only 3 games he hit .333 to close out his professional career. After his last season he returned to Los Angeles, worked as a janitor in the school system for thirty years, and retired.

Summers, Smith (Tack)
Career: 1923–29   Positions: lf, cf, rf, *2b, 3b*
Teams: Toledo Tigers ('23), Cleveland Browns ('24), Cleveland Elites ('26), Cleveland Hornets ('27), Cleveland Tigers ('28), Chicago American Giants ('29), Homestead Grays ('30)

This outfielder spent most of his career with Cleveland-based teams, playing with four different Negro National League entries from Cleveland. With the Cleveland Elites in 1926, he hit .300 while batting in the seventh slot and accruing playing time in each of the outfield positions. The next season, with the Cleveland Hornets, he hit .333 to move up to the fifth spot in the batting order, and he settled in left field. In 1930 he appeared in a single game for the Homestead Grays.

Sunkett, Pete (Golden)
Career: 1943–45   Positions: p, lf, 2b
Team: Philadelphia Stars
Bats: Right   Throws: Right
Height: 6'1"   Weight: 200

A wartime player with the Philadelphia Stars, he began his career in 1943 as a reserve left fielder and second baseman but also pitched occasionally, winning both of his decisions. In 1944 the big right-hander turned his skills to the mound and closed out his career as a combination pitcher-outfielder, splitting 2 decisions in 1945. In the field he had good hands, average range, and an accurate arm, while at the plate he was a mediocre batter with average power, contact, and bunting skills. On the bases he had average speed but was not a good base stealer.

Susini, Antonio
Career: 1921   Positions: 2b, ss
Team: All Cubans ('21)

This middle infielder killed teammate Julio LeBlanc and was imprisoned to serve a sentence of ten to fifteen years.

Suttles, Earl
Career: 1950   Position: 1b
Team: Cleveland Buckeyes

A reserve first baseman with the Cleveland Buckeyes, he hit .174 in 10 games in 1950, when the Negro American League was struggling to survive the loss of players to organized baseball.

Suttles, George (Mule)
Career: 1918–44;   Positions: **1b, lf**, rf, 1948   manager, umpire
Teams: Birmingham Black Barons ('23–'25), **St. Louis Stars** ('26–'31), Baltimore Black Sox ('30), Detroit Wolves ('32), Washington Pilots ('32), Cole's American Giants ('33–'35), **Newark Eagles** ('36–'40, '42–'44), Indianapolis ABCs ('39), New York Black Yankees ('41–'42)
Bats: Right   Throws: Right
Height: 6'3"   Weight: 215
Born: Mar. 2, 1901, Brockton, La.
Died: 1968, Newark, N.J.

A great power hitter who swung for distance while still maintaining a good average, Suttles, using a big 50-ounce bat, generated as much power as anyone in black baseball. Exemplifying this accomplishment are his stats after joining the St. Louis Stars in 1926, where he is credited with 26 home runs, a .432 batting average and a 1.000 slugging percentage, and his 1930 season statistics, showing a .384 batting average to pair with a .837 slugging percentage, which produced a home-run for each 10.1 at-bats.

At St. Louis, Stars' Park, with the trolley-car barn in left field, was an inviting target for a right-handed pull hitter, but Suttles was so strong that he didn't need the benefit of the short left-field fence and accumulated his impressive power totals without pulling the ball.

A free-swinger who struck out frequently, Suttles was a low-ball hitter with a big, powerful swing who hit towering tape-measure home runs that are still remembered by his teammates. The players would yell "Kick Mule!" and he would "kick" it out of the park. In Havana's Tropical Park, the center-field fence is 60 feet high and more than 500 feet from the plate. Teammate Willie Wells recalled a gargantuan drive that carried over the heads of the soldiers on horseback riding crowd control duty behind the fence, a total of about 600 feet. Afterward, a marker was placed at the spot, commemorating the prodigious homer.

Leon Day remembers the day Suttles hit one over the center-field fence in Washington's Griffith Stadium, and Ray Dandridge recalls a game in Louisville when one of Suttles's towering flies traveled more than 500 feet but was caught in deepest center field. Another teammate told of a game in 1929 when Suttles hit 3 home runs in a single inning against the Memphis Red Sox, and the next time he came to the plate, the Memphis team walked off the field.

With limited mobility, the hulking slugger's play afield was not impressive, either at first base or in the outfield. However, while not a graceful first sacker, he did handle everything he could reach, and his fielding was more than sufficient to complement his batting prowess.

The big right-hander's heavy hitting solidified his presence in the heart of the lineups of some of black baseball's best teams. As an outfielder for the St. Louis Stars Suttles hit .355 in 1929, and he supplied the power for the Stars to win championships in 1928, 1930, and 1931. In the 1928 championship playoffs against the Chicago American Giants he had a excellent Series at the plate and helped slug the Stars to a championship.

The 1931 pennant was the last in the history of the first Negro National League, with the league falling victim to the Depression, and the Stars' own demise closely following. After the Stars disbanded, Suttles jumped from one team to another, playing with the Washington Pilots and the Detroit Stars before eventually joining Robert A. Cole's Chicago American Giants. In

Chicago, manager Dave Malarcher corrected the slugger's tendency to overswing, and Suttles responded with a .315 batting average while generating a home run for each 13.5 at-bats to help power the club to the 1933 championship. During the ensuing winter he continued his power production, counting 14 home runs among his hits on the way to a .325 batting average in the Cuban League.

When financial difficulties befell the American Giants in 1936, Suttles joined the Newark Eagles as a first baseman and became a part of the celebrated "million-dollar infield" of 1937, while hitting .356 and averaging a homer for each 12.7 at-bats. Obviously the slugger had found a second home, and his numbers indicate the success he enjoyed in Newark. His marks show a .396 batting average and 36 home runs in 1936, a .420 batting average and 26 home runs in 1938, and a .325 average in 1939.

These marks earned the slugger two more East-West All-Star appearances to go with the three he had made with Chicago. He was also picked for the 1938 All-Star game but was withheld from the contest by the Eagles, and when the East lost, second-guessers were furious. Suttles, who liked to hit in clutch situations and was considered by teammate Willie Wells to be the best 1-run hitter ever, was one of the first All-Star game heroes, clouting 2 homers in dramatic fashion.

In the inaugural game, he hit the first home run in All-Star competition to lead the West to victory. Two years later, Suttles resorted to trickery to set the stage for an even more dramatic home run. In the eleventh inning, with Josh Gibson at the plate, 2 outs, and the winning run on second base, Suttles had pitcher Sug Cornelius kneel in the on-deck circle to fool the East brain trust into thinking he was the next batter, so they would intentionally walk Gibson. The ploy worked and Gibson was purposely passed to pitch to Cornelius. But it was really Suttles who was the next batter, and he provided the crowd with a Hollywood ending, with a towering shot off Martin Dihigo for another West victory. Although Suttles, who usually swung from the heels, was not a high-contact hitter, the totals for his five years of All-Star competition show a .412 batting average and an incredible .883 slugging percentage.

In April 1939 he was "loaned" to the Indianapolis ABCs to play a game against the Homestead Grays. Their owner, Cum Posey, was incensed at the tactic and protested vehemently. Suttles was also often sought for barnstorming tours. In an exhibition game against major-leaguers with Chicago Cubs' pitcher Big Jim Weaver on the mound, Suttles singled, doubled, and tripled. When he came up to bat for the fourth time, Weaver asked shortstop Leo Durocher how to pitch to the big slugger and Durocher answered, "Just pitch and pray." The advice was well founded, as Suttles is credited with a .374 lifetime batting average in exhibitions against major-leaguers.

The prodigious home runs hit by the big Louisiana native were powered by muscles developed in the coal mines of Birmingham, where Suttles played semipro ball on the mining teams of the area. These teams would form the nucleus for the Birmingham Black Barons in later years, and Suttles' older brother Charles was also a good player but broke his leg in the mines the same year that he was supposed to report to the Negro National League. Suttles was more fortunate and began his professional career at age seventeen. He played twenty-six years before bowing out as an active player, leaving behind a .338 lifetime average in league play. His longevity may be attributed to his outlook on life, which he expressed, "Don't worry about the Mule going blind, just load the wagon and give me the lines."

In 1941 the Eagles traded Suttles to the New York Black Yankees during the summer, but he returned during the next season, and in 1943 he was given the Eagles' managerial reins. As a manager he controlled his emotions on the field and was a patient hitting instructor. Off the field he was a gentle person, but jovial and frequently joking and kidding around. After retiring from baseball he lived in Newark until he died from cancer in 1968. He told the younger players, "When I die, have a little thought for my memory, but don't mourn too much."

Sutton
Career: 1929   Position: player
Team: Nashville Elite Giants

He appeared in a game with the Nashville Elite Giants in 1929, but his position is uncertain.

Sutton, Leroy
Career: 1941–45   Position: p
Teams: New Orleans-St. Louis Stars ('41), Chicago American Giants ('42–'44), Birmingham Black Barons ('43), Cincinnati-Indianapolis Clowns ('45), *Boston Blues ('46)*
Bats: Right   Throws: Right
Height: 6'2"   Weight: 190

A two-pitch hurler with average control of a mediocre curve and fastball, he was a second-line pitcher for the 1941 St. Louis Stars but was regarded as a good pitching prospect and was fighting hard for a starting berth on the club. He left the Stars and pitched with the Chicago American Giants for a season, then joined the Birmingham Black Barons in 1943, posting a 5–3 record before returning to the American Giants in 1944, suffering a 2–9 season. Finally, in 1945, he closed out his career with the Clowns. Aside from his pitching, he was an average fielder but a poor hitter.

Swallis
Career: 1921   Position: p
Team: Cuban Stars

He pitched briefly with the Cuban Stars in 1921, when they were playing as the Cincinnati entry in the Negro National League.

Swan
Career: 1933   Position: ss
Team: Akron Tyrites

This light-hitting shortstop played as a part-time starter, batting at the bottom of the order when in the lineup, for the Akron Tyrites in 1933, his only year in black baseball. The team was of marginal quality but combined with the Columbus Blue Birds to form the Cleveland Giants, a second-half entry in the Negro National League.

Swancy
Career: 1924   Position: p
Team: Indianapolis ABCs
He pitched briefly with the Indianapolis ABCs in 1924, his only year in the Negro Leagues.

Sweatt, George Alexander (Never, Sharkey, The Teacher)
Career: 1921–27   Positions: cf, 1b, rf, 3b, 2b, lf
Teams: *military service ('18–'19)*, Kansas City Monarchs ('21–'25), Chicago American Giants ('26–'27), *Chicago Giants ('28)*
Bats: Right   Throws: Right
Height: 6'2"   Weight: 195
Born: Dec. 12, 1893, Humboldt, Kan.
Died: July 19, 1983, Los Angeles, Calif.

This versatile player was at home in either the outfield or the infield, and played seven years in the Negro Leagues, beginning with the Kansas City Monarchs in 1921. During his last four years he became the only regular player to appear in each of the four World Series played between the Negro National League and the Eastern Colored League. The first two years he played with the Kansas City Monarchs against Hilldale, and the last two years he played with the Chicago American Giants against the Bacharach Giants. In these four World Series he recorded batting averages of .278, .150, .289, and .212, respectively, and was on the winning team each time except in 1925.

During the regular seasons of these four years, he hit .259, .235, .262, and .254 while usually batting in the fifth or sixth slot in the batting order. The tall, lanky utility man was the starting center fielder for the Monarchs during the 1924 season and switched to first base for the next year. In 1926 he was playing at second base when he was traded to the American Giants for Cristobal Torriente, and moved

back to the outfield, starting in center field that year and switching to right field in 1927.

An all-around athlete at Humboldt High School, he also played on the local white town team, and with a nearby town's black team called the Iola Gold Devils. After graduation in 1912, he continued his athletic pursuits, starring in football, basketball, track, and baseball while attending Pittsburg, Kansas, Normal College. In his last year in college, he also pitched with a semipro team. After completing his college studies, he accepted a teaching position in Coffeyville, Kansas.

Both his careers, in education and in baseball, were interrupted by military service during World War I. He was with the 816th Pioneer Infantry Division, which arrived in France only two weeks before the Armistice. After his discharge the following year, he returned to both of his careers, teaching and playing semipro baseball.

His batting performance against John Donaldson of the touring All Nations ballclub earned Sweatt a spot with the Kansas City Monarchs. He was placed at thirdbase. His fielding left much to be desired, but his hitting earned him a spot on the roster. He was a good 2-strike hitter and never swung at the first pitch. After being traded to the American Giants, Foster changed his batting stance. After Foster became incapacitated, the team ownership was transferred to William E. Trimble in 1927.

When the new owner did not offer Sweatt a raise for the 1928 season, he left the franchise and began working full time in the Postal Service. On weekends he managed Joe Green's Chicago Giants for a season before managing a lesser semipro team, Jimmy Hutton's All-Stars, for an additional six years. Two years later, in 1936, he moved to Evanston, Illinois, and was active in civic, church, and Scouting activities for young people. He also liked to sing and bowl and, after retiring from the Postal Service in 1957, he continued to pursue his hobbies, even bowling a 153 game at age eighty. In the latter years of his life he moved to California and lived with his son until his death only a few months short of his ninetieth birthday.

Sykes, Franklin J. (Frank, **Doc**)
a.k.A. Melvin
Career: 1915–26   Positions: **p,** *1b*
Teams: Philadelphia Giants ('13), Brooklyn Royal Giants ('14–'16), New York Lincoln Stars ('15–'17), **Hilldale Daisies** ('17–'18, '22–'23), Baltimore Black Sox ('20–'24), New York Lincoln Giants ('26)
Bats: Right   Throws: Right
Height: 6'2"   Weight: 185
Born: Apr. 10, 1892, Decatur, Ala.
Died: Nov. 10, 1986, Baltimore, Md.

This long-legged spitballer was an off-speed pitcher with three speeds—slow, slower, and slowest. He had superb control and once pitched a perfect game. His father, Sol, was an embalmer, and as the sixth child in a family of a dozen, the youngster learned early to fend for himself, working as a redcap at Union Station Washington, D.C. and learning the value of an education. While pitching for the Lincoln Stars and Hilldale in the '10s, he continued his education while playing professional baseball. He attended Atlanta Baptist College (now Morehouse College) for one year before enrolling at Howard University in 1912 to study dentistry for five years, graduating in 1918.

During this time he pitched in college and with the New York Lincoln Giants, Brooklyn Royal Giants, and Lincoln Stars, playing with whatever team was easiest to correlate with his studies in the university. Doc Wiley, a catcher, dentist, and Howard graduate, was responsible for him going to the Lincoln Giants the first time he was with the ballclub. In 1915 he pitched briefly with the Philadelphia Giants but joined the Lincoln Stars in mid-June. The following year he was with Howard University in April, pitched with the Brooklyn Royal Giants during the summer, and was back to college again in September. The next year, after leaving Howard, he played with the Lincoln Stars and the Brooklyn Royal Giants before joining Hilldale in mid-June.

After graduation he set up a dental office in Anniston, Alabama, but moved his practice to Baltimore in 1920 so he could earn extra money by pitching with the Baltimore Black Sox. In 1921 he had a 13–3 record, following in 1922 with an 18–4 record, including a no-hitter against the Bacharachs. The Black Sox finished with a home record of 49–12 and won the title Champions of the South. In 1923 his playing time was lessened and he split half a dozen pitching decisions. The following summer, Sykes was released by Black Sox manager Pete Hill because his dentistry practice prohibited him from traveling with the team.

During his career he occasionally played first base, and he recorded batting averages of .164, .245, and .231 in 1921–22 and 1926. After one last fling with Hilldale in 1926, he retired from the diamond and moved back to Decatur, Alabama, to practice dentistry.

Five years later he was involved in the infamous Scottsboro Case as a witness at the trial. Sykes's parents were born slaves but, without benefit of a formal education, they taught him truth, honesty, and respect. These lessons served him well during his testimony at the trial. Afterward, receiving related threats to his life and his family's welfare, he moved back to Baltimore in 1937 and reestablished his dental practice. Settling down to the life of a professional, he counted Paul Robeson among his circle of friends. Sykes died of complications from pulmonary pneumonia in Baltimore in 1986.

Sykes, Joe
a.k.a. Siki
Career: 1942   Positions: p, of
Team: Ethiopian Clowns

In 1942, he pitched and played outfield with the Ethiopian Clowns, an independent team that was on a par with league teams. His Clown name was Siki.

T

Tabor
Career: 1910   Position: 2b
Team: St. Louis Giants

This infielder appeared as a second baseman with the St. Louis Giants in 1910, the second season after the team was organized.

Taborn, Earl (Mickey)
Career: 1946–50   Position: c
Teams: Kansas City Monarchs ('46–'51), *minor leagues* ('49), Mexican League ('51–'61)
Bats: Right   Throws: Right
Height: 6'0"   Weight: 175
Born: July 21, 1922, Carrie Mills, Ill.

As a receiver he was outstanding behind the plate, with a strong and accurate arm, but he was slow on the bases and, although a tough out for some pitchers, he was generally an average hitter for both consistency and power, usually hitting in the eighth slot for the Monarchs. Joining Kansas City in 1946, he shared the catching duties with Joe Greene for the Monarch's last pennant-winning ballclub but hit only .206. While Greene was a better hitter, Taborn was the top receiver on the squad and was charged with handling the Monarchs' superb mound corps. After another year of sharing the catching spot with Greene, Taborn took over sole possession of the starting position in 1948, and responded with a batting average of .301. Two years later he batted .345.

Between these two prime seasons with the Monarchs, he spent some time with Newark in the International League, batting only .247. Beginning in 1951, when he hit .247 with Mexico City, he began eleven straight seasons in the Mexican League. His best year was in 1957 with Nuevo Laredo, when he hit .314 with 27 home runs. The next year was also a good year with the club, and he hit .274 with 17 home runs. Prior to joining Nuevo Laredo he played with Veracruz, compiling marks of .289 with 15 home runs and .279 with 12 home runs in 1955–56. He finished his career in 1961 with Puebla, hitting .267. During his years in Mexico, the light-complexioned catcher was sometimes mistaken for a Mexican.

Talbert, Dangerfield (**Danger**, Tal, Old Reliable)
Career: 1900–1911   Positions: **3b**, ss, 2b
Teams: Chicago Unions ('00), Chicago Union Giants ('01–'02, '04), Algona Brownies ('03), Cuban X-Giants ('05), Leland Giants ('06–'09), Chicago Giants ('10–'11)
Bats: Right   Throws: Right
Born: Mar. 8, 1878, Platte City, Mo.

One of the top guardians of the hot corner during the first decade of the century, he spent almost his entire career with Chicago-based ballclubs owned by Frank Leland. He began playing baseball at age sixteen, as a catcher on his public high-school team in Omaha, Nebraska, and began his professional career in 1900 when he signed as a third baseman with Peters' Chicago Unions. The next season, when owner Frank Leland consolidated the team with the Columbia Giants to become the Chicago Union Giants, Talbert remained as part of the new ballclub. During his stint with the Union Giants, the infielder was a regular at third base (1901), shortstop (1902), and second base (1904), but left for a season to hold down the hot corner of the Algona (Iowa) Brownies in their championship 1903 season.

In 1905 he played both second base and third base for the Philadelphia-based Cuban X-Giants, but returned to Chicago the following season to reunite with Frank Leland on the new team bearing the owner's name, the Leland Giants. Talbert played at second base that season, but returned to his more familiar territory at third for the next three seasons under manager Rube Foster. In 1909, with Talbert doing his usual great work at the hot corner and hitting .309, the Lelands won the City League championship. His fielding and hitting equalled those of any other man on the team, earning him the nickname "Old Reliable" among his teammates for his dependability and the timeliness of his contributions.

When Leland and Foster went their separate ways in 1910, Talbert went with Leland and his new team, the Chicago Giants. The owner described his expectations for his veteran infielder, saying that Talbert would be "found in the infield as usual picking them up with either hand and slugging sweet curves that are most to his liking." An all-around player, he was a good batter, was good on the double play, and could "deliver the goods." After two years with the Chicago Giants, he retired from the baseball diamond after a dozen seasons with the top clubs of the era.

Talbert, James
Career: 1946–48   Position: c
Team: Chicago American Giants

He joined the Chicago American Giants in 1946 and was a backup catcher during his three years with the team, batting in the lower part of the order when in the lineup and posting averages of .128 in 1946 and .217 in 1948, his last season.

Talley
Career: 1932–34   Position: p
Teams: Atlantic City Bacharach Giants ('32), New York Black Yankees ('34)

A pitcher with the New York Black Yankees in 1934, he had appeared with the Bacharach Giants two years previously.

Tampos
Career: 1916   Position: 1b
Team: Cuban Stars

He played as a first baseman with the Cuban Stars in 1916, his only year in black baseball.

Tapley, John R.
Career: 1933   Position: 3b
Team: Akron Tyrites

In 1933 he was a part-time starter at third base with the Akron Tyrites, and usually hit in the second slot in the batting order when in the lineup. The Tyrites was an independent team that merged with the Columbus Blue Birds, who dropped out of the Negro National League after the first half to form the Cleveland Giants' ballclub as a replacement entry in the second half of the Negro National League season. His brother, Townsend also played with Akron.

Tapley, Townsend
Career: 1933   Position: ss
Team: Akron Tyrites

In 1933 he played shortstop with the Akron Tyrites, a marginal independent team that merged with the Columbus Blue Birds, who dropped out of the Negro National League after the first half to form the replacement ballclub, the Cleveland Giants. His brother, John, also played with Akron.

Tate
Career: 1914   Position: p

Teams: New York Lincoln Giants ('14), *Philadelphia Giants ('18)*

A marginal pitcher during the '10s, he made his first appearance with the Lincoln Giants in 1914, winning his only recorded decision. In 1918 he pitched with the Philadelphia Giants after the team had declined in its quality of play.

Tate, George

Career: 1922   Positions: owner, officer

Team: Cleveland Tate Stars (*'18–'22*)

The owner of the Cleveland ballclub incorporated his name into that of his team, the Cleveland Tate Stars, and entered them in the Negro National League in 1922, their only year in the league. He also served as the vice president of the league that season.

Tate, Roosevelt (Speed)

Career: 1931–37   Position: of

Teams: Knoxville *Giants* ('31), Louisville White Sox ('31), Louisville Black Caps ('32), Birmingham Black Barons ('32), Nashville Elite Giants ('32), Memphis Red Sox, Cincinnati Tigers ('37), Chicago American Giants ('37),

Bats: Both   Throws: Right

This speedy outfielder spent his seven seasons with southern teams except for 1937, when he played with the Chicago American Giants. An occasional starter in center field that season, he batted in the leadoff spot when in the lineup.

Tatum, Reece (Goose)

Career: 1941–49   Positions: 1b, of

Teams: Birmingham Black Barons ('41–'42), Cincinnati Clowns ('43), Cincinnati-Indianapolis Clowns ('45), Indianapolis Clowns ('46–'49), Minneapolis-St. Paul Gophers, *Detroit Stars ('58)*

Bats: Right   Throws: Right

Height: 6'6"   Weight: 190

Better known as a member of the world-famous Harlem Globetrotters' basketball team,

Tatum was also a flashy-fielding showman with the Indianapolis Clowns. At first base he provided a big target for infielders and entertained the fans with his long arms and a bit stretch. Although better known for his glovework, Tatum started the 1947 All-Star game for the West squad and banged out 2 hits in 4 times at the plate. The next spring he was incapacitated when stricken with appendicitis and hit only .226 for the year.

Although gaining most of his baseball recognition with the Clowns, he began his professional career with the Birmingham Black Barons in 1941 and spent two seasons in Birmingham before joining the Clowns when they were located in Cincinnati. His hitting was not exceptional, with batting averages of .250 and .282 in 1945–46, but the Philadelphia Phillies wanted to sign him and offered him $1,000 per month. However, they planned to send him to the minor leagues, and he declined their offer. Tatum was considered very moody, and once stabbed Kansas City Monarchs' pitcher Hilton Smith with a screwdriver. While recognized as a great basketball player, he was only mediocre on the baseball diamond.

Taylor

Career: 1910   Position: p

Team: Kansas City Giants

He was a pitcher with the Kansas City, Kansas, Giants in 1910, the year of their strongest team.

Taylor

Career: 1922   Positions: p, of

Team: Harrisburg Giants

He pitched and played outfield with the Harrisburg Giants in 1922, when they were still an inndependent team.

Taylor

Career: 1940   Position: p

Team: Newark Eagles

This pitcher appeared briefly, without a decision, for the Newark Eagles in 1940.

Taylor, Alfred

Career: 1933   Position: 1b
Team: Akron Tyrites

In 1933 he played first base with the Akron Tyrites, a marginal independent team that merged with the Columbus Blue Birds, who dropped out of the Negro National League after the first half to form the replacement ballclub, the Cleveland Giants.

Taylor, Benjamin

Career: 1947   Position: p
Team: New York Black Yankees

He was a pitcher with the New York Black Yankees in 1947, his only season in the Negro Leagues.

Taylor, Benjamin H. (Ben)

Career: 1910–40   Positions: **1b**, p, manager, umpire

Teams: *Birmingham Giants ('08–'09)*, West Baden Sprudels ('10, *'13*), St. Louis Giants ('11–'12), New York Lincoln Giants ('12), Chicago American Giants ('13–'14), **Indianapolis ABCs** ('14–'18, '20–'22), Hilldale Daisies ('19), New York Bacharach Giants ('19), Washington Potomacs ('23–'24), Harrisburg Giants ('25), Baltimore Black Sox ('26–'28), Atlantic City Bacharach Giants ('29); *California Stars ('30), Silver Moons ('31)*, Washington Pilots ('32), *Baltimore Stars ('33)*, Brooklyn Eagles ('35), *Winston-Salem Eagles ('38)*, Washington Black Senators ('38), *Washington Royals ('39)*, New York Cubans ('40), *Edgewater Giants ('41)*
Bats: Left   Throws: Left
Height: 6'1"   Weight: 190
Born: July 1, 1888, Anderson, S.C.
Died: Jan. 24, 1953, Baltimore, Md.

One of the early stars of the game, this smooth-fielding, sharp-hitting member of the famous Taylor family was considered the best first baseman in black baseball prior to the arrival of Buck Leonard. Throughout his career Taylor was one of the most productive players offensively, ending with a .334 lifetime batting average. He was good on ground balls and could make all the plays at first, making the other infielders look good by digging out low throws and making difficult plays with such ease that they appeared routine. Always a heads-up player, Taylor was an ideal man to have on a ballclub.

Taylor began his playing career in 1908 as a pitcher with th Birmingham Giants, and recorded an impressive 22–3 ledger in 1909. Two years later, with St. Louis, he is credited with a 30–1 pitching record against all levels of opposition. Although he continued with his pitching for several years afterward, it was with his bat and play at first base that he earned his most notoriety. He was a scientific batter, drilling line drives to all fields, and he could execute the hit-and-run play.

When his brother C. I. Taylor assumed the managerial reins of the West Baden, Indiana, Sprudels in 1910, Ben moved North with him and, playing as a combination pitcher-first baseman, won a disputed team batting title. Although he was still regarded primarily as a pitcher, his baseball acumen was beginning to attract the attention of baseball's top teams. He spent the 1911–12 seasons with the St. Louis Giants, but had a brief stint the latter year with the New York Lincoln Giants. During these formative seasons he turned in some solid performances as a moundsman, often showing flashes of brilliance. But he also continued his early hitting promise, registering as .379 average in 1912 to warrant interest from Rube Foster.

At Chicago he joined his brothers Jim and Johnny, and after a season as Foster's first baseman on the 1913 Chicago American Giants, Taylor gained his greatest fame while playing with the Indianapolis ABCs (1914–22), Managed by his brother C. I. Taylor. In his first year with the ABCs, Ben Taylor stepped into the cleanup slot, hit a robust .333, and remained in that batting slot as long as he was with the ABCs. In his second season with the team he turned in another solid performance, with available stats showing a .308 average as the ABCs fought their way toward the top. The following year, management difficulties produced a schism between owner Thomas Bowser and manager C. I. Taylor, with two different ABCs squads being fielded during the first half of the season. However, Taylor's ABCs regrouped during the second half to get the championship from Foster's team. Taylor, a left-hander both in the field and at the plate, batted .335 and fashioned an MVP-level performance to lead the surge to the championship.

Sandwiched between the 1915 and 1916 seasons Taylor made a sojourn to Cuba, where he left behind an impressive .500 average for his stint on the island before returning to the ABCs with his hot bat. He remained with the ABCs through 1918, leaving for a season with the New York Bacharach Giants in 1919 for his first excursion into managerial waters. He returned to the ABCs in 1920 and, already an established veteran, the hard-hitting first sacker easily made the transition from the deadball era to the lively ball. Continuing to hit with authority, he compiled averages of .323, .407, and .358 in his last three seasons (1920–22) with the ABCs.

Following the death of his brother C. I. Taylor in 1922, he managed the ABCs for a season before leaving the team in the spring of 1923 to travel East again for another venture into management. He assumed the responsibility of organizing the Washington Potomacs ballclub and hired his brother Steel Arm Johnny Taylor as pitching coach to help with instruction in baseball fundamentals. After assembling the team, Ben Taylor guided his charges for one season as an independent ballclub. During their maiden season Taylor tried twenty-eight different players in the lineup, but for the most part they were not of major-league caliber, and he retained only six of this group for the 1924 season, when they were admitted to the Eastern Colored League ranks.

Taylor was credited with hitting over .300 in fifteen of his first sixteen years in baseball, but with the managerial pressures to produce a winning team in 1924, he had what he considered his worst offensive year but still led his team in batting average (.314) and home runs (15). Although the skipper personally forged respectable statistics, the ballclub had a disappointing season, and when the Potomacs were scuttled, he joined forces with Oscar Charleston at Harrisburg for the 1925 season and hit for a .328 average as playing manager.

From there he moved to the Baltimore Black Sox, again as playing manager, replacing Pete Hill in midsummer of 1926. The team was suffering with disciplinary problems, and Taylor's stay there was troubled. After assuming the managerial reins, he quickly dispatched free-spirited slugger John Beckwith to Harrisburg in a trade in an effort to instill a semblance of discipline. The following summer, Taylor suffered cuts that required twenty stitches when he and several other Black Sox players were injured as a cement truck sideswiped their team automobile. Despite being past his prime, and the hardships he encountered during his three seasons in Baltimore, he still stroked the ball for averages of .242, .307, and .336.

Prior to the start of the 1929 season, in a trade of managers, he was traded to the Atlantic City Bacharach Giants for Dick Lundy and signed what was thought to be the highest salary in black baseball. With the Bacharachs, at age forty-one, he still hit .322 to close both the decade and his playing career, finishing with a .334 lifetime batting average in black baseball.

After he ended his career as an active player, he continued in baseball in various capacities. He umpired in both the East-West League in 1932 and the Negro National League in 1934. He also managed and coached with several teams at different levels of competition, including the Baltimore Stars in 1933, where he tutored Buck Leonard on the finer points of playing first base.

Modest, easygoing, and soft-spoken, Taylor was a true gentleman who maintained a fair and professional demeanor, and he was an excellent teacher of young players. It was from him that Buck Leonard learned to polish and refine his skills as a first baseman.

In the latter years of his life Taylor operated

a poolroom for a time, but broke his left arm in a fall and, when it was not properly set, he lost the arm to amputation. He remained active in baseball, securing rights to print and distribute game programs and scorecards at Bugle Field when the Baltimore Elite Giants played there. In January 1953, three years after giving up his enterprise, he died of pneumonia. Highly regarded by his peers, smooth in the field, and with no weakness at the plate, Ben Taylor is well deserving of his niche among the greats in black baseball history.

Taylor, Charles Isham (**C. I.**)
Career: 1904–22   Positions: 2b, **manager**; officer (NNL)
Teams: Birmingham Giants ('04–'09), West Baden Sprudels ('10–'13), **Indianapolis ABCs** ('14–'21)
Bats: Right   Throws: Right
Height: 5'11"   Weight: 175
Born: Jan. 20, 1875, South Carolina
Died: Feb. 23, 1922, Indianapolis, Ind.

Acknowledged along with Rube Foster as one of the two greatest managers of all time, contemporaries said that C.I. trained the players and Rube signed them. On the field, the master builder from Carolina was a strict disciplinarian and a great teacher who brought out the best in his players. At times he would put on a show for the fans by "clowning" in the third-base coaching box by eating grass or jumping up and down and yelling about a pitcher's fastball offerings. His crowd-pleasing comedic antics contrasted with his off-field behavior, where C.I., the son of a Methodist minister, was a perfect gentleman and demonstrated exemplary character. He was civic-minded and as a member of the Masonic Lodge, he held the honor of being a thirty-third-degree Mason.

After attending Clark College in Atlanta and serving in the Spanish-American War, he began his nineteen-year managerial career in 1940 with the Birmingham Giants, where he was a player-manager. After five seasons in the South's steel center, he moved the team North to West Baden, Indiana, where he played second base and managed the West Baden Sprudels in 1910. In 1914 he again transferred the team, this time to Indianapolis, where the club was sponsored by the American Brewing Company and called the ABCs. Immediately his baseball acumen was evident as he built and nurtured a team that was recognized as a perennial power.

His greatest success came in 1916 when, featuring such stalwarts as Oscar Charleston, Ben Taylor, Bingo DeMoss, and Dizzy Dismukes, the ABC's captured the western championship by defeating Rube Foster's Chicago American Giants. The previous year, the ABCs had lost a hard-fought championship series to the American Giants. Although well past his prime, Taylor still made an occasional appearance, primarily as a pinch hitter, and had a composite .200 batting average for the 1915–16 teams. After having fought their way to the top, the ABCs were decimated by the draft in World War I, losing seven men to military service. Taylor, a patriotic veteran of the Spanish-American War, took his draftees to Washington, D.C., and showed them the buildings in the country's seat of government.

Always a proud man, he was equally proud of his team, and under his management the ABCs always fielded a classy ballclub. His teams traveled first-class and were dressed well on the field. He maintained his composure with umpires, even when he thought they were wrong. On one occasion, after being barraged by bad calls from an umpire, he called for a time-out and walked out to the offending umpire and said, "If I were a cursing man, I would curse you," then turned and walked back to the bench.

When the Negro National League was formed in 1920, the ABCs were charter members and C.I. was installed as the league's vice president, serving in that capacity until his death in 1922. In reinforcing his roster for the initial season of league competition, he signed half a dozen players from the San Antonio Black Aces, including Biz Mackey and Henry Blackman. Taylor knew how to handle men, and under his tutelege the ABCs played winning baseball during the first two seasons in the league. But Taylor's brilliant career was abruptly terminated when he died at the relatively young age of 47. Even after his untimely death, his presence remained in evidence through the players he had schooled in the finer points of baseball—players whose characters were shaped in the Taylor kiln and who bore the indelible imprint of the C. I. Taylor philosophy of baseball.

Taylor, C. I., Mrs.
Career: 1922–24   Position: officer
Team: Indianapolis ABCs

After her husband's death in February 1922, his widow continued to run the ballclub for three years. In the first season, with C.I.'s younger brother Ben handling the managerial reins, the team challenged Rube Foster's American Giants with a strong second-place finish in 1922. But without C.I.'s presence to hold the team together, after the formation of the Eastern Colored League, many players left for other teams. This exodus to the East included Ben Taylor, who had differences with Mrs. Taylor regarding management of the team. The raids from the East were devastating to the franchise and the decline was rapid, with the team eventually being forced to discontinue operations after the 1926 season.

Taylor, Cyrus G.
Career: 1924–25   Position: of
Teams: New York Lincoln Giants ('24), Harrisburg Giants ('25)

A reserve outfielder for two years during the mid-'20s, he appeared with the New York Lincoln Giants and the Harrisburg Giants.

Taylor, George
Career: 1889–1906   Positions: 1b, c, of, ss
Teams: *minor leagues ('90),* Page Fence Giants ('95, '97–'98), Chicago Union Giants ('03–'06), Leland Giants ('05)

During the late 1890s, he played first base and shortstop with the Page Fence Giants, one of the best black teams of the era. A good

hitter, he batted .350 in 1895, his first year with the team. Earlier in his career he played in predominantly white leagues, including a season as the left fielder for the Lincoln, Nebraska, Giants in 1890, and stints with Beatrice in the Nebraska State league and both Aspen and his hometown Denver in the Colorado State League. After the turn of the century he played with the Chicago Union Giants prior to joining the Leland Giants as the starting first baseman in their first season, 1905. After his single season with the Lelands, he returned to the Union Giants for his last year with a top black team.

Taylor, H. C.
Career: 1887   Position: player
Team: *Boston Resolutes*

He played with the Boston Resolutes, one of eight teams that were charter members of the League of Colored Baseball Clubs in 1887. However, the league's existence was ephemeral, lasting only a week. His position is uncertain.

Taylor, James Allen (Candy Jim)
Career: 1940–48   Positions: **3b**, 2b, ss, *p*, **manager**, officer; league official
Teams: Birmingham Giants ('04'–08), Leland Giants ('09), St. Paul Gophers ('09–'10), Chicago Giants ('10), St. Louis Giants ('11), *West Baden Sprudels ('12),* Chicago American Giants ('12–'13), Indianapolis ABCs ('14–'19), '31–'32), Louisville White Sox ('15), Bowser's ABCs ('16), Dayton Marcos ('19–'21), Cleveland Tate Stars ('22), Toledo Tigers ('23), St. Louis Stars ('23–'29), Cleveland Elites ('26), Detroit Stars ('26, '33), Memphis Red Sox ('30), Nashville Elite Giants ('33–'34); Columbus Elite Giants ('35), Washington Elite Giants ('36), Baltimore Elite Giants ('48), Chicago American Giants ('37–'39, '41–'42, '45–'47), Birmingham Black Barons ('40), Homestead Grays ('43–'44)
League: Negro National League

Bats: Right Throws: Right
Height: 5'9" Weight: 185
Born: Feb. 1, 1884, Anderson, S.C.
Died: Apr. 3, 1948, Chicago, Ill.

A member of the famous Taylor family, "Candy Jim" was a good-hitting infielder and a quick thinker who played mostly at third base prior to becoming a successful manager. As a player he was a member of three championship teams: the 1909 St. Paul Gophers, the 1912 Chicago American Giants, and the 1916 Indianapolis ABCs. As a manager he piloted another pair of teams to a championship. He directed the St. Louis Stars to the 1928 Negro National League championship, and a during a wartime stint with the Homestead Grays, he managed the team to a pair of World Series victories over the Birmingham Black Barons in 1943–44. A master strategist with excellent managerial ability, he began his helm experience in 1919 as playing manager, and he was with sixteen different teams during a forty-five-year career as player and manager that spanned virtually the entire existence of the black baseball era.

He attended Greeley Institute in his hometown of Anderson, South Carolina, and learned the game of baseball on the local sandlots, making his debut at age thirteen, but did not play with an organized team until 1901, when he joined an amateur ballclub in his hometown as a catcher. The next two years he played with different clubs in South Carolina, and in 1904 he went to Birmingham, Alabama, where his brother C. I. Taylor was managing. Assigned to the hot corner, Candy Jim handled the job well, making only 3 errors in 55 games for the remainder of the season. In addition to his exceptional fielding he posted batting averages of .290, .306, .298, .340, and .316 for the seasons of 1904–08 with the Birmingham Giants. He continued with that team for the next five years, until early in the 1909 season, when he moved North to join the St. Paul Gophers, who defeated the Leland Giants for the western championship.

In 1910 he moved to Chicago to play third base with Frank Leland's newly formed Chicago Giants, but after a year he joined the St. Louis Giants, batting fifth in the lineup while holding down the third-base slot. Leaving again after only one year, he signed on with Rube Foster's Chicago American Giants in 1912, and stepped into the cleanup spot in his first year with the team. The American Giants proved to be the top team in the West, and one of Foster's best teams ever. The next season Candy Jim's brother Ben joined him on the American Giants, who retained their place atop the western independents.

In 1914 the two brothers joined their other pair of brothers, C. I. and Steel Arm Johnny, on the Indianapolis ABCs. Candy Jim batted third and Ben fourth, while Johnny was a star hurler and C. I. was the manager and pinch hitter in the ABCs' first year as a major-league-caliber ballclub. After a season in Louisville. Candy Jim returned to the ABCs and slipped back into the third slot in the batting order, hitting .315 as the ABCs defeated Rube Foster's Chicago American Giants for the western championship in 1916. The next season he split his time afield between third base and second base but was hampered by injuries, dropping to a .235 batting average for the year. In 1918 he played at second base while Dave Malarcher moved into the third-base spot. He left the ABCs in 1919 to join the Dayton Marcos, batting in the heart of the order while playing every infield position except first base.

Embarking on his managerial career, he spent the next few seasons at the helm of faltering franchises that slipped in and out of the Negro National League in short order. The 1920 Marcos was the first team he guided in league play. Leaving the Marcos, he signed on as manager of the Cleveland Tate Stars in 1922, and was the third baseman and cleanup hitter, but the team also dropped out of the league after a year. His next stop with a fringe ballclub was with the Toledo Tigers, who lasted only half a season in the league.

Finally he took the reins of an established team, signing with the St. Louis Stars in 1923 and remaining as player-manager through 1929 except for the 1926 season, when he managed the Cleveland Elites and the Detroit Stars. As a player he posted batting averages of .287, .342, .186, .317, and .389 in 1923–27. By the middle of the decade his emphasis was on managing, and he had adjusted to a reserve status as a player. Taylor had a reputation of being a good judge of young talent, but according to one source, he made a colossal mistake in one instance. In 1930, while managing the Memphis Red Sox, he picked up a youngster named Josh Gibson for a game in Scranton, Pennsylvania, and afterward said that he would never be a catcher.

After a year at the helm of the Red Sox and with a batting average of .250 at age forty-six, he returned to Indianapolis to try to reestablish the ABCs after four years without a ballclub in the city. After two years he became part owner and the franchise moved to Detroit, playing in 1933 as the Stars. But falling victim to the economy of the Depression, the ballclub folded after the season. Following he demise of his team, he resumed his helm-hopping, making stops with the Nashville Elite Giants, Columbus Elite Giants, Brooklyn Royal Giants, Washington Elite Giants, Chicago American Giants, Birmingham Black Barons, Homestead Grays, and Baltimore Elite Giants.

Beginning in 1935 he was a nonplaying manager, and he was the manager of the Negro National League All-Star team that easily won the *Denver Post* Tournament in 1936. During his association with baseball he also served as the vice chairman of the Negro National League. He began the 1948 season as manager of the Baltimore Elite Giants, but after an extended illness, he passed away in the spring before the start of the regular season.

Taylor, Jim

Career: 1896   Position: of
Team: Cuban Giants

In 1896 he was an outfielder with the Cuban Giants, the first black professional team, which was organized in 1885.

Taylor, John (Big, **Red**)

Career: 1920–25   Position: p
Teams: Chicago Giants ('20–'21), Kansas City Monarchs ('21–'22), Gilkerson's Union Giants, New York Lincoln Giants ('24–'25), *Pennsylvania Red Caps of New York ('26–'28)*

This emery ball pitcher began his career with the Chicago Giants in 1920, the first year of the Negro National League, and posted a 4–11 mark in his second season in the league. The next season he joined the Kansas City Monarchs, where he was called "Big" Taylor, and after leaving the Monarchs, he had one of his best years, with the New York Lincoln Giants in 1924, but slipped back to a 1–7 mark in 1925. He was the brother-in-law of pitcher Luther Farrell, and while Farrell was with the champion Bacharachs, Taylor spent the next three seasons with the Pennsylvania Red Caps of New York, a team of lesser status. He also played with Gilkerson's Union Giants, and is reported to have played for San Francisco in the Pacific Coast League under an assumed name.

Taylor, John (**Johnny,** Schoolboy)

Career: 1935–45   Position: p
Teams: **New York Cubans** ('35–'38, '40, '42, '45), *semipro ball ('37)*, Pittsburgh Crawfords ('38), Toledo Crawfords ('39), *Mexican League ('39–'41, '45–'46), voluntarily retired ('43–'44), military service ('42–'44), minor leagues ('49)*
Bats: Right   Throws: Right
Height: 5'11"   Weight: 165
Born: Hartford, Conn.

A stringy young right-hander with a big leg kick, he was a star pitcher for the New York Cubans during the late 1930s. He had a good fastball and curve, with a pretty good change-up, and his drop was regarded as the best in the league in 1937. That season he injured his arm while pitching for a Hartford semipro team in his hometown. But after his recovery he gained his first notoriety when he tossed a no-hitter at the Polo Grounds for the Negro National League All-Stars against Satchel Paige's Dominican All-Stars. Despite losing a rematch to Satchel a week later, his sterling performance had made him a hot property and he was sought by several teams in 1938. He initially decided in favor of the Cubans, but during the season he joined the Pittsburgh Crawfords. Taylor earned a spot on the East squad for the East-West All-Star game, yielding 3 hits in 2 scoreless innings in the contest, a 5–4 victory for the West.

Taylor broke in with the New York Cubans in 1935, with a 4–3 league ledger, as the Cubans captured the second-half title in the Negro National League's split season, and extended the Pittsburgh Crawfords to 7 games in the championship playoffs before bowing in defeat. After pitching two years with the team and also pitching in the Cuban winter league, the popular young hurler became a favorite around New York. When he jumped the Cubans in 1939 for the big money in Mexico, he was rated as a "sure-fire" prospect.

In his first season in Mexico, pitching with Cordoba, he registered an 11–1 record, an 1.19 ERA, and 92 strikeouts in 105 innings. In 1940 he left the Mexican League to pitch again with the Cubans for most of the season, but after a disappointing 1–7 record, he returned to Mexico and pitched in 4 games with a 3–1 record for Jorge Pasqual's Vera Cruz team. In 1941 he returned to the same team and they walked away with the championship. Taylor contributed a 13–10 record with a 4.40 ERA despite having severe control problems, walking 150 batters in 190 innings.

During the next three seasons he stayed home in Hartford, pitching for the Cubans on weekends in 1942, but choosing not to play at all for the next two seasons. He didn't pitch in Mexico again until 1945, when he hurled for Vera Cruz. After World War II he split 4 decisions in 1946 and was still having some difficulty with his control. Unfortunately, he hurt his arm while bearing down too hard in striking out 3 straight batters in an inning, and the injury cut his season short after only two weeks.

He again remained out of baseball until 1949, when he pitched in his hometown with Hartford's Eastern League team. Taylor had a 6–7 record with a 3.39 ERA, but his arm was not the same as before the injury. During his career he had all the skills necessary for stardom, but his lack of stamina inhibited him from pitching complete games. Consequently he consistently tired in late innings, with a correlating loss in sharpness.

Taylor, Johnny
Career: 1943–45   Position: of
Team: Birmingham Black Barons

A wartime player, he appeared as a reserve outfielder with the Birmingham Black Barons for the last three seasons before the end of World War II.

Taylor, Jonathan Boyce (John, Steel Arm Johnny)
Career: 1903–25   Positions: p, manager, coach
Teams: Birmingham Giants ('03'–09), St. Paul Gophers ('09), Chicago Giants ('10), West Baden Sprudels ('10, '13), St. Louis Giants ('11), New York Lincoln Giants ('12), Chicago American Giants ('13), Indianapolis ABCs ('14, '16, '20), Louisville Sox ('15), Bowser's ABCs ('16), Hilldale Daisies ('17), Bacharach Giants ('19), Washington Potomacs ('24)
Bats: Right   Throws: Right
Height: 5'10"   Weight: 170
Born: 1879, Anderson, S.C.

The second oldest of the five famous members of the Taylor clan, he began his baseball career early in life, but pitched his first games of any note in the spring of 1898, when he pitched for Biddle University of Charlotte, North Carolina, against Shaw University at Latta Park, his home field. A sportswriter for the *Charlotte Observer*, a white daily newspaper, was so impressed with his exceptional speed that he dubbed Taylor "Steel Arm

Johnny.'' After school was out for the summer, he played with two teams in South Carolina, first for two months with the Greenwood Red Stockings, and the remainder of the season with Greenville. The next two seasons, 1899–1900, he pitched for his hometown team, Anderson, South Carolina, winning 90 percent of his games.

In 1903 he journeyed to Alabama, joining the Birmingham Giants, managed by his older brother C. I. Taylor. During the next six years John always pitched thirty to forty games a season and never lost more than 7 games in any year. Taylor could also hit the ball, was a good defensive player, and had the reputation of being a smart, steady pitcher who pitched to the corners. In addition to his lightning fastball, he had a good assortment of curves, and in 1908 he and another great fastball artist, Smokey Joe Williams, hooked up in a pitching duel in San Antonio, Texas. While holding a tenuous 1–0 lead with the bases filled and none out in the bottom half of the ninth inning, Steel Arm Johnny struck out the side to preserve his precarious victory.

Leaving Birmingham in the spring of 1909, he joined the St. Paul Gophers and pitched them to a western championship. That season he pitched a total of 43 games, fashioning a 37–6 record for the season. He carried a 9–3 mark with him for Birmingham and added a 28–3 ledger with St. Paul for his total. He was the pitching ace for St. Paul, and in the playoffs that season against the Leland Giants, he pitched in 3 games, winning 2 and losing 1. His second win was the clinching victory over Dougherty in the final game.

He signed with Leland's Chicago Giants in 1910 and, in excellent health, was expected to give a good account of himself. Once during the season, he was even pressed into service as a replacement catcher in an emergency situation, and acquitted himself quite well. Leaving after only one year in Chicago, he spent a year each with the St. Louis Giants and the New York Lincoln Giants before returning to Chicago to pitch for Rube Foster's Chicago Amer-

ican Giants in 1913. Leaving Chicago again after only a season, he played with the ABCs for a year and then managed the Louisville White Sox in 1915. Altogether he pitched for seventeen years, and frequently served as a manager and coach as well.

Taylor often coached college teams, beginning in the spring of 1899, when he coached the Biddle University team. He returned to that post again in 1905, and also coached the M & I College team of Holly Springs, Mississippi, in 1908, developing players who later went into the professional ranks. This included a battery with the Birmingham Giants—Pinson, a pitcher, and Cobb, who did the brunt of the backstopping in the 1909 season.

As a coach, Taylor emphasized clean living and hard work, and set an example for his players, abstaining from the use of both alcohol and tobacco in any form. He was a hard worker and possessed a sweet baseball disposition. When his younger brother Ben Taylor was appointed manager of the Washington Potomacs in 1924, Johnny was asked to go with him as the pitching coach.

Taylor, Joseph Cephus (**Joe**, Cash)
Career: 1949–50　　Positions: c, of
Teams: Chicago American Giants ('49–'50), *minor leagues ('50–'63), Canadian League ('51–'52)*, major leagues ('54, '57–'59) *Mexican Leagues ('63)*
Bats: Right　　　Throws: Right
Height: 6'1"　　Weight: 185
Born: Mar. 2, 1926, Chapman, Ala.

This power-hitting outfielder had a fourteen-year career in professional baseball, including parts of four seasons in the major leagues, but he began as a catcher with the Chicago American Giants in 1949. At that time the Negro American League was struggling to survive the loss of players to organized baseball, and during the 1950 season he became one of the defectors, playing with Winnipeg in the Mandak League and batting .237 in 34 games. During the next two seasons he played in the Provincial League, batting .360 and .308, and adding

25 home runs in 120 games the latter season. He split 1953 between Williamsport in the Eastern League and Ottawa in the International League, showing consistency in his hitting with averages of .324 and .313.

After playing most of the next season in Ottawa, showing a .323 average and 23 home runs, he earned his first shot at the major leagues. Playing in 18 games with the Philadelphia Athletics, he hit .224 with a single homer, and was back in AAA ball in 1955, splitting the season between the Pacific Coast League and the International League. Again he showed consistency in his hitting, with averages of .295 and .286 in the respective leagues. The next two seasons, were spent primarily with Seattle, and after marks of .260 with 24 homers and .304 with 22 homers in the Pacific Coast League, he earned another shot in the majors. This time he went up with the Cincinnati Reds in the National League, and hit .262 with 4 home runs in 33 games.

In 1958 he played with three clubs, one in each major league sandwiched around a stint with Omaha of the American Association. He began the season with the Cardinals and was hitting .304 before being farmed to Omaha, and then finished the season with Baltimore in the American League, where he hit .273. The next season he started with the Orioles but after only 14 games and a .156 batting average, he was back to the Pacific Coast League, which was to be his home through 1962.

Beginning with a .292 average and 23 homers for the remainder of 1959 with Vancouver, he maintained good offensive production, although with a different team each year. He had seasons of .291 and 30 homers with Seattle and .268 and 26 homers with San Diego in 1960–61. The next season his skills began to fade, as his average dropped to .246 and his home-run production dwindled to 13, half of the previous year. In 1963 he left the Coast League and played his final year in professional baseball in the Mexican League, with Puebla and Mexico City, and managed a combined .309 batting average in closing out his career.

Taylor, Leroy R. *(Ben)*
Career: 1925–36   Positions: **rf**, lf, cf, 1b
Teams: Chicago American Giants ('25), Indianapolis ABCs ('26), **Kansas City Monarchs** ('28–'30, '32, '34), Homestead Grays ('32), Detroit Wolves ('32), Detroit Stars ('33), Cleveland Red Sox ('34)
Bats: Right   Throws: Right
Height: 5'11"   Weight: 175

This outfielder had good speed on the bases, was adept at stealing bases, and was proficient on either end of the hit-and-run-play. At the plate he was a mediocre batter with little power but was a skillful bunter. In the field he was only an average performer except for his strong arm.

He began his career with the Chicago American Giants in 1925 but could not break into the strong starting outfield. The next year he signed with the Indianapolis ABCs, playing center field, batting leadoff, and hitting .239. The ABCs disbanded after the 1926 season, and he joined the Kansas City Monarchs in 1928. A year later he was the starting right fielder and hit .355 while batting fifth in the order as the Monarchs won the Negro National League championship. In 1930 he hit .277 and the Monarchs disbanded after the season, but formed again during the second half of the 1931 season. Taylor rejoined the team in 1932 and also played with the Detroit Wolves and the Homestead Grays but was unable to win a starting position with any of the teams. In 1933 he was a substitute right fielder with the Detroit Stars under manager Jim Taylor, and closed out his career with the Cleveland Red Sox in 1934.

Taylor, O.
Career: 1935   Position: p
Team: Columbus Elite Giants

He was a pitcher with the Elite Giants during the 1935 season, when the franchise was located in Columbus.

Taylor, Olan (**Jelly,** Satan)
Career: 1934–46   Positions: **1b** *c,*
                              manager
Teams: Birmingham Black Barons, ('34), Pittsburgh Crawfords ('35), Cincinnati Tigers ('36–'37), **Memphis Red Sox** ('38–'42, '45–'46) *military service ('43–'45)*
Bats: Left   Throws: Left
Height: 5'10"   Weight: 190
Born: July 7, 1910, London, O.

This left-handed first baseman was noted more for his fancy fielding than for his hitting, and he kept the fans entertained with his comical antics and flashy glovework around the initial sack. The line-drive hitter did not hit for power and hit only .258 for the independent Cincinnati Tigers in 1936. The next season the Tigers entered the Negro American League and made a good showing but dropped from league competition at the end of the season. Taylor signed with the Memphis Red Sox for the 1938 season, and they batted the Atlantic Black Crackers for the title. The slick fielder and Atlanta's flashy first sacker Red Moore were the subjects of an ongoing argument about who was better defensively. Taylor was fat and had short arms, earning him the nickname "Jelly," and his appearance belied his ability afield. He also earned the nickname "Satan" because he "played like the Devil." But his mother did not approve of the latter name, and Jelly was the moniker that stuck.

Meanwhile, the Red Sox won the first-half title but the Black Crackers copped the second half, necessitating a playoff. The Red Sox won the first two games before the Series was cancelled because of disagreements between the managements of the two teams about money and scheduling.

As the regular first baseman with the Red Sox, he played in the next three All-Star games, 1939–41. After the Japanese attack on Pearl Harbor, he was one of the first players from the Negro Leagues inducted into the Army during World War II, and was batting .286 in 1942 when he was called into the service. After returning from military service in 1945, he did not play substantially but hit .345 for the remainder of the season. He was appointed playing manager for the 1946 season, and hit .274 in his last year in the Negro Leagues.

Taylor, Raymond (Broadway)
Career: 1931–44   Positions: **c,** of
Teams: **Memphis Red Sox** ('31–'37), Indianapolis ABCs ('38), St. Louis ('39, '41), New Orleans-St. Louis Stars ('40), New York Black Yankees ('42), Cincinnati Buckeyes ('42), Cleveland Buckeyes ('43), Kansas City Monarchs ('44), *Cleveland Clippers ('46)*
Bats: Right   Throws: Right
Height: 5'11"   Weight: 165
Born: 1910

This hustling catcher was a fine backstop with a great throwing arm, slow afoot, and a fairly consistent hitter, credited sometimes with hitting over .300, but without significant power. He began his professional baseball career in his hometown, with the Memphis Red Sox in 1931. After seven seasons in Memphis he joined the Indianapolis ABCs for the 1938 season, remaining with the franchise when it shifted to St. Louis and became the new St. Louis Stars. With the Stars he shared the catching duties while hitting in the eighth spot.

When the Stars folded following the 1941 season, he was among many ex-Stars who journeyed eastward to join the Black Yankees in New York. But after a brief stay, he located with the Cincinnati Buckeyes for two seasons as their regular catcher, batting in his usual eighth spot. With World War II taking the Kansas City Monarchs' regular catcher, he signed on with Kansas City for the 1944 season, providing depth as a backup receiver and batting .385 in only 10 league games. He closed out his career with the Cleveland Clippers in the United States League in 1946.

Taylor, Rip (Zeke)
Career: 1931   Position: of
Team: Hilldale Daisies

He was listed as an outfielder with Hilldale

in 1931, when the team was playing as an independent ballclub.

Taylor, Robert (Lightning)
Career: 1938–42   Position: c
Teams: Indianapolis ABCs ('38), St. Louis Stars ('39), New Orleans-St. Louis Stars ('40), New York Black Yankees ('42)

A catcher with the ABCs in 1938, he moved to St. Louis with the franchise shift the following season and then to the Black Yankees when the franchise folded following the 1941 season.

Taylor, S.
Career: 1912, 1931   Positions: p, manager
Teams: St. Louis Giants ('12), *Little Rock Black Travelers ('31)*

A pitcher with the St. Louis Giants in 1912, he managed the Little Rock Black Travelers, a team of lesser quality, in 1931.

Taylor, Shine
Career: 1939   Positions: lf, rf
Team: Toledo Crawfords

He split his playing time between left field and center field as a part-time starter with the Toledo Crawfords in 1939, batting eighth in the order.

Taylor, T.
Career: 1909   Position: 2b
Team: Kansas City Royal Giants

In 1909 he was a second baseman with the Royal Giants of Kansas City, Missouri.

Taylor, William
[see Tyler, William (Steel Arm, Bill)]

Taylor, Zachary
Career: 1937   Position: p
Team: Memphis Red Sox

A fringe player, he pitched briefly with the Memphis Red Sox in 1937.

Teasley, Ronald (**Ron**, School Boy, Roomie)
Career: 1948   Positions: of, 1b

Teams: *Toledo Cubs ('45), minor leagues ('48–'51),* New York Cubans ('48)
Height: 5'11"   Weight: 177
Bats: Right   Throws: Right
Born: Jan. 26, 1927, Detroit, Mich.

He played in the outfield with the New York Cubans for about two months in 1948 after being released by a farm team of the Brooklyn Dodgers' organization, the Olean team of the Pony League. He and Sammy Gee were released by the Dodgers at the same time, although both were doing pretty well. Teasley, playing first base, had 3 homeruns in 23 games. Both returned to the Negro Leagues with the Cubans, but Teasley was still depressed about being let go at Olean and did not perform well. Later he played with Carman in the Mandak League, batting .299 in 1950, and was selected to the All-Star team twice in 1950 and 1951.

As a youngster he played with semipro teams in Detroit, Toledo, and Ypsilanti and toured Michigan playing teams from the Negro Leagues. One of these teams, the Motor City Giants of Detroit, was an independent semipro team aspiring to become a member of the ill-fated United States League. In college at Wayne State University, Teasley finished with a .500 batting average. After his baseball career ended, he returned to the university, earning a degree in education, and began a second career as a high-school teacher and coach in Detroit. In 1986 was inducted into Wayne State University's Hall of Fame.

Tenney, William
Career: 1910   Position: c
Team: Kansas City Giants

He was a catcher for the Kansas City, Kansas, Giants in 1910.

Teran, Julian (**Recurbon**)
a.k.a. Recurvon
Career: 1916–24   Positions: **2b**, 3b
Teams: Cuban Stars (East) ('16–'24), Cuban Stars (West) ('24)

This second baseman began his career as the leadoff batter for owner Alejandro Pompez's

New York based Cuban Stars in 1916. The next season, still based in New York, the team played as the Havana Cuban Stars, but returned to their original designation in 1918. The infielder continued with the Cubans for seven more seasons, usually batting in the sixth slot, while splitting his playing time between second base and third base.

Terrell, Lawrence
Career: 1924–25   Position: p
Team: Detroit Stars

He pitched without distinction for the Detroit Stars for two seasons during the midtwenties.

Terrell, S. M.
Career: 1928   Position: officer
Teams: Cleveland Stars

He was an officer with the Cleveland Stars in 1928, when they made their only entry into the Negro National League.

Terrill, Windsor W. (George)
Career: 1887–96   Positions: ss, ut
Teams: *Boston Resolutes ('87),* Cuban Giants ('90, '91), Cuban X-Giants ('96)

He was shortstop with the Boston Resolutes, one of eight teams that were charter members of the League of Colored Baseball Clubs in 1887. However, the league dissolved after only a week and he later became a utility player with the Cuban Giants when they represented York, Pennsylvania, in the Eastern Interstate League in 1890 and Ansonia in the Connecticut State League in 1891. After the ballclub splintered into two different clubs, he played shortstop with the Cuban X-Giants in 1896.

Terry, John
Career: 1931–36   Positions: 2b, 3b
Teams: Indianapolis ABCs ('31), Homestead Grays ('32–'33, '36), Newark Dodgers ('33, '35), Cincinnati Tigers ('34)

This infielder played for six seasons as a part-time starter and substitute infielder, mostly with the Homestead Grays. As a sometime starter at second base in 1933, he batted third

when in the lineup. Incomplete statistics show a .238 batting average for the season and a .313 average for 1936.

Tevera
Career: 1924   Position: 2b
Team: Cuban Stars (West)

He played as a second baseman in 1924 with the Cuban Stars (West) in the Negro National League.

Thomas
Career: 1904–11   Positions: 1b, p
Team: Philadelphia Giants

He made his first appearance with the Philadelphia Giants in 1904 as a reserve first baseman. In his next appearance in 1911, he also pitched with the Giants.

Thomas
Career: 1919–25   Positions: 1b, lf
Team: Pennsylvania Red Caps of New York

He was a reserve first baseman for the Pennsylvania Red Caps of New York in 1919–20. The Red Caps were a marginal team in 1919 and had dropped to a lesser status during the '20s, when he played in the outfield.

Thomas
Career: 1928   Position: 2b
Team: Philadelphia Tigers

He was a second baseman for the Philadelphia Tigers in 1928, their only year in the Negro National League.

Thomas, Alfred (Buck)
Career: 1944–49   Position: p
Team: Chicago American Giants

During the late '40s, he pitched with the Chicago American Giants for half a dozen seasons.

Thomas, Arthur
Career: 1886–91   Positions: c, 1b, of
Teams: Cuban Giants ('86–'90), New York Gorhams ('91)
Born: Dec. 10, 1864, Washington, D.C.

Beginning his amateur career in his hometown of Washington, D.C., in 1880, he was the catcher for the Manhattan Club of that city. For the next two years, 1881–82, he was a catcher with th West End ballclub of Long Branch, New Jersey, another amateur team.

In 1886 he began his professional career with the Cuban Giants and, in late June of his first professional season, representatives from the Athletics ballclub in Philadelphia tried to sign him but he declined, remaining with the Cuban Giants through the 1890 season. During his tenure with the ballclub, they represented cities in white leagues, including Trenton, New Jersey, of the Middle States League in 1887 and 1889, and York, Pennsylvania, of the Eastern Interstate League in 1890. In 1891, in his last year of professional baseball, he played with the New York Gorhams, one of the top clubs of the nineteenth century.

Thomas, Boy
[see Thomas, Herb. (Boy)]

Thomas, C. W.
Career: 1918   Position: 3b
Teams: *Philadelphia Giants ('16), Dayton Marcos ('18)*

He was a third baseman with marginal teams, generally of lesser quality than league teams, including the Dayton Marcos in 1918, two years before they entered the Negro National League.

Thomas, Charles
[see Thomason, Charles (Charlie)]

Thomas, Charley
Career: 1916–22   Positions: c, manager
Team: Baltimore Black Sox

Playing with the Baltimore Black Sox during their formative years, he was the regular catcher and hit fifth in the batting order for four seasons 1916–19. Afterward he assumed a reserve role, batting .298 and .267 in his last two seasons as a player, 1921–22 while being appointed manager of the independent Black Sox the former year.

Thomas, Clinton Cyrus (**Clint**, Hawk, Buckeye)
Career: 1920–38   Positions: **cf**, rf, 2b
Teams: *military service ('18–'19)*, Brooklyn Royal Giants ('20), Columbus Buckeyes ('21), Detroit Stars ('22), **Hilldale Daisies** ('23–'28), Atlantic City Bacharach Giants ('28–'29), New York Lincoln Giants ('30), New York Harlem Stars ('31), Indianapolis ABCs ('32), **New York Black Yankees** ('32–'35, '37–'38), Newark Eagles ('36), Philadelphia Stars
Bats: Right   Throws: Right
Height: 5'8"   Weight: 180
Born: Nov. 25, 1896, Greenup, Ky.

A complete ballplayer, he hit for average and with power, was an outstanding center fielder defensively with an outstanding arm, and was a fast and skillful base runner. In a career that spanned nineteen seasons, he earned the nickname "Hawk" because of his sharp eye at the plate and his speed and agility as a ball hawk in the outfield.

In 1910, as the oldest of eight children, Thomas dropped out of school after the eighth grade and left home at age fourteen to seek employment in Columbus, Ohio. Once there the youngster worked in a restaurant and grocery store and also began playing amateur ball until joining the Army during World War I. After his discharge in 1919, he returned to Columbus and played semipro ball with the Bowers Easters, where one of his teammates knew John Henry Lloyd and arranged a tryout for Thomas with the Brooklyn Royal Giants. Lloyd was favorably impressed, and Thomas began his professional career as a second baseman with the Royals in 1920.

The next year, Lloyd was named manager of the Columbus Buckeyes and took the youngster with him. In his only season there, Thomas batted .281 before joining the Detroit Stars in 1922. During his only season in Detroit, manager Bruce Petway gave him a new position and a new nickname. After moving from second base to right field, Thomas earned the sobriquet "Hawk" for his play at the new position. He responded to the change with an .342 batting average. In the off-season he worked in a Ford plant, but when the Eastern Colored League organized for the 1923 season, Thomas jumped to the Hilldale ballclub, along with three other Detroit players—Peter Hill, Frank Warfield, and Bill Holland.

With Hilldale he was reunited with manager John Henry Lloyd, and in his first year with the team he hit .373 with 23 home runs and 56 stolen bases to help Hilldale win the first Eastern Colored League pennant. The next two years he hit .363 and .351 as the team captured two more league flags and subsequently played in the first two World Series, facing the Negro National League champion Kansas City Monarchs each year. After losing a tough, hardfought, best-of-nine World Series to the Monarchs in 1924, Hilldale gained a measure of revenge by defeating the Monarchs in five of six games to win the rematch the following year. Rebounding from a .211 average in the 1924 Series, he hit a respectable .273 in the 19–25 Series, chipping in a pair of doubles and a pair of stolen bases.

Thomas, who usually played left field and batted fifth in the order for Hilldale, hit .306 and .279 in 1926–27, and topped the league with 23 stolen bases the former season. Including exhibitions in addition to league games, he was credited with 28 home runs that year. When the Eastern Colored League broke up in 1928, he joined the Bacharach Giants in the American Negro League for the 1929 season and responded to his new surroundings with a .342 batting average.

In the '20s, Thomas played winter ball in Cuba, where his team won three consecutive championships under the tutelage of former major-leaguer Dolph Luque. In the winter of 1925–26 Thomas hit .335 and, during his six seasons (1923–31) on the island, he compiled a lifetime .310 batting average. During one of his winters on the island, Thomas hit a home run off a young pitching prospect named Fidel Castro, who would later lead a revolution and become president of Cuba.

The ballhawking outfielder played against major-leaguers both in the California winter league and in postseason barnstorming exhibitions. In one 1934 encounter against Dizzy Dean, Thomas tripled in the ninth inning and stole home to win the game, 1–0.

The graceful center fielder gained further acclaim in the "Big Apple," playing with the New York Lincoln Giants in 1930 and batting .351 from the leadoff spot in the franchise's final year. After a year with John Henry Lloyd's Harlem Stars, where he batted in the heart of the lineup, he joined the New York Black Yankees in 1932, their first year of existence. While playing his home games in Yankee Stadium, Thomas hit .293 in his first season with the Black Yankees, and covered centerfield with such ease that in the later '30s the even-tempered team player earned the sobriquet "the black Joe DiMaggio." Thomas carried a .343 average through late June 1937, and a month later he was credited with his 367th career home run. That was the last full season of his career, as he retired after playing briefly in 1938. He finished as a lifetime .300 hitter.

After his baseball career was completed, he worked four years as a guard at the Brooklyn Navy Yard, followed by thirty years as a custodian and staff supervisor in the West Virginia Department of Mines and the State Senate. Thomas was reared in Greenup, Kentucky, and his eightieth birthday party celebration in that town turned into the first Negro Leagues reunion; it became an annual event for several years.

Thomas, Dan
Career: 1921–28   Positions: **2b**, ss, 3b,
                         1b, of
Teams: Indianapolis ABCs ('21), Kansas City Monarchs ('22), St. Louis Stars ('23–'24), Cleveland Hornets ('27), Memphis Red Sox ('28)

A reserve infielder for most of his career, playing with five teams during his eight years in the Negro National League, he could play any nonbattery position, but his best spot was at second base. Beginning his career in 1921 with the Indianapolis ABCs, he closed out with the Memphis Red Sox in 1928.

Thomas, Dan

Career: 1936–40   Positions: of, p
Teams: Cincinnati Tigers ('36), Chicago American Giants ('36–'37), Jacksonville Red Caps ('38–'39), Birmingham Black Barons ('40)

He was a pitcher-outfielder with the Chicago American Giants but played exclusively in the outfield with all other teams. After leaving Chicago, he was the left fielder with the Jacksonville Red Caps, batting in the sixth slot, and in 1940 he was the center fielder and leadoff batter for the Birmingham Black Barons.

Thomas, David (Showboat)

Career: 1928–46   Position: **1b** *of,*
                                        manager
Teams: *Montgomery Grey Sox ('23), Atlanta Black Crackers ('26), Chattanooga Black Lookouts ('27), Nashville Elite Giants ('28),* Birmingham Black Barons ('29–'30, '46), Brooklyn Royal Giants ('30, '39–'40), Baltimore Black Sox ('30–'32), New York Black Yankees ('32–'36), **New York Cubans** ('35–'37, '40'–46), *Santo Domingo ('37),* Washington Black Senators ('38), Ethiopian Clowns ('41)
Bats: Left   Throws: Left
Height: 6'0"   Weight: 178
Born: Mar. 22, 1905, Mobile, Ala.

A flashy-fielding, left-handed first baseman, he handled everything thrown to him and dazzled the fans. His movements were described as being filled with classic grace. The "fancy Dan" used a small glove and played far off the base, and often caught the ball behind his back, especially on a 3–6–3 double play. Also called the classiest first baseman of all time, he was well deserving of his nickname "Showboat." Despite his outstanding glove and footwork at the initial sack, he did not have a strong arm nor good speed. Rated among the best prospects, the popular but

aging field general was scouted by Branch Rickey during the mid-1940s, but was rejected, along with Terris McDuffie, after an impromptu Dodger tryout in 1942.

After learning his baseball in Mobile, Alabama, from an older brother, who was a first baseman, Thomas graduated from high school in 1921 and embarked upon a professional career in his hometown. He played with the Caulfield Ads in 1922 and then joined the Mobile Tigers for two seasons, also appearing with the Montgomery Grey Sox in 1923. For the next four seasons he continued to make the rounds of the southern teams, playing a season each with the Atlanta Black Crackers, The Chattanooga Black Lookouts, the Nashville Elite Giants, and the Birmingham Black Barons. After beginning his second season with the Black Barons in 1930, he jumped to the Baltimore Black Sox.

Early in his career he was a weak hitter, as evidenced by batting averages of .178, .233, and .192 in 1931–32 and 1934, with the Baltimore Black Sox and the New York Black Yankees. But as his career progressed he improved his stickwork and developed into a respectable hitter, with averages of .260 and .287 in 1935–36 with the New York Cubans and .312 in the 1936–37 Cuban winter league.

The flamboyant first baseman played on the New York Cubans' team that won the 1935 Negro National League second-half championship, only to lose the playoff to the Pittsburgh Crawfords. In 1937 he jumped the Cubans to play in Santo Domingo with Martin Dihigo's Aguilas Cibaenas club, batting only .158 with little power and a high strikeout frequency. After returning to the United States he played on manager Ben Taylor's Washington Black Senators in 1938, followed by a two-year stint with the Brooklyn Royal Giants, and hit in the third slot each year.

In 1941 he became playing manager for the Ethiopian Clowns for a season, before rejoining the New York Cubans the following year. With the Cubans for the remainder of his career, he hit in the second slot, registering averages of .235 and .333 in 1942–43. During the last two years of World War II he served as a special officer at the Port of Embarkation in New York City, while also playing part-time with the Cubans and posting batting marks of .212 and .393 in 1945–46, his last years in the Negro Leagues.

Thomas, Frank
Career: 1945   Position: p
Team: Birmingham Black Barons

A wartime player, he pitched briefly with the Birmingham Black Barons in 1945, his only year in the Negro Leagues.

Thomas, Hazel
Career: 1935   Position: p
Team: Cole's American Giants

In 1935 he pitched briefly with owner Robert A. Cole's Chicago American Giants.

Thomas, Henry
Career: 1931   Position: of
Team: Harlem Stars ('31)

A fringe player, he was listed as an outfielder with manager John Henry Lloyd's Harlem Stars in 1931.

Thomas, Herb (Boy)
Career: 1929–30   Position: p
Teams: New York Lincoln Giants ('29), Hilldale Daisies ('30)

Pitching with the New York Lincoln Giants in the American Negro League in 1929, he fashioned a 3–1 work sheet, and with Hilldale the following season, he lost his only decision with the independent ballclub.

Thomas, J.
Career: 1887   Position: player
Team: *Louisville Falls Citys*

He was a player with the Louisville Falls Citys, one of eight teams that were charter members of the League of Colored Baseball Clubs in 1887. However, the league's existence was ephemeral, lasting only a week. His position is uncertain.

Thomas, J.
Career: 1932, 1938   Positions: ss, 2b
Teams: Indianapolis ABCs ('32), Detroit Stars ('37)

This middle infielder was the regular second baseman for the Indianapolis ABCs in 1932, usually batting leadoff, and was a reserve shortstop with the Detroit Stars in 1937.

Thomas, Jack (Jules, Jule, Home Run)
Career: 1909–28   Positions: cf, lf, rf, 1b
Teams: Brooklyn Royal Giants ('09–'11, '13–'14, '24, '26), St. Louis Giants ('12), **New York Lincoln Giants** ('14–'25, '28), Atlantic City Bacharach Giants ('17), *Pennsylvania Red Caps of New York ('26–'27, '30–'31)*
Bats: Right   Throws: Right

He was one of the biggest men in baseball, and his great bulk made him a good power hitter, but the big outfielder also hit for a high average. In the field he had a wide range and an outstanding glove, making spectacular running catches and shoestring catches, but making them look natural. He showed very good speed on the bases and considerable skill as an accomplished base stealer. He was a self-made but underpublicized ballplayer and a good man "when he wants to be," but despite his accomplishment, he was not swellheaded.

He began his career with the Brooklyn Royal Giants in 1909, as they claimed consecutive eastern championships in 1909–10. The following season he stepped into the cleanup spot in the lineup, leaving for a year to fill the same spot in the lineup with the St. Louis Giants and help them to a city championship in 1912. He returned to the Royals for two more years before signing with the New York Lincoln Giants late in the 1914 season.

For the next decade Thomas was playing center field and hitting in the heart of the order for the Lincolns and was called "Home Run" Thomas. In 1917, playing against all levels of opposition, statistics show an incredible .517 batting average and a .833 slugging percentage. In 1918–19 he followed with seasons of .316 and .340. His heavy hitting continued on into the lively-ball era, but the veteran was released by the New York Lincoln Giants in the spring of 1924, along with Smokey Joe Williams, Doc Wiley, and others, in a housecleaning youth movement. He was still a fair outfielder and, after being dropped, he signed on again as a center fielder with the Brooklyn Royal Giants, batting .312 and .372 for the 1924–25 seasons, and closing out his career with top teams in 1928. He continued with the Pennsylvania Red Caps of New York, a team of lesser quality, through 1931.

Thomas, Jerome
Career: 1887   Position: player
Team: *Washington Capital Citys*

He played with the Washington Capital Citys, one of eight teams that were charter members of the League of Colored Baseball Clubs in 1887. However, the league's existence was ephemeral, lasting only a week. His position is uncertain.

Thomas, John
Career: 1946–47   Position: of
Team: Birmingham Black Barons

He was a reserve center fielder for the Birmingham Black Barons for two post–World War II seasons, batting .314 in limited play in 1946.

Thomas, John
Career: 1950   Position: p
Team: Cleveland Buckeyes

He began his career as a pitcher with the Cleveland Buckeyes in 1950, when the Negro American League was struggling to survive the loss of players to organized baseball. He appeared in 3 games without a decision.

Thomas, Jules
see Thomas, Jack (Jules, Jule, Home Run)

Thomas, L.
Career: 1928–30   Positions: of, 1b, c
Teams: Nashville Elite Giants ('28), Birmingham Black Barons ('29–'30)

He played three seasons at three positions with southern teams, the last two with the Birmingham Black Barons in the Negro National League, and hit .346 as a first baseman in 1930, his last season.

Thomas, Lacey
Career: 1934–39   Positions: of, p
Teams: Jacksonville Red Caps ('34–'38), Cleveland Bears ('39), Chicago American Giants ('35)
Bats: Left   Throws: Right
Height: 6'2"   Weight: 170
Born: Apr. 26, 1910, Meridian, Miss.

He started his baseball career in 1928 with a lesser team, the Cubans of Tampa, Florida, and joined the Jacksonville Red Caps in 1934. The tallest man on the club and a popular player, he was a hard hitter and could hit the long ball, being credited with a mark close to .300 in 1937. In the field, he had a strong and accurate "steel" arm and threw out base runners with "strikes" from the farthest corners of the outfield. When the franchise moved to Cleveland in 1939, he relocated with the team, playing as the Bears. He also played briefly with the Chicago American Giants.

Thomas, M. (Rube)
Career: 1918–19   Position: p
Team: New York Lincoln Giants

For two years, 1918–19, he was on the mound staff of the New York Lincoln Giants, headed by Smokey Joe Williams, and won his only recorded decision in the former season.

Thomas, Nelson
Career: 1947   Position: p
Team: Newark Eagles

He pitched with the Newark Eagles in 1947, splitting 4 decisions, in his only season in the Negro Leagues.

Thomas, Orel (Little Dean)
Career: 1937   Position: p
Team: Detroit Stars

He pitched briefly with the Detroit Stars in

1937, the first year of the Negro American League.

Thomas, Walter Lewis (Bancy, Banzai)
Career: 1936–47   Positions: p, of
Teams: Kansas City Monarchs ('36, '44–'45), Detroit Stars ('37), St. Louis Stars ('37), Memphis Red Sox ('46), Chicago American Giants ('46), Birmingham Black Barons ('47) *minor leagues ('48)*
Bats: Left   Throws: Right
Height: 5'10"   Weight: 165

He began his career as a pitcher but quickly began acquiring additional playing time as an outfielder, eventually leaving the mound completely by the time he closed his career. During the last two years of World War II he stepped into the Kansas City Monarchs' starting lineup as the regular right fielder, batting .279 and .241. A steady, consistent fielder, he had an accurate arm developed from his pitching years that made opposing runners hesitant to attempt taking an extra base. He had good speed, and although considered dangerous at the plate, he was only an average hitter with fair power, batting .279 and .241 in 1944–45 while usually hitting sixth in the order. For the next two seasons he played with the Chicago American Giants, Memphis Red Sox, and Birmingham Black Barons, batting .220 in 1946. After the color line was removed, he played in organized baseball with Wilkes-Barre in 1948, batting .268 in 12 games.

Thomason, Charles (Charlie)
a.k.a. Thomas
Career: 1941–44   Positions: of, *3b*
Team: Newark Eagles

A wartime reserve outfielder with the Newark Eagles, batting in the lower part of the order when he was in the lineup, he hit .174 in only 6 league games in 1942.

Thompson
Career: 1906–1914   Position: p
Team: Famous Cuban Giants

He was a pitcher with the Famous Cuban Giants, one of the various Cuban Giants ballclubs that flourished during the early years of the century and appropriated a variation of the Cuban Giants' name as their own.

Thompson
Career: 1917   Position: 1b
Team: Cuban Giants

He played as a first baseman with the Cuban Giants in 1917.

Thompson
Career: 1940–41   Position: p
Teams: Baltimore Elite Giants ('40), Kansas City ('41)

He pitched in both the Negro National League and Negro American League during his two years in black baseball, beginning with the Baltimore Elite Giants in 1940 and moving to the Kansas City Monarchs in 1941.

Thompson, (Copperknee)
Career: 1942   Positions: 3b, ss, 2b
Teams: Ethiopian Clowns ('42), *Minneapolis-St. Paul Gophers ('42)*

In 1942, the infielder's only year with a top club, he played with both the Ethiopian Clowns, an independent team playing a caliber of baseball on a par with the league teams, and the Minneapolis-St. Paul Gophers, a team of lesser quality.

Thompson, Frank (Groundhog)
Career: 1945–50   Position: p
Teams: *New Orleans Black Pelicans ('45)*, Birmingham Black Barons ('45, *'52–'54*), Homestead Grays ('46–'48), Memphis Red Sox ('49–'54)
Bats: Left   Throws: Left
Height: 5'2"   Weight: 135

This scrappy, diminutive left-handed pitcher held his own against bigger opponents. Short and squat, he was built like a fire hydrant, and had a harelip, walleye, and chipped tooth. His physical appearance sometimes made him the object of ridicule. Josh Gibson kidded him about his looks and put him on his "all-ugly" team. Once during a game he lost the cap off his gold tooth and halted the game while he got down on his knees on the mound looking for his treasured item. On another occasion, in a card game on the Grays' team bus, he and gigantic Luke Easter were accusing each other of cheating and Easter threatened to hit him. Unintimidated, Thompson responded by pulling his knife on Easter and threatening to "cut you down to my size."

He joined the Grays in 1946, fashioned a 7–3 record in 1947, and was on their pitching staff in 1948 when they copped the last Negro National League pennant and defeated the Birmingham Black Barons in the World Series. After the Negro National League folded, he left the Grays to play with the Memphis Red Sox in the Negro American League, posting a 7–7 ledger in 1950. By then the league was suffering from the loss of players to organized baseball and was no longer a quality league, but he continued with the Red Sox and Black Barons for another half-dozen seasons. His last team in the Negro American League was his first, having broken in with the Black Barons in 1945 with a 2–3 record.

Thompson, Frank P.
Career: 1885   Position: organizer
Teams: *Argyle Hotel Athletics ('85),* Cuban Giants ('85)

In 1885, Thompson, the headwaiter at Long Island's Argyle Hotel in Babylon, New York recruited players from the Philadelphia Keystones to work at the hotel as waiters and form a baseball team to play for the entertainment of the summer guests. After the end of the tourist season he added more players, from the Philadelphia Orions and the Manhattans of Washington, D.C., to form the Cuban Giants, the first black professional team.

Thompson, (Gunboat)
Career: 1916–20   Positions: **p**, of, 1b
Teams: New York Lincoln Stars ('16), Pennsylvania Red Caps of New York ('17), Atlantic City Bacharach Giants ('17), Chicago American Giants ('18), Pittsburgh Stars of Buffalo ('19), Detroit Stars ('20)

In 1918 he was signed by Rube Foster as a replacement for the players the American Giants lost to the World War I draft. Without a wealth of raw talent, he pitched with his head, exploiting the batters' weaknesses. He had an excellent change of pace and good control, but was not a power pitcher and preferred just to keep the batters off-stride and let his fielders help instead of trying for a strikeout. He is credited with a win in his only recorded decision for Foster's team.

A big, raw hurler from the mines of West Virginia, he began his career pitching in the regular rotation for the Lincoln Stars in 1916. Although primarily a pitcher, he was also a good man at the plate and occasionally played in the outfield or at first base, but was not a good fielder and had difficulty fielding bunts when on the mound. When the Stars disbanded prior to the 1917 season, Thompson was among the ex-Stars signing with the Pennsylvania Red Caps of New York, and he also pitched part of the season with the Bacharachs. Later he joined the Pittsburgh Stars of Buffalo, a team of lesser status, where he also played first base. He closed out his career with the Detroit Stars in 1920, as a pitcher-outfielder.

Thompson, Harold
Career: 1949   Position: p
Team: Kansas City Monarchs

He began his career with the Kansas City Monarchs in the 1950 season, when the Negro American League was struggling to survive the loss of players to organized baseball.

Thompson, Henry Curtis (**Hank,** *Ametralladora*)
Career: 1943–48   Positions: **2b, rf, lf**, ss
Teams: **Kansas City Monarchs** ('43, '45–'48), *military service ('44–'45), Mexican league ('45), major leagues ('47–'49, '56), minor leagues ('49, '51, '57)*
Bats: Left   Throws: Right
Height: 5'9"   Weight: 171

Born: Dec. 8, 1925, Oklahoma City, Okla.
Died: Sept. 30, 1969, Fresno, Calif.

This hard-hitting Kansas City Monarch was versatile afield, playing both the infield and the outfield but, although he had a good throwing arm, he was only an average fielder. He was fast afield and on the bases, and always a solid hitter—the left-handed swinger hit with power and for average. In his first year with the Monarchs, in 1943, as a seventeen-year old youngster, available statistics indicate a .314 batting average with a slugging percentage of .514. Following his rookie year, he entered military service in 1944, and when he was discharged, he split the remainder of the 1945 season between Kansas City and Tampico in the Mexican League, playing largely in Mexico, where he hit .264 but drew a high percentage of walks. Back with the Monarchs in 1946, he played second base and hit .287 while batting leadoff as the Monarchs won the Negro American League pennant, and hit .296 in the ensuing World Series loss to the Newark Eagles.

The next year he moved into the shortstop position in the field and into the third slot in the batting order, hitting .344 during regular-season play and gaining a shot at the major leagues with the Browns when he and Monarchs teammate Willard Brown were signed by Bill Veeck. He and Brown were questionable types who didn't fit the Jackie Robinson pattern. After having "a cup of coffee" in the majors and batting .256 in 27 games, he and Brown were unconditionally released. Thompson thought they should have been farmed out for an adjustment period, as the Dodgers had done with Jackie Robinson. But instead, he returned to the Monarchs to hit .344 for the remainder of the season.

In 1948 he hit .375 with a slugging percentage of .633 to earn another chance with the major leagues, this time with the Giants. He began the 1949 season at Jersey City, with Monte Irvin as a teammate, and hit .295 to earn a promotion to the New York Giants. With the Giants he hit .280 and remained with the Giants for eight years as a third baseman-out-fielder. He had his best major-league season in 1953, when he hit .302 with 24 home runs. During his nine-year major-league career, Hank played in two World Series, 1951 and 1954, batting .364 in the latter Series victory over the Cleveland Indians. His last season in the majors was 1956, and he played one more season with Minneapolis in the American Association before ending his baseball career.

During his career he played three winter seasons in Cuba, where he earned the nickname "Ametralladora," which means "machine gun." In Cuba he demonstrated consistency, hitting .320, .318, and .321 for the years 1946–49 while also demonstrating good power and speed. He led the league in RBIs in the middle season to lead Havana to the championship, and led the league in triples in each of the other seasons.

Thompson came from a tough home environment in Dallas, Texas, and as a youngster his mother had to put her rowdy son in reform school. Later in life, after he had begun his baseball career, he shot and killed a man who was trying to force his affections on Thompson's sister. He was sometimes described as a "hoodlum" and continued to carry a gun, even after arriving in the major leagues.

Thompson, James (**Sandy**)
a.k.a. Tompkins
Career: 1920–33 Positions: lf, cf, rf, 1b, c
Teams: Dayton Marcos ('20), Milwaukee Bears ('23), Birmingham Black Barons ('24–'25, '27), Chicago American Giants ('26, '28–'30), Chicago Columbia Giants ('31), Cole's American Giants ('32), Cuban Stars (East) ('33)
Bats: Left Throws: Right

After two seasons with the Birmingham Black Barons, with batting averages of .322 and .341, this tall, fast outfielder joined the Chicago American Giants in 1926, under manager David Malarcher's leadership, playing left field and hitting .306 while batting fifth in the lineup. His batting consistency helped the

American Giants win the second-half title, defeat the Kansas City Monarchs in the playoff for the Negro National League pennant, and defeat the Bacharach Giants in the World Series to claim the championship.

The next season he returned to the Black Barons, playing center field and batting second in the order. A left-handed batter, he won the batting title in 1927 with an average of .441, leading the Black Barons to the second-half Negro National League title, but losing to his former teammates in the playoffs as the Black Barons dropped 4 straight.

Rejoining the American Giants in 1928, in his third year with the team, he slipped to a .243 batting average in 1930. He played with Malarcher's charges as they played under the banners of the Columbia American Giants and Cole's American Giants. They won the Negro Southern League flag in 1932, as Thompson hit .322 while still batting in the heart of the order. He played hurt, with a sore leg skinned raw from sliding, and lost his speed. In 1933 he closed out a career that started as a reserve right fielder with the Dayton Marcos in 1920.

Thompson, Jimmy
Career: 1945   Position: umpire
League: Negro American League

He served as an umpire in the Negro American League during a wartime season.

Thompson, Lloyd P.
Career: 1910–17,
1922–30   Positions: ss, of, officer
Team: Hilldale Daisies

A slick-fielding shortstop, he played with Hilldale in the earliest years after its origin as a ballclub for youngsters and remained with the team as the participants became older and more skilled in the rudiments of the game. These players, who were with the club when functioning at a semipro level, were instrumental in forming the nucleus for the evolving professional club. Thompson doubled as the business manager in 1912, and when the team became stronger and entered league play, he served as an officer for the ballclub.

Thompson, Marshall
Career: 1887   Position: manager
Team: *Boston Resolutes*

He was the manager of the Boston Resolutes, one of eight teams that were charter members of the League of Colored Baseball Clubs in 1887. However, the league's existence was ephemeral, lasting only a week.

Thompson, S.
Career: 1933–1935   Position: p
Teams: Cuban Stars ('33), Brooklyn Eagles ('35)

This pitcher made two appearances in the Negro Leagues, first with the Cuban Stars in 1933 and then with the Brooklyn Eagles in 1935.

Thompson, Sammy (Runt)
Career: 1931–38   Positions: 2b, *manager*
Teams: Memphis Red Sox ('31), Cleveland Stars ('32), Atlanta Black Crackers ('35, '38), *Little Rock Black Travelers* ('31)

In 1938 this diminutive second baseman was on the spring roster for the Atlanta Black Crackers, but after being "struck down by an ailment," he was not given a fair shake by the Black Crackers and was released in early May. Although he made his home in Chicago, he had previously been with Atlanta, having been fired as manager of th Black Crackers three years earlier after only a few weeks in that role.

Thompson, Samuel **(Sad Sam,** Tommy, Long Tom)
Career: 1931–42   Positions: **p,** *of*
Teams: Kansas City Monarchs ('31–'32), Monroe Monarchs ('32), Indianapolis ABCs ('32), Detroit Stars ('33), Nashville Elite Giants ('34), Columbus Elite Giants ('35), **Philadelphia Stars** ('36–'40), Chicago American Giants ('41–'42)

Bats: Right Throws: Right
Height: 6'1" Weight: 185

An average hurler with moderate control and a standard three-pitch repertory, he had a mediocre fastball and change-up, with a fair curve. He began his career with the Kansas City Monarchs in 1931, when the team formed again for the second half of the season after having disbanded for half a season. During black baseball's chaotic Depression years, he bounced around with half a dozen teams before settling in Philadelphia for five seasons with the Stars. After a modicum of success in Philly, typified by a 2–3 record in 1940, he closed out his career with the Chicago American Giants in 1941–42.

Thompson, Sandy
[see Thompson, James (Sandy)]

Thompson, Wade
Career: 1922–26 Position: **p**
Teams: *Richmond Giants ('22)*, Baltimore Black Sox ('22), Harrisburg Giants ('23, '26)

During his first two years in black baseball, he pitched with teams just one year away from entry into the Eastern Colored League, first in 1922 with the Baltimore Black Sox and then in 1923 with the Harrisburg Giants.

Thompson, Will
Career: 1949–50 Position: p
Team: Philadelphia Stars

He began his career with the Philadelphia Stars in 1949, in the team's first season in the Negro American League after the demise of the Negro National League the previous season, and pitched with the Stars for two years when the league was struggling to survive the loss of players to organized baseball. In his last season, 1950, he was winless while suffering 7 defeats.

Thompson, William
Career: 1887–1900 Position: c
Teams: *Louisville Falls Citys ('87),* Genuine Cuban Giants ('00)

He was a catcher with the Louisville Falls Citys, one of eight teams that were charter members of the League of Colored Baseball Clubs in 1887. However, the league's existence was ephemeral, lasting only a week. Years later he played with the Genuine Cuban Giants, one of the various ballclubs that flourished during the early years of the century and that appropriated a variation of the Cuban Giants' name as their own.

Thomson
a.k.a. Thompson
Career: 1941 Positions: of, 3b
Team: Newark Eagles

A light hitter, he was a reserve player with the 1941 Newark Eagles, playing outfield and third base and hitting .231 in 9 league games.

Thornton
Career: 1928 Position: c
Team: Philadelphia Tigers

He was a catcher with the Philadelphia Tigers in 1928, their only season in the Eastern Colored League.

Thornton, Charles
Career: 1887 Position: player
Team: *Pittsburgh Keystones*

He appeared with the Pittsburgh Keystones, one of eight teams that were charter members of the League of Colored Baseball Clubs in 1887. However, the league's existence was ephemeral, lasting only a week. His position is uncertain.

Thornton, H.
Career: 1931 Position: of
Team: Memphis Red Sox

This outfielder played with the Memphis Red Sox in 1931, his only season in black baseball.

Thornton, Jack
Career: *1932–38* Positions: p, 2b, 1b
Team: Atlanta Black Crackers

In 1938 he was on the spring roster as a first baseman for the new Atlanta Negro American

League team. During the previous fall, the former football and basketball star at Morris Brown College and Atlanta University was playing professional football in his hometown of Chicago. The handsome ballplayer was a veteran at the hot corner and was considered to be a welcome addition if he could "get back to old-time form." Although he hit only .238 in 1937 with the Atlanta Black Crackers, he hit well in the clutch (.396) and was aggressively pursued by the Atlanta franchise. However, in mid-May he was playing with the Athens Red Sox, a semipro team, and showing no inclination toward signing a contract with the Black Crackers for the 1938 season.

Thornton, Jesse
Career: 1937   Position: officer
Team: Indianapolis Athletics

He was an officer with the Indianapolis Athletics in 1937, the franchise's only year in the Negro American League.

Thorpe, Clarence **Jim**
Career:1928–1934   Position: p
Teams: Hilldale Daisies ('28), Atlantic City Bacharach Giants ('34)

Possessing nowhere near the athletic skills of his namesake, he made two appearances in the Negro Leagues, playing 3 games with Hilldale in 1928 and hitting an even .200, and making another appearance with the Bacharachs in 1934, their last year of existence.

Thrilkill
[see Trealkill, Clarence Harvey]

Thurman
Career: 1937   Position: 1b
Team: St. Louis Stars

He was a first baseman with the St. Louis Stars in 1937, the inaugural year of the Negro American League.

Thurman, Jim
Career: 1932–33   Positions: **p**, of

Teams: Louisville Black Caps ('32), Columbus Turfs ('32), Columbus Blue Birds ('33)

He was a marginal player who pitched for teams struggling to play in the black major leagues. He began the 1932 season with the Louisville Black Caps in the Negro Southern League, but the franchise was replaced at the end of the first half by the Columbus Turfs, who finished the season. At the beginning of the next season Columbus was represented in the Negro National League by the Columbus Blue Birds, but they also folded after only half a season.

Thurman, Robert Burns (**Bob**)
Career: 1946–49   Positions: p, rf
Teams: *military service ('42–'45),* Homestead Grays ('46–'48), Kansas City Monarchs ('49), *minor leagues ('49–'52, '57, '59–'61), suspended list ('53–'54),* major leagues ('55–'59)
Bats: Left   Throws: Left
Height: 6'1"   Weight: 198
Born: May 14, 1917, Kellyville, Okla.

While the big, broad-shouldered, muscular Homestead Grays' pitcher-outfielder was best known as a pitcher in the Negro Leagues, he was an outfielder during his stint in the major leagues. As a pitcher he was only moderately effective, with a mediocre fastball and curve, and a fair change-up counted in his standard three-pitch repertory.

During World War II he enlisted in the Army and served in the Pacific Theater, in New Guinea, and Luzon. He was discovered while playing baseball in the Philippines with an Army team, and after the war he joined the Grays. In his first year, 1946, he was only 1–2 as a pitcher against league teams but hit .408. He was a good power hitter who could pull the ball, and he was fast on the bases. The following season, playing more in the outfield, he hit .338 and exhibited some home-run power, with 6 in 157 at-bats. In 1948 he hit .341 as the Grays won the last Negro National League pennant and defeated the Birmingham Black Barons in the World Series.

His display of power (18 home runs) with

Santurce in the Puerto Rican winter league attracted attention, and with the Negro National League already folded following the 1948 World Series, Thurman joined the Kansas City Monarchs in the Negro American League for the beginning of the 1949 season. With the color line eradicated, Thurman misrepresented his age, shaving off four years for the benefit of major-league scouts. He was soon in organized baseball as an outfielder, playing with Newark in the International League that same year and hitting .317. A hand injury prevented him from possibly moving up to the parent New York Yankees.

In 1950 he dropped to .269 but still showed sufficient power at the plate and he was assigned to San Francisco in the Pacific Coast League, where he spent two seasons, batting .274 and .280 while continuing to demonstrate good power. In 1953 he was placed on the suspended list and he was not in organized ball for two years, but he continued to play, in Puerto Rico, batting .281 and .323 for the 1953–55 winters and his speed and power remained evident, as he hit 14 homers in the latter season.

The next spring, at age thirty-eight, he made his first trip to the major leagues, with Cincinnati, counting seven homers among his .217 batting average while playing in only about half of the games. The Reds had a strong outfield and in 1956 he again was relegated to part-time duty, responding with a .295 average and 8 homers. In 1957, although splitting the season between Seattle and Cincinnati, he had his best home-run production, with 16 in 190 at-bats. He remained with the Reds in 1958, but not playing full-time, and after a few pinch-hitting appearances in 1959 he was sent back to the minors.

In 1960, with Charleston in the American Association, he hit .274 with 10 homers and, reverting back to his beginnings with the Grays, also pitched, but without a decision. The next year, with Charlotte in the South Atlantic League, was his last in baseball, and he finished his career with a lifetime .246 average

for his five years in the major leagues. After ending his active career, he served as a scout for the Cincinnati Reds and Kansas City Royals before becoming a scout for the Major League Scouting Bureau.

Thurston
Career: 1938   Position: p
Team: Birmingham Black Barons

He pitched briefly with the Black Barons in 1938, his only year in the Negro American League.

Thurston, Bobby
Career: 1911   Position: of
Team: Chicago Giants

The outfielder played briefly with Frank Leland's Chicago Giants in 1911, the first year after Leland separated from Rube Foster and formed a new team.

Tiant, Luis Eleuterio, Sr. (Lefty, Sir Skinny)
Career: 1930–47   Position: p
Teams: Cuban Stars (West) ('30–'32), Cuban House of David ('34), New York Cubans ('35–'36, '39–'40, '43, '45–'47)
Bats: Left   Throws: Left
Height: 5'11"   Weight: 175
Born: Aug. 27, 1906, Havana, Cuba
Died: Dec. 12, 1977

The father of the former major-league pitcher of the same name, Luis Tiant appeared in two East-West All-Star games twelve years apart, in 1935 and 1947. He earned his first All-Star selection with an 8–4 league ledger during the New York Cubans' best season, when they copped the Negro National League's second-half title before losing to the Pittsburgh Crawfords in a hard-fought 7-game playoff. Tiant suffered the loss in the closely contested 8–7 finale.

His second All-Star selection came at age forty, while weaving a regular-season 10–0 record with 3 shutouts to lead the New York Cubans to the 1947 Negro National League pennant. He then started 2 World Series games as the Cubans defeated the Negro American

League Cleveland Buckeyes for the championship.

Almost thirty years later, in 1975, after not having seen his son in fifteen years, Tiant and his wife were allowed by Fidel Castro to leave Cuba to see their son pitch in the major-league World Series for the Boston Red Sox at Fenway Park. His son was a different type of pitcher, but the elder Tiant had taught him how to throw a curve and sinker when he was a youngster.

Deliberate on the mound and throwing with a herky-jerky motion but an easy release that lent itself to deception, the crafty Cuban was a master at changing speeds and mixed his vast repertory of off-speed ''junk'' expertly to become one of the most successful pitchers of his era. He had outstanding control and an excellent curve and slider and a good fastball, but it was for his superior pickoff move and screwball that the wily veteran is best known. So effective was his move that the lanky left-hander once struck out a batter while throwing to first base.

He began pitching in Cuba with the Almendares Blues in 1926, and pitched on the 1929 championship Ciefuegos team. The following year he began his Negro League career, with an ignominious 4–13 record for the Cuban Stars. Within two seasons he had improved to a 5–1 mark with the Cubans when they entered the East-West League. During the early years of the Depression the Stars sometimes played as the Cuban House of David team, and Tiant was called the ''black Lefty Grove.'' At other times, more appropriately, he was called the ''Cuban Carl Hubbell.'' In the spring of 1935 he defeated the St. Louis Cardinals in a masterful 11-inning, 2–1 contest played in Havana, and in a pair of postseason exhibitions against the Babe Ruth All-Stars in October, he won both games by scores of 6–1 and 15–3, and held the Bambino to only a single.

In 1937 he jumped the New York Cubans to play with Martin Dihigo's Aguilas Cabaenas team in Santo Domingo, posting a 1–3 mark as his club lost the championship to Trujillo's

ballclub, featuring Satchel Paige and Josh Gibson. In 1941 Tiant again left the Cubans, this time to pitch with Aguila in the Mexican League, where he posted a 2–5 record with a 5.05 ERA.

After rejoining Pompez's New York Cubans, statistics are very sketchy, showing him as a .500 pitcher during the '40s, until his perfect 1947 performance. However, one game of note during this period was on Easter Sunday in 1945, when he beat the defending champion Birmingham Black Barons, 3–1, in New Orleans. Called the ''grand master of mound wizardry,'' he stayed in goods shape by pitching in the Cuban winter league, and was selected for the 1945–46 All-Cubans team. He was a very intelligent pitcher, but he was skinny and, as the years passed, he tired in late innings because his legs were not strong. In his latter years the aging veteran would sometimes be the subject of good-natured ribbing from younger teammates when he would go to sleep on the bus and his false teeth would fall out.

Finally, in 1948, at age forty-two, he retired from baseball and pooled his money with his brother-in-law to buy a truck and became a furniture mover.

Tindle, Levy
Career: 1933   Position: officer
Team: Detroit Stars

During the Detroit Stars' last season in the Negro National League, 1933, he served as an officer with the club.

Tinker, Harold
Career: 1931   Position: of
Team: Pittsburgh Crawfords ('29–'31)

He played with the Pittsburgh Crawfords when they were a semipro team consisting primarily of younger and less talented players, before Gus Greenlee opened his purse strings and began recruiting and signing top players. In 1929 Tinker was the captain and comanager of the Crawfords and was responsible for recruiting a youthful Josh Gibson. Tinker was still with the team in 1931, the year of transition to a major-league club, transformed primarily when Greenlee signed Satchel Paige during the summer.

Titus, James
Career: 1937   Position: officer
Team: Detroit Stars
He was an officer with the Detroit Stars in 1937, the inaugural season of the Negro American League and the last season for the Stars.

Toledo Crawfords
Duration: 1939   Honors: None
Affiliation: Negro American League
The Pittsburgh Crawfords switched both their home city and their league, moving to Indianapolis in 1939 and entering the Negro American League as a replacement team for the Indianapolis ABCs during the second half of the season.

Toledo Tigers
Duration: 1923   Honors: None
Affiliation: Negro National League
In their only season of league playa, they fielded a team in the Negro National League in 1923, but disbanded in mid-July.

Tolbert, Jake
Career: 1946   Position: p
Team: New York Black Yankees
In his only year in the Negro Leagues, he pitched briefly with the New York Black Yankees.

Tolbert, James
[see Talbert, James]

Tolliver
Career: 1921   Position: p
Team: *Pittsburgh Keystones*
He was a pitcher with the Pittsburgh Keystones in 1921, a year before they entered the Negro National League.

Tomm
a.k.a. Town

Career: 1917–18   Position: of
Teams: Atlantic City Bacharach Giants ('17), Brooklyn Royal Giants ('18), *Philadelphia Giants ('18)*
He was a part-time starter, batting sixth in the order and playing center field for the Bacharachs in 1917, their second season in Atlantic City. He split the next season between the Brooklyn Royal Giants and the Philadelphia Giants, a team of lesser quality.

Tompkins
Career: 1921   Position: p
Team: Baltimore Black Sox
He split 2 decisions while pitching with the Baltimore Black Sox in 1921, when they were still an independent team.

Tompkins
[see Thompson, James (Sandy)]

Tone, Eddie
Career: 1942   Position: player
Team: Newark Eagles
He appeared briefly with the Newark Eagles in 1942, but his position is uncertain.

Toney, Albert
Career: 1901–16   Positions: ss, 2b, of
Teams: Chicago Union Giants ('01, '04, '08), Algona Brownies ('02–'03), Leland Giants ('06), Chicago American Giants ('12), Chicago Giants ('13–'16)
Beginning his career in 1901 with the Chicago Union Giants as a center fielder, he moved to the infield with the Algona Brownies, playing third base in 1902 and shortstop in 1903, when they won the western championship. He remained at shortstop for the next three seasons, while changing teams, going back to the Chicago Union Giants in 1904 and then joining the Leland Giants. In 1912 he was a reserve shortstop for the Chicago American Giants, but after only one season he joined the Chicago Giants. During his second season with the team he was the regular right fielder and

batted sixth in the order, before resuming a reserve hole in his last two seasons.

Torres
Career: 1916   Position: c
Team: Long Branch Cubans

He was a catcher with the Long Branch Cubans in 1916.

Torres, Armando
Career: 1939   Position: p
Team: New York Cubans

He was a member of the New York Cubans' pitching staff in 1939, his only year in the Negro Leagues.

Torriente, Cristobal
a.k.a. Christobel (Carlos) Torriente
Career: 1913–28   Positions: **cf**, lf, rf, p, 3b, 1b
Teams: Cuban Stars ('13–'18), All Nations ('13, '16–'17), **Chicago American Giants** ('18–'25), Kansas City Monarchs ('26), Detroit Stars ('27–'28), *Gilkerson's Union Giants ('30), Atlanta Black Crackers ('32), Cleveland Cubs ('32)*
Bats: Left   Throws: Left
Height: 5'9"   Weight: 190
Born: 1895, Cuba
Died: 1938, New York, N.Y.

The slugging superstar of Rube Foster's great Chicago American Giants of 1918–25, he was also an outstanding fielder with great range and a strong, accurate arm. This muscular left-handed power hitter was the only legitimate slugger on Foster's team, and although primarily a pull hitter, he hit with power to all fields. A notorious bad-ball hitter, any pitch that left the pitcher's hand was likely to end up against the outfield wall. The stocky center fielder combined exceptional power with deceptive speed, and was an accomplished base stealer who could fit into Foster's bunt-and-run mold when the need presented itself.

In the first three years of the newly formed Negro National League, 1920–22, Torriente led the American Giants to consecutive championships, with averages of .411, .338, and .342. He claimed the league batting title mark in 1920 and again in 1923, when he topped the league with a .412 average. Setting the table for the slugger during these years were several players from Rube Foster's stable of race-horses, including Bingo DeMoss, Jimmy Lyons, Jelly Gardner, and Dave Marlarcher. Torriente, Gardner, and Lyons formed one of the fastest and best defensive outfields of all time.

In postseason play Torriente is credited with a .302 average for the 1921 playoffs. The following season, the Cuban superstar lost playing time due to an injury, but Foster had acquired the services of slugger John Beckwith, who picked up the slack until Torriente got back into the lineup. In addition to his tremendous hitting, the Cuban superstar, who began his career as a pitcher and had a 15–7 lifetime league ledger, often displayed his versatility by taking a turn on the mound.

Torriente's predilection for "nightlife" contributed to his being traded to the Kansas City Monarchs in 1926, where his team-leading .381 batting average sparked the team to the first-half championship. His temperament manifested itself again in mid-August, when he quit the Monarchs after being refused reimbursement by the owner for a lost diamond ring. His absence during this dispute was critical and may have cost the Monarchs the second-half title, as they lost out to the Chicago American Giants. In the playoff against his old teammates, the burly outfielder hit for a .407 average in a losing effort. His difficulties with the Monarchs' management facilitated his exit from Kansas City, and he signed with the Detroit Stars, where he hit .339 and .320 during his two seasons (1927–28) in the Motor City.

As the '30s approached, Torriente was winding down a career that started during the dead-ball era with two independent ballclubs, the Cuban Stars and the All Nations team. Rube Foster coveted the stocky Cuban's skills and secured his services for a short time in 1914, before landing him to stay in 1919. That year,

Torriente hit .325 and paired with Oscar Charleston in the American Giants' outfield to form a deadly duo.

Jocko Conlan, a Hall of Fame umpire who barnstormed against black teams as a player, regarded Torriente as a great hitter. A lifetime .333 hitter in the Negro Leagues, he also recorded a lifetime average of .352 for thirteen seasons in the Cuban winter league. Other than his first year (1913), when he hit .265 and his last year (1927), when he hit .222, he batted over .300 in every season except one. Counting two batting titles among his credits while playing in his homeland, he put together a string of seasons with averages of .337, .387, .402, .360, .296, .350, .346, .380, .344, and .375. Torriente, along with Dihigo and Mendez, are considered the greatest of the Cuban players from the Negro Leagues, and Torriente was among the first group of ten players elected to the Cuban Hall of Fame.

The Cuban slugger also hit for an average .313 against major-league competition in exhibitions. One series played in Cuban in the winter of 1920 is particularly noteworthy. Almendares, with Torriente, played a nine-game series against the New York Giants, who had added Babe Ruth to their roster for the tour of the island. Torriente outhit Ruth. 378, to .345, outhomered him 3 to 2, and compiled a .757 slugging percentage as Almendares edged the Ruth-assisted Giants by a 1-game margin.

A complete ballplayer with superb talent, if he were playing today he would be considered "the franchise" of any team on which he played. Indianapolis ABCs' manager C. I. Taylor, stated, "If I should see Torriente walking up the other side of the street, I would say, 'There walks a ballclub.' " The New York Giants, recognizing the potential impact his talents would have on a ballclub, scouted the light brown Torriente and would have signed him to play in the major leagues except for the rough texture of his hair.

After his skills began fading he played with teams of lesser quality, including Gilkerson's Union Giants, the Cleveland Cubs, and the Atlanta Black Crackers. Torriente left baseball in the mid-1930s but while making his home in Ybor City, Florida, in 1938, he was being sought by Black Crackers' acting manager Don Pelham to play again in Atlanta. However, there is no record that Pelham was successful in his quest, and the greatest Cuban home-run hitter in baseball history faded into obscurity as a lonely, impoverished alcoholic. He was reported to have died in New York City of tuberculosis a short time afterward, and his body was returned to his homeland draped in a Cuban flag for interment.

Torrin
Career: 1920　　　Position: p
Team: St. Louis Giants

He pitched with the St. Louis Giants in 1920, the inaugural season of the Negro National League.

Town
[see Tomm]

Trabue
Career: 1924　　　Position: p
Team: Indianapolis ABCs

He pitched briefly with the Indianapolis ABCs in 1924, his only season in the Negro National League.

Trammel, Nat
Career: 1930–32　　　Positions: 1b, rf, *p*
Teams: Birmingham Black Barons ('30), Brooklyn Royal Giants ('32)
Bats: Left　　　Throws: Right
Height: 6'0"　　　Weight: 175

An Army man, he played baseball with the 24th Infantry team before embarking on a short professional career. He was a good fielder, had average speed as a base runner, and was a line-drive hitter with average power, batting .309 in 1930. But eventually the competition was too strong for him as a hitter. He played as a first baseman with the Birmingham Black Barons, was a right fielder with the Brooklyn

Royal Giants, and even took a turn as a pitcher when the circumstances dictated a need.

Trawick, Joe
Career: 1950   Position: 2b
Team: Cleveland Buckeyes

This second baseman started his career with the Cleveland Buckeyes in 1950, when the Negro American League was struggling to survive the loss of players to organized baseball, but league statistics do not confirm his playing time.

Treadway, Ted
Career: 1939–40   Position: p
Teams: Kansas City Monarchs ('39), Toledo Crawfords ('39), Indianapolis Crawfords ('40)
Bats: Right
Throws: Right
Height: 6'   Weight: 170

A fringe player, this righthander pitched without distinction for two seasons in the Negro American League, with the Monarchs and Crawfords.

Treadwell, Harold
Career: 1919–28   Positions: **p,** *of*
Teams: New York Lincoln Giants ('19), Brooklyn Royal Giants ('19), **Atlantic City Bacharach Giants** ('20–'23), Harrisburg Giants ('23), Chicago American Giants ('24–'28), Detroit Stars ('24, '26), Cleveland Browns ('24), Indianapolis ABCs ('25), Dayton Marcos ('26)
Bats: Right   Throws: Right
Died: 1971, Chicago, Ill.

An underhand pitcher with good control, he had a good curve and fastball and sometimes also used a sidearm delivery. In 1920 he pitched with the Bacharachs, starting the year as the team's number two pitcher behind Dick Redding, but during the course of the season, he was passed by Red Ryan. The Bacharachs were playing an independent schedule, and incomplete statistics show wins in both of his decisions against league teams.

Pitching in the 1921 playoffs against the Chicago American Giants, he entered the record books when he pitched a complete game but lost a reknowned 1–0 contest in 20 innings. Leaving the Bacharachs in 1923, he was one of the top hurlers for the Harrisburg Giants. The next season he was with three different teams, including Rube Foster's Chicago American Giants. In the early spring of 1925 he was released by Foster to the Indianapolis ABCs. In 1926, despite being winless in league play against 6 losses, he was a leading pitcher for the Dayton Marcos.

Although he was considered a good-hitting pitcher, he batted only .167 for his year with the Marcos. In 1928 he returned to the Chicago American Giants, now managed by David Malarcher, to close out his career. Treadwell had a cordial relationship with his teammates but had a drinking problem and, more than forty years after his baseball career ended, he was found dead in an alley in Chicago.

Trealkill, Clarence Harvey
a.k.a. Thrilkill
Career: 1929–31   Positions: ss, of
Team: Nashville Elite Giants

Although used primarily as a shortstop, he played in both the infield and the outfield with the Nashville Elite Giants during his three-year career. In 1930 the Elite Giants were in the Negro National League, sandwiched between two years in the Negro Southern League. In his first year with the Elite Giants he batted .231 while playing in only 5 games, and in his last year with the team, he was a part-time starter in center field, batting at the bottom of the order when in the lineup.

Trent, Theodore (**Ted**, *Highpockets, Stringbean, Big Florida*)
Career: 1927–39   Position: p
Teams: **St. Louis Stars** ('27–'31), Washington Pilots ('32), Detroit Wolves ('32), Homestead Grays ('32), Baltimore Black Sox ('32), Kansas City Monarchs ('32, '36), New York Black Yankees ('33–'34), Cole's American Giants ('33–'35), **Chicago American Giants** ('36–'39)
Bats: Right   Throws: Right

Height: 6'3"   Weight: 185
Born: Dec. 17, 1903, Jacksonville, Fla.
Died: Jan. 10, 1944, Chicago, Ill.

A big right-hander with an even bigger curve and a good slider, Trent was an ace on the outstanding St. Louis Stars teams of 1927–31, winners of three Negro National League pennants. Actually, Trent had three distinctly different curves, breaking a long curve, a short curve, and a shorter curve. He also had a good fastball and a drop that broke like it was falling off a table. On the mound, he was a level-headed master with control of all his pitches, and once struck out Bill Terry four times in an exhibition game. The tall, slim hurler had a straight overhand delivery and needed an extra day between starts, but was the Stars' "Sunday pitcher" for five years.

His best season came in their first pennant-winning season, 1928, when, he posted a 21–2 record, and won 3 more games in the playoffs against the Chicago American Giants, defeating Willie Foster in the finale. This was sandwiched between seasons of 15–11 and 12–8, and in the Stars' second championship season, 1930, he crafted a 12–2 mark, adding 2 more wins against a single loss in the playoffs with the Detroit Stars. The next season the Stars captured the final flag before the demise of the Negro National League. Records for the season are imcomplete but show Trent with a 3–1 mark.

One of the tallest players in black baseball, he was also one of the best right-handers in the game for more than a decade, and after the breakup of the St. Louis Stars he pitched for four teams during the 1932 season, compiling a composite 5–4 mark. Signing with the Chicago American Giants, he starred for the American Giants' teams of the '30s, appearing in the East-West All-Star game four consecutive years (1934–37), including two starting assignments. His first starting assignment was in the second All-Star contest, in 1934, when he pitched shutout ball for three innings, leaving the game in a scoreless deadlock. The next season he topped all pitchers in the balloting.

His highest win total during his stay in Chicago came in 1936, when they were playing as an independent team and he posted a 29–5 record against all levels of competition. In the two previous seasons he had a combined 8–11 record in league play, and after the American Giants joined the Negro American League in 1937, he is credited with seasons of 8–2, 6–4, and 2–2 in his last three years of his career. He also pitched in Cuba during the winter of 1928–29 and in the California winter league in 1930–31.

The big Floridian began his professional career in 1924 at St. Augustine, Florida, and pitched for the Bethune-Cookman College baseball team in 1925–26. After school was out the latter season, he joined Jimmy Reel's West Palm Beach Giants. Reel and Morty Clark recommended Trent to the St. Louis Stars, who signed him for the 1927 season.

Always a hard drinker, this weakness and the difficult traveling conditions eventually took their toll and contributed to his contracting tuberculosis. Four years after retiring from baseball, Trent fell ill and died a few weeks past his fortieth birthday.

Trice, Robert Lee (**Bob**, Bill)
Career: 1948–50   Positions: p, of
Teams: Homestead Grays ('48–'50), *Canadian League ('50–'52), minor leagues ('52–'55),* Major Leagues ('53–'55), *Mexican League ('56–'58)*
Bats: Right   Throws: Right
Height: 6'2"   Weight: 190
Born: Aug. 28, 1926, Newton, Ga.
Died: Sept. 16, 1988, Wierton, W. Va.

This big right-hander pitched for the Homestead Grays in 1949 and 1950 before becoming the first black to play for the Philadelphia A's, in 1953. During his three partial years in the major leagues, he split 18 decisions, but between leaving the Grays during the 1950 season and signing with the A's, he pitched for three seasons in the Canadian Provincial League. His first two seasons with Farnham produced seasons of 5–3 and 7–12, but in

1952, with St. Hyacinthe, he posted a 16–3 record with a 3.49 ERA.

The next stop was Ottawa in the International League, where his success (21–10, 3.10 ERA) earned him his first shot at the parent A's, and in 3 games he won 2 against a lone defeat. The next year was also split between the same two teams but with different results, 7–8 with the A's and 4–8 with Ottawa. In 1955 the Athletics moved to Kansas City and he had one last try at the major leagues, but pitched poorly without a decision in only four outings. His work was not impressive at either of his other two stops that season. The last three years were spent in the Mexican League with the Mexico City Reds, and he had an aggregate 14–15 ledger for these seasons, ending his career after the 1958 season.

Throughout his career he showed some ability with the bat, leaving a .288 major-league average behind and a pattern of good averages in even seasons, .297 in 1952, .298 in 1954, and .289 in 1956. His hitting also showed good power, with 7 home runs in each of his three years in Mexico, and 4 homers in each of his two seasons with Ottawa.

Trimble, William E.

Career: 1927–32   Position: owner, officer
Team: Chicago American Giants

A white businessman who owned a racetrack in Peoria, Illinois, he became the owner of the Chicago American Giants in 1927 after Rube Foster became incapacitated. He was also a gambler, and when he had a substantial wager on his baseball team, he always wanted Willie Foster to pitch. He served as an officer with the team through 1932, when Robert Cole purchased the franchise.

Triplett

Career: 1917–18   Position: cf
Team: Hilldale Daisies

He was a reserve center fielder with Hilldale in the team's early years as a professional ballclub.

Trouppe, Quincy Thomas (Big Train, Baby Quincy, El Roro)

a.k.a. Quincey Troupe
Career: 1930–49   Positions: c, of, 2b, p, manager
Teams: St. Louis Stars ('30–'31, '39), Detroit Wolves ('32), Homestead Grays ('32), Kansas City Monarchs ('32, '34–'36), Chicago American Giants ('33, '48), Bismarck, N.D., Cubs ('33–'36), voluntarily retired ('37), Indianapolis ABCs ('38–'39), Mexican League ('39–'44, '50–'51), Cleveland Buckeyes ('44–'47), New York Cubans ('49), Canadian League ('49), major leagues ('52)
Bats: Both   Throws: Right
Height: 6' 3"   Weight: 210
Born: Dec. 25, 1912, Dublin, Ga.
Died: Aug. 10, 1993, Creve Coeur, Mo.

A smart receiver and a superior handler of pitchers, this switch-hitter had power from both sides of the plate, but more from the right side. Consequently the pull hitter received a substantial number of free passes from opposing pitchers. He used a heavy bat and was a good curveball hitter, but he did not have much speed on the bases. Trouppe played in five All-Star games for the West squad over a ten-year period.

He was the youngest of ten children and learned early in life to watch out for himself. He was a Golden Gloves boxer before he began playing baseball, and he also attended Lincoln College in Missouri. The strong-armed catcher broke in with the Negro National League champion St. Louis Stars in 1931 as an eighteen-year-old youngster. In 1932 he played with the Homestead Grays and Kansas City Monarchs, and the following year he played as a reserve with another championship team, the Chicago American Giants.

After a three-year tour with Bismarck, North Dakota (1934–36), he was out of baseball for a season. But the big receiver returned to the diamond with the Indianapolis ABCs in 1938 before traveling to Mexico, where he spent five years (1939–44) plying his trade while also acquiring and polishing his managerial skills. In each of these seasons he hit over .300, registering averages of .307, .337, and .306 with Monterrey and .364 and .301 with Mexico City. The next year, during the height of World War II, he encountered difficulty with his draft board in securing a passport to return to Mexico. Seeking assistance, he contacted Mexican League president Jorge Pasquel, who quickly made arrangements for eighty thousand Mexican workers to be exchanged so Trouppe and Theolic Smith could leave their defense jobs and play baseball in Mexico.

Late in the 1944 season, Trouppe was contacted about managing the Cleveland Buckeyes for the 1945 season. He returned to the United States and played a few games at the end of the season with the Buckeyes to evaluate the personnel, and became playing manager for the Buckeyes in 1945, replacing Red Parnell, who remained as captain. With his able knowledge of the game and his own playing ability, he led his team to the Negro American League pennant. Although batting only .245 during the regular season, he hit .400 in the ensuing World Series as the Buckeyes swept the Negro National League champion Homestead Grays in 4 straight games. He continued his hot hitting into the next two seasons, with averages of .313 and .352 in 1946–47. In the latter year the Buckeyes won another pennant under his leadership, but lost the World Series to the New York Cubans.

The next season, Trouppe played with the Chicago American Giants, hitting a robust .342 with 10 home runs. Leaving after one year, he traveled to Canada to play with Drummondville in the Provincial League, batting .282 for the 1949 season. In 1950 he returned to the Mexican League for a second, short stay, hitting .283 and .252 and 1950 and 1951 with Guadalajara.

Afterward he signed with the Cleveland Indians and played briefly in the major leagues in 1952. During his short time with the Indians the veteran catcher proved to be a hard worker, good on blocking balls, and a very good receiver with an excellent arm who called a good

game. After only 10 at-bats and 1 major-league hit, he was assigned to Indianapolis in the American Association, and he completed the season with a .259 batting average.

Throughout his career Trouppe frequently played baseball year-round, logging twelve years of winter ball, including six All-Star seasons. He played in Puerto Rico (1941–42, 1944–45, 1947–50), Cuba (1950–51), Venezuela (1945–47, 1951–53) and Colombia (1953–54). Among his accomplishments in Puerto Rico was managing his Caguas team to a championship in the 1947–48 winter league.

During his career, summer and winter, he played with about two dozen different teams over twenty-three years, during seventeen of which he was an All-Star, and seven years were spent as a catcher-manager. He went to the East-West All-Star game five times, and every year that he played, his team won. When he closed his career he had a lifetime average in the Negro Leagues of .311. For his eight years in the Mexican League he showed a .304 average, and for three winters in Cuba he finished with a .254 average. After retiring from baseball he was a scout for the St. Louis Cardinals for ten years.

Troy, Donald
Career: 1944–45   Position: p
Team: Baltimore Elite Giants

He was a wartime player with the Elites Giants, and his pitching career consisted of the last two seasons, 1944–45, during World War II. He lost his only decision.

Trusty, Job
Career: 1896   Position: 3b
Team: Cuban Giants

In 1896 he was a third baseman for the Cuban Giants, the first black professional team, organized in 1885 as an extension of the Argyle Hotel Athletics.

Trusty, Shepard (**Shep**)
Career: 1885–89   Positions: **p**, of

Teams: *Philadelphia Orions ('84), Argyle Hotel Athletics ('85),* Cuban Giants ('86–'89)
Born: May 10, 1863, Philadelphia, Pa.
Died: Trenton, N.J.

A tall, slender hurler with bewildering curves and superb overall pitching skills, in 1886 the phenom was championed by many observers, including two different newspapers, as ''unquestionably'' the best colored pitcher in the country. That season, pitching with the Cuban Giants, he pitched two notable games against major-league opposition, a six-hitter against the Philadelphia league club and a seven-hitter against the New York Metropolitans.

He began his baseball career playing with Millville, New Jersey, and the Orions of Philadelphia. In 1885 he was a member of the Argyle Hotel Athletics, organized by Frank P. Thompson, the headwaiter at Long Island's Argyle Hotel in Babylon, New York, to play for the entertainment of the summer guests. After the end of the tourist season, the team added some more players from the Orions and the Manhattans of Washington D.C., to form the Cuban Giants, the first black professional team. Trusty was the first player signed by owner Walter Cook when he bought the team in May 1886.

He continued to pitch other significant games during the Cuban Giants' first season. Pitching against St. Louis while still recovering from an injury, he pitched commendably despite losing, 9–3. In another outing, on June 9, he faced Philadelphia of the American Association, a major league at the time, and held them hitless until the game was called after 4 innings due to rain, with the Cubans behind, 3–0, on 3 unearned runs. The next month, on July 26, he pitched excellent ball as he defeated the National League's Kansas City team, 3–2. The next day, pitching without rest at his own request, he was knocked out by the same Kansas City squad and lost, 13–4. Later in the summer he lost to Newark 3–1, despite a brilliant performance on his part.

For the next four years he continued pitching with the Cuban Giants, who often played as representatives of a host city in a regular league. In 1887 and 1889 they represented Trenton, New Jersey, in the Middle States League. At an undetermined date, the first black pitching star died in Trenton of tuberculosis.

Tuck
Career: 1934   Position: of
Team: Atlantic City Bacharach Giants

He appeared with the Bacharach Giants in 1934, their last year in the Negro National League.

Tucker, Henry
Career: 1916–22   Positions: owner, officer
Team: Atlantic City Bacharach Giants

He was one of the two businessmen responsible for the Duval Giants leaving Jacksonville, Florida, in 1916 to relocate in Atlantic City as the Bacharach Giants. As co-owner, he served as an officer with the Bacharachs during the ballclub's formative years, before they entered the Eastern Colored League.

Tucker, Orval
Career: 1930   Positions: **2b**, ss, 3b
Teams: Baltimore Black Sox ('30), Hilldale Daisies ('30), *Boston Royal Giants ('42)*

Primarily a second baseman, he could play any infield position, and was a reserve infielder with the Baltimore Black Sox and Hilldale in 1930, batting .367 in limited play in his only season with top ballclubs. A dozen years later he played with the Boston Royal Giants, a lesser team.

Tugerson, Leander
Career: 1950   Position: p
Team: Indianapolis Clowns ('50–'52), Minor Leagues ('53)
Bats: Right   Throws: Right

He began his career in 1950, when the Negro American League was struggling to survive the loss of players to organized baseball.

After pitching briefly with the Clowns, he also entered organized ball, playing one season with Knoxville, where he had an undistinguished 3–5 record with a 5.55 ERA.

Turner

Career: 1930   Position: 1b
Team: Kansas City Monarchs

He was a reserve first baseman with the Kansas City Monarchs in 1930, batting but .196 in his only year in the Negro Leagues.

Turner, B. (Aggie)

Career: 1914–17   Positions: 1b, 2b, of, c
Teams: Indianapolis ABCs ('11–'14), Chicago Union Giants ('16), Chicago Giants ('16–'17), All Nations ('17)

Beginning his career with the Indianapolis ABCs in 1911, when they were in their formative stages, he was a reserve infielder with the team in 1914, their first year as a major-league-caliber team. Leaving the ABCs, he joined the Chicago Union Giants, splitting his playing time between first base and second base and batting in the leadoff spot in 1916. Later in the season he moved to the Chicago Giants, playing second base and batting third in the order when in the lineup. He began the next year in Chicago but left during the season to travel with the All Nations team.

Turner, E.C. (Pop)

Career: 1925–32, 1937 Positions: **3b**, ss, 2b,
                    umpire
Teams: Brooklyn Royal Giants ('25–'28), Homestead Grays ('29), Birmingham Black Barons ('30), Cleveland Cubs ('31), New York Black Yankees ('31), Cole's American Giants ('32)

Bats: Right   Throws: Right

Beginning his career with the Brooklyn Royal Giants in the Eastern Colored League, he left when the league broke up and signed on as a substitute infielder with the Homestead Grays in the replacement American Negro League in 1929, batting .279 for the season. He was a good third baseman with an arm

good enough to get the batter by a step. At the plate he had no power and lacked speed, but he was a smart, alert base runner. He was highly intelligent and used his mind more than his body, while also helping the team as a teacher for younger players.

When the American Negro League folded after only a year, he joined the Birmingham Black Barons and hit .248 while playing third base. In 1932 he was the regular shortstop and, although usually batting in the lower part of the order, he hit .302 for Cole's American Giants as they captured the Negro Southern League championship. After his active playing days were over, he began a second career in baseball as an umpire in the Negro National League.

Turner, Etwood

Career: 1923   Position: cf
Team: Toledo Tigers

He played center field with the Toledo Tigers in 1923 before they disbanded and dropped out of the Negro National League in midseason.

Turner, Henry (Dad, **Flash**)

Career: 1938–43   Positions: c, 2b, 1b, lf,
                         rf
Teams: Jacksonville Red Caps ('35–'38, '41–'42), Cleveland Bears ('39–'40), Homestead Grays ('39), Harrisburg-St. Louis Stars ('43), Cleveland Buckeyes ('43)

Bats: Right   Throws: Right
Height 5'11"   Weight: 172
Born: Sept. 1, 1913, Lloyd, Fla.

An exceptionally hard hitter and considered very tough in the clutch, he was called one of the best right-handed hitters in the South. He began playing baseball with the St. Petersburg Stars and joined the Jacksonville Red Caps in 1935, when they were in the Negro Southern League, leading the team to seasons of 70–16, 77–26, and 44–28. In the latter year, 1937, he registered a .310 batting average while developing into a fine receiver with an accurate peg to second base. The following season he was being called "Dad" and batting cleanup as the team joined the Negro American League.

When the franchise moved to Cleveland for the 1939–40 seasons, he retained his cleanup spot in the order while dividing his playing time between catcher and the outfield. After two years in Cleveland the franchise returned to Jacksonville, and Turner retained his same position in the lineup until the Red Caps dropped out of the league in July 1942. His next team, the Harrisburg-St. Louis Stars, also dropped out of league play, leaving early in the spring to go barnstorming against a team headlined by Dizzy Dean. Turner signed on with the Cleveland Buckeyes as an outfielder for the remainder of the 1943 season, his last in the Negro Leagues.

Turner, J. O.
Career: 1887   Position: player
Team: *Philadelphia Pythians*

He played with the Philadelphia Pythians, one of eight teams that were charter members of the League of Colored Baseball Clubs in 1887. However, the league's existence was ephemeral, lasting only a week. His position is uncertain.

Turner, (Little Lefty)
Career: 1940–42   Position: 1b
Teams: Indianapolis Crawfords ('40), Baltimore Elite Giants ('42)

This light-hitting little ballplayer began his career in 1940, batting in the seventh slot as the regular first baseman of the Negro American League's Indianapolis Crawfords. The Crawfords dropped out of the league at the end of the season, and his last year in the Negro Leagues was spent as a backup for George Scales with the Baltimore Elite Giants in 1942. He hit a meager .100 in that capacity, and on those occasions when he took a turn in the starting lineup, he batted at the bottom of the order.

Turner, Robert (Bob)
Career: 1946, 1950   Position: c

Bats: Right   Throws: Right
Born: 1927
Teams: Kansas City Monarchs ('46), Houston Eagles ('50), *minor leagues ('49, '52–'53)*

A light hitting third-string catcher with the Monarchs in 1946, he later played in organized ball with Berick in the North Atlantic League in 1949, batting .259 in only a dozen games. The next year he was back with a black team, playing briefly with the Houston Eagles. But two years later he had another tour of duty in organized ball, playing with Porterville in the Southwest International League and hitting .265 with modest power. In 1953 he played with Carman in the Mandak League, hitting .204 with only a single homer in 54 games.

Turner, Ted
Career: 1948   Position: p
Team: Birmingham Black Barons
Bats: Right   Throws: Right

This rangy right-hander from St. Augustine, Florida, won a position on the pitching staff with the Birmingham Black Barons in the spring of 1948, and the Black Barons went on to win the Negro American League pennant before losing to the Homestead Grays in the World Series.

Turner, Thomas
Career: 1947   Position: 1b
Team: Chicago American Giants

He was a backup first baseman with the Chicago American Giants in 1947.

Turner, Tuck
Career: 1919, 1923,
1928   Position: p
Teams: Chicago American Giants ('19), St. Louis Stars ('23, '28)

He began his career in 1919 as a marginal member of the pitching staff for the Chicago American Giants and was a sporadic member of the St. Louis Stars' pitching staff in the '20s.

Turnstall, Willie
Career: 1950   Position: p
Team: Cleveland Buckeyes

He began his pitching career in the 1950 season when the Negro American League was struggling to survive the loss of players to organized baseball.

Tut, King
[see King, Richard]

Twyman
Career: 1916   Position: of
Team: New York Lincoln Stars
He appeared briefly as an outfielder with the Lincoln Stars in 1916.

Tye, Dan
Career: 1930, 1936 Positions: **3b**, ss, p
Teams: Memphis Red Sox ('30), Cincinnati Tigers ('36)
He played third base for the Memphis Red Sox in 1930 and played with the Cincinnati Tigers in 1936, a year before the team entered the Negro American League.

Tyler, Charles H.
Career: 1934–35 Position: officer
Team: Newark Dodgers
He was an officer with the Newark Dodgers during the ballclub's two-year existence.

Tyler, Edward
Career: 1925–26 Positions: p, rf
Teams: St. Louis Stars (25), Hilldale Daisies ('26), *Brooklyn Cuban Giants ('28)*
He played one year each in the Negro National League and the Eastern Colored League. He was a reserve outfielder in 1925 with the St. Louis Stars and a pitcher in 1926 with Hilldale. He lost his only decision in 1926, but also pitched in 1928 with the Brooklyn Cuban Giants, an independent team of lesser status.

Tyler, Eugene
Career: 1943   Positions: ss, c, lf, 3b
Teams: *Chicago Brown Bombers ('42–'43),* Kansas City Monarchs ('43)
He was a reserve infielder-outfielder with the Monarchs in 1943, playing both shortstop and

left field. Prior to joining the Monarchs he was a shortstop-catcher with the Chicago Brown Bombers, a strong independent team but of lesser status than the league teams.

Tyler, Roy
Career: 1925–27 Positions: p, of
Teams: Chicago American Giants ('25–'26), Cleveland Elites ('26), Cleveland Hornets ('27)
His three seasons in the Negro National League was divided between Chicago and Cleveland. He began his pitching career in 1925 with the Chicago American Giants and closed it out with the two Cleveland entries in the Negro National League, the Elites in 1926 and the Hornets in 1927.

Tyler, William (**Steel Arm,** Bill)
a.k.a. Taylor
Career: 1925–32 Positions: **p,** *of*
Teams: Memphis Red Sox ('25, '27–'28), Chicago American Giants ('26), Kansas City Monarchs ('27), Detroit Stars ('29–'30), Cole's American Giants ('32)
This pitcher began his career with the Memphis Red Sox in 1925 and posted a 7–8 record in 1927. He was signed by the Chicago American Giants in early 1926, and returned to Chicago in 1932 to close out his career. In the interim he played a year with the Monarchs and two years with the Detroit Stars, where he compiled marks of 7–7 an 2–0 for league play. He was reputed to have killed a white man, and consequently he had a problem with the law.

Tyms
Career: 1923   Position: of
Team: Chicago American Giants
He was with the Chicago American Giants briefly as an outfielder in 1923.

Tyree, Ruby
a.k.a. Tyrees
Career: 1916–24 Position: p
Teams: *Tennessee Rats ('16),* All Nations ('16), Chicago American Giants ('16–'17), *Chicago Union Giants ('17), Lost Island*

Giants ('17), St. Louis Giants ('17), Cleveland Browns ('24)

Bats: Right   Throws: Right

He was in the playoffs for Chicago American Giants against the Indianapolis ABCs in 1916, and during the ensuing winter he played with Rube Foster's team representing the Royal Poinciana Hotel in the Florida winter league. The little right-handed pitcher and catcher George Dixon were called the ''pony battery'' when they were signed by the Chicago American Giants in April 1917. After being showcased in the first game, and winning his first 2 decisions, he was released to St. Louis in early May and later played with the Chicago Union Giants, a lesser team. Prior to signing with the Chicago American Giants, he played with the Lost Island Giants, the Tennessee Rats, and the All Nations team. With the Lost Island Giants in later June 1917, he struck out 14 batters in a game against the Tennessee Rats and struck out 21 batters against the Lennox, South Dakota, team.

Tyrees, Ruby
[see Tyree, Ruby]

Tyson
Career: 1945   Position: 1b
Team: New York Black Yankees

He was briefly a wartime reserve first baseman with the New York Black Yankees in 1945, his only year in the Negro Leagues.

Tyson, Armand Cupree (Cap)
Career: 1936–40   Positions: c, 3b
Team: Birmingham Black Barons
Bats: Right   Throws: Right

He began his career with the Birmingham Black Barons in 1936 as a catcher and closed at the hot corner in 1940.

Tyus, Julius, Jr.
Career: 1947   Position: p
Team: Philadelphia Stars

He pitched very briefly with the Philadelphia Stars in 1947, his only year in the Negro Leagues.

U

Underhill, Bob
Career: 1924   Position: p
Team: Hilldale Daisies

In his only season in the Negro Leagues, he was a member of the pitching staff for the Eastern Colored League champion Hilldale ballclub in 1924 but saw little action.

Underwood, Ely
Career: 1937   Positions: lf, rf
Team: Detroit Stars

This light-hitting outfielder was a part-time starter, playing in both side pastures, with the new Detroit Stars' franchise, charter members in the Negro American League in 1937, their only year in the league. Available statistics show a meager .105 batting average for the season, and his career ended with the demise of the franchise.

Underwood, Ray
Career: 1937   Position: p
Team: Detroit Stars

He was a lesser member of the Detroit Stars' pitching staff in 1937, when the new franchise became charter members in the Negro American League. In limited mound duty, there is no record of a decision, and his career did not extend beyond the demise of the franchise at the end of the season.

V

Vactor, John
Career: 1887–88   Positions: p, of
Teams: *Philadelphia Pythians ('87),* New York Gorhams ('87–'88)

This nineteenth-century player played with two of the best-known early black teams, the Philadelphia Pythians and the New York Gorhams, both of which were among the eight teams that were charter members of the League of Colored Baseball Clubs in 1887. Although the league was short-lived, lasting only a week, the clubs continued to operate as independent teams.

Valdes, Fermin (Strico, Swat)
a.k.a. Valdez
Career: 1931–44   Positions: **2b,** ss, *p*
Teams: Cuban Stars ('31–'32), Atlanta Black Crackers ('32), New York Cubans ('38–'39), Cincinnati-Indianapolis Clowns ('44)

A middle infielder with the Cuban Stars during the '30s, he was the starting second baseman with the Stars when they also played as the Cuban House of David in 1931–32; he usually hit in the lower part of the batting order, but sometimes batted in the first two spots at the top of the order. He was the regular second baseman with the New York Cubans in 1938–39, and he shared the starting assignments at second base and hit .240 for the Cincinnati-Indianapolis Clowns in 1944.

Valdez, Rogelio
a.k.a. Valdes

Career: 1905–11   Positions: **of,** 2b
Team: All Cubans

This light-hitting Cuban outfielder spent most of his baseball career in his native country, playing only two seasons (1905 and 1911) in the United States. In a 14-year Cuban career spent mostly with Havana and Almendares, he registered a paltry lifetime batting average of only .195. His best year was 1908, when he hit for a .258 average. Although not particularly noted for his extra-base power, he led the league in each extra-base category at some time in his career (triples in 1900, doubles in 1903, and homers in 1910). In the latter year he played left field with Almendares against the Detroit Tigers in a winter exhibition series and, while batting in the eighth slot, hit .133.

While lacking punch at the plate, he was an excellent defensive player, who was regarded as the best Cuban outfielder of his time. Very fast afoot, he had exceptional range and a strong throwing arm, described as a "whip of steel." His speed was also evident on the bases, and he was an excellent base stealer. A durable player, he led the league in the most games played on four occasions (1900, 1901, 1904, 1907), and was elected to Cuban Hall of Fame in 1946.

Valdez, Tony
a.k.a. Valdes
Career: 1910–20   Positions: of, 1b, p
Teams: Stars of Cuba ('10), Cuban Stars (West) ('11–'20)

Beginning his career with the Stars of Cuba in 1910, he batted leadoff and split playing time between first base and left field. The following season he was one of half a dozen players, including José Mendez, to join Tinti Molina's strong Cuban Stars. With the Stars he played left field and batted in the eighth spot. His career linked the deadball era, when the Stars were touring as an independent team, and the beginning of the Negro National League in 1920. The league's first year was his last year, and he played in the outfield and pitched for the Stars while closing out a career that spanned a decade.

Valentine
Career: 1915–19   Position: of
Teams: Philadelphia Giants ('15–'17), Hilldale Daisies ('18–'19), *Madison Stars ('21)*

He was an outfielder for five seasons during the late '10s with Philadelphia-based teams of marginal quality, primarily the declining Philadelphia Giants and Hilldale in their formative years.

Valos
Career: 1917   Position: 3b
Team: *Cuban Giants*

In 1917 he was a third baseman with the Cuban Giants, a team of lesser quality.

Van Buren
Career: 1931   Position: of
Team: *Memphis Red Sox*

He was an outfielder with the 1931 Memphis Red Sox, but they were not in the Negro National League that season.

Vance, Columbus (Luke)
Career: 1927–34   Positions: **p**, of
Teams: Birmingham Black Barons ('27–'31), Indianapolis ABCs ('32), Homestead Grays ('32), Detroit Wolves ('32), Detroit Stars ('33)
Bats: Right   Throws: Left
Height: 5'10"   Weight: 168

This left-hander's best pitch was a "jumping" curveball, but he also had a good slider

and a fair fastball. He pitched with several teams during the late '20s and early '30s but is best identified with the Birmingham Black Barons, where he posted an 8–11 record in 1930. In his first year with the Black Barons, he contributed a 3–0 league mark as the team captured the Negro National League's second-half title before losing to the Chicago American Giants in the 1927 championship playoff.

The hurler was from Honolulu, but the Black Barons discovered him while he was pitching with the 24th Infantry baseball team at the nearby Army post. He left Birmingham, when the Negro National League folded following the 1931 season, and pitched with three teams in 1932, including the Homestead Grays, where he lost his only 2 league contests. After joining the Detroit Stars the following season, he finished with a 6–7 record for the year.

Vandever, Bobby
Career: 1944   Position: if
Team: Kansas City Monarchs

He was a wartime reserve infielder with very limited playing time for the Kansas City Monarchs in 1944.

Van Dyke, Fred
a.k.a. Vandyke
Career: 1895–97   Positions: p, of
Teams: Page Fence Giants

A native of Vandalia, Michigan, he pitched and played outfield for the Page Fence Giants in the late '90s, losing all 3 of his mound decisions and batting .171 in 1895.

Vargas, Guillermo
Career: 1949   Position: of
Teams: New York Cubans ('49), *Canadian League ('52)*
Bats: Right   Throws: Right
Height: 5'11"   Weight: 140
Born: 1919

This outfielder played with the Cubans in 1949, hitting .276 in his only year in the Negro Leagues. In 1952 he played with Drummondville in the Canadian Provincial League, batting .282 with average power.

Vargas, Juan Estando (**Tetelo**)
a.k.a. Estanto José Vargas, Juan Esteban Vargas Marcano
Career: 1927–44   Positions: rf, lf, cf, ss, 2b
Teams: Cuban Stars ('27–'31), **New York Cubans** ('38–'39, '41–'44), *Mexican League ('52–'53)*
Bats: Right   Throws: Right
Height: 5'10"   Weight: 160
Born: Apr. 11, 1906, Santo Domingo de Guzman, Dominican Republic
Died: 1971, Guayama, Puerto Rico

A good all-around player, this hustling New York Cubans' center fielder hit for average and with power, excelled defensively, had a good arm, and was a good base stealer who had a sprinter's stride and could "run like a deer," especially when going from first base to third base on a hit. He starred for the Cubans during the early 1940s, hitting in the heart of the batting order, and made back-to-back All-Star appearances in 1942–43.

He began his career in the Negro Leagues as a reserve shortstop with Alejandro Pompez's Cuban Stars in 1927 and had won the starting shortstop position and was batting leadoff for the team in 1931. In 1939 he had moved to the outfield and was the star of Pompez's New York Cubans. In 1941 he paired with Frank Coimbre to provide the offensive thrust to help the Cubans take the second-half title before losing to the Homestead Grays in the playoff for the Negro National League championship.

He also played in Puerto Rico, batting .410 in the winter of 1943–44, then stringing together consecutive seasons of .382 and .362 in 1946–48 and finally batting .301 in 1949–50. He also excelled in Mexico, batting .297 and .355 in 1952–53 with the Estraellas Orientals ballclub.

In 1923 he and two older brothers (Guagua and Juan) were ballplayers on the Escogido team in Santo Domingo, with Tetelo playing shortstop. Thirty years later, at age forty-six, while playing in the 1953 winter league in his home country, he batted over .350 to outhit Ray Dandridge and win the batting title. Tetelo Vargas remains one of the best baseball players of all time from the Dominican Republic.

Vargas, Roberto Enrique
a.k.a. Robert
Career: 1948   Position: p
Teams: Chicago American Giants ('48), *minor leagues ('51–'54, '56–'59)*, Dominican League ('53), major leagues ('55), *Mexican Leagues ('59–'61)*
Bats: Left   Throws: Left
Height: 5'11"   Weight: 175
Born: May 29, 1929, Santurce, Puerto Rico

This left-handed pitcher was a light-complected Puerto Rican but was considered black. In his only year in the Negro Leagues he posted a 6–8 record with a 3.09 ERA for the Chicago American Giants in 1948. He pitched for nine years in organized ball, including an 18–8 season for Lakeland in 1951 in the Florida International League.

Seasons of 13–10 and 12–13 with Reading in the Eastern League in 1952 and 1954 lead to his solitary season in the major leagues, as he pitched with the Milwaukee Braves in 1955, appearing in 25 games without a decision while compiling an unimpressive 8.64 ERA. However, he did get a hit in his 2 at-bats to give him a lifetime .500 major-league batting average.

For the next four seasons he pitched with five different teams and in four different leagues, with his most successful season coming with Macon in the South Atlantic League in 1958, when he fashioned a 9–4 record with a 1.79 ERA. The next year, after washing out with Montreal and Houston, he jumped south to Poza Rica in the Mexican League to finish his career, with seasons of 13–3 and 6–8 in 1960–61.

Varona, Gilberto (**Gilbert**)
Career: 1950   Position: 1b

Teams: Memphis Red Sox ('50–'55), *minor leagues ('54)*
Bats: Right   Throws: Right
Born: Cuba

He was a first baseman for the Memphis Red Sox in 1950, hitting .211 without demonstrable power but with a high strikeout incidence. He continued with the Red Sox for another five seasons, after the decline of the Negro Leagues. In 1954 he had a brief unproductive stint with Del Rio in the Big State League, batting only .176.

Varona, Orlando Clemente
[see Clemente Verona, Orlando]

Vasquez, Armando
Career: 1944–48   Positions: 1b, of, 2b, 3b, ss
Teams: Cincinnati-Indianapolis Clowns ('44), Cincinnati Clowns ('45), Indianapolis Clowns ('46–'52), *Havana La Palomas ('47),* New York Cubans ('48), *Canadian League ('49–'51), minor leagues ('54), Mexican League ('55)*
Bats: Left   Throws: Left
Height: 5'8"   Weight: 160
Born: Aug. 20, 1922, Juines, Cuba

A light-hitting left-handed line-drive hitter with modest power, this Cuban first baseman began his career during the wartime era as a regular with owner Syd Pollock's Clowns, hitting .239 and .246 in 1944–45. A smooth fielder, he stayed with the franchise as it relocated in Indianapolis, but left after the 1946 season.

Prior to joining the Clowns, he had gained professional experience playing with Almendares in the Cuban winter league after having been discovered playing semipro ball in Olbay Cerato. After joining the Clowns he played with the Havana La Palomas team in 1947, and the following season he was a utility player with the New York Cubans.

After the demise of the Negro National League following the 1948 season, he traveled North to Canada for three seasons, hitting .244

and .209 in the first two seasons and returning to the Clowns early in 1952, when Hank Aaron was the shortstop. In 1954 he played with Thibodaux in the Evangeline League and hit .259, and played briefly with the Mexico City Tigers the following season, batting .250 in 16 at-bats to close out his career.

Vaughn, Harold
Career: 1926–27   Position: cf
Team: Kansas City Monarchs

He was a seldom-used reserve outfielder for two seasons (1926–27) with the Kansas City Monarchs.

Vaughn, Slim
Career: 1933–34   Positions: p, *lf*
Teams: Newark Browns ('31), Newark Dodgers ('33–'34)

He pitched with two Newark teams, beginning with the Browns in 1931, and joining the Dodgers late in 1933, when they were first organized.

Vazquez, Armando
[see Armando, Vasquez]
Velasquez, José Luis
Career: 1948   Position: p
Team: Indianapolis Clowns
Bats: Right   Throws: Right

This right-handed pitcher played with the Indianapolis Clowns in 1948, his only season in the Negro Leagues.

Velasquez, Laru
Career: 1948–50   Position: p
Team: Indianapolis Clowns
Bats: Right   Throws: Right

A right-handed pitcher, he played with the Indianapolis Clowns for three seasons, beginning in 1948, when he was 1–4 with a 3.63 ERA, and ending with a brief appearance in 1950, when the Negro American League was struggling to survive the loss of players to organized baseball.

Veney, Jerome
Career: 1908–17   Positions: of, manager
Team: *Homestead Grays*

He was with the Homestead Grays during their formative years, when they were still a semipro team.

Ventura
Career: 1929   Position: p
Team: Cuban Stars (West)

He pitched briefly with the Negro National League Cuban Stars (West) during the 1929 season but did not register a decision.

Vernal, Sleepy
Career: 1941   Position: p
Team: New York Cubans

He was a pitcher with the 1941 New York Cubans, but his playing time was restricted.

Verona, Orlando Clemente
a.k.a. Varona
Career: 1948–50   Positions: **ss**, 3b
Teams: Memphis Red Sox ('48–'52, '55), *minor leagues ('52, '54)*
Bats: Right   Throws: Right
Height: 6'   Weight: 170
Born: Dec. 8, 1926, Havana, Cuba

This Cuban shortstop's batting improved each season with the Memphis Red Sox, with averages of .176, .226, and .273 for the years 1948–50. He failed to demonstrate more than a modicum of power or speed during this time, but continued with the Red Sox for two more seasons in the declining years of the Negro Leagues before he entered organized baseball. He played with Tampa in the Florida International League in 1952, batting .211, and with Abilene in the West Texas-New Mexico League in 1954, batting .278. In the winters he spent four seasons (1950–54) with Havana, where he compiled a lifetime .230 batting average.

Vierira, Chris
Career: 1949   Position: of
Team: New York Black Yankees

He was an outfielder with the New York Black Yankees in 1949, a year after the demise of the Negro National League, when the team was playing an independent schedule.

Villa, Roberto (**Bobby**)
Career: 1910–22   Positions: rf, lf, 2b, ss, p
Teams: Stars of Cuba ('10), Cuban Stars (West) ('11, '15–'18, '22), All Cubans ('21)

Beginning his career with the Stars of Cuba in 1910, he batted sixth in the order and split playing time between second base and right field. The following season he was one of half a dozen players, including José Mendez, to leave the team and join the Cuban Stars. Beginning in 1912 he joined Cristobal Torriente in the heart of the batting order for five consecutive seasons.

Villafane, Vicente
Career: 1947   Positions: if, of, c
Team: Indianapolis Clowns
Bats: Right   Throws: Right

This infielder served as a utility player for a short time with the Indianapolis Clowns in 1947.

Villazon
Career: 1913   Positions: p, ut
Team: Long Branch Cubans

This pitcher also served as a utility player with the Long Branch Cubans in 1913.

Villodos, Luis (King Kong)
Career: 1946–47   Position: c
Teams: Baltimore Elite Giants ('46–'47), Dominican Republic ('51), *minor leagues ('54–'55)*
Bats: Right   Throws: Right
Height: 6'2"   Weight: 190
Born: 1925, Ponce, Puerto Rico

In 1946 this big, husky Puerto Rican youngster was impressive in spring training with the Baltimore Elite Giants and provided support as a backup catcher, batting .274 with good power. The following season he was one of a trio of catchers who shared playing time at the position, but his production dropped, both in consistency (.224 BA) and in power (no extra-base hits in 76 at-bats).

Prior to joining the Elite Giants, he had hit .400 in a partial season with Mayagüez in the Puerto Rican winter league, and eight years later, he managed only a .118 average with Ponce in the same league. However, coming off the weak winter output, the slow-footed free-swinger earned the nickname "King Kong" during the following two summers (1954 and 1955), while playing in the West Texas-New Mexico League with Borger and Abilene, hitting .354 (.507 slugging percentage) and .327 (.487 slugging percentage).

In 1951 with Aquilas Cibaenas in the Dominican Republic, he led the league in batting and is credited with hitting the longest home run ever hit at Cabio Park.

Vincent, Irving B. (**Lefty**)
Career: 1934　　　Position: p
Team: Pittsburgh Crawfords
Bats: Left　　　　Throws: Left
Born: 1909
Died: October 1977, St. Louis, Mo.

This left-hander pitched briefly with the Pittsburgh Crawfords in 1934 without registering a decision.

Vines, Eddie
Career: 1940　　　Positions: 3b, 1b, p
Teams: Birmingham Black Barons, Chicago American Giants ('40)

He was a reserve player who saw duty for the Birmingham Black Barons at both corners in 1940. He also played for the Chicago American Giants that year.

Vivens
Career: 1929　　　Position: p
Team: St. Louis Stars

In 1929 he pitched briefly with the St. Louis Stars without registering a decision.

W

Waddy, Irving (**Lefty**)
Career: 1932–33   Position: p
Teams: Indianapolis ABCs ('32), Detroit Stars ('33)
Bats: Left   Throws: Left

This left-hander pitched with a pair of teams during the early Depression years, beginning with the Indianapolis ABCs in the Negro Southern League in 1932, when it was recognized as a major league, and joining the Detroit Stars in the first year of the second Negro National League in 1933, where he posted a 1–4 record.

Wade, Lee
Career: 1909–19   Positions: **p**, of, 1b
Teams: Cuban Giants ('09), Philadelphia Giants ('10–'11), St. Louis Giants ('12, '16), New York Lincoln Giants ('13, '15, '17), Chicago American Giants ('14), New York Lincoln Stars ('15), Brooklyn Royal Giants ('18), G.C.T. Red Caps ('18–'19), Pennsylvania Red Caps of New York ('19)

Pitching most of his career in the East, with New York-based teams, his limited career in the West included one season with Rube Foster's strong Chicago American Giants, where he posted a 10–2 record in 1914. The American Giants won the western title and swept the Brooklyn Royal Giants, the top team in the East, to claim the championship. This marked his second consecutive championship team, as he had pitched with the great Lincoln Giants

the previous season, with partial statistics showing a 6–3 ledger.

After his season in Chicago, he returned to New York in 1915, playing with both the Lincoln Giants and the Lincoln Stars. In 1916 he made his second stop with the St. Louis Giants, having pitched there part of the 1912 season. The next season he was back in New York, with incomplete statistics showing marks of 3–2 with Joe Williams's Lincoln Giants in 1917 and 3–0 with the G.C.T. Red Caps the following season. His entire career was spent during the deadball era, as his last season in black baseball was in 1919, when he pitched with two teams ostensibly composed of Red Caps from two of the major train terminals in New York City, the G.C.T. Red Caps and the Pennsylvania Red Caps.

Wagner, Bill
Career: 1921–31   Positions: **ss**, 2b, 3b, manager
Teams: New York Lincoln Giants ('21), **Brooklyn Royal Giants** ('21–'27), Harlem Stars ('31)

One of the best-fielding shortstops in the league, this young man played shortstop for the Brooklyn Royal Giants in the early '20s but also could play second base. A fair base runner and a fair batter, he hit .177 and .243 in 1924–25 and usually batted in the lower part of the order, except in 1925–26, when he batted in the second slot. He began his career as a reserve third baseman with the New York Lincoln Giants and closed it with a brief appearance in a reserve capacity with the replacement team for the Lincoln Giants, the Harlem Stars. He knew the game and was a smart ballplayer, becoming a manager later in his baseball career.

Wagner, J.
Career: 1927   Positions: 2b, 1b
Teams: Atlantic City Bacharach Giants, Hilldale Daisies

He split the 1927 between the two top teams in the league, playing second base with the Bacharachs and first base with Hilldale.

Waites, Arnold (Tommy)
a.k.a. Waite
Career: 1936–37   Position: p
Teams: Homestead Grays ('36–'37), Washington Elite Giants ('37)
Bats: Right   Throws: Right
Height: 6'0"   Weight: 180

This fastballer pitched with the Homestead Grays and the Washington Elite Giants in 1937. The following season he was sought by the Atlanta Black Crackers but apparently was not signed. Instead he pitched with the San Angelo Shepherds and shut out the Kansas City Monarchs, 5–0, on 3 hits. Aside from his mound skills he was an average fielder and a weak hitter.

Wakefield, Bert
Career: 1899–1915   Positions: **1b**, 2b
Team: *minor leagues ('95–'98),* Chicago Unions ('99–'01), Algona Brownies ('02), Kansas City Monarchs ('08), Kansas City Giants ('08)

He was the regular first baseman with the Chicago Unions for three seasons, bridging the turn of the century, leaving the team to assume the same role with the Algona Brownies in 1902. During his career he also played with the Monarchs of Kansas City, Missouri, and the Giants of Kansas City, Kansas. The first sacker was also one of the last black players to play in a white league before the color line was firmly established, playing with Salina and Emporia in the Kansas State League and making his last appearance in 1898.

Waldon, Allie (Ollie)
Career: 1944   Position: of
Teams: Chicago American Giants, Kansas City Monarchs

A wartime player, he played briefly as an outfielder with the Chicago American Giants and the Kansas City Monarchs in 1944, batting .260 in his only season in the Negro American League.

Walker
Career: 1896   Position: player
Team: Page Fence Giants

He was a member of the Page Fence Giants in 1896, their championship season, but his position is uncertain.

Walker
Career: 1905   Position: c
Team: Brooklyn Royal Giants

He was a catcher with Brooklyn Royal Giants during the deadball era, playing with the team in their first season.

Walker, A.
Career: 1923–27   Position: p
Teams: Milwaukee Bears ('23), Kansas City Monarchs ('27)

Making his first mound appearance with the Milwaukee Bears in 1923, the franchise's only season in the Negro National League, he posted a 3–2 league ledger with the Kansas City Monarchs in 1927, his only other appearance in league play.

Walker, A.
Career: 1933   Position: of
Team: Newark Dodgers

He played briefly as an outfielder with the Newark Dodgers, when the team was first formed late in the 1933 season.

Walker, A. M.

Career: 1937   Position: manager
Team: Birmingham Black Barons

In 1937 he managed the Birmingham Black Barons in their inaugural season in the Negro American League.

Walker, Casey

Career: 1935, 1937   Position: c
Teams: Newark Dodgers ('35), Indianapolis Athletics ('37)

His seasons in black baseball were spent with fringe teams, beginning his career with the Newark Dodgers before Abe Manley bought the franchise and consolidated it with the Brooklyn Eagles to create the Newark Eagles, and ending his career as a reserve catcher with the Indianapolis Athletics in 1937, the team's only season in the Negro American League.

Walker, Charlie, Jr.

Career: 1930–34   Positions: owner, officer
Team: Homestead Grays

Walker became a co-owner of the Homestead Grays in 1930, when Cum Posey needed greater financial backing for his team. The partnership paid immediate dividends, and the Grays won the Eastern championship during the first two years of the partnership. Together they assembled the personnel of the 1931 ballclub, which is often called the greatest black team of of all time.

In his first year of ownership, the team traveled in two nine-passenger automobiles, and while speeding to make a game in Shreveport, Louisiana, the team came close to disaster when both cars were involved in an accident. Walker and Oscar Charleston were the drivers of the two vehicles, with Charleston in the lead. While racing down the highway, Charleston's car blew a tire and rolled over three times, with the players being thrown out into a ditch, miraculously unhurt. Walker, speeding along in an effort to overtake Charleston, also turned over; again, nobody was injured.

Surviving this near-disaster, the team enjoyed tremendous success until Gus Greenlee's raids on the Grays robbed the franchise of many of their top ballplayers and knocked them off the top perch in the East. Walker was second only to Posey as a major force behind the development of the Homestead Grays as a dominant team in black baseball.

Walker, Edsall (Big, *The Catskill Wild Man*)

Career: 1936–45   Position: p
Teams: *Zulu Cannibal Giants ('34), Albany Black Giants ('35),* **Homestead Grays** ('36–'45), Philadelphia Stars ('42), Newark Eagles ('42), New York Black Yankees ('42)
Bats: Right   Throws: Left
Height: 6'0"   Weight: 215
Born: Sept. 15, 1913, Catskill, N.Y.

A member of the Homestead Grays' pitching staff during their dynasty period of the late '30s and early '40s, he played on eight of their nine straight pennant winners, missing only the 1942 season, when he worked at the shipyards in Baltimore. That season he pitched with the Philadelphia Stars and any other team that came into Baltimore, including the Grays. The left-hander had a wicked sinking fastball that he used to mow down batters for ten years in the Negro Leagues. Throughout his career he used his fastball almost exclusively, keeping the ball low and inside to right-handed batters and, contrary to percentage baseball, was much more effective against right-handers. This anomaly was partially caused by the measure of difficulty he encountered with his control when facing a left-handed batter.

Walker and Raymond Brown formed a lefty-righty pair of aces in 1938, pitching the Grays to their best record of their dynasty period. During the season the pair made a bet about who would lose fewer games. Late in the season, neither hurler had lost a game, when Walker lost his first and only game of the season. Shortly afterward, Brown lost a game to the Elites in the first game of a doubleheader and angrily demanded to pitch the second game as well. Much to his chagrin, he lost that contest, too, giving him two losses for the season. Neither pitcher lost another game, and Walker won the wager. That season he was credited with 8 league victories and earned the distinction of being the starting pitcher for the East squad in his only appearance in the East-West All-Star classic.

Walker continued his impressive work, posting a 10–5 record in 1940 as the Grays copped another pennant, even without Josh Gibson. The first World Series between the Negro National League and the Negro American League was played in 1942, the only year that Walker was not with the Grays. But after fashioning league marks of 8–3 and 4–3 in 1943–44, he pitched in 2 games in each of the 1943 and 1944 World Series. Facing the Negro American League's Birmingham Black Barons in both Series, he won his only decision while recording a composite 0.70 ERA.

The Grays had two pitchers named Walker, and they were called "Big Walker" and "Little Walker," with Edsall being the "Big" half. A typical Homestead Grays' pitcher, he was a pretty good hitter with good power and sometimes was used as pinch hitter, batting .297 and .190 in 1943–44. He could field his position, but on the bases his speed was at best average.

As a teenager in Catskill, New York, he was an all-around athlete, playing football and pitching semipro ball for the Mohawk Giants in Albany in the late '20s. He played briefly with Charlie Henry's Zulu Cannibal Giants in 1934, a team that combined "show biz" and baseball in the same vein as the Ethiopian Clowns. The next season he played with the Albany, New York, Black Giants. When he signed with the Grays in August 1936 for $150 a month, the press referred to him as "The Catskill Wild Man" because of the lack of control he had with his fastball.

During his decade in the Negro Leagues, he was usually categorized among the top left-handers in the Negro National League, but he never made more than $500 a month. During his prime his services were sought by teams in both Mexico and Cuba, but he chose not to play in the Latin American winter leagues. After retiring from baseball he returned to the Catskills area, living in Albany, New York, and managing a Little League team in Albany's South End neighborhood for twenty years.

Walker, George T. (Little, Schoolboy)
Career: 1937–50   Position: p
Teams: Homestead Grays ('37–'38), **Kansas City Monarchs** ('39–'43, '45–'52), *minor leagues ('52)*
Bats: Right   Throws: Right
Height: 5'11"   Weight: 185
Born: Feb. 5, 1915, Waco, Tex.
Died: Aug. 19, 1967, Waco, Tex.

Although he was above average in size, he was called "Little" Walker because he was smaller than Edsall, the other Walker on the Grays' pitching staff, who was called "Big" Walker. He was a power pitcher with a good fastball and drop, but his best pitch was his curve. He also had a slider, a screwball, a change of pace, and better-than-average control. As a twenty-two-year-old with a "buggy-whip arm" playing with the San Angelo Shepherds, he was "burning up" the Texas League and was unsuccessfully sought by the Atlanta Black Crackers in the spring. Later in the year he was playing in Waco when, with the recommendation of See Posey as a "sure-fire winner," he joined the Grays in 1937. During his two seasons with the team, the Grays won their first two of nine straight pennants.

Leaving the Grays in 1939, he joined the other dark dynasty of the time, the Kansas City Monarchs, and was credited with marks of 5–0 and 4–0 in his first two seasons. The Monarchs were the Negro American League counterparts of the Grays and, although Walker's contributions to the pennant chase declined markedly, the Monarchs won four straight pennants after he joined the team. The last one culminated in a victory over his former teammates in the first Negro World Series between the Negro National League and Negro American League.

In 1943 his record was an unimpressive 3–4

and, although the Monarchs captured another pennant in 1946, his performance was not a primary factor in the team's success. His next big season was in 1950, when he posted a 12–3 record with a 1.98 ERA. He remained with the Monarchs through 1952, after the Negro American League was in decline, before signing with Tucson in the Arizona-Texas League, where he pitched poorly in his only game. Aside from his pitching, he had average speed and was a pretty good fielder but a weak hitter.

Walker, H.

Career: 1932   Positions: c, lf
Team: Monroe Monarchs

In 1932, the only season when the Negro Southern League was recognized as a major league, he was a catcher with the Monroe Monarchs.

Walker, Jack

Career: 1940–43   Position: p
Teams: Newark Eagles ('40), Philadelphia Stars ('41), Harrisburg-St. Louis Stars ('43)

Beginning in 1940 with the Newark Eagles and pitching briefly without a decision, he continued in the Negro National League during the early '40s. His most active season was in 1941, when he posted a 3–6 record with the Philadelphia Stars. He made his last league appearance with the Harrisburg-St. Louis Stars in 1943, before they withdrew from the league in the spring to accompany Dizzy Dean's team on a barnstorming tour.

Walker, Jesse (Hoss, Deuce)

a.k.a. Aussa
Career: 1929–50   Positions: ss, 3b, manager
Teams: Atlantic City Bacharach Giants ('29–'30), Cleveland Cubs ('31), Nashville Elite Giants ('31–'34), Columbus Elite Giants ('35), Washington Elite Giants ('36–'37), Baltimore Elite Giants ('38–'39, '48–'49), Memphis Red Sox ('38), New York Black Yankees ('40–'41), Birmingham Black Barons ('41–'43, '53–'54), Ethiopian Clowns ('42), Cincinnati Clowns ('43), Cincinnati-Indianapolis Clowns ('44–'45), Indianapolis Clowns ('46–'47), *Nashville Cubs ('48), Detroit Stars ('55)*
Bats: Right   Throws: Right
Height: 5'11"   Weight: 190
Born: 1922, Austin, Tex.

In general he was an average player in each phase of the game, but he made the most of his abilities to build a long career in baseball. He was a pull hitter with a little power, an average gloveman with good arm strength and accuracy, and he possessed moderate speed on the base. But he was a good baseball man, and he remained in baseball for twenty-two years, including several stints as a manager.

He began his career as a shortstop, joining Tom Wilson's Elite Giants early in his career, when they were based in Nashville, playing as a substitute in 1931 before earning a starting position in 1933 despite a weak stick that placed him at the bottom of the batting order and yielded only a .154 batting average for the season. The franchise moved to Columbus in 1935 and on to Washington the following season, with Walker enjoying one of his better years at the plate, with a .309 average in 1936. After two years in the capital city, the Elite Giants made their final move, relocating in Baltimore, but the new surroundings were not a help to his offensive production, being credited with averages of .194 and .210 in 1938–39.

In the former year he shared playing time at third base, but after the season, Memphis Red Sox manager Ted "Double Duty" Radcliffe added Walker and the Birmingham Black Barons's David Whatley to the Red Sox roster for the Negro American League playoff against the Atlanta Black Crackers. He played shortstop in the 2 games that were played before the Series was canceled because of disagreements between the managements of the two teams.

After being relegated to substitute status in 1939, he played one full season with the New York Black Yankees, batting only .148, before joining the Birmingham Black Barons early in 1941, where he raised his average to .231 while sharing starting assignments at shortstop. Throughout most of his career he hit in the lower part of the batting order, but in 1942 he was often inserted into the second slot. During a stint with Birmingham, he also appeared with the Clowns while maintaining his residence in Nashville.

In 1944 he was appointed manager of the Cincinnati-Indianapolis Clowns, guiding the team to a second-place finish. The Clowns had been admitted to the Negro American League a year earlier, and had eliminated most of their "clowning" routines in league games, although they still performed their acts in exhibition games. Walker remained at the helm for three years, remaining with the franchise as it shifted from one home city to another, and batting .230, .240, and .130 for the 1944–46 seasons. But after his initial managerial success, his teams dropped to losing records the last two years and he was replaced as manager, although playing another year as an infielder.

During the 1948 season he joined the Baltimore Elite Giants as manager, replacing interim manager Henry Kimbro, who had taken charge of the team following the illness and death of Candy Jim Taylor. After the Negro National League folded at the end of the season, the Elite Giants joined the Negro American League's Eastern Division.

After leaving the Elite Giants, Walker became a bench manager and continued managing into the '50s, although the league was in decline and was strictly a minor-league operation by then. After leaving the dugout he entered front-office management during the latter part of his career.

Walker, Larry
[see Doby, Larry]

Walker, Moses Fleetwood (**Fleet**)
Career: 1883–89   Positions: c, of, 1b
Teams: *minor leagues ('83, '85–'89),* major leagues ('84)
Bats: Right   Throws: Right

Born: Oct. 7, 1857, Mt. Pleasant, O.
Died: May 11, 1924, Steubenville, O.

Tall, slender, handsome, and intelligent, he became the first black player to play in the major leagues when he played 42 games with the Toledo Blue Stockings of the American Association in 1884, batting .263 for the season. A catcher with the ballclub, later in the year he was joined by his brother, Weldy Walker, who joined the team as a replacement outfielder for an injured player. The previous season Fleet had batted .251 in 60 games with the team when they were in the Northwest League, which did not enjoy major-league status. In general he was well received by players and spectators except in two southern cities, Baltimore and Louisville. He suffered a broken rib from a foul tip in mid-July and was released by the team later in the season amid threats of bodily harm from anonymous sources.

In 1887 he played with Newark in the International League, where he and George Stovey formed the first black battery, and Walker hit .263 and stole 36 bases for the season. The superstar of the era, Cap Anson, refused to play in the game because of their presence, setting the stage for future exclusion of blacks from the established leagues. Before the color line was established, Walker also played with Cleveland in the Western League in 1885, but the team folded in June and he joined the Waterbury team, which played in both the Southern New England League and the Eastern League, during the remainder of the season. In 1886 he hit .209 with Waterbury, and he joined Newark in 1887. When the Newark team folded in the fall, he was signed by Syracuse of the International League, and after the 1889 season he was out of baseball.

The son of a doctor, he was born at a way station on the underground railway for fugitive slaves on their way to Canada, and as a youngster his parents moved to Steubenville, Ohio, where he attended integrated schools and played on integrated baseball teams. At age twenty he entered Oberlin College, attending for five years, the first two in preparatory school, and studied the standard academic curriculum of the era. In 1881, his last year, he played on the school baseball team as a catcher, with his brother also playing on the team. Leaving Oberlin before graduation, Fleet played baseball with the University of Michigan baseball team for two seasons, 1882–83. Later in the 1883 season he turned professional, joining the Toledo team.

Later in life, after leaving baseball, he became a businessman, inventor, newspaper editor, and author. Embittered, he became an advocate of racial separation, supporting a "back to Africa" policy for American blacks.

Walker, Moses L.
Career: 1928–31   Position: officer
Team: Detroit Stars

He was an officer with the Detroit Stars during the last four years of the first Negro National League.

Walker, Pete (Lottie)
Career: 1923–26   Positions: p, of, 2b, 3b
Team: Homestead Grays

Although primarily a pitcher, he was an all-purpose player with the Homestead Grays during the '20s.

Walker, R. A.
Career: 1887   Position: player
Team: *Boston Resolutes*

He was a player with the Boston Resolutes, one of eight teams that were charter members of the League of Colored Baseball Clubs in 1887. However, the league's existence was ephemeral, lasting only a week.

Walker, Robert Taylor (R. T.)
Career: 1945–49   Position: p
Teams: *St. Louis Stars ('44)*, Homestead Grays ('45–'49), *Boston Blues ('46)*
Bats: Right   Throws: Right
Height: 6'1"   Weight: 197
Born: Aug. 20, 1914, Arboa, Fla.

In general he was an ordinary pitcher with a good fastball and average control. He did not have a change-up but used his curve and drop as off-speed pitches. In 1944 he was one of the leading pitchers in the West with the St. Louis Stars, who were not then a major-league club, but in the spring of 1945 he was declared a free agent by the two league presidents, and the Homestead Grays outbid the other clubs for his services. In 1947 he had a 4–1 league ledger, and the following year he was on the Grays' pitching staff as they won the last Negro National League pennant and defeated the Birmingham Black Barons in the World Series.

Unlike most Grays' pitchers, he was not a good hitter and did not fit the Grays' mold for a pitcher, but was a pretty good fielder and an adequate base runner. His mother named him after the movie actor Robert Taylor but, as described by a teammate, he "looked like King Kong," and Josh Gibson kidded him about his countenance and put him on his "all-ugly" team. Despite the jesting, he considered himself a ladies' man.

Walker, Tom (Tony)
Career: 1945   Position: p
Team: Baltimore Elite Giants

A wartime player, he pitched with the Baltimore Elite Giants in 1945 without a decision.

Walker, W.
Career: 1932   Positions: of, c
Team: Monroe Monarchs

After playing with the Monroe Monarchs in the Negro Southern League in 1931, he was the irregular left fielder, batting in the seventh spot in the lineup, in 1932, the only year that the league was recognized as being a major league.

Walker, Welday Wilberforce (Weldy)
Career: 1884–87   Positions: of, c, 2b
Teams: major leagues ('84), *minor leagues ('85–'87)*
Born: July 27, 1860, Steubenville, O.
Died: Nov. 23, 1937, Steubenville, O.

The brother of Fleet Walker, he attended

Oberlin College and played on the school base-ball team as a right fielder. In 1884, when the Toledo team of the American Association found itself shorthanded in the outfield due to injuries, he joined his brother on the ballclub, making him the second black player ever with a major-league team. Playing in only 5 games, he hit .222 with Toledo, and never played in the major leagues again. He did play with minor-league teams, including Akron in the Ohio State League and Cleveland in the Western League.

He also played as an outfielder with the Pittsburgh Keystones, one of eight teams that were charter members of the League of Colored Baseball Clubs in 1887. However, the league folded within a week.

Walker, William
Career: 1937   Position: of
Team: St. Louis Stars

In 1937 he was a reserve outfielder with the St. Louis Stars in the first year of the Negro American League.

Wall, Eddie
[see Walls, Eddie]

Wallace, Felix **(Dick)**
Career: 1906–21   Positions: **ss**, 2b, 3b,
                                                  manager
Teams: Cuban Giants ('06–'07), St. Paul Gophers ('08–'09), Leland Giants ('10), **St. Louis Giants** ('11–'13, '15–'16, '19–'21), Atlantic City Bacharach Giants ('16), New York Lincoln Giants ('14, '17–'18), Brooklyn Royal Giants ('18), Hilldale Daisies ('19)
Bats: Right   Throws: Right
Born: 1884, Owensboro, Ky.

A consistent hitter, good base runner, and marvelous infielder, he was fast afield and excelled as a middle infielder, playing on either side of the keystone sack. He was one of the greatest shortstops of the second decade of the century and also had no superior as a second baseman.

He started his baseball career in 1903 as a

third baseman for the Paducah Nationals of Paducah, Kentucky. After three years he moved East in 1906, playing with the Cuban Giants of New York City for two years. In 1908 Wallace joined the St. Paul Gophers of St. Paul, Minnesota, playing second base. He captained the Gophers in 1909, when his work around the keystone sack against manager Rube Foster's Leland Giants at St. Paul in the playoff for the western championship was largely responsible for the Gophers' victory over the Lelands. Consequently Foster recruited Wallace to play with the Lelands in their postseason exhibition series against the Chicago Cubs, and he had 2 hits in each game against the Cubs' celebrated ace Mordecai "Three Finger" Brown.

In 1910, he joined the Leland Giants, playing at Auburn Park in Chicago. Splitting his playing time between third base and shortstop, he batted in the fifth slot but hit only .191 for the year. In 1911 he joined the St. Louis Giants and played most of the next dozen seasons with that team, while hitting in the second slot. His stay in St. Louis was interrupted by intermittent stints with ballclubs in New York City, including the Lincoln Giants, where he batted .348 in 1914 and .235 and .275 in 1917–18.

Wallace, Jack
Career: 1926–31   Positions: 3b, 2b, ss, rf
Teams: Atlantic City Bacharach Giants ('26), *Chappie Johnson's Stars ('27), Philadelphia Colored Giants of New York ('28),* Cleveland Cubs ('31)

Most of this infielder's career was spent with marginal teams; he made only two appearances with top clubs, both times as a reserve player. His first appearance was with the Bacharachs in 1926, when he hit .267 in limited play, and after five years with lesser ballclubs, he was a substitute third baseman with the Cleveland Cubs before they disbanded in 1931.

Wallace, James (Bo)
Career: 1948–49   Position: c
Teams: Newark Eagles ('48), Houston Eagles

('49), *minor leagues ('50), military service ('51–'52)*

A bright catching prospect with the Newark Eagles, this two-time All-State baseball player joined the team in June 1948 and was credited with a .321 batting average and 11 home runs against all levels of opposition. He remained with the franchise when the team was relocated in Houston in 1949, batting .228 in league competition. The next year, as a catcher-outfielder, he played in organized baseball with Bridgeport in the Colonial League, batting .303, and with Ottawa in the Border League, where he hit .278. Before the start of the next season, the young ballplayer was drafted during the Korean War and entered military service in 1951. Tragically, he suffered the loss of part of his left hand from a grenade explosion, which effectively ended his baseball career. Afterward he worked as a bartender at Don Newcombe's club.

Waller

Career: 1906   Position: ss
Team: Cuban Giants

He played shortstop with the Cuban Giants in 1906, his only season in black baseball.

Walls, Eddie

a.k.a. Wall
Career: 1925–27   Position: p
Teams: St. Louis Stars ('25), Cleveland Elites ('26), Cleveland Hornets ('27)

A marginal player, he pitched for three seasons in the Negro National League, beginning with the St. Louis Stars in 1925 and continuing with the two Cleveland entries in the league, losing both of his league decisions in 1926.

Walsh

Career: 1913   Position: player
Team: Long Branch Cubans

He was listed with the Long Branch Cubans in 1913, but his position is not known.

Walsh

Career: 1916   Position: 2b
Team: Bacharach Giants

He appeared briefly as a reserve with the Bacharachs in 1916, their first year in Atlantic City.

Walters

Career: 1923–24   Position: p
Teams: Milwaukee Bears ('23), Cleveland Browns ('24)

He appeared in two seasons with marginal teams in the Negro National League, pitching briefly with the Milwaukee Bears and the Cleveland Browns during the '20s.

Walton

[see Watters]

Walton

Career: 1948   Position: of
Team: Indianapolis Clowns

A reserve outfielder with the Indianapolis Clowns, he appeared briefly in 1948, his only season in the Negro Leagues.

Walton, Fuzzy

Career: 1930, 1938   Position: of
Teams: Baltimore Black Sox ('30), Pittsburgh Crawfords ('38)

He was a reserve outfielder with the Baltimore Black Sox in 1930, and appeared again briefly as a reserve outfielder with the Crawfords in 1938, their last season in Pittsburgh.

Ward, Britt

Career: 1944   Position: c
Team: Kansas City Monarchs

A wartime player, he appeared briefly with the Kansas City Monarchs as a reserve catcher in 1944.

Ward, C. (Pinky)

a.k.a. Ward Gillespie
Career: 1924–35   Positions: lf, cf, rf, *3b*
Teams: Washington Potomacs ('23), Indianapolis ABCs ('24), **Memphis Red Sox** ('24–'29), Birmingham Black Barons ('27), Chicago Columbia Giants ('31), Louisville Black Caps

('32), Atlantic City Bacharach Giants ('33), Cincinnati Tigers ('34), Brooklyn Eagles ('35)
Bats: Left   Throws: Right

This left-handed batter was a good hitter and played for a dozen years as an outfielder with several teams, primarily in the West. After starting with Ben Taylor's Washington Potomacs in 1923, he joined the Indianapolis ABCs for a short time and then joined the Memphis Red Sox for most of the '20s, hitting .260 in 1927 and in 1929, and batting cleanup the former year. That year he also played part of the season with the Birmingham Black Barons, winners of the second-half Negro National League title. After leaving the Red Sox, he was a reserve outfielder with David Malarcher's Columbia American Giants in 1931. Two years later, playing under his real name of Gillespie, he was a part-time starter in right field with the 1933 Bacharachs, when the team was in decline, and he was batting seventh in the order. He was given the nickname "Pinky" despite a very dark complexion, and he earned a reputation as a thief by stealing from his own teammates.

Ward, Ira
Career: 1922–27   Positions: ss, 1b
Team: Chicago Giants

The infielder played with the Chicago Giants after the team had declined in quality to a marginal status.

Ware, Archie V.
Career: 1940–50   Position: 1b
Teams: Chicago American Giants ('40), Kansas City Monarchs ('41), Cincinnati Buckeyes ('42), **Cleveland Buckeyes** ('43–'48), Louisville Buckeyes ('49), Indianapolis Clowns ('50–'51), *Canadian League ('51), minor leagues ('52)*
Bats: Left   Throws: Left
Height: 5' 9"   Weight: 160
Born: June 19, 1918, Greenville, Fla.

This flashy-fielding first baseman began his career with the Chicago American Giants in 1940, remaining with them until the latter part of the 1941 season, when he joined the Negro American League champion Kansas City Monarchs. Leaving Kansas City, he was a mainstay of the Cincinnati Buckeyes in 1942, missing only one game due to an injury, and led the team in RBIs despite being credited with an average of only .221. The next year the franchise moved to Cleveland and his batting improved: He hit .267, .296, and .276 in 1944–46 while hitting either second or fifth in the batting order. In each of these years he was selected as the starting first baseman on the West squad in the East-West All-Star game, in which he compiled a composite batting average of an even .300.

During his middle season as an All-Star, Ware provided leadership and good defense to the Buckeyes in their championship season of 1945, when they won the Negro American League pennant and then swept the Homestead Grays in the World Series. With Ware hitting .349 and leading the league with 99 hits, the Buckeyes won the Negro American League pennant again in 1947, but lost the World Series to the New York Cubans.

Ware duplicated his batting average in 1948, again hitting .349, but slipped to .226 when the franchise moved to Louisville in 1949. The next year he played with the Indianapolis Clowns, batting .277 in his last full year in the Negro Leagues. In 1951 he played with Farnham in the Canadian Provincial League, batting .257, and in 1952 he played with Lewiston in the Western International League, batting .286 in only 15 games.

At the plate he was a good contact hitter with moderate power, with few home runs counted among his extra-base hits. In both championship seasons he batted in the second slot in the order, but earlier in his career he usually batted fifth or sixth in the order. On the bases he had good speed and would steal his share of bases. Temperamentally he was a gentleman and never complained.

Ware, Joe (Showboat)
Career: 1932–36   Positions: of, 1b, 3b, 2b

Teams: Pittsburgh Crawfords ('32), Cleveland Stars ('32), Cleveland Giants ('33), Akron Tyrites ('33), Newark Dodgers ('35), Memphis Red Sox ('36)

In 1932, after playing second base with the Cleveland Stars until the East-West League broke up, he appeared as a reserve right fielder with the Pittsburgh Crawfords. A light hitter, he batted in the lower part of the order, as he did the following season, when he was a part-time starter in center field with the Akron Tyrites, a team that consolidated with the Columbus Blue Birds to form the Cleveland Giants entry in the Negro National League for the second half of the 1933 Negro National League season. He also appeared briefly with the Newark Dodgers and the Memphis Red Sox before closing out his career in 1936.

Ware, William (Willie)
Career: 1924–26   Positions: 1b
Team: Chicago American Giants
Bats: Right   Throws: Right

A good-fielding but light-hitting first baseman with the Chicago American Giants during the '20s, he played with a lot of pep and enthusiasm. He was playing on Wiley College's baseball team in the spring of 1924 when he was discovered and signed by the American Giants. During his first season with Chicago he shared the first-base duties with veteran Leroy Grant and earned the starting position the following season, hitting near the bottom of the batting order. In 1926 he was a reserve, batting .212 while playing behind Jim Brown, with occasional starts during the American Giants' pennant-winning season. But his hitting wasn't sufficient for him to stay with the club in 1927.

Warfield, Francis Xavier (**Frank**, The Weasel)
Career: 1915–32   Positions: **2b**, ss, 3b,
                            of, manager
Teams: St. Louis Giants ('14–'16), Indianapolis ABCs ('15, '17–'18), Bowser's ABCs ('16), Dayton Marcos ('19), Detroit Stars ('19–'22), Kansas City Monarchs ('21), **Hilldale Daisies**

('23–'28), **Baltimore Black Sox** ('29–'31), Washington Pilots ('32)
Bats: Right   Throws: Right
Height: 5'7"   Weight: 160
Born: 1895, Indianapolis, Ind.
Died: July 24, 1932, Pittsburgh, Pa.

An outstanding fielder in every aspect, he had wide range, good hands, and a good arm, with a unique underhand snap throw that helped him in turning double plays. At the plate he was a good contact hitter, skilled at the hit-and-run play, a master of the sacrifice bunt, and above the norm as a hitter, augmenting his average power by salvaging numerous leg hits to the infield. With a studied eye at the plate, he was skilled at waiting and worrying pitchers into free passes and, utilizing his exceptional speed and baserunning ability, move himself into scoring position with a stolen base. Best known for his skills afield and on the bases, he nevertheless compiled a .304 batting average over four winter seasons in Cuba.

Although sometimes referred to as "always quiet and modest" and "unassuming," he was an intense competitor and frequently used sarcasm and made caustic and threatening remarks to teammates. He was also known to carry a knife, and was not very popular with some of his fellow players, who nicknamed him "The Weasel." The little infielder was tough with a streak of meanness and always was ready to fight. In Cuba, in an altercation evolving from a dice game, he and fiery-tempered superstar Oliver Marcelle engaged in a vicious fight in which Warfield bit off part of Marcelle's nose. The incident began when Warfield, who was winning, refused Marcelle's request to borrow $5, which led to an argument that escalated into a fight when Marcelle hit Warfield in the mouth.

Despite his temperament he was an intelligent player and, as a successful manager, proved to be a clever strategist, guiding Hilldale to consecutive Eastern Colored League pennants in 1924–25, including a World Series victory in the latter season. He also managed the Baltimore Black Sox to the only American Negro League pennant, in 1929. His spirited play and quick temper made him quick to engage in arguments with umpires or to castigate a player in view of spectators, which caused some resentment. Rookie shortstop Jake Stevens and Warfield played side by side for more than a year without speaking to each other. Regardless of his management methods, his results were good, and his success extended to Cuba, where he managed the 1924 Santa Clara team to the championship.

A native of Indianapolis, he began his career in 1914 with the St. Louis Giants, but appeared briefly as a reserve left fielder with C. I. Taylor's ABCs in 1915. He spent most of the next season back with the St. Louis Giants as a shortstop, usually hitting third in the batting order. After only a year in St. Louis, C. I. Taylor engineered his return to the ABCs, where the middle infielder played for two seasons, one each at second base and shortstop.

In the first season, during a heated contest against Rube Foster's Chicago American Giants, in a pickoff attempt at second base, Warfield slid back in hard with spikes high, opening a gash on John Henry Lloyd's knee that required two stitches to close.

Although hobbled by a sprained ankle during the latter year, he hit .240 and .324 in 1917–18 while batting in the lower half of the lineup with the ABCs. In 1919 he joined Tenny Blount's Detroit Stars as part of an aggregation that was probably the greatest team in Detroit's history. Beginning in 1920, with the first year of the Negro National League, Warfield batted leadoff for the Stars, hitting .271, .269, and .342 for the 1920–22 seasons.

In 1923 the Eastern Colored League was organized, and the star second sacker was among the players traveling East to join it. After arriving with Hilldale, he played under John Henry Lloyd for a season, batting a solid .339 and stealing a team-high 67 bases. But he was among the dissident players who caused Lloyd to be fired as manager, even though he had

just won an eastern championship. When Lloyd moved to Atlantic City with the Bacharachs, Warfield was elevated to the position of manager with the Hilldale club.

Upon assuming the managerial reins, he moved Judy Johnson from shortstop to third base and put light-hitting but far-ranging and smooth-fielding Jake Stephens at shortstop. The change paid dividends as the young playing manager won pennants in each of his first two seasons at the Hilldale helm. After each pennant they faced the Kansas City Monarchs in the World Series, losing the initial Series, but defeating the Monarchs in a rematch in 1925. While penciling himself in the number two position in the batting order, he hit for averages of .243 and .261 in the Series, after regular-season averages of .342 and .314. After the pennant-winning seasons, he dropped to batting marks of .255, .274, and .198 in 1926–28.

In 1929 he was traded to the Baltimore Black Sox with Red Ryan for Crush Holloway and Workie Jackson. With the Black Sox he succeeded Ben Taylor as manager, who had been traded to the Bacharachs for Dick Lundy. Warfield and Lundy teamed with Oliver Marcelle and Jud Wilson to form the Baltimore Black Sox' famous "million-dollar infield" a decade before the Newark Eagles' great infield of the same name. With the superior defense in place, in his initial season at the helm Warfield led the Black Sox to the American Negro League pennant in the league's sole year of existence.

He remained at the helm for three seasons, batting .221, .214, and .154 as a player, and without winning another title. Although his playing skills were beginning to erode, he was in his prime as a manager, and he signed to manage the 1932 Washington Pilots in the East-West League. He was always looking ahead and, in anticipation of forthcoming conditions, was prepared for situations as they occurred. When the East-West League began going under during the season, he had already booked games four weeks in advance. The team was in Pittsburgh for a series with the Pittsburgh Crawfords in late July, and Warfield, who was batting .233, had yielded his starting position at second base to a youthful Charlie Hughes several weeks earlier and had become a bench manager.

He was still officially serving in the capacity of playing manager when he died of a heart attack under vague circumstances. A known ladies' man who liked to flash big money rolls, he was in the company of a woman when he was rushed to the hospital, bleeding. His death was almost instantaneous after suffering an internal hemorrhage. Webster McDonald succeeded him as manager of the Washington Pilots.

Warmack, H.
Career: 1910–11   Position: 1b
Team: St. Louis Giants

He was a reserve first baseman during the formative years of the St. Louis Giants in 1910–11, missing only their first year of existence.

Warmack, Sam
Career: 1929–33   Positions: lf, cf, 3b
Teams: *Richmond Giants ('22–'23), Chappie Johnson's Stars ('25, '28),* Washington Pilots ('32), Hilldale Daisies ('29, '32), Atlantic City Bacharach Giants ('33–'34), Indianapolis ABCs, *Louisville Black Colonels ('38)*

With Hilldale in 1929, he hit .336 as a substitute, and his career was spent mostly in a reserve role or as a regular player on a lesser team. At the beginning of the 1932 season he was a substitute center fielder with the Washington Pilots, batting in the sixth spot when in the lineup, but he switched to the new Hilldale club, playing third base and outfield, after the original Hilldale club folded in midseason. Later he moved to the Bacharachs, where he played outfield and batted cleanup in 1933–34.

Warren, Cicero
Career: 1946–47   Position: p

Teams: Memphis Red Sox ('46), Homestead Grays ('46–'47)

A pitcher for two post-World War II seasons, he lost both of his decisions with the Homestead Grays in 1947.

Warren, Jesse
Career: 1940–47   Positions: 3b, 2b, of
Teams: Memphis Red Sox ('40), New Orleans-St. Louis Stars ('41), Birmingham Black Barons ('42), Chicago American Giants ('47), *Washington Black Senators ('47)*
Bats: Right   Throws: Right

Beginning his career as a reserve infielder for the Memphis Red Sox in 1940, he could play infield and outfield equally well, and in 1941 this utility man earned a regular spot in left field, batting leadoff for the Stars when they were sharing hometown honors with New Orleans. He was relegated to a reserve role again in 1942 with the Birmingham Black Barons, but after World II he won the starting spot at second base with the Chicago American Giants in 1947, batting leadoff for the team.

Warwick
a.k.a. Warrick
Career: 1903–05   Positions: p, of
Teams: Philadelphia Giants ('03–'04), Brooklyn Royal Giants ('05)

Beginning his career with the Philadelphia Giants in 1903, after two years in Philadelphia he joined the Brooklyn Royal Giants as a pitcher for their first year of existence and his last season with a top black baseball club.

Washington
Career: 1910   Position: p
Team: St. Louis Giants

He was a pitcher with the St. Louis Giants in 1910, the team's second year of existence.

Washington
Career: 1929   Position: c
Team: *Nashville Elite Giants*

He was a catcher with the Nashville Elite

Giants in 1929, a year before the team entered the Negro National League.

Washington
Career: 1935   Positions: **p**, lf
Team: Philadelphia Stars

A pitcher with the Philadelphia Stars in 1935, he also played in left field, performing with mediocrity at both positions.

Washington, Blue
[see Washington, Edgar (Ed, Blue)]

Washington, Edgar (Ed, **Blue**)
Career: 1915–20   Positions: p, 1b
Teams: Chicago American Giants ('15–'16), Kansas City Monarchs ('20)

He began his career in 1915 as a pitcher with Rube Foster's Chicago American Giants and closed it out as a first baseman with the Kansas City Monarchs during the Negro National League's inaugural season, 1920. A resident of Los Angeles, he also gained recognition in the motion picture industry, appearing in silent films with Buster Keaton. His son, Kenny Washington, earned his own fame as a football All-American at UCLA, and was also a good semipro baseball player.

Washington, Fay
[see Washington, Lafayette (Fay)]

Washington, I. Jasper (**Jap**)
Career: 1922–37   Positions: 3b, 1b, of,
                                  umpire
Teams: Pittsburgh Keystones ('22), **Homestead Grays** ('22–'29, '32–'33), Pittsburgh Crawfords ('31), Newark Browns ('32)
League: Negro National League
Bats: Right   Throws: Right
Height: 6'3"   Weight: 230

Although best known as a first baseman, the big Homestead Grays' captain during the 1920s was at home at either corner. A popular player, he was a fixture in the lineup, usually batting cleanup, but in 1928, when Martin Dihigo and John Beckwith joined the team, he dropped to the sixth spot in the order. The big first sacker projected a mean image and was as tough as he looked. Once in infield practice, a line drive hit him in the mouth and knocked out his teeth, but he just shook it off and was not even knocked down.

He batted .378 in 1929, when the Grays entered the American Negro League, but when the Grays loaded up with talent in 1930–31, he was displaced by Oscar Charleston and left the fold for a couple of seasons before returning in 1932. In limited play in 1933, incomplete statistics show a batting average of .280. However, by the '30s his playing skills were beginning to erode, and after his active days on the diamond were ended, he became an umpire in the Negro National League.

Washington, Isaac
Career: 1928   Position: officer
Team: Atlantic City Bacharach Giants

In 1928, the year of the Eastern Colored League's collapse and demise, he was an officer with the Atlantic City Bacharach Giants.

Washington, John G. (**Johnny**)
Career: 1933–50   Positions: **1b**, 3b
Teams: Montgomery Grey Sox ('33), Birmingham Black Barons ('34), Pittsburgh Crawfords ('36–'38), New York Black Yankees ('38–'40), Baltimore Elite Giants ('41, '46–'48), *military service ('42–'45),* Houston Eagles ('49–'50), *New Orleans Eagles ('51)*
Bats: Left   Throws: Right
Height: 6'2"   Weight: 185

A good hitter with extra-base power, he was capable afield, with a good throwing arm. The lanky first baseman from Montgomery, Alabama, was personally groomed by Oscar Charleston as his replacement. As a rookie, after replacing the aging superstar at first base for the strong Pittsburgh Crawfords' ballclub, he was credited with a .480 batting average and made his first All-Star appearance in the 1936 East-West game.

In 1938, partial statistics show a batting average of .403, and after owner Gus Greenlee divested himself of the Crawfords, Washington joined the New York Black Yankees, where he usually batted in the heart of the order and proved to be a good fielder and a consistent .300 hitter with power, as shown by his .367 batting average in 1940. In 1941 he joined the Baltimore Elite Giants and, batting in the third slot in the lineup, hit .362 while leading the team with 129 hits and 13 triples and also contributing 21 doubles. Although having only average speed, he also tied for the team lead with 18 stolen bases.

He was just reaching his prime when World War II interrupted his diamond accomplishments, but after returning from four years of military service, he still ranked among the league's best. Usually batting fifth or sixth in the order, he slipped to a .252 batting average in his first year back, but by mid-July 1947 he was leading the league in batting with a .406 mark, with 78 hits in 51 games. He suffered an eye injury shortly afterward and missed two weeks in August, yet still finished with a regular-season batting average of .392 for the Elite Giants and again appeared in the East-West All-Star game. The veteran left the Elite Giants after hitting .308 in the 1948 season and signed with the Eagles, who had moved to Houston, batting .345 and .351 in 1949-50 and making a final All-Star appearance in 1950, representing the new Eagles' ballclub.

Washington, Lafayette **(Fay)**
Career: 1940–45   Position: p
Teams: New Orleans-St. Louis Stars ('40), St. Louis Stars ('41), Chicago American Giants ('43), Birmingham Black Barons ('44–'45), Cincinnati-Indianapolis Clowns ('45), Kansas City Monarchs ('45)
Bats: Right   Throws: Right
This right-hander began his career in 1940 with the St. Louis Stars and was called a good pitcher, but in 1941 he was a second-line pitcher fighting hard for a starting berth on the club. After the Stars folded, he pitched in his hometown of Chicago with the American Giants before joining the Birmingham Black

Barons during the last two wartime seasons. In 1944 he posted a 3–2 mark for the Black Barons, and in his last season he also pitched for the Clowns and Monarchs before closing out his career.

Washington, Lawrence (Trickshot)
Career: 1945   Position: 1b
Team: New York Black Yankees
Height: 6'4"   Weight: 215
A tall, towering youngster, he was a newcomer with the New York Black Yankees in 1945 and earned the nickname "Trickshot" because of the clever way he handled himself at the initial sack. While his fielding was satisfactory, his hitting prowess became the determining factor in his quest to make the grade in the Negro Leagues.

Washington, Namon
Career: 1920–31   Positions: of, ss, c, 2b, 3b
Teams: *San Antonio Black Aces ('20),* Indianapolis ABCs ('20–'24), Hilldale Daisies ('25–'27), *Brooklyn Cuban Giants ('28),* Philadelphia Tigers ('28), New York Lincoln Giants ('29), Brooklyn Royal Giants ('30–'31)
A good fielder with a strong arm, this little outfielder could also play infield or catch. But he was a light hitter and usually batted in the lower part of the order, although he sometimes hit in the second slot. He began his professional career in Texas with the San Antonio Black Aces, but moved North in 1920 as a reserve left fielder with the Indianapolis ABCs, and worked his way into the lineup as a part-time starter the following season.

After five years with the ABCs, he moved, East and joined the defending Eastern Colored League champion Hilldale ballclub as a substitute and part-time starter in the outfield and at shortstop. He batted .225 for the season as Hilldale captured another pennant and defeated the Kansas City Monarchs in the World Series. In 1926 he was a regular with Hilldale, batting .279 and playing left field, but the following season he returned to his reserve role and a

.189 batting average. The next season was the last for the Eastern Colored League and he played with the Philadelphia Tigers in their only year in league play.

In 1929 the American Negro League operated as a replacement league for a season, and he was the regular left fielder with the Lincoln Giants, hitting .323 while batting second. In the next two seasons there was no Eastern Colored League, and he played with the Brooklyn Royal Giants, who followed an independent schedule.

Washington, Peter (**Pete**, Joe)
Career: 1923–35   Positions: cf, lf
Teams: Washington Potomacs ('23–'24), Wilmington Potomacs ('25), New York Lincoln Giants ('25), **Baltimore Black Sox** ('27–'33), Philadelphia Stars ('33–'35)

A very fast outfielder with exceptional range afield, he got a great jump on the ball and was one of the best defensive outfielders in the East during the '20s and early '30s. However, his offensive punch was not equal to his glovework, and he usually batted in the lower half of the batting order throughout his career.

The North Carolinian was playing with Albany, Georgia, when he was obtained by the Washington Potomacs in the spring of 1923, but the first impression he gave was not a positive one, with reports indicating that he "looked awful." But by hard work and expert instruction by manager Ben Taylor, he became a top outfielder within a year. Taylor projected him as a potential future rival to Oscar Charleston. In 1924, playing left field with the Potomacs, he hit .280 with 14 home runs, the second-best total on the team, earning him selection to some all-star teams that season. The next season the Potomacs moved to Wilmington and folded early in the season, with Washington finishing the season with the Lincoln Giants and batting .297 for the year.

After leaving the Lincolns he signed with the Baltimore Black Sox, and in August 1927 he and other Black Sox players were involved in an automobile accident, but Washington es-

caped serious injury, suffering only from some cuts. During his seven seasons with the Sox, his best year came in their championship season of 1929, when he hit .349 as the team annexed the American Negro League's only pennant. In 1933 he left the Black Sox to join Webster McDonald's new team, the Philadelphia Stars, and in 1934 Washington was the regular left fielder on the team, batting .231 as they won the Negro National League pennant and then defeated the Chicago American Giants in a seven-game playoff for the championship. The ball-hawking outfielder remained with the Stars in 1935, closing out his career as a part-time starter after thirteen seasons in the Negro Leagues.

Washington, Tom
Career: 1904–11   Positions: **c**, of
Teams: Philadelphia Giants ('04–'05, '08), Cuban X-Giants ('06), Chicago Giants ('11), *Pittsburgh Giants ('10)*

A reserve player, this little catcher was with the Philadelphia Giants during the ballclub's best years, in the first decade of the century.

Washington Black Senators
Duration: 1938   Honors: None
Affiliation: Negro National League

One of the worst teams ever to play in the Negro Leagues, they were entered in the Negro National League in 1938, finishing the first half of the season with only a single victory against 20 losses for a .050 winning percentage. The team did not finish the second half of the season.

Washington Elite Giants
Duration: 1936–37   Honors: First-half title ('36)
Affiliation: Negro National League

Tom Wilson's franchise, which originated in Nashville and had an interim season in Columbus, Ohio, came to Washington in 1936–37 before finally locating in Baltimore. In their first season in the nation's capital, the Elite Giants won the first-half Negro National League championship with a 14–10 record, but dropped to the cellar in the second half with a 7–14 record, yielding a losing record for the whole season. There was no conclusive playoff between the Elite Giants and the Pittsburgh Crawfords, winners of the second half, to determine a league champion. In 1937 the Elite Giants again posted a losing record, and relocated in Baltimore the following season.

Washington Pilots

Duration: 1932   Honors: None
Affiliation: East-West League

In 1932 the Pilots were entered in the ill-fated East-West League for part of the league's brief existence, as the league folded in June.

Washington Potomacs

Duration: 1923–24   Honors: None
Affiliations: Independent ('23), Eastern Colored League ('24)

This team was formed by Ben Taylor in 1923, and after playing a year as an independent ballclub, they entered the Eastern Colored League in 1924, finishing seventh in the eight-team league, with a record of 21–37 for a .362 winning percentage. After the disappointing season, the ballclub dropped out of league competition, and team owner Robinson moved the franchise to Wilmington, Delaware, where it played as the Wilmington Potomacs for part of the 1925 season.

Waters

[see Watters]

Waters, George

Career: 1887   Position: player
Team: *Boston Resolutes*

He was a player with the Boston Resolutes, one of eight teams that were charter members of the League of Colored Baseball Clubs in 1887. However, the league's existence was ephemeral, lasting only a week.

Waters, Ted

Career: 1920   Positions: of, p

Teams: Chicago Giants ('20), Brooklyn Royal Giants ('25), *Chappie Johnson's Stars ('27)*, Hilldale Daisies ('27), Philadelphia Tigers ('28)

He began his career as a pitcher with the Chicago Giants but finished it as an outfielder with Hilldale and the Philadelphia Tigers.

Waters, Dick

Career: 1916   Position: manager
Team: St. Louis Giants

He served as manager of the St. Louis Giants in 1916, with the team temporarily dissolving in the spring of 1917.

Watkins

Career: 1913   Position: p
Team: Chicago American Giants

He was a pitcher with Rube Foster's Chicago American Giants in 1913, his only year with a top black ballclub.

Watkins, G. C.

Career: 1937   Position: officer
Team: Indianapolis Athletics

He was an officer with the Indianapolis Athletics during their entry into the Negro National League in its inaugural season.

Watkins, John (**Pop**)

Career: 1899–22   Positions: c, 1b,
                                         manager
Teams: Cuban Giants ('99–'04), Genuine Cuban Giants ('05–'06), Brooklyn Royal Giants ('07–'09), Havana Red Sox ('15), *Pop Watkins Stars ('08)*
Died: Feb. 28, 1923, Durham, N.C.

Beginning his career before the turn of the century, this scrappy player caught for the original Cuban Giants for many of his fifteen years as an active player. A popular player, he served as team captain for many years. In 1907 the ex-captain was still a popular figure in New York City, and he became a manager in the latter years of his career, managing the Brooklyn Royal Giants in 1907–09; taking the helm of the Havana Red Sox of northern New York;

being named as manager of new baseball team in New York City in 1917; and guiding his own team, the Pop Watkins Stars, for many years. He had been in failing health for several months but was with his club in spring training, preparing for another summer, when he died.

Watkins, Maurice (**Murray**, Skeeter)
Career: 1941–50   Positions: **3b**, 2b, ss
Teams: Philadelphia Stars ('41, '46–'50), Indianapolis Clowns ('42), Newark Eagles ('42–'46), *Canadian League ('51–'53)*
Bats: Left   Throws: Right
Height: 5'4"   Weight: 135
Born: Oct. 16, 1915, Towson, Md.

An eagle-eyed leadoff batter who drew numerous walks and combined good speed and extra hustle to become a good base stealer, he was a contact hitter with average power. The popular little pepperpot was brilliant in the field and, although he had appeared in one game each in 1941 and 1942, he was still regarded as a rookie in 1943. He was considered the best defensive third baseman in the league but had only average range at the hot corner. The left-handed swinger was a good drag bunter, a capable hit-and-run man, and a place-hitter who hit to left field and rarely struck out.

He began playing baseball with the Orangeburg Red Sox in 1932, along with his two brothers. Placed in center field, he badly misjudged two fly balls and was moved to the infield. He next joined Doc Thomas's Baltimore Colts, a semipro team, and began honing his diamond skills. In 1942 he left his job in a steel mill at Sparrow's Point to barnstorm through the Midwest with the Ethiopian Clowns for two weeks.

The next season he joined Abe Manley's Newark Eagles and hit .260, .271, and .276 in 1943–45 while playing third base. The little infielder led the league in stolen bases in 1945, warranting his selection to the first of his two consecutive East-West All-Star games. He had 1 at-bat in each All-Star game and produced hits both times. After the end of World War II

he moved to the Philadelphia Stars, where he batted .265 and .294 in 1946–47. He rated a look by the Dodgers in 1948, and although he failed to sign with the organization, the exposure led to a barnstorming tour with Jackie Robinson's All-Stars during the following winter, 1948–49. In his last two seasons in the Negro Leagues, 1949–50, his batting average dropped to .202 and .108, respectively.

Afterward he played in Manitoba, Canada, for three years, 1950-52, and learned to pull a ball for the first time in his baseball career. Abe Saperstein contacted him about playing in South America, and Watkins played there for about two months before being sent back to the United States. After baseball he worked in the Baltimore school system until he retired in 1980.

Watkins, Richard
Career: 1950   Position: if
Team: Memphis Red Sox

This infielder began his career with the Memphis Red Sox in 1950, when the Negro American League was struggling to survive the loss of players to organized baseball.

Watson, Amos
Career: 1945–50   Position: p
Teams: Cincinnati-Indianapolis Clowns ('45), Indianapolis Clowns ('46), Kansas City Monarchs ('46), Baltimore Elite Giants ('47)
Bats: Right   Throws: Right
Height: 6'0"   Weight: 170
Born: 1926, Lake Alfred, Fla.

In 1944, this Florida teenager played with Jimmy Hill's All-Stars, posting a 27–3 record with 5 shutouts. After this impressive showing, he was signed by the Negro American League Cincinnati-Indianapolis Clowns, and posted league marks of 4–3, 3–6, and 7–5 for the 1945–47 seasons.

Watson, David
Career: 1923   Position: p
Team: *Birmingham Black Barons*

He was a pitcher with the Birmingham Black

Barons in 1923, a year before they entered the Negro National League.

Watson, Everett
Career: 1931   Position: officer
Team: Detroit Stars

During the last season of the first Negro National League, he served as an officer with the Detroit Stars.

Watson, George Johnny
Career: 1922–26   Position: of
Team: Detroit Stars

An outfielder with the Detroit Stars during the '20s, he was the regular left fielder in 1926, batting seventh in the order and hitting .201 for the year.

Watson, Robert (Jimmy)
Career: 1950   Position: p
Team: New York Cubans

He split a pair of decisions while pitching with the New York Cubans in 1950, when the Negro American League was struggling to survive the loss of players to organized baseball.

Watson, William
Career: 1926–26, 1931 Positions: of, 1b
Teams: Brooklyn Royal Giants ('24–'25), *Pennsylvania Red Caps of New York ('26),* Atlantic City Bacharach Giants ('31)

Beginning his career with the Brooklyn Royal Giants in 1924, he hit .234 the following year and then played with the Pennsylvania Red Caps of New York, a team of lesser quality, surfacing again with the Bacharachs in 1931, his last appearance in the Negro Leagues.

Watters
a.k.a. Waters; Walton
Career: 1916   Position: ss
Team: Chicago Giants

This infielder was the regular shortstop with the Chicago Giants in 1916, hitting in the seventh slot.

Watts, Andrew (Andy, Sonny, Big Six)
Career: 1946, 1950   Position: 3b
Teams: *military service ('44–'45),* Cleveland Buckeyes ('46), Birmingham Black Barons ('50), *Indianapolis Clowns ('52)*
Born: Aug. 20, 1922, Ensley, Ala.
Died: Jan. 31, 1991, Inkster, Mich.

With only semipro experience before entering the Navy during World War II, he became a member of the Great Lakes Naval Training Station championship baseball team in 1944. A year later he was stationed in Guam and playing on a team there. After his discharge from the Navy he played briefly with the Cleveland Buckeyes in 1946 and hit a home run the first time he played in Cleveland Stadium. His next appearance in league play was in 1950, when he hit .299 as an outfielder with the Birmingham Black Barons. Two years later he played with the Indianapolis Clowns, but at that time the Negro Leagues were struggling to survive the loss of players to organized baseball and were no longer of major-league quality.

Watts, Eddie
Career: 1924–27   Positions: 2b, ss, 1b, 3b
Teams: St. Louis Stars ('24–'25), Cleveland Elites ('26), Cleveland Hornets ('27)

Primarily a middle infielder, he could play any infield position. Beginning his career in 1924, he played two years with the St. Louis Stars, and two years with the Cleveland entries in the Negro National League. In 1926 he batted at the bottom of the order and hit .256 with the Elites. He hit .169 with the Hornets in 1927.

Watts, Herman (Lefty)
Career: 1941–42   Position: p
Teams: New York Black Yankees ('41), Jacksonville Red Caps ('41), Cincinnati Buckeyes ('42)
Bats: Left   Throws: Left

This pitcher from Indianapolis, Indiana, pitched without a decision with the New York Black Yankees in 1941 while splitting the season with the Jacksonville Red Caps. The following season, playing with the Cincinnati Buckeyes, he was hospitalized after being injured in an automobile accident while returning home after a series with the Black Yankees. On September 7, 1942, he was one of five passengers in a car driven by teammate Ulysses Brown that was struck from behind by a truck, with Brown and Raymond "Smoky" Owens being killed instantly. Watts was among four others who were injured, with Eugene Bremmer also being hospitalized, while Alonzo Boone and owner Wilbur Hayes escaped with minimal injuries. The accident occurred at 3:00 A.M. just west of Geneva, Ohio, when their car was reentering a highway after they had stopped to change a flat tire.

Watts, Jack
Career: 1914–19   Positions: **c**, 1b
Teams: *Louisville Cubs ('13),* Chicago American Giants ('14–'15), Indianapolis ABCs ('14–'17), Bowser's ABCs ('16), Dayton Marcos ('18–'19), *Madison Stars ('20)*

He was a backup for the Chicago American Giants in 1914–15; Incomplete statistics show averages of .220 and .194, but in the latter year he quit baseball to box professionally. However, his retirement was soon rescinded, and he was playing with the Indianapolis ABCs in August of the same season. In 1916 he was still struggling at the plate, and batted only .163 for the year. In the late fall of the following year he suffered a tragic accident, when his little finger on his right hand was torn almost completely off in the October playoff between the American Giants and the ABCs. It was feared that he would never be able to use it again, but he returned to the ABCs in 1917 and played with the Marcos in 1918.

Watts, Richard (Dick)
Career: 1949–50   Position: p
Team: Birmingham Black Barons

This hurler began his career with the Birmingham Black Barons in 1949–50, when the Negro American League was struggling to survive the loss of players to organized baseball.

Webb
Career: 1917–19   Position: p
Team: New York Lincoln Giants

He pitched with the New York Lincoln Giants for three seasons in the latter years of the deadball era, beginning in 1917, when he had no recorded decision.

Webb, James (Baby)
Career: 1910   Position: c
Team: Chicago Giants

He was a reserve catcher in 1910 with the Chicago Giants, a team formed by owner Frank Leland after he and Rube Foster went their separate ways.

Webster, Charles
Career: 1950   Position: of
Team: Birmingham Black Barons

He was listed as an outfielder with the Birmingham Black Barons in 1950, when the Negro American League was struggling to survive the loss of players to organized baseball, but league statistics do not confirm his playing time.

Webster, Daniel (**Jim**, Double Duty)
Career: 1933–37   Positions: **c**, p
Teams: Detroit Stars ('33, '37), Kansas City Monarchs ('36), *Louisville Black Colonels ('38)*

A combination pitcher-catcher, he appeared briefly with the Detroit Stars and the Kansas City Monarchs during the '30s.

Webster, Pearl F.
[see Webster, William (Speck, West)]

Webster, William (**Speck**, West)
a.k.a. Pearl F. Webster
Career: 1911–26   Positions: c, 1b, of
Teams: Chicago American Giants ('11, '18), **Brooklyn Royal Giants** ('12–'17), Chicago Giants, Mohawk Giants ('13), New York Lincoln Giants ('14, '18, '24), St. Louis Giants

('15), Jewell's ABCs ('17), Indianapolis ABCs ('18), G.C.T. Red Caps ('18), Hilldale Daisies ('18), Atlantic City Bacharach Giants ('18, '23), *military service ('19),* Dayton Marcos ('20), Detroit Stars ('21), *Brooklyn Cuban Giants ('26–'28)*

Another of the good catchers of the '10s, he played for the eastern champion Brooklyn Royal Giants in 1914. That winter in Cuba, he hit a solid .330, and partial statistics show averages of .292 and .283 in 1917–18. Although best identified with the Brooklyn Royal Giants, during his sixteen-year career he also played with a dozen other clubs, including the Lincoln Giants and the Bacharachs. Nicknamed "Speck" because of his freckles, he was captain of the Camp Dix baseball team, which included the best New York players drafted into service during World War I.

Weeks, E.
Career: 1921–24   Position: 3b, ss, 2b, of
Teams: *Pennsylvania Giants ('18), Madison Stars ('20–'21),* Hilldale Daisies ('21, '24), Harrisburg Giants ('22–'24), Brooklyn Royal Giants ('23), *Pittsburgh Stars of Buffalo ('20–'21)*

After playing with marginal teams for three years, he spent parts of four seasons as a reserve infielder with teams that played in the Eastern Colored League after its formation. In 1921 he advanced from the Madison Stars, a team of lesser status that served as a farm team, to the Hilldale ballclub. Over the next three seasons he also appeared with the Harrisburg Giants and the Brooklyn Royal Giants.

Weeks, William
Career: 1922   Position: officer
Team: Atlantic City Bacharach Giants

During the Bacharachs' last season as an independent team before joining the Eastern Colored League, he served as an officer with the ballclub.

Weems
Career: 1936   Position: of
Team: Memphis Red Sox

In 1936, before the team joined the Negro American League, he appeared as an outfielder with the Memphis Red Sox.

Weidel
Career: 1916   Position: p
Team: All Nations

He was a pitcher on the All Nations baseball club in 1916, one of the team's peak seasons.

Welch, Winfield Scott (Gus, Moe)
Career: 1926–49   Positions: player, **manager**
Teams: *New Orleans Black Pelicans ('26), Monroe Monarchs, Shreveport Giants,* Cincinnati Buckeyes ('42), Birmingham Black Barons ('42–'45), *Cincinnati Crescents,* New York Cubans, Chicago American Giants ('49, '51)

His playing days were spent with lesser teams, but he was a better manager than player and earned his baseball reputation after his playing career had ended. A good tactician, he was appointed manager of the Brimingham Black Barons in 1942 and managed the team to consecutive Negro American League championships in 1943–44. After a losing season in 1945, he was replaced at the helm but later managed with the Chicago American Giants in the latter years of the Negro Leagues as viable major leagues.

Wellman
Career: 1939   Position: p
Team: Homestead Grays

He pitched briefly with the Homestead Grays in 1939 but was an undistinguished member of their mound corps.

Wells
Career: 1918   Positions: 2b, c
Teams: New York Lincoln Giants, *Pennsylvania Giants*

In 1918 he appeared briefly as a second baseman with the New York Lincoln Giants but was a catcher with the Pennsylvania Giants, a lesser team, for the remainder of the season.

Wells, I.
Career: 1948   Position: p
Team: Memphis Red Sox

He pitched briefly with the Memphis Red Sox in 1948, splitting a pair of league decisions.

Wells, Willie Brooks (**Junior**)
a.k.a. Willie Wells, Jr.
Career: 1944–50   Positions: ss, 3b, 2b
Teams: Memphis Red Sox ('44–'50), *minor leagues ('50), New Orleans Eagles ('51)*
Bats: Right   Throws: Right
Height: 5'5"   Weight: 158
Born: Oct. 23, 1922, Austin, Tex.

The son of shortstop superstar Willie Wells, this infielder played in his father's shadow, and often under his father's management, throughout his career. As an infielder with the Memphis Red Sox, he lacked the defensive skills and especially the offensive punch that his father displayed. In his first two years (1944–45) with the Red Sox, he batted only .120 and .196, but by 1948 he had raised his average to .251. After leaving the Negro Leagues early in 1950, he also played with his father at Winnipeg in the Mandak League, batting .212.

Wells, Willie James (The Devil, El Diablo, *Chico, Bubbles*)
Career: 1924–49   Positions: ss, 3b, 2b, p, manager
Teams: *San Antonio Black Aces ('23),* **St. Louis Stars** ('24–'31), Detroit Wolves ('32), Homestead Grays ('32), Kansas City Monarchs ('32, '34), Cole's American Giants ('33–'35), **Newark Eagles** ('36–'39, '42, '45), *Mexican League ('40–'41, '43–'44),* Chicago American Giants ('44), New York Black Yankees ('45–'46), Baltimore Elite Giants ('46), Indianapolis Clowns ('47), Memphis Red Sox ('44, '48), *Canadian League ('49–'51),* Birmingham Black Barons ('54)
Bats: Right   Throws: Right
Height: 5'8"   Weight: 160
Born: August 10, 1905, Austin, Tex.
Died: Jan. 22, 1989, Austin, Tex.

The best shortstop in black baseball during the 1930s and early 1940s, Wells was outstanding both in the field and at the plate. Possessing good range, sure hands, and an accurate arm, Wells compensated for a weak arm by a quick release and knowledgeable positioning based on a studied analysis of the hitters. His stellar defensive play earned him a spot in the Newark Eagles' "million-dollar infield" in the late 1930s, where in addition to his defensive prowess he hit for averages of .386, .330, and .343 in 1937–39.

He began playing baseball on the sandlots of Texas and, while playing with San Antonio Black Aces in 1923, he was discovered by both Rube Foster of the Chicago American Giants and St. Louis Stars' owner Dr. George Keys. Wells chose to sign with the Stars and began playing with the St. Louis club in 1924. Early in his career, through hard work and diligence, he made himself a good hitter, compiling averages of .378 and .346 in 1926–27 while establishing a single-season record in the former year when he hit 27 home runs in 88 games. His hitting continued to sizzle as he annexed consecutive batting titles in 1929–30 with averages of .368 and .404. With Wells paving the way, the St. Louis Stars won Negro National League championships in 1928, 1930, and 1931.

His early stardom in St. Louis ended when the Stars folded along with the Negro National League, and Wells had a short vagabound period until settling with the Chicago American Giants. In Chicago he led the American Giants to consecutive pennants in two different leagues, capturing the Negro Southern League title in 1932 and the first flag of the new Negro National League in 1933. The latter season he hit .300, provided the leadership that sparked the team to the championship, and was selected to the West squad's starting lineup in the first annual East-West All-Star classic, where he contributed 2 hits to the West's victory. His selection to the All-Star team established a tradition that was maintained for years, and in the eight All-Star games in which he appeared,

Willie recorded a .281 batting average and a .438 slugging percentage.

In September 1934 Dan Daniel wrote in the *New York World-Telegram,* "Lloyd's current counterpart is Wee Willie Wells of the Chicago American Giants. He is hitting .520, fielding 1,000 and stealing bases almost as regularly as Cool Papa Bell." Two years later, in 1936, when the American Giants' management had financial difficulties; Wells left Chicago for the Newark Eagles, where he joined Ray Dandridge, providing a pair of Gold Glove winners on the left side of the infield. Opponents threw at Wells so much that he became a pioneer in wearing a batting helmet. When Baltimore's ace spitballer Bill Byrd hit him in the temple, knocking him unconscious, he was advised not to play for the remainder of the series. Disregarding the doctor's advice, he played in the next contest, wearing a modified construction worker's hard hat. The catalytic star continued playing with the Eagles for the remainder of the decade, batting .357, .386, .396, and .346 over the last four seasons.

Wells also spent several winter seasons in Latin American leagues, primarily in Cuba, where he had a .320 lifetime average in his seven years there. He played on the 1929–30 championship Cienfuegos team. His final two seasons on the island, playing with Almendares, are indicative of his playing ability and team value as he won the team MVP in 1938–39 and, in his farewell season, hit .328 to lead his team to the championship, earning a spot on the All-Star team and being voted the league's MVP award. With the onset of the new decade, Wells traveled to Mexico, where the master shortstop became affectionately known as "El Diablo." Records there show batting averages of .345 and .347 in 1940 and 1941, while playing with Vera Cruz, leading them to the pennant during the former season.

During the ensuing winter he played his only season in Puerto Rico, batting .378 with Aquadilla. With the advent of World War II, rather than return to Mexico, Wells opted to return to the United States, and four days after the Japanese attack on Pearl Harbor, he wrote Abe Manley, offering to return to Newark as a player-manager for $315 per month. Manley was glad to have his star shortstop back, and Wells, an intelligent player and an excellent teacher of younger players, become a playing manager at Newark in 1942. As a manager he was respected by his players, just as he had been respected as a player by his peers. Leading by example, he had a sensational season, hitting a resounding .361, being selected to Cum Posey's annual All-American dream team, and being identified as one of the top five players in the game when prospects qualified to go to the major leagues were discussed.

In 1943, after a disagreement with Mrs. Manley, he returned to Mexico, where he batted .295 with Tampico. The next year he batted .294, after replacing Rogers Hornsby as manager of the Mexico City ballclub after Hornsby allegedly served an ultimatum to get rid of Wells and three other blacks and was fired himself. Manley, wanting his star players back, had devised a plan to get Wells and Ray Dandridge back from Mexico by having their draft exemptions revoked. But Wells stayed in Mexico for two more years before he again returned to the United States, and although past his prime, "The Devil" still retained enough magic in his bat to hit for averages of .320 and .297 in 1945–46.

During the intervening winter, when an all-star team was picked to tour Venezuela, Jackie Robinson, then a rookie shortstop with the Kansas City Monarchs, was selected instead of the veteran Wells, who despite his age was still considered the best in the Negro Leagues. Soon afterward it was learned that Robinson had been signed by the Dodgers, and his presence on the all-stars was a way of showcasing him. Later, when Robinson was moved to second base with Montreal, Wells helped tutor him on the art of making the pivot.

In late May of 1946, Wells was released by the New York Black Yankees and signed by the floundering Baltimore Elite Giants to play third base. During the remainder of the '40s, the wily veteran also served stints with Memphis and Indianapolis, batting .328 in 1948 at age forty-three. In the early '50s Wells traveled to Canada to assume the duties as playing manager with the Winnipeg Buffaloes, spending most of his final years in baseball in that country. He returned to the United States in 1954 as manager of the Birmingham Black Barons. When he finally hung up the spiked shoes, he left behind some impressive credentials. Against regular Negro League competition he recorded a lifetime .334 batting average, and against major-leaguers in exhibition games he hit for a .392 average.

After retiring from baseball Wells worked in New York City as a delicatessen for thirteen years before moving back to Austin, Texas, in 1973 to help care for his aging mother. After she passed away, he continued living in the same house where he was reared, until he died from congestive heart failure in 1989.

Welmaker, Roy Horace (Snook, Lefty)
Career: 1936–45   Position: p
Teams: *Atlanta Black Crackers ('30, '33–'35), Macon Black Peaches ('31–'32),* **Homestead Grays** ('36–'39, '42, '44–'45), Toledo Crawfords ('39), Philadelphia Stars ('39–'40), *Mexican League ('40–'41), military service ('42–'44), Venezuelan League ('46–'48), minor leagues ('49–'53)*
Bats: Both   Throws: Left
Height: 5'11½"   Weight: 190
Born: Dec. 6, 1913, Atlanta, Ga.

This hard-throwing left-hander was sneaky fast with a good curve, a fair drop, and remarkable control. In 1945 he finished with a 12–4 regular-season record with the Negro National League pennant-winning Homestead Grays, and pitched a scoreless stint in the All-Star game. In the World Series he lost a pair of heartbreakers to the Jefferson brothers, losing the opener, 2–1, to Willie and the third game, 4–0, to George as the Grays were swept by the upstart Negro American League Cleveland Buckeyes.

Altogether, Welmaker pitched in a total of 7 World Series games in 1942, 1944, and 1945. In the 1942 Series he was the starting pitcher in the opening game against Satchel Paige and the Kansas City Monarchs and suffered the loss. He relieved in two other games without a decision as the Grays were swept in the Series. He also started the second game of a doubleheader against the Monarchs at Yankee Stadium, but by mutual consent of the owners, the contest was designated as an exhibition game. In 1944, after being released from military duty in August, he notched a 3–0 record down the stretch as the Grays annexed another pennant, and won both of his starts in the ensuing World Series as the Grays defeated the Birmingham Black Barons for the championship.

One of the Grays' good-hitting pitchers, Welmaker batted .321 in 1945 and often was used as a pinch hitter. He also had sufficient power, good speed on the bases, and he could field his position. He began his professional career in 1930 for the hometown Atlanta Black Crackers in the Negro Southern League, followed by two years with the Macon Black Peaches, before returning to the Black Crackers in 1933. While playing summers with the Black Crackers, he also played football and baseball at Clark University, and was discovered by the Grays when they trained in Atlanta in 1936. When school was out, he joined the Grays for the remainder of the season. During his first two full seasons in a Grays' uniform, the team won the first two of nine straight Negro National League flags, with the left-hander being credited with a single loss in his first full season, while splitting four decisions in 1938.

In 1939 he played a few games with the Toledo Crawfords, but owner Hank Rigney returned him to the Grays by the end of July. Soon afterward he signed with the Philadelphia Stars, and posted a 2–2 mark in 1940 before jumping the Stars to play in Mexico. With Torreon in 1941, he finished the season with an 11–16 record, a 5.27 ERA, and the second-highest strikeout total in the Mexican League

(131 strikeouts in 225 ⅓ innings). Unfortunately, he had 117 walks, also the second-highest in the league, but he contributed a .292 batting average for the season.

He returned to Homestead for the 1942 season, posting a 5–4 record as the Grays captured the pennant and faced the Kansas City Monarchs in the first World Series between the two rival leagues. Soon afterward his career was interrupted by military service in World War II. While stationed at Fort Benning, Georgia, he struck out 39 batters in back-to-back games on successive days, and took the mound in a third game within two days to extend his strikeouts to 49 in 23 innings.

After his Army discharge, he returned to the Grays and was selected for the All-Star team that toured Venezuela during the winter of 1945. Welmaker won all eight of his decisions during the trip and opted to remain in Venezuela afterward. He was accustomed to pitching in Latin American climates, having played in Puerto Rico earlier in his career, when he fashioned an 8–2 record with Ponce in the 1939–40 winter. In Venezuela he pitched with Vargas and Maracaibo for the next three seasons, leading the league with a 2.80 ERA while posting a 12–8 record in the 1946–47 winter season.

Two years later, after returning from Venezuela in the spring of 1949, he walked into the Cleveland Indians' training camp in Phoenix and asked for a tryout. In two outings he made a favorable showing, yielding only 1 hit in 4 innings and gaining a victory in his only decision. Manager Lou Boudreau was highly impressed, and the left-hander was signed by the Cleveland organization.

In 1949 he led Wilkes-Barre in the Class A Eastern League in victories (22–12, 2.44 ERA) and was promoted to San Diego in the Pacific Coast League in 1950, where he continued to pitch winning baseball (16–10, 4.27 ERA). However, the next three seasons in the Pacific Coast League—with San Diego, Hollywood, and Portland—were not as impressive, as he dropped to marks of 3–4, 4–8, and 4–2. He closed out his professional career after the

1953 season and located in Los Angeles, where he owned and operated a service station until his retirement.

Wesley, Charles (Charlie, Connie, Two Sides)
Career: 1921–38   Positions: **of, 2b**, 1b, 3b, manager
Teams: Columbus Buckeyes ('21), Pittsburgh Keystones ('22), St. Louis Stars ('22), Birmingham Black Barons ('23–'24, '28–'29), Memphis Red Sox ('25–'27, '29), Louisville White Sox ('30–'31), Louisville Red Caps ('32), Atlanta Black Crackers ('38), Indianapolis ABCs.

During the '20s he played with several teams, mostly southern ballclubs, including the Memphis Red Sox and the Birmingham Black Barons. A versatile player, he was at home in either the outfield or the infield, and with the Red Sox he demonstrated his ability at both places. In 1925 he was the regular right fielder for the Red Sox, hitting fifth in the batting order, and two years later he was their starting second baseman, hitting second in the order. Partial statistics show anemic batting averages of .162 and .183 for 1927 and 1929, respectively.

Beginning his career with the Columbus Buckeyes in 1921, he played with Louisville teams a decade later before playing with lesser teams. Frequently playing in the Negro Southern League, he was a member of the Atlanta Black Crackers who captured southern championships in the early '20s. In 1938, when Atlanta was in the Negro American League, he was added to the Black Crackers' roster as a second baseman and also was utilized as a coach to steady the youngsters on the team.

Wesley, Edgar
Career: 1918–31   Position: 1b
Teams: Chicago American Giants ('18), **Detroit Stars** ('19–'23, '25–'27), Harrisburg Giants ('24), Cleveland Hornets ('27), Atlantic City Bacharach Giants ('31)
Bats: Left   Throws: Left
This power-hitting first sacker for the Detroit

Stars teamed with Turkey Stearnes to give the Motor City team an outstanding pair of sluggers, with Wesley usually batting cleanup behind Stearnes. Wesley was dangerous in a pinch and, although noted for his hitting prowess, the big, rangy Texan was a capable first baseman and had good speed on the bases.

He joined Detroit in 1919, after a stint with Rube Foster's American Giants. Before joining the American Giants, he was a first baseman with the Texas All-Stars in July 1918, when Foster acquired him late in the season as a replacement for Leroy Grant, who had been drafted. Wesley was called a natural first baseman who played in big-league style. He used proper footwork, was "reasonably sure" on grounders and pop-ups, and handled bad throws adequately. He was also considered to be a "boy of excellent habits" who was admired for his quiet, unassuming manner on and off the field.

He was predicted to have a bright future, but was one of the players Foster used to stock the Detroit franchise in 1919, accompanying Pete Hill, Frank Duncan, Bruce Petway, José Mendez, and Frank Wickware from the American Giants to form the nucleus of a strong Detroit squad. Wesley remained with Detroit during most of his career, making use of his power in the accommodating Mack Park to record impressive power statistics during his tenure there. Beginning with the lively-ball era in 1920, he posted averages of .277, .290, .344, .338, .266, .424, .300, and .421 through the 1927 season. With the exception of the 1924 season, which was spent with Harrisburg in the Eastern Colored League, and the 1927 season, spent mostly with the Cleveland Hornets, the other years were with Detroit. During his season in the East, he was regarded as one of the best first basemen in the league. Seven years later he returned to the East to close out his career with the Bacharach Giants in 1931.

Wesson, Les
Career: 1948–49   Position: p
Team: New York Black Yankees

He was a pitcher with the New York Black Yankees in the last year of the Negro National League and the first year of their play as an independent team after the league's demise.

West, Charlie
Career: 1942   Position: of
Team: Birmingham Black Barons

This outfielder played briefly with the Birmingham Black Barons in 1942.

West, James (**Jim**, Shifty)
Career: 1930–47   Positions: **1b**, of, *2b*
Teams: Nashville Elite Giants ('30, '33–'34), Birmingham Black Barons ('30, '32, '47), Memphis Red Sox ('30, '32), Cleveland Cubs ('31), Columbus Elite Giants ('35), Washington Elite Giants ('36–'37), **Baltimore Elite Giants** ('38–'39), **Philadelphia Stars** ('39–'45), New York Black Yankees ('47)
Bats: Both   Throws: Right
Height: 6'2"   Weight: 218
Born: 1912, Mobile Ala.
Died: 1970, Philadelphia, Pa.

A stylish, smooth-fielding first baseman with fancy footwork around the initial sack, West took throws one-handed, using a floppy old glove, and made plays look easy. His fielding was the best part of his game as he was encumbered with a slow, "stumbling" stride on the bases and was not a consistent hitter in the early part of his career. A big, powerful hitter, he was rated as one of best prospects in the Negro Leagues, but during his career he was usually overshadowed by the Homestead Grays' great first baseman Buck Leonard. However, West appeared in two All-Star games, in 1936 and 1942, for the Elite Giants and Philadelphia Stars, respectively, and finally broke into the top ten batters in the league in 1944 with a .350 average while also leading the league with 7 triples.

He began his career in 1930, playing with southern teams, including Tom Wilson's Nashville Elite Giants, batting .262 for the year. In his early years with the Elite Giants he did not produce impressive numbers, being credited with averages of .211 and .215 in 1931 and 1933, respectively. But in his last season in Nashville he registered a .422 average in 1934. The franchise was shifted to Columbus, where he hit .278, and then relocated in Washington, where he hit .403 and .374 in his two seasons in the capital city, earning his first trip to the All-Star game in his first year. The Elite Giants' search for a satisfactory home city ended in 1938, when they relocated to Baltimore. West responded to his new location with a .403 batting average. In the past, the first sacker had usually been ensconced in the lower half of the batting order, but he had worked his way up to the fifth slot in 1937–38.

In 1939 he joined the Philadelphia Stars, usually batting in the fifth slot, as he had in his last two years with the Elite Giants. He hit for averages of .255, .356, .218, and .303 in his first four seasons with the Stars and earned his second All-Star appearance in the latter season. During the war years he moved into the cleanup spot for three seasons, 1943–45, hitting .317, .350, and .272, respectively. West wrapped up his eighteen-year career with the New York Black Yankees in 1947, batting .242 in his last season in the Negro Leagues.

After retiring from baseball, he worked as a bartender in Philadelphia. One night an armed holdup man entered the bar and, as West wrestled for control of the pistol while trying to disarm him, he was shot and killed by the gunman.

West, Ollie Ernest (Bill)
Career: 1942–46　　　Position: p
Bats: Right　　　Throws: Right
Teams: Chicago American Giants ('42–'45), Homestead Grays ('43), Birmingham Black Barons, *Pittsburgh Crawfords ('46)*

A pitcher with the American Giants for most of his career, he began with the team in 1942 under manager Candy Jim Taylor. When Taylor signed to manage the Homestead Grays in 1943, he took West with him, but the American Giants protested, and West had to return to the Negro American League. During his short stint

with the Grays, he lost his only recorded decision. Back in Chicago, he split 2 league decisions in 1945, his last year with the American Giants, and closed out his career the following season in the U.S. League.

Weston
Career: 1930　　　Position: p
Team: Hilldale Daisies

He appeared briefly as a pitcher with Hilldale in 1930, when the team was playing as an independent ballclub.

Weston, Issac (Deacon)
Career: 1949　　　Position: p
Team: Louisville Buckeyes

He was listed as a pitcher with the Louisville Buckeyes in 1949, when the Negro American League was struggling to survive the loss of players to organized baseball, but his participation was restricted.

Weyman, J. B.
Career: 1887　　　Position: player
Team: *Baltimore Lord Baltimores*

He was a player with the Baltimore Lord Baltimores, one of eight teams that were charter members of the League of Colored Baseball Clubs in 1887. However, the league's existence was ephemeral, lasting only a week. His position is uncertain.

Wharton
Career: 1922–23　　　Position: of
Team: Kansas City Monarchs

He appeared briefly as a reserve outfielder with the Kansas City Monarchs in 1922–23.

Whatley, David (Dave, Speed, Hammerman)
Career: 1936–45　　　Position: of
Teams: Birmingham Black Barons ('36–'38), Memphis Red Sox ('38), Jacksonville Red Caps ('39), Cleveland Bears ('39), **Homestead Grays** ('39–'44), New York Black Yankees ('44–'45), *Pittsburgh Crawfords ('46)*
Bats: Left　　　Throws: Right
Height: 5'10"　　　Weight: 170

Nicknamed "Hammerman" while with the Birmingham Black Barons, after joining the Homestead Grays he picked up the moniker "Speed" because he was exceptionally fast going from the batter's box to first base. Aside from Cool Papa Bell, he was the fastest man on the Homestead Grays during the early 1940s. Usually batting in the leadoff position, the right fielder was one of the team's best base stealers and was skilled on either end of the hit-and-run play. He could either bunt or slug an extra-base hit when needed, although his power was not exceptional. Generally a contact hitter whose average did not widely deviate from the norm, the hard-hitting, left-handed batsman provided an extra dimension at the top of the batting order for the Grays.

He began his career with the Black Barons in 1936, batted cleanup in 1937, and was picked up by Memphis Red Sox manager "Double Duty" Radcliffe in 1938 to play for the Sox against the Atlanta Black Crackers in the Negro American League championship series. The next season he was signed by the Grays and quickly established himself as a star. A fixture in right field, he hit for averages of .285, .290, .241, and .214 on their championship teams for the next four years, 1939–42. The latter season marked the first World Series between the Negro American League and the Negro National League, and the Grays faced the Kansas City Monarchs in the matchup of the two dominant dark dynasties of the era. The Monarchs swept the Series, but earlier in the season, when the two teams faced each other in August, Whatley had 3 hits off Satchel Paige, including a two-out single in the twelfth inning to knock in the winning run, giving the Grays a 3–2 victory.

During the 1944 season, with his propensity for alcoholic consumption and the acquisition of veteran Cool Papa Bell for the outfield the previous year, Whatley became expendable and was released outright by the Grays. However, he was picked up by the New York Black Yankees and played two more seasons in the Negro National League in a reserve role. In 1946 he closed out his baseball career with the new Pittsburgh Crawfords, a team of lesser quality.

Weatherspoon
Career: 1917   Position: p
Team: Atlantic City Bacharach Giants

He appeared briefly as a pitcher with the Bacharachs in 1917, during their formative years.

Wheeler, Joe (Jodie)
Career: 1922–28   Position: p
Teams: *Washington Braves ('21)*, Baltimore Black Sox ('21–'23), Atlantic City Bacharach Giants ('22), Homestead Grays ('24), *Brooklyn Cuban Giants ('28)*, Wilmington Potomacs ('25), *Chappie Johnson's Stars ('25–'26)*

During the '20s he pitched with several teams, including the Baltimore Black Sox, and posted a record of 11–1 with the Black Sox in 1921, when they were still playing as an independent team. In the next two seasons his marks showed more limited success, with a combined 2–1 ledger. After leaving the Black Sox he pitched with the Homestead Grays, Wilmington Potomacs, and Chappie Johnson's Stars, a team of lesser status.

Wheeler, Sam
Career: 1948   Position: lf
Teams: *Harlem Globetrotters ('47)*, New York Cubans ('48)

After a season with the Harlem Globetrotters' baseball team, he was the regular left fielder with the 1948 New York Cubans, hitting fifth in the batting order.

White
Career: 1913, 1916   Position: p
Teams: Mohawk Giants ('13), Chicago Union Giants ('16)

During the deadball era, he pitched a season each with the Mohawk Giants in the East and the Chicago Union Giants in the West.

White
Career: 1925   Position: p
Team: Indianapolis ABCs

He was a pitcher with the Indianapolis ABCs in 1925, his only year in the Negro Leagues.

White, Arstando Artemis (Art, **Ladd**)
Career: 1947–48   Position: p
Teams: Memphis Red Sox ('47–'48), Indianapolis Clowns ('48), *minor leagues ('49), Canadian League ('50)*
Bats: Left   Throws: Right

This right-handed pitcher began his career with the Memphis Red Sox in 1947 and posted a 1–3 record in 1948 while splitting his playing time between Memphis and the Indianapolis Clowns. The following season he pitched unimpressively with Leavenworth (3–9, 5.16 ERA). He played with Drummondville in the Canadian Provincial League (9–12, 3.77 ERA) in 1950.

White, Arthur
Career: 1934   Position: p
Team: Newark Dodgers

He was a pitcher with the Newark Dodgers in 1934, the first full season for the franchise.

White, Bill
[see White, Eugene (Bill)]

White, Burlin
Career: 1915–28; 1942 Positions: c, 1b,
                          manager
Teams: *West Baden Sprudels ('15),* Bowser's ABCs ('16), Chicago American Giants ('16–'17), Atlantic City Bacharach Giants ('17, '23), *Madison Stars ('20),* New York Lincoln Giants ('21, '25), *Philadelphia Royal Stars,* Harrisburg Giants ('23), *Philadelphia Giants ('25–'28), Wilmington Quaker Giants ('30),* Cuban Stars (East) ('33), *Boston Royal Giants ('42)*

This burly catcher began his career with the Sprudels of West Baden, Indiana, in 1915, and played briefly with Thomas Bowser's ABCs the following season before signing with Rube Foster's Chicago American Giants as one of the receivers stacked behind Bruce Petway. Leaving Foster's team in 1917, White traveled East to join the Bacharach Giants and, as a better receiver but a lesser batter than the other catcher, shared the regular catching assignments for the year. While in the East he also played with the Lincoln Giants in 1921 and the Harrisburg Giants in 1923. With Harrisburg he shared a starting position, accruing playing time at both first base and catcher while batting at the bottom of the order when in the lineup.

He also played with several marginal teams and became a manager later in his career, serving at the helm of the Philadelphia Giants and the Boston Royal Giants. After retiring from baseball he settled in Boston's South End, along with pitcher Will Jackman.

White, Butler
Career: 1920–23   Position: 1b
Team: Chicago Giants

When the Chicago Giants entered the Negro National League in 1920, its inaugural season, he was the team's regular first baseman and hit sixth in the batting order. He continued with the Giants even after they dropped out of league play.

White, Chaney *(Reindeer, Liz)*
Career: 1919–36   Position: of
Teams: Hilldale Daisies ('19–'22, '28, '30–'32), Chicago American Giants ('20), **Atlantic City Bacharach Giants** ('23–'29), Washington Potomacs ('24), Wilmington Potomacs ('25), Quaker Giants, Homestead Grays ('30), Philadelphia Stars ('33–'35), Baltimore Black Sox ('32), New York Cubans ('36)
Bats: Right   Throws: Left
Height: 5'10"   Weight: 195
Born: Dallas, Tex.
Died: 1965, Philadelphia, Pa.

A star center fielder on the Eastern Colored League champion Bacharach Giants of 1926–27, Chaney White was an aggressive player at bat, on the bases, and in the field. Using his excellent speed and spikes-high slide, he was a terror on the bases. One opponent described White by saying that he was "built like King Kong but runs like Jesse

Owens.'' He was reputed to run 100 yards in 10 seconds, and once circled the bases in 14 seconds on a sprained ankle.

His hard-nosed approach earned him a reputation as a ''dirty'' ballplayer, and he made no distinctions about who was on the receiving end of his flashing spikes. He once opened a wound on catcher Larry Brown's leg above the knee that required eight stitches to close, and in another play at home plate, he cut the chest protector and shin guards off Josh Gibson.

White's style of play contrasted with his demeanor off the field, where he was quiet and slow-talking, with a girlish laugh. His movements were languid, making him appear lazy and lackadaisical, but he was described as a gentleman and a scholar.

Although a right-handed batter, he was a left-handed thrower with a weak arm, but with good hands and great range in the field. A very good hitter, he had a composite .347 batting average for three winter seasons in Cuba, and finished his eighteen-year career in the Negro Leagues with a .302 lifetime batting average.

The Texan began playing baseball in the Lone Star State, and was with the Dallas-Fort Worth team before joining Hilldale. He made his first appearance with Hilldale in 1919, and after an unsuccessful trial with Rube Foster's Chicago American Giants in 1920, he returned to Hilldale and became their regular left fielder that season. In 1921–22 he moved into the third slot in the lineup, batting .369 and .349 against all competition as Hilldale pursued an independent schedule. In 1923 the Eastern Colored League was organized and White joined the Bacharachs, playing left field and batting leadoff while hitting .385, .352 and .358.

He had some problems during his early years in Atlantic City, stemming from leg injuries. He started the 1924 season in center field for the Bacharachs, but suffered from bad legs and in mid-June was released to the Washington Potomacs. There he became their regular centerfielder until late in the season, when he suffered a bad knee injury and was unable to return to his previous form and had to be rested.

In 1925 he returned to the Bacharachs, and beginning in 1926 he moved to center field and began batting in the heart of the lineup as the Bacharachs captured two consecutive Eastern Colored League pennants in 1926–27 but, unfortunately, lost each World Series to the Negro National League champion Chicago American Giants. In the 1926 Series he stole 5 bases in 6 attempts. His averages during the two pennant seasons were lower than subsequent years, as he posted marks of .295 and .274. But he followed with a pair of good seasons, batting .338 and .357 in 1928–29.

In 1930, with no league in the East, he joined the aggregation of talent that Cum Posey had attracted to the Homestead Grays, but left before the end of the season to return to Hilldale, recording a composite .333 average for the year. For the next two seasons he remained with Hilldale, batting in the third and fourth spots in the order and registering an average of .276 in 1931. In 1932, when the East-West League failed and the Hilldale club folded, he switched to the Baltimore Black Sox for the remainder of the season. In 1933 he joined Webster McDonald's Philadelphia Stars as their right fielder and third-place batter, compiling averages of .273, .284, and .256 in 1933–35. In the middle year of his three-year stint, the Stars won the Negro National League pennant, defeating the Chicago American Giants in the playoff for the championship.

In 1936 he closed out his career with the New York Cubans, hitting .319. His all-around skills were recognized by those who competed against him, and he was selected by John Henry Lloyd as the left fielder on his all-time team for a national magazine in 1953.

White, Charles, Jr. (**Charlie**)
Career: 1950　　　　　　Positions: 3b, c
Teams: Philadelphia Stars ('50), *minor leagues ('51–'53, '55–'63, '65),* major leagues ('54–'55), *voluntarily retired ('64)*
Bats: Left　　　　　　Throws: Right

Height: 6'0"   Weight: 196
Born: August 12, 1928, Kinston, N.C.

A major-league catcher for two seasons, he began his career as a third baseman with the Philadelphia Stars in 1950, batting .256 in his only year in the Negro Leagues. The next year he played briefly with Winnipeg in the Mandak League before joining Toronto in the International League. During his second year with Toronto he began catching in addition to playing third base, and he followed the same pattern at San Antonio in 1953, where he batted .274.

In 1954 he made his first appearance in the major leagues, joining the Milwaukee Braves as a catcher. He hit .237 that year and followed with a .233 average the next season before being farmed out to Rochester. Although he would play ball for another decade, he would never return to the major leagues.

In 1956 he was with Wichita in the American Association, hitting .279, and then began five seasons with Vancouver in the Pacific Coast League, with averages of .277, .291, .273, .259, and .268. After two more years in the Coast League, with Hawaii, and a year away from baseball, he returned to Vancouver for 6 hitless-at-bats in 1965 to close out his career.

White, Clarence (Red)
Career: 1928–32   Positions: **p**, 2b
Teams: Memphis Red Sox ('28), Nashville Elite Giants ('29–'30), Louisville White Sox ('30–'31), Monroe Monarchs ('32), Montgomery Grey Sox ('32)

Playing with five teams in a five-year career, he played exclusively with southern teams. Beginning with the Memphis Red Sox in 1928 and posting a combined 2–9 record for his two seasons with the Nashville Elite Giants in 1929–30, he closed out his career in 1932 after stints with Negro Southern League teams in Louisville, Montgomery, and Monroe.

White, Edward (Eddie)
Career: 1944   Position: p
Team: Homestead Grays

A wartime player, he pitched without distinction for the Homestead Grays in 1944, his only year in the Negro Leagues.

White, Eugene (Bill)
Career: 1935–36   Position: 3b
Teams: Brooklyn Eagles ('35), Newark Eagles ('36)

He was a third baseman with the Brooklyn Eagles in 1935, and when Abe Manley consolidated the team with the Newark Dodgers to form a single team, White was among the players taken for the Newark Eagles in 1936. However, the starting third baseman, Ray Dandridge, came from the Dodgers, and White was relegated to a reserve role.

White, Henry (Lefty)
Career: 1940   Position: p
Team: Cleveland Bears

After the Jacksonville Red Caps moved to Cleveland to represent the city under the banner of the Cleveland Bears, he pitched with the team in 1940, their second and last season.

White, Ladd
[see White, Arstando Artemis (Art, Ladd)]

White, Lawrence (Eugene)
Career: 1950   Positions: ss, 2b
Teams: Chicago American Giants ('50), *minor leagues ('53–'54)*

He was listed as a player with the Chicago American Giants in 1950, during the Negro American League's declining years, when the teams were struggling to survive the loss of players to organized baseball. However, league statistics do not confirm his playing time.

With the color line eradicated, he played briefly with Portsmouth in the Piedmont League in 1953 and with Fort Walton Beach in the Alabama-Florida League in 1954, where he hit .245 with average power and a high incidence of walks and strikeouts.

White, M.
Career: 1886–87   Position: p
Team: *New York Gorhams*

He was a pitcher with the New York Gorhams, one of the earliest quality black teams and one of eight teams that were charter members of the League of Colored Baseball Clubs in 1887. However, the league's existence was ephemeral, lasting only a week.

White, R. W.
Career: 1887   Position: player
Teams: *Washington Capital Citys,* Cuban Giants

He was a player with the Washington Capital Citys, one of eight teams that were charter members of the League of Colored Baseball Clubs in 1887. However, the league was short-lived, lasting only a week, and he joined the Cuban Giants, the premier black team of the era.

White, Robert
Career: 1922–23   Positions: 2b, 3b
Teams: *Madison Stars ('20–'21),* Pittsburgh Keystones ('22), St. Louis Stars ('22), Toledo Tigers ('23)

A marginal infielder, his Negro Leagues career consisted of two years as a reserve infielder, playing second base and third base with the Pittsburgh Keystones and the St. Louis Stars in 1922 and with the Toledo Tigers until the team folded in mid-July of 1923. Before joining the Keystones, he played two years with the Madison Stars, a lesser team.

White, Soloman (Sol)
Career: 1887–1912,
1920–26   Positions: **2b**, 3b, 1b,
ss, of, **manager**,
coach, officer
Teams: *minor leagues ('87, '95),* Pittsburgh Keystones ('87, '92), Washington Capital Citys ('87), New York Gorhams ('89), Cuban Giants ('89–'91, '93–'94), Genuine Cuban Giants, [Philadelphia] Big Gorhams ('91), Page Fence Giants ('95), Cuban X-Giants ('96–'99, '01), Columbia Giants ('00), **Philadelphia Giants** ('02–'09), Brooklyn Royal Giants ('10), New York Lincoln Giants ('11), *Boston Giants*

('12), *Quaker Giants ('09),* Columbus Buckeyes ('20), Cleveland Browns ('24), Newark Stars ('26)
Bats: Right   Throws: Right
Height: 5'9"   Weight: 170
Born: June 12, 1868, Bellaire, Ohio.
Died: August 1955, New York, N.Y.

While still enrolled at Wilberforce University (1886–90), he began his baseball career in 1887, as a nineteen-year-old second baseman for the Pittsburgh Keystones, one of eight teams that were charter members of the League of Colored Baseball Clubs in 1887, and was batting .308 when the league folded after only a week. He then joined the Wheeling, West Virginia, Green Stockings in the Ohio State League, batting .371 as a rookie third baseman.

From this first experience, White continued to play in organized white leagues, either as an individual player, as he did in 1895, when he hit .385 with Fort Wayne, Indiana, in the Western Interstate League, or as a member of a black team representing a host city in an otherwise all-white league, as he did with the Cuban Giants and the New York Gorhams. The Gorhams played in the Middle States League in 1889, and the Cubans represented York, Pennsylvania, in the Eastern Interstate League in 1890 and Ansonia in the Connecticut State League in 1891. During those three seasons, White posted batting averages of .324, .356, and .375, respectively, giving him a lifetime average of .356 in organized baseball.

In addition to playing in the white leagues, he made significant contributions to black baseball, playing with many of the premier teams of the era, including ten championship teams. Those banner-winning ballclubs are the New York Gorhams (1889), the Big Gorhams (1891), the Cuban Giants (1894), the Cuban X-Giants (1897 and 1899), the Columbia Giants (1900), and the Philadelphia Giants (1904–07). He also played with the Page Fence Giants in 1895, their first full season, and batted .404 during his stint with the team.

However, it is with the Philadelphia Giants that he is best identified. He and Walter

Schlichter, a white sportswriter, organized the Philadelphia Giants in 1902, with White holding down the shortstop position as playing manager. A year later the team was in the playoff with the Cuban X-Giants for the eastern championship, but lost the Series, 5 games to 2, with the Cubans' pitching ace, Rube Foster, leading the way. The next season, White lured Foster to Philadelphia, and the playoff results were reversed as Foster won both Philadelphia victories to take the best-of-3 series for their first championship. The ballclub, under White's direction, added three more titles, making four consecutive eastern championships. By then he had moved to first base and was not playing full-time. In 1907 he chronicled his experiences in a small volume titled *History of Colored Baseball,* which covered events through the 1906 season.

An intense player when in action on the diamond, he otherwise demonstrated a calm disposition that served him well as a manager. After leaving Philadelphia, he signed with the Brooklyn Royal Giants for the 1910 season and, when Jess McMahon organized the New York Lincoln Giants the following year, he became their first manager. Later in the season, he gave way to John Henry Lloyd, and retired from baseball in 1912.

After pursing other activities for the next eight years, he returned to black baseball when the Negro National League was formed in 1920, as secretary of the league's Columbus Buckeyes, leaving to manage the Cleveland Browns when they entered the Negro National League in 1924. His last year in baseball was as a coach with the Newark Stars in the Eastern Colored League in 1926, making him an active participant in the first three black leagues formed, beginning with the League of Colored Baseball Clubs in 1887. After his retirement from the baseball diamond, he wrote a column for the *Amsterdam News.*

Whitfield, Lefty
Career: 1950   Position: p
Team: Baltimore Elite Giants

He was listed as a pitcher with the Baltimore Elite Giants in 1950, after they had joined the Negro American League, and the teams were struggling to survive the loss of players to organized baseball. League statistics do not confirm his playing time.

Whitley
[see Whitney, Carl]

Whitlock
Career: 1926   Position: 1b
Team: Dayton Marcos

A light-hitting part-time starter, he batted in the lower part of the order when in the lineup with the Dayton Marcos in 1926, their last season in the Negro National League.

Whitney, Carl
a.k.a. Whitley
Career: 1942   Positions: of, *p*
Team: New York Black Yankees
Bats: Left   Throws: Left
Height: 5'11"   Weight: 170

An infrequently used reserve outfielder with the New York Black Yankees during the 1942 season, this lefthander was an ordinary player who was an average fielder but with a light bat, and had a modicum of speed but was not a basestealing threat.

Whitworth, Richard (Big)
Career: 1915–25   Position: p
Teams: **Chicago American Giants** ('15–'19, '22, '24–'25), Chicago Union Giants ('17), New York Bacharachs ('19), Hilldale Daisies ('20–'21), Chicago Giants ('22–'23)
Bats: Right   Throws: Right
Height: 6'4"   Weight: 215

This tall, light-complexioned hurler was a classy pitcher and Rube Foster's ace during the latter part of the '10s. The big hurler's money pitch was a sinking fastball, and he was a power pitcher who liked to strike out batters. He was also regarded as a fairly good hitter for a pitcher, showing averages of .141, .125, .250, and .227 for the seasons 1916–19. However, he was slow afoot and not a good base runner.

Beginning his career in 1915 with Rube Foster's Chicago American Giants, he pitched a no-hitter in his first season while posting an 8–4 work sheet, second only to Frank Wickware on the staff. In a hotly contested series against the Indianapolis ABCs, the American Giants emerged victorious to claim the western championship. The next year he again paired with Wickware to pitch the American Giants into the playoffs against the ABCs, but this time C. I. Taylor's charges copped the honors. Earlier in the season Whitworth had pitched the opening-game victory in a challenge series against the Lincoln Stars, the top team in the East.

In 1917 Whitworth played with both the Chicago American Giants and the Chicago Union Giants, with incomplete records showing him with a 6–1 ledger. After finishing with a 16–4 mark the following season, he was ranked among the best pitchers in black baseball and was compared to Rube Foster and Smokey Joe Williams. In 1919 the American Giants' ace held out for more than a month in a salary dispute, and the press observed "he caught a cold in his salary arm," but he returned in time to post a sterling 10–1 record and retain his reputation as the ace of the pitching staff.

"Big" Whitworth traveled East in 1920, joining Hilldale for two seasons. In 1921 his record was 15–8, with a 2.94 ERA. In 1922 he returned to the Midwest, pitching with the Chicago American Giants before switching to the Chicago Giants later in the season. By then he was well past his prime, and the debilitating effects of his heavy drinking were beginning to show. Even in his prime, on days when he was scheduled to pitch, he would go under the stand and consume some whiskey before he took the mound. Nearing the end of his career, he returned to the American Giants in 1924 and was unconditionally released by Foster in the spring of 1925, along with a large number of other veteran players, in a youth movement.

Whyte, William T. (**Billy**)
a.k.a. White
Career: 1885–94   Positions: **p**, of, 2b
Teams: Cuban Giants ('85–'90, '94)
Born: Apr. 10, 1860, Providence, R.I.
Died: Sept. 27, 1936, Trenton, N.J.

One of the top pitchers from the nineteenth century, this Providence native sported a handlebar mustache, and played for the St. Louis Black Stockings and the Resolutes of Boston before turning professional. In 1885 he joined the Cuban Giants, the first black professional team, and traveled through the South with the team during the winter season. In later years, the Cubans represented cities in otherwise all-white leagues, including Trenton, New Jersey, in the Middle States League in 1887 and 1889, and York, Pennsylvania, in the Eastern Interstate League in 1890.

While with the Cuban Giants, he faced the 1887 National League champion Detroit team and was leading, 4–2, after seven innings. Unfortunately, his teammates committed 4 errors and allowed 4 unearned runs, 2 in the eighth inning to tie the game and another pair in the last inning to lose, 6–4. He also pitched against two teams from the other major league, the American Association, tying the New York Metropolitans but losing to the Philadelphia Athletics. After these pitching exhibitions against the top white teams of the era, he coached the Columbia College baseball team following the 1888 season.

Wicks
Career: 1921, 1923   Positions: 3b, ss
Teams: Hilldale Daises ('21), Harrisburg Giants ('23)

After appearing in one game with Hilldale in 1921, the youngster joined the Harrisburg Giants in 1923 and started the season at third base.

Wickware, Frank (*Smokey, Rawhide, The Red Ant, Big Red, Smiley*)
a.k.a. Wigware
Career: 1910–25   Position: p
Teams: *Dallas Giants ('09),* Leland Giants ('09–'10), **Chicago American Giants** ('11–'12, '14–'18, '20–'21), Brooklyn Royal Giants ('12–'14), Mohawk Giants ('13–'14), Louisville White Sox ('14), New York Lincoln Stars, Indianapolis ABCs ('16), Jewell's ABCs ('17), *Chicago Giants ('17), military service ('18–'19),* Detroit Stars ('19), *Norfolk Stars ('20),* New York Lincoln Giants ('20, '25), *Canadian League ('21),* St. Louis Giants, Philadelphia Giants
Bats: Right   Throws: Right
Born: 1888, Coffeeville, Kan.
Died: 1967, Schenectady, N.Y.

An angular right-hander with a blazing fastball, Frank Wickware was a formidable pitcher during the second decade of the century. Arriving on the Chicago baseball scene in 1910, after previously having played with the Dallas Giants, a team of lesser status, he took the town by storm. Posting an 18–1 record for Rube Foster's great Leland Giants' ballclub, he quickly developed into the ace of the staff, supplanting Foster and Pat Dougherty. During the season Wickware told the press that he had never had to extend himself, and experienced diamond observers called him "the most sensational pitcher seen for some time."

At age twenty-two, Wickware was already noted for his velocity, mound presence, coolness under pressure, and smooth delivery. A big winner with the Chicago American Giants, he also pitched two winter seasons in Cuba. While pitching with the Fe ballclub in 1912, he led the Cuban league with 10 victories, and registered a composite 12–8 record on the island.

He was a star gate attraction and in demand by all the leading teams of the era, and remained a formidable pitcher throughout the decade. In a game in July 1913, after jumping to the Mohawk Giants of Schenectady, New York, he excited the crowd when he called in his outfield with two outs in the ninth inning and struck out the last batter to end the game. A month later the Chicago Cubs came to town for a scheduled exhibition game with the Rutland, Vermont, team. Rutland had hired Wickware as a ringer to pitch against the Cubs, but the Cubs remembered him from Chicago and refused to play if he pitched.

Another recorded incident, while he was with the Mohawks, serves as a clear indicator of Wickware's value to a team. Foster's western champion Chicago American Giants and the eastern champion New York Lincoln Giants were in a playoff for the colored championship, and both teams signed Wickware as a "ringer" to pitch for them in the championship series. When each of the opposing managers learned of his counterpart's plans, an argument ensued over who had the legal claim to Wickware, and the game was protested.

Always in demand and without hesitation to jump for more money, during the 1914 season he pitched for four different teams and was credited with no-hitters against both the Indianapolis ABCs and the Cuban Stars. However, he gained his most notoriety when he outdueled Walter Johnson 2 out of 3 games in 1913 and 1914, when both hurlers were in their prime. One of those victories, a 1–0 game called on account of darkness after five innings, came in October 1913, with Johnson just having completed a sensational season with a 34–7 record and a 1.09 ERA. Johnson and Wickware shared the same hometown—Coffeeville, Kansas—and Wickware was often called the black Walter Johnson.

Statistics from his prime seasons are fragmented, partly because of his continued changing of teams, but scattered box scores show a composite 15–14 ledger against quality teams. In addition to his willingness to jump a team for more money, his personal habits, both on and off the playing field, had become too much for some managers to tolerate, and Wickware's brilliant career was cut short because of his fondness for the bottle. Although he remained active, the dissipation robbed him of his previous effectiveness, and with it the possibility of a plaque at Cooperstown. In 1917 he was with the Chicago Giants, a team in decline, and at that time a ballclub of lesser quality. His pitching was erratic, with a glaring lack of control, and his performance indicated that he might be about "over the hill." But by late summer he had joined the Chicago American Giants and was back in form for a time. The next season his personal decline manifested itself again by another incident, where he was thrown out because he quit running on a ground ball, when he would have beaten the throw. Wickware's career, already in disrepair, was further affected by his stint in the Army during World War I.

As a new decade began, both his skills and his gate appeal faded. He drifted around during these years, with his location not completely documented for the decade. He made a pitching appearance with the Calgary Black Sox in 1921, and in 1925, at age thirty-seven, he was with the New York Lincoln Giants for his last year in black baseball. In April he and Oliver Marcelle were with teammate Dave Brown on the night when Brown killed a man in a barroom fight. Although not involved in the incident, the next day at the ballfield, he and Marcelle were picked up but later released. In the latter years of his career, he was referred to as "Rawhide" Wickware, and served briefly as manager in New Bedford, Massachussetts, in 1930. After he left baseball, he lived in Schenectady during the '40s, but faded into obscurity and died in 1967.

Wiggins, Joe
a.k.a Cheavier
Career: 1930–34   Positions: **3b**, ss
Teams: Nashville Elite Giants ('30–'32), Cleveland Cubs ('31), Baltimore Black Sox ('32), Hilldale Daisies ('32), Atlantic City Bacharach Giants ('32–'34), New York Black Yankees ('34)

Beginning his career with Tom Wilson's Nashville Elite Giants, he accompanied the franchise to Cleveland in 1931, when they played as the Cubs. In 1932 he was originally with the Baltimore Black Sox in the East-West League, but in the summer, when the league started breaking up, he signed with the new Hilldale franchise, leaving them in turn to play third base with the Bacharachs for the remainder of the season. For the next two seasons he was the regular at the hot corner and hit in the third slot with the Bacharachs.

Wiggins, Maurice
Career: 1920   Position: ss
Team: Chicago American Giants

He appeared briefly as a reserve shortstop for the Chicago American Giants in 1920, the first season of the Negro National League.

Wigware
Career: 1930   Positions: ss, 3b
Team: Nashville Elite Giants

A reserve infielder, he appeared briefly with the Nashville Elite Giants, playing on the left side of the infield.

Wigware
[see Wickware, Frank]

Wilbert, Art
a.k.a. Mofike
Career: 1942   Position: lf
Teams: Ethiopian Clowns, *Minneapolis-St. Paul Gophers*

He played left field with the Ethiopian Clowns in 1942, using the Clown name Mofike, and also appeared with the Minneapolis-St. Paul Gophers, a team of lesser status.

Wiley
Career: 1919   Position: 1b
Team: Detroit Stars

In 1919 he played first base with Tenny Blount's first Detroit Stars team, but was not the regular at that position.

Wiley, F

Career: 1922–27   Positions: **p**, 2b, of
Teams: *Pennsylvania Red Caps of New York ('20–'21, '26–'27)*, New York Lincoln Giants ('22–'25, '27)

A pitcher during the '20s, he played with the New York Lincoln Giants for five seasons, but began and ended his career with the Pennsylvania Red Caps of New York, a team of lesser quality. In addition to pitching, he could play in the infield or the outfield.

Wiley, Joe

Career: 1947–50   Positions: 3b, 2b
Died: March 13, 1993
Teams: *Cincinnati Crescents ('45), New Orleans Black Pelicans ('45)*, Baltimore Elite Giants ('47–'49), Memphis Red Sox ('50)

An infielder with the Baltimore Elite Giants in 1947, he shared the second-base position with a young Junior Gilliam, batting seventh in the order and hitting .223 for the season. The next season he was relegated to a reserve role behind Gilliam. After leaving the Elite Giants he joined the Memphis Red Sox, but his playing time was severely restricted.

Wiley, S.

Career: 1910   Position: 3b
Team: West Baden Sprudels

He was the regular third baseman under manager C. I. Taylor with the Sprudels of West Baden, Indiana, in 1910, their strongest season.

Wiley, Wabishaw Spencer (**Doc**, Bill, Washeba)

Career: 1910–24   Positions: **c**, 1b, of, *p*
Teams: West Baden Sprudels ('10), Brooklyn Royal Giants ('11–'12, '18), Mohawk Giants ('13), **New York Lincoln Giants** ('13–'24), Philadelphia Giants ('18), *military service ('18–'19)*, Atlantic City Bacharach Giants ('19)
Bats: Right   Throws: Right
Height: 6'0"   Weight: 190
Born: Feb. 1, 1892, Muskogee, Okla.
Died: Essex County, Va.

One of the best catchers of his era, an early highlight of his fifteen-year career was when he batted .398 while catching for the 1913 eastern champion New York Lincoln Giants, a team that featured such greats as John Henry Lloyd, Spot Poles, Louis Santop, Home Run Johnson, Joe Williams, and Dick Redding. Owner Jess McMahon insisted that his team that year could have won the pennant in either the American League or the National League.

The big Oklahoman was part Indian, and began his career in 1910 as a catcher with the West Baden Sprudels, under manager C. I. Taylor, but moved to New York the following year and remained there for most of his career. After two seasons with the Brooklyn Royal Giants, batting in the lower part of the batting order, he joined the Lincoln Giants and spent a dozen seasons with the club. In 1914 he hit .418 and moved into the third slot in the batting order, becoming a fixture in both the batting order and behind the plate, catching Cyclone Joe Williams. A smart catcher, he was very skilled at handling pitchers, and was a good clutch hitter with power, batting in the heart of the order for the Lincoln Giants for almost a decade. Incomplete statistics show batting averages of .241, .441, and .343 for the years 1917–19, and in 1920 the big, jolly six-footer was still swinging a hefty bat, playing a "stellar" game afield, and was very popular with the fans at the Protectory Oval.

As a young man he attended Arkansas Baptist College and Wiley University before graduating from the Howard University School of Dentistry. Before completing the schoolwork for his diploma, he attended college during the off-season, and was also the catcher on the school's baseball team. In 1916 he was catching with the Howard University team in April but joined the Lincoln Giants when the regular season started and even took a few turns on the mound during the latter months of the season. After he earned his degree, he began practicing Dentistry in addition to playing baseball, setting up offices in Newark and East Orange, New Jersey.

During World War I he volunteered for military service and was commissioned a first lieutenant in the Army Dental Corps. After his discharge in 1919, he began spending more time with his dental practice prior to being released by the Lincoln Giants in a housecleaning in the spring of 1924. Finally retired from baseball, he was able to devote a greater part of his time and energy to his profession. However, he kept active in baseball by coaching the East Orange Police Department's baseball team. He was also an expert trap and skeet shooter and belonged to both a gun club and to professional dental organizations. He died at an early age but had made good business investments and left his wife financially secure.

Wilkes, Barron
Career: 1919   Position: officer
Team: New York Bacharach Giants

When the Bacharachs moved from Atlantic City to New York City in 1919, he served as an officer with the ballclub.

Wilkes, *James E.* (**Jimmy**, Seabiscuit)
Career: 1945–50   Positions: **cf**, rf, lf
Teams: Newark Eagles ('45–'48), Houston Eagles ('49–'50), *minor leagues ('50–'52), Indianapolis Clowns ('52)*
Bats: Both   Throws: Right
Height: 5'8"   Weight: 160

A batter with only modest power, this fleet-footed center fielder was the leadoff hitter for the 1946 Negro National League champion 1946 Newark Eagles, and hit .272 in the regular season and .280 in the ensuing World Series victory over the Kansas City Monarchs. He hit .317 the previous year as a rookie, and a .234 the following season. A hustler, he was an excellent defensive player, with outstanding range and a good arm. He had a good eye at the plate, was a pretty good contact hitter, had excellent speed, and was a good base stealer, which made him a good leadoff batter. While with the Eagles, the little speedster was given the nickname "Seabiscuit" after the famous racehorse.

After a change in ownership, the Eagles

moved to Houston in 1949, and Wilkes batted .254 for the year. In 1950 he started slowly, batting only .199 with the Eagles before entering organized baseball. He split the remainder of the season between Elmira in the Eastern League, where he hit .281, and Three Rivers in the CanAm League, where he managed only a minuscule .180 average. The next season he again split the year between two teams, hitting .273 with Elmira and .231 with Lancaster. In 1952 he played only 4 games with Great Falls in the Pioneer League before returning to the Negro Leagues to play with the Indianapolis Clowns for the remainder of the year.

Wilkins, Wesley (Wes)
Career: 1910–16   Position: of, p
Teams: Kansas City, Kansas Giants ('10), All Nations ('16)

Beginning as a left fielder with the Kansas City, Kansas, Giants in 1910, he later appeared as a pitcher with the All Nations club in 1916.

Wilkinson
Career: 1931   Position: 2b
Team: Atlantic City Bacharach Giants

In 1931, in his only appearance in the Negro Leagues, he was a reserve second baseman with the Bacharach Giants.

Wilkinson, James Leslie (**J.L.**)
Career: 1909–48   Positions: officer, **owner**, secretary (NNL), treasurer (NAL)
Teams: All Nations, **Kansas City Monarchs** ('20–'47)
Born: 1874, Perry, Ia.
Died: Aug. 21, 1964, Kansas City, Mo.

A white businessman, he pioneered black baseball as the founder and owner of the Kansas City Monarchs, directing the team's destiny from the team's entry in the Negro National League in its inaugural season, 1920, through the 1947 season. During this time the franchise had two dynasty periods, one in the '20s in the first Negro National League, and the other during the first decade of the Negro American League, beginning in 1937. During the interim, the Monarchs toured as an independent team, traveling across the Midwest, into Canada, and even into Mexico, ''scuffling'' to remain solvent during the depths of the Depression.

Wilkinson's father was the president of Algona Normal College, and as a youngster in Des Moines, Iowa, he played baseball until suffering an injury that ended his baseball participation as an active player. Retaining his interest in baseball, he entered the management end of the game, beginning with the All Nations team, which included players of various nationalities and ethnic backgrounds. After securing sponsorship from a Des Moines business establishment, the team toured the Midwest, playing top semipro and black ballclubs. Since the best players on the team were black, the ballclub eventually evolved into the Kansas City Monarchs, although for a short time he tried to maintain both franchises. Although the All Nations team faltered and folded, the Monarchs went on to a long and successful existence. When he first organized the Monarchs in 1920, Casey Stengel recommended several players from the 25th Infantry team at Fort Huachuca to Wilkinson, and they formed a nucleus for his early teams.

Under Wilkinson's guidance the Monarchs captured ten Negro league pennants (1923–25, 1929, 1937, 1939–1942, and 1946) and two of the four Negro World Series in which they competed as representatives of their league. Wilkinson's Monarchs won the first Negro World Series played in each of the two eras when Series were played between the two competing leagues. In 1924 they defeated Hilldale in the first Series held between the Negro National League and the Eastern Colored League, and in 1942 they swept the Homestead Grays in the first Series between the Negro American League and the new Negro National League.

During the Depression, between the two eras when a Negro World Series was played, Wilkinson helped pioneer night baseball, installing a portable lighting system on the beds of trucks in 1930. The initial $50,000 system proved so successful that it was paid for during the team's spring training tour of the Southwest.

After the color line in major-league baseball was eradicated, the Monarchs eventually sent 27 players into the major leagues, more than any other black team. Among those players were Jackie Robinson, Satchel Paige, Ernie Banks, and Elston Howard.

Ailing, almost blind, and recognizing the inevitable end of the Negro Leagues, Wilkinson ended his twenty-eight years at the head of the Monarchs by selling his remaining half interest to Tom Baird in February 1948. Baird was a longtime associate who began working with Wilkinson in 1919 and who had served in many capacities prior to becoming a partner with Wilkinson.

During his years with the franchise, Wilkinson traveled with the team and looked after the best interests of his players, providing the best travel accommodations available and compensating the players generously. He was well liked and respected for his honesty by both his players and executives from other teams.

Willas, S.
Career: 1887   Position: player
Team: *New York Gorhams*

He was a player with the New York Gorhams, one of eight teams that were charter members of the League of Colored Baseball Clubs in 1887. However, the league's existence was ephemeral, lasting only a week. His position is uncertain.

Willburn
Career: 1926   Position: p
Team: Baltimore Black Sox

He pitched briefly with the Baltimore Black Sox in 1926, his only season in the Negro Leagues.

Willett, Pete
Career: 1923–28   Positions: 3b, ss, of
Teams: New York Lincoln Giants ('23), Cleve-

land Browns ('24), Homestead Grays ('25), Cleveland Tigers St. Louis ('28)

After beginning his career in 1923 as a substitute shortstop with the Lincoln Giants, he played as a reserve third baseman with two Cleveland teams, the Browns and the Tigers, during each team's only year in league play. He also played briefly with the Homestead Grays in 1925, when they were still playing an independent schedule.

Willetts
Career: 1933   Position: p
Team: Philadelphia Stars

He pitched with the Philadelphia Stars in 1933, the team's first year of existence, when they were playing as an independent ballclub before entering league play in 1934.

Williams
Career: 1910   Position: 2b
Team: St. Louis Giants

In 1910, during the team's formative years, he was a second baseman with the St. Louis Giants.

Williams
Career: 1914   Position: ss
Team: Philadelphia Giants

In 1914 he was a shortstop with the Philadelphia Giants when that once-proud team was already suffering a decline in quality.

Williams
Career: 1923   Position: rf
Team: Homestead Grays

He was a right fielder with the Homestead Grays in 1923, when they were still playing an independent schedule.

Williams
Career: 1930   Position: 1b
Team: Baltimore Black Sox

He appeared briefly as a first baseman with the Baltimore Black Sox in 1930, when they were playing as an independent ballclub.

Williams, A. D.
Career: 1925   Position: officer
Team: Indianapolis ABCs

In the years after C. I. Taylor's death, he served as an officer with the Indianapolis ABCs as they struggled to survive. The franchise folded a year after his short stay as an executive with the team.

Williams, A. N.
Career: 1922   Position: officer
Team: Pittsburgh Keystones

He served as an officer with the Pittsburgh Keystones in 1922, the team's only year in the Negro National League.

Williams, Al Sidney
Career: 1943–45   Position: p
Team: Newark Eagles

A wartime player, he pitched sparingly with the Newark Eagles for three seasons, losing his only decision in 1945.

Williams, Andrew (**Stringbean**)
Career: 1914–25   Positions: **p**, *of,*
                                    manager
Teams: **Brooklyn Royal Giants** ('14–'17, '21, '23), St. Louis Giants ('15), Indianapolis ABCs ('17–'18), Pennsylvania Red Caps of New York ('18), *Philadelphia Giants ('18),* Chicago American Giants ('19), Dayton Marcos ('19), Atlantic City Bacharach Giants ('20–'22, '24), Washington Potomacs ('23–'24), New York Lincoln Giants ('25)

This quiet, elongated hurler had a good curve and was a leading pitcher during the last five seasons of the deadball era, but his effectiveness diminished when the lively-ball era began. Beginning his career with the Brooklyn Royal Giants in 1914, when the Royals captured the eastern championship, he spent most of his career in the East but had stints in the West with the St. Louis Giants, the Indianapolis ABCs, and the Chicago American Giants before returning to the East Coast to finish his career. He also played in the Florida winter hotel league during his prime years, and matched Smokey Joe Williams in effectiveness during his stints in Palm Beach.

In August 1917 he left New York City and joined the ABCs, but during the next season he moved back to New York, with partial statistics showing a combined 11–11 record for the two seasons. In 1919 he jumped again, signing with Rube Foster's Chicago American Giants, where he had a 4–2 mark before leaving to join the Dayton Marcos for the remainder of the season. In 1920 he was back East for the remainder of his career, pitching with the Bacharachs for the first three years. In 1921 he split 4 decisions, but when Ben Taylor organized the Washington Potomacs in 1923, Williams jumped teams again. After pitching for the Potomacs until June of the following year, he jumped back to the Bacharachs and had a good season after his return. That year the Bacharachs' veteran hurler was second in age only to Smokey Joe Williams. In 1925 Stringbean Williams closed out his career with the New York Lincoln Giants, losing both of his decisions.

Williams, B.

Career: 1931–39   Position: of
Teams: Montgomery Grey Sox ('31), Indianapolis ABCs ('32, '39)

He was the regular center fielder, batting in the sixth slot, for the Indianapolis ABCs in 1932, when they played in the Negro Southern League. The franchise moved to Detroit the following year, but seven years later he made another appearance with the new ABCs franchise, but again the team relocated after the season.

Williams, Bilbo (**Biggie**)

Career: 1942–43   Position: rf
Teams: *Chicago Brown Bombers ('42)*, Baltimore Elite Giants ('43)

A wartime player, he was a reserve right fielder with the Baltimore Elite Giants in 1943, after having played the previous year with the Chicago Brown Bombers, a team of lesser status.

Williams, Bill

Career: 1899–1900   Position: p
Teams: Cuban X-Giants ('99), Genuine Cuban Giants ('00)

His pitching career consisted of two years, one in each century, pitching with the champion Cuban X-Giants in 1899 and the Genuine Cuban Giants in 1900.

Williams, Buck

Career: 1920   Position: p
Team: New York Lincoln Giants

In 1920 he was a reserve pitcher for the New York Lincoln Giants, but pitched with minimal effectiveness.

Williams, Charles

Career: 1887   Position: player
Team: *Boston Resolutes*

He was a player with the Boston Resolutes, one of eight teams that were charter members of the League of Colored Baseball Clubs in 1887. However, the league's existence was ephemeral, lasting only a week. His position is uncertain.

Williams, Charles Arthur (**Charlie**)

Career: 1924–33   Positions: ss, 2b, 3b
Teams: Memphis Red Sox ('25), Chicago American Giants ('26–'30), Chicago Columbia Giants ('31), Indianapolis ABCs ('31)
Born: 1908
Died: July 1931, Chicago, Ill.

One of the many players who learned baseball on the sandlots of Mobile, Alabama, as a chunky teenage middle infielder he began his professional career in 1925 playing shortstop with the Memphis Red Sox, but moved North to Chicago in 1926 to play with the Chicago American Giants. In 1927 he earned a starting position on the team, playing as the regular shortstop and batting in the lower part of the batting order. In his first two seasons with the team he fielded his position well and hit .223 and .252 as the American Giants won the Negro National League pennant each year and defeated the Eastern Colored League champion Bacharach Giants in both World Series. He continued with the American Giants for three more seasons, hitting .248 and .255 in 1929–30.

The next season was to be his last year in baseball and the last year of his life. Following Rube Foster's death in 1930, the American Giants encountered some financial difficulties under the new ownership, and the slick shortstop joined Dave Malarcher's Chicago Columbia Giants. However, early in the 1931 season he left to play with the Indianapolis ABCs, where he paired with second baseman John Henry Russell as a keystone tandem and batted in the fifth slot. With a bright future ahead of him, in July 1931 he died at the age of twenty-three of ptomaine poisoning.

Williams, Charles Henry (**Lefty**)
Career: 1915–34   Positions: p, *of*
Teams: **Homestead Grays** ('15–'34), Detroit Wolves ('32)
Bats: Left   Throws: Left
Height: 5'6"   Weight: 165
Born: Sept. 24, 1894, Madison County, Va.
Died: Apr. 26, 1952, Homestead, Pa.

Although slight in stature, this small curveballer accomplished big results and was one of the Homestead Gray's all-time best pitchers. The dependable left-hander pitched for the Grays for the entirety of his twenty-year career, during which he is credited with 540 wins out of 625 games pitched against all levels of competition. Included in these wins are 17 no-hitters, one of which was a perfect game. He was a mainstay on the Grays' teams of 1930–31, with the latter aggregation often considered the best black team of all time. In 1930 Williams won every game he pitched, logging a 29–0 record, including a key victory against the New York Lincoln Giants in the playoff for the eastern championship.

The Grays' ace disliked pitching under the lights and, despite his incredible success on the barnstorming trail, his record against league opponents was not as impressive. When owner Cum Posey joined the American Negro League in 1929, Williams finished the season with a 6–4 mark against league teams. After the 1930 season he was credited with a combined record of 4–2 against league opposition.

In the summer of 1932 Posey consolidated the Grays and the Detroit Wolves into a single franchise, and the Grays played out the remainder of both teams' schedules. Extra work never bothered Williams, and throughout his long career the rubber-armed hurler never had a sore arm. In addition to his expertise on the mound, he was also skilled at pocket billiards and was one of the dedicated card players on the Grays, loving to play the game of hearts almost as much as baseball.

Williams, Chester Arthur (**Chet**)
Career: 1930–43   Positions: **ss**, 2b, 3b
Teams: **Pittsburgh Crawfords** ('31– 38), Homestead Grays ('32–'33, '41–'42), Toledo Crawfords ('39), Philadelphia Stars ('39–'41), *Mexican League ('40),* Memphis Red Sox ('43), Chicago American Giants ('43)
Bats: Right   Throws: Right
Height: 5'9"   Weight: 180
Died: Dec. 25, 1952, Lake Charles, La.

The sparkplug of the infield for the Pittsburgh Crawfords in the '30s, this quick, flashy shortstop was one of the first quality players whom Gus Greenlee added to his roster after purchasing the team in 1931, and he remained an essential part of the nucleus of the great Crawford teams that sent five players to the Hall of Fame. An outstanding fielder, he could play either shortstop or second base equally well. On the bases he had both speed and quickness and posed a threat to steal. A solid hitter with appreciable power, he hit for averages of .302, .301, .319, .247, and .381 during the Crawfords' glory years, 1932–36. A ballplayer's ballplayer, the scrappy infielder "came to play," and his team value was recognized by teammates and opponents alike. His style of play was also appreciated by the fans, and he was selected to play in four consecutive East-West All-Star games in 1934–37.

With the defection of Satchel Paige, Josh

Gibson, Cool Papa Bell, and other players from the Crawfords in 1937, the halcyon years passed. Williams, who had previously been placed in the lower part of the batting order, was moved into the second slot for his last two seasons with the Crawfords, and he responded by hitting .348 in 1938. When the franchise left Pittsburgh to relocate in Toledo, the slick-fielding shortstop soon took his glove elsewhere, signing with the Philadelphia Stars, where he hit .291 while batting in the second slot. But his stay with the Stars was short, and in 1940 he jumped the team to play with Torreon in the Mexican League, where he hit .344 with 13 doubles, 5 triples, 7 home runs, and only 9 strikeouts in 74 games.

Returning to the United States after only one season in Mexico, he soon connected with Cum Posey, who sought him to fill a hole at shortstop for the Homestead Grays. Although he was past his prime, he fielded his position as expected and contributed a .250 batting average as the Grays annexed another Negro National League pennant. After a winter with Aquadilla in the Puerto Rican League, the veteran infielder split his playing time between shortstop and second base in 1942. As a part-time starter, his offensive production was reduced to a meager .160 batting average, but the Grays won their sixth straight pennant and played in the first World Series between the Negro National League and the Negro American League.

In 1943 he closed out his career, when he batted .270 while splitting his season between the Memphis Red Sox and the Chicago American Giants in the Negro American League. He also played in the Cuban League and averaged .298 during two winters on the island. Throughout his career he was a free spirit and often was involved in off-the-field escapades that could have resulted in serious consequences. Fewer than ten years after he played his last baseball game, the former All-Star shortstop was shot to death in a bar in Texas on Christmas Day 1952.

Williams, Clarence

Career: 1885–1912   Positions: c, ss, 3b, of, manager

Teams: *minor leagues ('85, 90)*, **Cuban Giants** ('85–89, '91, '92–'94), New York Gorhams ('91), Philadelphia Giants ('02), Cuban X-Giants ('03–'05), *Colored Capital All-Americans,* Smart Set ('12)

Bats: Right   Throws: Right

Born: Jan. 27, 1868, Harrisburg, Pa.

He joined the Cuban Giants, the first black professional team, in the latter part of their first season, and was their regular catcher for a decade. The Cuban Giants were the colored champions in 1887 and 1888, and were considered the top ballclub of the era, often playing as representatives of a host city in an otherwise all-white league. In 1887 and 1889 they represented Trenton, New Jersey, in the Middle States League, and in 1891 they represented Ansonia in the Connecticut State League. In 1890 Williams and Frank Grant defected to the Harrisburg team in the Eastern Interstate League. Altogether he hit an even .300 for his three seasons in organized baseball.

He began playing baseball as a teenager in his hometown of Harrisburg, Pennsylvania, playing left field for the local ballclub in 1882. The next season he became a catcher for the Middletown baseball club of Pennsylvania and progressed to the Williamsport professional baseball club in the early part of 1885 before joining the Cuban Giants.

He joined Sol White's Philadelphia Giants in 1902, their initial season, but jumped to the rival Cuban X-Giants the following year. In addition to his catching, he played infield and outfield positions and appeared with the Colored Capital All-Americans of Lansing, Michigan. Later in his career he became a manager, guiding the Smart Set as playing manager in 1912, his last season in black baseball.

In 1909 he was among a group of former Cuban Giants' players, including Frank Grant, George Williams, and Ben Holmes, who made plans to play a benefit game for an ailing Bud

Fowler, baseball's first black professional player.

Williams, Clarence
Career: 1938–40   Positions: p, of
Teams: Washington Black Senators ('38), Baltimore Elite Giants ('39–'40)

Beginning his career in 1938 with the ill-fated Washington Black Senators' franchise that folded during the second half of the season in their only year in the Negro National League, he pitched with the Baltimore Elite Giants for the next two seasons, posting a 4–0 mark in 1940.

Williams, Clyde (Lefty)
Career: 1947–50   Position: p
Team: Cleveland Buckeyes
Bats: Left   Throws: Left

Pitching with the Negro American League champion Cleveland Buckeyes in 1947, he registered a 2–0 league record. Although he was listed with the Buckeyes through the 1950 season, league statistics do not confirm his playing time.

Williams, Cotton
[see Williams, Robert (Bob, Cotton)]

Williams, E.
Career: 1929   Position: p
Teams: Chicago American Giants ('29), Homestead Grays ('29)

A pitching prospect with a good fastball, soon after arriving in Chicago to play with the Chicago American Giants, he ran afoul of the law and left town, joining the Homestead Grays. He was the brother of Charlie Williams.

Williams, E.
Career: 1943   Positions: rf, 3b, 2b, ss
Team: Newark Eagles

A wartime player, he could play in either the outfield or the infield, and was a utility reserve with the Newark Eagles in 1943.

Williams, E. J.
Career: 1887   Position: player
Team: *Washington Capital Citys*

He was a player with the Washington Capital Citys, one of eight teams that were charter members of the League of Colored Baseball Clubs in 1887. However, the league's existence was ephemeral, lasting only a week. His position was uncertain.

Williams, Eli (Eddie)
Career: 1943–45   Position: lf
Teams: Harrisburg-St. Louis Stars ('43), Kansas City Monarchs ('45)

A wartime player, this left fielder played with the Harrisburg-St. Louis Stars in 1943, before the team withdrew from league play to barnstorm with Dizzy Dean's All-Stars. Two years later he was a reserve outfielder with the Kansas City Monarchs, batting .270 in his last season in the Negro Leagues.

Williams, Elbert
Career: 1931–35   Position: p
Teams: Louisville White Sox ('31), Detroit Stars ('31), Monroe Monarchs ('32–'34), Brooklyn Eagles ('35)

Beginning his career in 1931, he split a pair of decisions while dividing the season between the Louisville White Sox and the Detroit Stars. He joined the Monroe Monarchs in the Negro Southern League in 1932, the only year the league was accorded major-league status, and made a final appearance in 1935 with the Brooklyn Eagles, posting a 2–1 record to close out his career.

Williams, F.
Career: 1927   Position: rf
Team: Birmingham Black Barons

He appeared briefly as a reserve right fielder with the 1927 Birmingham Black Barons, winners of the Negro National League's second-half title.

Williams, Felix (Jeff)
Career: 1950   Positions: 2b, 3b, of

Teams: Houston Eagles ('49–'50), Kansas City Monarchs ('50–'53)

Breaking in with the Houston Eagles in 1949, after the franchise moved from Newark to Texas, this infielder's best position was second base. After joining the Kansas City Monarchs, he also played third base in 1950 and outfield in 1953. By then the Negro American League was struggling to survive the loss of players to organized baseball and was strictly a minor-league operation.

Williams, Frank (Shorty)
Career: 1942–46   Position: of
Team: Homestead Grays ('42–'43, '46)

Beginning his career during the World War II years, this little line-drive hitter from Cincinnati was a reserve right fielder with the Homestead Grays in 1946, occasionally batting leadoff when in the lineup.

Williams, Fred
Career: 1922–25   Position: c
Teams: Brooklyn Royal Giants ('22), Washington Potomacs ('24), Harrisburg Giants ('24), Indianapolis ABCs ('25)

A backup catcher from Dallas, Texas, he was a very good receiver but weak on throwing and hitting, managing only a .161 batting average in 1924 as the third-string catcher with the Washington Potomacs. During the season, he was sent to Harrisburg as a temporary replacement after their regular catcher, Pepper Daniels, jumped the team. Later in the season he was recalled by Potomacs' manager Ben Taylor, but was not reserved by the club for 1925. After his first experience in league play, he made a final appearance with the Indianapolis ABCs in 1925 in a reserve capacity.

Williams, G.
Career: 1939   Position: ut
Team: Baltimore Elite Giants

In his only season in the Negro Leagues, he was a utility player with the Baltimore Elite Giants in 1939.

Williams, George
Career: 1928   Position: ss
Team: Cleveland Tigers

Playing with the last Cleveland entry in the Negro National League in 1928, he was a shortstop with the Tigers in their only season in league play.

Williams, George
Career: 1885–1902   Positions: **2b**, **1b**, 3b, of
Teams: *Argyle Athletics ('85)*, **Cuban Giants** ('86–'90), New York Gorhams ('91), Cuban X-Giants ('02)

One of the original players recruited by Frank P. Thompson to play on the ballclub at the Argyle Hotel in Babylon, New York, for the entertainment of the summer guests, he continued with the team after the end of the tourist season, as the team added more players to form the Cuban Giants, the first black professional team. Having gained experience with the Philadelphia Orions, a top amateur club, he ranked among the better players on the Cuban Giants, and although playing both infield and outfield, he was at his best as a second baseman. While he was with the team, the Cuban Giants were the colored champions in 1887 and 1888 and were considered the top ballclub of the era.

During his years with the Cuban Giants, the team often played as representatives of a host city in an otherwise all-white league. They represented Trenton, New Jersey, in the Middle States League in 1887 and 1889, and York, Pennsylvania, in the Eastern Interstate League in 1890. His career spanned eighteen seasons, and he also played with the other two top black teams of the era, the New York Gorhams and the Cuban X-Giants, before retiring from the diamond.

Williams, George W.
Career: 1886–88   Position: c
Team: Cuban Giants

A catcher from Philadelphia, he played with the first black professional team, the Cuban

Giants, for three years. His first game with the ballclub was June 9, 1886, when the Cubans played the major-league Philadelphia Athletics of the American Association in a contest that was rained out before enough innings had been played to be counted as an official game. At that time he was considered the team's best all-around player and coach, and he left the team after the 1888 season to coach the baseball team at Philadelphia Institute. Many years later, acting in conjunction with Frank Grant, Clarence Williams, and Ben Holmes, he planned to play a benefit game for an ailing Bud Fowler in 1909.

Williams, Gerard

Career: 1921–26   Positions: **ss**, 2b
Teams: Indianapolis ABCs ('21–'23), New York Lincoln Giants ('24–'25), Homestead Grays ('25–'26)

In 1924 the New York Lincoln Giants' pepperbox shortstop lacked an abundance of natural ability, but compensated for this shortcoming with his "indomitable spirit." Veteran manager Ben Taylor declared that it was "impossible for him to be quiet on the ballfield." He was a very good shortstop, good on ground balls, and had one of the best arms in baseball. He was only a fair hitter, but because of his speed on the bases and the compressed strike zone from his diminutive size combined with a camera eye and superior pitch selection, he was an excellent leadoff batter. With the Lincolns he also sometimes batted in the third slot, hitting .323 for the 1924 season.

The youngster began his career with the Indianapolis ABCs in 1921 as a reserve player, but after three seasons in Indianapolis and the death of C. I. Taylor, he jumped to the East when the new league was established. In 1925, the little shortstop left the New York Lincoln Giants to play with the Homestead Grays, and batted in the second slot for Cum Posey's team. In 1926 Williams was sought by Rube Foster, a superior judge of ability, who wanted to sign him for the Chicago American Giants.

However, Foster's efforts to negotiate satisfactory terms of transfer with the Grays were unsuccessful.

Williams, Graham H.

Career: 1929–32   Positions: **p**, 3b
Teams: Homestead Grays ('32), Monroe Monarchs ('32), *New Orleans Crescent Stars ('34)*

Pitching primarily with southern teams during his career in the early '30s, he also appeared at third base with the Homestead Grays in 1932.

Williams, Hank

Career: 1911–13   Positions: 3b, 2b, 1b
Teams: Brooklyn Royal Giants ('11), Mohawk Giants ('13)

A light-hitting infielder, he batted in the ninth position as a part-time starter at third base for the Brooklyn Royal Giants in 1911. He could also play first base and second base. After leaving the Royal Giants he played with the Mohawk Giants in 1913, when they fielded one of their stronger teams.

Williams, Harry

Career: 1917–22   Position: 3b
Team: Baltimore Black Sox

He began his diamond career with the Baltimore Black Sox when they were in their formative years. In 1917 he played third base and batted cleanup and remained in the starting lineup, batting in the heart of the order through the 1920 season. But as the team attained major-league status, he was dropped from the roster.

Williams, Harry

Career: 1931–46, 1950 Positions: **3b**, 2b, ss,
of, c, manager
Teams: Pittsburgh Crawfords ('31–'32, '36–38), New York Black Yankees ('32, '41–'44; '50), Baltimore Black Sox ('33), Homestead Grays ('33–'34, '42), Brooklyn Eagles ('35), Newark Eagles ('36), *Santo Domingo ('37)*, Toledo Crawfords ('39),

Venezuelan League ('39), Mexican League ('41), Harrisburg-St. Louis Stars ('43), Baltimore Elite Giants ('45), New York Cubans ('46; '50), *New Orleans Creoles ('47–'50)*
Bats: Right   Throws: Right
Height: 5'10"   Weight: 185

An underrated ballplayer, this hard-hitting Pittsburgh native could play any infield position. He had good speed and hustle, was slightly above average in the field, and was a pretty good hitter with about average power. The versatile infielder was always willing to make a jump that would prove more financially advantageous, and he played for ten different teams during his career.

He first began playing baseball with a sandlot team, the Pittsburgh Black Sox, and in 1928 was recruited along with his brother Roy, to play with the Pittsburgh Crawfords, then still a semipro team comprised of mostly young players. By 1931 he was one of only three remaining on the Crawfords from 1928 as the team continued to recruit new and more talented ballplayers.

Playing with the Crawfords in 1932, he was batting .268 when he left to join the New York Black Yankees for the remainder of the season, playing third base and batting second in the order. After a season in New York he moved sequentially to the Baltimore Black Sox and the Homestead Grays, where he played shortstop and batted second in the order in 1934. In 1935 he joined the Brooklyn Eagles, batting .339, and was a member of the Newark Eagles the following season, when owner Abe Manley consolidated the Brooklyn franchise with the Newark Dodger franchise. During the season, after less than a full year in Newark, he was traded back to the Crawfords, and was credited with a combined batting average of .229 for the season.

That winter, 1936–37, he played in Cuba with Santa Clara and led the league in both hitting and stolen bases, with a .349 batting average and 15 successful steals. Returning to the Crawfords in the spring, he jumped along

with Satchel Paige to Santo Domingo to join the Ciudad Trujillo team, but he batted only .227 while playing about half of the games. Back with the Crawfords in 1938, he played second base, batted fifth in the order, and hit a robust .403. But a year later he jumped the Crawfords again, this time to play in Venezuela, where he was a teammate of Ray Dandridge.

In 1941 he played 24 games with Tampico in the Mexican League, batting .270, before returning to the United States to finish the season. A decade after his first appearance in a Black Yankees' uniform, he returned to the New York aggregation, playing second base, shortstop, and third base while batting in the heart of the order and hitting an even .300 for the remainder of the 1941 season. After leaving the Black Yankees he played with the Baltimore Elite Giants in 1945, batting .248, and the New York Cubans in 1946, his last year as a player with a top Negro League team. He played with the New Orleans Creoles before ending up back with the Black Yankees in 1950 as a manager.

Williams, Henry (Flick)
Career: 1922–31   Positions: **c**, 2b, of, *1b, ss*
Teams: Kansas City Monarchs ('22–'23), Indianapolis ABCs ('24–'25, '31), St. Louis Stars ('26–'30)

This Oklahoman began his career in 1922 as a catcher with the Kansas City Monarchs, leaving after two seasons to join the Indianapolis ABCs and leaving again after two years to join the St. Louis Stars. With the Stars he found a home for five seasons, sharing the catching assignments while batting in the lower part of the order and hitting .293, .194, .297, and .309 for the years 1926–30, exclusive of 1928.

Williams, Honey
Career: 1938   Position: player
Team: Atlanta Black Crackers

He was added to the Atlanta Black Crackers'

roster in late June 1938 but had only a brief stay with the team.

Williams, James (Jim, **Big Jim**)
Career: 1936–48   Positions: **of,   1b,**
manager
Teams: New York Black Yankees ('36–'37, '40–'41, '44), Newark Eagles ('37), Homestead Grays ('37–'38), Toledo Crawfords ('39), Cleveland Bears ('40), New York Cubans ('42), Birmingham Black Barons, Atlanta Black Crackers, *Durham Eagles ('48)*
Bats: Right   Throws: Right
Height: 6'1"   Weight: 200

Big, strong, and fast, he could run, hit, and hit with power, but his fielding was unexceptional and his throwing arm was a bit lacking. A hard-playing competitor, he was termed aggressive by some but was called a dirty player by other observers. The hard-hitting outfielder batted behind Josh Gibson and Buck Leonard for the Homestead Grays in 1938, rapping the ball for a .363 average as the Grays easily won both halves of the split season, finishing with their highest winning percentage during their skein of nine consecutive Negro National League pennants. The following season he moved to the Toledo Crawfords in the Negro American League, where, batting in the third slot for manager Oscar Charleston, his performance earned him a spot in the 1939 East-West All-Star game.

Williams first joined the Grays in 1937, after brief stints with two other teams during the season. Beginning the year with the New York Black Yankees, he was sold to the Newark Eagles in April, but soon arrived with the Grays to fill a need in the batting order and to enable Raymond Brown to concentrate more on his pitching.

In 1940 he left the Crawfords to take the managerial reins of the Cleveland Bears, who were the transplanted Jacksonville Red Caps. He placed himself at first base and in the fifth slot in the batting order, but he was displaced at the helm before the season was over and returned to the Black Yankees. Back in New

York, he resumed the right-field position and his fifth spot in the batting order, but partial statistics show uncharacteristically low averages of .200 and .245. The next season he moved to the New York Cubans, batting cleanup, as he did when he returned for his third stint with the Black Yankees in 1944, when he hit .294 for the season.

Williams' remaining seasons were spent with southern ballclubs, including the Durham Eagles, a team of lesser quality. He closed out his dozen seasons in the Negro Leagues in 1948.

Williams, Jesse
Career: 1944–47   Positions: c, ss, of
Teams: Cleveland Buckeyes ('44–'47), Chicago American Giants ('44)
Born: Opelika, Ala.

Not to be confused with the shortstop of the Kansas City Monarchs of the same name, this player was signed off the Dayton, Ohio, sandlots in 1944 by the Cleveland Buckeyes. After being traded to the Chicago American Giants, he was released, and signed again by the Buckeyes as a utility man for the next three years. The Buckeyes won the Negro American League pennant in two of those years, 1945 and 1947. In the latter season he batted .222 as a reserve outfielder to close out his career in the Negro Leagues.

Williams, Jesse Harold
Career: 1939–50   Positions: ss, 2b, 3b, of
Teams: **Kansas City Monarchs** ('39–'47, *'51), Mexican League ('46),* Indianapolis Clowns ('48–'50), *minor leagues ('52–'54)*
Bats: Right   Throws: Right
Height: 5'11"   Weight: 160
Born: June 22, 1913, Henderson, Texas
Died: Feb. 27, 1990, Kansas City, Mo.

A Kansas City Monarchs' shortstop during the 1940s, Jesse was a flashy fielder with excellent range and who could go to either his left or his right for grounders. He had the best throwing arm in the league and had quick hands, getting the ball away fast. He was compared to major-league shortstop Eddie Miller by some observers. He was good at turning a double play and, considered one of classiest keystone performers, could play either side of the second sack. This versatility was manifested when he played in the East-West All-Star games in 1943 and 1945, playing both shortstop and second base while batting an even .500 with 4 RBIs in the two contests. He was a good bunter and was especially adept at the squeeze play. Although only a mediocre hitter with modest power, he was regarded as a dangerous hitter with with men on base, and in the 1942 World Series he was the leading hitter with a .471 average.

An all-around athlete, he played halfback on the Jackson High School Bears football team, winners of three straight Texas State championships in the late '20. He began his professional baseball career with the Black Spiders of Mineola, Texas, and joined Kansas City in 1939. After a year as a utility man, he assumed the starting shortstop position in 1940 and played on three straight Negro American League championship teams (1940–42), batting .217 and .236 the latter two years. During this time he usually batted near the bottom of the order, but during the war years he moved to the leadoff position for three seasons (1943–45), batting .259 and .253 the latter two years. During the 1945 season he moved over to second base to allow rookie Jackie Robinson to play shortstop.

Following the 1945 season, he jumped to San Luis of the Mexican League and afterward played in the Cuban winter league, batting .264. After returning to the United States, the tough competitor was plagued by bad luck. During a tour of the South by the Kansas City Monarchs, he suffered a blood clot in his right arm when hit by a ball in a night game, but he refused to leave the game. The next day in Waco, Texas, he broke his left arm in the fourth inning but completed the game despite the injury. However, he eventually had to make concessions to his injuries, and he lost substantial playing time as a result.

In 1948 he joined the Indianapolis Clowns and played with them for three years before returning to the Monarchs for the 1951 season. That winter he played with Chet Brewer's Kansas City Royals in the 1951 California winter league, and he entered organized baseball in 1952, after being sold to Vancouver in the Western International League, where he hit .251. Two years later he had 6 at-bats and 1 hit with Beaumont in the Texas League to close out his career.

Williams, Jim
Career: 1934–35   Positions: of, 1b
Teams: Newark Dodgers ('34–'35)

An outfielder-firstbaseman, he played with the Newark Dodgers in their two full seasons of existence, 1934–35.

Williams, Jim (Bullet)
Career: 1929–32   Position: p
Teams: Nashville Elite Giants ('29–'30), Cleveland Cubs ('31), Detroit Wolves ('32)

This fastball pitcher began his career in 1929 with owner Tom Wilson's Nashville Elite Giants, and accompanied the franchise to Cleveland in 1931, when they played as the Cubs. After the demise of the Negro National League at the end of the season, he joined the Detroit Wolves in the East-West League, winning both of his recorded league decisions before the collapse of the league.

Williams, Joe
Career: 1941   Position: ss
Team: Homestead Grays

He appeared as a shortstop with the Homestead Grays in 1941.

Williams, Joe
Career: 1946   Positions: of, 3b
Team: New York Black Yankees

He appeared as an outfielder with the New York Black Yankees in 1946.

Williams, John (Big Boy)
Career: 1926–38   Positions: **p, lf**, rf, 3b,
                                    cf, 1b

Teams: Dayton Marcos ('26), St. Louis Stars ('27–'31), Indianapolis ABCs ('31–'32), Detroit Stars ('33), Homestead Grays ('33–'34), Columbus Elite Giants ('35), Jacksonville Red Caps ('38)

During the five years that he pitched with the St. Louis Stars, the team captured three Negro National League pennants, 1928 and 1930–31. In the 1930 season he was in the regular rotation and was credited with a 7–3 league record. However, his best season was the previous year, when he finished with a 18–5 ledger for 1929. In his first year with the Stars, 1927, he posted a 4–2 league mark. He began his career with the Dayton Marcos in 1926, with a 2–7 mark for the weaker team. After leaving the St. Louis Stars, he played with the Indianapolis ABCs for two years and then had stops with the Detroit Stars, the Homestead Grays, and the Columbus Elite Giants. He also played in the outfield and at the corners, showing batting averages of .259 in 1927 and identical marks of .319 in both 1929 and 1930.

Williams, John (Joe)
Career: 1948   Positions: **1b**, of
Teams: Chicago American Giants ('48), *Indianapolis Clowns ('54–'55), Birmingham Black Barons ('55, '58)*

In 1948 he was the regular first baseman with the Chicago American Giants, batting in the sixth slot and hitting .234 for the season. After the decline of the Negro American League he played with the Indianapolis Clowns and Birmingham Black Barons on into the '50s, but the league was strictly a minor-league operation at that time.

Williams, John (**Johnny**, Nature Boy)
Career: 1944–48   Position: p
Teams: *Shreveport Sports ('35–'36), Cleveland Buckeyes ('37), Palmer House All-Stars ('40–'43), Chicago Brown Bombers ('42–'43),* Cincinnati-Indianapolis Clowns ('44–'45), Indianapolis Clowns ('46–'48), Kansas City

Monarchs ('46), *Chicago American Giants ('51–'52), minor leagues ('51–'55)*
Bats: Right   Throws: Right
Height: 6'2"   Weight: 208
Born: 1916, Shreveport, La.

Considered the ace of the pitching staff for the Indianapolis Clowns in 1946, this big right-hander posted a 5–4 league ledger and made his only All-Star appearance in that season's East-West game, yielding only 1 hit in a 2-inning stint. In the preceding two seasons he had years of 6–4, 2.00 ERA and 5–9, 3.40 ERA, while in 1948 he posted a 3–7 record and a 5.40 ERA. Before joining the Clowns the Chicago resident had pitched with teams of lesser caliber in the Chicago area, including the Palmer House All-Stars and the Chicago Brown Bombers.

In 1951 he embarked on a five-year career in organized baseball, with an 8–10, 2.57 ERA season with Elmira in the Eastern League. In each of the next two seasons he pitched only briefly with Elmira while playing with Hornell in the Pony League, where he posted a mark of 13–9 with a 2.13 ERA in 1952, and with Fond du Lac in the Wisconsin State League, where he showed a 9–5 record with a 3.93 ERA. During 1954–55 he pitched in only a handful of games before closing out his baseball career.

Williams, Joseph (Joe, **Smokey Joe,** Cyclone, Yank)
Career: 1905–32   Positions: **p**, *of*, *1b*, manager
Teams: *San Antonio Black Bronchos ('07–'09),* Chicago Giants ('10), **New York Lincoln Giants** ('11–'23), Mohawk Giants ('13), Chicago American Giants ('14), Atlantic City Bacharach Giants ('16), Hilldale Daisies ('17), Brooklyn Royal Giants ('24), **Homestead Grays** ('25–'32), Detroit Wolves ('32)
Bats: Right   Throws: Right
Height: 6'4"   Weight: 190
Born: April 6, 1885, Seguin, Tex.
Died: Mar. 12, 1946, New York, N.Y.

During the first half of its existence, Smokey

Joe Williams was to black baseball what Satchel Paige was to the latter half. Indeed, Williams made the footprints in which Satchel later walked. Old-timers who saw him play remember him as Satchel's equal, if not his superior.

With a fastball that earned him the nicknames "Cyclone" and "Smokey Joe," he was a dominant force in black baseball from his first appearance in the big time with Frank Leland's Chicago Giants in 1910 until his retirement from the Homestead Grays in 1932, a period of more than twenty years. In addition to his blinding speed, the tall fireballer had exceptional control and was a smart pitcher who in his later years compensated for his loss of velocity with cunning and know-how.

The big, hawk-nosed hurler, who was part Indian, reached his peak from 1912–23 while playing primarily for the New York Lincoln Giants. A 20-strikeout game was not uncommon during his prime, with his top effort coming when he engaged in a famous pitcher's duel against Chet Brewer in 1930 and "smoked" 27 batters while 1-hitting the Kansas City Monarchs in a 12-inning night game. Despite his success, Joe actually did not like pitching under the lights. Existing records indicate that his best all-around season came in 1914 when, pitching against all levels of competition, he registered 41 wins against only 3 losses. His record against black teams of major-league caliber was 12–2, with 100 strikeouts in 17 games. Statistics reconstructed from box scores show records of 8–2 and 18–3 for the 1912–13 seasons. During the latter year, the big Lincoln Giants' hurler averaged better than a strikeout per inning. He pitched with the Fe Stars for the winter of 1913–14, but went back to the New York Lincoln Giants for the regular season.

Ty Cobb considered him to be a "sure 30-game winner" if he had been able to pitch in the major leagues. This evaluation was well justified, as Joe compiled a lifetime record of 20–7 in exhibitions against major-league competition. Three of these games serve to showcase his exceptional talent, as each time he dueled the National League champions in post-season play. The first showdown was in 1912, when he shut out the world champion New York Giants, 6–0. A second matchup was in 1915, when he struck out 10 batters while throwing a 3-hit shutout at Grover Cleveland Alexander and the Philadelphia Phillies, winning by a score of 1–0. Joe's third extraordinary performance occurred in 1917, when he struck out 20 batters while no-hitting the New York Giants, although he lost the game, 1–0, on an error. Some sources indicate that during this game Hall of Famer Ross Youngs gave him the nickname "Smokey Joe." Another source indicates that the name originated from the 27-strikeout performance against the Kansas City Monarchs. Other sources suggest that he picked up the nickname because of Smokey Joe Wood of the Boston Red Sox, or from his appearance with the Homestead Grays in Pittsburgh, the Smokey City.

Wherever the origin of the moniker, it was an appropriate one. Joe Fero, a longtime semi-pro player-manager-owner, insisted that Williams was faster than Bob Feller, and described games that he, Fero, had witnessed involving the dark speedball artist. In one game, he pitched a no-hitter, with 25 strikeouts, but lost the game in the ninth inning on walks and errors. In another game he lost a 26-inning game against the Bushwicks on a "dinky hit and error." Fero also maintained that Williams beat the New York Giants twice in a 3-game series in the mid-teens.

The tall, dark Texan began his career around the ball diamonds in San Antonio, Texas, in 1905 and fashioned a five-year ledger (1905–09) of 28–4, 15–9, 20–8, and 32–8; at one stretch in his Texas career, Williams was credited with 20 straight wins. Only the 1906 season, spent with Austin, and the latter part of 1909, when he finished with the Birmingham Giants, were not played with the San Antonio Black Bronchos. The Bronchos often played the Birmingham Giants, owned by C. I. Taylor, and Williams frequently hooked up in a pitcher's duel against Johnny "Steel Arm" Taylor. Those game were classic mound duels, with a single run often making the difference in the score. Williams joined the Birmingham team in 1909 but soon got homesick and returned to Texas.

In the autumn, the big, hard-throwing youngster signed to play during the winter season with the Trilbys of Los Angeles, California, where he remained until he joined the Chicago Giants for the 1910 season. Owner Frank Leland described the new hurler for the homefolks, "If you have ever witnessed the speed of a pebble in a storm you have not even seen the equal of the speed possessed by this wonderful Texan Giant. He is the king of all pitchers hailing from the Lone Star State and you have but to see him once to exclaim, 'That's a-plenty!'

In the winter of 1911–12, Williams traveled to Cuba, where he finished with a 10–7 mark for the season and sported a lifetime 22–15 mark in Cuban League action. In the spring of 1912 he pitched with the Chicago American Giants on their western tour and compiled a 9–1 work sheet, which included victories over every Pacific Coast League team except Portland. Williams left Chicago to join the New York Lincoln Giants in 1912, teaming with Dick Redding for the first time, and pitched with the Lincolns through the 1923 season. A good hitter with power, he often played outfield or first base when not pitching and, during his tenure there, batted .320, .299, and .175 in 1912–14 and .281 in 1917.

He also served as captain and manager for several seasons. In 1919 he pitched an opening-day no-hitter against Dick Redding; the next year, he and Redding feuded and refused to shake hands with each other for a photographer. In 1921, Williams fashioned an 18–2 record through mid-August, and in 1922 he married a Broadway showgirl in New York. However, in the spring of 1924 Williams was released during a youth movement housecleaning, although he was still one of the best pitchers in the league. Signing with the Brook-

lyn Royal Giants, he again teamed with Dick Redding and, although Williams was the top pitcher for the Royals, he was released after the season and signed with the Homestead Grays.

In 1929 Grays' owner Cum Posey entered the team in the Negro American League, and Williams accrued a 12–7 record. The league folded after a single season, and the Grays returned to play as an independent ballclub. In 1930 the Grays added a new young catcher, Josh Gibson, to their lineup and the team won the eastern championship by winning a challenge series over the Lincoln Giants. The following season, with Gibson, Oscar Charleston, Jud Wilson providing the power and Williams as their ace pitcher, the Grays fielded what many consider to be the greatest black team of all time.

Williams added a dignity to the game and, in a 1952 survey conducted by the *Pittsburgh Courier,* he outpolled Satchel Paige by a single vote, 20–19, as the all-time best pitcher in the Negro Leagues. Of all the players who ever played in the era of Black baseball, Smokey Joe Williams is the greatest player not yet enshrined in the National Baseball Hall of Fame.

Williams, L.
Career: 1905–09   Position: of
Team: Cuban Giants ('06)

He was an outfielder with the Cuban Giants for five years during the first decade of the century.

Williams, L. C.
Career: 1939–42   Position: of
Teams: Ethiopian Clowns ('39), New York Cubans ('42)

He was in the starting outfield with the New York Cubans in 1942, usually batting fifth in the order. Earlier in his career he played with the Ethiopian Clowns.

Williams, Lefty
Career: 1938   Positions: p, *manager*
Teams: Atlanta Black Crackers, *Atlanta Lincoln Giants*

He was on the roster for the Atlanta Black

Crackers in mid-March of 1938 but may not have played with them in a league contest. Making his home in Atlanta, he was described as a former local semipro and organized baseball pitching star. Later in the spring of the 1938 season, after Mike Schaine sold the Atlanta Black Crackers, Williams became the manager of Schaine's Atlanta Lincoln Giants.

Williams, Lem

Career: 1923   Position: umpire
League: Negro National League

He was an umpire in the Negro National League in 1923.

Williams, Lemuel

Career: 1937–39   Position: p
Teams: St. Louis Stars ('37), Chicago American Giants ('39)

He pitched with the St. Louis Stars during the first season of the Negro American League, and with the Chicago American Giants in 1939.

Williams, Leonard (Len)

Career: 1950   Positions: 1b, of, 3b, p, ss, 2b

Teams: Indianapolis Clowns ('50–'51), *minor leagues ('52–'59)*
Bats: Right   Throws: Right
Height: 5'10"   Weight: 185
Born: 1928

A free-swinging power hitter, he played with the Indianapolis Clowns in 1950–51, during the declining years of the Negro American League. He could play in either the infield or the outfield, and when he entered organized baseball in 1952, he played first base and shortstop with Hartford in the Eastern League and compiled a .253 average in his first year. During the next three years with Evansville in the Three-I League, he played outfield and all infield positions while batting .306, .270, and .311.

The next two seasons represented the best offensive production of his career. In 1956 he hit .352 with Boise in the Pioneer League, and in 1957 he powered 43 home runs while hitting .316 with 113 RBIs and 115 strikeouts with

Topeka in the Western League. The next two seasons reversed the trend of the previous two years. In 1958, splitting the year with Charlotte in the Sally League and Fort Worth in the Texas League, his home-run power was down drastically—he managed only a combined 5 in 324 at-bats. In 1959, his last season, his average went down as well, as he hit a meager .161 with Lancaster in a brief stint with that club.

Williams, Leroy

Career: 1947–50   Positions: ss, 2b
Teams: Newark Eagles ('47–'48), Kansas City ('50–'51) *minor leagues ('50)*
Bats: Right   Throws: Right
Height: 5'10"   Weight: 169
Born: 1928

This middle infielder joined the Newark Eagles in 1947, when they were the defending champions of the Negro National League, and batted .215 for the year. Indirectly he owed his playing time to Monte Irvin and Larry Doby, who had been the keystone combination the previous season. In 1947 Irvin split his playing time between shortstop and center field, with Williams filling in at shortstop when Irvin was in the outfield. Later that year Doby signed with the Cleveland Indians, and in 1948 Williams became the regular second baseman, batting eighth in the order but showing good speed on the bases. In 1950, he began the season with the Kansas City Monarchs, hitting .308 with moderate power but also showing a high incidence of strikeouts for his short stint with the club. Most of that season was spent with Springfield in the Mississippi-Ohio Valley League, where he batted .280 for the remainder of the year before returning to the Monarchs in 1951.

Williams, M.

Career: 1931   Position: ss
Team: Pittsburgh Crawfords

In 1931 the Pittsburgh Crawfords began the season as a semipro team, but in midseason owner Gus Greenlee began stocking the team with quality talent. Williams was a shortstop with the team during this year of transition.

Williams, M.

Career: 1939–43   Position: p
Teams: Baltimore Elite Giants ('39), Newark Eagles ('43)
Bats: Right   Throws: Right

This right-hander pitched briefly in the Negro Leagues, making his first appearance with the Baltimore Elite Giants in 1939. He pitched again during the war years, with the Newark Eagles in 1943.

Williams, Marshall

Career: 1927–29   Positions: c, of
Teams: *Mobile Bears ('21–'24), Montgomery Grey Sox ('25), Memphis Red Sox ('26), Birmingham Black Barons ('26), Pittsburgh Crawfords ('27),* Homestead Grays (27), Detroit Stars ('28–'29), *Mobile Giants ('34)*
Born: Dec. 23, 1906, Whistler, La.
Bats: Right   Throws: Right
Height: 5'9"   Weight: 180
Born: Nov. 23, 1906, Mobile, Ala.

A catcher with a light bat and without long-ball power, he was a good bunter, but it was for his defensive skills that he was best known. He seldom had a passed ball and could throw from a squat. He had a good arm and is credited with throwing out Cool Papa Bell in their few encounters. He played baseball for more than thirty years, almost entirely with semipro or minor-league teams, but occasionally he would be "loaned out" to more prominent clubs, including the Memphis Red Sox and the Birmingham Black Barons, and he played briefly with the Homestead Grays and the Detroit Stars during the '20s. In later years, in the late '30s, he was picked up by the Grays to back up Josh Gibson for a few games when the star catcher was indisposed. A decade later he was sometimes picked up by Satchel Paige to catch in exhibition games that Satchel was pitching. But on these occasions he was a "ringer" and not on the regular roster.

He got his start in baseball in 1921 as a fourteen-year-old catcher with the Mobile Bears, when he volunteered to replace the injured regular receiver. After catching several games on a temporary basis, he became the regular catcher during the next season, and was called the "kid catcher" in the Negro Southern League. In 1925 he signed with the Montgomery Grey Sox, owned by Mr. Bird, a white official of the International Paper Mill. He played with the Pittsburgh Crawfords in 1927 as Josh Gibson's backup catcher, when the team was still a semipro outfit of youthful aspirants, but left the team after a few months to join the Homestead Grays in a reserve capacity.

In 1928 he played with the Detroit Stars and later played with several semipro teams in the Detroit area but always was available to travel when the opportunity presented itself. He is the uncle of Hall of Famer Billy Williams.

Williams, Marvin (Tex, Coqueta)

Career: 1943–50   Positions: 2b, 3b, 1b, of
Teams: Philadelphia Stars ('43–'46, '49), *Mexican League ('45, '48–'49, '51–'52, '59), Venezuelan League ('47),* Cleveland Buckeyes ('50), *minor leagues ('50, '52–'61)*
Bats: Right   Throws: Right
Height: 6'0"   Weight: 190
Born: Feb. 12, 1923, Houston, Tex.

A good hitter with power, this Philadelphia Stars' second baseman hit .338 in 1944 and appeared in the East-West All-Star game. The next spring, a year before Rickey signed Jackie Robinson, Williams joined Robinson and Sam Jethroe in a tryout with the Red Sox, but although they performed impressively, nothing resulted from their efforts. Returning to the Stars for the first part of the 1945 season, he recorded a .393 batting average and a .732 slugging percentage before jumping to the Mexico City Reds in the Mexican League, where he hit .362 and slugged .633 for the remainder of the year.

Playing with Vargas in the Venezuelan winter league, he led the league in doubles the next two winters. Back with Mexico City, he continued his offensive production with a .381 batting average and a .583 slugging percentage in 1948, and a .316 batting average and a .534

slugging percentage in 1951. He was selected to the Mexican All-Star team each of these seasons, batting a perfect 3-for-3 in the 1951 game. He split the 1950 season between the Cleveland Buckeyes of the Negro American League and the Sacramento of the Pacific Coast League, recording identical .250 batting averages in each.

For the next decade he continued his baseball journeys through organized baseball, winning batting titles with Chihuahua in 1952 (.401) and Vancouver in 1954 (.360). At Chihuahua he also led the league in home runs (45) and had 131 RBIs while being walked 117 times in 117 games. In 1956–58 he played with Tulsa in the Texas League, hitting .322, .253, and .294 before taking another trip south of the border in 1959, where he hit .310 and led the league with 29 home runs. After his Mexican finale, he played two more years in the Texas League before retiring after the 1961 season. Altogether he played with a dozen different teams in organized baseball but never in the major leagues.

Williams, Mathis (**Matt**, Rod)
Career: 1922   Positions: ss, 3b
Teams: Pittsburgh Keystones ('21–'22), Cleveland Tate Stars ('22–'23)

Playing on marginal teams, this infielder began his career with the Pittsburgh Keystones but joined the Negro National League's Cleveland Tate Stars as the regular shortstop during the 1922 season, hitting seventh in the batting order; he played third base with the team in 1923.

Williams, Morris (Stringbean)
Career: 1920–21   Positions: p
Teams: *San Antonio Black Aces ('20)*, Indianapolis ABCs ('20–'21)

This tall hurler began his professional career in Texas with the San Antonio Black Aces in 1920, but joined the Indianapolis ABCs that same season. Pitching with the ABCs in the first two seasons of the Negro National League,

he posted a 1–3 league mark in 1921, his last season with a top club.

Williams, Nelson M.
Career: 1887   Position: manager
Team: *Washington Capital Citys*

He managed the Washington Capital Citys, one of eight teams that were charter members of the League of Colored Baseball Clubs in 1887. However, the league's existence was ephemeral, lasting only a week.

Williams, Norm
Career: 1930   Position: of
Team: Nashville Elite Giants

He was an outfielder with the Nashville Elite Giants in 1930, their first season in the Negro National League.

Williams, Peanuts
Career: 1910   Position: 3b
Team: Kansas City Royal Giants

A good bunter, he played third base with the 1910 Kansas City Royal Giants.

Williams, Phil (**Pete**, Bo)
Career: 1931–39   Positions: 2b, 3b
Teams: Baltimore Black Sox ('31), Jacksonville Red Caps ('34), Toledo Crawfords ('39)

A marginal player, he had a checkered career in the Negro Leagues, beginning his career as a reserve third baseman with the Baltimore Black Sox in 1931, playing third base with the Jacksonville Red Caps in 1934, and closing out his career as a reserve second baseman with the Toledo Crawfords in 1939.

Williams, Phillip
[see Cockrell, Phil]

Williams, Poindexter
Career: 1921–33   Positions: c, 1b, manager
Teams: Chicago American Giants ('21), Detroit Stars ('21–'22), **Birmingham Black Barons** ('23–'29), Louisville White Sox ('30–'31),

Nashville Elite Giants ('30, '32–'33), Homestead Grays ('33)

Bats: Right   Throws: Right
Height: 6'0"   Weight: 200

A catcher with a good arm and a fair hitter, he registered batting averages of .381, .309, and .308 in 1927, 1929, and 1930, respectively. Beginning his career in 1921, he was locked in as a backup catcher with Rube Foster's Chicago American Giants, and made the jump to the Detroit Stars, where he broke into the starting lineup and batted in the sixth slot. After leaving the Stars he found a home with the Birmingham Black Barons, batting in a power slot while playing both catcher and first base with the franchise throughout the remainder of the decade. He was credited with a batting average of .389 in 1925 with the Black Barons. In 1930 he joined Tom Wilson's Nashville Elite Giants briefly. He served a stint with the Louisville White Sox as their catcher and cleanup hitter in 1931, their only year in the Negro National League. In 1933 he joined the Homestead Grays as a backup receiver.

Williams, Ray

Career: 1933–39   Position: p
Team: New York Black Yankees

He pitched with the New York Black Yankees during the '30s and is credited with seven seasons with the ballclub.

Williams, Ray

Career: 1950   Positions: p, of
Team: New York Black Yankees

His career began during the 1950 season, when the New York Black Yankees were playing as an independent team and struggling to survive the loss of players to organized baseball. In addition to pitching, he could play in the outfield.

Williams, Rhiny (Red)

Career: 1926, 1938   Positions: ss, manager
Team: Indianapolis ABCs

Appearing briefly as a shortstop for the Indianapolis ABCs in 1926, the last season of the

franchise before its demise, he batted .278 in only 4 league contests. A dozen seasons later, in 1938, he returned to Indianapolis at the helm of the new ABCs franchise in the Negro American League.

Williams, Robert (Bob, **Cotton**)

a.k.a. Cotton; Coton
Career: 1943–50   Positions: **p**, of, 3b, ss, 2b

Teams: Newark Eagles ('43–'48), Houston Eagles ('49–'50), *New Orleans Eagles ('51), Philadelphia Stars ('51)*

Bats: Right   Throws: Right
Height: 5'9"   Weight: 165

In 1943 this rookie from Maryland came to training camp as an infielder, but threw so hard the other infielders complained, and manager Mule Suttles decided to convert him to a pitcher. After watching him pitch two games, the skipper was convinced that he would make a successful pitcher. However, while he had a good fastball, his other pitches failed to match his velocity, and his improvement as a moundsman was not substantial. Although he never became a front-line pitcher, he posted a 6–4 mark in 1947. Throughout his career he continued to play other positions, often filling in as an outfielder or at third base, and in limited play in 1947 he hit .216. Sometimes he was listed in the box scores only as Cotton.

Williams, Robert Lawns (**Bobby**)

Career: 1918–34, 1945 Positions: **ss**, 2b, 3b, *of*, manager

Teams: *Dayton Giants ('17),* **Chicago American Giants** ('18–'25, '28), *military service ('18–'19),* Indianapolis ABCs ('26, '32), Homestead Grays ('26–'27), Cleveland Tigers ('28), Atlantic City Bacharach Giants ('30), Pittsburgh Crawfords (*'30–*'32), Columbus Blue Birds ('33), Akron Tyrites ('33), Cleveland Giants ('33), Cleveland Red Sox ('34)

Bats: Right   Throws: Right
Height: 5'5"   Weight: 145
Born: Sept. 30, 1895, New Orleans, La.
Died: Dec. 30, 1978, Chicago, Ill.

A great little shortstop for the 1920–22 champion Chicago American Giants, this slick fielder could play any infield position and, although a weak hitter, he was a good bunter, and his exceptional speed on the bases often made things happen, fitting nicely into Rube Foster's racehorse brand of baseball. Williams, who had attended Xavier College in New Orleans with David Malarcher, played semipro ball with the New Orleans Eagles and was picked up by Foster to replace John Henry Lloyd. After a good showing in the winter hotel league in Palm Beach, Florida, he was inserted into the starting lineup for the 1918 season. The media publicized him heavily as Lloyd's replacement, and the public was receptive to his scrappy style of play. A headfirst slide into first while attempting to beat out a bunt demonstrated characteristics of his style that old-timers loved to see.

Once during the season, Williams failed to show up for one game and was seen before the game wandering unsteadily down a local street, which caused some alarm about the possibility of an "abduction." But despite such problems, he was off to a good start for the 1918 season when he was drafted into service in midsummer and finished with a .224 batting average. While he was in France with the 803rd Pioneer Infantry, he was replaced in the American Giants' lineup by former great pitcher José Mendez, who had extended his playing career as an infielder.

Discharged in March, Williams was back in the lineup for the 1919 season, and continued as the starting shortstop with the American Giants as they annexed the first three Negro National League pennants, 1920–22. In the latter season he was working in the post office and did not make the trip South with the American Giants for spring training. However, he remained with the club, usually batting at the bottom of the order. In 1925 he was placed in the second slot by Foster, before Williams left the following March with Bingo DeMoss, who was handed the reins as the new manager of the Indianapolis ABC's. Before the season was over, Williams had jumped to Cum Posey's Homestead Grays and batted leadoff after joining the team. After another full season as the Grays' regular shortstop in 1927, he returned to the Chicago American Giants in 1928 in a reserve capacity.

Moving back East, he was playing with the Bacharach Giants when Gus Greenlee signed him to manage the Pittsburgh Crawfords in 1930. Williams brought in his old friends with him, while playing second base and third base himself, and that marked the beginning of the Crawfords' rise to prominence. However, as Greenlee brought in more talent in 1932, the veteran infielder and his .185 batting average became expendable, and he was replaced as manager. He remained as a player-coach for part of the season, but that proved to be his last year in Pittsburgh. He then played with some of the marginal teams, in Ohio who were trying to establish a quality league ballclub and survive the Depression. Included among these teams were the Columbus Blue Birds, the Akron Tyrites, the Cleveland Giants, and the Cleveland Red Sox. Williams played third base with Akron and second base for the other teams.

Williams, Roy K.
Career: 1931–41   Position: p
Teams: Pittsburgh Crawfords ('31–'32), Homestead Grays ('31), Columbus Blue Birds ('33), Baltimore Black Sox ('33), Philadephia Stars ('33), Brooklyn Royal Giants ('34), Brooklyn Eagles ('35), *voluntarily retired ('36–'37)*, New York Black Yankees ('38–'40), Baltimore Elite Giants ('40–'41)
Bats: Right   Throws: Right
Height: 6'0"   Weight: 180
Born: 1909
Died: April 1944

Williams was a pal of Josh Gibson and was with the Grays prior to signing again with the Crawfords in 1932. Owner Gus Greenlee signed him as an inducement to get Gibson also to jump to the Crawfords. Williams played with the Pittsburgh Black Sox, a local semipro team, and was recruited along with his brother Harry in the late '20s to play with the Pittsburgh Crawfords. By 1931 he was one of only three players remaining on the team from 1928 as Greenlee continued to recruit new players, and Williams himself left before the end of 1931. But he was lured back into the fold by Greenlee's ploy, and responded with a 4–2 record for the 1932 season.

After leaving the Crawfords he pitched with a series of teams without significant success, posting a mark of 7–8 in 1933 with the Philadelphia Stars. After stints with the Brooklyn Royal Giants and the Brooklyn Eagles, he suffered an arm injury in 1936 and retired. Later he tried to make a comeback, appearing with the Black Yankees and the Baltimore Elite Giants, posting marks of 6–2 and 7–3 with the Elites in 1940–41. Aside from his pitching he was an average fielder, and as a batter he did not hit with power.

Williams, *Sidney*
[see Williams, Al Sidney]

Williams, Samuel C. (**Sam,** Sammy)
Career: 1947–50   Position: p
Teams: Birmingham Black Barons ('47–'52), *minor leagues ('52–'56), Mexican League ('57–'58)*
Bats: Left   Throws: Right
Height: 6'1"   Weight: 155
Born: 1923

In his second season with the Birmingham Black Barons, he fashioned a 6–3 record with a 3.21 ERA as they copped the Negro American League pennant. The team lost to the Negro National League Homestead Grays in the last World Series between the two leagues. The next two seasons he posted records of 8–6 with a 3.21 ERA and 13–7 with a 3.81 ERA.

After starting the 1952 season with the Black Barons, he pitched with Brandon in the Mandak League and Wisconsin Rapids of the Wisconsin State League. In 1953 and 1954 he pitched with Pampa of the West Texas-New Mexico League, registering seasons of 25–12

(5.13 ERA) and 15–10 (4.64 ERA). Between the years 1954 and 1957 he also pitched with teams in the Texas League, the Northwest League, the Midwest League, and the California League, with his best season coming with San Jose (15–9, 3.10 ERA) in 1956. In 1957 he pitched most of the year with Vera Cruz in the Mexican League, splitting 16 decisions, and finished his career in Mexico the following year with a 9–11 mark with Poza Rico.

Williams, Shorty
Career: 1945   Position: player
Team: Homestead Grays

A native of Cincinnati, he joined the military service from the Grays' roster, apparently before actually appearing in a game. His position is uncertain.

Williams, Stringbean
[see Williams, Andrew (Stringbean)]

Williams, Stuart
Career: 1950   Positions: ss, 2b
Team: Cleveland Buckeyes

This middle infielder batted .267 while playing both keystone positions with the Cleveland Buckeyes in 1950, when the Negro American League was struggling to survive the loss of players to organized baseball.

Williams, T.
Career: 1896–1905   Positions: **c**, of
Team: Cuban X-Giants

For a decade, bridging the turn of the century, he was a catcher for the Cuban X-Giants, one of the dominant teams of the era.

Williams, Thomas (**Tom**)
Career: 1916–25   Position: p
Teams: Atlantic City Bacharach Giants ('16, '22), **Chicago American Giants** ('16–'18, '20–'25), Hilldale Daisies ('18–'19), New York Lincoln Giants ('18, '22), Brooklyn Royal Giants ('18), Chicago Giants ('25), Detroit Stars ('24)

Bats: Right   Throws: Right
Died: Jan. 25, 1937, Chicago, Ill.

He was one of Rube Foster's top pitchers with the Chicago American Giants for a decade, and his career spanned the deadball era and the lively-ball era. Beginning his career in 1916, while he was still a student at Morris Brown College, he pitched until being released in 1925. The right-handed hurler was a very smart pitcher, changed speeds well, and utilized a varied repertory that included a good assortment of curves to complement a drop, spitter, fastball, and slow "floater." He also had good pickoff moves to both first base and second base, utilizing a snap throw to either station.

After making appearances with both the Bacharachs and the American Giants the preceding season, he joined the American Giants in early May 1917, posting a 10–2 mark for the season. In 1918 he began with the American Giants, but moved East and pitched with a trio of teams—Hilldale, the Lincoln Giants, and the Brooklyn Royal Giants—showing a combined record of 10–0 for the year. He pitched another year with Hilldale, 1919, before returning to the American Giants' fold, where he posted marks of 12–7 in 1921, 6–1 in 1923, and 9–4 in 1924. The following spring he was unconditionally released by Foster, along with a large number of other veteran players, in a youth movement.

Williams, V.
Career: 1929   Position: c
Team: St. Louis Stars

He was a reserve catcher with the St. Louis Stars in 1929, his only season in the league.

Williams, Vinicius J. (**Nish**, Zeke)
Career: 1927–39   Positions: **c**, rf, lf, 3b, 1b, 2b, manager
Teams: **Nashville Elite Giants** ('27–'34), Cleveland Cubs ('31), Columbus Elite Giants ('35), Washington Elite Giants ('36–'37), Birmingham Black Barons ('37–'38), Atlanta Black Crackers ('38), Indianapolis ABCs ('39)

Bats: Left   Throws: Right
Height: 6'2"   Weight: 185
Born: Atlanta, Ga.
Died: Sept. 2, 1968, Atlanta, Ga.

A catcher whose only liability was a weak throwing arm, he was better known as a good clutch hitter. Strictly a fastball hitter, he was a pull hitter and could hit the long ball. Playing primarily with the Elite Giants, his bat kept him in the Negro Leagues for thirteen years. During his career he also played in both the infield and the outfield, and he is the father of former major-leaguer Donn Clendenon.

In 1938 he was still under contract to Tom Wilson's Elite Giants, but was selected to manage the new Negro American League Atlanta team and secured his release from the Elites by letting Wilson have his pick of any Atlanta player. At that time, there were two teams in Atlanta, with Williams and Don Pelham, the manager of the Atlanta Black Crackers, competing for the best playing talent in the area. Fortunately, Williams was able to get the better end of the split. When the Harden-Baker owner combination bought out Atlanta Black Crackers' owner Mike Schaine and took the name Black Crackers, Williams was retained as manager of the consolidated team.

Born in Atlanta, he attended Morehouse College and was a favorite with fans and liked by his players. But as a rookie manager he was subjected to much second-guessing and interference by owners John Harden and W. B. Baker. In mid-June, as the problems mounted and friction increased, he was given his unconditional release as manager by owner John Harden, and was replaced by a Lundy-Pelham brain trust for the remainder of the first half. At the beginning of the second half, Dick Lundy chose to play with the Newark Eagles, and Gabby Kemp returned from the Jacksonville Red Caps and took the helm. Williams returned to Nashville after his dismissal, but played with the Birmingham Black Barons for the second half of the 1938 season, as an outfielder and first baseman, while batting in the heart of the order. In 1939, when the Atlanta Black Crackers moved to Indianapolis and played as the ABCs, he shared the catching duties and batted third in the order.

Williams, Walter
Career: 1898   Position: p
Team: *Celeron Acme Colored Giants*

He was a pitcher with the all-black Acme Colored Giants' team that played in the Iron and Oil League as representatives of Celeron, New York, in 1898. Both the team and the league folded in July, and it was to be the last time a black team played in a white league.

Williams, Walter
Career: 1939   Position: p
Team: Newark Eagles

He pitched briefly with the Newark Eagles in 1939, his only appearance in the Negro Leagues.

Williams, Willie
[see Williams, Woodrow Wilson (Woody, Willie)]

Williams, Willie
Career: 1929–33   Positions: ss, 2b
Teams: Atlantic City Bacharach Giants ('29), Brooklyn Royal Giants ('30–'33)

He began his career as a shortstop with the Bacharach Giants in 1929, and played second base with the Brooklyn Royal Giants during the early '30s. Although the comparison may have been exaggerated, he prided himself on being called the black Hans Wagner.

Williams, Willie C. (**Curley**)
Career: 1945–50   Positions: **ss**, 3b, 2b, of
Teams: Newark Eagles ('45–'48), Houston Eagles ('49–'50), *New Orleans Eagles ('51), minor leagues ('51–'53)*
Bats: Left   Throws: Right
Height: 5'10"   Weight: 175
Born: 1923, Holly Hill, SC

This Newark Eagles' infielder had disparate seasons in 1945 and 1947, with batting and slugging averages of .333 and .621 in 1945 compared to .215 and .280 in 1947. In 1948 the little infielder was the regular shortstop for the Eagles, batting second in the order. While adequate afield, he was a light hitter and not a good base runner. When the Eagles moved to Houston he compiled averages of .290 and .292 in 1949–50, with a slugging percentage of .488 the latter year. In 1951 he entered organized baseball, with Colorado Springs, hitting .297, and then split the next year between Toledo in the American Association (.234) and Scranton in the Eastern League (.268). His last season was with Carman in the Mandak League in 1953, where he hit .286 with 12 home runs.

Williams, Wilmore
Career: 1943   Position: of
Team: Newark Eagles

A wartime player, he appeared as an outfielder with the Newark Eagles in 1943.

Williams, Woodrow Wilson (**Woody**, Willie)
Career: 1933–41   Position: p
Teams: Akron Tyrites ('33), Washington Elite Giants ('37), Baltimore Elite Giants ('38–'39), Birmingham Black Barons ('41)
Bats: Left   Throws: Left

A left-handed pitcher, he joined the Elites Giants in 1937, when they were based in Washington, and he moved with the franchise to Baltimore in 1938. He pitched creditably in 1939 and early 1940, but came up with a sore arm and was out for the remainder of the season. He had made an undistinguished appearance with the Akron Tyrites in 1933 and closed his career with the Birmingham Black Barons in 1941.

Williams, Zeke
[see Williams, Vinicius J. (Nish, Zeke)]

Williamson
Career: 1916   Positions: lf, rf
Team: Atlantic City Bacharach Giants

In 1916, during the team's formative years,

he was a reserve outfielder with the Bacharach Giants.

Willis, Jim (Cannonball)

Career: 1927–39   Positions: **p**, of
Teams: **Nashville Elite Giants** ('27–'34), Birmingham Black Barons ('28), Cleveland Cubs ('31), Philadelphia Stars ('33), Columbus Elite Giants ('35), Washington Elite Giants ('36–'37), Baltimore Elite Giants ('38–'39)
Bats: Right   Throws: Right

This right-handed fastball pitcher spent most of his career with Tom Wilson's Elite Giants at four different franchise locations, posting marks of 2–5 and 5–8 in 1929–30, when the team was in Nashville. His only stints away from Wilson's teams were in 1928, with the Birmingham Black Barons, and in 1933, when he joined Webster McDonald's Philadelphia Stars in their first season. Pitching with the Stars, he finished with a 4–6 composite record for the 1933 season.

Willis, S.

Career: 1887   Position: player
Team: *New York Gorhams*

He was a player with the New York Gorhams, one of eight teams that were charter members of the League of Colored Baseball Clubs in 1887. However, the league's existence was ephemeral, lasting only a week. His position is uncertain.

Wilmington Potomacs

Duration: 1925   Honors: None
Affiliation: Independent ('25)

Formerly the Washington Potomacs, the franchise moved to Wilmington in 1925 and attempted to survive as an independent ballclub, but folded early in the year.

Wills

Career: 1911   Position: 3b
Team: Brooklyn Royal Giants

He was listed as a third baseman for the Brooklyn Royal Giants in 1911. This may possibly be the same player as Hank Williams.

Wilmore, Alfred Gardner (**Al**, Apples)

Career: 1946–50   Position: p
Teams: *military service ('43–'46)*, Philadelphia Stars ('46–'47), Baltimore Elite Giants ('48–'50)
Bats: Right   Throws: Right
Height: 6'1"   Weight: 180
Born: Nov. 15, 1924, Philadelphia, Pa.

An overhand pitcher with the three basic pitches in his repertory, his best pitch was a fastball. After beginning his career with the Philadelphia Stars in 1947, he pitched with the Baltimore Elite Giants for the next three seasons. In the spring of 1949 he was considered the most improved pitcher on the staff and fashioned a 10–6 record for the year and earned a trip to the East-West All-Star game. He could field his position and was a fair slap hitter, but he lacked power and had difficulty hitting the curveball, as evidenced by his .105 batting average in 1950.

After leaving the Stars, he pitched with Winnipeg in the Mandak League in 1951. The next year he became one of the first black players to sign with the Philadelphia Athletics, and played with their farm team in Lincoln, Nebraska. During the spring he was in a group of three players who became the first black players to appear in the ballpark at Savannah, Georgia. Later in the season he suffered a rotator cuff injury but chose not to have the recommended operation. Instead, he returned to Philadelphia and tended bar for several years, until gaining employment at the Philadelphia Housing Authority, where he worked for twenty years until his retirement in 1989.

Born and reared in Philadelphia, he picked up the nickname "Apples" at a very young age, when he would use his money to buy apples instead of candy, and then eat the entire apple, seeds and all, except for the stem. In high school he was small for his size, but began pitching on the playgrounds in South Philly, and after several no-hitters was discovered by Philadelphia Stars' manager Goose Curry.

However, in 1943 he went into the Army,

serving in the South Pacific with the 595th field artillery unit in the 93rd Division but pitching for the 369th Infantry baseball team. Another Negro League player, Charlie Biot, was on the team. Wilmore matured in the service, and after his discharge he joined the Philadelphia Stars. While with the Stars and the Elite Giants, he played two winters in Latin American leagues, playing in Cuba in 1949–50, and in Panama the previous year under manager Buster Haywood. That winter he hurt his arm for the first time, while carrying a no-hitter into the ninth inning with two outs before losing his bid for the elusive gem.

Wilson
Career: 1917   Position: ss
Team: Atlantic City Bacharach Giants

He appeared as a shortstop with the Bacharach Giants in 1917, his only year in black baseball.

Wilson
Career: 1927   Position: c
Team: Harrisburg Giants

His brief appearance as a reserve catcher with the Harrisburg Giants in 1927 marked his only year in the Negro Leagues.

Wilson
Career: 1946   Position: c
Team: Philadelphia Stars

He was listed as a reserve catcher with the Philadelphia Stars in 1946, his only year in the Negro Leagues.

Wilson
Career: 1950   Position: p
Team: Cleveland Buckeyes

In 1950, when the Negro American League was struggling to survive the loss of players to organized baseball, he pitched in a game with the Cleveland Buckeyes and suffered the loss.

Wilson, Alec
Career: 1939   Position: of
Team: New York Black Yankees

In 1939, his only year in the Negro Leagues, he appeared briefly as an outfielder with the New York Black Yankees.

Wilson, Andrew
Career: 1923   Positions: of, p
Teams: *New Orleans Crescent Stars ('22)*, Milwaukee Bears ('23), *Chicago Giants ('24–'27)*

He played center field and pitched with the Milwaukee Bears in 1923, their only season in the Negro National League. Previously he played left field for the New Orleans Crescent Stars in 1922, and later he was with the Chicago Giants, although the ballclub had dropped out of league competition.

Wilson, Arthur Lee (**Artie**)
Career: 1944–48   Position: ss
Teams: **Birmingham Black Barons** ('44–'48), *minor leagues ('49–'57, '62)*, major leagues ('51)
Bats: Left   Throws: Right
Height: 5'10"   Weight: 160
Born: Oct. 28, 1920, Springville, Ala.

The Birmingham Black Barons' crack shortstop Artie Wilson was an ideal leadoff batter. A left-handed opposite-field hitter, he notched averages of .346 in 1944 and .374 in 1945, finishing second to Sam Jethroe each time. Wilson slipped to .288 in 1946 before finally winning batting titles of his own in 1947–48 with averages of .370 and .402, respectively.

The speedster was also an asset on the bases, finishing among the leaders in stolen bases each season. A superior defensive shortstop who was a master at the double play, he was generally regarded as the best shortstop in black baseball during the '40s. In his five years in the Negro American League (1944–48) he appeared in four East-West All-Star games, missing only the 1945 contest, and helped the Black Barons win three pennants (1943–44 and 1948). Unfortunately, the Black Barons lost the World Series to the Negro National League champion Homestead Grays in each instance.

As a youngster, Wilson taught himself to hit with a rubber ball and broomstick, and as he got older, he would play with a ball made from wrapping thread around a golf ball. He bought his first uniform for $2.98, earning the money by shining shoes. At age sixteen he began attending school three days a week and working at the Acipico Pipe Company two days a week. While working there he lost his thumb in an accident. But he also honed his baseball skills playing semipro baseball with the company's team in the Birmingham Industrial League prior to signing with the Black Barons.

He left the Negro Leagues and made the transition to the major leagues with the New York Giants after the color barrier was lifted. During this time he and Luis Marquez were the center of a controversy between the New York Yankees and the Cleveland Indians, but Commissioner Happy Chandler resolved the disagreement on May 13, 1949, by ruling that Wilson was the property of the Yankees.

The circumstances surrounding the controversy began after he led the Negro American League in batting in 1948 and spent the ensuing winter as player-manager in Mayagüez, Puerto Rico. He was hitting about .370 in the latter part of January when he was scouted by Yankee scout Tom Greenwade. Wilson was making $750 per month at Birmingham, but when approached about signing an AAA contract for a maximum of $500 per month with the Yankees, he responded that he was just interested in getting a chance at the major leagues and that "salary is not important." Acting in good faith, the Yankees' Larry MacPhail negotiated with Tom Hayes, Jr., owner of the Black Barons, who accepted the terms for transferring the contract. However, Wilson changed his mind, wanting a higher salary and a portion of the sale price, and in February both Wilson and Hayes wired MacPhail that the deal was off. Subsequently Hayes entered into an agreement with Abe Saperstein, representing the Cleveland Indians, to sell Wilson's contract for a higher amount. Chandler declared this to be null and void and that he was the property of the Yankees' Newark farm team.

After the financial maneuverings were settled, Wilson entered organized baseball in 1949, and had two seasons in the Pacific Coast League of .348 and .312 batting averages, earning a place on the New York Giants' roster in 1951. Always a left-field hitter, while with the Giants, opposing teams used a shift on him like he was a right-handed pull hitter, and he just could not pull the ball to overcome the shift. Used sparingly, he hit an uncharacteristically low .182 in only 22 major-league at-bats. Some observers felt that in the early years of baseball desegregation, there was an unwritten quota system, and when Willie Mays was brought up to the Giants, Wilson was farmed out.

The remainder of 1951 was spent with three different teams in the three highest minor leagues. Finally he settled in the Pacific Coast League and hit for averages of .316, .332, .336, .307, .293, and .263 for the years 1952–57, while leading the league in hits (in 1952) and in triples in consecutive seasons (1953 and 1954). But he never got another look at the big leagues. His best years came in Seattle, but he also played with Portland, Oakland, and Sacramento. After four years away from baseball, he returned to Portland in 1962, but the layoff was too much to overcome, and he finished the season with Kennewick in the Northwest League. After retiring with a .312 lifetime batting average in the minors, he opened a car dealership in Portland.

Wilson, Benjamin (Benny)
Career: 1923–28   Positions: rf, lf, cf
Teams: New York Lincoln Giants ('23–'25), Pennsylvania Redcaps of New York ('26–'28)

This little right fielder for the 1924 New York Lincoln Giants was a very good fielder, fast on his feet, above average at bat, and one of the smallest men in baseball, with a corresponding strike zone, making a difficult target for pitchers.

Wilson, Carter (Coltie)
Career: 1920–23   Position: of

Teams: *Peters' Union Giants ('20, '22–'23), Gilkerson's Union Giants ('21)*, Chicago Giants ('20–'21)

An outfielder with marginal teams during the early '20s, he played mostly with Peters' Union Giants, an independent traveling team, but made an appearance with the Chicago Giants.

Wilson, Charles

Career: 1920–22   Positions: **p**, of

Teams: *Dayton Giants ('17)*, Dayton Marcos ('20), Columbus Buckeyes ('21), Detroit Stars ('21–'22)

This pitcher began his Negro National League career in 1920 with the Dayton Marcos, and spent most of his short career with struggling franchises, playing with the Columbus Buckeyes before landing with the Detroit Stars and posting a 5–7 record in 1921.

Wilson, Charles

Career: 1948–49   Positions: of, 3b

Team: Indianapolis Clowns

An outfielder and occasional third baseman, he played two seasons in the late '40s with the Indianapolis Clowns, batting .313 in only 13 games in 1948.

Wilson, Daniel Richard (**Dan**)

Career: 1937–47   Positions: **lf, rf**, 2b, 3b, ss

Teams: Pittsburgh Crawfords ('37–'38), St. Louis Stars ('39), *Mexican League ('40)*, New Orleans-St. Louis Stars ('41), New York Black Yankees ('42, '44), Harrisburg-St. Louis Stars ('43), Homestead Grays ('46), Philadelphia Stars ('47)

Bats: Both   Throws: Right
Height: 5'10"   Weight: 170
Born: 1913
Died: Dec. 23, 1986, St. Louis, Mo.

A good hitter with good speed on the bases and in the field, this outfielder represented the St. Louis Stars on the West squad in 1939 and 1941, and represented the New York Black Yankees on the East squad in 1942 in the an-

nual East-West All-Star game. Wilson batted .333 in All-Star play, and he slammed a dramatic 3-run homer to win the 1939 contest. From that height of glory he eventually fell to the bottom, dying from a fire he had built to keep warm, while a homeless derelict living out of a shopping cart.

He began his career in 1937 with the Pittsburgh Crawfords, batting in the fifth slot in the order while playing right field and second base. The following season he moved up to the second slot in the batting order and registered a .370 average. In 1939 he moved West to join the St. Louis Stars for his All-Star heroics, before succumbing to the lure of Mexico for a season. In the Mexican sun he batted .333 for Monterrey before returning to the Stars for another All-Star season in 1941, while playing both right field and shortstop during the year.

In 1942 the Stars' franchise broke up and he was among the ex-Stars traveling East to join the New York Black Yankees, playing left field and hitting .293 while batting in the third slot. The next season the St. Louis product was back with the Stars and was considered the top man on the team, playing alternately at second base and in left field while batting in the first two spots in the order. But early in the spring the ballclub withdrew from the Negro National League to barnstorm against Dizzy Dean's team. His last two years in the Negro Leagues was spent in the outfield with the Homestead Grays and the Philadelphia Stars. With the Grays he played in the side pastures, hitting sixth in the order and batting .260 for the 1946 season. The next year he was with the Stars, usually batting in the lower part of the lineup, and his hitting dropped to a .227 average for his final season.

Wilson, Ed

Career: 1896–1905   Positions: 1b, of

Teams: Cuban X-Giants ('96, '99–'03), Page Fence Giants ('97), *Lansing, Michigan, Colored Capital All-Americans*

Beginning as a first baseman with the Cuban X-Giants during the latter part of the nineteenth century, he joined the Page Fence Giants during their brief but successful existence and played with the Colored Capital All-Americans of Lansing, Michigan. During his career he sometimes also played in the outfield, before closing out his decade in black baseball in 1905.

Wilson, Edward

Career: 1898   Position: p
Team: *Celeron Acme Colored Giants*

He pitched with the all-black Acme Colored Giants, representing Celeron, New York, in the Iron and Oil League. Both the team and the league folded in July, and it was to be the last time a black team played in a white league.

Wilson, Elmer

Career: 1921–26   Position: 2b, 3b
Teams: Detroit Stars ('21–'24), St. Louis Stars ('24–'25), Dayton Marcos ('26)

A light-hitting infielder during the '20s, he shared the second-base assignments for the St. Louis Stars in 1925, batting at the bottom of the order when in the lineup. He began his career in 1921, and played with the Detroit Stars before joining St. Louis. He closed his career as a reserve second baseman with the Dayton Marcos in 1926.

Wilson, Emmett Dabney

Career: 1937–46   Positions: lf, rf, cf
Teams: Pittsburgh Crawfords ('37–'38), Satchel Paige's All-Stars ('38), Cincinnati Buckeyes ('42), Cincinnati Clowns ('43), *military service ('44–'45), Boston Blues ('46)*

This fleet-footed but light-hitting outfielder played with the Pittsburgh Crawfords in 1937, sharing a starting outfield position while batting in the lower part of the order. That season he and his brother, All-Star outfielder Dan Wilson, played in the same outfield. Leaving the Crawfords the next season, he barnstormed with Satchel Paige's All-Stars before joining the Cincinnati Buckeyes in 1942, their first year in the Negro American League. As a part-time starter in left field for the Buckeyes, he

hit in one of the two top spots in the batting order when in the lineup, and finished with a .212 average for the season. After a year with the Cincinnati Clowns he was with the New York Black Yankees for part of the 1944 season, batting .186 in only 15 games before entering military service. After the end of World War II he played with the Boston Blues of the United States League in 1946, and after the season he toured with Jackie Robinson's All-Star team.

Wilson, Ernest Judson (**Jud**, Boojum)

Career: 1922–45   Positions: **3b, 1b,** 2b,
                                         ss, of, manager
Teams: *military service ('18),* **Baltimore Black Sox** ('22–'30), **Homestead Grays** ('31–'32, '40–'45), Pittsburgh Crawfords ('32), **Philadelphia Stars** ('33–'39)
Bats: Left   Throws: Right
Height: 5'8"   Weight: 185
Born: Feb. 28, 1899, Remington, Va.
Died: June 26, 1963, Washington, D.C.

A savage, pure hitter who hit with power and was at this best in the clutch, Wilson could hit anything thrown to him and would have been an ideal designated hitter. Cum Posey considered him to be the most dangerous and consistent hitter in black baseball, calling him one of the stars of all time, and placed him on the all-time All-American team for a national magazine in 1945. So intense was his disdain and lack of respect for pitchers that he actually dared them to throw the ball. The left-handed slugger hit all varieties of pitching styles and all pitchers, including Satchel Paige, who considered him one of the two best hitters ever in black baseball.

The records bear this out as he consistently hit in the high .300s and even topped the .400 level on occasion. Beginning with a league-leading .373 batting average in 1923, he is credited with averages of .377, .395, .346, .469, .376, .350, .372, .323, .356, .354, .342, .324, .315, and .386 through the 1937 season. His career covered a quarter of a century, ending after the 1945 season, with a .345 lifetime average. He starred in Cuba for six winters, and his records there show a .372 lifetime average and two batting titles. Playing with Havana, he topped the league with averages of .403 and .441 during the winters of 1925–26 and 1927–28. His lifetime statistics in the Negro Leagues show an impressive .345 batting average, and against major-leaguers in exhibitions the ledger shows a .442 average.

A product of the Washington, D.C., sandlots in the Foggy Bottom section of town, Wilson had a big upper body, a small waist, and was slightly bowlegged and pigeon-toed. Although he was awkward, he was fast and sure afield and, while lacking form, could play adequately at either corner. The rugged Wilson played third base by keeping everything in front of him, knocking the ball down with his chest, and then throwing the batter out, and was described as "a crude but effective workman."

A fierce competitor, hard loser, and habitual brawler, the bull-necked Wilson was fearless, ill-tempered, and known for his fighting almost as well as he is known for his hitting. Teammates, opponents, and umpires all feared the fury of the fiery-eyed, quick-tempered strongman. He was considered one of the "Big Four of the big badmen" of black baseball. The others accorded this designation were Chippy Britt, Oscar Charleston, and Vic Harris. Although his on-field conduct improved slightly as he got older, he never eliminated his need to exercise greater restraint in his behavior. He had the reputation as "the toughest man to handle in baseball." In 1925 this reputation led to his arrest on a "frame-up" assault charge. He was mean and nasty on the field, but when the uniform came off, he was a genial person off the field. He roomed with little Jake Stephens on the Homestead Grays, Pittsburgh Crawfords, and Philadelphia Stars, and they became very good friends. When he was in the last days of his life and unable to recognize anyone else, he recognized Jake by name.

But his good friend and roommate sometimes caused him problems. Once, when the pair were playing together with the Philadel-phia Stars, Stephens was arguing with an umpire about a call, and Wilson intervened by positioning himself between the two parties as a buffer, keeping Stephens behind him and away from the ump. Stephens reached around him and hit the ump in the face, but the arbiter thought it was Wilson and put him out of the game. Wilson exploded, and the police had to come onto the field to subdue his fury. It took three policemen, freely using their blackjacks, to put him inside the patrol wagon and take him to jail. After being released he threatened to kill his little friend, and Stephens was so scared that he left town.

On another occasion, after the East-West All-Star game in Chicago, Stephens came back to the room at about 2:00 A. M. after a night of carousing, and awoke the sleeping Wilson, who grabbed his little roomie and held him out of the sixteenth-story window by the leg while Stephens kicked his arm with his free foot. Wilson just changed hands, like a gunfighter's "border shift," with Stephens kicking and screaming sixteen stories above the pavement.

On the field, Wilson was vicious, and especially rough on umpires. Once he became so angered at umpire Phil Cockrell, a former player, because of a call that he made in a game against the Grays, that he grabbed the arbiter by the skin of his chest and lifted him off the floor, berating him for cheating them out of a game. His fury did not abate until his teammate Crush Holloway picked up a bat and interceded on behalf of the umpire. Only then did Wilson gain control of his temper and let the umpire go.

Wilson hated the bench almost as much as he hated umpires, and often refused to leave the lineup, even continuing to play with injuries that should have kept him out of action. In June 1924 he was playing first base for the Baltimore Black Sox and was hobbled by a bad ankle, but he insisted on playing. He crowded the plate when batting and was frequently hit by pitches. In the late summer of 1926 he was hit by pitched ball and suffered a cracked bone in his right elbow and was declared to be out for the season. But against his doctor's advice, he was back in the lineup two weeks later and slammed 2 hits. A year later he suffered cuts when he and other Baltimore Black Sox players were in an automobile accident, but he refused to stay out of the lineup. But in June 1937 he failed to "dodge the bullet" when the Philadelphia Stars' team bus was hit by a car and his injury necessitated him missing an extended amount of playing time. Consequently his swing was impaired through the early part of the 1938 season. His distaste for being away from the action never abated, and on another occasion he played with three broken ribs. As late in his career as May 1940 he was injured and impatiently hurried his return to the lineup.

The esteem that he was accorded as a player is shown by a rumored trade that gained credibility in 1929, which would have sent him to the Homestead Grays in exchange for both Martin Dihigo and John Beckwith, two of black baseball's premier players.

When Wilson had his tryout with the Baltimore Black Sox, he earned the nickname "Boojum" because of the sound his line drives made when they hit the fence during batting practice. In later years he was described by the press as "probably the hardest hitter Negro baseball has seen." In 1922, his first year with the Black Sox, they were the champions of the South with a record 49–12, and he peppered the walls with base hits, batting a fantastic .522 through mid-August. Although the youngster was homesick and wanted to go back to Foggy Bottom at one point in the season, he stayed with the club for nine years.

During his career he was an integral part of teams that are easily identifiable as some of the greatest teams in black baseball history. During a six-year stretch he starred with the 1929 Baltimore Black Sox, the 1931 Homestead Grays, the 1932 Pittsburgh Crawfords, and the 1934 Philadelphia Stars. All four were championship teams, with the Black Sox winning the American Negro League pennant, the Stars taking the Negro National League pennant, the Crawfords claiming an unofficial championship, and the Grays winning a playoff for their championship. Wilson captained this Grays' team, which is considered by many to be the greatest black team of all time.

The demand for his baseball talents is exemplified by the 1932 season, when he began the year as the playing manager of the Homestead Grays but switched in turn to the Baltimore Black Sox and the Pittsburgh Crawfords in the regular season. Then, in the latter part of the season, he played with Black Sox again in a series of exhibitions against a major-league all-star team while being sought by the Kansas City Monarchs to go with them on their Mexican tour. The next season the East-West All-Star game was inaugurated, and he was selected to the starting lineup for the first three classics after its inception, getting 5 hits in the games for a .455 All-Star batting average.

He was appointed playing manager of the Stars in 1937 and, as would be expected, was a strict disciplinarian who did not tolerate loafing or grandstanding on the field. He hit a home run off the center-field fence to break a tie and win his first game as manager, and at the end of the first half of the season he was hitting .356. As a player he gave his best performance regardless of who was the manager, and he expected the same from the players under his authority. That season he beat Hall of Famer Ray Dandridge by a narrow margin in the All-Star vote but did not play in the contest due to an injury. The next season, 1938, he lost to Dandridge by 27 votes, but Rev Cannady actually played in the East-West game.

After a .373 batting average in 1939 and three seasons under his belt as a manager, he left the Stars and joined the Homestead Grays during their glory years of the '40s. The grizzled veteran was past his prime and didn't play full time in the latter years, but still hit for averages of .282, .340, .255, .350, .417, and .288 for the years 1940–45, as the Grays captured Negro National League pennants every year after his arrival.

In the latter stages of his career he was afflicted with epilepsy and had to be hospitalized. In one World Series contest, the game had to be halted because he was in the field at third base, drawing little circles in the dirt with his finger and completely oblivious to his surroundings. After retiring from baseball, he worked for a road crew building Washington, D.C.'s, Whitehurst Freeway.

With a thirst for victory and a hunger for hitting, on the playing field Jud Wilson took a backseat to no one. His intense will to win and aggressiveness on the diamond added another dimension to his team value.

Wilson, Felton

Career: 1932–37   Position: c
Teams: Cleveland Stars ('32), Akron Tyrites ('33), Detroit Stars ('37)

After reserve roles with marginal Negro National League teams in the early '30s, he shared the regular catching assignments with the Detroit Stars in 1937, the first season of the Negro American League and the last season for the Stars.

Wilson, Fred

a.k.a. Sardo
Career: 1934–45   Positions: **cf, lf, rf,** p, *manager*
Teams: Miami ('34–'37), Ethiopian Clowns ('38–'42), New York Black Yankees ('38), Newark Eagles ('39–'40), Cincinnati Clowns ('43), *military service ('44)*, Cincinnati-Indianapolis Clowns ('45)
Bats: Left   Throws: Right
Height: 6'1"   Weight: 195
Born: 1909, Hastings, Fla.

A very talented player, he was one of the hardest hitters in the Negro Leagues, hitting for both average and with power. And he was a good fielder with a strong arm, but he had a bad disposition and a quick temper, which partially offset his contributions to a club. He was also a fast base runner but had "bad wheels" and was always complaining about his feet hurting.

With the Newark Eagles he hit .327 in 1939, but soon rejoined the Ethiopian Clowns. During the 1943 season, the team's first in Cincinnati, he replaced Bunny Downs at the helm, and the new playing manager was sent to the East-West All-Star game as an utility outfielder. The next year he played with the baseball team at Fort Benning, Georgia, but returned to the Clowns as a player in 1945, resuming his accustomed third-place spot in the batting order while playing right field. While with the Clowns he sometimes pitched with a limited degree of effectiveness, posting marks of 1–5 and 0–2 in 1943 and 1945, respectively.

As a batter he was often a target for opposing pitchers, who would throw at him. Despite getting hit in the head, he refused to duck, insisting that the pitchers should learn better control. Eventually the beanings took their toll, and once his skills had eroded and he could no longer be productive offensively, he was released. In 1945, his last year with the Clowns, he managed only a .200 batting average.

He began his baseball career in 1934, playing with independent teams, including the Clowns when they were still based in Miami. He had a late start in league play because of his propensity for getting in trouble with the law, and was in jail in Miami when Abe Manley signed him. He had written to Manley earlier from Miami offering to join the Newark Eagles in 1939 and to bring other players with him. Wilson had an evil demeanor and would frequently exhibit bizarre behavior. Sometimes he would pull his switchblade and say to a teammate, "I'm going to stick you to see if you bleed." On one occasion he carried through with his threat and knifed the Clowns' ace pitcher Dave Barnhill in the side after an argument. Years later, after Wilson was dropped from the Clowns' roster, he returned to Miami, where he became involved in an altercation and was stabbed to death.

Wilson, George H.

Career: 1895–1905   Positions: **p,** of

Teams: *minor leagues ('95)*, Page Fence Giants ('95–'98), Columbia Giants ('99–'00), Chicago Union Giants ('01–'05)

As a nineteen-year old from Palmyra, Michigan, he pitched in a game with the Page Fence Giants in 1895 but did not figure in the decision. The remainder of the year he played with Adrian in the Michigan State League, posting a 29–4 record while batting .327 and also playing in the outfield. He rejoined the Page Fence Giants, and after the 1898 season, when the team disbanded, he was among the players from the ballclub who formed the Columbia Giants. He was an ace pitcher with the Chicago-based team for the two seasons of their existence, and when Frank Leland combined the team with the Chicago Unions to form the Chicago Union Giants, he also pitched with the new aggregation. After he was no longer with top teams in the United States, he pitched with the Havana team in the Cuban winter league in 1907.

Wilson, Harvey
Career: 1939   Position: inf
Team: Toledo Crawfords

He appeared as a reserve infielder with the Toledo Crawfords in 1939, after Gus Greenlee sold the team and the franchise relocated in a new city and in a new league.

Wilson, Herb
Career: 1928–29   Position: p
Team: Kansas City Monarchs

His two years on the pitching staff of the Kansas City Monarchs included the 1929 season, when the Monarchs copped the Negro National League pennant, with him contributing a 6–1 mark to the effort.

Wilson, J. H.
Career: 1887   Position: player
Team: *Baltimore Lord Baltimores*

He was a player with the Lord Baltimores, one of eight teams that were charter members of the League of Colored Baseball Clubs in 1887. However, the league's existence was ephemeral, lasting only a week. His position is uncertain.

Wilson, James
Career: 1947   Position: p
Team: Memphis Red Sox

He pitched briefly with the Memphis Red Sox in 1947, his only season in the Negro Leagues.

Wilson, James
Career: 1940   Positions: of, 2b, 3b
Team: Indianapolis Crawfords

While playing both infield and outfield, he was the leadoff batter for the Crawfords in 1940, after the team had relocated in Indianapolis. This was his only season in the Negro Leagues and the Crawfords' last year.

Wilson, James (Chubby)
Career: 1929–33   Position: of
Teams: Atlantic City Bacharach Giants ('29), Newark Dodgers ('33)

He was an outfielder with the Bacharach Giants in 1929 and appeared again with the Newark Dodgers when they were organized late in the 1933 season.

Wilson, John E. (Johnny)
Career: 1948–49   Position: of
Team: Chicago American Giants

Obtained in a trade, the pitcher from St. Louis was with the 1948 Chicago American Giants.

Wilson, Joseph
Career: 1887   Position: player
Team: *Washington Capital Citys*

He was a player with the Washington Capital Citys, one of eight teams that were charter members of the League of Colored Baseball Clubs in 1887. However, the league's existence was ephemeral, lasting only a week. His position is uncertain.

Wilson, Jud
[see Wilson, Ernest Judson (Jud, Boojum)]

Wilson, Lefty
[see Brown, Dave]

Wilson, M.
Career: 1926   Position: if
Team: Chicago American Giants

The infielder signed with the 1926 Chicago American Giants, but his playing time was very limited.

Wilson, Percy Lawrance (**Pete**)
Career: 1923–24   Positions: 1b, of
Teams: *New Orleans Crescent Stars ('22)*, Milwaukee Bears ('23), Baltimore Black Sox ('24)
Bats: Both   Throws: Right
Born: Mar. 3, 1889, New Orleans, La.

This switch-hitting first baseman began playing baseball in 1914 as a pitcher at Leland University in New Orleans. The following year he joined the New Orleans Red Sox as a first baseman and continued playing with ballclubs in the New Orleans area, including the New Orleans Crescent Stars, until 1923, when he signed with the Negro National League's Milwaukee Bears. Although the team did not finish the season, manager Pete Hill remembered the fleet-footed first sacker after taking the helm in Baltimore in 1924 and gave him a chance with the Black Sox, but Wilson was not able to hold down a starting position.

Wilson, Ray
Career: 1902–10   Positions: 1b, p
Teams: Cuban X-Giants ('02–'06), Philadelphia Giants ('07–'10)

After beginning his career in 1902 with the Cuban X-Giants, he switched to their biggest rival of the early years of the century, the Philadelphia Giants, and served as the team captain. In his prime he was considered the best first baseman in black baseball, but after moving to Philadelphia he was assigned to a spot near the bottom of the batting order. In 1909 the veteran suffered a badly wrenched foot in the season's playoffs against the Leland Giants. The next season the first baseman-manager was

absent from the Giants' starting lineup and was being called the "grand old man of baseball."

Wilson, Robert (**Bob**, Bill, Horace)
Career: 1947–50   Positions: **3b**, of
Teams: Newark Eagles ('47–'48), Houston Eagles ('49–'50), *minor leagues ('51–'60)*, major leagues ('58)
Bats: Right   Throws: Right
Height: 5'11"   Weight: 197
Born: Feb. 22, 1925, Dallas, Tex.
Died: April 23, 1985, Dallas, Tex.

This third baseman began his career with the Newark Eagles in 1947, hitting .276 while also seeing some duty in the outfield. He was a good prospect, with sufficient speed and power potential, and made good contact at the plate. After the Eagles moved to Houston, he hit for a .352 average in 1949 and played in the East-West All-Star game. The next year he hit .359 with good power (a .558 slugging percentage) before entering organized baseball, with Elmira, during the season. In 1951 he played the entire year with Elmira and batted .313.

Advancing to AAA ball with St. Paul in the American Association, he hit .334 and .317 in 1952–53, and knocked in 117 runs his first year there. In 1954 he began with Oakland in the Pacific Coast League but moved to Montreal for most of the season. That was the beginning of a four-year tenure with the International League team, during which he recorded batting averages of .306, .317, .306, and .290. After the first year he was moved to the outfield for the last three seasons, and responded by leading the league in hits in his first full season (1955) and in doubles twice (1955 and 1956).

After these four productive years, he finally got a chance in the major leagues, but his time there was very brief. In 1958 he played in 3 games, with a hit in 5 at-bats, as an outfielder with the Los Angeles Dodgers. But the remainder of his season was spent with St. Paul, where he hit. 349. He was back in the International League in 1959, splitting his time between Montreal and Toronto while batting a combined .325. The next season, 1960, was his last in baseball, splitting the year between Toronto and Dallas-Ft. Worth in the American Association, with a combined .226 batting average.

Wilson, Thomas T. (**Tom,** Smiling Tom)
Career: 1921–47   Positions: owner, officer
Teams: *Nashville Standard Giants ('18–'20),* **Nashville Elite Giants** ('21–'34), Cleveland Cubs ('31), Columbus Elite Giants ('35), Washington Elite Giants ('36–'37), **Baltimore Elite Giants** ('38–'47)
Born: 1883
Died: May 17, 1947, Nashville, Tenn.

A prominent sportsman, businessman, and numbers banker in Nashville, Tennessee, he organized the Nashville Elite Giants in 1921 and shepherded the ballclub through difficult times, playing variously in the Negro Southern League and the Negro National League, and moving the franchise to Cleveland, Columbus, Washington, and Baltimore in search of diamond success and solvency. He owned the Paradise Ballroom in Nashville, providing him with a legitimate source of income to invest in his ballclub.

In addition to being an owner and team officer, he served as a league officer in assorted positions, including secretary and president of the Negro Southern League and vice chairman, treasurer, and president (1936–46) of the Negro National League. He also was credited as a primary force behind organizing the first East-West All-Star game, in 1933.

He began his association with baseball teams in 1909 with the Nashville Maroons and, four years later, connected with a team called the Elites in 1913. Later he was with the Nashville Standard Giants. During his involvement with baseball he acquired the nickname ''Smiling Tom.''

Wilson, W. **Rollo**
Career: 1929–34   Positions: officer, commissioner

Leagues: American Negro League, Negro National League

A sportswriter, he held positions in each of the black major leagues of his time, serving as secretary of the American Negro League and as commissioner of the Negro National League.

Wilson, William H.
Career: 1887   Position: ss
Team: *Pittsburgh Keystones*

He was a shortstop with the Pittsburgh Keystones, one of eight teams that were charter members of the League of Colored Baseball Clubs in 1887. However, the league's existence was ephemeral, lasting only a week.

Wilson, Woodrow (**Lefty**)
Career: 1931–40   Position: p
Teams: Cuban Stars ('31), Kansas City Monarchs ('36–'37), Memphis Red Sox ('37–'40), Baltimore Elite Giants ('38), New York Cubans
Bats: Left   Throws: Left
Height: 6'2"   Weight: 190

After an appearance with the Cuban Stars in 1931, he next played in the Negro Leagues with the Kansas City Monarchs in 1936. During the next season he moved to the Memphis Red Sox and was credited with a 2–1 pitching record as they copped the Negro American League's first-half championship in 1938. He had average control and a mediocre curve and change-up, but his fastball lacked sufficient velocity. After his first appearance with Memphis, he pitched briefly with the Baltimore Elites and the New York Cubans in the East before returning to the Red Sox to close out his career.

Winfield
[see Wingfield]

Wingfield
a.k.a. Winfield
Career: 1920–23, 1931 Positions: of, 2b, ss, p
Teams: Dayton Marcos ('20), Detroit Stars

('21), *Washington Braves ('21)*, Toledo Tigers ('23), Memphis Red Sox ('31)

An all-purpose player with teams in the Midwest during the early '20s, he played both outfield and infield, and made a final appearance in 1931 with the Memphis Red Sox.

Wingo, Doc

Career: 1944   Positions: c, ss
Team: Kansas City Monarchs
Bats: Right   Throws: Right
Height: 5'9"   Weight: 155

A wartime player, he was one of four catchers on the Kansas City Monarchs' roster in 1944, and also could play shortstop. He had good speed, a wide range afield, and a good arm, but he had a light bat, hitting .128 in his only year in the Negro Leagues.

Winston, Clarence (Bobby)

Career: 1905–23   Position: of
Teams: *Norfolk Red Stockings ('05)*, Philadelphia Giants ('05), Cuban X-Giants ('05–'06), Leland Giants ('07–'09), **Chicago Giants** ('10–'21)
Born: 1880, Richmond, Va.

For most of the first quarter of the twentieth century, he was a superior base stealer and a star outfielder with great range and outstanding defensive ability, playing primarily with the Chicago Giants. As a youngster playing with Havana in the Cuban National League in the winter of 1908, he hit .266 and showcased his speed and daring baserunning by stealing 33 bases in only 177 official at-bats, establishing a record that is still standing, although Sam Jethroe came close to equaling his record with 32 steals in the winter of 1948–49.

Winston began playing professional ball in 1900 as captain and manager of the Reformers All-Stars of Richmond, Virginia. In 1905 he signed with the Norfolk Red Stockings and, in August of the same year, joined the Cuban X-Giants, remaining with them through 1906. The following year Winston traveled West to Chicago for a three-year stint with the Leland Giants, during which he won the hearts of the

fans with his ability on the baseball diamond, especially with his exploits on the bases. In 1909, his last year with the Lelands, he hit .240 and continued his basestealing heroics, swiping 11 bases in 50 at-bats. When owner Frank Leland and manager Rube Foster parted company before the 1910 season, Winston went with Leland's Chicago Giants, playing left field and batting leadoff while batting .333 for the year. For the next seven seasons he batted in the second slot and played left field for Leland's Chicago Giants. His play afield was described as "destroying three-baggers of all hitters who may chance to hit the ball to his territory." In the last year of this string of seasons, 1917, he batted .227 for the season.

When the Giants entered the Negro National League in 1920, the aging veteran continued with the team, still hitting in the number two spot. The Giants dropped out of league play after two seasons, and Winston closed out his career in 1923.

Winston, James

Career: 1931   Positions: p, of
Teams: *Chicago Giants ('29–'30)*, Chicago Columbia Giants ('31), Detroit Stars ('31), *Atlanta Black Crackers ('32)*

Beginning his career in 1929 with the Chicago Giants, a lesser team, he joined the pitching staff of David Malarcher's Chicago Columbia Giants in 1931, but left during the season to join the Detroit Stars' staff, where he was not credited with a decision. The next season he appeared with the Atlanta Black Crackers in the Negro Southern League as an outfielder.

Winters, Jesse (Nip, Nipper, Jim)

Career: 1920–33   Positions: **p**, 1b, of
Teams: *Norfolk Stars ('19–'21)*, Baltimore Black Sox ('20, '29), Atlantic City Bacharach Giants ('21–'22, '31–'33), *Washington Braves ('21)*, **Hilldale Daisies** ('22–'28, '31), New York Lincoln Giants ('28–'29), Homestead Grays ('28), Newark Browns ('31), Washing-

ton Pilots ('32), Philadelphia Stars ('33), Harrisburg Giants
Bats: Left　　　　　Throws: Left
Height: 6'5"　　　　Weight: 225
Born: 1899, Washington, D.C.
Died: December 1971, Hockessin, Del.

The best pitcher in the Eastern Colored League's history was a tall, left-handed curveballer named Nip Winters. Although he had good speed to go with his outstanding curve, he was somewhat wild, especially early in his career. The Hilldale ace pitched his team to pennants in the first three years of the league's existence, including a World Series victory in 1925. In 1923 Winters registered a sensational 32–6 record on the mound while pitching against all competition. He fashioned records of 19–5 in 1924 and 21–10 in 1925 in league play, including a no-hitter the former season. In the 1924 World Series he pitched 4 complete games, including a shutout, and won 3 games in accruing a 1.16 ERA. However, his brilliant effort was negated, as the Kansas City Monarchs emerged victorious. In the 1925 World Series he added another complete-game victory and a 2.00 ERA to gain a measure of revenge as Hilldale prevailed against the Monarchs.

In 1926–27 he posted records of 15–5 and 14–8 with Hilldale but was suspended during the latter season for "not trying." Possibly the team's disenchantment with his play was partly related to his excessive drinking. Whatever the cause, in April 1928 he was traded with George Carr to the New York Lincoln Giants for Red Ryan and Rev Cannady. Later in the season he was released by the Lincoln Giants and picked up by the Homestead Grays in late September, but he returned to the Lincolns' fold in 1929. By then his fastball was no longer effective, and his marks for the two years were 8–7 and 3–5.

He started his professional career with Chappie Johnson's Norfolk Stars in 1919 and, except for a short stint with the Baltimore Black Sox in 1920, remained with the Stars until joining the Bacharach Giants in 1921. That season he posted a 3–2 mark against top black teams, and in the playoffs for the championship against Rube Foster's Chicago American Giants, Winters won the opening game with a 2-hit shutout. The next season he posted a record of 4–3, but left the Bacharachs in 1923 until almost a decade later, when he returned to Atlantic City in the twilight of his career, posting marks of 1–5 and 1-1 in 1931 and 1932, and ending his career in a Bacharachs' uniform in 1933. Afterward he went to Canada and remained through 1940.

A good hitter, he sometimes pinch hit or played first base, and he showed averages of .345 and .314 in 1925 and 1926. He also often played in exhibition games against major-leaguers and, playing against Babe Ruth's All-Stars, he split 2 decisions with the Philadelphia Athletics' great lefthander Lefty Grove. Winters' three winters in the Cuban League, 1923–26, were less distinguished, as he posted an unimpressive 4–12 composite mark. Much of his poor performance on the island can be attributed to an extreme lack of control, a problem he battled throughout his career. After closing out his baseball career he worked sporadically as a handyman and continued to cultivate his excessive drinking habits.

Wirestone
Career: 1910　　　　Position: lf
Team: Chicago Giants

In 1910 he appeared very briefly as a left fielder with the Chicago Giants, in his only season in black baseball.

Wise, Russell
Career: 1940　　　　Position: 1b
Team: Indianapolis Crawfords

He appeared briefly as a first baseman with the Indianapolis Crawfords in 1940, their last season in league play.

Witherspoon, Lester
Career: 1948–49　　　　Positions: p, of
Teams: Indianapolis Clowns ('48–'49), Homestead Grays ('49), *minor leagues ('50–'55)*

Bats: Both   Throws: Right
Height: 6'1"   Weight: 190
Born: 1927

In the Negro Leagues he was a pitcher-outfielder with the Indianapolis Clowns in 1948–49, and also played briefly with the Homestead Grays after they had dropped out of league play. After entering organized baseball he no longer pursued a pitching career, playing outfield and first base. With Porterville in the Southwest International League he hit .363 with balanced power (27 doubles, 14 triples, 16 home runs) and also demonstrated good speed (17 stolen bases) in 93 games. At the end of the season he had a 7-game stint with San Diego in the Pacific Coast League, but managed an unimpressive .154 average and did not return the next year. The next three years were spent with Salem in the Western International League (.331), Lakeland in the Florida International League (.331), and Texas City in the Big State League (.303), but he was not advancing toward higher classifications and he closed out his career after the 1955 season.

Wolfolk, Lewis William
Career: 1923–25   Position: p
Team: Chicago American Giants

After pitching with the Chicago American Giants in 1923, his participation was lessened in 1924 and he was unconditionally released by manager Rube Foster in spring of 1925, along with a large number of veteran players.

Womack, James
Career: 1928–33   Positions: **1b**, 3b, 2b, of
Teams: *Richmond Giants ('28)*, Cleveland Tigers ('28), Indianapolis ABCs ('31), Cuban Stars (West) ('32), Atlantic City Bacharach Giants ('32), Columbus Turfs ('32), Columbus Blue Birds ('33), Baltimore Black Sox ('33)

Playing primarily at the infield corners, he played with struggling teams for half a dozen seasons, usually as a part-time starter or as a substitute. During the tumultous early Depression years he played with the Columbus Turfs in 1932, when the team was in the Negro Southern League for the first half of the season. Later in the year he played third base with the Bacharachs and as a reserve first baseman with the Cuban Stars. In 1933 he played first base with the Baltimore Black Sox early in the year, and he played right field with the Columbus Blue Birds when that team was in the Negro National League for the second half of the season. In each instance, when in the lineup he usually hit in the lower half of the batting order. He began his well-traveled professional career as a second baseman with the Richmond Giants, a team of lesser status.

Wood
Career: 1897   Position: cf
Team: Adrian Page Fence Giants

He was a center fielder with the Adrian Page Fence Giants in 1897, his only season in black baseball.

Woodard
Career: 1928   Position: inf
Team: Cleveland Tigers

He was a reserve infielder with the Cleveland Tigers in 1928, their only season in the Negro National League.

Woods
Career: 1916   Position: p
Team: Chicago American Giants

In 1916, his only season in black baseball, he pitched briefly with the Chicago American Giants.

Woods, Ed
Career: 1891–98   Positions: **p**, 1b
Teams: Cuban Giants ('91), Chicago Unions ('95–'98)

He pitched with the Cuban Giants when they represented Ansonia in the Connecticut State League in 1891. After this first appearance, he played with the Chicago Unions for four years, 1895–98. During the first two seasons he pitched and also was the starting first baseman when not on the mound, but in the latter two seasons he devoted his time to pitching.

Woods, Parnell
Career: 1933–49   Positions: 3b, manager
Teams: Birmingham Black Barons ('33–'38, '40), Jacksonville Red Caps ('38, '41), Cleveland Bears ('39–'40), Cincinnati Buckeyes ('42), **Cleveland Buckeyes** ('43–'48), *minor leagues ('49)*, Louisville Buckeyes ('49), Memphis Red Sox ('50), *Chicago American Giants ('51)*
Bats: Right   Throws: Right
Height: 5'9"   Weight: 170
Born: Feb. 26, 1912, Birmingham, Ala.
Died: July 22, 1977, Cleveland, O.

A team leader, he was a fighter, a strong hitter, a successful base stealer, and a good fielder whose only liability was a weak arm. He was selected to the West squad for the East-West All-Star game four consecutive years, 1939–42, each time representing a different club. In 1942 he had become the youngest manager in the Negro Leagues, with the Cincinnati Buckeyes, and when the franchise moved to Cleveland in 1943, both the Buckeyes and Woods found a home. Batting in the third slot he hit .288, .329, and .335 in 1943–45. Although he was replaced by Quincey Trouppe as manager in 1945, he remained as the team captain and moved into the cleanup spot in the batting order to help the Buckeyes to a Negro American League championship and a sweep of the Homestead Grays in the World Series.

He began his career in Birmingham, playing with the Black Barons in 1933–38, posting batting averages of .269 and .256 in 1937–38, and joining the Jacksonville Red Caps during the latter season. In 1939 the Red Caps moved the franchise to Cleveland and, while based there for two years, played as the Cleveland Bears. After batting .343 for the Bears in 1939, he left the team during 1940 to play with Birmingham for the remainder of the season, batting .318. He returned to the Red Caps in 1941 and started the 1942 season with Jacksonville, but was signed by the Buckeyes in June as playing manager. He hit for a combined .343 average that season, and in the spring of 1943 was called from spring training to report for

military service. However, he was rejected by the military and returned to his spot at the hot corner for the Buckeyes.

In 1949 he signed with Oakland in the Pacific Coast League, batting .275 for 40 games, but split the season with the relocated Buckeyes in Louisville. In 1950 he was still in the Negro American League, with the Memphis Red Sox, batting an anemic .174 as the years began to show. The next season, at age thirty-nine, he played with the Chicago American Giants, but by then the league was strictly of minor-league quality.

During his prime years he played winter ball in Puerto Rico, Cuba, and Venezuela. With Ponce in the Puerto Rican League in 1939–40 he batted .269; in the Venezuela League in 1946–47 he hit .354 while leading he league in doubles; and in the Cuban League in 1947–48 he hit .258. After ending his baseball career, he served as business manager for the Harlem Globetrotters for twenty-seven years.

Woods, Robert
Career: 1902   Position: p
Team: Algona Brownies

He was a pitcher with the Algona, Iowa, Brownies in 1902, when they were one of the top teams in black baseball.

Woods, Sam (Buddy)
Career: 1946–50   Position: p
Teams: Cleveland Buckeyes ('46), Memphis Red Sox ('47–'54), *minor leagues ('55–'57)*
Bats: Right   Throws: Right
Height: 6'2"   Weight: 205
Born: 1922
Died: Philadelphia

After a 3–1 season with the Cleveland Buckeyes in 1946, this Texan joined the Memphis Red Sox, where he had records of 4–6, 1–8, and 10–6 with corresponding ERAs of 3.80, 5.93, and 4.06 for the years 1948–50. He continued his Negro Leagues career with the Red Sox through 1954, although the Negro American League was no longer of major-league quality. In 1955 and 1956 he pitched with Pampa in the West Texas-New Mexico

League, posting records of 10–11 and 14–10 despite having an ERA of over 5.00 each year. In 1957 he split the season among three teams in three different leagues without achieving a winning record with any team, and he had a combined record of 7–12 for his last year in baseball.

Woods, Tom
Career: 1945   Position: 3b
Team: Philadelphia Stars ('45)
A wartime player, he was a reserve third baseman with the Philadelphia Stars in 1945, his only season in the Negro Leagues.

Woods, William
Career: 1887   Position: ss
Team: *Philadelphia Pythians*
He was a shortstop with the Philadelphia Pythians, one of eight teams that were charter members of the League of Colored Baseball Clubs in 1887. However, the league's existence was ephemeral, lasting only a week.

Woods, William J.
Career: 1919–26   Position: of
Teams: Brooklyn Royal Giants ('19, '23, '26), Indianapolis ABCs ('21), Columbia Buckeyes ('21), St. Louis Stars ('22), Washington Potomacs ('23–'24), Atlantic City Bacharach Giants ('25), Chicago American Giants ('21), *Chappie Johnson's All-Stars ('27)*
An outfielder during the '20s, he began his career in the last season of the deadball era, as a reserve outfielder with the Brooklyn Royal Giants. He had good speed but was a light hitter, usually batting in the lower part of the batting order, but occasionally in the top two spots, when in the lineup. Most of his career was spent as a part-time starter or substitute.
Following a winter with the Los Angeles White Sox, he shared a starting outfield position with the Indianapolis ABCs in 1921, batting in the second slot. After a season with the St. Louis Stars he returned to the Brooklyn Royal Giants to share an outfield position before joining Ben Taylor's Washington Poto-

macs, where he continued his usual role, sharing the regular center-field position during the 1924 season. After the Potomacs disbanded, he signed with the Bacharachs as a substitute right fielder in 1925 before returning to the Brooklyn Royal Giants to close out his career with the same team and in the same capacity as he began his career.

Woolridge, Edward
Career: 1926, 1928   Positions: ss, 1b, of
Teams: Cleveland Elites ('26), Cleveland Tigers ('28)
He began his career as a shortstop with the Cleveland Elites in 1926, batting .179 in limited play, and played first base and outfield with the Cleveland Tigers in 1928.

Wright
Career: 1923   Position: of
Team: Atlantic City Bacharach Giants
He appeared briefly as a reserve outfielder with the Bacharachs in 1923, his only season in black baseball.

Wright
Career: 1931   Position: p
Team: Atlantic City Bacharach Giants
He appeared briefly as a pitcher with the Bacharach Giants in 1931, when they were playing as an independent ballclub and were only a season away from their last year of existence.

Wright
Career: 1946   Position: 3b
Team: New York Cubans
He appeared briefly in a reserve role as a third baseman with the New York Cubans in 1946.

Wright, Burnis (**Bill**, Wild Bill)
Career: 1932–45   Positions: **cf, rf,** lf
Teams: Nashville Elite Giants ('32–'34), Columbus Elite Giants ('35), Washington Elite Giants ('36–'36), **Baltimore Elite Giants**

('38–'39, '42, '45), **Mexican League** *('40–'41, '43–'44, '46'–'56)*
Bats: Both   Throws: Right
Height: 6'4"   Weight: 220
Born: June 6, 1914, Milan, Tenn.

This big, strong, swift Elite Giants' star was a wide-ranging center fielder with a strong though not always accurate arm. One of the fastest men in the league, he was also the cleanup hitter and could hit the long ball when needed. A switch-hitter who was best in the clutch, he had a compact swing and was a good contact hitter but hit better from the left side. Selected seven times to the East-West All-Stars squad, beginning with five consecutive appearances (1935–39), and adding two more in 1942 and 1945, he rapped the Negro American League's best pitchers for a .318 average in All-Stars competition.

One of the top all-around players in the league, he began pitching when he was five years old, but it was another ten years before he made his professional baseball debut in 1931. A Tennessee teenager with a lingering passion for pitching, he played with a local team, the Milan Buffaloes, in his hometown. In those early years he earned the nickname "Wild Bill" because of his lack of control. Later, when he had a tryout in Nashville with the Elite Giants, he hurt his arm throwing too hard in the cold weather and was switched to the outfield. In 1932, his rookie year, the Elites were in the Negro Southern League, which was designated as a major league that season. Wright remained with Tom Wilson's Elite Giants as they joined the Negro National League and relocated in Columbus, Washington, and finally in Baltimore, where the team found a home until the demise of the Negro Leagues.

He also played with Wilson's Royal Giants in the winter league of 1935, batting .351. During his twelve years with Wilson's club, the big outfielder was credited with averages of .300, .244, .300, .244, .293, .410, .316, and .488 for his first eight seasons, 1932–39. Those were the halcyon years for the Elites, with

1939 being especially notable because they defeated the Homestead Grays in a postseason playoff. The team's offensive thrust that season was led by Wright, who copped the Negro National League batting title with his fabulous .488 average.

After succumbing to the lure of Mexico in 1940, the perennial all-star returned for an additional two seasons in Baltimore during World War II, due to his draft status. In 1942 he was hitting a league-leading .416 in August and finished the season with a .303 mark. And in 1945, his last year in the Negro Leagues, he registered a slugging percentage of .517 while hitting .371, for a lifetime average in the Negro Leagues of .361.

In Mexico he quickly became one of the most productive and most popular players in the country, registering averages of .360, .390, .366, .335, .301, .305, .326, .282, .299, and .362. Wright's versatility was demonstrated by the diversity of the statistical categories in which he topped the league. In 1940, his first season, he tied for the lead in doubles while also ranking fifth in batting average. In 1941 he led the league in both stolen bases and batting average, with Hall of Famers Josh Gibson and Ray Dandridge finishing in the next two spots behind him in the batting race, and also finished third in home runs, behind league leader Gibson.

But his ultimate accomplishment came in 1943, when he won the Triple Crown. The honors did not come easily, as he was embroiled in a heated but friendly battle with Ray Dandridge that went down to the wire. In the final analysis, Wright barely edged Dandridge for the batting title, and the two ended in a dead heat for the top spot in RBIs. Wright was also engaged in a tight race for the league lead in both home runs and stolen bases, surpassing Roy Campanella by one homer to complete the coveted triad, while missing the stolen-base crown by a single theft.

Wright could circle the bases in 13.2 seconds. He was adept at pushing a bunt down the third-base line, and was a superior drag bunter, employing both in conjunction with his speed to avoid a prolonged batting slump by getting a leg hit when he needed one.

The third time he left the Elites for Mexico was in 1946, when the Pasquel brothers were recruiting major-leaguers for their Mexican League team. Wright hit well against major-league pitchers, both in Mexico and in the California winter league, batting. 371 in competition against major-leaguers including Bob Feller, Dizzy Dean, Ewell Blackwell, Max Lanier, and Bobo Newsome.

Sometimes called a dirty ballplayer, Wright could be temperamental and occasionally showed flashes of a mean streak, but in a game in Mexico in 1950 these attributes probably saved the life of his teammate Rufus Lewis. After Lewis had hit Lorenzo Cabrera with a pitched ball, the batter rushed to the mound with a bat and knocked Lewis unconscious. While Cabrera stood over the fallen pitcher with his bat raised to hit him again, Wright came out of his dugout with a bat to protect Lewis and struck Cabrera first, rendering him unconscious. Had Wright not stepped in when he did, Lewis may have been killed.

However, this incident contrasts with his other experiences in his adopted country, and Wright decided to move from Los Angeles to Mexico to continue a *baseball career* that spanned a quarter century as a player (1931–56) and an additional three seasons as a coach. Wright had decided to retire after the 1951 season, but after being convinced by manager Lazaro Salazar to reconsider, he helped his team win the championship that year. After finally retiring from the game, the popular outfielder opened a restaraunt, *Bill Wright's Dugout*, in Aquascalientes, Mexico, and the sojourn that started as a respite from the rigors of travel in the Negro Leagues became an unplanned permanent home. Wright enjoyed a long career and attained legendary status on the baseball diamonds south of the border, and in recognition was elected to the Mexican Hall of Fame.

In 1958, shortly after Roy Campanella's tragic accident that left him paralyzed, Wright appeared as one of the surprise guests on television's *This Is Your Life* show when Campy was the spotlighted celebrity; he was Campy's first roomie. That was Wright's last visit to the United States until 1990, when he attended a reunion of Negro League players.

Wright, Charley
Career: 1931   Position: p
Team: *Birmingham Black Barons*

In 1931 he was a pitcher with the Birmingham Black Barons, a year after they dropped out of the Negro National League.

Wright, Clarence (Buggy)
Career: 1898   Position: 1b
Team: *Celeron Acme Colored Giants*

He was a first baseman with the Acme Colored Giants, which played in the Iron and Oil League as representatives of Celeron, New York. Both the team and the league folded in July, and it was to be the last time a black team played in a white league.

Wright, Ernest (Ernie)
Career: 1941–49   Positions: owner, officer
Teams: *Cleveland White Sox ('41)*, Cincinnati Buckeyes ('42), Cleveland Buckeyes ('43–'48), Louisville Buckeyes ('49)

The owner of the Cleveland Buckeyes, he located the franchise in Cincinnati during their first season, 1942, and in Louisville during his last year of ownership, 1949. Otherwise the team played with Cleveland as their home city. In addition to being a club officer, he also served as the vice president of the Negro American League. Wright was the owner of the Pope Hotel in Erie, Pennsylvania, and was a well-known sportsman in the area prior to purchasing the franchise.

Wright, George Ed
Career: 1905–13   Positions: ss, 2b
Teams: *Norfolk Red Stockings ('04)*, Brooklyn Royal Giants ('05–'06, '13), Philadelphia

Quaker Giants ('06), Leland Giants ('07–'09), Chicago Giants ('10), New York Lincoln Giants ('11–'12)
Bats: Right   Throws: Right
Born: Aug. 1, 1882, Norfolk, Va.

A middle infielder during the early years of the century, he hit for averages of .326 and .355 for the Lincoln Giants in 1911 and 1912, respectively. He began his baseball career in his hometown in 1904, playing with the Norfolk Red Stockings, a professional team of lesser status. In 1905 he joined the Brooklyn Royal Giants in their first season of existence, as their regular shortstop, and started the next season with the team before finishing the season with the Philadelphia Quaker Giants. In 1907, he began three seasons as the shortstop for the Leland Giants, more properly known as the Leland Giants Baseball and Amusement Association.

In 1910, when owner Frank Leland and manager Rube Foster went their separate ways, each forming his own team, Wright chose to play with Leland's Chicago Giants. In late June he was forced out of the lineup due to an illness and was sent to Hot Springs, Arkansas, to recuperate. Upon returning to the team for the remainder of the season, he was moved from shortstop to second base. The next season, 1911, he traveled back to the East, signing on with Jess McMahon's newly organized New York Lincoln Giants, again playing second base after yielding the shortstop position to John Henry Lloyd. Wright hit in the sixth slot for two years with the champion Lincoln Giants, but returned to the Brooklyn Royal Giants in 1913 to close out his career with the Royals, where he had begun his career with top clubs eight years earlier.

Wright, Henry L. (Red, Howard)
Career: 1928–35   Positions: **p**, lf
Teams: **Nashville Elite Giants** ('28–'34), Cleveland Cubs ('31), Columbus Elite Giants ('35), Birmingham Black Barons

A pitcher with Tom Wilson's Nashville Elite Giants, he began his career in 1928 and posted marks of 5–3 and 6–11 in 1929–30 and 3–4 in 1933. He also sometimes played the outfield, batting .267 in 1930. He closed out his career in 1935, after the Elites had moved to Columbus. His son, Henry, Jr., also played in the Negro Leagues, beginning his career twenty years after the father's debut.

Wright, Henry L., Jr. (**Red**)
Career: 1948   Position: c
Team: Baltimore Elite Giants

His father was a pitcher with the Elite Giants when the team was based in Nashville, and he was a catcher with the Elite Giants in 1948, after owner Tom Wilson had moved his team to Baltimore.

Wright, John Richard, Sr. (**Johnny,** *Needle Nose*)
Career: 1937–48   Position: p
Teams: Newark Eagles ('37–'38), Atlanta Black Crackers ('38), Pittsburgh Crawfords ('38), Toledo Crawfords ('39), Indianapolis Crawfords ('40), **Homestead Grays** ('41–'43, '45, '47–'48), *military service ('44–'45), minor leagues ('46)*
Bats: Right   Throws: Right
Height: 5'11"   Weight: 175
Born: Nov. 28, 1916, New Orleans, La.
Died: May 10, 1990, Jackson, Miss.

This willowy right-hander's poise, blazing fastball, assortment of sharp-breaking curves, and good control caught Branch Rickey's attention and led to his becoming the second black player signed by the Dodger organization. Joining Jackie Robinson in the Dodgers' spring training camp in 1946, Wright could not withstand the pressures unrelated to the baseball diamond and was sent to Montreal, where he pitched in only 2 games without a decision before being shipped to Three Rivers in the CanAm League. Although he completed a winning season (12–8, 4.14 ERA) there and had a successful winter in Puerto Rico (8–5, 1.50 ERA) with Ponce, he left organized baseball to return to the comforting familiarity of the Homestead Grays.

As a member of the outstanding Homestead Grays' teams of the 1940s, he pitched in the World Series of 1942, 1943, and 1945. In Wright's first World Series against the Kansas City Monarchs, he made 2 relief appearances without distinction, but pitched brilliantly in the 1943 Series, in which he started 4 games, including 2 shutout victories over the Birmingham Black Barons. He was credited with a 31–5 slate against all competition during the regular season in 1943, and in recognition of his starring role in the Grays' championship that year, he was selected to pitch in his first East-West All-Star game.

Before the next season began, Wright entered military service during World War II, and while serving in the Navy, he pitched for both the Great Lakes Naval Station team and the Floyd Bennett Air Field team. After his discharge in 1945 he returned in time to pitch at the end of the season, winning all 3 of his decisions. Unfortunately, in the ensuing World Series the Grays were swept by the Cleveland Buckeyes.

After his fling with organized ball he returned to the Grays, posting an 8–4 league record during the 1947 season and making his second All-Star game appearance, yielding 3 hits in the only inning he worked. In 1948, his last year with the Grays, they won the Negro National League's last championship and defeated the Black Barons again in the World Series, although Wright failed to appear in the Series.

Originally from New Orleans, after a season in the sandlots of his hometown he began his career with the Newark Eagles in 1937 without being involved in a league decision. The following spring the Eagles loaned both Wright and Mule Suttles to the Atlanta Black Crackers to play against the Homestead Grays. The Grays protested the practice of a Negro National League team loaning players to other teams, and Wright was returned to Newark until traded to the Pittsburgh Crawfords later in the year. Earning a spot in the starting rotation, he finished the season with a 4–5 record,

and pitched with the Crawfords for three years, with the franchise located in a different city each season, until signing with the Grays in 1941.

Unlike most Grays' pitchers, he was not a good hitter, frequently striking out, but he showed a modicum of power when he did make contact. He also demonstrated the ability to field his position and was an adequate base runner. He continued in baseball into the early '50s, pitching in Puerto Rico in 1953 and 1954 with Escojido and Aquilas Cibaenas, respectively.

Wright, L.
Career: 1932   Position: of
Team: Nashville Elite Giants

He was an outfielder with the Nashville Elite Giants in 1932, when the Negro Southern League was recognized as a major league.

Wright, Robert
Career: 1915   Position: c
Team: Chicago American Giants

He appeared briefly as a reserve catcher with the Chicago American Giants in 1915, his only season in black baseball.

Wright, Zollie
Career: 1931–43   Position: rf
Teams: Memphis Red Sox ('31), Monroe Monarchs ('31–'32), *New Orleans Crescent Stars ('33–'34)*, Columbus Elite Giants ('35), Washington Elite Giants ('36–'37), New York Black Yankees ('38–'40, '43), Washington Black Senators ('38), Baltimore Elite Giants ('39), Philadelphia Stars ('41)
Bats: Right   Throws: Right
Height: 5'9"   Weight: 190
Born: Sept. 17, 1909, Milford, Tex.

A big, strong, powerful hitter, a good base runner, and an outstanding fielder with a strong throwing arm, Wright was a balanced ballplayer. Playing right field and batting cleanup for Tom Wilson's Elite Giants during their two years in Washington, D.C., the outfielder hit .296 in 1936 and was selected to the East-West All-Star team, responding with a 2-RBI single in his only time at bat. The previous year, when the team was based in Columbus, he posted a .288 batting average for the 1935 season.

Before joining the Elite Giants he attended Paul Quinn College for a year, played with the Dallas Black Giants in 1930, and moved up in competition to the Memphis Red Sox, Monroe Monarchs, and New Orleans Crescent Stars in 1931–34. During the winter of 1935 he played with Tom Wilson's Royal Giants, leading him to Columbus in the regular 1935 season. After his seasons with the Elite Giants he played with both the Washington Black Senators and the New York Black Yankees, batting in the heart of the order, with limited statistics showing a .333 batting average for the 1938 season. During the '40s Wright played mostly with the New York Black Yankees but also played with the Philadelphia Stars in 1941, sharing a starting position in the outfield and batting cleanup when in the lineup. However, his offensive productivity deteriorated rapidly, with marks of .120, .152, and .152 in 1940–41 and 1943, respectively.

Wyatt

Career: 1929   Position: c
Team: Detroit Stars

In 1929 this catcher appeared in a game with the Detroit Stars, going hitless in 2 at-bats.

Wyatt

Career: 1941   Position: p
Team: New York Black Yankees

In 1941, his only year in the Negro Leagues, he pitched with the New York Black Yankees without a decision.

Wyatt, David (Dave)

Career: 1896–1903;
1920   Positions: ss, 2b, rf
Teams: Chicago Unions ('98), Chicago Union Giants ('02–'03)

This middle infielder was the regular shortstop with the Chicago Unions in 1898. After the Unions were combined with the Columbia

Giants by Frank Leland in 1901, creating the Chicago Union Giants, he was the regular at two positions in successive seasons. He started at second base in 1902 and started in right field in 1903. Later in life he was tapped by Rube Foster to be a codrafter of the constitution of the Negro National League.

Wyatt, Ralph Arthur (Pepper)

Career: 1941–46   Positions: ss, 2b
Teams: **Chicago American Giants** ('41–'46), Homestead Grays ('43), Cleveland Buckeyes ('46)
Bats: Right   Throws: Right
Height: 5'11"   Weight: 162
Born: Sept. 17, 1920, Chicago, Ill.

A slick-fielding shortstop, he broke in with the Chicago American Giants in 1941 as a reserve middle infielder, but earned a starting position in 1942, hitting .224 while batting in the seventh slot. The next season he moved into the leadoff position and remained there for the next three years, batting .267 and .230 in 1944–45. In 1943, when "Double Duty" Radcliffe was loaned to the Negro American League's Birmingham Black Barons for the World Series, Wyatt was loaned to the Negro National League's Homestead Grays as a counterbalance for the Series. In 1946, his last season, he began the year with the Chicago American Giants under manager Candy Jim Taylor, batting third in the order, but finished the year with the Cleveland Buckeyes.

Wylie, Steve Enloe

Career: 1944–47   Position: p
Teams: Memphis Red Sox ('44), Kansas City Monarchs ('44–'47)
Bats: Right   Throws: Right
Height: 6'0"   Weight: 180
Born: May 7, 1911, Crossville, Tenn.
Died: Oct. 23, 1993, Clarksville, Tenn.

This big right-hander began as a wartime pitcher in 1944, posting a 1–4 mark with the Kansas City Monarchs. He appeared to have "come into his own" and was considered a valuable commodity in 1945. In fulfilling the expectations of Monarchs' manager Frank Duncan, he used a blazing fastball and a sharp-breaking curve to fashion a 7–3 record in 1946 as the Monarchs won the Negro American League pennant before losing to the Negro National League's Newark Eagles in the World Series. The next season, 1947, was his last.

Wynder, Clarence
Career: 1950   Position: c
Team: Cleveland Buckeyes

This catcher began his career with the Cleveland Buckeyes in 1950, when the Negro American League was struggling to survive the loss of players to organized baseball, but league statistics do not confirm his playing time.

Wynn, Calvin
Career: 1949   Position: of
Team: Louisville Buckeyes

He was listed as an outfielder with the Louisville Buckeyes in 1949, but his actual participation is not confirmed.

Wynn, Willie M. (Fourteen)
Career: 1944–50   Position: c
Teams: **Newark Eagles** ('44–'48), New York Cubans ('49–'50)
Bats: Right   Throws: Right

Height: 5' 10"   Weight: 175
Born: 1918, Windsor, N.C.
Died: July 14, 1992, Camden, N.J.

Breaking in with the Newark Eagles during the World War II years, he earned a starting position in 1944 and hit .222 while batting second in the order. After the war ended he remained with the team as a backup until 1948, when he shared playing time with three other players fighting for the starting position. He was a fair receiver but did not have a good arm, and was weak at the plate.

A good all-around athlete, he learned to play ball in his hometown of Windsor, North Carolina, and played basketball at Howard University, but baseball was his most enduring sport. Altogether he spent twenty-five years playing baseball, both in the Negro Leagues and with semipro teams. After settling in Camden, New Jersey, in 1956, he worked in a meat-packing plant and played baseball with the Camden Giants, earning the nickname ''Fourteen'' from the uniform number he wore. Later he worked in a metal shop and coached Little League baseball teams. Earlier in his life, while playing with the Camden Giants in the late '30s, he was offered a contract with the Philadelphia A's by Connie Mack if he would pass as a Latin American, but he refused the offer.

X

X-Giants
[see Cuban X-Giants]

Y

Yancey
Career: 1911   Position: cf
Team: Philadelphia Giants

He played center field for the Philadelphia Giants in 1911, when that once-proud franchise was in decline.

Yancey, William James (**Bill**, Yank)
Career: 1927–36   Positions: **ss**, 2b, 3b, 1b, of
Teams: *Philadelphia Giants ('23–'26), Boston Giants ('23)*, Hilldale Daisies ('27, '31), *Philadelphia Quaker City Giants ('28)*, Philadelphia Tigers ('28), New York Lincoln Giants ('29–'30), New York Black Yankees ('32–'34), Brooklyn Eagles ('35), New York Cubans ('35), *Atlantic City Bacharach Giants ('36)*, Philadelphia Stars ('36)
Bats: Right   Throws: Right
Bats: Right   Weight: 165
Born: Apr. 2, 1904, Philadelphia, Pa.
Died: Apr. 13, 1971, Moorestown, N.J.

A sparkplug shortstop with a strong, accurate arm, he was a solid right-handed hitter and possessed good speed on the bases. Although small, during the off-season he was a star guard on the great Renaissance Five basketball team that was inducted into the Basketball Hall of Fame as a unit in 1963.

Playing primarily with teams in Philadelphia and New York, he was reared in Philadelphia and, as a youngster, attended Central High School but was not permitted to play either basketball or baseball with the school teams. However, during his sophomore year, in 1919, he began playing baseball as a utility man with the semipro Pelham Silk Sox, and a year after graduating from high school, he had a tryout with the Philadelphia Giants, owned by Ziegfeld Follies star Bert Williams. The teenage prospect was sent to the Boston Giants for more seasoning, but after acquiring additional polish he returned to the Giants for four seasons. In 1927 he joined Hilldale, playing shortstop, third base, and first base, and batting .278 in his utility role. That season Hilldale defeated Connie Mack's Athletics in a post-season match-up.

After leaving Philadelphia for New York, he began playing basketball with the Rens and played shortstop for the strong Lincoln Giants' ballclub managed by John Henry Lloyd. Acknowledged as an all-time great, Lloyd taught the aspiring shortstop the key elements necessary for mastery of the position, showing him the proper way to pivot when turning double plays and how to make cutoffs. His all-around team play made him invaluable to the team's success, and he hit for averages of .269 and .335 in 1929 and 1930. During the latter season Yancey became the first black player to set foot in Yankee Stadium. When the Lincolns were scheduled to play in "the house that Ruth built," he ran out on the field early, and pretended to catch fly balls in right field like Babe Ruth and took swings at home plate, pretending to hit homers into the right-field stands like the Babe. Yancey counted playing in the Stadium as one of his biggest thrills in baseball.

After the Lincoln Giants' franchise folded, he rejoined Hilldale in 1931 as their regular shortstop, but batting at the bottom of the order, as he had with the other ballclubs. The next season he returned to New York to play with the Black Yankees for three years. After leaving the Black Yankees his skills faded, and he spent his last two seasons with four teams, batting only .194 in 1935 and closing out his active career in 1936.

A smart player, after ending his active career "Yank" managed in Latin America, traveling to Colón, Panama, in 1937 and coaching the Olympic team and serving as director of the YMCA there through the 1943 season. In 1945 he returned to the United States as the manager of the Atlanta Black Crackers, and years later he scouted for the New York Yankees and the Philadelphia Phillies. He served as a member of the Hall of Fame's Special Committee for the Negro Leagues.

Yank

[see Deas, James Alvin (Yank)]

Yarbrough

Career: 1940   Position: p
Team: Newark Eagles

He appeared as a member of the Newark Eagles' pitching staff in 1940, his only season with the club.

Yokely, Laymon Samuel (Norman, Corner Pocket, The Mysterious Shadow)

Career: 1926–44   Position: p
Teams: **Baltimore Black Sox** ('26–'33), Atlantic City Bacharach Giants ('34), Philadelphia Stars ('34–'37, '39),
Washington Black Senators ('38), *Edgewater Giants ('40–'43)*, Baltimore Elite Giants ('44)
Bats: Right   Throws: Right

Height: 6'2"   Weight: 210
Born: May 30, 1906, Winston-Salem, N.C.
Died: January 1976, Baltimore, Md.

The ace of the great Baltimore Black Sox staff of the late 1920s and early 1930s, Yokely was Leon Day's boyhood hero. The fastballer was credited with six no-hitters for the Black Sox. In 1929 he won 17 games to pitch the Sox to the American Negro League pennant. After his comeback from a sore arm, he appeared with the 1934 Negro National League champion Philadelphia Stars. In 1939 Yokely was credited with 25 wins with the Stars after already winning 15 with the semipro Bacharachs, giving him a total of 40 victories against all levels of competition for the season.

He attended Livingstone College in Salisbury, North Carolina, in 1925, and while in college he often hooked up in pitching duels with Bun Hayes, who pitched for J. C. Smith University in Charlotte, North Carolina. Both hurlers were scouted and signed by the Baltimore Black Sox for the following season. Yokely continued his education in the off-season and was on the Black Sox' reserved list in 1929 while still in school in March of that season.

He was so popular with fans that he was called a matinee idol, and in 1926 he acquired the nicknames "Corner Pocket" Yokely and "The Mysterious Shadow." A downside to his popularity was that because so many fans wanted to see him pitch, he may have been overworked, shortening his career. After a few seasons of throwing his fastball at too-frequent intervals, his arm started to go bad. Initially the problem was manifested by an inability to pitch complete games, but soon progressed to a point where he began to lose effectiveness. Beginning in 1930, his decline in effectiveness accelerated, and within two years his arm was so bad that he was benched. Then he began pitching for the Baltimore Red Sox, a sandlot semipro team, and rumors abounded that he was "washed up," but he vowed to make a comeback. Black Sox skipper Dick Lundy promised him a chance, and in October 1932

Yokely faced his old college adversary Bun Hayes. Neither pitcher finished the game, but Yokely struck out 8 while allowing 11 hits in 6 innings. Although his team lost the game and he failed to reclaim his previous level of performance, he proved he could still pitch at a major-league level.

After his years with the Philadelphia Stars he pitched with the Edgewater Giants, a team of lesser status. In 1943 he won 13 straight games and earned a final shot with a league team in 1944, when he appeared with the Baltimore Elite Giants in 1944. The next season he formed his own ballclub, Yokely's All-Stars, and continued to operate the club until 1959, when he retired from baseball and opened Yokely's Shine Parlor on Pennsylvania Avenue.

Yokum
Career: 1922   Position: p
Team: Kansas City Monarchs

A pitcher from Ash Grove, Missouri, he was with the Kansas City Monarchs briefly in 1922.

York, Jim
Career: 1919–23   Positions: c, of
Teams: Hilldale Daisies ('19–'21), *Norfolk Stars ('21), Atlantic City Bacharach Giants ('23)*

A good hitter with power, this catcher hit .356 against all opposition in 1921. Beginning his career with Hilldale in 1919, he was always in a backup role, and he made his last appearance in the Negro Leagues with the Bacharach Giants in 1923, the first year of the Eastern Colored League.

Young
Career: 1930   Position: ss
Team: New York Lincoln Giants

He appeared as a shortstop with the New York Lincoln Giants in 1930, the last season for the franchise.

Young, Berdell
Career: 1922–28   Positions: **rf**, lf, 1b
Teams: Atlantic City Bacharach Giants ('22,

'24–'25), *Philadelphia Giants ('23–'24)*, New York Lincoln Giants ('25–'28)

A part-time starter for three seasons with the New York Lincoln Giants under manager John Henry Lloyd, he played right field and also logged some playing time at first base while batting in the leadoff spot. Before joining the New York ballclub he played with the Bacharachs and the Philadelphia Giants, beginning in 1922. However, he was relegated to a reserve role with the Bacharachs until 1925, when he hit .317 while batting in the seventh spot as the regular left fielder before joining the Lincolns during the season.

Young, Bob
Career: 1950   Positions: ss, 2b, 3b
Team: Cleveland Buckeyes

A utility infielder with the Cleveland Buckeyes when the Negro American League was struggling to survive the loss of players to organized baseball, his playing time was severely restricted and is not confirmed by league statistics.

Young, Edward (Ed, **Pep**)
Career: 1936–47   Positions: c, 1b, 3b, of
Teams: **Chicago American Giants** (36–'43, '46), Kansas City Monarchs ('44), Homestead Grays ('47)
Bats: Right   Throws: Right
Height: 6'2"   Weight: 210

Although he was primarily a catcher, he also played extensively as a first baseman. He was an average player offensively and defensively but was not a good base runner. Breaking in with the Chicago American Giants in 1936, he spent most of his career there, with his most productive seasons coming in 1939–40, when he played first base and batted cleanup. In 1944 he was listed as a reserve catcher with the Kansas City Monarchs. After the end of World War II he returned to the Chicago American Giants for another season before closing out his career with the Homestead Grays in 1947 as one of the catchers used in an effort to replace Josh Gibson, who had died the previous winter. When Buck Leonard suffered a broken hand during the season, Young filled in at first base until Leonard's injury healed.

Young, Frank A. **(Fay)**
Career: 1939–48   Position: officer
League: Negro American League
Died: November 1957

A leading sportswriter and editor for the *Chicago Defender* for many years, he also served as the secretary of the Negro American League for a decade.

Young, John
Career: 1923–24   Position: p
Teams: St. Louis Stars ('23), Memphis Red Sox ('23–'24)

He pitched for two seasons in the Negro American League, with the St. Louis Stars and the Memphis Red Sox.

Young, Leandy
Career: 1944–45   Position: of
Teams: Kansas City Monarchs ('40, '45), Birmingham Black Barons ('44–'45)

After leaving his hometown of Dallas, Texas, he played in Shreveport, Louisiana, prior to making a brief appearance with the Kansas City Monarchs in 1940. His next stint with a Negro American League team was during World War II, when he played as a reserve left fielder and utility man for the Birmingham Black Barons in 1944–45. He returned to the Monarchs in the latter part of 1945 to close out his Negro League career.

Young, Maurice (Doolittle)
Career: 1927   Position: p
Team: Kansas City Monarchs
Bats: Left   Throws: Left

This left-handed pitcher joined his brother, catcher Tom Young, to form a brother battery for the Monarchs in 1927.

Young, Norman **Harvey** (Pep)
Career: 1941–44   Positions: ss, 3b, 2b
Teams: New York Black Yankees ('41–'42),

Atlanta Black Crackers ('43), Baltimore Elite Giants ('43),
Cleveland Buckeyes ('44), *Nashville Cubs ('46)*
Bats: Right   Throws: Right

A light hitter but a sensational fielder, he was the regular third baseman with the New York Black Yankees in 1941, batting at the bottom of the lineup. After leaving the Black Yankees he played shortstop for the 1943 Atlanta Black Crackers in the Negro Southern League and was considered the infield cement that held it together. His glovework in Atlanta earned him another chance with a top club, and he joined the Baltimore Elite Giants in 1943, allowing Felton Snow to move back to the hot corner. When Pee Wee Butts rejoined the Elite Giants the next year, Young because expendable in Baltimore and switched leagues to fill a reserve role with the Cleveland Buckeyes before finishing his career with lesser ballclubs in the South.

Young, Roy
Career: 1942–45   Position: umpire
League: Negro American League

He served as an umpire for four seasons in the Negro American League during World War II.

Young, Thomas Jefferson (T. J., **Tom**, Shack Pappy)
Career: 1925–41   Positions: **c**, of
Teams: **Kansas City Monarchs** ('25–'35, '41), St. Louis Stars ('31), Detroit Wolves ('32), Homestead Grays ('32), Pittsburgh Crawfords ('37), New York Cubans ('38), *Mexican League ('39)*, Newark Eagles ('41)
Bats: Left   Throws: Right
Height: 6'0"   Weight: 190

A good left-handed pull hitter who made pretty consistent contact, he was an average receiver with a good arm. He was a good hustler, but with only mediocre speed on the bases, he was no threat to steal. Most of his career was spent with the Kansas City Monarchs, including the Depression years when they were playing as an independent ballclub and touring throughout the Midwest and Canada. Playing in an exhibition against Dizzy Dean's All-Star team during Diz's prime years with the St. Louis Cardinals, Young batted cleanup for Kansas City and had four hits, including a double off Diz and a triple off Paul Dean.

He began his career with the Monarchs as a backup catcher, but by 1927 he was sharing the catching assignments with Frank Duncan while batting in the lower part of the batting order. That season he was joined on the Monarchs by his brother, Maurice, a pitcher, forming a brother battery. When the Monarchs disbanded following the 1930 season, Tom signed with the St. Louis Stars in 1931 and was their regular catcher, batting in the sixth spot. Although the club was the class of the Negro National League, he left the Stars in the late summer to sign again with the Monarchs when they reorganized for the second half of the season. In 1932 he moved into the cleanup spot for the Monarchs, who were barnstorming following the demise of the first Negro National League.

He left the Monarchs in 1936, playing with the Pittsburgh Crawfords and the New York Cubans before traveling to Mexico to ply his trade, where he caught a no-hitter hurled by ex-Monarch teammate Chet Brewer in 1939.

Young, W. H., *Dr.*
Career: 1949–50   Position: officer
Team: Houston Eagles
He was an officer with the Eagles after the franchise had been purchased from Effa Man-

ley and relocated in Houston in an effort to save the financially floundering franchise.

Young, Wilbur
Career: 1945   Position: p
Team: Birmingham Black Barons
A wartime player, he pitched with the Black Barons in 1945, his only year in the Negro Leagues.

Young, William
Career: 1927   Position: p
Team: Kansas City Monarchs
He was a pitcher with the Kansas City Monarchs in 1927, his only year in the Negro Leagues.

Young, William P. (Pep)
Career: 1918–34   Positions: c, of
Teams: G.C.T. Red Caps of New York ('18), Homestead Grays ('19–'34)
During most of his career he was a backup catcher, playing primarily with the Homestead Grays during the '20s, when they were building into a power. Earlier in his career he had played left field for the G.C.T. Red Caps of New York.

Yvanes, Armando
Career: 1949–50   Position: ss
Team: New York Cubans
He batted .311, with average power, as the regular shortstop with the New York Cubans in 1950, when the Negro American League was struggling to survive the loss of players to organized baseball.

Z

Zapp, James (**Jim**, Jimmy, Zipper)
Career: 1945–50   Positions: lf, rf, *3b*
Teams: *military service ('42–'45)*, Baltimore Elite Giants ('45–'46, '50–'51, '54), *Nashville Cubs ('46), Atlanta Black Crackers ('47)*, Birmingham Black Barons ('48, '54), *semipro teams ('49–'50), minor leagues ('52–'55)*
Bats: Right   Throws: Right
Height: 6'2"   Weight: 208
Born: Apr. 18, 1924, Elyria, Ohio.

After this big, hard-hitting outfielder slugged 11 homers with the Negro Southern League's Atlanta Black Crackers in 1947, he attracted the attention of the Birmingham Black Barons and won an outfield position with the team the following spring. His bat helped Birmingham nail down the Negro American League title when, in the fifth game of the league championship series against the Kansas City Monarchs, he homered in the bottom of the ninth inning to tie the ball game, opening the door for another Black Baron tally in the last frame to win a 4–3 thriller and give Birmingham a 1-game edge in the playoffs.

During the regular season, Black Barons' manager Piper Davis had given Zapp a rest and inserted a teenage rookie named Willie Mays in his left-field spot for the second game of a doubleheader. Later in the season, when center fielder Norman Robinson broke his leg, Mays stepped into the breach and used the opportunity to demonstrate his defensive skills on an everyday basis. Although Mays had trouble hitting a curve and was not a significant offensive factor, his fielding earned him the starting position in center field. When Robinson eventually returned to the lineup, he was inserted into left field to utilize his speed and glove, and Zapp was displaced from the starting lineup for a short time. Fortunately, he returned in time to deliver the big blow in the playoffs. After securing the pennant, the Black Barons lost the World Series to the Negro National League champion Homestead Grays.

During the next two seasons he played with semipro teams in the Nashville area, including the Morocco Stars in 1949 and the Nashville Stars in 1950. During the latter part of the 1950 season he returned to the Baltimore Elite Giants when they were in the Negro American League after a realignment, and remained with them in 1951. Zapp had begun his professional career with the Elite Giants in 1945, when they were in the Negro National League, after his discharge from the Navy. He had begun playing baseball in 1942 while stationed in Hawaii, and his Navy team won back-to-back championships in 1943–44.

In 1952 he entered organized baseball with Paris in the Mississippi-Ohio Valley League, where he hit .330 and slammed 20 home runs with 136 RBIs. His temperament, which had always contributed to problems while he was playing, continued to plague him after leaving the Negro Leagues. In his second season in the Mississippi-Ohio Valley League he began with

Danville but played only briefly before joining Lincoln in the Western League, also for a brief time. But in 1954 and 1955 he enjoyed two more big seasons, batting .290 with 32 home runs in 90 games and .311 with 29 home runs in 89 games, with Big Springs in the Longhorn League. In the latter season he also played with Port Arthur in the Big State League, adding another 8 homers in 39 games to close out his organized baseball career.

In 1954 the slugging outfielder went back to the Negro American League for the latter part of the season, playing with the Elite Giants and the Black Barons during the last month of the season. By then, however, the Negro American League was no longer a major-league operation.

Ziegler, William (Doc)
Career: 1921, 1927–29 Positions: p, of
Teams: Detroit Stars ('21), *Chicago Giants ('27–'29)*

In his only year with a top team, he pitched briefly without a decision for the 1921 Detroit Stars. Later in the decade he played as an outfielder with the Chicago Giants when the ball-club was of marginal quality.

Zimmerman, George
Career: 1887   Position: c
Team: *Pittsburgh Keystones*

This nineteenth-century player was on the roster of the Pittsburgh Keystones, one of eight teams that were charter members of the League of Colored Baseball Clubs in 1887. However, the league's existence was ephemeral, lasting only a week.

Zomphier, Charles (Zomp)
Career: 1926–31   Positions: **2b**, 3b, ss, 1b, rf, lf, p, umpire
Teams: Cleveland Elites ('26), Cleveland Hornets ('27), Birmingham Black Barons ('27), Cuban Stars (West) ('27), St. Louis Stars ('27), Cleveland Tigers ('28), Detroit Stars, Memphis Red Sox ('30), Cleveland Cubs ('31)

League: Negro American League
Bats: Right   Throws: Right
Born: 1905, St. Louis, Mo.
Died: Jan 31, 1973, St. Louis, Mo.

This hustling second sacker learned his baseball on the sandlots of St. Louis but was soon discovered by the professional teams and joined their ranks in 1926, batting second in the order for the Negro National League Cleveland Elites. He played with the various league teams representing Cleveland for most of his Negro League career and ended his career as the third-place hitter with the Cleveland Cubs in 1931. The versatile and much-traveled infielder also played with the St. Louis Stars, Memphis Red Sox, Birmingham Black Barons, Cuban Stars, and Detroit Stars during his half-dozen seasons with league teams. In one season he is alleged to have hit .480, but this has not been confirmed.

After his playing days were over he embarked on a second career, as an arbiter. He umpired in the Negro American League and in semipro ball in the St. Louis area, and he organized the St. Louis Umpires' Association in 1940. In recognition of his contributions to sandlot baseball, he was inducted into the Greater St. Louis Amateur Baseball Hall of Fame.

Zulu Cannibal Giants
Duration: 1934–37   Honors: None
Affiliation: Independent

A touring independent baseball team that combined baseball and entertainment, they were forerunners of the Indianapolis Clowns. Organized by Charlie Henry and playing primarily in the '30s, they filled essentially the same role with their comedy skits and clowning activities to amuse the crowds. The players dressed in grass skirts over basketball shorts and wore red wigs and face paint, making it difficult to distinguish among the players. Consequently sometimes only the four best hitters would bat, with the opposition rarely noticing the difference.

Appendix

Human Resources

Former players from the Negro Leagues who contributed to the information included in this volume are as follows:

Robert Abernathy
Russell Awkward
Otha Bailey
David Barnhill
Ernest Barnwell
Cool Papa Bell
Gene Benson
William Beverly
Charlie Biot
Joe Black
Garnett Blair
Lyman Bostock, Sr.
Chet Brewer
William Bridgeforth
Johnny Britton
Willard Brown
Bill Bruton
Allen "Lefty" Bryant
Buddy Burbage
Bill Byrd
Roy Campanella
Marlin Carter
Bill Cash
Orlando Cepeda
Buz Clarkson
Jim Cohen
Rogelio Crespo
Jimmy Crutchfield
Ray Dandridge

Rudolpho Fernandez
Wilmer "Red" Fields
Charles Gary
Josh Gibson, Jr.
Stanley Glenn
Wiley Griggs
Napoleon Gulley
Sam Hairston
Perry Hall
Ed Hamman
Bob Harvey
Sammy Haynes
Bill Harvey
Jehosie Heard
Jimmy Hill
Cowan "Bubba" Hyde
Monte Irvin
Sam Jethroe
Clarence Israel
Byron Johnson
Connie Johnson
Josh Johnson
Judy Johnson
Casey Jones
Cecil Kaiser
Henry Kimbro
Larry Kimbrough
James "Lefty" LaMarque
Buck Leonard

Cy Morton
Don Newcombe
Willie O'Kelley
Buck O'Neill
Bill Owens
Ted Page
Pat Patterson
Frank Pearson
Alonzo Perry
Nate Pollard
Leonard Pigg
Ted "Double Duty" Radcliffe
Dick Powell
Othello "Chico" Renfroe
Bobbie Robinson
Tommy Sampson
Pat Scantlebury
Joe Scott
Joe Burt Scott
Eugene Smith
Ford Smith
Hilton Smith
Lonnie Summers
Frank "Doc" Sykes
Johnny Taylor
Mickey Tabor
Ron Teasley
Bob Thurman
Quincey Trouppe

Johnny Davis
Piper Davis
Saul Davis
Leon Day
Wesley "Doc" Dennis
Lou Dials
Mahlon Duckett
Jake Dunn
Bill Evans
Felix "Chin" Evans
Al Fennar

Lester Lockett
Henry McCall
"Jeep" McClain
Rufus Lewis
Butch McCord
Fred McDaniel
Clyde McNeal
John Miles
Orestes Minoso
Juanelo Mirabal
James "Red" Moore

James "Bo" Wallace
Murray Watkins
Tweed Webb
Edsall Walker
Enloe Wiley
Willie Wells
Jesse Williams
Al Wilmore
Artie Wilson
Bill Wright
Jim Zapp

Bibliography

Books

Books dedicated exclusively to the subject of the Negro Leagues that were used as sources of information contained in this volume are as follows:

Title	Author	Publisher	City	Year
All-Time All-Stars of Black Baseball	Riley, James A.	TK Publishers	Cocoa, Fla.	1983
Black Diamonds	Holway, John B.	Meckler Books	Westport, Ct.	1989
Blackball Stars	Holway, John B.	Meckler Books	Westport, Ct.	1988
Blacks in Baseball	Hardwick, Leon	Pilot Hist. Assoc.	Los Angeles, Calif.	1980
Dandy, Day and the Devil	Riley, James A.	TK Publishers	Cocoa, Fla.	1987
Get That Nigger off the Field	Rust, Art, Jr.	Delacorte Press	New York, N.Y.	1976
Invisible Man	Rogosin, Donn	Atheneum	New York	1093
Josh Gibson	Brashler, William	Harper & Row	New York, N.Y.	1978
Josh and Satch	Holway, John B.	Meckler Books	New York, N.Y.	1991
Kansas City Monarchs, The	Bruce, Janet	University Press of Kansas	Lawrence, Kan.	1985
Man and His Diamonds, A	Whitehead, Charles	Vantage Press	New York, N.Y.	1980
Maybe I'll Pitch Forever	Paige, Satchel	Double-day & Company	Garden City, N.Y.	1961
Negro Baseball Leagues	Dixon, Phil	Amereon	Mattituck,	1992

		House	N.Y.	
Only the Ball Was White	Peterson, Robert	Prentice-Hall	Englewood Cliffs, N.J.	1970
Pictorial Negro League Legends Album	Retort, Robert D.	Retort Enterprises	New Castle, Pa.	1992
Pitchin' Man	Paige, Satchel	Cleveland News	Cleveland, O.	1948
Pittsburgh Crawfords, The	Bankes, James	Wm. C. Brown	Dubuque, Ia.	1991
Sandlot Seasons	Ruck, Rob	University of Illinois Press	Chicago, Ill.	1987
Sol White Baseball Guide	White, Sol	Camden House	Columbia, S.C.	1984
Twenty Years Too Soon	Trouppe, Quincy	S & S Enterprises	Los Angeles, Calif.	1977
Voices from the Great Black Baseball Leagues	Holway, John B.	Dodd, Mead & Company	New York, N.Y.	1975

Booklets

Booklets dedicated exclusively to the subject of the Negro Leagues that were used as sources of information contained in this volume are as follows:

Title	**Author**	**City**	**Year**
Ben Taylor Memorial	Bolton, Todd	Baltimore, Md.	1992
Bullet Joe and the Monarchs	Holway, John B.	Washington, D.C.	1984
Frank Leland's Chicago Giants Baseball Club	Leland, Frank	Chicago, Ill.	1910
Lou dials: Life in Baseball's Negro Leagues	Dials, Lou	Ashland, Ky.	1987
Memorial Observance for John (Bud) Fowler	Davids, Bob	Manhattan, Kan.	1987
Negro Baseball Yearbook	Sepia Sports Publishers	Washington, D.C.	1946
Rube Foster: The Father of Black Baseball	Holway, John B.	Washington, D.C.	1981
Smokey Joe and the Cannonball	Holway, John B.	Washington, D.C.	1983

Reference Books

Reference books with a portion of the contents dedicated to the subject of the Negro Leagues that were used as sources of information contained in this volume are as follows:

Title	Author	Publisher	City	Year
Ballplayers, The	Shatzkin, Mike	Arbor House	New York, N.Y.	1990
Baseball Chronology, The	Charlton, James	Macmillan Publishing Company	New York, N.Y.	1991
Baseball's Best: Hall of Fame Gallery	Appel, Martin	McGraw-Hill Book Company	New York, N.Y.	1980
Biographical Dictionary of American Sports: Baseball	Porter, David L.	Green-wood Press	Westport, Ct.	1987
Biographical Dictionary of American Sports: 1989–92 Supplement	Porter, David L.	Green-wood Press	Westport, Ct.	1992
Baseball Encyclopedia, The, 8th ed.	Wolff, Rick	Macmillan Publishing Company	New York, N.Y.	1990

Periodicals

A compete list of all pereiodicals or newspapers that had infrequent articles appearing about the Negro Leagues is too voluminous to make a listing practical. Periodicals with regular features dedicated to the subject of the Negro Leagues that were used as sources of information contained in this volume are as follows:

Title	Publisher	City	Year
Diamond, The	FANS Publishing, Inc.	Scottsdale, Ariz.	1993–94
National Pastime, The	Society of American Baseball Research	Cleveland, O.	1975–94
Oldtyme Baseball News	McKinstry Brothers Publishing Group, Inc.	Petoskey, Mich.	1988–94

SABR Journal Society of American Cleveland, O. 1982–94
Baseball Research

Newspapers

Newspapers most frequently utilized as sources of information contained in this volume are as follows:

Afro-American *Cleveland Call and Post* *Newark Herald News*
Amsterdam News *Indianapolis Freeman* *Patriot*
Atlanta Daily World *Indianapolis Ledger* *People's Voice*
Atlantic City Daily Press *Kansas City Call* *Philadelphia Tribune*
Birmingham News *Memphis Commercial Appeal* *Pittsburgh Courier*
Chicago Defender *New York Age* *St. Louis Argus*

Special Collections

Special collections that were examined for contents relating to the Negro Leagues and that served as appreciable sources of information included in this volume are as follows:

A.B. Chandler Oral History Project, University of Kentucky
Black Sports in Pittsburgh Collection, University of Pittsburgh
Effa Manley Collection, Newark Public Library
Library of Congress, Washington, D.C.
Negro League Files, National Baseball Hall of Fame Library
Philadelphia Afro-American Library
Schomberg Center for Research in Black Culture, New York Public Library
Western Historical Manuscript Collection, University of Missouri

About the Author

James A. Riley received the Macmillan-SABR Research Award for the first edition of *The Biographical Encyclopedia of the Negro Baseball Leagues* in 1994. Since the publication of this landmark volume, the author has continued his scholarship on the history of black baseball as a researcher, writer and lecturer. He has written three more books on the subject, collaborating on the autobiographies of two Hall-of-Famers, *Buck Leonard: The Black Lou Gehrig* (1995) and *Monte Irvin: Nice Guys Finish First* (1996), and authoring *The Negro Leagues* (1997) in the African-American Achievers Series.

He has contributed to many compilations including, *Biographical Dictionary of American Sports: Supplement for Baseball, Football, Basketball and Other Sports* (1995), *African-American Sports Greats: A Biographical Dictionary* (1995), *Biographical Dictionary of American Sports: Baseball II* (2000) and *The Scribner Encyclopedia of American Lives, Volumes 3 and 4* (2001), as well as forthcoming compilations *The Encyclopedia of New York State*, and *Scribners Encyclopedia of American Lives - Sports Volume*.

He has also contributed to *All-Star Game: Official Major League Baseball Program* (1993, 1994), *The Diamond: Official Chronical of Major League Baseball* (1993, 1994), *Negro Leagues Baseball Museum Yearbook* (1993, 1994), *Athloon Baseball* (1994, 1995), *Oldtyme Baseball News* (1994-97), *SABR Baseball Research Journal* (1997), *Don't Forget About Josh* (MSNBC on the Internet, 1998), *Ted Williams Museum Yearbook* (1998, 1999), and *Home Run* (1999).

He was a guest speaker at Smithsonian Associates in Washington, D.C. (1995), was a session chair at the Bethune-Cookman symposium *Breaking Baseball's Color Line: Jackie Robinson & Fifty Years of Integration* (1996), was a member of the Florida Humanities Council Speakers Bureau (1996-2001), and maintains an award-winning website <www.blackbaseball.com>.

He was honored by SABR's Negro Leagues Committee with the *Lifetime Achievement Award* (1998) and the *Robert Peterson Recognition Award of Honor* (1999), and received the East Tennessee State University *National Alumni Association Award of Honor* (2000).

The author currently holds the position of Director of Research for the Negro Leagues Baseball Museum in Kansas City, Missouri, and is past president of the Society for American Baseball Research (SABR). He and his wife, Dottie, have two sons and two grandsons, and currently reside in Holly Springs, Georgia.

Index

Introductory Notes for the Addendum

Publication of the first editon of *The Biographical Encyclopedia of the Negro Baseball Leagues* stimulated much public interest in this segment of baseball history and, more especially, in the players who were compelled by circumstance and tradition to display their talent in the relative obscurity of the Negro leagues. It has virtually become the Roots of the baseball world, with families taking and unprecedented interest in a family member whose contributions to baseball had long lain dormant or remained undiscovered. Many letters poured in, either expressing appreciation for helping to preserve the memories of a specific player, or seeking information on a player who was not included. One special letter from Los Angeles emphasized that the book had brought generations together, as they discovered a father or grandfather whose baseball career formed a common bond.

Walk through any cemetary in the United States and almost invariably you will see headstones on the graves, each bearing the name of the person interred followed by two dates separated by a hyphen. The birthdate and deathdate form the endpoints of the hyphen, the beginning and ending of his life, with all in between his birth and death - his entire life - reduced to a hyphen. In the first edition of this volume, more emphasis was placed on the hyphen - especially that portion of the hyphen representing his baseball career - than on the endpoints of the hyphen. In this edition more of the endpoints for entries are provided, along with some new data on the subjects, and even some new players have been revivified from this era.

Unfortunately, verification has not yet been found for some players who are thought to have played briefly in the Negro Leagues. However, some new players have been identified, and they are marked with and asterisk (*) following their name in the entries. When additional or corrective data (i. e. height, weight, birthdate, deathdate) is included for players previously listed, the page of the original entry is listed in brackets following the respective player's name in the addendum for quick reference to correlate with the original information.

Acknowledgments

In the intervening years since the first publication of this reference volume, I have received assistance of varying degrees from several researchers, historians and Negro League aficionados. I thank all those who have helped, especially Don Motley and Raymond Doswell of the Negro Leagues Baseball Museum in Kansas City, Mo., and Scott Mondore of the National Baseball Hall of Fame and Museum in Cooperstown, New York. Also deserving special recognition are Carlos Bauer, Fred Brilhart, Roy Campanella II, Ralph J. Christian, Rory Costello, Paul Debono, Bill Dunstone, Jan Finkel, Frank Keetz, Ted Knorr, Gary Krause, Barry Mednick, John Pardon, Alan Pollock, Bill Plott, Kazuo Sayama, Jay Sanford, David Skinner, Barry Swanton, and Eduardo Valero.

James A. Riley
November 6, 2001

Addendum

A

Acosta, Jose [p. 26]
Died: Nov. 16, 1977, Havana, Cuba

Alberts *
Career: 1923   Position: p
Teams: Washington Potomacs

Allen, Toussaint L'Ouvertre **(Tom)** [p. 33]
Height: 5' 9"   Weight:180

Almeida, Rafael D. (Mike) [p. 33]
Died: March 19, 1968, Havana, Cuba

Anderson, Theodore M. **(Bubbles)** [p. 35]
Born: Nov. 4, 1904, Denver, Colorado`
Died: March 14, 1943, Denver, Colorado

Anderson, William Albert **(Bill)** [p. 35]
Born: January 25, 1913, Brevard, NC

Armour, Alfred **(Buddy**, Al) [p. 38]
a.k.a. Buddy Wilson
Born: April 27, 1915, Jackson, Mississippi
Died: April, 1974, Carbondale, Illinois

Armstead *
Career: 1925   Position: p
Teams: Atlantic City Bacharach Giants

Armstead, Jimmie [p. 38]
Height: 5' 11" Weight: 180
Born: Sept. 18, 1919, Birmingham, Ala.

Armstrong, Bill *
Career: 1945   Position:player
Teams: Indianapolis Clowns

Arnold, Paul [p. 39]
Height: 5' 9"   Weight: 160
Born: 1906, Hopewell, NJ

Arrington, Luther *
Career: 1928   Position: p
Teams: Atlantic City Bacharach Giants

Ascanio, Carlos (Earthquake) [p. 39]
Born: 1916, Venezuela
Died: Feb. 27, 1998, Caracas, Venezuela

Augustus *
Career: 1937   Position: p
Teams: St. Louis Stars

B

Baker, Eugene Walter (**Gene**) [p. 45]
  Died: Dec. 1, 1999, Davenport, Iowa

Baker, Rufus (Scoop) [p. 46]
  Born: Sept. 20, 1918, Bridgeport, Conn.
  Died: June 22, 1992, Bridgeport, Conn.

Barbee, John Quincy Adams (**Bud**) [p. 56]
  Career: 1935-49   Position: **p, 1b**, of
  Teams: Newark Eagles ('36), **New York Black Yankees** ('37–'38, '40–'41, '46–'49), Brooklyn Royal Giants ('39), Baltimore Elite Giants ('40, '43), *Mexican League ('41)*, Philadelphia Stars ('42), *Military Service ('43-'46) Canadian League ('49-'51, '54)*, Minor Leagues ('52-'55)
  Height: 6' 0"   Weight: 204
  Born: March 16, 1914, Durham, NC
  Died: Jan. 14, 2000, Durham, NC
  Although he was primarily known as a pitcher, he was also a good hitter with power. As a pitcher he relied on a fastball and curve. In the original volume, the entires for him and his brother Walter were inter-mingled and substantively reversed.

Barbee Walter Bratcher (**Lamb**) [p. 55]
  Career: 1942-49   Position: **of**, 1b
  Teams: Ethiopian Clowns ('42), Cincinnati-Indianapolis Clowns ('45), Indianapolis Clowns (46), New York Black Yankees, Louisville Buckeyes ('49)
  Height: 6' 0"   Weight: 195
  Born: April 30, 1916, Durham, N. C.
  Died: Aug. 1, 1986,
  Durham, N. C.
  He played briefly as an outfielder with the Louisville Buckeyes in 1949. Earlier in his career he played with the Clowns ballclub in the 1940s.

Barber, Sam [p. 56]
  Died: April 18, 1999, Birmingham, Ala.

Barnes, Harry (Mooch, Tackhead) [p. 59]
  Died: December 1993, Birmingham, Ala.

Barnes, John (**Fat,** Tubby) [p. 60]
  Born: Feb. 12, 1904
  Died: Sept. 5, 1977, St. Louis, Mo.

Barnes, William (Bill, Jimmy) [p. 60]
  Born: Feb. 20, 1921, Birmingham, Ala.

Barnhill, Herbert Edward (**Herb**) [p. 62]
  Born: July 2, 1913, Hazlehurst, Ga.

Barnwell, Ernest (Gator) [p. 63]
  Died: Dec. 8, 1996, Fort Pierce, Fla.

Battle, William James (**Bill**) [p. 66]
  Career: 1938-40   Position: 3b, ss, 2b, p, of
  Teams: Chicago American Giants ('38, '40), *Schenectady Mohawk Giants ('39), Homestead Giants ('47)*
  Bats: Both   Throws: Right
  Height: 5' 8"   Weight: 150
  Born: Feb. 20, 1908, Savannah, Ga.
  Died: Oct. 21, 1995, Edgewater, Fla.
  He was a good fielder, a fast baserunner, and a punch hitter who sprayed the ball to all fields.

Baxter, James *
  Career: 1944   Position: 2b
  Teams: Baltimore Elite Giants

Beckwith, John [p. 69]
  Born: June 20, 1902, Louisville, Ky.
  Died: Jan. 4, 1956, New York, N. Y.

Beitia, Cosme *
  Career: 1926   Position: of
  Team: New York Lincoln Giants

Bejerano, Augustin (Pijini) [p. 70]
Born: May 16, 1909, Manzanilla, Cuba

Bell, Clifford (**Cliff,** Cherry, Clarence) [p. 71]
Height: 5'10" Weight: 180
Born: July 2, 1897, Kildare, Texas
Died: April 13, 1952, Los Angeles, Calif.

Bell, William, Sr. (**W**, Bill) [p. 74]
Born: August 31, 1897, Lavaca County, Tex.
Died: March 16, 1969, El Campo, Tex.

Benjamin, Jerry Charles (Ben) [p. 75]
Died: Nov. 23, 1974, Detroit, Mich.

Bennett, James (**Jim**) [p. 76]
Born: Sept. 15, 1919, Indianapolis, Ind.
Died: June 3, 1991, Indianapolis, Ind.

Bennett, Sam [p. 77]
Born: March 7, 1884, St. Louis, Mo.

Benson, Eugene (**Gene**, Spider) [p. 77]
Died: April 6, 1999, Philadelphia, Pa.

Bibbs, Junius A. (**Rainey**, Sonny) [p. 82]
(Died: Sept. 11, 1980, Indianapolis, Ind.

Binder, James (**Jimmy**) [p. 83]
Born: Aug. 2, 1902, Bessemer, Ala.
Died: July 1, 1979, Pittsburgh, Pa.

Biot, Charles Augustus (**Charlie**) [p. 84]
Died: March 10, 2000, East Orange, N. J.

Blair, Garnett E. (Schoolboy) [p. 88]
Died: Jan. 12, 1996, Midlothian, Va.

Blaylock, Fred *
Career: 1945 Position: p

Teams: Homestead Grays
Height: 6'1" Weight: 194

Bond, Theodore H. (**Timothy,** Ted) [p. 92]
Born: Jan. 25, 1904
Died: Dec. 18, 1997, Chicago, Ill.

Booker, James (**Pete**) [p. 93]
Died: Sept. 27, 1922, Chicago, Ill.

Boone, Alonzo D. (Buster) [p. 93]
Born: Jan. 13, 1908, Decatur, Ala.

Bowman, Emmett (**Scotty**) [p. 97]
Died: Feb. 28, 1912, Corapolis, Pa.

Bowman, George *
Career: 1916 Position: player
Teams: Chicago American Giants ('16)

Bracken, Herbert (Herb, **Doc**) [p. 99]
a.k.a. Alphonso Bragana; Alfredo Bragana
Born: May 12, 1915, Paducah, Ky.
Died: Feb. 17, 1994, St. Louis, Mo

Bradley, Province **Frank** (Red, Dick) [p. 100]
Born: Oct. 22, 1907, Shreveport, La.

Braithwaite, Alonzo [p. 102]
Career: 1948 Position: 2b, ss
Teams: Philadelphia Stars ('48), *Canadian League ('51–'55), Minor Leagues ('55–'58), Mexican League ('59)*
Born: Feb. 18, 1932, Panama
In the original volume, the career of the two Panamanian Braithwaites were combined.

Braithwaite, Archie [p. 102]
Career: 1944-48 Position: rf, cf, 1b
Teams: Newark Eagles ('44), Philadelphia Stars ('47–'48), *Mexican League ('51, '53–'54), Minor Leagues ('55–'58)*

Born: Aug. 23, 1919, Colon, Panama

Although an average player in the field, on the bases and at the plate, he could hit with power. In the original volume, the career of the two Panamanian Braithwaites were combined.

Bremer, Eugene Joseph, Sr. **(Gene)** [p.104]
Died: June 19, 1971, Cleveland, Ohio

Briggs, Otto (*Mirror*) [p.108]
Born: April 5, 1891, Kings Mountain, N. C.

Brodie, Milledge *
Career: 1917   Position: p
Team: Atlantic City Bacharach Giants

Brooks, Ameal [p.112]
Born: June 3, 1904, New Orleans, La.
Died: Nov. 1, 1971, Bronx, N. Y.

Brown, Barney (Brinquitos) [p.115]
Born: Oct. 23, 1908, Hartsville, S. C.
Died: Oct. 1, 1985, Philadelphia, Pa.

Brown, Lawrence James **(Lefty)** [p.123]
Height: 5' 4"   Weight: 140
Born: Jan. 16, 1910, Memphis, Tenn.

Brown, Raymond (Ray) [p.124]
Died: 1965, Canada
Brown, Thomas Jefferson [p.126]
Ht: 5' 6"   Wt: 170

Brown, Willard Jesse (Home Run) [p.127]
Died: Aug. 8, 1996, Houston, Texas

Bruton, William Haron **(Bill)** *
Career: 1949   Position: of

Teams: *Philadelphia Stars ('49),* Major Leagues ('53–'64)
Bats: Left   Throws: Right
Height: 6' 0"   Weight: 165
Born: Dec. 22, 1925, Panola, Ala.
Died: Dec. 5, 1995, Marshalton, Del

Buckner, Harry (Green River, Doc) [p.131]
Died: April 1, 1938, Milwaukee, Wisc.

Bumpus, Earl (Bump) [p.132]
Born: April 14, 1914, Evansville, Ind.
Died: May 1, 1985, Uniontown, Ky.

Burbage, Knowlington O. **(Buddy)** [p.132]
Born: June 23, 1907, Salisbury, Md.

Burgin, John **(Johnny)** *
Career: 1928   Position: player
Teams: Hilldale

Burns *
Career: 1930   Position: lf
Teams: Memphis Red Sox

Burton, (Shorty) *
Career: 1918-26   Position: of, c
Teams: Atlantic City Bacharach Giants ('18), Newark Stars ('26)

Butts, Thomas A. (Tommy, **Pee Wee**) [p.139]
Born: Aug. 28, 1919, Sparta, Ga.
Died: Dec. 30, 1972, Atlanta, Ga.

Byas, Richard Thomas **(Subby,** Prof) [p.140]
Height: 5' 8"   Weight: 165
Born: March 19, 1910, Pineland, Texas
Died: Oct. 2, 1985, Chicago, Ill.

C

Cain, Marlon (**Sugar**, Ben) [p. 144]
　Bats: Right　Throws: Right
　Born: Feb. 14, 1914, Macon, Ga.

Calhoun, Walter (Walt, **Lefty**) [p. 145]
　Born: Aug. 21, 1911, Union City, Tenn.
　Died: Oct. 2, 1976, Cleveland, Ohio

Campbell, William (**Zip,** Bill, Bullet) [p. 149]
　Bats: Right　Throws: Right
　Height: 5' 9"　Weight: 180
　Born: March 26, 1896, Boston, Mass
　Died: July, 1973, Boynton Beach, Fla.

Cannady, Walter (**Rev**) [p. 150]
　Died: Dec. 3, 1981, Ft. Myers, Fla.

Carr, Charley *
　Career: 1924　Position: p
　Team: Baltimore Black Sox ('24)

Carr, George Henry (**Tank**) [p. 153]
　Died: Jan. 14, 1948, Los Angeles, Calif.

Carreras, Clemente Gonzalez (**Sungo**) [p. 154]
　Died: Nov. 19, 1989

Carter, Marlin Theodore (Pee Wee) [p. 157]
　Died: Dec. 20, 1993, Memphis, Tenn.

Cepeda, Pedro Anibal (**Perucho**) [p. 162]
　Born: Jan. 31, 1906, Catano, Puerto Rico
　Died: April 27, 1955, San Juan, Puerto Rico

Chapman, Leonardo Medina [p. 164]
　Team: Baltimore Elite Giants ('44)

Charleston, Oscar McKinley (Charlie) [p. 164]
　Died: Oct. 5, 1954, Philadelphia, Pa.

Charleston, Porter [p. 166]
　Born: Jan. 8, 1904
　Died: June 1, 1986, Chester, Pa.

Christopher, Thadist (Thaddeus) [p. 170]
　Born: Dec. 24, 1912, Tampa, Fla.
　Died: 1973, La Tigera, Calif.

Clark, Charles B. (Charley, **Sensational**) *
　Career: 1925　Position: p
　Teams: Indianapolis ABCs ('25), Homestead
　Grays ('25), Atlantic City Bacharach Giants ('25)

Clark, Cleveland Chiflan [p. 172]
　Born: 1918, Havana, Cuba

Clark, Morten (**Morty,** Specs) [p. 173]
　Born: Aug. 19, 1889, Bristol, Tenn.

Clarke, Robert (**Eggie,** Bob, Kike) [p. 174]
　Died: May 1, 1972, Norfolk, Va.

Clarkson, James Buster (**Bus**) [p. 175]
　Born: March 13, 1913, Hopkins, S. C.

Clay, John *
　Career: 1925　Position: of
　Teams: Atlantic City Bacharach Giants

Clayton, Leroy Watkins (**Zack**) [p. 177]
　Born: April 17, 1917, Gloester, Va.
　Died: Nov. 20, 1997, Philadelphia, Pa.

Cleveland, Howard (**Duke**) [p. 179]
　Bats: Left　Throws: Right
　Height: 6' 1"　Weight: 196

Cockrell, Phillip (**Phil,** Fish) [p. 182]
　Born: June 26, 1898, Augusta, Ga.

Colas, Carlos Celestino Suce (Charlie) [p. 184]
Height: 5' 9 1/2"   Weight: 170
Born: Dec. 4, 1917, Havana, Cuba

Collins, Arthur *
Career: 1923-24   Position: p
Teams: Harrisburg Giants

Collins, Frank *
Career: 1924   Position: p
Teams: Baltimore Black Sox

Colzie, James (**Jim**) [p. 189]
Teams: Ethiopian Clowns ('37, '42), *Military Service ('42–'45)*, Indianapolis Clowns ('46–'47)
Bats: Right   Throws: Right
Height: 6 0"   Weight: 155
Born: July 12, 1920, Montezuma, Ga.
His son, Neal Colzie, played professional football in the NFL.

Cooper, Andrew L. (**Andy**, Lefty) [p. 190]
Born: April 4, 1896, Waco, Texas
Died: June 3, 1941, Waco Texas

Cooper, Daltie (Dolly, Dudley) [p. 192]
Height: 6' 2"   Weight: 190

Copeland, Lawrence *
Career: 1935   Position: p
Teams: Brooklyn Eagles

Corbett, Charles (Geech, **Geechie**) [p. 193]
Bats: Right   Throws: Right

Cornelius, William McKinley (**Sug**) [p. 193]
Height: 5' 7"   Weight: 175
Born: Sept. 4, 1908, Atlanta, Ga.
Died: Oct. 30, 1989, Chicago, Ill.

Craig *
Career: 1935   Position: player
Teams: Brooklyn Eagles

Crowder *
Career: 1920   Position: p
Teams: Madison Stars, New York Lincoln Giants

Cummings, Napoleon (**Chance**) [p. 204]
Died: April, 1974, Atlantic City, N. J.

Currie, George Rueben (**Rube**) [p. 206]
Born: July 17,1898, Kansas City, Mo.
Died: Sept., 1968, Minneapolis, Minn.

Curry, Homer (**Goose**) [p. 206]
Born: May 19, 1905, Mexia, Texas
Dallard, William (Eggie, Bill, Will [p. 208]
Born: May 6, 1899, Elm, N. J.
Died: November 26, 1933, Philadelphia, Pa.

D

Dallard, William (**Eggie**, Bill, Will) [p. 208]
Born: May 6, 1899, Elm, N. J.
Died: November 26, 1933. Philadelphia, Pa.

Dandridge, Raymond Emmitt (**Ray**) [p. 209]
Died: Feb. 12, 1994, Palm Bay, Fla.

Daniels, Leon (**Pepper**) [p. 211]
Born: Aug. 20, 1902, Valdosta, Ga.

Davenport, Lloyd (Ducky, Bear man) [p. 212]
Died: 1988, New Orleans, La.

Davis, Babe (Atlas, Country, *Dave*) [p. 214]
Teams: Atlanta Black Crackers, Homestead Grays

Davis, Edward A. (**Peanuts**, Nyassas) [p. 215]
Born: Jackson, Miss.

Davis, Lorenzo (**Piper**) [p. 217]
Died: May 21, 1997, Birmingham, Ala.

Davis, Saul Henry, Jr. (Sol, Rareback) [p. 220]
Died: Feb. 8, 1994, Minot, N. D.

Day, Leon [p. 223]
Died: March 13, 1995, Baltimore, Md.
He was inducted into the National Baseball Hall of Fame in 1995.

Day, Wilson C. (**Connie**) [p. 224]
Born: Dec. 30, 1900, Lima, Ohio

Dennis, Wesley L. (**Doc**) [p. 229]
Died: March 6, 2001, Nashville, Tenn.

Dials, Oland Cecil (**Lou**) [p. 231]
Born: Jan. 10, 1904, Hot Springs, Ark.
Died: April 1, 1994, Modesto, Calif.

Dismukes, William (**Dizzy**) [p. 236]
Height: 6' 0"   Weight: 180

Dixon, George (Tubby) [p. 238]
Bats: Left   Throws: Right

Dougherty, Lon (Leon) *
Career: 1934-35   Position: p
Teams: Kansas City Monarchs, Brooklyn Eagles
Bats: Left   Throws:
Height: 6' 2"   Weight: 190

Douglas, Fred *
Career: 1945   Position: p
Team: Indianapolis Clowns

Douglas, Jesse Warren [p. 245]
Born: March 27, 1916, Longview, Tex.

Douglass, Edward (**Eddie**) [p. 246]
Born: Aug. 9, 1891, Dallas, Texas
Died: Nov. 1, 1979, Suffolk, N. Y.

Downs, McKinley (**Bunny**) [p. 246]
Born: March 7, 1894
Died: June 1, 1973, Eller, North Carolina

Duany, Claro [y Hiedra] [p. 250]
Died: March 30, 1997, Evanston, Ind.

Dukes, Thomas (**Tommy**, Dixie) [p. 252]
Born: Sept. 24, 1906, Picayner, Miss.

E

Eggleston, Macajah Marchand (**Mack**) [p. 264]
Died: Sept. 1, 1980, Baltimore, Md.

Everett, James William, Sr. (**Jim,** Dean) [p. 272]
Bats: Right   Throws: Right`
Height: 5' 11"   Weight: 190
Born: July 4, 1908, Jacksonville, Fla.
Died: May 3, 1996, Miami, Fla.

Ewing, William Monroe (**Buck**) [p. 272]
Bats: Right   Throws: Right
Height: 6' 2"   Weight: 190
Born: Jan. 31, 1903, Massillon, Ohio
Died: Sept. 1, 1979, Schenectady, N. Y.

F

Fabre, Isidro (Papi) [p. 273]
Height: 5' 6"   Weight: 155
Born: May 15, 1895, Havana, Cuba

Fennar, Albertus Avant (Al, **Cleffie**) [p. 276]
Died: June 15, 2001, Palm Bay, Fla.

Fernandez, Rodolfo (Rudy) [p. 278]
Died: Sept. 6, 2000, New York, N. Y.

Ferrell, Howard **Leroy** (Toots) [p. 279]
Born: Sept. 21, 1929, Chestertown, Md.

Fiall, Thomas (**Tom**) [p. 280]
Born: June 20, 1894
Died: June 1, 1978, Cape Fear, N. C.

Figarola, Jose [p. 282]
Career: 1904–15   Position: **c**
Teams: All Cubans ('04), Stars of Cuba ('10),
Cuban Stars (West) ('11–'15)
Died: Oct. 22, 1915, Havana, Cuba
   In the fall of 1915, he was killed when struck
over the heart by a pitch from Jose Mendez.

Figarola, Rafael *
Career: 1916-18   Position:1b
Teams: Cuban Stars (West) ('16), Brooklyn
Royal Giants ('18)

Finley, Thomas (**Tom,** James) [p. 283]
Died: Sept. 9, 1933, New York, N.Y.

Fisher *
Career: 1917   Position: p
Teams: Atlantic City Bacharach Giant

Flournoy, Jesse Willis (**Pud**) [p. 285]
Height: 6' 2"   Weight: 180

Forbes, Franklin Tidwillington (**Frank**, Strangler)
[p. 287]
Career: 1929-43   Position: bus. mgr., ump
Born: May 30, 1891, Philadelphia, Pa.
Died: Aug. 19, 1983, Philadelphia, Pa.

Forbes, Joe *
Career: 1913-19   Position: ss, 3b, of, 2b, p
Teams: Philadelphia Giants ('13, '22), Lincoln
Stars ('14), New York Lincoln Giants ('15-'18),
Pennsylvania Red Caps of New York ('18-20)
Atlantic City Bacharach Giants ('17, '19),
Chappie Johnson's Stars ('27)
Bats: Right   Throws: Right
Height: 5' 9"   Weight: 179
He is the brother of Frank Forbes.

Ford, James (**Jimmy,** Jim) [p. 288]
Height: 5' 8"   Weight: 185
Born: Oct. 16, 1912, Memphis, Tenn.

Foreman, F. Sylvestor (**Hooks**) [p. 289]
Bats: Right   Throws: Right
Died: Aug. 23, 1940, Kansas City, Mo.

Foster, William Hendrick (**Willie,** Bill) [p. 292]
He was inducted into the National Baseball Hall
of Fame at Cooperstown, N. Y. in 1996.

Franklin *
Career: 1917   Position: cf, ss
Teams: Atlantic City Bacharach Giants

Franks, Bobby *
Career: 1933   Position: p
Teams: Philadelphia Stars

G

Galeto *
Career: 1924   Position: c
Teams: Cuban Stars (East)

Garcia, Silvio [y Rendon] [p.304]
Died: Aug. 28, 1977, Cuba

Gardner, Floyd (**Jelly**) [p.305]
Died: March 1, 1977, Chicago, Ill.

Gaston, Robert (**Rab Roy**) [p.308]
Born: March 19, 1910, Chattanooga, Tenn.
Died: Feb. 11, 2000, Pittsburgh, Pa.

Gatewood, William (**Bill,** Big Bill) [p.309]
Born: Aug. 22, 1881, Columbia, Mo.`
Died: Dec. 1, 1962, Columbia, Mo.

Gerard, Alphonso (Al, Piggy) [p.311]
Born: Jan. 22, 1916, St. Croix, Virgin Islands
Died: St. Croix, Virgin Islands

Gibbons, John **Bay** *
Career: 1941   Position: p
Teams: Philadelphia Stars ('41), New York Black
Yankees ('41), *Harlem Globetrotters ('46)*
Bats: Right   Throws: Right
Height: 5' 9"   Weight: 135
Born: April 16, 1922, Milan, Ga.
    In the original volume his career was combined, with the career of his brother Walter.

Gibbons, Walter Lee [p. 312]
Career: 1948-49   Position: p
Teams: Indianapolis Clowns ('48–'49), *Mandak
League ('49–'50, '52–'54), Military Service
('50–'51)*
Bats: Left   Throws: Right
Height: 5' 6"   Weight: 175
Born: Oct. 13, 1928, Tampa, Fla.

Gibson *
Career: 1933   Position: rf
Teams: Philadelphia Stars

Gilyard, Luther [p. 320]
Born: Feb. 20, 1910
Died: Sept. 1, 1976, Detroit, Mich.

Gipson, Alvin (**Bubber,** Skeet) [p. 320]
Born: Dec. 11, 1913, Shreveport, La.
Died: Nov. 21, 1992, Shreveport, La.

Glass, Carl Lee (Butch, Lefty) [p. 322]
Died: Oct. 19, 1972, Lexington, Ky.

Glenn, Hubert (Country) [p. 322]
Born: July 13, 1916, Lewisville, N. C.

Gonzales, Miguel Angel (**Mike**) [p. 326]
Bats: Right   Throws: Right
Height: 6' 1"   Weight: 200
Born: Sept. 24, 1890, Havana, Cuba

Gould *
Career: 1917   Position: of
Teams: Atlantic City Bacharach Giants

Govern, Stanislaus Kostka (**S. K.**, Cos) [p. 328]
Born: Oct. 16, 1854, St. Croix, Virgin Islands
Died: Nov. 3, 1924, Hot Springs, Va.

Grace, William (**Willie,** Fireman) [p. 329]
Born: June 30,1919, Memphis, Tenn.

Grant, Charles (**Charlie,** Tokahoma) [p. 330]
Born: Aug. 31, 1874, Cincinnati, Ohio
Died: July 9, 1932, Cincinnati, Ohio

Gray, Emerson *
Career: 1917   Position: p

Teams: Shang Johnson's All-Stars, Atlantic City Bacharach Giants, Brooklyn Royal Giants

Gray, G. E. (**Dolly,** Willie, Lefty) [p. 333]
Bats: Left   Throws: Left

Green, Leslie, Sr. (**Chin**) [p. 336]
Born: Feb. 8, 1914, St. Louis, Mo.

Greene, James Elbert (**Joe**, Pea, Pig) [p. 337]
Died: July 17, 1989, Stone Mountain, Ga.

Grier, Claude (**Red**) [p. 340]
Height: 5' 11" Weight: 190

Grimes, Eugene *
Career: 1947   Position: p-of
Team: Cleveland Buckeyes

Grimes, Lionel [p. 342]
Teams: Cleveland Buckeyes ('47)
Born: Dec. 28, 1918
Died: Feb. 6, 1993, Alliance, Ohio

Guilbe, Juan (Telo) [p.343]
Died: April 21, 1994, Ponce, Puerto Rico

H

Haines *
Career: 1926   Position: p
Teams: New York Lincoln Giants

Hairston, Samuel Harding (**Sam**) [p. 346]
Died: Oct. 31, 1997, Birmingham, Ala.

Hall *
Career: 1945   Position: of
Teams: Kansas City Monarchs

Hall, Perry [p. 348]
Born: April 18, 1901, Hogansville, Ga.
Died: Feb. 3, 1993, Chicago, Ill.

Handy, William Oscar (**Bill**) [p. 352]
Died: April, 1945, New Orleans, La.

Hardy, Arthur Wesley (Art, Bill) [p. 354]
Died: Sept. 20, 1980, Buffalo, N. Y.

Harrison, Abraham (Abram, **Abe**) [p. 365]
Born: March 4, 1867, Norristown, Pa.
Died: May 1, 1932, Hamilton, N. J.

Hawkins, Lemuel (**Lem,** Hawk) [p. 369]
Bats: Left   Throws: Left
Height: 5' 10" Weight: 185
Born: Oct. 2, 1895, Macon, Georgia
Died: Aug. 10, 1934, Chicago, Ill.

Hayes, Burnalle James (**Bun**) [p. 369]
Bats: Right   Throws: Right
Height: 5' 11" Weight: 170
Born: Aug. 2, 1905, Louisburg, North Carolina
Died: Nov. 29, 1969, Louisburg, North Carolina

Hayes, Johnny William (John) [p. 370]
Died: Nov. 16, 1988, Auburn Park, Ill.

Haynes, Sam (**Sammie**) [p. 371]
Died: Nov. 11, 1997, Los Angeles, Calif.

937

Haywood, Albert (**Buster,** Wahoo) [p. 372]
Born: Jan. 12, 1910, Portsmouth, Va.
Died: April 19, 2000, Los Angeles, Calif.

Heard, Jehosie (Jay) [p. 373]
Died: Nov. 18, 1999, Birmingham, Ala.

Henderson, Arthur Chauncey (**Rats**) [p. 374]
Died: Sept. 8, 1988, East End, Va.

Henry, Leo (**Preacher**) [p. 377]
Born: March 10, 1911, Inverness, Fla.
Died: May 16, 1992, Jacksonville, Fla.

Heredia, Ramon (Napoleon) [p. 377]
Born: March 3, 1917, Matanzas, Cuba

Hill, Joseph Preston (**Pete**) [p. 381]
Born: Oct. 12, 1880, Pittsburgh, Pa.
Died: Nov. 26, 1951, Buffalo, N. Y.

Holloway, Christopher Columbus (**Crush**) [p. 388]
Died: June 24, 1972, Baltimore, Md.

Holtz, Eddie [p. 390]
Died: July 15, 1924, St. Louis, Mo.

Hooker, Leniel Charlie (**Lennie,** Len) [p. 391]
Died: Dec., 1977, Newark, N. J.

Hoskins, William Charles (**Bill**) [p. 394]
Born: March 14, 1916
Died: March, 1975

Houston, Nathanial (**Jess**) [p. 395]
Bats: Right   Throws: Right
Height: 5' 10 1/2"   Weight: 172
Born: July 17, 1910, Montgomery, Ala.

Howard, Carranza (Schoolboy) [p. 395]
Born: Dec. 16, 1920, Daytona Beach, Fla.
Died: October 16, 1993, Clair Mel City, Fla.

Hubbard, Jesse James (Mountain) [p. 397]
Died: 1982, Los Angeles, Calif.

Huber, John Marshall (Bubber) [p. 397]
Height: 5' 9" Weight: 170
Born: April 26, 1908, Lexington, Ky.

Hutchinson, Willie (Ace) [p. 404]
Born: April 23, 1920
Died: October, 1992, Denver, Colo.

I

Israel, Elbert Willis [p. 410]
Born: April 19, 1927, Rockville, Md.
Died: Oct. 22, 1996, Rockville, Md.

J

Jackson *
Career: 1930   Position: 3b
Teams: Memphis Red Sox

Jackson, Norman (**Jelly**) [p. 414]
Born: Sept. 13, 1909, Washington, D. C.

Jackson, Thomas Walton, (**Tom,** Jack) [p. 417]
Born: Feb. 23, 1904, Mobile, Ala.
Died: May 29, 1996, St. Louis, Mo.

Jefferson, George Leo (Jeff) [p. 420]
Died: Sept. 1, 1985, Erie, Pa.

Jefferson, Willie (Bill) [p. 421]
Died: Sept. 22, 1979, Harris, Texas

Jeffries, Henry *
Career: 1943-44   Position: c
Teams: Indianapolis Clowns, Chicago
American Giants

Jeffries, James C. [p. 422]
Born: May 18, 1893, Nashville, Tenn.

Jenkins, James Edward (**Pee Wee**) [p. 424]
Born: March 15, 1925, Hampden Sydney, Va.

Jessup, Joseph **Gentry** (Jeep) [p. 425]
Born: July 4, 1914, Mount Airy, N. C.
Died: March 26, 1998, Springfield, Mass.

Jethroe, Samuel (**Sam,** The Jet) [p. 426]
Born: Jan. 20, 1917, East St. Louis, Ill.
Died: June 16, 2001, Erie, Pa.

Johnson, Arthur John (**Jack**) [p. 436]
Height: 6' 0"   Weight: 200
Born: March 31, 1878, Galveston, Tex.
Died: June 10, 1946, Franklinton, N. C.

Johnson, C. *
Career: 1924   Position: 1b
Teams: New York Lincoln Giants, *Brooklyn Cuban Giants*

Johnson, George Washington (Dibo) [p. 434]
Height: 6' 1"   Weight: 180

Johnson, Joshua (**Josh,** Brute) [p. 438]
Born: Jan. 25, 1913, Evergreen, Ala.
Died: Aug. 12, 1999, Springfield, Ill.

Johnson, Mamie (**Peanut**) [p. 440]
Born: Sept. 27, 1935, Ridgeway, S. C.

Johnson, Oscar (**Heavy**) [p. 440]
Born: Nov. 2, 1896, Atchison, Kan.
Died: Jan., 1964, Cleveland, Ohio

Johnson, Peter, (**Pete,** Perly) [p. 441]
Born: 1902, Palata, Md.
Died: Dec. 19, 1991, Boston, Mass.

Johnson, William Julius (**Judy,** Jing) [p. 444]
Born: Oct. 26, 1899, Snow Hill, Md

Johnston, William **Wade** [p. 445]
Born: April 9, 1897, Columbus, Ohio
Died: March 8, 1978, Steubenville, Ohio

Jones, Clinton (**Casey**) [p. 447]
Died: Nov. 17, 1998, Memphis, Tenn.

Jordan, Henry (Hen) [p. 452]
Died: June 1, 1928

Joseph, Walter Lee (Newton, **Newt**) [p. 453]
Died: Jan. 18, 1953, Kansas City, Mo.

K

Kellman, Edric **Leon** [p. 457]
  Born: July 11, 1921, Gatun, Panama Canal Zone

Kemp, James Allen (**Gabby,** Mouth) [p. 459]
  Born: April 9, 1919
  Died: Oct. 21, 1993, Atlanta, Ga.

Kerry *
  Career: 1929   Position: ph
  Teams: Atlantic City Bacharach Giants

Kimbro, Henry Allen (Kimmie, Jumbo) [p. 462]
  Died: July 11, 1999, Nashville, Tenn.

Kimbrough, Larry Nathaniel [p. 463]
  Died: Jan. 31, 2001, Philadelphia, Pa.

Kincannon, Harry (Tincan) [p. 464]
  Born: July 30, 1909
  Died: October 1, 1965

Klep, Edward Joseph (**Eddie**) [p. 466]
  Born: Oct. 12, 1918, Erie, Pa.
  Died: Nov. 21, 1981, Los Angeles, Calif.

Kranson, Floyd Arthur [p. 467]
  Born: July 24, 1913
  Died: Sept. 1, 1967
  Lackey, Obie Ezekial [p. 468]
  Born: October 6, 1903, Stony Point, N. C.
  Died: Dec. 1, 1979, Philadelphia, Pa.

L

Lackey, Obie Ezekial [p. 468]
  Born: October 6, 1903, Stony Point, N. C.
  Died: Dec. 1. 1979, Philadelphia, Pa.

Lamar, Clarence (Horacio, Lemon) [p. 468]
  Bats: Right   Throws: Right
  Height: 5' 10"   Weight: 175

LaMarque, James Harding (**Lefty**, Jim) [p. 469]
  Died: Jan. 15, 2000, Kansas City, Mo.

Larkins *
  Career: 1933   Position: c
  Teams:Philadlephia Bacharach Giants

Laurent, Milfred Stephen (Milt, **Milton**) [p. 471]
  Died: Nov. 21, 1995, New Orleans, La.

LeBlanc, Jose V. (**Julio**) [p. 473]
  Died: Feb. 6, 1922, Havana, Cuba

Leonard, Charlie *
  Career: 1936   Position: inf.
  Teams: Newark Eagles
  He is the brother of Buck Leonard.

Leonard, Walter Fenner (**Buck**) [p. 476]
  Died: Nov. 27, 1997, Rocky Mount, N. C.

Lewis, Joe (Sleepy) [p. 480]
  Height: 5' 11 1/2"   Weight: 195
  Born: Jan. 17, 1896, Drakes Branch, Va.
  Died: Oct. 1896, Portsmouth, Va.

Lewis, Rufus (Lew) [p. 481]
  Died: Dec. 17, 1999, Southfield, Mich.

Ligon, Rufus C. [p. 482]
Born: May 6, 1903, Memphis, Tenn.
Died: Sept. 24, 1992, Dunlay, Texas

Lindsey, Charles Clarence (**Bill**) [p. 484]
Career: 1920-34   Position: ss, 2b, 3b, of
Teams: *Philadelphia Giants of New York ('20),*
New York Lincoln Giants ('20, '25–'26),
Richmond Giants ('22–'23), Baltimore Black
Sox ('23–'24, '28), Washington Potomacs ('24),
Wilimngton Potomacs ('25), Dayton Marcos
('26), *Pennsylvania Red Caps of New York
('26–'27, '30-'32),* Hilldale Daisies ('28),
Atlantic City Bacharach Giants ('29)

Lindsay, William Hudson (**Bill**, Red) [p. 485]
Career: 1931-34   Position: ss, 2b, 3b
Teams: Philadelphia Bacharach Giants ('31-'34),
Washington Pilots ('32-'33)
Bats: Right   Throws: Right
Born: April 15, 1905, Spartanburg, S. C.
In the original volume his career was com-
bined with the career of Charles Lindsey.

Lloyd, John Henry (Pop, El Cuchara) [p. 486]
Died: March 19, 1964, Atlantic City, N. J.

Locke, Clarence Virgil (Dad) [p. 489]
Born: March 25, 1911, Kansas City, Mo.

Longley, Wyman (**Red,** Ray) [p. 493]
Height: 5' 9"   Weight: 205
Born: Sept. 7, 1909, Little Rock, Ark.
Died: July 1, 1977, Memphis, Tenn.

Lopez, Candido Justo (**Cando**) [p. 493]
Born: October 15, 1902, Cuba
Died: September, 1979, Puerto Rico

Lyles, John [p. 499]
Born: March 18, 1912, St. Louis, Mo.
Died: July 15, 1991

Lyons, James (**Jimmie**) [p. 500]
Born: Nov. 6, 1892, Chicago, Ill.
Died: October, 1963, Chicago, Ill.

M

Mackey, James Raleigh (**Biz**) [p. 502]
Died: Sept. 22, 1965, Los Angeles, Calif.

Malone *
Career: 1944   Position: p
Teams: Kansas City Monarchs

Malone, William H. [p. 508]
Died: May 10, 1917, Saginaw, Mich.

Manley, Abraham L. (**Abe**) [p. 508]
Born: Dec. 22, 1885, Hartford, N. C.
Died: Dec. 9, 1952, Germantown, Pa.

Manley, Effa Brooks (Effie) [p. 508]
Born: March 27, 1900, Philadelphia, Pa.
Died: April 16, 1981, Los Angeles, Calif.

Markham, John Matthew (Johnny) [p. 512]
Born: Oct. 12, 1908, Shreveport, La.
Died: 1977, Hutchison, Kan.

Marshall, William James (**Jack**, Boisy) [p. 516]
Died: Aug. 31, 1990, Chicago, Ill.

Martinez, Horacio (Rabbit) [p. 518]
Height: 5' 9"   Weight: 155
Born: May 20, 1912, Santiago, Santo Domingo

Mason, Charles (Corporal, Charlie) [p. 519]
Bats: Right   Throws: Right
Height: 6' 2"   Weight: 200

Massingale *
Career: 1944   Position: c
Teams: Kansas City Monarchs

Matchett, Jack (Zip) [p. 520]
Born: Feb. 3, 1906, Palestine, Texas

Mathews, Francis Oliver (**Fran,** Matty) [p. 520]
Born: Nov. 2, 1916, Barbados, West Indies
Died: Aug. 24, 1999, Los Angeles, Calif.

Mathis, Verdell (Lefty) [p. 521]
Died: Oct. 30, 1998, Memphis, Tenn.

Mays *
Career: 1917   Position: ss, p
Teams: Atlantic City Bacharach Giants

Mayweather, Eldridge E. (Chili, Ed) [p. 524]
Born: Feb. 26, 1909, Shreveport, La.
Died: Feb. 19, 1966, Kansas City, Mo.

McAdoo, Tulous Dudley (**Tully**) [p. 525]
Born: July 9, 1903
Died: Feb. 1, 1987, Waurika, Okla.

McDaniels, Booker Taliaferro [p. 531]
Born: Sept. 13, 1913, Blackwell, Ark.

McDonald, Luther (Vet, Old Soul) [p. 532]
Born: Feb. 6, 1906
Died: May 1, 1976, St. Louis, Mo.

McDuffie, Terris Chester (Speed) [p. 534]
Died: May. 1968, New York, N. Y.

McHenry, Henry (Cream) [p. 537]
Born: April 3, 1910
Died: Feb. 9, 1981, Brooklyn, N. Y.

McKinnis, Gready (Gread, Lefty) [p. 538]
Died: March 8, 1991, Chicago, Ill.

McLaurin, Felix [p. 539]
Born: Sept. 5, 1921, Jacksonville, Fla.
Died: May 1, 1972

McLloyd *
Career: 1923   Position: p
Teams: Atlantic City Bacharach Giants

McNeal, Clyde Clifton (Junior) [p. 541]
Died: April 14, 1996, San Antonio, Tex.

Medina, Lazarus (**Lazaro**, Leonardo) [p. 543]
Born: Oct. 3,1922, Havana, Cuba

Merchant, Henry Lewis (Frank, Speed) [p. 546]
Born: Feb. 17, 1918, Birmingham, Ala.
Died: Aug. 23, 1982, Cincinnati, Ohio

Meredith, Buford (**Geetchie**) [p. 547]
Died: Jan. 20, 1932, Birmingham, Ala.

Minoso, Saturnino **Orestos** Arrieta Armas
(Minnie) [p. 554]
Born: Nov. 29, 1925, Perico, Cuba

Mirabal, Juanelo [p. 555]
Died: 1989, Elizabeth, N. J.

Missouri, James (**Jim**) [p. 556]
Born: May 29, 1917
Died: July 4, 1989, Capitol Heights, Md.

Mitchell *
Career: 1931   Position: inf
Teams: Homestead Grays

Mitchell, George (Big, Toad) [p. 557]
Born: Dec. 20, 1898, Sparta, Ill.
Died: 1964, New Jersey

Mitchell, Robert (Pud) [p. 558]
Born: Dec. 20, 1898, Sparta, Ill.
Died: June 1, 1974, Dallas, Texas

Montgomery, Grady (**Monty**) *
Career: 1948-50
Teams: Baltimore Elite Giants ('48), Chicago American Giants ('49–51) *Indianapolis Clowns* ('52)
Born: Aug. 8, 1931, Gastonia, N. C.

Moody, Lee [p. 562]
Born: May 14, 1917, East St. Louis, Ill.
Died: July 4, 1998, Ferguson, Mo.

Moody, Willis [p. 562]
Bats: Left   Throws: Left
Born: 1898, Clarksburg, W. Va.

Moore, Clarence *
Career: 1928   Position: 1b
Teams: Atlantic City Bacharach Giants
Bats: Left   Throws: Left

Moore, Walter (**Dobie,** Freckles, Scoops) [p. 566]
Born: Feb. 27, 1890, Rome, Ga.
Died: April 1, 1963, Rome, Ga.

Morales, Paredo *
Career: 1917   Position: p
Teams: Atlantic City Bacharach Giants

Moreland, Nathaniel Edmund (**Nate**) [p. 567]
Height: 6' 1"   Weight: 195
Born: April 22, 1917, England, Ark.
Died: Nov. 27, 1973, Alemada County, Calif.

Morgan, Constance Enola (**Connie**) [p. 568]
Died: Oct. 14, 1996, Philadelphia, Pa.

Morney, Leroy [p. 568]
Height: 5' 10"   Weight: 170
Born: May 13, 1909
Died: Nov., 1980, Oak Forest, Ill.

Morris, Barney (Big Ad) [p. 569]
Born: June 3, 1913, Shreveport, La.

Morris, Harold (**Yellowhorse**) [p. 570]
Bats: Right   Throws: Right
Height: 5' 11"   Weight: 169
Born: Feb. 16, 1896, Oakland, Calif.
Died: Oct. 10, 1970, S. San Francisco, Calif.

Morton, John *
Career: 1935   Position: p
Teams: Brooklyn Eagles
Throws: Right

Morton, Sydney Douglas (**Sy,** Cy) [p. 571]
Born: Dec. 19, 1921, Washington, N. C.

Moss, Porter (Ankleball) [p. 571]
Born: June 10, 1910, Cincinnati, Ohio
Died: July 16, 1944, Jackson, Tenn.

Mothel, Carroll Ray (**Dink,** Deke) [p. 572]
Died: April 24, 1980, Topeka, Kan.

Murry, Richard (Dick)
Career: 1943–44   Position: p
Teams: Cincinnati Clowns

N

Napier, Euthumn (**Eudie**) [p. 576]
    Born: Jan. 3, 1913, Baldwin County, Ga.
    Died: March, 1933, Allegheny, Pa.

Neil, Raymond (**Ray**) [p. 578]
    Born: Oct. 12, 1920, Apopka, Fla.

Nelson, Clyde [p. 578]
    Born: Sept., 1921, Bradenton, Fla.

Nelson, Ike *
    Career: 1918 Position: of
    Teams: Atlantic City Bacharach Giants

Newberry, James (**Jimmy**) [p. 581]
    Born: June 9, 1922, Birmingham, Ala.

Noble, Rafael Miguel [y Magee] (**Ray**) [p. 584]
    Died: May 9, 1998, New York, N. Y.

O

Oliver, James F. (Pee Wee) [p. 587]
    Died: Dec. 15, 1971, St. Petersburg, Fla.

Orange, Grady Diploma (Dip, Gerber) [p. 590]
    Born: March 22, 1900, Terrell, Texas
    Died: Sept. 21, 1946, Alexandria, La.

Owens, Roosevelt *
    Career: 1927 Position: p
    Teams: New York Lincoln Giants

Owens, William John (**Bill,** Willie) [p. 593]
    Born: Nov. 14, 1900, Indianapolis, Ind.
    Died: May 5, 1999, Indianapolis, Ind.

P

Padron, Juan **Luis** [p. 594]
    Height: 6' 0" Weight: 185

Page, Theodore Roosevelt (**Ted**) [p. 596]
    Born: April 22, 1903, Glasgow, Ky.

Pages, Pedro Armando (Gamo) [p. 597]
    Born: Feb. 21,1913, Mantanzas, Cuba

Palm, Robert Clarence (**Spoony**) [p. 600]
    Born: Oct. 6, 1914, Clarendon, Ark.
    Died: July 17, 1976, St. Louis, Mo.

Palmore, Morris (Pop Nyassis) *
    Career: 1936-42   Position: of, p, mgr.
    Team: Ethiopian Clowns
      He was the playing manager of the original
Clowns in 1936. In 1938 he won 17 consecutive

games for the Clowns and hit .389, while playing in the outfield when not pitching.

Parker, Thomas (**Tom,** Big Train) [p. 603]
Born: Feb. 12, 1912, Alexandria, La.

Parnell, Roy (**Red**) [p. 605]
Born: Sept. 17, 1905, Austin, Texas
Died: June 1, 1969, Terrell, Texas

Partlow, Roy (Silent Roy) [p. 607]
Born: June 8, 1911, Washington, Ga.

Patterson, Andrew Lawrence (**Pat**) [p. 608]
Died: May 16, 1984, Houston, Texas

Payne, Andrew H. (**Jap**) [p. 610]
Died: Aug., 1942, New York, NY

Pearson, Frank [p. 612]
Died: Aug. 11, 1997, Memphis, Tenn.

Pearson, Leonard Curtis (**Lennie**) [p. 612]
Died: Dec. 9, 1980, Newark, N. J.

Pendleton, James Edward (**Jim**) [p. 616]
Died: March 20, 1996, Houston, Tex.

Perry, Alonzo Thomas [p. 620]
Died: Oct. 13, 1982, Birmingham, Ala.

Pettus, William Thomas (**Bill,** Zack) [p. 622]
Died: Aug. 22, 1924, New York City, N. Y.

Philadelphia Bacharach Giants *
Duration: 1931-34   Honors: None
Affiliation: Independent ('31-'33), NNL ('34)

Phillips, John (Lefty) [p. 626]
Died: Jan. 12, 2001, Chicago, Ill.

Pigg, Leonard Daniel (Len, Fatty) [p. 627]
Died: Aug. 22, 1993, Seattle, Wash.

Poindexter, Robert (Albert) [p. 630]
Died: June, 1930, Washington, D. C.

Poles, Edward (Possum, **Googles**) [p. 631]
Died: Jan. 23, 1932, Baltimore, Md.

Pollard, Nathaniel Hawthorne (**Nat**) [p. 632]
Born: Jan. 8, 1915, Alabama City, Ala.
Died: Nov. 23, 1996, Dolemite, Ala

Pope, David (**Dave**) [p. 634]
Born: June 17, 1921, Talladega, Ala.
Died: Aug. 28, 1999, Cleveland, Ohio

Porter, Merle McKinley (Bugs Bunny) *
Career: 1949-50   Position: 1b
Team: Kansas City Monarchs
Born: Jan. 19, 1921, Little Rock, Ark.
Died: Oct., 2000, Los Angeles, Calif.

Posey, Cumberland Willis, Jr. (**Cum**) [p. 636]
Born: June 20, 1890, Homestead, Pa.

Posey, Seward Hayes (**See**) [p. 638]
Born: Oct. 3, 1887, Munhill, Pa.

Powell, Melvin (**Put**) [p. 639]
Born: May 30, 1908, Edwards, Miss.
Died: Feb., 1985, Chicago, Ill.

Powell, William Henry (**Bill**) [p. 639]
Born: May 8, 1919, Birmingham, Ala.
Quinones, Tomas Planchardon [p. 646]
Born: July 17, 1914, Puerto Rico
Died: November, 1980, New York, N. Y.

Q

Quinones, Tomas Plancherdon [p. 646]
Born: July 17, 1914, Puerto Rico
Died: November, 1980, New York, N. Y.

R

Ramsey *
    Career: 1947   Position: p
    Teams: Memphis Red Sox

Rector, Cornelius (**Connie**) [p. 653]
    Born: June 15, 1891, New York`
    Died: May 1, 1963

Redus, Wilson R. (**Frog**) [p. 655]
    Died: March, 23, 1979, Tulsa, Okla.

Reid, Allen *
    Career: 1940   Position: p
    Teams: Newark Eagles

Reid, Ambrose (Kid) [p. 658]
    Born: Dec. 13, 1897
    Died: April, 1966, Philadelphia, Pa.

Richmond, Morton *
    Career: 1935   Position: p
    Teams: Brooklyn Eagles

Riddle, Marshall Lewis (Jit) [p. 663]
    Born: April 22, 1918, St. Louis, Mo.
    Died: Sept. 2, 1988,St. Louis, Mo.

Rile, Edward (Ed, **Huck**) [p. 665]
    Born: June 30, 1900
    Died: June 1, 1971, Columbus, Ohio

Rios, Herman(Matias) [p. 665]
    Died: July, 1924, Havana, Cuba

Rivero, Manuel (**Manny**)
    Career: 1933   Position: 3b, of
    Teams: Cuban Stars

Roberts, Elihu [p. 668]
    Born: Sept. 2, 1897, Atlanta, Ga.
    Died: March 1, 1975, Atlantic City, N. J.

Robinson, Cornelius Randall (**Neil**) [p. 670]
    Died: July 23, 1983, Cincinnati, Ohio

Robinson, Henry **Frazier** (Pep, Sloe) [p. 671]
    Born: May 30, 1910, Birmingham, Ala.
    Died: Oct. 15, 1997, Kings Mountain, N. C.

Robinson, Norman Wayne (Bobby) [p. 673]
    Bats: Both
    Height: 5' 10" Weight: 180
    Born: April 1, 1913, Oklahoma City, Okla.
    Died: March 26, 1984, Panorama City, Calif.

Robinson, William L. (**Bobbie**) [p. 675]
    Born: Oct. 25, 1903, Whistler, Ala.

Rodriguez, Jose [p. 676]
    He is not the same Jose Rodriquez who is in the
    Cuban Hall of Fame.

Rogan, Wilber (**Bullet**) [p. 677]
He was inducted into the National Baseball Hall of Fame in Cooperstown, NY in 1998.

Rogers, William Nathaniel (**Nat**) [p. 679]
Died: December, 1981, Memphis, Tenn.

Rosselle, Basilio (Brujo) [p. 683]
Born: March 14, 1902, Los Arabas, Matanzas, Cuba

Ruffin, Charles **Leon** (Lassas) [p. 684]
Born: Feb. 11, 1912, Portsmouth, Va.
Died: Aug. 14, 1970, Portsmouth, Va.

Russ, Pythias [p. 685]
Born: 1904, Cynthiana, Ky.
Died: Aug. 9, 1930, Cynthiana, Ky.

Ryan, Merven John (**Red,** Carnarsie) [p. 687]
Born: July 11, 1897, Brooklyn, N. Y.
Died: Aug., 1969, New York, N.Y.

S

Sadler, William A. (**Bill,** Bubby) [p. 689]
Died: Nov. 10, 1987, Delaware City, Del.

Sampson, Thomas (**Tommy,** Toots) [p.692]
Born: Aug. 31, 1912, Calhoun, Ala.

Sanford *
Career: 1925   Position: c
Teams: Harrisburg Giants

Saqua *
Career: 1909   Positions: p
Teams: Cuban Stars

Saylor, Alfred (Greyhound) [p. 699]
Height: 6' 1"   Weight: 175
Born: Dec. 31, 1911, Blytheville, Ark.

Scales, George Walter (Tubby) [p. 699]
Died: April 15,1976, Los Angeles, Calif.

Scantlebury, Patricio Athelstan (**Pat**)
Died: May 24, 1991, Glen Ridge, N. J.

Schofield, (**Lefty**) *
Career: 1935   Position: p
Teams: Pittsburgh Crawfords

Scott, Ed   *
Career: 1939   Position: player
Teams: Ethiopian Clowns
Later he became a scout and helped sign Hank Aaron for the Clowns.

Scott, Joseph (**Joe**) [p. 704]
Died: Jan. 12, 1997, Los Angeles, Calif.

Selden, William H. (**Willie**) [p. 707]
Born: Oct. 10, 1866, Norfolk, Va.
Died: Aug. 26, 1926, Boston, Mass.

Serrell, Bonnie Clinton (Barney) [p. 708]
a.k.a. William C.
Born: March 9, 1920, Bayou Natchez, La.
Died: Aug.1, 1996, East Palo Alto, Calif.

Shively, George Anner (Rabbit) [p. 712]
Born: 1893, Lebanon, Ky.
Died: June 7, 1962, Bloomington, Ind.

Singer, Orville (**Red**) [p. 716]
Born: Dec. 27, 1898
Died: June 1, 1985, Dorset, Ohio

Smalls *
Career: 1935   Position: c
Teams: Brooklyn Eagles

Smith, Allen (Nicodemus) *
Career: 1936-38   Position: 1b,p
Teams: *Miami Giants ('35),* Ethiopian Clowns
('36-'38), *Poinciana Royals ('40)*
Bats: Right   Throws: Right
Height: 5' 10" Weight: 165
Born: Oct. 13, 1914, Key West, Fla.
He and "Cheever" Smith were brothers and
teammates on the original Clowns ballclub.

Smith, Clarence *
Career: 1918   Position: p
Teams: Atlantic City Bacharach Giants

Smith, Eugene (**Cheever,** Goat) *
Career: 1936-47   Position: 3b, ss, 2b, 1b, of
Teams: *Miami Giants ('35),* Ethiopian Clowns
('36–'42), Military Service ('43–'45), Cleveland
Buckeyes ('46–'47)
Bats: Right   Throws: Right
Height: 5' 8 1/2"   Weight: 135
Born: Nov. 28, 1911, Key West, Fla.
    Smith was a versatile player and could play
any position but played primarily at third base.
He played with the original Clowns until 1943,
when he was drafted into the Army and served in
a combat battalion on Saipan. Following his dis-
charge, he played two years with the Cleveland
Buckeyes before retiring from the diamond.

Smith, Eugene F. (**Gene**, Genie) [p. 721]
Born: April 23, 1917, Ansley, La.

Smith, Henry [p. 723]
Born: Dec. 13, 1914, Houston, Texas

Smith, Hilton [p. 723]
He was inducted into the National Baseball Hall
of Fame in Cooperstown, N.Y. in 2001.

Smith, O. *
Career: 1918   Position: cf
Teams: Atlantic City Bacharach Giants

Smith, Theolic (Fireball, Theo) [p. 728]
Died: Nov. 3, 1981, Compton, Calif.

Snead, Sylvestor Alonzo (Bo Gator) [p. 730]
Born: 1911, Quincy, Fla.
Died: May 21, 1995, Perry, Fla.

Snow, Felton (Mammy, Skipper) [p.730]
Died: March 16, 1974, Louisville, Ky.

Souell, Herbert (**Herb,** Baldy) [p. 731]
Died: July 12, 1978, Los Angeles, Calif.

Spearman, Charles (Crock) [p. 733]
Bats: Both   Throws: Right

Sproul *
Career: 1927   Position: p
Teams: New York Lincoln Giants

Stearnes, Norman Thomas (**Turkey**) [p. 739]
He was inducted into the National Baseball Hall
of Fame in Cooperstown, N. Y. in 2000.

Steele, Edward D. (**Ed**, Stainless) [p. 740]
Born: Aug. 8, 1915, Selma, Ala.
Died: February, 1974, Birmingham, Ala.

Stewart, Riley [p. 744]
Born: March 14, 1919, Benton, La.
Died: Dec. 10, 2000

Stone, Toni [p. 746]
a.k.a. Marcenia Lyle Alberga [her real name]
Born: July 17,1931, St. Paul, Minn.
Died: Nov. 2, 1996, Almeda, Calif.

Stovey, George Washington [p. 746]
   Born: 1866, Williamsport, Pa.
   Died: March 22, 1936, Williamsport, Pa.

Strong, Joseph Tarleton (**Joe,** J.T.) [p. 749]
   Born: Aug. 4, 1902, Jackson, Ky.
   Died: Nov. 12, 1986, Middleton, Ohio

Strong, Theodore Reginald (**Ted,** T. R.) [p. 750]
   Born: Jan. 2, 1914, South Bend, Ind.
   Died: March 1, 1978, Chicago, Ill.

Strothers, Tim Samuel (**Sam**) [p. 751]
   Died: Aug., 1942, Chicago, Ill.

Summers, Lonnie (Carl) [p.752]
   Died: Aug. 24, 1999, Los Angeles, Calif.

Suttles, George (**Mule**) [p.753]
   Born: March 31, 1900, Brockton, La.
   Died: July 9, 1966, Newark, N. J.

T

Taborn, Earl (Mickey) [p. 758]
   Died: Dec. 21, 1997, San Antonio, Texas

Tatum, Reece (**Goose**) [p. 760]
   Born: May 3, 1921, Eldorado, Ark.
   Died: Jan. 18, 1967, El Paso, Texas

Taylor, Charles Isham (**C. I.**) [p. 763]
   Born: Jan. 20, 1875, Anderson, S. C.

Taylor, John Arthur (**Johnny**) p. [766]
   Born: Feb. 4, 1916, Hartford, Conn.
   Died: June 15, 1987, Hartford, Conn.

Taylor, Jonathan Boyce (**Steel Arm** Johnny) [p. 767]
   Born: Aug. 18, 1880, Anderson S. C.
   Died: March 25, 1956, Peoria, Ill.

Taylor, Leroy (Ben) [p. 769]
   Born: Aug. 11, 1902, Marshall, Texas
   Died: March 7, 1968, Los Angeles, Calif.

Taylor, Olan (**Jelly,** Satan) [p. 770]
   Died: October, 1976, Cleveland, Ohio

Taylor, Raymond (Broadway) [p. 770]
   Born: 1910, Memphis, Tenn.

Taylor, Robert R. (Lightning) [p. 771]
   Born: May 25, 1916, Binghampton, N. Y.
   Died: May 16, 1999, Binghampton, N. Y.

Thomas, Clinton Cyrus (**Clint**) [p. 773]
   Died: Dec. 2, 1990, Charleston, W. Va.

Thomas, Davy (Kid)   *
   Career: 1928   Position: p
   Teams: New York Lincoln Giants

Thomas, Walter Lewis [p. 778]
   Born: Oct. 21, 1913, Mobile, Ala.
   Died: Feb. 9, 1991, Garland City, Ark.

Thompson, Frank (**Groundhog**) [p. 778]
   Born: Oct. 23, 1918, Maryville, La.

Thompson, Samuel (**Sad Sam**) [p. 781]
   Born: May 27, 1908, Sulligent, Ala.
   Died: 1978, Los Angeles, Calif.

Thompson, William *
Career: 1926   Position: ss
Teams: Brooklyn Royal Giants

Thurman, Robert Burns (**Bob**) [p. 783]
Died: Oct. 31, 1998, Wichita, Kansas

Tiant, Luis Eleuterio, Sr. (Lefty) [p. 784]
Died: Dec. 10, 1976, Milton, Mass.

Torriente, Cristobal [p. 787]
Born: 1893, Cienfuegas, Cuba

Turner *
Career: 1935   Position: p
Teams: Pittsburgh Crawfords

Turner, E. C. (**Pop,** Honus Wagner) [p. 794]
a.k.a. Wagner
    Early in his career with the Brooklyn Royal Giants, he played under the name "Wagner", possibly to protect his amateur standing.

U

Underwood, Ely
Born: Jan. 29, 1908, Ohio
    His great-nephew Blair Underwood, an actor, played Jackie Robinson in the HBO movie "Soul of the Game."

V

Vincent, Irving B. (Lefty) [p. 804]
Born: Feb. 26, 1909, Nashville, Tenn.
Died:Aug.25,1977,St.Louis,Mo.

W

Walker, Edsall Elliott (Big) [p. 807]
Died: Feb. 19, 1997, Albany, N.Y.

Walker, Jesse (**Hoss,** Deuce) [p.809]
Born: Sept. 23, 1912, Austin, Texas
Died: Jan. 26, 1984, San Antonio, Texas

Wallace, James (**Bo**) [p. 812]
Born: April 7, 1930, Elizabeth, N. J.
Died: April 14, 2000, Elizabeth, N. J.

Ware, Archie Virgil [p. 814]
Died: Dec. 13, 1990, Los Angeles, Calif.

Warren *
Career: 1918   Position: 2b
Team: Atlantic City Bacharach Giants

Washington, John G. (**Johnny**) [p. 818]
Born: Jan. 9, 1915, Montgomery, Ala.
Died: 1999, Chicago, Ill.

Washington, Namon [p. 819]
Born: June 20, 1894
Died: May, 1971, Brooklyn, N. Y.

Washington, Peter (**Pete**, Joe) [p. 820]
Height: 6' 0" Weight: 165
Born: 1933, Camden, N. J.

Watkins, John (**Pop**) [p. 821]
Born: 1857, Augusta, Ga.

Watkins, Maurice Clifton (**Murray**) [p. 822]
Died: March 26, 1987, Bolton Hills, Md.

Webster, Pearl F. [p. 824]
Career: 1912-18   Position: c, of
Teams: **Brooklyn Royal Giants** ('12-'17),
Hilldale ('17-'18), *Military Service ('19)*
Died: 1919, France
He reportedly died of in France during WWI.

Webster, William (**Speck**, West) [p. 824]
Career: 1911-26   Position: c, 1b, of
Teams: Chicago American Giants ('11), St. Louis
Giants ('12, '15–'16, '21), New York Lincoln
Giants ('14, '18, '24), *Jewell's ABCs ('17)*
Indianapolis ABCs ('18–'19), *Military Service
('18–'19)*, G.C.T. Redcaps ('18), Atlantic City
Bacharach Giants ('18, '23), Dayton Marcos
('20), Detroit Stars ('21), *Brooklyn Cuban Giants
('28)*

He was nicknamed "Speck" because of his
freckles. In 1918 he was the leftfielder for the
Bacharachs, but missed several games when his
wife became ill.

Welding *
Career: 1920   Position: cf
Team: Atlantic City Bacharach Giants

Wells, Willie Brooks (**Junior**) [p. 826]
Died: Jan. 1, 1994, Austin, Texas

Wells, Willie James (Devil, El Diablo) [p. 826]
He was inducted into the National Baseball Hall
of Fame at Cooperstown, N. Y. in 1997.

Welmaker, Roy Horace (Snook, Lefty) [p. 828]
Died: Feb. 3, 1998, Decatur, Ga.

Wesley, Edgar (Ed) [p. 829]
Died: July, 1966, Detroit, Mich.

West, James (**Jim**, Shifty, Hinkey) [p. 830]
Born: Aug. 9, 1911, Mobile, Ala.
Died: June, 1970, Philadelphia, Pa.

Whatley, Claude **David** (Dave, Speed) [p. 831]
Born: Nov. 10, 1914, Griffin, Ga.
Died: May, 1992, Cedarton, Ga.

White, Chaney (Reindeer, Liz) [p. 833]
Born: April 15, 1894, Dallas, Texas
Died: Feb. 1, 1967, Philadelphia, Pa.

Wickware, Frank [p. 840]
Born: March 8, 1888, Coffeeville, Kan.
Died: Nov. 2, 1967, Schenectady, N. Y.

Wiggs, Leonard *
Career: 1934   Position2b, of
Teams: Cleveland Red Sox
Died: June 29, 2000, Tampa, Fla.

Wilkes, James Eugene (**Jimmy**) [p. 842]
Bats: Left   Throws: Left
Born: Oct. 1, 1925, Philadelphia, Pa.

Wilkinson, James Leslie (**J. L.**) [p. 842]
a.k.a. Joe Green
Born: May 14, 1878, Perry, Iowa

Williams, Joseph (Smokey **Joe,** Cyclone) [p. 854]
Born: April 6, 1886, Seguin, Tex.
Died: Feb. 25, 1951, New York, N.Y.
He was inducted into the National Baseball Hall
(of Fame at Cooperstown, N. Y. in 1999.

Williams, Marvin (Tex, Coqueta) [p. 858]
Died: Dec. 23, 2000, Conroe, Texas

Williams, Vinicius J. (**Nish**, Zeke) [p. 863]
Born: Feb. 29, 1904, Atlanta, Ga.

Wilson, Arthur Lee (**Artie,** Snoop) [p. 866]
Born: Oct. 28, 1916, Springville, Ala.

Wilson, Daniel Richard (**Dan**) [p. 868]
Born: Sept. 13, 1913, St. Louis, Mo.

Winters, James H., Jr. (Jesse, **Nip**) [p. 876]
Born: April 29, 1899
Died: December 12, 1971

Witherspoon, (Reds) *
Career: 1917   Position: p
Teams: Atlantic City Bacharach Giants

Wright, Burnis (**Bill,** Wild Bill) [p. 880]
Died: Aug. 3, 1996, Aquascalientes, Mexico

Wright, Zollie [p. 884]
Died: April, 1976, Philadelphia, Pa.

Wyatt, Ralph Arthur (Pepper) [p. 885]
Died: March 1, 1990, Auburn Park, N. Y.

Wynn, Sydney *
Teams: Miami Giants, Indianapolis Clowns,
Kansas City Monarchs

X-Y

Young, Thomas Jefferson (T. J., **Tom**) [p. 891]
Born: 1906, Wichita, Kan.

Z

Zomphier, Charles (Zomp) [p. 894]
Born: Feb. 16, 1906, St. Louis, Mo.